THE PALESTINE QUESTION IN
INTERNATIONAL LAW

THE PALESTINE QUESTION
IN INTERNATIONAL LAW

Compiled and Edited by
VICTOR KATTAN

**British Institute of
International and
Comparative Law**

Published and Distributed by
British Institute of International and Comparative Law
Charles Clore House, 17 Russell Square, London WC1B 5JP

© British Institute of International Law and the various contributors, 2008

British Library Cataloguing in Publication Data
A Catalogue record of this book is available from the British Library

ISBN 978-1-905221-30-1

The views expressed in the contributions to this work are those of their authors and do not necessarily reflect the views either of the editor of the work or of the British Institute of International and Comparative Law (BIICL). BIICL is a registered charity and an independent research institute committed to supporting high standards of scholarship in all aspects of international and comparative law.

Typeset by Cambrian Typesetters
Camberley, Surrey
Printed in Great Britain by Biddles Ltd
King's Lynn

Foreword

The Palestine–Israel conflict is a dispute about land and people, about competing territorial claims and about the rights and duties of peoples that live in the former mandated territory of Palestine. It is primarily a political dispute but at the same time it is a legal dispute, a dispute whose principle features are characterized by legal argument. To mention just some of the legal questions that arise: is the 1948/9 Armistice Line (the 'Green Line') the border between Israel and Palestine? Or is the border to be fixed by the wall Israel is presently constructing in the West Bank? Do Palestinian refugees enjoy a right of return to Israel? Does Gaza remain occupied territory following the withdrawal of Israeli settlers and army in 2005? Are Israeli settlements in the West Bank and Jerusalem unlawful colonial enterprises? Is Israel bound by international human rights conventions in the Occupied Palestinian Territory? Is the Fourth Geneva Convention on civilians in armed conflict binding on Israel in the Occupied Palestinian Territory? Do Palestinians have a right of self-determination? Is the targeted killing of Palestinian militants, the demolition of houses, sonic booms, the destruction of power plants, the closure of schools and the obstruction of health care contrary to international humanitarian law?

Legal disputation is a regular feature of international discourse. The absence of a compulsory system of adjudication in international law allows parties to debate competing claims without, in most cases, fear of legal contradiction. But the Palestine–Israel debate is different. Although there is no binding judicial decision on questions of the kind raised above, the international community has spoken on many of these issues through authoritative organs charged with the task of interpreting and pronouncing on international law. The International Court of Justice in its 2004 Advisory Opinion has held the wall presently being built by Israel in Palestinian territory to be illegal, and given approval to the Green Line as the lawful border. In its Opinion it has also held the Fourth Geneva Convention and international human rights conventions to be binding on Israel in the Occupied Palestinian Territory. And it has unanimously held settlements to be illegal. The finding that the Fourth Geneva Convention and international human rights conventions are applicable to the Occupied Palestinian Territory provides answers to many of the questions concerning the violation of human rights and humanitarian law. The Security Council has spoken on the illegality of settlements and the annexation of East Jerusalem. And the International Committee of the Red Cross, the body charged with the task of monitoring the Fourth Geneva Convention has likewise judged many of Israel's actions in the Palestinian Territory to be unlawful.

Although many of the legal questions surrounding the Palestinian issue have been convincingly answered, important questions remain about the consequences of illegal situations and actions. In addition there is need to portray the reasoning that leads to many conclusions and the historical and political context in which the legal questions have arisen. Herein lies the value of the present work edited by Victor Kattan. It places the Palestine–Israel conflict squarely in a legal context and demonstrates how legal norms inform the debate on subjects such as the rights of refugees, borders, the status of East Jerusalem, self-determination, access to water, the occupation of Palestine, statehood, the construction of the wall in Palestine and the negotiations for a peaceful settlement of the dispute. The essays selected provide clear evidence of the extent to which international law itself has become a casualty of the Palestine–Israel conflict. Moreover, as scholarly writings, they present this evidence in a reasoned and balanced manner.

Despite the evidence of Israeli illegal actions, many governments and individuals prefer to accept Israel's expansive security justification for its actions or to ignore these illegal actions on the ground that geo-political considerations override international law. This is a dangerous attitude as it not only undermines respect for the rule of law in international relations but at the same time provides a precedential shield for other international wrongdoers. This is evident in the decision-making of the UN Human Rights Council, where the failure of the West to take a firm line on Israeli violations of international law has led to the refusal of the developing world to cooperate in the condemnation of human rights violations by other States.

Clearly nothing will change until there is a change in public opinion. The present carefully selected essays, which provide a broad overview of the legal issues surrounding the Palestine–Israel conflict, will contribute to a greater awareness of the legal debate and, hopefully, to a change in public opinion. They may—should—also make it clear that a negotiated settlement in the region that is not premised on international law and ignores the normative dimension is destined to fail—as sadly illustrated by the failure of the Oslo Accords of 1993/1994.

JOHN DUGARD

Contents

Acknowledgments

Cover photo © Anne Paq/Activestills.org. The Wall in Abu Dis, 2005.

Maps courtesy of the Palestinian Academic Society for the Study of International Affairs (PASSIA).

Jean Allain, 'Orientalism and International Law: the Middle East as Underclass of the International Legal Order' originally published in (2004) 17 Leiden Journal of International Law 391–404 and reprinted with the permission of the Leiden Journal of International Law.

Michael Akehurst, 'The Arab-Israeli Conflict in International law' originally published in (1973) 5 New Zealand Universities Law Review 231–249 and reprinted with the permission of Thomson Brookers and the editorial board of the New Zealand Universities Law Review.

John B Quigley, 'Displaced Palestinians and a Right of Return'. First printed in Volume 39 of the Harvard International Law Journal. Copyright © 1998 The President and Fellows of Harvard College and the Harvard International Law Journal.

Iain Scobbie, 'The Responsibility of Great Britain in Respect of the Creation of the Palestine Refugee Question' originally published in (2003–4) 11 Yearbook of Islamic and Middle Eastern Law 39-58 and reprinted with the permission of Brill.

Victor Kattan, 'The Nationality of Denationalized Palestinians' originally published in (2005) 74 Nordic Journal of International Law 67–102 and reprinted with the permission of Brill.

Michael Lynk, 'The Right to Compensation in International Law and the Displaced Palestinians' originally published in (2003) 21 Refuge 96–113 and reprinted with the permission of Refuge.

Lex Takkenberg, 'The protection of Palestinian Refugees in the Territories Occupied by Israel' originally published in (1991) 3 International Journal of Refugee Law 414–34 and reprinted with the permission of Oxford University Press.

Martha Roadstrum Moffett, 'Perpetual Emergency: A Legal Analysis of

Israel's Use of Defence (Emergency) Regulations, 1945, in the Occupied Territories' originally published in [1989] Al Haq and reprinted with the permission of Al Haq.

Antonio Cassese, 'Legal Considerations on the International Status of Jerusalem' originally published in (1986) 3 Palestine Yearbook of International Law 13–39 and reprinted with the permission of Brill.

Ardi Imseis, 'Facts on the Ground: An Examination of Israeli Municipal Policy in East Jerusalem' originally published in (2000) 15 American University International Law Review 1039–69 and reprinted with the permission of The American University International Law Review.

John McHugo, 'Resolution 242: A Legal Reappraisal of the Right-Wing Israeli Interpretation of the Withdrawal phrase with Reference to the conflict between Israel and the Palestinians' originally published in (2002) 51 International & Comparative Law Quarterly 851–82 and reprinted with the permission of the International and Comparative Law Quarterly.

Adam Roberts, 'The Palestinians, the Uprising and International Law' originally published in (1989) 2 Journal of Refugee Studies 26–39 and reprinted with the permission of Oxford University Press.

Jamal L El-Hindi, 'The West Bank Aquifer and Conventions Regarding Laws of Belligerent Occupation' originally published in (1989–90) 11 Michigan Journal of International Law 1400–23 and reprinted with the permission of the Michigan Journal of International Law.

Samira Shara, 'On the Road to Apartheid: The Bypass Road Network in the West Bank' originally published in (1997) 29 Columbia Human Rights Law Review 221 and reprinted with the permission of the Columbia Human Rights Law Review.

Ardi Imseis, 'On the Fourth Geneva Convention and the Occupied Palestinian First printed in Volume 44 of the Harvard International Law Journal. Copyright © 2003 The President and Fellows of Harvard College and the Harvard International Law Journal.

Orna Ben Naftali, Aeyal M Gross and Keren Michaeli, 'Illegal Occupation: Framing the Occupied Palestinian Territory' © 2005 by the Regents of the University of California. Reprinted from Berkeley Journal of International Law Vol 23 Bo 3 pp 551–614, by permission of the Regents of the University of California.

Iain Scobbie, 'An Intimate Disengagement: Israel's withdrawal from Gaza, the Law of Occupation and of Self-Determination' originally published in (2004–5) 11 Yearbook of Islamic and Middle Eastern Law 3–41 and reprinted with the permission of Brill.

Francis Boyle, 'The Creation of the State of Palestine' originally published in (1990) 1 European Journal of International Law 301–6 and reprinted with the permission of the European Journal of International Law.

James Crawford, 'The Creation of the State of Palestine: Too much too soon?' originally published in (1990) 1 European Journal of International Law 307–13 and reprinted with the permission of the European Journal of International Law.

Roger O'Keefe, 'Legal Consequences of the Construction of a Wall in the Occupied Palestinian Territory: A Commentary' originally published in (2004) 37 Revue Belge de Droit International 92–149 and reprinted with the permission of Revue Belge de Droit International.

Pieter HF Bekker, 'The World Court's Ruling Regarding Israel's West Bank Barrier and the Primacy of International Law: An Insider's Perspective' originally published in (2005) 38 Cornell International Law Journal 553–68 and reprinted with the permission of the Cornell Journal of International Law.

Aeyal M Gross, 'The Construction of a Wall between The Hague and Jerusalem: The Enforcement and Limits of Humanitarian Law and the Structure of Occupation' originally published in (2006) Leiden Journal of International Law 1–48 and reprinted with the permission of the Leiden Journal of International Law.

Victor Kattan, 'The Legality of the West Bank Wall: Israel's High Court of Justice v The International Court of Justice' originally published in (2007) 40 Vanderbilt Journal of Transnational Law 1425–1521 (© 2007) and reprinted with the permission of the Vanderbilt Journal of Transnational Law.

Omar M Dajani, 'The Role of International Law in Palestinian–Israeli Peace Talks' originally published in (2007) 32 Yale Journal of International Law 189–252 and reprinted with the permission of the Yale Journal of International Law.

List of Contributors

MICHAEL AKEHURST spent most of his career in the Department of Law at Keele University. He studied law at Emmanuel College, Cambridge (MA, LLB) and was a Docteur de L'Université de Paris. He was awarded the Diploma of the Hague Academy of International Law in 1965 and spent his early career with the United Nations Relief and Works Agency for Palestine Refugees in the Near East (UNRWA) in Beirut. He was a member of the Editorial Committee of the *British Yearbook of International Law*, where he published most of his work. He was the author of *A Modern Introduction to International* Law (now *Akehurst's Modern Introduction to International Law*, by Peter Malanczuk), which has appeared in seven editions (1970–97) and is one of the most successful student texts ever published. In the foreword to a *Gedenkschrift* published in his memory he was described as 'one of the most gifted international lawyers of his generation.' He died in Crewe on 4 October 1989, at the age of 49.

JEAN ALLAIN is Senior Lecturer in Public International Law at Queen's University of Belfast and the co-editor of the *Irish Yearbook of International Law*. He previously taught at the American University in Cairo, where he wrote *International Law in the Middle East: Closer to Power than Justice* (Ashgate, Aldershot, 2004), which considers, inter alia, the Palestinian refugee question and the establishment of the State of Israel. Dr Allain's 2002 public lectures at the Ibrahim Abu-Lughod Institute of International Studies, Birzeit University, were published by the Institute as a booklet entitled: *On Achieving Palestinian Statehood: Concepts, Ends and Means from the Perspective of International Law*; as was a 2005 Strategic Paper entitled: *Beyond the Armed Struggle: the Relationship of International Law and International Organizations to the Palestinian Cause*. He received his doctorate from the Graduate Institute of International Studies, University of Geneva.

ORNA BEN-NAFTALI holds a law degree from Tel-Aviv University Law Faculty and advanced degrees from Harvard University and the Fletcher School of Law and Diplomacy. She served at the Department of Peacekeeping Operations/UN, and currently heads the International Law Division at the Law School, the College of Management Academic Studies, Israel. She is member of the executive board of B'tselem: The Israeli Information Center for Human Rights in the Occupied Territories; and of the editorial board of the *European Journal of International Law*. She has published numerous scholarly articles on the Israel–Palestine conflict in English and Hebrew.

PIETER BEKKER is a Partner in the International Dispute Resolution Group at McDermott Will & Emery LLP in New York. His practice focuses on public international law advice and international arbitration. He is a former staff lawyer in the Registry of the International Court of Justice (ICJ) and serves on the Executive Council of the American Society of International Law. He chairs the Committee on Intergovernmental Settlement of Disputes within the American Branch of the International Law Association. Dr Bekker, who holds Dutch citizenship, has basic and doctoral degrees in International Law from Leiden University (The Netherlands) and a Masters degree from Harvard Law School. The author of three books and over 100 articles in leading journals, he is an Adjunct Professor at Fordham University School of Law in New York. Dr Bekker served as Senior Counsel to Palestine in the ICJ advisory proceeding concerning *Legal Consequences of the Construction of a Wall in the Occupied Palestinian Territories.*

FRANCIS BOYLE is a Professor of International Law at the University of Illinois, College of Law. He received a JD degree *magna cum laude* in political science from Harvard University. Before moving to Illinois he was a teaching fellow at Harvard and an associate at its Center for International Affairs. He also practised tax and international tax with Bingham, Dana & Gould in Boston. Professor Boyle served as Legal Advisor to the Palestine Liberation Organization on the Palestinian Declaration of Independence and the Creation of the State of Palestine from 1987 to 1989, including the accession by Palestine to the Geneva Conventions and Protocols. He then served as Legal Advisor to the Palestinian Delegation to the Middle East Peace Negotiations from 1991 to 1993. He continues to serve as sometime Legal Advisor to the Provisional Government for the State of Palestine on various issues, including its prospective membership in the United Nations Organization. He is the author of *Palestine, Palestinians and International Law* (Clarity Press, Atlanta, 2003), an Arabic language version of which was published by Sharouk International in 2004.

ANTONIO CASSESE is a Professor of International Law at the University of Florence, Italy, previously Professor of International Law at the University of Pisa and the European University Institute. He was the first President of the International Criminal Tribunal for the former Yugoslavia from 1993 to 1997. In 2004 he was appointed by the UN Secretary-General to be the Chairman of an International Commission of Inquiry that visited Darfur in the Sudan. He is a member of the Italian delegation to the UN Commission on Human Rights, the Council of Europe Steering Committee on Human Rights, and the Council of Europe Committee Against Torture. He is the co-founder and co-editor of the *European Journal of International*

Law, and the Founder and Editor-in-Chief of the *Journal of International Criminal Justice*, as well as the author of numerous books and articles on international human rights law, humanitarian law, and international criminal law.

JAMES CRAWFORD SC, FBA, LLD is Whewell Professor of International Law, Director of the Lauterpacht Centre for International Law and a Fellow of Jesus College, Cambridge. He was a member of the United Nations International Law Commission from 1992 to 2001 and Special Rapporteur on State Responsibility (1997–2001). In addition to scholarly work on statehood, self-determination, collective rights and international responsibility, he has appeared frequently before the International Court of Justice and before other international tribunals, and is actively engaged as expert, counsel and arbitrator in investment arbitration, including many cases under the NAFTA. He appeared before the ICJ as counsel to Palestine in the 2004 advisory opinion on the *Legal Consequences of the Construction of a wall in the Occupied Palestinian Territory*.

OMAR DAJANI is a Visiting Professor of Law at the University of California, Hastings College of the Law, and an Associate Professor at the University of the Pacific, McGeorge School of Law, where he has taught since 2004. Previously, he was based in the occupied Palestinian territories, where he served, first, as legal adviser to the Palestinian team in peace talks with Israel and, subsequently, on the peace team of United Nations Special Envoy Terje Roed-Larsen. Prior to working in the Middle East, he clerked for Judge Dorothy Nelson on the US Court of Appeals for the Ninth Circuit and was a litigation associate at the Washington office of Sidley & Austin. He received his BA in History and American Culture from Northwestern University and his JD from Yale Law School. He is a member of the State Bar of California, the Council on Foreign Relations, the International Institute of Strategic Studies and the 21st Century Trust.

JOHN DUGARD SC is an honorary professor of law at the University of Leiden and the Centre for Human Rights of the University of Pretoria. He is a graduate of the University of Stellenbosh (BA, LLB) and the University of Cambridge (LLB, LLD). He is a member of the International Law Commission (1999–present) and was Special Rapporteur to the Commission on the subject of diplomatic protection from 1999 to 2006. He has sat as an ad hoc judge on the International Court of Justice. Since 2001 he has served as Special Rapporteur to the UN Human Rights Council (previously Commission on Human Rights) on the human rights situation in the Occupied Palestinian Territory.

JAMAL EL-HINDI is a senior official in the Financial Crimes Enforcement Network (FinCEN) of the US Department of the Treasury, where he oversees the development, implementation and enforcement of US anti-money laundering and counter-terrorism finance regulations. Before joining Treasury in December 2000, Mr El-Hindi was an associate at Patton Boggs LLP in Washington, DC, where his legal practice focused on US regulation of international business transactions, representation of foreign sovereigns and international banking litigation. He is a past president and current advisory board member of the Washington Foreign Law Society. He received his JD and a master's degree in Modern Middle Eastern & North African Studies from the University of Michigan. He also holds a Diploma in International Relations from the London School of Economics & Political Science, and an undergraduate degree in Journalism from the University of North Carolina. His additional work on water issues with respect to Israel and Palestine includes the article 'Compensation as Part of Equitable Utilization in the Israel–Palestinian Water Context' (2000) 22 Arab Studies Quarterly 113.

AEYAL GROSS teaches at the Tel-Aviv University Faculty of Law. He received his LLB from Tel-Aviv University and his SJD from Harvard Law School. He was awarded the Diploma in Human Rights by the European University Institute and, in 1995, was an intern with the European Commission on Human Rights. Dr Gross served on the board of the Association for Civil Rights in Israel. He was also a board member at the Concord Center for the Interplay between International Norms and Israeli Law in the College of Management, and at the Academic Committee of the Minerva Center for Human Rights at Tel-Aviv University. He has taught at Columbia University's School of International and Public Affairs and was a fellow at the Stellenbosch Institute for Advanced Studies in South Africa. He is currently a visiting fellow with the Institute for Advanced Legal Studies, and is teaching at SOAS, both at the University of London.

ARDI IMSEIS LLM (Columbia), LLB (Dalhousie), BA Hons (Toronto) of Osgoode Hall, Barrister-at-Law, is a Legal Officer with UNRWA, West Bank Field Office, Jerusalem, Occupied Palestinian Territory. Since 2002 he has served with UNRWA as a policy and legal advisor to the Office of the Commissioner-General in the Gaza Strip and the office of the Director of UNRWA Operations in the West Bank. Imseis is also an Assistant Professor of public international law at Birzeit University and his work has been published in numerous law reviews and journals. He is a former Human Rights Fellow and Harlan Fiske Stone Scholar, Columbia University School of Law, and Social Sciences and Humanities Research Council of Canada Doctoral Fellow.

VICTOR KATTAN is a Research Fellow in Public International Law at the British Institute of International and Comparative Law (BIICL) on the project on Human Rights in International Law and Iran. Prior to this he was a Visiting Fellow there. He has an LLB (Hons) from Brunel University, an LLM from Leiden University, and is currently a doctoral candidate at the School of Oriental and African Studies, University of London where he was awarded a scholarship from the Arts and Humanities Research Council to undertake a study on the partition of territory in international law. He has been an Editor of the *Yearbook of Islamic and Middle Eastern Law* with HH Eugene Cotran and Professor Martin Lau since 2005 and has published articles in international law journals in the United States and Europe. In 2003–4, he worked in the Occupied Palestinian Territories as UN Development Programme TOKTEN consultant to the BADIL Resource Centre for Palestinian Residency and Refugee Rights. He has also worked on projects for BADIL as an external consultant.

MICHAEL LYNK is Associate Professor at the Faculty of Law, The University of Western Ontario, London, Ontario, where he teaches labour, human rights and constitutional and administrative law. He has also taught labour law at the University of Ottawa and Victoria University of Wellington (New Zealand). Professor Lynk is a graduate of Dalhousie University (LLB) and Queens University (LLM) Before becoming an academic, he practised labour law in Ottawa and Toronto for a decade. He is a senior co-editor of the *Labour Law Casebook* (7th edn), which is the national casebook used in law schools across the country. Professor Lynk is also an editor of the *Canadian Labour and Employment Law Journal*. In addition to his labour law activities, he has worked with UNRWA in the West Bank, and has written law review articles and media commentary on political and legal developments in that region.

JOHN McHUGO is an English solicitor and a consultant to Trowers & Hamlins where he was head of public international law until he retired in early 2007. He was listed as Counsel for Bahrain at the ICJ in 1994 during the jurisdiction and admissibility proceedings in the case concerning Maritime Jurisdiction and Territorial Questions between Qatar and Bahrain. During 2001–2 he was an honorary visiting fellow at the Scottish Centre for International Law at Edinburgh University. He studied Arabic at Oxford University and the American University in Cairo and is a specialist on legal documentation in Arabic.

KEREN MICHAELI is a DPhil candidate at St Antony's College, the University of Oxford. She is a graduate of Georgetown University (LLM) and the Law School, the College of Management Academic Studies, Israel

(LLB). She is currently a tutor in public international law, international human rights law and the law of war at the University of Oxford.

MARTHA ROADSTRUM MOFFETT received her BA from Smith College in the field of political science and a law degree from Boston University School of Law. She served as a trial lawyer with the United States Department of Justice in Washington, DC, where she worked in the Antitrust Division and as a Special Assistant United States Attorney prosecuting federal crimes. After three years, she went into private practice with the Washington, DC law firm of Hogan & Hartson. While her husband was assigned to the Middle East for *The Christian Science Monitor*, based in Jerusalem, she worked for Al Haq, where she wrote an article on the British Defence Emergency Regulations of 1945, as reproduced in this book. Subsequently, she became Jerusalem staff attorney for the New York-based Lawyers Committee for Human Rights. In 1994 she left her law work to become a Christian Science Practitioner and Lecturer.

ROGER O'KEEFE, BA, LLB (Hons) (Sydney), LLM, PhD (Cantab), is University Lecturer in Law and Deputy Director of the Lauterpacht Centre for International Law at the University of Cambridge, as well as Fellow and College Lecturer in Law at Magdalene College, Cambridge. He has published articles in numerous international law journals and is a member of the Conseil scientifique of the *Revue Belge de Droit International*. In 2003 he was a member of an expert panel convened in Brussels by the European Coordinating Committee of NGOs on the Question of Palestine to provide informal advice on the legal means at the disposal of the European Union and its Member States to ensure respect by Israel of its international commitments. He was a speaker at the conference *Palestine and International Law*, hosted in 2005 by the School of Oriental and African Studies, University of London.

JOHN QUIGLEY is President's Club Professor in Law at the Ohio State University in Columbus, Ohio USA. Prior to joining the Ohio State Faculty in 1969, he was a research scholar at Moscow State University and a research associate in comparative law at Harvard Law School, from which he holds an LLB degree. He has published numerous scholarly articles on the Arab–Israeli conflict as well as on the law of State responsibility, war and peace, the United Nations and human rights. His books in international law include *The Case for Palestine: An International Law Perspective* (Duke University Press, Durham, 2005) and *The Genocide Convention: An International Law Analysis* (Ashgate, Aldershot, 2006).

SIR ADAM ROBERTS was Montague Burton Professor of International Relations at Oxford University and a Fellow of Balliol College, from 1986 to 2007. He is a Fellow of the British Academy. He did a BA degree in History at Oxford, and was a Lecturer in International Relations at LSE from 1968 to 1981 before returning to Oxford. He has a long-standing interest in the study of resistance movements (both non-violent and violent) in response to external control. His books include (edited with Benedict Kingsbury), *United Nations, Divided World: The UN's Roles in International Relations* (2nd edn, OUP, Oxford, 1993) and (edited with Richard Guelff), *Documents on the Laws of War* (3rd edn, OUP, Oxford, 2000). He has written extensively on Middle East problems. He co-authored a report, *Academic Freedom under Israeli Military Occupation*, International Commission of Jurists, London and Geneva, 1984 and is the author of 'Prolonged Military Occupation: The Israeli-occupied Territories Since 1967'(1990) 84 American Journal of International Law 44–103.

IAIN SCOBBIE is the Sir Joseph Hotung Research Professor in Law, Human Rights and Peace Building in the Middle East at the School of Oriental and African Studies, University of London. Professor Scobbie studied at the Universities of Edinburgh and Cambridge, and at the Australian National University. He is a member of the Executive Board of the European Society of International Law, and of its International Legal Theory interest group; of the Governing Board of the Scottish Centre for War Studies, which is based in the University of Glasgow; of the Lieber Society on the Law of Armed Conflict; and of the International Advisory Council of Diakonia's International Humanitarian Law Programme, which is based in Jerusalem. He is also a member of the Scientific Advisory Board of the *European Journal of International Law*. He has published widely on the question of Palestine in international law journals.

SAMIRA SHAH is a Senior Attorney in the litigation department at Cravath, Swaine & Moore LLP in New York. She received her AB in Near Eastern Languages and Civilizations (1992) and her MA in Middle Eastern Studies (1993) from the University of Chicago. She was awarded a Fulbright grant to study in Syria at *L'Institut Français d'Etudes Arabes de Damas* (1994–5). While in Syria, she interned at the United Nations High Commission for Refugees (1995). She earned her JD from Columbia University School of Law in New York (1998), where she was a Harlan Fiske Stone Scholar. While in law school, she was awarded a Human Rights Internship Grant during the summer of 1996 to intern at Al-Haq in Ramallah. At Al-Haq, she studied the impact of the bypass road network on the West Bank and its legality under international law. After receiving her law degree, she clerked for the Honorable William H Walls in the United States District Court for the District of New Jersey (1998–9) before working as an associate at Cravath, Swaine & Moore LLP.

LEX TAKKENBERG is General Counsel of UNRWA in Jerusalem. He earned degrees in Dutch law (1980 and 1985) and international law (1983) from the University of Amsterdam. In 1997, he obtained a doctorate in international law from the Katholic University of Nijmegen. His doctoral dissertation, *The Status of Palestinian Refugees in International Law,* was published in English (1998) and Arabic (2003) and is recognized as the leading text on the subject. Lex joined UNRWA in 1989 as a Refugee Affairs Officer in Gaza. He then served in Gaza as Deputy, Field Relief & Social Services Officer (1990–2) and in Syria as Chief, Relief and Social Service Programme (1993–4). He returned to Gaza as Chief, Field Relief and Social Services Programme (1992–7) and Deputy Director of UNRWA Operations (1997–2000). He subsequently held the positions of Deputy Director of UNRWA Affairs (2000–4) and Director of UNRWA Affairs (2004–6) in Syria.

Introduction

Sixty years since the creation of the State of Israel and the demise of the British Mandate of Palestine, many of the underlying legal issues of controversy that have affected the ensuing Arab–Israeli conflict have withstood the passage of time: the Palestinian refugee question, the denial of Palestinian self-determination and the legal status of Jerusalem. Since 1967, Israel's occupation has raised additional questions of international law due to its prolonged nature and the establishment of Israeli settlements in those territories. Israel's construction of a wall around those settlements, which has all the hallmarks of an act of de facto annexation, was found to be contrary to international law by the International Court of Justice (ICJ) in its 9 July 2004 advisory opinion.[1] And yet despite these intricate legal issues, almost all attempts that have been made towards an Arab–Israeli accommodation have sidelined these substantive legal questions or have left them to final-status negotiations which at the time of writing have not yet commenced. Although Israel and the Palestinians recently agreed at Annapolis 'to immediately launch good-faith bilateral negotiations in order to conclude a peace treaty, resolving all outstanding issues, including all core issues without exception, as specified in previous agreements', there was no explicit mention of international law in the joint statement they released to the press.[2] As the ICJ concluded in its advisory opinion:

> The Court considers that it has a duty to draw to the attention of the General Assembly, to which the present Opinion is addressed, to the need for these efforts to be encouraged with a view to achieving as soon as possible, *on the basis of international law*, a negotiated solution to the outstanding problems and the establishment of a Palestine State, existing side by side with Israel and its other neighbours, with peace and security for all in the region (emphasis added).[3]

Of course the parties are free to negotiate a solution to their outstanding problems and international law will not always provide an answer. But it

---

[1] International Court of Justice, *Legal Consequences of the Construction of a Wall in the Occupied Palestinian Territory* (2004) 43 International Legal Materials 1009–56, para 121 ('The Court considers that the construction of the wall and its associated régime create a "fait accompli" on the ground that could well become permanent, in which case, and notwithstanding the formal characterization of the wall by Israel, it would be tantamount to *de facto* annexation.').

[2] See Annapolis agreement: full text, *The Guardian* (27 Nov 2007), available online at <http://www.guardian.co.uk/israel/Story/0,,2217946,00.html> (last accessed 6 Dec 2007).

[3] *Wall* advisory opinion (n 1) 1054, para 162.

can provide a general framework through which an Arab–Israeli peace can be negotiated. As Omar Dajani has argued, recourse can be made to international law to buttress unpopular decisions reached by political leaders in the interests of peace so as to insulate themselves from the dissatisfaction of their constituents.[4] In other words, concessions can be justified by recourse to international law. For example, in the context of the Arab–Israeli conflict, the government of Israel could always advance the argument, at least hypothetically, that it was ceasing support for the settlement movement because the settlements are contrary to international law and Israel wants to improve its image and standing in the world.[5]

Due to the sheer number of articles published on the Arab–Israeli conflict over the years, it was thought necessary to publish a select number on a range of topical issues, to aid the reader in coming to terms with this complex and difficult subject. With the enormous growth in online databases, it is becoming increasingly difficult to locate the very best scholarship on the Palestine question which this collection of essays attempts to do. Some of the articles reproduced in this book have been published recently and others in the distant past. The article by Michael Akehurst[6] on the origins of the conflict, though dated, remains a classic which is still cited in some of the more recent literature. It is also not available on any electronic database. As the origins of the conflict have not changed so much in the last six decades it was thought appropriate to include it. Similarly, the article by Antonio Cassese on the status of Jerusalem is not currently available on any electronic database, and though it was published in 1986 is still very relevant.[7] To accompany his article, Ardi Imseis provides a more recent perspective on the status of Jerusalem today[8] and how the eastern side of that city (that is, the Arab side) is being neglected and colonized by Jewish settlements.[9] The article by Martha Roadstrum Moffett on Israel's use of the Defence (Emergency) Regulations from 1945 in the occupied territories is possibly the only article that has ever been published on this topic and is

---

[4] OM Dajani, 'Shadow or Shade? The Roles of International Law in Palestinian–Israeli Peace Talks' (2007) 32 Yale Journal of International Law 61–124.

[5] Alas, days after the Annapolis Peace Conference Israel's Housing Ministry announced that it has plans to build 307 new homes in the settlement of Har Homa in East Jerusalem. See R McCarthy, 'Israel to build in East Jerusalem' *The Guardian* (5 Dec 2007).

[6] M Akehurst, 'The Arab–Israeli Conflict in International law' (1973) 5 New Zealand Universities Law Review 231–49.

[7] A Cassese, 'Legal Considerations on the International Status of Jerusalem' (1986) 3 Palestine Yearbook of International Law 13–39.

[8] For a fascinating book on Israeli policy towards East Jerusalem, see A Cheshin, B Hutman and A Melamed, *Separate and Unequal: The Inside Story of Israeli Rule in East Jerusalem* (Harvard University Press, Cambridge MA, 1999).

[9] See A Imseis, 'Facts on the Ground: An Examination of Israeli Municipal Policy in East Jerusalem' (2000) 15 American University International Law Review 1039–69.

essential reading.[10] In addition, we have included a number of articles on the Palestinian refugee question which have been published in the last decade or so to take into account the impact of recent Israeli historiography concerning the causes and consequences of the Palestinian exodus in 1948.[11] The Israeli occupation is also covered with articles covering the period from the first Palestinian *intifada* (uprising) in 1987[12] to the onset of Al-Aqsa *intifada* after the failed negotiations at Camp David in the summer of 2000 and Israel's decision to redeploy its troops from Gaza in 2005.[13] In connection with this, we have included an article by three Israeli international lawyers, who have characterized Israel's decades' long occupation of the West Bank and Gaza as illegal.[14] The question of Palestinian statehood, although widely discussed, is still not a reality despite the 'vision' of US President George W Bush in June 2002. Israel's decision to construct a wall around the West Bank settlements makes any prospect of a viable and contiguous Palestinian State even more remote, despite efforts to rekindle the peace process. Therefore articles on the wall and Palestinian statehood have been included as well as Omar Dajani's article on the failed peace talks between Israelis and Palestinians that began in Oslo in the early 1990s, and which he participated in, in the late 1990s.[15]

Victor Kattan

[10] M Roadstrum Moffett, 'Perpetual Emergency: A Legal Analysis of Israel's Use of the British Defence (Emergency) Regulations, 1945, in the Occupied Territories' (1989) Al Haq Pamphlet.

[11] See, eg, JB Quigley, 'Displaced Palestinians and a Right of Return' (1998) 39 Harvard International Law Journal 171–229; I Scobbie, 'The Responsibility of Great Britain in Respect of the Creation of the Palestine Refugee Question' (2003–4) 11 Yearbook of Islamic and Middle Eastern Law 39–58; and V Kattan, 'The Nationality of Denationalized Palestinians' (2005) 74 Nordic Journal of International Law 67–102.

[12] A Roberts, 'The Palestinians, the Uprising and International Law' (1989) 2 Journal of Refugee Studies 26–39.

[13] See I Scobbie, 'An Intimate Disengagement: Israel's withdrawal from Gaza, the Law of Occupation and of Self-Determination' (2004–5) 11 Yearbook of Islamic and Middle Eastern Law 3–41.

[14] See O Ben Naftali, AM Gross, and K Michaeli, 'Illegal Occupation: Framing the Occupied Palestinian Territory' (2005) 23 Berkeley Journal of International Law 551–614.

[15] See Dajani (n 4) and F Boyle, 'The Creation of the State of Palestine' (1990) 1 European Journal of International Law 301–6; J Crawford, 'The Creation of the State of Palestine: Too much too soon?' (1990) 1 European Journal of International Law 307–13; OM Dajani, 'Stalled between Seasons: the International Legal Status of Palestine during the Interim Period' (1997) 26 Denver Journal of International Law & Policy 27–92; R O'Keefe, 'Legal Consequences of the Construction of a Wall in the Occupied Palestinian Territory: A Commentary' (2004) 37 Revue Belge De Droit International 92–149; PHF Bekker, 'The World Court's Ruling Regarding Israel's West Bank Barrier and the Primacy of International Law: An Insider's Perspective' (2005) 38 Cornell International law Journal 553–68; AM Gross, 'The Construction of a Wall between The Hague and Jerusalem: The Enforcement and Limits of Humanitarian Law and the Structure of Occupation' (2006) 19 Leiden Journal of International Law 393–440; and V Kattan, 'The Legality of the West Bank Wall: Israel's High Court of Justice v The International Court of Justice' (2007) 40 Vanderbilt Journal of Transnational Law 1425–1521.

Palestine and International Law: An Historical Overview

Victor Kattan

This chapter will provide the reader with a sketch of the major international documents that are pertinent to the conflict. As many of these issues will be dealt with in more depth in the numerous articles republished throughout this book, only a brief recap of some intricate factual and legal issues will be provided in the following historical overview.

Although the origins of political Zionism can be traced to developments in 19th-century Europe, the first documents of any international legal significance appertaining to the century-long conflict between the Arabs and the Zionists was the 'Hussein-McMahon correspondence', concerning Arab support for the Allied cause in their struggle against Austria-Hungary, Germany and the Ottoman Empire.[1]

I. THE HUSSEIN–McMAHON CORRESPONDENCE

During the First World War (1914–1918), Great Britain entered into an exchange of correspondence with the Sherif of Mecca, Hussein Ibn Ali, over his support for the allied cause in the struggle against the Ottoman Empire. In the correspondence, the Sherif and Sir Henry McMahon, the British High Commissioner in Cairo, exchanged their views on the future disposition of Ottoman territory in the event of an allied victory. In a letter from McMahon, which was to cause the British Government much embarrassment in later years, he pledged that his government was 'prepared to recognise and support the independence of the Arabs in all the regions within limits demanded by the Sherif of Mecca' with the exception of the two districts of Mersina and Alexandretta (situated in modern-day Turkey) and portions of the Levant (that is Lebanon and Syria) lying to the west of the districts of Damascus, Homs, Hama and Aleppo (which are situated today in Syria, the territories lying to the west of those cities being in Lebanon).[2] The Sherif had demanded independence in those territories which today comprise Israel/Palestine, Iraq, Jordan, Saudi Arabia and Syria.

---

[1] See Correspondence between Sir Henry McMahon, GCMG, GCVO, KCIE, CSI, His Majesty's High Commissioner in Cairo and the Sherif of Mecca, 5957 Command Paper (1939) 3–18, 27 Great Britain House of Commons, Parliamentary Publications, Sessional Papers 1938–9, vol 27.

[2] ibid, letter of 24 Oct 1915.

As was clear from the passage quoted above from McMahon, Palestine was not explicitly excluded from his pledge. The grammatical and ordinary sense of the words he used was clear and he used no terminology to suggest that Britain had a special interest in Palestine. As McMahon explained to Sir Edward Grey, the British Foreign Secretary:

> 4. I have been definite in stating that Great Britain will recognise the principle of Arab independence in purely Arab territory, this being the main point of which agreement depends, but have been equally definite in excluding Mersina, Alexandretta and those districts *on the northern coast of Syria*, which cannot be said to be purely Arab, and where I understand that French interests have been recognised (emphasis added).[3]

At no point in the 20th century was Palestine situated 'on the northern coast of Syria'. The only reasonable conclusion one can deduce from the correspondence is that McMahon did not intend to exclude Palestine from his pledge and that it was not excluded from the territory promised to the Sherif in which he was to create his 'Arab Caliphate of Islam'.

The question as to whether the correspondence between McMahon and Hussein was legally binding is an interesting one and has not been explored much in legal literature.[4] It is suffice to say at this point that agreements between Britain and Arab sheikhs had been referred to as treaties before.[5] In fact, in one letter from McMahon to Hussein he expressly referred to 'our existing treaties with Arab chiefs' and of course an exchange of notes

---

[3] See the telegram from Sir Henry McMahon to Sir Edward Grey, informing the latter about his pledge to Hussein, 26 Oct 1915, Cairo, File No 163832, FO 371/2486.

[4] For a detailed analysis of the correspondence see V Kattan, *From Coexistence to Conquest: International Law and the Origins of the Arab–Israeli Conflict 1891–1949* (Pluto Press, London, forthcoming 2009).

[5] For examples of treaties concluded by Britain with Ibn Saud of Arabia and the Idrisi Sayyid of Sabya concluded in the same year as McMahon was in negotiations with the Sherif see JC Hurewitz (ed), *Diplomacy in the Near East: A Documentary Record, Volume II* (D Van Nostrand Co, Princeton, 1956) 12–13 and 17–18. See also, C Parry (ed), (1915–1916) 221 The Consolidated Treaty Series 66–7, for the treaty between Great Britain and the Idrisi. For examples of treaties with the Trucial Sheikhdoms, see *Case Concerning Maritime Delimitation and Territorial Questions Between Qatar and Bahrain, (Qatar v Bahrain), (Merits),* 16 Mar 2001 [2001] ICJ Rep, paras 38–40. See also, *Treaties, Agreements, and Engagements, Between the Honorable East India Company and the Native Princes, Chiefs and States, in Western India: The Red Sea; the Persian Gulf; etc. Also Between Her Britannic Majesty's Government, and Persia, Portugal, and Turkey, compiled under instructions from the Government of Bombay, by R. Hughes Thomas, Uncovenanted Assistant to the Chief Secretary, with Notes and Memoranda by the Compiler* (Education Society's Press, Bombay, 1851). For even more examples, see See CU Aitchison, BCS, *A Collection of Treaties, Engagements and Sanads Relating to India and Neighbouring Countries, Vol. XI Containing the Treaties, & c., Relating to Aden and the South Western Coast of Arabia, the Arab Principalities in the Persian Gulf, Muscat (Oman), Baluchistan and the North-West Frontier Province* (Manager of Publications, Delhi, 1933).

may amount to a treaty.[6] In all the debates which took place over the legal effects of correspondence in later years, Britain never advanced the argument that it was not binding.[7] Rather, the British Government said that it did not intend to include Palestine in the Arab State they pledged to award the Sherif for his assistance in defeating the Turks.[8]

II. THE SYKES–PICOT AGREEMENT

After the exchange of correspondence with the Sherif, Britain concluded another secret treaty on 16 May 1916 with the French Government. In this agreement Britain and France agreed to carve up Turkey's former possessions in the Middle East into respective spheres of European influence, without consulting the peoples of those territories.

What became known as the Sykes–Picot agreement, named after Sir Mark Sykes, a distinguished British orientalist and M Charles François Georges-Picot, formerly French Consul in Beirut, envisaged giving the French control of parts of southern Turkey, Kurdistan, Syria, Lebanon and a part of what was then referred to as Mesopotamia (ie Iraq); the British control of the remainder of Iraq, including Basra and Baghdad; the Italians control of southern Turkey; and the Russians control of the Caucasus and Armenia.[9] Substantial parts of what is known today as Syria, Jordan and the remainder of Iraq were to become an 'independent Arab State' or a 'confederation of States', under the suzerainty of an Arab chief whereby Britain and France would supply 'advisers or foreign functionaries' with a view to administering the territory. An international administration was to

---

[6] See Permanent Court of International Justice, Advisory Opinion, *Customs Régime between Germany and Austria*, 5 Sept 1931, Series A/B, 47. See also, *Case Concerning the Temple of Preah Vihear (Cambodia v Thailand) (Preliminary Objections)*, judgment of 26 May 1961, [1961] ICJ Rep 31.

[7] Sir Michael McDonnell, who served as Chief Justice in the Supreme Court of Palestine from 1927 to 1937, argued that in his opinion it was sufficiently clear from reading the Hussein–McMahon correspondence that Palestine was to be included in the Arab State. See statement by Sir Michael McDonnell on certain legal points arising out of the Lord Chancellor's statement at the second meeting of the committee on 24 February in *Report of a Committee Set Up to Consider Certain Correspondence between Sir Henry McMahon and the Sharif of Mecca in 1915 and 1916*, Presented by the Secretary of State for the Colonies to Parliament by Command of His Majesty, Mar 1939, Command Papers, 5974.

[8] See 'Juridical Basis of the Arab Claim to Palestine' (attaches a memorandum discussing the main points on which the Arab legal claim is based, to which answers may be required), 21 Dec 1938, Political Eastern, Palestine and Transjordan (1939), FO 371/23219. However, see Letter to HF Downie, Esq OBE, Colonial Office, 19 Jan 1939, (E6/6/31), FO 371/23219 ('. . . after going into the whole question of the McMahon–Hussein correspondence again, our position in regard to this correspondence seems to me even weaker than it did before').

[9] See The Sykes–Picot Agreement, 16 May 1916, reproduced in J Norton Moore (ed), *The Arab–Israeli Conflict, Volume III: Documents* (Princeton University Press, New Jersey, 1974) 24–8.

be established in Palestine, the form of which was to be decided upon after consultation with Russia, the other allies and the representatives of the Sherif of Mecca.

The Sykes–Picot agreement was exposed by the Bolsheviks after they removed Kerensky from power in the revolution of 7 November 1917 (25 October on the Julian calendar) as evidence of what they saw as Western and Tsarist imperialism.

III. THE BALFOUR DECLARATION

On 2 November 1917, Britain's Foreign Secretary Arthur James Balfour addressed a letter to Lord Rothschild (a British banker and zoologist) in which the British Government viewed:

> . . . with favour the establishment in Palestine of a national home for the Jewish people . . . it being clearly understood that nothing shall be done which may prejudice the civil and religious rights of existing non-Jewish communities in Palestine . . . [10]

Although this declaration was of considerable political importance, legally it merely expressed a promise to a private person as to future British policy in Palestine.[11] Although declarations made by way of unilateral acts can produce legal obligations under international law, this is only so if it is the intention of the State making the declaration that it should become bound according to its terms.[12] Usually, this intention is expressed in clear and precise terms and is addressed to the international community or to another State.[13]

---

[10] A copy of the original Balfour Declaration is photographically reproduced in Moore, ibid 885.

[11] For further reading and analysis, particularly in the light of the incorporation of the Balfour Declaration into the British Mandate of Palestine, see WT Mallison, Jr, 'The Balfour Declaration: An Appraisal in International Law' in I Abu Lughod (ed), *The Transformation of Palestine: Essays on the Origin and Development of the Arab–Israeli Conflict—with a fore-word by Arnold J. Toynbee* (2nd edn, Northwestern University Press, Evanston, 1987) 61–111. It should be said that although there was no legal obligation on the part of Great Britain to create a home for the Jewish people in the declaration itself, the Treaty of Peace signed at Sèvres between the Allied Powers and Turkey on 10 August 1920 did provide in Article 95 that 'the Mandatory will be responsible for putting into effect' the Balfour Declaration. This treaty was, however, never ratified by the Turkish parliament. Turkey renounced all claims to Palestine at the Treaty of Lausanne. See *The Treaties of Peace 1919–1923*, vol II (Carnegie Endowment for International Peace, New York, 1924) 789 (Sèvres) and 959 (Lausanne).

[12] On the legal effects of unilateral declarations made by government officials see *Nuclear Tests Case (Australia v France)*, 20 Dec 1974 [1974] ICJ Rep, paras 43–6.

[13] ibid para 51 (where the ICJ analysed a number of statements made by the French

In this respect, it may be questioned whether Britain gave an undertaking to be bound by the Balfour Declaration in November 1917, especially since His Majesty's Government (HMG) only viewed 'with favour the establishment in Palestine of a national home for the Jewish people', and only agreed to use its 'best endeavours' to achieve this objective. In contrast, when it came to the civil and religious rights of the 'existing non-Jewish communities in Palestine', HMG wanted it to be 'clearly understood that nothing shall be done' which may prejudice their rights. In other words the promise to establish a Jewish home was *conditional* upon safeguarding the rights of the indigenous population of Palestine.

IV. THE COVENANT OF THE LEAGUE OF NATIONS

During the Paris Peace Conference at the end of the First World War a decision was made to create a new international organization called the League of Nations. A Covenant was subsequently drafted.[14] Of particular interest was Article 22 which provided:

To those colonies and territories which as a consequence of the late war have ceased to be under the sovereignty of the States which formerly governed them and which are inhabited by peoples not yet able to stand by themselves under the strenuous conditions of the modern world, there should be applied the principle that the well-being and development of such peoples form a sacred trust of civilisation and that securities for the performance of this trust should be embodied in this Covenant.

The best method of giving practical effect to this principle is that the tutelage of such peoples should be entrusted to advanced nations who by reason of their resources, their experience or their geographical position can best undertake this responsibility, and who are willing to accept it, and that this tutelage should be exercised by them as Mandatories on behalf of the League'.

The character of the mandate must differ according to the stage of development of the people, the geographical situation of the territory, its economic conditions and other similar circumstances.

Certain communities formerly belonging to the Turkish Empire have reached a stage of development where their existence as independent nations can be provisionally recognised subject to the rendering of administrative advice and assistance by a Mandatory until such time as

---

Government to the effect that it would cease atmospheric nuclear testing at its Centre d'experimentations du Pacifique in the territory of French Polynesia, after a complaint submitted to the Court by Australia).

[14] Covenant of the League of Nations (1920) 1 League of Nations Official Journal 3–12.

they are able to stand alone. The wishes of these communities must be a principal consideration in the selection of the mandatory.[15]

In an earlier draft of the first paragraph of Article 22 presented to the Paris Peace Conference, the territories which were to form a 'sacred trust of civilisation' were explicitly mentioned. These included Armenia, Kurdistan, Syria, Mesopotamia, Palestine and Arabia.[16] All of these territories were considered 'A-class' mandates which signified that they were on the verge of independence.[17]

In essence, this 'sacred trust of civilisation' was a device borrowed from Anglo-Saxon common law.[18] Great Britain, as the mandatory power, had undertaken to act 'on behalf of the League' as a fiduciary.[19] Although not entirely analogous to the concept of trusts in English equity, it is evident that the draftsmen of the Covenant were greatly influenced by the trust concept of English and American law.[20] And although the trust was not a tool common to civil law countries, there was nothing original in the concept of a mandate which traced its origins to Roman law.[21] As Sir Arnold McNair commented in his Separate Opinion on the *International Status of South-West Africa*:

The trust has frequently been used *to protect the weak and the dependent, in cases where there is 'great might on the one side and unmight on the other'*, and the English courts have for many centuries pursued a vigorous policy in the administration and enforcement of trusts.[22]

Article 22 explicitly provided that those communities formerly belonging to the Ottoman Empire had reached a stage of development where their exis-

---

[15] ibid 9.

[16] See D Hunter Miller, *The Drafting of the Peace Treaties*, vol II (GP Putnam's Sons, New York, 1928) 552.

[17] See MF Lindley, *The Acquisition and Government of Backward Territory, Being a Treatise on the Law and Practice of Colonial Expansion* (Longmans, Green & Co, London, 1921) 257.

[18] See D Campbell Lee, *The Mandate for Mesopotamia and the Principle of Trusteeship in English Law* (St Clements Press, London, 1921).

[19] As Judge MM Bustamante opined in his Separate Opinion concerning the preliminary objections in the *South-West Africa* cases: 'In an objective sense the achievement of the purposes of the Mandate is entrusted, *as a fiduciary attribution of responsibility*, to an advanced nation in the capacity of Mandatory' (emphasis added). See *South-West Africa cases (Ethiopia v Liberia; Liberia v South Africa) (Preliminary Objections)*, 21 Dec 1962 [1962] ICJ Rep 319.

[20] See *International Status of South-West Africa (Advisory Opinion)*, 11 July 1950, Separate Opinion by Sir Arnold McNair [1950] ICJ Rep 148.

[21] For a brief comment on the concept of trusts and mandates see JL Brierly, 'Trusts and Mandates' (1929) 10 British Yearbook of International Law 217–19.

[22] (n 20) 149 (emphasis added).

tence as independent nations was provisionally recognized. The only proviso was that Britain and France had the right to render administrative advice and assistance until the time when they were able to stand alone (that is, attain independence). Paragraph four of Article 22 of the Covenant provided that: 'The wishes of *these communities* must be a principal consideration in the selection of the Mandatory' (emphasis added). According to the construction of this paragraph, 'these communities' could only refer to Palestine's indigenous inhabitants, which included established communities of Christians, Jews, Muslims and others.

Although decolonization was not explicitly referred to in the Covenant, the overall concept behind Article 22 could be regarded as the first manifestation of the ultimate goal to abrogate colonial systems that were still being pursued by many European States at the time.[23] After all, the mandate system—just as the UN Charter system—did not explicitly promote continued or new colonial power. And it was the idea underlying the concept of the mandate and its 'sacred trust' that would eventually work its way into the Trusteeship System of the United Nations. In fact, the principle of the 'sacred trust' as it was enshrined in the Covenant of the League of Nations had its origins in the Conference of Berlin of 1884–5 and was intimately connected with 'the duty of civilisation'.[24]

V. THE BRITISH MANDATE OF PALESTINE

During the drafting of the British Mandate of Palestine, the Zionists succeeded in lobbying the Principal Allied Powers to insert a number of clauses pertaining to the 'Jewish national home'. Consequently, the final draft of the Palestine Mandate included the following phrases which converted the original Balfour Declaration of November 1917 from a statement of intention into a legally binding obligation:

> Whereas the Principal Allied Powers have also agreed that the Mandatory should be responsible for putting into effect the declaration originally made on November 2nd, 1917 by the Government of His Britannic Majesty, and adopted by the said Powers, in favour of the establishment in Palestine of a national home for the Jewish people, it being clearly understood that nothing should be done which might prejudice the civil and religious rights of existing non-Jewish communities in Palestine, or the rights and political status enjoyed by Jews in any other country and

[23] See N Matz, 'Civilization and the Mandate System under the League of Nations as Origin of Trusteeship' (2005) 9 Max Planck Yearbook of United Nations Law 55.
[24] See CH Alexandrowicz, 'The Juridical Expression of the Sacred Trust of Civilisation' (1971) 65 American Journal of International Law 149–59, 154.

> Whereas recognition has thereby been given to the historical connection of the Jewish people with Palestine and to the grounds for reconstituting their national home in that country . . .
>
> . . .
> *Article 2*
> The Mandatory shall be responsible for placing the country under such political, administrative and economic conditions as will secure the establishment of the national home, as laid down in the preamble, and the development of self-governing institutions, and also for safeguarding the civil and religious rights of all the inhabitants of Palestine, irrespective of race and religion.[25]

In early drafts of the mandate the Zionists wanted to include the phrase: 'The reconstitution of Palestine as *the* national home' (emphasis added).[26] And during the negotiations over the terms of the mandate, they hoped the High Contracting Parties would 'recognise the historic *title* of the Jewish people to Palestine' (emphasis added).[27] However, they were unsuccessful with these endeavours as the final draft of the mandate only mentioned the words 'establishment' and 'the national home' and merely recognized 'the historical connection [note, not title] of the Jewish people with Palestine and to the grounds for reconstituting their national home *in* that country' (emphasis added). Evidently, these statements could hardly be considered as declarations of statehood or a promise to provide the Zionists with one. This is because rather than Palestine being reconstituted as the national home as the Zionists desired, the national home was to be reconstituted *in* Palestine.

It would therefore seem from its plain and ordinary meaning that the declaration envisaged granting the 'Jewish people' some sort of autonomy *within* Palestine. Hence in early drafts of the mandate the Zionists desired 'the creation of an autonomous commonwealth'.[28] But even this was restricted by Article 3 of the mandate which provided: 'The Mandatory shall, *so far as circumstances permit*, encourage local autonomy.'[29]

---

[25] See Annex 391, British Mandate for Palestine (1922) 3 League of Nations Official Journal 1007–12.

[26] The *travaux préparatoires*, which include the various drafts agreed upon between the Zionist organization and the Political Section of the British Peace Delegation, are available at the National Archives. See Peace Conference (British Delegation) Eastern Mission (Turkey) Files 76–91 (1920). CO 733/248/19.

[27] See, eg, 'Proposal for Palestine Mandate: On behalf of the Zionist Organisation in Paris transmits a draft scheme for the above, Mr Frankfurter to Col Meinertshagen', 20 Mar 1919, FO 608/100.

[28] See Proposal for Palestine Mandate (on behalf of the Zionist Organisation in Paris transmits a draft scheme for the above), 20 Mar 1919, FO 608/100.

[29] Emphasis added.

In his White Paper of 1922, Winston Churchill, then Secretary of State for the Colonies, provided an authoritative interpretation of what was meant by the phrase 'the development of the Jewish National Home in Palestine'. According to the Paper, this was 'not the imposition of a Jewish nationality upon the inhabitants of Palestine as a whole, but the further development of the existing Jewish community, with the assistance of Jews in other parts of the world, in order that it may become a centre in which the Jewish people as a whole may take, on grounds of religion and race, an interest and a pride.'[30] Churchill made it clear that the British Government 'never contemplated, at any time, the disappearance or the subordination of the Arabic population, language or culture in Palestine.'[31] After all, as he pointed out, the Balfour Declaration did not contemplate that 'Palestine as a whole should be converted into a Jewish National Home, but that such a Home should be founded in Palestine.'[32]

VI. THE PARTITION OF PALESTINE

On 29 November 1947, the General Assembly voted by a 33 to 13 majority with 10 abstentions to recommend the partition of Palestine with economic union.[33] The plan proposed to create an Arab state and a Jewish state with Jerusalem and Bethlehem established as a *corpus separatum* (that is, a separate body) which was to be administered by the UN.

According to figures provided by the United Nations Special Committee on Palestine (UNSCOP), in the proposed Arab state there would have been 10,000 Jews and almost 1 million Arabs. In the proposed Jewish state there would have been 498,000 Jews and 435,000 Arabs.[34] However, the figures used by the UNSCOP did not include the Bedouin population. A more accurate British figure estimated that the population figures would have been 509,780 Arabs and 499,020 Jews in the Jewish state, which meant the Arabs, would have remained a majority.[35]

---

[30] See Command Paper 1700, Great Britain House of Commons (1922) 23 Sessional Papers 17–21.
[31] ibid.   [32] ibid.
[33] UN General Assembly 181 (II), 29 Nov 1947. For the voting record see UN Doc A/PV 128.
[34] The figure provided for by the UNSCOP was 407,000. See Official Records of the Second Session of the General Assembly, Supplement No 11, United Nations Special Committee on Palestine, Report to the General Assembly, Volume 1 (Lake Success, New York, 1947,) UN doc A/364, 3 Sept 1947. However, for a more accurate figure see the population statistics in UN doc A/AC.14/SR 32, 25 Nov 1947.
[35] See Official Records of the Second Session of the General Assembly, Ad Hoc Committee on the Palestinian Question, 25 Sept–25 Nov 1947, UN doc A/AC 14/32 and Add 1, 11 Nov 1947, paras 61–6.

Although persons of the Jewish faith only constituted 33 per cent of the population of Palestine at that time (a figure which included Jewish immigrants), they were to have received approximately 56–60 per cent of Palestine's land mass.[36] And according to the document circulated by a British delegate at a UN Sub-Committee, 84 per cent of cultivable land was to be allocated to the Jewish state, with only 16 per cent of it going to the Arab state.[37] This left 80 per cent of agricultural land in the Jewish state, which would have devastated the Arab citrus industry, as this was their largest export.[38] In the Negev, where 15 per cent of the land was privately owned (14 per cent by the Arabs and 1 per cent by the Jews) the Jewish state got the lot, even though only 1,020 Jews inhabited the area as opposed to 103,820 Arabs.[39]

It was therefore hardly surprising that the Palestine Arabs rejected the plan. Ernest Bevin, Britain's Secretary of State for Foreign Affairs, also thought it was 'manifestly unfair to the Arabs'.[40] Less surprisingly, the Jewish Agency accepted the plan but only as 'the indispensable minimum'.

Regarding the question as to whether the UN General Assembly resolution was binding or not, it is instructive to note that UN Secretary-General Trygve Lie thought that the resolution was legally binding because it constituted a decision taken by the General Assembly, which as a successor to the Council of the League of Nations had in his opinion the competence to partition a mandated territory.[41] The Government of Israel also argued that it was binding and based its claim to statehood on the basis of the strength of the partition plan.[42] The District Court at Haifa actually referred to the partition plan as 'a document having validity under international law.'[43]

However, despite the opinions of these authorities, the better view would seem to be that although the resolution was drafted with the intention that the partition plan would actually be implemented, since it expressly referred to Articles 39 and 41 of the UN Charter, the resolution was ultimately only

[36] See the speech by Khan in UN doc A/PV.126, 28 Nov 1947 (citing 60 per cent although the figure 56 per cent is usually used).
[37] See speech by Khan, ibid.
[38] ibid.
[39] ibid. For exact figures see Ad Hoc Committee on the Palestinian Question Report of Sub-Committee 2, UN Doc A/AC 14/32, 11 Nov 1947, para 65.
[40] See Bevin Memorandum, 18 Sept 1947, CP (47) 259, Cab 129/21.
[41] See AW Cordier and W Foote (eds), *Public Papers of the Secretaries-General of the United Nations*, vol 1, *Trygve Lie, 1946–1953* (Columbia University Press, New York, 1969) 106–15.
[42] See Declaration of the Establishment of the State of Israel, 14 May 1948 (1948) 1 Laws State of Israel 3–5.
[43] See *Attorney-General of Israel v El-Turani, Israel*, District Court of Haifa, 21 Aug 1951, (1957) 18 International Law Reports 167. ('From the point of view of international law, the demilitarized zone is included within the Partition Resolution, which is a document having validity under international law.')

a recommendation and not a legally binding decision.[44] This is because according to Articles 10–14 of the UN Charter, the General Assembly can only make recommendations. This view is supported by the fact that both the Security Council[45] and the Mandatory Power[46] refused to enforce the partition plan when they could have done so.[47] Ultimately, it is only the Security Council which can make legally binding decisions under Article 25 of the UN Charter and enforce them by invoking its enforcement powers which are provided for in Chapter VII (principally, Articles 39, 41 and 42).[48] The General Assembly does not have the power to enforce its recommendations or to make law, as it is not a legislative body.[49]

It is, however, apparent that the plan to partition Palestine was not entirely without its faults for it faced several objections on legal, moral and political grounds. To begin with, the plan was inequitable[50] in that the Jewish state was to have received the majority of the land even though most of it was owned by the inhabitants of the putative Arab state. One would have thought that in marking the frontier between the Jewish state, the Arab state and the *corpus separatum* (Jerusalem and Bethlehem), the boundary commission would have taken into consideration those areas in which the land was predominantly Arab-owned and partitioned it from those areas where it was predominantly Jewish-owned (or alternatively partitioned those areas in which Arabs formed a majority of the population from those parts where Jews were preponderant). Yet, as was evident from the plan, most of the land that was awarded to the Jewish state was owned by the Arabs and it seems that a majority of the inhabitants in the Jewish state would have also been Arab.

[44] See J Castañeda, *Legal Effects of United Nations Resolutions*, trans Alba Amoia (Columbia University Press, New York, 1969) 73 and 132–3.

[45] See the statement of Warren Austin at 271st meeting of the Security Council, UN Doc S/PV.271, 19 Mar 1948. See also, UN Press Release PAL/145, 12 Mar 1948.

[46] See the statement by Ernest Bevin in House of Commons, Parliamentary Debates, 12 Dec 1947, col 1396.

[47] See C Eagleton, 'Palestine and the Constitutional Law of the UN' (1948) 42 American Journal of International Law 397–9.

[48] Although there is some doctrinal debate as to whether this might also apply to decisions made under Chapter VI of the Charter. See R Higgins, 'The Advisory Opinion on Namibia: which UN resolutions are binding under Article 25 of the Charter?' (1972) 21 International & Comparative Law Quarterly 270–86, 281–2. In referring to UN resolutions on the Namibia question, Higgins writes: 'The binding or non-binding nature of those resolutions turns not upon whether they are to be regarded as 'Chapter VI' or 'Chapter VII' resolutions ... but upon whether the parties intended them to be 'decisions' or 'recommendations'.'

[49] See, eg, M Virally, 'The sources of international law' in M Sørensen (ed), *Manual of Public International Law* (Macmillan, London, 1968) 160–2.

[50] On the question of equity in boundary disputes generally, see, eg, M Miyoshi, *Considerations of Equity in the Settlement of Boundary Disputes* (Martinus Nijhoff, Dordrecht, 1993). This book which was based upon a University of London PhD thesis was supervised by Sir Francis Aime Vallat, who was one of the Foreign Office legal advisers during the partition of Palestine.

One possible explanation for this anomaly is that the UNSCOP wanted to ensure that there would be enough space for those Jewish refugees from Europe who had survived the *Shoah* to emigrate to the envisaged Jewish state to settle there and develop the land.[51] However, it is noteworthy that this issue had already been looked into in some detail by the Anglo-American Committee of Enquiry of 1946[52] whose members toured the concentration camps of Europe, after which they recommended that whilst some refugees (approximately 100,000) should be allowed into Palestine, its territorial integrity should be kept intact.[53]

In this regard it is intriguing that in the Armenia–Turkey Boundary case of 1920, the arbitrator concluded that where:

> the requirements of a correct geographic boundary permitted, all mountain and valley districts along the border which were predominantly Kurdish or Turkish have been left to Turkey rather than assigned to Armenia, unless trade relations with definite market towns threw them necessarily into the Armenian State. Whenever information upon tribal relations and seasonal migrations was obtainable, the attempt was made to respect the integrity of tribal groupings and nomad pastoral movements.[54]

In addition, the arbitrator suggested to the boundary commission, in regard to one portion of the frontier, 'the desirability of consulting with the local inhabitants with a view to possible modification' of the boundary.[55]

During the partition of Ireland a boundary commission was asked to 'determine in accordance with the wishes of the inhabitants, so far as may be compatible with economic and geographic conditions, the boundaries between Northern Ireland and the rest of Ireland . . .'.[56] The three-man commission interpreted its terms of reference so that an inhabitant was some-

[51] See UNSCOP Report (n 49) ('The proposed Jewish State leaves considerable room for further development and land settlement').

[52] See Report of the Anglo-American Committee of Enquiry regarding the problems of European Jewry and Palestine, Miscellaneous No 8 (1946), Lausanne, 20 Apr 1946 (HMSO Cmd 6808, London).

[53] The Committee's Recommendation No 2 was that 100,000 certificates be authorized for the admission into Palestine of Jews who had been victims of Nazi persecution. However, in Recommendation No 1, the Committee concluded that 'Palestine alone cannot meet the emigration needs of the Jewish victims of Nazi and Fascist persecution. The whole world shares responsibility for them and indeed for the resettlement of all 'Displaced Persons.' In Recommendation No 3 they advised that Palestine 'shall be neither a Jewish state nor an Arab state'. See Anglo-American Committee of Enquiry, ibid 1–4.

[54] See *Armenia–Turkey Boundary* Case of 1920, 22 November 1920, (1920) 1 Digest of International Law, 715.

[55] ibid.

[56] See Article XII of the Treaty between Great Britain and Ireland, signed at London, 6 December 1921 (1924) 26 League of Nations Treaty Series.

one who had a permanent connection to the area concerned and in order to assess the wishes of the inhabitants they made use of the census returns of 1911, showing the religious denominations to which the inhabitants belonged.[57] It was taken for granted that members of Protestant denominations wanted to be in Northern Ireland and that Roman Catholics preferred to be in the Irish Free State.[58]

In the *Jaworzina* case of 1923, which concerned a section of the frontier between Poland and Czechoslovakia, the Permanent Court of International Justice (PCIJ) affirmed that the question of its delimitation had been settled by a decision of the Conference of Ambassadors (which was comprised of the USA, the British Empire, France, Italy, Japan and the Principal Allied and Associated Powers).[59] In that decision the Conference of Ambassadors had established a Frontier Delimitation Commission which was empowered to propose 'any modifications which it may consider justified by reason of the interests of individuals or of communities in the neighbourhood of the frontier line and having regard to settled local circumstances'.[60]

Moreover, the boundary commission that was established by the British Government to partition the Punjab after the decision to partition British India had been announced was instructed to 'demarcate the Boundaries of the two parts of the Punjab on the basis of ascertaining the contiguous majority areas of Muslims and non-Muslims'.[61]

It therefore seemed that the UNSCOP was departing from established practice in that it neither consulted the Arab population of Palestine (although this may have been because the Arab Higher Committee boycotted the commission), nor took into consideration those areas in which they formed a majority of the population (or where they were the major landowners), in recommending partition. Then there was also the question of economic viability, which the arbitrator in the Armenia–Turkey boundary case considered of the utmost importance.[62] In this respect it was

---

[57] See Geoffrey J Hand (ed), *Report of the Irish Boundary Commission* (Irish University Press, Shannon, 1969) 30.

[58] ibid 30–1.

[59] See Question of *Jaworzina* (Polish–Czechoslovakian Frontier), Collection of Advisory Opinions, Series B, No 8, 6 Dec 1923, 6–57, 57.

[60] See Acts and Documents Relating to Judgments and Advisory Opinions Given by the Court, Series C, No 4 (13 Nov–6 Dec 1923), Documents Relating to Advisory Opinion No 8 (Jaworzina) 31 (referring to the Resolution of the Conference of Ambassadors on 28 July 1920).

[61] See MM Sadullah (ed), *The Partition of the Punjab 1947: A Compilation of Official Documents*, vol 1 (National Documentation Centre, Lahore, 1983) 80–1.

[62] (n 54). ('The conflicting territorial desires of Armenians, Turks, Kurds, and Greeks along the boundaries assigned to my arbitral decision could not always be harmonized. In such cases it was my belief that considerations of a healthy economic life for the future state of Armenia should be decisive').

highly questionable whether the Arab state—as opposed to the Jewish state—would be economically viable and this was one of the reasons why the Arab states opposed partition because they thought that the proposed Arab state would be dependent on handouts from the international community.[63]

It would also seem that the method through which Palestine was to be partitioned was contrary to the spirit of the UN Charter in that it would have had to be enforced by recourse to armed force[64] which is in direct contradistinction to the preamble and a number of purposes and principles enumerated in Articles 1 and 2. And in fact this was the principal reason why partition was not ultimately pursued by the UN as the mandatory power opposed enforcing it against the wishes of both the Arabs and the Jews.[65] The Americans also decided not to place the plan before the Security Council when they realized that any UN force sent to Palestine would have included Soviet troops as they did not want to give them a foothold in that part of the Middle East.[66] Moreover, every single country in the entire region and some beyond were also opposed to the partition plan in principle. Although the UN was created in the interests of international peace and security, the partition plan was so inequitable that it seemed self-evident that it would lead to conflict.

In this regard it is noteworthy that in the Indo-Pakistan Western Boundary Case, which concerned a part of the boundary that was not delimited by the boundary commission headed by Sir Cyril Radcliffe during the 1947 partition of British India, Gunnar Lagergren, the Chairman of the three-man tribunal took into account 'the paramount consideration of promoting peace and stability in the region' in determining the boundary between India and Pakistan in the Rann of Kutch (which is a salty marsh of some 10,000 square

---

[63] See Ad Hoc Committee on the Palestinian Question, 25 Sept–25 Nov 1947 (n 35) paras 80–3.

[64] In the General Assembly the argument was advanced that the problem of Palestine could not be dealt with under Art 14 of the UN Charter because what was being proposed was not the peaceful adjustment of a situation but the imposition by force of a settlement contrary to the wishes of the people concerned. If the General Assembly adopted the plan for partition, it would have to use force to carry it out. See *Repertory of Practice of United Nations Organs* (United Nations, New York, 1955) 471. According to the American historian Michael Cohen, Maj-Gen Alfred Greunther, head of the Joint Chiefs, estimated in a meeting with President Harry Truman that the implementation of partition by force would require a minimum of 80,000 and a maximum of 160,000 American troops. See MJ Cohen, *Palestine and the Great Powers: 1945–1948* (Princeton University Press, New Jersey, 1982), 340–1.

[65] 'I am, therefore, instructed to repeat explicitly that the United Kingdom Government cannot allow its troops and administration to be used in order to enforce decisions which are not accepted by both parties in Palestine', Sir Alexander Cadogan (United Kingdom), UN Doc A/PV 124, 26 Nov 1947.

[66] See Cohen (n 64) 34–67. See also, K Roosevelt, 'The Partition of Palestine: A Lesson in Pressure Politics' (1948) 2 The Middle East Journal 1–16.

miles).[67] He also invoked considerations of equity, in awarding territory to Pakistan since not doing so in the particular circumstances of the case 'would be conducive to friction and conflict'.[68] There were good reasons why the Swedish Chairman invoked considerations of equity in promoting peace and stability between India and Pakistan: the two countries have gone to war several times since over the Rann of Kutch, as well as over Jammu and Kashmir, most recently in the *Atlantique* incident.[69]

Moreover, in a dispute over the inter-entity boundary line in the Brčko area (which is a town located in a strategic location along the partitioned territories of Republika Srpska and the Federation of Bosnia and Herzegovina) the arbitral tribunal concluded that any 'simple solution' had to be rejected in favour of an approach 'that is consistent with law and equity and is designed gradually to relieve the underlying tensions and lead to a stable and harmonious solution'.[70]

The UNSCOP would perhaps have been wise to have taken into account considerations of equity, peace and stability when they recommended partitioning Palestine. In awarding so much territory to a minority community, many of whom had no legal connection to Palestine either through nationality (as many were foreign immigrants) or through habitual residency (as many had recently arrived), they added to Arab discontent and provided a recipe for a war that has since haunted the Middle East.

---

[67] See Rann of Kutch Arbitration (India and Pakistan), The Indo-Pakistan Western Boundary Case, constituted pursuant to the Agreement of 30 June, 1965, Award, 19 Feb 1968 (1968) 7 International Legal Materials 633–705.

[68] ibid 692.

[69] On 21 September 1999, the Islamic Republic of Pakistan filed in the Registry of the Court an Application instituting proceedings against the Republic of India in respect of a dispute relating to the destruction, on 10 August 1999, of a Pakistani aircraft. Pakistan asked the ICJ to adjudge and declare that India's action in shooting down the Pakistani aircraft constituted breaches of various obligations under the UN Charter, customary international law and a number of other treaties. The ICJ by a majority vote of 14 to 2 found that it had no jurisdiction to entertain the application filed by Pakistan. See *Case Concerning the Aerial Incident of 10 August 1999 (Pakistan v India) (Judgment of 21 June 2000)* [1999] ICJ Rep 835.

[70] See Arbitral Tribunal for Dispute over Inter-Entity Boundary in Brčko Area, *The Republika Srpska v The Federation of Bosnia and Herzegovina*, Award, 14 Feb 1997, (1997) 36 International Legal Materials 399–437, 421. In the Final Award the tribunal established a new institution under a new multi-ethnic democratic government known as 'The Brčko District of Bosnia and Herzegovina' under the exclusive sovereignty of Bosnia and Herzegovina. See *The Federation of Bosnia and Herzegovina v The Republika Srpska*, Arbitration for the Brčko Area, Final Award, 5 Mar 1999 (1999) 38 International Legal Materials 536–50. For commentary, see C Schreuer, 'The Brčko Award of 14 February 1997' (1998) 11 Leiden Journal of International Law 71–80 and the commentary by the same author on the Final Award in (1999) 38 International Legal Materials 534–5.

VII. THE 1948 WAR

When war broke out between the Zionists and the Arabs in the aftermath of the UN vote in favour of partition, the Zionists did not confine themselves to conquering the territories they were awarded in that plan.[71] In fact, Golda Meir had already come to an arrangement with King Abdullah of Transjordan over partitioning Palestine in the event of conflict.[72] In this respect the situation was not too dissimilar to that of Jammu and Kashmir which was partitioned between the Indian army and Pakistani tribal forces in 1948 without taking into consideration the wishes of the inhabitants of those territories.[73] In this respect the partition of Palestine was undertaken not under UN auspices but by the unilateral use of force.[74]

There were two phases to the war: during the first phase of the conflict, which lasted from December 1947 to May 1948, the conflict took place within the borders of the British Mandate of Palestine. It was during this period that many Palestinian Arabs were forced to flee their homes, through expulsion or fear of expulsion.[75] During the second phase the conflict acquired an international character with armed intervention from the neighbouring Arab countries. They claimed they were coming to the assistance of the Palestinian people, many of whom had already fled their homes during the first stage of hostilities, into the borders of those countries.[76] In this regard, it is arguable that the Arabs were acting under the rubric of self-defence[77] although there is evidence that King Abdullah of Transjordan had

---

[71] For a collection of articles on the 1948 war, see EL Rogan and A Shlaim, *The War for Palestine: Rewriting the History of 1948* (CUP, Cambridge, 2001).

[72] For the full story, see A Shlaim, *The Politics of Partition: King Abdullah, the Zionists and Palestine 1921–1951* (OUP, Oxford, 1990).

[73] See, eg, Security Council resolution 47, 21 Apr 1948. UN Doc S/726. There has never been a plebiscite.

[74] See, eg, I Pappé, *The Ethnic Cleaning of Palestine* (Oneworld Publications, Oxford, 2006).

[75] According to an internal assessment by the Israeli Defence Forces Intelligence Services approximately 390,000 Palestinians were displaced either through expulsion or fear of expulsion between December 1947 and May 1948. The document, which contains this assessment, was found in the private papers of Aharon Cohen, Director of Mapam in the Hashomer Hatza'ir Archive in Israel, and is officially entitled: 'The Emigration of the Arabs of Palestine in the period 1/12/1947–1/6/1948 (t'nu'at ha'hagira shel arvi' yei eretz yisrael ba't' kufa 1/12/1947–1/6/1948). According to this document, the operations undertaken by the Haganah, the Irgun and Lehi accounted for 70 per cent of the Arab exodus from Palestine. It is reproduced and analysed by Benny Morris in 'The Causes and Character of the Arab Exodus from Palestine: the Israel Defence Forces Intelligence Service Analysis of June 1948' in B Morris, *1948 and After: Israel and the Palestinians* (Clarendon Press, Oxford, 1990) 69–8, 72.

[76] See Res 85, The Policy of the Arab States Towards the Question of Palestine, translated and reproduced in M Khalil (ed), *The Arab States and the Arab League: A Documentary Record, Vol. II International Affairs* (Khayats, Beirut, 1962) 166.

[77] See UN doc S/748, 17 May, cablegram from King Abdullah of Transjordan to the Secretary-General of the UN and Press Release PAL/167, 16 May 1948; cablegram from the

territorial ambitions in Palestine which were tacitly encouraged by the Zionists and by the British Government, the latter having commanding officers in the Arab Legion.[78]

As with most conflicts, gross violations of humanitarian and human rights law occurred during the fighting with expulsions, random executions, kidnappings, massacres and even rapes committed by both sides.[79] However, the most tragic outcome of the war was the exodus of the predominantly but not exclusively Arab population of Palestine.[80] According to UN estimates more than 750,000 Palestinian Arabs fled the fighting by the time the conflict ended.[81] This amounted to the overall displacement of up to 85 per cent of the Palestinian Arab population living in the territory that became the State of Israel.[82] In many instances, whole Palestinian communities were uprooted from their ancestral villages and expelled (over 400 villages in total).[83] Counte Folke Bernadotte, who was the UN Mediator for Palestine in 1948, mentioned numerous reports—from what he described as 'reliable sources'— of large scale looting, pillaging and plundering, and of instances of the destruction of villages without apparent military necessity.[84]

On 11 December 1948 the UN General Assembly passed resolution 194 (III), of which paragraph eleven provided:

Egyptian government to the UN Secretary-General UN doc S/743, 15 May 1948 and cablegram from the Secretary-General of the Arab League to the UN Secretary-General UN doc S/745, 15 May 1948. See also, Special Appendix Relating to Palestine (conferring upon it a special status in the Arab league) and Art 6 Pact of the League of Arab States on collective self-defence, signed at Cairo, on 22 March 1945. Filed and recorded at the request of Egypt on 29 August 1950 (1950), 70 United Nations Treaty Series, 238–47 (in Arabic), and 248–62 (in English and French). The Arabic text is the official text.

[78] See generally, Shlaim (n 72) and MC Wilson, *King Abdullah, Britain and the Making of Jordan* (CUP, Cambridge, 1987). One of the British commanding officers in the Arab Legion was known as 'Glubb Pasha'. See Lieutenant-General Sir John Bagot Glubb, *A Soldier with the Arabs* (Hodder and Stoughton, London, 1957).

[79] For a description of events, see eg M Palumbo, *The Palestinian Catastrophe the 1948 Expulsion of a People from their Homeland* (Quartet, London, 1989); G Karma and E Cotran (ed), *The Palestinian Exodus, 1948–1998* (Ithaca, London, 1999); and especially Pappé (n 74).

[80] Approximately 17,000 Jews were also registered as displaced in 1948. See United Nations Conciliation Commission for Palestine Final Report of the Economic Survey Mission for the Middle East, Part 1, UN doc A/AC.25/6, 28 Dec 1949, 18. ('No one knows exactly how many refugees there are. After considering all available information, the Economic Survey Mission estimates that the total number of refugees does not exceed 774,000, including 48,000 in Israel, of whom 17,000 are Jews').

[81] ibid.

[82] According to demographic projections by Abu Lughod, between 890,000 and 904,000 Palestinians would have been living in the territories that became the state of Israel if not displacement had taken place in 1948. See J Abu-Lughod, 'The Demographic Transformation of Palestine', in Lughod (n 11) 159.

[83] See W Khalidi, *All the Remains: The Palestinian Villages Occupied and Depopulated by Israel in 1948* (Institute of Palestine Studies, Washington DC, 1993).

[84] See the Progress Report of the UN Mediator, GAOR, 3rd session, supp 11, UN doc A/648 16 Sept 1948, at Chapter V entitled 'Refugees' para 7.

... that the refugees wishing to return to their homes and live at peace with their neighbours should be permitted to do so at the earliest practicable date, and that compensation should be paid for the property of those choosing not to return and for loss of or damage to property which, under principles of international law or in equity, should be made good by the Governments or authorities responsible.[85]

To date, the vast majority of those displaced Arabs have been prevented from returning.[86] Nor have they been compensated.[87] There is an ongoing debate, as reflected in some of the articles reproduced in this book, on whether Israel is under a legal obligation to repatriate the Palestinian Arabs displaced from their homes as a result of that conflict.[88]

It is noteworthy that in 1946 the 1907 Hague Regulations were held by the Nuremberg Tribunal to reflect customary international law.[89] And although the four Geneva Conventions did not enter into force until 21 October 1950, by which time the fighting in mandatory Palestine was already over, many of its provisions embodied pre-existing law.[90] In this regard it has been said that the practice of deportations was not discussed at Hague Peace Conferences because the practice was thought to have been alien to modern warfare.[91] It would also seem that the expulsion of so many people to the surrounding Arab countries violated their sovereignty and territorial integrity.[92] Many of the actions undertaken by Israeli forces would probably be described in modern parlance as 'ethnic cleansing' akin to the atrocities committed in the Balkans in the 1990s.[93]

---

[85] UN doc A/Res/194 (III), 11 Dec 1948.

[86] See B Morris, _The Birth of the Palestinian Refugee Problem Revisited_ (CUP, Cambridge, 2004) 334 and following chapter at 341–413.

[87] See, eg, M Lynk, 'The Right to Restitution and Compensation in International Law and the Displaced Palestinians' (2003) 21 Refuge 96–113.

[88] See, eg, JB Quigley, 'Displaced Palestinians and a Right of Return' (1998) 39 Harvard International Law Journal 171–229.

[89] See the 'Trial of the German Major War Criminals' (1947) 41 American Journal of International Law 248–9 ('by 1939 these rules laid down in the Convention were recognized by all civilized nations, and were regarded as being declaratory of the laws and customs of war...') and the _Cessation of vessels and tugs for navigation on the Danube_ case (1921) 1 Reports of International Arbitral Awards 104.

[90] See, eg, the comments regarding Art 49 (1) of Geneva Convention IV by JS Pictet, _Commentary: IV Geneva Convention Relative to the Protection of Civilian Persons in Time of War_ (International Committee of the Red Cross, Geneva, 1958) 279 ('The Hague Regulations do not refer to the question of deportations; this was probably because the practice of deporting persons was regarded at the beginning of this century as falling into abeyance. The events of the last few years have, however, made it necessary to make more detailed provisions on this point which may be regarded today as having been embodied in international law').

[91] See John HE Fried, 'Transfer of civilian manpower from Occupied Territory' (1946) 40 American Journal of International Law, 307–9 (analysing Second World War precedents).

[92] Art 2 (4) UN Charter.

[93] As described by a former mayor of Jerusalem. See Meron Benvenisti, _Sacred Landscape_

In 1949, armistice agreements were concluded between Egypt, Lebanon, Syria, Jordan and the newly created State of Israel which brought that conflict to an end.[94]

VIII. THE CREATION OF ISRAEL

Sometime between 14 May 1948 and 24 February 1949, when Israel signed an armistice agreement with Egypt, the State of Israel was born in the midst of its war with the Arabs of Palestine and the neighbouring Arab States.[95] Israel formally proclaimed its 'independence' at midnight on 14/15 May by making reference to the General Assembly's partition resolution, even though it did not exercise effective control over the territory allocated to it in that plan. Within a few hours of this proclamation, the President of the United States, Harry Truman recognized 'the Provisional Government [of Israel] as the de facto authority of the new State of Israel.'[96] Two days later, the Soviet Union 'decided to recognize officially the State of Israel and its Provisional Government'.[97]

From these statements it was apparent that whereas America merely recognized the fact that Israel had declared its independence and recognized its existence as a fact, the Soviet Union went further. In the words of one commentator:

The Soviet Union, acting as a kind of godfather, accorded a diplomatic baptism to the newborn infant and thus assumed by implication a benign interest and responsibility for the child's welfare. President Truman did not imply anything more than the acknowledgement of the child's existence and its *de facto* guardians.[98]

Ernest Gross, the State Department's legal adviser, counselled the White House that any premature recognition of a new State's existence would be wrongful in international law because it would constitute an unwarranted

the Buried History of the Holy Land since 1948 (University of California Press, Berkeley, 2000) 145.

[94] See the Egyptian–Israel armistice agreement, UN doc S/1264/Corr 1, 23 Feb 1949; the Israel–Jordan armistice agreement, UN doc S/1302/Rev 1, 3 Apr 1949; the Israel–Lebanon armistice agreement, UN doc S/1296, 23 Mar 1949; and the Israeli–Syrian General armistice agreement, UN doc S/1353, 20 July 1949.

[95] J Crawford, *The Creation of States in International Law* (Clarendon Press, Oxford, 2006) 433. ('Israel must be considered to have met that standard [of secessionary independence] by 24 February 1949, when the Egyptian-Israel Armistice Agreement was signed'.)

[96] See (1963) 2 Digest of International Law 167–9, 168.

[97] See P Marshall Brown, 'The Recognition of Israel' (1948) 42 American Journal of International Law 620.

[98] ibid 622.

interference in the affairs of the previously existing State.[99] In a legal memorandum he wrote that the policy of the State Department on the recognition of Israel should be based on three factors: (a) de facto control of the territory and the administrative machinery of state, including the maintenance of public order; (b) ability and willingness of a Government to discharge its international obligations; and (3) general acquiescence of the people of a country in the Government in power.[100]

In stark contrast to the position adopted by the US and the Soviet Union, Great Britain, which as the Mandatory Power was then in the process of evacuating its troops from Palestine, announced that it would not recognize Israel 'for the time being' because in its opinion it did not fulfil the 'basic criteria' of an independent state.[101] It was evident that Israel could not claim to be an independent State on 14 May because on that date British troops were still occupying Palestine (they did not complete their evacuation until 29 June 1948). Britain also opposed Israel's application to the UN because in its opinion the Jewish State's frontiers were not clearly defined and because it did not exercise effective control over the territories it claimed for itself.

In a letter to Alexander Cadogan, Britain's UN representative, dated 18 August 1948, Aubrey Eban argued that after the evacuation of British troops Israel fulfilled the conditions to secure admission to the UN because it satisfied its criteria: (a) it was a State; (b) it was a peace-loving State; (c) it was willing to accept the obligations contained in the UN Charter; and (d) it was able and willing to carry out those obligations.[102] Eban claimed that the Provisional Government of Israel exercised effective control in the areas allocated to it in the partition resolution and in those areas of Palestine where its militias had 'repelled attacks launched by the armies of the Arab states.'[103] In support of Israel's application, Eban pointed out that Israel has become 'a signatory to the Geneva Convention' and had 'been invited to send a delegation to the Conference of the International Red Cross'.[104]

A paper prepared by the Foreign Office rejected this contention:

---

[99] See J Snetsinger, *Truman, the Jewish Vote and the Creation of Israel* (Hoover Institution Press, Stanford, 1974) 109.

[100] See Memorandum of Legal Opinions on Recognition of the Palestine State, prepared by Ernest A. Gross, State Department legal adviser, 13 May 1948. Gross's opinions were attached to a memorandum from CH Humelsine, Office of the Secretary of State, 14 May 1948, Clifford Papers. This is cited in Snetsinger, ibid 109, endnote 24.

[101] See 'Recognition of the Jewish State', FO 371, Eastern, Palestine (1948).

[102] See Letter to the Right Hon Sir Alexander Cadogan, 18 Aug 1948 from Aubrey S Eban, Representative of the Provisional Government of Israel, File 6090, FO 371, Eastern, Palestine (1948).

[103] ibid.   [104] ibid.

In the case of the Jewish authorities in Palestine it is by no means clear what are the exact boundaries of the area which they at present administer. In any event this area is not identical with that which they claim for permanent inclusion within their State. Originally they maintained their right to establish a State within the frontiers recommended by the General Assembly of the United Nations last November. Statements are now being made, however, which show that the Jewish leaders no longer regard themselves as bound by the General Assembly recommendation, and that they will in due course present claims to additional territory. The limits of these claims have not yet been precisely stated.[105]

The British Government also thought that 'the effectiveness of the authority claimed over the Jewish population of Palestine by its present leaders' had not yet been 'sufficiently demonstrated'.[106] This was because 'the right-wing dissident military organization known as Irgun Zvai Leumi' did not accept 'the authority of Mr Ben Gurion [the leader of the Provisional Government of Israel and its first Prime Minister] and his colleagues'.[107] In this respect, Britain pointed out that five British subjects had been kidnapped by that organization and that Mr Ben Gurion's men had only been able to secure their release by making concessions in which two of the five British subjects were put on trial despite the 'illegal action' which led to their kidnapping:

> It thus appears that there is no certainty either about the extent of Jewish territory or about the effectiveness of the control exercised by the authorities in Tel Aviv. In present circumstances, therefore, H.M.G. do not propose to recognize the Jewish State.
> It follows that H.M.G. will not support the application of this State for membership of the United Nations.[108]

In any event, by 1949 when Israel had signed armistice agreements with Egypt, Syria, Jordan and Lebanon, Britain decided that Israel had fulfilled the conditions necessary to support its application to the UN subject to its acceptance of the UN General Assembly's resolutions on partition and refugees.[109] Upon a recommendation from the Security Council which was opposed by Egypt and in which Britain abstained from voting, it was decided that Israel was a 'peace loving State' that was 'able and willing to carry out the obligations contained in the Charter'.[110] Accordingly, the General Assembly decided to admit Israel to membership in the UN on 11 May 1949.[111]

---

[105] See 'Recognition of the Jewish State' (n 101). [106] ibid.
[107] ibid. [108] ibid.
[109] See the armistice agreements (n 94). [110] See SC Res 69 (1949), 4 Mar 1949.
[111] See GA Res 273 (III), 11 May 1949.

IX. THE 1967 WAR

In June 1967, armed conflict broke out again between Israel and its Arab neighbours.[112] Initially, Israel alleged that it had been attacked by the Egypt only to subsequently change its story by arguing that it had effectively acted in 'anticipatory' self-defence.[113] It is, however, highly questionable whether this was the case as an Egyptian attack against Israel was clearly not imminent because the Egyptian Government was in talks with the US over resolving their dispute over the Straits of Tiran when Israel launched its *blitzkrieg*.[114] Charles Yost, a senior American diplomat had succeeded in obtaining from Nasser an undertaking not to physically block the Gulf of Aqaba, pending a decision on its status by the International Court of Justice; to effect a partial withdrawal of Egyptian forces from the Sinai; to cooperate in the reinstatement of a Military Mixed Armistice Commission on both sides of the Egypt–Israel border; and to send his vice-president to Washington on 7 June to tie up these assurances in a formal agreement.[115] It was therefore apparent that Nasser did not want to go to war and that diplomatic methods had not been exhausted. Yitzhak Rabin, who was then Chief of Staff of the Israeli army, and one of the key architects of the 1967 war, was clearly aware of this. He told a French newspaper:

> I do not believe that Nasser wanted war. The two divisions he sent into Sinai on May 14 would not have been enough to unleash an offensive against Israel. He knew it and we knew it.[116]

In any event, Article 51 of the UN Charter predicates the right to act in self-defence on the existence of an 'armed attack'. Yet when Israel launched its attack on Egypt the only aircraft airborne at the time was a training flight of four unarmed aircraft flown by an instructor and three trainees.[117] It is therefore difficult to view Israel's actions as consistence with the right of self-defence as enshrined in Article 51 of the UN Charter. Moreover, it seems doubtful whether the removal of the UN Emergency Force from the Sinai Peninsula could in itself amount to an

---

[112] With the exception of Lebanon which was not involved in that conflict.

[113] Compare statement by Mr Rafael (Israel), UN Doc S/PV 1347/Rev1, 5 June 1967 to statement of Mr Eban (Israel) UN Doc S/PV 1348, 6 June 1967.

[114] See D Rusk, *As I Saw It: A Secretary of State's Memoirs* (IB Tauris, London, 1991) 330–1.

[115] See A Schleifer, *The Fall of Jerusalem* (The Bertrand Russell Peace Foundation, Nottingham, 1972) 149 citing DG Nes, 'Sharm el-Sheikh Block the Way to Peace' (1971) Middle East International (June).

[116] *Le Monde* (29 Feb 1968).

[117] See RS Churchill and WS Churchill, *The Six Day War* (Heinemann, London, 1967) 78.

armed attack.[118] Although the closure of the Straits to strategic Israeli cargo (such as oil and weapons) may have been a tactical blunder by Nasser as it gave Israel a *casus belli* which it could invoke in the battle for public opinion, it was not an armed attack. The most that could perhaps be said of Israel's attack is that it amounted to 'pre-emptive self-defence' which is really just a synonym for an act of aggression.[119] There was certainly nothing anticipatory about its strike on 12 Egyptian airfields which practically wiped out the entire Egyptian air force whilst it was still grounded at 7.45 am on 5 June.[120] Numerous statements made by the Israeli Generals who planned that war seem to support the view that Israel's actions in June 1967 amounted to an act of aggression rather than an act of self-defence.[121] Israel was certainly not faced with an existential threat. As General Matitiahu Peled told the Israeli newspaper *Maariv*:

To claim that the Egyptian forces concentrated on our borders were capable of threatening Israel's existence not only insults the intelligence of anyone capable of analysing this kind of situation, but is an insult to Zahal [the Israeli army].[122]

Nor was there ever any doubt in Jerusalem, London, Moscow or Washington DC that in the event of an Arab–Israeli conflict, Israel would emerge victorious.[123] As Robert McNamara, who was then the US Secretary of Defence, recalled:

A meeting between President Johnson and British Prime Minister Harold Wilson had long been planned for June 2, to review our common interests around the world. When the day arrived, the imminent Arab–Israeli war had crowded all other issues off the agenda. We compared our intelligence estimates and our conclusions about the conflict's outcome. We agreed on all points, including who would win: Israel—beyond a shadow of a doubt. One side, I recall, anticipated an Israeli victory within ten days; the other expected it within seven.[124]

[118] For an account depicting events which led up to and included the removal of UNEF from Sinai, see M-G Indar Jit Rikhye, *The Sinai Blunder* (Frank Cass, London, 1980).

[119] On the difference between self-defence, anticipatory self-defence and pre-emption see N Shah, 'Self-defence, Anticipatory Self-defence and Pre-emption: International Law's Response to Terrorism' (2002) 12 Journal of Conflict and Security Law 95–126.

[120] On the facts, see Churchill and Churchill (n 117) 78.

[121] See Art 3 of the Definition of Aggression annexed to General Assembly resolution 3314 (XXIX) of 14 December 1974 for a list of acts that amount to aggression.

[122] *Maariv*, 24 Mar 1972, quoted in D Hirst, *The Gun and the Olive Branch: The Roots of Violence in the Middle East* (Faber & Faber, London, 1977) 211, n 13.

[123] See Rusk (n 114) 329.

[124] See, eg, RS McNamara, *In Retrospect: The Tragedy and Lessons of Vietnam* (Random House, New York, 1995) 278. They were both wrong. Israel did it in six days.

And Major General Ezer Weizmann, Chief of Operations in the 1967 war, boasted:

> Had the Egyptians attacked first, they would have also then suffered a complete defeat. The only difference is that the war then would have been prolonged; to command control of the air, maybe thirteen hours would have been needed instead of three . . .[125]

During the conflict an estimated 550,000 Palestinians fled their homes, many for the second time, having already been displaced from their homes inside what became the State of Israel in 1948.[126] The Security Council in resolution 237 called on the Government of Israel to ensure the safety, welfare and security of the inhabitants of the areas where military operations have taken place and to facilitate the return of those inhabitants who have fled the areas since the outbreak of hostilities.[127] Although the Israeli Government permitted some refugees to return, only 14,000 could do so as the borders were only open for 13 days, from the 18 August until 31 August 1967.[128]

In resolution 242 the Security Council affirmed that the principles of the UN Charter required the 'withdrawal of Israel armed forces from territories occupied in the recent conflict.'[129] Regarding which territories Israel was required to withdraw from, and which is dealt with in some detail in the article by John McHugo in this book, Dean Rusk, then US Secretary of State, had this to say:

> We wanted that [the withdrawal phrase in resolution 242] to be left a little vague and subject to future negotiation because we thought the border along the West Bank could be 'rationalized'; certain anomalies could easily be straightened out with some exchanges of territory, making a more sensible border for all parties. We also wanted to leave open demilitarisation measures in the Sinai and the Golan Heights and take a fresh look at the City of Jerusalem. But we never contemplated any significant grant of territory to Israel as a result of the June 1967 war. On that point we and the Israelis to this day remain sharply divided.[130]

---

[125] *Ha'aretz*, 29 Mar 1972, quoted in JK Cooley, *Green March, Black September: The Story of the Palestinian Arabs* (Frank Cass, London, 1973) 162.

[126] This figure includes persons displaced from the West Bank to Jordan, the Golan Heights to Syria and those who had fled from Gaza and the Sinai to Egypt. This figure does not, however, include persons with lost ID permits, or deportees, spouses and descendants. See Report of the Commissioner-General of the United Nations Relief and Works Agency for Palestine Refugees in the Near East, Official Records of the General Assembly, Twenty-second Session, Supplement No 13, 1 July 1966–30 June 1967 UN doc A/6713.

[127] 14 June 1967.

[128] International Committee for the Red Cross Annual Report (Geneva, 1967) 10–11.

[129] 22 Nov 1967.   [130] See Rusk (n 114) 333.

At the end of the war Israel was in effective control of East Jerusalem, the West Bank, the Gaza Strip, the Golan Heights and the Sinai Peninsula. Israel has remained a belligerent occupant in those territories ever since June 1967 with the exception of the Sinai Peninsula from which it withdrew after concluding a peace treaty with Egypt.[131] In the 40 years that have transpired since then, Israel has transferred some 400,000 Jewish settlers into the occupied territories contrary to Article 49 (6) of Geneva Convention IV.[132] Although Israel redeployed its troops from the Gaza Strip between August and September of 2005, it would seem that it still exercises effective control there as the occupying power.[133]

X. THE EGYPT–ISRAEL PEACE TREATY

On 26 March 1979, Egypt and Israel concluded a Treaty of Peace, which was witnessed by Jimmy Carter, then President of the United States.[134] The treaty does not mention the Palestinian people by name in any of its provisions. The preamble does, however, mention that the parties are 'convinced of the urgent necessity of the establishment of a just, comprehensive and lasting peace in the Middle East in accordance with Security Council resolutions 242 and 338'. According to Articles I (2) and II:

> Israel will withdraw its armed forces and civilians from the Sinai behind the international boundary between Egypt and mandated Palestine . . .
>
> The permanent boundary between Egypt and Israel is the recognised international boundary between Egypt and the former mandated territory of Palestine . . . without prejudice to the issue of the status of the Gaza Strip . . .

The Gaza Strip thus remained under Israeli occupation subject to Geneva Convention IV, its status to be resolved in future peace talks between Israel, the Palestinians and those Arabs States with an interest in the Palestine question (principally, Egypt, Jordan, Lebanon and Syria).

---

[131] See Treaty of Peace between the Arab Republic of Egypt and the State of Israel, 26 Mar 1979, reproduced in (1979) 18 International Legal Materials 362.

[132] 75 United Nations Treaty Series (1950) 287.

[133] See I Scobbie, 'An Intimate Disengagement: Israel's withdrawal from Gaza, the Law of Occupation and of Self-Determination' (2004–5) 11 Yearbook of Islamic and Middle Eastern Law 3–41.

[134] See (n 131).

XI. THE ISRAEL–JORDAN PEACE TREATY

In the Treaty of Peace between Israel and Jordan[135] the Palestinians are explicitly mentioned in Article 8 on Refugees and Displaced Persons. This provides in part:

1. Recognizing the massive human problems caused to both Parties by the conflict in the Middle East, as well as the contribution made by them towards the alleviation of human suffering, the Parties will seek to further alleviate those problems arising on a bilateral level.
2. Recognizing that the above human problems caused by the conflict in the Middle East cannot be fully resolved on the bilateral level, the Parties will seek to resolve them in appropriate forums, in accordance with international law, including the following:
   a. in the case of displaced persons, in a quadripartite committee together with Egypt and the Palestinians:
   b. in the case of refugees.
      i. in the framework of the Multilateral Working Group on Refugees.
      ii. in negotiations, in a framework to be agreed, bilateral or otherwise, in conjunction with and at the same time as the permanent status negotiations pertaining to the Territories referred to in Article 3 of this Treaty . . .

Article 3 refers to the boundary between Israel and Jordan 'without prejudice to the status of any territories that came under Israeli military government control in 1967', namely the West Bank which includes East Jerusalem.[136] Article 9 on Places of Historical and Religious Significance and Interfaith Relations, provides in part:

1. Each Party will provide freedom of access to places of religious and historical significance.
2. In this regard, in accordance with the Washington Declaration, Israel respects the present special role of the Hashemite Kingdom of Jordan in Muslim Holy shrines in Jerusalem. When negotiations on the permanent status will take place, Israel will give high priority to the Jordanian historic role in these shrines . . .

It should be said that in 1988, King Hussein of Jordan publicly renounced in an address to the nation on behalf of his government, all claims to East

---

[135] (1995) 34 International Legal Materials 46–66.   [136] Art 3 (2), ibid.

Jerusalem and the West Bank in favour of Palestinian self-determination and the status of the Palestine Liberation Organization (PLO) as the 'sole legitimate representative of the Palestinian people'.[137]

XII. THE OSLO ACCORDS

The Oslo Accords refer to a series of bilateral agreements between Israel and the PLO which can be traced to the secret back-channel negotiations that took place between them in the capital city of Norway in the early 1990s.[138] These talks undercut the more public series of meetings which were taking place between Israeli officials and prominent Palestinians from the occupied territories in Washington DC, a process which had begun during the 1991 Madrid Peace Conference.[139] The PLO had been excluded from the Washington process by the US Government although they were in daily contact with members of the Palestinian negotiating team (and as would later be revealed with some members of the Israeli Government).[140] The Palestinians negotiating in Washington were not privy to the Oslo process and threatened to resign when it became known.[141] They complained that Arafat had not given them decision-making powers in Washington and had excluded them from the secret negotiations in Oslo.[142] They also questioned the wisdom of his decision to defer the question of Israeli settlements and Jerusalem to final status talks in his negotiations

---

[137] See Jordan: Statement Concerning Disengagement from the West Bank and Palestinian Self-Determination', Address by His Majesty King Hussein to the Nation, 31 July 1988 (1988) 27 International Legal Materials 1637–45.

[138] For literature on the political developments which led to the Oslo Accords by some of those who participated in it see M Abbas, *Through Secret Channels* (Garnet, Reading, 1995) 103–41; A Qurie ('Abu Ala'), *From Oslo to Jerusalem: The Palestinian Story of the Secret Negotiations* (IB Tauris, London, 2006); S Peres, *Battling for Peace: A Memoir* (Random House, New York, 1995); and U Savir, *The Process: 1,100 Days that Changed the Middle East* (Vintage Books, New York, 1999). See also, M Heikal, *Secret Channels: The Inside Story of Arab–Israeli Peace Negotiations* (HarperCollins, London, 1996) 433–46; and J Corbin, *Gaza First: The Secret Norway Channel to Peace between Israel and the PLO* (Bloomsbury, London, 1994).

[139] For insights into the Washington DC talks, see R Shehadeh, *From Occupation to Interim Accords: Israel and the Palestinian Territories* (Kluwer Law International, The Hague, 1997) 104–31, 259–71.

[140] The Palestinian negotiating team in Washington DC included prominent Palestinian personalities such as Dr Haider Abdel-Shafi, Faisal Husseini, Saeb Erekat and Hanan Ashrawi, amongst others.

[141] J Rowland, 'Arafat rejects peace team resignations' *The Guardian* (13 Aug 1993) 8.

[142] See P Ford and L Andoni, 'Palestinian negotiators resign in rift with PLO' *Christian Science Monitor* (9 Aug 1993) 2; D Makovsky and B Hutman, 'Husseini–Arafat showdown expected in Tunis over decision-making in peace talks' *Jerusalem Post* (9 Aug 1993); and B Hepburn, 'Palestinian negotiators set to quit in fight with Arafat' *Toronto Star* (9 Aug 1993) A10.

with the Israelis.[143] The Israeli negotiators in Washington also felt slighted
that they had been excluded by their government from the Oslo process and
refused to participate in a meeting where President Clinton endorsed the
breakthrough.[144]

On 13 September 1993, Yasser Arafat, then Chairman of the PLO, and
Yitzhak Rabin, then Israeli Prime Minister, signed a Declaration of
Principles[145] on the White House lawn in the presence of US President Bill
Clinton. The Principles provided that the aim of the Israel–PLO negotiations were 'to establish a Palestinian Interim Self-Government Authority,
the elected Council, for the Palestinian people in the West Bank and the
Gaza Strip, for a transitional period not exceeding five years, leading to a
permanent settlement based on Security Council resolutions 242 and
338.'[146] What was meant by the term 'permanent settlement' was left
deliberately ambiguous and would cause difficulty in the ensuing years. The
Palestinians evidently aspired to create a Palestinian state in East Jerusalem,
the West Bank and the Gaza Strip. The Israeli Government, however, had
other ideas. As Prime Minister Yitzhak Rabin told the Knesset (Israel's
Parliament) upon ratification of the Israeli–Palestinian Interim
Agreement[147] on 5 October 1995:

We view the permanent solution in the framework of State of Israel [*sic*]
which will include most of the area of the Land of Israel as it was under
the rule of the British Mandate and alongside it a Palestinian *entity*
which will be a home to most of the Palestinian residents living in the
Gaza Strip and the West Bank.

We would like this to be an entity *which is less than a State* and which
will independently run the lives of the Palestinians under its authority.
The borders of the State of Israel, during the permanent solution, will be
beyond the lines which existed before the Six Day War. *We will not
return to the 4 June 1967 lines.*[148]

[143] ibid.
[144] E Bronner, 'Israel–PLO deal imminent as talks weigh details' *Boston Globe* (2 Sept 1993)
20. ('The Israeli chief negotiator, Elyakim Rubinstein, also felt insulted and did not go to
Washington this week. It was unclear whether he would resign').
[145] Declaration of Principles on Interim Self-Government Arrangements, Israel–Palestine
Liberation Organization, 13 Sept 1993 (1993) 32 International Legal Materials 1525–44.
[146] ibid Art 1.
[147] See the Israeli–Palestinian Interim Agreement on the West Bank and Gaza Strip, with
selected Annexes (1997) 36 International Legal Materials 551–649.
[148] Address to the Knesset by Prime Minister Rabin on the Israel–Palestinian Interim
Agreement, 5 Oct 1995 reprinted in Mero Medzini (ed), *Israel's Foreign Relations: Selected
Documents, 1995–1996, Volume 15* (Ministry of Foreign Affairs, Jerusalem, 1997) 322–9,
323 (emphasis added).

Rabin was speaking to the Knesset after his government had signed the most important of the Olso Agreements from the legal point of view (and also the most detailed). Amongst other matters, the Israeli–Palestinian Interim Agreement provided for the redeployment of Israeli military forces from areas populated by Palestinians in the West Bank (known as Areas A and B),[149] the deployment of Palestinian policemen into those areas and the retention of Israeli forces in Area C (which is the largest area where the settlements and bypass roads are located).[150] The Agreement also provided that Israel was obliged 'to continue to carry out the responsibility for external security, as well as the responsibility for overall security for Israelis for the purpose of safeguarding their internal security and public order.'[151] This included responsibility for providing security in the settlements.[152] Article XI, which is of interest in the light of Israel's 2005 redeployment from Gaza, provided that

1. The two sides view the West Bank and the Gaza Strip as a single territorial unit, the integrity and status of which will be preserved during the interim period.

The other agreements concluded in the 1990s and which are collectively referred to as the 'Oslo Accords', included the Arafat–Rabin–Holst Letters,[153] and the Agreement on the Gaza Strip and the Jericho Area[154] which includes the Paris Economic Protocol,[155] the Agreement on the Preparatory Transfer of Powers and Responsibilities,[156] the Protocol Concerning the Redeployment in Hebron,[157] the Wye River Memorandum[158] and the Sharm el-Sheikh Memorandum on

---

[149] Protocol Concerning Redeployment and Security Arrangements, Art 1.1 (n 147) 569.

[150] Appendix 2, Deployment of Palestinian Policemen, ibid 589.

[151] Chapter 2, Redeployment and Security Arrangements, Art X, para 4, 561, ibid.

[152] Arrangements for Security and Public Order, Art XII, para 1, 562, ibid.

[153] Israel–PLO Recognition: Exchange of Letters between Arafat, Holst and Rabin, 9 Sept 1993, reproduced in M Cherif Bassiouni (ed), *Documents on the Arab–Israeli Conflict: The Palestinians and the Israeli-Palestinian Peace Process, Volume 2* (Transnational Publishers, New York, 2005) 888–9.

[154] Israel–Palestine Liberation Organization Agreement on the Gaza Strip and Jericho Area, 4 May 1994 (1994) 33 International Legal Materials 622–39 (excluding protocols).

[155] Protocol on Economic Relations between the Government of the State of Israel and the PLO, representing the Palestinian People, 29 Apr 1994 (Annex IV to the Gaza–Jericho Agreement) (1994) 33 International Legal Materials 696–720.

[156] Israel–Palestine Liberation Organization: Agreement on Preparatory Powers and Responsibilities, 29 Aug 1994 (1995) 34 International Legal Materials 455–81.

[157] Israel–Palestine Liberation Organization: Protocol Concerning the Redeployment in Hebron and Note for the Record (1997) 36 International Legal Materials 650–66.

[158] Israel–Palestine Liberation Organization: Wye River Memorandum (Interim Agreement), 23 Oct 1998 (1998) 37 International Legal Materials 1251–7.

Implementation Timeline of Outstanding Commitments of Agreements Signed and Resumption of Permanent Status Negotiations.[159]

It has been convincingly argued that these agreements amounted to legally binding treaties between the parties[160] and that they are still in force, even though they were not considered by the ICJ in its 2004 advisory opinion in *Wall*.[161]

XIII. THE 2004 ICJ ADVISORY OPINION

In 2002 Israel began constructing a vast concrete and wire barrier of several hundred kilometres in length in the West Bank. Ostensibly, the 'wall' as it came to be known, is being constructed by Israel to prevent the infiltration of Palestinian suicide bombers into its city centres.[162] Although there is no question that the barrier has a security function, the fact that it effectively incorporates the West Bank settlements into Israel raised some eyebrows. The Palestinians argued that if Israel was solely concerned about its security it could have constructed the wall on or close to the 1949 ceasefire lines. They said the fact that the wall protruded into the occupied territories, in some places for several kilometres, meant that the wall was effectively annexing territory to Israel. Worried that the construction of the wall inside the occupied territories would prejudice the creation of an independent, democratic and viable Palestinian State as envisaged in the 'Roadmap',[163] Nasser Al-Kidwa, the Permanent Observer of Palestine to the United Nations, wrote a letter to UN Secretary-General Kofi Anan.[164] In the letter he specifically called on the Security Council

> to immediately take the necessary measures, consistent with the Charter of the United Nations, international humanitarian law and the Council's

[159] Israel–Palestine Liberation Organization: The Sharm El-Sheikh Memorandum (1999) 38 International Legal Materials 1465–8.

[160] See, eg J Quigley, 'The Israel–PLO Interim Agreements: Are they Treaties?' (1997) 30 Cornell International Law Journal 717–40 and GR Watson, *The Oslo Accords: International Law and the Israeli–Palestinian Peace Agreements* (OUP, Oxford, 2000) 55–102 (both arguing that they are binding).

[161] For criticisms of the ICJ's opinion on this point, see G Watson, 'The Wall 'Decisions' in Legal and Political Context' (2005) 99 American Journal of International Law 6–26, especially 22–4.

[162] For a description of the structure see Question of the Violation of Human Rights in the Occupied Arab Territories, including Palestine, UN doc E/CN.4.2004/6, 8 Sept 2003, paras 6–16.

[163] The Performance-Based Roadmap to a Permanent Two-State Solution to the Israel–Palestine Conflict is contained in the annex to a letter dated 7 May 2003 from the Secretary-General of the United Nations Kofi Anan addressed to the President of the Security Council in UN doc S/2003/539.

[164] UN doc A/58/399, S/2003/929, 1 Oct 2003.

own previous relevant resolutions, to address this grave matter and to bring to a halt these illegal actions by the occupying Power.[165]

Subsequently, a draft resolution was submitted to the UN Security Council by Guinea, Malaysia, Pakistan and the Syrian Arab Republic that declared the wall illegal and asked Israel to cease and reverse its construction.[166] The draft resolution was, however, vetoed by a permanent member of the Security Council on 14 October 2003.[167] Thirteen days later, a number of European States acting in concert introduced a resolution in the General Assembly in the context of the Tenth Emergency Special Session which

> *Demands* that Israel stop and reverse the construction of the wall in the Occupied Palestinian Territory, including in and around East Jerusalem, which is in departure of the Armistice Line of 1949 and is in contradiction to relevant provisions of international law.[168]

This resolution also requested the UN Secretary-General to report on Israel's compliance with the resolution within a month. On 24 November 2003, his report was submitted to the General Assembly.[169] It concluded that Israel was not in compliance with the Assembly's demand to stop building the wall.[170] On receipt of this report, the Assembly requested the ICJ to urgently render an advisory opinion on the following question

> What are the legal consequences arising from the construction of the wall being built by Israel, the occupying power, in the Occupied Palestinian Territory, including in and around East Jerusalem, as described in the report of the Secretary-General, considering the rules and principles of international law, including the Fourth Geneva Convention of 1949, and relevant Security Council and General Assembly resolutions.[171]

On 23 February 2004, oral pleadings before the ICJ began. Palestine, 12 States (Algeria, Bangladesh, Belize, Cuba, Indonesia, Jordan, Madagascar, Malaysia, Saudi Arabia, Senegal, South Africa and the Sudan) and two international organizations (League of Arab States and the Organization of the Islamic Conference) sent representatives to appear before the Court. Israel refused to participate. The pleadings concluded on 25 February when the ICJ began its deliberation. On 9 July 2004, the ICJ delivered its advisory

---

[165] ibid.
[167] ibid, veto (US).
[169] UN doc ES-10/248, 24 Nov 2003.
[171] GA Res ES-10/14 (A/ES-10/L.16), 8 Dec 2003.

[166] UN doc S/20003/980, 14 Oct 2003.
[168] GA Res ES-10/13, 27 Oct 2003.
[170] ibid 7.

opinion[172] which was broadly welcomed by the international community, although it was condemned by Israel.[173]

The ICJ's *dispositif* was as follows:

THE COURT,

(1) Unanimously,
    Finds that it has jurisdiction to give the advisory opinion requested;
(2) By fourteen votes to one,
    Decides to comply with the request for an advisory opinion;
    IN FAVOUR: *President* Shi; *Vice-President* Ranjeva; *Judges* Guillaume, Koroma, Vereshchetin, Higgins, Parra-Aranguren, Kooijmans, Rezek, Al-Khasawneh, Elaraby, Owada, Simma, Tomka;
    AGAINST: *Judge* Buergenthal;
(3) *Replies* in the following manner to the question put by the General Assembly:
A. By fourteen votes to one,
    The construction of the wall being built by Israel, the occupying Power, in the Occupied Palestinian Territory, including in and around East Jerusalem, and its associated régime, are contrary to international law;
    IN FAVOUR: *President* Shi; *Vice-President* Ranjeva; *Judges* Guillaume, Koroma, Vereshchetin, Higgins, Parra-Aranguren, Kooijmans, Rezek, Al-Khasawneh, Elaraby, Owada, Simma, Tomka;
    AGAINST: *Judge* Buergenthal;
B. By fourteen votes to one,
    Israel is under an obligation to terminate its breaches of international law; it is under an obligation to cease forthwith the works of construction of the wall being built in the Occupied Palestinian Territory, including in and around East Jerusalem, to dismantle forthwith the structure therein situated, and to repeal or render ineffective forthwith all legislative and regulatory acts relating thereto, in accordance with paragraph 151 of this Opinion;
    IN FAVOUR: *President* Shi; *Vice-President* Ranjeva; *Judges* Guillaume, Koroma, Vereshchetin, Higgins, Parra-Aranguren, Kooijmans, Rezek, Al-Khasawneh, Elaraby, Owada, Simma, Tomka;
    AGAINST: *Judge* Buergenthal;
C. By fourteen votes to one,

---

[172] See International Court of Justice, Legal Consequences of the Construction of a Wall in the Occupied Palestinian Territory (2004) 43 International Legal Materials 1009–56.

[173] See C McGreal, 'Sacred right to fight terror overrides court, says Sharon' *The Guardian* (12 July 2004). (Ariel Sharon: 'On Friday, the sacred right of the war on terrorism received a slap in the face by the ICJ after it decided that the terrorism-prevention fence is illegal and that Israel must dismantle it'.)

Israel is under an obligation to make reparation for all damage caused by the construction of the wall in the Occupied Palestinian Territory, including in and around East Jerusalem;

IN FAVOUR: *President* Shi; *Vice-President* Ranjeva; *Judges* Guillaume, Koroma, Vereshchetin, Higgins, Parra-Aranguren, Kooijmans, Rezek, Al-Khasawneh, Elaraby, Owada, Simma, Tomka;

AGAINST: *Judge* Buergenthal;

D. By thirteen votes to two,

All States are under an obligation not to recognize the illegal situation resulting from the construction of the wall and not to render aid or assistance in maintaining the situation created by such construction; all States parties to the Fourth Geneva Convention relative to the Protection of Civilian Persons in Time of War of 12 August 1949 have in addition the obligation, while respecting the United Nations Charter and international law, to ensure compliance by Israel with international humanitarian law as embodied in that Convention;

IN FAVOUR: *President* Shi; *Vice-President* Ranjeva; *Judges* Guillaume, Koroma, Vereshchetin, Higgins, Parra-Aranguren, Rezek, Al-Khasawneh, Elaraby, Owada, Simma, Tomka;

AGAINST: *Judges* Kooijmans, Buergenthal;

E. By fourteen votes to one,

The United Nations, and especially the General Assembly and the Security Council, should consider what further action is required to bring to an end the illegal situation resulting from the construction of the wall and the associated régime, taking due account of the present Advisory Opinion.

IN FAVOUR: *President* Shi; *Vice-President* Ranjeva; *Judges* Guillaume, Koroma, Vereshchetin, Higgins, Parra-Aranguren, Kooijmans, Rezek, Al-Khasawneh, Elaraby, Owada, Simma, Tomka;

AGAINST: *Judge* Buergenthal.

The ICJ's *dispositif* is slightly misleading in that it appears as though Judge Buergenthal dissented from the opinions of the rest of his colleagues. This was not so. Judge Buergethal appended a Declaration to the advisory opinion, not a Dissenting Opinion. He did not participate in the deliberations because in his opinion the Court did not have before it the requisite factual information to make a determination as to whether the wall was contrary to international law, although it is telling that Judge Owada did not quite agree with him on this point.[174] In his Declaration Judge Buergenthal said that his negative votes in the *dispositif*

---

[174] See Declaration of Judge Buergenthal in *Wall* (n 172) para 1. Contrast this with the Separate Opinion of Judge Owada in *Wall* (n 172) para 24. ('it would seem reasonable to

should not be seen as reflecting my view that the construction of the wall by Israel on the Occupied Palestinian Territory does not raise serious questions as a matter of international law. I believe it does, and there is much in the Opinion with which I agree.[175]

Buergenthal agreed with all of the major legal issues raised by his colleagues in the advisory opinion. He thought that Geneva Convention IV was applicable to the occupied Palestinian territories; Israel's practice of settling its own population into that territory was contrary to Article 49 (6) of that Convention; the Palestinian people's right to self-determination was an obligation *erga omnes*; and human rights law was also applicable.[176]

The issue that really seems to have irked Judge Buergenthal was the question of self-defence. He objected to the Court's narrow interpretation of Article 51 of the UN Charter as did some of the other judges.[177] However, whereas Judge Higgins ultimately voted in favour of this narrow interpretation of Article 51, although with some reservations, Buergenthal lambasted the Court for failing 'to address any facts or evidence specifically rebutting Israel's claim of military exigencies or requirements of national security.'[178] In this regard, it will be recalled that Israel did not enter a plea on the merits of the case in its written statement. Nor did it participate in the oral pleadings before the Court. Moreover, none of the States that submitted written statements or made oral pleadings before the Court supported Israel's claim that the construction of the wall was justified as a measure of self-defence under Article 51 of the UN Charter.[179] In fact, many argued that it was inapplicable. This may explain why the ICJ's interpretation of Article 51 was brief as self-defence was not pleaded before it as an exculpatory justification for building the wall. As Israel was the State pleading self-defence, was it not obliged to produce evidence to the effect that the wall had to be built in the occupied territories, and that the 1949 ceasefire lines could not be defended? How can the ICJ be expected to address any facts that might rebut Israel's claims of military exigencies or requirements of national security when Israel did not provide any information as to why the wall had to be built in the occupied territories?

---

conclude on balance that the political, social, economic and humanitarian impacts of the construction of the wall, *as substantiated by ample evidence supplied and documented in the course of the present proceedings*, is such that the construction of the wall would constitute a violation of international obligations under various international instruments to which Israel is a party'). Emphasis added.

[175] Judge Buergenthal, ibid para. 1.
[176] Declaration of Judge Buergenthal, ibid.
[177] See also, the Separate Opinion of Judge Higgins in *Wall* (n 172) paras 33–5.
[178] See Declaration of Judge Buergenthal in *Wall* (n 172) para 7.
[179] See I Scobbie, 'Words My Mother Never Taught Me: 'In Defense of the International Court' (2005) 99 American Journal of International Law 77, n 6.

It is telling that Israel's Supreme Court, acting as a High Court of Justice, delivered a decision responding to a petition complaining about the wall nine days before the ICJ rendered its advisory opinion.[180] In the *Beit Sourik* case, which was evidently delivered to coincide with the ICJ's advisory opinion, and which was translated into English[181] (something the HCJ does not normally do), three Israeli judges ruled that the wall could be constructed in the occupied territories and that it was not contrary to the laws of belligerent occupation.[182] Responding to the argument raised by the petitioners that the route of the wall was motivated by political reasons so as to incorporate Israeli civilian settlements established inside the West Bank into Israel, the HCJ held:

> . . . it is the security perspective—and not the political one—which must examine a route based on its security merits alone, *without regard for the location of the Green Line* (emphasis added).[183]

Evidently, the HCJ could only reach this conclusion by not answering the question as to whether Article 49 (6) of Geneva Convention IV was applicable to the West Bank. This is because this article prohibits an occupying power from transferring its civilian population into the territory it occupies.[184] In *Mara'abe v The Prime Minister of Israel*, which was delivered after the ICJ's advisory opinion, the HCJ stuck to its guns holding that the wall was not contrary to international law.[185] Yet again it refused to address the issue of whether Geneva Convention IV was applicable to the occupied territories which allowed it to avoid a finding that the settlements,

---

[180] HCJ 2056/04 *Beit Sourik Village Council v the Government of Israel* (2004) translated in (2004) 43 International Legal Materials 1099–128, hereafter cited as *Beit Sourik*.

[181] For commentary, see I Scobbie, 'Regarding/Disregarding: The Judicial Rhetoric of President Barak and the International Court of Justice's Wall Advisory Opinion' (2006) 5 Chinese Journal of International Law 269–300, 287.

[182] *Beit Sourik* (n 180) para 32. However, they held that in a number of sections the wall's route did not satisfy the proportionality test established by the HCJ.

[183] *Beit Sourik*, ibid, para 30.

[184] Geneva Convention Relative to the Protection of Civilian Persons in Time of War (12 Aug 1949) 75 United Nations Treaty Series 287. See JS Pictet (ed), *Commentary on the Geneva Conventions of 12 August 1949: IV Geneva Convention Relative to the Protection of Civilian Persons in Time of War* (ICRC, Geneva, 1958) 283. In 1967, Theodor Meron, who was then working as the legal counsel to Israel's Foreign Ministry, wrote in a 'Top Secret' Memorandum: 'My conclusion is that civilian settlement in the administered territories contravenes the explicit provisions of the Fourth Geneva Convention.' See G Gorenberg, *The Accidental Empire: Israel and the Birth of the Settlements, 1967–1977* (Henry Holt, New York, 2006) 99–102. Since the 1970s, Legal advisors at the US State Department have accepted that the settlements contravene Article 49(6) of Geneva Convention IV. See Letter of HJ Hansell, Legal Advisor, USDOS to House Communication on International Relations, 21 Apr 1978, in (1978) 17 International Legal Materials 777.

[185] HCJ 7957/04 (2005), translated in (2006) 45 International Legal Materials, 202–45, hereafter cited as '*Mara'abe*'.

which it admitted the wall is designed to protect, are contrary to international law.[186] However, as a result of developments since the *Mara'abe* case, several justices of the Israel Supreme Court have castigated the Israeli Government for misleading it as to the true reasons underlying the wall's route.[187] It would seem that some Israeli Government ministers were under the impression that the HCJ was actually establishing Israel's borders.[188] If this is indeed the case, then it would seem that the Government of Israel is trying to have its cake and eat it too: it wants to protect its citizens, hence the construction of the wall, but at the same time it desires to acquire more territory for itself, hence the wall's route incorporates the settlements into Israel, an act tantamount to de facto annexation.[189]

XIV. CONCLUSIONS

The Palestine question has been on the agenda of the United Nations since 3 April 1947.[190] Since then there have been six major confrontations[191] between Israel and its Arab neighbours (the 1948 conflict, the 1956 Suez war, the 1967 Arab–Israeli war, the 1973 October war, and Israel's invasion of Lebanon in 1978 and in 1982) and two Palestinian *intifadas* (the first from 1987 to 1993 and the second from 2000 to 2005, although it has not really ended). Each conflict concluded with a peace of sorts, but they did not solve the underlying dispute between Arabs and Jews in the Holy Land. The Egypt–Israel Peace Treaty was widely seen as a sell out by the Arab world, which Anwar Sadat paid for with his life. Similarly, the road from Oslo was effectively blocked by the assassination of Yitzhak Rabin and the election of Binyamin Netanyahu who did his utmost to stall implementing

---

[186] ibid para 21.

[187] *Ha'aretz* reported that Justices Aharon Barak, Dorit Beinisch, and Ayala Procaccia severely criticized the government for concealing in earlier High Court hearings that the existing route was determined partly by a master plan for expanding the settlements, and not solely for security considerations. See Yoaz Yuval, Court orders section of separation fence torn down, *Ha'aretz* , 16 June 2006. See also, HCJ 2732/05May 2005 translation provided courtesy of Michael Sfard, Adv (on file with author).

[188] Tzipi Livni, who was Israel's Minister of Justice said the wall would serve as 'the future border of the State of Israel' and that the HCJ in its rulings 'is drawing the country's borders'. See Yuval Yoaz, Justice Minister: West Bank fence is Israel's future border, *Ha'aretz*, 1 Dec 2005.

[189] See *Wall* advisory opinion (n 172) para 121.

[190] See Question of Palestine, Letter from the United Kingdom Delegation at the United Nations to the Acting Secretary-General of the United Nations, UN doc A/286, 3 Apr 1947.

[191] Excluding last summer's conflict between Israel and Hezbollah which is analysed in V Kattan, 'The Use and Abuse of Self-Defence in International Law: The Israel–Hezbollah Conflict as a Case Study' (2005–6) 12 Yearbook of Islamic and Middle Eastern Law 31–50. See also, G Redsell, 'Illegitimate, Unecesssary and Disproportionate: Israel's Use of Force in Lebanon' (2007) 3 Cambridge Student Law Review 70–85.

the agreements.[192] The negotiations at Camp David ended in failure, as did the talks at Taba in the following year.[193] The Roadmap and all the other peace initiatives floated in the media (such as the Geneva Accords) have come to nought.[194] Similarly, the Arab world's gesture towards a two-state solution, first made in Beirut in 2002 and reiterated in Algiers in 2005 has fallen on deaf ears. In August–September 2005, Israel unilaterally withdrew from Gaza, an act inconsistent with the Interim Agreement of 1995, and which has left Gaza starved and cut off from the outside world leaving a power vacuum that has been filled by the Muslim brotherhood.

It may at this juncture be difficult to see what role international law can play in the path towards peace but it seems clear that any 'peace' which ignores international legal principles such as justice and equity, will be no peace at all. The international community needs to think of more creative ways of achieving their vision of two viable and independent sovereign states living side by side in peace and security. It is self-evident that the parties cannot do this between themselves without serious third-party intervention, assistance and encouragement. Whether the rekindling of the 'peace process' at Annapolis will deliver results, time will only tell.

---

[192] Although he eventually agreed to the Wye River Memorandum, after much pressure from the US.

[193] For further reading, see C Enderlin, *Shattered Dreams: The Failure of the Peace Process in the Middle East, 1995–2002* (Sudan Fairfield trans, New York, Other Press 2003); CE Swisher, *The Truth about Camp David: The Untold Story about the Collapse of the Middle East Peace Process* (Nation Books, New York, 2004); and H Agha and R Malley, 'Camp David: The Tragedy of Errors' *New York Review of Books* (9 Aug 2001) 59.

[194] On the Geneva Accords, see N Kardahji, *The Geneva Accord: Plan or Pretence?* (PASSIA, Jerusalem, 2004).

PALESTINE MAPS

Sykes-Picot Agreement, 1916

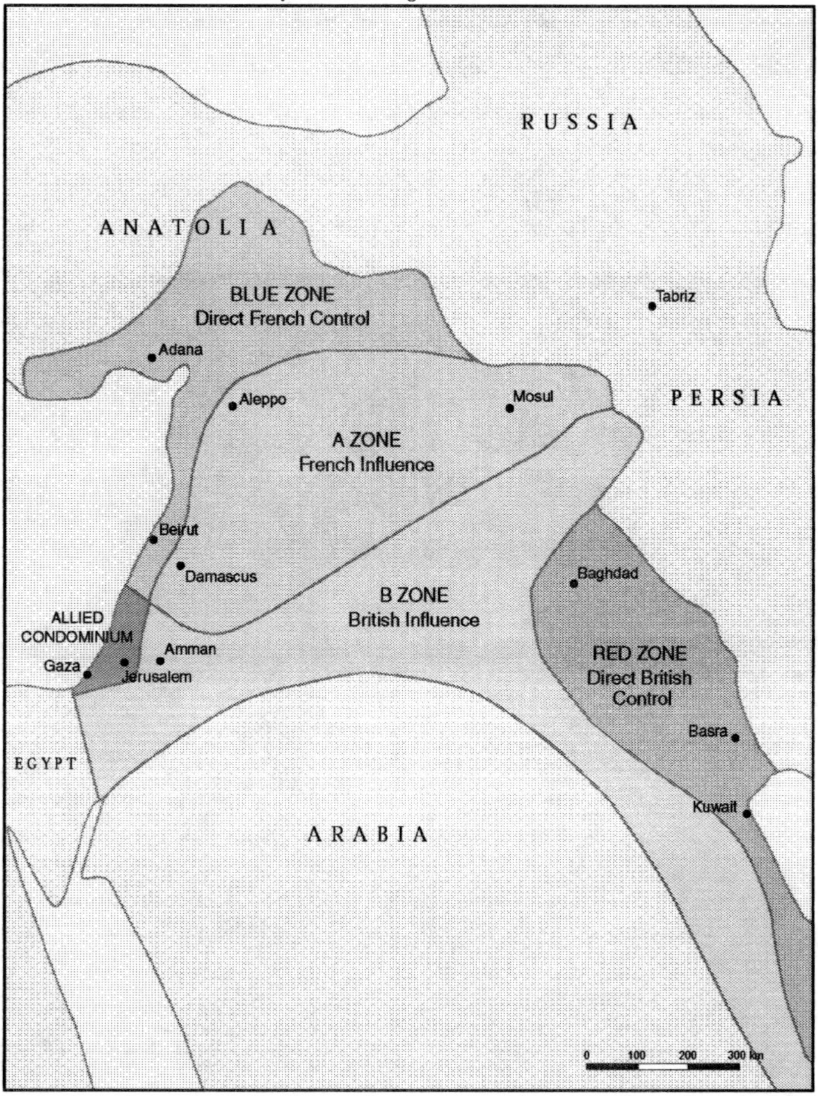

RUSSIA

ANATOLIA

BLUE ZONE
Direct French Control

Tabriz

Adana

Aleppo

Mosul

PERSIA

A ZONE
French Influence

Beirut

Damascus

Baghdad

ALLIED
CONDOMINIUM

Amman

B ZONE
British Influence

RED ZONE
Direct British
Control

Gaza

Jerusalem

EGYPT

Basra

Kuwait

ARABIA

0   100   200   300 km

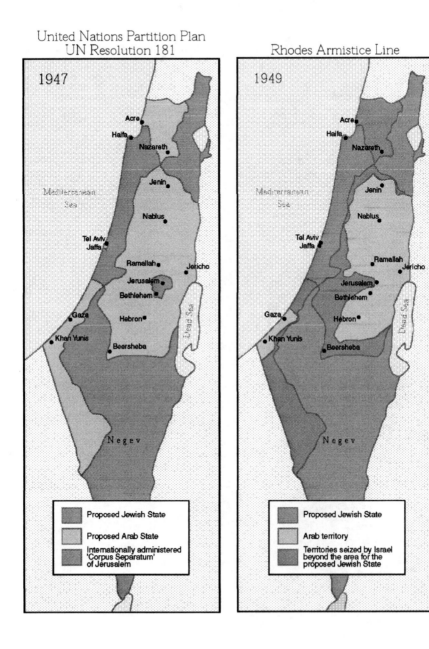

United Nations Partition Plan
UN Resolution 181

Rhodes Armistice Line

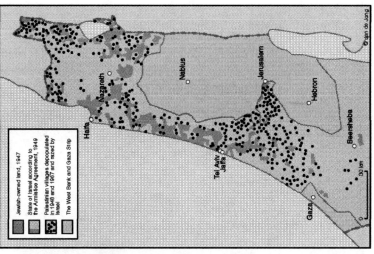

Palestinian Villages Depopulated in 1948 and 1967, and Razed by Israel

Jewish-owned land, 1947

State of Israel according to the Armistice Agreement, 1949

Palestinian villages depopulated in 1948 and 1967 and razed by Israel

The West Bank and Gaza Strip

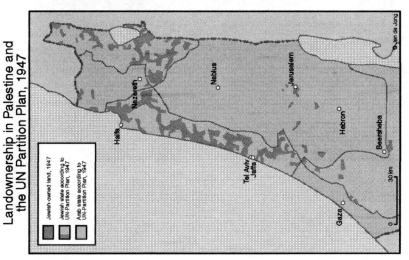

Landownership in Palestine and the UN Partition Plan, 1947

Jewish-owned land, 1947

Jewish state according to UN-Partition Plan, 1947

Arab state according to UN-Partition Plan, 1947

The Near East after the 1967 June War

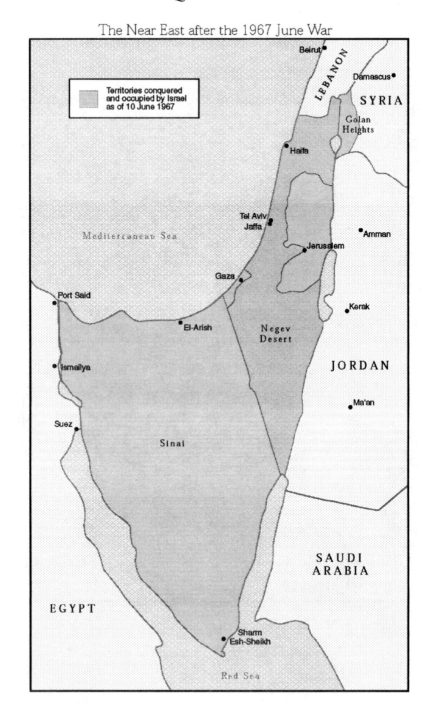

Oslo II, 1995

0   20 km

Jenin

GANIM

Tulkarem

SHAVEI
SHOMRON

Nablus

ELON MOREH

Qalqilya

ALFEI
MENASHE

ARIEL

MA'ALE
EPHRAIM

RIMONIM

PSAGOT

Ramallah

SHA'AI
ZE'EV

Jericho

Jerusalem

MA'ALE
ADUMIM

KALYA

ISRAEL

Bethlehem

ETZION
BLOC

Green Line

KIRYAT ARBA

Dead Sea

Hebron

Area A - Palestinian cities

Area B - Palestinian villages

Area C - Israeli settlement,
military areas and state lands

▲ Main Israeli settlements

The Gaza Strip, 2000

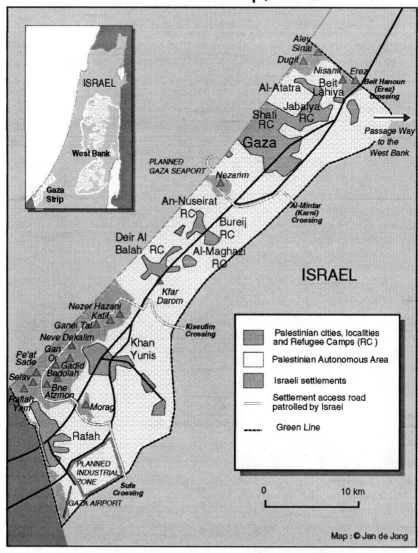

Map : © Jan de Jong

REFUGEES

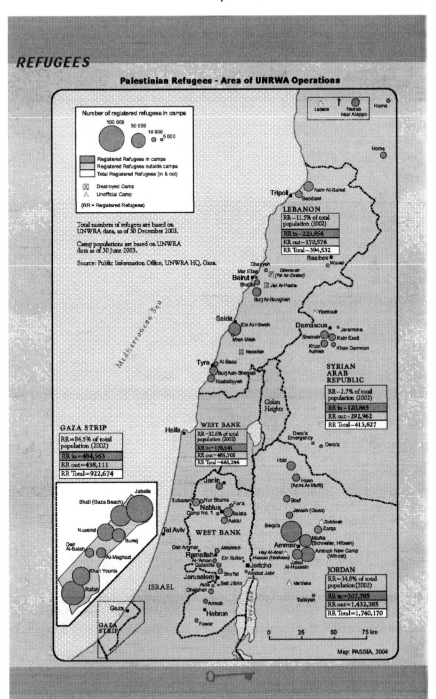

Palestinian Refugees - Area of UNRWA Operations

Number of registered refugees in camps

100 000   50 000   10 000   5 000

Registered Refugees in camps
Registered Refugees outside camps
Total Registered Refugees (in & out)

☒ Destroyed Camp
⚊ Unofficial Camp

(RR = Registered Refugees)

Total numbers of refugees are based on
UNWRA data, as of 30 December 2003.

Camp populations are based on UNWRA
data as of 30 June 2003.

Source: Public Information Office, UNWRA HQ, Gaza.

LEBANON
RR – 11.5% of total
population (2002)
RR in – 223,956
RR out – 170,576
RR Total – 394,532

SYRIAN ARAB REPUBLIC
RR – 2.7% of total
population (2002)
RR in – 120,865
RR out – 292,962
RR Total – 413,827

GAZA STRIP
RR = 84.5% of total
population (2002)
RR in = 484,563
RR out = 438,111
RR Total = 922,674

WEST BANK
RR – 32.6% of total
population (2002)
RR in – 179,541
RR out – 485,705
RR Total – 665,246

JORDAN
RR = 34.8% of total
population (2002)
RR in = 307,785
RR out = 1,432,385
RR Total = 1,740,170

Map: PASSIA, 2004

West Bank Wall - Map 2006

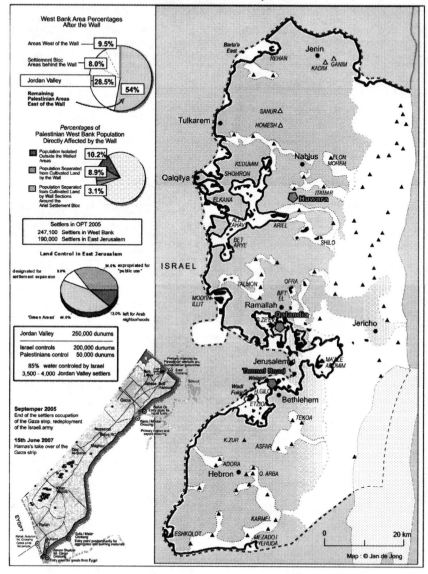

Map : © Jan de Jong

The Gaza Strip 2007

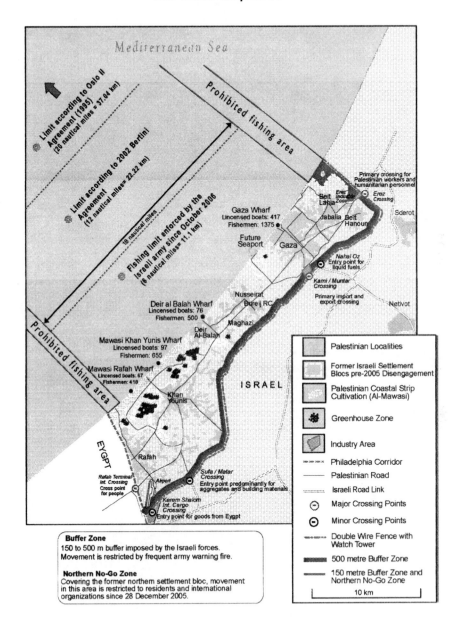

Part I

INTERNATIONAL LAW IN THE MIDDLE EAST

Leiden Journal of International Law, 17 (2004), pp. 391–404
© Foundation of the Leiden Journal of International Law   Printed in the United Kingdom   DOI: 10.1017/S0922156504001864

Orientalism and International Law: The Middle East as the Underclass of the International Legal Order

JEAN ALLAIN*

Abstract

Taking Edward Said's 'orientalist' thesis as a starting point, this piece considers the manner in which the 'Orient' has been transformed by the West into a zone wherein the dictates of international law need not hold. By giving voice to a number of cases – the regime of the Suez Canal, the creation of the state of Israel, aggression during the Lebanese and two gulf wars, UN-imposed Iraqi sanctions, and states of emergency in Syria and Egypt – it becomes evident that international law has been utilized in an instrumental manner. The outcome is a region which has been treated as the underclass of the international community, wherein international law has been, in fundamental instances, interpreted arbitrarily, applied selectively, and enforced punitively.

Key words

international legal theory; Middle East; orientalism; post-colonialism; third-world approach

No other publication has had as much impact on area studies in the last 25 years as that of the late Edward Said's *Orientalism*. In his 1978 work, Said sought to demonstrate how European cultural imperialism of the late eighteenth and nineteenth centuries paved the way for what would follow: the European colonization after the First World War of 85 per cent of the globe.[1] What Said demonstrated is the manner in which the orientalist – those individuals who wrote about the Orient (i.e. Africa, Asia, and the Middle East), such as travellers and scholars – determined and, hence, established Western 'knowledge' regarding these areas. If we take Said's thesis seriously and ask ourselves the extent to which there is interplay between the discipline of international law and manifestations of 'orientalism', I believe that a much clearer understanding emerges of the manner in which the stage was set to allow international law to be utilized in an instrumental manner so as to achieve the continuing subjugation of various regions of the world. What follows is a *tour d'horizon* which seeks to demonstrate the qualitatively different manner in which

---

* Assistant Professor of Public International Law, American University in Cairo. The following is an amplification of the orientalist theme which underlies, in part, the thesis of my monograph, *International Law in the Middle East: Closer to Power than Justice* (2004). I wish to thank, with appreciation, Steven Blockmans, who approached me after I presented a lecture on the issue at the Asser Institute in August 2002, for inviting me to submit a piece to the *Leiden Journal of International Law* on my understanding of the manner in which international law is perceived in the Middle East.
1. E. Said, *Orientalism: Western Conceptions of the Orient* (1995), 122.

international law has been applied and interpreted in one such region – the Middle East – as a result of the effects of orientalism. What emerges is a sense that much as the underclass in a domestic legal system feels the punitive, repressive, and selective nature of law, so, too, the local population of the Middle East experiences international law not as a shield but as a sword. As a result, international law in the Middle East lacks legitimacy.

When this lack of legitimacy in superimposed on one of the most highly militarized regions of the world, the result is a powder keg with an extremely short fuse. As the various undertakings of international law are the only future-orientated limitations to which sovereign states have consented in their interaction on the international plane, the de-legitimization of international law means that few constraints exist on state action in the Middle East. As a result, the history of the modern Middle East is one fraught with bloodshed brought on by an unwillingness to accept the fundamental tenets of international law: the peaceful settlement of international disputes and the prohibition on unilateral use of force. While international law may be perceived in the Western world as neutral and benign, as a legitimate means of regulating and maintaining international order, in the Middle East it is understood to be little more than a tool of the powerful, used to coerce and oppress. This short piece seeks, by examining international law through the lens of the Middle East, to understand the qualitatively different manner in which international law continues to be applied and interpreted in the region: not in the interest of the local inhabitants, but in line with the wishes and/or dictates of the West.

1. ORIENTALISM AND INTERNATIONAL LAW

To what extent has international law played its part in the 'long and slow process of appropriation by which Europe, or European awareness of the Orient, transformed itself from being textual and contemplative into being administrative, economic, and even military'?[2] While Edward Said is interested in the front-end of the European imperialist venture – the writings of the 'orientalists' of the late eighteenth and nineteenth centuries whose studies and writings projected the East as backward, degenerate, and uncivilized, thus giving justification to European colonial and imperial ventures – the role of international law is to be manifest in the outcome of that process: the actual, physical, taking of the Orient. International law, in the guise of capitulation agreements, the League of Nations mandate system, and even in the UN Security Council sanctions regime, has been a major factor in turning the Orient 'from alien into colonial space'.[3] Where a nexus exists between the orientalist thesis and international law it is to be found in the use of 'facts' propagated by orientalists which allowed for the great divide to emerge in international law between 'civilized nations' and 'backward territories'.[4] Such justifications lent weight to the

---

2.   *Ibid.*, at 210.
3.   *Ibid.*, at 211.
4.   For instance, less than eighty years ago, M. F. Lindley could explain that such backward territories were understood to extend, at the extreme, to those that were 'entirely uninhabited; and it clearly includes

development of an arsenal of legal justifications for, what in polite company might be called, 'appropriation': including *terra nullius*, protectorates, mandates, and trusteeships. As such, the orientalist project laid the groundwork by demeaning those foreign to the West – the 'other' – so that imperial ventures could persist unimpeded. That realpolitik should manifest itself in actual terms in this region more than elsewhere is testament to the manner in which orientalism has paved the way for a calculus of state action devoid of any consideration of the interests and aspirations of the people who actually live in the Middle East.

Edward Said's thesis emphasizes the Gramscian concept of 'hegemony' wherein ideas are not enforced through coercion, but through consent. 'In any society not totalitarian', Said explains, 'certain cultural forms predominate over others, just as certain ideas are more influential than others.'[5] Orientalist writings of past centuries have thus built a twofold consensus which persists to this day: one, 'the ideal of European identity as a superior one in comparison with all the non-European peoples and cultures', and two, that European knowledge about the Orient overrides 'the possibility that a more independent, or more sceptical, thinker might have had different views on the matter'.[6] Beyond the intellectual debt owed to Antonio Gramsci, Said also pointed to the work of Michel Foucault, and especially to his concept of 'discourse', to show how the orientalist venture was established as the West's 'corporate institution for dealing with the Orient'. Said elucidates: 'dealing with it [the Orient] by making statements about it, authorizing views of it, describing it, by teaching it, settling it, ruling over it: in short, *Orientalism as a Western style for dominating, restructuring, and having authority over the Orient*'.[7]

The impact of Edward Said's orientalist thesis, it has been noted, is that it 'single-handedly inaugurates a new area of academic inquiry: colonial discourse',[8] while acting as a catalyst for the development of postcolonial theory.[9] Postcolonial theory, for its part, as Leela Gandhi notes, 'is a form of resistance to the mystifying amnesia of the colonial aftermath. It is a disciplinary project devoted to the academic task of revisiting, remembering and, crucially, interrogating the colonial past'.[10] Fundamentally, orientalism forces one to go back and re-evaluate those things which appear benign and neutral and to consider them critically so as to flush out any

---

territory inhabited by natives as low in the scale of civilization as those of Central Africa'. See M. F. Lindley, *The Acquisition and Government of Backward Territory in International Law: Being a Treatise on the Law and Practice Relating to Colonial Expansion* (1926), v.

5.   Said, *supra* note 1, at 7.
6.   *Ibid.*
7.   *Ibid.*, at 3 (emphasis added). To make this clear, Said later writes:

> Now because Britain, France and recently the United States are imperial powers, their political societies impart to their civil societies a sense of urgency, a direct political infusion as it were, where and whenever matters pertaining to their imperial interest abroad are concerned. I doubt that it is controversial, for example, to say that an Englishman in India or Egypt in the later nineteenth century took an interest in those countries that was never far from his status in his mind as British colonies. To say this may seem quite different from saying that all academic knowledge about India and Egypt is somehow tinged and impressed with, violated by, the gross political fact – and yet *that is what I am saying* in this study of Orientalism. (*Ibid.*, at 11 (emphasis in original)).

8.   P. Williams and L. Chrisman (eds.), *Colonial Discourse and Post-Colonial Theory: A Reader* (1994), at 5.
9.   See L. Gandhi, *Postcolonial Theory: A Critical Introduction* (1998), 64.
10. *Ibid.*, at 4.

institutional bias. Whereas critical legal scholarship at the municipal level has sought to change and, in many ways, has been successful in changing laws which were demonstrably biased against, for instance, racial groups or women, a critical examination regarding issues of international law appears to be at a more primitive stage, where, before strategies of change can be considered and given effect, first what needs to transpire is a simple exposition of institutional bias. To that end, the 'third-world approach' to international law has been instrumental in seeking to bring to the fore, very much in line with the postcolonial project, previously suppressed narratives of history to allow for an expanded space in which international law can be considered and critiqued. Thus the value of the third-world approach, and of the insights of Said's *Orientalism,* is that they seek to expand the limits of the discipline of international law so as to incorporate voices and understanding that go beyond the eurocentric origins of public international law, thus making the discipline truly 'international'. With the third-world approach, new historical veins are mined, and those facts are placed against the international legal standards of the day to seek to challenge the dominant discourse and to demonstrate the manner in which international law has been used and abused. Karin Mickelson explains:

> identifying a Third World approach as a theoretical position within international legal discourse means reclaiming a voice that has long been there, but to which very little serious attention has been paid. It is essential to bear in mind that the Third World approach to international law must be seen as lying at the intersection of two different discourses. One is the discourse of traditional international law and international legal scholarship. Here it is part of the story of the development of international law. The other discourse is that of decolonization: the full, broad panoramic view of a history of oppression and transformation. Here it can be seen as part of the story of anti-colonial and post-colonial struggle. In some ways, a Third World approach to international law is the untold part of both these stories. That which has remained somewhat marginal, while not entirely overlooked.[11]

Where the Middle East is concerned, this task of focusing on suppressed narratives has been easier of late, for instance, with regard to the creation of the state of Israel and the plight of Palestinian refugees. The 'New Historiography' movement in Israel has fundamentally rewritten the history of both the 1948 war and the forced transfer and expulsion of Palestinians during the consolidation of the state of Israel during the period of 1947–9.[12] In other instances, it has meant piecing together from various

---

11. K. Mickelson, 'Rhetoric and Rage: Third World Voices in International Legal Discourse', (1998) 16 *Wisconsin International Law Journal* 361–2. Writings within this stream include: C. Weeramantry and N. Berman, 'The Grotius Lecture Series', (1999) 14 *American University International Law Review* 1516–69; and A. Anghie, 'Finding the Peripheries: Sovereignty and Colonialism in the Nineteenth-Century International Law', (1999) 40 *Harvard International Law Journal* 1–80. On the Middle East, see G. Bisharat, 'The Legal Foundations of Peace and Prosperity in the Middle East: Peace and the Political Imperative of Legal Reform in Palestine', (1999) 31 *Case Western Reserve Journal of International Law* 253–89; and A. Shalakany, 'Privatizing Jerusalem: Or of Law, Religion and Garbage Collection', (2002) 14 *Leiden Journal of International Law* 431–44. Finally, see T. Ruskola, 'Legal Orientalism', (2002) 101 *Michigan Law Review* 179–234.

12. See the chapter entitled 'The New Historiography: Israel and its Past', in B. Morris, *1948 and After: Israel and the Palestinians* (1994); and more generally E. Rogan and A. Shalim (eds.), *The War for Palestine: Rewriting the History of 1948* (2001).

sources threads which, when brought together, form a coherent narrative to which legal standards of the day can be applied. When these two streams converge – the subjugation of 'other' through the orientalist project and the raising of suppressed narratives – what emerges is a sense that, as a result of the establishment of an orientalist substructure, international law in the Middle East has been applied and interpreted in a qualitatively different manner. Even if one were to apply a pure positivist interpretation of the law – that international law is simply what states say it is – the application of international law in the Middle East fails. As a result of the lack of consistent and uniform application and interpretation of international law in the Middle East, in essence de-legitimatizing its fundamental, normative, tenets, the law has failed to gain a semblance of regulating the region. This lack of uniformity which contributes to seeing a qualitatively different manner of application and interpretation of international law in the region is manifest in the following examples which have made of the region the underclass of the international legal order. First, consideration is given to the selective manner in which the Suez Canal was governed under tutelage of the United Kingdom from 1888 to 1956, as well as to that state's disregard for international law in imposing its Zionist policy in the 'special' case of Palestine. In these two cases, vestiges of orientalist language lingered and provided justification for the projection of the British will on to the region. Orientalism, having laid the groundwork, allowed the Middle East to develop into an underclass of the international community wherein the laws can be enforced in a selective manner, imposed punitively, and, where 'oriental despots' are concerned, passed over in silence. Examination thus turns to a number of issues: to the selective enforcement of international law by the UN Security Council as against the prohibition regarding aggression; to the punitive nature of the UN sanctions regime imposed on Iraq; and, finally, to the ability of Egypt and Syria to maintain perpetual states of emergency and to torture with impunity is also considered to demonstrate how, as with the other items noted, the law in the books dictates one outcome, while the reality – and realism – of a Middle East variety, in effect, creates another.

2. THE DEVELOPMENT OF THE UNDERCLASS

The ramifications of this lack of uniform application of international law in the Middle East means that law is to be considered instrumental in nature and simply another political tool of statecraft used by the strong against the weak. This alignment of international law in the Middle East closer to power than justice means that law loses much of its independence from international politics. No longer can one clearly identify, in this region, a set of principles which should be acted on – a normative framework. Instead of there being applied overriding legal principles – acting in good faith, the exclusion of the unilateral projection of uses of force, the peaceful settlement of disputes, and so on – the region is left, instead, to its own devices, to the whims of each state's perceived interest. In an anecdotal manner, this is best exemplified by the reaction to the claim by Boutros Boutros-Ghali, when he was acting as the Egyptian Minister of State for Foreign Affairs in 1978, that the forcing down of a Kenyan civilian airliner, in retaliation for the storming of an Egyptian aircraft in Nairobi, was tantamount to piracy. The Egyptian Prime Minister at the time, Mahduh Salim, rebuked him: 'Dr. Boutros, forget that you were a professor; international problems are not handled by international law'![13] And yet such instinctive reactions to the problem of international relations appear to be the bedrock of actions in the region. This should come as little surprise if one considers the evolution in the region of the disregard for fundamental principles of international law.

2.1. Selective application and interpretation

When legal scholars today consider the regime of the Suez Canal as manifested in the 1888 Constantinople Convention, little do they realize that it only truly gains effective legal footing more than 90 years after its signing. Although the maritime powers of the late 1800s were prepared to ratify an international agreement regulating transit through the Suez Canal, Britain effectively suspended the coming into force of the 1888 Constantinople Convention by attaching a reservation, to which France objected, meant to allow for the compatibility of provisions of the Convention with its occupation of Egypt. The 'exceptionalism' of the application of international law, which is a hallmark of events which take place in the Middle East, is manifest in the fact that it took the Entente Cordiale of 1904 between France and Britain – wherein they agreed to settle *their* outstanding claims with regard to Morocco and Egypt – to allow the coming into force of the Constantinople Convention. Yet the 1904 agreement simply allowed Britain to consolidate its control over Suez and to treat the canal as an imperial asset, having been in military occupation of Egypt since 1882. In this manner, Britain did not feel compelled to follow the dictates of the Convention; instead it governed the canal in line not with the 1888 Convention but with its imperial interest. Thus it allowed Italy to use the Canal in pursuit of its invasion of Abyssinia, despite Italy having been branded the aggressor by the League of Nations. Britain would then about-turn and exclude Italy from transiting the Isthmus of Suez, as it would the Central, and later Axis, Powers during the two world wars, effectively opening the Suez Canal to enemy attack. Despite the introduction of prohibitions against the use of force found in the Charter of the United Nations, Britain would maintain an imperial attitude towards 'its' Canal in the wake of Egyptian independence, as it masterminded with France and Israel an act of tripartite aggression against Egypt. Despite Egypt being well within its legal right in nationalizing the Suez Canal Company in 1956, the United Kingdom was prepared to forgo the fundamental building block of the international system – the prohibition against aggression – so as to attempt to re-establish its privileged position in the Middle East.[14]

---

13. B. Boutros-Ghali, *Egypt's Road to Jerusalem: A Diplomat's Story of the Struggle for Peace in the Middle East* (1997), 64.
14. Ultimately, it was not until the coming into force of the 1979 peace treaty between Egypt and Israel that the 1888 Constantinople Convention truly became operational, that is as per its Article 1: 'free and open, in time of war as in time of peace, to every vessel of commerce or of war, without distinction of flag'.

The extent to which the orientalist project denigrated the local inhabitants in the eye of the British can be seen, for example, as the basis for policy decisions by Anthony Eden's administration during the Suez crisis. The Orient, as Said noted, is something which remains 'fixed in time and place for the West',[15] and as such the binary opposition which has developed through Western projections of the East, of the 'European' and the 'other', allowed the British to disregard Egypt's right of nationalization, and instead seek to justify its actions on the basis of Egyptian incompetence and lack of a civilized demeanour. The day after the nationalization of the Suez Canal Company by the Egyptian president, Gamal Abdel Nasser, the British Cabinet met. The minutes of that meeting reflect that the Cabinet understood that Nasser had been acting legally, that from 'a narrow legal point of view his action amounted to no more than a decision to buy out the shareholders'. The minutes of the Cabinet meeting continue:

> Our case must be presented on wider international grounds: our argument must be that the canal was an important international asset and facility and that Egypt could not be allowed to exploit it for a purely internal purpose. The Egyptians had not the technical ability to manage it effectively; and their recent behaviour gave no confidence that they would recognize their international obligations in respect of it.[16]

This being the case, the British sought to establish various justifications for military intervention, including the initiation of 'Operation Pile-up', which sought to demonstrate that Egyptians were incapable of managing the Suez Canal. On 16 November 1956, the British sent 50 ships to the Mediterranean terminus 'in an attempt to swamp the piloting system' of the Canal. British historians relate, however, that the operation 'was a failure as the Egyptian pilots proved capable of clearing this increased Canal traffic in a day'.[17]

The orientalist project having for more than two hundred years established the 'other' as inferior, whose 'behaviour gave no confidence', meant that Britain could consider the Canal as its – imperial – asset and manage it in its interest, regardless of the dictates of international law. In situations where the Canal functioned in line with the Constantinople Convention, it was due to the Convention being in line with British colonial policy, not the other way around. The groundwork of the orientalist project, having been set down for centuries, allowed Eden and his Cabinet to continue to project the orient as backward and open to appropriation. But in the case of Britain's masterminding of the 'tripartite aggression' (the term, quite correctly, given in the Middle East to the UK, French, and Israeli invasion which, in the West, is given the benign designation of 'the Suez Crisis') aimed at the Suez Canal in 1956, the use of force proved to be at its peril.

---

15. Said, *supra* note 1, at 108.
16. See Document 3.1, Cabinet Discussion of Initial Reactions to the Nationalization of the Suez Canal, 27 July 1956, in A. Gorst and L. Johman, *The Suez Crisis* (1997), 58.
17. *Ibid.*, at 84; see also D. A. Farnie, *East and West of Suez: The Suez Canal in History, 1854–1956* (1969), 719, 743.

2.2. Blatant disregard

The British attitude during the evolution of the legal regime of the Suez Canal is indicative of the qualitative exceptionalism of the application and interpretation of international law as it relates to the Middle East. That is to say, where the interests of European powers, such as those of Britain, collided with their obligations under international law, more often than not they did not let those obligations limit their action; instead such powers were willing to forgo the standards of behaviour established by international law. This willingness to forgo legal obligations is brought home to us again when consideration is given to the manifest disregard for international law demonstrated by Britain in support of a Zionist policy in Palestine as part of its larger imperial aims in the region. With the acquiescence of the leading states during the interwar period, Britain imposed its Zionist policies in Palestine in clear disregard of the dictates of international law. Britain's willingness to give voice to the Balfour Declaration in 1920-3, despite not having settled the peace with Turkey, meant that, in Palestine, Britain was in violation of the laws of occupation. From the 1920 San Remo Conference – which determined that Britain would gain a League of Nations' mandate for the region – onwards, Britain no longer felt compelled to heed the dictates of the laws of occupation, instead treating Palestine as territory under its control. It was only after the ratification of the 1923 Treaty of Lausanne by Turkey that Britain received the seal of approval of the League of Nations to continue its Zionist policies, as it was officially granted the mandate for Palestine which incorporated the Balfour Declaration in its preamble.

The orientalist undertones of the mandate system itself were manifest in the description of the system as seeking to assist those 'peoples not yet able to stand by themselves under the strenuous conditions of the modern world' by providing them with the tutelage of 'advanced nations who by reason of their resources, their experience or their geographical position can best undertake this responsibility'. Yet where the mandate for Palestine was concerned, the British did not feel that they had even to respect the obligations of Article 22 of the Covenant of the League of Nations, which required that Britain ensure the 'well-being and development' of the people of Palestine, thus forming 'a sacred trust of civilization' between itself and the local inhabitants. In the case of Palestine, Britain forwent the interests of the vast majority of the local population in order to accommodate the wishes and aspirations of European Jewry to establish a national home in the shadow of the biblical Mount Zion. The imposition of Britain's Zionist policy meant that by the end of the Palestine mandate and the proclamation of the state of Israel in 1948, a critical mass of Jewish immigrants had established themselves in Palestine. The ability of Israelis to fight off the challenge by Arab states in 1948, coupled with recognition by key states of the international community, meant that Israel had constituted itself as an independent state. While the establishment of the state of Israel as a member of the international community of states took place well within the boundaries of international law, the alignment of international law with the wishes of the Western states meant that Britain's Zionist policies could be undertaken in clear disregard for the principles and the wording of various international instruments. This realization was evident to those formulating British foreign policy, as is made plain by the following letter from Arthur Balfour to his Foreign Secretary, George Curzon, in August 1919:

> The contradiction between the letters of the Covenant and the policy of the Allies is even more flagrant in the case of the 'independent nation' of Palestine than in that of the 'independent nation' of Syria. For in Palestine we do not propose even to go through the form of consulting the wishes of the present inhabitants of the country, though the American [King-Crane] Commission has been going through the form of asking what they are.
>
> The Four Great Powers are committed to Zionism, and Zionism, be it right or wrong, good or bad, is rooted in age-long traditions, in present needs, in future hopes, of far profounder importance than the desire and prejudices of 700,000 Arabs who now inhabit that ancient land.
>
> In my opinion that is right...
>
> I do not think that Zionism will hurt the Arabs, but they will never say they want it. Whatever the future of Palestine it is not now an 'independent nation', nor is it yet on the way to become one. Whatever deference should be paid to the views of those living there, the Powers in their selection of a mandatory do not propose, as I understand the matter, to consult them. *In short, so far as Palestine is concerned, the Powers have made no statement of fact which is not admittedly wrong, and no declaration of policy which, at least in the letter, they have not always intended to violate.*[18]

The seeds of orientalism found in the mandate system itself point to Western projection of the other as uncivilized, but particularly with respect to British foreign policy. In Palestine, Balfour speaks for the 'Arabs', professing to know what is best for 'them', which means going 'against the desire and prejudices of 700,000 Arabs', since Britain's wishes (and those of the 'civilized' world) are of a 'far profounder importance'. If this means blatantly disregarding the dictates of international law, so be it, as the civilizing process must proceed unhampered.

2.3. Selective enforcement

The manifestations of the orientalist project linger to this day, as it allows for a special form of realism to be acted upon, one which, having established a distinction between West and East, civilized and uncivilized, and so on, frees states to act, more often than not, in pure self-interest. Yet for those living in the Middle East the question remains: what normative framework holds: the exceptionalism made possible by an orientalist substructure or the dictates of international law? One need not look too far, since the fundamental underpinning of the international legal order – the prohibition against aggression – has been selectively dealt with in the Middle East. Consider the ten-year period between the start in 1980 of the first Gulf War, that between Iran and Iraq, and the lead-up to the UN-approved campaign of the US-led coalition against Iraq in the second Gulf War. The differing responses of the UN Security Council in reaction to invasions and occupation demonstrate the extent to which the application of international law in this region is subservient to the geopolitical interests of Western states, above all, those of the United States (which replaced Britain as the dominant external actor in the region after the Suez debacle of 1956). During the first Gulf War – the Iran–Iraq War (1980–8) – the Iraqi

---

18. See D. Ingrams, *Palestine Papers, 1917–1922: Seeds of Conflict* (1972), 73 (emphasis added).

invasion of Iran was met with a muted response by the international community, which, for the longest time, was unwilling to act to restore international peace and security. Despite the war having started in 1980, the Security Council only acted under the rubric of Chapter VII of the UN Charter, which authorized the use of any means to restore international peace and security, by passing Resolution 589 in 1988. Although this resolution ultimately led to the cease-fire which ended the conflict, during the interim eight years of inaction more than a million people died and major violations of both *jus ad bellum* and *jus in bello* transpired.

In contrast to the passive neglect of the Security Council during the Iran–Iraq War, its neglect during the 1982 Israeli invasion and subsequent occupation of Lebanon was active, as the United States blocked, through recourse to its veto power on nine separate occasions, any move by the Council to seek to restore international peace.[19] In this situation, where Israel's aggression continued, through its occupation of southern Lebanon, until 2000, the region witnessed the UN Security Council being forced to forfeit its collective security obligations through the active policy of the United States seeking to exclude Lebanon from the UN agenda. By contrast, Iraq's invasion of Kuwait in 1990 marked a watershed in the ability of the Security Council to deal with issues of international peace and security. Not only did a Security Council resolution authorize a US-led multinational force to evict Iraqi forces from Kuwait in 1991, it also imposed various measures such as an economic embargo, a disarmament regime, and the establishment of the Iraq–Kuwait border, in a bid to restore international peace and security. The irony was that throughout the subsequent decade, when the Security Council was asserting itself in an overwhelming manner against Iraq for its occupation of Kuwait, Israel remained in occupation of southern Lebanon. Such selectivity in enforcement reinforces the perception regarding the qualitative exceptionalism of the Middle East, whereby the dictates of the powerful (given self-legitimacy through the orientalist project) are to override agreed norms of behaviour as established by international law.

2.4. Punitive nature

The punitive nature of international law is to be seen in the UN sanctions regime imposed on Iraq as a result of its invasion of Kuwait in 1990. While law may be a coercive tool meant to modify the behaviour of states, the cumulative effects of the UN sanctions regime imposed on Iraq went beyond what could be considered as justifiable punishment, as the effects of the sanctions regime appeared to transgress the *jus cogens* imperative prohibiting crimes against humanity. The comprehensive sanctions regime imposed by the UN Security Council via Resolution 661 had originally been maintained to force Iraq out of Kuwait; when that was achieved in 1991 by force of arms, the sanctions were seen as a part of the attempt by the Security Council to restore international peace and security in the region. By 1997, the regime had been held hostage by the United States, which indicated that the sanctions would remain in place until the Iraqi president, Saddam Hussein, was

---

19.   See A. Patil, *The UN Veto in World Affairs, 1946–1990: A Complete Record and Case Histories of the Security Council's Veto* (1992).

replaced as the head of state. The sanctions imposed on Iraq in 1990 were in the guise of a comprehensive embargo that originally allowed only for an exception for medical supplies. After the Second Gulf War, as a result of a UN report that found that the coalition bombing had relegated Iraq 'to a pre-industrial age', the Security Council modified its regime to allow for the import of food, agricultural equipment, and items related to water purification and sanitation.[20] Further, the Security Council introduced the 'oil-for-food' programme in an attempt to mitigate the effects of the sanctions on the general populace. Although this programme, which allowed for the selling of oil to assist Iraq in purchasing items which were exempt from the embargo, was established in 1991, it only became operational in 1996. Despite these modifications to the sanctions regime, the UN Secretary-General noted in a March 2000 report that even if the oil-for-food programme was 'implemented perfectly, it is possible that the efforts will prove insufficient to satisfy the population's needs'.[21]

While the needs of the population had been dire, as it became clear that hundreds of thousands, if not millions, of Iraqi deaths were a direct result of the sanctions regime, the modifications to the sanctions under the oil-for-food programme simply ended the free fall of the population from affluence to poverty and, to a large extent, stabilized the effect of sanctions at their 1996 level. This did not preclude what amounted to a children's holocaust whereby between 1991 and 1998 it was estimated that the death of at least 100,000, but more probably 227,000, children under five took place, of which three-quarters could be attributed to the consequences of UN sanctions.[22] Although the ability to impose sanctions is well within the rights of the UN Security Council as the principal agent for ensuring international peace and security, by their cumulative effect the sanctions went beyond being punitive to being criminal. This is so since the effects of sanctions transgressed the *jus cogens* prohibition regarding the committing of crimes against humanity. It appears that the effects of the sanctions regime were of such magnitude that they most resembled the crime against humanity known as 'extermination', as elaborated in the Statute of the International Criminal Court. A 'crime against humanity', as spelled out at Article 7 of the Statute, is to be considered an act which is 'committed as part of a widespread or systematic attack directed against any civilian population'; while the concept of 'extermination' includes the 'intentional infliction of conditions of life ... calculated to bring about the destruction of part of a population'. Although the Security Council attempted to mitigate the worst elements of the humanitarian catastrophe which the sanctions regime had brought about, its own studies made it clear that these modifications did not reverse what has been the humanitarian plight of the Iraqis for more than a

---

20. UN Security Council, Report to the Secretary-General on Humanitarian Needs in Kuwait and Iraq in the Immediate Post-crisis Environment by a Mission to the Area Led by Mr. Martti Ahtisaari, Under-Secretary-General for Administration and Management, dated 20 March 1991, annexed to a letter from the Secretary-General addressed to the President of the Security Council, UN Doc. S/22366, dated 20 March 1991, para. 8.
21. As quoted in Commission on Human Rights, The Adverse Consequences of Economic Sanctions on the Enjoyment of Human Rights: Working Paper Prepared by Mr Marc Bossuyt, UN Doc. E/CN.4/Sub.2/2000/33, 21 June 2000, para. 62.
22. D. Cortright and G. Lopez, *The Sanctions Decade: Assessing UN Strategies in the 1990s* (2000), 46.

decade. When the definition of extermination as 'intentional infliction of conditions of life ... calculated to bring about the destruction of part of a population' is
considered, it is clear that, after more than a decade of sanctions which killed anywhere from hundreds of thousands to nearly two million people, the regime imposed
on Iraq went beyond simply being punitive to being what can rightly be considered
a crime against humanity.

That the international community was actively complicit in this crime and that
the United Nations was the medium by which Anglo-American coercion was imposed speaks volumes as to the manner in which the orientalist project denigrated,
and to an extent dehumanized, the Iraqi people. The projections of the Orient as
being 'out there', as being alien, meant that these Western states could carry out
with little discomfort a near-genocidal campaign against a community which was
seen as being in direct opposition to themselves. As such, the normative values even
of a non-derogable nature could be sidestepped in order to teach – as a parent does a
child – Saddam Hussein a lesson.

2.5. Internalization of the precepts of international law

Having examined the way in which international law has been used in an instrumental manner by states outside the Middle East, consideration now turns to how
states in the region have internalized the lessons learnt regarding the application
and interpretation of international law. To consider the human rights records of two
Middle East states which have maintained near-permanent states of emergency in
violation of their international obligations is to reinforce the notion that, to use
Karl Marx's term, 'oriental despots' live in a world apart – the uncivilized world –
where respect for human rights need be of no consequence to the West.[23] Thus,
without a serious attempt to hold Middle East states accountable, the human rights
situation in the region is lamentable. In the same manner in which power trumps
the dictates of international law on the international plane, it is clear that the same
lack of respect for the rule of law exists when one examines the record of various administrations in the region. The situations in Egypt and Syria, for instance,
highlight the extent to which the governing elite suppresses individual human
rights so as to ensure the maintenance of their rule, in their case by reference to a
perpetual state of emergency. By considering the standards which the UN Human
Rights Committee has established in its General Comment 29 regarding derogation from human rights in states of emergency,[24] it is clear that both Egypt and
Syria maintain states of emergency in violation of their obligations under the International Covenant on Civil and Political Rights, and yet are perpetually allowed to
do so.

Such perpetual states of emergency have allowed for the growth, in both Egypt
and Syria, of an extra-constitutional security apparatus which is immune from judicial oversight. As a result, mass and systematic violations of the non-derogable

---

23. See Said, *supra* note 1, at 153.
24. See Human Rights Committee, General Comment No. 29 – States of Emergency (Article 4), UN. Doc.
CCPR/C/21/Rev.1/Add.11, 31 Aug. 2001.

rights enshrined in Article 4(2) of the International Covenant on Civil and Political Rights take place with growing sophistication. In both Egypt and Syria the imposition of states of emergency has allowed the Assad and Mubarak administrations to consolidate and maintain power by closing off peaceful means of political change. Using the threat of 'Islamists' as a basis, both Egypt and Syria have sought to criminalize dissent and to subject those who oppose their administrations to the worst types of human rights abuses. Under perpetual states of emergency, there has been a transformation of the institution of government in both states whereby power is vested disproportionately in the executive organ at the expense of the judiciary. As a result judges have a diminished ability to oversee the work of the 'security forces' – that arm of the executive branch which, in effect, acts to ensure the survival of the status quo. The result of this limited judicial oversight in both Egypt and Syria has lead to systematic and widespread violations of non-derogable rights including the right to life and the prohibition against torture. The work of the various actors within the UN system of human rights protection when combined with reports from non-governmental organizations documents, in no uncertain terms, the manner in which Egypt and Syria have perpetuated long-term states of emergency and have killed and tortured with impunity, all in violation of the most fundamental, non-derogable, human rights established.[25] Yet such actions have been allowed to persist despite the dictates of international law, since international standards need not apply to the administrations of these oriental despots.

3. CONCLUSION

While this *tour d'horizon* cannot truly do justice to the issues concerned, I believe that an overall framework exists to make the argument that the Middle East has developed as the underclass of the international legal order wherein international law has been, with respect to formative events, selectively applied and enforced, blatantly disregarded, or used in a punitive manner. Much in the same manner as the inability to predict the implosion of the Soviet Union forced those in international relations to move beyond the simply theoretical paradigm of realism/liberalism, the events of 11 September 2001 require international jurists to take the Middle East seriously and to move beyond self-delusion. The fact that, on balance, international law has been outweighed by the interests of the powerful during the evolution of the modern Middle East has been translated into a legacy of war, dispossession, and repression, whereby the people of the region feel frustrated by the abuse and have been willing, at their most extreme, to take the type of drastic measures which were visited upon New York and Washington in order to change the tide of affairs. Law can

---

25. See, e.g., Commission on Human Rights, Civil and Political Rights Including the Question of Torture and Detention, Report of the Special Rapporteur, Sir Nigel Rodley, Submitted Pursuant to Commission on Human Rights Resolution 2000/43, UN Doc. E/CN.4/2001/66, 25 Jan. 2001; or Human Rights Committee, Consideration of Reports Submitted by States Parties under Article 40 of the Covenant: Second Periodic Report States Parties Due in 1984: Syrian Arab Republic, UN Doc. CCPR/C/SYR/2000/2, 25 Aug. 2000. As for nongovernmental reports, see annual country reports from both Amnesty International and Human Rights Watch.

never be divorced from politics. This is especially true of international law, which, because of its decentralized nature, lacks a central determination, application, or enforcement system. Yet for any system of justice to prevail, law must show itself to be insulated as much as possible from the dictates of power. Where the Middle East is concerned, international law has failed to dissociate itself from the worst excesses of those dictates, in effect creating of the region an underclass of international legal society. It should thus come as little wonder, as Thucydides wrote two thousand years ago, in his *History of the Peloponnesian War*, that 'having destroyed a principle that is to the general good of all men' should result in repercussions that have been felt beyond the region. The legacy of the manner in which international law has been applied in the region is not a pretty one, but it is one worth recounting, as it makes clear that the issues which remain unsettled to this day – in Iraq or in Palestine – did not emerge in a vacuum, but were the result of political machinations which managed to impose the current realities of the Middle East on its people at the expense of transgressing the common standards of behaviour agreed to by all states: international law.

Part II

ORIGINS OF THE ARAB–ISRAELI CONFLICT

THE ARAB-ISRAELI CONFLICT AND
INTERNATIONAL LAW

By Michael Akehurst*

I. Origins of the Arab-Israeli Conflict

Even in Biblical times the Jews were never the only people living
in Palestine. After a series of unsuccessful revolts against the
Romans, the Jews were expelled from Palestine by the Romans in
A.D. 133; the population which remained was a mixture of Philis-
tines, Canaanites, Greeks, Romans, etc. After the Arab conquest in
A.D. 637 most of the inhabitants came to speak Arabic and were
converted to Islam and intermarried with the invaders, although
some of them remained Christians. The Crusades and the Turkish
conquest in 1517 had little effect on the composition of the
population.

The Zionist movement[1] started towards the end of the nineteenth
century, but it got off to a slow start. It is estimated that in 1880
there were 24,000 Jews in Palestine, out of a total population of
500,000, and as late as 1918 the Jews numbered no more than
56,000, out of a total population which by this time had risen
to approximately 700,000.

In 1917 the British government issued the Balfour Declaration,
which said the British government "view with favour the establishment in Palestine of a national home for the Jewish people, it
being clearly understood that nothing should be done which might
prejudice the civil and religious rights of existing non-Jewish communities in Palestine". Two comments are worth making at this

---

* M.A., LL.B. (Cantab.), Docteur de l'Université de Paris, Senior Lecturer
in Law at the University of Keele and one time Legal Officer for the
United Nations Relief and Works Agency for Palestine Refugees in the
Near East. This article reflects the author's private views (which do not
necessarily coincide with those of the United Nations), and is based on
lectures given by the author while he was a visiting lecturer at the
University of Otago in 1972.
[1] The Zionist movement sought to create a Jewish state, so that the Jews
could be safe from persecution by the Gentiles. It was a secular movement,
not a religious movement; it was a product of late nineteenth century
nationalism. Despite the religious significance of Palestine for the Jews,
the Zionist movement at one time came very close to choosing Uganda
instead of Palestine as the site of the future Jewish state.
  Palestine contains many Jewish, Muslim and Christian holy places, but
it is a mistake to regard the Arab-Israeli conflict as a religious struggle
between Muslims and Jews. A number of Arabs are Christians; many
Israelis are not practising Jews; and not all practising Jews are Zionists.

stage. First, the declaration spoke of *a* national home for the Jews, not *the* national home; it was never intended that all the Jews in the world should move to Palestine. Second, the reference to "existing non-Jewish communities" seems a rather odd way of referring to people who at that time formed ninety-two percent of the population of Palestine.

After the first world war Palestine was detached from the Turkish empire and administered by the United Kingdom under a mandate granted by the League of Nations. The provisions of the mandate incorporated the terms of the Balfour Declaration and stated that Jewish immigration and naturalisation should be encouraged. The Jewish population of Palestine rose from about 56,000 (out of a total population of about 700,000) in 1918 to 83,794 (out of a total of 757,182) in 1922, and to 608,000 (out of a total of 1,972,560) in 1946; this increase was almost entirely the result of Jewish immigration from Europe. The Permanent Mandates Commission, a League of Nations organ which supervised the administration of mandated territories, criticised the British for not allowing more Jewish immigration into Palestine. On the other hand, the Palestinian Arabs rioted on a number of occasions in protest against Jewish immigration. Dissension between the Arab and Jewish communities in Palestine prevented the establishment of representative government in Palestine.

Sympathy for the appalling sufferings of the Jewish people during the Nazi holocaust caused public opinion in many countries to look with favour on the establishment of a Jewish state in Palestine. The Arabs protested that it was unfair to make the Arabs pay for Germany's crimes (indeed, over the centuries the Jews had been far better treated in Arab countries than they were in Europe— until the formation of the state of Israel caused the Jews to be regarded in some, but not all, Arab countries as potential fifth columnists); but these protests fell on deaf ears. The Zionists began an armed struggle for independence from British rule in October 1945. The United Kingdom, unable to satisfy the conflicting demands of the Jewish and Arab communities in Palestine, referred the problem to the United Nations in the hope that the United Nations would have greater success in solving it. On 29 November 1947 the General Assembly passed a resolution proposing the partition of Palestine into a Jewish state and an Arab state, which would be joined together in an economic union; Jerusalem and its environs would be administered by the United Nations. Although the Jews formed less than a third of the population of Palestine, the partition resolution allotted them fifty-seven percent of the area of Palestine, including most of the fertile coastal plain. The Zionists accepted the partition resolution (reluctantly, because they would have liked an even greater share of the area of Palestine), but the Arabs rejected it; the Arabs wanted Palestine to be a single state in which they would have formed the majority. (They proposed that Palestine should be a federal state, composed of Jewish and Arab cantons, with a constitution modelled on that of the United States.[2])

After the passing of the partition resolution, clashes between the Arabs and Jews began in Palestine and soon developed into all-out war. The British gradually withdrew, leaving the two communities to fight it out. The mandate came to an end at midnight 14/15 May 1948, but even before then there had been considerable foreign intervention in the fighting; volunteers from other Arab states went to help the Palestinian Arabs, and the Zionists obtained money, weapons and men from Jewish communities overseas.

With superior organisation and leadership, the Zionists got the upper hand and seized territory exceeding the amount allotted to the Jewish state under the partition plan. By the time the mandate ended, 300,000 Arab refugees had fled from territory occupied by the Zionists. Some of them fled simply in order to escape the fighting, but others were deliberately expelled by the Zionists; and the massacre of the entire population of the village of Deir Yassin by Zionist extremists on 9 April 1948 caused the inhabitants of the surrounding area to flee in panic.

The formation of the state of Israel was proclaimed a few hours before the mandate ended, and almost immediately several Arab states sent their armies to help the Palestinian Arabs. Israel drove the Arab armies back and seized more Palestinian territory, aggravating the refugee problem. Fighting continued off and on until early 1949, with short bursts of fighting being separated by lengthy truces. On 29 May 1948 the Security Council recommended a four-weeks truce, which lasted from 11 June 1948 till 7 July 1948. After further fighting in July 1948, the Security Council passed a resolution on 15 July 1948 *ordering* a truce under article 40 of the Charter; and this resolution was obeyed, apart from short outbursts of fighting in the south in October and December 1948 and March 1949. Israel concluded armistice agreements with her Arab neighbours during 1949.

The result of this first Arab-Israeli war was to give Israel about eighty percent of the territory of Palestine. Only 50,000 Arabs were left in the territory occupied by Israel, and between 650,000 and a

---

[2] Details may be found in *Yearbook of the United Nations* (1947–1948), 246.

million were refugees. On 31 May 1967 1,344,576 refugees were registered with the United Nations Relief and Works Agency for Palestine Refugees (the increase in numbers between 1949 and 1967 was mainly caused by a high birth rate among the refugees). The popular belief that the refugee problem has been artificially kept alive by the Arab governments is only partly true; some (but not all) Arab governments have made considerable efforts to find jobs for the refugees, but this has not been easy, because a rapidly expanding population has caused unemployment in most Arab states. Even so, by 1966 a third of the refugees who were capable of work had found jobs.

II. LEGAL ASPECTS OF THE EVENTS OF 1947–1949

Henry Cattan, an international lawyer who is himself a Palestinian Arab refugee, argues in Appendix XI of his book *Palestine, the Arabs and Israel* that sovereignty over Palestine has always been vested in the original inhabitants of Palestine. However, as a general rule in international law sovereignty can only be vested in a state, and not in a people.

But the special status of Palestine as a mandated territory under the League of Nations Covenant may make it an exception to the general rule. Palestine was covered by article 22 (4) of the Covenant, which provided: "Certain communities formerly belonging to the Turkish empire have reached a stage of development where their existence as independent nations can be provisionally recognised subject to the rendering of administrative advice and assistance by a Mandatory until such time as they are able to stand alone . . ." This provision, which was the legal basis of the administration of Palestine under the mandate, recognises that the population of Palestine had, if not sovereignty, at least very considerable rights under international law.[3] Moreover, the advisory opinions on South West Africa given by the International Court of Justice in 1950 and 1971[4] indicate that the legal position created by the mandate was not altered by the dissolution of the League in 1946.

It is unclear whether the partition resolution of 1947 was intended to be a mere recommendation or whether it was intended to have dispositive effect in the sense of creating title to territory in Palestine. Normally General Assembly resolutions are merely

---

[3] In ,1931 the Institut de Droit International passed a resolution describing the communities under mandate as subjects of international law (26 *American Journal of International Law,* (1932), 91).
[4] I.C.J. Reports (1950), 128, and (1971). 16.

recommendations, but there might be something in the mandate system which would give the General Assembly increased powers. In 1950 the International Court of Justice advised that the status of the mandated territory of South West Africa could only be altered by South Africa with the consent of the United Nations (acting as successor to the League).[5] When it referred the Palestine problem to the United Nations, the United Kingdom committed itself in advance to accept any solution to that problem which the United Nations was able to reach. It could therefore be argued that the partition resolution represented an agreement between the United Nations and the mandatory, which, on the authority of the 1950 advisory opinion on South West Africa, was capable of altering the status of Palestine. But, even if the International Court of Justice meant to imply that the United Nations and South Africa could alter the status of South West Africa against the wishes of its inhabitants (a point to which the court did not apparently direct its mind), it by no means follows that the wishes of the inhabitants of Palestine could be disregarded in like manner. South West Africa was a "C" mandate; Palestine was an "A" mandate. The Covenant of the League of Nations described the "A" mandates as "communities" whose "existence as independent nations can be provisionally recognised", and required that "the wishes of these communities must be a principal consideration in the selection of the Mandatory" (which surely implies by analogy that the wishes of the communities could not be ignored when the fate of the mandated territories after the expiry of the mandates was being determined). All this is very different from the provisions of the Covenant concerning the "C" mandates, which are simply described as "territories [not communities] . . . which . . . can be best administered under the laws of the Mandatory as integral portions of its territory". It is submitted, therefore, that the Covenant conferred rights on the inhabitants of Palestine which could not be revoked without their consent, in the same way that a treaty can sometimes confer an irrevocable right on a third state.[6]

The best way of giving effect to the rights of the inhabitants of Palestine would have been to let them decide, by a referendum, what the legal status of Palestine should be after the end of the mandate. Elihu Lauterpacht argues[7] that the partition resolution "was in fact a direct application of the principle [of self-determination]. The Jews were not to determine the future of the Arabs, nor were the Arabs to determine the future of the Jews.

[5] I.C.J. Reports (1950), 128 at 141–143.
[6] Article 37 (2) of the Vienna Convention of the Law of Treaties, 1969.
[7] *Jerusalem and the Holy Places* (1968), 18.

Each group was to determine its own future". But to allow a minority of the population to partition the country against the wishes of two-thirds of the population seems to be a very odd way of giving effect to rights which the Covenant regarded as being vested in the population as a whole, particularly since there was no clear geographical division between Arab and Jewish areas in Palestine. The partition plan not only allotted fifty-seven percent of Palestine to the "Jewish" state, despite the fact that the Jews constituted less than a third of the population; it also would have meant that over 400,000 Arabs would have been living in the "Jewish" state (compared with only 10,000 Jews in the "Arab" state), so that those Arabs would have been forced to choose between living under alien rule and migrating to another part of Palestine. Altogether, the partition plan represented such a clear sacrifice of the interests of the majority for the benefit of the minority that it cannot be regarded as compatible with the rights which the Covenant had conferred on the population of Palestine as a whole.

The legal problems discussed above affect the character and legality of the hostilities of 1947–1949. From the point of view of Israel, and of anyone who recognises that the state of Israel came into being on 14 May 1948, the attack by the Arab states on Israel was a clear breach of article 2 (4) of the United Nations Charter.

But the Arab states have always regarded the formation of the state of Israel as a nullity from the point of view of international law because it infringed the legal rights of the population of Palestine (or, rather, of the Arabs who formed the majority of the population of Palestine).[8] In Arab eyes, the struggle of 1947–1949 was more in the nature of a civil war than of an international war (this applies both to events before the end of the mandate and to those afterwards); a minority of the population of Palestine, with foreign assistance, was trying to secede from or dominate or expel the majority.

Arab statements to the Security Council in 1948 about the help which they were giving to the Palestinian Arabs refer indiscrimin-

---

[8] Normally a state exists for the purposes of international law if it fulfils the factual requirements of territory, population and government. But if the creation of a state is a breach of international law, it is a nullity in the eyes of international law until it has been recognised by other states. Thus western states do not recognise East Germany because they regard its creation by the Soviet Union as contrary to the Soviet Union's obligations under the Potsdam and other agreements. See also Hersch Lauterpacht, *Recognition in International Law* (1947), chapter 21.

Quaere whether Israel fulfilled even the factual requirements of statehood in May 1948, in view of the confused nature of the struggle between the Arab and Jewish communities in Palestine—although obviously it fulfilled those requirements in subsequent years.

ately to the Zionists as a rebellious minority and to Zionist aggression. The description of the Zionists as a rebellious minority reflects the idea that the struggle in Palestine was a civil war, but the reference to Zionist aggression might suggest at first sight that Israel was a *state* attacking her neighbours, although obviously the Arabs did not mean to imply that Israel was a state. What the Arabs really had in mind was the idea of subversion or indirect aggression, such as can occur during a civil war: the Jewish community in Palestine was being used by foreign interests to commit indirect aggression against Palestine. The Arab states were protecting Palestine against such subversion; it is generally agreed that one state may protect another against subversion, under the rule of collective self-defence. The Zionist victory was due in no small measure to the money, weapons and men which the Zionists received from overseas. It is true that this help came mainly from private individuals and private organisations rather than from governments, and most instances of collective self-defence against subversion relate to subversion by foreign governments; but common sense suggests that a state should have as much right to defend another state against subversion from foreign private interests as it has to defend another state against subversion from foreign governments, particularly as private interests are often as powerful as governments. For instance, during the early 1960s a number of states regarded the assistance allegedly given by western capitalists to the secessionary movement in Katanga as a form of subversion, and claimed a right to defend the Congo against such subversion.

III. The Legal Status of Palestine after 1949

The Arab states continue to regard the creation of the state of Israel as a nullity because it was contrary to international law; they do not recognise Israel because recognition would cure the illegality of Israel's origin. However, in 1949 Egypt, Transjordan, Syria and Lebanon signed armistice agreements with Israel, which placed them under a legal obligation not to attack Israel. One only has to think of armistice agreements made during a civil war to realise that an armistice agreement is binding in international law even though it is made with a body which is not recognised as a state.

Other states have recognised Israel and have thereby precluded themselves from arguing that the creation of the state of Israel was contrary to international law. But recognition of a state does not necessarily connote recognition of all the territorial claims made by that state. In particular, many states (including the United States of America, United Kingdom, USSR, France, Australia and New Zealand) which recognise Israel regard Israel as having only de facto authority (not sovereignty) over those parts of Jerusalem which are on the Israeli side of the 1949 armistice line. Under the partition plan Jerusalem was supposed to be administered by the United Nations, and the states in question apparently regard the United Nations as still having some vestige of title to Jerusalem.

Israel claimed to annex all the territory on the Israeli side of the 1949 armistice line, which included not only part of Jerusalem but also much of the territory which had been ear-marked for the Arab state under the partition plan. Elihu Lauterpacht argues[9] that the Arab attack on Israel in 1948 was aggressive and therefore gave the Arab states no right to annex any part of Palestine; there was therefore a "sovereignty gap" which Israel was entitled to fill. More precisely, he argues that Israeli forces moved into some of the areas ear-marked for the Arab state while exercising a right of self-defence against the attack by the Arab states, and, because there was a sovereignty gap, Israel was entitled to stay there and fill the sovereignty gap. This argument is fallacious even if we concede that the Arab states were the aggressors and that Israel acted in self-defence. The Arab states were not trying to annex any part of Palestine in 1948, but to set up an Arab state in Palestine, which surely had at least as much right to exist as a Jewish state. Moreover, the whole idea of a sovereignty gap is incompatible with the rights which the Covenant of the League of Nations conferred on the population of Palestine, because it implies that the relevant portions of Palestine were *terra nullius,* open to occupation by *any* state.

Nor can Israel argue that self-defence gives her the right to acquire territory by conquest. The better view nowadays is that no state, whether it is the aggressor or acting in self-defence, can acquire territory by conquest. This view would not have been generally accepted in 1949, but, since it is regarded nowadays as a logical corollary of the prohibition on the use of force in the United Nations Charter,[10] we can, with the benefit of hindsight, consider that this rule has been valid since the Charter came into force on 24 October 1945. However, such defects in a state's title to territory can be cured by general recognition by other states—and this makes it
• important to consider what attitudes other states have adopted towards Israel's territorial claims.

[9] *Jerusalem and the Holy Places* (1968), 44–45.
[10] e.g. *International Legal Materials,* vol. 9 (1970), 1292 at 1294.

Apart from reservations about Jerusalem, most states seem to regard territory on the Israeli side of the armistice line as subject to Israeli sovereignty for practical purposes. Such recognition is usually accompanied by the statement that the frontiers of Israel have not yet been finally determined, but, since no one knows where those frontiers will be, the practical solution has been to regard all territory on the Israeli side of the armistice line as Israeli territory pending the conclusion of a peace settlement between Israel and her neighbours. This is rather surprising, considering that the armistice agreements all say that the armistice lines are not to be construed as political or territorial boundaries.

The areas of Palestine on the Arab side of the armistice lines consist of the Gaza strip and the West Bank of the Jordan.

The legal status of the Gaza strip has caused little controversy. Egypt never annexed it, but treated it as an area of Palestine under temporary Egyptian military administration.

The West Bank united with Transjordan to form the Kingdom of Jordan in 1950; a general election on both banks of the Jordan in 1950 produced a Parliament which voted in favour of union. Jordan's title rests, not on conquest, but on the consent of the inhabitants. The United Kingdom granted de jure recognition to the union, but many other states withheld de jure recognition (although they may have granted de facto recognition). In particular, the other Arab states denounced the union as a betrayal of the Palestinian cause and as a breach of a resolution passed by the League of Arab States prohibiting the annexation of any part of Palestine. Eventually a compromise was reached: Jordan declared that the annexation of the West Bank was without prejudice to the final settlement of the Palestine issue, and this was accepted by the other Arab states.

Even the United Kingdom's recognition of the merger was accompanied by reservations to the effect that the United Kingdom recognised that Jordan had only de facto authority over eastern Jerusalem and that the frontiers between Israel and Jordan had not been finally determined. This mirrors the United Kingdom's attitude to the territorial claims made by Israel.

IV. THE SIX DAYS WAR OF 1967 AND ITS SEQUEL

Following clashes on the Israeli-Syrian armistice line, Israel threatened in May 1967 to "attack Damascus and change its government". Threats of this sort are often made in Arab-Israeli relations as morale-boosters for domestic public opinion and are usually not taken seriously by the other side.[11] On this occasion, however, the Israeli threats were repeated by Israeli diplomats in private conversations with journalists and foreign (especially Soviet) diplomats, which led the Soviet Union and Egypt to conclude that the threats were made in deadly earnest. Egypt moved troops up to the Israeli-Egyptian armistice line, claiming that she thereby intended to deter an Israeli attack on Syria, but Israel interpreted the Egyptian move as a prelude to an Egyptian attack on Israel.[12]

The Egyptian army asked the United Nations Emergency Force, which had been patrolling the Israeli-Egyptian armistice line, to stand aside so that Egyptian forces could be stationed on the armistice line. U Thant has been criticised for withdrawing the force in response to this request, but it could be argued that Egypt had the right to demand the withdrawal of the force at any moment.[13] When Israel protested at the withdrawal of the force, U Thant suggested that the force should operate on the Israeli side of the armistice line instead, but Israel rejected this suggestion as "entirely unacceptable". Israel was quite within her rights in doing so, since the force had no right to enter the territory of any state without that state's consent, but Israel's attitude shows that the withdrawal of the force did not constitute a serious threat to Israel's security. In any case, the force was never intended to resist full-scale invasions across the armistice line, and the fact that it never numbered more than 6,000 men would have made such a role totally impracticable. It was authorised only to shoot in order to defend itself, and its function was to patrol the armistice line and to *report* any infiltration taking place across the line; it was quite successful in performing this function, because for more than ten years its mere presence was enough to deter all but a few guerilla raids across the armistice line.

---

[11] Cf. the empty Arab threat to drive the Israelis into the sea.

[12] For a more detailed analysis of the events leading up to the Six Days' War, see the articles by Charles Yost in *Foreign Affairs,* vol. 46 (1968), 304 and by Rosalyn Higgins in the *Journal of Contemporary History,* vol. 3 (1968), 253.

[13] The force was not allowed to enter the territory of any state without that state's consent. Egypt had made an agreement with the United Nations giving her consent to the presence of the force on Egyptian territory. U Thant said in 1967 that this agreement only covered the initial entry of the force into Egyptian territory and had no bearing on the question of withdrawal. Rosalyn Higgins, in her article cited in the previous note, has shown convincingly that U Thant was wrong in this respect. However, it is one thing to prove that the agreement was applicable and another thing to interpret it; the provisions of the agreement concerning the circumstances in which Egypt was entitled to revoke her consent were remarkably ambiguous. The full text of the agreement is printed in Rosalyn Higgins' book, *United Nations Peacekeeping,* vol. 1 (1969), 337.

Israel attacked Egypt on 5 June 1967. Jordan and Syria came to Egypt's defence, but within six days the Israeli Army had overrun the Gaza strip, the Sinai peninsula (i.e. all Egyptian territory on the east side of the Suez Canal), the West Bank of the Jordan and part of Syria (the Golan Heights).

At first Israel claimed that the Arab armies had attacked her first, but nobody believes this nowadays; the Israeli air force seems to have taken the Arabs by surprise.

If this Israeli claim is false, why did Israel tell a lie? This question can best be answered by asking another question: supposing Israel had admitted striking the first blow, how could she have justified her action legally? Many writers argue that article 51 of the United Nations Charter should be interpreted broadly so as to permit states a right of anticipatory self-defence (i.e. if a state thinks it is about to be attacked by another state, it is allowed to forestall that attack by striking the first blow), but this interpretation (which the present writer regards as wrong) is not often invoked by states in practice.[14] If Israel had claimed to be using a right of anticipatory self-defence, several states might have denied that any such right existed. India, for instance, said as much during the General Assembly debate following the Six Days' War.

Indeed, the Six Days' War shows the danger of arguing in favour of anticipatory self-defence. The Six Days' War was probably a war which neither side wanted; each side miscalculated the intentions of the other side.[15] To argue in favour of anticipatory self-defence in a situation of acute tension, when each side suspects the other of being about to attack it, is to add a match to gunpowder: each side is encouraged to attack first, and this means that wars will occur which could have been avoided. A restrictive interpretation of article 51 would encourage states to be more cautious, thus preventing some wars.

There is another lesson to be learned from the Six Days' War; it underlines the wisdom of the (often forgotten) fact that the United Nations Charter forbids the threat as well as the use of force. In theory one can separate the two, but in practice they can merge into one another; threats of force (such as were made by both sides in the few weeks preceding the Six Days' War) are very dangerous because they can provoke the other side into anticipatory

[14] Akehurst, *A Modern Introduction to International Law* (2nd ed., 1971), 314–317. When Israel attacked Egypt in 1956 she did not invoke anticipatory self-defence; rather, she claimed to be acting in response to past attacks (or to a single *continuing* attack) by Egyptian feda'ayin (guerillas).
[15] This is the conclusion reached by Yost in his article cited above.

self-defence. Even if anticipatory self-defence is illegal, there is still much to be said for prohibiting acts which will provoke other states into acting illegally.

One result of the Six Days' War was a further aggravation of the refugee problem. About 1,100,000 people were living on the West Bank of the Jordan before the Six Days' War, and about 250,000 of them fled to the East Bank of the Jordan during and immediately after the war. This was partly the effect of a general panic caused by the retreat of the Jordanian army, but Israel deliberately helped to increase the flow of refugees, by deportations in individual cases and by demolishing Arab towns like Qalqilya and Emmaus after the end of the fighting. Very few of these refugees have been allowed to return by Israel.

The United Nations has been virtually unanimous in declaring that Israel has no right to annex any of the territory which it occupied in 1967, and so far Israel has not annexed any of this territory, although Eastern Jerusalem (which was under Jordanian administration until June 1967) has been merged with Western Jerusalem for local government purposes only. It seems reasonable to maintain that Israel is entitled to remain in possession of the occupied territory as a belligerent occupant until there is a peace settlement between the Arab states and Israel; but the powers of a belligerent occupant over territory are much less than the powers of a state possessing sovereignty over territory.

V. OUTLINE OF A SETTLEMENT— SECURITY COUNCIL RESOLUTION 242

In November 1967 the Security Council passed resolution 242 recommending, in outline, the terms of a settlement of the Arab-Israeli conflict. This resolution has been accepted by Egypt, Jordan and (after considerable delay) Israel. (The text of the resolution is printed as an appendix to the present paper.) The resolution contains only an outline of a solution, and so far it has proved impossible to reach agreement on detailed rules giving effect to the principles laid down in the resolution (indeed, the resolution would probably never have been passed if it had not papered over major differences between the parties with ambiguous phrases). However, it represents the closest that anyone has ever come towards reaching a peaceful settlement of the Arab-Israeli conflict in the last twenty years, and for that reason, if for no others, it merits close study.

Paragraph 1 of the resolution would require both the Arab states and Israel to make an enormous concession. The Arab states would have to make peace with Israel[16] and acknowledge her sovereignty, i.e. recognise her. Recognition would not need to be accompanied by entry into diplomatic relations, but it would, by its very nature, represent a waiver by the Arab states of their claims that the creation of the state of Israel was a legal nullity because it was contrary to international law. Since these claims reflect very deep feelings on the part of the Arab states and are based on legal considerations which are by no means frivolous, their waiver would constitute a very big concession by the Arab states. In return, Israel would be required to withdraw from territories occupied in 1967. The implementation of the resolution has so far been prevented by arguments as to whether withdrawal by Israel should precede, accompany or follow recognition of Israel by the Arab states; in addition, the Arab states maintain that the resolution requires withdrawal by Israel from all the territories occupied in 1967, whereas Israel says that it requires withdrawal from only some of the territories, so that Israel would be able to retain Eastern Jerusalem and perhaps other areas as well. The Israeli interpretation is based mainly on the fact that the resolution talks of "withdrawal from territories", not "withdrawal from *the* territories"; but the French text of the resolution does say "withdrawal from *the* territories". In any case, an ambiguity of this sort can be resolved by referring to the preamble of the resolution, "emphasising the inadmissibility of the acquisition of territory by war"—a principle which is now accepted by the vast majority of states as a correct statement of international law.[17]

Many of Israel's needs could be met in other ways which would not involve the annexation of territory. For instance, the return of Eastern Jerusalem to Jordan could be accompanied by guarantees enabling Israelis to visit the Western [Wailing] Wall and other Jewish holy places in Eastern Jerusalem. Security against attack is an even greater preoccupation for Israel, because the 1967 cease-fire lines are much easier for Israel to defend than the 1949 armistice lines. Paragraph 2 (c) of resolution 242 mentions the establishment of demilitarised zones as one means whereby states could be preserved from attack by other states. The stationing of United Nations forces on the border between Israel and her Arab neighbours could be another means of doing the same thing. In order to perform this function, a United Nations force would have to be given a more extensive right to use force than UNEF possessed (probably such

---

[16] Termination of the state of war between Israel and the Arab states need not necessarily take the form of a peace treaty; the states concerned could reach the same result by issuing unilateral declarations (29 British Year Book of International Law, (1952) 435).

[17] Ante, page 238.

a force could only be set up by the Security Council, and not by the General Assembly); it would also have to be very much larger. Such a force would be useless if the host state had a right to require it to leave at any moment; the agreement between the United Nations and the host state would therefore have to make clear that the host state's consent to the presence of the force was irrevocable, or else the force would have to be established by the Security Council under Chapter VII of the Charter (member states of the United Nations have agreed in advance, in articles 25 and 48 of the Charter, to accept decisions made by the Security Council under Chapter VII as binding, so that a force created under Chapter VII would be legally entitled to enter and remain in the territory of a member state regardless of that state's wishes).

Paragraph 2 (a) of resolution 242 lays down the principle of freedom of navigation through international waterways in the area. This is designed to remove a long-standing Israeli grievance against Egypt: Egypt prevented Israeli ships, and ships carrying goods (or at least certain types of goods) to Israel, from using the Suez Canal and the Straits of Tiran.[18] The question whether Egypt was entitled to act in this way gives rise to a host of fascinating legal issues about which much might be said on both sides; but the question is only of historic interest, because Egypt has not had the means of pursuing this policy since 1967, and, if resolution 242 is implemented, it will not have the right to do so. There is a certain circularity in the use of the term "international waterways"; in the past Egypt argued (probably wrongly) that the Gulf of Aqaba was a historic bay and that the Straits of Tiran were thus not an international waterway. This is a point which needs to be clarified in future discussions before a settlement can be reached.

Paragraph 2 (b) of resolution 242 lays down the principle of "a just settlement of the refugee problem". This is probably the issue on which it will be hardest to reach agreement; what seems just to one side will not seem just to the other side. If Israel withdraws from the territories occupied in 1967, the refugees who fled across the Jordan in 1967 will be able to return to the West Bank; but a solution to the problem of the 1948 refugees and their descendants will be as far away as ever. Israel would never agree to the return

---

[18] Egypt pursued this policy consistently since 1948, except that the interference with ships in the Straits of Tiran was suspended during 1957–1967, while UNEF occupied Sharm esh-Sheikh, the headland commanding the entrance to the Straits. The Egyptian announcement that it would close the Straits upon the withdrawal of UNEF in 1967 was one of the factors which provoked Israel to attack Egypt; but Israel did not cite the Egyptian announcement (which was never implemented) as a legal justification for the attack.

of all the 1948 refugees and their descendants, because the presence of a large Arab population in Israel would contradict the whole raison d'être of the Zionist movement, which is that the Jews should have a Jewish state; it is therefore unprofitable to consider whether international law places an obligation on Israel to let the refugees return. The most that could be hoped for is that Israel might let a few of the refugees return and pay compensation to the rest. International law is very relevant to the question of compensation. Israel is under an obligation to pay compensation for the property which the refugees left behind in 1948, even if we assume that the territory on which such property was situated was Israeli territory in 1948 (this is a very big assumption, because Israel had no definite boundaries in 1948); the traditional rule of international law is that a state may not expropriate foreign-owned property without compensation. Israel might argue that this property was taken during a war, and that she is entitled to seize enemy-owned property in wartime without compensation. It is true that compensation need not be paid during the war, but the better view is probably that after the war the property must be returned or compensation paid.[19] At all events, Israel has declared that she would be willing to pay "compensation for abandoned lands and property" as part of a general peace settlement.[20]

VI. PROCEDURE FOR REACHING A SETTLEMENT

One obstacle to a peaceful settlement between Israel and the Arab states is that the parties disagree as to the procedure by which such a settlement should be reached. The Arab states refuse to enter into direct negotiations with Israel because they fear that entry into direct negotiations would be construed as implied recognition of Israel; in their eyes recognition is a big concession which should be made in return for similar concessions by Israel during the final stage of the search for a settlement, instead of being made gratuitously at the beginning of the search for a settlement. No international lawyer would regard entry into negotiations as implying recognition, but public opinion in Arab countries would, and it is doubtful whether any Arab leader who entered into direct negotiations with Israel

---

[19] Such points are usually settled by peace treaties, so that the customary law on the subject is uncertain for lack of precedents. The issue came before the International Court of Justice in the *Nottebohm* and *Interhandel* cases (ICJ Reports (1955), 4, and (1959), 6), but was not decided, because the court dismissed the claims on preliminary objections.

[20] *The Times,* 11 March 1971.

without getting anything in return would survive. Israel, on the other hand, tends to insist on direct negotiations, partly because this is the only thing on which the Israeli cabinet can agree; Israel has a coalition government who do not agree among themselves about the *terms* of a settlement with the Arab countries. This deadlock has only been partly broken by the appointment of Gunnar Jarring as the Secretary-General's Special Representative in the Middle East under paragraph 3 of resolution 242; Israel has frequently argued that Gunnar Jarring should act as a go-between only during the early stages of the search for a settlement, and that thereafter direct negotiations should take place.

One suspects, however, that both sides are using this argument about procedure as a means of cloaking their unwillingness to make the necessary concessions concerning the *substance* of a settlement. Even if they agreed about the procedure, the chances of a settlement would be as small as ever. The deadlock concerning the substance of a settlement could probably be broken only if a settlement was imposed on the parties by the great powers or by the United Nations. The chances of the Soviet Union and the United States agreeing on the terms of a Middle East settlement may seem very remote, but the chances of the Arab states and Israel reaching agreement without external pressure are even more remote. The Arab states tend to favour the idea of an imposed settlement, because they hope that pressure from the great powers will offset Israel's military superiority over them; conversely, Israel opposes the idea of an imposed settlement because she wishes to retain the bargaining strength which she derives from her military superiority over the Arabs.

Would it be lawful for the great powers to impose a settlement on Israel and the Arab states?

The Security Council is sometimes regarded as an institutionalised form of the great powers; certainly it is a great coincidence that the five permanent members of the Security Council happen to be the five nuclear powers. But it seems that the United Nations Charter does not authorise the Security Council to *impose* a settlement on parties to a dispute, as opposed to merely *recommending* a settlement. The Security Council can issue orders under articles 40 and 41 of the Charter, but an order under article 40 must be "without prejudice to the rights, claims or position of the parties concerned", and an order under article 41 can only require a state to take non-military enforcement action, not to accept a particular solution to a dispute. It has sometimes been suggested that the Security Council could decide that the refusal by a state to accept particular terms for settling a particular dispute constituted a threat to the peace, and take enforcement action against that state. The Security Council toyed with the idea of enforcing the partition resolution in this way in 1947–1948 (by taking enforcement action against any attempt to obstruct by force the settlement contained in the partition resolution), but it soon abandoned the idea; Senator Austin, the United States representative, said that such action would be contrary to the Charter. Recommendations for the peaceful settlement of disputes under Chapter VI are not binding, and it would be improper to try to evade this rule by imposing sanctions under Chapter VII on a state which did not comply with such a recommendation.[21]

The great powers would therefore have to act outside the Security Council if they wanted to impose a settlement on the Arab states and Israel. In the nineteenth century the great powers, assembled in a conference, often imposed settlements of disputes between small powers. The legal form in which the settlement is accepted by the state or states concerned is laid down in article 35 of the Vienna Convention on the Law of Treaties: "An obligation arises for a third state from a provision of a treaty if the parties to the treaty intend the provision to be the means of establishing the obligation and the third state expressly accepts that obligation in writing".

It would be tempting to say that such a treaty is a treaty in form only, and that in substance it reflects an assertion of competence by the great powers to legislate for the international community. A state which refuses to accept a settlement dictated by the great powers runs the risk of having all sorts of unpleasant things done to it by the great powers. But suppose it takes that risk and refuses to accept the settlement, is it bound by the terms of the treaty containing the settlement? Probably not. There have been cases in which small states have successfully defied the great powers. For instance, at the end of the Cuban missiles crisis in 1962 the United States and the Soviet Union agreed that the United States should

---

[21] In the *Namibia* case (ICJ Reports (1971), 16, 51–54) the International Court of Justice advised that the Security Council possessed, in addition to the specific powers mentioned in Chapters VI, VII, VIII and XII of the Charter, general powers which included the power to pass mandatory resolutions, in so far as that was necessary for the maintenance of international peace and security. The court's ruling on this point was condemned as erroneous by all four of the Western European states represented on the Security Council in 1971. However, even if the court's ruling is accepted as correct, the arguments set out in the main text above would still preclude the Security Council from imposing a peaceful settlement of the Arab-Israeli conflict under its "general powers"; the rule that recommendations for the peaceful settlement of disputes under Chapter VI are not binding would be meaningless if the Security Council could pass binding resolutions for the peaceful settlement of disputes under its "general powers".

send inspectors to Cuba to verify the departure of the Soviet missiles; Cuba refused to accept this arrangement, and no United States inspectors went to Cuba. So it seems more realistic to say that the great powers have no legislative power over the international community and that a state is not bound by a treaty unless it consents.

Of course, the consent given by a state to a settlement imposed by the great powers might be given unwillingly, under various forms of pressure from the great powers. But the unwillingness might be partly feigned; if a settlement is unpopular in the eyes of a state's public opinion, the government may try to retain popularity by pretending that it has been forced into accepting the settlement by foreign pressure, although it may secretly welcome the settlement. This is particularly true of many Arab countries, where public opinion on the Arab-Israeli dispute is often more extreme than governmental opinion.

Pressure of various kinds might have to be used by the great powers in order to impose a settlement on Israel and the Arab states. Would a treaty entered into under such pressure be invalidated by the pressure? The answer depends partly on the type of pressure employed. Article 52 of the Vienna Convention on the Law of Treaties, 1969, says that a treaty is void if it is procured by the threat or use of force contrary to the United Nations Charter; but the Vienna Conference rejected proposals to apply the same rule to treaties procured by economic or political coercion (the so-called "unequal treaties").

But, over and above the distinction between military coercion and economic and political coercion, a distinction must be made between treaties imposed by individual states and treaties imposed by (or with the approval of) the international community as a whole. There is no legislature in international law, and often a state will not agree to a change in its rights unless it is forced to. In the nineteenth century, when all treaties imposed by force were valid, there was no legal obstacle to forcing states to agree to changes which were in the public interest—or to changes which were not. The modern rule invalidating treaties procured by military force is a welcome innovation in so far as it prevents changes which are not in the public interest; it will seem less desirable if it is also applied so as to prevent changes which *are* in the public interest. How does one decide whether a change is in the public interest? The answer lies in that difficult but crucial area of international law, recognition. A treaty procured by military force is invalid, but that invalidity will be cured if the treaty is recognised as valid by the vast majority of states—which is likely to happen if the treaty is imposed by the great powers acting together and if the treaty brings about changes which are generally regarded as being in the public interest. If this were not so, no peace treaty concluded after a modern war could ever be valid.

APPENDIX

TEXT OF RESOLUTION 242

THE SECURITY COUNCIL,

Expressing its continuing concern with the grave situation in the Middle East,

Emphasising the inadmissibility of the acquisition of territory by war and the need to work for a just and lasting peace in which every State in the area can live in security,

Emphasising further that all Member States in their acceptance of the Charter of the United Nations have undertaken a commitment to act in accordance with Article 2 of the Charter,

1. *Affirms* that the fulfilment of Charter principles requires the establishment of a just and lasting peace in the Middle East which should include the application of both the following principles:

   (i) Withdrawal of Israeli armed forces from territories occupied in the recent conflict;

   (ii) Termination of all claims or states of belligerency and respect for and acknowledgement of the sovereignty, territorial integrity and political independence of every State in the area and their right to live in peace within secure and recognised boundaries free from threats or acts of force;

2. *Affirms further* the necessity

   (a) For guaranteeing freedom of navigation through international waterways in the area;

   (b) For achieving a just settlement of the refugee problem;

   (c) For guaranteeing the territorial inviolability and political independence of every State in the area, through measures including the establishment of demilitarised zones;

3. *Requests* the Secretary-General to designate a Special Representative to proceed to the Middle East to establish and maintain contacts with the States concerned in order to promote agreement and assist efforts to achieve a peaceful and accepted settlement in accordance with the provisions and principles in this resolution;

4. *Requests* The Secretary-General to report to the Security Council on the progress of the efforts of the Special Representative as soon as possible.

Part III

PALESTINIAN REFUGEES

Displaced Palestinians and a Right of Return

John Quigley*

> These unfortunate people [the displaced Palestinians] should not
> be made pawns in the negotiations for a final settlement .
> —Dean Rusk, December 3, 1948[1]

Displacement of population has become a frequent item of action in
international bodies in recent years. The hostilities in the Balkans
provide only one example among many of military conflicts accompanied by flight of population.[2] International pressure has compelled the
development of new state practice on this issue of wartime displacement.

The issue of population displacement has surfaced within the context
of projected settlement negotiations between Israel and the Palestine
Liberation Organization (P.L.O.). These discussions are aimed at resolving the outstanding Arab-Israeli issues,[3] including the status of Palestinians displaced from their homeland as a result of the Arab-Israeli
conflict.[4] On the displacement issue, the Palestinians[5] assert a right to
return, a claim to which Israel demurs. On the one end of the spec-

---

* Professor of Law, Ohio State University. A.B., Harvard College, 1962; LL.B., Harvard Law
School, 1966; M.A., Harvard University, 1966. The author is grateful for comments on an early
draft to Professors Sally V. Mallison, W. Thomas Mallison, and Abdullah Abu-Eid. The author
is grateful for consultation to his colleague Professor Michael Kindred. Translations from non-
English sources are by the author. Professor W. Thomas Mallison passed away shortly before the
publication of this Article. The issue raised in the Article was one close to his heart. To him the
Article is dedicated.

1. *Summary Records of Meetings 21 September–8 December 1948*, U.N. GAOR, 3d Sess., pt.1, C.1,
at 909, U.N. Doc. A/C.1/SR.226 (1948).

2. *See generally infra* notes 244–248.

3. *See* Declaration of Principles on Interim Self-Government Arrangements, Sept. 13, 1993,
art. 5, 32 INT'L LEGAL MATS. 1525, 1529 (agreement between Israel and Palestine Liberation
Organization to negotiate on "final status" issues, including refugees).

4. This Article will use the term "displaced Palestinians," rather than the more common term
"refugee," to refer to the this class of persons. Whereas "refugee" refers to people seeking asylum
in another state, it is the author's contention that "displaced Palestinians" seek not to stay abroad
but to return to their territory of origin. *See, e.g.*, Vojin Dimitrijevic, *Legal Position of Palestine
Refugees*, 19 REV. INT'L AFF. 427 (1968) (discussion of this terminological issue).

5. For the purposes of this Article, "Palestinian" refers to Arabs formerly or presently inhabiting the territory of interwar Palestine, as well as their direct descendants.

trum, the Palestinian version contends that the displaced Palestinians were forced out by direct military action, or by fear instilled by atrocities. In contrast, the Israelis argue that they did not, directly or indirectly, force the Palestinians to leave. Thus, analysis of the wartime displacement issue is complicated by the fact that the two parties disagree not only over the law but also over the facts, holding radically different assessments of the .circumstances of the Palestinians' departure.

The sharp difference in view between Arabs and Israelis regarding Palestinian displacement makes it appropriate, in anticipation of the negotiations, to analyze both the factual and legal aspects of the issue. Given the difference in views, the Article will examine the rights of the displaced Palestinians on the factual premise maintained by each party. Briefly stated, it will be argued that the question whether the Palestinians are entitled to return to their territory as a matter or right, does not hinge on the factual perspective.

To this end, Part I of this Article will sketch out the factual context for the discussion, laying out the historical genesis of the conflict, as well as the contrasting Israeli and Palestinian views of the circumstances of the displacement. Part II will first explore the international reaction to the Palestinian displacement, and then will inquire whether the United Nations has deemed the Palestinians entitled to a right of return. Parts II, III, and IV will assume the Israeli view of the Palestinian flight, i.e., that it was not a deliberately coerced event. Under this premise, the Article will derive theories for the right of return based on several alternative principles of international law in Part III, and examine the arguments that have been asserted to refute that right in Part IV. Part V will shift the factual assumptions, and will propose a further basis for the right of return, one that rests on the factual premise of the coerced departure of the Palestinians. Lastly, Parts VI and VII will address the issue of remedies for the violation of the right of return, as well as situate the alternate justifications[6] for the Palestinian right of return within the terms of the ongoing Israeli-PLO negotiations. To restate, the Article will maintain that the displaced Palestinians bear an entitlement to return as a matter of right, one that

---

6. This Article will not address an additional possible basis for a Palestinian return, namely, one based on the right of self-determination, which arguably is exercisable by them in the territory that constitutes the state of Israel. This basis is here ignored because the Article focuses on the return issue as it will be addressed in the Israel-P.L.O. negotiations, where the P.L.O. recognizes Israel's right to the territory it holds and seeks a return for Palestinians under circumstances in which they would fall under Israeli sovereignty. *See generally* JOHN QUIGLEY, PALESTINE AND ISRAEL: A CHALLENGE TO JUSTICE (1990) (addressing the issue of Palestinian self-determination in the territory held by Israel).

rests on several alternate grounds, and one that withstands Israeli arguments to the contrary.

I. FACTS OF THE PALESTINIANS' DEPARTURE

Palestinians were displaced from their home areas at various times beginning in 1948, with two major episodes of hostilities marking the greatest periods of Palestinian flight in 1948 and 1967.[7] In 1948, Palestinians left territory being taken to establish a Jewish state. Consequently, the home areas of the Palestinians displaced at that time are in what later became Israel. In 1967, Palestinians left the two sectors of Palestine (the Gaza Strip, and the West Bank of the Jordan River) that remained outside Israel's control after 1948; since 1967 Israel has controlled these two sectors on the basis of belligerent occupation.[8] This Part examines the circumstances surrounding the flight, which define both the Israeli view of non-coerced exodus, as well as the Palestinian claim of forced displacement.

A. The Palestinian Exodus of 1948

A large number of Palestinians, probably three quarters of a million, were displaced during the hostilities of 1948.[9] Because of the magnitude of the 1948 flight, this Article will first survey the historical facts surrounding the exodus, and then posit some reasons for the displacement.

1. The Facts of the 1948 Flight

Confrontation began when Palestinians, protesting a recommendation by the U.N. General Assembly to partition Palestine, staged a commercial strike and street demonstrations.[10] Groups of Palestinians

---

7. Most were present in their home areas during the hostilities and departed at that time. Others, however, were temporarily absent during the hostilities and have been prevented by the government of Israel from returning. In this Article the term "displaced Palestinians" includes Palestinians who left during or following the hostilities, and those who were absent.

8. This Article focuses on Palestinians seeking admission to territory in Israel. However, a similar analysis would be applicable to Palestinians seeking admission to the Gaza Strip or West Bank of the Jordan River. Pending negotiations, it is unclear who will have decision-making power regarding admission to these territories.

9. The following paragraphs are intended to show what caused Palestinians to depart. They are not an overall account of the hostilities. *See generally* EDGAR O'BALLANCE, THE ARAB ISRAELI WAR, 1948, 147 (1956, reprinted 1981).

10. *See* G.A. Res. 181, U.N. GAOR, 2d Sess., U.N. Doc. A/519 (1947) (resolution of Nov. 29, 1947, recommending partition of Palestine); Sam Pope Brewer, *Palestine's Arabs Kill Seven Jews, Call 3-day Strike,* N.Y. TIMES, Dec. 1, 1947, at A1 (Arab Higher Committee calls for strike); Sam Pope Brewer, *Palestine Strife Widens, Grips Jaffa-Tel Aviv Area; Arabs Rebuff Peace Plan,* Dec. 4, 1947, at A1 (strike continues); *see also* ILAN PAPPÉ, THE MAKING OF THE ARAB ISRAELI CONFLICT 1947–1951, 77 (1992) (citing view of Sir Alan Cunningham, British High Commis-

attacked Jews, and Jews responded in kind, resulting in casualties on both sides.[11] Palestinian irregulars also attacked transport convoys carrying supplies to Jewish settlements, resulting in Jewish casualties.[12]

Two Jewish militias, the Irgun Zvai Leumi, (IZL), and LEHI, threw bombs at Arab shops and street crowds and attacked Arab civilians in their villages.[13] Attacks on Arab civilians were also carried out by the Haganah, a militia of the Jewish Agency.[14] According to the U.S.

---

sioner for Palestine, that the Arab strike was aimed against the partition recommendation, not against Jewish population).

11. *See* Sam Pope Brewer, *Palestine's Arabs Kill Seven Jews, Call 3-day Strike*, N.Y. TIMES, Dec. 1, 1947, at A1 (15 Arabs and Jews killed); Sam Pope Brewer, *Jerusalem Torn By Rioting; Arabs Use Knives, Set Fires; Jews Reply, Haganah In Open*, N.Y. TIMES, Dec. 3, 1947, at A1 (8 Jews and 6 Arabs killed); Sam Pope Brewer, *Palestine Strife Widens, Grips Jaffa-Tel Aviv Area; Arabs Rebuff Peace Plan*, N.Y. TIMES, Dec. 4, 1947, at A1 (10 Jews and 5 Arabs killed); Sam Pope Brewer, *Arabs Make Roads New Battlefields; Rake Bus Convoys*, N.Y. TIMES, Dec. 5, 1947, at A1; Sam Pope Brewer, *Jews Carry Fight to Arabs, Palestine Adds 28 to Dead*, N.Y. TIMES, Dec. 13, 1947, at A1 ("The Jews again appeared today to be on the offensive, roughly two-thirds of the incidents being initiated by them, and in their operations they showed evidence of planning, something absent in general from the Arab attacks"); Sam Pope Brewer, *Irgun Attacks In Palestine; 21 Arabs, 3 Jews Are Slain*, N.Y. TIMES, Dec. 14, 1947, at A1 ("The day's total casualties were twenty-one Arabs and three Jews killed . . . . More than eighty Arabs were wounded and three Jews were seriously wounded.").

12. *See* Sam Pope Brewer, *Arabs Make Roads New Battlefields; Rake Bus Convoys*, N.Y. TIMES, Dec. 5, 1947, at A1; *see also* J. BELL, THE LONG WAR: ISRAEL AND THE ARABS SINCH 1946, at 76 (1969); ARTHUR KOESTLER, PROMISE AND FULFILLMENT: PALESTINE 1917–1949, at 154 (1983).

13. *See* LT. COL. NETANEL LORCH, THE EDGE OF THE SWORD: ISRAEL'S WAR OF INDEPENDENCE, 1947–1949, at 57 (1961); MICHAEL PALUMBO, THE PALESTINIAN CATASTROPHE 35 (1987); MAJ. R.D. WILSON, CORDON AND SEARCH WITH 6TH AIRBORNE DIVISION IN PALESTINE 156 (1949) (describing "bestial attacks [by LEHI] on Arab villages, in which they showed not the slightest discrimination for women and children, whom they killed as opportunity offered."); Sam Pope Brewer, *Jews Carry Fight to Arabs, Palestine Adds 28 To Dead*, N.Y. TIMES, Dec. 13, 1947, at A1 (reporting 13 killed in Irgun attack on Tireh village); Sam Pope Brewer, *Arab Legion Force in Palestine Kills 14 Jews in Convoy*, N.Y. TIMES, Dec. 15, 1947, at A1 (describing Irgun actions of Dec. 14 as "terrorist bombings of Arabs."); *see also* MENACHEM BEGIN, THE REVOLT 337–38 (1951) ("For three days, from 11th to 13th December [the Irgun] hammered at concentrations of rioters and their offensive bases [Arab villages] . . . we attacked at Haifa and Jaffa; at Tireh and Yazar. We attacked again and again in Jerusalem . . . . Enemy casualties in killed and wounded were heavy.").

14. The Agency was recognized by the United Nations as representing the Jewish community of Palestine. *See, e.g.,* JON & DAVID KIMCHE, BOTH SIDES OF THE HILL: BRITAIN AND THE PALESTINE WAR 83 (1960); CHRISTOPHER SYKES, CROSSROADS TO ISRAEL 337 (1973) (describing the attack on Khissas as a "Haganah crime," stating that it was "part of a considered policy which had been preceded by debate, and was finally ordered by the highest authorities of the Jewish Agency Haganah," and commenting that the attack showed that "something of the evil spirit of the terrorists [a reference to Irgun and LEHI] was entering Haganah"); Sam Pope Brewer, *Haganah kills 10 in Raid on Arabs*, N.Y. TIMES, Dec. 20, 1947, at A8 (Haganah killed five adults and five children); Sam Pope Brewer, *Irgun Shoots Down 2 British Soldiers, Arabs Get Warning*, N.Y. TIMES, Dec. 22, 1947, at A1 (attack by Palmach, an elite unit of the Haganah, on Khissas village, Jewish Agency condemned the action); Sam Pope Brewer, *Haganah Attacks a 2nd Arab Village*, N.Y. TIMES, Dec. 21, 1947, at A1 (dynamiting of house of village elder with occupants inside, number of casualties undetermined); *14 More Arabs Die in Haganah Blasts; Zionist Militia Dynamites 3 Houses Around Safad, Says It Blew Up Jerusalem Hotel*, N.Y. TIMES, Jan. 6, 1948, at A6; *see*

Central Intelligence Agency, these Haganah attacks were "terrorist raids against the Arabs similar in tactics to those of the Irgun Zvai Leumi and the Stern Gang [LEHI]."[15] The Haganah justified the raids as reprisals for Palestinian attacks on Jews.[16]

Violent attacks against Palestinians continued and resulted in Palestinian flight from the affected areas. LEHI bombed a building in the city of Jaffa where Palestinian civilians had taken refuge from attacks on their villages.[17] Other attacks included a Haganah bombing of a Palestinian hotel in west Jerusalem and the shelling[18] of Palestinian neighborhoods. These acts generated enough flight from Jerusalem that Jewish Agency leader, David Ben Gurion, began to direct the settlement of Jews in abandoned Arab housing.[19] Haganah personnel drove loudspeaker vans through Palestinian neighborhoods, ordering residents to evacuate.[20] By early April 1948, Palestinian flight from various sectors of Palestine had assumed substantial proportions.[21]

In April 1948, the Irgun and LEHI killed 250 civilians in the village of Deir Yassin, near Jerusalem, after capturing the village.[22] LEHI paraded Deir Yassin survivors in trucks through Jerusalem, as a dem-

also Benny Morris, *The Harvest of 1948 and the Creation of the Palestinian Refugee Problem*, 40 MIDDLE EAST J. 671, 672 (1986).

15. Report by the Central Intelligence Agency: Secret: Possible Developments in Palestine, 1948 (5) FOR. REL. U.S. 666, 672 (1948).

16. *See* LORCH, *supra* note 13, at 59; Sam Pope Brewer, *Irgun Shoots Down 2 British Soldiers, Arabs Get Warning, supra* note 14, at A1 (Jewish Agency gave its approval for reprisal raids on Arab villages, expressed regret over the killing of five Arab children in raid on an Arab village); *Shooting in Jerusalem*, LONDON TIMES, Dec. 22, 1947, at 4 ("While the Jews are suffering mainly through sniping at their road convoys, the Arabs have lost many lives through Jewish assaults on their villages.").

17. *See* LORCH, *supra* note 13, at 59; BENNY MORRIS, THE BIRTH OF THE PALESTINIAN REFUGEE PROBLEM, 1947 - 1949, at 46 (1987); PALUMBO, *supra* note 13, at 83–84; Sam Pope Brewer, *Palestine Blasts Rip Arab Offices, Kill at Least 34*, N.Y. TIMES, Jan. 5, 1948, at A1; *14 More Arabs Die in Haganah Blasts; Zionist Militia Dynamites 3 Houses Around Safad, Says it Blew up Jerusalem Hotel*, N.Y. TIMES, Jan. 6, 1948, at A6.

18. *See* MORRIS *supra* note 17, at 50; Sam Pope Brewer, *British Condemn Haganah 'Murders'*, N.Y. TIMES, Jan. 7, 1948, at A1 (British government condemned the hotel attack, which resulted in 26 deaths, as a "dastardly and wholesale murder of innocent people.").

19. *See* MORRIS, *supra* note 17, at 50–52.

20. *See id.* at 52 (occurring in Feb. 1948 after a Jewish woman was shot, and reporting that many Arabs left in fear of the consequences); Erskine B. Childers, *The Wordless Wish: From Citizens to Refugees, in* THE TRANSFORMATION OF PALESTINE: ESSAYS ON THE ORIGIN AND DEVELOPMENT OF THE ARAB ISRAELI CONFLICT 165, 186 (Ibrahim Abu-Lughod ed. 1971).

21. *See* DAVID BEN GURION, REBIRTH AND DESTINY OF ISRAEL 237 (1954) (statement of Ben Gurion Apr. 6, 1948: "villages have been emptied in panic, even from Haifa one-third of its Arabs have fled."); MORRIS, *supra* note 17, at 41, 52, 59 (stating that the mass exodus of Arabs was the result of attacks on Arabs led by Jewish extremists composed of the Haganah, Irgun, and LEHI).

22. *See* Dana Adams Schmidt, *200 Arabs Killed, Stronghold Taken*, N.Y. TIMES, Apr. 10, 1948, at A6 (eyewitnesses said killings of civilians occurred after fighting for the village ended). *But see* BEGIN, *supra* note 13, at 162–65 (Irgun claimed it killed the inhabitants while taking houses).

onstration to Jerusalem's .Palestinians.[23] The Deir Yassin killings instilled fear in the Palestinian population and accelerated their flight
from the country.[24]

   Subsequent tactics employed by the Jewish militias as they captured
the major towns of Palestine further accelerated the flight of Palestinians. In Tiberias, the Haganah used barrel bombs and loudspeaker
warnings.[25] The Haganah and Irgun, attacking Haifa, lobbed mortars
into densely populated neighborhoods and rolled barrel bombs into
alleys.[26] The Irgun, attacking Jaffa,[27] shelled residential districts, setting the population to flight.[28] In the Galilee, the Palmach, an elite

---

23. *See* HARRY LEVIN, I SAW THE BATTLE OF JERUSALEM 57 (1950).
   24. *See* NAFEZ NAZZAL, THE PALESTINIAN EXODUS FROM GALILEE 1948, at 34, 44, 52, 90
(1978); ARNOLD TOYNBEE, A STUDY OF HISTORY 290 (1954); Michael Akehurst, *The Arab-Israeli
Conflict in International Law,* 5 N.Z. U. L. REV. 231, 233 (1973) (all three sources indicating that
many Arabs, particularly in unprotected rural areas, left the country soon after the Deir Yassin
incident, out of concern that it might be repeated in their areas).
   25. *See* PALUMBO *supra* note 13, at 107; *Arab Exodus From Tiberias,* PALESTINE POST, Apr. 19,
1948, at 1 (reporting the hasty exodus of Arabs from Tiberias that continued throughout the
day); *see also* Leo Heiman, *All's Fair . . .,* MARINE CORPS GAZETTE, June 1964, at 37, 39
(explaining that the Haganah sent barrel bombs "crashing into the walls and doorways of Arab
houses" to encourage the residents to flee. Haganah personnel driving jeeps with loudspeakers
then broadcast tape-recorded "shrieks, wails, and anguished moans of Arab women, interrupted
by a sepulchral voice calling out in Arabic: . . . . 'Run for your lives in the name of Allah!'").
   26. *See* LYNNE REID BANKS, TORN COUNTRY: AN ORAL HISTORY OF THE ISRAELI WAR OF
INDEPENDENCE 116 (1982) (quoting Ben Zion Inbar, a Haganah commander at Haifa, "we
manned the biggest mortar which our forces had at that time—a three-inch mortar—and when
all the Arabs gathered in this area we started firing on them. When the shells started falling on
them, they rushed down to the boats and set off by sea for Acre."); *cf.* Kurt René Radley, *The
Palestinian Refugees: the Right to Return in International Law,* 72 AM. J. INT'L L. 586, 589 (1978)
(stating that Arabs left Haifa because local Arab leaders decided to evacuate to avoid living under
Zionist rule). *But see* Walid Khalidi, *The Fall of Haifa,* 35 MIDDLE EAST F. 22, 24–25, 32 (Dec.
1959); *see also* BEGIN, *supra* note 13, at 165 (reporting that some Haifa residents shouted "Deir
Yassin" as they left); Childers, *supra* note 20, at 189; MORRIS, *supra* note 17, at 85–86 (British
officials reporting "indiscriminate and revolting machinegun fire" by Haganah "on women and
children" as they ran for the docks, and "hysterical and terrified Arab women and children and
old people on whom the Jews opened up mercilessly with fire."); PALUMBO, *supra* note 13, at
69–70 (both indicating that Arab leaders in Haifa met with Haganah only after population was
in flight); IDF, Intelligence Branch, *The Emigration of the Arabs of Palestine in the Period 1/12/1947–
1/6/1948,* June 30, 1948, *in* Benny Morris, *The Causes and Character of the Arab Exodus from
Palestine: the Israel Defence Forces Intelligence Branch Analysis of June 1948,* 22 MIDDLE EASTERN
STUD. 5, 6 (1986) (citing assessment by Haganah Intelligence Branch that the "barrages making
loud explosive sounds" and the "loudspeakers in Arabic . . . proved their great efficacy when used
properly (as in Haifa particularly)"); *Haifa's Pivotal Points Fall To Haganah After 30-hour Battle,*
PALESTINE POST, Apr. 23, 1948, at 1 (stating, "In whatever transport they could find, many of
them on foot—men, women, and children—moved in a mass exodus toward the port area."),
WILSON, *supra* note 13, at 193 (Haganah fired on departing Arabs to keep them moving).
   27. *See* PALUMBO, *supra* note 13, at 93; Gene Currivan, *Haganah, Irgun Unite for Action; Joint
or Separate Operations Agreed To—British Bar Jewish Capture of Haifa,* N.Y. TIMES, Apr. 28, 1948,
at A14; Gene Currivan, *Jews Split Jaffa, Reach Sea; RAF Planes Strife Zionists; Irgunists Press Assault
on Port as Haganah Captures 2 Villages to Isolate Defense—Spitfires Strike at Near-By Colony,* N.Y.
TIMES, Apr. 29, 1948, at A1.
   28. *See* MORRIS, *supra* note 17, at 96–97; *see also* BEGIN, *supra* note 13, at 363; *Flight Psychosis
Among Arabs,* PALESTINE POST, May 4, 1948, at 1 (reporting a "mass exodus" out of Jaffa, by

unit of the Haganah, shelled residential neighborhoods in capturing the towns of Safad[29] and Beisan.[30] By mid-May 1948, when the Jewish Agency declared a Jewish state, the Palestinians were "in panic flight,"[31] approximately 300,000 having left.[32] As the Jewish Agency declared statehood, Haganah loudspeaker vans in Jerusalem were urging the remaining Palestinians to leave.[33]

As indicated, Jewish militia attacks culminated with the Jewish Agency's declaration of statehood. The declaration occurred as Great Britain withdrew, thus ending its administration on the basis of a League of Nations mandate. Thereafter, expulsion of Palestinians was carried out openly. Haganah intelligence, referring to the expulsions of this period, stated that "British withdrawal freed our hands."[34] By July, the three Jewish militias had merged to form the Israeli Defense Force, (I.D.F.). Their combined efforts resulted in the capture of the twin cities of Ramleh and Lydda. Immediately after the capture, David Ben Gurion, as the provisional prime minister, ordered the expulsion of Ramleh and Lydda inhabitants. The I.D.F. executed the order, forcing out 60,000 Palestinians.[35] The I.D.F. expelled the inhabitants of Gali-

---

sea and overland); *Jaffa Capitulates; An Open City,* PALESTINE POST, May 11, 1948, at 1 (reporting evacuation of 70,000 Arabs from Jaffa).

29. *Arabs Flee Safad,* PALESTINE POST, May 3, 1948, at 1 (Arab residents fled when the fall of Safad was imminent); *Haganah Wrests Safad from Iraqis and Syrians,* PALESTINE POST, May 11, 1948, at 1 (reports flight of "the last of the 8,000 Arab inhabitants of Safad."); *see also* URI AVNERY, MY FRIEND, THE ENEMY 264 (1986) (quoting Palmach commander Yigal Allon regarding Palmach assault on Safad: "The Arab population fled. We did everything to encourage them to flee."); PALUMBO, *supra* note 13, at 113; MORRIS, *supra* note 17, at 107–08.

30. *See* MORRIS, *supra* note 17, at 107; PALUMBO, *supra* note 13, at 116 (shelling led some Arabs to flee; after taking the town Palmach expelled most of the rest).

31. *See Jerusalem 'Cease Fire' Exacted by British from Foreign Arab Chieftains,* PALESTINE POST, May 9, 1948, at 1.

32. *See* Childers, *supra* note 20, at 193; Morris, *supra* note 26, at 6–7; Akehurst, *supra* note 24, at 233.

33. *See* HARRY LEVIN, JERUSALEM EMBATTLED: A DIARY OF THE CITY UNDER SIEGE, MARCH 25TH, 1948–JULY 18TH, 1948, at 160 (1950) (reporting loudspeaker message as: "Take pity on your wives and children and get out of this bloodbath . . . . Surrender to us with your arms. No harm will come to you. Or get out by the Jericho road [which leads out of Palestine to Jordan], that is still open to you. If you stay, you invite disaster.").

34. *See* IDF, Intelligence Branch, *The Emigration of the Arabs of Palestine in the Period 1/12/1947– 1/6/1948,* June 30, 1948, in Morris, *supra* note 26, at 9; *see also* O'BALLANCE, *supra* note 9, at 147 (stating that after the statehood declaration Israel's policy "was now openly one of clearing out all the Arab civil population before them."); Uri Avnery, *Les Réfugiés Arabes, Obstacle à la Paix,* LE MONDE, May 9, 1964, at 1, 2 (author, a Haganah officer, referring to period following declaration of statehood, states: "The evacuation of Arab civilians had become a war aim.").

35. *See* FOUZI EL ASMAR, TO BE AN ARAB IN ISRAEL 4–13 (1978); KIMCHE, *supra* note 14, at 227–28; GEORGE KIRK, THE MIDDLE EAST 1945–1950, at 281 (1954); BENNY MORRIS, 1948 AND AFTER: ISRAEL AND THE PALESTINIANS 2 (1994) (reporting order issued July 12, 1948, by Lt.-Col. Yitzhak Rabin: "The inhabitants of Lydda must be expelled quickly without attention to age. They should be directed towards Beit Nabala . . . . Implement immediately," and a similar simultaneous order relating to adjacent town of Ramleh); MORRIS, *supra* note 17, at 207; O'BALLANCE, *supra* note 9, 147 (reporting I.D.F. forced nearly the entire population of the two

lee villages,[36] demolishing many of the villages to prevent a return.[37] When it captured the Negev desert, the I.D.F. forced out most of the Arabs.[38] It expelled the population of Beersheeba, the Negev's largest town.[39] An I.D.F. unit, capturing a village near Hebron, killed several hundred civilians.[40]

2. Reasons for the Palestinian Exodus of 1948

The Israeli response to allegations of mass expulsions was varied. First, Israeli international representatives claimed that Israel was trying to stop the flight.[41] The legal adviser to Israel's foreign ministry said that the flight was organized by Arab leaders as part of their war plan.[42] Israel's U.N. delegate claimed that the Palestinians left because they

---

towns to march east to an area under Jordanian control, firing mortars to force the inhabitants along the road out of town); Reja-e Busailah, *The Fall of Lydda, 1948: Impressions and Reminiscences*, 3 ARAB STUD. Q. 123, 128 (1981); Benny Morris, *Operation Dani and the Palestinian Exodus from Lydda and Ramle in 1948,* 40 MIDDLE EAST J. 82, 96 (1986); David K. Shipler, *Israel Bars Rabin From Relating '48 Eviction of Arabs*, N.Y. TIMES, Oct. 23, 1979 at A3 (reporting Yitzhak Rabin's statement that Ben Gurion ordered the expulsion).

36. *See* NAZZAL, *supra* note 24, at 75 (reporting I.D.F. airplanes dropped barrel bombs, metal fragments, nails, and glass on a village, population fled in panic); MORRIS, *supra* note 17, at 200 (expulsion from Galilee town of Saffuriya); *see generally* Nafez Abdullah Nazzal, *The Zionist Occupation of Western Galilee, 1948*, 3 J. PALESTINE STUD. 58 (1974) (attacks in July 1948).

37. *See* MORRIS, *supra* note 17, at 148; PAPPÉ, *supra* note 10, at 97 ("From October 1948 on the Israelis did their utmost to create a *fait accompli* that would render repatriation impossible. The prime objective was to demolish what was left of the abandoned Palestinian villages, almost 350 in all, so that the term itself would become meaningless."); Benny Morris, *Yosef Weitz and the Transfer Committees, 1948–49*, 22 MIDDLE EASTERN STUD. 522, 530–31; Benny Morris, *The Crystallization of Israeli Policy Against a Return of the Arab Refugees: April–December 1948*, 6 STUD. IN ZIONISM 86, 103, 109; *see also Progress Report of the United Nations Mediator on Palestine*, U.N. GAOR, 3d Sess., Supp. No. 11, at 14, U.N. Doc. A/648 (1948) (Mediator Bernadotte stated that the demolitions were undertaken "without apparent military necessity.").

38. *See* PALUMBO, *supra* note 13, at ix–xii, 173; WALTER SCHWARZ, THE ARABS IN ISRAEL 158 (1959).

39. *See* LORCH, *supra* note 13, at 357–59; MORRIS, *supra* note 17, at 221 (action of Oct. 22, 1948); PALUMBO, *supra* note 13, at xi.

40. *See* U.N. SCOR, 3d Sess., Supp. for Nov. 1948. at 6, U.N. Doc. S/1068 (1948) (*Cablegram dated 3 November 1948 from the Secretary-General of the League of Arab States to the Secretary-General Concerning Alleged Truce Violations by Jewish Forces in Galilee*, claiming massacre of women, children, elderly by I.D.F. in village of Dawaymeh; *id.* (*Cabled corrigendum to the cablegram dated 3 November 1948 from the Secretary-General of the League of Arab States to the Secretary-General*, correcting mistake as to location of village). *Cf.* U.N. SCOR, 3d Sess., Supp. for Nov. 1948, at 11–12, U.N. Doc. S/1073 (1948) (*Letter dated 8 November 1948 from the representative of the Provisional Government of Israel to the President of the Security Council concerning a letter from the Secretary-General of the League of Arab States (S/1068)*, claiming that Arab population had abandoned Dawaymeh prior to its occupation by I.D.F.); PALUMBO, *supra* note 13, at xii, xiv (action of Oct. 28, 1948 in Dawaymeh).

41. "The government of Israel must disclaim any responsibility for the creation of this [refugee] problem. The charge that these Arabs were forcibly driven out by Israeli authorities is wholly false; on the contrary, everything possible was done to prevent the exodus." *See* PAPPÉ, *supra* note 10, at 214, *citing* Israel State Archive 73/4 (Comay to Jessup, July 24, 1949).

42. *See* Shabtai Rosenne, *The Israel Nationality Law and The Law of Return 5710–1950*, 81 J. DU DROIT INT'L 4, 8–9 (1954).

were "in imminent danger of being caught in a clash between the invading Arab armies and those of its Jewish neighbours."[43]

One U.N.-appointed mediator concluded that the "exodus of Palestinian Arabs resulted from panic created by fighting in their communities, by rumors concerning real or alleged acts of terrorism, or expulsion."[44] Haganah intelligence concluded that the "main cause of the movement of population" was "hostile operations," which, it said, accounted for fifty-five percent of the flight.[45] It attributed another fifteen percent to fear engendered by prior attacks on civilians.[46] Despite the more limited Israeli explanation regarding the exodus, the U.S. member of the U.N. Conciliation Commission for Palestine held Israel responsible for all the displaced Palestinians but said that Israel had "particular responsibility for those who have been driven out by terrorism, repression and forcible ejection."[47]

U.N. mediator Bernadotte reported that "almost the whole of the Arab population fled or was expelled from the area under Jewish occupation."[48] In the area the I.D.F. occupied in 1948, there had been 900,000 Arabs, but according to the first Israeli census, only 120,000 remained.[49]

. The Arab Higher Committee for Palestine charged that attacks by Jewish militia, and later the I.D.F., on Arab civilians were designed to frighten them into departing. It said that "[t]he aim of Jewish terrorism against the Arabs was to drive the Arabs out of their homes and their country."[50] There are indications of an organized effort to expel the Palestinian Arabs.[51] Ben Gurion, speaking to the Haganah leadership in December 1947, urged a "major offensive against the Arabs"

---

43. *See Summary Records of Meetings 21 September–8 December 1948* U.N. GAOR, 3d Sess., pt.1, C.1, 715, U.N. Doc. A/C.1/SR.208 (1948).

44. *Progress Report, supra* note 37, at 14, ¶ 6.

45. Note that while the Haganah intelligence report is not entirely clear as to what the category "hostile operations" encompasses, it does state that another 15% were induced by fear of *prior* attacks. Thus, the implication may be that the 55% fled due to *ongoing* "hostile operations."

46. *See* Morris, *supra* note 26, at 9; *see also* Kaiwan v. Minister of Defence, 8 P.D. 301, 20 INT'L L. RPTS. 1953 51 (1957) (holding that a person who had been illegally expelled from Israel who returned without permission was to be regarded as one who had never left, and thus a national of Israel under the 1952 Nationality Law).

47. *The Ambassador in France (Bruce) to the Secretary of State*, 1949 (6) FOR. REL. U.S. 1124 (1949) (message written by Mark Ethridge, U.S. member of Palestine Conciliation Commission).

48. *Progress Report, supra* note 37, at 47.

49. *See* Janet Abu-Lughod, *The Demographic Transformation of Palestine, in* THE TRANSFORMATION OF PALESTINE: ESSAYS ON THE ORIGIN AND DEVELOPMENT OF THE ARAB-ISRAELI CONFLICT 139, 160 (Ibrahim Abu-Lughod ed. 1971).

50. *See Summary Records of Meetings 21 September–8 December 1948,* U.N. GAOR, 3d Sess., pt.1, C.1, at 698, U.N. Doc. A/C.1/SR.207 (1948).

51. *See, e.g.,* I.F. Stone, *Holy War,* N.Y. REV. BOOKS, Aug. 3, 1967, at 10 ("Jewish terrorism, not only by the Irgun, in such savage massacres as Deir Yassin, but in milder form by the Haganah, itself 'encouraged' Arabs to leave areas the Jews wished to take over for strategic or demographic reasons. They tried to make as much of Israel as free of Arabs as possible.").

that, he said, would "greatly reduce the percentage of Arabs in the population of the new state."[52] The Haganah's tactical plan for taking Palestine, developed in early 1948, called for the destruction of Palestinian villages and for Jewish settlement on their sites.[53]

As the Palestinian exodus from Jerusalem began, Ben Gurion expressed satisfaction. "Since Jerusalem's destruction in the days of the Romans," he said, "it hasn't been so Jewish as it is now." In "many Arab districts" in Jerusalem, he said, "one sees not one Arab. I do not assume that this will change." Furthermore, he stated, "what had happened in Jerusalem [flight of Palestinians] . . . could well happen in great parts of the country . . . [c]ertainly there will be great changes in the composition of the population in the country."[54]

In addition to acts of violence, the Israeli forces used psychological warfare to promote flight.[55] The Jewish Agency organized "whispering campaigns," encouraging Jews to advise Palestinian neighbors to leave for their own safety.[56] Haganah radio broadcast false rumors that cholera and typhus would break out in Palestinian areas.[57]

The idea of a Jewish state encompassing the territory of Palestine, as the Agency envisaged, was, moreover, impossible so long as Jews remained a minority. In the 1930s the Jewish Agency established a Population Transfer Committee, which devised schemes to remove the Palestinians by securing land for them in neighboring states, or by having Britain remove them.[58] An emissary for U.S. President Franklin Roosevelt reported:

---

52. MICHAEL BAR-ZOHAR, BEN GURION: THE ARMED PROPHET 103 (1967) (Ben Gurion's speech of Dec. 26, 1947, and further, indicating Ben Gurion's belief that the fewer Arabs in the new Jewish state, "the better he would like it."); *see also* PALESTINE POST, May 6, 1948, at 1 (Ben Gurion, in a speech to the Jewish National Council stated that "the Arabs had left 100 villages, and 150,000 of them were on the move," and cited these facts as evidence of "the success of Jewish arms").

53. *See* SIMHA FLAPAN, THE BIRTH OF ISRAEL: MYTHS AND REALITIES 42 (1987); MORRIS, *supra* note 17, at 63; PAPPÉ, *supra* note 10, at 93 (stating that Plan D was "the principal explanation for the departure of most of the Arabs of Palestine."); *see also* MORRIS, *supra* note 35, at 21 ("In conformity with . . . Plan D, . . . the Haganah cleared various areas completely of Arab villages—the Jerusalem corridor, the area around Mishmar Ha'emek, and the coastal plain.").

54. MORRIS, *supra* note 17, at 52; *see* TOM SEGEV, 1949: THE FIRST ISRAELIS 25 (1986).

55. *See* MORRIS, *supra* note 35, at 21 ("In several areas, Israeli commanders successfully used psychological warfare ploys to obtain Arab evacuation."); O'BALLANCE, *supra* note 9, at 64 ("it was deliberate Jewish policy to encourage the Arabs to quit their homes, and they used psychological warfare extensively in urging them to do so."); Childers, *supra* note 20, at 192–93 (quoting Palmach commander Yigal Allon as saying that the Haganah "saw the need to clean inner Galilee . . . [in order] . . . to cause the tens of thousands of sulky Arabs who remained in Galilee to flee . . ."); Radley, *supra* note 26, at 594 ("the Jews certainly played on Arab fears").

56. *See* IDF, Intelligence Branch, *The Emigration of the Arabs of Palestine in the Period 1/12/1947–1/6/1948*, June 30, 1948, in Morris, *supra* note 26, at 10.

57. *See* Childers, *supra* note 20, at 183; Walid Khalidi, *Why Did the Palestinians Leave? An Examination of the Zionist Version of the Exodus of '48*, 35 MIDDLE EAST F. 21 (July 1959).

58. *See* PALUMBO, *supra* note 13, at 4; CHAIM SIMONS, INTERNATIONAL PROPOSALS TO TRANSFER

the Zionist organization in Palestine {Jewish Agency} has indicated its commitment to an enlarged program for (1) a sovereign
Jewish state which would embrace Palestine and probably Transjor-
dania, (2) an eventual transfer of the Arab population from Palestine to Iraq, ...[59]

Ben Gurion expressed himself as favoring "transferring the Arab populations with their consent or without."[60]

B. 1967: Exodus on a Smaller Scale

During the brief war of 1967, 350,000 Palestinians were displaced,
representing one-quarter of the population of the two sectors.[61] Israel
denied causing this exodus,[62] but according to a U.S. State Department
account, Israeli aircraft "hit many civilian targets on the West Bank
where there are absolutely no military emplacements,"[63] causing thousands to flee.[64] In some West Bank localities, using loudspeakers, the

---

ARABS FROM PALESTINE, 1947–1985: A HISTORICAL SURVEY 163–76 (1988) (Jewish leadership
favored compulsory transfer of Arabs, but hoped Britain might carry it out).

59. *Brigadier General Patrick J. Hurley, Personal Representative of President Roosevelt, to the President,*
May 5, 1943, 1943 (4) FOR. REL. U.S. 776, 777.

60. ILAN HALEVI, SOUS ISRAEL LA PALESTINE 138 (1978); MORRIS, *supra* note 17, at 25 (letter
from David Ben Gurion to Amos Ben Gurion, Oct. 5, 1937: "We must expel Arabs and take
their places."); PALUMBO, *supra* note 13, at 23, at 32; SIMONS, *supra* note 58, at 10–17, 247–48
(on Ben Gurion's views).

61. *See* SYDNEY D. BAILEY, THE MAKING OF RESOLUTION 272, 172 (1985); Janet Abu-Lughod, *The Continuing Expulsions From Palestine: 1948–1985, in* PALESTINE: CONTINUING DISPOS-
SESSION 17, 20, 32 (Glenn E. Perry ed. 1986); *Palestinian Emigration and Israeli Land Expropriation
in the Occupied Territories,* 3 J. PALESTINE STUD. 106, 106–07 (no. 1, 1973).

62. *See Report by the Secretary-General to the Security Council in pursuance of operative paragraph 3
of the Council's resolution 237,* U.N. SCOR, 22d Sess., Annex I ("Note verbale" dated 22 June
1967, addressed to the Secretary-General by the Representative of Israel), Supp. of April–June
1967, at 301, U.N. Doc. S/8021 (1967) ("Any allegation that Israel has been expelling residents
from their homes and thus creating a new refugee problem is untrue . . . ."); *cf.* Sholomo Gazit,
Early Attempts at Establishing West Bank Autonomy, 3 HARV. J. L. & PUB. POL'Y 129, 132 (1980)
(author and former Israeli coordinator of government operations in the occupied territories
between 1967 and 1974, explained the exodus thus: "Afraid that they might be indefinitely
separated from their families on the East Bank, immediately after the cessation of hostilities some
150–200,000 refugees left their West Bank homes and moved to the East Bank. Most were
joining relatives who worked on the East Bank or in Kuwait, Saudi Arabia or the other Gulf
Emirates.").

63. DONALD NEFF, WARRIORS FOR JERUSALEM: THE SIX DAYS THAT CHANGED THE MIDDLE
EAST 228–29 (1984) (quoting report from U.S. embassy in Jordan).

64. *See* PETER DODD & HALIM BARAKAT, RIVER WITHOUT BRIDGES: A STUDY OF THE
EXODUS OF THE 1967 PALESTINIAN ARAB REFUGEES 40 (1969), *id.* at 46 (in survey, 57% of
West Bank Arabs who took refuge in Jordan during 1967 war cited aerial bombardment as reason
for departing); FRED J. KHOURI, THE ARAB-ISRAELI DILEMMA 150 (1976); Dana Adams Schmidt,
100,000 in Jordan Said to Have Fled Across River, N.Y. TIMES, June 12, 1967, at A19 ("the 60,000
inhabitants of the three big United Nations camps around Jericho were attacked by planes on
the second day of the fighting. They are now the biggest single group among the refugees who
have arrived [in Jordan].").

IDF encouraged or ordered inhabitants to leave their homes and villages.[65]

C. Facts: A Summation

The factual analysis thus creates a scenario, where the hostilities surrounding the 1948 and 1967 events, may be susceptible to two readings. On the one hand, a reading that is most favorable to the Israeli position holds that the hostilities at least created powerful incentives for the Palestinian exodus, thereby accelerating the exodus. On the other, the facts can also evidence a concerted Israeli effort to remove the Palestinians from their territory, whether by force or other means of coercion and encouragement.

As noted earlier, the following discussion will assume these contrasting factual postures, and advance theories for a Palestinian right of return within the terms of each position. The first cluster of parts analyzes the U.N. position on the Palestinian displacement, and develops international law right of return theories based on the Israeli reading of non-coerced flight.

II. U.N. REACTION TO THE PALESTINIANS' DEPARTURE: DECLARATION AND AFFIRMATION OF THE RIGHT OF RETURN

A. Resolution 194

The first U.N. official to assess the situation of the displaced Palestinians was its mediator, Count Bernadotte. He advised the General Assembly:

> no settlement can be just and complete if recognition is not accorded to the right of the Arab refugee to return to the home from which he has been dislodged by the hazards and strategy of the armed conflict between Arabs and Jews in Palestine. The majority of these refugees have come from territory which, under the Assembly resolution of 29 November [1947], was to be included in the Jewish State . . . . It would be an offence against the principles of elemental justice if these innocent victims of the conflict were denied the right to return to their homes while Jewish immigrants flow into Palestine, and, indeed, at least offer the threat of permanent replacement of the Arab refugees who have been rooted in the land for centuries.[66]

---

65. *See* DODD & BARAKAT, *supra* note 64, at 47 KHOURI, *supra* note 64, at 150; NEFF, *supra* note 63, at 293; Schmidt, *supra* note 64 (reports use by I.D.F. of loudspeaker vans announcing buses available to take Arabs to Jordan).

66. *Progress Report of the United Nations Mediator on Palestine, supra* note 37, at 14 (stating that

The seriousness of what had befallen the displaced Palestinians was not lost on the General Assembly. The French delegate said [paraphrase],

> Many of the villages which they had been obliged to leave had been partly demolished by systematic action which was still continuing . . . . It was unthinkable that the horrors perpetrated during the war against the Jewish populations in Europe should be repeated or should be reproduced in respect of the Arab population. Such a situation, which was a disgrace to mankind, must be brought to a close.[67]

Acting on the mediator's report, the General Assembly included in a resolution seeking an overall settlement of the Palestine question (Resolution 194) a paragraph 11 on the displaced persons. This provision:

> [r]esolves that the refugees wishing to return to their homes and live at peace with their neighbours should be permitted to do so at the earliest practicable date, and that compensation should be paid for the property of those choosing not to return and for loss of or damage to property which, under principles of international law or in equity, should be made good by the Governments or authorities responsible.[68]

To press for a settlement and to seek implementation of other aspects of Resolution 194, the General Assembly created a three-member U.N. Conciliation Commission for Palestine, composed of representatives of Turkey, France, and the United States.[69] The Commission asked Israel to implement the General Assembly's call for the repatriation of displaced Palestinians.[70] Israel admitted 8,000 Palestinians on the basis

---

"[t]he liability of the Provisional Government of Israel to restore private property to its Arab owners and to indemnify those owners for property wantonly destroyed is clear, irrespective of any indemnities which the Provisional Government may claim from the Arab States."); *see* Morris, *Yosef Weitz and the Transfer Committees, 1948–49, supra* note 37, at 532–33, 543–44 (stating that Israel systematically settled Jews in areas left vacant by displaced Palestinians); Morris, *The Crystallization of Israeli Policy Against a Return of the Arab Refugees: April–December 1948, supra* note 37, at 106, 109 (stating that Israel settled Jews in the homes of displaced Palestinians).

67. U.N. GAOR, 3d Sess., 184th plen. mtg., at 945–46, U.N. Doc. A/PV.184 (1948) (Mr. Schuman, France).

68. G.A. Res. 194, U.N. GAOR, 3d Sess., ¶ 11, U.N. Doc. A/810 (1948).

69. *See* G.A. Res. 194, U.N. GAOR, 3d Sess., ¶ 2, U.N. Doc. A/810 (1948); *see also* 1948 U.N.Y.B. 176 (appointing Turkey, France, U.S. members of the Palestine Conciliation Commission).

70. *See The Ambassador in France (Bruce) to the Secretary of State*, Top Secret, June 12, 1949, 6 FOR. REL. U.S. 1124 (1949) (message written by Mark Ethridge, U.S. member of Palestine Conciliation Commission, while at Lausanne conference: "Commission members, particularly US Representatives, have consistently pointed out to Prime Minster, Foreign Minister, and Israeli delegation that key to peace is some Israeli concession on refugees."); *see also* MARK TESSLER, A HISTORY OF THE ISRAELI-PALESTINIAN CONFLICT 311 (1994) (referring to the view of the

of reuniting split families,[71] and offered to admit 100,000 more, but when U.N. officials pressed Israel to admit a larger number it withdrew the offer.[72] The U.S. member of the U.N. Conciliation Commission for Palestine, frustrated at the failure of his efforts to convince Israel to repatriate, said that Israel's "attitude toward [the Palestinian] refugees is morally reprehensible . . . . Her position as conqueror demanding more does not make for peace."[73]

B. Israeli Recalcitrance and its Justifications

Even as the United Nations pressed for repatriation, Israel, in 1949 and for several years thereafter, forced additional Palestinians out of the country. It expelled particularly from the Galilee region,[74] trucking Palestinians to the armistice line and forcing them to cross.[75] In some cases Israel claimed that it expelled Palestinians due to security considerations, while in others it cited a need to make room for Jewish immigrants.[76] In 1950, citing security considerations, it expelled 14,000 residents of Majdal (Ashkelon) by trucking them to the nearby border with the Gaza Strip and forcing them to cross.[77] It continued expulsions into 1951,[78] and for several years thereafter forced out thousands of Palestinian bedouins from the Negev Desert.[79]

Shortly after the 1967 hostilities, Israel readmitted 14,000 of the Palestinians displaced in that year.[80] However, Israel's reluctance to

---

international community 1948–49: "there was broad agreement that the return of the Palestinians was a necessary ingredient in any peace plan.").

71. *See* Radley, *supra* note 26, at 603.

72. *See* HENRY CATTAN, THE PALESTINE QUESTION 65 (1988); PAPPÉ, *supra* note 10, at 231; TESSLER, *supra* note 70, at 314; *Major General John H. Hildring to Secretary of State*, July 25, 1949, 6 FOR. REL. U.S. 1249, 1250 (1949) (reporting that, at U.S. President Harry Truman's request, he conveyed message to Foreign Minister Moshe Sharett about the need for concessions on the issue of displaced Palestinians).

73. *The Ambassador in France (Bruce) to the Secretary of State*, Top Secret, June 12, 1949, *supra* note 70, at 1125.

74. *See* MORRIS, *supra* note 17, at 239–42; SEGEV, *supra* note 54, at 61; SABRI JIRYIS, THE ARABS IN ISRAEL 81 (1976); M. Cherif Bassiouni & Eugene Fisher, *The Arab-Israeli Conflict—Real and Apparent Issues: An Insight into Its Future from the Lessons of the Past*, 44 ST. JOHN'S L. REV. 399, 453 (1970); *see generally* ELIAS CHACOUR, BLOOD BROTHERS 52 (1984).

75. *See* ROSEMARY SAYIGH, PALESTINIANS: FROM PEASANTS TO REVOLUTIONARIES 85, 88–89, 103 (1979); Charles Kamen, *The Arab Population in Palestine and Israel, 1946–1951*, NEW OUTLOOK, Oct.–Nov. 1984, at 36, 38.

76. *See* SEGEV, *supra* note 54, at 52.

77. *See* JIRYIS, *supra* note 74, at 82; Bassiouni & Fisher, *supra* note 74, at 453; SEGEV, *supra* note 54, at 62.

78. *See* JIRYIS, *supra* note 74, at 82; Bassiouni & Fisher, *supra* note 74, at 453; RAFIK HALABI, THE WEST BANK STORY 204 (1982).

79. *See* SCHWARZ, *supra* note 38, at 158–59; Ghazi Falah, *How Israel Controls the Bedouin*, 19 J. PALESTINE STUD. 35, 41 (1985); SAYIGH, *supra* note 75, at 99.

80. *See* U.N. SCOR, 22d Sess., 1375th mtg., at 9, U.N. Doc. S/PV.1375 (1967) (Mr. Rifa'i, Jordan).

repatriate the displaced Palestinians in greater numbers has drawn continuing condemnation from the U.N. General Assembly. In reaction to the General Assembly's stance, some analysts have argued that Israel's position is consistent with Resolution 194, because of ambiguity in that resolution. Five separate points have been raised that might lead to a conclusion that Israel is not in violation of Resolution 194. These arguments converge on the conclusion that Resolution 194 did not conceive of Palestinian return as a matter of right. To these ends, it has been argued that: (1) final settlement is a condition precedent for Palestinian repatriation; (2) Resolution 194 only required repatriation of those displaced Palestinians who are willing to live in peace with their Israeli neighbors; (3) since Resolution 194 did not speak of any specific date for repatriation, it did not conceive of it as a right; (4) Resolution 194 is couched in discretionary language of "should" rather than more mandatory terms; (5) subsequent U.N. actions have indicated that it did not view repatriation as a right. Ultimately, however, these arguments are unpersuasive, and thus fail to undermine the authority of Resolution 194 for the Palestinian right of return.

1. Repatriation only upon an Overall Settlement

Some analysts have commented that the General Assembly contemplated that repatriation would occur only as part of an overall settlement, and therefore that it imposed no obligation to repatriate prior to that time.[81] Thus, Israel put the onus on the Arab states to conclude peace with it before it would discuss repatriation.[82] Under this view, the General Assembly did not regard return as a matter of right.

This issue was debated in the General Assembly's First Committee, where a draft of what became Resolution 194 was introduced by the United Kingdom.[83] Guatemala proposed to amend the paragraph on repatriation by adding the words "after the proclamation of peace by the contending parties in Palestine, including the Arab states," so that repatriation would have been required only after peace agreements.[84] Guatemala explained that it was concerned that there would be "constant friction between the Arabs and Jews" if the displaced returned

---

81. *See* Ruth Lapidoth, *The Right of Return in International Law, with Special Reference to the Palestinian Refugees*, 16 Isr. Y.B. on H.R. 103, 116 (1986); Radley, *supra* note 26, at 602.

82. *See* Tessler, *supra* note 70, at 312. Armistices were concluded in 1949 with neighboring Arab states, but no peace agreements.

83. *See Annexes to the Summary Records of Meetings*, U.N. GAOR, 3d Sess., pt.1, at 61, U.N. Doc. A/C.1/394.Rev.2 (1948).

84. *See Annexes to the Summary Records of Meetings*, U.N. GAOR, 3d Sess., pt.1, at 69, U.N. Doc. A/C.1/398.Rev.2 (1948).

"while war was continuing."[85] Israel supported the Guatemalan amendment,[86] but the United States opposed it [paraphrase]:

> His delegation could not accept the proclamation of peace as a prerequisite for the return of refugees and hoped that the Assembly would not make this a condition. It was recognized that the bulk of the refugees could only return in peaceful circumstances. However, they need not wait for the proclamation of peace before beginning. These unfortunate people should not be made pawns in the negotiations for a final settlement.[87]

Egypt made the same point, stating that the Guatemalan amendment "gave the Jews an opportunity to use the status of the Arab refugees as a bargaining point in the settlement of the Palestine question."[88]

Guatemala countered that the displaced Palestinians, if they returned before a peace agreement, "would not obey the Government," and that "their return could only create new difficulties and bloodshed."[89] The U.K. replied that:

> There were minorities in many countries which disputed the rights of their Governments or indeed of their State to exist. The United Kingdom delegation could not, and hoped that the Assembly would not, subscribe to the thesis that such minorities should be driven out as refugees into other countries because of differences of political opinion with the Governments of the countries in which they lived.[90]

The Guatemalan amendment was put to a vote in the First Committee and was defeated, thirty-seven votes to seven, with five abstentions.[91] Thus, the Committee considered and rejected the idea that return might be delayed pending peace agreements. After Resolution 194 was adopted, the U.N. Conciliation Commission for Palestine pressed Israel for immediate repatriation, thereby reconfirming that the

---

85. *See Summary Records of Meetings 21 September–8 December 1948*, U.N. GAOR, 3d Sess., pt.1, C.1, at 904, U.N. Doc. A/C.1/SR.226 (1948) (Mr. García Granados, Guatemala).

86. *See Summary Records of Meetings 21 September–8 December 1948*, U.N. GAOR, 3d Sess., pt.1, C.1, at 906, U.N. Doc. A/C.1/SR.226 (1948) (Mr. Eban, Israel).

87. *Summary Records of Meetings 21 September–8 December 1948*, U.N. GAOR, 3d Sess., pt.1, C.1, at 909, U.N. Doc. A/C.1/SR.226 (1948) (Mr. Rusk, U.S.A.).

88. *Summary Records of Meetings 21 September–8 December 1948*, U.N. GAOR, 3d Sess., pt.1, C.1, at 904, U.N. Doc. A/C.1/SR.226 (1948) (Mr. Fawzi Bey, Egypt).

89. *Summary Records of Meetings 21 September–8 December 1948*, U.N. GAOR, 3d Sess., pt.1, C.1, at 910, U.N. Doc. A/C.1/SR.226 (1948) (Mr. García Granados, Guatemala).

90. *See Summary Records of Meetings 21 September–8 December 1948*, U.N. GAOR, 3d Sess., pt.1, C.1, at 910, U.N. Doc. A/C.1/SR.226 (1948) (Mr. Beeley, U.K.).

91. *See Summary Records of Meetings 21 September–8 December 1948*, U.N. GAOR, 3d Sess., pt.1, C.1, at 912, U.N. Doc. A/C.1/SR.226 (1948).

Assembly had not intended that repatriation should await peace agreements.[92]

2. Only Palestinians Wishing to "Live at Peace"

Some analysts have argued that Resolution 194 called for the repatriation of only those displaced Palestinians "wishing to . . . live at peace with their neighbors,"[93] and that this formulation limited the return to Palestinians so inclined, thus not to all the displaced Palestinians.[94] Analysts have further asserted that the determination as to which Palestinians wished to live in peace could be made unilaterally by Israel.[95] Analysts who focus on the "live at peace" language read the resolution as falling short of recognizing a return as a right for the displaced Palestinians.

The phrase "live at peace" was not explained in debates leading to the adoption of Resolution 194. It is, however, open to another interpretation consistent with return as a right. The Assembly anticipated that some of the displaced Palestinians might not be disposed to return to live under Israeli sovereignty. The phrase "wishing to live at peace" provided a way to refer to those who were disposed to return to live under Israeli sovereignty. Those not wishing to live in peace with their neighbors referred to those who might remain abroad. The choice would be that of each displaced Palestinian. Under this interpretation, Resolution 194 would recognize a right of return.

Whatever the proper meaning of Resolution 194 in this regard, the General Assembly in resolutions in later years omitted the phrase "wishing to live at peace." Subsequent U.N. resolutions on the topic establish that Palestinians may return to their homelands *as a matter of right.* In 1974, for example, the General Assembly referred to "the inalienable right of the Palestinians to return to their homes and property from which they have been displaced and uprooted."[96] Thus, any ambiguity in Resolution 194 as to whether the Assembly viewed return as a matter of right was resolved in later resolutions.

---

92. *See The Top Ambassador in France (Bruce) to the Secretary of State,* Top Secret, June 12, 1949, *supra* note 70.

93. G.A. Res. 194, U.N. GAOR, 3d Sess., ¶ 11, U.N. Doc. A/810 (1948).

94. *See* Radley, *supra* note 26, at 602.

95. *See* Yoav Tadmor, *Comment: The Palestinian Refugees of 1948: The Right to Compensation and Return,* 8 TEMPLE INT'L & COMP. L.J. 434 (1994) (stating that, under G.A. Res. 194, return is "contingent upon Israel's assessment of the refugees' ability to live in peace").

96. G.A. Res. 3236, U.N. GAOR, 29th Sess., Supp. No. 31, ¶ 2, U.N. Doc. A/9631 (1974).

3. Date of Implementation

Resolution 194 calls for a return "at the earliest practicable date."[97] Some analysts have argued that this formulation meant less than immediate repatriation and thus that Resolution 194 did not conceive of return as a right.[98]

However, it would seem that the General Assembly was concerned that Israel would not implement repatriation promptly, in particular that it not delay until peace agreements were signed.[99] The Assembly contemplated that return would be effectuated by diplomatic means through the U.N. Conciliation Commission for Palestine and assumed that the logistics of a return would require a period of time.[100]

The U.K. draft resolution had used the phrase "earliest possible date."[101] After floor debate, the U.K. delegate changed "possible" to "practicable" in the English text, in order, as he said, "to make clearer the intention of the proposal,"[102] and as a partial response to concern expressed by the Israeli delegate that a return prior to peace agreements would create security problems.[103]

Curiously, the French text of paragraph 11, which, like the English, read "as soon as possible [*le plus tôt possible*] in the original U.K. draft, was not changed on the floor.[104] Thus, in the resolution as adopted by the General Assembly, the phrase is "as soon as practicable" in English, and "as soon as possible" in French. Evidently, the change made in the English text was not deemed sufficiently great to require a change in the French text. As finalized, the phrasing implies a sense of immediacy to the obligation, i.e., that repatriation must be accomplished as soon as it can be done.

4. "Should" as Not Implying a Legal Obligation

It was also objected that the General Assembly resolution did not mention a "right" to return, but instead said that the refugees "should

---

97. G.A. Res. 194, *supra* note 93.

98. *See* Radley, *supra* note 26, at 602.

99. *See supra* notes 83–92.

100. *See* W. Thomas Mallison & Sally V. Mallison, The Palestine Problem in International Law and World Order 179–80 (1986).

101. *Annexes to the Summary Records of Meetings*, U.N. GAOR, 3d Sess., pt.1, ¶ 11, U.N. Doc. A/C.1/394.Rev.2 (1948).

102. *Summary Records of Meetings 21 September–8 December 1948*, U.N. GAOR, 3d Sess., pt.1, C.1, at 910, U.N. Doc. A/C.1/SR.226 (1948) (Mr. Beeley, U.K.).

103. *See Summary Records of Meetings 21 September–8 December 1948*, U.N. GAOR, 3d Sess., pt.1, C.1, at 906, U.N. Doc. A/C.1/SR.226 (1948) (Mr. Eban, Israel).

104. G.A. Res. 194, *supra* note 68, ¶ 11 (final text in French).

be permitted" to return.[105] Thus, it was said that the General Assembly did not recognize a right for the Palestinians to return.[106]

As the resolution was debated in the General Assembly, the delegate of the United Kingdom, the resolution's drafter, called the provision on displaced persons a "precise directive," a characterization that makes sense only if it is a call for repatriation.[107] The U.S. delegate said that the draft resolution "aimed at facilitating the repatriation and resettlement of refugees."[108] In the First Committee debate, no state, other than Israel,[109] questioned repatriation as of right. Delegates who addressed the issue were consistent in either stating or assuming that Israel was required to repatriate.[110]

The issue would seem to be moot, however, since in subsequent resolutions the General Assembly referred to a Palestinian return as a matter of right. In one resolution, for example, it "[r]eaffirm[ed] also the inalienable right of the Palestinians to return to their homes and property from which they have been displaced and uprooted, and call[ed] for their return."[111]

Other U.N. bodies have also said that displaced Palestinians have a right to return. Secretary-General U Thant said: "people everywhere, and this certainly applies to the Palestinian refugees, have a natural right to be in their homeland."[112] The United Nations Commission on Human Rights determined that human rights norms required Israel to

---

105. *See* Lapidoth, *supra* note 81, at 116; Radley, *supra* note 26, at 601 ("It would seem clear enough that the phraseology 'should be permitted' does not amount to 'must be permitted.'").

106. *See* Donna E. Arzt, *Palestinian Refugees: The Human Dimension of the Middle East Peace Process*, PROC. AM. SOC. INT'L L. 372 (1995) (pointing to the use of "should" in Res. 194 and stating that it "nowhere uses the word 'right.'").

107. *See* U.N. GAOR, 3d Sess., 184th mtg. at 948, U.N. Doc. A/PV.184 (1948) (Mr. McNeil, U.K.).

108. U.N. GAOR, 3d Sess., 184th mtg. at 954, U.N. Doc. A/PV.184 (1948) (Mr. Dulles, U.S.A.).

109. *See Summary Records of Meetings 21 September–8 December 1948*, U.N. GAOR, 3d Sess., pt.1, C.1, at 646, U.N. Doc. A/C.1/SR.200 (1948) (Mr. Shertok, Israel: "It [Israel] believed that serious thought should be given to the re-settling of the Arab refugees in neighbouring territories.").

110. *See Summary Records of Meetings 21 September–8 December 1948*, U.N. GAOR, 3d Sess., pt.1, C.1, at 683, U.N. Doc. A/C.1/SR.205 (1948) (Mr. Jessup, U.S.A.: "The United States Government believed that those who wished should be returned to their homes."); *id.* at 686 (Mr. Liu Chieh, China, referring to "the rights of the Arab refugees to return to their homes."); *Summary Records of Meetings 21 September–8 December 1948*, U.N. GAOR, 3d Sess., pt.1, C.1, at 724, U.N. Doc. A/C.1/SR.209 (1948) (Mr. Urdaneta Arbelaez, Colombia: "they should have the right to choose between receiving compensation or returning to their homes."); *id.* at 729 (Mr. Parodi, France: "Substantial aid must be given to those refugees to enable them to return home or, if they so preferred, to settle elsewhere."); *see also* Christian Tomuschat, *State Responsibility and the Country of Origin, in* THE PROBLEM OF REFUGEES IN THE LIGHT OF CONTEMPORARY INTERNATIONAL LAW ISSUES 59, 69 (Vera Gowlland-Debbas ed., 1996) (stating that in resolution 194, the General Assembly asserted a right to return).

111. G.A. Res. 3236, U.N. GAOR, 29th Sess., Supp. No. 31, ¶ 2, U.N. Doc. A/9631 (1974).

112. *Introduction to the Annual Report of the Secretary-General on the Work of the Organization*, U.N. GAOR, 22d Sess., Supp. No. 1A, at 7, U.N. Doc. A/6701/Add.1 (1967).

allow the displaced Palestinians to return. In a 1987 resolution, the Commission found a "right of the Palestinians to return to their homeland Palestine and their property, from which they have been uprooted by force."[113] There would thus seem to be little basis for concluding that the United Nations does not view a Palestinian return as legally required.

5. A Possible United Nations Retreat from Insisting on Right of Return

During the 1950s and 1960s, the General Assembly, in a series of resolutions, urged Arab states to resettle displaced Palestinians in their own territory.[114] This effort, it was argued in support of Israel's refusal to repatriate, denoted an assessment by the United Nations that the situation of the displaced Palestinians could be resolved in a fashion other than repatriation, and thus that the U.N. did not view Israel as being obliged to repatriate:

> In addition to a perfunctory reaffirmation of Resolution 194, the General Assembly in the years 1952 through 1968 annually reaffirmed Resolution 513, emphasizing public works projects by which the refugees might be resettled and reintegrated into the Arab communities where they were.[115]

The General Assembly's insistence on a Palestinian repatriation continued, however, through the 1950s and 1960s, the period when, according to the critics, the General Assembly ignored the subject. In a 1957 resolution, for example, the General Assembly called for action by relevant U.N. agencies to implement the return called for in its 1948 resolution.[116]

---

113. E.S.C. Res. 1987/4, U.N. ESCOR, 43d Sess., 28th mtg., Supp. No. 5, at 21, U.N. Doc. E/1987/18 (1987).

114. *See* G.A. Res. 513, U.N. GAOR, 6th Sess., Supp. No. 20, at 12, U.N. Doc. A/2119 (1951).

115. Radley, *supra* note 26, at 603–04. *See also* G.A. Res. 513, U.N. GAOR, 6th Sess., Supp. No. 20, at 12, U.N. Doc. A/2119 ("For many years following the adoption of Resolution 194 in 1948, the focus of General Assembly attention with respect to the Palestinian problem drifted from repatriation toward resettlement as a solution."); *see* Eyal Benvenisti & Eyal Zamir, *Private Claims to Property Rights in the Future Israeli-Palestinian Settlement*, 89 AM. J. INT'L L. 295, 326 (1995) ("Subsequent [to G.A. Res. 194] resolutions . . . indicated the understanding . . . that unrestricted repatriation of refugees was neither a feasible option nor the preferred one. At the same time that it repeatedly reaffirmed Resolution 194(III), the General Assembly advocated programs that would include the resettlement of the refugees in Arab countries.").

116. *See* G.A. Res. 1018, U.N. GAOR, 11th Sess., Supp. No. 17, ¶ 4, U.N. Doc. A/3572 (1957) (requesting U.N. Relief and Works to continue consultations with U.N. Palestine Conciliation Commission to implement G.A. Resolution 194, paragraph 11).

A more plausible reading of the General Assembly's Resolution 513[117] is that the Assembly viewed resettlement in Arab states as a complement, not an alternative, to repatriation. The longer the displaced Palestinians remained abroad, the more would they develop ties in the states of refuge, and thus more could be expected to desire to remain. The U.N. Conciliation Commission for Palestine reported, following discussions with Arab governments, that

> it would be necessary to take into account the possibility that not all the refugees would decide to return to their homes. The Commission believed, therefore, that the Arab States should agree in principle to the resettlement of those refugees who did not desire to return to their homes.[118]

The General Assembly was also concerned that the United Nations might not be financially able to sustain its relief work and hoped that the Arab states would assume some of the financial burden. Thus, in a 1950 resolution the General Assembly stated that it

> 4. Considers that, without prejudice to the provisions of paragraph 11 of General Assembly Resolution 194 (III) of 11 December 1948, the reintegration of the refugees into the economic life of the Near East, either by repatriation or resettlement, is essential in preparation for the time when international assistance is no longer available, and for the realization of conditions of peace and stability in the area;
> 5. Instructs the [U.N. Relief and Works] Agency [for Palestine Refugees in the Near East] to establish a reintegration fund which shall be utilized for projects requested by any government in the Near East and approved by the Agency for the permanent re-establishment of refugees and their removal from relief.[119]

And again in 1957, the General Assembly called on host governments "without prejudice to paragraph 11 of General Assembly Resolution 194 (III)" to plan projects to support the displaced Palestinians.

The United Nations reaffirmed its position on return of displaced Palestinians after more were displaced in 1967, calling on Israel to repatriate the Palestinians displaced in the hostilities of that year. The Security Council, in its Resolution 237, urged Israel to "facilitate the

---

117. *See* G.A. Res. 513, U.N. GAOR, 6th Sess., Supp. No. 20, at 12, U.N. Doc. A/2119 (1951).

118. *General Progress Report and Supplementary Report of the United Nations Conciliation Commission for Palestine,* U.N. GAOR, 5th Sess., Supp. No. 18, at 12, U.N. Doc. A/1367/Rev.1 (1951).

119. G.A. Res. 393, U.N. GAOR, 5th Sess., Supp. No. 20, at 22, U.N. Doc. A/1775 (1950).

return without delay of those inhabitants who have fled the areas since the outbreak of hostilities."[120]

Another Security Council resolution of 1967, Resolution 242, is cited by some analysts as an indication that the United Nations did not regard repatriation of the displaced Palestinians as legally required, or that if it once deemed it legally required it abandoned that view.[121] Israel and the P.L.O. have accepted Resolution 242 as a basis for their negotiations on final status issues, including that of the displaced Palestinians.[122] According to one view:

> The weakness of the claim to a legal right of return and repossession is reinforced by United Nations resolutions on the settlement of the refugee problem in the Middle East. Security Council Resolution 242 . . . calls for "a just settlement of the refugee problem."[123]

These analysts state, appropriately, that the term "just settlement" must be read in light of prior U.N. statements as to a just outcome but then, relying on their view that the U.N. had moved from repatriation to resettlement, they find that "just settlement" meant the latter. On this analysis, they conclude that "[t]he acceptance of Resolution 242 in the [Israel-P.L.O.] accords [of 1993] seems to reject a general right of return and repossession."[124]

The Security Council's insistence on a "just settlement," however, is more plausibly read as affirming a right for the Palestinians to return. Resolution 242 was a global resolution seeking an overall settlement of the Arab-Israeli conflict. It was not a resolution whose primary focus was the displaced Palestinians. "Just settlement" probably referred to what the United Nations had found since 1948 to be a just outcome, namely, return for displaced Palestinians.[125] It would be hazardous to

---

120. S.C. Res. 237, U.N. SCOR, 22d Sess., at 5, U.N. Doc. S/INF/22/Rev.2 (1967); *see also* G.A. Res. 2452A, U.N. GAOR, 23d Sess., Supp. No. 18, at 22, U.N. Doc. A/7218 (1968) (calling on Israel "to take effective and immediate steps for the return without delay of those inhabitants who have fled the areas since the outbreak of hostilities.").

121. *See* S.C. Res. 242, U.N. SCOR, 22d Sess., at 8, U.N. Doc. S/INF/22/Rev.2 (1967).

122. *See Declaration of Principles on Interim Self-Government, September 13, 1993, supra* note 3, art. 1 (stating that "negotiations on the permanent status will lead to the implementation of Security Council Resolutions 242 and 338"). *But see* Sarah Honig & David Makovsky, *Religious Issues Delay Coalition Deal,* JERUSALEM POST, June 17, 1996, at 1 (indicating that government of Prime Minister Benjamin Netanyahu appeared to retract Israel's position that Resolution 242 would form basis for negotiations with P.L.O.).

123. Benvenisti & Zamir, *supra* note 115, at 326.

124. *See id.*

125. *See* MALLISON & MALLISON, *supra* note 100, at 188 (analyzing "just settlement of the refugee problem" language of S.C. Res. 242: "There are no elements of such a just settlement stated in the resolution and the only authoritative principles adopted by the United Nations on

construe use of the phrase "just settlement" as a repudiation of the U.N. position that repatriation was required. Statements by delegates in Security Council discussion before and after the adoption of Resolution 242 are consistent with repatriation as the intended meaning, although no delegate analyzed the matter in detail.[126]

Beginning in the 1970s, the U.N. General Assembly viewed the Palestinians as entitled to self-determination and thus to return on that additional legal basis.[127] However, the Assembly continued to reiterate its call to Israel to implement Resolution 194 and thus reaffirmed its view that individual Palestinians had a right to return, apart from the collective rights of the Palestinians as a people.[128]

To recapitulate, U.N. Resolution 194 affirms a Palestinian right of return. The General Assembly's position remains undiluted either by the Israeli view of the Palestinian flight as non-coerced, or by the arguments that try to remove the obligatory element from the repatriation resolution. The General Assembly's position reflected a principle found in general international law that guarantees the right of inhabitants of a territory to reside there. The next Part will retain the Israeli factual perspective, and will derive theories for the right of return from these three bodies of international law: state-state law, human rights law, and humanitarian law.

III. INTERNATIONAL LAW AS A SOURCE OF THE RIGHT OF RETURN: OBLIGATION TO ADMIT NATIONALS

The issue of the rights of inhabitants, and, in particular, the resident minority groups, upon the formation of new states was one the international community had faced before. It had dealt with the matter

---

this subject remain the General Assembly resolutions which have been considered above [G.A. Res. 194 and its progeny].").

126. *See* U.N. SCOR, 22d Sess., 1375th mtg., at 11, U.N. Doc. S/PV.1375 (1967) (Mr. Rifa'i, Jordan); *id.* at 14 (Mr. Tarabanov, Bulgaria); U.N. SCOR, 22d Sess., 1377th mtg., at 4, U.N. Doc. S/PV.1377 (1967) (Lord Caradon, U.K.); *id.* at 7 (Mr. Goldberg, U.S.A.); *id.* at 8 (Mr. Goldberg, U.S.A.); U.N. SCOR, 22d Sess., 1379th mtg., at 3, U.N. Doc. S/PV.1379 (1967) (Lord Caradon, U.K.); U.N. SCOR, 22d Sess., 1381st mtg., at 6–7, U.N. Doc. S/PV.1381 (1967) (Mr. Kuznetsov, U.S.S.R.); U.N. SCOR, 22d Sess., 1382d mtg., at 2, U.N. Doc. S/PV.1382 (1967) (Mr. Tomeh, Syria).

127. *See* G.A. Res. 3089(D), U.N. GAOR, 28th Sess., Supp. No. 30, at 27, U.N. Doc. A/9030 (1974) (the Assembly resolved "that the enjoyment by the Palestine Arab refugees of their right to return to their homes and property, recognized by the General Assembly in resolution 194 (III) of 11 December 1948, which has been repeatedly reaffirmed by the Assembly since that date, is indispensable for the achievement of a just settlement of the refugee problem and for the exercise by the people of Palestine of its right to self-determination.").

128. *See id.*; *cf.* DONNA E. ARZT, REFUGEES INTO CITIZENS: PALESTINIANS AND THE END OF THE ARAB-ISRAELI CONFLICT 25 (1997) (stating, without providing substantiation, that in the U.N. view, an exercise of self-determination in the West Bank and Gaza Strip would substitute for repatriation to Israel).

primarily through the concept of nationality. In various ways, the law on nationality protected members of minorities, as well as others, from being evicted from, or refused admission to, their homelands.

Nationality rights are ordinarily implemented in routine fashion and draw little attention.[129] When, however, populations move, or territory changes hands, or a state seeks to exclude a group it does not want, the principle of nationality comes to the fore.

A state must accept absent nationals into its territory. This obligation exists at two levels. First, at the state-to-state level, it is an obligation to states where the absent nationals are located. Second, it is an obligation running from the state to its national as a protected human right. The latter category may be alternatively derived from human rights law or humanitarian law. The following sections will lay out the three sources of the right of return; Part IV will discuss the arguments that dispute these obligations.

A. An Obligation to Other States to Admit a National

The obligation to admit a national has become "an inherent duty of States resulting from the conception of nationality."[130] A state's refusal to admit its national may violate the rights of the state in which the national is present. The state of nationality bears an obligation toward a state where its absent national sojourns, because the state of sojourn is entitled to control residence in its territory by aliens.[131]

The state of sojourn being under no obligation to admit the alien, or to allow the alien to remain, the alien's state of nationality must grant admission.[132] Accordingly, the Havana Convention Regarding the Status of Aliens provides, "States are required to receive their nationals expelled from foreign soil who seek to enter their terri-

---

129. *See* LOUIS SOHN & THOMAS BUERGENTHAL, THE MOVEMENT OF PERSONS ACROSS BORDERS 39–40 (1992) (states have a duty to admit a national and ordinarily do so); RICHARD PLENDER, INTERNATIONAL MIGRATION LAW 73 (1972) (on constitutional provisions in some states protecting a right of entry for nationals).

130. P. WEIS, NATIONALITY AND STATELESSNESS IN INTERNATIONAL LAW 47 (1979).

131. PLENDER, *supra* note 129, at 71 ("The proposition that every state must admit its own nationals to its territory is so widely accepted that it may be described as a commonplace of international law.").

132. *See, e.g.*, Charles Dupuis, *Règles générales du droit de la paix*, 32 HAGUE ACAD. DROIT INT'L, RECUEIL DES COURS 5, 156 (1930, II) ("It is acknowledged, in principle and without difficulty, that a state may not expel its nationals, that this would violate the respect it owes to other states if it would attempt to get rid of its subjects, citizens, or *ressortissants* that it deems undesirable, in a way that forces them onto the other state." [The French *ressortissants* is explained in WEIS, *supra* note 130, at 7–9]. Although Dupuis is discussing expulsion, the same conclusion applies by necessary implication to a refusal to admit); H.C. 698/80, Kawasme et al. v. Minister of Defence et al. [second phase], 35(1) P.D. 617, 639–45 (Cohn J., dissenting, *excerpted in* 11 ISR. Y.B. ON H.R. 349, 353 (1981): finding in customary international law a prohibition against expulsion of nationals).

tory."[133] If the state of nationality refuses to admit its national, it is liable to the state of sojourn and has an obligation to restore the *status quo ante*,[134] specifically, to admit its national. A state's obligation to admit its nationals applies even if the national has never set foot in the state's territory.[135]

A state's obligation to admit its national applies as well if the state revokes the nationality. If a state revokes the nationality of a national located abroad, it must repatriate the person despite the revocation.[136] As provided in the Harvard Law Research draft Convention on Nationality:

> A state may not refuse to receive into its territory a person, upon his expulsion by or exclusion from the territory of another state, if such person is a national of the first state or if such person was formerly its national and lost its nationality without having or acquiring the nationality of any other state.[137]

A state may not, by revoking nationality, force another state to accept its national.[138]

---

133. Convention Regarding the Status of Aliens, Havana, Feb. 20, 1928, art. 6, 46 Stat. 2753, 132 L.N.T.S. 301.

134. *See* CLYDE EAGLETON, THE RESPONSIBILITY OF STATES IN INTERNATIONAL LAW 182 (1928); Chorzów Factory (Ger. v. Pol.), 1928 P.C.I.J. (ser. A) No. 13, at 47; International Law Commission, *Report of the International Law Commission on the work of its forty-eighth session*, U.N. GAOR, 51st Sess., Supp. No. 10, at 142, U.N. Doc. A/51/10 (1996), draft articles on state responsibility, art. 43.

135. WEIS, *supra* note 130, at 53 ("the State of nationality is also under an obligation to admit a national born abroad who never resided on its territory if his admission should be demanded by the State of residence.").

136. *See* John Fischer Williams, *Denationalization*, 8 BRIT. Y.B. INT'L L. 45, 61 (1927) ("a state cannot, whether by banishment or by putting an end to the status of nationality, compel any other state to receive one of its own nationals whom it wishes to expel from its own territory. There will also be general agreement that a state is bound to receive back across its frontiers any individual who possesses its nationality."); *id.* at 56 ("The duty of a state to receive back its own nationals is laid down by the accepted authorities in the most general terms and is in accordance with the actual practice of states.").

137. Research in International Law, Harvard Law School, *Nationality, Responsibility of States, Territorial Waters: Drafts of Conventions Prepared in Anticipation of the First Conference on the Codification of International Law, The Hague, 1930*, The Law of Nationality, art. 20, 23 AM. J. INT'L L. 13, 16 (Supp. 1929) [hereinafter "The Law of Nationality"].

138. *See* PLENDER, *supra* note 129, at 87 ("a state may not justify its expulsion or non-admission of its own former nationals by drawing attention to the fact that it first took the precaution of denaturalizing them."); for examples of revocation, see Mario Modiano, *Prof Papandreou Loses Greek Nationality*, LONDON TIMES, Aug. 14, 1971, at 5 (Greece revoked nationality for political activity, refused admission); *Czech Emigre Loses Citizenship*, LONDON TIMES, Apr. 13, 1974, at 6 (Czechoslovakia revoked nationality for political activity, refused admission).

B. A Right of Admission in Human Rights Law

The right of admission found in the law of nationality runs between states. If the state of sojourn is willing to accept another state's national, then it waives its right to insist on repatriation by the state of nationality.[139] However, in this situation the individual may have a right to return under rules of law that protect the individual. Such a right would be independent of the will of the state of sojourn and thus would attach even if the state of sojourn does not ask the state of nationality to admit the individual.

States must, once they recognize an individual as a national, admit that person to their territory. This right is commonly referred to as a right of return.[140] In human rights instruments one finds a right for nationals to be admitted.[141] Under the Universal Declaration of Human Rights, "Everyone has the right to leave any country, including his own, and to return to his country."[142] Under the International Covenant on Civil and Political Rights, to which Israel is a party,[143] "no one shall be arbitrarily deprived of the right to enter his own country."[144] Under the International Convention on the Elimination of All Forms of Racial Discrimination, to which Israel is also a party,[145] a state may not deny, on racial or ethnic grounds, the opportunity "to return to one's country."[146]

Regional human rights treaties similarly protect a right of entry to one's country. Protocol No. 4 to the European Convention for the Protection of Human Rights and Fundamental Freedoms states that "no one shall be deprived of the right to enter the territory of the State

---

139. *See* PLENDER, *supra* note 129, at 72 ("If the state of nationality refuses to admit the national, the state of residence may acquiesce in the refusal, and so forfeit its right to repatriate him.").

140. *See* Lapidoth, *supra* note 81, at 108 (as in the law of nationality the right applies even if the national has never been in the state of nationality); *see supra* note 135 (for the corresponding rule in the law of nationality).

141. *See* HURST HANNUM, THE RIGHT TO LEAVE AND RETURN IN INTERNATIONAL LAW AND PRACTICE 56–59 (1987).

142. Universal Declaration of Human Rights, G.A. Res. 217A, art. 13, ¶ 2, at 71, U.N. Doc. A/810 (1948); *Les Transfers Internationaux des Populations*, 44(2) ANNUAIRE DE L'INSTITUT DE DROIT INT'L 138, 146 (1952) (stating that the Declaration "excluded rather clearly any form of pressure or threat to convince a population to abandon the territory on which it is located").

143. *See Multilateral Treaties Deposited with the Secretary-General* (status as at 31 December 1995), at 121 U.N. Doc. ST/LEG/SER.E/14 (1996) (entered into force for Israel Oct. 3, 1991).

144. International Covenant on Civil and Political Rights, 999 U.N.T.S. 171, art. 12, ¶ 4.

145. *Multilateral Treaties Deposited with the Secretary-General*, *supra* note 143, at 95 (entered into force for Israel Jan. 3, 1979).

146. International Convention on the Elimination of All Forms of Racial Discrimination, 660 U.N.T.S. 195, art. 5(d)(ii). The Convention, art. 1, defines "racial discrimination" to mean "any distinction, exclusion, restriction or preference based on race, colour, descent, or national or ethnic origin" that has the effect of depriving a person of a right.

of which he is a national."[147] The American Convention on Human Rights states that "no one can be expelled from the territory of the State of which he is a national or be deprived of the right to enter it."[148] The African Charter on Human and Peoples' Rights states that "every individual" is entitled "to return to his country."[149]

Rights provisions framed in more general terms may protect the right to enter one's country. The European Commission of Human Rights, hearing a case in which Protocol No. 4 had not been ratified by the state in question, found nonetheless a right of admission for nationals in treaty provisions forbidding degrading treatment and ethnic discrimination and guaranteeing security of the person.[150] As in the law of nationality, so in human rights law, a state may not evade its obligation to admit nationals by depriving them of nationality.[151]

C. A Right of Admission in Humanitarian Law

The territory to which some of the displaced Palestinians seek return is, as indicated, territory that falls under Israel's belligerent occupation. Another body of law, humanitarian law, guarantees a spectrum of rights to persons who inhabit territory that is occupied by a foreign power. One such right is repatriation of those entitled to it.[152]

Several propositions in humanitarian law point in this direction. The Hague Regulations on the law of war[153] require an occupant to respect

---

147. European Convention for the Protection of Human Rights and Fundamental Freedoms, 1963, Protocol No. 4, art. 3, ¶ 2, 46 Eur. T.S.

148. Organization of American States, *Official Records*, OEA/SER.K/XVI/1.1, Doc. 65, Rev. 1, Corr. 1, Jan. 1, 1970, art. 22, ¶ 5.

149. *African Charter on Human and Peoples' Rights*, 21 Int'l Leg. Mats. 58, 61 (1982).

150. *See East African Asians: Twenty-Five Applications against the United Kingdom*, 36 Eur. Comm'n on H.R. 92, 122 (1971) (making a threshold finding that applicants have stated a case under the European convention provisions on degrading treatment and race discrimination, as well as on security of the person and equality of treatment); *Thirty-One Applications of East African Asians v. U.K.*, 15 Hum. Rts. L.J. 215 (1994) (finding violations on the merits of Article 3 (degrading treatment) and Article 14 (race discrimination), but not of Article 5 (the security of the person) or of the equality of treatment guarantees).

151. *See* Hannum, *supra* note 141, at 156, Strasbourg Declaration on the Right to Leave and Return, Nov. 26, 1986, art. 6, ¶ B ("No person shall be deprived of nationality or citizenship in order to exile or to prevent that person from exercising the right to enter his or her country."); *Draft Principles on Freedom and Non-Discrimination in respect of the Right of Everyone to Leave Any Country, including His Own, and to Return to His Country*, U.N. Sub-Commission on Prevention of Discrimination and Protection of Minorities, Jan. 14 to Feb. 1, 1963, Res. 2B(XV), ¶ II(b) at 44, 46, U.N. Doc. E/CN.4/846 (1963) ("No one shall be arbitrarily deprived of his nationality . . . as a means of divesting him of the right to return to his country.").

152. *See* Quincy Wright, *Legal Aspects of the Middle East Situation*, 33 Law & Contemp. Probs. 5, 19 (1968) (stating, with reference to Palestinians displaced from occupied territory, "The law of war, applicable to all *de facto* hostilities, requires the occupant to spare the civil population, and refusal to allow repatriation . . . would violate that law.").

153. *See* Convention Respecting the Laws and Customs of War on Land, Oct. 18, 1907, Annex: Regulations Respecting the Laws and Customs of War on Land [hereinafter "Hague Regula-

and maintain the "public life" of the territory.[154] The repatriation of nationals or non-national residents who happen to be abroad for whatever reason when the occupant enters into control would seem necessary in this regard.

The 1949 Geneva Civilians Convention, to which Israel is a party, directly addresses repatriation of absent nationals or residents. It requires a belligerent occupant to ensure the rights of "protected persons," which the Convention defines as "those who, at a given moment and in any manner whatsoever, find themselves . . . in the hands of a[n] . . . Occupying Power of which they are not nationals."[155] The phrase "in the hands of" covers persons temporarily absent, as evidenced by two other provisions of the Geneva Civilians Convention. A provision setting the closing dates for application of the Convention specifies that, even after the closing date, the Convention continues to apply with respect to "protected persons whose . . . repatriation . . . may take place after such dates."[156] The convention's denunciation provision precludes a denunciation from taking effect "until after operations connected with . . . repatriation . . . of the person protected by the present Convention have been terminated."[157]

IV. ANALYSIS OF THE CHALLENGES TO ISRAEL'S OBLIGATION TO ADMIT PALESTINIANS AS DISPLACED NATIONALS

An obligation to admit nationals, as found in the law of nationality, human rights law, and humanitarian law, would seem to apply *prima facie* to the displaced Palestinians. The obligation in the law of nationality would apply, because the Palestinians are prevented from entering their original territory, and the states where the Palestinians have found refuge, in particular the Arab states, have made strenuous efforts to convince Israel to admit them. The obligation in the law of human

---

tions"], 36 Stat. 2277, 2295; *also in* 1 BEVANS, TREATIES AND OTHER INTERNATIONAL AGREE-
MENTS OF THE UNITED STATES OF AMERICA 1776–1949 631, 643 (1968).

154. Hague Regulations, *supra* note 153, art. 43. Art. 43 requires an occupier to maintain *la vie publique* in the occupied territory. The French text is the only official text. This phrase is incorrectly rendered in the English translation of the Regulations, found in 36 Stat. 2277, 2295, as "public order and safety." *See* Edmund H. Schwenk, *Legislative Power of the Military Occupant under Article 43, Hague Regulations*, 54 YALE L. J. 393, 398 (1945) (construing *l'ordre et la vie publique* to mean "general safety and social functions and ordinary transactions which constitute daily life."); Yoram Dinstein, *The Israel Supreme Court and the Law of Belligerent Occupation: Deportations* 23 ISR. Y.B. ON H.R. 1, 19–20 (1993) (noting that Israel Supreme Court has stated that the English text is wrong).

155. Convention Relative to the Treatment of Civilian Persons in Time of War, Aug. 12, 1949, 75 U.N.T.S. 287.

156. Convention Relative to the Treatment of Civilian Persons in Time of War, *supra* note 155, art. 6, ¶ 4.

157. *Id.*, art. 158, ¶ 3.

rights would seem to apply, because the Palestinians have manifested a desire to return to their areas of origin. For the Palestinians of the West Bank and Gaza Strip, humanitarian law would apply, since Israel is in belligerent occupation there.

However, it has been suggested, in support of Israel's stance, that the obligation to repatriate is subject to limitations, and that various of these limitations negate a right of return for the displaced Palestinians. Six possible limitations will be addressed: (1) that the admission of the displaced Palestinians would threaten Israel's security; (2) that Israel may suspend the right of return during a declared emergency; (3) that the displaced Palestinians are not entitled to return because they are not Israeli nationals; (4) that there is no obligation in international law binding on Israel to admit members of large displaced populations; (5) that Israel is not obliged to admit those Palestinians who have acquired a new nationality; (6) that Israel may deny repatriation to the Palestinians if Arab states mistreat their Jewish inhabitants.

A. A Return as a Potential Threat to Israel's Security

In July 1948, U.N. Mediator Bernadotte asked Israel to repatriate the displaced Palestinians, but it declined.[158] Foreign Minister Moshe Sharett wrote Bernadotte that "the war brought in its wake a mass exodus, mostly spontaneous," and that

> the return during the truce of thousands of displaced Arabs to the State of Israel which is still beset by enemy armies . . . would in fact gravely prejudice our rights and position . . . . When the Arab States are ready to conclude a peace treaty with Israel, the question will come up for a constructive solution as a part of the general settlement, with due regard to our counterclaim . . . .[159]

Another Israeli official explained:

> While a state of war continues to exist between Israel and the surrounding Arab states, it would gravely prejudice the security and defense of Israel if its borders were flung open to an unrestricted influx of Arabs from those states, who would be a disruptive element in the maintenance of internal law and order, and a

---

158. See PALUMBO, supra note 13, at 147; Morris, supra note 22, at 145–47; AVI SHLAIM, COLLUSION ACROSS THE JORDAN: KING ABDULLAH, THE ZIONIST MOVEMENT, AND THE PARTITION OF PALESTINE 283–84 (1988).

159. U.N. SCOR, 3d Sess., Supp. for Aug. 1948, at 106, 108, U.N. Doc. S/949 (Letter from the Foreign Minister of Israel to the Mediator, July 30, 1948). The reference to a counterclaim is to damage caused by intervening Arab armies.

formidable fifth column for external enemies. It must be appreciated that a truce is not peace, ...[160]

Israel's expressed concern was that since the Palestinians and the Arab states did not recognize Israel, a large-scale influx of Palestinians would threaten Israel's continued existence as a state.[161] The legal adviser to Israel's foreign ministry argued that Israel could legitimately exclude from its nationality Palestinians who fled in 1948, since their flight reflected disloyalty to Israel, the flight, according to his account, having been organized by Arab leaders.[162]

Some legal commentators have found Israel's invocation of security considerations a legitimate reason to refuse to admit the Palestinians, at least with respect to rights under human rights law:

[T]he general limitation clause of Article 29 of the [Universal] Declaration [of Human Rights] permits the non-application of the right; the influx of more than one and a half million mostly hostile refugees would without doubt violate "the rights and freedoms of others" in Israel, and it would damage "public order and the general welfare in a democratic society."[163]

The quoted language comes from Article 29 of the Universal Declaration of Human Rights, which specifies limitations that a state may impose on the rights provided in the Declaration:

> In the exercise of his rights and freedoms, everyone shall be subject only to such limitations as are determined by law solely for the purpose of securing due recognition and respect for the rights and freedoms of others and of meeting the just requirements of morality, public order and the general welfare in a democratic society.[164]

In U.N. practice, however, invocation of security considerations to evade an obligation to repatriate has been discouraged. With Namibia, which, like Palestine, had been under a League of Nations mandate, a process for the return of displaced Namibians was set in motion by the

---

160. *Acting United States Representative at the United Nations (Jessup) to the Secretary of State*, July 27, 1948, 1948(5) FOR. REL. U.S. 1248 (giving text of letter received from Michael Comay, Provisional Government of Israel).

161. *See* TESSLER, *supra* note 70, at 308 ("The Israeli case begins with the assertion that by demanding repatriation, the Arabs were knowingly and explicitly calling for the destruction of the Jewish state.").

162. *See* Rosenne, *supra* note 42, at 8–9.

163. Lapidoth, *supra* note 81, at 114; *see also* Radley, *supra* note 26, at 613 ("the return of potentially some one and one-half million Palestinians of doubtful allegiance to a state whose population itself numbers only somewhat more than three million is as valid a threat to that state's 'general welfare' as there is likely to exist.").

164. Universal Declaration of Human Rights, *supra* note 142, art. 29, ¶ 2.

U.N. Security Council, even though many of these Namibians had gone abroad to take up arms to drive South Africa out of Namibia.[165] The Security Council specified by resolution that repatriation of Namibians should be implemented by South Africa "pending the transfer of power," without awaiting a political settlement.[166]

Moreover, the International Covenant on Civil and Political Rights, unlike the Universal Declaration of Human Rights, has no general limitations clause. In the International Covenant, certain rights, including those found in Article 12 (freedom of movement), may be suspended during a declared emergency.[167] In certain articles of the International Covenant, one finds limitations provisions applicable to that article alone. Article 12 contains some limitations language:

> 1. Everyone lawfully within the territory of a State shall, within that territory, have the right to liberty of movement and freedom to choose his residence.
> 2. Everyone shall be free to leave any country, including his own.
> 3. The above-mentioned rights shall not be subject to any restrictions except those which are provided by law, are necessary to protect national security, public order (*ordre public*), public health or morals or the rights and freedoms of others, and are consistent with the other rights recognized in the present Covenant.
> 4. No one shall be arbitrarily deprived of the right to enter his own country.

The structure of Article 12 makes it plain that the limitations language found in paragraph 3 applies only to the rights enumerated in paragraphs 1 and 2. The limitations language does not apply to the right specified in paragraph 4, namely, the right to enter one's country. Thus, the International Covenant, unlike the Universal Declaration, does not permit a state to condition the right of admission on security considerations.

Under Article 12, paragraph 4, only one qualification applies to the obligation to permit entry. Return can be refused if the refusal is not arbitrary. This qualification has been invoked in support of Israel's

---

165. *See Letter dated 10 April 1978 from the Representatives of Canada, the Federal Republic of Germany, France, the United Kingdom of Great Britain and Northern Ireland, and the United States of America to the President of the Security Council*, U.N. SCOR, 33d Sess., Supp. for Apr.-June 1978, at 17, 18 ¶ 7(c) & (d), U.N. Doc. S/12636 (1978) (these five states, which had been asked by the Council to make recommendations, said that displaced Namibians should be allowed to return).

166. S.C. Res. 385, ¶ 11(d), U.N. SCOR, 31st Sess., *Res. & Dec.* 8, U.N. Doc. S/INF/32 (1977).

167. *See infra* note 173.

refusal to admit displaced Palestinians.[168] The term "arbitrarily" potentially gives a state of nationality great latitude to exclude nationals. However, the drafting history suggests that such was not the intent.

"Arbitrarily" was inserted into Article 12, paragraph 4, for a particular purpose that leaves its meaning quite narrow. Some states participating in the drafting used exile as a penal sanction in their domestic law and were therefore reluctant to accept a flat obligation to grant entry. It was proposed then to require a state to grant entry with an exception for nationals who had been exiled.

However, many states deemed exile unlawful as a penal sanction and were unwilling to provide expressly that exile as a penal sanction was permitted. As a result, language was sought to accommodate the use of exile as a penal sanction but without saying so directly, and the term "arbitrarily" was inserted to that end.[169] Beyond this circumstance, no other was viewed as permitting a state to expel or deny entry to a national.[170]

Israel's security argument is potentially relevant to a claim of return under human rights or humanitarian law, but it is not relevant under the law of nationality. States of sojourn of displaced persons need not accommodate a state with security problems. States of sojourn have no obligation to keep displaced persons, even if the state of nationality might experience security difficulties by repatriating them.

B. Delay of Return During Israel's Declared Emergency

It has been argued, again with respect to Israel's potential obligation under human rights law, that Israel may lawfully delay repatriation while in a state of emergency.[171] "There is not doubt," runs this argument, "that Israel is still in a time of public emergency."[172]

The International Covenant does allow states to derogate from certain Covenant obligations during a declared emergency.[173] The theory

---

168. *See* Lapidoth, *supra* note 81, at 115.

169. *See* MANFRED NOWAK, U.N. COVENANT ON CIVIL AND POLITICAL RIGHTS: CCPR COMMENTARY 219 (1993) ("In light of the historical background, there can be no doubt that the limitation on the right to entry expressed with the word 'arbitrarily' ('*arbitrairement*') is to relate exclusively to cases of *lawful exile as punishment* for a crime."); MARC BOSSUYT, GUIDE TO THE "TRAVAUX PRÉPARATOIRES" OF THE INTERNATIONAL COVENANT ON CIVIL AND POLITICAL RIGHTS 260–63 (1987) (giving relevant quotations during drafting process).

170. Even though exile as a penal sanction would appear to be permitted under art. 12, it is questionable whether it is permitted in light of the human right to a nationality, at least if exile would render the person stateless. In addition, a state may, by exiling a person as a penal sanction, require another state to accept the person.

171. *See* Lapidoth, *supra* note 81, at 114–15 (*citing* International Covenant on Civil and Political Rights, *supra* note 144, art. 4).

172. Lapidoth, *supra* note 81, at 115.

173. International Covenant on Civil and Political Rights, *supra* note 144, art. 4, ¶ 1.

is that in certain extreme situations, a state is justified in taking measures that are not warranted in normal times. Derogation is not permitted from certain guarantees, like the protection against torture,[174] but is permitted from many others, including the freedom to leave a country, or to enter.[175]

Israel's declared emergency is based on its relations with neighboring states. In May 1948 its provisional parliament declared a state of emergency,[176] and that declaration remains in force. Thus, Israel has considered itself to be in a state of emergency continuously since May 1948. In 1991, when Israel ratified the International Covenant on Civil and Political Rights, it made a formal communication to explain its emergency. The declaration read:

> Since its establishment, the State of Israel has been the victim of continuous threats and attacks on its very existence as well as on the life and property of its citizens.
>
> These have taken the form of threats of war, of actual armed attacks, and campaigns of terrorism resulting in the murder of and injury to human beings.
>
> In view of the above, the State of Emergency which was proclaimed in May 1948 has remained in force ever since. This situation constitutes a public emergency within the meaning of article 4(1) of the Covenant.
>
> The Government of Israel has therefore found it necessary, in accordance with the said article 4, to take measures to the extent strictly required by the exigencies of the situation, for the defence of the State and for the protection of life and property, including the exercise of powers of arrest and detention.
>
> In so far as any of these measures are inconsistent with article 9 of the Covenant, Israel thereby derogates from its obligations under that provision.[177]

This communication mentions only Article 9, which relates to detention and arrest, as a provision from which Israel derogated. The communication did not mention Article 12, paragraph 4, which guarantees a right to enter one's country. In order to take advantage of the option of derogating from Covenant-protected rights, a state must indicate in its declaration the specific Covenant provisions from which

---

174. *Id.*, art. 4, ¶ 2.

175. *See* THEODOR MERON, HUMAN RIGHTS LAW-MAKING IN THE UNITED NATIONS 91 (1986); THEODOR MERON, HUMAN RIGHTS IN INTERNAL STRIFE: THEIR INTERNATIONAL PROTECTION 57 (1987).

176. Law and Administration Ordinance, art. 9(a), 1 LAWS OF THE STATE OF ISRAEL 7 (1948) (date of enactment May 19, 1948).

177. *Multilateral Treaties Deposited with the Secretary-General, supra* note 143, at 142 (Israel's declaration of Oct. 3, 1991).

it derogates.[178] Since Israel did not specify Article 12, paragraph 4, it has not sought to justify a delay in repatriation of the displaced Palestinians on its declared emergency.

It would, however, be open to Israel, in principle, to file a new communication in which it might indicate a need to derogate from Article 12. A state may file such a communication at any time, so long as it can recite appropriate reasons, with respect both to the existence of an emergency and to the need to derogate from particular provisions.

Were Israel to file a new communication adding Article 12, paragraph 4, as another provision from which it derogates, however, the validity of such a communication would be open to doubt. Israel would have to recite in such a communication why keeping the Palestinians out was "required by the exigencies of the [emergency] situation,"[179] an assertion that might be difficult to sustain.

In human rights law, moreover, an emergency must be temporary. Israel's long-term state of emergency is without parallel in contemporary international practice. The Human Rights Committee that administers the International Covenant on Civil and Political Rights[180] has said that an emergency may not be declared for an indefinite period. One case before the Committee involved the validity of an emergency declared by the government of Chile that appeared to be open-ended. The Committee criticized Chilean authorities for using the declaration of a state of emergency as a pretext for the lengthy imposition of restrictions.[181]

The situations in which other states have declared emergencies, and which have been ascertained by decision-making bodies as appropriate, have involved ongoing civil armed conflict of limited duration. The European Court of Human Rights administers the European human rights treaty,[182] which contains derogation provisions similar to those of the International Covenant.[183] The European Court has defined an emergency as "an exceptional situation of crisis or emergency which affects the whole population and constitutes a threat to the organised life of the community of which the State is composed."[184] It found a

---

178. *See* International Covenant on Civil and Political Rights, *supra* note 144, art. 4, ¶ 3.

179. International Covenant on Civil and Political Rights, *supra* note 144, art. 4, ¶ 1.

180. The Committee is the official monitoring body for the Covenant. It is established in the Covenant itself. International Covenant on Civil and Political Rights, *supra* note 144, art. 28.

181. *Report of the Human Rights Committee*, U.N. GAOR, 34th Sess., Supp. No. 40, at 20, U.N. Doc. A/34/40 (1979).

182. Convention for the Protection of Human Rights and Fundamental Freedoms, Nov. 4, 1950, art. 19, 213 U.N.T.S. 222, Eur. T.S. No. 5.

183. *Id.*, art. 15 ("In time of war or other public emergency threatening the life of the nation any High Contracting Party may take measures derogating from its obligations under this Convention to the extent strictly required by the exigencies of the situation, provided that such measures are not inconsistent with its other obligations under international law.").

184. Lawless Case (Rep. of Ireland), 1961 Y.B. EUR. CONV. ON H.R. 438, 472–74; *see also id.* at 473–75 for the French text of the quoted language, which states more clearly that the situation

validly declared emergency in Ireland in 1956-57, because of Irish Republican Army activities over a nine-month period.[185] In a later case, the Court found a validly declared emergency in Northern Ireland, again on the basis of military activities of the Irish Republican Army.[186] In a third case, however, the European Commission of Human Rights, which also adjudicates violations under the European human rights treaty,[187] found invalid an emergency declared in Greece, because, unlike the situation in Northern Ireland, there was no military activity at the time.[188]

By the standard reflected in these European cases, the Israeli declaration of emergency would probably be invalid. The factual assertion on which Israel's continuing declaration of emergency relies, namely, that Israel has on a continuing basis been the object of armed attacks from outside, is difficult to sustain.[189] Even if the assertion were accurate for the earlier period of Israel's existence, it would not seem to be so in an era of actual and anticipated peace agreements with neighboring Arab states.

C. Displaced Palestinians as Non-Nationals of Israel

Under a 1952 Israeli nationality statute, only those Palestinians who in 1948 remained within the territory that became Israel, and stayed until 1952, acquired Israeli citizenship.[190] This provision excluded from citizenship the Palestinians of the 1948 exodus. Thus, Israel does not deem the displaced Palestinians to be its nationals. This fact, according to some analysts, negates any right for the displaced Palestinians to return to the territory that became Israel.[191]

---

must pose imminent danger (*"une situation de crise ou de danger exceptionnel et imminent"*). The French text, not the English, was the authentic text.

185. *Id.* at 474.

186. Ireland v. United Kingdom, 1978 Y.B. EUR. CONV. ON H.R. 602, 608.

187. Convention for the Protection of Human Rights and Fundamental Freedoms, *supra* note 183, art. 19.

188. Greek Case (European Commission of Human Rights), 12 Y.B. EUR. CONV. ON H.R. 72, 76, 100 (1969) (stating also that Greece had the burden to prove an emergency).

189. *See* QUIGLEY, PALESTINE AND ISRAEL: A CHALLENGE TO JUSTICE, *supra* note 6, at 57–65, 156, 161–67, 195, 159–200 (finding Israel not to have been the target of aggression in the hostilities of 1948, 1956, 1967, 1973, and 1982).

190. *See* Nationality Law, art. 3, 6 LAWS OF THE STATE OF ISRAEL 50 (1952) (deeming as well to be citizens those Palestinians who returned legally between 1948 and 1952).

191. *See* Lapidoth, *supra* note 81, at 114 ("The right probably belongs only to nationals of the State, and at most to permanent residents. The Palestinian Arab refugees have never been nationals or permanent residents of Israel."); *see also* Radley, *supra* note 26, at 613–14 ("The Palestinian refugees are, of course, not Israeli nationals, not by that state's definition, and significantly, also, not according to the refugees' own self-identity; they make no claim to Israeli nationality or allegiance. The right of a national under Article 13, paragraph 2 [of the Universal Declaration of Human Rights] to return to 'his country' is, therefore, irrelevant to the question whether a right exists on the part of the Palestinian refugees to return to Israel.").

Since after 1948 Palestine nationality had little meaning,[192] Israel's 1952 law had the effect of depriving those Palestinians who were nationals of Palestine at the time of the 1948 hostilities, of the nationality of their homeland.[193] Revocation, as indicated above, may not justify a refusal to admit a national.[194] From Israel's perspective, it did not revoke nationality, it merely refused to offer it. This situation is not unprecedented. On the basis of cases in which sovereignty has changed, a body of practice has developed regarding the nationality of inhabitants.

1. Nationality of Inhabitants upon a Change in Sovereignty

The issue of nationality for inhabitants of new, or newly configured, states, arose in the wake of World War I. States were carved out of the territories of the defeated parties, and substantial minority populations resulted in many of them. The allies conferring at Versailles over the new dispensation for Europe understood that the governments of these new states might not look favorably on some of these minorities.[195] The allies therefore demanded that these states conclude treaties in which they agreed to protect their minorities. A major element in that protection was recognition of the link between these populations and the territory. Minority rights treaties following World War I recognized this link, giving the minorities a right to nationality,[196] and requiring the newly created states to extend their nationality to the minorities.[197]

When sovereignty changes, the state taking the territory, or a new state if it is such, must respect the nationality rights of the inhabitants. A state achieving sovereignty in a territory may not deprive the inhabitants of nationality by refusing to offer them its nationality. The obligation of a state acquiring territory to extend its nationality has been affirmed recently by a working group established by the Interna-

---

192. *See* Hussein v. Governor of Acre Prison, 6 P.D. 897 (1952) [Supreme Court of Israel] 17 INT'L L. RPTS. 112 (1950) (stating that Palestine citizenship "no longer exists").

193. *See* Dimitrijevic, *supra* note 4, at 18. ("At the moment when the refugees left their part of Palestine, it was still 'their land.'").

194. *See supra* notes 136–138.

195. *See* Advisory Opinion on certain questions arising out of the application of Article 4 of the Polish Minorities Treaty, 1923 P.C.I.J. (ser. B) No. 7, at 15 ("One of the first problems which presented itself in connection with the protection of the minorities was that of preventing these States from refusing their nationality, on racial, religious or linguistic grounds, to certain categories of persons, in spite of the link which effectively attached them to the territory allocated to one or other of these States.").

196. *See id.* at 16 ("Though, generally speaking, it is true that a sovereign State has the right to decide what persons shall be regarded as its nationals, it is no less true that this principle is applicable only subject to the Treaty obligations referred to above.").

197. *See* Minorities Treaty between the Principal Allied and Associated Powers and Poland (Versailles), June 28, 1919, art. 4, 225 CONSOL. T.S. 412.

tional Law Commission to analyze nationality upon state succession.[198] The working group stated as a preliminary conclusion that a new state must extend its nationality to the inhabitants.[199]

Under this rule, an inhabitant of territory coming under new sovereignty acquires the nationality of the new sovereign,[200] unless the inhabitant opts for the nationality of the former sovereign.[201] If the new state declines to offer its nationality, international law infers it.[202] This proposition was accepted by the Tel Aviv District Court in a 1951 case, in which the court said: "every individual who, on the date of the establishment of the State of Israel was resident in the territory which today constitutes the State of Israel, is also a national of Israel."[203] The court said that following the transfer of territory, "every individual and inhabitant of the ceding State becomes automatically a national of the receiving State."[204] One purpose of the rule that nationality transfers is to avoid statelessness.[205] Another is to accord fair treatment to the inhabitants.[206]

The principle that the inhabitants assume the new nationality, received reinforcement from the law of human rights, when it emerged in the mid-twentieth century. With individuals now regarded as bearers of rights, the inhabitants of a territory undergoing a sovereignty

---

198. *See Report of the International Law Commission on the Work of its Forty-Seventh Session*, U.N. GAOR, 50th Sess., Supp. No. 10, at 68, U.N. Doc. A/50/10 (1995); *see also* Robert Rosenstock, *The Forty-Seventh Session of the International Law Commission*, 90 AM. J. INT'L L. 106, 113–14 (1996).

199. *See Report of the International Law Commission on the Work of its Forty-Seventh Session*, U.N. GAOR, 50th Sess., Supp. No. 10, at 271, 272–75, U.N. Doc. A/50/10 (1995).

200. *See* 2 CHARLES HYDE, INTERNATIONAL LAW 1090 (1945) ("Whenever a State acquires from another a part of its territory, the inhabitants of the area transferred, who were nationals of the former sovereign, are, in the absence of agreement, collectively naturalized."); 1 L. OPPENHEIM, INTERNATIONAL LAW 598 (1948) ("the inhabitants of the subjugated and the ceded territory acquiring *ipso facto* by the subjugation or cession the nationality of the State which acquires the territory," and referring to this rule as being "settled by the customary Law of Nations").

201. CHARLES ROUSSEAU, DROIT INTERNATIONAL PUBLIC 271–72 (1953); *see also* Joseph L. Kunz, *L'Option de Nationalité*, 31 HAGUE ACAD. DROIT INT'L, RECUEIL DES COURS 111, 121 (1930) (inhabitant may retain prior nationality).

202. *See* The Law of Nationality, *supra* note 137, at 61 ("international law assumes that the successor state confers its nationality upon the nationals of the predecessor state residing in the annexed territory at the time of the annexation").

203. A.B. v. M.B., 3 P.M. 263, 272 (1950-1951) [Dist. Ct., Tel Aviv] 17 INT'L L. RPTS. 110, 111 (1950).

204. *Id.*

205. *See* The Law of Nationality, *supra* note 137, at 61.

206. *See* Ian Brownlie, *The Relations of Nationality in Public International Law*, 39 BRIT. Y.B. INT'L L. 284, 325 (1963) ("Sovereignty denotes responsibility, and a change of sovereignty does not give the new sovereign the right to dispose of the population concerned at the discretion of the government."); *see also* Daniel D.N. Nsereko, *The Right to Return Home*, 21 INDIAN J. INT'L L. 335, 343 (1981) (stating, "the fact that territorial sovereignty over a territory has, whether rightly or wrongly, changed hands should not affect the inhabitants' right to reside thereon or to return thereto.").

change were viewed as possessing a right to a nationality. Thus, the International Convention on the Elimination of All Forms of Racial Discrimination guarantees a "right to a nationality,"[207] meaning that a denial of nationality grounded on a racial distinction is invalid as a violation of the rights of the individual. Also, the Universal Declaration of Human Rights guarantees a "right to a nationality" and states that no one may be arbitrarily deprived of it.[208] The attachment of the individual to the territory provides the basis for the individual's right.[209] A right based on that attachment is not circumvented by a political change resulting in the creation of a new state.[210]

2. Nationality in a State Formed from Mandate Territory

The foregoing analysis of acquisition of nationality by inhabitants depends on a change in sovereignty from a "predecessor state" to a "successor" state. The formation of Israel, however, involved not the assumption of sovereignty by one state from another, but the creation of a state in territory under a mandate from the League of Nations.

This factual difference yields no difference in result as regards the acquisition of nationality. If anything, when a state emerges from mandate territory, the rationale for requiring an offer of nationality is stronger. The nationality status of inhabitants of a League of Nations mandate territory was a topic on which the authorities struggled for clarity.[211] On the one hand, these inhabitants were not nationals of the administering power, which served as a "trustee," caring for the terri-

---

207. International Convention on the Elimination of All Forms of Racial Discrimination, *supra* note 146, art. 5(d)(iii), at 220.

208. *See* Universal Declaration of Human Rights, *supra* note 142, art. 15, at 74. The International Covenant on Civil and Political Rights, *supra* note 144, has no comparable general provision on a right to nationality but does provide for a right to nationality for children. (art. 24) A right to nationality for children is also provided by the Convention on the Rights of the Child, Nov. 20, 1989, art. 7, *reprinted in* 28 INT'L LEGAL MATS. 1457, 1460 (1989), to which Israel is a party. *Multilateral Treaties Deposited with the Secretary General, supra* note 143, at 198 (entered into force for Israel Oct. 3, 1991).

209. *See* PAUL HADROSEK, THE NATURAL RIGHTS OF PEOPLES TO THEIR NATIVE SOIL: SURVEY AND CRITICISM OF THE JURIDICAL DISCUSSION 62–68 (1969) (The author uses *Heimat* in German, *sol natal* in French, and native soil in English to indicate the territory in which an individual has a right); *see also Les Transfers Internationaux des Populations, supra* note 142, at 171 (Herbert Kraus reporting that in 1950 the Association of German Professors of International Law adopted a resolution in support of a human right to a *Heimat*).

210. *See* Christian Tomuschat, *Das Recht Auf Die Heimat, Neue Rechtliche Aspekte, in* DES MENSCHEN RECHT ZWISCHEN FREIHEIT UND VERANTWORTUNG—FESTSCHRIFT FÜR KARL JOSEF PARTSCH ZUM 75. GEBURTSTAG 183, 192 (Jürgen Jekewitz et al. eds., 1989) (stating that a change in sovereignty does not override the right of a refugee to describe the state from which he has been exiled as "his own country."); *see also* ANNUAIRE DE L'INSTITUT DE DROIT INT'L, *supra* note 142, at 183 (Walter Schätzel stating that "no state has the right to rid itself of a population that was already located on the territory before the creation of the state.").

211. *See* WEIS, *supra* note 130, at 24 ("The position of these persons is somewhat anomalous.").

tory and its population pending their acquisition of a future new status. The new status in the case of the "A" class mandates, of which Palestine was one, was to be political independence.[212] Britain followed this rule in Palestine; Britain did not deem inhabitants of Palestine to be British nationals.[213]

On the other hand, inhabitants of mandate territory were not stateless. The administering power could provide diplomatic protection for them in any controversy involving another state,[214] and some kind of nationality.[215] Britain did so for the inhabitants of Palestine, who previously had been nationals of the Ottoman Empire, but who lost that status following the Ottoman Empire's defeat in World War I and its withdrawal from Palestine.[216] Britain created a Palestine nationality and issued a passport denominated "British passport—Palestine."[217]

Sovereignty in territory under mandate, it was said, was "in abeyance."[218] But a community under mandate was a "subject of international law," as the beneficiary of the trust arrangement.[219] International subjectivity gains evidence from the fact that Palestine was, in its own name, a party to a number of treaties during the two and a half decades of its existence.[220]

---

212. See LEAGUE OF NATIONS COVENANT, art. 22 ("Certain communities formerly belonging to the Turkish Empire have reached a stage of development where their existence as independent nations can be provisionally recognized subject to the rendering of administrative advice and assistance by a Mandatary until such time as they are able to stand alone.").

213. See The King v. Ketter, 1 K.B. 787 (1940) (finding that status as citizen of Palestine did not make the appellant a British subject).

214. See Brownlie, supra note 206, at 317.

215. See Mandate for Palestine, art. 7, 8 League of Nations O.J. 1007, 1008 (1922), reprinted in Terms of League of Nations Mandates: Republished by the United Nations, U.N. Doc. A/70 (1946), also in Convention between the United States and Great Britain Concerning Palestine, Dec. 3, 1924, 44 Stat. 2184 ("The Administration of Palestine shall be responsible for enacting a nationality law.").

216. Kunz, supra note 201, at 135 (stating that, "As for 'A' mandates [of which Palestine was one], it is certain that the inhabitants of these countries lost their Turkish nationality; but in turn they did not acquire the nationality of the mandatory power; they possess a separate nationality; . . . Palestinian nationality.").

217. Palestinian Citizenship Order in Council, 1925, S.R. & O., no. 777, at 474; see also Norman Bentwich, Nationality in Mandated Territories Detached from Turkey, 7 BRIT. Y.B. INT'L L. 97, 102 (1926); and Nationality Law, supra note 190, art. 3 (referring to "a person who, immediately before the establishment of the state, was a Palestinian citizen," thus recognizing a Palestinian citizenship during the mandate period).

218. International Status of South-West Africa, 1950 I.C.J. 128, 150 (July 11) (separate advisory opinion of Judge McNair).

219. See Institute of International Law, Resolution on Mandates, 1931, para. 6, in James Brown Scott, The Two Institutes of International Law, 26 AM. J. INT'L L. 87, 91 (1932).

220. See J.L., The International Status of Palestine, 90 J. DROIT INT'L 964 (1963); see, e.g., Exchange of Notes constituting a Provisional Commercial Agreement, June 6 & 21, 1928 Egypt-Palestine, 80 L.N.T.S. 277; Agreement Concerning the Exchange of Postal Parcels, May 15, 1929, Palestine-Switz., 95 L.N.T.S. 395.

The creation of Israel did not involve the substitution of one sovereignty for another, instead it was a state emerging from a mandate. Its formation involved not a transfer of sovereignty but the emergence of actual sovereignty in territory in which sovereignty was suspended.[221] Thus, the rule of customary law that, upon a substitution of sovereignty, the inhabitants acquire the nationality of the new state, obtains as well when a state is formed in mandate territory. Israel's nationality law followed this practice, at least with respect to Arab nationals of mandate Palestine who were physically present at the time of transfer and who remained there after the transfer.[222]

3. Nationality for Persons Absent at the Time of Transfer

As indicated, however, Israel's Nationality Law did not extend nationality to Arab nationals of Palestine who were abroad at the time of the transfer, or who left after the transfer. Most of the Palestinians who departed in 1948 did so after the date on which Israel became a state, and thus were resident in Israel for a time. On that basis, they deserved to be nationals of the new state. Less clear is the position of the smaller, though significant, number of Palestinians departed in the weeks preceding Israel's formation: one may inquire whether the inference of nationality would apply to them, since they were abroad when Israel declared itself sovereign.

State practice suggests that the inference of nationality applies to all who carry the nationality of the prior state, regardless of their whereabouts on the date of transfer of sovereignty.[223] The International Law Commission's working group has said that the inference of nationality applies to all nationals of the former state, regardless of where they reside.[224] The inference thus would apply to Palestinians absent at the time Israel entered into sovereignty.

This result gains confirmation from the fashion in which the U.N. General Assembly treated nationality in its proposal for two states in Palestine, one Jewish and one Arab. The General Assembly anticipated that Jews living in the Arab state would hold its nationality, and that Arabs living in the Jewish state would hold its nationality.[225] The

---

221. *See* International Status of South-West Africa, *supra* note 218, (stating, "if and when the inhabitants of the Territory obtain recognition as an independent State . . . sovereignty will revive and vest in the new State.").

222. *See* sources cited *supra* note 191.

223. *See, e.g.,* An Act to Provide a Government for the Territory of Hawaii, ch.339, 31 Stat. 141 (1900) ("all persons who were citizens of the Republic of Hawaii on August twelfth, eighteen hundred and ninety-eight, are hereby declared to be citizens of the United States").

224. *See Report of the International Law Commission on the Work of its Forty-Seventh Session,* U.N. GAOR, 50th Sess., Supp. No. 10, at 271, 272-275 (Annex: Report of the Working Group on State Succession and its Impact on the Nationality of Natural and Legal Persons).

225. *See* Rosenne, *supra* note 42, at 9.

Assembly anticipated that the Jewish state would include substantial numbers of Arabs.[226] The constitution of each state, according to the proposal, was to guarantee "equal and non-discriminatory rights in civil, political, economic and religious matters and the enjoyment of human rights and fundamental freedoms."[227] One such right would have been that to nationality.

D. Return for Members of a Displaced Group

Another factor that might negate a Palestinian right of return relates to the scope of the right of return. Some have suggested that the right of return does not apply to the displaced Palestinians, because the right protects individuals, but not persons who were part of a "mass relocation."[228]

1. The Scope of the Right of Return in International Instruments

This objection has arisen in particular with respect to Article 12, paragraph 4, of the International Covenant, the provision that requires a state to admit its nationals. It has been argued that Article 12, paragraph 4, "is structured as an individual right and not a collective or group right," and therefore provides members of displaced groups like the Palestinians no right of return.[229]

Article 12, paragraph 4, is structured as an individual right, but that is true of most rights in international human rights instruments. Rights enumerated in the International Covenant are ostensibly designed to protect individuals, but no reason exists to read them narrowly. Even if a numerical distinction were admissible in principle, it is difficult to imagine how one might meaningfully set a cutoff number.

Both the Universal Declaration and the International Covenant guarantee a right of entry, without indicating that the right applies only to isolated individuals. Nonetheless, it has been argued that the drafters did not intend to protect persons displaced as part of a mass

---

226. *See Estimated Population of Palestine as of 31 December 1946* (Appendix I), Ad Hoc Committee on the Palestine Question, Summary Records of Meetings 25 September–25 November 1947, U.N. GAOR, 2d Sess., at 304, U.N. Doc. A/AC.14/32 (1947) (estimating that in the proposed Jewish state there would be a large number of Arabs).

227. G.A. Res. 181, U.N. GAOR, 2d Sess., Pt.1B, art. 10, ¶ d, U.N. Doc. A/519 (1947).

228. *See* Benvenisti & Zamir, *supra* note 115, at 325 (stating that a right of return for large groups "is not recognized in human rights instruments such as the Universal Declaration of Human Rights and the International Covenant on Civil and Political Rights, and that it is yet to be generally accepted as part of customary law"); *see also* Lapidoth, *supra* note 81, at 114 ("the right of return is limited to nationals, or at most to permanent residents; it does not apply to masses of displaced people.").

229. *See* Donna E. Arzt, *Palestinian Refugees: The Human Dimension of the Middle East Peace Process*, PROC. AM. S. INT'L L. 372 (1995).

movement, "particularly where those seeking to return are not nationals of the state of destination."[230]

The drafting history of the International Covenant does not show any discussion of the question of applicability to members of displaced populations.[231] There is a hint that the drafters may have assumed that the return of displaced populations, in particular to territory whose sovereignty had changed, would receive discussion in some other body of law.[232]

The text of Article 12, paragraph 4, of the International Covenant implies no numerical limitation. A number of analysts, however, have concluded that the text means what it says, namely, that it applies to all nationals of a state, regardless of their numbers.[233] Even if the drafters did not consider mass dislocations, or thought that some other body of law would handle them, it is the words used in a treaty that reflect the agreement of the parties.[234] Drafting history comes into play only if the text "leaves the meaning ambiguous or obscure," or "leads to a result which is manifestly absurd or unreasonable."[235] Here the text leaves no ambiguity because the text contains no exceptions regarding groups. The result flowing from the text's language is not absurd or unreasonable. The drafting history does not provide evidence that members of displaced groups did not enjoy the right of entry.

2. State Practice on the Return of Members of Displaced Groups

The international community has had ample occasion to react to group displacement. A survey of international practice will begin first

---

230. HANNUM, *supra* note 141 at 59–60; *see also* STIG JAGERSKIOLD, *The Freedom of Movement*, *in* THE INTERNATIONAL BILL OF RIGHTS 166, 180 (1981) ("This right [to enter one's own country] is intended to apply to individuals asserting an individual right. There was no intention here to address the claims of masses of people who have been displaced as a byproduct of war or by political transfers of territory or population, such as the relocation of ethnic Germans from Eastern Europe during and after the Second World War, the flight of Palestinians from what became Israel, or the movement of Jews from the Arab countries.").

231. *See* Tomuschat, *supra* note 210, at 190; *see also* U.N. GAOR, 10th Sess., Annexes, Agenda item 28-II, at 39, U.N. Doc. A/2929 (1955).

232. *See* Tomuschat, *supra* note 210, at 190; *cf.* HANNUM, *supra* note 141, at 60 n.175, suggesting that such persons might be entitled to a right of return under the law of self-determination, and that their situation is more appropriately analyzed under that rubric; *Les Transfers Internationaux des Populations*, *supra* note 142, at 159 (E.M. van Asbeck, stating that Declaration art. 13 "was not aimed at measures taken for the general welfare of groups of persons such as the transfer of population," but finding, *id.* at 156, that expulsion of groups is forbidden under general international law unless done in the interests of maintaining international peace).

233. *See* Tomuschat, *supra* note 210, at 191; *see also* NOWAK, *supra* note 169, at 220 (stating that art. 12 applies "even if masses of people are claiming this right").

234. *See* Vienna Convention on the Law of Treaties, art. 31, ¶ 1, 1155 U.N.T.S. 331 ("A treaty shall be interpreted in good faith in accordance with the ordinary meaning to be given to the terms of the treaty in their context and in the light of its object and purpose.").

235. *Id.*, art. 32.

with respect to human rights treaties, then with respect to humanitarian law, and finally with respect to United Nations action.

a. Practice under Human Rights Treaties

In treaty interpretation, state practice implementing a treaty provision is relevant in establishing the intent of the parties.[236] With many of the instances of state practice on nationality upon a change in sovereignty, one finds no reference to treaty provisions. Thus it is not always clear that states taking a position on the issue of nationality do so on the basis of treaty obligations.

Some state practice includes specific reference to Article 12, paragraph 4. The U.N. Subcommission on Prevention of Discrimination and Protection of Minorities invoked Article 12, paragraph 4, when it said that

> practices of forcible exile, mass expulsions and deportations, population transfer, 'ethnic cleansing' and other forms of forcible displacement of populations within a country or across borders deprive the affected populations of their right to freedom of movement.[237]

Authoritative bodies have construed the European and American human rights conventions to give a right of admittance to nationals in cases in which large groups sought to exercise the right. The European Commission of Human Rights found that under the European Convention, the right of admittance for nationals applied in the case of a large group. Asian nationals of the United Kingdom, that Uganda had expelled, sought admission to the United Kingdom, and the Commission found in their favor, even though thousands sought the right to reside in the United Kingdom.[238] Similarly, the Inter-American Human Rights Commission, citing the provision on right of entry in the American Convention on Human Rights,[239] said that this provision required Nicaragua to permit the return of Miskito Indians whom the Nicaraguan government had forced out of their native area.[240]

---

236. *See id.*, art. 31, ¶ 3 ("There shall be taken into account, together with the context: . . . (b) any subsequent practice in the application of the treaty which establishes the agreement of the parties regarding its interpretation.").

237. U.N. Subcommission on Prevention of Discrimination and Protection of Minorities, Res. 1995/13, U.N. ESCOR, 50th Sess., at 20, U.N. Doc. E/CN.4/Sub.2/1995/L.11/Add.3 (1995).

238. *East African Asians: Twenty-Five Applications against the United Kingdom*, 36 EUR. COMM'N ON H.R. 92, 102 (1971) (noting substantial increase in numbers entering U.K. from East African Dependencies late 1960s as a result of Africanization policies); *id.* at 122 (finding that complaints were admissible).

239. *See supra* note 148.

240. *See* Inter-American Commission on Human Rights, *Report on the Situation of Human Rights*

The Committee on the Elimination of Racial Discrimination, established to monitor compliance with the International Convention on the Elimination of All Forms of Racial Discrimination, found a violation of the Convention by Serb authorities in Bosnia, for forcing out Muslims.[241] The Committee called for "the voluntary return of displaced people."[242] The Committee found

> that any attempt to change or to uphold a changed demographic composition of an area, against the will of the original inhabitants, by whichever means is a violation of international law and demanded that persons be given the opportunity to return safely to the places they inhabited before the beginning of the conflict.[243]

b. Practice of the U.N. Political Organs

In a number of conflicts that have come before the United Nations, displacement of large numbers of civilians has occurred. In every such instance, the return of the displaced has represented a key element in the solution the United Nations proposed. While U.N. bodies have not always made it clear whether they acted on the basis of human rights law or humanitarian law, language in U.N. documents indicates that the nations based their calls for return on the understanding of an international-legal obligation to repatriate.

After Turkey occupied the northern part of Cyprus in 1974, thousands of Greek Cypriots fled to the south, and thousands of Turkish Cypriots in the south moved into the northern sector. Turkey said that the Greek Cypriots who fled south had no right to return. The U.N. General Assembly, however, "call[ed] for . . . urgent measures for the voluntary return of the refugees to their homes in safety."[244]

---

of a Segment of the Nicaraguan Population of Miskito Origin, at 112, OEA/ser.L/V/II.62, Doc. 26 (1984) (referring to American Convention's statements on the right to residence), *id.* at 119 (stating that Nicaragua must allow the return of those so desiring), *id.* at 120 (stating, "massive relocation of population groups may be juridically valid if done with the consent of the population involved.").

241. *See Report of the Committee on the Elimination of Racial Discrimination*, U.N. GAOR, 50th Sess., Supp. No. 18, at 47–48, ¶ 219, U.N. Doc. A/50/18 (1995).

242. *Id.; see also* Tomuschat, *supra* note 210, at 191 (citing discussion in Human Rights Committee of Afghanis displaced from Afghanistan during civil hostilities in which certain Committee members stated that the Afghanis had a right to return under International Covenant on Civil and Political Rights, art. 12, ¶ 4).

243. *Report of the Committee on the Elimination of Racial Discrimination, supra* note 241, ¶ 26.

244. G.A. Res. 37/253, U.N. GAOR, 37th Sess., Supp. No. 51, at 48, U.N. Doc. A/37/51 (1983); S.C. Res. 365, U.N. SCOR, 29th Sess., *Res. & Dec.* 11, U.N. Doc. S/INF/30 (1975) (endorsing G.A. Res. 3312, which stated, ¶ 6, "that all the [Cypriot] refugees should return to their homes in safety" and called upon the parties concerned "to undertake urgent measures to that end.").

In a statement on the conflict of the early 1990s in Abkhazia, the Security Council adopted a similar stance. It "reaffirm[ed] the right of all refugees and displaced persons affected by the [Georgian-Abkhaz] conflict to return to their homes in secure conditions in accordance with international law."[245] The use of the term "persons affected" indicates that a right of return applies not only to persons who left a place of residence, but as well to those who, for any other reason, could not return to their homes, thus including persons temporarily abroad during the hostilities. Moreover, the reference to international law manifests an understanding (*opinio juris*) that the return is a matter of right.

In a resolution on Croatia, the Security Council addressed the displacement of minority Serbs from their home areas. The Council not only called on Croatia to repatriate these Serbs but referred to repatriation as being required by law, demanding that Croatia,

> in conformity with internationally recognized standards . . . respect fully the rights of the local Serb population including their rights to remain, leave or return in safety . . . [and] create conditions conducive to the return of those persons who have left their homes.[246]

In dealing with the conflict in the Abkhazia sector of Georgia, a situation that generated a substantial population flight, the U.N. Security Council similarly found a right of "refugees and displaced persons to return to their homes."[247] With the conflict in Namibia, the Security Council called on South Africa to "accord unconditionally to all Namibians currently in exile for political reasons full facilities for return to their country."[248]

The pattern of Security Council resolutions referring to return as a right constitutes strong evidence of state practice that members of displaced groups are entitled to return to their home territory. The Security Council has not differentiated between persons expelled and

---

245. *See Security Council Says Unilateral Act to Establish 'Sovereign Abkhaz Entity' Violates Commitment For Political Settlement of Georgian-Abkhaz Conflict*, Federal News Service, Dec. 5, 1994, *available in* LEXIS, News Library, Fednew File; *see also* S.C. Res. 779, U.N. Doc. S/RES/779 (1992) (stating, regarding Bosnia, that "all displaced persons have the right to return in peace to their former homes"); *and* S.C. Res. 787, U.N. Doc. S/RES/787 (1992) ("insist[ing] [regarding Bosnia] that all displaced persons be enabled to return in peace to their former homes.").

246. *See* S.C. Res. 1009, U.N. Doc. S/RES/1009 (1995); *see also* S.C. Res. 1019, U.N. Doc. S/RES/1019 (1995) (the Council, again referring to Serbs displaced from Croatia, demanded that Croatia "respect fully the rights of the local Serb population including their right to remain or return in safety," and called on Croatia "to lift any time-limits placed upon the return of refugees to Croatia to reclaim their property.").

247. S.C. Res. 876, U.N. Doc. S/RES/876 (1993).

248. S.C. Res. 385, U.N. SCOR, 31st Sess., *Res. & Dec.* 8, U.N. Doc. S/INF/32 (1976).

those otherwise displaced. Nor has it differentiated between international and internal wars.[249] Anyone displaced as a result of hostilities would seem to enjoy a right to return.

E. Acquisition of Third-State Nationality

Many displaced Palestinians went to neighboring Arab states and took up residence there, either in refugee camps or in the general community. Among these states Jordan alone extended its nationality to displaced Palestinians. As indicated above, as a state-to-state obligation, the prohibition against refusing admission to a national is premised on injury to the state of sojourn, since a refusal to admit requires the state of sojourn either to admit the person or to find a third state willing to do so.[250] A grant of nationality by the state of sojourn would ordinarily amount to acceptance of the person and would thus relieve the state from which the displacement occurred of any liability. Thus, Jordan's grant of nationality might be taken to indicate its consent to the Palestinians' admission, and thus its waiver of any right resulting from Israel's wrong in refusing to admit them.

As a human rights matter, the right of admission into one's state of nationality is rationalized, in part, on the need to avoid rendering persons stateless. Since Jordan granted nationality, these persons were not left stateless. Seeking nationality elsewhere might be taken as a waiver of the individual's right to his original nationality.

However, the circumstances suggest that Jordan's extension of nationality to the Palestinians affected neither Jordan's claim against Israel for the Palestinians' admission, nor the human rights claims of individual Palestinians for admission. Jordan's grant of nationality to the Palestinians resulted from its annexation of the West Bank in 1950. Jordan granted nationality both to the Palestinians inhabiting the West Bank, and to those residing elsewhere in Jordan (the East Bank).

In its resolution approving the annexation of the West Bank, Jordan's parliament specified: "Arab rights in Palestine shall be protected. Those rights shall be defended with all possible legal means and this unity shall in no way be connected with the final settlement of Palestine's just cause within the limits of national hopes, Arab cooperation

---

249. *See* Protocol Additional to the Geneva Conventions of 12 August 1949, and relating to the Protection of Victims of Non-International Armed Conflicts, Protocol II, art. 17, June 8, 1977, 1125 U.N.T.S. 609 ("The displacement of the civilian population shall not be ordered for reasons related to the conflict unless the security of the civilians involved or imperative military reasons so demand . . . . Civilians shall not be compelled to leave their own territory for reasons connected with the conflict.").

250. *See supra* text accompanying notes 130–138.

and international justice."[251] Thus, Jordan's annexation was subject to the future emergence of a Palestinian state of which the West Bank might be a part. "One might thus conclude," wrote one analyst, "that the Palestinians are only provisionally placed under Jordanian sovereignty."[252]

The nationality Jordan granted was of a provisional character as well. In 1988, deferring to a decision of the Palestine National Council to declare a Palestinian state, Jordan renounced its claim to the West Bank.[253] In that connection, it phased out the nationality it had accorded to West Bank Palestinians.

Jordan's grant of nationality would not seem to negate a Palestinian's right to return. The grant reflected no intent on the part of the Palestinians in question to renounce a connection with Palestine, and no intent on the part of Jordan to interfere in the Palestinians' connection with their state of origin.

F. *Treatment of Jews in Arab States*

When Israel was asked in 1948 to repatriate the displaced Palestinians, it said that before it would do so, it would consider whether Jews were being mistreated in Arab states. "Such future consideration [of a return of displaced Palestinians]," an Israeli official said, "will take into account the position and treatment of Jewish minorities in the Arab countries."[254] The question of the propriety of the treatment of Jews in Arab states would require extended discussion,[255] but Israel's position can be addressed in the abstract, since ill treatment could in principle occur at any time.

A state is permitted under international law to violate the rights of another state in response to a violation by the latter state of rights of the former. Thus, State A may respond to a violation of its rights by

---

251. *Decision of the Council of Representatives and the Council of Notables in Joint Session on April 24, 1950, Concerning the Union of Eastern and Western Jordan, in* HELEN MILLER DAVIS, CONSTITUTIONS, ELECTORAL LAW, TREATIES OF STATES IN THE NEAR AND MIDDLE EAST 265–66 (2d ed. 1953), *also in* Albion Ross, *Amman Parliament Vote Unites Arab Palestine and Transjordan,* N.Y. TIMES, Apr. 25, 1950, at 1, 14 (where translation varies slightly, stating that Jordan's parliament acted "without prejudicing the final settlement of Palestine's just case within the sphere of national aspirations, inter-Arab cooperation and international justice.").

252. G. Feuer, *Les accords passés par les gouvernements jordanien et libanais avec les organisations palestiniennes (1968–1970),* 16 ANNUAIRE DE L'INSTITUT DE DROIT INT'L 177, 189 (1970).

253. John Kifner, *Hussein Surrenders Claims on West Bank to the P.L.O.,* N.Y. TIMES, Aug. 1, 1988, at A1 (King Hussein announcing, "We respect the wish of the P.L.O . . . [for] an independent Palestinian state").

254. *Acting United States Representative at the United Nations (Jessup) to the Secretary of State,* July 20, 1948, 1948(5) FOR. REL. U.S., pt. 2, 1249 (giving text of letter to Jessup from Michael Comay, Provisional Government of Israel, the quoted language appearing in the letter).

255. *See* QUIGLEY, PALESTINE AND ISRAEL: A CHALLENGE TO JUSTICE, *supra* note 6, at 99–102.

State B with an act that violates the rights of State B. This is called a countermeasure.[256] Countermeasures are, however, subject to limitations. One limitation is that a countermeasure may be directed only at a state that has violated the rights of the acting state.[257] Thus, an act by one Arab state would not provide a basis for Israel to take countermeasures against another Arab state. The implication of the quoted 1948 statement is that Israel might deny return to displaced Palestinians in one Arab state in response to violations of the rights of Jews in another Arab state. This would not be a proper countermeasure. Israel, owing an obligation to Arab state A, where displaced Palestinians have sought refuge, to repatriate those persons, may not decline to do so because of the violation of the rights of Jews by Arab state B.

A second limitation relates to the magnitude of the violation. A countermeasure must be proportional to the gravity of the act of the other state.[258] If Arab state A violates the rights of Jews in some fashion, Israel cannot necessarily respond by denying return to Palestinians.

A third limitation is that a state may take action as a countermeasure only in response to a wrongful act by another state that affects adversely the former state. Thus, a state must be a victim of a violation of its rights before it may take action as a countermeasure.[259] If Arab states violate the rights of their Jewish inhabitants, it is not clear that the rights of Israel as a state are violated, despite the role claimed by Israel with respect to world Jewry.[260]

A fourth limitation on countermeasures is that, regardless of what another state has done, a state may not, as a countermeasure, violate "basic human rights," or violate a so-called "peremptory norm of general international law."[261] While neither of these two categories admits of easy definition, the right of entry to one's state probably qualifies as "basic." Further, it is doubtful that states may, by treaty, allocate individuals between them (so-called forcible "population ex-

---

256. International Law Commission, Draft Articles on State Responsibility, art. 47, *Report of the International Law Commission on the Work of its Forty-Eighth Session*, U.N. GAOR, 51st Sess., Supp. No. 10, at 144, art. 47, ¶ 3, U.N. Doc. A/51/10 (1996).

257. *Id.*

258. *Id.*, art. 49.

259. *See Report of the International Law Commission on the Work of its Forty-Eighth Session*, U.N. GAOR, 51st Sess., Supp. No. 10, at 155, U.N. Doc. A/51/10 (1996) (stating that there must be "an internationally wrongful act, infringing a right of the State taking the countermeasure.").

260. *See* 4 LAWS OF THE STATE OF ISRAEL 114, ¶ 1 (1949/50) (giving "[e]very Jew" a "right to come to this country . . . .").

261. International Law Commission, Draft Articles on State Responsibility, *Report of the International Law Commission on the Work of its Forty-Eighth Session*, U.N. GAOR, 51st Sess., Supp. No. 10, at 145, art. 50, U.N. Doc. A/51/10 (1996).

change"),[262] and if that is so, then the right of return is a peremptory norm.

Thus, a refusal by Israel to repatriate on the basis of the treatment of Jews in Arab states is not sustainable as a countermeasure. As a countermeasure, such a refusal is directed against the wrong party. Arabs have not been displaced in the numbers of the Palestinians displaced. Any mistreatment of Jews in Arab states is not a cognizable harm to Israel as a state. Finally, the norm requiring admission to inhabitants is not one that can be violated by way of a countermeasure.

V. LEGAL CONSEQUENCES OF A COERCED DEPARTURE

To this point, this Article has addressed the issue of return for displaced Palestinians irrespective of the circumstances of their departure, assuming the Israeli view of non-coerced departure. If the Palestinians' departure, as the Palestinians claim, involved wrongful conduct on Israel's part, then return might be required on the additional basis of a state's obligation to reverse the consequences of an unlawful act. The obligation would run both to the states of sojourn and directly to the displaced Palestinians. The legal norms involved in a coerced departure, as applicable to the Palestinian departure, are explored in this section.

A. *Expulsion as a Violation of the Law of Nationality*

One basis for the illegality of expulsion is that it violates the rights of the states to which the persons are expelled, because those states are under no obligation to accept them.[263] The United States protested to Russia in 1891 over the expulsion by Russia of Jews of Russian nationality. U.S. President Benjamin Harrison explained:

> The banishment, whether by direct decree or by no less certain indirect methods, of so large a number of men and women is not a local question. A decree to leave one country is, in the nature of things, an order to enter another—some other. This consideration, as well as the suggestions of humanity, furnishes ample ground for the remonstrances which we have presented to Russia.[264]

---

262. *See infra* text accompanying notes 288–294.
263. *See* Dupuis, *supra* note 132, at 156.
264. *Message of the President to the Senate and House of Representatives*, Dec. 9, 1891, 1891 FOR. REL. U.S., at xiii (referring as well, as a reason to protest the expulsion, to "principles of international law and eternal justice").

State-to-state liability attaches not only when the flight is a result of actual expulsion, but as well when the state mistreats its nationals in such a way that either those mistreated, or others fearing similar treatment, decide to flee. The United States protested to Romania in 1902 over ill treatment by Romania that led Romanian Jews to seek admission to the United States, even absent actual expulsion. The United States took the view:

> Whether consciously and of purpose or not, these helpless people, burdened and spurned by their native land, are forced by the sovereign power of Roumania upon the charity of the United States. This Government cannot be a party to such an international wrong. It is constrained to protest against the treatment to which Jews in Roumania are subjected, not alone because it has unimpeachable ground to remonstrate against the resultant injury to itself, but in the name of humanity.[265]

B. Expulsion as a Human Rights Violation

Mass expulsion is also unlawful as a violation of the rights of those expelled.[266] "Simple expulsion [of population]," wrote one analyst, "is inconceivable under a regime of international law and irreconcilable with respect for human rights."[267] The Charter of the International Military Tribunal defined "crimes against humanity" to include "deportation,"[268] and the U.N. General Assembly subsequently endorsed the principles of law found in the Charter of the International Military Tribunal.[269] At Nuremberg, acts of expulsion of population from ter-

---

265. *Jews in Roumania—Discussion of proposed naturalization convention between the United States and Roumania: Discriminations, in the latter country, against Jews, condition of helplessness to which they are reduced, and objection of United States Government to immigration of such persons*, 1902 FOR. REL. U.S. 910, 914 (Mr. Hay to Mr. Wilson, July 17, 1902).

266. *See* 2 RESTATEMENT (THIRD) OF THE LAW: FOREIGN RELATIONS LAW OF THE UNITED STATES § 702 cmt. m at 167 (1987) (characterizing "mass uprooting of a country's population" as a human rights violation); Alfred M. de Zayas, *International Law and Mass Population Transfers*, 16 HARV. INT'L L.J. 207, 257 (1975) ("Mass expulsions in any context violate important principles of international and/or municipal law . . . . The persons unjustly deported have a right to compensation and also the right to return to their homeland.").

267. *Les Transfers Internationaux des Populations*, *supra* note 142, at 167–68 (statement of Max Huber); *id.* at 169 (statement of Herbert Kraus finding "unilateral transplanting of population" to be unlawful); *id.* at 172 (Herbert Kraus, stating: "I do not see that the U.N. Declaration [of Human Rights] leaves any place for a transfer of multitudes of persons from their country, a transfer which, moreover, has as a consequence the loss of nationality that these persons had before their expulsion.").

268. Charter of the International Military Tribunal, Agreement for the Prosecution and Punishment of the Major War Criminals of the European Axis, Aug. 8, 1945, art. 6(c), 82 U.N.T.S. 279, 288.

269. *Affirmation of the Principles of International Law recognized by the Charter of the Nürnberg Tribunal*, G.A. Res. 95, U.N. GAOR, 1st Sess., at 188, U.N. Doc. A/64/Add.1 (1946).

ritories occupied by Germany were charged as crimes, as well as acts of expulsion from Germany of non-German groups. The expulsion of Slovenes from Germany was prosecuted as a crime against humanity,[270] as was the forced emigration of Jews from Austria.[271] When Israel tried Adolf Eichmann for atrocities committed as a Nazi leader, it included charges of expulsions,[272] characterizing them as "war crimes" and as "crimes against humanity."[273]

The International Law Commission regards expulsions as a "mass violation of human rights."[274] The U.N. Subcommission on Prevention of Discrimination and Protection of Minorities, basing itself on customary law, has found expulsion unlawful, stating that it

> 1. [a]ffirm[ed] the right of persons to remain in peace in their own homes, on their own lands and in their own countries;
> 2. [a]lso affirm[ed] the right of refugees and displaced persons to return in safety and dignity, to their country of origin and/or within it, to their place of origin or choice.[275]

The U.N. Human Rights Commission has also found expulsion to violate human rights.[276] Expulsion violates the same human rights norms as those analyzed above that are involved in a denial of return, since expulsion implies an intent to forbid return.[277]

C. Expulsion as a Violation of Humanitarian Law

Expulsion also violates humanitarian law. A belligerent occupant may not force inhabitants out. The Geneva Civilians Convention prohibits expulsion by a belligerent occupant.[278] Both the General Assem-

---

270. *See* 8 TRIAL OF THE MAJOR WAR CRIMINALS BEFORE THE INTERNATIONAL MILITARY TRIBUNAL at 254–55 (1947).

271. *See* 22 TRIAL OF THE MAJOR WAR CRIMINALS BEFORE THE INTERNATIONAL MILITARY TRIBUNAL at 574 (1947).

272. Attorney-General of the Government of Israel v. Adolf Eichmann, 36 INT'L L. RPTS. 5, 8–9 (D.C. Jm, 1961) (counts 3, 5, 8, 9, 10, 11, 12 of the indictment); *see id.* at 95–102 (reciting facts of expulsions found to have been carried out or planned by Eichmann).

273. *Id.* at 9.

274. *Report of the International Law Commission on the Work of its Forty-Third Session*, U.N. GAOR, 46th Sess., Supp. No. 10, at 250, U.N. Doc. A/46/10 (1992) (Draft Code of Crimes against the Peace and Security of Mankind, "deportation or forcible transfer of population" listed in art. 21, which is headed "systematic or mass violations of human rights").

275. U.N. Subcommission on Prevention of Discrimination and Protection of Minorities, Res. 1994/24, U.N. ESCOR, 49th Sess., at 4, U.N. Doc. E/CN.4/Sub.2/1994.L.11/Add.3 (1994).

276. *See Human Rights and Mass Exoduses*, Commission on Human Rights Res. 1995/88, art. 3, U.N. ESCOR, 50th Sess., *Report of the Commission on Human Rights on Its Fifty-first Session*, Supp. No. 4, at 259, 261, U.N. Doc. E/1995/23, E/CN.4/1995/176 (1995) (deploring policies of intolerance towards ethnic groups as a cause of "forced migratory movements.").

277. *See supra* text accompanying notes 230–235.

278. Geneva Convention Relative to the Protection of Civilian Persons in Time of War, Aug.

bly and Security Council have declared Israel's expulsion of inhabitants from occupied territory to violate this provision.[279] A commission appointed by the allies after World War I to explore criminal responsibility for acts committed during the war composed a list of offenses that it deemed prohibited by the customary law of war. The commission included "deportation of civilians" and "attempts to denationalize the inhabitants of occupied territory."[280]

D. *Standard of Responsibility for Wrongfully Inducing Departure*

Under the rules on state responsibility, liability attaches well beyond the obvious situation in which a state purposely violates internationally protected rights. A state answers as well for harm committed by its agents, on a respondeat superior basis. It answers for harm committed with its support by private parties, a rule that has been applied in the case of expulsions.[281] A state formed as a result of hostilities is deemed to ratify the acts of the military forces that brought it into being.[282]

12, 1949, art. 49, 75 U.N.T.S. at 287, 318 ("Individual or mass forcible transfers as well as deportations of protected persons from occupied territory to the territory of the Occupying Power or to that of any other country, occupied or not, are prohibited, regardless of their motive."); *see id.*, art. 158 at 392 (forbidding denunciation of the Convention by a party during a conflict until it has repatriated protected persons; this provision seems to assume an obligation to repatriate protected persons).

279. G.A. Res. 36/147, U.N. GAOR, 36th Sess., Supp. No. 51, at 88, U.N. Doc. A/35/51 (1982) (criticizing the "evacuation, expulsion, deportation, displacement and transfer of Arab inhabitants of the occupied territories and denial of their right to return"); S.C. Res. 607, U.N. SCOR 43d Sess., *Res. & Decs.* 1, U.N. Doc. S/INF/44 (1988) *and* S.C. Res. 608, U.N. SCOR 43d Sess., *Res. & Decs.* 2, U.N. Doc. S/INF/44 (1988) (both Security Council resolutions calling on Israel to cease deportations).

280. *Commission on the Responsibility of the Authors of the War and on Enforcement of Penalties: Report Presented to the Preliminary Peace Conference*, 14 AM. J. INT'L L. 95, 114 (1920), crimes list *reprinted in* INTERNATIONAL CRIMINAL LAW: CASES AND MATERIALS 24 (Jordan Paust, M. Cherif Bassiouni et al. eds. 1996) (listing, in a chapter headed "Violations of the Laws and Customs of War," offenses deemed to be prohibited by the customary law of war). Leading experts on international law served on the commission, which was appointed by the U.S.A., U.K., France, Italy, and Japan. The original publication (which, unlike the version in the *American Journal of International Law*, includes a lengthy annex listing examples of violations of the laws of war committed during the war) is *Violation of the Laws and Customs of War: Reports of Majority and Dissenting Reports of American and Japanese Members of the Commission of Responsibilities, Conference of Paris, 1919* (Carnegie Endowment for International Peace, Division of International Law, 1919) where the list of crimes appears at 18.

281. *See* Application of the Convention on the Prevention and Punishment of the Crime of Genocide (Bosnia & Herz. v. Yugo.), 1993 I.C.J. 3 (interim order of Apr. 8, 1993), *reprinted in* 87 AM. J. INT'L L. 505 (1993) (enjoining Yugoslavia from promoting acts of ethnic cleansing undertaken by non-state groupings).

282. *See* IAN BROWNLIE, STATE RESPONSIBILITY, PART I 178 (1983) (finding "a categorical imposition of responsibility for all acts of the insurgent forces"); International Law Commission, Draft Articles on State Responsibility, art. 15, ¶ 2, *Report of the International Law Commission on the Work of its Forty-Eighth Session*, U.N. GAOR, 51st Sess., Supp. No. 10, at 142, U.N. Doc. A/51/10 (1996); EAGLETON, *supra* note 134, at 147 ("the government set up by successful revolutionists must accept responsibility for their acts as insurgents from the beginning, a

Responsibility attaches when an expulsion is carried out by agents of a state, even if the state has set no policy that they should do so, and even if the agents exceed their authority under domestic law.[283] This principle applies in particular where the agents are military forces. Because of the potential for military forces to cause harm, a state bears a high standard of care in controlling them.[284] In one arbitration case, a state was held responsible for acts of its armed forces, even where the armed forces acted recklessly, as opposed to purposely, in causing harm:

> [I]t is mistaken action, error in judgment, or reckless conduct of soldiers for which a government in a given case has been held responsible. The international precedents reveal the application of principles as to the very strict accountability for mistaken action.[285]

If expulsion of population is occurring in a state, the state must try to prevent it, whether the expulsion is being carried out by its own agents or by non-state parties, since in any event the rights of neighboring states will be infringed by the exodus.[286] Another state has no obligation to accept persons coming into its territory, and therefore a state must endeavor to prevent an exodus.[287]

E. Coerced Departure by Agreement among States

One does find in the state practice of the first half of the twentieth century instances in which states agreed by treaty to exchange populations, regardless of the will of the individuals involved. The two major instances involved Greece and Turkey in the 1920s, and the forced emigration of German nationals after World War II. Neither

---

conclusion logically deducible from the fact that the acts of the insurgents have now become the acts of the government, for which it must accept responsibility."); Rousseau, *supra* note 201, at 380 ("The decisions base this principle on the fact that victorious revolutionaries are taken to represent, by reason of their victory, the national will from the beginning of the conflict; there is also a kind of retroactive confirmation of the action of the insurgents, based on their ultimate success").

283. *See Report of the International Law Commission on the Work of its Forty-Eighth Session*, U.N. GAOR, 51st Sess., Supp. No. 10, at 128, U.N. Doc. A/51/10 (1996) (stating that there is responsibility "even if, in the particular case, the organ exceeded its competence according to internal law or contravened instructions concerning its activity.").

284. *See* BROWNLIE, *supra* note 282, at 140 (stating, "it is probably the case that a higher standard of prudence in their [armed forces] discipline and control is required, for reasons which are sufficiently obvious"); 5 RPTS. INT'L ARB. AWARDS 516, 529 (1929) (Cairo Claim; a state must exercise superior vigilance over acts of military personnel).

285. 4 RPTS. OF INT'L ARB. AWARDS 575, 579 (1930) (Kling Claim, op. of Commissioner Nielsen).

286. *See* Luke T. Lee, *The Right to Compensation: Refugees and Countries of Asylum*, 80 AM. J. INT'L L. 532, 553 (1986).

287. *Id.* at 553.

instance, however, stands as state practice for the propriety of forced transfer, as in each case the agreement to evict populations came only after a period of unilateral expulsion.

Greece and Turkey agreed on an exchange of Turks from Greece for Greeks from Turkey,[288] but only after Turkey had expelled Greeks unilaterally.[289] The exchange was arranged not on the basis of the propriety of such an arrangement, but rather as a way of providing relief to Greece.[290]

After World War II, the United Kingdom, United States, and U.S.S.R. approved in an agreement reached at Potsdam the compulsory migration of several million Germans to Germany from Czechoslovakia, Romania, Yugoslavia, Hungary, and from eastern German provinces that Germany was forced to cede to Poland.[291] Here too, however, unilateral expulsions came first, Germans being expelled from the named states, often under conditions of great cruelty. The Potsdam agreement approved additional compulsory transfers, but on condition that they be carried out humanely.[292] The Potsdam agreement in fact registered disapproval of unilateral expulsions.[293]

Whatever the position under earlier law, compulsory population transfer would seem to be at odds with human rights concepts that entered the law in the second half of the twentieth century, in particular norms on right of entry and right of nationality. It is doubtful that an agreed compulsory population transfer would be lawful in contemporary law.[294]

---

288. Convention concerning the Exchange of Greek and Turkish Populations (Lausanne), Jan. 30, 1923, art. 1, 32 L.N.T.S. 75 ("As from the 1st May, 1923, there shall take place a compulsory exchange of Turkish nationals of the Greek Orthodox religion established in Turkish territory, and of Greek nationals of the Moslem religion established in Greek territory. These persons shall not return to live in Turkey or Greece respectively without the authorisation of the Turkish Government or of the Greek Government respectively.").

289. *See* STEPHEN P. LADAS, THE EXCHANGE OF MINORITIES: BULGARIA, GREECE AND TURKEY 338 (1932) (quoting four-power statement that one reason for their support of compulsory transfer was that it represented the "most efficacious way of dealing with the grave economic results which must result from the great movement of populations which has already occurred" [a reference to fact that expelled Greeks had no means of livelihood in Greece, and that by forcing out Turks, land would be made available to these Greeks]).

290. *See* E. Reut-Nicolussi, *Displaced Persons and International Law*, 1948 HAGUE ACAD. DROIT INT'L, RECUEIL DES COURS 1, 29 (referring to the forced transfer of Turks from Greece under the Lausanne convention as "compensation" gained by Greece for Turkey's prior forcible expulsion of Greeks).

291. *See generally* ALFRED DE ZAYAS, NEMESIS AT POTSDAM (2d ed., 1979).

292. Berlin (Potsdam) Conference, Aug. 2, 1945, sec. XII, 3 Bevans 1207, 1220 (calling for transfer to Germany of German populations in Poland, Czechoslovakia, Hungary).

293. Potsdam Conference Protocol, *supra* note 292, sec. XII (noting an ongoing influx of Germans from Poland, Czechoslovakia, and Hungary, and stating "The Czechoslovak Government, the Polish Provisional Government and the Control Council in Hungary are at the same time being informed of the above and are being requested meanwhile to suspend further expulsions pending an examination by the Governments concerned of the report from their representatives on the Control Council.").

294. *See Report of the International Law Commission on the Work of its Forty-seventh Session,* U.N.

F. Israel's Responsibility in the Palestinian Departure

As recounted above, some Palestinians left their home areas virtually at gunpoint, some left as their home areas came under bombardment, and some left out of fear instilled by atrocities committed elsewhere.[295] It has been said that there was no "master plan" behind the expulsions from the Israeli side.[296] As the previous section indicates, it is not necessary that there be a "master plan" for state responsibility to attach. Under the principles adduced in this section, Israel would seem to be responsible for wrongfully inducing the departure of those Palestinians who left under direct compulsion, or out of fear instilled by acts calculated to create fear.[297] This would include the vast majority of the Palestinians displaced in both 1948 and 1967.[298] Regarding 1948, responsibility lies for the coerced departures occurring both before and after the date of declaration of Israeli statehood, because of the responsibility of a state for acts of successful insurgents.

VI. MODALITIES OF A RETURN

Given that a right to return for the Palestinians exists under customary international law, the question of proper remedies is in order. A state that violates rights is required under international law to restore the situation as it was before the illegal act.[299] Repatriation is the remedy that comes closest to restoring the *status quo ante*, even after the passage of decades and changes in the demography of the areas in question.[300]

The duty to restore the pre-existing situation requires Israel to repatriate the Palestinians it dispossessed. This means allowing them to return to their original areas. The General Assembly's 1948 resolution gives the choice between repatriation or compensation to the

---

GAOR, 50th Sess., Supp. No. 10, *Report of the Working Group on State Succession and its Impact on the Nationality of Natural and Legal Persons*, at 271, 276, U.N. Doc. A/50/10 (1995) (referring to human rights as a basis for concluding that states may not by treaty attribute nationality to persons against their will).

295. *See supra* notes 13–40; *see also* MORRIS, *supra* note 35, at 21 ("[I]n most cases, expulsion orders were unnecessary; the inhabitants had already fled, out of fear or as a result of Jewish attack."); *see also* Dimitrijevic, *supra* note 4, at 18 (explaining that Palestinians who fled out of fear of Israeli army "may be considered to have been expelled by force, exiled.").

296. *See* MORRIS, *supra* note 35, at 17.

297. *See* Alfred de Zayas, *The Illegality of Population Transfers and the Application of Emerging International Norms in the Palestinian Context*, 6 PALESTINE Y.B. INT'L L. 17, 44–46 (1991).

298. *See* Mohammed Bedjaoui, Inaugural Address Before the Seminar of Arab Jurists on Palestine in THE PALESTINE QUESTION: SEMINAR OF ARAB JURISTS ON PALESTINE, ALGIERS, 22–27 July, 1967 (1968) at 3, 6 ("Can it be . . . [that these] . . . repeated acts of theft and violence [by Israeli military units against Palestinian civilians] conferred some right on those who committed them?").

299. *See* EAGLETON, *supra* note 134, at 182; *see also* Chorzów Factory (Ger. v. Pol.), 1928 P.C.I.J. 47 (ser. A) No. 13, at 47.

300. *See* Reut-Nicolussi, *supra* note 290, at 52–55 (discussing repatriation as the preferred solution after World War II for persons displaced during and before the war).

individual refugee, not to Israel.[301] The U.N. Committee on the Exercise of the Inalienable Rights of the Palestinian People[302] specified that the Palestinians' right of return "should be absolute for every Palestinian and must have priority over any other form of substitute arrangements, such as compensation."[303] The Committee's view is consistent with the right of return; a displaced person cannot be forced to remain abroad with an offer of compensation.

Repatriation of the Palestinians is complicated by the fact that Israel has settled others in their home areas. It destroyed and built over Arab villages and gave their land to kibbutzim and moshavim or to other users. The U.N. Conciliation Commission for Palestine said in this regard: "The areas from which the refugees came are no longer vacant, and any movement of return would have to be carefully worked out and executed with the active co-operation of the Government of Israel."[304] After the passage of half a century from the first displacement, a perfect restoration of the *status quo* is not possible. However, repatriation could be accomplished.[305]

Israel has maintained that it has no room to accommodate returning Palestine Arabs. Israel has, however, endeavored in recent years to attract Jews to settle in Israel. Through arrangements with the former Soviet government in the 1980s, it granted large numbers of visas to emigrating Jews, and when some of these Jews tried to migrate to states other than Israel, Israeli authorities intervened to force them to Israel.[306] Thus, it appears that Israel has room for additional population.

In another case, an argument of lack of capacity to absorb persons entitled to enter a state was rejected.[307] The right of entry prevailed. Large-scale repatrations may well present difficulties, but a number of

---

301. *See* G.A. Res. 194, ¶ 11, U.N. Doc. A/810 (1948) ("[T]hat the refugees wishing to return to their homes . . . should be permitted to do so . . . and that compensation should be paid for the property of those choosing not to return.").

302. *See* G.A. Res. 3376, U.N. GAOR, 30th Sess., Supp. No. 34, at 3, U.N. Doc A/10034 (1975) (establishing the committee).

303. *Report of the Committee on the Exercise of the Inalienable Rights of the Palestinian People* U.N. SCOR, 31st Sess., at 8, U.N. Doc. S/12090 (1976).

304. *Progress Report of the U.N. Conciliation Commission for Palestine*, U.N. GAOR, 6th Sess., Supp. No. 18, at 5, U.N. Doc. A/1985 (1951).

305. *See Report of the Committee on the Exercise of the Inalienable Rights of the Palestinian People*, *supra* note 303, at 8 (recommending to the Security Council a two-stage plan that called for the return, first, of the 1967 refugees, and, second, of the 1948 refugees).

306. *See* Menachem Shalev, *Massive Exodus of Soviet Jews Predicted: Secret Report States that U.S. Curbs Will Cause Many to Come to Israel*, JERUSALEM POST INT'L ED., Apr. 8, 1989, at 1.

307. *See East African Asians: Twenty-Five Applications Against the United Kingdom*, 36 EUR. COMM'N ON H.R. 92, 102–03 (1971) (stating that U.K. was unable to absorb the numbers of East African Asians who sought admission); *id.* at 122 (stating that the European Commission's position that the complaints of the applicants for entry to the U.K. were nonetheless admissible).

displaced population groups have been resettled in recent times in their home territory.[308]

VII. THE REPATRIATION ISSUE IN THE ISRAEL-P.L.O. NEGOTIATIONS

To recapitulate, Palestinians are entitled to return to their home areas as a matter of right, not as a matter of Israeli grace. This right exists irrespective of whether one adopts the Israeli factual assumptions of non-coerced exodus, or the Palestinian view of forced flight. Furthermore, this right is independently based on the law of nationality, human rights law, and humanitarian law, and is recognized by U.N. practice. As shown, the reasons advanced by Israel in opposition to that right are weak. Those reasons have, moreover, been seriously undermined by the concessions of the 1990s from the Palestinians and the Arab states, in particular: the P.L.O.'s recognition of Israel,[309] the deletion from the P.L.O. covenant of language expressing opposition to Israel as a state,[310] and Israel's concluded and anticipated peace agreements with neighboring states. The P.L.O. will presumably agree that returnees would live under Israel's sovereignty, and there would be little chance that returnees would view the matter in any other fashion. Any remaining factual basis for Israel's security concern is tenuous.

Perhaps recognizing that the security rationale is not convincing, the government that assumed power in Israel in 1996 gave a new and

---

308. *See* Reut-Nicolussi, *supra* note 290, at 31, 42–43 (discussing repatriation of persons forced to Germany as slave labor during World War II). *See also* JOSEPH SCHECHTMAN, POPULATION TRANSFERS IN ASIA 51–70 (1949) (describing the repatriation to Soviet Armenia in 1946–47 of Armenians displaced during World War I). *See also* V.M. Broshevan, *Deportatsiia zhitelei Kryma [The Deportation of the Inhabitants of Crimea]*, *in* KRYMS'KI TATARY: ISTORIIA I SUCHASNIST' (DO 50-RICHCHIA DEPORTATSII KRIMS'KO-TATARS'KOGO NARODU): MATERIALY MIZHNARODNOI NAUK-OVOI KONFERENTSII, KYIV, 13–14 TRAVNIA 1994 R. [THE CRIMEAN TATARS: HISTORY AND THE PRESENT DAY (TOWARDS THE 50TH ANNIVERSARY OF THE DEPORTATION OF THE CRIMEAN TATAR PEOPLE): MATERIALS OF THE INTERNATIONAL SCHOLARLY CONFERENCE KIEV, 13–14 MAY 1994] 44 (I. Kuras ed. 1995) (reporting how Tatars of Crimea, deported internally by U.S.S.R. government for allegedly collaborating with Germany during World War II, were repatriated in the 1990s); *see also* Neubauer *Welcomes Estonian President's Call as Model for Czechs*, CTK [Czech News Agency] National News Wire, Oct. 10, 1995, *available in* LEXIS, Nexis Library, CTK File (reporting offer by Lennart Meri, President of Estonia, to repatriate Baltic Germans, and their descendants, who were forced out of Estonia and Latvia under 1939 agreements with Germany); *see also* S.C. Res. 1030, U.N. SCOR, 50th Sess., ¶ 14, U.N. Doc. S/RES/1030 (1995) (noting success in repatriating persons displaced from Tajikistan during that country's civil war).

309. *See Letter from P.L.O. Chairman Yasser Arafat to Israeli Prime Minister Yitzhak Rabin* (Sept. 9, 1993), *in* 7 PALESTINE Y.B. INT'L L. 230 (1994) ("The P.L.O. recognizes the right of the State of Israel to exist in peace and security.").

310. *See* Serge Schmemann, *P.L.O. Ends Call for Destruction of Jewish State*, N.Y. TIMES, Apr. 25, 1996, at A1.

different rationale for refusing repatriation to the displaced Palestinians, namely, "demographic security."[311] The evident meaning is that the government of Israel does not want to see a diminution of Israel's Jewish majority. The new government indicated it would oppose "the right of return of Arab populations to any part of the Land of Israel west of the Jordan River,"[312] a position that would preclude repatriation either to Israel, or to the Gaza Strip or West Bank. This position eschews the legal objections to return that have been considered in this Article, basing the denial rather on patently impermissible ethnic grounds. No arguable legal principle permits a denial of repatriation to those so entitled on the basis of their ethnicity.[313]

If Israel successfully insists on a settlement regarding the displaced Palestinians that does not satisfy their legitimate expectations, the consequences could be serious. While for Israel, such a settlement may appear advantageous, in the long term it might be quite disadvantageous, because it would fail to resolve this major outstanding issue between the two parties. Hostility would persist, and peace could not be assured.[314]

There is a risk that if the negotiations are left to the parties alone, the outcome will be one that does not meet the Palestinians' legitimate expectations. It is incumbent on the two convening powers, the United States and Russia, to ensure an appropriate outcome. The same obligation falls on the United Nations. The U.N. Security Council, to be sure, has continued to play a role to bring the peace process to a successful conclusion.[315] The United States likewise must remain engaged.[316]

---

311. *See* Sarah Honig & David Makovsky, *Religious Issues Delay Coalition Deal*, JERUSALEM POST, June 17, 1996, at 1 (quoting unnamed aide to Prime Minister-elect Benjamin Netanyahu).

312. Eric Silver, *Netanyahu Hits First Crisis Over Cabinet Line-up*, INDEPENDENT, June 19, 1996, at 10; Elaine Ruth Fletcher, *Peace Talks Will Hinge on Israeli Elections: Likud Party Would Try to Impose More Controls on Palestinians*, S.F. EXAMINER, May 5, 1996, at A15 (indicating that Likud position is to oppose return of displaced Palestinians to Israel, to West Bank, and to Gaza Strip).

313. *See* International Convention on the Elimination of All Forms of Racial Discrimination, *supra* note 146.

314. *See* SALIM TAMARI, PALESTINIAN REFUGEE NEGOTIATIONS: FROM MADRID TO OSLO II 58 (1996) (stating the author's concern that the issue of the displaced "will be further marginalized and neglected by Israeli negotiators, until the time when it becomes an explosive and destabilizing issue in relations between Israel and the Palestinians, as well as betweeen the P[alestinian] A[uthority] and the Palestinian diaspora." The author was coordinator of the Refugee Working Group for the Palestinian team in multilateral negotiations held under the interim arrangements, and a member of the Quadripartite Committee on Displaced Persons, established in the Declaration of Principles to discuss "modalities for the admission of 1967 displaced persons to the West Bank and Gaza.").

315. *See* S.C. Res. 1073, U.N. Doc. S/RES/1073 (1996).

316. *See* Steven Erlanger, *Mideast Accord: The Mediator—Dennis B. Ross; A Political Survivor Who Travels Light Finally Wins the Trust of the Untrusting*, N.Y. TIMES, Jan. 16, 1997, at A8 (making

If the final status negotiations are to produce a settlement that enjoys the respect of the parties, and of the people who make up their constituencies, the issue of the displaced Palestinians must be resolved in a way that satisfies legitimate expectations. The parties would do well to recall the 1948 advice quoted above of the U.N. mediator, Count Bernadotte, who did not question Israel's existence as a state but who thought, nonetheless, that "it would be an offence against the principles of elemental justice if these innocent victims of the conflict were denied the right to return to their homes."[317]

---

reference to U.S. role in bringing about agreement on an Israeli partial withdrawal from the West Bank town of Hebron).

317. *Progress Report of the United Nations Mediator on Palestine, supra* note 37, at 14.

The Responsibility of Great Britain in Respect of the Creation of the Palestine Refugee Question

*Iain Scobbie**

This article examines the question of whether Great Britain bears responsibility for the creation of the Palestinian refugee question. In international affairs, responsibility for a situation may take many forms: for instance, the moral, political or legal responsibility of a State, or group of States, for a given incident or situation may each be explored depending on the focus of the analysis. This article examines only questions of responsibility under international law: in other words, did Great Britain violate any of its obligations under international law in such a way that this gave rise to or contributed to the creation of the refugee situation? Accordingly, the argument presented here is narrowly legal and does not address either the moral or political dimensions of the matter. Further, the article can do no more than indicate some of the legal considerations relevant to determining whether Great Britain bears responsibility, under international law, for the creation of Palestinian refugees. It cannot conclude whether, or not, Great Britain's responsibility was engaged, as this would require a close examination of the facts and evidence which goes well beyond the bounds of this article.[1] Finally, because this examines the creation of the Palestinian refugee question, the focus of the analysis is

---

* Sir Joseph Hotung Research Professor in Law, Human Rights and Peace Building in the Middle East, School of Oriental and African Studies, University of London.

1 Apart from the difficulties that might arise in fulfilling evidential requirements in international litigation, the question of the genesis of the Palestinian refugee question is, to a degree, contested, especially given the emergence of the "new" or revisionist Israeli historians. In connection with the refugee question, perhaps the most important revisionist work is Morris, B., *The birth of the Palestinian Refugee Problem Revisited* (Cambridge University Press, Cambridge, 2004): see also the interview conducted with Morris by Ari Shavit, entitled "On ethnic cleansing", *26 New Left Review* 37 (2004). It must be acknowledged that the actual truth need not coincide with the "truth" established judicially, or with the "truth" established by historians. For an interesting discussion of these issues within an Israeli context, see the articles by Abraham, Maoz and Moglen in 18/3 *Law and History Review* (2000), Moaz, A., "Historical adjudication: courts of law, Commissions of Inquiry, and 'historical truth'" at 559; Abraham, D., "Where Hannah Arendt went wrong" at p. 607; Moglen, E., "Making history: Israeli law and historical demarcation" at p. 613; and Moaz, "Law and history – a need for demarcation" at p. 619. These papers are available online at <www.historycooperative.org/journals/lhr/18.3/>.

historical. Contemporary standards of international law are irrelevant: the question of legal responsibility must be gauged by reference to international law as it stood during the first half of the 20th century.

This article falls into two broad sections. The first outlines the legal framework that has to be applied to determine whether Britain bears responsibility for the creation of the Palestinian refugee question. This deals with structural questions: regardless of the specific obligations that might be involved, how does international law regulate the attribution of responsibility to States? The second section applies this framework to the specific issue of the creation of the Palestinian refugee question. As any analysis of this question must cover a range of issues, a convenient way to keep these manageable is to try to determine how the United Kingdom would approach any claim that it bore responsibility under international law for the creation of the Palestine refugee question. This has the advantage that it should identify the points that the United Kingdom thinks would be fundamentally in its favour, and therefore the key issues at which any contrary argument should be directed.

1 FRAMEWORK OF RESPONSIBILITY

An examination of the legal framework that should be employed to decide whether Britain bears responsibility for the creation of the Palestinian refugee question principally requires the identification of the relevant principles of the law of State responsibility. These principles are, however, structural. They create the framework to decide whether a State's responsibility for an internationally wrongful act has been engaged, and the resultant legal consequences, but do not themselves identify the specific obligation or obligations whose breach gives rise to responsibility. The focus of this analysis is historical as it refers to events that occurred while Britain administered the Mandate for Palestine between July 1922 and May 1948. To evaluate historic events, the law that must be applied is the law that existed at that time – this is known as the application of inter-temporal law. This is equally applicable to structural rules of international law, such as the rules of State responsibility, as it is to the law's substantive content.

1.1 The inter-temporal rule

The inter-temporal rule, sometimes expressed in the Latin maxim *tempus regit factum*, is a well-established rule of international law.[2] Although subject to

---

2 See, for instance, Judge Huber in the *Island of Palmas arbitration* (US and Holland: 1928), 4 *Annual Digest of Public International Law Cases* (1927-28) 3 at p. 4 (also 22 *American Journal of International Law* 867 (1928) at 883; *Namibia advisory opinion*, ICJ Reps, 1971, 16 at pp.31-32, para. 53; separate opinion of Judge de Castro, *Western Sahara advisory opinion*, ICJ Reps, 1975, 12, 127 at pp.168-169; and *Aegean Sea continental shelf* case, ICJ Reps, 1978, 3 at pp. 29-34, paras. 71-80. For commentary, see Greig D., *Intertemporality and the Law of Treaties* (British Institute of International and Comparative Law: London, 2001); Higgins, R., "Some observations on the inter-temporal rule in international law", in Makarczyk, J. (Ed), "Theory of international law

further jurisprudential development,[3] the classic enunciation of this doctrine is that of Judge Huber in the *Island of Palmas arbitration.* He stated:

> a juridical fact must be appreciated in the light of the law contemporary with it, and not of the law in force at the time such dispute in regard to it arises or falls to be settled.[4]

Nevertheless, he qualified the force of this *dictum* by adding:

> As regards the...the so-called "inter-temporal" law ... a distinction must be made between the creation of rights and the existence of rights. The same principle which subjects the act creative of a right to the law in force at the time the right arises, demands that the existence of the right, in other words its continued manifestation, shall follow the conditions required by the evolution of law.[5]

The relationship between these passages is uneasy to some degree,[6] but is generally understood as meaning that treaties are to be interpreted in the light of general rules of international law in force at the time of their conclusion. As the International Court affirmed in the *Namibia advisory opinion,* attention should be paid to "the primary necessity of interpreting an instrument in accordance with the intentions of the parties at the time of its conclusion".[7]

Nonetheless, the interpretation of an instrument cannot be insulated from subsequent legal developments where the concepts employed are themselves subject to change. For instance, in the *Aegean Sea continental shelf* case, the International Court ruled:

> Once it is established that the expression "the territorial status of Greece" was used ... as a generic term denoting any matters comprised within the concept of territorial status under general international law, the presumption necessarily arises that its meaning was intended to follow the evolution of the law and to correspond with the meaning attached to the expression by the law in force at any given time.[8]

Further, in the *Namibia advisory opinion,* in its consideration of the inter-temporal rule, the International Court held that "an international instrument must be interpreted and applied within the overall framework of the juridical system in force at the time of the interpretation".[9] If accepted at face value, this ruling goes too far: as Judge Higgins comments, the Court appears not to have realised that "the inter-temporal issue as it arises for treaties generally is very much more complex".[10]

---

at the threshold of the 21st century: essays in honour of Krzysztof Skubuszewski"(Kluwer: The Hague, 1996), p. 173; Jennings, R. Y. and Watts, A. D., *Oppenheim's International Law* (Longman: London: 1992, 9th Edn.) 1281, §633.11; and Rosenne S, *Developments in the Law of Treaties* (Cambridge University Press, Cambridge, 1989) p.76 *et seq.*

3   Judge Higgins' analysis addresses both the international and European dimensions of this development – see Higgins, 1996, *passim*: for instant purposes, only the international aspects are relevant.

4   22 *American Journal of International Law* 883 (1928).

5   *Loc. cit.,* and also 4 Annual Digest (1927-28) 4.

6   A detailed exposition of their relationship is found in Higgins, 1996.

7   ICJ Reps, 1971, p. 31, para. 53.

8   ICJ Reps, 1978, p. 32, para. 77.

9   ICJ Reps, 1971, p. 31, para. 53.

10 Higgins, 1996, p. 177.

For present purposes, in order to provide a legal evaluation of past events that arose under a treaty régime which has long been terminated, the law applicable must be that which was current at the time those events happened. There can be no question of assessing past events using contemporary standards. Expectations based on contemporary international law will not necessarily give an accurate picture of the historic content of international law. It cannot be denied that the application of inter-temporal law can give rise to legal evaluations that may be perceived as unjust. Our perceptions of international law, and of its content, are often informed by legal concepts that simply did not exist in the past. In relation to the creation of the Palestinian refugee question, expectations derived from modern human rights law are, on the whole, irrelevant. In broad terms, apart from the protection of minorities, human rights law simply did not exist in the first half of the 20th century. The development of modern human rights law stems from the 1948 Universal Declaration of Human Rights, but in 1948 this was only a recommendation adopted by the General Assembly and not a binding instrument.[11] Evaluation must employ the specific substantive content of the applicable legal standards which existed at the relevant historical moment. Accordingly, the application of the inter-temporal rule to the question of British responsibility for the creation of the Palestinian refugee question requires consideration of the doctrine of the critical date.

1.2 Doctrine of the critical date

This is a doctrine primarily associated with cases involving the determination of title to territory.[12] With regard to the assessment of British responsibility, this doctrine should be applied analogously, to provide the legal "historical context"[13] for that assessment. Although the doctrine of the critical date principally concerns the admissibility of evidence, with facts subsequent to that date being irrelevant to the determination of the dispute, it is also a matter of substance:[14]

> In any dispute a certain date, or several dates, will assume prominence in the process of evaluating the facts. The choice of such a date, or dates, is within the province of the tribunal seized of the dispute and will depend in some circumstances on the inevitable logic of the law applicable to the particular facts and, in other cases, on the practical necessity of confining the process of decision to relevant and cogent facts and thus to acts prior to the existence of the dispute. In the latter context the tribunal is simply employing judicial technique in the use of evidence and more especially the exclusion of evidence consisting of self-serving acts of parties at a stage

---

11 For a history of the drafting of the Universal Declaration, see Glendon, M.A., *A World Made New: Eleanor Roosevelt and the Universal Declaration of Human Rights* (Random House, New York, 2001).

12 For a good account of the doctrine in the context of territorial disputes, see the *Dubai-Sharjah border arbitration*, 91 *International Law Reports* 543 at p. 590 *et seq.*

13 See *Western Sahara advisory opinion*, ICJ Reps, 1975, 38, para.76.

14 See Jennings and Watts, 1992, 711.

when it was evident that a dispute existed ... There are several types of critical date, and it is difficult and probably misleading to formulate general definitions.[15]

With regard to the question of British responsibility for the creation of the Palestinian refugee issue, the initial issue that must be addressed in order to determine the content of the applicable law is the date at which British responsibility should be assessed. Surely this must be the period of the Mandate.

1.3 Legal Foundations of State Responsibility

Determination of the critical date is not only decisive for the identification of the content of the relevant substantive law, but also for the content of the relevant principles of State responsibility.

In 2001, the International Law Commission issued its Articles on the Responsibility of States for Internationally Wrongful Acts.[16] Although these provide a useful and convenient restatement of the core rules of the law of State responsibility, the Articles themselves are contained in a non-binding instrument which is seen as a possible basis for subsequent conversion into a treaty.[17] Also, the Articles attempt to develop international law to an extent, as well as to codify established customary international law. Accordingly, the 2001 Articles cannot be employed blindly to determine questions of British responsibility during the period of the Mandate as they do not fit the requirements of the inter-temporal rule, except insofar as these Articles express principles of customary international law applicable at the critical date. It is necessary to refer to legal materials produced at that time to determine the applicable law – such as the 1927 Institut de Droit International Resolution on International Responsibility of States for injuries on their territory to the person or property of foreigners;[18] the 1929 Harvard Law School draft Articles on The Law of Responsibility of States for damage done in their territory to the person or property of foreigners;[19] and the work on the Responsibility of States for damage caused in their territory to the person or property of foreigners associated with the 1930 Hague Conference for the Codification of International Law, which was convened by the League of Nations.[20]

---

15 Brownlie I, *Principles of Public International Law* (Oxford University Press, Oxford, 2003, 6th Edn.), pp. 125-126, notes omitted.

16 The Articles, and the International Law Commission's commentary upon them, are reprinted in Crawford, J., *The International Law Commission's Articles on State Responsibility: Introduction, Text and Commentaries* (Cambridge University Press, Cambridge, 2002).

17 On this aspect of the Articles, see Crawford 2002, pp. 58-60.

18 Reproduced in 22 *American Journal of International Law*, Document Supplement at p. 330 (1928).

19 Reproduced in 23 *American Journal of International Law*, Document Supplement at p. 131 (1929).

20 For contemporary accounts of the work of the Hague Codification Conference on State responsibility, see Borchard, E., "'Responsibility of States', at the Hague Codification Conference", 24 *American Journal of International Law* 517 (1930); and Hackworth, G. H., "Responsibility of States for damages caused in their territory to the person or property of foreigners: the Hague Conference for the Codification of International Law", 24 *American Journal of International Law* 500 (1930). See also 24 *American Journal of International Law*, Document Supplement 46 (1930); and Brownlie, I., *System of the Law of Nations: Part One, State Responsibility* (Clarendon Press, Oxford, 1983), pp. 10-13.

Continued overleaf

The fundamental principle of State responsibility, codified in Article 1 of the 2001 Articles, is that every internationally wrongful act of a State engages its international responsibility.[21] This principle was clearly and comprehensively expressed in the first paragraph of Article I of the 1927 Institut de Droit International resolution:

> The State is responsible for injuries caused to foreigners by any action or omission contrary to its international obligations, whatever be the authority of the State whence it proceeds: constitutional, legislative, governmental, administrative, or judicial.[22]

This principle was also repeatedly affirmed by the Permanent Court of International Justice in the inter-war period,[23] and undoubtedly forms part of the inter-temporal law relevant to the question of British responsibility. At that time, moreover, international law did not recognise any notion of obligations *erga omnes* (or obligations owed to the international community as a whole to employ the phrase used by the International Law Commission in the 2001 Articles)[24] and, effectively, the right to invoke the responsibility of a State for its violation of an international obligation lay with the State or States to whom that obligation was owed.[25]

To engage a State's responsibility, the delictual conduct must be attributable, or imputable, to that State. Article 2 of the International Law Commission's 2001 Articles formulates this principle as follows. There is an internationally wrongful act of a State when conduct consisting of an action or omission:

No final text was adopted by the Committee on Responsibility of States at the Hague Codification Conference because it became apparent that a two-thirds majority vote in favour of the Articles it had drafted could not be obtained. This was principally because of objections to an Article, which was nevertheless thought to reflect customary international law, imposing responsibility on States which had failed to take adequate measures to prevent or punish private individuals which caused injury to aliens – see Borchard, 1930, at p. 518 and pp. 535-538; and Hackworth, 1930, pp. 511-514.

21 For the International Law Commission's commentary on Article 1 of the 2001 Articles, see Crawford, 2002, at p. 77 *et seq.*

22 On the unanimous affirmation of this principle by the Committee on Responsibility of States at the Hague Codification Conference, see Borchard, 1930, at pp. 518-520; and Hackworth, 1930, at pp. 501-502, and pp. 501-505 generally.

23 See, for instance, *S.S. Wimbledon*, PCIJ Ser.A, No.1 (1923) 15 at 30; *Chorzów factory* case: *preliminary objections judgment*, PCIJ, Ser.A, No.9 (1927) 21; *Chorzów factory* case: *merits judgment*, PCIJ, Ser.A, No.17 (1928) 29; *Phosphates in Morocco* case: *preliminary objections judgment*, PCIJ, Ser.A/B, No.74 (1938) 10.

24 This is subject to the possible exception of general international servitudes, such as the internationalisation of the Kiel Canal, the implications of which were in issue in the *Wimbledon* case: see, in particular, the dissenting opinion of Judge Schücking, *Wimbledon* case: *merits judgment*, PCIJ, Ser.A, No.1 (1923), 15 at 43. It should be noted that servitudes need not be to the benefit of the entire international community but can be limited in effect to a single or restricted group of States: see, for instance, the *German railway station at Basle* case (1928), 4 Annual Digest, pp. 136-138, and also the *Canton of Thurgau v. Canton of St Gallen* case, 4 Annual Digest 420 at 420-421: but compare the dissenting opinion of Judge Moreno Quintana, *Right of passage over Indian territory* case: *merits judgment*, ICJ Reps, 1960, 6, 88 at 90.

25 As a measure of progressive development, Article 48 of the International Law Commission's 2001 Articles envisions the invocation of responsibility by an "interested" State, that is, a State not directly injured by the breach of an international obligation, in a circumscribed set of circumstances; for instance, if the obligation breached is owed to the international community as a whole, see Crawford, 2002, pp. 276 *et seq.*

    i. is attributable to the State under international law; and

    ii. constitutes a breach of an international obligation of the State.[26]

Again, this principle was recognised in the jurisprudence of the Permanent Court, and by other international tribunals, in the inter-war period.[27] The notion of attribution, or imputability, simply means that the conduct giving rise to the violation of an international obligation must have been committed by, or on behalf of, the delinquent State by its organs or officials.[28] Article 3 of the Harvard Draft contains a relevant formulation of the scope of attribution to the issue in hand:

> A State is not relieved of responsibility because an injury to an alien is attributable to one of its political subdivisions ... For the purposes of this article, a dominion, a colony, a dependency, a protectorate, *or a community under mandate*, which does not independently conduct its foreign relations, is to be assimilated to a political subdivision.[29]

The third principle relevant to the question of British responsibility for the creation of Palestinian refugees is that the breach of an obligation gives rise to a duty to make reparation. This was authoritatively enunciated by the Permanent Court of International Justice in the *Chorzów factory* litigation in the 1920s. In the preliminary objections judgment, the Court proclaimed this basic duty:

> It is a principle of international law that the breach of an engagement involves an obligation to make reparation in an adequate form. Reparation therefore is the indispensable complement of a failure to apply a convention and there is no necessity for this to be stated in the convention itself.[30]

---

26 For commentary, see Crawford, 2002, p. 81 *et seq.*

27 For instance, see the *Phosphates in Morocco* case: *preliminary objections judgment*, PCIJ, Ser.A/B, No.74 at 28, and the award of the Mexico-United States General Claims Commission in the *Dickson Car Wheel Company case* (1931), 4 Reports of International Arbitral Awards 669 at p. 678. See also Brownlie, 1983, pp. 36-37.

28 For an exposition of the "standard" attribution to a State of the acts of its organs and officials, see Brownlie 1983 Chapter VII. In certain circumstances, States may also be responsible for the acts of private individuals, but given the broad question in issue here, this question need not detain us, apart from recalling the terms of Article 13.b of the Harvard Draft. This provided: "In the event of a successful revolution, the state whose government is established thereby is responsible ... if an injury to an alien has resulted from a wrongful act or omission of the revolutionists committed at any time after the inception of the revolution."

    As noted above, the efforts of the Hague Codification Conference failed because of disagreement regarding the State's responsibility for the acts of individuals, and the 1927 Institut de Droit International resolution expressly refused to take a position on responsibility for the acts of successful insurgents. Article VII provided, in part: "The question of the degree to which a State is responsible for acts of insurgents ... in case they have become the government of the country, is reserved."

29 Emphasis added. For commentary on this Article, which expressed customary international law, see 23 *American Journal of International Law*, Document Supplement 145 (1929); see also *Basis of Discussion 15, Point VI* placed before the Hague Codification Conference, 24 *American Journal of International Law*. Document Supplement 59-60 (1930); and compare Article IX of the 1927 Insitut de Droit International resolution, 22 *American Journal of International Law*. Document Supplement 331-332 (1928).

30 PCIJ, Ser.A, No.9 (1927) 21. This principle was also expressed in Article X of the 1927 Institut de Droit International resolution and in Article 1 of the 1929 Harvard Draft (for commentary, see 23 *American Journal of International Law*. Document Supplement 140-142 (1929).

In the subsequent merits phase of this case, the Court elaborated the content
of the obligation to make reparation:

> The essential principle contained in the actual notion of an illegal act – a principle
> which seems to be established by international practice and in particular by the
> decisions of arbitral tribunals – is that reparation must, so far as possible, wipe out all
> the consequences of the illegal act and reestablish the situation which would, in all
> probability, have existed if that act had not been committed. Restitution in kind, or,
> if this is not possible, payment of a sum corresponding to the value which a restitution
> in kind would bear; the award, if need be, of damages for loss sustained which would
> not be covered by restitution in kind or payment in place of it – such are the principles
> which should serve to determine the amount of compensation due for an act contrary
> to international law.[31]

These are the basic principles which should be applied as a matter of inter-
temporal law to determine whether Britain was responsible, in whole or in
part, for the creation of the Palestinian refugee situation. The first question
that accordingly arises is, what were the international obligations that might
Britain have breached which would have engaged its responsibility?

1.4 Probable attitude of the United Kingdom

It is sensible to assume that the United Kingdom would deny that it bore any
responsibility under international law for the creation of Palestinian refugees.
It would presumably argue that, in 1948, it was under no duty under
international law to prevent the creation of a refugee problem and that there
then existed no prohibition on population transfers. On the contrary, the
United Kingdom could well argue that post-conflict population transfers were
a recognised method of dealing with potential national or ethnic problems.

Further, the United Kingdom would probably claim that the Mandate had
been terminated and it had withdrawn from Palestine at the time the refugee
question arose. Accordingly, as it no longer had any legal obligations in regard
to the territory, how could its responsibility be engaged?

Finally, the United Kingdom would undoubtedly argue that any obligations
it did owe in relation to Mandate Palestine were not owed to its inhabitants,
or to future States created in the territory of Mandate Palestine, but to the
League of Nations and its Member States. It has used this strategy before in
litigation bearing on territory over which it exercised powers of international
administration, namely, in the *Northern Cameroons* case before the International
Court of Justice in the early 1960s.

1.5 Population transfers and international law

To base its claim that the creation of displaced populations was not unlawful
under international law in 1948, the United Kingdom would undoubtedly
point to the expulsion of ethnic German populations from Eastern European
States after Word War II. At that time, the British Prime Minister, Winston
Churchill, stated:

---

31 PCIJ, Ser.A, No.17 (1928) 47.

The Palestine Question in International Law   109

Palestine Refugee Question. The Responsibility of Great Britain?   47

Expulsion is the method which, in so far as we have been able to see, will be the most satisfactory and lasting. There will be no mixture of populations to cause endless trouble. A clean sweep will be made.[32]

Exchange of populations, as the 1937 Peel Commission Report noted, was also the method used to soothe ethnic tensions between Greece and Turkey after World War I.[33] Further, in the inter-war period, a number of cases before the Permanent Court of International Justice bore directly upon questions arising from population transfers, but neither the States appearing before the Court, nor the Court itself, suggested that these were contrary to international law.[34] Regarding the political situation in Mandate Palestine, the Peel Commission Report observed:

The Arabs of Palestine, it has been admitted, are as fit to govern themselves as the Arabs of Iraq or Syria. The Jews of Palestine are as fit to govern themselves as any organised and educated community in Europe. Yet, associated as they are under the Mandate, self-government is impracticable for both peoples. The Mandate cannot be fully implemented nor can it honourably terminate in the independence of an undivided Palestine unless the conflict between Arab and Jew can be composed.[35]

The method suggested to resolve this conflict was population transfer as part of a Partition solution for Palestine – "If Partition is to be effective in promoting a final settlement it must mean more than drawing a frontier and establishing two States. Sooner or later there should be a transfer of land and, as far as possible, an exchange of population".[36] After examining the Peel Commission Report, the Permanent Mandates Commission of the League of Nations, which

---

32 Parliamentary Debates, House of Commons, 15 December 1944, quoted in Schechtman, J., *Postwar Population Transfers in Europe 1945-1955* (University of Pennsylvania Press, Philadelphia, 1962), p. 186.

33 See UK summary of the Peel Commission Report distributed to the League of Nations, League document C.495.M.336.1937.VI (30 November 1937), Chapter XXII, section 10, available on <http://domino.un.org/unispal.nsf> (the UN Information System on the Question of Palestine).

  The authoritative scholarly account of the post-World War I exchange of populations between Greece and Turkey, and the comparable exchange of minorities between Greece and Bulgaria, is Ladas, S., *The exchange of Minorities: Bulgaria, Greece and Turkey* (MacMillan, New York, 1932). These exchanges had been foreshadowed by population exchange agreements concluded in 1913 between Turkey and Bulgaria and in 1914 between Greece and Turkey – see Ladas, 1932, pp. 18-23. For an assessment of the legality of population transfers in the immediate post World War II period, see Fried JHE, "Transfer of civilian manpower from Occupied Territory", 40 *American Journal of International Law* 303 (1946) at pp. 304-305.

34 See, for instance, *Exchange of Greek and Turkish populations advisory opinion*, PCIJ Ser.B, No.10 (1925); see also *Expulsion of the Ecumenical Patriarch: Minute of the Court noting that the request for an advisory opinion was withdrawn*, PCIJ, Ser.C, Vol.9-II, 10 (1925); *German settlers in Poland advisory opinion*, PCIJ, Ser.B, No.6 (1923); *Greco-Bulgarian communities advisory opinion*, PCIJ, Ser.B, No.17 (1930); *Interpretation of the Bulgarian-Greek (Molloff-Caphandaris) Agreement of 9 December 1927 advisory opinion*, PCIJ, Ser.A/B, No.45 (1932); and *Polish agrarian reform and the German minority case: Order (interim protection) of 29 July 1933*, PCIJ, Ser.A/B, No.58 (1933) – proceedings terminated due to Germany's withdrawal from the League of Nations, see *Order (termination) of 2 December 1933*, PCIJ, Ser.A/B, No.60 (1933).

35 UK summary of the Peel Commission Report, Chapter XVIII.

36 UK summary of the Peel Commission Report, Chapter XXII, section 10.

supervised the Mandates system,[37] declared that it was favourable in principle to examining a solution involving partition, but was opposed to the immediate creation of two new independent States.[38]

It could, of course, be counter-argued that mass deportations or population transfers were condemned as criminal by the 1945 London Charter which established the International Military Tribunal at Nuremberg. Article 6.b defined war crimes as 'violations of the laws and customs of war' which included "deportation to slave labour or for any other purpose of civilian population of or in occupied territory", while Article 6.c specified that the deportation of "any civilian population" constituted a crime against humanity. The Tribunal ruled that deportations were illegal, which is perhaps not surprising as it admitted that it was bound by the definitions of crimes against humanity and war crimes set out in the London Charter.[39] In the aftermath of the Nuremberg judgment, the Diplomatic Conference convened to draft the Geneva Conventions of 1949 unanimously agreed on the insertion of Article 49 into Convention IV, on the protection of civilian populations in time of war. Article 49.1 provides:

> Individual or mass forcible transfers, as well as deportations of protected persons from occupied territory to the territory of the Occupying Power or to that of any other country, occupied or not, are prohibited, regardless of their motive.[40]

The International Committee of the Red Cross's commentary to Article 49.1 notes that the 1907 Hague Regulations, which were held by the Nuremberg Tribunal to embody customary international law,[41] had not referred to

---

37 The final paragraph of Article 22 of the Covenant of the League of Nations made provision for the Permanent Mandates Commission, stating: "A permanent Commission shall be constituted to receive and examine the annual reports of the Mandatories and to advise the [League] Council on all matters relating to the observance of the mandates."

38 See U.N. Division for Palestinian Rights, *The origins and evolution of the Palestine problem: 1917-1988*, text to note 119: available on <http://domino.un.org/unispal.nsf>. See, generally, Section VIII of this report, which is entitled *Palestine and the League of Nations*.

39 See the *Trial of the Major German War Criminals* (1946) 41 *American Journal of International Law* 172 (1947): Article 6 of the London Charter is reproduced at pp. 174-75; the Tribunal ruled that it was bound by the terms of the Charter at pp. 175, 216 and 248; and it discussed deportation for the purpose of slave labour at pp. 239-243. On Germany's deportation policy during World War II, see Fried 1946 312-315. He also argues that the deportation of civilians from territories falling under the régime of belligerent occupation, as this is defined in Article 42 of the 1907 Hague Regulations – namely territory "actually placed under the authority of the hostile army" – was unlawful from at least the early 20th century, see Fried 1946 305 *et seq.*

40 Article 147 of the Fourth Convention further provides that a violation of Article 49.1 is a grave breach of the Convention. Under Article 146, each High Contracting Party is:
under the obligation to search for persons alleged to have committed, or to have ordered to be committed, such grave breaches, and shall bring such persons, regardless of their nationality, before its own courts. It may also, if it prefers, and in accordance with the provisions of its own legislation, hand such persons over for trial to another High Contracting Party concerned, provided that such High Contracting Party has made out a *prima facie* case.

41 This position was first set out in the *Cessation of vessels and tugs for navigation on the Danube* case, 1 Reports of International Arbitral Awards 83 (1921) at 104, and authoritatively endorsed by the International Military Tribunal at Nuremberg in the *Trial of the German major war criminals*, 41 *American Journal of International Law* 172 (1947) at pp. 248-249. As far as Israeli law is concerned, the Nuremberg ruling was expressly endorsed by then-President Shamgar of the Israel High Court in *Affo v. IDF Commander in the West Bank*, 83 International Law Reports 122 at p. 163.

The Palestine Question in International Law 111

Palestine Refugee Question. The Responsibility of Great Britain? 49

deportations, because the practice was then thought to be "so alien to modern warfare that it was not even discussed at the Hague Conferences".[42] World War II, however, made it necessary to include an express provision prohibiting deportations "which may be regarded today as having been embodied in international law".[43]

The United Kingdom would, however, respond that any rules of international humanitarian law which prohibited deportations at the end of World War II were irrelevant to any consideration of its legal responsibility for the creation of the Palestinian refugee question simply because Mandate Palestine was not occupied territory. Rather, by concluding the Mandate agreement, the League of Nations had granted Great Britain the right to administer Palestine on behalf of the League, pursuant to Article 22 of the Covenant of the League of Nations.[44] Moreover, at the relevant time, Great Britain was not involved in any international armed conflict on that territory, and thus there could be no question of its responsibility being engaged on the basis of war crimes, crimes against humanity, or grave breaches of the Fourth Geneva Convention. Finally, the United Kingdom would undoubtedly observe that the Fourth Geneva Convention was concluded after the refugee question arose, and only entered into force on 21 October 1950.[45] Accordingly, consideration of the provisions of this instrument was irrelevant as these could not form part of the applicable inter-temporal law.

1.6 What obligations did Britain bear for Mandate Palestine?

As has been indicated, Britain would argue that there existed no international obligation upon States to prevent population displacement in 1948, and also that when the Palestinian refugee question was created it had withdrawn from Mandate Palestine and could no longer be legally responsible for matters arising in that territory. Accordingly, any examination of British responsibility must concentrate on the period during which Britain was in lawful control of Mandate Palestine and, in particular, focus upon whether Britain discharged its obligations under the Mandate for Palestine in such a way that it did not contribute to the subsequent creation of Palestinian refugees. This, *ex facie*, would require an examination of whether Britain properly fulfilled its obligations under Articles 2, 6, and 17 of the Mandate, but it must be remembered that one function of the Mandate was to implement the Balfour Declaration. The second preambular paragraph of the Mandate stated:

---

42 See Fried, 1946, pp. 307-308: quotation at p. 307.

43 Pictet, J. (Ed), *Commentary to the Fourth Geneva Convention Relative to the Protection of Civilian Persons in Time of War* (ICRC, Geneva, 1958), p. 279.

44 On this distinction, see Greenwood, G, "The administration of occupied territory in international law", in Playfair, E. (Ed), *International law and the administration of occupied territories* (Clarendon Press: Oxford: 1992) 241 at 250-251.

45 See the Swiss Government's website at <http://www.eda.admin.ch/eda/f/home/foreign/intagr/train/iprotection.Par.0003.UpFile.pdf/mt_040602_genf49_f.pdf>.

Whereas the Principal Allied Powers have also agreed that the Mandatory should be responsible for putting into effect the declaration originally made on November 2nd, 1917, by the Government of His Britannic Majesty, and adopted by the said Powers, in favour of the establishment in Palestine of a national home for the Jewish people, it being clearly understood that nothing should be done which might prejudice the civil and religious rights of existing non-Jewish communities in Palestine, or the rights and political status enjoyed by Jews in any other country.

This perceived need to draw a balance between Jewish and non-Jewish interests in Palestine was expressed in other Articles of the Mandate, thus Article 2 provided:

The Mandatory shall be responsible for placing the country under such political, administrative and economic conditions as will secure the establishment of the Jewish national home, as laid down in the preamble, and the development of self-governing institutions, and also for safeguarding the civil and religious rights of all the inhabitants of Palestine, irrespective of race and religion.

Similarly, Article 6 also provided that a balance should be maintained:

The Administration of Palestine, while ensuring that the rights and position of other sections of the population are not prejudiced, shall facilitate Jewish immigration under suitable conditions and shall encourage ... close settlement by Jews on the land...

Article 17 provided, in part:

The Administration of Palestine may organise on a voluntary basis the forces necessary for the preservation of peace and order, and also for the defence of the country, subject, however, to the supervision of the Mandatory...

These obligations were, of course, subject to the over-riding requirement of Article 22 of the Covenant of the League of Nations that, to the populations of Mandated territories, "there should be applied the principle that the well-being and development of such peoples form a sacred trust of civilisation". In this connection, it should be remembered that in paragraph 88 of the advisory opinion on the *Legal consequences of the construction of a wall in the Occupied Palestinian Territories*, the International Court re-affirmed:

that in 1971 it emphasized that current developments in "international law in regard to non-self-governing territories, as enshrined in the Charter of the United Nations, made the principle of self -determination applicable to all [such territories]". The Court went on to state that "These developments leave little doubt that the ultimate objective of the sacred trust" referred to in Article 22, paragraph 1, of the Covenant of the League of Nations "was the self -determination ... of the peoples concerned" (*Legal Consequences for States of the Continued Presence of South Africa in Namibia (South West Africa) notwithstanding Security Council Resolution 276 (1970), Advisory Opinion, I.C.J. Reports 1971*, p. 31, paras. 52 -53).[46]

To assess whether Britain bears any responsibility under international law for the creation of the Palestinian refugee question, it must be determined not only whether it struck a correct balance between the interests of the different sectors of the Mandate Palestine population, as it was required to do under

---

46 43 International Legal Materials 1009 (2004) at 1034.

The Palestine Question in International Law   113

Palestine Refugee Question. The Responsibility of Great Britain?   51

the Mandate, but also whether it properly maintained order in the territory so that the Palestinian population was not prejudiced. Did it properly fulfil its obligation to ensure that the civil rights of all inhabitants of Palestine were safeguarded? – in other words, did Britain administer the territory in such a way that the seeds of the subsequent population displacement were not planted during its administration?

It cannot be denied that the ethnic population balance and patterns of land ownership and land use drastically changed during the duration of the Mandate over Palestine. This could perhaps be seen as contributing at least indirectly to the creation of the refugee question, but it is probable that the United Kingdom would argue that these changes did not breach the Mandate but were in fact required by it. For instance, the United Kingdom would point to its duty to facilitate Jewish immigration under the terms of Article 6 of the Mandate.

To this it could be counter-argued that Great Britain had failed to observe the other requirements of Article 6, that "the rights and position of other sections of the population" were not prejudiced by Jewish immigration, or that immigration had not been undertaken "under suitable conditions". If Britain's regulation of Jewish immigration could be shown to be in breach of Article 6, and perhaps also linked to a demonstration that it had failed to exercise due diligence to maintain proper order in the territory, then this might provide the basis of a claim that Britain had acted in breach of the Mandate which, *prima facie*, would give rise to its responsibility for the creation of the Palestinian refugee question.

This, however, raises the question, to whom did Britain owe the obligations it assumed under the Mandate? Who could invoke Britain's responsibility and hold it accountable for any breach of the terms of the Mandate?

1.7 To whom were Britain's obligations owed?

Even if it were established that Britain did not discharge its duties under the Mandate properly, and that it violated its obligations towards the non-Jewish population of the territory, it would undoubtedly defend itself by arguing that it owed no responsibility towards that population but only towards the League of Nations, as preambular paragraph 6 of the Mandate provides:

> Whereas His Britannic Majesty has accepted the mandate in respect of Palestine and undertaken to exercise it on behalf of the League of Nations in conformity with the following provisions;

Further, the United Kingdom could argue that this had been recognised by the League's Permanent Mandate Commission in 1936, which had affirmed:

> The mandate defines the obligations assumed by the Mandatory Power towards the League of Nations, on whose behalf the territory is administered. These obligations themselves are derived from the Balfour Declaration of 2 November 1917, and from the provisions of Article 22 of the Covenant, to which the United Kingdom Government, in accepting the mandate, undertook to give effect.[47]

---

47 U.N. Division for Palestinian Rights, *The origins and evolution of the Palestine problem: 1917-1988*, text to note 118.

The United Kingdom might argue that because the League of Nations did not complain about its administration of Mandate Palestine, not only does this indicate that no breach giving rise to international responsibility had occurred, but also that no one else has the right to complain. The duty in question was owed exclusively to the League of Nations, and thus no other entity has the right to try to enforce the provisions of the Mandate or allege breach.

The United Kingdom has previously employed this argument in relation to its administration of territory placed under its control by international organisations – namely, in relation to Northern Cameroons which it held first under a Mandate, which was then converted to a Trust Territory after the demise of the League of Nations and the creation of the United Nations.

When Northern Cameroons was joined to Nigeria for the purpose of independence, Cameroun complained that Britain's administration of the territory had prevented the free expression of the population of Northern Cameroons for the purposes of self-determination. Cameroun thought that this should have resulted in Northern Cameroons being assigned to it, and not Nigeria. It raised proceedings before the International Court of Justice seeking a judgment that Britain had violated it obligations under its Trusteeship Agreement with the United Nations by virtue of its maladministration.

The *Northern Cameroons* case[48] was intertwined with the concurrent *South West Africa* litigation,[49] given the virtual identity of the *compromis* involved in each. The jurisdictional title employed in the *South West Africa* cases was Article 7.2 of the Mandate for South West Africa, which provided:

> The Mandatory agrees that, if any dispute whatever should arise between the Mandatory and another Member of the League of Nations relating to the interpretation or the application of the provisions of the Mandate, such dispute, if it cannot be settled by negotiation, shall be submitted to the Permanent Court of International Justice provided for by Article 14 of the Covenant of the League of Nations.[50]

Article 12.1 of the Mandate for Northern Cameroons had been cast in identical terms,[51] but by the time the complaint in the *Northern Cameroons* case was filed, this Article had been replaced by Article 19 of the Trusteeship Agreement, which provided:

> If any dispute whatever should arise between the Administering Authority and another Member of the United Nations relating to the interpretation or application of the provisions of this Agreement, such dispute, if it cannot be settled by negotiation or other means, shall be submitted to the International Court of Justice provided for in Chapter XIV of the United Nations Charter.[52]

---

48 ICJ Reps, 1963, 15.
49 ICJ Reps, 1962, 319; and ICJ Reps, 1966, 6.
50 *South West Africa* Pleadings, vol.I, 201 at p. 202.
51 See *Northern Cameroons* Pleadings 114 at p. 117.
52 *Northern Cameroons* Pleadings 87 at pp. 91-92.

The application initiating proceedings before the International Court in the *Northern Cameroons* case was filed by Cameroun on 30 May 1961;[53] the judgment in the *1962 South West Africa* cases was delivered on 21 December 1962. The United Kingdom's counter-memorial in *Northern Cameroons* was dated 14 August 1962,[54] and thus could not take account of that judgment, whereas the Cameroun's written observations, which examined the preliminary objections against the Court's jurisdiction raised by the United Kingdom, were filed on 27 June 1963.[55] Cameroun's observations relied heavily on the Court's rulings in the 1962 *South West Africa* judgment.

Cameroun had complained that the United Kingdom had breached Articles 3, 5, 6 and 7 of the Trusteeship Agreement[56] which dealt with the administration of the territory. This complaint was analogous to the allegations made by Liberia and Ethiopia against South Africa in the *South West Africa* proceedings. For instance, Cameroun's claim that Article 3 of the Trusteeship Agreement was equivalent to Liberia and Ethiopia's allegation that South Africa had breached the "sacred trust" embodied in the Mandate, as Article 3 provided:

> The Administering Authority undertakes to administer the territory in such a manner as to achieve the basic objectives of the international trusteeship system laid down in Article 76 of the United Nations Charter ...[57]

In its written observations on the United Kingdom's preliminary objections, Cameroun addressed the objection that Article 19 of the Trusteeship Agreement did not allow another U.N. member to implead the United Kingdom before the International Court regarding the conduct of its administration of Northern Cameroons, as this was only intended to allow judicial recourse by individual members regarding obligations specifically assumed in relation to other U.N. members and their nationals in Articles 9-13.[58] Cameroun stated that this question had been argued in detail in the *South West Africa* proceedings, and that the 1962 judgment was of great importance in the instant proceedings as the United Kingdom's argument was essentially that advanced by South Africa.[59] Cameroun emphasised the similarity between the *compromis* invoked in both cases, and between the Mandate and Trusteeship systems.[60]

The core of Cameroun's argument was that the *1962 South West Africa* judgment drew a distinction between administrative supervision by the League, and judicial supervision by the Court at the instance of any League member.[61] It claimed that the Mandate and Trusteeship systems on the points in issue in the *Northern Cameroons* proceedings were such that the transposition of principles from one to the other was apparent.[62] Cameroun continued that

---

53 See *Northern Cameroons* case, ICJ Reps, 1963, p. 17.
54 *Northern Cameroons* Pleadings, p. 54.
55 *Northern Cameroons* Pleadings, p. 185.
56 *Northern Cameroons* Pleadings 197, p. 206.
57 Reproduced *Northern Cameroons* Pleadings, p. 88.
58 *Northern Cameroons* Pleadings 59, 61-62, 287-289, 303 and 385: see also 308, 393-396 and 398.
59 *Northern Cameroons* Pleadings, pp. 198-199, 206 and 346.
60 *Northern Cameroons* Pleadings, pp. 199-203.
61 On this distinction, see ICJ Reps, 1962, pp. 336 and 344.
62 *Northern Cameroons* Pleadings, 200-201, pp. 204, 346, 348-349 and 366.

just as judicial protection was the ultimate protection against violations of the Mandate System,[63] so it was for the Trusteeship, because the political nature of General Assembly supervision could sacrifice legal rights in pursuit of political expediency.[64]

On this basis, Cameroun concluded that it was entitled to submit to the Court a dispute concerning the way in which the United Kingdom had discharged its obligations under the Trusteeship Agreement, and that no distinction could be drawn between its various provisions. As a U.N. member, Cameroun claimed that it had a legal interest with regard to the trusteeship system as a whole. Accordingly, it could appear before the Court even though it claimed no particular actual or tangible interests in issue.[65] Cameroun, however, conceded that it could be objected that it did not defend interests different from those which could be espoused by any other State, but noted that the Court had not yet ruled in the *South West Africa* proceedings with the argument that:

> behind the present dispute [between Liberia and Ethiopia and South Africa] there is another and similar disagreement ... between the respondent on the one hand, and the other Members of the United Nations, holding identical views with the applicants, on the other.[66]

The United Kingdom declared this dichotomy between administrative and judicial supervision to be irrelevant because United Nations political organs took all aspects, including the legal aspects, into account when dealing with a dispute.[67] From the outset, the United Kingdom had argued that, as Administering Authority of the Trust Territory of Northern Cameroons, it was not the proper destination of complaints made by Cameroun regarding the administration and supervision of the Territory. Rather, by virtue of Article 75 of the Charter, responsibility for administration and supervision lay with the United Nations which was the proper forum for members' complaints.[68] Further it argued that Cameroun was simply attempting to re-open a question which had been settled by the General Assembly and thus have that action judicially reviewed. The core of this argument was that if individual United Nations members were capable of utilising the Court in this way, then this would disrupt the finality of decisions taken by the General Assembly.[69]

There can be little doubt that the United Kingdom would make a similar argument should its responsibility be invoked for the creation of Palestinian refugees. It would argue that any obligations it owed under the Mandate were owed to the League of Nations, which had supervised its administration of the territory, and which had not called it to account for its administration of

63 Relying on *South West Africa* cases, 1962 ICJ Repts, p. 336.
64 *Northern Cameroons* Pleadings 191, pp. 200, 204-206, 209, 228, 342-343 and 351-366.
65 *Northern Cameroons* Pleadings, pp. 202 and 207; see also pp. 343-346.
66 Quoted in *Northern Cameroons* Pleadings 204 from ICJ Reps, 1962, 345; see also *Northern Cameroons* Pleadings, pp. 332-333 and pp. 412-413.
67 Pleadings, p. 378.
68 See Pleadings, pp. 56-57, 61-62 and 287-288.
69 See Pleadings, pp. 59-60, 62-63, 284, 293, 375, 395 and 399.

The Palestine Question in International Law   117

Palestine Refugee Question. The Responsibility of Great Britain?   55

the territory. Accordingly, its obligations had been fully discharged under the Mandate and the question could not be re-opened.

It is possible, however, that this argument might not prevail. A subsequent case appears to open the possibility that a former Mandated territory, which has become an independent State, may raise proceedings before the International Court against the Mandatory Power for breach of the provisions of the Mandate. On 19 May 1989, Nauru filed an application instituting proceedings against Australia before the International Court. It alleged that Australia had breached the trusteeship obligations it had accepted in relation to Nauru under Article 76 of the United Nations Charter and under Articles 3 and 5 of the Trusteeship Agreement, as well as obligations owed under general international law, by failing to rehabilitate land from which phosphate was extracted before Nauru achieved independence in 1968. Australia was not the sole trustee of Nauru. Article 2 of the Trusteeship Agreement provided:

> The Governments of Australia, New Zealand and the United Kingdom (hereinafter the "Administering Authority") are hereby designated as the joint Authority which will exercise the administration of the Territory.[70]

This mirrored the arrangements made in the tripartite 1919 Nauru Island Agreement which was concluded between these States to regulate the implementation of the Mandate granted over Nauru by the League of Nations in favour of "His Britannic Majesty". Nauru achieved independence on 31 January 1968.

On 19 September 1990, Australia filed preliminary objections against both the Court's jurisdiction and the admissibility of the claim. In its preliminary objections judgment of 26 June 1992,[71] the International Court ruled that the case was admissible and that it had jurisdiction to hear the merits of Nauru's claim.

Two of the Australian objections are relevant to the question in hand. One alleged that the Nauran Local Government Council had waived its rehabilitation claim before independence. The Court disposed of this by reference to the facts, finding that no clear and unequivocal waiver had been made. It expressly abstained from examining the legal issues implicit in this argument – in particular whether any pre-independence waiver by Nauruan authorities would be opposable to the Republic of Nauru.[72] Judge Oda, the sole dissenter on this point,[73] employed precisely the same materials to reach a diametrically opposed conclusion.

The judgment also rejected the Australian objection that the Nauruan claim was inadmissible because termination of the Trusteeship precluded allegations of breaches of the Trusteeship Agreement being examined by the Court.

---

70 The Trusteeship system was the mechanism which the United Nations adopted to replace the Mandate system after the dissolution of the League of Nations. Article 77.1.a of the United Nations Charter provides: "The trusteeship system shall apply to such territories in the following categories as may be placed thereunder by means of trusteeship agreements: a. territories now held under mandate;..."

71 *Certain phosphate lands in Nauru* case: *preliminary objections judgment,* ICJ Reps, 1992, 240.

72 ICJ Reps, 1992, p. 247, para.13.

73 See the dissenting opinion of Judge Oda, ICJ Reps, 1992, 303 at pp. 304-311, paras. 5-13.

Australia claimed that in the absence of an express finding at the time of termination that a breach of the trusteeship by the Administering Authority subsisted, termination operated as a complete discharge for the Administering Authority from all further responsibility. Nauru could not ask the Court to review the performance of the Trusteeship to overrule and contradict the conclusions reached and decisions taken by the competent United Nations organs in their supervision of the Trusteeship Agreement.

Following the *Northern Cameroons* case, the Court noted that General Assembly resolution 2347(XXII), 19 December, had "definitive legal effect" in terminating the Trusteeship over Nauru.[74] Conceding that this might open the possibility that the application was inadmissible, the Court then proceeded to reserve the question of principle:

> the Court does not consider it necessary to enter into this debate and will confine itself to examining the particular circumstances in which the Trusteeship for Nauru was terminated.[75]

The Court established that the question of rehabilitation had been raised in competent United Nations bodies, and that General Assembly resolutions had directed the Administering Authority to rehabilitate the island.[76] Although resolution 2347 contained no express provision on rehabilitation, its preamble recalled the earlier resolutions.[77] Further, the Court found that when the Trusteeship was terminated, "everyone was aware of subsisting differences of opinion" between the Nauruan representatives and the Administering Authority regarding rehabilitation. Therefore, although resolution 2347 was silent on rehabilitation, "the Court cannot view that resolution as giving a discharge to the Administering Authority with respect to such rights" and, by 12 votes to one, rejected the objection.[78] Again Judge Oda was the lone dissenter on this point, and again he employed the same materials used by the Court to reach the opposite conclusion.[79]

The International Court did not adjudicate on the merits of the *Certain Phosphate lands in Nauru* case. The proceedings were discontinued by the agreement of the parties[80] after the preliminary objection judgment as Australia entered into a compensation agreement with Nauru.[81] Article 3 of this Agreement provided in part:

---

74 ICJ Reps, 1992, p. 251, para. 23, relying on *Northern Cameroons*, ICJ Reps, 1963, p. 15 at 32.
75 ICJ Reps, 1992, p. 251, para. 23.
76 See ICJ Reps, 1992, 251-253, paras. 24-28; this direction was contained in General Assembly resolutions 2111(XX)(21 December 1965) and 2226(XXI)(20 December 1966).
77 ICJ Reps, 1992, p. 253, para. 29.
78 ICJ Reps, 1992, p. 53, para. 30.
79 See the dissenting opinion of Judge Oda, ICJ Reps, 1992, pp. 312-322, paras. 14-25.
80 See *Order (discontinuance of proceedings), 13 September 1993*, ICJ Reps, 1993, p. 322.
81 10 August 1993 Agreement between Australia and the Republic of Nauru for the Settlement of the Case in the International Court of Justice concerning Certain Phosphate Lands in Nauru, available at <http://www.austlii.edu.au/au/other/dfat/treaties/1993/26.html>, and also 32 International Legal Materials 1471 (1993).

The Palestine Question in International Law   119

Palestine Refugee Question. The Responsibility of Great Britain?   57

> The Republic of Nauru agrees that it shall make no claim whatsoever, whether in the International Court of Justice or otherwise, against all or any of Australia, the United Kingdom of Great Britain and Northern Ireland and New Zealand, their servants or agents arising out of or concerning the administration of Nauru during the period of the Mandate or Trusteeship or the termination of that administration ...

Subsequently it was reported that Australia sought contributions in respect of the compensation paid to Nauru from the United Kingdom and New Zealand, because they were co-administrators of Nauru during the Trusteeship and Mandate periods.[82]

Accordingly, the *Certain Phosphate lands in Nauru* proceedings indicate that it may be possible for territories formerly under a Mandate to raise an action against the former Mandatory Power for breach of the terms of the Mandate. As indicated above, however, in relation to the creation of the Palestinian refugee question, the United Kingdom might well argue that it had fulfilled rather than breached the terms of the Mandate.

1.8 Balfour Declaration

As a final consideration, even if it were assumed that Great Britain did not breach the terms of the Mandate, does it not bear legal responsibility for the root cause of the Palestinian refugee question, namely its promulgation of the Balfour Declaration on 2 November 1917? This provided:

> His Majesty's Government view with favour the establishment in Palestine of a national home for the Jewish people, and will use their best endeavours to facilitate the achievement of the object, it being clearly understood that nothing shall be done which may prejudice the civil and religious' rights of existing non-Jewish communities in Palestine, or the rights and political status enjoyed by Jews in any other country.[83]

It must be doubted whether the Balfour Declaration provides a solid basis for ascribing legal responsibility to Great Britain for the creation of the Palestinian refugee question. In the first place, it was a non-binding instrument expressing only a statement of policy. It contained no legal undertaking to "create a national home for the Jewish people". As such, it is difficult to see what rule of international law could have been breached by promulgation of the Declaration in 1917. In the second place, the Balfour Declaration only gained legal force when it was embodied in preambular paragraph 2 of the Mandate for Palestine. Only at that point did Great Britain assume a legal obligation to implement the Declaration, but this was a duty imposed on it by, and owed to, the League of Nations. Even then any obligation imposed was legally weak, as it was not cast in imperative terms. It was only required that Great Britain "*should* be responsible for putting into effect the [Balfour] declaration".[84]

---

82 See the introductory note to the 1993 Australia-Nauru Agreement, *32 International Legal Materials* 1471 (1993) at 1472.

83 The text of the declaration is available on the U.N. Information System on the Question of Palestine, <http://domino.un.org/unispal.nsf>.

84 Emphasis added.

Further, the 1939 MacDonald White Paper, which was the last major British policy statement on Palestine issued before World War II, made clear that the British government thought that the extent of this obligation was circumscribed by the terms of the Mandate. The White Paper observed:

> His Majesty's Government believe that the framers of the Mandate in which the Balfour Declaration was embodied could not have intended that Palestine should be converted into a Jewish State against the will of the Arab population of the country
>
> ...
>
> His Majesty's Government therefore now declare unequivocally that it is not part of their policy that Palestine should become a Jewish State. They would indeed regard it as contrary to their obligations to the Arabs under the Mandate, as well as to the assurances which have been given to the Arab people in the past, that the Arab population of Palestine should be made the subjects of a Jewish State against their will.[85]

2 FUTURE PROSPECTS

It is to be expected that the United Kingdom would argue that, legally, it bears no responsibility for the creation of the Palestinian refugee question. It should be acknowledged that the United Kingdom could deploy some substantive arguments in its favour. Further, should the question be referred to international adjudication, whether before the International Court of Justice or some other international tribunal, the United Kingdom should be expected to raise objections in an attempt to prevent the court from deciding the case. On the other hand, the *Certain Phosphate lands in Nauru* proceedings perhaps indicate that former Mandatory Powers might be willing to provide compensation for events that occurred during their international administration of territory. The terms of the *Phosphate lands* settlement are worth noting. Article 1 of the 1993 Australia-Naura Agreement expressly stated that this was "without prejudice to Australia's long-standing position that it bears no responsibility for the rehabilitation of the phosphate lands". Formally, this marks a shift from legal discourse to a recognition of moral or political responsibility for past events. Non-legal avenues for redress provide less determinate solutions than the ascription of responsibility under international law, but nonetheless are important and should also be pursued.

---

85 Quoted U.N. Division for Palestinian Rights, *The origins and evolution of the Palestine problem, 1917-1988*, text to note 109.

Nordic Journal of International Law **74**: 67–102, 2005.
© 2005 *Koninklijke Brill NV. Printed in the Netherlands.*

The Nationality of Denationalized Palestinians

VICTOR KATTAN*

Abstract. One in three refugees in the world today is Palestinian. The majority of these refugees have no nationality because they were denationalised by Israel's Nationality Law in 1952 after they had fled or been expelled from their homeland in 1948. Israel has refused to allow the majority Palestinian refugees, being displaced in 1948, the right to return to their homes in contravention of U.N. General Assembly Resolution 194 (III). Israel has also refused to allow the majority of Palestinians displaced in 1967 the right to return to their homes despite appeals from the International Committee of the Red Cross and despite calls from the UN Security Council. Since then Israel has manipulated the laws of occupation by transferring its civilian population into the territory it occupies whilst subjecting the indigenous Palestinian population to military law. In 2003, Israel enacted racially discriminatory legislation in the form of the Nationality and Entrance into Israel Law which the U.N. Human Rights Committee has specifically requested Israel revoke. This legislation restricts nationality and residency rights for Arabs resident in the Occupied Palestinian Territories whilst specifically excluding Jewish settlers from its application. These are some examples of the lengths to which the State of Israel is prepared to go – in order to maintain a Jewish majority in the country – even if they violate international law. This paper will examine whether the forced displacement and denationalization of Palestine's original non-Jewish inhabitants – including an examination of Israel's Nationality and Entrance into Israel Law (2003) – are compatible with the basic principles of international law today.

1. Introduction

In 1948, the year of the Palestinian *Nakbah*,[1] Hersch Lauterpacht wrote an article entitled the "Nationality of Denationalized Persons".[2] His article was about the former Jewish citizens of Germany denationalized by the National Socialist

---

* LL.B (Hons.) Brunel University and LL.M Leiden University is a member of Badil's Global Legal Support Network. The U.N. Development Program of Assistance to the Palestinian People (PAPP) funded his research work at the Badil Resource Center for Palestinian Residency and Refugee Rights (<www.badil.org>) in Bethlehem from May–August 2003 and from November–February 2004 where he carried out research at the Hebrew University of Jerusalem and at Birzeit University. He has also carried out research at the Peace Palace in The Hague, at the Institute for Advanced Legal Studies, at the School of Oriental and African Studies (SOAS) and at the Weiner Library in London.

[1] *Nakbah* means catastrophe in Arabic.
[2] *Jewish Yearbook of International Law* (1948) pp. 164–185.

Party in 1935 and in 1941.[3] Lauterpacht expressed concern about the effect of denationalization decrees on Jews who sought refuge in the United Kingdom, France, Switzerland and elsewhere.[4] In the 1930s and 1940s millions of Jewish immigrants fled the *Shoah*[5] for Palestine as the doors to Great Britain and the United States were shut to them.[6] This paper is about the nationality of the former Arab citizens of the British Mandate of Palestine who just like their Jewish counterparts were denationalized but under different circumstances.

During the British mandate (1922–1948) Palestine was not a sovereign nation.[7] The Treaty of Xvres, the Treaty of Lausanne, the Covenant of the League of Nations or the British mandate did not provide for sovereignty.[8] Sovereignty had been suspended. It had no application to mandated territory.[9] According to Judge McNair this is because sovereignty in mandated territory is in abeyance, "if and when the inhabitants of the Territory obtain recognition as an independent State . . . sovereignty will revive and vest in the new State".[10] Essentially what matters are the rights and duties of the mandatory power regarding the administration of territory rather than who has sovereignty.

The rights and duties of the mandatory in Palestine included responsibility for enacting a nationality law which included provisions to facilitate the acquisition of Palestinian citizenship by Jews who took up their permanent residence in Palestine.[11] Britain, however, was not the first power to facilitate Jewish

---

[3] *See* Dr. P. Weis 'The Undermining of the Nationality Concept by German Law' which is an extract from the author's unpublished study on 'The Legal Status of German and Austrian Refugees in Great Britain'. This is a Microfilm 454/75, 15 February, 1943. It can be viewed in the Wiener Library, 4 Devonshire Street, London W1W 6BH.

[4] Lauterpacht was particularly concerned about the effect of war time legislation in the UK which defined any German as an "enemy national" which included Jews denationalized by the National Socialist Party's racial purity laws.

[5] *Shoah* means catastrophe in Hebrew.

[6] For further reading *see* L. London, *Whitehall and the Jews 1933–1948 British Immigration Policy and the Holocaust* (Cambridge University Press, Cambridge, 2000); and D.S. Wyman, *The Abandonment of the Jews America and the Holocaust 1941–1945*, with a new introduction by E. Wiesel (Pantheon Books, New York, 1985).

[7] For arguments to the contrary *see* H. Cattan, *Palestine, The Arabs and Israel* (Longman, London, 1969) pp. 242–275.

[8] Although the Balfour Declaration was incorporated into the Treaty of Xvres in Article 95, the treaty made no mention of the transfer of sovereignty. *See* Part III Political Clauses, Treaty Series No. 11 (1920) signed at Xvres, August 10, 1920 (London: HMSO) p. 26. The Treaty of Peace with Turkey signed at Lausanne on 24 July 1923 made no reference to the establishment of the Jewish national home in Palestine. It also contained no provisions for the transfer of sovereignty. *See* The Treaty of Peace with Turkey signed at Lausanne, 24 July, 1923. *Treaties of Peace 1919 (1923, Vol. II)* (Carnegie Endowment for International Peace, New York, 1924).

[9] *See International Status of South West Africa*, ICJ Reports (1950) p. 150.

[10] *Ibid.*

[11] *See* Article 7 of the British mandate of Palestine. Reproduced in W. Laqueur, *The Israel/Arab Reader A Documentary History of the Middle East Conflict* (Weidenfeld & Nicolson, London, 1969) pp. 34–42.

immigration to Palestine and their subsequent naturalization as citizens: the Ottomans had also facilitated the immigration of Jews into Palestine.[12] Jews who became naturalized as Palestinian citizens had the same civil and political rights as Christian and Muslim Arab Palestinians, and other minorities.[13]

In 1947 the U.N. General Assembly proposed to partition Palestine to pave the way for two distinct States, one Arab, and the other Jewish, with Jerusalem established as a *Corpus Separatum*.[14] The Partition Resolution narrowly gained the required majority of two-thirds – 33 in favour, 13 opposed and 10 abstaining.[15] Britain, the mandatory power, abstained from the vote and the partition plan was never enforced.[16] The plan was referred to the U.N. Security Council but it too refused to enforce it.[17] Attempts were made by the Arab Higher

[12] The Ottomans agreed to grant special facilities to Jews wishing to become Ottoman subjects under Article 4 of the Ottoman Nationality Law, whereby the five years residence requirement could be waived in exceptional circumstances. *See* N.J. Mandel, *The Arabs and Zionism before World War 1* (University of California Press, Berkeley, 1976) pp. 171–172. This book is based on Mandel's 1965 Oxford Doctorate thesis entitled *Turks, Arabs and Jewish Immigration into Palestine: 1882–1914. See also* the Ottoman Law of Nationality, January 19, 1869, in R.W. Flournoy Jr. and M.O. Hudson (eds.), *A Collection of Nationality Laws of Various Countries as Contained in Constitutions, Statutes and Treaties* (Oxford University Press, New York, 1929) pp. 568–569.

[13] According to Article 8 of the Palestine Citizenship Order "[a] person to whom a certificate of naturalization is granted by the High Commissioner shall, subject to the provisions of this order, be entitled to all political and other rights, powers and privileges and be subject to all obligations, duties and liabilities to which a Palestinian citizen is entitled or subject". *See* R.H. Drayton, *The Laws of Palestine* Vol. III (Waterlow and Sons, London, 1934), and the *Official Gazette* 16 September 1925 pp. 460–478.

[14] *See* U.N. General Assembly Resolution No. 181 (II) of 29 November 1947 in G.J. Tomeh (ed.), *United Nations Resolutions on Palestine and the Arab-Israeli Conflict Volume One 1947–1974* (Institute for Palestine Studies, Washington D.C. 1988).

[15] Included in the countries that switched their votes between November 25 to November 29 to provide the two-thirds majority were Liberia, the Philippines, and Haiti. All heavily dependent on the United States financially, they had been lobbied to change their votes. *See* J. Quigley, *Palestine and Israel A Challenge to Justice* (Duke University Press, Durham, 1990) p. 37.

[16] The British Government had rejected the partition plan which had been proposed ten years earlier by the Peel Commission in 1937. "His Majesty's Government, after careful study of the Partition Commission's report, have reached the conclusion that this further examination has shown that the political, administrative and financial difficulties involved in the proposal to create independent Arab and Jewish States inside Palestine are so great that this solution of the problem is impracticable". British Statement of Policy November 1938. Reproduced in Laqueur, *The Israel/Arab, supra* note 11, pp. 62–63.

[17] Mr. Austin (USA): "From what has been said in the Security Council and in consultations among the several members of the Security Council, it is clear that the Security Council is not prepared to go ahead with efforts to implement this plan [the partition plan] in the existing situation. We had a vote on that subject, and only five votes could be secured for that purpose". Security Council, Two Hundred and Seventy-First Meeting, U.N. Doc. S/PV.271, 19 March 1948. *See also* U.N. Press Release PAL/145, 12 March 1948.

Committee and the Arab States to refer the legality of the partition resolution
to the International Court of Justice for an advisory opinion but the votes necessary for this purpose could not be mustered at the General Assembly.[18] The
majority of the inhabitants in Palestine at the termination of the British mandate on 14 May 1948 were Palestinian Arab. In discussing the U.N. resolution
to partition Palestine, the Palestinian jurist and legal representative to the
Arab Higher Committee Henry Cattan noted that:

> "In terms of population, the Jews in 1947 constituted less than one-
> third of the inhabitants of Palestine: 608,230 Jews out of a total pop-
> ulation of 1,972,560. What is more, only one-tenth of the Jews were
> original inhabitants; the rest were immigrants originating mostly
> from Poland, the U.S.S.R., and central Europe. *And only one-third of*
> *these immigrants had acquired Palestinian citizenship.* The Jewish
> community then existing in Palestine was, therefore, composed
> mainly of foreigners – both by origin *and nationality.* Nowhere,
> except in Palestine, have foreign immigrants been allowed to break
> up the territorial integrity of the country in which they came to live
> [emphasis added]."[19]

The creation of Israel occurred in the midst of the mass displacement and
expulsion of the predominantly but not exclusively Arab population of mandatory Palestine.[20] This allowed the Zionists to create their Jewish State called
Eretz-Israel or the land of Israel. In 1967 there was a further exodus of
Palestinians from their homeland when Israel captured vast swathes of territory in excess of that which the British had controlled during the mandate
period. The majority of Palestinians sought refuge in the surrounding Arab
States where they have remained ever since. This article will focus on Israel's
denationalization of the former non-Jewish citizens of the British mandate of
Palestine who were forced to flee their homeland in 1948. Today it is recognized that the right to a nationality is a human right and yet the majority of

---

[18] *See* Syria: Draft Resolution Concerning Reference of Certain Legal Questions to the ICJ,
U.N. GAOR, 2nd sess., UN Doc A/AC.14/25, p. 241 Annex 17 (1947); and Egypt: Draft
Resolution Concerning Reference of a Legal Question to the ICJ, U.N. GAOR, 2nd sess. UN
Doc A/AC.14/24, p. 240, Annex 16 (1947). U.N. GAOR, 2nd sess. UN Doc A/AC.14/32, p. 273
(1947); *Yearbook of the United Nations* 1947–8 (1949) p. 241.

[19] *See* H. Cattan, 'Recollections on the United Nations Resolution to Partition Palestine', 4
Palestine Yearbook of International Law (1987–1988) pp. 260–264 at p. 263.

[20] Approximately 17,000 Jews were registered as displaced in 1948. *See Final Report of the*
U.N. Economic Survey Mission for the Middle East (January 1950). *See* United Nations
Conciliation Commission for Palestine Final Report of the Economic Survey Mission for the
Middle East Part 1. The Final Report and Appendices (United Nations Lake Success New York)
U.N. Doc. A/AC.25/6, 28 December 1949, p. 18.

Palestinians have no nationality as they remain stateless. As nationality is an attribute of statehood the nationality of the Palestinian refugees is inextricably linked to the right of return.[21] This paper will examine whether the forced displacement and denationalization of Palestine's original non-Jewish inhabitants is compatible with the basic principles of international law today.

2. Denationalization in International Law

Denationalization is the process by which an individual is stripped of his or her nationality and in some cases rendered stateless – which would occur if the individual does not acquire a new nationality. As nationality is the link between the individual and the State, denationalization often results in breaking that link. A person without nationality would have no civil or political rights. Such persons would not be entitled to diplomatic protection, nor would they be entitled to a passport making it virtually impossible for them to travel outside the territory where they reside. Their rights to reside and work would be severely curtailed as these would be at the discretion of the host country. It is a most unpleasant phenomenon.

The legality of denationalization has long been in dispute.[22] On denationalization Lauterpacht wrote "[t]here is no clear rule of international law at present which limits the freedom of action of States in this respect, but it is submitted that the indiscriminate exercise by a State of the right of denationalizing its subjects, when coupled with the refusal to receive them when deported from a foreign country, constitutes an abuse of rights which could hardly be countenanced by an international tribunal".[23] In the eighth edition of *Oppenheim's International Law* it was said "[i]n so far as such deprivation of nationality results in statelessness, it must be regarded as retrogressive. That it is not dictated by any vital national interest may be seen from the fact that, subject to certain insignificant exceptions, it finds no place in the laws of other States . . .".[24] According to Schwarzenberger "[f]or purposes of his own municipal law, a territorial sovereign may deny groups of inhabitants, such as

---

[21] *See* V. Kattan 'The Right of Return Revisited', Special Edition 8 *Mediterranean Journal of Human Rights* (2004) pp. 293–321.

[22] For a review of the legal arguments advanced as to whether or not denationalization was prohibited by international law during and between the two great wars *see* P. Abel 'Denationalization', 5 *Modern Law Review* (1942) pp. 57–68.

[23] H. Lauterpacht, *The Function of Law in the International Community* (Clarendon Press, Oxford, 1933) p. 301.

[24] *See* the eighth edition of *Oppenheim's International Law* edited by H. Lauterpacht (Longmans, Green and Co, London, 1955) p. 658.

aborigines or gypsies, all or most rights of citizenship, yet still consider himself entitled to protect them in relation to other subjects of international law. If other States accept this claim, the meaning of nationality in international law and municipal law need not be the same".[25]

If the denationalization occurs within the State then the act will not be illegal. This is because nationality has long been considered a matter solely to be determined by municipal law. This position was established by the Permanent Court of International Justice in the *Tunis and Morocco Nationality Decrees* which held:

> "The question whether a certain matter is or is not solely within the jurisdiction of a State is an essentially *relative* question; it depends upon the development of *international relations*. Thus, *in the present state of international law*, questions of nationality are, in the opinion of this Court, *in principle* within this reserved domain [emphasis added]."[26]

This judgement was delivered in 1923. The Permanent Court had recognized then that the answer to that "essentially relative question" may change over time. Since 1923 international relations have changed considerably and developments since that time show that international law today plays a greater role in restricting what States can and cannot do in conferring and withdrawing nationality.[27] If the deprivation is part and parcel of a breach of an international duty then the act of deprivation would be illegal.[28] This would occur where a group of persons were wrongfully expelled from State A to State B. State B would have no obligation to recognise the delictual conduct of State A. Consequently State B has no obligation to grant its nationality to persons from State A.

The legality of such measures is especially questionable where the denationalization of persons affects relations between States or where the denationalization affects particular groups of persons on account of their race or religion. Van Panhuys writing in 1959 noted that "strong feelings are aroused . . . if deprivation of nationality is based on grounds which are gener-

---

[25] G. Schwarzenberger, *A Manual of International Law* (Professional Book Limited, Milton, 1976) p. 113.

[26] Tunis and Morrocco Decrees (U.K. v. Fr.), 1923 P.C.I.J., Ser. B, No.4 (7 February) p. 24.

[27] At the Hague Codification Conference of 1930 the First Committee stated in its report that although nationality "is primarily a matter for the municipal law of each state it is nevertheless governed to a large extent by principles of international law". *League of Nations, Conference for the Codification of International Law, Acts of the Conference, II, Report of the 1st Committee* (1930) V.8. 2–3.

[28] *See* I. Brownlie, 'The Relations of Nationality in Public International Law', 39 *British Yearbook of International Law* (1963) pp. 339–340.

ally deemed rejectable, such as race discrimination. This is particularly true if it is applied on a *large scale*" [emphasis added].[29] However, D.P. O'Connell takes a more cautious view. According to O'Connell it is the expulsion that is illegal and not the denationalization as such.[30] This is because whilst denationalization is abhorrent it did occur throughout the twentieth century in various forms in Russia, Germany, Italy, Japan, Pakistan, Bhutan and South Africa.[31]

This all began to slowly change after the Second World War. The U.N. was established to promote (among other things) universal respect for human rights and fundamental freedoms.[32] Human rights law began to play a more prominent role in international relations after a series of international bills and covenants were concluded by the international community. A European Court of Human Rights was established in Strasbourg. *Ad Hoc* international tribunals were set up to try suspected war criminals in Arusha, The Hague, Nuremberg and Tokyo. It would therefore seem highly unlikely that mass denationalization would be tolerated in this day and age. Hence it is hardly surprising to find Chen arguing that "[i]n spite of past assertions by such distinguished authors . . . that international law sets no limit on the competence of States to deprive individuals of nationality, general community expectations today would appear to be moving toward curtailing such allegedly 'unlimited' competence".[33] It is therefore submitted that racially discriminatory mass denationalization, especially when *coupled* with the expulsion or transfer of a civilian population from their homeland to the neighbouring States, is hardly

---

[29] V. Panhuys, *The Role of Nationality in International Law* (Sijthoff, Leiden, 1959) p. 163.

[30] D.P. O'Connell, *International Law* Vol. 2 (Stevens and Sons, London, 1970) p. 684.

[31] For the situation in Russia *see* J. Fischer Williams, 'Denationalization', 8 *British Yearbook of International Law* (1927) pp. 45–61; for the situation in Germany *see* Lauterpacht, *supra* note 2, and Weis, *supra* note 3; for the situation in Japan *see* C.-ll Chee, 'Japan's Post-War Mass Denationalization of the Korean Minority in International Law', 10 *Korean Journal of Comparative Law* (1982) pp. 19–52; for the situation in Pakistan *see* S. Sen 'Stateless Refugees and the Right to Return: The Bihari Refugees of South Asia', 11 *International Journal of Refugee Law* (1999) pp. 625–645; for the situation in Bhutan *see* T. Lay Lee, 'Refugees from Bhutan: Nationality, Statelessness and the Right to Return', 10 *International Journal of Refugee Law* (1998) pp. 118–155; and for the situation in South Africa *see* J. Dugard 'South Africa's 'Independent' Homelands: An Exercise in Denationalization', 10 (1) *The Denver Journal of International Law and Policy* (1980) pp. 11–36; and by the same author 'The Denationalization of Black South Africans in Pursuance of Apartheid', 22 *International Commission of Jurists* (1984) pp. 49–60.

[32] *See* Article 55 and 56 of the U.N. Charter. This can be viewed in I. Brownlie (ed.), *Basic Documents in International Law* (Oxford University Press, Oxford, 2002) pp. 14–15.

[33] *See* L. Chen, *An Introduction to Contemporary International Law* (Yale University Press, New Haven, 2000) p. 175.

something that would be countenanced in this day and age by an international tribunal and would be in breach of a State's, international obligations.[34]

3. The Palestinian *Nakbah*

3.1. *The Expulsion of the Palestinians in 1948*

On 14 May 1948 the State of Israel was born in the midst of a war with the Arabs of Palestine and the neighbouring Arab States.[35] There were two phases to this war. The first phase of the war began on 29 November 1947 and lasted until 14 May 1948 when Israel came into being and declared independence.[36] The second phase of the war, when the Arab States intervened on behalf of the Palestine Arabs, lasted from 15 May 1948 until the termination of hostilities on 7 January 1949.[37] The exodus of Palestine's Arabs coincided with the phases of the war, and the hostilities that began in December 1947 and lasted until March 1948 triggered the beginning of the exodus of Palestine's Arabs.[38] During the first phase of the conflict over 50 per cent of the indigenous Palestinian Arab population and three per cent of the Jewish population were displaced.[39] This would result in the overall displacement of up to 85 per cent of the indigenous Palestinian Arab population living in the territory that became the State of Israel.[40] In December 1947 the Haganah waged a series of

[34] Generally *see* G.S. Goodwin-Gill, 'The Limits of the Power of Expulsion in Public International Law', 47 *British Yearbook of International Law* (1974–1975) pp. 55–156; A.M. De Zayas, 'International Law and Mass Population Transfers', 16 *Harvard International Law Journal* (1975) pp. 207–258; and J. Quigley 'Mass Displacement and the Individual Right of Return', 68 *British Yearbook of International Law* (1997) pp. 65–125.

[35] For further reading *see* M. Palumbo, *The Palestinian Catastrophe the 1948 Expulsion of a People from their Homeland* (Quartet 1987); Karma and Cotran (ed.), *The Palestinian Exodus 1948–1998* (Ithaca 1999); Rogan and Shlaim (eds.), *The War for Palestine Rewriting the History of 1948* (Cambridge University Press 2001).

[36] For the text of Israel's Proclamation of Independence *see* Laqueur, *supra* note 11, pp. 125–128.

[37] *See* A. Shlaim, *The Iron Wall Israel and the Arab World* (Penguin Books 2000) pp. 28–41.

[38] *See* B. Morris, *The Birth of the Palestinian Refugee Problem 1947–1949* (Cambridge University Press 1987) pp. 41–131. *See also* by Morris, *Righteous Victims A History of the Zionist-Arab Conflict 1881–1999* (Alfred A. Knopf 1999) pp. 252–258.

[39] *See supra* note 20 and S.H. Abu-Sitta, *From Refugees to Citizens at Home* (Palestine Land Society and Palestinian Return Centre London (2001) p. 7.

[40] According to demographic projections by Abu Lughod, between 890,000 and 904,000 Palestinians would have been living in the territories that became the State of Israel if no displacement had taken place in 1948. *See* I. Abu Lughod, 'The Demographic Transformation of Palestine', in Abu Lughod (ed.), *The Transformation of Palestine* (Northwestern University Press, Evanston, 1971) p. 159.

attacks against Lifta, Romeima and Sheikh Badr.[41] These villages were strategically located at the entrance to Jerusalem on the main road to Tel Aviv and were therefore cleared of "potentially hostile Arab elements".[42] The expulsions which led to the exodus formed part of a military blueprint drawn up by the Haganah called "Tochnit Dalet" or Plan D.[43] According to Ilan Pappé, Senior Lecturer in the Department of Political Science at Haifa University:

> "Plan D was put into full operation in April and May [of 1948]. It had two very clear objectives, the first being to take swiftly and systematically any installation, military or civilian, evacuated by the British . . . The second, and far more important, objective of the plan was to cleanse the future Jewish State of as many Palestinians as possible. The main military force was the Haganah, which had several brigades. Each brigade received a list of villages it was to occupy. Most of the villages were destined to be destroyed, and only in very exceptional cases were the soldiers ordered to leave them intact."[44]

Counte Folke Bernadotte, who was the U.N. Mediator for Palestine in 1948, mentioned numerous reports from what he described as "reliable sources" of large scale looting, pillaging and plundering, and of instances of the destruction of villages without apparent military necessity.[45] Two Arab towns, Acre and Jaffa, which were supposed to be in the Arab State envisaged in the 1947 partition resolution, were subsequently attacked, occupied and depopulated by the Haganah.[46] Meron Benvenisti, a former deputy mayor of Jerusalem, characterized the expulsions which took place in 1948 as coming "dangerously close to fitting the definition of 'ethnic cleansing'".[47] He continued by saying,

---

[41] *See* N. Krystall, 'The Fall of the New City 1947–1950' in Salim Tamari (ed.), *Jerusalem 1948 The Arab Neighbourhoods and their Fate in the War* (The Institute of Jerusalem Studies & Badil Resource Center 2002) pp. 84–141.

[42] Krystall *Ibid.* p. 92.

[43] *See* W. Khalidi's essay 'Plan Dalet: Master Plan for the Conquest of Palestine' in the *Middle East Forum*, November 1961, reprinted in 18 *Journal of Palestine Studies* (1988) pp. 4–70.

[44] I. Pappé, *A History of Modern Palestine, One Land, Two Peoples* (Cambridge University Press 2004) p. 130. *See also* Pappé, *The Making of the Arab Israeli Conflict 1947–1951* (I.B. Tauris, London, 1994) and *see* A. Shlaim, 'The debate about 1948', pp. 171–192; B. Morris, 'The causes and character of the Arab exodus from Palestine: the Israeli defence forces intelligence service analysis of June 1948', pp. 193–210; and N. Masalha, "A critique on Benny Morris" pp. 211–220 all in Pappé, *The Israel/Palestine Question (Re-writing Histories)* (Routledge, London, 1999).

[45] *See* the Progress Report of the U.N. Mediator, GAOR, 3rd session, supp. 11, U.N. Doc. A/648 16 September 1948, at Chapter V entitled "Refugees" para. 7.

[46] *See* D. Gilmour, *Dispossessed* (Sidgwick and Jackson 1980) pp. 59–76 at 62.

[47] *See* M. Benvenisti, *Sacred Landscape the Buried History of the Holy Land since 1948* (University of California Press 2000) p. 145.

"[a]lthough not as severe as in the case of Bosnia, atrocities that could be defined as war crimes did occur".[48] In a recent interview with *Ha'aretz* newspaper Professor Benny Morris of Ben Gurion University said that twenty four massacres took place in Palestine during the inter-war years perpetrated by Zionist forces, the worst cases being in Saliha, Deir Yassin, Lod, Dawayima, Abu Shusha, Jaffa, Arab al Muwasi, Safsaf, Jish, Eilaboun, Deir al Asad, Majdal Krum and Sasa.[49] In the light of recent evidence it is also thought that a further massacre took place at Tantura and as each year passes more and more evidence comes to light of these atrocities.[50] In preparation for a new edition of his book, based on original documents from the archives of the Israel Defence Forces, Morris discovered that there were "far more Israeli acts of massacre than I had previously thought. To my surprise, there were also many cases of rape".[51] What Morris and many Israeli academics today acknowledge is what many Palestinian survivors of the war have been saying for decades: that they there were expelled from their homeland.[52] The difference is that Morris disputes the argument that Plan D was a "master plan" for the expulsion of the Palestine Arabs.[53] However, Arab (and even some Israeli historians) argue that the Zionists knew they could not have established a Jewish State in Palestine, without transferring its indigenous Palestinian Arab population from the area allocated to the Jewish State in the U.N. partition resolution, because there would have been more Arabs living in that territory than Jews.[54] Now one of Israel's leading Zionist historians admits that Ben Gurion, (who would become Israel's first Prime Minister), knew that there could be no

---

[48] *Ibid.*

[49] *See* the B. Morris interview "Survival of the Fittest' in *Haaretz Friday Magazine* 9 January 2004 and his new book *The Birth of the Palestinian Refugee Problem Revisited* (Cambridge University Press 2004).

[50] *See* I. Pappé, 'The Tantura Case in Israel: The Katz Research and Trial' and 'Eye-Witness Testimonies of the Tantura Massacre, 22–23 May 1948'; both in the 30 (3) *Journal of Palestine Studies* (2001) pp. 5–39.

[51] According to Morris at *supra* note 49, "[i]n Operation Hiram there was an unusually high concentration of executions of people against a wall or next to a well in an orderly fashion. That can't be by chance. It's a pattern. Apparently, various officers who took part in the operation understood that the expulsion order they received permitted them to do these deeds in order to encourage the population to take to the roads. The fact is that no one was punished for these acts of murder. Ben-Gurion silenced the matter. He covered up for the officers who did the massacres."

[52] Morris *Ibid.*: "A Jewish state would not have come into being without the uprooting of 700,000 Palestinians. Therefore it was necessary to uproot them. There was no choice but to expel that population."

[53] *See* B. Morris, 'For the Record', *The Guardian*, 14 January 2004.

[54] *See* N. Masalha *The Expulsion of Palestinians: The Concept of Transfer in Zionist Political Thought 1882–1948* (Institute for Palestine Studies, Washington D.C. 1992); and S. Flapan, *The Birth of Israel* (Pantheon Books 1987) pp. 13–118.

Jewish State "with a large and hostile Arab minority in its midst" and that "an atmosphere of population transfer" was in the air.[55]

Israel has always disputed the arguments that it was responsible for the chain of events which led to the exodus of Palestine's indigenous Arab population.[56] Initially, Israel claimed that the Palestinians left because they were ordered to, and deliberately incited into panic, by their own leadership who wanted the field clear for the 1948 war.[57] It was also argued that there would have been no Palestinian refugees had the Arab States not attacked the Jewish State on 15 May 1948.[58] Abba Eban argued that "[t]he problem of the Arab refugees was caused by a war of aggression launched by the Arab States against Israel in 1948".[59] According to this version of events the 1948 war was a defensive war and the Arab States were the aggressors.[60] On 24 June 1949, Chaim Weizmann sent a letter to Harry S. Truman where he wrote that:

[55] In the interview with Shavit, *supra* note 49, Morris said, "[f]rom April 1948, Ben-Gurion is projecting a message of transfer. There is no explicit order of his in writing, there is no orderly comprehensive policy, but there is an atmosphere of [population] transfer. The transfer idea is in the air. The entire leadership understands that this is the idea. The officer corps understands what is required of them. Under Ben-Gurion, a consensus of transfer is created . . . Ben Gurion was a transferist. He understood that there could be no Jewish State with a large and hostile Arab minority in its midst. There would be no such State. It would not be able to exist."

[56] *See* the arguments advanced by A. Dershowitz, *The Case for Israel* (John Wiley and Sons 2003) pp. 78–90. This book is however very controversial. Professor N.G. Finkelstein of De Paul University accused the Harvard scholar of concocting a fraud. In a televised debate on the Democracy Now! an independent daily radio and TV program in the U.S., Finkelstein told Dershowitz that his book was "a collection of fraud, falsification, plagiarism and nonsense." On p. 80 of his book Dershowitz says that Benny Morris "estimates that between two and three thousand Arabs fled their homes during this phase of Arab-initiated fighting". In fact Morris said that 2–3 *hundred thousand* Arabs had fled. You can see the debate on video and a transcript of the discussion at <www.democracynow.org/article.pl?sid=03/09/24/1730205>, web site last visited 27 October 2004.

[57] On 12 May 1961 Erskine Childers wrote an article called 'The Other Exodus' which was published in the *Spectator* (London) where he examined Arab broadcasts from the period in the British museum. He wrote, "[a]s none of the other stock quotations in Israeli propaganda are worth comment, I next decided to test the undocumented charge that the Arab evacuation orders were broadcast by Arab-radio which could be done thoroughly because the BBC monitored all Middle Eastern broadcasts throughout 1948 . . . There was not a single order, or appeal, or suggestion about evacuating from Palestine from any Arab radio station, inside or outside Palestine, in 1948. There is repeated monitored record of Arab appeals, even flat orders, to the civilians of Palestine to stay put." Childers' article is also mentioned by I.F. Stone in "Holy War" the *New York Review of Books* 3 August 1967 which is reproduced in Laqueur, *supra* note 11, at p. 317.

[58] The difficulty with this argument is that the expulsion of the Palestinians began before 15 May 1948.

[59] *See* A. Eban, *The Voice of Israel* (Faber and Faber 1958) p. 169.

[60] *See* J. Stone, *Israel and Palestine Assault on the War of Nations* (John Hopkins University Press 1981) pp. 51–53. Stone argues that Israel's war in 1948 was a war of self-defence against

"[i]t was not the birth of Israel which created the Arab refugee problem, as our enemies now proclaim, but the Arab attempt to prevent
that birth by armed force. These people are not refugees in the sense
in which that term has been sanctified by the martyrdom of millions
in Europe – they are part of an aggressor group which failed and
makes no secret of its intention to resume aggression."[61]

In recent years an old argument has resurfaced.[62] Morris, for instance, now
argues that what occurred was a population exchange.[63] He cites the exchange
of populations that occurred between Greece and Turkey to buttress his
claims that what Israel did was justified.[64] Others have mentioned the

---

the Arab-aggressor. According to Stone, "Israel's presence in all of these areas pending negotiations of new borders is entirely lawful".

[61] *See* Letter to Harry S. Truman, Washington, (Rehovot, 24 June 1949) in B. Litvinoff and
A. Klieman (eds.), *The Letters and Papers of Chaim Weizmann / Series A Letters XXIII August
1947–June 1952* (Transaction Books, Rutgers University, Israel Universities Press 1980)
p. 314. *See also* Letter to James De Rothschild, London, (Rehovot, 1 December 1948) where
Weizmann wrote at p. 234, "[e]veryone seems to think that they [referring to the Palestine Arab
refugees] have gone for good, and that with the exception of about 70,000 who are here and who
never left, the Arab population has to all intents and purposes disappeared". *See also* Weizmann's
correspondence with Lady Violet Bonham-Carter, (later Baroness Asquith), London (Rehovot,
13 March 1949) where Weizmann tries to justify what happened to the Palestinian refugees
p. 265. Regarding Weizmann's comments that Palestinian refugees are "not refugees in the sense
in which that term has been sanctified by the martyrdom of millions in Europe", *see* S. Hadawi,
Bitter Harvest A Modern History of Palestine (Olive Branch Press Interlink 1991) on the Arab
refugee problem at pp. 134–148.

[62] *See* the arguments advanced by Abba Eban on 18 November before the U.N. General
Assembly's *Ad Hoc* Political Committee in early propaganda pamphlets provided by Israel's
Office of Information in New York: *Arab Refugees – Road to a Solution* (1955); M. Comay, *The
Future of the Arab Refugees* (1954) and G. Meir, *Arab Refugee Problem Towards a Solution*
(1961). One of the myths advanced in these pamphlets is that the Palestinians abandoned their
properties while "fleeing" to surrounding Arab countries, which in retaliation expelled their
Jewish citizens and confiscated their properties. For a summary of the situation of Jews in Arab
countries in the 1940s, 1950s and 1960s see Jan Abu Shakrah "Deconstructing the link:
Palestinian refugees and Jewish immigrants from Arab countries" in Naseer Aruri (ed.)
Palestinian Refugees the Right of Return (Pluto Press, 2001), pp. 208–216.

[63] *See* B. Morris, "In '48, Israel did what it had to do", *L.A. Times* 26 January 2004.

[64] Morris *Ibid.*, "Israel's decision was not unprecedented, nor was it necessarily immoral.
Something similar had happened in the early 1920s when a Greek invasion of the Turkish main-
land triggered a Turkish counterattack, in which almost all the Greeks living in Asia Minor were
expelled. In response, in northern Greece, the Turkish minority was uprooted and expelled to
Turkey. For centuries, Turks had oppressed Greeks, and Greeks and Turks had slaughtered one
another. The mutual uprooting of these minority communities removed major bones of contention and, ever since, the two peoples have lived in relative peace. While the 'population
exchange' was no doubt traumatic, in the long run both peoples have vastly benefited."

Sudetenland in this context.[65] However, the Greek and Turkish exchange of populations which Morris refers to were specifically provided for in the Treaty of Lausanne whereas no such treaty was ever concluded between Israel and the Arab States in 1948.[66] Instead, in 1949, a series of cease fire agreements were concluded between the former belligerents but these agreements did not mention anything about an exchange of populations.[67] As for the Sudetenland justification, there are no parallels between German Sudets and Palestinian refugees.[68] At Potsdam, the victors of the Second World War recognized "that the transfer to Germany of German populations, or elements thereof, remaining in Poland, Czechoslovakia and Hungary, will have to be undertaken", whereas in Palestine the international community never condoned the expulsion of the Palestinian people.[69] Instead on 11 December 1948, the U.N. General Assembly in resolution 194 (III) set up a U.N. Conciliation Commission for Palestine (composed of France, Turkey and the USA) whose task included facilitating the repatriation, resettlement and economic and social rehabilitation of the refugees and the payment of compensation.[70] Paragraph 11 of this resolution provided:

> "that the refugees wishing to return to their homes and live at peace with their neighbours should be permitted to do so at the earliest practicable date, and that compensation should be paid for the property of

[65] *See* the *Jerusalem Post's* supplement on Palestinian refugees. This can be located at <http://info.jpost.com/C003/Supplements/Refugees/>, last visited on 27 October 2004.

[66] *See* Convention concerning the Exchange of Greek and Turkish Populations, signed in Lausanne on 30 January 1923, *supra* note 8, pp. 1036–1044 or at 23 *League of Nations Treaty Series* 76. For further reading on population exchanges *see* C. Meindersma, 'Legal Issues Surrounding Population Transfers in Conflict Situations', 41 *Netherlands International Law Review* (1994) pp. 31–83; and by the same author, 'Population Exchanges: International Law and State Practice', 9 *International Journal of Refugee Law* (1997) at pp. 335–364 and pp. 613–653.

[67] *See* the corrigendum to the cablegram from the Acting Mediator, R.J. Bunch, to the Secretary-General transmitting the text of an armistice agreement between Egypt and Israel U.N. Doc. S/1264/Corr.1, 23 February 1949; Lebanon and Israel U.N. Doc. S/1296, 23 March 1949; Hashemite Jordan Kingdom and Israel U.N. Doc. S/1302/Rev.1 3 April 1949; and between Israel and Syria U.N. Doc. S/1353, 20 July 1949.

[68] For further reading on the Sudetenland *see* A.M. De Zayas, "International Law and Mass Population Transfers", 16 *Harvard International Law Journal* (1975) pp. 207–258 at 227–242.

[69] The allies agreed that any transfers that took place "should be affected in an orderly and human manner." As De Zayas points out (*ibid.*, p. 235) "conditions of the expulsions were neither orderly nor humane." *See* Article XII of the Berlin (Potsdam) Conference, 17 July–2 August 1945 (a) Protocol of the Proceedings, 1 August 1945 entitled "Orderly Transfer of German Populations." This can be viewed on the web site of the Avalon Project at Yale Law School at <www.yale.edu/lawweb/avalon/decade/decade17.htm>, last visited on 28 October 2004.

[70] *See* U.N. Doc. A/Res/194 (III), 11 December 1948.

those choosing not to return and for loss of or damage to property which, under principles of international law or in equity, should be made good by the Governments or authorities responsible."[71]

Whilst this resolution does not provide a binding legal right *per se* it is evidence of the will of the international community in 1948.[72] In stark contrast to the Sudetenland scenario, where the uprooting of German Sudets from the homeland was specifically sanctioned by the allied powers, in the case of Palestinian refugees, the international community adopted the recommendations of the U.N. Mediator's Progress Report.[73] In this report the U.N. Mediator wrote that "[t]he liability of the Provisional Government of Israel to restore private property to its Arab owners and to indemnify those owners for property wantonly destroyed is clear, irrespective of any indemnities which the Provisional Government may claim from the Arab States".[74] He also wrote that it would be "an offence against the principles of elemental justice if these innocent victims of the conflict were denied the right to return to their homes while Jewish immigrants flow into Palestine, and, indeed, at least offer the threat of permanent replacement of the Arab refugees who have been rooted in the land for centuries".[75] In his "specific conclusions" Bernadotte concluded that, "[t]he right of the Arab refugees to return to their homes in Jewish-controlled territory at

---

[71] Due to the fact that Jews were also displaced during the 1948 war, drafters of U.N. General Assembly Resolution 194 (III) used non-discriminatory language that reaffirmed the right of all refugees and displaced persons to return to their homes. *See* United Nations Conciliation Commission for Palestine, *Analysis of Paragraph 11 of the General Assembly's Resolution of 11 December 1948* (Working Paper Prepared by the Secretariat). U.N. Doc. A/AC.25/W.45, 15 May 1950.

[72] For differing arguments on the interpretation of this resolution and the right of return *see* K. René Radley 'The Palestinian Refugees: the Right of Return in International Law', 72 *American Journal of International Law* (1978) pp. 586–614; K. Lawand, 'The Right to Return of Palestinians in International Law', 8 *International Journal of Refugee Law* (1996) pp. 532–568; and J. Quigley, 'Displaced Palestinians and a Right of Return', 39 *Harvard International Law Journal* (1998) pp. 171–229. *See also* W. Thomas Mallison and S.V. Mallison, *The Palestine Problem in International Law and World Order* (Longman 1986) pp. 174–206; H. Cattan, *Palestine, The Arabs and Israel the Search for Justice* (Longmans 1969) pp. 39–54; and Badil Occasional Bulletin No. 11 (April 2002) The meaning of U.N. General Assembly Resolution 194 (III), 11 December 1948 (The Right of Return) at <www.badil.org/Publications/Bulletins/Bulletin-11.htm>, last visited 7 November 2004.

[73] For the Progress Report *see supra* note 45.

[74] *Ibid.*, para. 7 (Chapter V). For further reading on the situation of Jews in Arab countries in the 20th century see. M. Gat The Jewish Exodus from Iraq 1948–1951 (London: Cass, 1997) and A. Shiblack The Lure of Zion: The Case of Iraqi Jews (London: Al Saqi, 1986); R. Ahroni, Jewish Emigration from Yemen, 1951–98: Carpet Without Magic (Richmond: Curzon 2001); and K. Schulze, The Jews of Lebanon between Coexistence and Conflict (Brighton: Sussex Acdemic Press 2001).

[75] *Ibid.*, para. 6.

the earliest possible date should be *affirmed* by the United Nations, and their repatriation, resettlement and economic and social rehabilitation, and payment of adequate compensation for the property of those choosing not to return, should be supervised and assisted by the United Nations conciliation commission . . .".[76]

Israel's first application for membership of the U.N. was rejected on 29 November 1948 precisely because the question of boundaries, settlements *and refugees* had not been settled.[77] On 4 March 1949 the U.N. Security Council decided to recommend to the General Assembly that it admit Israel to membership in the U.N.[78] On 11 May 1949, Israel was admitted to membership in that organization subject to the declarations and explanations made by the representative of the Government of Israel before the *Ad Hoc* Political Committee.[79] On 5 May 1949, Abba Eban in Lake Success, New York rejected Arab assertions that Israel was responsible for the exodus but said that the Government of Israel would nevertheless be ready to make its own contribution to a solution to the refugee problem, though he said "it was not yet ascertainable *how many Arabs wished to return* under conditions that might be prescribed by the Assembly or how many Arabs *Israel could receive* in the light of existing political and economic considerations [my emphasis]".[80] Israel and the Arab States never did come to an agreement at the Lausanne Peace Conference in 1949 and so the 1948 Palestinian refugees would remain in camps administered by the U.N Relief and Works Agency for Palestinian Refugees in the Near East (UNRWA).[81]

3.2. *The Expulsion of the Palestinians in 1967*

In six days in June 1967 Israel captured the West Bank, the Gaza Strip, the Golan Heights and the Sinai Peninsula in the war with Egypt, Jordan and Syria.

---

[76] *Ibid.*, Chapter VIII entitled "Conclusions" at 4 (i).

[77] *See* H. Cattan, *The Palestine Question* (Croom Helm 1988) pp. 86–89.

[78] *See* U.N. Doc. S/Res/69 S/1277, 4 March 1949 (UK abstained. Egypt voted against).

[79] *See* U.N. General Assembly resolution A/RES/273 (III), 11 May 1949.

[80] *See* U.N. Doc. A/AC.24/SR.45, 5 May 1949.

[81] UNRWA was established by U.N. General Assembly resolution A/RES/302 (IV), 8 December 1949. According to Article 1 (d) of the U.N. Convention Relating to the Status of Refugees, "[t]his Convention shall not apply to persons who are at present receiving from organs or agencies of the United Nations other than the United Nations High Commissioner for Refugees protection or assistance. When such protection or assistance has ceased for any reason, without the position of such persons being definitely settled in accordance with the relevant resolutions adopted by the General Assembly of the United Nations, these persons shall *ipso facto* be entitled to the benefits of this Convention." Palestinian refugees do not fall under the ambit of the UNHCR's mandate because they are presently receiving assistance (but not protection) from another agency of the U.N. The text of this Convention can be read in Cotran, Pearle and Onslow-Cole (eds.), *Butterworths Handbook on Immigration Law*

Between 300,000 to 400,000 Palestinians were expelled or fled their homes to become refugees.[82] Many Palestinians displaced in this war became refugees for the second times in their lives. Having been displaced from their original homes inside Israel in 1948, they were then displaced from the areas that Israel captured in the war of 1967.[83] Although it has been argued that the sheer size of the exodus was due to a general panic caused by the retreat of the Jordanian army, Israel took advantage of the situation to increase the flow of refugees by deportations in individual cases and by demolishing Arab towns like Qalqilya and Emmaus after the end of the fighting.[84] Israel permitted some of the refugees to return to their homes, but only 14,000 could do so as the borders were only open for thirteen days, from the 18 August until 31 August 1967.[85] The International Committee for the Red Cross appealed to the Israeli gov-

---

(Butterworths 2001) pp. 921–946. However in this regard *see* S.M. Akram and T. Rempel, 'Temporary Protection as an Instrument for Implementing the Right of Return', 22 *Boston University International Law Journal* (2004) pp. 1–162. For further reading on Palestinian Refugees *see* B. Schiff, *Refugees unto the Third Generation* (Syracuse University Press 1995). On the Lausanne conference *see* N. Masalha, "The PLO, Resolution 194 and the 'right of return': evolving Palestinian attitudes towards the refugee question from the 1948 *nakba* to the Camp David summit of July 2000", 7 *Yearbook of Islamic and Middle Eastern Law* (2000–2001) pp. 137–138.

[82] Figures for refugee displacement in 1967 vary considerably depending on whether refugees from 1948 as well as 1967 (persons made refugees twice) are included. According to the U.N. the number of persons who had fled from the areas under Israeli occupation during and after the June hostilities is estimated at 550,000. This figure includes persons displaced from the West Bank to Jordan, the Golan Heights to Syria and those who had fled from Gaza and the Sinai to Egypt. This figure does not however include persons with lost ID permits, or deportees, spouses and descendants. *See* Report of the Commissioner-General of the United Nations Relief and Works Agency for Palestine Refugees in the Near East, Official Records of the General Assembly, Twenty-second Session, Supplement No. 13, 1 July 1966–30 June 1967 U.N. Doc. A/6713. New York: United Nations, 1967. The figure 300–400,000 takes into account various estimates from Palestinian, Israeli and U.N. sources. *See Survey of Palestinian Refugees and Internally Displaced Persons 2002* (Badil Resource Center for Palestinian Residency and Refugee Rights, Bethlehem, 2002).

[83] On 14 June 1967, the U.N. Security Council adopted resolution 237 that called upon the Government of Israel "to ensure the safety, welfare and security of the inhabitants of the areas where military operations have taken place and *to facilitate the return of those inhabitants who have fled the areas since the outbreak of hostilities* . . ." [emphasis added] Mr. George Brown, Secretary of State for Foreign Affairs of the United Kingdom, said at a meeting before the U.N. General Assembly that "it is imperative, if feelings are not to be further inflamed, or a settlement made more remote, that the Arab communities whose lands have been overrun should be allowed to stay where they are, or to return if they have fled and wish to come back . . ." See UN Doc. A/PV, 21 June 1967.

[84] *See* M. Akehurst, 'The Arab-Israeli Conflict and International Law', 5 *New Zealand Universities Law Review* (1972–1973) p. 242. Dr. Michael Akehurst used to work in the Lebanon for the UNRWA.

[85] International Committee for the Red Cross Annual Report (Geneva: 1967) pp. 10–11.

ernment requesting it to extend the time limit to enable all those wishing to return to their homes to do so, but the Israeli government rejected this appeal.[86] Since 1967 Israel has been a belligerent occupant in East Jerusalem, the West Bank, the Gaza Strip and the Golan Heights. As Weiler notes, Israel's status as a belligerent occupant in the Palestinian territories is being manipulated as it presents those who wish to retain the territory with the preferred position: "You exercise control over the territory (as a belligerent occupant) but you are able to deny the local citizens any political rights since they do not become citizens of the occupying State – and all this with the penumbra of legality accorded to this status in international law. Legally you get the land without the people".[87]

4. The Denationalization of the Palestinians

4.1. *Israeli Case Law*

In the early days of the Jewish State the Tel Aviv District Court held that with the termination of the British Mandate of Palestine, former Palestine citizens lost their citizenship without acquiring any other.[88] The decision of the Court was an attempt not to grant citizens of the British Mandate of Arab decent nationality in the new State. However, interestingly, in another decision of the Tel Aviv District Court it was held that:

> "the point of view according to which there are no Israeli nationals is not compatible with public international law. The prevailing view [based on Oppenheim, Schwarzenberger, and Lauterpacht] is that, in the case of transfer of a portion of the territory of a State to another State, every individual and inhabitants of the ceding State becomes automatically a national of the receiving State . . . If this is the case, is it possible to say that the inhabitants of part of a State which is transformed into an independent State are not *ipso facto* transformed into the nationals of that State? So long as no law has been enacted

---

[86] *Ibid.*

[87] J.H.H. Weiler, 'Israel, The Territories and International Law: When Doves are Hawks' in A.E. Kellermann (ed.), *Israel Amongst the Nations: International and Comparative Law Perspectives on Israel's 50th Anniversary* (Kluwer Law International, The Hague, 1998) p. 390.

[88] *Oseri* v. *Oseri* (1953) 8 PM 76 at 78. According to Justice Kennet, "[c]itizenship is the grant of personal status to the citizen and it creates a bond of loyalty between the State and the national. The loyalty which had been created by the [Palestine Citizenship Order] was towards the Mandatory power, which has now disappeared, and it is difficult to reach a deduction that the very law which established a bond of loyalty between the Mandatory Power and its inhabitants can now create a new nationality and a new bond of loyalty between the State of Israel and its inhabitants. Such a bond cannot automatically devolve".

providing otherwise, my view is that every individual who, on the date of the establishment of the State of Israel was resident in the territory which today constitute the State of Israel, is also a national of Israel. Any other view must lead to the absurd result of a State without nationals – a phenomenon the existence of which has not yet been observed."[89]

This decision was subsequently overruled by the Israel Supreme Court in *Hussein* v. *Governor of Acre Prison* where the Court held that Palestinian citizenship had come to an end, and that former citizens of the British Mandate of Palestine had not become Israeli citizens.[90] Former Palestine citizens were held to be stateless during the period between the establishment of the State and the entry into force of the Israel's Nationality Law.[91] It is submitted that the decision of the Tel Aviv District Court in *A.B.* v. *M.B.* accords with international law as it had been widely recognized that upon a succession of States persons habitually resident in the territory of the new State *ipso facto* become nationals of that State.[92] Williams writing in 1927, concluded that "a State cannot, whether by banishment or by putting an end to the status of nationality, compel any other State to receive one of its own nationals whom it wishes to

---

[89] *A.B.* v. *M.B.* 17 ILR 110 (1950).

[90] (1952) 6 PD 897, 901; 17 ILR 111(1950); also cited in G. Goodwin Gill, *The Refugee in International Law* (Clarendon Press, Oxford, 1998) pp. 242–243.

[91] For further reading *see* M.D. Gouldman, *Israel Nationality Law* (The Hebrew University of Jerusalem Faculty of Law – Institute for Legislative Research and Comparative Law, Jerusalem, 1970). According to Gouldman, Palestine citizenship ceased to exist on the day of the establishment of the State, although the Palestine Citizenship Orders were not specifically repealed until later.

[92] *See* Article 30 of the 1923 Treaty of Lausanne, *supra* note 8. *See also* Article 18 of the Draft Conventions Prepared in Anticipation of the First Conference on the Codification of International Law, the Hague 1930, Research in International Law Harvard Law School, April 1929. Draft Conventions and Comments on Nationality, Responsibility of States for Injuries to Aliens, and Territorial Waters, Prepared by the Research in International Law of the Harvard Law School, 23 *American Journal of International Law* (1929) pp. 1–79. According to Ian Brownlie the evidence is overwhelmingly in support of the view that the population follows the change of sovereignty in matters of nationality. Brownlie supports his view in citing the Treaties of Versailles, St Germaine, Trianon, and Paris: "It is thought that the precedent value of such provisions is considerable in view of their uniformity and the international character of the deliberations preceding the signature of these treaties." *See* I. Brownlie, *Principles of Public International Law* (Oxford University Press, Oxford, 1998) p. 657. According to Article 5 of the International Law Commissions Draft Articles on the Nationality of Natural Persons in Relation to the Succession of States prepared on the basis of a request addressed to the International Law Commission by the General Assembly in paragraph 8 of its resolution 51/160 of 16 December 1996 and adopted at its 51st session "persons concerned having their habitual residence in the territory affected by the succession of States are presumed to acquire the nationality of the successor State on the date of such succession".

expel from its own territory".[93] Brownlie has noted that if a new State, in this case it could be Israel, relying on the absence of municipal law, tried to deport a part of its permanent population, it would be acting in clear breach of its legal duties and might even involve its government in acts punishable as genocide.[94]

4.2. *Israel's Nationality Law 1952*

After having been wrongfully expelled from their homeland in 1948 the Palestinians were denationalized by section 3 of Israel's Nationality Law of 1952 which provides:

"3. (a) A person who, immediately before the establishment of the State, was a Palestinian citizen and who does not become an Israeli national under section 2, shall become an Israeli national with effect from the day of the establishment of the State if –

(1) he was registered on the 4th Adar, 5712 (1st March 1952) as an inhabitant under the Registration of Inhabitants Ordinance, 5709–1949; and

(2) he is an inhabitant of Israel on the day of the coming into force of this Law; and

(3) he was in Israel, or in an area which became Israeli territory after the establishment of the State, from the day of the establishment of the State to the day of the coming into force of this law, or entered Israel legally during this period.

(b) A person born after the establishment of the State who is an inhabitant of Israel on the day of the coming into force of this Law, and whose father or mother becomes an Israel national under subsection (a), shall become an Israel national with effect from the day of his birth."[95]

It becomes immediately apparent that section 3 (a) only applies only to Palestinian Arabs. This is because Jews would have all acquired Israeli

---

[93] Fischer Williams, *supra* note 31, p. 61.

[94] *See* I. Brownlie, *Principles of Pubic International Law, supra* note 92, p. 400. In a lecture at the Hague Academy of International Law, Rosayln Higgins noted that, "no non-ratifying state could claim to be free to commit genocide because it was not a party to that legal instrument. The prohibition against genocide clearly pre-existed the Convention as a prohibition of customary international law". *See* R. Higgins, "International Law and the Avoidance, Containment and Resolution of Disputes", *Recueil Des Cours* (1991) V, (230) p. 56.

[95] Nationality Law 5712 – 1952. Published in *Sefer Ha-Chukkim* No. 95, April 8, 1952, p. 146; LSI Vol. XI, at 50. The laws of Israel from the early days of the Jewish State can be viewed in J. Badi (ed.), *Fundamental Laws of the State of Israel* (Twayne, New York, 1961).

nationality under section 2. Section 2 refers to Israel's 1950 Law of Return which of course only applies to Jews.[96] It should be noted that in the intervening four years (1948–1952) Palestinian Arabs in Israel were stateless. Israel was then in the process of consolidating the Jewish State. It was not until 1952 after millions of Jewish immigrants had entered the country vastly outnumbering the Palestinian Arabs that the Jewish State felt comfortable giving them Israeli nationality. The situation was so acute that Israel had to house these Jewish immigrants in abandoned Arab houses.[97]

The Nationality Law of 1952 sets out three conditions that Palestinian Arabs in Israel must satisfy to acquire Israeli nationality. The first condition is that the Arab be registered on the 1 March 1952 under the Registration of Inhabitants Ordinance Law 1949.[98] This law requires that every inhabitant who has attained the age of 16 years and is in the territory conforming to the State of Israel is to notify his particulars at a registration office. He or she has 30 days to do this from the date of the publication of the Ordinance. The second condition is that the Arab must be an inhabitant of Israel on the day of the coming into force of this law. As Israel had engineered the removal of most of the Arab inhabitants in the land that it captured during the war, Israel's Nationality Law applied only to the few Arab inhabitants who remained in the newly created State of Israel. This, and the following provision, ensured that no Arabs outside Israel, including those that might have somehow returned to Israel, could

---

[96] Israel's 1950 Law of Return allows any Jew in the world to come to Israel and obtain Israel Nationality automatically. The only criterion is that the person is Jewish. *See* Law of Return 5710–1950; Law of Return (Amendment 5714–1954); and Law of Return (Amendment No. 2) 5730–1970. These laws can be viewed in English, in the Laws of the State of Israel (hereafter *'L.S.I.'*). *See also* Nancy Caren Richmond, 'Israel's Law of Return: Analysis of Its Evolution and Present Application', 12 *Dickinson Journal of International Law* (1993–1994) pp. 95–133. It is submitted that the Law of Return confuses the laws of immigration with the laws of nationality. Immigration laws concern the entry of foreign nationals to and from a particular State, whereas nationality is the link between the individual and the State. The Law of Return is effectively a blend of immigration and nationality law for it confers nationality automatically on foreign immigrants. It also confers Israeli nationality on the children of Israeli parents regardless of where they are born and irrespective of whether or not they desire Israeli nationality. In this respect the Law of Return is inconsistent with the doctrine of the real and effective link established by the International Court of Justice in the *Nottebohm* Judgement. *See Nottebohm* Case (second phase) Judgement of 6 April ICJ Reports 1955 p. 4 [*Liechtenstein* v. *Guatemala*].

[97] *See* 'Israel's Initial Absentee Policy' and 'Absorption of Absentee Property' in D. Peretz, *Israel and the Palestine Arabs* (The Middle East Institute, Washington D.C. 1958) pp. 141–191.

[98] Registration of Inhabitants Ordinance 5709–1949, Published in *Iton Rishmi* No. 48, Supplement I, 4 February, 1949, p. 164; LSI Vol. II, pp. 103.

claim its nationality.[99] The third condition is that the Palestinian Arab was in Israel, or in an area which became Israeli territory after the establishment of the State, from the day of the establishment of the State to the day of the coming into force of this law, or entered Israel legally during that period. Only the few remaining Palestinian Arab inhabitants of the newly created State of Israel who resided there *continuously* from 14 May 1948 until 14 July 1952 could become Israeli nationals. All those who had left in the meantime or who were resident abroad could not become nationals. This included 750,000 Palestinian Arab refugees. It is important to point out that Palestinian Arabs had to satisfy all three conditions in order to qualify for Israeli nationality.

4.3. *Israel and Occupied Palestinian Territory*

In 1967 Israel captured the West Bank, the Gaza Strip, the Golan Heights and the Sinai Peninsula.[100] However Israeli nationality was not conferred upon persons resident in these territories. Were Israel to have done this there would be as many Arabs with Israeli nationality as there are Jews in Israel today. The laws governing the resort to the use of armed force (*jus in bello*) which is sometimes referred to as international humanitarian law applicable in armed conflict, are consequently applicable to Israel's military occupation of these territories. The two most relevant conventions governing the *jus in bello* in the Occupied Palestinian Territories are the 1907 Hague Regulations Respecting the Customs of War on Land (*hereinafter 'Hague Regulations'*) and the 1949

---

[99] In *Shaya v. Minister of the Interior* (1960) 45 P'sakim (Elyon) 308, the petitioner had spent a considerable part of the said period outside the boundaries of Israel. The authorities were held to be justified in their refusal to recognize him as a national and not to grant him a passport.

[100] Jordan annexed the West Bank in 1950 and administered it until 1967. Its Palestinian inhabitants acquired Jordanian nationality. Palestinians maintained their Jordanian nationality after June 1967 (when Israel captured it from Jordan) although they could not exercise their full rights as they were (and are) subject to Israel's belligerent military occupation. In 1988, Jordan severed its legal and administrative links with the West Bank effectively denationalizing Palestinians for the second time. It had become apparent to King Hussein of Jordan that the Palestine Liberation Organisation (hereafter 'PLO') was making preparations to declare the establishment of an independent Palestinian State in the West Bank and Gaza with Jerusalem as its capital. This occurred at the 19th emergency session of the Palestine National Congress in Algiers on 15 November 1988. *See* U.N. Doc. A/43/827 (18 November 1988) and J.L. Prince, 'The International Legal Implications of the November 1988 Palestinian Declaration of Statehood', 25 *Stanford Journal of International Law* (1989) pp. 681–708. Only those Palestinians in the West Bank, which Jordan annexed in 1950, lost their nationality. All those Palestinians in the East Bank (or in Jordan-proper) retained their Jordanian nationality. The West Bank is still occupied and as Palestinians no longer have Jordanian nationality and as there is still not a Palestinian State, they are stateless.

Fourth Geneva Convention relative to the protection of Civilian Persons in Time of War (hereinafter 'Fourth Geneva Convention').[101]

Israel has not conferred its nationality on the inhabitants of the West Bank and the Gaza Strip because Israel does not want to become a binational State or a State where the majority of the population are non-Jews. In this particular instance, it happens to be in Israel's interest to abide by international law.[102] On the other hand, Israel is transferring its citizens into the territory it is occupying which is prohibited by Article 49(6) of the Fourth Geneva Convention.[103] As Weiler points out, Israel is manipulating the *jus in bello* by refraining from imposing its nationality on the inhabitants that it occupies, which is in accordance with international law, while at the same time transferring its citizens into the territory it occupies which is prohibited by international law.[104] Israel has been manipulating the law in this way for the last 37 years.[105] Israel wants to change the demography of the West Bank in the hope that parts of it can be annexed in the not to distant future.[106] It is no coincidence that the construction

[101] Hague Convention (IV) Respecting the Laws and Customs of War on Land, and Annex: Regulations Respecting the Laws and Customs of War on Land, T.S. No. 539, 1 Bevans 631, signed at the Hague, 18 October 1907, entry into force 26 January 1910. Geneva Convention (IV) Relative to the Protection of Civilian Persons in Time of War, 12 August 1949, 75 *UN Treaty Series* 287 (entered into force 21 October 1950).

[102] *Ibid. see* Article 45 of the Hague Regulations and Article 67 of the Fourth Geneva Convention.

[103] This provides that the Occupying Power shall not deport or transfer parts of its own civilian population into the territory it occupies.

[104] *See* Weiler, *supra* note 87.

[105] On 6 May 2004, the U.N. General Assembly affirmed that, "the status of the Palestinian territory occupied since 1967, including East Jerusalem, remains one of military occupation, and affirms, in accordance with the rules and principles of international law and relevant resolutions of the United Nations, including Security Council resolutions, that the Palestinian people have the right of self-determination and to sovereignty over their territory and that Israel, the occupying power, has only the duties and obligations of an occupying power under the Fourth Geneva Convention and the Regulations annexed to the Hague Convention Respecting the Laws and Customs of War of 1907". *See* U.N.G.A. resolution A/58/L.61/Rev.1. This resolution was adopted with 140 States in favour to six against (Israel, Marshall Islands, Micronesia, Nauru, Palau and the U.S.A.) with 11 abstentions (Australia, Costa Rica, Dominican Republic, Guatemala, Honduras, Nicaragua, Peru, Serbia and Montenegro, Solomon Islands, Tonga and Tuvalu).

[106] This was summed up in the words of Israel's deputy Prime Minister, Ehud Olmert, in a recent interview with David Landau in Ha'aretz newspaper as 'Maximum Jews Minimum Palestinians', *Ha'aretz*, 5 December 2003, <www.haaretz.com/GA/pages/shArtGA. jhtml?itemNo=360533>, last visited 30 March 2005. According to Olmert "[t]here is no doubt in my mind that very soon the government of Israel is going to have to address the demographic issue with the utmost seriousness and resolve. This issue above all others will dictate the solution that we must adopt. In the absence of a negotiated agreement – and I do not believe in the realistic prospect of an agreement – we need to implement a unilateral alternative".

of the wall[107] closely corresponds with those areas in the Occupied Palestinian Territory with a heavy concentration of Jewish settlements.[108]

4.4. *Israel's Nationality and Entry into Israel Law 2003*

In May 2003, the Knesset enacted the Nationality and Entry into Israeli Law, which suspends, for a renewable one year period, the possibility of family reunification, subject to limited and subjective exceptions especially in the cases of marriages between an Israeli (Arab) citizen and a person (Arab) residing in the Occupied Palestinian Territories.[109] The law directly discriminates between Arabs resident in the Occupied Palestinian Territories and Jews resident in the Occupied Palestinian Territories as it only applies to Arabs; Jews are excluded from its application. Section 2 of this law limits citizenship and stay in Israel:

> "During the period in which this law shall remain in force, despite what is said in any legal provision, including Article 7 of the Nationality law, the Minister of Interior shall not grant the inhabitant of an area nationality on the basis of the Nationality law, and shall not give him a license to reside in Israel on the basis of the Entry into Israel Law, and the Area Commander shall not grant a said inhabitant, a permit to stay in Israel, on the basis with the security legislation in the area."[110]

This means, in effect, that the normal conditions for non-Jews to obtain Israeli nationality, such as marriage between a Palestinian resident in the Occupied Palestinian Territories, and a Palestinian with Israeli nationality i.e. 'Israeli Arabs', no longer apply. Therefore were a Palestinian woman to marry a

---

[107] This is the terminology used by the U.N. General Assembly and by the International Court of Justice to describe a system of walls, fences, ditches, trenches, watchtowers, and barriers in and around East Jerusalem, and in substantial parts of the West Bank. According to the Court: "the 'Wall' in question is a complex construction, so that the term cannot be understood in a limited physical sense. However, the other terms used, either by Israel ("fence") or by the Secretary-General ("barrier"), are no more accurate if understood in the physical sense. In this Opinion, the Court has therefore chosen to use the terminology employed by the General Assembly". See para. 67 of the ICJ's advisory opinion on the legal consequences of the construction of a Wall in the Occupied Palestinian Territory. This can be viewed on the Court's website at: <www.icj-cij.org/icjwww/idocket/imwp/imwpframe.htm>, last visited 27 March 2005.

[108] For further reading *see* the report by the U.N. Special Rapporteur, Professor John Dugard, at U.N. Doc. E/CN.4/2004/6/Add.1, 27 February 2004. This report focused on the Wall.

[109] The Nationality and Entry into Israel Law (temporary provision) 5763–2003 can be viewed on the web site of the Knesset at <www.knesset.gov.il/laws/special/eng/citizenship_law.htm>, last visited 8 November 2004.

[110] *Ibid.*

Palestinian man, say from Haifa, who has Israeli nationality, neither the Palestinian woman nor her children would obtain Israeli nationality. However Jewish nationals of Israel residing also in the Occupied Palestinian Territories are *not* subject to this law. The Nationality and Entry into Israel Law is drafted to apply to Arabs only. It applies both to Arabs in Israel and to Arabs in East Jerusalem. It has a two fold purpose: to limit the number of Arabs obtaining Israeli nationality and to limit the number of Arabs obtaining residency rights in East Jerusalem. Its enactment was necessitated by demographic concerns. The Jewish State fears that its Jewish character is at threat. In its seventy-eighth session, the Human Rights Committee set up to monitor the Covenant on Civil and Political Rights concluded that, "[t]he State party [Israel] should revoke the Nationality and Entrance into Israel Law (Temporary Order) of 31 July, 2003, which raises serious issues under Articles 17, 23 and 26 of the Covenant. The State party should reconsider its policy with a view to facilitating family reunification of all its citizens and permanent residents . . .".[111] In July 2004 the Government of Israel decided to renew this law for a further year despite protests by human rights organizations.[112]

5. Conclusions

Simply put, for the purposes of international law Palestinians have no nationality. They are for the most part stateless persons. The reason for this is that Palestinians were denationalized by Israel in 1952, after Israel wrongfully evicted them from their homeland. Section 3 of Israel's 1952 Nationality Law was specifically drafted to denationalize Palestinian Arabs *en masse* on a racially discriminatory basis. This occurred after Israel had wrongfully expelled the Palestinian Arabs from their homes. Since 1967 Israel has manipulated international humanitarian law by transferring its civilian population into the territory it occupies whilst the indigenous Palestinian population

---

[111] *See* the Concluding Observations of the Human Rights Committee: Israel 21/08/2003. CCPR/CO/78/ISR, para 21.

[112] *See* the Briefing Note by the *Mossawa* Center, The Advocacy Center for Arab Citizens of Israel, Haifa, Israel. Their web page can be viewed at <www.mossawacenter.org> According to *Mossawa*, this law "will not only prevent newly married couples from being able to live together, but will also affect couples who have been married for years, and whose requests for residence permits are still pending. This bill clearly discriminates against Israeli citizens of Palestinian origin and their spouses . . . This bill does not affect marriages between Israeli citizens and other foreign spouses. As a result, this law permits discrimination on grounds of ethnicity and national origin and clearly violates international human rights law, treaties and domestic laws which Israel has ratified to uphold. According to Israeli government statistics, *over 21,000 couples are currently effected by this legislation* [emphasis added]. Failing to comply with this new law, the spouse could be subject to deportation by the State at any time".

remains subject to military law.[113] Israel has furthermore enacted racially discriminatory legislation in the form of the Nationality and Entrance into Israel Law (2003), which the Human Rights Committee (set up to monitor the Covenant on Civil and Political Rights) has requested Israel to revoke. Whilst commentators were unclear as to the illegality of mass denationalization under international law in the first half of the twentieth century, today it is generally accepted that expulsion and populations transfer when combined with racially discriminatory mass denationalization contravene international law.

According to the law of State responsibility, "[a]n act of a State does not constitute a breach of an international obligation unless the State is bound by the obligation in question at the time the act occurs".[114] Yet even in 1952, the year Israel enacted its Nationality Law, it was clear that a State could not, whether through expulsion or other means, compel another State to receive one of its own nationals whom it has expelled from its own territory. It was State practice before 1948 that persons habitually resident in a State undergoing succession *ipso facto* acquired the nationality of the successor State.[115] Molony wrote in 1934 that "in the post-war Peace Treaties the principle of domicile or habitual residence is the criterion most favoured for the acquisition of nationality".[116] The 1919 Rumanian Minorities Treaty provided that, "Rumania undertakes to recognize as Rumanian nationals *ipso facto* and without requirement of any formality Jews inhabiting any Rumanian territory who do not possess another nationality".[117] This principle was also applied to Palestine in 1925 under Article 30 of the Treaty of Lausanne which provided that "[t]urkish subjects habitually resident in territory which in accordance with the provisions of the present Treaty is detached from Turkey will become *ipso facto*, in the conditions laid down by the local law, nationals of the State to which such

---

[113] For an Israeli military perspective see Uri Shalom "The Principle of Legality and the Israeli Military Government in the Territories" 153 *Military Law Review* (1996) pp. 245–273.

[114] *See* Article 13 of the International Law Commission's Draft articles on Responsibility of States for Internationally Wrongful Acts adopted at its fifty-third session (2001). *Official Records of the General Assembly, Fifty-sixth session, Supplement No. 10* (A/56/10), chp.IV.E.1). This can also be viewed in Brownlie *Basic Documents, supra* note 32, pp. 300–310.

[115] Kunz, Oppenheim, Keith, Lawrence, Gettys, Fauchille, Mann, McNair, Brownlie and others have all asserted that there is a rule of international law that upon a change of sovereignty the inhabitants of the territory lose the nationality of the predecessor State and become *ipso facto* nationals of the successor State. The Treaties of Versailles, St Germaine, Trianon, Paris and Lausanne are examples of this.

[116] *See* W. O'Sullivan Molony, *Nationality and the Peace Treaties* (George Allen and Unwin, London, 1934) p. 85.

[117] *See* the Rumanian Minorities Treaty signed on 9 December 1919, in force as from 4 September 1920, and placed under the guarantee of the League of Nations on 30 August 1921, concluded in pursuance of Article 60 of the St. Germain Treaty and Article 46 of the Trianon Treaty. *See* Molony *ibid.* p. 129.

territory is transferred".[118] Israel did not grant persons habitually resident in Palestine in 1948 its nationality because the Zionists wanted to create a Jewish State, one where the majority of the population in the State would be Jewish. This could not have been accomplished without expelling the Arabs from Palestine. This expulsion, – and the population transfer that has been taking place on an almost continuous basis since the establishment of the State of Israel, (in particular since 1967 in the Occupied Palestinian Territories), is today contrary to international law.[119] Similarly, Israel's continuous obstruction of the Palestinians right of return is also prohibited by international law. This is because Israel's refusal to allow Palestinian refugees the right of return imposes a burden on the adjoining States to provide refuge to persons wrongfully expelled from their homeland, violating their territorial sovereignty and Statehood. The deportation or forcible transfer of a civilian population is nowadays considered a crime against humanity.[120]

According to the rule of intertemporal law, a juridical fact must be appreciated in the light of the law contemporary with it, and not of the law in force at the time when a dispute in regard to it arises or falls to be settled. However, according to Judge Huber a distinction must be made between the creation of rights and the existence of rights, "[t]he same principle which subjects the act creative of a right to the law in force at the time the right arises, demands that the existence of the right, in other words its continued manifestation, shall follow the conditions required of law".[121] In other words, rights acquired in a valid manner according to the law contemporaneous with that creation may be lost if not maintained in accordance with the changes brought about by the development of international law.[122] This definition corresponds to that of the

---

[118] *See supra* note 8.

[119] By population transfer I am referring to the transfer of Jewish-Israeli settlers into colonies in the Occupied Palestinian Territories that according to the International Court of Justice's advisory opinion on the Wall have been established in breach of international law (para. 120).

[120] Article 7 (1) d of the Rome Statute of the International Criminal Court lists the deportation or forcible transfer of population as a crime against humanity. According to Article 7 (2) d of the Statute "'Deportation or forcible transfer of population' means forced displacement of the persons concerned by expulsion or other coercive acts from the area in which they are lawfully present, without grounds permitted under international law". The Rome Statute can be viewed at <www.un.org/law/icc/statute/romefra.htm>, last visited 30 October 2004. *See also* A. De Zayas, 'The Illegality of Population Transfer and the Application of Emerging International Norms in the Palestinian Context', 6 *The Palestine Yearbook of International Law* (1990–1991) pp. 17–55.

[121] *See Island of Palmas* case (Netherlands v. United States) 2 E. Int'l Arb. Awards pp. 831 and 845.

[122] *See* T.O. Elias, 'The Doctrine of Intertemporal Law', 74 *American Journal of International Law* (1980) p. 286; and E. McWhinney, 'The Time Dimension in International Law, Historical Relativism and Intertemporal Law' in J. Makarczyk (ed.), *Essays in Honour of Judge Manfred Lachs* (Martinus Nijhoff, The Hague, 1984) pp. 179–199.

International Law Commission's Draft Articles on Responsibility of States for Internationally Wrongful Acts regarding the extension in time of an international obligation. Article 14 (2) provides "[t]he breach of an international obligation by an act of a State *having a continuing character extends over the entire period* during which the act continues and remains not in conformity with the international obligation [emphasis added]".[123] It was the intention of the international community in drafting U.N. General Assembly resolution 194 (III) in 1948 that Palestinian refugees should have the right to choose whether or not to return to their homes or to receive compensation.[124] In his Progress Report the U.N. Mediator concluded that:

> "[t]he Arab inhabitants of Palestine are not citizens or subjects of Egypt, Iraq, Lebanon, Syria and Transjordan, the States which are at present providing them with a refuge and the basic necessities of life. As residents of Palestine, a former mandated territory for which the international community *has a continuing responsibility* until a final settlement is achieved, these Arab refugees understandably look to the United Nations for effective assistance [emphasis added]."[125]

Israel's obligation towards the Palestinian refugees continues from the date of their expulsion until the present day and will continue so long as Israel is not in conformity with its international obligations.[126]

As the grant of nationality is an attribute of Statehood, and as there is not yet a Palestinian State which can grant the Palestinians its nationality, Palestinians remain stateless.[127] If there were a Palestinian State in the West Bank and the Gaza Strip with East Jerusalem as its capital then the Palestinians

---

[123] *See supra* note 114.

[124] *See* the report of the U.N. mediator Counte Folke Bernadotte who thought that "their [the Palestinian refugees] unconditional right to make a free choice should be fully respected", *supra* note 45. Higgins attaches importance to the intention of the parties in the application of the intertemporal rule of international law. She draws attention to the practice of the European Court of Human Rights to emphasize the need to interpret human rights by reference to developing ideas. *See* R. Higgins "Some Observations on the Inter-Temporal Rule in International Law" in J. Makarezyk (ed.), *Theory of International Law at the Threshold of the 21st Century Essays in Honour of Krzystof Skubiszwski* (Kluwer Law International, The Hague, 1996) pp. 173–181.

[125] *See* the Progress Report at (c) entitled "Assistance to Refugees" VI. Conclusions 1 (d), *supra* note 45. *See also* E.H. Buehrig, *The UN and the Palestinian Refugees* (Indiana University Press 1971) p. 11.

[126] For further reading *see* J. Pauwelyn, "The Concept of a 'Continuing Violation' of an International Obligation: Selected Problems", 66 *British Yearbook of International Law* (1995) pp. 415–450.

[127] For further reading on the status of Palestinian refugees *see* S. M. Akram and G. Goodwin-Gill, *Brief Amicus Curiae* prepared for the United States Department of Justice Executive Office for Immigration Review, Board of Immigration Appeals, Falls Church, Virginia. This was reproduced in 11 *Palestine Yearbook of International Law* (2000/2001) pp. 185–260.

will have a State where they can exercise their right to self-determination and statehood in accordance with U.N. Security Council resolutions 242 (1967), 338 (1973), 1397 (2002) and 1515 (2003). However these resolutions, with the exception of resolution 242, make no mention of the Palestinian refugees.[128] Having said this, U.N. Security Council resolution 1515 endorses, "the Quartet Performance-based Roadmap to a Permanent Two-State Solution to the Israeli-Palestinian conflict" and this document does mention that a final and comprehensive permanent status agreement will include "an agreed, just, fair and realistic solution to the refugee issue".[129] However, there is no reference to the norms of principles of international law regarding the refugee question in that document. Moreover, since 14 April 2002, Israel has been constructing a wall in substantial parts of the West Bank, including in and around East Jerusalem, in what is Occupied Palestinian Territory.[130] The wall, which the International Court in July 2004 held to be unlawful, poses a direct challenge to the Roadmap and to the Palestinian people's legitimate aspirations for independence and statehood.[131]

According to John Dugard, the U.N. Special Rapporteur for Human Rights in the Occupied Palestinian Territories, the wall is likely to lead to a new generation of refuges or internally displaced persons.[132] More refugees and I.D.P.'s

[128] *See* U.N. Security Council resolution 242, 22 November 1967. This resolution affirms "the necessity for achieving a just settlement of the refugee problem".

[129] *See* U.N. Doc. S/2003/529, 7 May 2003.

[130] *See* the Report of the Secretary-General prepared pursuant to General Assembly resolution ES-10/13, U.N. Doc. A/ES-10/248, 24 November 2003.

[131] On 1 October 2003, Mr. Nasser Al-Kidwa, the Permanent Observer of Palestine to the U.N. sent a letter to Mr. Kofi Annan the Secretary-General, expressing concern that the construction of the Wall inside Occupied Palestinian Territory would interfere with the creation of "an independent, democratic and viable Palestinian State" as envisaged in the Roadmap. *See* U.N. Doc. A/58/399, S/2003/929, 1 October 2003. Subsequently, the U.N. General Assembly adopted a resolution requesting the International Court of Justice to urgently render an advisory opinion on the legal consequences arising from the construction of the Wall. *See* U.N.G.A resolution ES-10/14 (A/ES-10/L.16), 8 December 2003. James Crawford in his oral pleading before the International Court pointed out that that the Wall being constructed by Israel was not mentioned in the Road Map. He pointed out that, "the Wall, if allowed to be completed, will destroy the Road Map." *See* the Statement by James Crawford para. 32. This can be viewed at the web site of the International Court of Justice at <www.icj-cij.org/>. The International Court agreed and found the Wall and its associated regime contrary to international law. *See* the opinion on the web site at para. 142 and subparagraph 3 A of the *dispositif.* On 8 May 2004, President George W. Bush decided to unilaterally abandon the timetable set out in the Roadmap for the creation of a Palestinian State (which was supposed to be in 2005) in an interview he gave to an Egyptian newspaper. In an interview with Ibrahim Nafie the editor-in-chief of the Egyptian daily *Al-Ahram* President George W. Bush said that, "2005 may be hard (to have an independent and viable Palestinian State), since 2005 is right around the corner".

[132] *See* the summary of his report in U.N. Doc. E/CN.4/2004/6, 8 September 2003 p. 2. He

are, however, precisely what Palestinians do not need at this moment in time, for it is estimated that there are already seven million Palestinian refugees and I.D.P.'s, out of a world wide population of nine million Palestinians.[133] What Palestinians need is a State and for their rights enshrined in international law to be respected and upheld. It is clear that U.N. General Assembly resolution 194 (III) affirms the right of refugees "wishing to return to their homes and live at peace with their neighbours should be permitted to do so at the earliest practicable date, and that compensation should be paid for the property of those choosing not to return . . .". To date Palestinian refugees have neither been compensated; nor offered any right to return to home. Resolution 194 (III) is recalled annually in the U.N. General Assembly by overwhelming majorities.[134] Moreover, the Treaty of Peace concluded between the States of Israel and Jordan make it abundantly clear that the Palestine refugee question is to be solved according to the principles, and norms, of international law.[135] Today, according to the general principles of international law, and in particular the multilateral human rights treaties the right to a nationality is recognised as a human right.[136] The right to a nationality was first recognised in Article 15 of the 1948 Universal Declaration of Human Rights, adopted by the U.N. General

wrote, "Over 210,000 Palestinians will be seriously affected by the Wall. Palestinians living between the Wall and the green line will be effectively cut off from their farmlands and workplaces, schools, health clinics and other social services. This is likely to lead to a new generation of refugees or internally displaced persons". In his report of December 2004, Dugard notes under the heading, "Forced Exodus" that one of the purposes of the Wall is "to compel Palestinian residents in the so-called 'Seam Zone' between the Wall and the Green Line and those adjacent to the Wall, but seperated from their lands by the Wall, to leave their homes and start a new life elsewhere in the West Bank, by making life intolerable for them". See UN Doc. E/CN.4/2005/29, 7 December 2004 at para. 35. This was also acknowledged by the International Court of Justice in para. 133 of its advisory opinion.

[133] *See* the *Survey of Palestinian Refugees and Internally Displaced Persons 2002* (Badil Resource Centre for Palestinian Residency and Refugee Rights (2003) p. 34.

[134] The last reaffirmation of resolution 194 (III) was in U.N. General Assembly resolution A/RES/58/91 of 9 December 2003. This resolution was adopted by 167 States in favour to one against (Israel) with eight abstentions. *See* U.N.G.A. resolution 59/117, 15 December 2004 where 167 States voted in favour, 11 abstained and 1 (Israel) voted against; and U.N.G.A. resolution 59/120, 15 December 2004 where 161 States voted favour, 9 abstained and 6 voted against. *See also* U.N.G.A. resolution 59/118, 15 December 2004, which refers to persons displaced as a result of the 1967 war, where 162 States voted in favour, 9 abstained and 6 voted against.

[135] *See* U.N. Doc. A/50/73 S/1995/83, 27 January 1995. Article 8 (2) of the Treaty provides "that the above human problems [referring to the Palestinian refugees] caused by the conflict in the Middle East *cannot be fully resolved on the bilateral level*, the Parties will seek to resolve them in appropriate forums, *in accordance with international law* [my emphasis]".

[136] *See* J.M.M. Chan, 'The Right to a Nationality as a Human Right', 10 *Human Rights Law Journal* (1991) pp. 1–14.

Assembly the day before it passed Resolution 194 (III).[137] Since this time
the right to a nationality has been recognized in the 1961 Convention on the
Reduction of Statelessness, the 1966 International Convention on the
Elimination of All Forms of Discrimination, the 1966 International Covenant
on Civil and Political Rights and the 1989 Convention on the Rights of the
Child.[138] Israel, Lebanon, Syria and Jordan, countries with large populations of
Palestinian refugees, have all signed and ratified those conventions but with the
noticeable exception of the Convention on the Reduction of Statelessness.[139]
Yet the right to a nationality, including the right to independence and statehood,
is something continuously denied to Palestinians.

According to the law of State responsibility, full reparation for the injury
caused by the internationally wrongful act shall take the form of restitution,
compensation and satisfaction, either singly or in combination.[140] Restitution
is the primary form of reparation.[141] It involves a return to the *status quo ante*,
provided and to the extent that restitution: (a) is not materially impossible; (b)
does not involve a burden out of all proportion to the benefit deriving from
restitution instead of compensation.[142] It is submitted that allowing Palestinian
refugees the right to choose whether to remain in their states of refuge, or to
return home is neither materially impossible, and nor does it involve a burden
out of all proportion to the benefit that they would receive from being able to
return home.[143] Should the Palestinian refugee[s] choose not to return home,

---

[137] This was adopted by the U.N. General Assembly on 10 December 1948. *See* U.N. Doc.
A/811, 10 December 1948.

[138] *See* Article 5 (d) (iii) of International Convention on the Elimination of All Forms of
Discrimination. This was adopted on 20 November 1963 by the U.N. General Assembly in
resolution 1904 (XVIII) 3 *International Legal Materials* (1964) p. 164 and *Yearbook of the
United Nations* (1963) p. 330; For the International Covenant on Civil and Political Rights *see*
Article 24 (3) U.N. General Assembly resolution 2200A (XXI), U.N. Doc. A/6316 (1966), 999
United Nations Treaty Series 171; and for the Convention on the Rights of the Child *see* Article
7 of the annex to U.N. General Assembly resolution A/44/49 (1989) 1577 *United Nations Treaty
Series* 3.

[139] *See* Article 1 and 10 of the Convention on the Reduction of Statelessness which was
adopted on 30 August 1961 by a conference of plenipotentiaries which met in 1959 and reconvened in 1961 in pursuance of General Assembly resolution 896 (IX) of 4 December 1954
(entered into force 13 December 1975) *see* 989 *United Nations Treaty Series* 175.

[140] *See* Article 34 of the ILC's Draft Articles, *supra* note 114. The U.N. Mediator's concluded
his Progress Report (*supra* note 45) on a personal note by saying that he believed "that for the
international community to accept its share of responsibility for the refugees of Palestine is one
of the minimum conditions for the success of its efforts to bring peace to that land".

[141] *See* Third Report on State Responsibility by Mr. James Crawford Special Rapporteur U.N.
Doc. A/CN.4/507/Add.1, 30 May 2000 paras. 124, 135, 143.

[142] *See* Article 35, *supra* note 114.

[143] There is no reason in principle why Palestinian refugees should not be allowed to exercise their right of return. Many of the homes and villages that were destroyed in 1948 remain

the State responsible for the international wrongful act, which in this case is the State of Israel, is nevertheless under an obligation to compensate Palestinian refugees for the damage caused, insofar as such damage is not made good by restitution.[144] Compensation, which is specifically referred to in U.N. General Assembly resolution 194 (III), should cover any financially assessable damage including loss of profits, insofar as they can be established, and the interest runs from the date when the principal sum should have been paid until the date the obligation to pay is fulfilled.[145] According to the Draft Articles, "[s]atisfaction may consist in an acknowledgement of the breach, an expression of regret, a formal apology or another appropriate modality".[146] To date, the State of Israel has never formally apologized or expressed regret for its role in the Palestinian tragedy.

Under international law the Arab States also have obligations towards Palestinian refugees resident in their territory, in particular to the descendents of Palestinian refugees. After all, Jordan, Lebanon and Syria, like Israel, have all signed multilateral human rights treaties which include provisions on nationality.[147] However, of all the Arab States only Jordan has offered Palestinian refugees (from the West Bank) Jordanian nationality.[148] This is due to a law passed by the League of Arab States in 1954 which prohibits dual-nationality in the Arab world.[149] Unless this Agreement is annulled it would not

---

uninhabited. In some situations Palestinian refugees in UNRWA camps in the West Bank can actually see their former farms and homes. They are however prohibited from returning. It would seem that the real issue underlying Israel's rejection of the Palestinian right of return is that, according to Israel, allowing so many ethnic Arabs the right to return to their homes inside Israel would 'dilute' the Jewish character of the State, (if they chose to return), which is an entirely political argument. When I asked former Prime Minister of Israel, Ehud Barak, whether some of the Palestinian refugees from 1948 and their descendants should have the right to return to their former homes in Israel, he responded by saying in a live question and answer session with Haaretz newspaper (<www.haaretzdaily.com>) on 19 July 2004 "The principle we set at Camp David and which in fact existed even prior to this, that not a single Palestinian can have a *political* right of return, should remain a cornerstone of our position [my emphasis]".

[144] *See* Article 36 of the ILC Draft Articles *supra* note 114.

[145] *See* Article 36 (2) and 38 (2) of the ILC Draft Articles *ibid*. U.N. General Assembly resolution 194 (II) says, "that compensation should be paid for the property of those choosing not to return and for loss of or damage to property which, *under principles of international law or in equity*, should be made good by the Governments of authorities responsible [my emphasis]."

[146] *See* Article 37 of the ILC Draft Articles, *supra* note 114.

[147] According to Article 7 (1) of the Convention on the Rights of the Child, *supra* note 138, "[t]he child shall be registered immediately after birth and shall have the right from birth to a name, *the right to acquire a nationality* and, as far as possible, the right to know and be cared for by his or her parents [my emphasis]".

[148] This is because Jordan occupied and annexed East Jerusalem and the West Bank from 1950–1967. Only two states formally recognized this: Pakistan and the United Kingdom.

[149] On 5 April 1954 the League of Arab States agreed to a number of provisions on nationality in the Arab world. According to Article 6 of the Nationality Agreement, "[a] national of one

be possible for Palestinian refugees to be nationals of their host country and of a future Palestinian State.[150] Having said this, primary responsibility for the Palestinian refugee problem does rest with Israel. Had the Palestinian not been expelled or forced to flee Palestine they would never have ended up in refugee camps in Lebanon, Syria and Jordan.[151] Article 14 (2) of the International Law Commissions Draft Articles on Nationality of Natural Persons in Relation to the Succession of States requires that, "[a] state concerned shall take all necessary measures to allow persons concerned who, because of events connected with the succession of states, *were forced to* leave their habitual residence on its territory *to return thereto* [emphasis added]".[152]

The question of Palestine can only be solved when the predicament of the Palestinian refugees is taken fully into consideration. Any negotiated solution must be based on international law. Palestinian refugees should be given a choice as whether to return to their homes or to accept compensation as stipulated in U.N. General Assembly resolution 194 (III), the principal document embodying their rights enshrined in international law. It will take a combined effort by the international community including Israel, the P.L.O., and the Arab States most affected by the Palestinian refugee problem to solve it; and any solution must take into account the legitimate aspirations of the refugees whose voices must be heard.[153] This was the very essence of Counte Folke

Member State of the Arab League shall not, except with the approval of his Government, acquire by naturalization the nationality of another Member State of the League; on his so acquiring the new nationality his former nationality shall abate." *See* M. Khalil, *The Arab States and the Arab League a Documentary Record in Two Volumes* (Vol. II) (Khayats, Beirut 1962) p. 128.

[150] On 31 August 2004 I interviewed Dr. Lex Takkenberg in Damascus. Takkenberg is currently Director-General of UNRWA's Syrian Field Office. He told me that the agreement on the prohibition of dual-nationality in the Arab world might be reconsidered in the context of a political solution to the question of Palestine, making it possible for (former) Palestinian refugees to acquire the nationality of both Palestine and their host country. For further reading *see* L. Takkenberg, *The Status of Palestinian Refugees in International Law* (Oxford University Press 1998).

[151] According to UNRWA statistics there are 1,740,170 Palestinian refugees registered as living in Jordan; 394,532 in Lebanon; 413,827 in Syria; 665,246 in the West Bank; and 922,674 in the Gaza Strip (Public Information Office, UNRWA Headquarters Gaza, March 2004).

[152] In the commentary to the draft articles it says, "[p]aragraph 2 addresses the problem of habitual residents in the specific case where the succession of States is the result of events leading to the displacement of a large part of the population. The purpose of this provision is to ensure the effective restoration of the status of habitual residents as protected under paragraph 1. The Commission feels that, in light of recent experience in Eastern Europe, it was desirable to address explicitly the problem of this vulnerable group of persons." It is submitted that recent experiences in Eastern Europe are not too dissimilar to past experiences in Palestine. The commentary and draft articles can be viewed at <www.un.org/law/ilc/reports/1999/english/chap4.htm>, last visited 30 October 2004.

[153] Dr. Karma Nabulsi, Prize Research Fellow at Nuffield College, Oxford University is cur-

Bernadotte's last progress report which he submitted to the U.N. General Assembly the day before his assassination on Friday 17 September 1948.[154]

Author's Note

The Israeli-Palestinian conflict is not just about territory; it is also about the people who inhabit that territory. Whilst Israel succeeded in engineering the removal of Palestine's indigenous inhabitants in 1948 and 1967, from land it acquired through war to create the Jewish State, it has been losing its "demographic battle" with the Palestinians ever since. On 28 February 2005, the U.S. Department of State released their "Country Report on Human Rights Practices" in Israel and the Occupied Palestinian Territories for the year 2004.[155] According to this report there are 1.4 million Palestinians living in the Gaza Strip, 2.4 million Palestinians living in the West Bank (not including East Jerusalem), 237,185 Palestinians living in East Jerusalem and 1.3 million Palestinians (also known as "Israeli Arabs") living in Israel. In other words, there are 5,377,185 Palestinians living in Israel and the Occupied Palestinian Territories (i.e. in territory conforming to the British Mandate of Palestine).[156]

---

rently undertaking a civic needs assessment of Palestinian refugees entitled "Civitas". The project was developed in collaboration with the European Commission of External Relations, through a series of reports and workshops run at Nuffield College, the European University Institute, and exile Palestinian communities over the last four years. The purpose of Civitas is to facilitate Palestinian refugees and exile communities outside the West Bank and Gaza, so they deliberate on the mechanisms and structures they need in order to communicate effectively with their representatives; the PLO, the host countries, humanitarian agencies that serve them, and other refugee communities, through participatory methodology. The communities will run these debates themselves. Visit <www.civitas-online.org> for further information.

[154] "The ruthless assassination of Count Folke Bernadotte, United Nations Mediator in Palestine, and of United Nations Observer Colonel Andre Serot of the French Air Force, in Jerusalem on Friday, 17 September 1948, was the result of a deliberate and planned attack aimed at the person of the Mediator and at the authority of the United Nations in Palestine. Assassinations occurred in Territory controlled and administered by armed forces and officials of the provisional government of Israel. Foreign Minister of provisional government has informed me by letter dated 19 September 1948 that "as there seems to be little doubt that the group calling itself Hazit Hamoledet (fatherland front), which was acknowledged the authorship of the crime, is an arm of the dissident organization, Lohame Herut Israel (fighters for the freedom of Israel), the provisional government has proceeded to take action against this organization and its members". *See* the Report Regarding the Assassination of the U.N. Mediator, U.N. Doc. S/1018 28 September 1948, para. 1.

[155] The report can be located at the State Department's web site: http://www.state.gov/g/drl/rls/hrrpt/2004/41723.htm, last visited 8 March 2005.

[156] There are also a further 290,000 people classified as minorities such as Druze, Bedouin and Circassians. These minority groups would be classified as non-Jewish.

According to the same report, there are 5.2 million Jews living in Israel, including Jews living in settlements in East Jerusalem, the West Bank and the Gaza Strip.[157] On the basis of these figures; Palestinians outnumber Jews in the land between the Jordan River and the Mediterranean Sea. If this is right, then it is the first time since the 1948 exodus that Palestinian Arabs have outnumbered Israeli Jews in the Holy Land. One should bear in mind that these figures don't include Palestinian refugees nor Palestinians who emigrated elsewhere, or their descendents. And one should not forget that these people have not waived their rights regarding return, repatriation, restitution and compensation for they have been *prevented* from exercising them.

Israeli demographers Arnon Sofer,[158] Professor in the Department of Geography at Haifa University, and Sergio Della Pergola, of the Institute of Contemporary Jewry at the Hebrew University of Jerusalem, have been highlighting this demographic trend (i.e. the surge in the Palestinian population) for a number of years and are said to have influenced the current policies of Israel's Prime Minister, Ariel Sharon.[159] Their findings may partly explain why, in recent years, the State of Israel has been taking drastic measures such as building a Wall in Occupied Palestinian Territory that loops around large, densely populated, Jewish settlement blocs in the West Bank, combined with a plan to unilaterally "disengage" from some parts of the Gaza Strip.[160] Bearing in mind that the number of settlers in Gaza, at approximately 7,500 persons, roughly represent 2% of all Jewish settlers in Occupied Palestinian Territory[161]

---

[157] According to a source in the US Embassy in Tel Aviv who wishes to remain anonymous, these figures were drawn from the Israeli Central Bureau of Statistics and include Israeli Jews living inside the "Green Line" (i.e. in settlements).

[158] Sometimes spelt "Soffer".

[159] *See* the Interview with Arnon Soffer, "One on one: It's the demography stupid!" with Ruthie Blum in the *Jerusalem Post* 20 May, 2004. According to Soffer: "Unilateral separation doesn't guarantee 'peace' – it guarantees a Zionist-Jewish state with an overwhelming majority of Jews; it guarantees the kind of safety that will return tourists to the country; and it guarantees one other important thing: Between 1948 and 1967, the fence was a fence, and 400,000 people left the West Bank voluntarily. This is what will happen after separation. If a Palestinian cannot come into Tel Aviv for work, he will look in Iraq, or Kuwait, or London. I believe that there will be movement out of the area".

[160] For further reading *see* "Legal Aspects of Israel's Disengagement Plan under International Humanitarian Law" a Policy Brief by the *Harvard Program on Humanitarian Policy and Conflict Research*. You can read this brief (PDF file) at the following web site: http://www.ihlre-search.org/opt/pdfs/briefing3466.pdf, last visited 24 March 2005.

[161] Settler statistics in the OPTs vary. In 2002, according to the Applied Research Institute in Jerusalem there were 405,000 settlers in OPT. Of these, 195,000 live in East Jerusalem and 6,500 in Gaza. According to the Palestine Central Bureau of Statistics, in 2002 there were 412,785 set-

(including East Jerusalem); and that the ratio of Palestinians to settlers in the Gaza Strip is 187 to 1, it would seem likely that Machiavellian reasons rather than humanitarian gestures underlie Israel's sudden decision to dismantle settlements and carry out a qualified military redeployment from parts of the Gaza Strip.[162] It has suddenly dawned upon the political hierarchy in Israel that to maintain the Jewish character of the State, Israel must withdraw from parts of the Occupied Palestinian Territories (i.e. densely populated Palestinian areas).[163] Israel has probably concluded that it is in its best interests to get out of Gaza, one of the most densely populated places on earth, which accounts for only 1.25% of the land of mandatory Palestine, whilst consolidating its control over the West Bank.[164] In other words, Israel may lose Gaza but it will gain the West Bank. All Israel loses is what it already considers "lost"; a small amount of land populated by the "wrong" kind of people. It would therefore be naïve to think that Israel's Wall and its "disengagement plan" have anything to do with a "peace process". Rather, they represent Israel's last ditch attempt at "self-preservation" by trying to maintain a Jewish majority in a Jewish State, whilst thwarting Palestinian aspirations for independence and statehood, and

tlers in OPT of which 224,693 live in the West Bank, 180,792 in East Jerusalem and 7,300 in Gaza. According to the Yesha Settler Council, in 2002 there were 226,028 settlers in the West Bank alone, with 213,672 in East Jerusalem. In January 2004, according to the Foundation for Middle East Peace there were 7,576 settlers in the Gaza Strip. *See also* the Palestinian Academic Society for the Study of International Affairs (PASSIA) for a detailed report (PDF file) on Israeli settlements and the Wall at: <www.passia.org/publications/bulletins/settlements2004/settlements-wall.pdf>, last visited 10 March 2005.

[162] Excluding the Philadelphi corridor, known to Arabs as the Salah al-Din corridor, which is between the Gaza Strip and Egypt.

[163] *See* the "disengagement plan" on the web site of the Israeli Prime Minister's Office at http://www.pmo.gov.il/PMOEng/Communication/DisengagemePlan/, last visited 30 March 2005.

[164] For the purpose of international humanitarian law the test is one of *effective* control to determine who has responsibility for Occupied Territory. *See* the policy brief by the *Harvard Program on Humanitarian Policy and Conflict* Research, supra note 157 at p. 6: "The test is not *per se* the military presence of the occupying forces in all areas of the territory, but the extent to which the Occupying Power, through its military presence, is exerting effective control over the territory and limiting the right of self-determination of the occupied population." According to U.N. Special Rapporteur John Dugard, "Israel intends to portray this (i.e. its unilateral withdrawal from Gaza) as the end of the military occupation of Gaza, with the result that it will no longer be subject to the Fourth Geneva Convention in respect of Gaza. In reality, however, Israel does not plan to relinquish its grasp on the Gaza Strip. It plans to retain ultimate control over Gaza by controlling its borders, territorial sea and airspace. Consequently, it will in law remain an Occupying Power still subject to obligations under the Fourth Geneva Convention". *See* U.N. Doc. E/CN.4/2005/29, 7 December 2004 at p. 2.

postponing any discussion of final status issues (water, settlements, Jerusalem, refugees and borders) to some as-of-yet unidentified date in the future when the "facts on the ground" favour Israel.[165]

---

[165] On 5 April 2004, the BBC quoted Israeli Prime Minister Ariel Sharon telling the Hebrew language Israeli newspaper *Yediot Aharonot* that "In the unilateral plan, there is no Palestinian state . . . When you fence areas and communities in the West Bank, you end a lot of dreams . . . My plan is tough on the Palestinians. A mortal blow". In an interview with Ari Shavit in *Ha'aretz Friday Magazine* "The Big Freeze" 8 October 2004, Dov Weisglass, a senior advisor to Ariel Sharon said: "The disengagement is actually formaldehyde. It supplies the amount of formaldehyde that's necessary so that there will not be a political process with the Palestinians . . . The disengagement plan makes it possible for Israel to park conveniently in an interim situation that distances us as far as possible from political pressure. It legitimizes our contention that there is no negotiating with the Palestinians. There is a decision here to do the minimum possible in order to maintain our political situation . . . The political process is the evacuation of settlements, it's the return of refugees, it's the partition of Jerusalem. And all that has now been frozen . . .".

The Right to Restitution and Compensation in International Law and the Displaced Palestinians

MICHAEL LYNK

Abstract

In any final settlement between Israel and the Palestinians, compensation for the material and moral losses of the Palestinian refugees will be a central feature. The parties have ostensibly agreed that compensation will be paid, but differ significantly on the principles that will determine the global amount of compensation, the valuation of losses, and the method of distribution to the recipients. Compensation for refugees, for victims of human rights violations, and for property loss have become well-grounded features in contemporary international law. The author argues that these international law principles should shape the compensation agreement that will settle the conflict, because fairness and transitional justice, rather than unequal bargaining power, will more readily hasten the healing of the many wounds that the Palestinians and Israelis have endured.

Résumé

Un aspect central de tout accord final entre Israël et les Palestiniens sera la compensation pour les pertes matérielles et morales subies par les réfugiés palestiniens. En apparence, les deux parties sont d'accord pour que des compensations soient être versées, mais un certain écart les sépare encore sur la question des principes qui serviront à déterminer la somme globale de la compensation, la façon d'évaluer les pertes et les méthodes de distribution aux bénéficiaires. Le droit international contemporain reconnaît pleinement aujourd'hui le droit aux compensations pour les réfugiés, les victimes de violations des droits humains et pour ceux qui ont subi des pertes

de biens. L'auteur soutient que ce sont ces mêmes principes de droit international qui devront façonner l'accord de compensation qui clôturera le conflit, car c'est l'équité et la justice transitionnelle plutôt que le pouvoir de marchandage inégal, qui ont le plus de chances de guérir les nombreuses blessures que Palestiniens et Israéliens ont eu à subir

I. Introduction

Reaching a final, durable, and equitable resolution of the Middle East conflict requires the comprehensive settlement of the Palestinian refugee issue.[1] In its cornerstone pronouncement on the conflict, the United Nations Security Council in 1967 called for the just settlement of the refugee problem.[2] Israel and the Palestine Liberation Organization acknowledged, in their 1993 Declaration of Principles, that the refugee issue is one of the most intractable problems at the heart of their aspirations for peace, and postponed its resolution until the future initiation of final status negotiations.[3] Israel has agreed, in its 1994 peace treaty with Jordan, that the persistence of the refugee issue over the past five decades has caused massive human problems in the region, and the settlement of the issue is to be in accordance with international law.[4] Beyond this, there has been little substantive progress by the parties towards a final settlement of the fate of the Palestinian refugees, and little consensus between them as to the requirements of international law. At the centre of the issue is the national and individual status of the majority of the estimated 7.6 million Palestinians in the world today: the 3.9 million Palestinian refugees who were displaced, personally or by family lineage, from their homes, properties, and lands by the 1947-49 and 1967 Middle East wars. The irresolution of their fate perpetuates the largest, longest-running and most destabilizing refugee problem in the world today.

Contemporary legal, political, and diplomatic analyses of the Palestinian refugee issue have focused on three principal components: repatriation, resettlement, and compensation. In current settlement proposals, these three components are intimately interlinked, but they are each capable and deserving of stand-alone analysis. *Repatriation* focuses on the generally accepted right in international law of refugees to choose whether to return to their homeland and their homes following the cessation of conflict or persecution.[5] Palestinians claim their capacity to exercise this right of return extends to Israel as well as to a future state of Palestine,[6] while the most liberal position articulated by official and semi-official Israeli spokespersons have argued that any more than a very modest number of refugees returning to their ancestral homes within its borders would threaten its existential character as a Jewish state.[7] *Resettlement* is the strongly maintained Israeli solution, which would see all, or almost all, of the estimated 3.9 million registered Palestinians refugees required to accept permanent civil status of some form in their present homes in Syria, Lebanon, and Jordan, return to a truncated Palestinian state, or accept relocation elsewhere.[8] Palestinians resist this option, arguing that it would abolish their legal right to return and negate their decades of suffering in exile.[9]

The third issue, *compensation*, focuses on the individual and collective claims of the Palestinian refugees and the displaced for the restitution of, and/or indemnification for, their lost homes and properties in present-day Israel, as well as monetary damages for related losses. Both sides agree that compensation should be part of a final peace agreement, but for quite different reasons which would lead to quite different results. Israel prefers a global collective fund that would be primarily used for refugee resettlement elsewhere and financed largely by international donors. Its contributions would be made *ex-gratis*, without assuming any official liability.[10] On the other hand, the Palestinians advance the compensation issue as a right recognized in international law that would obligate Israel to return, or pay for, the refugee properties expropriated or destroyed in 1948 and afterwards. As well, they argue that Israel must pay damages for pain and suffering, and for its use of Palestinian properties over the past five decades.[11]

These differences on compensation are significant. The gap between the parties goes to a number of issues, including: (i) the legal basis for compensation; (ii) the number of potential claimants; (iii) the range of compensation categories; (iv) methods of calculation; (v) whether restitution forms part of the compensation issue; (vi) whether the

compensation should be awarded collectively or individually; and (vii) the status of related issues, such as the compensation claims of (a) the Arab countries that have hosted the Palestinian refugees for five decades, and (b) the Arab Jews who left behind property in their home countries such as Iraq and Egypt in the 1950s. The differences on compensation have never been publicly expressed in dollar figures by Israel or the Palestine Liberation Organization, but recent assessments by scholars and researchers range from \$5-10 billion (US) by Shlomo Gazit,[12] to \$15-20 billion in a Harvard refugee project led by Joseph Alpher and Khalil Shikaki,[13] to \$271 billion by Atif Kubursi.[14]

This article focuses on the issue of compensation, which for these purposes includes restitution.[15] Whether the Palestinian refugee issue is eventually resolved through repatriation or resettlement, or some combination of both, compensation will inevitably be a significant feature of the final agreement. However, if this final agreement is to be durable, it must reflect the fair aspirations of both parties. As such, it will have to be anchored in the principles of international law, and not simply reflect the starkly unequal bargaining strengths between Israel and the Palestinians. Indeed, if compensation and restitution are to play a forward-looking role towards healing the transparent wounds of the decades-long conflict, and building the foundation for a prosperous and secure future in the region, then the available rules found in international law are both the principled and the most constructive road to follow.[16]

II. The Dimensions of the Issue

A. An Historical Précis to 1948

On 29 November 1947, with the British Mandate in Palestine collapsing, the United Nations General Assembly passed Resolution 181(II).[17] It recommended the termination of the Mandate, the partition of Palestine into independent Arab and Jewish states, and a special international status for Jerusalem. Following months of civil violence, the State of Israel declared its independence on 14 May 1948, and a larger war involving the neighbouring Arab countries ensued. This larger war alternated between periods of intense conflict and unstable truces until the signing of the Rhodes armistice agreements in 1949. At the conclusion of the war, Israel was victorious and its land size had expanded from the 54 per cent of Mandate Palestine allocated to the Jewish state by UNGA resolution 181(II) to 78 per cent of the territory.

Between December 1947 and September 1949, approximately 725,000 Palestinians – more than half of the Arab population of Palestine – were driven from, or fled, their homes in that part of Palestine that became Israel.[18] They sought refuge primarily in the neighbouring Arab countries, including the West Bank of the Jordan River (occupied by Jordan after 1949), Jordan, Syria, Lebanon, and the Gaza Strip (administered by Egypt after 1949). The first UN Mediator for Palestine[19] and modern historians of the period[20] have observed that the Palestinians fled for the same mixture of reasons that have caused most mass population displacements in the twentieth century: forced expulsions, a widespread fear of harm from advancing armies, and panic after credible reports of civilian massacres by Israeli militias.

In his September 1948 progress report to the UN Secretary-General, the Mediator for Palestine, Count Folke Bernadotte, urged the United Nations to affirm that the Palestinian refugees had the right to return to their homes at the earliest practicable date: "It is, however, undeniable that no settlement can be just and complete if recognition is not accorded to the right of the Arab refugee to return to the home from which he has been dislodged by the hazards and strategy of the armed conflict between Arabs and Jews in Palestine."[21] In his listing of the basic premises for an equitable resolution of the conflict, Count Bernadotte recommended that those refugees choosing not to return should be paid "adequate compensation" for their properties.[22] (This echoed the United Nations' stipulation in Resolution 181(II) the year before that "full compensation" was to be paid for the expropriation of any Arab land by the Jewish state.)[23] Moreover, he added in his report that Israel bore the responsibility to indemnify those owners whose property had been wantonly destroyed during the conflict, with no qualification as to whether they returned from their exile or not.[24] The day after delivering his report, Count Bernadotte and an aide were assassinated by the Stern Gang, an extremist Jewish militia.

The United Nations General Assembly adopted the thrust of the Bernadotte report in December 1948 in UNGA Resolution 194.[25] In Paragraph 11, the General Assembly endorsed the report's recommendations on the right of return and compensation:

> The General Assembly, having considered further the situation in Palestine...[r]esolves that the refugees wishing to return to their homes and live at peace with their neighbours should be permitted to do so at the earliest practicable date, and that compensation should be paid for the property of those choosing not to return and for loss of or damage to property which, under principles of international law or in equity, should be made good by the Governments or authorities responsible.

In its resolution, the General Assembly spoke to four primary features of the compensation question, all of which flowed directly from the Bernadotte report. First, it stated that those refugees willing to live at peace with their neigh-

bours were entitled to the restitution of their homes at the earliest practicable time. Second, those refugees not returning home should be entitled to compensation for their lost property. Third, those refugees who do return home and find their properties damaged or destroyed should be compensated for their losses. And fourth, it explicitly grounded its direction that the refugees were entitled to repatriation, restitution, and compensation based upon the principles of international law and equity. Ironically, while these features of Resolution 194 would significantly influence the rights in international law that refugees and victims of human rights abuses elsewhere could claim in the years to come, these entitlements have been largely unavailable for the intended recipients.

B.   After 1948

The homes, lands, and properties left behind by the flight of the Palestinians between 1947 and 49 were substantial. The United Nations Conciliation Commission for Palestine (created by Resolution 194 to resolve the outstanding issues between Israel, the Palestinians, and the neighbouring Arab countries)[26] estimated in 1951 that almost 80 per cent of Israel's total area of 20,850 square kilometres represented abandoned Arab lands, although only about 28 per cent of that land was cultivable.[27] Approximately 400 Arab villages and towns, representing most of the Palestinian communities in the territory assigned to, or captured by Israel, were occupied and depopulated during the war.[28] The transfer of wealth to Israel in the form of Palestinian lands, homes, assets, and property was crucial to the new state's ability to survive and develop in its formative years.[29] Between 1948 and 1953, 350 of the 370 new Jewish settlements created in Israel were on former Arab property. Don Peretz has estimated that, by 1954, more than one-third of the Israeli Jewish population were living on former Arab lands, and an additional 250,000 Israeli Jews, including one-third of the new immigrants, lived in abandoned Arab urban property.[30] In the countryside, where most Palestinians had lived prior to 1948, enormous tracts of citrus, olive, and other cultivable properties were expropriated by Israel and turned over to Jewish agricultural settlements. The importance of these agricultural lands was critical to the fledging Israeli economy: to cite one example, exports of citrus products from expropriated Arab groves provided nearly 10 per cent of Israel's foreign currency earnings in 1951.[31]

Israel subsequently legalized the land and property expropriations through legislation that vested broad powers in the state-appointed Custodian of Absentee Property, who was to hold all of the abandoned properties of the "absentees" in trust.[32] An absentee was defined expansively as any Arab in Palestine who left his or her home after 29

November 1947, and the burden of proof that a claimant was not an absentee fell on the former owner.[33] Eventually, much of the expropriated Palestinian lands and properties held by the Custodian were transferred via a purchase agreement to an Israeli state development authority, which allowed the Israeli government to maintain that these properties were acquired legally (*i.e.*, through payment), even though the Palestinians owners never received any money.[34] This authority, in turn, turned these properties over to the Jewish National Fund, whose charter explicitly prohibited it from selling, leasing, or returning the lands to non-Jews. These steps had the effect of completely severing the proprietary link between the absentees and their lands.[35] Although Palestinian refugees living in exile and even those displaced within Israel sought to have their properties returned to them, very few ever succeeded.[36] By the early 1950s, Israel had so significantly transformed the emptied Palestinian properties through irreversible steps – such as the levelling of villages, the settlement of Jewish immigrants into abandoned homes, and the establishment of *kibbutzim* and *moshavim* (Jewish agricultural settlements) on cultivated Arab farms – that there was increasingly little of the lands and homes of the displaced Palestinians which remained in its original state.[37]

During these early years, Israel was prepared to address the question of compensation for the abandoned Palestinian properties, but tied its commitment to a number of pre-conditions that amounted to deal-breakers.[38] At the centre of its position was its insistence that it would not accept the return of the refugees, and that there would be no restitution of abandoned Palestinian properties. After 1950, the Israeli authorities developed the argument that the Jews who left behind their properties in Iraq and other Middle East countries when they emigrated to Israel constituted a population exchange, which settled any compensation or restitution obligations which it might have owed to the displaced Palestinians.[39] The position of the Arab countries on compensation was starkly different.[40] At the heart of their argument was the fulfilment of Resolution 194 and the right to repatriate. Only after the free choice of refugees as to whether to return was exercised, the Arab states maintained, could the subsequent issue of compensation be determined and implemented. There should be no linkage with the compensation claims of the Arab Jews, since their claims had no direct nexus with the Palestinians. Thus, while both sides accepted the premise of compensation, no progress was made towards a settlement because of the larger, intractable issue of repatriation.[41] With no agreement, the unresolved fate of the displaced Palestinians was left to fester as an open political sore that would spark four more wars, two sustained popular uprisings, and chronic regional instability over the next five decades.[42]

III. The Right to Compensation and Restitution in International Law

A. Introduction

Compensation for refugees and displaced persons, and for victims of the abuse of internationally recognized human rights, has evolved into the status of a right in international law. It has acquired that status because it satisfies the criteria that are commonly accepted as the formal sources of international law.[43] Applying these criteria, the obligation to pay compensation to refugees and displaced persons is evident in the requirements of regional treaties, conventions, and agreements; in the domestic and international practice of states; in the rulings of international judicial bodies; in the consensus among scholars of international law; and in the repeated pronouncements of the international community as expressed in the relevant bodies and organs of the United Nations. While the modern body of rights for refugees and displaced persons emerged only after the Second World War, the antecedents of the right to compensation and restitution are evident even in the nascent years of international law.

The policy justifications for articulating the principle of compensation and restitution as a right for refugees and displaced persons in international law are at least five-fold. First, since modern international law forbids the mass expulsion of civilian populations even during wars and civil conflict[44] and prohibits the domestic conditions of persecution that create large-scale refugee displacements,[45] compensation is regarded as a potent tool to deter potential states of origin from domestic actions that would generate refugees.[46] Second, as a principle of equity, countries should not benefit from proceeds reaped through violating the human rights of minorities or the nationals of other countries.[47] Third, compensation and restitution serve to repair some of the individual and/or group dignity lost by the refugee through the violation of her or his human rights by mass displacement.[48] Fourth, where compensation is assessed and collected against a refugee-generating state, both the international community and the individual refugees will have their financial burdens reduced. This would be a particularly important benefit for refugees, whose movable and immovable property they lost through the conflict or persecution they fled from invariably represents the sum total of their meagre personal wealth.[49] And fifth, the compensation principle may assist with the reconciliation of the parties or groups to the conflict that sparked the mass population displacement, as part of a broader range of restorative remedies, such as a frank apology, the revelation of the truth, substantial reforms to political and social institutions, public educational campaigns to transform attitudes, and substantial changes to employment patterns.[50]

B. The Origins of the Right to Compensation in International Law

Prior to the emergence of modern human rights, humanitarian, and refugee law in the immediate aftermath of the Second World War, compensation and restitution for displaced persons had already been a regular practice in international treaties and state practice (although not in a consistent manner nor with the agreed-upon compensation obligations always being honoured). For example, in the aftermath of the American War of Independence, 60,000 American colonialists loyal to the British crown fled their homes and properties in the newly independent United States. In the 1794 *Treaty of Amity, Commerce and Navigation* (the "Jay Treaty")[51] between Great Britain and the United States, the Americans agreed that the Loyalists could claim either the restitution of their properties or compensation for their property and commercial losses.[52] However, the subsequent deterioration of political relations between the two countries resulted in the American abdication of any responsibility to pay the Loyalist claims.

Similar examples of early European and international treaties and laws that recognized compensation and/or restitution claims for displaced civilians include the 1648 *Treaty of Westphalia* that ended the Thirty Years War;[53] the 1678 *Treaty of Nimmegeun* between Spain and France that ended the war over the Spanish Netherlands;[54] and the 1839 *Treaty of London* that guaranteed the independence and neutrality of Belgium,[55] among others.[56] Even treaties that legitimized mass displacement of civilians and population exchanges (actions that are now prohibited by international law[57]) – such as the 1920 *Treaty of Neuilly* between Greece and Bulgaria,[58] and the 1923 *Treaty of Lausanne* between Greece and Turkey[59] – contained provisions to compensate civilians who lost properties.

The modern basis for compensation and restitution in international law has been decisively shaped by the seminal 1928 ruling of the Permanent Court of International Justice in *Chorzow Factory*.[60] In the aftermath of World War One, the Polish government expropriated a German-owned factory on Polish territory, and the German government sought reparations on behalf of the owners. In its lead ruling on the merits, the World Court stated that state responsibility applies in the case of an act or omission in violation of an international legal obligation:

> It is a principle of international law, and even a general conception of law, that any breach of an engagement invokes an obligation to make reparation. [R]eparation is the indispensable complement of a failure to apply a convention, and there is no necessity for this to be stated in the convention itself.[61]

Regarding damages, the Court endorsed the principle of restitution first, and full compensation for the property owners where restitution was unobtainable. In addition, it stated that awards for other damages not covered by restitution and compensation were also available:

> The essential principle contained in the actual notion of an illegal act – a principle which seems to be established by international practice and in particular by the decisions of arbitral tribunals – is that reparation must, as far as possible, wipe out all the consequences of the illegal act and re-establish the situation which would, in all probability, have existed if the act had not been committed. Restitution in kind, or, if this is not possible, payment of a sum corresponding to the value which a restitution in kind would bear; the award, if need be, of damages sustained which would not be covered by restitution in kind or payment in place of it – such are the principles which should serve to determine the amount of compensation due for an act contrary to international law.[62]

Although *Chorzow Factory* was decided as a commercial property action in private international law, its articulation of the principles on compensation have since been widely endorsed in various public international law decisions. These endorsements include leading judgments on damages for injuries to United Nations personnel[63] and reparations for human rights violations,[64] as well as by a seminal United Nations study on compensation for human rights violations.[65]

C. Resolution 194 and the Articulation of the Right to Compensation

United Nations General Assembly Resolution 194, which established the availability of return, compensation, and restitution for the Palestinian refugees, was the world community's first affirmation of these principles in the context of a displaced population. Resolution 194 is commonly cited by refugee law scholars as a primary international law source for the right of refugees and displaced persons anywhere in the world to compensation and restitution.[66] Two particular features of Resolution 194 embed it with an international law importance that distinguishes it from the limited legal scope of an ordinary General Assembly resolution.

First, Resolution 194 explicitly states that the repatriation, compensation and restitution of the refugees should be made according to "… principles of international law or in equity." Luke Lee argues that, by deliberately choosing this particular drafting, the General Assembly clearly signalled that it was *restating* pre-existing law on the principle of compensating wrongs in international law, rather than simply establishing a new legal obligation.[67] As such, the resolution moves beyond the recommendatory and political character of most General Assembly resolutions and acquires a legal, binding nature. Its binding effect arises not from the resolution itself, but from the declared law, which is then obligatory upon all states, whether they voted in favour of the resolution or not.[68]

Second, the resolution has been repeatedly affirmed by the General Assembly. Since 1948, Resolution 194 has been reaffirmed or referred to, by near unanimous majorities, at least 140 times.[69] For instance, UNGA Resolution 53/51, voted on 3 December 1998, expressly cited Resolution 194 when endorsing the entitlement of Palestinian refugees "to their property and to the income derived therefrom, in conformity with the principles of justice and equity."[70] Resolution 53/51, like its many predecessor resolutions, was passed by an overwhelming majority, in this case 156 member countries in favour and only two (Israel and the United States) in opposition. International law scholars have stated that, in specific circumstances, the repeated affirmation of a resolution by unanimous or overwhelming majorities of the General Assembly endows it with an acquired legal character, particularly when it reflects the parallel development of state practice on the issue.[71] Leading judgments of the World Court have endorsed this approach.[72]

D. General Principles of Domestic Law

A leading source for international law are the general principles of domestic law widely accepted by the developed legal systems, insofar as they apply to international rights and obligations.73 The principles of compensation and restitution have been cornerstone features of most domestic legal systems for centuries,[74] and constitute the primary remedial response to repair proven damages and instances of unjust enrichment. For example, the English common law courts have long applied the principle; in *Fibrosa Spolka Akcyjna* v. *Fairbairn Lawson Combe Barbour Ltd.*, Lord Wright stated in 1943 that:

> It is clear that any civilized system of law is bound to provide remedies for cases of what has been called unjust enrichment or unjust benefit, that is to prevent a man from retaining the money of or some benefit derived from another which it is against conscience that he should keep.[75]

Similarly, the American Law Institute, in its seminal restatement of the domestic law on restitution, has established that: "A person who has been unjustly enriched at the expense of another is required to make restitution to that other."[76]

E. International Treaties and Conventions

Through treaties and conventions, international law has accepted the cornerstone principle that a state which has violated a legal obligation is required to end the violation and to make reparation, including restitution and compensation for loss and injury in the appropriate circumstances.[77] These international instruments also stipulate that those whose human rights have been breached are to have access to meaningful remedies. Article 8 of the *Universal Declaration of Human Rights* states that every individual is entitled to an "effective remedy,"[78] a requirement that is repeated in the *International Covenant on Civil and Political Rights*[79] and the *Declaration on the Elimination of all Forms of Racial Discrimination*.[80] Other human rights instruments are even more specific: the *American Convention on Human Rights* refers to a "right to be compensated in accordance with the law"[81] and provides that "no one shall be deprived of his property except upon payment of just compensation,"[82] while the *African Charter on Human and Peoples' Rights* establishes the "right to an adequate compensation."[83] The *International Covenant on Civil and Political Rights*[84] and the *European Convention on Human Rights*[85] both refer to the "enforceable right to compensation." The 1998 *Treaty of Rome*,[86] which established the International Criminal Court, has directed the new court to establish principles of restitution, compensation, and rehabilitation for victims of international war crimes. Other international treaties and conventions contain similar remedial requirements.[87]

Theo van Boven, a Special Rapporteur for the United Nations Commission on Human Rights, issued a comprehensive final report in 1993 on international law remedies arising from the violation of human rights norms.[88] After reviewing a number of international treaties and conventions, he stated: "the principal right [that human rights] victims are entitled to under international law is the right to effective remedies and just reparations."[89] In his conclusion, the Special Rapporteur said: "it is…an imperative norm of justice that… the rights of the victims be sustained to the fullest possible extent."[90] These remedies included restitution, compensation, rehabilitation and guarantees of non-repetition,[91] and would be claimed against the state perpetrating the violations. Among the human rights and fundamental freedoms – whose gross violation would trigger a claim for remedies under international law – that van Boven listed were "deportation or forcible transfer of population".[92] The Special Rapporteur also maintained that international law contains no statute of limitations for claims regarding human rights reparations.[93]

F. Contemporary International Law Rulings

Decisions by international legal courts and tribunals, particularly since the 1980s, have affirmed that compensation and restitution are available remedies for displaced persons and victims of human rights abuses. Using both the 1928 World

Court decision in *Chorzow Factory* and international human rights treaties as the legal foundation for the principle, such international judicial bodies as the Inter-American Court of Human Rights and the European Court of Human Rights have ruled that violations of international obligations which result in harm create an obligation to compensate for and repair the damages. The Inter-American Court has stated that:

> It is a principle of international law, which jurisprudence has considered "even a general concept of law", that every violation of an international obligation which results in harm creates a duty to make adequate reparation. Compensation, on the other hand, is the most usual way of doing it.[94]

In 1989, the Inter-American Court ruled in *Velasquez-Rodriguez* v. *Honduras*,[95] a case under the *American Convention on Human Rights*[96] involving state responsibility for the disappearance of Honduran citizens, that international law requires restitution of the *status quo ante* where possible, and compensation where it is not possible.[97] After finding Honduras liable for human rights violations, the Court held that the claimants were entitled to a broad range of compensation headings under international law, as per the "fair compensation" criteria in Article 63(1) of the *Convention*. These headings included damages for lost salaries, based on probable future earnings, and moral damages, based upon the emotional harm suffered by the families of the victims. The Court emphasized that the "fair compensation" criteria must be applied in "sufficiently broad terms in order to compensate, to the extent possible, for the loss suffered."[98] These compensation principles have been regularly applied by the Inter-American Court in subsequent decisions.[99]

In a similar manner, the European Court of Human Rights has ruled under the *European Convention on Human Rights*[100] that the deprivation of property and human rights obligates the offending state to provide restitution and compensation for the claimant. In *Loizidou* v. *Turkey*,[101] a Greek Cypriot national with property holdings in the northern part of Cyprus occupied by Turkey since 1974 complained that she was prevented from returning to her lands and peacefully enjoying them. The Court found that Turkey was responsible, as the occupying power, for breaching the *Convention*, and rejected its arguments that its stated need to rehouse displaced Turkish Cypriot refugees justified the negation of Ms. Loizidou's property rights. At the remedial stage,[102] the European Court ruled that the claimant was still the legal owner of the property, and entitled to reclaim her lands at any time. As reparations, it awarded compensation for ground rent (based on the market value earnings that could have been realized but for

the occupation), moral damages for the loss of property enjoyment, and costs and interest.

More recently, the European Commission of Human Rights issued a 1999 report[103] on Cyprus, where it applied the principles in *Loizidou* regarding the claims of other displaced Greek Cypriots to property restitution and compensation. The Commission unanimously found that Turkey remained in continuing breach of the *European Convention on Human Rights* because of its ongoing refusal to allow Greek Cypriots to return to their homes in northern Cyprus. It also ruled that Turkey's refusal to pay compensation for its interference with the claimants' property rights breached the *Convention*. Turkey's defence that property succession legislation enacted by the Turkish Republic of North Cyprus invalidated the property claims was rejected by the Commission, as was its argument that property restitution and compensation should await a future global settlement of the Cyprus issue.[104]

G. Contemporary State and International Practice

Recent state and international practice have provided rich examples of restitution and compensation for violations of property and human rights. Many modern treaties and agreements that ended international or internal conflicts have included these principles in the final settlement. Similarly, most countries in Eastern and Central Europe in the 1990s have offered restitution and compensation for those who lost properties or suffered human rights abuses under fascism or communism. As well, there are a number of contemporary domestic examples where these remedial principles have been applied as a restorative step to address a troubled history between majority and minority populations.

The template for the modern international obligation to compensate for unilateral property confiscations and widescale human rights abuses has been the post-war German and European reparations for Jewish and other victims of Nazi persecution.[105] Following the 1952 *Luxembourg Agreement*[106] between the Federal Republic of Germany, Israel, and the Conference on Jewish Material Claims against Germany, the West German government enacted a series of laws to provide compensation for gross violations of human rights (such as loss of life, loss of health, forced labour, deportation, imprisonment, maltreatment, and degradation) and for property losses (including immovable and moveable property, capital, income, securities, mortgages, pensions, copyright and patents) for victims or their heirs.[107] These compensation payments have amounted to DM 100 billion up to the year 2000, payable to Holocaust survivors, both individually and through the State of Israel. The range of compensable claims for Nazi victims has been steadily widened through the decades to include Swiss bank accounts, European insurance policies, looted works of art, and slave labour.[108] Other European countries, such as Austria, Norway, Denmark, and the Netherlands have also undertaken to offer compensation to Jewish and other victims of Nazism.[109] And with the fall of communism in Eastern Europe, procedures have been created in a number of countries – including Hungary, Poland, Slovakia, and the Czech Republic – to restore property confiscated either by fascist or communist regimes to Jewish and other dispossessed owners.[110] After German reunification in 1990, the German parliament enacted legislation to restore confiscated Jewish properties in the former East Germany to their original owners or heirs, and to award the proceeds from the sales of communal and unclaimed Jewish property to the Jewish Claims Conference in order to aid needy Holocaust survivors worldwide.[111]

In Bosnia, a centrepiece of the 1995 *Dayton Peace Agreement*[112] that brought the first war in the former Yugoslavia to an uneasy end was the provision that all refugees and displaced persons would have the right to return home and have their properties restored to them. Alternatively, compensation for properties was available for those that either could not, or did not wish to, return to them.[113] The *Dayton Agreement* established a Commission for Displaced Persons and Refugees, later renamed the Commission for Real Property Claims of Displaced Persons and Refugees, to adjudicate real property claims, including the return of the confiscated property, or, in lieu of return, the awarding of "just compensation."[114] Compensation may be awarded in the form of money or in the form of a bond for the future purchase of real property elsewhere in Bosnia. For a variety of international and inter-ethnic reasons, the Dayton compensation provisions have been only implemented in a piecemeal fashion, as the legal structures to adjudicate the claims await the realization of political will.[115] In a related legal process, an international human rights chamber in Sarajevo has declared that displaced property owners in Bosnia are entitled to be compensated for the unlawful eviction from their residence, through declaratory relief and moral damages, based upon the *European Convention on Human Rights*.[116]

As part of the recent resolution of other international and domestic conflicts, compensation and restitution have been integral parts of the settlement process. In the aftermath of the Second Gulf War in 1990–91, the United Nations established a compensation commission to process claims and pay out compensation for property, personal, and moral losses resulting from the Iraqi invasion and occupation of Kuwait.[117] The Iraq-Kuwait compensation experience built upon the lessons of the Iran-United States

Claims Tribunal, created in 1981 to adjudicate the American claims for property and material losses following the 1979 Islamic revolution in Iran.[118] In Guatemala, the agreements in the early 1990s that brought an end to the four-decades-old civil war stipulated property restitution and compensation to land owners who fled the country during the armed conflict.[119] Domestically, compensation has played a role in repairing the civil rights violations of Japanese-Americans[120] and Japanese-Canadians[121] for their arbitrary detention and property confiscation during the Second World War. Similarly, the tools of compensation and property restoration have shaped the modern attempts of the United States,[122] Canadian,[123] Australian,[124] and New Zealand[125] governments to restitute their aboriginal peoples for the centuries of land alienation and social harm that these states inflicted upon them. After the fall of oppressive military dictatorships in Chile, Argentina, Uruguay, and Uganda, the new democratic governments enacted legislation that offered compensation and, where possible, restitution for victims of human rights abuses and property losses by the previous regimes.[126]

IV. Restitution, Compensation and the Palestinians

International law authoritatively establishes that restitution and compensation are available remedies for those who have been displaced or turned into refugees through acts contrary to international treaties and conventions, for those who have suffered gross violations of their internationally recognized human rights, and for those who have lost homes or property through the breach of internationally established standards. In the case of the Middle East conflict, the Palestinians who became refugees, who lost properties, or who suffered other legally recognized damages as a consequence of the various upheavals in the region – and particularly the 1947–49 and 1967 wars – also have an established legal grounding for restitution and compensation in the substantial body of United Nations resolutions that specifically refer to their claims. Indeed, it would be difficult to find another community of disadvantaged people for whom the modern principles of international law – especially in the fields of human rights and refugee law – so clearly buttress their claim either to have their properties restored to them or to receive appropriate compensation for their losses.

Establishing the entitlement to compensation and restitution as a right in international law is one matter. Articulating the detail of substance and procedure that must invariably accompany the realization of this right is quite another. As a body of principles, international law has become a mature legal system, deserving of the considerable respect it enjoys in the modern world because of its impressive assembly of the values that the international community has declared it wishes to live by. But, as a guide to the efficacious application of these principles, the practice of international law has been considerably less sophisticated. Its application of these principles has been an inchoate array of uneven experiences, shaped by two primary factors: (i) the poverty of political will to implement these principles in a manner consistent with the international rule of law; and (ii) the wide variety and real differences among the many contemporary experiences where the application on international law has been attempted. Developing the practical rules to implement an international right – such as the entitlement to restitution and compensation – has, in many cases, been an original creation, an *ad hoc* arrangement. Yet, increasingly, this need not be so. The accumulation of international experience has reached the point where sufficient precedents and rules exist, particularly on restitution and compensation, to productively and equitably craft their implementation in any contemporary situation.

The Palestinian claims for restitution and compensation are neither exceptional nor insurmountable. The only substantive obstacle is political will. While the circumstances of the Palestinians present some particular challenges – which is unsurprising, given their massive displacement, their enormous personal, property, and moral losses, the subsequent transformation of their homes and lands, the array of international political actors involved, and the extraordinary length of time involved – recent international and domestic practice from elsewhere points to applicable rules that can be successfully adapted to untie this Gordian knot. In anticipation that the negotiations between the Israeli and Palestinian representatives will eventually turn to the issues of compensation and restitution, five aspects of the issue stand out that will form a significant feature of the parties' final settlement of the rights of the Palestinians. While these five aspects are all worthy of an extended discussion, they can, for the purposes of this essay, only be reviewed briefly.[127]

A.   Return and Compensation

Modern international law, beginning with the proclamation of the *Universal Declaration of Human Rights* in December 1948, has insisted that refugees and displaced persons, as well as their descendants, have the right to return to their homes, if that is their freely determined choice.[128] The Human Rights Committee, the United Nations body responsible for interpreting the *International Covenant on Civil and Political Rights*, stated in 1999 that "there are few, if any, circumstances in which deprivation of the right to enter one's own country could be reasonable."[129] The right to return survives even when sovereignty over the lands from

where the displaced had fled is contested or has changed hands. Those unable to return to a former home because it is occupied by an innocent third party or has been destroyed are entitled to choose return to the vicinity or to receive compensation. However, international law holds that compensation is not a substitute for the right to return to one's home.[130] To that end, the ensuing discussion on restitution and compensation is to be seen in the context of remedies adjacent to the right to return, not in place of it.

B.   Types of Compensation

According to international law and practice, the Palestinians eligible for restitution and compensation have a range of remedies available to them, including: (i) the restitution of their confiscated movable and immovable properties; (ii) compensation for the damages to their restituted properties; (iii) compensation for the income derived from the use of their restituted properties; (iv) compensation for those refugees and displaced who choose not to return; and (v) damages for a spectrum of non-material losses, including lost earnings and opportunities, and social and moral damages. In addition, collective restitution claims are available for: (i) expropriated religious, educational, communal, and public lands; and (ii) the use and depletion of natural resources, such as water, minerals, and forests. Technically, the accomplishment of these remedies within the regional context is feasible, because the extensive historical documentation on property and ownership in Palestine has been largely preserved. The land records assembled by the British Mandate authority, the United Nations CCP, the Israeli Custodian of Absentees' Property, and the Israeli Lands Authority, as well as the personal records of the families of the displaced and refugees, would make compensation an easier technical task in comparison to the successful claims achieved in recent years by victims of European fascism and by the aboriginal nations in North America, Australia, and New Zealand.

Politically, the types of compensation awarded would depend on the prior determination of how many of the displaced Palestinians would achieve the right to return to Israel and have their original properties restored to them. Palestinian researchers have maintained that the total compensation pricetag would be significantly reduced if a greater number of displaced and refugees were able to return to their homes inside Israel.[131] However, discussions within the *status quo* framework indicate that a final settlement on the Palestinian refugee issue will consist largely of compensation in exchange for the negation of the large-scale right to return. The leading example is the 1995 Beilin-Abu Mazan agreement,[132] where a future Israeli justice minister and a senior advisor to the Palestinian Authority developed an unofficial, but influential, template for a final status settlement. It accepted the right of the displaced Palestinians to compensation and rehabilitation for their material and moral losses, while excluding any significant return of, or to, their properties within Israel. The issue of restitution was raised at the January 2001 final status talks in Taba, where the Israelis rejected any return of refugee property.133 How the parties to the final status negotiations will square any agreement that dissolves the right of Palestinian refugees to return to their original lands with the cornerstone principle in international refugee and human rights law that refugees have a right to freely choose repatriation back to their homeland will be a closely observed matter.

C. Valuation of Losses

International law requires that compensation for internationally recognized losses should, as much as remedies can, place the claimants back in the position that they would have been in, had the breach of the legal right not occurred. Beyond that, it has not spoken with particular clarity regarding the precise formula to use, employing at different times the terms "full," "just," "fair," and "adequate" to describe the compensation required. While "full compensation" is an appropriate yardstick in international claims of small and medium size, large-scale claims – because their size creates problems of efficiency, fairness, and cost – have tended towards less-than-global "attainable justice" standards. Indeed, the larger and more complex the potential claim, the more likely it has been that the final compensation arrangement will be a judicious mixture of political feasibility (*i.e.*, available financial resources and domestic public reaction) and the requirements of justice (*i.e.*, international legal obligations, international pressure, and the cost of ongoing dissent by the aggrieved party). "Attainable justice," while necessarily falling short of "full compensation," is an acceptable and appropriate standard in large-scale international claims where: (i) the aggrieved party freely agrees to the settlement or it is the result of a legal process that the aggrieved party has freely agreed to adhere to; (ii) the compensation addresses all of the recognized losses; (iii) internationally accepted means of valuation for the losses are employed; and (iv) the party responsible for the compensation of the losses undertakes a guarantee of non-repetition. However, with whatever valuation standard is chosen, international law requires that it is to be given a broad application, so that the restorative purposes of human rights remedies – which include justice, equity, acknowledgement of responsibility, deterrence, reconciliation, and social harmony – are achieved.

D. Creating an Appropriate Compensation Regime

A number of issues arise in choosing the modalities of a compensation regime for resolving the Middle East conflict. The principal issues include:

1. *The group of claimants.* The choices for appropriate claimant groups would include:
   a. The 1948 property owners and their heirs, which would award those who suffered direct losses, but would disproportionally benefit land-owners, and disadvantage the poor and women (who frequently could not own or inherent property),134 as well as require personal documentary evidence which may not always exist;
   b. The extended family or villages, which reflects the traditional rural social units and may resolve some problems surrounding claims over collective lands, but could create problems in determining membership, and would not address the landless or gender inequity issues;
   c. Per capita awards for all the displaced, regardless of property ownership, which would address the inequality and gender issues, but would still require a determination of eligibility; or
   d. A collective claim made on behalf of the displaced by the Palestinian state, which would create a national fund for future public works, but would not likely provide the kind of political and emotional closure for the displaced that an individual compensation scheme should provide.

2. *Formula.* The choices among appropriate compensation formulas would include:
   a. A claims-based system that bases compensation upon the value of the lost property, which would most directly link the financial remedies to the actual losses, but would also likely recreate the inequalities of pre-1948 Palestinian society;
   b. A modified claims-based system that creates several compensation categories based upon size of claim, which would be more efficient and award more progressive remedies than the pure claims-based system, but would also still be biased towards larger property owners;
   c. A pure per capita payment system that would award equal payments to all refugees, thereby achieving efficiency and eliminating the social inequalities of the previous proposals, but would diminish the link between payments and scale of losses; or
   d. A modified per capita payment system that would create several categories of claimants based upon a generational or returnee v. non- returnee status, which would still be efficient and relative equitable,

but which could also create social tension between the categories.

3. *Mechanism*. What forms would compensation be awarded? Among the choices would be:
   a. Cash payments, which are efficient to administer, but may not have significant macro-social or economic benefits;
   b. Services or vouchers for individuals or families, which can be directed towards more focused public benefits plans, but are less flexible for the recipients and weaken the link between the compensation and actual losses;
   c. Investment in community development, which also promotes public benefit plans, but weakens the link between the displaced and the purpose of the compensation; or
   d. A equity scheme involving refugee ownership in collective development projects, which more directly connects the displaced to public plans, but does not strongly address the personal needs for closure.

4. *Administrative Process*. How should the compensation fund be administered and distributed? Several politically feasible types of bodies are possible, including:
   a. Palestinian state, which may build up the governing expertise of the future state, but which also raises issues of accountability and fairness;
   b. A bilateral body made up of Palestine and Israel, which would involve the main parties to the conflict, but would invite administrative gridlock because of their historical animosity;
   c. A trilateral commission, involving Palestine, Israel and another party, which would lessen but not likely eliminate the problems of a bilateral commission; or
   d. An international commission of parties acceptable to Palestine and Israel, or a United Nations commission, which would likely avoid gridlock, but would not be directly accountable to the direct stakeholders.

4. *Compensation Determination*. How should a global figure be determined? Among the approaches would include:
   a. A politically determined number that is largely shaped through the course of the final status negotiations by the amount of money that the international community and Israel are willing to pay. While this is doubtlessly the easiest method to achieve a global figure, it would have little to do with the international legal obligation to provide fair compensation;
   b. A macro-economic survey that would evaluate the assets as a prelude to determining an estimated value.

While this approach would approximate a fair value of the Palestinian losses, it also underestimates the degree of economic loss by minimizing the appreciation of value over the years since dispossession, as well as downplaying moral losses; or
   c. A multiplier approach, which would start with the estimated value and scale of the confiscated properties in 1948, and then add accepted appreciation factors to determine present-day value. This approach would come the closest to the "fair compensation" requirements, but, given the scale of Palestinian losses, it would doubtlessly be the most difficult method to fund.

At the unsuccessful Taba final status talks in January 2001, the Palestinian and Israeli negotiators agreed on several of the less contentious issues pertaining to compensation.[135] Within the context of a comprehensive agreement, an International Commission and an International Fund would be created to conclusively settle all outstanding compensation issues pertaining to Palestinian material and non-material losses. Also agreed upon would be a multi-track assessment system, where smaller claims below a certain monetary ceiling would be determined through a fast-track procedure. As well, Israel would accept some moral and financial responsibility for compensation, although no amount was seriously discussed. However, left unsettled by the time the Taba talks broke down was any agreement on the central questions of how the overall amount of compensation would be calculated, who would fund it, how the funds would be equitably distributed, and whether there would be separate parcels of funds for individual compensation and national projects.

E. Who Should Pay?

International law provides that the state, body, or individual who causes the damage or harm in breach of an internationally recognized obligation is liable for the restitution and compensation. In this case, Israel would bear the primary responsibility for compensation, because it either created and perpetuated the Palestinian refugee problem in defiance of international law, or on the lesser ground that – regardless of moral blame – it has been unjustly enriched through its expropriation and use of Palestinian properties, homes, and lands. Payments by Israel to meet its compensatory obligations could take the form of direct restitution (the return of homes and properties, which would likely lessen its potential total liabilities), the handing over of the settlements, roads, and other structures built in the West Bank and Gaza, and the financial contribution to a compensation fund. While Israel is an economically advanced nation – with a per capita income of over $18,000 (U.S.), it is almost twenty times the level of the Palestinian economy – even its financial capacity is unlikely to entirely satisfy the requirements of a final compensation fund by itself. For a variety of complex *real-politik* and practical reasons, the international community (primarily Europe and North America) would likely contribute to a compensation fund, which would enhance their voice in shaping the modalities of the compensation regime.

V. Conclusion

To satisfy the direction of the international community that the Palestinian refugee problem is to be settled in accordance with the principles of justice and equity, international law mandates that they are entitled to restitution and compensation for their losses. These losses attributable to Israel in violation of its international law obligations are substantial, and arise from: the expulsion or flight of over half of the Palestinian population; the confiscation of approximately 16,000 square kilometres of land, representing almost 80 per cent of Mandate Palestine; the large-scale expropriation or destruction of Palestinian property; the refusal to allow the refugees to return to their homes; the suffering caused by the losses and the decades in exile; and unjust enrichment from the use of the confiscated properties. Although international law does not speak with precision regarding the formulas to be applied in such a large-scale and complex claim, it has clearly stipulated a number of principles that are directly applicable in any future final-status agreement between Palestine and Israel, including: (i) Restitution of the wrongly acquired property enjoys primacy, with compensation available for property damage and unjust enrichment; (ii) Compensation in place of restitution is acceptable, but only where restitution has become impossible for practical reasons; (iii) Compensation is available for both individual and community losses, and covers remedies for the loss or damage to immovable and movable property; for loss of actual income and future earning potential; for moral damages, including emotional harm; for unjust enrichment; for the costs of rehabilitation; and for an undertaking that such actions will not be repeated; (iv) however the legal formula for compensation has been phrased – be it "full," "fair," "adequate," etc. – it is to be given a sufficiently broad application so that the restorative purposes of human rights remedies are fulfilled; (v) The state actor that displaced the indigenous population and unjustly benefited from the confiscated properties is the party responsible for restitution and compensation; and (vi) The responsible state actor cannot argue that the difficulties of process – those caused by the passage of time, the magnitude of potential claimants, the determination of worthy claimants, the calculation of outstanding damages, the existence of subsequent domestic legislation that has transferred legal title, the hostile mood among the domestic political constituency, or the lack of a comprehensive settlement to the wider conflict – are justifiable barriers to satisfying an otherwise established claim for restitution and compensation.

The lessons of reconciliation in the modern world are profound. Those on both sides of an historical wound benefit immensely from a genuine effort to acknowledge, remember, and restore. While full justice may not have been achieved even in the template cases of post-war Europe or contemporary South Africa, the transformation of relations and the flourishing of new values among these former nemeses have been substantially aided by the restorative remedies of restitution and compensation. In the Middle East, the closure of the decades-long conflict will require no less. For Israelis, offering these remedies will finally allow a reckoning with the uncomfortable history that still stares out from among the ruined homes and wild olive groves that can be found in every corner of their country. For Palestinians, accepting the remedies of restitution and compensation will not return some past Eden, but it will address not only the sufferings they have endured and the material possessions they have lost, but also provide the tools for a productive national future. The requirements of an enduring regional peace require no less.

Notes

1. This essay uses the term "displaced Palestinians" to include the Palestinian refugees of the 1948 and 1967 wars and their descendants, as well as those Palestinians, whether refugees or not, who suffered compensable losses arising from the conflict in Israel/Palestine. While the Palestinian refugees will likely be the primary beneficiary of any compensation plan that emerges from a settlement of the Middle East conflict, there are Palestinians who do not qualify as refugees within the applicable United Nations definition who nevertheless have claims for lost lands and properties that were expropriated by Israel at some point over the past five decades.

2. UNSC Res. 242, 22 November 1967: "The Security Council...affirms further the necessity...(b) for achieving a just settlement of the refugee problem."

3. *Declaration of Principles on Interim Self-Government Arrangements*, 13 September 1993, Government of Israel – Palestine Liberation Organization [1993] 33 I.L.M. 1525.

4. *Treaty of Peace Between the State of Israel and the Hashemite Kingdom of Jordan*, 26 October 1994, [1994] 34 ILM 43. See Article 8(2), where the parties commit to resolving the "massive human problems" of the refugees and displaced persons "in accordance with international law."

5. The centrepiece of the right to return is generally cited as Article 13(2) of the *Universal Declaration of Human Rights*, U.N. Doc. A/811: "Everyone has the right to leave any country, including his own, and to return to his country." On the

application of the right to the Palestinian/Israeli conflict, see J. Quigley, "Displaced Palestinians and a Right to Return" (1998) 39 *Harvard International Law Journal* 171; and K. Lawand, "The Right to Return of Palestinians under International Law" (1996) 8 *International Journal of Refugee Law* 533.

6. The current Palestinian position is expressed in the Palestinian negotiating paper submitted during the final status talks with Israel at Taba, Egypt, in January 2001: "In accordance with the United Nations General Assembly Resolution 194 (III), all refugees who wish to return to their homes in Israel and live at peace with their neighbours have the right to do so"; online: <www.monde-diplomatique.fr/cahier/proche-orient/refuge espal -en> (date accessed: 18 December 2002).

7. See the "non-paper" produced by the European Union envoy Miguel Moratinos (the "Moratinos Document") which summarized the discussions between the Israeli and Palestinian delegations at the Taba talks in January 2001; online: <http://www.arts.mcgill.ca/MEPP/PRRN/papers/moratinos .html (date accessed: 18 December 2002). For a summation of the Israeli position on the right to return, see S. Gazit, *The Palestinian Refugee Problem* (Tel Aviv: Jaffee Center for Strategic Studies, 1995).

8. Gazit, *ibid.* at 27.

9. Palestinian National Authority, *Palestinian Refugees and the Right to Return* (Jerusalem: Ministry of Information, 1995). Also see E. Zureik, *Palestinian Refugees and the Peace Process* (Washington, D.C.: Institute for Palestine Studies, 1996).

10. See "Private [Israeli] Response on Palestinian Refugees;" online: <http://www.monde-diplomatique.fr/cahier/proche-orient/isra elrefugees-en> (date accessed: 18 December 2002).

11. The Palestinian negotiating paper issued at the Taba talks in January 2001 called for the restitution of real property, and compensation in today's values for loss of property, for moral suffering, and for rehabilitation. The paper maintained that: "The rights of return and compensation are independent and cumulative. A refugee's exercise of his or her right of return to Israel shall not prejudice his or her right to receive compensation [for loss of property], nor shall a refugee's receipt of compensation prejudice his or her right of return...." *Supra* note 6.

12. *Supra* note 7.

13. J. Alpher & K. Shikaki, *The Palestinian Refugee Problem and the Right of Return* (Cambridge, Mass.: Weatherhead Center for International Affairs, 1998).

14. A. Kubursi, "Palestinian Losses in 1948 in 1999 Dollars" (unpublished, 1999). For an overview of earlier cost estimates, see T. Rempel, "The Ottawa Process: Workshop on Compensation and Palestinian Refugees" (1999) 29 *Journal of Palestine Studies* 36.

15. For definitions of compensation and restitution, see V. Condé, *A Handbook of International Human Rights Terminology* (Lincoln: University of Nebraska Press, 1999). (Compensation: "Money...paid...to extinguish a state's legal obligation by the payment of monetary damages to those whose human rights

have been...violated under international law"; Restitution: "A judicial remedy...to return property to another person from whom it was unlawfully taken or damaged.")

16. Other recent studies of the Middle East final status negotiations on the Palestinian refugees emphasize the same point. For example, see the 1998 report of the Harvard Joint Working Group on Israeli-Palestinian Relations: J. Alpher & K. Shikaki, *The Palestinian Refugee Problem, supra* note 13.

17. Unless otherwise noted, this historical précis is drawn from the following: W. Khalidi, ed., *All That Remains* (Washington, D.C.: Institute of Palestine Studies, 1992); B. Morris, *Righteous Victims* (New York: Knopf, 1999); B. Morris, *The Birth of the Palestinian Refugee Problem, 1947–1949* (Cambridge: Cambridge University Press, 1987); I. Pappé, *The Making of the Arab-Israeli Conflict, 1947–1951* (London: I.B. Tauris, 1992); and A. Shlaim, *The Iron Wall* (New York: W.W. Norton & Co., 1999).

18. The 1948 Palestinian refugee figures are highly contested. Official Israeli estimates place the number of refugees at 590,000. Palestinian estimates range from 745,000 to 850,000, while British and American estimates in the early 1950s put the number between 810,000 and 875,000. The United Nations adopted a figure of 726,000 in 1949, and has commonly used figures in that vicinity since. For the purposes of this essay, I rely on the United Nations figure. See E. Zureik, *Palestinian Refugees, supra* note 9 at 17.

19. F. Bernadotte, "Progress Report of the United Nations Mediator on Palestine," UN GAOR, 3rd sess., Supp. No. 11, UN Doc. A/648, at 16.

20. See in particular the writings of Israeli historian Benny Morris cited in note 16.

21. Bernadotte, *supra*, note 18 at 16.

22. *Ibid.*, at p. 20: "The right of innocent people, uprooted from their homes by the present terror and ravages of war, to return to their homes, should be affirmed and made effective, with assurance of adequate compensation for the property of those who may choose not to return."

23. UN GA Res. 181(II), 29 November 1947, Part I, C, chap. 2, para. 8.

24. *Supra* note 19 at 16:

     There have been numerous reports from reliable sources of large-scale looting, pillaging and plundering, and of instances of destruction of villages without apparent military necessity. The liability of the Provisional Government of Israel to restore private property to its Arab owners and to indemnify those owners for property wantonly destroyed is clear, irrespective of any indemnities which the Provisional Government may claim from the Arab States.

25. UN GA Res. 194 (III), 3 UN GAOR, pt. 1, Res. at 21, 24, UN Doc. A/810 (1948).

26. For a general history of the UNCCP, see: D. Forsythe, *United Nations Peacekeeping: The Conciliation Commission for Palestine* (Baltimore: Johns Hopkins University Press, 1972).

27. UNCCP, *Historical Survey of Efforts of the United Nations Conciliation Commission for Palestine to Secure the Implemen-*

tation of Paragraph 11 of General Assembly Resolution 194 (III), A/AC.25/W.81/Rev.2, 2 October 1961, at para. 92. Also see M. Fischbach, "The United Nations and Palestinian Refugee Property Compensation" (2002) 31 *Journal of Palestine Studies* 35.

28. Estimates of the number of Palestinian villages emptied between 1947–49 vary. See B. Morris, *The Birth of the Palestinian Refugee Problem, supra* note 17 at 297–98, who suggests 370; W. Khalidi, ed., *All That Remains, supra* note 17, who estimates the number to be 418; and I. Pappé, *The Making of the Arab-Israeli Conflict, supra* note 17, who offers a figure of 400.

29. D. Peretz, *Palestinian Refugee Compensation* (Washington, D.C.: Center for Policy Analysis on Palestine, 1995) at 12–13.

30. D. Peretz, *Palestinians Refugees and the Middle East Peace Process* (Washington, D.C.: U.S. Institute for Peace, 1993) at 87.

31. D. Peretz, *Palestinian Refugee Compensation, supra* note 29 at 13. Also see F. Lewis, "Agricultural Property and the 1948 Palestinian Refugees: Assessing the Loss" (1996) 33 *Explorations in Economic History* 169.

32. D. Artz, *Refugees into Citizens: Palestinians and the End of the Arab-Israeli Conflict* (New York: Council of Foreign Relations, 1997), at p. 16.

33. I. Kershner, "The Refugee Price Tag" *The Jerusalem Report* (17 July 2000) 22–23.

34. *Ibid.* at 23. Also see Rempel, *supra* note 14.

35. E. Benvenisti & E. Zamir, "Private Claims to Property Rights in the Future Israeli-Palestinian Settlement" (1995) 89 *American Journal of International Law* 295. Also see T. Rempel, "Dispossession and Restitution" in S. Tamari, ed., *Jerusalem 1948* (Jerusalem: Institute of Jerusalem Studies, 1999) 189.

36. Peretz, *Palestinian Refugee Compensation, supra* note 29 at 7; Artz, *supra* note 32 at 16; also see D. Kretzmer, *The Legal Status of the Arabs in Israel* (Boulder: Westview Press, 1990), ch. 4.

37. B. Morris, *The Birth of the Palestinian Refugee Problem, supra* note 17 at 155, states that these developments included:

> …the gradual destruction of the abandoned Arab villages, the cultivation and/or destruction of Arab fields and the share-out of the Arab lands to Jewish settlements, the establishment of new settlements on abandoned lands and sites and the settlements of Jewish immigrants in empty Arab housing in the countryside and in urban neighbourhoods. Taken together, they assured that the refugees would have nowhere, and nothing, to return to.

38. The principal Israeli pre-conditions, as summarized in the mediation conferences organized between 1949 and 1952 by the UNCCP, were: (i) compensation must be part of a general peace settlement; (ii) there would be no restitution of property; (iii) compensation would not be paid for individual claimants, but only to a collective fund, which would be utilized for the resettlement of the refugees elsewhere; (iv) Israel would maintain the right to raise its own claims for property damages and losses; (v) its contributions to a compensation fund would be limited by its ability to pay; (vi) it accepted no moral or political responsibility for the creation of the refugee problem; and (vii) the resolution of abandoned Jewish property claims

in Iraq, and, subsequently, to Jewish property left behind in other Arab countries. See UNCCP, *supra* note 27 at paras. 62–65, 72–75, 99–101; Peretz, *Palestinian Refugee Compensation, supra* note 29 at 10–11; R. Zweig, "Restitution of Property and Refugee Rehabilitation: Two Case Studies" (1993) 6 *Journal of Refugee Studies* 56.

39. In March 1951, Moshe Sharett, the Israeli Foreign Minister, told the Knesset that:

> We…have an account with the Arab world – namely, the account of the compensation that accrues to the Arabs who left the territory of Israel and abandoned their property…The act now committed by the Kingdom of Iraq… forces us to link the two accounts…We will take into account the value of the Jewish property that has been frozen in Iraq with respect to the compensation we have undertaken to pay the Arabs who abandoned property in Israel.

Quoted in Yehouda Shenhav, "The Jews of Iraq, Zionist Ideology, and the Property of the Palestinian Refugees of 1948: An Anomaly of National Accounting" (1999) 31 *International Journal of Middle East Studies* 605 at 619.

40. At the UNCCP conferences, the position of the Arab states focused on the following: (i) the Palestinian refugees had to be given a free choice about returning to their homes, and only then could compensation be determined as between those returning and those resettling elsewhere; (ii) compensation was to be paid to individual claimants; (iii) compensation should reflect the true value of the property; (iv) Israel bore the principal responsibility for paying the compensation, and if it is unable to pay the full amount, the United Nations also bore responsibility because of its role in the 1948 partition; and (v) the refugees must be represented at the different stages of negotiations. UNCCP, *supra* note 27 at paras. 102–5.

41. E. Buehrig, *The UN and the Palestinian Refugees* (Bloomington: Indiana University Press, 1971) 21–25.

42. The United States Assistant Secretary of State, George McGhee, presciently foresaw the consequences of leaving the Palestinian issue unresolved, during testimony given to the House Committee of Foreign Affairs in February 1950:

> The presence of three-quarters of a million idle, destitute people – a number greater than the combined strength of all the standing armies of the Near East – whose discontent increases with the passage of time, is the greatest threat to the security of the area which now exists.

U.S. Congress, House, Committee on Foreign Affairs, *Hearings on Palestine Refugees,* 81st Cong., 2nd Sess. S. J. Res. 153, 16–17 February 1950 (Washington, D.C.: USGPO, 1950) 9.

43. The accepted starting point for the sources of international law is Article 38(1) of the *Statute of the International Court of Justice.* It directs the Court to apply: (i) international conventions, whether general or particular; (ii) international customary law; (iii) general principles of law, which include principles commonly accepted by various domestic legal systems, and principles of equity; (iv) judicial decisions; and (v)

scholarly views. Other accepted sources of international law include the frequent restatement of principles by international organizations, particularly by the United Nations. See generally I. Brownlie, *Principles of Public International Law,* 5th ed. (Oxford: Oxford University Press, 1998) 1–30.

44. A. de Zayas, "Population, Expulsion and Transfer" in R. Bernhardt, ed., 8 *Encyclopaedia of Public International Law* (Amsterdam: North Holland Publishing Co., 1992) 438 at 443. ("As a fundamental denial of the right to self-determination and in the light of the Nuremberg principles, the Genocide Convention and the developing body of human rights law, population expulsion must be seen as incompatible with modern international law.")

45. International Law Association, *Declaration of Principles of International Law on Compensation to Refugees,* Cairo, April 1992. Reprinted in (1993) 6 *Journal of Refugee Studies* 69. Also see H. Garry, "The Right to Compensation and Refugee Flows: A 'Preventative Mechanism' in International Law?" (1998) 10 *International Journal of Refugee Law* 97; L. Lee, "The Right to Compensation: Refugees and Countries of Asylum" (1986) 80 *American Journal of International Law* 532.

46. International Law Association, *ibid.* Principle 1 states:

    The responsibility for caring for the world's refugees rests ultimately upon the countries that directly or indirectly force their own citizens to flee and/or remain abroad as refugees. The discharge of such responsibility by countries of asylum, international organizations (e.g., UNHCR, UNRWA, IOM) and donors (both governmental and non-governmental), pending the return of refugees, their settlement in place, or their resettlement in third countries, shall not relieve the countries of origin of their basic responsibility, including that of paying adequate compensation to refugees.

47. Such a principle has been a policy centrepiece for organizations dedicated to the material restitution of human rights victims. For example, a founding principle of the Jewish Restitution Successor Organization, which played a significant role in the recovery of heirless property owned by Jewish victims of the Holocaust, stated: "that a nation may not retain property that it gained by the mass spoliation of minorities whom it persecuted on racial or religious grounds." See S. Kagan & E. Weismann, *Report on the Operations of the Jewish Restitution Successor Organization, 1947–1972* (New York: J.R.S.O., 1972) at 6.

48. While serious violations of human rights such as mass population displacements are, at one level, irreparable, since no remedy can perfectly restore the victim to her or his position prior to the violation, the United Nations Special Rapporteur for Human Rights has nonetheless argued that "reparation for human rights violations has the purpose of relieving the suffering of, and affording justice to, victims by removing to the extent possible the consequences of the wrongful acts." T. van Boven, Special Rapporteur, *Study Concerning the Right to Restitution, Compensation and Rehabilitation for Victims of Gross*

Violations of Human Rights and Fundamental Freedoms, UN Doc. E/CN.4/Sub.2/1993/8 (2 July 1993) at para. 137.

49. L. Lee, "The Right to Compensation," *supra* note 45.

50. E. Marx, "Refugee Compensation" in J. Ginat & E. Perkins, eds., *Palestinian Refugees: Old Problems – New Solutions* (Norman: University of Oklahoma Press, 2001).

51. 19 November 1794, 8 Stat. 116.

52. *Ibid.,* Article 9: "It is agreed, that British Subjects who now hold lands in the Territories of the United States…shall continue to hold them according to the nature and Tenure of their respective Estates and Titles therein, and may grant Sell or Devise the same to whom they please, in like manner as if they were Natives…"

53. K. Schwerin, "German Compensation for Victims of Nazi Persecution" (1972) 67 *Northwestern University Law Review* 479.

54. United Nations, "Historical Precedents for Restitution of Property or Payment of Compensation to Refugees," UN Doc. A/AC.25/W.81/Rev.2, March 1950.

55. *Ibid.*

56. For other historical examples besides the treaties mentioned, see K. Schwerin, *supra* note 53.

57. *Fourth Geneva Convention of 1949,* 75 U.N.T.S. 287, Article 49 ("Individual or mass forcible transfers, as well as deportations of protected persons from occupied territory to the territory of the Occupying Power or to that of any other country, occupied or not, are prohibited, regardless of their motive.")

58. *Convention Respecting Reciprocal Emigration,* 27 November 1919, 1 LNTS 68.

59. *Convention Respecting the Exchange of Populations,* 30 July 1923, 2 *The Treaties of Peace, 1919–1923* 653 (New York: Carnegie Endowment for International Peace, 1924).

60. (Merits) 1928 P.C.I.J. (Ser. A.), No. 17.

61. *Ibid.* at 29.

62. *Ibid.* at 47.

63. Reparations for Injuries Suffered in the Service of the United Nations, Advisory Opinion, I.C.J. Reports 1949, 184.

64. *Valesquez Rodriguez Case (Compensatory Damages),* (1989), 7 Inter-Am. Ct. H.R. (ser. C).

65. T. van Boven, *Preliminary Report, Study Concerning the Right to Restitution, Compensation and Rehabilitation for Victims of Gross Violations of Human Rights and Fundamental Freedoms,* U.N. Doc. E/CN.4/Sub.2/1990/10 (26 July 1990).

66. E. Rosand, "The Right to Compensation in Bosnia: An Unfulfilled Promise and a Challenge to International Law" (2000) 33 *Cornell International Law Journal* 113; H. Garry, "The Right to Compensation and Refugee Flows," *supra* note 45; L. Lee, "The Preventative Approach to the Refugee Problem" (1992) 28 *Willamette Law Review* 811; L. Lee, ""The Right to Compensation," *supra* note 45.

67. Lee, "The Preventative Approach," *ibid.* at 829.

68. Lee, "The Right to Compensation," *supra* note 45 at 544.

69. For a comprehensive collection of the relevant UN resolutions on the Middle East conflict, see the five-volume series: *United Nations Resolutions on Palestine and the Arab-Israeli Conflict*

(Washington, D.C.: Institute for Palestine Studies, 1975, 1988, 1988, 1993, 1999).

70. *Ibid.*, vol. 5, 211–12.

71. B. Sloan, "General Assembly Resolutions Revisited (Forty Years After)" (1987) 58 *British Yearbook of International Law* 39; J. Castaneda, *Legal Effects of United Nations Resolutions* (New York: Columbia University Press, 1969); S. Bleicher, "The Legal Significance of Re-Citation of General Assembly Resolutions" (1969) 63 *American Journal of International Law* 444; R. Falk, "On the Quasi-Legislative Competence of the General Assembly" (1966) 60 *American Journal of International Law* 782; R. Higgins, "The Development of International Law through the Political Organs of the United Nations" in *Proceedings of the 59th Annual Meeting of the American Society of International Law* 116.

72. See in particular the oft-cited dissenting opinion of Judge Tanaka in the *South West Africa Cases* (Second Phase), 1966 ("What is required for customary international law is the repetition of the same practice; accordingly, in this case resolutions, declarations, etc., on the same matter in the same, or diverse, organizations must take place repeatedly."), reproduced in I. Brownlie, ed., *Basic Documents on Human Rights*, 3rd ed. (Oxford: Clarendon Press, 1992) at 575. Also see *Military and Paramilitary Activities In and Against Nicaragua* [1986] I.C.J. Rep. 99–100; *Namibia Advisory Opinion*, [1971] I.C.J. Rep. 50.

73. *Statute of the International Court*, Art 38(1)(c).

74. The Roman lawyer and legislator Pomponius stated in the second century A.D. that: "For this by nature is equitable, that no one be made richer through another's loss."; quoted in J.P. Dowson, *Unjust Enrichment: A Comparative Analysis* (Boston: Little, Brown and Co., 1951), at 3.

75. [1943] A.C. 32, at 61. In the Third World, a similar view was stated by Mr. Justice Guha Roy of India in 1961: "That a wrong done to an individual must be redressed by the offender himself or by someone else against whom the sanction of the community may be directed is one of those timeless axioms of justice without which social life is unthinkable." "Is the Law of Responsibility of States for Injuries to Aliens a Part of Universal International Law?" (1961) 55 *American Journal of International Law* 863.

76. American Law Institute, *Restatement of the Law of Restitution, Quasi-Contract and Constructive Trusts* (St. Paul: American Law Institute Publishers, 1937) at 12.

77. T. van Boven, *Revised Set of Basic Principles and Guidelines on the Right to Reparation for Victims of Gross Violations of Human Rights and Humanitarian Law*, U.N. Doc. E/CN.4/Sub.2/1996/17, 24 May 1996. Also see: (Third) Restatement of the Law, 901 (Redress for Breach of International Law).

78. *Supra* note 5.

79. Art. 2(3)(a), G.A. Res. 2200A (XXI), 21 U.N. GAOR Supp. (No. 16) at 52.

80. Art. 6, G.A. Res. 2106 (XX), B, 20 U.N. GAOR.

81. Art. 10, O.A.S., Treaty Series No. 36, 1144 U.N.T.S. 123.

82. Art. 21(2), *ibid.*

83. Art. 21(2), O.A.U. Doc. CAB/LEG/67/3 rev.5.

84. *Supra* note 79 at Article 9(5).

85. Article 5(5), E.T.S. No. 5, Rome, 4.XI. 1950.

86. Article 75, [1998] 37 I.L.M. 999.

87. *Convention against Torture and Other Cruel, Inhuman or Degrading Treatment or Punishment*, G.A. Res. 39/46, Annex, 39 UN GAOR Supp. No. 51 at 97, art. 14(1) ("an enforceable right to fair and adequate compensation, including the means for as full rehabilitation as possible"); *Declaration on the Protection of All Persons from Enforced Disappearance*, G.A. Res. 47/133, 47 UN GAOR, Supp. No. 49 at 207, art. 19 ("the victims of acts of enforced disappearance and their families shall obtain redress and have the right to adequate compensation, including the means for as complete a rehabilitation as possible"); *Convention Concerning Indigenous and Tribal Peoples in Independent Countries* (I.L.O. No. 169), 72 I.L.O. Official Bull. 59, Article 16(5) ("full compensation for any loss or injury").

88. *Supra* note 48.

89. *Ibid.* at para. 45.

90. *Ibid.* at para. 131.

91. *Ibid.* at para. 137.

92. *Ibid.* at para. 137.

93. *Ibid.* at para. 135.

94. *Velasquez-Rodriguez* v. *Honduras (Compensatory Damages)* (1989), 7 Inter-Am C.H.R. (ser. C), at para. 25. Also see D. Shelton, *Remedies in International Human Rights Law* (Oxford: Oxford University Press, 1999), ch. 8. The UNCHR Special Rapporteur (van Boven) study, *ibid.* notes, at para. 81, that the European Court had, by 1993, awarded "just satisfaction" of a pecuniary nature in far over one hundred cases.

95. *(Merits)* (1988), 4 Inter-Am Ct.H.R. (ser. C); *(Compensatory Damages)*, (1989), *ibid*; *(Interpretation of the Judgement on Compensatory Damages)* (1990), 9 Inter-Am Ct.H.R. (ser. C).

96. *Supra* note 81.

97. *(Merits)*, *supra* note 95 at para. 26: "Reparation for harm brought about by the violation of an international obligation consists in full restitution (*restitutio in integrum*), which includes the restoration of the prior situation, the reparation of the consequences of the violence, and indemnification for patrimonial and non-patrimonial damages, including emotional harm."

98. *(Interpretation of the Judgement on Compensatory Damages)*, *supra* note 95 at para. 27.

99. See D. Shelton, "Reparations in the Inter-American System" in D. Harris & S. Livingstone, *The Inter-American System of Human Rights* (Oxford: Clarendon Press, 1998), ch. 6.

100. *Supra* note 85, Article 8 states that: "Everyone has the right to respect for…his home."

101. (1997), 23 E.H.R.R. 513 (E.C.H.R.).

102. (1998), 26 E.H.R.R. C.D.5 (E.C.H.R.).

103. *Cyprus* v. *Turkey* (Application 25781/94) (8 September 1999).

104. *Ibid.* at para. 321.

105. J. Mickletz, "An Analysis of the $1.25 Billion Settlement Between the Swiss Banks and Holocaust Survivors and Ho-

locaust Victims' Heirs" (1999) 18 *Dickinson Journal of International Law* 199; S. Denburg, "Reclaiming Their Past: A Survey of Jewish Efforts to Restitute European Property" (1998) 18 *Boston College Third World Law Journal* 233; R. Zweig, *German Reparations and the Jewish World: A History of the Claims Conference* (Boulder: Westview Press, 1987); K. Schwerin, *supra* note 52; N. Balabkins, *West Germany Reparations to Israel* (New Brunswick, N.J.: Rutgers University Press, 1971).

106. [1953] BGB1. II 35. See generally Schwerin, *supra* note 53.

107. According to Balabkins, *supra* note 105 at 153, the primary German legislation, the *Federal Indemnification Law* of 1953, provided for "compensation for loss of life, damages to body and health, including medical costs, reduction of income, loss of freedom, incarceration, arrest, property losses, capital losses, discriminatory taxes, impairment of economic and professional advancement, etc."

108. Conference on Jewish Material Claims against Germany, *Restitution Guide*, online: <http://www.claimscon.org/CC_content.html> (date accessed: 26 November 2000). Also see the testimony of U.S. Deputy Treasury Secretary Stuart Eizenstat to the U.S. Senate Foreign Relations Committee, 5 April 2000, online: <http://www.usis.it/wireless/wfa00405/A0040508.htm> (date accessed: 26 November 2000).

109. *Restitution Guide, ibid.*

110. I. Pogany, *Righting Wrongs in Eastern Europe* (Manchester: Manchester University Press, 1997); M. Henry, *The Restitution of Jewish Property in Central and Eastern Europe* (New York: American Jewish Committee, 1997).

111. *Restitution Guide, supra* note 108.

112. *The General Framework Agreement for Peace in Bosnia and Herzegovina* (1996), 35 I.L.M. 1171.

113. *Ibid.*, Annex 7, Article I: "All refugees and displaced persons have the right freely to return to their homes of origin. They shall have the right to have restored to them property of which they were deprived in the course of hostilities since 1991 and to be compensated for any property that cannot be restored to them." Further, Article XII(5) permits all refugees and displaced persons the choice between return and compensation, and ensures that the owner has the right to compensation in lieu of return.

114. *Ibid.*, Annex 7, Article XI.

115. E. Rosand, *supra* note 66; M. Cox, "The Right to Return Home: International Intervention and Ethnic Cleansing in Bosnia and Herzegovina" (1998) 47 *International and Comparative Law Quarterly* 599.

116. "*Kevesevic v. Federation of Bosnia and Herzegovina*" (1998) 20 *Human Rights Law Journal* 318; (1999) 20 *Human Rights Law Journal* 326.

117. R. Lillich, ed., *The United Nations Compensation Commission* (Irvington: Transitional Publishers Inc., 1995); D. Beterman, "The United Nations Compensation Commission and the Tradition of International Claims Settlement" (1994) 17 *New York University Journal of International Law and Politics* 1.

118. N. Wuehler, "The Iran-United States Claims Tribunal: Ten Years of Arbitration at Work" (1991) 8 *Journal of International Arbitration* 5; W. Mapp, *Iran-US Claims Tribunal* (Manchester: Manchester University Press, 1990).

119. A. Painter, "Property Rights of Returning Displaced Persons: The Guatemalan Experience" (1996) 9 *Harvard Human Rights Journal* 145.

120. *The Civil Liberties Act of 1988*, 50 U.S.C. app. 1989 (b)-4; which authorized payments of $20,000 (US) to each person who suffered as a consequence. Also see E. Yamamoto, "Racial Reparations: Japanese American Redress and African American Claims" (1998) 40 *Boston College Law Review* 477.

121. M. Omatsu, *Bittersweet Passage: Redress and the Japanese Canadian Experience* (Toronto: Between The Lines, 1992).

122. N. Newton, "Compensation, Reparations, and Restitution: Indian Property Claims in the United States" (1994) 28 *Georgia Law Review* 453; M. Ferch, "Indian Land Rights: An International Approach to Just Compensation" (1992) 2 *Transitional Law and Contemporary Problems*" 301.

123. W. Henderson & D. Ground, "Survey of Aboriginal Land Claims" (1994) 26 *Ottawa Law Review* 187; K. Coates, ed., *Aboriginal Land Claims in Canada* (Toronto: Copp Clark Pitman Ltd., 1992).

124. R. Bartlett, "The Landmark Case on Aboriginal Title in Australia: *Mabo v. State of Queensland*" in S. Corrigan & J. Sawchuk, eds., *The Recognition of Aboriginal Rights* (Brandon: Bearpaw, 1996) 132.

125. B. Gilling, "The Maori Land Court in New Zealand: An Historical Overview" in S. Corrigan & J. Sawchuk, eds., *The Recognition of Aboriginal Rights, ibid.*, 121.

126. See generally N. Kritz, ed., *Transitional Justice: How Emerging Democracies Reckon with Former Regimes* (Washington, D.C.: U.S. Institute of Peace Press, 1995).

127. This part of the essay draws from the papers presented at a workshop held in Ottawa, Canada, in July 1999 on the role of compensation as part of a comprehensive solution to the Palestinian refugee issue. For a further review of the shape of these workshop discussions, see "Final Report, Workshop on Compensation," online: <http://www.arts.mcgill.ca/MEPP/PrrN/prcomp3.html> (date accessed: 18 December 2002); and T. Rempel, "The Ottawa Process," *supra* note 14.

128. *Supra* note 5. It is probable that the right to return had already achieved customary status in international law by the time the *Universal Declaration* was declared. See G. Boling, "Palestinian Refugees and the Right to Return: An International Law Analysis," BADIL Brief No. 8 (Bethlehem: January 2001).

129. United Nations Human Rights Committee, *General Comment #27: Freedom of Movement: Article 12*, 2 November 1999, CCPR/C/21/Rev.1/Add.9, para. 21. In para. 19, the Committee states: "The right to return is of utmost importance for refugees seeking voluntary repatriation. It also implies prohibition of enforced population transfers or mass expulsions to other countries."

The Right to Restitution and Compensation in International Law

130. For an articulation of the right in the context of the Middle East, see Human Rights Watch, "Letter to Israeli Prime Minister Ehud Barak," 22 December 2000, online <http://www. hrw.org/press/2000/12/isrpab1222.htm> (date accessed: 18 January 2001): "As in the cases of all displaced people, those unable to return to a former home because it is occupied or has been destroyed, or those have lost property, are entitled to compensation. However, compensation is not a substitute for the right to return to the vicinity of a former home, should that be one's choice."

131. BADIL Resource Centre for Palestinian Residency and Refugee Rights, "The Impact of Return on Compensation", paper presented to the July 1999 Ottawa Workshop on Compensation.

132. *Ha'aretz*, 21 September 2000.

133. The Moratinos Document, *supra* note 7, stated that: "The Palestinian side raised the issue of restitution of refugee property. The Israeli side rejected this."

134. For a thoughtful discussion of the issue of compensation and Palestinian women, see N. Abdo, "Engendering Compensation: Making Refugee Women Count!" (March 2000), online: <http://www.arts.mcgill.ca/MEPP/PRRN/abdo.html> (date accessed: 18 December 2002).

135. See the Moratinos Document, *supra* note 7.

Michael Lynk teaches at the Faculty of Law, the University of Western Ontario, London, Ontario, Canada. Prior to teaching, he practised law in Ottawa, and in 1989, served as a refugee affairs officer with the United Nations Relief and Works Agency on the West Bank. Prof. Lynk would like to thank Jill Tansley for her invaluable assistance, advice and encouragement during the writing of this paper, Lance Ceaser for his deft research, and the Law Foundation of Ontario for its financial assistance during the research stage. For space purposes, this article has used shortened footnotes. The full text version of endnotes is to be published in the online version of this paper available on the Refuge web site: <www.yorku. ca/crs/refuge>.

The Protection of Palestine
Refugees in the Territories occupied
by Israel

LEX TAKKENBERG*

1. Introduction

In many ways Palestine refugees differ from other groups of refugees,
for their former homeland no longer exists since the creation of the
State of Israel. Although the majority of the refugees have expressed
an interest in returning to their places of origin—an interest formally
recognized by the international community[1]—very few have been able
to do so. Local integration has not been a viable alternative, either in
the eyes of the refugees or of the Arab States. The same applies to
resettlement elsewhere, considered as a solution promoted by the
international community. For more than forty years it has been
impossible to find a durable solution for this group.

In the years following the end of the Second World War, the international community decided not to include the refugees from
Palestine in the mandate of the United Nations High Commissioner
for Refugees (UNHCR)[2], but to create a special UN organization to
take care of this group. Thus in 1950 the United Nations Relief and
Works Agency for Palestine Refugees in the Near East (UNRWA)
was created to take care of needy Palestine refugees in its areas of
operation.[3] Consequently, in 1951 it was also decided to exclude

* Deputy Field Relief & Social Services Officer, Gaza Field Office, United Nations Relief and
Works Agency for Palestine Refugees in the Near East (UNRWA). The author wishes to thank
Christian Berger, Gilbert Jaeger, Thomas Kramer, Christine MacCallum, Austin McGill,
Douglas Ross and Marco Sassoli for their helpful comments and generous assistance. The views
expressed are the writer's own, and are not necessarily shared by the United Nations or by
UNRWA. The information in the present text covers UN developments till 31 December 1990.

[1] Cf. UNGA res. 194(III), 11 Dec. 1946; see below, section 2.   [2] See below, section 2.
[3] Ibid.

Palestine refugees who were assisted by UNRWA from the 1951 Convention relating to the Status of Refugees.[4] As a result—combined with the fact that none of the 'UNRWA countries' (except Israel) are party to the 1951 Convention—Palestine refugees registered with UNRWA and residing in its areas of operation lack the special protection provided for in that Convention, as well as the international protection provided by UNHCR.

For a long time this has not been a serious problem. Protection against *refoulement*—the most crucial element of refugee protection—has never been an issue. The asylum States allowed the refugees to reside legally on their territory, while basic services were provided by UNRWA.[5]

In 1967, after the Six-Day War, two areas where many Palestinians had found refuge—the Gaza Strip and the West Bank—came under Israeli (military) control. The status of these areas now having changed to that of 'occupied territory', the status of the refugees also changed. In addition to being refugees, they now also became persons protected by international humanitarian law.[6] In this respect international protection has been provided by the International Committee of the Red Cross (ICRC).[7]

After more than 20 years living under occupation, the bitterness and despair over the lack of any sign of movement towards resolving the problems of the inhabitants of the occupied territories came to the surface in late 1987. Incidents that took place in early December 1987 spread quickly throughout the Gaza Strip and then to the West Bank. What at first seemed clearly to be a spontaneous uprising by the inhabitants turned into a broader confrontation characterized by increasingly frequent and varied incidents between the Palestinians and the occupation authorities. During only the first six months,

---

[4] 1951 Convention Relating to the Status of Refugees, signed at Geneva, 28 July 1951: 189 UNTS 150; text in UNHCR, *Collection of International Instruments Concerning Refugees*, (1979), 10 (hereafter referred to as '1951 Convention').

[5] According to one commentator, the Arab world has a long-standing tradition of granting asylum to refugees; see Arnaout, G., *Asylum in the Arab-Islamic Tradition*, Geneva, UNHCR, 1987. See also in this volume, Elmadmad, K., 'An Arab Convention on Forced Migration: Its Desirability and Possibilities,' below, pp. 461–81.

[6] Although not explicitly mentioned in the definition of protected persons in article 4 of the Fourth Geneva Convention, refugees are generally accepted as benefiting from the protection provided for in this Convention. Article 73 of the 1977 First Additional Protocol to the Geneva Conventions of 12 August 1949 states explicitly: 'Persons who, before the beginning of hostilities, were considered as stateless persons or refugees under the relevant international instruments accepted by the parties concerned or under the national legislation of the State of refuge or State of residence shall be protected persons within the meaning of Parts I and III of the Fourth Convention, in all circumstances and without any adverse distinction.' Cf. Patrnogic, J., *International Protection of Refugees in Armed Conflicts*, UNHCR, (1981); reprinted from *Annales de Droit International Médical*, July 1981.

[7] On ICRC's mandate in the occupied territories, see below, section 3

nearly 200 Palestinians had been killed and thousands injured as the authorities employed a variety of tough measures in their efforts to quell the uprising or *intifada*, the Arabic word by which the movement has widely come to be known.[8]

Since the beginning of the occupation but in particular since the beginning of the *intifada*, Palestinians have raised numerous complaints about human rights violations by the occupying power, the most frequently heard being,

Harsh methods of riot control including random and capricious violence against individuals;

Imposition of prolonged curfews and their inhumane enforcement;

The practice of administrative detention and the occurrence of routine violence in detention centres;

Harsh interrogation techniques used by the General Security Services (known as Shin Beth);

The taking of land in the occupied territories, especially for Israeli settlements, and the privileged access that these settlements are given to water supplies;

Deportations and other violations of the rights of the individual, including the blocking of family reunions;

Interruption of education through the closing of schools and universities and the denial of laissez-passers for an adequate period to Palestinian students pursuing higher education in other countries;

The demolition and/or sealing of houses belonging to (the family or relatives of) persons suspected of security offences;

Shortcomings in the judicial system, the obstacles placed in the way of the defence, usually on security grounds, and the lack of a fair hearing for Palestinians in the higher Israeli courts;

Economic discrimination against the territories, with the purpose of hindering their agricultural and industrial development and keeping them as a captive market and source of cheap labour for Israel.[9]

In view of these allegations it becomes clear that the fact that the international community had never provided for international protection for this group of refugees (other than the protection offered by the ICRC), made them particularly vulnerable. Several suggestions to introduce some form of international protection were made, *inter alia*, by the Security Council of the United Nations.[10]

---

[8] Cf. Report of the Commissioner-General of UNRWA to the 43rd Session of the General Assembly, GAOR, Supplement No. 13: UN doc. A/43/13, p. 9.

[9] Cf. Report submitted to the Security Council by the Secretary-General in accordance with resolution 605 (1987): UN doc. S/19443, 4–7. For a well documented review of human rights violations in the occupied territories, see Al-Haq, *A Nation under Siege, Annual Report on Human Rights in the Occupied Palestinian Territories*, 1989, Ramallah, Al-Haq (West Bank affiliate of the International Commission of Jurists), 1990.

[10] See, for example, UNSC res. 605 (1987), 22 Dec. 1987, discussed below in section 4. Other calls for (increased) international protection were made after the incidents following the killing

This article deals with the protection of Palestine refugees (as well as non-refugee Palestinians), residing in the territories occupied by Israel. In particular, it examines what protection Palestinians enjoy under international law, and what efforts have recently been made to provide them with additional international protection.

2. Historical Background

On 29 November 1947 the General Assembly of the United Nations adopted resolution 181(II), supporting the partition of Palestine into two States, one Jewish and one Arab. As a consequence of the resulting tension, followed by the first Israeli-Arab war immediately after the proclamation of the State of Israel in May 1946, some 600,000–760,000 Palestinian Arabs fled between December 1947 and September 1949.[11]

While a United Nations Mediator on Palestine and a Palestine Conciliation Commission tried to work towards a political solution of the crisis, on 19 November 1948 the UN General Assembly established the United Nations Relief for Palestine Refugees (UNRPR) to take care of the immediate needs of the refugees.[12] Three weeks later the General Assembly stipulated that 'the refugees wishing to return to their homes and live in peace with their neighbours should be permitted to do so at the earliest practicable date,'[13] thus clearly supporting voluntary repatriation as a solution to the refugee crisis. The UNRPR began to provide direct relief to the refugees in January-February 1949, through its operating agencies, the International Committee of the Red Cross, the League of Red Cross Societies, and the American Friends Service Committee.

In the course of 1949 it became clear that no immediate solution to the crisis was forthcoming. Therefore continued assistance, to be carried out directly by the United Nations would be necessary. On

of seven Palestinians near Tel Aviv by an Israeli gunman on 20 May 1990, and after the violence on 8 October 1990 at the Al Haram Al Shareef and other Holy Places of Jerusalem, which resulted in over twenty deaths, see below, section 4. An earlier attempt to increase the level of international protection was made in 1984, when the PLO Representative in New York seriously canvassed an amendment to UNHCR's Statute, to entitle Palestinians, like other refugees, to the protection of that Office. This failed to materialize for various reasons, including the fear of some contributing States that to involve UNHCR in this way could politicize its role.

[11] For a detailed study on the origins of this refugee problem, see Morris, B., *The Birth of the Palestinian Refugee Problem, 1947–1949*, Cambridge, Cambridge University Press, 1987. The estimates of the number of Palestinian Arabs who became refugees are taken from this work. More accurate figures do not exist, and these numbers have long been the subject of dispute between Israel and the Arab States.

[12] UNGA res. 212(III), 19 Nov. 1946.

[13] UNGA res. 194(III), 11 Dec. 1946.

8 December 1949 the General Assembly established the United Nations
Relief and Works Agency for Palestine Refugees in the Near East,

(a) To carry out in collaboration with local governments the direct relief and
works programmes as recommended by the Economic Survey Mission;
(b) To consult with the interested Near Eastern Governments concerning
measures to be taken by them preparatory to the time when international
assistance for relief and works projects is no longer available.[14]

Continued assistance for the relief of the Palestine refugees was considered necessary 'to prevent conditions of starvation and distress
among them and to further conditions of peace and stability.' The
General Assembly hoped that direct relief could be terminated by the
end of 1950.[15] However, it appeared that refugee needs could not be
solved by short-term relief, and their integration into the economic life
of the Near East was not feasible, either by repatriation or resettlement. After forty year still no durable solution has been found. The
UNRWA mandate was thus repeatedly extended, most recently until
30 June 1993.

At the time UNRWA was preparing its operations, the General
Assembly was busy with the drafting of the Statute of the UNHCR,
and it was decided not to include Palestinian refugees being assisted
by UNRWA within the mandate of the new High Commissioner for
Refugees. Paragraph 7 of the Statute declares that the competence of
the High Commissioner shall not extend to a person 'who continues to
receive from other organs or agencies of the United Nations protection
or assistance'.[16] The fact that UNRWA was only intended to provide
assistance and that, as a consequence of this provision, the
Palestinians would lack international protection, was not considered.
It was also not considered what 'level' of assistance would be sufficient to exclude the Palestinians from the jurisdiction of UNHCR.

The 1951 Convention on the Status of Refugees, drafted between
January 1950 and July 1951, also excludes Palestinians being assisted
by UNRWA, using identical wording to that in the UNHCR Statute:

This Convention shall not apply to persons who are at present receiving from

---

[14] UNGA res. 302(IV), 8 Dec. 1949.
[15] The main difference between UNRWA and UNRPR was that UNRWA not was only to
provide direct relief, but also to instigate work programmes aimed at reintegrating the refugees
in the economic life of the Middle East and thereby removing them from the relief rolls. For this
purpose, the Agency was provided with a considerable reintegration fund. Some attempts were
also made to resettle refugees elsewhere in the region. For example, UNRWA and the Egyptian
government carried out a survey on possible resettlement of 10,000 refugee families from Gaza to
the northwestern part of the Sinai Peninsula. See *Survey Report: Northwest Sinai Project Republic of
Egypt*, prepared by UNRWA and the Permanent Council for Development of National Production of the Republic of Egypt, Cairo, 1955.
[16] The UNHCR Statute is annexed to UNGA res. 428(V), 3 Dec. 1949. Text in UNHCR,
Collection, (1979), 3.

organs or agencies of the United Nations other than the United Nations High Commissioner for Refugees protection or assistance.[17]

However, the 1951 Convention takes into consideration the possibility that the special UN assistance might come to an end. The second sentence of paragraph D stipulates:

When such protection or assistance has ceased for any reason, without the position of such persons being definitively settled in accordance with the relevant resolutions adopted by the General Assembly of the United Nations, these persons shall *ipso facto* be entitled to the benefits of this Convention.[18]

Among the reasons for excluding Palestinian refugees was the desire not to create overlapping competence, as well as the reluctance of the Arab countries to be confronted with the burden of these refugees as long as the United Nations was caring for them.[19] Several Arab countries were also concerned that Palestinian refugees, whose reasons for flight were largely the responsibility of the United Nations, should not be included within the general provisions on refugees, but should receive the special attention due to them.

UNRWA began its operations in May 1950. Originally set up as a temporary organization, pending a solution to the Palestine issue, UNRWA started by providing emergency assistance: food, shelters, clothing and basic health care. The needs of the refugees and consequently the responses of the Agency, constantly changed over the years. Today, education takes up two-thirds of the annual budget, health 20 percent and relief services only 10 percent.[20]

UNRWA provides assistance to Palestine refugees who are residing in Jordan, Lebanon, Syria and the territories occupied by Israel.[21]

---

[17] Article 1, paragraph D.

[18] Article 1 D of the 1951 Convention has proven to be a serious obstacle for Palestine refugees who, after having resided in one of UNRWA's areas of operation, have attempted to seek asylum and protection as refugees elsewhere, particularly in Western Europe. A number of West European governments interpret article 1 D in a very restrictive way, maintaining that Palestinians previously resident in one of UNRWA's areas of operation may only be recognized as refugees under the 1951 Convention if they can prove that either UNRWA has ceased to assist them, or that they were no longer allowed to stay in the area concerned. Consequently very few Palestinians have been able to obtain full refugee status in Western Europe. See Nicolaus, P. and Saramo, P., 'Zu den Voraussetzungen und der Anwendbarkeit des Artikels 1 Abschnitt D Absatz der Genfer Flüchtlingskonvention,' ZAR 2/1989, 67–72.

[19] Cf. Robinson, N., *Convention relating to the Status of Refugees, Its History, Contents and Interpretation*, New York, Institute of Jewish Affairs, 1953, 63–4. See also Takkenberg L. and Tahbaz, C. C., *The Collected Travaux Préparatoires of the 1951 Geneva Convention Relating to the Status of Refugees*, Amsterdam, Dutch Refugee Council, 1989 (three volumes), in particular volume III.

[20] For an overview of the development of UNRWA's operations throughout the years of its existence, see the UNRWA publication *UNRWA · Past, Present and Future*, Vienna, 1986.

[21] UNRWA's working definition of a Palestine refugee reads: 'A Palestine refugee is a person whose normal residence was Palestine for a minimum of two years preceding the conflict in 1948, and who, as a result of this conflict, lost both his home and his means of livelihood and took refuge in 1946 in one of the countries where UNRWA provides relief. Refugees within this definition and the direct descendants of such refugees are eligible for Agency assistance if they

Currently, some 2.5 million refugees are registered with UNRWA, one third of whom live in sixty-one refugee camps. Some 350,000 pupils attend six hundred and thirty-five UNRWA schools, and more than one hundred health installations are available to the refugee community.

The six-day war in 1967 brought another upheaval. Refugees in southern Syria were displaced for the second time when Israeli forces occupied the Golan Heights and the Quneitra area. Many moved towards Damascus and some to Dera'a further south. About 150,000 registered refugees from the West Bank and some 38,500 refugees from the Gaza Strip fled to east Jordan, where they were joined by another 200,000 non-refugee former residents of the West Bank and the Gaza Strip, fleeing for the first time.

After the occupation of the West Bank and the Gaza Strip, the Israeli government explicitly requested UNRWA to continue its assistance to the Palestine refugees. Relevant agreements were laid down in an exchange of letters between UNRWA and Israel which became known as the Comay-Michelmore Agreement.[22] It was agreed that UNRWA would 'continue its assistance to Palestine refugees in the areas with the full cooperation of the Israeli authorities', and that the Israeli Government would 'facilitate the task of UNRWA to the best of its ability subject only to regulations or arrangements which may be necessitated by considerations of military security'. It was also stipulated that these restrictions 'will be removed as soon as considerations of military security permit this'.

3. Applicable International Norms and their Implementation

Three areas of international law are relevant to the protection of Palestinians residing in the occupied territories: international refugee law, international humanitarian law and international human rights law. Israel is a party to the 1951 Convention and the 1967 Protocol relating to the Status of Refugees.

It is questionable whether the 1951 Convention is applicable to occupied territory. Most of the provisions of the Convention grant rights to refugees residing or staying in the territory of a contracting State. From article 40 it appears that territory in this context concerns primarily metropolitan territory, not automatically including so-called dependent territories. However, in the view of the present

are: registered with UNRWA; living in the area of UNRWA operations; and in need.' See below, note 23; on the origins of the definition, see below, note 49.

[22] Exchange of letters constituting a provisional agreement between UNRWA and Israel concerning assistance to Palestine Refugees, Jerusalem, 14 June 1967, UNTS, 8955.

writer, the territories occupied by Israel, which have been under that State's effective jurisdiction for more than twenty years, should be considered 'territory' in the context of the 1951 Convention. Such an approach is in line with the evolution of international (human rights) law, in which increasing emphasis is placed on the State exercising (territorial) jurisdiction, rather than on the traditional concept of territorial sovereignty.

This is of mainly theoretical relevance to Palestinians residing in the occupied territories, for the 1951 Convention is not applicable to those Palestinian refugees who 'are at present receiving' assistance from UNRWA.

However, not all Palestinian refugees residing in the occupied territories are being assisted by UNRWA. A considerable number have either never been eligible for UNRWA assistance, or are no longer eligible.[23] In principle, and if they should wish to do so, these Palestinians could request the application of the 1951 Convention as well as international protection from UNHCR.[24] In practice Palestinians residing in the areas of UNRWA operations have not requested the application of the 1951 Convention and have not directly made requests for protection to UNHCR; for reasons of expediency or otherwise, the High Commissioner also has not sought to extend UNHCR activities to Palestinians in these areas, that is, to Palestinians who are not excluded from competence under paragraph 7(c) of the Statute.

With regard to international humanitarian law, a consensus exists among jurists and governments, including that of Israel, that the Regulations annexed to the 1907 Hague Convention (IV) Respecting the Laws and Customs of War on Land are applicable to the occupied territories.[25] Israel has consistently maintained the position that it does not accept formally the *de jure* applicability of the Fourth Geneva Convention Relative to the Protection of Civilian Persons in Time of War of 12 August 1949,[26] but since 1967 it has decided that it will respect the humanitarian provisions of the Convention *de facto*. It has, however, never defined these.[27]

---

[23] See UNRWA, *Consolidated Eligibility Instructions*, Rev. 7/63, January 1984. Palestine refugees who have never been eligible, for example, are those who originally fled into Egypt and only at a later stage established themselves in the occupied territories. Palestine refugees no longer eligible for assistance, for example, include refugee women marrying non-refugees.

[24] UNHCR has an office in Jerusalem.

[25] Reprinted in Schindler, D. & Toman, J., *The Laws of Armed Conflicts*, Martinus Nijhoff, The Netherlands, (3rd rev. ed., 1988). See also Al-Haq, above note 9, at p. 5. On acceptance of the Hague Regulations by Israel, Al-Haq cites Cohen, E.R., *Human Rights in the Israeli-Occupied Territories, 1967–1982*, Manchester, Melland Shill Fund, (1985), 58.

[26] Reprinted in ICRC, *The Geneva Conventions of August 12, 1949*, Geneva, 1987.

[27] Israel justifies this position, *inter alia*, by the legalistic argument that the Convention applies only where the Power ousted from the territory in question was a legitimate sovereign,

The Israeli position is not accepted by the ICRC, and it has not been endorsed by the other High Contracting Parties to the Fourth Convention.[28] Under that Convention, each Contracting State undertakes a series of unilateral engagements, vis-à-vis itself and at the same time vis-à-vis the others, of legal obligations to protect those civilians who are found in occupied territories following the outbreak of hostilities. This is why article 1 states that 'The High Contracting Parties undertake to respect and to ensure respect for the present Convention *in all circumstances*' (emphasis supplied). The phrase 'in all circumstances' is intended to include declared or undeclared war, recognized or unrecognized state of war, partial or total occupation with or without armed resistance, or even under certain circumstances when the opponent is not a contracting party.[29] The Convention applies automatically upon the outbreak of hostilities, and its application in territories occupied by the belligerents is not subject to the requirement that the ousted Power is the legitimate sovereign of the territories lost. Humanitarian considerations are the fundamental basis of the Geneva Conventions.

As a consequence of Israel's position on the Fourth Geneva Convention, the mechanism for international supervision and protection laid down in the Convention could not be implemented. The Convention provides for the possibility to appoint Protecting Powers whose duty it is to safeguard the interests of the Parties to the conflict, including the interests of its citizens.[30] In the case of the occupied territories, no Protecting Power has been appointed. None of the States party to the 1967 war, including Israel, made approaches to neutral States with a view to appointing such a Protecting Power. In addition, Israel as an occupying power failed to request a neutral State or an impartial organization to act as Protecting Power under the Convention.

In 1972, Israel did not accept an offer made by the ICRC to act as official substitute for a Protecting Power.[31] Israel recognizes the

---

and that neither Jordan nor Egypt was the sovereign power, in the West Bank and the Gaza Strip respectively, during the years preceding the 1967 war. See, for example, statement by the Permanent Representative of Israel in the Security Council, 16 Dec. 1967: UN doc. S/PV.2774, p. 74.

[28] In 1981, UNGA res. 35/122A, dealing specifically with the applicability of the Convention to the Occupied Territories, the General Assembly voted 141 in favour to one (Israel) against; only Guatemala abstained. In resolution 662 (1990), adopted unanimously on 12 Oct. 1990, the Security Council called upon Israel to abide scrupulously by its legal obligations and responsibilities under the Fourth Geneva Convention, stating that that Convention is applicable to all the territories occupied by Israel since 1967. In response to requests for clarification of that reference, the Council President said that these words included Jerusalem (UN doc. SC/5021).

[29] Cf. article 2.   [30] Cf. article 9.

[31] See ICRC, *ICRC Annual Report*, 1972, pp. 62–63. The ICRC made the same formal presentation to Egypt, Jordan, Lebanon and Syria, none of whom gave affirmative responses. Cf. Al-Haq, above, note 9, at p. 665, n. 18.

presence of the ICRC in the occupied territories but does not accord it
the status of an organization discharging the humanitarian functions
of a Protecting Power in accordance with article 11 of the Fourth
Geneva Convention. The ICRC is therefore not entitled to perform
the general monitoring and supervising functions of a Protecting
Power. In its 1970 annual review, the ICRC described its role in the
occupied territories:

> ... the functions of scrutiny entrusted to Protecting Powers or their sub-
> stitutes by the Geneva Conventions have not been, in the Middle East
> conflict, entrusted to the ICRC. Its action in this conflict is based on contrac-
> tual provisions setting out explicitly some of its particular duties as well as on
> the general article (Article 10) which recognizes its right to take action with
> respect to humanitarian activities other than those explicitly provided for.[32]

Furthermore, the role of the ICRC in the occupied territories is
limited by the extent to which Israel is willing to co-operate. The
ICRC addresses all matters deemed necessary in accordance with the
provisions of the Fourth Geneva Convention on a bilateral and con-
fidential basis.[33] The responses depend on an arbitrary choice made
by the Israeli authorities, which defines some of these provisions as
'political', thus rejecting their humanitarian character.

Finally, with regard to human rights law, the Israeli authorities
maintain that the occupied territories are administered in accordance
with the 1950 Agreement on the Importation of Educational, Scientific and Cultural Materials, the 1960 Convention Against Discrimination in Education, and the 1966 International Convention on the
Elimination of all Forms of Racial Discrimination.[34] Israel maintains
that other human rights conventions are applicable only in times of
peace. This position is strongly contested by various authors.[35]

4. Recent Initiatives by the United Nations

On 22 December 1987 the Security Council adopted resolution 605

---

[32] 10 *International Review of the Red Cross*, 429 (1970), cited in Al-Haq, above note 9, at p. 647.

[33] Another restriction faced by ICRC is its self-enforced policy of confidentiality. As in its
other areas of operation, the ICRC does not, and cannot, disclose to the High Contracting
Parties detailed information about human rights violations in the occupied territories. Only
exceptionally does the organization protest in public about practices in the occupied territories,
as happened for example in April 1989, after Israeli armed forces in the occupied territories shot
dead several people and wounded some 30 others during an incident in the West Bank village of
Nahalin, near Bethlehem; see ICRC *Bulletin*, May 1989, No. 160.

[34] 1984 Memorandum from the Office of the Legal Advisor to the Israeli Foreign Ministry.
Cited in Roberts, A., 'The Israeli-Occupied Territories 1967–1988: The International Legal
Framework of a Prolonged Occupation,' in Playfair, E., (ed.), *The Administration of Occupied
Territories: The Case of the West Bank and Gaza, 1967–1987*, Oxford, Oxford University Press,
forthcoming. See also Al-Haq, above note 9, at p. 5.

[35] See, for example, Robertson, A., *Human Rights in the World*, (1972), pp. 174–5.

(1987), the first resolution relating to the Palestinian issue since the beginning of the *intifada*. The resolution 'strongly deplores' the Israeli violations of the human rights of the Palestinian people in the occupied territories, and in particular 'the opening of fire by the Israeli army, resulting in the killing and wounding of defenceless Palestinian civilians.' The resolution also calls once again upon Israel 'to abide immediately and scrupulously' by the Fourth Geneva Convention and 'to desist forthwith from its policies and practices that are in violation of the provisions of the convention.' Finally, the resolution requests the Secretary-General 'to examine the present situation in the occupied territories by all means available to him, and to submit a report no later than 20 January 1988 containing his recommendations on ways and means for ensuring the safety and protection of the Palestinian civilians under Israeli occupation.'

A report prepared by the Secretary-General in accordance with this request was submitted to the Security Council on 21 January 1988.[36] The Secretary-General stressed, first, that in the long run, the only certain way of ensuring the safety and protection of the Palestinian people in the occupied territories, and of the people of Israel, is the negotiation of a comprehensive, just and lasting settlement of the Arab-Israeli conflict acceptable to all concerned. In addition, as the most important interim measure, the Secretary-General recommended that the international community 'should make a concerted effort to persuade Israel to accept the *de jure* applicability of the Fourth Geneva Convention to the occupied territories and to correct its practices in order to comply fully with that Convention.'

Consequently the Secretary-General discussed different ways and means that might be available to the international community in order to help ensure the civilian population's protection. In this respect, the Secretary-General considered four different concepts of 'protection':

(a) 'Protection' can mean physical protection, i.e. the provision of armed forces to deter, and if necessary fight, any threats to the safety of the protected persons;

(b) 'Protection' can mean legal protection, i.e. intervention with the security and judicial authorities, as well as the political instances, of the occupying Power, by an outside agency, in order to ensure just treatment of an individual or group of individuals;

(c) 'Protection' can also take a less well-defined form, called in this report 'general assistance', in which an outside agency intervenes with the authorities of the occupying Power to help individuals or groups of individuals to resist violations of their rights (e.g. land confiscations) and to cope with the

---

[36] See above, note 9.

day-today difficulties of life under occupation, such as security restrictions, curfews, harassment. bureaucratic difficulties and so on;

(d) Finally, there is the somewhat intangible 'protection' afforded by outside agencies, including especially the international media, whose mere presence and readiness to publish what they observe may have a beneficial effect for all concerned; in this report this type of protection is called 'protection by publicity'.[37]

Protection described under (a) is currently not practicable in the occupied territories, as United Nations peace-keeping operations require the prior consent of the parties to the conflict concerned, and the Israeli government has stated that it will not agree to any involvement of United Nations military personnel in the security of the territories.[38] Protection described under (b) has been provided since 1967 by the ICRC, subject, however, to the limitations above.

With respect to protection described under (c), the Secretary-General envisages an additional role for UNRWA:

In the case of the registered refugees, who number 818,983, or about 55 per cent of the Palestinian population of the occupied territories, UNRWA is clearly best placed to provide additional general assistance. UNRWA has been established on the ground for nearly 40 years; it knows well the refugees' problems; it is accepted by the Israeli authorities on the basis of an agreement signed in 1967; and it is trusted by the refugees. However, the number of UNRWA international staff in the field has declined over the years. Before the recent disturbances began, there were only 9 international staff in the West Bank (373,586 refugees and 19 camps) and only 6 in the Gaza Strip (445,397 refugees and 8 camps). In paying tribute to the invaluable service that UNRWA Palestinian staff have been rendering to the refugees in very difficult circumstances, I believe that international staff can at present play an especially valuable role. It is usually easier for them to gain access to Israeli authorities in emergency situations; and their mere presence at points of confrontation has a significant impact on how the civilian population (including UNRWA Palestinian staff) is treated by the security forces and helps it psychologically by making it feel less exposed.

I have therefore asked the Commissioner-General of UNRWA to examine the addition to UNRWA establishment in the occupied territories of extra international staff, within UNRWA existing administrative structures, to improve the general assistance provided to the refugee population . . . [39]

[37] UN doc. S/19443, p. 10.

[38] In his recent report to the Security Council—see below, note 53—the Secretary-General once again touched upon this subject: 'As regards the Palestinian appeals . . . for an impartial presence, properly mandated by the United Nations, this is a matter on which the Security Council would have to decide: the mandates for the United Nations personnel in the area, whether civilian or military, derive from the competent United Nations bodies and the Secretary-General does not have the competence to act on his own.'

[39] UN doc. S/19443, p. 12.

The Secretary-General's request did not remain without response. Shortly after the report went to the Security-Council, the first new additional international staff members arrived in the Gaza Strip and the West Bank. Neutrally titled 'refugee affairs officer' these international staff, accompanied by Palestinian assistants, were amongst other methods employed to provide the 'general assistance' envisaged by the Secretary-General.

More specifically the duties of the refugee affairs officers include, circulating throughout the West Bank and the Gaza Strip on a frequent (but unannounced) schedule for the purpose of observing and reporting to the Field Offices in Jerusalem or Gaza any unusual or abnormal circumstances; visiting UNRWA installations inside and outside of refugee camps to prevent use of these installations in a manner inconsistent with their status, and reporting any disruptions of Agency operations; visiting camps and other areas under curfew and reporting to the Field Office on any problems affecting the welfare of the population; assisting in defusing tense situations and averting incidents of maltreatment of the local population by members of the security forces; assisting in preventing interferences with the provision of Agency services, in particular health services; facilitating the delivery of food and medical assistance in times of curfew; liaising with local military governors and civil administrators on matters affecting UNRWA's operations or the welfare of the refugees.[40]

In carrying out these duties, the refugee affairs officers attempt to provide the 'general assistance' that the Secretary-General had in mind when reporting to the Security Council. Currently, nine refugee affairs officers are operational in Gaza; twelve in the West Bank. After more than two years it has become clear that the employment of a greater number of international staff has indeed had a considerable impact. Enabling the victims of alleged violations of human rights to report their story to international UN officers specifically assigned for this purpose, so that these events do not remain unnoticed, helps them, not least psychologically, to cope with the difficulties of life under occupation.[41]

In his report covering the period 1 July 1987–30 June 1988, the Commissioner-General of UNRWA informed the General Assembly of the introduction of the programme of general assistance and protection—as the programme was later named—as well as on its impact:

[40] For a detailed discussion of the duties of refugee affairs officers, see Viorst, M., *Reaching for the Olive Branch: UNRWA and Peace in the Middle East*, Washington D.C., Indiana University Press, 1989, 20–31. Several interviews with refugee affairs officers are also included. The present author was employed as a refugee affairs officer in the West Bank from Feb. 1989–Mar. 1990.

[41] Depending on the nature and seriousness of incidents or violations, these reports may lead to representations to the Israeli authorities at every level, from the local military commander up to the Ministries of Defence and Foreign Affairs.

UNRWA has sought to provide a greater measure of general assistance or protection to registered refugees. In the current situation, the presence of UNRWA international staff has served to support and reassure area staff in the performance of their duties under very difficult circumstances. At times Agency officials have also been able to ease tense situations and prevent ill treatment or injury to refugees and damage to their homes. UNRWA has noted physical ill-treatment of refugees and the destruction of their property, the sealing and demolition of houses, instances of intimidation, deportations and the application of collective punishment.

Additional staff were recruited to improve the Agency's capability to provide services. The refugee community has appreciated and welcomed the higher level of international staff presence.[42]

Commenting on the programme during a Symposium in the United Kingdom in 1988, A. Williams, UNRWA's Director of Relief and Social Services, observed

We have put into the West Bank and Gaza teams of international staff partnered with Palestinian colleagues from the Agency, whose job is to maintain a presence in the refugee camps and villages, to witness what is happening and to help where necessary, so that we can ensure clinics stay open, that assistance can be given to people. There have been numerous documented instances where that help was both necessary and effective. We also have documentary evidence that the presence of these international Refugee Affairs Officers, as we call them, has had a deterrent effect at points of confrontation. That is not to say that the beatings have stopped or that people have not been intoxicated by gas, or that there have been no miscarriages of justice. But there has been quite clear evidence that where a Refugee Affairs Officer has been present it has had an inhibiting effect on the behaviour of people with power to harm. That is something we will go on doing. We have also put into each of our Field offices a lawyer to keep us in mind of the relevant international legal provisions, and they have helped us with the reporting and in making our representations to the Israeli authorities, as we have done at every level from the local military commander right up to the Ministries of Defence and Foreign Affairs.[43]

From the report of the Commissioner-General to the General Assembly covering the period 1 July 1989–30 June 1990 it appears that the general assistance and protection activities have become a structural feature of UNRWA's programmes in the occupied territories, although still funded under the Agency's emergency budget. In a separate section on *Extraordinary measures of general assistance and protection*, the Commissioner-General remarked,

A further aspect of the Agency's emergency measures was the programme of general assistance and protection. The major component of this programme

---

[42] See above, note 8, at p. 16.

[43] Williams, A., 'UNRWA and the Occupied Territories,' 2 *J. Ref. Studies* 156–62 (1989), at 159–60.

was the assignment of 13 international staff members in the West Bank and 10 in the Gaza Strip as refugee affairs officers. They facilitated Agency operations and assisted the refugee population in their day-to-day life. The refugee affairs officers also helped, by their presence, to lower tensions and to prevent maltreatment of the refugees, especially vulnerable groups such as women and children. They helped to evacuate the wounded, to reduce interference with ambulances and to obtain the release of refugee children. They assisted the population as occasion arose, for example, to obtain permits to carry on essential services during curfew periods and to facilitate the movement of essential food and medical supplies to camps and other locations where needed. In performing these functions the refugee affairs officers sometimes succeeded in establishing a dialogue with Civil Administration officials and were able to assist on the spot in numerous matters affecting the welfare of the population. Refugee affairs officers continued to be of particular assistance to UNRWA local staff members who found it especially difficult to carry out their functions in the prevailing situation.[44]

Most of the duties of the refugee affairs officers are related to facilitating the delivery of UNRWA's services: health, education and relief and social services. However, a number of aspects of the work, in particular the 'general assistance' element envisaged by the Secretary-General, constitute an attempt by the Agency to meet changing demands for assistance.

This new dimension to UNRWA's work has not received a very warm welcome by the Israeli authorities. Israel has made it clear that it sees the operations (or at least some of the operations) of the refugee affairs officers as an unilateral transgression of UNRWA's mandate, extending beyond the terms of reference laid down in the Comay-Michelmore Agreement.[45] In this respect, the authorities have frequently accused the refugee affairs officers of monitoring and surveillance of Israeli troop movements and activities in the occupied territories, thereby obstructing the army's operations.[46]

In day to day practice this lack of acceptance of UNRWA's new role is translated into an increasingly unco-operative, at times even hostile behaviour on the part of the occupying forces on the ground. In this respect the Commissioner-General notes in his 1988–1989 annual report: 'Aggressive behaviour and physical harassment became more frequent also towards international staff and some were briefly detained during the performance of their official duties.'[47]

---

[44] Report of the Commissioner-General of UNRWA to the 45th Session of the General Assembly, GAOR, Supplement No. 13 (UN doc. A/45/13), p. 26. In addition to the assignment of refugee affairs officers, the programme of general assistance and protection also includes a low profile legal aid scheme.   [45] See above, note 22.

[46] See for example the article, 'Humanitarian Aid and More,' in the Israeli daily *Ha'aretz*, 15 Jan. 1990, in which the journalist Ori Nir confronts the UNRWA Commissioner-General with the various accusations of the Israeli Government. See also UN doc. A/SPC/45/SR.7, p. 10

The present writer does not consider that the Israeli criticism is well-founded. As a subsidiary organ of the United Nations General Assembly, established under article 22 of the Charter, the organization does not have the strict and well-defined mandate possessed by other international organizations established by treaty. As a subsidiary organ, UNRWA operates under the instructions of the principal organs of the United Nations, in particular, of the General Assembly. In late 1949, when the General Assembly adopted resolution 302(IV), it had a clear view as to what the organization was supposed to achieve; the reality of the Near East, however, has frequently obliged the General Assembly to modify the mandate or, explicitly or implicitly, to endorse adjustments initiated by the Commissioner-General of UNRWA to meet changing demands for assistance by the Palestinian community.[48]

For example, only three weeks after the Comay-Michelmore agreement came into force, the General Assembly in resolution 2252 (ES-V) endorsed '... the efforts of the Commissioner-General ... to provide humanitarian assistance, as far as practicable, on an emergency basis and as a temporary measure, *to other persons in the area who are at present displaced* and are in serious need of immediate assistance as a result of the recent hostilities' (emphasis supplied).[49] UNRWA's mandate therefore has to be reviewed pragmatically, and not as something cast in immutable terms forty years ago.

Moreover, the Comay-Michelmore agreement does not 'freeze' UNRWA's role in the occupied territories. The agreement states that UNRWA, at the request of the Israeli Government, 'would continue *its assistance* to the Palestine refugees' (emphasis supplied). Although it can be assumed that both parties had a clear idea of what that assistance included at the time, the nature of the agreement should be taken into consideration: an exchange of notes in the immediate after-

---

[47] Report of the Commissioner-General of UNRWA to the 44th Session of the General Assembly, GAOR, Supplement No. 13 (UN doc. A/44/13), p. 3.

[48] A list of relevant resolutions is annexed to the annual report of the Commissioner-General of UNRWA to the General Assembly. For the most recent list see above, note 44, Annex 11 at p. 50. A list of pertinent reports and other documents of the General Assembly and other United Nations bodies concerning UNRWA (notably those before 1987) can be found in *UNRWA at the United Nations (1948–1986)*.

[49] For an example of an explicit modification of the mandate by the General Assembly, see UNGA res. 1315(XIII), 12 Dec. 1958, in which UNRWA is requested 'to plan and carry out projects capable of supporting substantial numbers of refugees and, in particular, programmes relating to education and vocational training.' A tacit endorsement by the General Assembly of adjustments initiated by the Agency relates to UNRWA's definition of a Palestine refugee. Neither UNGA res. 302(VI) nor any subsequent resolution defined a Palestine refugee. During the first 10 years of its existence, however, UNRWA developed a working definition which was modified several times and ultimately finalized in UNRWA's *Consolidated Eligibility Instructions*. Although the wording of the various definitions was reported to the General Assembly on different occasions, that body never found it necessary to accord formal approval.

math of the 1967 war. It was never intended to prevent UNRWA from adapting its services to changed circumstances, adjusting its humanitarian services as needed.

Furthermore, in introducing new activities in the field of general assistance and protection, UNRWA is not entering alien territory. To promote and encourage respect for human rights and fundamental freedoms is one of the key purposes of the United Nations, laid down in article 1 of the UN Charter. Since 1982 the General Assembly has exhorted the Secretary-General, in consultation with the Commissioner-General of UNRWA, '. . . to undertake effective measures to guarantee the safety and security and the legal and human rights of the Palestine refugees in all the territories under Israeli occupation in 1967 and thereafter'.[50]

The programme of general assistance and protection resulted directly from the formal request of the UN Secretary-General to the Commissioner-General of UNRWA. It followed in turn on the Security Council's request to the Secretary-General to recommend 'ways and means for ensuring the safety and protection of the Palestinian civilians under Israeli occupation.' Neither the Security Council nor the General Assembly has considered it necessary formally to endorse the recommendation by the Secretary-General and later initiatives by UNRWA. During the last three sessions of the General Assembly, however, delegates of several major donor countries—which traditionally are also countries having a good relationship with Israel—have expressly commended UNRWA's emergency measures in the occupied territories, with special praise going to the programme of general assistance and protection. Similar support has been heard during several informal meetings of UNRWA's major supporters.[51]

The debate on the protection of Palestinians did not end with the adoption of Security Council resolution 605 (1987) and the introduction of UNRWA's programme of general assistance and protection. It was addressed at length by the Security Council following an incident on 20 May 1990 in which an Israeli gunman killed seven Palestinian workers and wounded eleven others at Rishon Lezion in Israel.[52] In

---

[50] See, for example, UNGA res. 39/99–1, 14 Dec. 1984.

[51] For example, such support was expressed during a meeting on 11–12 July 1989 in Vienna, attended by twenty-four countries and the European Community, representing the main contributors to UNRWA's budget, and the Arab States playing host to the refugees.

[52] Between December 1967 and May 1990 the Security Council has met on several occasions to consider the situation in the occupied territories, and has adopted resolutions specifically on the issue of deportations. See, for example, UN Security Council resolutions 607 (1988), 5 Jan. 1988; 608 (1988), 14 Jan. 1988; 636 (1989), 6 Jul. 1989 and 641 (1989), 30 Aug. 1989. In a statement by the President of the Council on 25 Aug. 1985 (UN doc. S/20156), the members of the Security Council declared their grave concern at the continued deterioration of the situation in the occupied territories since 1967, including Jerusalem.

the ensuing protest demonstrations, which erupted throughout the occupied territories, seventeen Palestinians were killed and more than 1,000 wounded by Israeli security forces.

During the Security Council debate in Geneva on 25 and 26 May 1990, and in New York on 31 May 1990, nearly every delegation that spoke, including members of the Council, emphasized the urgent need of the Palestinians for protection. However, a resolution which, *inter alia*, would have established a commission consisting of three Security Council members to examine the situation in the occupied territories and recommend ways and means for ensuring the safety and protection of the Palestinian civilians under Israeli occupation was not adopted, owing to the negative vote of the United States of America.[53]

Other calls for increased international protection were made following the violence on 6 October 1990 at the Al Haram Al Shareef and other Holy Places of Jerusalem, resulting in over twenty deaths. Following this incident, the UN Secretary-General decided once again to send a mission to the region, among other things, to look into 'ways to ensure the safety and protection of the Palestinian civilians under Israeli occupation.'[54] In resolution 662 (1990), adopted unanimously on 12 October 1990, the Security Council requested the Secretary-General to report before the end of October 1990 on his findings and conclusions arising from this mission.

The Israeli Government, however, rejected the resolution, and made clear it did not wish the mission to come. As a result, the Secretary-General informed the Security Council that he was not in a position to dispatch a mission, and on 24 October 1990, the Security Council, in resolution 673 (1990), deplored '... the refusal of the Israeli Government to receive the mission of the Secretary-General to the region', and urged Israel to reconsider its decision. This had no effect on the position of the Israeli Government, however, and on 31 October 1990 the Secretary-General reported without having been able to send the mission.[55]

The report reaffirmed the conclusions of that submitted on 21 January 1988.[56] The Secretary-General noted that his earlier recommendation on the addition of extra international staff to UNRWA's establishment in the occupied territories had been followed, and that they had 'helped to defuse tense situations, avert maltreatment of vulnerable groups, reduce interference with the movement of ambulances, and facilitate the provision of food and medical aid during curfews.'[57] The additional presence had 'been welcomed by the

---

[53] See *Report* submitted to the Security Council by the Secretary-General in accordance with res. 672 (1990): UN doc. S/21919, p. 7.   [54] See UN doc. SC/5221.

[55] See UN doc. S/21919, above, note 53.   [56] See above, note 9.

[57] See *Report*, above note 53, at p. 9.

Palestinians, but they add that, given the exceptional circumstances in which they are living, it has not had the necessary impact on the behaviour of the Israeli authorities.'[58]

The Secretary-General also stated that the numerous appeals to the Israeli authorities to abide by their obligations under the Fourth Geneva Convention had been ineffective. Realizing that for any measure of protection to be ensured, the co-operation of the Israeli authorities is absolutely essential, the Secretary-General, in an unprecedented appeal, suggested that the Security Council call for a meeting of the high contracting parties [of the Fourth Geneva Convention] to discuss possible measures that might be taken by them under the Convention.

In resolution 681 (1990), adopted unanimously on 20 December 1990, the Security Council reacted positively to this appeal, and requested the Secretary-General, in co-operation with the International Committee of the Red Cross, to develop further the idea of convening such a meeting, and to invite the submission of views on how the idea could contribute to the goals of the Convention and on other relevant matters, and to report to the Council. The Security Council also requested the Secretary-General 'to monitor and observe the situation regarding Palestinian civilians under Israeli occupation, making new efforts in this regard on an urgent basis, and to utilize and designate or draw upon the United Nations and other personnel and resources present there in the area and elsewhere needed to accomplish this task and to keep the Security Council regularly informed.'[59]

It is too early to determine whether this latest request will result in any improvement in the safety and protection accorded to the Palestinian population by the international community, but its wording provides another clear indication that UNRWA's initiatives with regard to general assistance and protection have the support of both the permanent and non-permanent members of the Security Council.[60]

---

[58] Ibid.

[59] The Secretary-General is requested to submit a first progress report to the Security Council by the first week of March 1991, and every four months thereafter. In a separate, non-binding statement by the President, the Security Council agreed that a properly timed and structured international conference should facilitate a lasting peace in the Arab-Israeli conflict. Following the adoption of resolution 681, the Secretary-General, during informal consultations of the Council on 21 Dec. 1990, referred to the Council's request that he monitor and observe the situation regarding Palestinian civilians under Israeli occupation, and said, 'In this connection, I will be asking the Commissioner-General of UNRWA to take the lead and to ask an appropriate number of his international staff serving in the area to provide me with the required information.'

[60] However, in a statement accompanying his vote in favour of resolution 681 (1990), the United States Permanent Representative to the United Nations made it clear that no formal

5. Conclusion

The Palestinian problem is one of the most tragic and compelling refugee crises of the post war era. In quantitative terms, it is overshadowed only by the Afghan refugee crisis; in terms of duration, complexity and political sensitivity, it is without precedent in modern history.

In the opinion of this author, the reasons advanced by the international community for excluding Palestinians from the general legal regime applicable to refugees are not very convincing. Given that this refugee problem could not be solved at short notice, and is today further from a solution than ever before, this decision should be considered a historic mistake. As a consequence, the legal position of the refugees concerned is extremely fragile.

In the occupied territories the non-applicability of the various instruments of international refugee law is neutralized to a large extent by the applicability of the Fourth Geneva Convention. However, the unilateral refusal of Israel to apply this Convention fully has shown, once again, the limitations of international law in effectively protecting the human rights of refugees. It is also to be regretted that the High Contracting Parties to the Fourth Geneva Convention have not utilized the means at their disposal to ensure respect for the Convention.[61] The Security Council has recently asked the Secretary-General to develop his idea of a meeting of the High Contracting Parties, and if this were realized it would constitute an unprecedented attempt by the international community to make one of its members abide by its obligations under international law.

In the face of the non-implementation of the mechanism for international supervision and protection laid down in the Fourth Geneva Convention, the initiative of the UN Secretary-General which led to the introduction by UNRWA of a programme of general assistance and protection should be considered as an important step to provide the Palestinians with additional international protection. As this article has shown, the assistance and protection provided have a

change to UNRWA's (and/or UNTSO's) mandate should be made: 'The United States strongly supports the ongoing efforts of the Secretary-General to monitor and report on the situation in the occupied territories. Nonetheless, my government wants to explain its view regarding the scope of the Council's request that the Secretary-General utilize available personnel of various UN organizations in the region and elsewhere for this purpose. UN personnel in the area are mostly employees of UNTSO and UNRWA, organizations with separate and well-defined mandates. No activity should be undertaken that would alter those mandates, which remain in force, and we would oppose any attempt to alter them.' See UN doc. SC/5247.

[61] Article 1 of the Fourth Geneva Convention states: 'The High Contracting Parties undertake to respect and *to ensure respect* for the present Convention in all circumstances' (emphasis added). On the obligations embodied in this article, see Stephens, M.T., *Enforcement of International Law in the Israeli-occupied Territories*, Al-Haq, Occasional Paper No. 7, Ramallah, 1989.

considerable impact and are highly appreciated by the Palestinian community. Given the exceptional circumstances, however, it has not been possible to put an end to the widespread pattern of human rights violations by the Israeli authorities.

In view of Israeli criticism of the programme, resulting in sometimes extremely difficult and even dangerous working conditions for the staff, it is very important that many governments have explicitly commended the work of the refugee affairs officers. There can be no other conclusion than that UNRWA is currently sufficiently mandated to carry out this important additional task.

Part IV

THE DEFENCE (EMERGENCY) REGULATIONS

PERPETUAL EMERGENCY:

A LEGAL ANALYSIS OF ISRAEL'S USE OF THE BRITISH DEFENCE (EMERGENCY) REGULATIONS, 1945, IN THE OCCUPIED TERRITORIES.

Martha Roadstrum Moffett

The author is an American lawyer currently living in Jerusalem

Acknowledgement: Editorial assistance for this study was provided by Mouin Rabbani, a volunteer researcher with al-Haq.

Al-Haq
1989

CONTENTS

I.   THE BRITISH DEFENCE REGULATIONS
     DURING THE BRITISH MANDATE . . . 3

II. BRITISH REVOCATION 6

III. THE JORDANIAN ADMINISTRATION:
     1948 - 1967 8

IV. ISRAEL'S REVIVAL OF THE
     DEFENCE REGULATIONS IN THE
     OCCUPIED TERRITORIES 11

     (A) Interpretation Order
         No. 160 11

     (B) Interpretation Order
         No. 224 14

V.   USE OF THE DEFENCE REGULATIONS
     IN ISRAEL: 1948 TO THE PRESENT . 17

VI. THE DEFENCE REGULATIONS UNDER
     INTERNATIONAL LAW 21

     (A) Application of
          International Humanitarian
          Law to the Occupied
          Territories 21

     (B) Application of
          International Humanitarian
          Law to Israel's Use of
          Deportation and House
          Demolition Under the
          Authority of the British
          Defence Regulations 26

          1. Deportation 26
             a. Israeli practice . . 26
             b. International law . . 28
          2. House Demolition 32
             a. Israeli practice . . 32

INTRODUCTION

During the first eighteen months of the Palestinian intifada (popular uprising) in the Israeli-occupied West Bank and Gaza Strip, the Israeli Government, in clear violation of international law, ordered the deportation of 51 Palestinians and totally demolished or sealed over 285 houses belonging to residents of the Occupied Territories.[1] Deportations and house demolitions, as well as various other measures used by the Israeli Government to counter Palestinian resistance to the Israeli occupation of the West Bank and Gaza Strip, are carried out under the authority of extraordinary legislation enacted by the British during their Mandate over Palestine, the British Defence (Emergency) Regulations, 1945.

The British Government revoked the Defence (Emergency) Regulations, 1945, at the end of the Mandate in May 1948, and Jordan did not consider these Regulations to be in effect during its administration of the West Bank from 1948 to 1967. Nevertheless, in 1967, shortly after taking control of the West Bank, the Israeli military authorities began using the British Defence Regulations against the population in the Occupied Territories, and have resorted to them with increasing frequency since the intifada began on December 9, 1987.[2]

Israel's justification of its continued use of the British Defence Regulations is essentially threefold. First, Israel asserts that the British Defence Regulations were never effectively revoked and thus remain part of the local law of the West Bank. Second, Israel contends that international law allows and even requires a military occupant to continue to apply the local law of the occupied territory. Third, Israel asserts that the measures it carries out under the authority of the British Defence Regulations, including deportation and house demolition, do not in fact violate relevant international law norms.

1

The purpose of this paper is to examine the validity of these three assertions. Section I discusses the British enactment of the Defence Regulations in 1945. Section II examines the subsequent British revocation of the Defence Regulations in May 1948. Section III reviews the status of the Defence Regulations during the Jordanian administration of the West Bank. Section IV examines Israel's revival of the Defence Regulations in the Occupied Territories beginning in 1967. Section V considers Israel's use of the Defence Regulations in the state of Israel from 1948 to the present. Section VI discusses the deportations and house demolitions carried out by the Israeli military forces in the West Bank and Gaza Strip under the authority of the British Defence Regulations, and considers the application of the Fourth Geneva Convention and the Hague Regulations to these measures. Section VII briefly examines other relevant portions of international human rights law.

The paper concludes that the British Defence Regulations do not constitute a part of the local law in the West Bank today and that the Israeli Government's continued use of these Regulations violates international law.[3]

I. THE BRITISH DEFENCE REGULATIONS
DURING THE BRITISH MANDATE

The British High Commissioner of Palestine enacted the Defence (Emergency) Regulations, 1945, on September 27, 1945 in the exercise of powers vested in him by the Palestine (Defence) Order in Council, 1937. The Palestine (Defence) Order in Council, 1937, was enacted by the King of England in Council and empowered the High Commissioner to

> make such regulations ... as appear to him in his unfettered discretion to be necesary or expedient for securing public safety, the defence of Palestine, the maintenance of public order and the suppression of mutiny, rebellion and riot, and for maintaining supplies and services essential to the life of the community.[4]

The Defence Regulations, as enacted, gave the High Commissioner extraordinary powers over the civilian population of Palestine, including the power to deport citizens of Palestine, to demolish houses, to impose curfews and town arrest, to censor newspapers and books, and to administratively detain, all without the necessity of judicial proceedings. These Defence Regulations actually revised and consolidated earlier and equally repressive emergency regulations enacted by the High Commissioner of Palestine into one volume.

The 1945 Regulations and the earlier emergency regulations were enacted in response to the virtual breakdown of civil authority in Palestine as first the Palestinians and then the Jews used violence as a tool to achieve political change.[5] At the height of the Arab Rebellion in 1938, for example, the British recorded 5,708 incidents of violence involving an estimated 16,000 armed Palestinian guerillas.[6] The British General Officer reported in August 1938 that "the situation was such that civil administration and control of the country was, to all practical purposes, non-existent".[7] According to official British

3

figures, between April 1936 and August 1939, 545 Jews, 126 British, and over 2,000 Palestinians were reported killed.[8]

During the period after World War II of Jewish opposition to the British Mandate, Jewish paramilitary organisations reportedly had an estimated strength of over 60,000 men under arms.[9] According to British statistics, between October 1 and November 18, 1946 alone, 99 British soldiers and policemen were killed.[10] In May 1947, the American Consul in Jerusalem reported that:

> with its officials attempting to administrate from behind masses of barbed wire, in heavily defended buildings, and with those same officials (minus wives and children evacuated some time ago) living in pathetic seclusion in 'security zones', one cannot escape the conclusion that the Government of Palestine is a hunted organization with little hope of ever being able to cope with conditions in this country as they exist today.[11]

The British Government responded to the escalating violence by enacting successive Orders in Council, which gave the British High Commissioner of Palestine broad authority to enact emergency regulations in the attempt to restore order.[12]

In spite of the extremely harsh measures imposed under the authority of these regulations, first during the Arab Rebellion and subsequently in response to Jewish violence, the deportations, house demolitions, mass arrests, curfews, sweeping searches, and collective fines were of questionable success in restoring order. Rather, they embittered the general population and made British rule even more unpopular.[13] The British progressively lost control of Palestine.[14]

4

On November 29, 1947, the United Nations General Assembly voted to partition Palestine. Almost immediately thereafter, civil war broke out between the Palestinian and Jewish communities.[15] The British Mandate came to an end on May 15, 1948.

II. BRITISH REVOCATION

On May 12, 1948, three days before the end of the British Mandate, the King of England enacted the Palestine (Revocations) Order in Council, 1948 (the "Revocations Order" - original text in Appendix A). The Revocations Order provides in pertinent part:

> The Orders in Council specified in the Schedule to this Order are hereby revoked to the extent specified in the second column of the Schedule.[16]

The last Order in Council listed in the attached Schedule is the "Palestine (Defence) Order in Council, 1937", under the authority of which the British Defence Regulations, 1945, had been enacted. The corresponding entry in the second column of the Schedule specifies "The whole Order".[17] The effect of the Revocations Order was therefore to revoke the Palestine (Defence) Order in Council, 1937, as well as the British Defence (Emergency) Regulations, 1945.

The Revocations Order was enacted "in exercise of the powers [granted] in this behalf by the Foreign Jurisdiction Act, 1890".[18] The Palestine (Defence) Order in Council, 1937, had also been enacted pursuant to the Foreign Jurisdiction Act, 1890.[19] Section 10 of the Foreign Jurisdiction Act, 1890, provides that:

> It shall be lawful for [His Majesty] in Council to revoke or vary any Order in Council made in pursuance of this Act.[20]

The Revocations Order specifies the day of "Coming into Operation" as "14th May, 1948".[21] The Interpretation Act of 1889, which was in effect at this time, provides:

> Where an Act passed after the commencement of this Act, or any Order in Council ... made, granted, or issued, under a power conferred by any such Act, is expressed to

6

come into operation on a particular
day, the same shall be construed as
coming into operation immediately on
the expiration of the previous
day.[22]

The Revocations Order therefore became
effective at midnight on May 13, 1948.[23]

III. THE JORDANIAN ADMINISTRATION:
1948 - 1967

Following the British withdrawal from Palestine at the termination of the Mandate on May 15, 1948, the Trans-Jordanian Army occupied the West Bank of the Jordan River. In April 1950, it was formally annexed by King Abdullah of Jordan. Jordan ruled the West Bank until its defeat by Israel in the 1967 June War.

On May 13, 1948, anticipating the end of the British Mandate two days later, King Abdullah issued an Addendum to the Trans-Jordan Defence Law of 1935. The Addendum provides that the Jordan Defence Law and all Regulations issued thereunder will apply to any country or area in which the Jordanian Arab Army is found or is entrusted with maintaining security and order.[24] The effect of the Addendum was to make the Jordanian Defence Law of 1935 and Defence Regulations issued thereunder applicable to the West Bank.

Article 2 of the Jordanian Defence Law provides that whenever there is an emergency necessitating the defence of Jordan or endangering public security or safety, the King may declare the Defence Law to be in effect. Article 4 empowers the King to enact Defence Regulations to ensure public security and the defence of Trans-Jordan.[25] On August 29, 1939, King Abdullah declared the Jordanian Defence Law to be in effect and enacted certain Defence Regulations thereunder.[26] The Jordanian Defence Law and Regulations provide, *inter alia*, for administrative detention, censorship, curfews, deportation, and house demolition.[27]

The Jordanian Defence Law of 1935 and Defence Regulations give the government of Jordan similar emergency powers to those granted to the British High Commissioner under the British Defence Regulations of 1945. However, the specific provisions of the two sets of laws differ in important respects. For example, while both sets of laws provide the power to order deportation and administrative detention, the British Defence Regulations

8

provide the right to appeal such orders while the Jordanian Defence Law and Regulations do not. Similarly, both sets of laws specify which courts will have jurisdiction over offences under the laws. However, the British Defence Regulations set up special military courts and provide detailed procedures by which these courts are to be governed. The Jordanian Defence Law relies on existing Jordanian courts and procedures.[28]

If the British Defence Regulations had still been in effect after the British left Palestine and Jordan took control of the West Bank, these Regulations would have been rendered unnecessary and superfluous by the Addendum of May 13, 1948 making the Jordanian Defence Law and Regulations applicable to the West Bank. There was no need for both sets of laws; moreover, since the provisions of the two sets of laws differ while conferring similar types of powers, to keep both sets of laws in effect would have resulted in inconsistency and confusion.

In fact, the Jordanian government (which was apparently unaware of the British revocation) considered the British Defence Regulations to have been repealed by virtue of the Addendum of May 13, 1948, and also by virtue of the following proclamation, issued by the Jordanian Military Commander in May 1948, making the Jordanian Defence Law and Regulations applicable to the West Bank:

> all Laws and Regulations in force in Palestine at the end of the Mandate, on 15 May 1948, shall remain in force ... save where that is inconsistent with any provision of the Defence of Trans-Jordan Law of 1935, or with any Regulations or Orders issued thereunder.[29]

Since important provisions of the Defence (Emergency) Regulations, 1945, are inconsistent with the Jordanian Defence Law and Regulations, the effect of this proclamation would have been to repeal the British Defence Regulations if they had not already been effectively revoked by the British.

In 1979, in <u>Abu Awad</u> v. <u>Commander of the Judea and Samaria Region</u>,[30] the Israel Supreme Court, sitting as the High Court of Justice, rejected a challenge to a deportation order issued under the authority of the British Defence Regulations. Petitioners argued that the Defence Regulations were no longer valid law in the West Bank. The Court considered the proclamation issued by the Jordanian Military Commander in May 1948, quoted above, and stated:

> We were not presented with any proof that the [British] Defence Regulations contradict the Jordanian Defence Law of 1935, thus the conclusion is that at the time of the Jordanian occupation of the West Bank in 1948, the above regulations remained valid.

As discussed above, there are important contradictions between the British Defence Regulations and the Jordanian Defence Law and Regulations. This conclusion is buttressed by an expert opinion submitted to the Israel Supreme Court in a different case by Palestinian lawyer Aziz Shehadeh (Appendix B). Advocate Shehadeh stated that "the provisions of [the British and Jordanian] regulations are contradictory", and concluded that "the [British] Defence Regulations ... were repealed and the same powers vested in the Jordanian King and his ministers by virtue of [the Addendum of May 13, 1948]".[31]

IV. ISRAEL'S REVIVAL OF THE DEFENCE
REGULATIONS IN THE OCCUPIED TERRITORIES

On June 7, 1967, after Israel occupied the West Bank and Gaza Strip, the Military Commanders of the West Bank and Gaza Strip issued the following proclamation:

> The Law in existence in the Region on June 7, 1967, shall remain in force, insofar as it does not in any way conflict with the provisions of this Proclamation or any Proclamation or Order which may be issued by me, and subject to modifications resulting from the establishment of government by the Israel Defence Forces in the Region.[32]

Israel contends that by means of this proclamation, the British Defence Regulations have remained in full force and effect in the West Bank and the Gaza Strip to the present day.

Apparently in anticipation of arguments that the Defence Regulations were revoked by the British prior to the end of the Mandate, or by the Jordanians during the Jordanian administration of the West Bank, two Interpretation Orders were issued. These orders will be discussed in turn.

(A) Interpretation Order No. 160

Interpretation Order No. 160 (Appendix C), issued by the Military Commander in 1967, provides:

> So as to remove any ambiguity, it is hereby decided that any Hidden Law does not have, or has ever had, any effect.

Article 1 of the same Order defines "Hidden Law" as:

11

any legislation, whatever it is, which was enacted between 29 November 1947 and 15 May 1948 and which was not published in the Official Gazette, in spite of the fact that it was the kind of legislation whose publication in the Official Gazette was required during that period whether by necessity or custom.[33]

The British Revocations Order, by which the British Defence Regulations were repealed prior to the end of the Mandate (see discussion in Section II, supra), was not in fact published in the Palestine Gazette, the official gazette in Palestine during the British Mandate.

In the 1985 Israel Supreme Court case of Nazzal et al. v. the IDF Commander of Judea and Samaria,[34] a deportation order issued under the authority of the British Defence Regulations was challenged on the grounds, inter alia, that the British Government had revoked the British Defence Regulations prior to the end of the Mandate. The Israel Supreme Court, sitting as the High Court of Justice, rejected this argument on the basis of Interpretation Order No. 160, quoted above, since the Revocations Order was not published in the Palestine Gazette.

In fact, the Palestine Gazette was not published at all after April 1948, due to civil war conditions prevailing in Palestine at that time.[35] However, there was no requirement under British law that the Revocations Order be published in the Palestine Gazette in order to be effective. Section 20 of Interpretation Ordinance No. 9 of 1945,[36] explains the requirement of publication in the Palestine Gazette as follows:

All regulations having legislative effect shall be published in the Official Gazette and, unless it be otherwise provided, shall take effect and come into operation as law on the date of such publication [Emphasis added.]

12

"Regulations" is defined in Section 2 of the same Interpretation Ordinance as:

> any regulations, rules, by-laws, proclamations, orders, directions, notifications, notices, or other instruments, made or issued by the High Commissioner ... under the authority of any Act or of any Order by His Majesty in Council ...

The requirement of publication in the Palestine Gazette therefore applied to legislation enacted by the High Commissioner of Palestine. There was no requirement that Acts or Orders in Council issued by the King of England in Council be published in the Palestine Gazette in order to be effective.

Requirements of publication for Orders in Council issued by the King at the time of the Revocations Order are set forth in the Statutory Instruments Act, 1946.[37]   The Statutory Instruments Act provides that:

> Where by any Act passed before the Commencement of this Act power to make statutory rules ... was conferred on any rule-making authority ... any document by which that power is exercised ... shall ... be known as a "statutory instrument" and the provisions of this Act shall apply thereto accordingly.

The Statutory Instruments Act goes on to provide that all such "statutory instruments" are to be published in the Statutory Instruments compilation. In accordance with the requirements of this Act, the Revocations Order was published in the Statutory Instruments compilation.[38] Thus the Supreme Court decision in the Nazzal case clearly appears to be in error in rejecting the British revocation on the grounds that it was not published in the Palestine Gazette.[39]

13

The British Government has confirmed the validity of the Revocations Order under British law and the fact that this Order effectively revoked the British Defence (Emergency) Regulations, 1945, in an April 22, 1987 letter to al-Haq. In this letter (Appendix C), the British Minister of State, Tim Renton, wrote:

> I confirm that, in view of the Palestine (Revocation) Order in Council 1948, the Palestine (Defence) Order in Council 1937 and the Defence Regulations 1945 made under it are, as a matter of English law, no longer in force.

(B) Interpretation Order No. 224

In 1968, the Military Commander issued Interpretation Order No. 224 (Appendix E), which provides:

DEFINITION

1. In this order, "emergency legislation" shall be understood as it is in Regulation No. 3 of the Defence (Emergency) Regulations, 1945.

METHODS TO REVOKE EMERGENCY LEGISLATION

2 (A). So as to remove all doubt, it is hereby clarified that emergency legislation is not rendered null and void by inference from later legislation which is not emergency legislation.

(B). Emergency legislation is rendered null and void solely by legislation which is not emergency legislation and which explicitly repeals it by name.

VALIDITY OF EMERGENCY LEGISLATION

3. Emergency legislation which was

14

in force in the area after 14 May
1948 shall remain in force from the
definitive date onward as if it had
been enacted as security
legislation, unless it was
explicitly revoked by name, as
stipulated in section 2(B), either
prior to or following the definitive
date.[40]

This interpretation order appears to have
been enacted to rebut claims that the British
Defence Regulations were implicitly revoked by
Jordan. The Addendum and Proclamation of May
1948 by means of which the Jordanian
government believed the British Defence
Regulations to have been repealed (see
discussion in Section III, supra) did not
"explicity revoke[]" the British Defence
Regulations "by name".

In the Nazzal case mentioned above, the
petitioners challenged three deportation
orders issued against residents of the West
Bank on the grounds, inter alia, that the
British Defence Regulations were implicitly
abolished by the May 1948 proclamation issued
by the Jordanian Military Commander. The Court
rejected this argument, citing Interpretation
Order No. 224, quoted above, and ruled that
the British Defence Regulations were still in
effect since they had never been explicitly
revoked.[41]

Of course, the British Defence
Regulations were explicitly revoked by name by
the British Revocations Order. (See discussion
in Section II, supra.) However, even as a
matter of Jordanian law, the Court appears to
be mistaken. The on-going validity of the
British Defence Regulations during the
Jordanian administration of the West Bank must
be determined as a matter of Jordanian law,
not subsequent Israeli legislation.[42] There is
no requirement under Jordanian law that
emergency legislation be explicitly revoked by
name.

In a letter to al-Haq dated June 25,
1988, the Jordanian Legal Commander in charge
of military justice confirms that, as a matter
of Jordanian law, the British Defence

Regulations, if still in effect, were repealed by the Addendum of May 13, 1948 and the Jordanian Proclamation of May 1948 (Appendix F). The letter states in pertinent part:

> the Jordanian legislator implicitly cancelled the Defence Regulations issued by the British Mandatory authorities in 1945...[citing both the Addendum of May 13, 1948 and the Jordanian Proclamation of May 1948].

Further commentary is provided in the expert opinion of Advocate Aziz Shehadeh, discussed above.[43]

In fact, during the course of the 19 years of Jordanian rule over the West Bank, the British Defence Regulations were never used by the Jordanian Government. This fact has been confirmed by a number of sources, including interviews with Palestinian lawyers who practiced in the West Bank during the period of Jordanian rule, and with officials of the Jordanian Ministries of Justice and Foreign Affairs.[44] As is pointed out in the above-quoted letter from the Jordanian Legal Commander:

> the Defence Regulations and orders which were issued during Jordanian rule were issued by virtue of the Jordanian Defence Law of 1935, not by virtue of the Defence (Emergency) Regulations of 1945.[45]

V. USE OF THE DEFENCE REGULATIONS
IN ISRAEL: 1948 TO THE PRESENT

While the main focus of this paper is Israel's on-going use of the British Defence Regulations in the Occupied Territories, it is interesting to note that Israel also considers the British Defence Regulations to still be in effect in Israel itself.

Shortly after the British withdrawal from Palestine, the Israel Provisional Council of State passed an ordinance which provided:

> The Law which existed in Palestine on the [14th of May 1948] shall remain in force, insofar as there is nothing therein repugnant to this Ordinance or to other laws which may be enacted by or on behalf of the Provisional Council of State, and subject to such modifications as may result from the establishment of the State and its authorities.[46]

It is on the basis of this ordinance that the British Defence Regulations are thought to have become a part of Israeli domestic law.[47]

Since the British revoked the Defence Regulations effective midnight May 13, 1948 (see discussion in Section II, supra), they were not in existence on May 14, 1948 and therefore could not be incorporated into Israeli law by this ordinance. However, while the use of the British Defence Regulations in the Occupied Territories has been challenged on the ground that these Regulations were revoked by the British, this has apparently never been the basis for a challenge to the use of the Defence Regulations in Israel.[48]

The new Israeli government first used the British Defence Regulations to arrest and administratively detain members of Jewish extremist groups.[49] In 1951, the Defence Regulations were used to arrest and administratively detain Orthodox Jews who protested against the conscription of women into the Army.[50] In addition, there have been other isolated incidents of the use of these

regulations against Jews in Israel. Their
principal use has, however, been against
Palestinian citizens of Israel.

Soon after the establishment of the State
of Israel, the Israeli authorities created a
military government to rule those areas of
Israel most densely populated with
Palestinians.[51] The Military Governor's
authority was based on the British Defence
Regulations.[52] Under the authority of Article
125 of the Regulations,[53] the entire area
under military government was divided into
numerous districts which were proclaimed to be
"closed areas". Palestinians living in one
closed area were not allowed to travel into
another closed area without obtaining a
special permit. There were reportedly over
fifty such closed areas in the Galilee
alone.[54]

The Israeli Government reportedly also
used Article 125 as one method of
appropriating Palestinian lands. Palestinians
who lived in one closed area and owned land in
another closed area were prohibited from
entering the second closed area to cultivate
their land. After several years without
cultivation, the land was confiscated by the
Israeli Government under the Cultivation of
Waste Lands Ordinance.[55]

Other provisions of the British Defence
Regulations used by the military government
during this time included Article 109
(empowering the military governor to order
anyone to remain at his residence and report
his movements to the authorities), Article 110
(allowing the military governor to require any
person to "reside within the limits of any
area" designated by the military governor and
remain at his residence from one hour after
sunset until sunrise), Article 111 (allowing
the administrative detention of any person for
a period not exceeding one year (subject to
renewal) without charge or trial), and Article
124 (allowing the military governor to place a
total or partial curfew on any village or
region).[56]

With the exception of administrative
detention under Article 111, none of the

18

above-listed sanctions were subject to any sort of judicial or administrative hearing or any type of appeal process. Moreover, restrictions imposed on entire Arab villages or areas were reportedly not enforced against Jews living in those same areas.[57]

In 1966, the system of military government was dismantled.[58] However, the British Defence Regulations were left in place and continue to be used today against the Palestinian population living in Israel.[59]

Several unsuccessful attempts have been made over the years to repeal all or part of the British Defence Regulations in Israel. In July 1949, a bill was introduced into the Knesset by the government itself to repeal the Defence Regulations. It did not pass, however.[60]

As the government legal advisor in 1950, Haim Cohn, later Justice of the Israel Supreme Court, suggested to the Knesset that the British Defence Regulations be abolished. According to Cohn, the Law Committee of the Knesset concluded that if there were to be such Regulations in effect in Israel, it was better that they be British.[61]

Repeal was again proposed in 1951. During the course of the debate, the Knesset passed a resolution declaring:

> the Defence (Emergency) Regulations, 1945, which have been effective since the time of the British Mandate, are incompatible with the principles of a democratic state...[62]

The Knesset delegated to its Constitution and Law Committee the responsibility of drafting a bill to repeal the Defence Regulations. However, the bill did not pass.[63]

In 1954, Meir Vilner of the Israeli Communist Party proposed that Article 125 of the Defence Regulations be abolished. He stated:

> [T]he Military Governors have lately

19

made a habit of declaring whole
villages and stretches of land
'closed areas' ... in order to
prevent Arab peasants from working
their land.

Vilner's proposal was crossed off the
agenda.[64]

According to Israeli legal scholar Baruch
Bracha, there are two main reasons that these
efforts to repeal the British Defence
Regulations in Israel have failed. The first
is that:

the special security situation in
Israel had necessitated the giving
of special powers which curb the
personal freedom of persons who may
endanger the State, although such
persons might possibly not be
convicted in the Courts on the basis
of the regular laws of evidence.

The second is that:

it was convenient for the Government
to attribute the blame for these
Regulations adversely affecting
individual liberties on the doorstep
of Mandatory legislation and thus
declare itself innocent.[65]

VI.THE DEFENCE REGULATIONS
UNDER INTERNATIONAL LAW

(A) Application of International Humanitarian Law to the Occupied Territories

For centuries it was assumed that a military occupant was the absolute owner of the occupied territory and could do whatever it wished with the inhabitants.   It is only relatively recently, beginning in the late nineteenth century, that it has come to be generally recognized that civilians under military occupation should be protected under international law.[66]

The two principal international conventions which set forth humanitarian law applicable to military occupations are the Convention (IV) Respecting the Laws and Customs of War on Land and appended Regulations ("1907 Hague Regulations"), particularly Articles 42 to 56, and the Geneva Convention Relative to the Protection of Civilian Persons in Time of War of August 12, 1949 ("Fourth Geneva Convention").[67]   Neither of these conventions sets forth lofty idealistic standards, impossible of application in the real world.   Rather, both conventions balance humanitarian concerns with the military needs of the occupant.[68]

The 1907 Hague Regulations have achieved the status of customary international law; they set forth norms of conduct applicable to all nations whether or not they have become parties to the convention.[69]   It is not yet clear whether the Fourth Geneva Convention, in its entirety, reflects customary international law, although many provisions of it certainly do.[70]   However, nearly all states are today parties to the Fourth Geneva Convention, including Israel, Jordan, and Egypt.[71]

Although as a party to the Fourth Geneva Convention Israel is bound to comply with its terms, Israel has not recognized the applicability of the Fourth Geneva Convention to its occupation of the West Bank and Gaza Strip.[72]   This position is based at least in

21

part upon Israel's contention that the Fourth Geneva Convention applies only where a legitimate sovereign power was ousted from the occupied territory.[73] Israel has never recognized that the West Bank was lawfully under the sovereignty of Jordan or that the Gaza Strip was lawfully under the sovereignty of Egypt prior to its occupation of these territories.[74]

In support of its position, Israel argues that the rules of belligerent occupation were created to protect the reversionary rights of the legitimate sovereign to the occupied territory.[75] Where no legitimate sovereign was ousted, the argument goes, the reasons for application of the Fourth Geneva Convention do not come into play, and, therefore, the Fourth Geneva Convention does not govern the occupation.[76]

It is correct that the rules of belligerent occupation were intended to protect the reversionary rights of the legitimate sovereign. However, these rules were also intended to protect the civilian population within the occupied territory.[77] In fact, it has been convincingly maintained that protection of the civilian population is the primary purpose behind the Fourth Geneva Convention.[78] In any event, to conclude that because there is no legitimate sovereign (assuming _arguendo_ that this is true) the civilian population is entitled to no protection under international law, is unsupportable. As noted by Jean Pictet of the International Committee of the Red Cross ("ICRC"): "[Humanitarian law] must be invoked to ensure at least a minimum of safeguards and of humanity to all men, in times of peace and in times of war alike".[79]

The reluctance of Israel to admit the applicability of the Fourth Geneva Convention to the Occupied Territories apparently stems, at least in part, from its concern that such an admission would be interpreted as a recognition of the sovereignty of Jordan over the West Bank, and of Egypt over the Gaza Strip.[80] The ICRC, which was responsible in large part for the drafting of the Fourth Geneva Convention, and which is charged with assisting the parties to the Convention in carrying out their obligations under the Convention, takes the position that the Fourth Geneva Convention applies where "territory under the authority of one of the parties passes under the authority of an opposing party", without regard to the question of sovereignty.[81]

And, indeed, Article 3 of the Fourth Geneva Convention provides: "The application of humanitarian law shall not affect the legal status of the parties to the conflict", thus indicating that Israel's recognition of the applicability of the Fourth Geneva Convention would not, under the terms of the Convention, constitute an admission of sovereignty.   In addition, Article 2 of the Convention provides that the provisions of the Convention shall apply "to all cases of partial or total occupation of the territory of a High Contracting Party..." Article 47 further states:

> Protected persons who are in occupied territory shall not be deprived, in any case or in any manner whatsoever, of the benefits of the present Convention by any change introduced, as the result of the occupation of a territory, into the institutions or government of the said territory, nor by any agreement concluded between the authorities of the occupied territories and the Occupying Power, nor by any annexation by the latter of the whole or part of the occupied territory.

"Protected persons" are defined in Article 4 as

> those who, at a given moment and in any manner whatsoever, find themselves, in case of conflict or occupation, in the hands of a party to the conflict or Occupying Power of which they are not nationals.

It seems then, that the clear intention was to have the widest possible application of the Convention, without regard for political considerations.

The International Committee of the Red Cross has from the outset maintained that the Fourth Geneva Convention does apply to Israel's occupation of the West Bank and Gaza Strip.[82] The United Nations Security Council, as well as most governments including that of the United States, have also asserted unequivocally the application of the Fourth Geneva Convention to Israel's occupation of the West Bank and the Gaza Strip.[83]

While continuing to maintain that Israel is not de jure bound to apply the provisions of the Fourth Geneva Convention to the Occupied Territories, Israel nevertheless has declared that it voluntarily complies with the humanitarian provisions of the Fourth Geneva Convention.[84] The former Attorney-General of Israel, Meir Shamgar (currently President of the Israel Supreme Court) has stated:

> By General Staff Orders of the Israeli Army, every soldier is bound to act according to the Fourth Geneva Convention which has been published as part of these Orders. Every soldier is obliged to respect the person, honor, family rights, religious convictions and practices, and manners and customs of the inhabitants of the Territories, and any action against these rules of behavior is punishable by virtue of the Israeli Military Justice Law.[85]

Israel also allows the ICRC access to detained prisoners within 14 days of arrest.[86]

The Israel Supreme Court has not ruled on the applicability of the Fourth Geneva Convention to the Occupied Territories. It has held that the Convention is non-justiciable since, as conventional rather than customary international law, it does not form a part of the municipal law of Israel, and could only become a part of this law if legislation to this effect were adopted by the Knesset.[87] The

24

Supreme Court has held, however, that the
Hague Regulations, as customary international
law, are binding on the military government in
the Occupied Territories.[88]

As Israeli legal scholar Theodore Meron
has aptly noted in this regard:

> If Israel is considered an occupying
> power for the purposes of the Hague
> Regulations, surely it must be an
> occupying power for the purposes of
> the Fourth Geneva Convention as
> well.[89]

Both treaties concern the application of
humanitarian law to military occupation.
Moreover, Israel's concern that recognition of
the applicability of the Fourth Geneva
Convention will be viewed as an admission of
the legitimacy of Jordan's and Egypt's
sovereignty over the Occupied Territories
should apply equally to the Hague Regulations,
since Article 43 of the Hague Regulations
states as its premise: "The authority of the
legitimate power having in fact passed into
the hands of the occupant ...."[90] Finally,
Israel's refusal to recognize the
applicability of any portion of the Fourth
Geneva Convention to the Occupied Territories
while at the same time admitting the
applicability of the Hague Regulations is
illogical since certain provisions of the
Fourth Geneva Convention merely restate
provisions of the Hague Regulations.[91]

The Government of Israel has allowed
various measures taken by the military
government in the Occupied Territories to be
tested in the Israel Supreme Court sitting as
the High Court of Justice under the standards
set forth in the Fourth Geneva Convention as
well as under the Hague Regulations.[92] For
this reason, and since the international
community does consider the Fourth Geneva
Convention to be binding on Israel, this paper
will next consider Israel's conduct in making
extensive use of the British Defence
Regulations in the Occupied Territories under
the standards set forth in both the 1907 Hague
Regulations and the Fourth Geneva Convention.

(B) Application of International Humanitarian Law To Israel's Use of Deportation and House Demolition Under the Authority of the British Defence Regulations

This section will examine two of the extrajudicial sanctions which the Israeli Government has imposed in the West Bank and Gaza Strip under the authority of the British Defence Regulations (deportation and house demolition), and will consider the application of international humanitarian law to these sanctions.

1. Deportation

a. Israeli Practice

Articles 108 and 112 of the British Defence Regulations empower the Military Commander "to issue an order ... for the deportation of any person in Palestine" if the Military Commander "is of the opinion that it is necessary or expedient to make the order for securing the public safety, the defence of Palestine, the maintenance of public order or the suppression of mutiny, rebellion or riot".[93] Since deportation is an administrative and not a judicial sanction, deportees are not formally charged with any crime nor afforded a trial prior to being expelled.

Under guidelines issued by the Israeli Government in 1977, prospective deportees have 48 hours to appeal the deportation order to a Military Advisory Committee and an additional 48 hours to appeal the Advisory Committee's decision to the Israel Supreme Court.[94] However, these rights of appeal are of limited value since deportation orders are typically made on the basis of secret evidence to which neither the prospective deportee nor his lawyer has access.[95]

In view of the very broad discretionary authority given to the Military Commander by the Defence Regulations to issue deportation orders, Supreme Court review of the Military

26

Commander's use of this discretion is
necessarily limited. As the Supreme Court,
sitting as the High Court of Justice,
explained in <u>Alyubi</u> <u>v</u>. <u>Minister</u> <u>of</u> <u>Defence</u>:

> The jurisdiction of this Court, in
> scrutinizing the competent
> authority's exercise of its power
> emanating from the Defence
> (Emergency) Regulations, 1945, is
> very limited. When the given
> Regulation empowers the competent
> authority to act against an
> individual in any case in which it
> 'thinks' or 'it seems to it' that
> there are conditions that require
> this, then that same Authority is
> the final Arbiter in determining the
> existence of these conditions. In
> such situations this Court's
> function is limited to examining
> whether the authority exceeded its
> power under the law by virtue of
> which it was empowered to act, if
> the said authority paid attention to
> the factors stated in the same law,
> and whether the authority acted in
> good faith. Since it is restricted
> to this limited jurisdiction, this
> Court is not to scrutinize the
> reasons encouraging the competent
> authority to issue the given
> Order.[96]

It is thus not surprising that the Supreme
Court has never overturned a deportation
order.

According to a report compiled for the
American Friends Service Committee, Israel
deported 1,156 Palestinians between 1967 and
1978.[97] There were few deportations between
1978 and 1984. In August 1985, Israel
announced it would again begin using
deportation and other administrative
punishment measures.[98] In 1985, Israel
deported 35 Palestinians; in 1986, 10; and in
1987, 8. Since the start of the intifada,
Israel has ordered the deportation of 60
Palestinians.[99]

In 1971, Meir Shamgar (then Attorney

General of Israel and currently President of the Supreme Court) described the Palestinians deported by Israel as "[s]aboteurs, members of terrorist organizations, and persons actively engaged on behalf of the Arab Governments in actions against security and public order". He went on to state:

> Most of the persons deported had been in administrative detention until their deportation; they were in detention for a long time prior to their deportation, and it would have been impossible to release them because of imperative reasons of security.[100]

More recently, Attorney-General Itzhak Zamir described Israel's criteria for deportation as follows:

> Typically, the recipient of a deportation order has a long history as a leader or officer of a terrorist organization; moreover, he has demonstrated that he will not be deterred by detention or lesser administrative measures.[101]

b. International Law

Article 49 of the Fourth Geneva Convention states with respect to deportations that:

> Individual or mass forcible transfers, as well as deportations of protected persons from occupied territory to the territory of the Occupying Power or to that of any other country, occupied or not, are prohibited, regardless of motive.

The *Commentary* of the International Committee of the Red Cross ("*ICRC Commentary*") notes that this prohibition against deportation

> is absolute and allows of no exceptions, apart from those stipulated in paragraph 2 [regarding

28

the evacuation of given areas for
security or military reasons].[102]

Article 76 of the Geneva Convention
further provides that:

> protected persons accused of
> offences shall be detained in the
> occupied country and, if convicted,
> they shall serve their sentences
> therein.

The ICRC Commentary emphasizes:

> ...as we are dealing with occupied
> territory, the protected persons
> concerned will benefit by the
> provisions of Article 49 and cannot
> be deported; they can therefore only
> be interned, or placed in assigned
> residence, within the frontiers of
> the occupied country itself.[103]

Israel justifies its deportations of
Palestinians under international law on two
grounds. First, it argues that deportations of
the nature carried out by Israel do not, in
fact, violate the Fourth Geneva Convention.
Second, Israel argues that both the Fourth
Geneva Convention and the Hague Regulations
allow and even require an occupying country to
continue to apply the local law of the
occupied territory. Israel maintains that the
Defence Regulations under the authority of
which deportation and house demolition are
carried out, continue to remain a part of the
local law of the Occupied Territories.

The first of these arguments will be
considered here; the second will be taken up
below after the discussion of house
demolitions in the next section, since the
analysis applies to both measures.

In an article published in 1971, Meir
Shamgar set forth two reasons why the deportations carried out by Israel do not
violate the Fourth Geneva Convention. These
two reasons were subsequently adopted and
developed by the Israel Supreme Court in
decisions upholding Israel's use of deportation under the Fourth Geneva Convention.

The first reason, according to Shamgar, is that

> Deportation of a person to Jordan
> is, according to the conceptions of
> the persons deported, neither
> deportation to the territory of the
> occupying power nor to the territory
> of another country. It is more a
> kind of return or exchange of a
> prisoner to the power which sent him
> and gave him its blessing and orders
> to act. There is no rule against
> returning agents of the enemy into
> the hands of the same enemy.[104]

The Palestinians here being referred to,
however, are not Palestinians who have entered
the Occupied Territories illegally. Where
"enemy agents" or "terrorist infiltrators"
have, in fact, crossed the border of the
Occupied Territories illegally, they may be
deported under the authority of Military
Orders Nos. 329 (West Bank) and 290 (Gaza
Strip), which allow the deportation of
individuals who have entered the Occupied
Territories illegally. Rather, the
Palestinians here referred to are legitimate
residents of the West Bank and the Gaza Strip.
Israel's characterization of the deportations
of these individuals as "a kind of return or
exchange of a prisoner to the power which sent
him and gave him its blessing and orders to
act" ignores the realities of the Palestinian
conflict, particularly since the start of the
Palestinian uprising in December 1987. In view
of the spontaneous character of the early
phases of the uprising, the Palestinians'
insistence on their right of self-
determination, their rejection of Jordanian
representation, Jordan's announcement that it
will not represent the Palestinians at any
upcoming peace conference and the break
between the PLO and Jordan, it cannot be
maintained that Palestinians who resist
Israeli occupation are agents of Jordan. This
argument also ignores the many recent
deportations to Lebanon. Most important, this
argument ignores the unequivocal language of
the Fourth Geneva Convention which prohibits
deportations "regardless of motive" and allows
no exceptions.

30

The second reason set forth by Meir
Shamgar is that: "[Article 49] was included in
the Convention against the background of the
specific and terrible experiences of World War
II". Shamgar cites the ICRC Commentary, which
includes this paragraph:

> There is doubtless no need to give
> an account here of the painful
> recollections called forth by the
> "deportations" of the Second World
> War, for they are still present in
> everyone's memory. It will suffice
> to mention that millions of human
> beings were torn from their homes,
> separated from their families and
> deported from their country, usually
> under inhumane conditions....[105]

Shamgar concludes:

> I venture to say that any comparison
> between deportation for the purpose
> of slave labor and the release of
> [a] saboteur to his fellows and
> commanders is out of context.[106]

In the Abu Awad case, mentioned above,
the Supreme Court of Israel, sitting as the
High Court of Justice, upheld a deportation
order against a challenge under Article 49 of
the Fourth Geneva Convention. The Court stated
that Article 49:

> is designed to protect civilians
> from arbitrary action of the
> occupying army, and its purpose is
> to prevent actions such as the
> horrors perpetrated by the Germans
> in the Second World War, in the
> course of which millions of
> civilians were deported from their
> homes for various reasons ... This
> matter has nothing in common with
> the deportations executed in the
> Second World War for the purpose of
> forced labor, torture and
> extermination.[107]

In Kawasma v. Minister of Defense, the Court
quoted Professor Stone approvingly:

31

It seems reasonable to limit the sweeping literal words of Article 49 to situations at least remotely similar to those contemplated by the draftsman, namely the Nazi World War II practices of large-scale transfers of populations ...[108]

As noted above, however, the language of the Fourth Geneva Convention could not be clearer or more absolute when it states that deportations "are prohibited, regardless of motive". The ICRC Commentary likewise leaves no room for doubt on this point. In light of the unequivocal language of the Convention, the Supreme Court's reading of Article 49 can only be viewed as an attempt to rewrite the Convention. As Justice Bach pointed out in a dissenting opinion in Nasser, Aziz, Affo v. The Commander of Forces in the West Bank:

> The Court should not depart from the clear and unambiguous meaning of the words where they do not contradict the purpose of the draftsman, and the literal meaning does not lead to unreasonable or absurd results.[109]

The United Nations, the International Committee of the Red Cross, the United States and others in the international community have consistently denounced Israel's deportations as clear violations of international law.[110]

2. House Demolition

a. Israeli Practice

Article 119 of the British Defence Regulations empowers the Military Commander to order the demolition of:

> (1) any house, structure or land from which he has reason to suspect that any firearm has been illegally discharged, or any bomb or incendiary article illegally thrown; or
>
> (2) any house, structure or land

situated in any area, town, village, quarter or street the inhabitants or some of the inhabitants or some inhabitants of which he is satisfied have committed, or attempted to commit, or abetted the commission of any offence against these Regulations involving violence or intimidation or any Military Court offence;

It is important to note that under the second criterion, a house may be demolished if the Military Commander is satisfied that residents of the village in which the house is located (not necessarily inhabitants of that particular house) have committed an offence against the Regulations.

House demolition, like deportation, is an administrative punishment. There are thus no judicial proceedings prior to issuance of a demolition order. Typically, houses of security suspects are demolished after their arrest but before they have been charged or tried.[111]

Unlike deportation, there is no formalized appeal procedure available to the residents of a house targeted for demolition. A petition challenging a house demolition order may be brought before the Israel Supreme Court sitting as the High Court of Justice.[112] However, in most cases there is no realistic possibility of appeal to the Court since residents are generally given no more than one half to two hours notice before the demolition takes place.[113] Recently, in reponse to a petition by the Association for Civil Rights in Israel, the Supreme Court ordered the Israel Defence Forces (IDF) to give residents of the West Bank Palestinian village of Beita 48 hours notice before demolishing additional houses. This was reportedly the first time that the Army committed to providing Palestinian families with a specific period of time to allow an appeal to the Supreme Court. The Court's order was, however, limited to residents of Beita and did not extend to the IDF's demolition of houses elsewhere in the Occupied Territories.[114]

Of those cases in which house demolition orders have been challenged in the Supreme Court and have reached a final decision, not one has been overturned by the Court.[115] This is not surprising in view of the standards by which the Supreme Court is governed in reviewing orders of this kind. (See the discussion in connection with the appeal of deportation orders, supra).

According to the West Bank Data Base Project, between 1967 and 1978 Israel demolished or sealed 1,224 homes in the West Bank.[116] Official Israeli government figures reflect that during the first 15 years of the occupation, 1,265 houses were demolished.[117] In the late 1970's and early 1980's, the Israeli government used this practice less frequently. In 1979, 9 homes were demolished and 9 sealed; in 1980, 19 were demolished and 11 sealed; in 1981, 17 were demolished and 17 sealed; in 1982, 32 were destroyed or sealed.[118] According to the records of al-Haq, which are admittedly incomplete, in 1983, six homes were demolished and in 1984 four houses were demolished.

In 1985, the Israeli Government announced that it would revive the use of administrative punishments in the West Bank[119] and from May to December 1985, 55 homes were demolished or sealed; in 1986, 48 were demolished or sealed; in 1987, 36 homes were demolished or sealed. From the beginning of the intifada until May 31, 1989, over 285 homes were totally demolished or sealed, and over 71 houses were partially demolished or sealed. These figures do not include houses which were demolished because their owners lacked the required building permit.[120]

In the past, Palestinians whose homes were demolished were suspected (not formally charged or tried) of having committed a political offence involving the use of weapons or explosives.[121] However, in January 1989, Israel Defence Minister Yitzhak Rabin announced that the homes of suspected stonethrowers would be demolished.[122]

b. International Law

Article 23(g) of the Hague Regulations provides:

[I]t is especially forbidden - ...
(g) To destroy or seize the enemies'
property, unless such destruction or
seizure be imperatively demanded by
the necessities of war;...[123]

Article 53 of the Fourth Geneva Convention specifically applies this general provision to military occupation:

Any destruction by the Occupying
Power of real or personal property
belonging individually or
collectively to private persons ...
is prohibited except where such
destruction is rendered absolutely
necessary by military operations.[124]

The ICRC Commentary states with respect to this section that "it will be for the Occupying Power to judge the importance of such military requirements".[125]

Meir Shamgar maintains that the demolition of houses is "rendered absolutely necessary by military operations" in two situations: (1) where the house is being used as a physical base for military action, as where a hand grenade is thrown from the house; and (2) to create effective military reaction: "The measure is of utmost deterrent importance..."[126] The International Committee of the Red Cross has taken the position that demolition of property as a punishment or deterrent is not allowed by Article 53 of the Fourth Geneva Convention. The ICRC has interpreted the term "military operations" in this article to mean "the movements, manoeuvres and other action taken by the armed forces with a view to fighting." (Emphasis in original.) The interpretation continues:

Destruction of property as mentioned
in Article 53 cannot be justified
under the terms of that article
unless such destruction is
absolutely necessary - i.e.

materially indispensible - for the
armed forces to engage in action,
such as making way for them. This
exception to the prohibition cannot
justify destruction as a punishment
or deterrent since to preclude this
type of destruction is an essential
aim of the article.[127]

Demolition of homes creates an additional
problem under international law. House
demolitions inevitably affect not only
individuals suspected of illegal activity, but
their families, relatives, landlords and/or
neighbors. Rarely do suspects in the West Bank
and Gaza live alone; and it is common for
extended families to live together. Demolition
of the house of a suspect who does not live
alone inflicts a cruel punishment on the other
residents of his house, who are not suspected
of wrongdoing.

Article 33 of the Fourth Geneva
Convention specifically forbids collective
punishments. It provides:

> No protected person may be punished
> for an offence he or she has not
> committed. Collective penalties and
> likewise all measures of
> intimidation or of terrorism are
> prohibited....Reprisals against
> protected persons and their property
> are prohibited.

The ICRC Commentary defines the term
"collective penalties" as:

> penalties of any kind inflicted on
> persons or entire groups of persons,
> in defiance of the most elementary
> principles of humanity, for acts
> these persons have not committed.

The ICRC Commentary explains:

> During past conflicts, the
> infliction of collective penalties
> has been intended to forestall
> breaches of the law rather than to
> repress them; in resorting to
> intimidatory measures to terrorise

the population, the belligerents hoped to prevent hostile acts. Far from achieving the desired effect, however, such practices, by reason of their excessive severity and cruelty kept alive and strengthened the spirit of resistance. They strike at guilty and innocent alike. They are opposed to all principles based on humanity and justice and it is for that reason that the prohibition of collective penalties is followed formally by the prohibition of all measures of intimidation or terrorism with regard to protected persons, whatever they may be.

Meir Shamgar has stated that:

Demolitions have been applied as personal punitive measures against a person in whose house acts of terrorism against the Army or the civilian population have been prepared or committed, or arms caches found.[128]

Colonel Dov Shefi, formerly Senior Staff Officer, Military Advocate General of the Israeli Defence Forces has stated that: "Demolition is never carried out as a collective punishment, but only and solely as a punishment of the individual involved".[129] However, these assertions ignore the realities of this particular form of punishment.

3. Local Law

In addition to asserting that the individual measures it carries out under the authority of the British Defence Regulations do not violate the Fourth Geneva Convention, Israel also points to provisions of the Fourth Geneva Convention and the Hague Regulations requiring the occupying power to continue to apply the law which was in existence in the occupied territory before the occupation began. Claiming that the Defence Regulations formed a part of the local law prior to the occupation, Israel contends that under international law it is entitled and perhaps even required to continue to apply them.[130]

Of course, the British Defence Regulations do not continue to form a part of the local law of the Occupied Territories since they were effectively revoked by the British. However, assuming _arguendo_ that they were still in force, this section will consider whether or not international law entitles or requires Israel to continue to apply them.

Article 43 of the 1907 Hague Regulations requires the Occupying Power to respect the laws of the occupied territory "unless absolutely prevented".[131]

Oppenheim comments with respect to this article:

> [I]n exceptional cases in which the law of the occupied State is such as to flout and shock elementary conceptions of justice and the rule of law, the occupying State must be deemed entitled to disregard it.[132]

Oppenheim further notes that during the military occupation of Germany by the Allied Powers following World War II, Nazi laws were suspended. He comments:

> It may be said without unduly straining the interpretation of Article 43, that the Western Powers were "absolutely prevented" from administering laws and principles the application of which within occupied territory was utterly opposed to modern conceptions of the rule of law.[133]

Following Oppenheim, the British Defence Regulations can certainly be said to be opposed to "modern conceptions of the rule of law". This is particularly so since portions of the British Defence Regulations clearly violate provisions of the Fourth Geneva Convention. Article 43 of the Hague Regulations cannot be read to require the occupying power to continue to apply local law which violates the Fourth Geneva Convention.

Moreover, Article 64 of the Fourth Geneva Convention provides:

> The penal laws of the occupied territory shall remain in force, with the exception that they may be repealed or suspended by the Occupying Power in cases where they constitute a threat to security or an obstacle to the application of the present Convention ... The Occupying Power may, however, subject the population of the occupied territory to provisions which are essential to enable the Occupying Power to fulfill its obligations under the present Convention, ...[134]

This provision has been interpreted to apply to civil as well as penal legislation.[135] Continuing to apply provisions of the British Defence Regulations which are prohibited by the Fourth Geneva Convention would certainly be "an obstacle to the application of the present Convention" and would prevent Israel from "fulfill[ing] its obligations under the present Convention". The ICRC Commentary notes concerning Article 64:

> the occupation authorities have the right to suspend or abrogate any penal provisions contrary to the Convention...[136]

Alan Gerson notes with respect to this commentary that "the occupant's right, [is] now expressly recognized to abrogate any legislation incompatible with humanitarian requirements".[137]

Thus, it cannot be said that the Fourth Geneva Convention or the Hague Regulations either entitle or require Israel to continue to apply the British Defence Regulations.

VII. INTERNATIONAL HUMAN RIGHTS
LAW AND THE BRITISH DEFENCE REGULATIONS

An examination of Israel's use of the British Defence Regulations would not be complete without reference to international human rights law and the ongoing state of emergency in both the Israel and the Occupied Territories. This subject will not be treated in any depth here. Rather, an attempt will be made to alert the reader to the fact that Israel's ongoing use of the British Defence Regulations raises serious questions about violations of basic human rights and fundamental freedoms recognized under international law.

The body of law concerning international human rights is distinct from the body of humanitarian law applicable to military occupations, which has been discussed above. A.H. Robertson explains:

> Human rights law relates to the basic rights of all human beings everywhere, at all times; humanitarian law relates to the rights of particular categories of human beings - principally, the sick, the wounded, prisoners of war - in particular circumstances, i.e. during periods of armed conflict.[138]

Human rights law and humanitarian law overlap at some points.[139] Nevertheless, the law of international human rights, taken by itself, continues to apply, although in modified form, even in times of military occupation or armed conflict.[140] Thus a military occupant must concern itself with both humanitarian law and international human rights law.

Numerous provisions of the British Defence Regulations infringe upon the human rights and fundamental freedoms recognized under international law. Thus, for example, the provisions of the Defence Regulations allowing administrative punishment, such as deportation and house demolition without formal charge or trial, appear to violate

Articles 9, 10, and 17 of the Universal Declaration of Human Rights ("UDHR"), and similar provisions of other major human rights treaties. Article 9 of the UDHR provides:

> No one shall be subjected to arbitrary arrest, detention or exile.

Article 10 provides:

> Everyone is entitled in full equality to a fair and public hearing by an independent and impartial tribunal, in the determination of his rights and obligations and of any criminal charge against him.

Article 17 provides:

> No one shall be arbitrarily deprived of his property.[141]

The broad censorship authority granted by the Defence Regulations violates Article 19 of the UDHR, which provides:

> Everyone has the right to freedom of opinion and expression; this right includes freedom to hold opinions without interference and to seek, receive and impart information and ideas through any media and regardless of frontiers.[142]

The observance of the full panoply of human rights is conditioned upon the existence of a peaceful state of society.[143] Nevertheless, even in times of public emergency a state is not free to completely abrogate all human rights. Rather, such abrogation must be necessary and proportional to the danger presented. Thus the International Covenant of Civil and Political Rights ("ICCPR") provides:

> In time of public emergency which threatens the life of the nation and the existence of which is officially proclaimed, the State Parties to the present Covenant may take measures

41

derogating from their obligations under the present Covenant to the extent strictly required by the exigencies of the situation, provided that such measures are not inconsistent with their other obligations under international law and do not involve discrimination solely on the ground of race, color, sex, language, religion or social origin.[144]

Three cases before the European Court of Human Rights challenging a nation's declaration of a state of emergency are informative on what constitutes a public emergency sufficient to justify some derogation from human rights. In the Cyprus case[145] the European Commission established that while a Government is entitled to "some margin of appreciation" in determining whether or not a state of emergency exists, nevertheless, the Commission has "the competence and the duty" to review the Government's decision and make an objective determination of whether or not such an emergency exists.

In the Lawless case, in which a state of emergency declared in Northern Ireland was challenged by an individual, the European Commission defined a public emergency as "an exceptional situation of crisis or emergency which affects the whole population and constitutes a threat to the organized life of the community of which the State is composed."[146]

In the Greek case,[147] Denmark, Norway, Sweden and the Netherlands challenged the declaration of a state of emergency by the Greek government, and suspension of various human rights, including the detention of large numbers of people without trial and censorship of the press.[148] The Commission held that a "public emergency" must:

(1) be actual or imminent;

(2) its effects must involve the whole nation;

42

(3) the continuance of the organized
life of the community must be
threatened; and

(4) the crisis must be exceptional,
in that the normal measures or
restrictions ... are plainly
inadequate.[149]

The Commission found that the burden was on
the Government, allowing for a "margin of
appreciation", to justify the state of
emergency.

Even if a public emergency is found to
exist, a state is not free to simply suspend
the observance of human rights until the
danger passes; rather, each derogation measure
which is taken must be "strictly required by
the exigencies of the situation," a limitation
which appears in each of the general human
rights treaties. This limitation means that
any derogation measures must be: (1)
proportional to the particular danger; (2)
temporary; and (3) necessary, in the sense
that no less restrictive alternative
exists.[150] In addition, each of the treaties
provides that derogation measures must be
consistent with a nation's other obligations
under international law, and both the American
Convention on Human Rights and the ICCPR
provide that derogation measures must not
involve discrimination.[151]

In short, derogation is the exception
rather than the rule; derogation is
justifiable only in the most extreme and
unusual circumstances of public emergency; and
even where such extreme and unusual
circumstances exist, wholesale derogation is
not permissible. Instead, derogation is
justifiable only as a last resort, and only to
the degree and for the period of time which is
absolutely necessary in order to return the
country to a more stable condition.

Emergency legislation, in the form of the
British Defence (Emergency) Regulations, 1945,
as well as other emergency laws, has been in
effect in Israel since 1948 and in the
Occupied Territories since 1967. A. Rubinstein
has noted:

43

[A] state of permanent emergency has become a feature of the Israeli situation and mentality. ... We have not followed the usual pattern of moving away from peacetime legislation to a short emergency-power period, and back again to peacetime law. We have had to live with both emergency and emergency laws ever since our creation.[152]

Whether or not the on-going state of emergency in Israel for the past 41 years and the Occupied Territories for the past 22 years has been fully justified is beyond the scope of this paper. Nevertheless, even if such a state of emergency were justified, every measure taken in derogation of the human rights of the Palestinians must be "strictly required by the exigencies of the situation". It seems doubtful that many of the measures taken by the Israelis under the authority of the British Defence Regulations could withstand scrutiny under this standard.

CONCLUSION

The British Defence Regulations, 1945, were enacted by the British during the Mandate in response to civil-war-like conditions in Palestine. In spite of the British military's extensive use of such administrative sanctions as deportations, house demolitions, and wide-ranging searches, the success of the British military forces in restoring order was very limited. Instead, use of these measures embittered the population and increased opposition to the Mandatory regime.

The British Government revoked the Defence Regulations prior to leaving Palestine in 1948. The effectiveness of this revocation was recently confirmed by the British Minister of State.

During its administration of the West Bank from 1948 to 1967, the Jordanian government never used the British Defence Regulations. A proclamation enacted by the Jordanian military commander in 1948 made Jordan's own Defence Law and Regulations applicable to the West Bank and simultaneously revoked the British Defence Regulations (which the Jordanians apparently did not realize had already been revoked by the British).

In spite of this rather clear history, the Israeli government today relies on the British Defence Regulations to justify the imposition of a number of administrative sanctions on residents of the West Bank, including deportation and house demolition.

Since the enactment of the Defence Regulations by the British in 1945, the Fourth Geneva Convention of 1949 was drafted. This Convention has been ratified by most nations in the world including Israel. The Fourth Geneva Convention sets forth standards of international law applicable to military occupations. Provisions of the Defence Regulations appear to clearly violate the standards set forth in the Fourth Geneva Convention as well as other applicable international law standards.

45

When the British Defence Regulations were enacted in 1945, Jews in Palestine strongly denounced them. The Jewish Bar Association, for example, passed the following resolutions:

> (1) The powers granted the authorities under the Defence (emergency) regulations deprive the Palestinian citizen of the fundamental rights of man. (2) These regulations undermine law and justice, and constitute a grave danger to the life and liberty of the individual, establishing a rule of arbitrariness without any judicial control. [The conference] demands the repeal of these laws ...[153]

In 1948, in **Herzel Cook and Ziborah Wienerski v. the Minister of Defence et al.**, the Tel Aviv District Court sitting as the High Court of Justice heard the first appeal concerning the use of the British Defence Regulations in Israel. The appeal concerned the administrative arrest of members of a Jewish paramilitary organization. Justice Shalom Kassan, expressing a minority view, stated:

> Everyone knows that the Jewish settlement in Palestine, and the Jewish people in exile, have protested violently against the defence regulations and have submitted petitions against them in the strongest possible language on every possible occasion... These laws and their aims are well known... Believing as I do that these laws are essentially invalid, I should not be asked to act against my conscience merely because the present government has not yet officially repealed them, though its members declared them illegal as soon as they were passed... If the court of the British Mandate did not cross these laws off the statute book, this court is honor bound to do so and to utterly eradicate them.[154]

The time is long overdue for the Israeli government to recognize that the British Defence Regulations no longer constitute valid law and to bring its occupation of the West Bank and Gaza Strip into compliance with international law.

ENDNOTES

1.   These figures, which come from the files of al-Haq, are as of May 31, 1989. According to al-Haq, during this same period over 71 houses were partially demolished or sealed, and many houses were structurally damaged because they were near houses which were demolished.

2.   For example, restrictions on the press, forced closure of shops, closure of professional organizations, outlawing of popular committees, and the imposition of curfews, are all based upon these Defence Regulations.

3.   This paper will not examine the status of the British Defence Regulations in the Gaza Strip since repeated attempts to contact the Egyptian Government concerning their administration of the Gaza Strip from 1948 to 1967 have not been successful. However, the examination of the history of the Defence Regulations during the British Mandate, the British revocation of the Regulations prior to the end of the Mandate, the Israeli Government's use of the Defence Regulations in the Occupied Territories after 1967, as well as the application of international law to the use of these Regulations applies equally to the Gaza Strip.

4.   Palestine Gazette No. 675, Supp. No. 2 (March 24, 1937), p. 267.

5.   From the outset of British rule in Palestine, tensions between the Arab and Jewish populations were high as Jews immigrated to and settled in Palestine. There were major Palestinian insurrections and/or disturbances in 1920, 1921, 1929, 1933, and from 1936 to 1939, the last of which is known as the Arab Rebellion. A.M. Lesch, Arab Politics in Palestine, 1917-1939: The Frustration of a Nationalist Movement (Ithaca: Cornell University Press, 1979), p. 199; H. Cattan, Palestine and International Law: The Legal Aspects of the Arab-Israeli Conflict (London: Longman, 1973), p. 17, and footnote 32.

Beginning in 1942 and 1943, Jewish extremist groups embraced violence as the only way to end the British Mandate in Palestine and replace it with a Jewish state. H. Sachar, <u>A History of Israel: From the Rise of Zionism to Our Time</u> (New York: Alfred A. Knopf, 1979), pp. 246-247.

6.   <u>Palestine and Transjordan</u> (London: Naval Intelligence Division Geographical Handbook Series, December 1943), p. 130.

7.   Lesch, <u>Arab Politics in Palestine</u>, p. 223; Y. Porath, <u>The Palestinian Arab National Movement, 1929-1939: From Riots to Rebellion</u> (London: Frank Cass, 1977), p. 238. During the Arab Rebellion, the Palestinian guerillas forced the British Civil Authorities out of many town and country districts, destroying police stations and government offices in Hebron, Jericho, Beersheba, Bethlehem, and Ramallah. British White Paper of 1939 reprinted in W. Khalidi, <u>From Haven to Conquest: Readings in Zionism and the Palestine Problem Until 1948</u> (Beirut: Institute for Palestine Studies, 1971), p. 461. By October 1938, the rebels had also gained control of the Old City of Jerusalem. A.W. Kayyali, <u>Palestine, A Modern History</u> (London: Croom Helm, 1978), p. 217.

8.   Cited in Khalidi, <u>From Haven to Conquest</u>, pp. 846-849.

9.   <u>Ibid.</u>, pp. 596-598 (citing the official text of the Anglo-American Commission of Enquiry Report).

10.   M. Cohen, <u>Palestine and the Great Powers, 1945 to 1948</u> (Princeton: Princeton University Press, 1982), p. 230. By the end of 1946, one Jewish paramilitary organisation claimed it had killed 373 people in Palestine, including 300 civilians. See C. Sykes, <u>Crossroads to Israel</u> (Bloomington: Indiana University Press, 1973), p. 307.

11.   Cited in Cohen, <u>Palestine and the Great Powers</u>, p. 250.

12.   The Orders in Council were enacted by the King of England in Council and defined the

scope of the High Commissioner of Palestine's powers to enact regulations to deal with the unrest. The first such order, Palestine Order in Council, 1922, (effective September 1, 1922) vested authority in the British High Commissioner of Palestine to execute his authority according to the Orders in Council relating to Palestine. The Laws of Palestine, (Revised Edition) Vol. III (London: Waterlow, 1934), p. 2569. Palestine (Defence) Order in Council, 1931, gave the High Commissioner the authority "in case of any public emergency, touching the public safety and defence of His Majesty's Empire or of Palestine on being proclaimed by the High Commissioner" to enact "Regulations for securing the public safety and the defence of Palestine". The Order in Council specifically authorized the regulations to include censorship, arrest, detention, and deportation. The Laws of Palestine pp. 2619, 2620. Following an outbreak of violent Palestinian demonstrations against the British in October 1933, the British High Commissioner proclaimed the Palestine (Defence) Order in Council, 1931, to be in effect and enacted Emergency Regulations. Palestine Gazette No. 399 (October 30, 1933), p. 1598. In February 1934, when the disturbances had come to an end, the High Commissioner withdrew the 1931 Order in Council and Emergency Regulations. Palestine Gazette No. 423, Supp. No. 2 (February 22, 1934), p. 143. Following new episodes of violence in 1936 the High Commissioner again declared the 1931 Order in Council to be in effect and enacted the Emergency Regulations, 1936, which contained similar powers to impose curfews, censorship, deportation, arrest without warrant, and gave broad powers of entry and search. Palestine Gazette No. 584, Supp. No. 2 (April 19, 1936), p. 259. On September 30, 1936, the Palestine Martial Law (Defence) Order in Council, 1936, was proclaimed which amended the 1931 Order by giving the High Commissioner the authority to enact regulations providing for "infliction of fines upon bodies of persons or upon corporations and the forfeiture and destruction of property as punitive measures whether actual offenders can or cannot be identified". Palestine Gazette No. 634 (September 30, 1936), p. 1070.

On March 24, 1937, the British Government enacted the Palestine (Defence) Order in Council, 1937, which revoked the 1931 and 1936 Orders in Council but retained the Emergency Regulations, 1936. This Order in Council broadened the High Commissioner's authority to enact emergency regulations. Palestine Gazette No. 675, Supp. No. 2 (March 24, 1937), p. 267. The High Commissioner thereafter amended and added to the Defence Regulations, 1936, until the enactment of the 1945 Regulations.

13. Sachar, A History of Israel, pp. 212-213, 218-219, 225-226. See also Kayyali, Palestine, A Modern History, pp. 195-202 and Lesch, Arab Politics in Palestine, p. 218.

14. Cohen, Palestine and the Great Powers, p. 229.

15. Ibid., pp. 301-302.

16. Statutory Instruments, 1948, Vol. 1, Part 1, No. 1004, p. 1350. Full text in App ˉix A.

17. Ibid., p. 1351.
18. Ibid., p. 1350.

19. Palestine Gazette No. 675, Supp. No. 2 (March 24, 1937), p. 267.

20. Halsbury's Statutes of England, Vol. 5 (53 & 54 Vict. c. 37) (London: Butterworth, 1929), p. 794. Section 3 of the Foreign Jurisdiction Act, 1890, further provides: "Every act and thing done in pursuance of any jurisdiction of [His Majesty] in a foreign country shall be valid as if it had been done according to the local law then in force in that country".

21. Statutory Instruments, p. 1350.

22. Halsbury's Statutes of England, Vol. 18 (52 & 53 Vict. c. 63), p. 992. This provision of the Interpretations Act applies to the Revocations Order since the Revocations Order is an Order in Council issued under a power conferred by an Act passed after the Interpretation Act, namely, the Foreign

Jurisdiction Act of 1890. **Statutory Instruments**, p. 1350.

23.   See also A. Rosenthal, "The 1945 Defence Regulations: Valid Law in the West Bank?" (unpublished paper, 1986).

24.   Addendum No. 20 of 1948, <u>Jordanian Official Gazette</u> No. 945 (May 16, 1948), p. 183.

25.   <u>Jordanian Official Gazette</u> No. 473 (March 19, 1935), p. 158.

26.   <u>Jordanian Official Gazette</u> No. 644 (August 29, 1939), p. 514.

27.   Article 4 provides that without limiting the King's powers, the Defence Regulations may provide for censorship, arrest, detention, deportation, search and seizure. Article 5 gives the King the authority (without the necessity of enacting Regulations) to deport anyone, to confiscate land and property, and to order the demolition of any structure. The Defence Regulations enacted under the authority of the Defence Law enable the Prime Minister, <u>inter alia</u>, to order the demolition of any building, impose curfews, and order administrative detention. <u>Jordanian Official Gazette</u> No. 473 (March 19, 1935), p. 158, and No. 644 (August 29, 1939), p. 514.

28.   <u>Jordanian Official Gazette</u> No. 473 (March 19, 1935), p. 158 and No. 644 (August 29, 1939), p. 514.

29.   <u>Compilation of Laws and Regulations Issued and in Force in the Hashemite Kingdom of Jordan until 1960</u>, Vol 3, p. 606 (in Arabic, 1961). Excerpted in English in the <u>Israel Yearbook of Human Rights</u> ("<u>IYHR</u>") vol. 9 (1979), p. 343.

30.   H.C. 97/79, 33 (3) P.D. 309; excerpted in English in <u>IYHR</u> vol. 9 (1979), pp. 343-345.

31.   The opinion was submitted in the case of <u>Kawasma v. Minister of Defence</u> (H.C. 698/80, 35 (1) P.D. 617).

32.   "Law and Administration Proclamation",

reprinted in English in "Territories Administered by Israel: Military Proclamations, Orders and Judicial Decisions: Extracts", IYHR vol. 1 (1971), p.419.

33.   Interpretation Order (Additional Orders)(No.1)(No.160), 1967 (in Hebrew and Arabic). Original text and English translation in Appendix C.

34.   H.C. 513/85, 39 (3) P.D. 645; excerpted in English in IYHR vol. 16 (1986), p. 329.

35.   See Government of Palestine, Legislation Enacted and Notices Issued Which Have Not Been Gazetted, 29th April-14th May 1948.

36.   Enacted by the High Commissioner, Palestine Gazette No. 1400, Supp. No. 1 (April 2, 1945), p. 48.

37.   39 Statutes 783 (9 & 10 Geo. 6, c. 36).

38.   Statutory Instruments, p. 1350.

39.   It is interesting to note that the Palestine Order in Council, 1948, enacted by the High Commissioner on April 29, 1948, dispensed with the requirement that Regulations passed by the High Commissioner be published in the Palestine Gazette in order to be effective, and left the manner of publication to the discretion of the High Commissioner. See Government of Palestine, Legislation Enacted and Notices Issued Which Have Not Been Gazetted, 29th April-14th May 1948. Thus, as a matter of British law, the previous requirement of publication in the Palestine Gazette was no longer in effect.

40.   Interpretation Order (Additional Provisions)(No.5)(Judea and Samaria)(No.224), 1968 (in Hebrew and Arabic). Original text and English translation in Appendix E.

41.   See also the Abu Awad case, cited above (footnote 30), in which the Supreme Court held that no implicit abolition could ever take place due to Interpretation Order No. 224.

42.   Of course, Israel could enact its own Defence Regulations and use the British

Regulations as a model. However, it could no longer claim that this legislation was inherited from the British Mandate. In addition, it would have to satisfy the requirements of the Hague Regulations and the Fourth Geneva Convention concerning the enactment of new legislation by an occupying power in occupied territory. Article 43 of the Hague Regulations requires the occupying power "to respect[], unless absolutely prevented, the laws in force" in the occupied territory. Article 64 of the Fourth Geneva Convention states: "The penal laws of the occupied territory shall remain in force, with the exception that they may be repealed or suspended by the Occupying Power in cases where they constitute a threat to its security or an obstacle to the application of the present Convention". Cited in A. Roberts and R. Guelff, ed., <u>Documents</u> <u>on</u> <u>the</u> <u>Laws</u> <u>of</u> <u>War</u> (Oxford: Clarendon Press, 1982), pp. 55-56, 293.

43. Advocate Shehadeh states: "the Palestine Defence Regulations ... were repealed and the same powers vested in the Jordanian King and his ministers by virtue of [the Addendum of May 13, 1948]". See also, United Nations Special Committee Report, Doc. A8089 (1970), pp. 57-60, reprinted in W. Khadduri, <u>International</u> <u>Documents</u> <u>on</u> <u>Palestine,</u> <u>1970</u> (Beirut: The Institute for Palestine Studies, 1973), pp. 581-617, particularly p. 597, in which the Jordanian Government, in response to questions put to it by a United Nations Special Committee in 1970, stated that the British Defence Regulations were "abolished" by the Addendum of May 13, 1948, making the Jordanian Defence Law and Regulations applicable to the West Bank.

44. May 7, 1988 interview with 'Awni Khasawneh, Director of Legal Department for the Jordanian Ministry of Foreign Affairs in Amman; May 7, 1988 interview with Attorney Majed Ranma at the Jordanian Ministry of Justice in Amman; May 2, 1988 interview with Attorney Dr. Hanna Naddy in Amman; May 1, 1988 interview with Attorney Ibrahim Bakr in Amman; several interviews in May and June 1988 with Attorney Fuad Shehadeh in Ramallah, West Bank.

(Austin, Texas: University of Texas Press, 1980), p. 124.

55. Lustick, Arabs in the Jewish State, pp. 177-178. See also the discussion in H. D. Nakkara, "Israeli Land Seizure Under Various Defense and Emergency Regulations", Journal of Palestine Studies No. 54 (Winter 1985), pp. 13, 15-16.

56. Jiryis, The Arabs in Israel, pp. 18-19.

57. Ibid., pp. 26-27. See also Davar, 28 March, 1969 (Interview with Eliahu Sasson, then-Minister of Police).

58. Lustick, Arabs in the Jewish State, p. 126.

59. The Defence Regulations are used not only in the areas which came under Israeli control in 1948, but also in East Jerusalem, which was annexed by Israel in 1967 and is subject to Israeli law. During the popular uprising, they were, for example, used to force East Jerusalem merchants to open their shops. The Jerusalem Post, April 26, 1988.

60. Knesset Debates (July 12, 1949), Vol. II, pp. 975-978, 998.

61. Remarks of H. Cohn made at the Symposium of the Association For Civil Rights on Administrative Punishment in the Administered Territories, December 10, 1985, Jerusalem.

62. Knesset Debates (May 22, 1951), Vol. 9, p. 1828.

63. Knesset Debates (June 6, 1951), Vol. 9, pp. 1966-1968, 1975-1976, 1978.

64. Knesset Debates (December 1, 1954), Vol. 17, pp. 241, 242, 243.

65. B. Bracha, "Restrictions of Personal Freedom", p. 318.

66. See for example L. Oppenheim, International Law: A Treatise, Vol. II (London: Longman, Green and Co., 1952), p. 432; D. Graber, The Development of the Law of

Belligerent Occupation, 1863-1914: A
Historical Survey (New York: Columbia
University Press, 1949), p. 13.

67.   Reprinted in Roberts and Guelff,
Documents on the Laws of War, pp. 44-59, 272-
337.

68.   See for example M. McDougal and F.
Feliciano, Law and Minimum World Public Order:
The Legal Regulation of International Coercion
(New Haven: Yale University Press, 1961), p.
75; Graber, The Development of the Law of
Belligerent Occupation, p. 290: "The motive
power for the changes which took place in the
1907 Hague Convention was the need for a law
which would give the maximum protection from
the rigors of war to the population of
occupied regions without hindering the
military objectives of the occupant".

69.   Oppenheim, International Law, pp. 234-
235; G. Von Glahn, "The Protection of Human
Rights in Time of Armed Conflicts", IYHR vol.1
(1971), pp. 208, 211; T. Meron, Human Rights
in Internal Strife: Their International
Protection (Cambridge: Grotius Publications,
1987), pp. 4-5.

70.   Oppenheim, International Law, p. 451; G.
Schwarzenberger, International Law as Applied
by International Courts and Tribunals, Vol.II
(London: Stevens & Sons, 1968), pp. 165-166.
T. Meron, Human Rights in Internal Strife, p.
6.

71.   Roberts and Guelff, Documents on the Laws
of War, pp. 326-330.

72.   See for example M. Shamgar, "The
Observance of International Law in the
Administered Territories", IYHR vol. 1 (1971),
pp. 262, 263.

73.   M. Shamgar, ed., Military Government in
the Territories Administered by Israel, 1967
-1980: The Legal Aspects (Jerusalem: Alpha
Press, 1982), p. 37.

74.   See for example Shamgar, "The Observance
of International Law", p. 263.

75. See for example Y. Blum, "The Missing Reversioner: Reflections on the Status of Judea and Samaria", Israel Law Review vol. 3 No. 1 (January 1968), pp. 279, 293-294.

76. Ibid., p. 293.

77. Oppenheim, International Law, p. 434; T. Kuttner, "Israel and the West Bank: Aspects of the Law of Belligerent Occupation", IYHR vol. 7 (1977), pp. 166, 169.

78. See for example S. Boyd, "The Applicability of International Law to the Occupied Territories", IYHR vol. 1 (1971), pp. 258, 260; T. Meron, "The West Bank and Gaza: Human Rights and Humanitarian Law in the Period of Transition", IYHR vol. 9 (1979), pp. 106, 109.

79. J. Pictet, Development and Principles of International Humanitarian Law (Dordrecht, The Netherlands: Martinus Nijhoff, 1985), p. 61.

80. See for example Shamgar, Military Government, p. 64; Meron, Human Rights in Internal Strife, p. 109.

81. Boyd, "The Applicability of International Law", p. 260, citing International Review of the Red Cross.

82. See Kuttner, "Israel and the West Bank", pp. 169-170.

83. United Nations Security Council Resolution 446 of March 22, 1979, for example, states: "Affirming once more that the Fourth Geneva Convention ... is applicable to the Arab territories occupied by Israel since 1967, including Jerusalem". See also Boyd, "The Applicability of International Law", p. 259.

84. Israel has never made clear which of the provisions of the Fourth Geneva Convention it considers to be "humanitarian" in nature. Jean Pictet, who apparently coined the phrase "humanitarian law", considers the entire Fourth Geneva Convention to be international humanitarian law. Pictet, Development and Principles of International Humanitarian Law,

pp. 1-2.

85. Shamgar, "The Observance of International Law", p. 271.

86. Meron, "The West Bank and Gaza", p. 108.

87. See for example The Military Prosecutor v. Zuhadi Saleh Hussein Zohar, 1 S.J.M.C. 545 (1968), excerpted in English in IYHR vol. 1 (1971), p. 453; the Beth El case, Ayoub v. Minister of Defence and Matweh v. Minister of Defence, H.C. 606/78 and 610/78 (1979) 33 (2) P.D. 113 (reprinted in English in Shamgar, Military Government, pp. 371-397, particularly pp. 379-381); and the Elon Moreh case, Izzat Muhamed Mustafa Dwaikat, et al. v. Government of Israel, et al., H.C. 390/79 (1980), 34 (1) P.D. 1 (reprinted in English in Shamgar, Military Government, pp. 404-441, particularly pp. 418-419).

Meron has noted: "[T]he failure of [Israel] to enact the necessary legislation [to make the Geneva Conventions part of Israeli domestic law] cannot affect its internal obligation to implement the Geneva Conventions ..." Meron, Human Rights in Internal Strife, p. 6.

88. See the Beth El and Elon Moreh cases, cited in Shamgar, Military Government, pp. 379-381, 419.

89. Meron, "The West Bank and Gaza", p. 111.

90. Roberts and Guelff, Documents on the Laws of War, pp. 55-56 (emphasis added).

91. J. Pictet, ed., Commentary ... IV Geneva Convention (Geneva: International Committee of the Red Cross, 1958) (hereafter "ICRC Commentary"), p. 615; Oppenheim, International Law, pp. 451-452.

92. Meron, "The West Bank and Gaza", p. 110.

93. British Defence (Emergency) Regulations, 1945, Articles 108 and 112, Palestine Gazette No. 1442, Supp. No. 2 (September 27, 1945), pp. 1055-1098.

94. Article 112B of the British Defence Regulations provides prospective deportees with a right of appeal. However, in 1976, the Israeli Government was criticized for not allowing two deportees the appeal rights provided in the Defence Regulations. In 1977 the Government issued its own guidelines concerning the appeal rights of prospective deportees. J. Hiltermann, Israel's Deportation Policy in the Occupied West Bank and Gaza (Ramallah: Al-Haq, 1986), pp. 46-47.

The Advisory Committee, to whom a prospective deportee may appeal, is set up by the Military Government and consists of three military officers. The Committee may but does not have to inform the prospective deportee of the place and time of the meeting so that he and his lawyer can attend. Even if allowed to attend the meeting, however, the prospective deportee and his lawyer are not allowed to see the secret evidence provided by the Israeli intelligence service, Shin Bet.

95. Hiltermann, Israel's Deportation Policy, pp. 46-55, 60-61.

96. H.C. 46/50, 4 P.D. 220, 227. Cited in Bracha, "Restrictions on Personal Freedom", p. 313. See also Haddad et al. v. Minister of Defence et al., H.C. 17/71, 25 (1) P.D. 141 (excerpted in English in IYHR vol. 8 (1978), p.315) in which the Supreme Court decided it did not have the power to examine the motivations behind the decision to deport.

97. This figure does not include two beduin tribes deported en masse in December 1967 and May 1969. A. Lesch, "Israeli Deportation of Palestinians from the West Bank and the Gaza Strip, 1967-1978", Journal of Palestine Studies No. 30 (Winter 1979), pp. 101-131, and No. 31 (Spring 1979), pp. 81-112.

98. Hiltermann, Israel's Deportation policy, p. 1; The Jerusalem Post, August 5, 1985.

99. The figure was supplied by al-Haq. The list compiled by al-Haq does not include detainees who have agreed to be deported in exchange for a reduction in their prison sentence.

100. Shamgar, "The Observance of International Law", pp. 273-274.

101. I. Zamir, "Deportation Orders in the Administrated Areas", (Jerusalem: Attorney General's Office, 1986).

102. Pictet, ICRC Commentary, p. 279.

103. Ibid., p. 368.

104. Shamgar, "The Observance of International Law", p. 274.

105. Pictet, ICRC Commentary, p. 278.

106. Shamgar, "The Observance of International Law", pp. 262-282, 275; see also D. Shefi, "The Reports of the UN Special Committees on Israeli Practices in the Territories, A Survey and Evaluation", in Shamgar, Military Government, pp. 285-334, particularly pp. 304-306.

107. H.C. 97/79, 33 (3) P.D. 309.

108. H.C. 698/80 35 (1) P.D. 617, quoting J. Stone, No Peace - No Law in the Middle East (Sydney, 1969), p. 17.

109. H.C. 785/87; H.C. 845/87; H.C. 27/88.

110. See for example United Nations Security Council Resolutions 468 of May 8, 1980 and 469 of May 20 1980.

111. According to al-Haq, in several cases the homes of suspects have been demolished before they are arrested.

112. E. Playfair, Demolition and Sealing of Houses as a Punitive Measure in the Israeli -Occupied West Bank (Ramallah: Al-Haq, 1987), p. 25.

113. Ibid. See also the remarks made by Moshe Negbi, former head of the international law section of the IDF Military Advocate-General's office, at a Seminar held by the Association for Civil Rights in Israel on December 10, 1985: "at least in the case of demolition of

houses we cannot talk about an effective possibility of appealing to the High Court of Justice". Ibid., p. 25.

114.   The Jerusalem Post, April 2, 1988. The Association for Civil Rights has filed a petition with the Supreme Court to extend the Beita ruling to all residents of the Occupied Territories.

115.   E. Playfair, Demolition and Sealing of Houses, p. 26.

116.   M. Benvenisti (with Z. Abu-Zayed and D. Rubinstein), The West Bank Handbook: A Political Lexicon (Jerusalem: The Jerusalem Post, 1986), p. 86.

117.   Playfair, Demolition and Sealing of Houses, p. 1; The Jerusalem Post, November 23, 1981.

118.   Benvenisti, The West Bank Handbook, p. 86.

119.   The Jerusalem Post, August 5, 1985.

120.   Information supplied by al-Haq. Al-Haq's records to date on demolitions and sealings in the Gaza Strip are incomplete.

121.   Playfair, Demolition and Sealing of Houses, p. 24.

122.   This policy is not entirely new. In the Beita incident in which an Israeli settler killed 2 Palestinians and 1 Israeli during a settler hike near the village of Beita, 13 houses of the Beita villagers suspected, though not formally charged, tried, or convicted, of throwing stones or "incitement" were demolished. An additional house was demolished at the same time for lack of a building permit. The residents were given one half to two hours notice. The Jerusalem Post, April 12, 1988 and April 20, 1988.

123.   Roberts and Guelff, Documents on the Laws of War, pp. 52-53.

124.   Ibid., p. 290.

125. Pictet, ICRC Commentary, p. 302.

126. Shamgar, "The Observance of International Law", p. 276.

127. From a November 25, 1981 Interpretation of Article 53 of the Fourth Geneva Convention signed by Jacques Moreillon and approved by Jean Pictet. Cited in Playfair, Demolition and Sealing of Houses, pp. 11-12.

128. Shamgar, "The Observance of International Law", p. 275.

129. D. Shefi, "The Protection of Human Rights in the Areas Administered by Israel: United Nations Findings and Reality", IYHR vol. 3 (1973) pp. 337, 346.

130. See, for example, D. Shefi, "The Reports of the U.N. Special Committees on Israeli Practices in the Territories", reprinted in Shamgar, Military Government, p. 285.

131. The full text of the Article provides:

> The authority of the legitimate power having in fact passed into the hands of the occupant, the latter shall take all the measures in his power to restore, and ensure, as far as possible, public safety, while respecting, unless absolutely prevented, the laws in force in the country.

(Cited in Roberts and Guelff, Documents on the Laws of War, pp. 44-59).

132. Oppenheim, International Law, p. 446.

133. Ibid., p. 447.

134. Cited in Roberts and Guelff, Documents on the Laws of War, p. 293. Emphasis added.

135. See also A. Gerson, Israel, The West Bank and International Law (London: Frank Cass, 1978), p. 122.

136. Pictet, ICRC Commentary, p. 336.

137.   Gerson, Israel, The West Bank and International Law, pp. 122-123. See also Justice Cohn's dissenting opinion in the High Court case of Christian Society for the Protection of Holy Places v. The Minister of Defence, et al. (H.C. 337/71, 26 (1) P.D. 481), in which he states that laws violative of the most fundamental human rights may be changed (discussed in Gerson, Israel, the West Bank, and International Law, p. 131). It should also be noted that Israel's argument on this point is inconsistent with the many new military orders which have been issued regulating and controlling economic life, land and water, tourism, etc. See, for example, R. Shehadeh, Occupier's Law: Israel and the West Bank (Washington, D.C.: Institute for Palestine Studies, 1988), pp. 72-73.

138.   A.H. Robertson, Human Rights in the World (London: Manchester University Press, 1972), p. 175; see also Pictet, Development of Principles of International Humanitarian Law, p. 3.

139.   See, for example, Meron, Humanitarian Rights in Internal Strife, pp. 14-28; Robertson, Human Rights, pp. 178-179.

140.   Robertson, Human Rights, p. 175;

141.   Cited in the Appendix to B.G. Ramcharan, ed., Human Rights: Thirty Years After the Universal Declaration (The Hague, The Netherlands: Martinus Nijhoff, 1979), p. 267.

142.   Ibid., p. 267.

143.   See for example von Glahn, "The Protection of Human Rights", pp. 213-214.

144.   International Covenant of Civil and Political Rights, Article 4(1). reprinted in P. Sieghart, The Lawful Rights of Mankind: An Introduction to the International Legal Code of Human Rights (Oxford: Oxford University Press, 1985), p. . The European Convention on Human Rights and Protocols, Article 15(1); the European Social Charter, Article 30(1), and the American Convention on Human Rights, Article 27(1) all contain nearly identical provisions.

145.   **Yearbook of the European Convention on Human Rights**, 1958-1959 (the **Cyprus** case), issued by the European Commission and European Court of Human Rights (The Hague: Martinus Nijhof, 1960).

146.   **Yearbook of the European Convention on Human Rights**, 1961 (the **Lawless** case), pp. 430-489, 472-473. See also the opinion of Messrs. Waldock, Berg, Faber, Crosbie, and Erim ("a situation of exceptional and imminent danger or crisis affecting the general public, as distinct from particular groups") in the **Report of the European Commission and European Court on Human Rights**, Series B, p. 82.

147.   **Yearbook of the European Convention on Human Rights**, 1969 (the **Greek** case).

148.   **Ibid.**, p. 17.

149.   **Ibid.**, p. 72.

150.   See for example C. Grossman, "A Framework for the Examination of States of Emergency Under the American Convention on Human Rights", **The American University Journal of Law and Politics**, Vo. 1 (1966), pp. 35, 50-53.

151.   International Covenant on Civil and Political Rights, Article 4(1); American Convention on Human Rights, Article 27(1).

152.   A. Rubinstein, "War and Rule of Law: The Israeli Experience", **IYHR** vol. 1 (1971), p. 322.

153.   **Hapraklit** ("The Lawyer"), Vol. 3, No. 2 (February 1946), p. 62 (in Hebrew).

154.   **Hamishpat** ("Justice"), 3 (1948/49): pp. 307, 321-326.

STATUTORY INSTRUMENTS

OTHER THAN THOSE OF A LOCAL, PERSONAL
OR TEMPORARY CHARACTER
FOR THE YEAR

1948

Volume I

(IN THREE PARTS)

comprising

PREFACE AND ALL TITLES
EXCEPT EMERGENCY LAWS AND
SUPPLIES AND SERVICES

together with

A NUMERICAL LIST OF ALL GENERAL AND
OF LOCAL PRINTED INSTRUMENTS, AN
APPENDIX OF PREROGATIVE ORDERS, ETC.,
A CLASSIFIED LIST OF LOCAL INSTRUMENTS,
TABLES SHOWING EFFECT OF LEGISLATION;
AND INDEX TO VOLUME I

PART I

Published by Authority

EXPLANATORY NOTE

(This Note is not part of the Order, but is intended to indicate its general purport.)

Under the provisions of the British Nationality Act, 1948, the Governor of Northern Rhodesia will be able to grant Imperial Certificates of Naturalization to aliens resident in the Territory. Hitherto, such persons were only eligible for the grant of local Certificates of Naturalization which were granted under the Northern Rhodesia Naturalization Orders in Council of 1914 and 1928. As no further local Certificates of Naturalization will now be granted in Northern Rhodesia it is desirable that these Orders in Council should be revoked.

---

6. PALESTINE

[See also PALESTINE, p. 3180 below.]

The Palestine (Revocations) Order in Council, 1948

1948 No. 1004

Made - - - -	*12th May, 1948*
Laid before Parliament	*12th May, 1948*
Coming into Operation	*14th May, 1948*

At the Court at Buckingham Palace, the 12th day of May, 1948

Present,

The King's Most Excellent Majesty in Council

11 & 12
Geo. 6. c. 27.   Whereas under section one of the Palestine Act, 1948, all jurisdiction of His Majesty in Palestine will, subject to the provisions of the Act, determine on the fifteenth day of May, 1948 (in that Act and in this Order referred to as the appointed day), and it is accordingly desirable to revoke certain provisions in Orders in Council relating to Palestine:

53 & 54
Vict. c. 37.   Now, therefore, His Majesty, by virtue and in exercise of the powers in this behalf by the Foreign Jurisdiction Act, 1890, or otherwise in His Majesty vested, is pleased, by and with the advice of His Privy Council, to order, and it is hereby ordered, as follows:—

1. This Order may be cited as the Palestine (Revocations) Order in Council, 1948, and shall come into force immediately before the appointed day.

2.—(1) References in the Palestine Orders in Council 1922 to 1947, to a Secretary of State, to the High Commissioner, and to instructions of His Majesty shall cease to have effect.

(2) The Orders in Council specified in the Schedule to this Order are hereby revoked to the extent specified in the second column of the Schedule.

(3) The Admiralty Offences (Colonial) Act, 1849, the Admiralty 12 & 13
ffences (Colonial) Act, 1860, and Part XIII of the Merchant Shipping Vict. c. 96.
ct, 1894 (which were applied to Palestine by Article 35 of the Palestine 23 & 24
rder in Council, 1922)(a) shall cease to apply to Palestine. Vict. c. 122,
57 & 58
Vict. c. 60.

3. Sub-section (2) of section 38 of the Interpretation Act, 1889, shall 52 & 53
ave effect in relation to any provision which is revoked or ceases to Vict. c. 63.
pply to or have effect in Palestine by or under this Order, as if such
rovision were an enactment repealed by Act of Parliament.

E. C. E. Leadbitter.

SCHEDULE

PROVISIONS OF ORDERS IN COUNCIL REVOKED

Order in Council	Extent of Revocation
alestine Order in Council, 1922 (as amended by the Palestine (Amendment) Order in Council, 1923(b), the Palestine (Amendment) Order in Council, 1933(c), the Palestine (Amendment) Order in Council, 1935(d), the Palestine (Amendment) Order in Council, 1939(e), the Palestine (Amendment) Order in Council, 1940(f), and the Palestine (Amendment) Order in Council, 1947)(g).	Articles 4 to 10 inclusive ; Article 14 ; Part III ; Article 35, para. (ii) ; Article 36 ; Article 44 ; Part VI ; Article 85 and Article 89.
alestine Order in Council, 1948(h).	The whole Order.
alestine (Appeal to Privy Council) Order in Council, 1924(i).	The whole Order.
alestine (Admiralty Jurisdiction) Order in Council, 1937(j).	The whole Order.
alestine (Defence) Order in Council, 1937(k).	The whole Order.

EXPLANATORY NOTE

(This Note is not part of the Order, but is intended to indicate its general purport.)

This Order in Council made under the Foreign Jurisdiction Act, 1890, revokes certain provisions of Orders in Council relating to Palestine. Another Order in Council, the Termination of Jurisdiction in Palestine (Transitional Provisions) Order in Council, 1948, has been made under the Palestine Act, 1948.

(a) S.R. & O. 1922 (No. 1282) p. 362.   (b) S.R. & O. 1923 (No. 619) p. 339.
(c) S.R. & O. 1933 (No. 312) p. 841.   (d) S.R. & O. 1935 (No. 151) p. 520.
(e) S.R. & O. 1939 (No. 603) II, p. 1651. (f) S.R. & O. 1940 (No. 2112) I, p. 403.
(g) S.R. & O. 1947 (No. 2770) I, p. 801.   (h) S.I. 1948 No. 106.
(i) S.R. & O. 1924 (No. 1243) p. 614.   (j) S.R. & O. 1937 (No. 739) p. 817.
(k) S.R. & O. 1937 (No. 225) p. 812.

APPENDIX B:

<u>**TEXE OF AFFIDAVIT SUBMITTED TO THE ISRAELI SUPREME COURT**</u>
<u>**BY ADVOCATE AZIZ SHEHADEH (1980)**</u>

I advocate Aziz Shehadeh make oath and say as follows:

I. When I was asked by Advocate Felicia Langer to submit a legal opinion on the subject of the deportation from Jordan it was my understanding that the intention was merely to state the contents of Article 9 (1) of the Jordanian Constitution without going into any detailed discussion thereof. Consequently in my affidavit I merely cited the said Article 9 (1) and added that Article 112 of the Defence (Emergency) Regulations of 1945 was repealed by Article 128 of the Jordanian Constitution. Upon reading the last affidavit of Dr. Meron, however, I noticed that he considers the brevity of my affidavit as an indication of the weakness of my argument. I also noticed that he commented negatively on my argument that the applicability or non-applicability of the Defence (Emergency) Regulations of 1945 is irrelevant since there is an article in the Jordanian Constitution which prohibits the deportation of any Jordanian citizen and considers any decision to carry out such an action null and void. Furthermore, Dr. Meron has commented on the fact that I did not refer to any Jordanian precedents to substantiate my statement that the Jordanian High Court of Justice followed the decision of the Council of State sitting as an administrative tribunal. I apologise for this brevity which was only due to the shortness of time in which I had to prepare the statement and which did not give me the opportunity to make reference to these precedents. I now respond to all these points to the best of my ability, in the circumstances, as follows:

1.   With reference to my statement that Article 128 of the Jordanian Constitution has repealed the Defence (Emergency) Regulations of 1945 (to which I shall hereinafter refer as the Palestine Defence Regulations) I hereby assert that these regulations were put into force by the High Commissioner in Palestine in accordance with Article 6 of the Palestine Order in Council (Defence) 1937, published in the Palestine Gazette, Vol. II, page 268 on 24/3/1937 and "by virtue and in exercise of the powers in this behalf by the Foreign Jurisdiction Act, 1890, or otherwise, in his Majesty Vested,... by and with the advice of His Privy Council". This Emergency Regulation and all the Palestine Defence Regulations and the Order in Council which give the powers to His Majesty or to the High Commissioner were repealed and the same powers were vested in the Jordanian King and his ministers by virtue of the following:

a.   On 13/5/1984 i.e. two days before the termination of the mandate, King Abdullah issued an addendum to the Trans-Jordan Defence Regulations 1935- No. 20/48 (page 183 of the Jordanian Gazette No.945, dated 16/5/1948) which stated that the provisions of the Trans-Jordan Defence Regulations 1935 and all orders and regulations issued in accordance therewith shall apply to the country or areas in which the Jordanian Arab Army shall be found or shall be entrusted with the security and order therein.

b.   After the Jordanian forces entered the West Bank, the Military Governor issued on 24/5/1948 Military Order No. 1 in which he stated that he was appointed Military Governor in accordance with Article 2 of the said addendum to the Jordanian Defence Regulations of 1935 No. 20/48, and that he will proceed to exercise his powers in accordance with the said law and orders and regulations issued by virtue thereof. The same day, i.e. 24/5/1948, he issued Military Order No. 2 which stated that all ordinances and regulations made thereunder that were in force in Palestine upon the termination of the mandate on 15/5/1948 shall remain in force in all the areas where the Jordanian Arab Army shall be found or shall be entrusted with the preservation of the safety and the security of the area with the exception of those provisions that are repugnant to any provisions of the Jordanian Defence Regulations 1935 or any order or provision issued by virtue thereof. In Cassation appeal No. 98/52 (page 157 Jordanian Law Reports Vol. 1) it was decided that these orders have the power of law and they are enforceable by virtue of Section 6 of the law amending the Law of Civil Administration in Palestine which I shall discuss hereafter. This judgement was followed in Cassation appeal No. 6/45 published on page 331 - Jordanian Law Reports Vol. 2.

c.   On 1/2/1949 the law amending the Law of Civil Administration in Palestine No. 48/49 (Jordanian Gazette No.

1002) was passed. Article 5 of the said law provides that all laws, regulations, and orders issued by virtue of the ordinances that were in force on the termination of the mandate over Palestine shall remain in force until they are amended or repealed. King Abdullah was granted by virtue of Article 2 of the said law the same powers that were vested in the King of Britain and the High Commissioner in Palestine by virtue of the Palestine Order in Council 1922 and all amendments thereto. It should be noted in this respect that the regulations that remained in force are those regulations which were issued by virtue of the Palestine Ordinances. These regulations however do not include those regulations that were put into force by virtue of the Palestine Orders in Council. It should also be noted, that the vesting in King Abdullah of the powers previously enjoyed by the King of Britain was to enable him to issue legislation over areas that were under the control of the Jordanian Arab Army, making it possible for him to achieve similar purposes for which the Palestine Order in Council (Defence) 1937 was put into force. According to Section 6 of Law No. 43/49 referred to above, the orders issued by the Jordanian Military Governor became enforceable and the Military Governor enjoyed the right to issue same by virtue of the powers from the Jordanian Law and not from the Orders in Council that were issued by the King of Britain.

d. On 16/9/1950 the law dealing with the laws and regulations in force in Palestine No. 28/50 - published on page 52 of the collection of Jordanian laws and regulations, vol. 1 was passed. Section 2 of said law provided that despite the unification of

72

both Banks of the Kingdom, the laws and regulations in force in each Bank shall remain in force until unified laws applicable to both Banks shall be passed. It should be noted in this respect that the reference was to 'laws' and not to 'Orders in Council'. The reference to regulations however refers to regulations that were in force on the eve of the passing of this law, i.e. on 16/9/1950, and these are the regulations that were passed in accordance with the Palestine   Ordinances   and   not in accordance with Orders in Council, as is evident from order No. 2 issued by the Jordanian Military Governor   to whom I referred   earlier,   with the   reservation   namely that these regulations shall not be repugnant to the Jordanian Defence Regulations of 1935 or any order   issued   in   accordance therewith.

e.   On 6/1/1952 the Jordanian Constitution was published in the Jordanian Gazette No. 1093 and came into force on the date of its publication. Section 123 of the Constitution provides that all laws and regulations and all other laws that were in force in the Hashemite Kingdom of Jordan on the eve of coming into force of the said Constitution shall remain in   force until they are amended or repealed by legislation passed by virtue thereof. It is to be noted that the said provision confined the laws   to those in force on the eve of the passing of the Constitution referred to and does not include all Palestinian legislation in general as indicated hereinbefore.

f.   The most striking indication that the Palestine Defence Regulations were not in force in the West Bank after the Jordanian Defence Regulations were applied in the West Bank is that it is illogical that [they would be in force] at the same time, firstly because the provisions of these regulations are contradictory and secondly because all Defence Regulations and orders issued during the Jordanian Regime were made by virtue of the Jordanian Defence Law of 1935 and never by virtue of the Palestine Defence Regulations of 1945. To support this argument I hereby append a list of the Defence Regulations that were issued by virtue of the 1935 Jordanian Defence Law published in Vol. 13 of the Collection of Jordanian Laws [not included here].   None of the regulations referred to in this list were issued by virtue of the Palestine Defence Regulations 1945. Had these regulations been in force, it is obvious that all Defence Regulations would have been passed by virtue thereof.

g.   In   conclusion I hereby submit that by virtue of the argument referred to above, the Palestine Defence Regulations were not in force in the West Bank during the Jordanian Regime.

II. There are numerous precedents of the Jordanian High Court of Justice relying on Egyptian precedents and I herebelow refer to but a few of them.

1. H.C. 72/55 published in the Jordanian Law Reports, 1956, on page 273.

2. H.C. 30/56 published in Jordanian Law Reports, 1956, on pages 474 and 475.

3. H.C. 3/1957 published in Jordanian Law Reports, 1957, page 325.

4. H.C. 108/1956 published in Jordanian Law Reports, 1957, page 403.

5. H.C. 36/1958 published in Jordanian Law Reports, 1958, page 560.

6. H.C. 6/1959 published in Jordanian Law Reports, 1958, page 864.

7. H.C. 57/1953 published in Jordanian Law Reports, 1954, pages 141 and 142.

I am ready to supply the court with the volumes in which these reports were published or photocopies of them if so requested.

III. As to the prohibition against issuing any legislation contravening any of the provisions of the Constitution, I wish to refer to an article by the scholar Abd El Razak Ahmad Sanhuri, the former president of the Egyptian Council of State, which was published in the publication of the Council of State Journal of 1952.

On page 55 he says that:

"Article 7 of the Egyptian Constitution states as follows:
"If a legislation is passed making it permissible to deport an

Egyptian from Egypt then such legislation shall be considered null and void for being repugnant to the Constitution. Deportation of an Egyptian and prohibiting him of his right of return after he leaves Egypt is also void for the same reason." It is to be noted that the Jordanian Courts do not enjoy the power of annulling any legislation for whatever reason because the Jordanian Courts have no sovereignty over the constitutionality of laws. For this reason the Jordanian legislator granted the High Court of Justice in sections (10) (3) (g) of the Constitution of the Regular Courts of 1952, which was referred to in my previous affidavit, the power of annulling any action taken by virtue of a regulation that is repugnant to the Constitution or to any law. They had no power to annul the Regulation or the law itself. I refer to a relevant decision delivered by the Jordanian High Court of Justice under No. 44/67, published on page 47 of the Jordanian Law reports for 1967. The court decided that if the legislative power passed an unconstitutional law, then it cannot force the judicial power to implement it nor can it apply any other legislation passed by any authorised body or passed contrary to the Constitution or the spirit of the Constitution. The court when faced with two conflicting legislations will apply the legislation passed by the highter body. That is to say that the Constitution is above all other laws and binds the Judge and the Legislator equally.

Furthermore, it does not seem reasonable to accept Dr. Meron's interpretation because that would mean that the Jordanian Constitution would allow deportation by virtue of laws passed previous to its promulgation, which allow deportation of a Jordanian while at the same time forbidding deportation in Article 9 (1) of the Constitution. In the decision of the Council of State which I have referred to above and which is published in the reports of the Council, Vol. 5, No. 357, on page 1099 , it was decided that whenever an action is taken contrary to the Constitution such as deportation, the Egyptian Court may not only annul the action but can directly declare the law on the basis of which it was taken as null and void on the grounds that it is contrary to the provisions of the Constitution. This is not the case, however, in Jordan where the High Court of Justice may only annul the action but has no jurisdiction to declare any regulation unconstitutional. The practical outcome is the same whether the court nullifies the law or regulation which is contrary to the Constitution or nullifies the set that was issued in accordance with such law or regulation.

The important principle is that in both cases the Constitution is considered as the highest legislation in the country. Despite the changes that occurred after the Socialist Revolution of 1952 in Egypt, the legal principles which the Council of State has applied and which the Jordanian High Court of Justice has followed have remained unchanged and are not affected by the decisions which the Egyptian Government took to remove Jews from Egyptian lands, which I consider to be outside the scope of our discussion. It is my suspicion that Dr. Meron's intention in bringing up this point is to win indirectly the sympathy of the Court. It may be worthwhile to mention here that there is no provision in Jordanian Law which obliges the Jordanian

Courts to follow Egyptian precedents. [The Courts are] merely guided by them. When it is remembered that the establishment of the High Court of Justice and the whole Corpus of Administrative Law was a novelty in Jordan at the time of the passing of the Jordanian Constitution and the Law of the Constitution of Regular Courts of 1952, it will be easy to appreciate the importance for the Jordanian Court of the decisions of the Egyptian Courts as guidelines. Similarly the High Court of Justice in Jordan also relied in arriving at its decisions on the principles adopted by the High Court of Justice in Palestine.

With respect to Dr. Meron's opinion that judgement No. 100/75 is not binding in the West Bank because it was passed in the East Bank eight years after the 1967 War, I submit that the date of the judgement is of no relevance. This is because the decision applies and explains legal principles which were in force prior to the 1967 War, which are that the Constitution is the highest legislation and that no decision can be taken contrary to it.

Aziz Shehadeh

* [This is the text of an affidavit submitted by Advocate Aziz Shehadeh to the Israeli High Court of Justice in 1980. Minor spelling and typing errors in the original text have here been corrected. Additionally, 12 appendices and all references thereto have been deleted.]

APPENDIX C2:

**OFFICIAL TEXT OF INTERPRETATION ORDER NO. 160 OF 5
NOVEMBER 1967 (IN HEBREW AND ARABIC)**

מנשרים, צווים ומינויים

של
ממקרת כוחות צה"ל באזור הגדה המערבית

مناشــير، أوامـر وتعيينـات

صادرة عن
قيادة قوات جيش الدفاع الاسرائيلي في منطقة الضفة الغربية

۲۷ كسليف ٥٧٢٨ (٢٩ كانون الأول ١٩٦٧)	مئ ٥ ـ العدد ٨	כ"ז בכסלו תשכ"ח (29 בדצמבר 1967)

جيش الدفاع الاسرائيلي

أمر رقم ١٦٠

أمر بشان تفاسير (تعليمات اضافية) (رقم ١)

استناداً الى الصلاحيات المخولة لي بصفتي قائد قوات جيش الدفاع الاسرائيلي في المنطقة ؛ اصدر الأمر التالي :

تعاريف

١ ـ في هذا الأمر :ـ

«الجريدة الرسمية» ـ حسب مدلولها في قانون التفاسير ، لسنة ١٩٤٥ .

«قانون خفيّ» ـ اي عمل تشريعي كان ، تخيلرا سنّ بصدد المنطقة في المدة الواقعة بين ١٦ كليف ٥٧٠٨ (٢٩ تشرين الثاني ١٩٤٧) وبين ٦ ايار ٥٧٠٨ (١٥ ايار ١٩٤٨) ولم ينشر في الجريدة الرسمية ، بالرغم من كونه محسوباً على نوع الأعمال التشريعية التي كان نشرها في الجريدة الرسمية ، يتحول الى تلك المدة ، من قبيل الواجب او العادة .

قانون خفيّ

٢ ـ منعاً لكل التباس يقرر بهذا ان كل قانون خفيّ ليس له ولم يكن له اطلاقاً اي مفعول .

الاسم

٣ ـ يطلق على هذا الأمر اسم «أمر بشان تفاسير (تعليمات اضافية) (رقم ١) (منطقة الضفة الغربية) (رقم ١٦٠) ، لسنة ٥٧٢٨ ـ ١٩٦٧» .

٢ حشوان ٥٧٢٨ (٥ تشرين الثاني ١٩٦٧)

الآلوف موزي زكيس
الآلوف القيادة الوسطى
وقائد قوات جيش الدفاع الاسرائيلي
في منطقة الضفة الغربية

צבא הגנה לישראל

צו מס' 160

צו בדבר פרשנות (הוראות נוספות) (מס' 1)

בתוקף סמכותי כמפקד כוחות צה"ל באזור, הנני מצווה בזה לאמור : —

הגדרות

1. בצו זה : —

"העתון הרשמי" — כמשמעותו בפקודת הפירושים, 1945.

"חוק נסתר" — מעשה חקיקה כל שהוא, שהיתו לחוקקו לגבי האזור בתקופה שבין ט"ז בכסלו תש"ח (29 בנובמבר 1947) ובין ר' באייר תש"ח (15 במאי 1948) ושלא פורסם בעתון הרשמי. למרות היותו נמנה עם סוג מעשי החקיקה שפרסומם בעתון הרשמי היה, עובר לאותה תקופה, חובה או מנהג.

חוק נסתר

2. כדי להסיר ספק, נאמר בזה כי חוק נסתר אין לו ומעולם לא היה לו כל תוקף.

השם

3. צו זה ייקרא "צו בדבר פרשנות (הוראות נוספות) (מס' 1) (אזור הגדה המערבית) (מס' 160), תשכ"ח—1967".

ב בחשון תשכ"ח (5 בנובמבר 1967)

עוזי נרקיס, אלוף
אלוף פיקוד המרכז
ומפקד כוחות צה"ל
באזור הגדה המערבית

ENGLISH TRANSLATION OF APPENDIX C1

Israel Defence Forces

Order No. 160

Explanatory Order
(Additional Instructions) (No. 1)

In accordance with the authority vested in me as Commander of the Israel Defence Forces in the Region, I issue the following Order:-

DEFINITIONS

1. In this Order:-

"Official Gazette" - As defined in the Explantory Law of 1945.

"Hidden Law"- Any legislation, whatever it is, which was enacted between 29 November 1947 and 15 May 1948 and which was not published in the Official Gazette, in spite of the fact that it was the kind of legislation whose publication in the Official Gazette was required during the period that period whether by necessity or custom.

HIDDEN LAW

2. In order to prevent any misunderstanding, it is hereby decided that Hidden Laws do not have nor ever had any force of law whatsoever.

TITLE

3. This Order will bear the title "Explanatory Order (Additional Instructions) (No. 1) (West Bank Region) of 1967.

5 November 1967
'Uzi Narkiss
Commander of the Central Region and Commander of the Israel Defence Forces in the West Bank Region

[TRANSLATION BY AL-HAQ]

LETTER TO AL-HAQ FROM THE BRITISH FOREIGN OFFICE OF 22 APRIL 1987

Foreign and Commonwealth Office

London SW1A 2AH

From The Minister of State   22 April 1987

Dear Mr. Shehadeh,

Thank you for your letter of 23 March concerning the validity of the British Emergency Powers (Defence) Regulations 1945.

I confirm that, in view of the Palestine (Revocation) Order in Council 1948, the Palestine (Defence) Order in Council 1937 and the Defence Regulations 1945 made under it are, as a matter of English law, no longer in force.

The status of the Defence Regulations under the law of any other State is a matter to be determined by the law of that State, and is therefore not one on which I would wish to express a view. In your letter, you take up the reference, in my letter of 2 January to Lord McNair, to the status of the Defence Regulations under Israeli law. This was in no way intended to imply acceptance (or otherwise) by us of the applicability of Israeli law to the Occupied Territories. By the same token, I cannot respond to your point about the status of the Regulations under Jordanian law. That law may be relevant, but it is our view that the matter cannot in any case be treated solely as a question of Jordanian law.

For these reasons, we have not raised with any other country the matter of the applicability of the Defence Regulations under the law of that country.

Nevertheless, I assure you that we share your concern about Israeli practices in the Occupied Territories, including deportation and house demolitions, which we regard as an obstacle to peace. We call for the withdrawal of the Israelis from territories occupied in 1967 and, pending this, urge them to fulfil their obligations as occupying power under the Fourth Geneva

/Convention.

Convention. We will continue to make our views very
clear in our regular contacts with the Israeli
authorities both here and through our Embassy in
Tel Aviv.

Yours sincerely,

Tim Renton

Tim Renton

Mr Raja Shehadeh
Al Haq
PO Box 1413
Ramallah
Via Israel

APPENDIX E:

OFFICIAL TEXT OF INTERPRETATION ORDER NO. 224 OF 20
FEBRUARY 1968 (IN HEBREW AND ARABIC)

מנשרים, צווים ומינויים
של
ממקרת אזור יהודה והשומרון

مناشير ، أوامـر وتعيينـات
صادرة من
قيادة قوات جيش الدفاع الاسرائيلي في منطقة الضفة الغربية

٢٠ سيلان ٥٧٢٨ (١٦ حزيران ١٩٦٨)   عدد ١٢ — العدد ١٢   כ׳ בסיון תשכ״ח 16 ביוני (1968)

جيش الدفاع الاسرائيلي

أمر رقم ٢٢٤

الأمر التفسيري (تعليمات اضافية) (رقم ٥)

استنادا الى الصلاحية المخولة لي بصفتي قائد المنطقة

اصدر الأمر التالي :

تعريف

١ . في هذا الأمر -

«تشريع الطوارىء» . حسب مدلوله في المادة ٣ من نظام الدفاع (الطوارىء) . لسنة ١٩٤٥ .

طرق البناء «تشريع الطوارىء»

٢ . (أ) منعا لحدوث اي التباس يوضح بهذا ان تشريع الطوارىء لا يلغى تلقائيا بواسطة تشريع لاخر ليس بتشريع الطوارىء .

(ب) لا يلغى تشريع الطوارىء الا بواسطة تشريع يحدد صراحة التشريع الملغي مع التنويه باسمه .

مفعول تشريع الطوارىء

٣ . ان تشريع الطوارىء. الذي كان ساري المفعول في المنطقة بعد تاريخ ٥ ايار ٥٧٠٨ (١١ ايار ١٩٤٨) يستمر ساري المفعول اعتبارا من اليوم المحدد (بالكسر) فصاعدا ، وكأنه سن كتشريع الأمن ، الا اذا الغي صراحة مع التنويه باسمه كما ذكر في المادة ٢ (ب) ، قبل اليوم المحدد (بالكسر) او بعده .

الاسم

٤ . يطلق على هذا الأمر اسم «الأمر التفسيري (تعليمات

اضافية) (رقم ٥) (الضفة الغربية) (أمر رقم ٢٢٤) ، لسنة ٥٧٠٨ - ١٩٦٨ .

٢١ شباط ٥٧٠٨ (٢٠ شباط ١٩٦٨)

الرؤوف بيثه رفائيل فاردي

قائد منطقة الضفة الغربية

צבא הגנה לישראל

צו מס' 224

צו בדבר פרשנות (הוראות נוספות) (מס' 5)

בתוקף סמכותי כמפקד האזור, הנני מורה בזה לאמר :

הגדרה

1. בצו זה —

"תחיקת שעת חירום" — כמשמעותה בתקנה 3 לתקנות ההגנה (שעת חירום), 1945.

דרכים לביטול תחיקת שעת חירום

2. (א) למען הסרת ספק מוצהר בזה, כי תחיקת שעת חירום אינה מתבטלת מכללא על-ידי תחיקה מאוחרת שאיננה תחיקת שעת חירום.

(ב) תחיקת שעת חירום מתבטלת רק על-ידי חקיקה הקובעת מפורשות, ותוך אזכור שמה, את דבר ביטולה.

תוקפה של תחיקת שעת חירום

3. תחיקת שעת חירום אשר היתה בתוקף באזור אחרי יום ה' באייר תש"ח (14 במאי 1948) תמשיך לעמוד בתוקפה מן היום הקובע ואילך, כאילו חוקקה כתחיקת בטחון, אלא אם בטלה מפורשות ותוך אזכור שמה כאמור בסעיף 2 (ב), לפני היום הקובע או אחריו.

השם

4. צו זה ייקרא "צו בדבר פרשנות (הוראות נוספות) (מס'

5) (יהודה והשומרון) (מס' 224), תשכ"ח–1968".

כ"א בשבט תשכ"ח (20 בפברואר 1968)

רפאל ורדי, אלוף-משנה
מפקד אזור
יהודה והשומרון

ENGLISH TRANSLATION OF APPENDIX E1

Israel Defence Forces

Order No. 224

Explanatory Order
(Additional Instructions) (No. 5)

In accordance with the authority invested in me as the commander of the region, I issue the following order:-

DEFINITION

1.   In this order, "emergency legislation" shall be understood as it is in Regulation No. 3 of the Defence (Emergency) Regulations, 1945.

METHODS TO REVOKE EMERGENCY LEGISLATION

2 (A). So as to remove all doubt, it is hereby clarified that emergency legislation is not rendered null and void by inference from later legislation which is not emergency legislation.

(B).   Emergency legislation is rendered null and void solely by legislation which is not emergency legislation and which explicitly repeals it by name.

VALIDITY OF EMERGENCY LEGISLATION

3.   Emergency legislation which was in force in the region after 14 May 1948 shall remain in force from the definitive date onward as if it had been enacted as security legislation, unless it was explicitly revoked by name, as stipulated in Section 2(B), either prior to or following the definitive date.

TITLE

4. This Order shall be entitled
Explanatory Order (Additional
Instructions) (No. 5) (West Bank) for
the year 1968.

20 February 1968
Rafael Vardi
Commander of the West Bank Region

[TRANSLATION BY AL-HAQ]

LETTER TO AL-HAQ FROM THE JORDANIAN DEPARTMENT OF
MILITARY JUSTICE OF 25 JUNE 1988 (IN ARABIC)

بسم الله الرحمن الرحيـــم

القيادة العامة للقوات المسلحة الاردنيـــة

مديرية القضاء العسكـــري

الرقـم / م ع /١١٠/١١ < ٤٠١٦ >

التاريخ / ذو القعدة ١٤٠٨

<< حزيران / ١٩٨٨

الساده لجنة القانون من أجل الانسان (الحـــق)

فرع لجنة الحقوقيين الدوليه ـ جنيـــــف ـ

الموضوع / أنظمة الدفاع التي أصدرتها سلطـــات

الانتداب البريطاني سنة / ١٩٤٥ .

أشير الى مذكرتكـــم رقم ٢٠٠٢ تاريـــخ ١٩٨٧/٧/٦م.

إن النقاط التي تضمنتها مذكرتكم المشار اليها اعلاه تمثل فعلاً الوضع في ظـــل
القانون الاردني ، فالشرع الاردني قـد ألغى شيئـــاً أنظمــة الدفـــاع التي أصدرتهـــا
سلطات الانتداب البريطاني سنة ١٩٤٥م للأسباب التاليـــة :ـ

أولاً :   في ١٣ مايو عام ١٩٢٨ ، صدر قانون يقضي بسريان قانون الدفـاع
الاردني لعام ١٩٢٥ ، على جميع المناطق التي تخضع للجيش الاردنـــي
وذلك مـــن أجل حفظ الأمن والنظـــام .

ثانياً :   في ١٠ مايو عام ١٩٢٨ ، أعلن القائد العسكري الاردني بأن السلطات
الاردنيه ستستمر في تطبيق جميع المراسيم واللوائح التي كانـــــت
ساريه المفعول في فلسطين أبان الانتداب البريطاني ، وذلـــــك
فيما عدا تلك التي تتناقض مع أي بند من بنود قانون الدفـــاع
الاردني لعام ١٩٢٥م.

ثالثاً :   نتيجة لعدم تطبيق أنظمة الدفاع ،، الطوارىء ،، لعام ١٩٤٥، وذلك
منذ عام ١٩٢٨ ، فإن الدستور الاردني الصادر سنة ١٩٥٢ لــــــم
يشر اليها إطلاقاً بما يفيد إلغاءها حتمـــاً .

رابعاً :   هنالك مؤشران يؤديان الى أن أنظمة الدفاع لعام ١٩٤٥ لم تعـــد
ساريه المفعول في الضفه الغربيه وذلك بعد سريان لوائـــــج
الدفاع الاردنيه :ـ

الاول : إن بنود أنظمة الدفاع لعام ١٩٤٥ ، متناقضة مع لوائـــــح
الدفاع الاردنيـــــــــة .

الثاني : إن لوائح الدفاع والاوامر التي صدرت في عهد النظام الاردنــي
صدرت وفقاً لقانون الدفاع الاردني لعام ١٩٣٥ ، وليس وفقـــــاً
لانظمة الدفاع ،، الطوارئ،، لعام ١٩٤٥م.

كذلك فإن أنظمة وأوامر الدفاع التي صدرت في عهد النظام الاردنـــــي
صدرت استناداً الى قانون الدفاع الاردني لسنة ١٩٣٥ وليس استناداً الى أنظمة الدفـــــاع
(الطوارئ) لسنة ١٩٤٥.

ومن ثم فإنه ليس لسلطات الاحتلال الاسرائيلي قانوناً حق تطبيــــق
أنظمة الدفاع (الطوارئ) لسنة ١٩٤٥ والتي صدرت عن سلطات الانتداب البريطانـــــي
في فلسطيــــن .

برجــــى العلــــم .

وتفضلوا بقبول وافر الاحترام .

اللواء الحقوقي
مدير القضاء العسكــــــري

APPENDIX F2

ENGLISH TRANSLATION OF APPENDIX F1 [1]

In the Name of God, Most Gracious,
Most Compassionate

General Command of the Jordanian Armed Forces
Department of Military Justice
Number Ma-1-10-24016
Date: 25 June 1988

Messrs. Law in the Service of Man (Al-Haq)
Affiliate of the International Commission of
Jurists - Geneva
Subject: Defence Regulations Issued by the
British Mandatory Authorities in 1945

I refer to your letter #2003 dated 6-6-1987.

The points mentioned in your letter do in
fact represent the present state of the
Jordanian law. It is true that the Jordanian
legislator implicitly cancelled the Defence
Regulations issued by the British Mandatory
authorities in 1945, and for the following
reasons:

1- On May 13, 1948, a law was issued
applying the Jordanian Defence Law of 1935
over all the areas which fall under the
control of the Jordanian army, for the
purpose of maintaining security and order.

2- On May 15, 1948, the Jordanian military
commander declared that the Jordanian
authorities would continue to apply all laws
and orders which were in effect in Palestine
during the British Mandate, except for those
which contradicted or conflicted with any of
the provisions of the Jordanian Defence Law
of 1935.

3- As a result of the cessation of the
operation of the Defence (Emergency)
Regulations of 1945, as of 1948, the
Jordanian constitution which was issued in
1952 did not refer at all to those
Regulations, indicating absolutely that they
had been cancelled.

4- There are two indicators which show that the Defence Regulations of 1945 were no longer operative in the West Bank after the application of the Jordanian Defence Law: firstly, that the provisions of the Defence Regulations of 1945 were in conflict with the Jordanian Defence Laws; and secondly, that the Defence Laws and orders which were issued during the period of Jordanian rule were issued in accordance with the Jordanian Defence Law of 1935, and not in accordance with the Defence (Emergency) Regulations of 1945.

Similarly the Defence Regulations and orders which were issued during Jordanian rule were issued by virtue of the Jordanian Defence Law of 1935, not by virtue of the Defence (Emergency) Regulations of 1945.

Therefore, it follows that the Israeli occupation authorities have no legal rights to apply the Defence (Emergency) Regulations of 1945 which were issued by the British mandatory authorities in Palestine.

We wish to bring the above to your attention.

Respectfully,

(Signature)

The Legal Commander in Charge of Military Justice
Taysir Na'na'

[TRANSLATION BY AL-HAQ]

Part V

THE LEGAL STATUS OF JERUSALEM

LEGAL CONSIDERATIONS ON THE INTERNATIONAL STATUS OF JERUSALEM

Antonio Cassese *

---

*   Professor of International Law, University of Florence and European Uni-
     versity Institute; visiting Fellow, All Souls College, Oxford 1979-1980;
     Director, Post-Graduate School of International Affairs, Florence 1980-
     1981; member of the Italian Government's delegation to various U.N.
     bodies, including the Commission on Human Rights 1972-1975 and the
     General Assembly; currently Chairman, Council of Europe "Steering
     Committee for Human Rights"-1974, 1975 and 1978.

     The present essay is a completely revised version of a paper given at a
     Conference convened in Vienna by the International Progress Organiza-
     tion in November 1980.

     The views expressed herein are those of the author and do not reflect
     those of any national or international agency.

I.   Introductory Remarks

It is not the purpose of this paper to review all the thorny questions relating to the international status of Jerusalem. I shall confine myself to discussing three points, which appear to be worthy of particular interest. They are: (i) the question of whether after the 1948-49 hostilities Israel and Jordan acquired sovereignty over Western and Eastern Jerusalem respectively; (ii) the legal status of Jerusalem after Israel occupied the whole city following the 1967 Arab-Israeli war, and (iii) the question of whether the United Nations is still legally responsible for deciding upon the status of the city, or whether authority on the matter has devolved upon the states concerned.

In briefly discussing these three issues I shall adopt a legal approach and shall only deal with *lex lata*. It is not within my province to look into *lex ferenda*, and make proposals for a change in the present situation. The choice of this approach raises two distinct problems. First, is it possible to make an unbiased legal assessment of the present situation in Jerusalem (or, for that matter, in the whole area)? Secondly, assuming that an even-handed approach is feasible, does international law have any role to play in this intricate and politically loaded subject, or is its role merely peripheral to any political settlement?

As for the first question, it is common knowledge that two schools of thought exist among jurists, one showing strong pro-Israeli leanings, [1] the other manifestly supporting Arab demands. [2] Save for rare exceptions [3] it would seem that one cannot avoid being decidedly influ-

---

1.   See, *e.g.* E. Lauterpacht, *Jerusalem and the Holy-Places* (1968); (hereinafter "Lauterpacht"); Stone, *No Peace No War in the Middle East* (1969); Schwebel, *What Weight to Conquest?*, 64 Am. J. Int'l L. 344 (1970 (hereinafter "Schwebel"); Blum, *The Juridical Status of Jerusalem* (1974) (hereinafter "Blum"); Stone, *Israel, the United Nations and International Law - Memorandum of Law,* UN doc A/35/316 (1980).

2.   See, *e.g.,* Cattan, *Palestine and International Law* (1973) (hereinafter "Cattan"); Hassan Bil Talal, *A Study on Jerusalem* (1979) (This study was written with the collaboration of G.I.A.D. Draper) (hereinafter "Hassan Bin Talal"); Mallison & Mallison, *The Palestine Problem in International Law and World Order,* 207-275 (1986) (hereinafter cited as "Mallison & Mallison").

3.   See, *e.g.,* Akehurst, *The Arab Israeli Conflict and International Law,* 5 New Zealand Univ. L. Rev. 231 (1973); Draper, *The Status of Jerusalem as a Question of International Law;* in Kochler (ed.), *The Legal Aspects of the Palestine Problem with Special Regard to the Question of Jerusalem,* 154 (1980).

   As for scholarly contributions which, although they do not specifically deal with the question of Jerusalem, take an original and unbiased stand, I shall mention, by way of illustration, Gerson, *Trustee - Occupant: The Legal*

enced by political feelings. Nevertheless, international scholars should at least try to be as little conditioned as possible by political prejudice. The idea that even the jurist must perforce adhere to one of the two camps would not only be contrary to the scholarly function but - and this is even more important - would make true dialogue, and compromise, impossible in this area. This I will not accept, if only because it would be contrary to the whole spirit of the fundamental principles governing international relations [4] and to the basic aspiration to the peaceful settlement of disputes laid down in the U.N. Charter.

Efforts should be made to look beyond the crystallized juridical positions of the two camps. The aim is thus not to present a partisan solution to the problem, but to show one possible way in which recourse to rules of international law may help to circumvent political obstacles. The fact that in considering each particular issue I will start from an examination of the legal views advanced by the pro-Israeli jurists should not be seen as contradicting the above; in fact, these views tend to be better argued and usually bolstered by sophisticated juridical reasoning.

We now turn to the second question, that is, the role law could play in this problem - area. Before embarking upon an analysis of the various legal issues relating to Jerusalem, one might be tempted to think that in this, as in all similar questions with a high political and military element, law inevitably plays a marginal role; at best it is used as a weapon in the hands of the opposing factions to buttress their respective political demands. Instead, I shall start from the assumption that even where international law has reached its "vanishing point" [5] in matters directly impinging upon force, one should not *a priori* discount the possible role of legal standards. In particular, one ought to shun generalizations, for everything depends on the way the legal framework of the world community responds to the strains of the specific situation. To put it differently, one should enquire, case by case, whether or not law is a remote and pointless entity, or whether it provides the guidelines for a feasible political settlement. One of the purposes of this paper is precisely this: to ascertain to what extent legal precepts - as they have evolved in the international community and are currently upheld by the majority of states - help in the search for peace in the Middle East.

Status of Israel's Presence in the West Bank, 14 Harv. Int'l L. J. (1973); Weiler, *Israel and the Creation of a Palestinian State - A European Perspective* (1985).

4.   On these principles, see Cassese, *International Law in a Divided World,* at 126 - 165 (1986).

5.   As used by H. Lauterpacht, *The Problem of the Revision of the Law of War,* 29 Brit Y. B Int'l at 360 (1952).

II. The Israeli and Jordanian Commitment Not to Change the Legal Status of Jerusalem Without U.N. Consent

It is not disputed that from 1517 to 1917 Jerusalem was part of the Ottoman Empire and therefore under its exclusive sovereignty. Similarly, no one questions the fact that in the period from 1917 to 1948 Jerusalem was actually controlled by the United Kingdom, first as a military occupant (during and after the first World War) then, after 1922, as the mandatory power under the League of Nations system. During these thirty-one years the United Kingdom did not, however, possess sovereign rights over the city. Although opinions on the general question where sovereignty over mandated areas lay differ widely, [6] in the case of Jerusalem the best view seems to be that "if the test of sovereignty rests in determining who had the power to dispose of any part of a territory under Mandate, the answer is that sovereignty lay in the League and the administering authority acting jointly". [7]

Who held sovereignty over Jerusalem after the Arab countries had refused the U.N. Partition Plan and a war erupted between Israel and the Arab countries is a matter of great controversy. [8] In particular,

---

6. See *e.g.*, I Oppenheim - Lauterpacht, *International Law, a Treatise* at 222, note 5. (Eighth ed., 1955).

7. Lauterpacht, at 13-14.

8. After the demise of the League of Nations, the question of Palestine was discussed by the U.N. General Assembly on the question of initiative of the United Kingdom which, in a letter dated April 2, 1947, had requested the convening of a special session of the Assembly; this body was called upon to make recommendations under Article 10 of the Charter. In operative para. 3 of Resolution 181 (II) A, containing the Partition Plan, adopted on November 29, 1947, the General Assembly *recommended* "to the United Kingdom, as the Mandatory Power for Palestine, and to all other Members of the United Nations the adoption and implementation, with regard to the future Government of Palestine, of the Plan of Partition with Economic Union" - 2 U.N. GAOR, Resolutions, 131 - 132, U.N. Doc. A/519 (16 Sept. - 29 Nov. 1947). Part III of the Partition Plan related to the City of Jerusalem provided that: "The City of Jerusalem shall be established as a *corpus separatum* under a Special International Regime and shall be administered by the United Nations. The Trusteeship Council shall be designated to discharge the responsibilities of the Administering Authority on behalf of the United Nations..."

The Resolution was substantially accepted by the United Kingdom, but rejected by the Arab States. The U.K., although it abstained from voting, declared that it would not obstruct the implementation of the Partition Plan, while Saudi Arabia, Pakistan, Iraq, Syria and Yemen denounced the Plan as being against the Charter, illegal and immoral, and stated that they did not feel bound by the Resolution.

Vol. III THE PALESTINE YEARBOOK OF INTERNATIONAL LAW (1986)

once the hostilities had ceased and the Armistice Agreement was signed by Israel and Jordan on 3 April 1949, [9] did Israel and Jordan gradually acquire a legal title over Western and Eastern Jerusalem respectively?

To answer this question it is necessary to determine who had the power to dispose of Palestine after the British had withdrawn from the area.

It is well known that before the League of Nations was dissolved on 18 April 1946 the last League Assembly adopted a resolution which took note of the "expressed intentions" of the League Members, then administering territories under mandate, to continue to administer them for the well-being and development of the peoples concerned "until other arrangements" had been "agreed between the United Nations and the respective mandatory Powers". [10] All the parties concerned therefore agreed that the mandatory powers were not free to dispose of mandated areas as they thought fit; the United Nations was to play a major role in the matter, in that it was to authorize any change of status for the areas. This authority did not flow from the U.N. Charter, but rather from an *agreement* reached outside the Charter. The agreement had been concluded by all the Member States of the League of Nations when they adopted the resolution referred to above. It should be stressed that it is not unusual for a group of states to enter into an internationally binding agreement by passing a resolution

---

What was the legal value of the Resolution? I submit that, since the General Assembly had special powers on mandated territories, its recommendations on the matter bore more weight that any ordinary resolution. In actual fact, they were *proposals* concerning the legal status of a territory. If accepted by the parties concerned, they would have given rise to an *international agreement* binding on the parties.

9.   42 U.N.T.S. 303 No. 656, Apr. 4, 1949.

10.   U.N.Y.B., 1946-47, at 575.

> The resolution, adopted unanimously (with Egypt abstaining) stated among other things the following:
>
> 3. [The Assembly] Recognizes that, on the termination of the League's existence, its functions with respect to the mandated territories will come to an end, but notes that Chapters XI, XII and XIII of the Charter of the United Nations embody principles corresponding to those declared in Art.22 of the Covenant of the League;
>
> 4. Takes note of the expressed intentions of the Members of the League now administering territories under mandate to continue to administer them for the well-being and development of the peoples concerned in accordance with the obligations contained in the respective mandates, until other arrangements have been agreed between the United Nations and the respective mandatory Powers.

17

within an international organization; [11] plainly, to ascertain whether the resolution is merely an ordinary recommendation or amounts to an international agreement one should look both into the intentions of the states concerned, as they are shown in their statements, and into the actual terms of the resolution. By virtue of this agreement, the Member States of the League of Nations administering mandated territories undertook not to relinquish their control over those areas without the consent of the United Nations; the remaining Member States of the League acquired a right to claim from the former compliance with the obligation just referred to. Besides, the United Nations was granted the right to authorize any transferral of power over the territories under mandate. This authority, it should be added, was tacitly accepted by the United Nations by its decision to deal with those territories, and, in the case of Palestine, by its decision to propose a settlement of the matter by means of the Partition Plan.

It is worth emphasizing that later on both Israel and Jordan tacitly "joined" the agreement. Israel did so as early as 1948. On 15 May, 1948, Mr Moshe Shertok, the Israeli Foreign Minister, sent a cable to the U.N. Secretary-General in which he recalled the proclamation issued by the National Council for the Jewish State declaring *inter alia* that "the State of Israel will be ready to co-operate with organs and representatives of the United Nations in the implementation of the resolution of [The General] Assembly of 29 November 1947" laying down the so-called 'Partition Plan'. He went on to state:

> Accordingly I beg [to] declare on behalf [of the] Provisional Government of [the] State of Israel its readiness to sign [the] declaration and undertaking provided for respectively in part I C and part I D of [the] resolution of [the] Assembly. [12]

These Israeli commitments made it clear that Israel implicity recognized the authority of the United Nations to propose a plan for Palestine which included Jerusalem. It seems that, in addition, Israel accepted, by implication, that decisions on Jerusalem should be initiated by the United Nations or, in any event, had to receive its consent.

After the rejection of the Partition Plan by the Arab States, the Israeli stand was reiterated and expressed in even clearer terms by the Israeli representative to the United Nations, Mr Abba Eban, in the

---

11.   See, *e. g.*, Castaneda, *Valeur juridique des resolutions des Nations Unies,* 129 Hague Recueil at 302 - 312 (1970 - I); Conforti, *Le role de l'accord dans le systeme des Nations Unies,* 142 Hague Recueil at 271 - 288 (1974 - II).

12.   U.N. Doc. S/747.

statement he made on 5 May, 1949, before the *Ad Hoc* Political Committee of the General Assembly, on the occasion of the discussion of Israel's application for admission to membership of the U.N. In the part of his lengthy statement concerning Jerusalem, Mr Eban made the following points: (a) Israel "had cooperated to the fullest extent with the Statute drawn up in November 1947", in an effort to implement the section of the General Assembly Resolution concerning Jerusalem; [13] (b) the failure of the United Nations scheme was therefore not to be blamed on Israel but on the Arab States and on the "refusal of United Nations organs to assume the obligations necessary for the fulfilment of the Statute"; [14] (c) in spite of the failure of the Partition Plan, Israel recognized that competence to decide on the status of Jerusalem still rested with the United Nations, and believed that a satisfactory solution of the question could only be reached "by international consent" within the United Nations. Indeed, the hostilities that ensued thereafter had created a new situation; in particular, they had brought about a "process of integration of the life of Jerusalem into the life of the neighbouring States which now exercised the *functions of administration* [of Jerusalem]". [15] However, although Western and Eastern Jerusalem had therefore been placed under the "administration" of Israel and Jordan respectively, and Israel suggested as the best proposal for a settlement a "functional internationalization" (i.e. an international regime for the Holy Places only - situated in the area under Jordanian control), nevertheless, Israel was ready to bow to an international decision on the matter if it was agreeable to her. As Mr Eban put it:

> The statement contained in the Lebanese draft resolution that the New City of Jerusalem [i.e. West Jerusalem] had been proclaimed as part of the State of Israel was false and malicious. The most salient feature of the Government of Israel's present attitude to the Jerusalem problem was its earnest desire to see the juridical status of the city satisfactorily determined by international consent. [16]

He later on stated the following:

> The Government of Israel would continue to seek agreement with the Arab interests concerned in the maintenance and preservation of peace and the reopening of blocked access

---

13. 3 U.N. GAOR, *Ad Hoc* Political Committee, Summary Records, 45th Meeting, at 235.

14. *Id.* at 236.

15. *Id.* at 232.

16. *Id.* at 233.

into and within Jerusalem. Negotiations on that subject would not, however, affect *the juridical status of Jerusalem, to be defined by international consent.* [17]

In particular, as for Israel's suggestions for a "functional internationalization" of Jerusalem, Mr Eban pointed out as follows:

> [I]t was for the Committee [i.e. the *Ad Hoc* Political Committee of the General Assembly] to decide whether it endorsed or did not endorse the views of the Government of Israel on the future status of Jerusalem. [18]

It is apparent from Mr Eban's statement that although it no longer felt bound by the Partition Resolution, Israel still recognized - quite explicitly - the *authority of the United Nations* in any decision concerning Jerusalem acceptable to the parties concerned, and that consequently, no final settlement of the matter could be reached without the approval or the endorsement of the United Nations. Thus Israel undertook to refrain from seeking any settlement of the question without United Nations consent. [19]

One could infer from the Israeli stand that she eventually joined the agreement concluded within the League of Nations on 18 April 1946. One could even see it as a "tacit accession" to that agreement, brought about by the statement made by Israeli representatives to the United Nations. Should this view appear formalistic or somewhat farfetched, the suggestion could be made that Israel undertook a commitment vis-a-vis the United Nations parallel to the 1946 agreement. It is worth noting that the Israeli commitment was very similar to that undertaken - in the view of the International Court of Justice - by the Union of South Africa vis-a-vis the United Nations, on the question of the status of South West

---

17. *Id.* at 236.

18. *Id.* at 234.

19. It should however be pointed out that Israel somewhat hardened its stand in November 1949. See for instance the statement made on November 2, 1949, in the General Assembly *Ad Hoc* Political Committee by the Israeli representative, Mr Sharett, GAOR *Ad Hoc* Political Committee, Forty-Fourth Meeting, at 261-264, and by Mr Eban, *Id.* Forty-Ninth Meeting, Nov. 29, 1949 at 293-300. Nevertheless, Israel still upheld the UN authority to consent to any definitive settlement. Thus, for instance, Mr Sharett stated the following: "As to the function of supervision in the area controlled by Israel, his delegation believed that the best way to ensure its effective discharge was through an agreement solemnly to be concluded, by virtue of a special resolution of the General Assembly, between the United Nations and the Government of Israel, providing for the obligations of that Government and for the prerogatives of the United Nations in that regard" *Id.* at 264, para. 72. As for the statement by Mr Eban, see for example, *Id.* paras. 41 at 297; 54 at 299; and 56.

Vol. III THE PALESTINE YEARBOOK OF INTERNATIONAL LAW (1986)

Africa. It is well known that in its Advisory Opinion on the *Status of South West Africa* (1950), when the Court tackled the question whether the Union of South Africa had the competence to modify unilaterally the international status of South West Africa, it denied this competence. Among other things, it noted that on 9 April 1946, before the Assembly of the League of Nations, the South-African representative had recognized the competence of the United Nations to consent to any change of status for South West Africa. The Court thus inferred from the commitment made by the Union of South Africa before the U.N. that the authority to determine and modify the international status of South West Africa rested "with the Union of South Africa acting with the consent of the United Nations". [20]

Whichever of these legal configurations seems preferable, what really matters is the ultimate result: the Israeli statements precluded Israel from making any decision on the status of Jerusalem without the approval of the United Nations. In particular, Israel was barred from acquiring sovereignty over Western or Eastern Jerusalem without United Nations approval. [21]

Jordan adopted a rather ambiguous attitude toward the United Nations 1947 scheme for Jerusalem in 1947-48. [22] Later on, by holding on Eastern Jerusalem, it manifested its rejection of the scheme. However, on 26 November 1949, in the *Ad Hoc* Political Committee of the U.N. General Assembly, the Jordanian representative, while insisting on the importance it attached to Jordanian control over the Eastern part of Jerusalem, bowed to U.N. authority on the general issue of Jerusalem; he indeed used words that should not be labelled as a merely hypocritical homage to U.N. prestige, but can be construed as conveying the idea that Jordan would answer to the U.N. for its control over Eastern Jerusalem. [23] Although the attitude of Jordan was rather

---

20. *International Status of South Africa,* Advisory Opinion of 11 July 1950, [1950] I.C.J. 128 at 143.

21. See also *infra,* Section V.

22. For an examination of Jordan's stand see Safaer, *The Political Status of Jerusalem in the Hashemite Kingdom of Jordan, 1948-1967,* Middle Eastern Studies at 75-77 (1978-79).

23. The Jordanian representative stated among other things that "The Government of the Hashemite Kingdom of the Jordan... had the greatest respect for the wishes for the international community represented in the United Nations" GAOR *Ad Hoc* Political Committee, 46th Meeting, November 26, 1949, para. 73, at 276. He also stated, while insisting on the fact that "the existing system of control and protection in Jerusalem could [not] be modified in any way", that his Government "hoped that the Committee would duly consider and appreciate the arguments it had submitted". *Id.* para. 77, at 277.

ambiguous and unclear for many years, once this country became a member of the United Nations, in 1955, it voted in favour of the various resolutions of the General Assembly on Jerusalem, particularly after 1967. It stands to reason that by supporting all the General Assembly resolutions calling upon Israel to rescind the measures adopted in Eastern Jerusalem after 1967, Jordan implicitly assented to the U.N.'s authority to determine - in agreement with the parties concerned - whether changes in the status of Jerusalem are internationally lawful. It follows that, like Israel, Jordan undertook an obligation vis-a-vis the United Nations along the lines of the 1946 agreement referred to above. Like Israel, Jordan was then barred from acquiring any title over Jerusalem without United Nations consent.

III.   Who Wielded Sovereignty over Jerusalem Between 1948 and 1967?

The rejection of the Partition Plan by most of the parties concerned and the consequent fighting in Palestine, left the General Assembly Resolution embodying the Plan a dead letter. However, although it was not implemented, it was never formally repealed by the General Assembly.

Can the contention be made that the actual occupation of Jerusalem by Jordan and Israel meant they acquired sovereign rights over Eastern and Western Jerusalem respectively?

A learned author has argued that, after 1952, both the General Assembly and the Security Council gradually abandoned any idea of internationalizing Jerusalem, although the "Secretariat and various individual Members of the U.N. continued, on occasion, to pay lip service to the idea"; [24] this was so much so that, in his view, one could safely contend that "the U.N. by its unconcern with the idea of territorial internationalization, as demonstrated from 1952 to the present date [1968], effectively acquiesced in the demise of the concept". [25] The whole complex situation that developed in Jerusalem was described by the same author as follows: since Jordan's occupation of Eastern Jerusalem in 1948 was in breach of Article 2 (4) of the U.N. Charter, it lacked any legal justification; consequently, Jordan was unable to acquire a legal title to sovereignty over the area. It merely performed a "prolonged *de facto* occupation" from 1948 to 1967. By contrast, Israel's occupation of Western Jerusalem was prompted by Jordan's attack;

---

24.   Lauterpacht, at 23. See also at 23-36.

25.   *Id.* at 36.

Vol. III THE PALESTINE YEARBOOK OF INTERNATIONAL LAW (1986)

Israel acted in self-defence, under Article 51 of the U.N. Charter. Her occupation of Western Jerusalem, being lawful, allowed Israel to acquire a legal title to that area. Acquisition of sovereignty was also possible because the United Nations did not challenge it; it acquiesced in the new legal situation. [26]

I shall not make a detailed analysis of the lawfulness of Jordan's invasion of Eastern Jerusalem-for the purposes of this paper it is sufficient to note that the better view is that the invasion was contrary to Article 2 (4) of the U.N. Charter and to the general principle arising out of it. As regards Israel, it seems that both assumptions on which the view quoted above rests, namely that Israel became the lawful sovereign of Western Jerusalem, and that the U.N. acquiesced in her sovereignty are questionable.

First, although Israel acted in self-defence under Article 51, this did not authorize her to annex territories under a "sovereignty vacuum" [27]. Indeed the view referred to above seems to rest on a misconception of self-defence. Self-defence only entitles states to use force to repel an unlawful armed attack; it does not legitimize the acquisition of territory. [28] The authors under consideration actually stretch the concept and the substance of self-defence to such an extent as substantially to distort this notion. To be sure, the victim of an "armed attack" could go so far as to occupy, temporarily, a territory in order to forestall the recurrence of armed attacks which might seriously jeopardize its territorial integrity and political independence. This occupation should, however, discontinue as soon as the United Nations steps in, and in any event does not entail acquisition of sovereignty over that territory. The situation cannot but be provisional; pending the cessation of the wrongful behaviour or a final settlement, the occupying power is only authorized to exercise *de facto* control over the territory. [29] At least since 1945, sovereignty cannot be acquired through military conquest, not even when the territory was previously unlawfully controlled by another state, or when force is resorted to in order to repel an unlawful attack. The ban on the use of force and military conquest, laid down in the Charter, [30] is too sweeping and drastic to make allowance for such

---

26. To this effect see also Blum, *The Missing Reversioner, Reflections on the Status of Judea and Samaria*, 3 Isr. L. Rev. 279, (1968); Schwebel.

27. Lauterpacht, at 41, 45.

28. Jennings, *The Acquisition of Territory in International Law*, 55 (1963).

29. See Articles 42-56 of the Regulations annexed to the Hague Convention IV Respecting the Laws and Customs of War on Land, 1907, 36 US Stat. 2227.

30. Article 2(4) of the U.N. Charter.

qualifications. Cogent arguments would be necessary to demonstrate that these qualifications are permissible. So far no international lawyer has advanced any. [31] By contrast, a great authority, Professor Robert Jennings (as he then was), wrote in 1963 that "conquest as a title to territorial sovereignty has ceased to be a part of the law" whether or not force used for the purpose of seizing territory was lawful or unlawful under the U.N. Charter". [32] In my view, a careful examination of the Charter system and its general purposes, as restated among other things in the 1970 Declaration of Friendly Relations [33] leads us to believe that "acquisition" of sovereignty as a result of military force *might perhaps* be allowed, but only on very strict conditions: (i) it must be *undisputed* that prior to the use of force *sovereignty* over the territory belonged to the same state which used force to expel the unlawful occupant; (ii) all possible means for a peaceful settlement of the dispute have been used before resorting to armed violence and, in particular, recourse has been made to the appropriate U.N. bodies, but they have failed to dispossess the *unlawful* occupant of the territory; and (iii) the use of force has not gone beyond the limited goal of restoring sovereign rights over the territory (it is apparent from these conditions

---

31. Schwebel, at 345, has argued that the notion that "defensive conquest" and "the taking of territory which the prior holder held [unlawfully]" legitimize the acquisition of sovereign rights over a territory "must be read in particular cases together with other general principles, among them the still more general principle of which it is an application, namely, that no legal right shall spring from a wrong, and the Charter principle that the Members of the United Nations shall refrain in their international relations from the threat or use of force against the territorial integrity or political independence of any state". With all due respect, it is submitted that this view is unsound. In the case at issue, the fact that Jordan unlawfully attacked Israel in 1948 and then in 1967 and that after the first conflict Jordan acquired control over Eastern Jerusalem, simply means that its resort to force was in breach of Article 2(4) of the Charter as well the corresponding general principle and that it did not acquire any sovereign rights over that territory. It does not follow at all from that premise that "Israel has better title in the territory" in hand. I cannot see why the fact that Jordan violated international Law and only gained *de facto* control over a territory could result in Israel acquiring a right over the same territory simply because of her acting in self-defence. The only logical and sound inference from the aforementioned premise is that neither Jordan nor Israel ever acquired sovereignty over Jerusalem.

32. Jennings, at 56, and see generally at 52-68.

33. Principle I, para. 10 of the Declaration (adopted on October 24, 1970 by consensus), provides that "No territorial acquisition resulting from the threat or use of force shall be recognized as legal". For the full text of the *Declaration on Principles of International Law Concerning Friendly Relations and Co - Operation among States in Accordance with the Charter of the United Nations,* see U.N. General Assembly, 25th Sess., Doc. ARES/2625(XXV).

that in the case under consideration it would be more correct to speak of "reacquisition" of territory).

If one looks at the question in the light of these conditions, it becomes clear that at least one of them is missing: before 1948 Israel could not claim to hold *sovereign rights* over Western Jerusalem.

The second criticism of the view referred to above is predicted upon the premise that it does not seem that after 1952 the U.N. ever endorsed Israeli (and, for that matter, Jordanian) alleged sovereignty over Jerusalem. It should be pointed out that U.N. silence on the question between 1952 and 1967 cannot amount, as such, to acquiescence in their acquisition of a legal title. U.N. inaction, clearly motivated by an inability to overcome the political impasse, can only mean that the world organization accepted and acquiesced in *de facto* control of Jerusalem by Jordan and Israel. The granting of a legal title or, to be more precise, the turning of *de facto* authority into fully-fledged sovereignty, could not be brought about by mere silence. In view of the enormous importance of the question at issue and of the impact that a solution could have on the very tricky problems of the Middle East, the issue of consent should not be taken lightly. How could one assume that the U.N. expressed its consent on such a complex and explosive matter by merely *keeping silent*? At least *a tacit manifestation of consent through conclusive acts* would have been necessary.

What has just been pointed out is corroborated by the action taken over the years by several prominent members of the United Nations, including the states more directly concerned. Thus, for instance, the United Kingdom, after granting in 1950 and 1951, *de facto* recognition only of Israel's and Jordan's control of Jerusalem, in contradistinction to its *de jure* recognition of Israel and Jordan, [34] did not appear to modify its position over the years. In addition, the U.S. Government consistently emphasized the need for Jerusalem to be given an international regime proving that it did not intend to recognize any sovereignty over Jerusalem. Suffice it to mention here a few U.S. statements. On 22 July 1952, in response to the proposed move of the Israeli Foreign Ministry from Tel Aviv to Jerusalem, the American Embassy stated:

> The Government of the United States has adhered and continues to adhere to the policy that there should be a special

---

34.   See Arab Bank *vs* Barclays Bank, L.R. [1954] A.C. 495, 498, reported in I Whiteman, *Digest of International Law*, at 699 (hereinafter "Whiteman"). See also the statement made in 1950 by Lord Henderson in the House of Lords and reported in Hassan Bin Talal, at 25 and n. 41.

CASSESE : *INTERNATIONAL STATUS OF JERUSALEM*

international regime for Jerusalem which will not only provide protection for the holy places but which will be acceptable to Israel and Jordan as well as the world community.

Since the question of Jerusalem is still of international importance, the U.S. Government *believes that the United Nations should have an opportunity to reconsider the matter* with a view to devising a status for Jerusalem which will satisfactorily preserve the interests of the world community and the States directly concerned. Consequently, the U.S. Government would not view favorably the transfer of the Foreign Office of Israel to Jerusalem. [35]

On 30 December 1958, in a despatch to the Secretary of State, the American Consul General at Jerusalem stated:

The majority of U.N. member nations, including the United States and the Soviet Union, have continued to respect the United Nations resolutions despite the *de facto* occupancy of the city of Jerusalem part by Israel and part by Jordan. As a result, an anomalous situation exists today embodied, in the case of the United States, by a Consulate General whose district is the 'international city' and certain adjacent areas on the Jordanian side. Other nations which maintain similar establishments are the United Kingdom, Turkey, Italy, Spain, Greece and Belgium. Many other countries mark their respect for the internationalization resolutions by establishing embassies in Tel Aviv thus avoiding recognition of Jerusalem as the capital of Israel and, by implication, as Israel's *de facto* sovereign territory. [36]

This stand was reaffirmed in 1960. On 5 April of that year the U.S. Ambassador at Amman, in a despatch to the Secretary of State, pointed out, *inter alia,* that:

The Government of the United States of America has adhered and continues to adhere to a *policy which respects the interest of the United Nations in the status of Jerusalem.* The United States Government therefore cannot recognize or associate itself in any way with actions which confer upon Jerusalem the attributes of a seat of government of a sovereign State, and are thus *inconsistent with this United Nations interest in the status of that city.* [37]

---

35.   Whiteman, at 595 (emphasis added).

36.   *Id.* at 594.

37.   *Id.* (emphasis added).

Vol. III THE PALESTINE YEARBOOK OF INTERNATIONAL LAW (1986)

As late as 1967 the U.S. reiterated its attitude. In a statement made on 28 June, the Department of State made it clear that:

> The United States has never recognized such unilateral actions by any of the States in the area as governing the international status of Jerusalem. [38]

Another important pronouncement was made in 1958 by the Italian Council of State (*Consiglio di Stato*), the supreme body of "administrative justice" responsible for reviewing the legality of executive acts either in contentious proceedings or at the request of other Italian State agencies. In an advisory opinion delivered on 9 December 1958 following a request of the Foreign Ministry, the Council had to pronounce upon the following issue: whether the Italian Consulate in Western Jerusalem had to pay rent to the Arab owner of the premises, who did not live in the city, or to the Israeli Custodian - the only entity authorized to receive the money under Israeli law. [39] The Italian Council held that since the Israeli law was applicable in Western Jerusalem, the Italian Consul was to conform to it and pay the rent to the Custodian. However, before reaching this conclusion the Council stated, *inter alia*, the following on the status of Jerusalem:

> The situation of the territory of Jerusalem is not at all clear from the point of view of public international law. To be sure, there exists an international law convention (*convenzione*) providing that the territory should be internationalized. However, it seems that this convention has not yet been implemented and sovereignty is *de facto* exercised by the State of Israel, although this state of affairs has not been legally recognized by the Member States of the United Nations, which are duty bound to abide by that convention. [40]

Thus the Italian *Consiglio di Stato* clearly pointed out that Israel had not acquired full sovereignty over Western Jerusalem. Also very significant appear the Council's remarks on the duty of all the Member States of the U.N. to comply with the General Assembly pronouncements on the matter by withholding recognition of the Israeli claim to sovereignty over Western Jerusalem. [41] Although the *Consiglio di Stato's*

---

38. Dep't. St. Bull., July 17, 1967, at 60.

39. On the authority of the Custodian under Israeli law, see 4 *Laws of the State of Israel*, (LSI) at 68 (1950), in particular, see Art. 2. See also *Israel Government Yearbook* 1958 at 235.

40. Text (in Italian) in *Rivista di diritto internazionale*, at 321 - 322 (1960).

41. On the advisory opinion of the *Consiglio di Stato* see Sereni, *La situazione giuridica di Gerusalemme*, Foro italiano, 1960, IV, 205 ff (who, however, takes a different view from this writer).

point on this issue was merely an *obiter dictum*, it can be considered indicative of the views of Italian State authorities, not only because the Foreign Ministry (which, as emphasized above, had requested the Council's advisory opinion) eventually upheld it but also because it is in line with other pronouncements by Italian authorities on the matter. [42]

It is apparent from all these statements that a great number of U.N. members did not intend to recognize any asserted acquisition of sovereignty either by Israel or by Jordan over Jerusalem; in addition, some of them strongly believed that the city should enjoy an international status. This being so, how could it be claimed that the United Nations acquiesced in the alleged transfer of sovereignty over Jerusalem? It is indeed difficult to dissociate the U.N. stand from that of the majority of its members. The attitude taken by the aforementioned states only confirms that U.N. inaction cannot be taken to mean a tacit acceptance of Israeli or Jordanian sovereignty over Jerusalem.

IV.   What Exactly Has the Legal Status of
       Jerusalem Been Since the 1967 War?

In 1967 Israel occupied Eastern Jerusalem in the course of armed hostilities started by Jordan, whereas during the conflict with Egypt and Syria, she had acted in "anticipatory self-defence". [43] On 27 June 1967, the Israeli Parliament (the Knesset) passed a law as a result of which in July of the same year the Israeli Government decreed that the whole of Jerusalem was incorporated into the municipal and administrative spheres of its government. [44] The administrative incorporation of Jerusalem into Israel was upheld by various Israeli courts in

---

42.   For the stand of Italian authorities on the question of the Middle East, see the statement quoted *infra*, note 54 as well as the various statements adopted by the Foreign Ministers or the Head of State of the EEC countries (see for example the one quoted *infra*, note 72).

43.   On this issue, see Malawer, *Anticipatory Self Defence Under Article 51 of the United Nations Charter and the Arab - Israeli War,* 1967 in *Problems,* Vol. VIII, no. 1-2 at 14 (June 1970). For the general legal criteria of anticipatory self - defence, see McDougal & Feliciano, *Law and Minimum World Orders* at 231 (1961).

44.   See text of the Law and Administrative Ordinance (Amendment No. 11) Law, 21 LSI at 75 (1967). Other Israeli Legislation affecting Jerusalem are Municipalities Ordinance (Amendment No.6) Law, *Id.* Protection of Holy Places Law, *Id.* at 76.

Vol. III THE PALESTINE YEARBOOK OF INTERNATIONAL LAW (1986)

the following years [45] and completed by a "Basic Law" passed on 30 July, 1980 by the Knesset. [46] On the strength of this law the whole of Jerusalem was actually made an integral part of the State of Israel, and indeed became her capital city.

It is submitted that the annexation of Jerusalem is contrary both to *conventional* and *general* international law. As to conventional law, it has already been emphasized before [47] that by implicitly joining the agreement concluded in 1946 within the last League of Nations Assembly, or at any rate by entering into a distinct but parallel agreement with the United Nations, both Israel and Jordan formally recognized the need for U.N. authorization or consent to any change in Jerusalem; they accordingly undertook to refrain from doing anything that would impinge upon the legal status of that city without prior U.N. approval. It is common knowledge that both in 1967 and in the following years, in particular in 1980, the Security Council, as well as the General Assembly, strongly condemned the Israeli annexation of Jerusalem and declared all the acts accomplished by Israel are null and void. [48] It should be stressed that the refusal to acknowledge the legality of Israeli action in Jerusalem was reiterated, both within and outside the United Nations, by various Western countries-normally more friendly, or at least less hostile to Israel than socialist and developing states. Thus, for instance, mention can be made of the U.S., [49] the United Kingdom, [50]

---

45. See, *e. g.*, the judgement delivered on Mar. 10, 1969 by the Supreme Court of Israel in the Hanzalis' case (French translation in 98 Journal de Droit International, 1971 at 345). See also the comments by Shaki, *Id.* at 356 - 357.

46. Basic Law: Jerusalem, Capital of Israel in 34 LSI at 209 (1980).

47. See *supra*, Section II.

48. For a survey of these resolutions, see Jones, *The Status of Jerusalem: Some National and International Aspects* in Moore (ed.), *The Arab - Israeli Conflict Readings and Documents* at 223 (1973); Cattan; at 202 and *passim;* Pfaff, *Jerusalem: a Keystone of an Arab - Israeli Settlement, Id.* at 273 and *passim;* Mallison & Mallison, at 211-228; Reddaway, *Jerusalem and International Organizations* (reneotyped), at 7 and *passim* (1979); Rostow, *Palestinian Self - Determination: Possible Futures of the Unallocated Territories of the Palestine Mandate,* Yale Studies in World Public Law, at 162 and *passim* (1980).

49. See, for example, 57 Dep't St. Bull. July 31, 1967 at 148; *Id.* July 28, 1969, at 76; *Digest of United States Practice in International Law* 1976, at 634-635; 1977, at 922-925; 1978, at 1557, 1579-1580; 1979 at 258.

50. See Brit.Y.B. Int'l. L. at 481 (1980); *Id.* at 514 - 517, (1981); *Id.* at 366, 531 - 534 (1982); *Id.* at 459, 538 - 539,(1983).

France, [51] the Federal Republic of Germany, [52] Belgium, [53] Italy, [54] the Netherlands, [55] Canada [56] and Japan. [57] All these pronouncements make it clear that the United Nations as a whole, as well as its individual member states, expressly withheld recognition of the Israeli annexation of Jerusalem. It follows that the consent required by the multilateral or bilateral agreements referred to above, was not given; consequently Israel never acquired a valid legal title.

Let us now consider whether such a title was acquired under customary international law. Can we maintain that Israeli sovereignty stems from a different source than treaty law, a more flexible source and which *ex hypothesi* could override treaty obligations? To put it differently, can we hold that - unlike treaty law, by definition better geared to the specific circumstances of individual cases - customary law, being more traditional and general, takes account of, and legitimates, the physical taking of Jerusalem by Israel coupled with her intention to annex it?

Two points need to be made. First, under customary international law, actual control over a territory attended by *animus possidendi* can only create a legal title to areas belonging to no one. [58] However, it would be both unsound and contrary to all evidence to suggest that Jerusalem became *terra nullius* after the British withdrawal. Hence, a legal title other than the one required for the acquisition of 'territories without master' is necessary. In the case at issue, the legal title should be granted by the previous holders of sovereignty, i.e. the League of

---

51.   See, *e.g.*, 26 *Annuaire francais de droit international*, at 919 - 920, (1980), *Id.* at 256, (1983).

52.   See 44 Zeitschrift fur auslandisches offentliches Recht und Volkerrecht, at 503 (1984).

53.   See 15 Revue Belge de droit international, at 616 (1980).

54.   See 3 The Italian Y.B. Int'l. L. at 418 (1977); 4 at 224 - 227, (1978 - 79); 5 at 301, (1980 - 81).

55.   See, *e. g.*, Netherlands Y.B. Int'l L. at 151, (1970) as well as The Times, Feb. 11, 1981.

56.   See 15 The Canadian Y.B. Int'l. L. at 346 (1977); 17 at 340-341 (1979).

57.   See Oda and Owada (eds.) 1982, *The Practice of Japan in International Law 1961- 1970*, at 6-7 (1982).

58.   See the Island of Palmas case (U.N., Reports of International Arbitral Awards, II, 838-856) the Clipperton Island case (*Id.* at 1108 - 111), and the Eastern Greenland case (P.C.I.J., Ser. A/B, no.53. In general, on this subject see the classical work by R. Ago, *le requisito dell'effetivita dell'occupazione in diritto internazionale* (Roma, 1934).

Nations (after 1946 by its successor, the U.N.) and the United Kingdom, as the former Mandatory State. Such transferral, however, has not been made, either through formal international instruments, or by implication (i.e. by the acquiescence of the U.K. and the U.N. in the alleged sovereignty of Israel and Jordan, or of Israel only). [59] Can acquisition of territory derive from a different title, namely "unlawful conquest"? It has been suggested that between 1948 and 1967 Eastern Jerusalem was under the unlawful control of Jordan and in 1967 occupied by Israel acting in self-defence against the wrongful attack by Jordan. According to various distinguished jurists [60] the lawful conquest of a territory illegally occupied by a state in breach of Article 2 (4) of the U.N. Charter creates a sovereign title in favour of the conquering state. Arguments advanced with respect to the status of Jerusalem in the period between 1948 and 1967 [61] could be repeated in this instance. General international law on territorial sovereignty has undergone a major change, at least since 1945: whenever a state appropriates a territory by using force (whether in breach of Article 2 (4) or by acting in self-defence under Article 51 of the U.N. Charter), no legal title over the territory can be acquired. The classical elements for transferral of sovereignty are no longer sufficient. Authority over the territory is internationally illegal (except as a belligerent occupant), until such time as the overwhelming majority of states (or the competent organs of the United Nations) decide legally to recognize the change of status of the territory. [62] However, U.N. approbation or consent have been refused in the case at issue.

In sum, while treaty law excludes any acquisition of sovereignty by Israel over Jerusalem, one cannot even fall back on customary law for the purpose of validating Israeli claims to sovereignty. As pointed out

---

59. In addition, as I have already pointed out above (Section II), the undertaking of Israel and Jordan serves to exclude the possibility of their acquiring sovereignty without U.N. assent, should the mistaken theory of Jerusalem as *terra nullius* be upheld. Indeed, assuming that Jerusalem became a "territory without sovereign" after the British authorities relinquished it, Israel and Jordan could not acquire sovereignty simply by meeting the requirements of general international law. For they had both assumed the *conventional* obligation vis - a - vis the United Nations and its Member States to refrain from changing the legal status of Jerusalem without the U.N. assent. This obligation would of necessity overrides customary international law to their advantage.

60. See, for instance, the works by Schwebel and Blum.

61. See *supra*, Section III.

62. It stands to reason that this recognition cannot be granted at whim, but should be motivated by special circumstances fully warranting an exception to the ban on acquisition of sovereignty by force.

above, at present general international law has departed markedly from the *principle of effectiveness: de facto* situations brought by force of arms are no longer automatically endorsed and sanctioned by international legal standards. At present the principle of legality is overriding - at least at the normative level - and effectiveness must yield to it. As it has already been emphasized, this is the consequence of a whole range of major changes that occurred in the world community after the adoption of the U.N. Charter.

V.　Does the United Nations Still Have a Role in Deciding Upon the Future of Jerusalem?

It is apparent from the above that the United Nations, although it has no "real" power of disposition over Jerusalem (certain *de facto* situations cannot be obliterated by merely legal means) does, however, have a decisive say in the matter and no international settlement can be lawfully reached without its approval. Admittedly, Israel has shown much reticence on this matter and at present in actual practice it denies the United Nations the authority to legalize any settlement acceptable to the parties concerned by its approbation. Nevertheless, Israel's refusal is contrary to her previous commitments vis-a-vis the United Nations - a commitment never nullified on any of the grounds for rendering agreements null and void (in particular, the clause *rebus sic stantibus* cannot validly be invoked, for, as stated above, Israel accepted U.N. authority even after the Partition Plan had been rejected by Arab countries). In addition, the Israeli refusal referred to above cannot produce any legal effects under customary international law, for the latter requires a set of conditions for the acquisition of a valid legal title to sovereignty that Israel does not fulfil.

However deep the cleavage between Israel on the one side, and the world community on the other, a settlement sanctioned by law must require the assent of the world community, as expressed by its representative body, the United Nations.

·VI.　Has the Idea of Territorial Internationalization Been Abandoned by the United Nations?

Let us now briefly look into the question of whether the U.N., given its authority over any settlement of the Jerusalem issue, has yet proposed a definite scheme, or whether it has refrained from taking any initiative on the matter.

One of the authors referred to above has suggested that recent U.N. resolutions do not reflect any intention on the part of the United

Nations "to resurrect the idea of the territorial internationalization of Jerusalem" and in particular that the "status of the city", about which some of these resolutions expressed concern, was not the status chosen by the General Assembly in 1947 for internationalization. [63] This contention rests on two elements: first, in the discussion before the passing of those resolutions, no mention was usually made of internationalization; second, no reference whatsoever to internationalization is to be found in the language itself of the resolutions. The conclusion is accordingly drawn that the United Nations now accept that Jerusalem should be divided into two parts, one under Israeli sovereignty, the other in a sort of legal vacuum as to sovereign rights - although, in the opinion of the author under consideration, after 1967 Israel may have come lawfully to exercise the powers of a belligerent occupant over Eastern Jerusalem [64] while other authors take the view that Israel lawfully acquired sovereignty over the whole of Jerusalem. [65]

Admittedly, the various resolutions passed by the United Nations since 1967 only refer, in terms, to the duty of Israel to cancel the measures it has taken in Eastern Jerusalem and, consequently, to withdraw to Western Jerusalem. Taken at their face value, they seem to indicate that the United Nations has abandoned any idea of internationalization. Indeed, a few authorities [66] have spoken of the "apparent ambiguity" or "lack of clarity" of these resolutions. Can we infer from their text that the United Nations has now come to accept a city divided into two parts, each under the sovereignty of a different state?

The somewhat obscure character of the resolutions and their deliberate openness to various interpretations, as well as the whole context of the United Nations' stand on the question of Jerusalem, point to the following conclusions.

First, the world organization never intended to endorse the occupation of Eastern Jerusalem by Israel, much less the alleged acquisition of sovereignty by that state.

Secondly, the United Nations never proposed a definite scheme for the final settlement of the question ; it has neither insisted on the idea of *internationalization,* nor has it favoured the *splitting* of the city into two parts, each under the sovereignty of a different state. The Organization has preferred to take a very cautious stand by leaving either solu-

---

63. Lauterpacht, at 34 - 36.

64. *Id.* at 47 - 51.

65. See, for example, the works by Schwebel and Blum.

66. Mallison and Mallison, at 228; Reddaway at 8-13.

tion open. In particular, it has avoided pronouncing either on the legal title required for either solution, or on which state would have a better title to sovereignty over all or part of Jerusalem.

Thirdly, the Organization has clearly shown its intention of retaining full power of disposition over the territory or, to put it in more accurate terms, to maintain its right to authorize, or consent to, any legal change in the status of Jerusalem.

This stand, which at first sight might appear ambiguous, hence open to criticism, is instead realistic and flexible. By not crystallizing its position in one rigid formula, the United Nations has left all the options open, thus showing its desire to take account of the evolving political and military realities in the area. It has adopted a wise and balanced course of action, by only insisting on one crucial point - the principle of United Nations authority over any final settlement.

It should be noted that the United Nations' attitude ultimately represents *a synthesis* of the differing views of some of its Members. A number of Member States still believe that the idea of *a corpus separatum* should be revived; suffice it to mention the statements made in Parliament by the Belgian Government in 1969 [67] and again in 1971 [68]

---

67.   In 1969, during the discussion on the Foreign Ministry's budget which took place in the Belgian Senate, the official position of the Belgian Government on the question of Jerusalem was set out as follows: "Dans son discours prononcé lors de la session extraordinaire de l'Assemblée générale des Nations Unies en 1967, le ministre des Affaires étrangères a exprimé la préoccupation du gouvernement belge quant au sort de Jérusalem. Il demeure favorable à l'établissement d'un statut international des lieux saints qui en garantirait le libre accès aux fidèles de toutes les religions". Report in Revue Belge de Droit International, at 278 (1971).

68.   In 1971, replying to a question from a Senator, the Belgian Foreign Minister declared in the Senate the following: "Je voudrais rappeler au Senat que la Belgique demeure fidèle à la décision du 29 novembre 1947 de l'Assemblée générale des Nations Unies qui prévoyait un territoire international pour Jerusalem *corpus separatum.* L'Assemblée générale des Nations Unies, en juillet 1967, c'est-à-dire après la reprise des conflits, et le Conseil de sécurité, le 21 mai et le 23 juillet 1969, ont invité l'Etat d'Israel à renoncer à l'annexion de Jerusalem et à s'abstenir de toute disposition visant à modifier le statut de la ville. La Belgique a approuvé ces dispositions du Conseil de sécurite et de l'Assemblée générale des Nations Unies.

Des lors, les principaux pays occidentaux: les Etats - Unis, la Grande - Bretagne, la France, l'Italie, l'Espagne, la Grèce et la Turquie maintiennent à Jerusalem des consuls généraux.

Respectant le principe du *corpus separatum*, l'exequatur n'est demandé ni aux Israeliens, ni aux Jórdaniens. Les autorités israeliennes ne sont guere favorables au maintien de ces consuls dans cette situation, mais qui est conforme à

Vol. III THE PALESTINE YEARBOOK OF INTERNATIONAL LAW (1986)

and by the Philippines in 1980 in the Security Council. [69] The same stand had already been taken in 1967 within the United Nations, following the Israeli occupation of Eastern Jerusalem, by twenty Latin American States, as well as by Spain. [70] A different view was expressed in 1979 by the British Foreign Minister, who proposed that "there should be an Arab Jerusalem and an Israeli Jerusalem, each exercising full sovereignty within its own territory, but with no barriers between them and no impediment in freedom of movement between them". [71] A looser formula was suggested by the EEC members. On 13 June 1980 the European Council, meeting in Venice, stated that the Nine (as they then were) did not accept any unilateral initiative aimed at changing the status of Jerusalem, and that any agreement on the status of the city should guarantee free access for all to the Holy Places. [72] The apparent implication is that the EEC members do not intend to recognize the alleged sovereignty of Israel over Eastern Jerusalem, and take the view

---

l'attitude que la plupart des gouvernements occidentaux, y compris le gouvernement belge, ont prise. Cette situation particulière explique le caractère délicat des fonctions de consul général à Jerusalem, puisque le titulaire doit entretenir des relations avec les autorités locales, qui sont israeliennes, sans pour autant reconafare l'annexion de la ville" Report in Revue Belge de Droit International, at 266 (1973).

69. See U.N.Y.B at 40 (1980).

70. On the occasion of the debate in the U.N. on the occupation of Eastern Jerusalem resulting from the June War, several States suggested that Jerusalem should be placed under permanent international administration, as a *corpus separatum*, with special guarantees for the protection of the Holy Places. This stand was taken by Argentina, Brazil and Spain (U.N.Y.B. at 210 (1967), which explicitly referred to G.A. Resolution 181 (II) of 29 November 1947, as well as by Uruguay and Venezuela, *Id.* Furthermore, twenty countries (Argentina, Barbados, Bolivia, Brazil, Chile, Colombia, Costa Rica, Dominican Republic, Ecuador, El Salvador, Guatemala, Guyana, Honduras, Jamaica, Mexico, Nicaragua, Panama, Trinidad and Tobago and Venezuela) put forward a proposal (draft resolution A/L.523 Rev. 1) which among other things reaffirmed, as in earlier recommendations, the desirability of establishing an international regime for the City of Jerusalem, for the consideration of the Assembly at its next session. True, this draft was not adopted because it failed to obtain the required two-thirds majority (it received 57 votes in favour, 43 against with 20 abstentions: *Id.*, at 220). Although it did not acquire the status of a General Assembly Resolution, that draft is of great importance at least in the following respect: it shows that the 20 co-sponsors, as well as other states which voted in favour of it, *clung to the idea of the internationalization of Jerusalem.*

71. See The Guardian, 27 Aug. 1979 as quoted by Hassan Bin Talal, at 49 and n. 86.

72. See EEC Bulletin, 1980, no. 6, para. 1.1.6 sub-para. 8.

that only through an international agreement can a final settlement be reached. It should be added that in 1980, in the Security Council, Cuba, Jordan and Turkey loosely referred to an international regime for Jerusalem under the aegis of the United Nations. Clearly, the existence of disparate or even opposed view-points among the member states of the United Nations helps to explain why the Organization has deemed it advisable since 1967 to shun any clear-cut scheme for the city, as long as the political situation remains fraught with danger and no solution acceptable to all the parties concerned is in sight [73].

VII.   Final Remarks

A)   Conclusions of the foregoing analysis

Under current international law it is ultimately for the United Nations, Israel and Jordan to make arrangements for the international status of Jerusalem. [74]However, by virtue of the general principle on the self-determination of people, these arrangements cannot be validly made without the participation of the legitimate representatives of the Palestinian people, who must be allowed to take part in the decision-making process, and express the aspirations of the Palestinians. Until such time as a general agreement is reached with the United Nations on the matter, Israel's present claim to sovereignty cannot produce any legal effects. Under international law, Israel only exercises *de facto* control over Jerusalem. And, as for her control over Eastern Jerusalem, it is clearly a breach of the international rules on military occupation, because it goes far beyond the limits assigned to the powers of a military occupant. [75]

---

73.   See U.N.Y.B. at 401 (1980).

74.   It seems that this position was to some extent adumbrated by the U.S. representative to the U.N. in the statement he made on September 25, 1971, in the U.N. Security Council. He said the following: "... In our view, the ultimate status of Jerusalem should be determined through negotiation and agreement between the Governments of Israel and Jordan in the context of an overall peace settlement, taking into account the interests of its inhabitants, of the international religious communities who hold it sacred, and of other countries in the area". Dept. St. Bull at 469 (1971).

75.   The legal consequences of the illegality of the Israeli annexation of Eastern Jerusalem were also drawn on the domestic plane. Thus, for instance, a Dutch Bill on naturalization was changed in the Netherlands Parliament to take account of the legal situation existing in Jerusalem. The Bill mentioned the place and date of birth of an applicant for naturalization as follows: "Jerusalem (Israel), June 20, 1923" (it actually concerned Eastern Jerusalem).

In concluding this study, one may try to advance a few general remarks on the role of law. It is submitted that current international law does not "freeze" the existing *de facto* situation in Jerusalem; it does not give it its 'blessing'. In the case of Jerusalem, we come face to face with a striking phenomenon: a *de facto* situation, brought about by force of arms and now solidly implanted in the daily life of the city, is not recognized by any other member of the world community, and consequently is not validated either under general international law or conventional law. [76] The principle of *effectiveness* is overriden by that of *legality*, although the United Nations, creator of and spokesman for international legality, is unable to enforce it. This schizophrenic state of affairs forces international law to confine itself to an essentially negative stand, that is to withholding its endorsement of the *de facto* situation; subject to what shall be suggested later, by and large international law does not seem to provide a solution in *positive* terms. Although a huge gap separates law from reality, law at least accomplishes the useful function of indicating *how* a solution can be reached. Under international law a definitive settlement can only be achieved by dint of agreement between the parties concerned and subject to the consent of the United Nations. In other words, although international law does not furnish a *fully-fledged substantive* settlement, at least it enjoins the *procedure* to be followed. It calls for a process of negotiation involving the two states of the area, the legitimate representatives of the Palestinian people, as well as the other members of the world community. It is a process that will necessarily require a number of mutual concessions by the parties concerned; besides it will have to take account of the keen interest of the whole international community in the safeguarding of the holy places in Jerusalem. It seems that only on these conditions can a solution acceptable to the world community, be achieved.

B)   Substantive guidelines for a possible settlement, stemming from international law and practice

One could object that a peaceful settlement along the procedural

---

In this connection the following observation was made in Parliament: "Since this annexation has never been formally recognized, it is hardly possible to state that, under international law, this zone belongs to Israel. In connection with this application for naturalization the Bill mentions that Jerusalem is situated in Israel. How this is to tally with the Minister's statement that these indications are based upon the present status under international law of the area concerned? The Government shared this view and the Bill was changed to the effect that "Jerusalem (Israel)" was replaced by "Jerusalem (old city, Jordan), presently under Israeli administration". See Netherland Y.B. Int'l. L. at 151, (1970).

76.   See *supra*, Section III.

lines suggested above is a chimera, like that house mentioned by Swift, so perfectly built in accordance with all the rules of symmetry and equilibrium that if a sparrow were to alight on it, it would immediately collapse. Indeed, considering the present rift between Israel and most Arab States, the tensions or dissensions both among the Arab countries and within the Palestine Liberation Organization, the deadlock at the U.N., the political inability of the Organization to smooth out the conflicts, a prompt solution through mutual concessions and trade-offs becomes highly problematical. This being so, it would seem all the more urgent to delve among the legal norms to see if one could at least postulate a *general scheme*. This, of course, could not impose itself by legal fiat, until it had been embodied in an agreement. Nevertheless, its mere existence would provide a *substantive* blueprint for action, thereby *facilitating* the achievement of a compromise.

It is submitted that international law and practice tend to suggest the following solution. In the first place, international practice seems to regard as feasible the possible granting to Israel of sovereign rights over Western Jerusalem. Indications to this effect can be drawn from three sets of circumstances. First, at the end of hostilities in 1948 the armistice line dividing Jerusalem corresponded more or less to the demographic situation of Arabs and Jews in Jerusalem: the Western sector of the city included the highest number of Jewish inhabitants. Second, after 1967, the U.N. has repeatedly called upon Israel to withdraw from the "occupied territories"; this expression could be taken to cover only those territories occupied in 1967. By implication, one might infer that since Western Jerusalem is not among such territories, the U.N. might be ready to accept that *de facto* control over the Western sector be turned into sovereign rights proper. Third, when concluding the Camp David Agreement [77] Egypt made a unilateral declaration on Jerusalem, whereby it implicitly accepted Israeli control over Western Jerusalem while rejecting any acquisition by Israel of rights over the Old City.

One could object that foreign embassies have been withdrawn from Western Jerusalem with ever increasing frequency after 1967, and particulary after 1980, when the whole of Jerusalem was annexed by Israel. However, this was primarily done in protest at the illegal incorporation of Jerusalem into the Israeli political, administrative and legal system. This seems to be the best way of accounting for the seeming contradiction between the probably implicit acceptance of Israeli control over

---

77. See text of the Agreements in The Camp David Summit (U.S. Dept. St. Pub. 8954, Sept. 1978).

the Western sector of the city after 1967 and the withdrawal of foreign embassies.

In the second place, international law seems to point in a different direction as far as sovereign rights over Eastern Jerusalem are concerned. They should be granted to the legitimate representative of the Palestinian people, for three reasons. First, in 1948 the ethnic majority in Eastern Jerusalem was Arab. Second, Jordanian control over Eastern Jerusalem in the period 1948-67 was never accepted as definitive by the world community, nor, indeed, by the Arab League which, as early as 12 April 1948, stated that Jordanian control in Palestine was temporary and that the country "should be handed [over] to its owners so that they may rule as they please". [78] Third, the right of people to self-determination requires that a home be granted to the Palestinian people, [79] and this could be brought about, amongst other things, by entrusting the Palestinians with full authority over Eastern Jerusalem. Of course, such authority should be made conditional on full enjoyment by everyone of the rights of access and worship in the Holy Places.

This substantive settlement may, or may not, be considered realistic. Be that as it may, one can say, in conclusion, that international law, faced with this highly complex political problem, can allow a flexible and constructive "response"; a response which is neither preposterous and overbearing nor blind to political realities. It points to one of the few paths that can lead to peaceful settlement. It is incumbent upon the parties concerned, and the international community at large, to tread one of these paths and, through a process requiring patience and reasonable trade-offs, bring about a compromise acceptable to all.

78.   See II, Khalil (ed.) (1962) *The Arab States and the Arab League - A Documentary Record,* at 166.

79.   There are many U.N. Resolutions confirming this right. See, *e.g.,* Resolution 2672 C on Dec. 8, 1970 in U.N. GAOR, Supp. 28 at 73 - 74; Res. 39/17, Nov. 23, 1984.

FACTS ON THE GROUND: AN EXAMINATION OF ISRAELI MUNICIPAL POLICY IN EAST JERUSALEM

ARDI IMSEIS[*]

---

* LLB., Dalhousie University; B.A. with honors, University of Toronto.

> We said things without meaning them, and we didn't carry them out, we
> said over and over that we would equalize the rights of the Arabs to the
> rights of the Jews in the city—empty talk. . . Never have we given them a
> feeling of being equal before the law. [As mayor of Jerusalem, I] nurtured
> nothing and built nothing [for the Arabs]. For Jewish Jerusalem I did
> something in the past 25 years. For [Arab] East Jerusalem? Nothing!
> What did I do? Nothing! Sidewalks? Nothing. Cultural Institutions? Not
> one. Yes, we installed a sewage system for them and improved the water
> supply. Do you know why? Do you think it was for their good, for their
> welfare? Forget it! There were some cases of cholera there, and the Jews
> were afraid that they would catch it, so we installed [a] sewage and a wa-
> ter system against cholera. . .[1]

INTRODUCTION

If Teddy Kollek's ("Kollek") comments regarding the quality of
municipal services in Jerusalem seem excessive, this is because the
city has stood at the center of one of the twentieth century's most
tumultuous political conflicts. Particularly disturbing about the former Israeli mayor's candid admission is the fact that for over a quarter-century he was not only "the most powerful actor in the city,"[2]
but was also viewed as a champion of Palestinian rights in Jerusalem.[3] Among other things, the glaring contradiction between his
reputation as a right-dealing moderate and his categorical acknowledgment of the role he played in perpetuating inequity amongst Jerusalem's inhabitants is indicative of the wider manner in which Israeli
municipal laws and policies have been employed by the Jewish State
since it conquered Arab East Jerusalem thirty-two years ago.

Although Israeli municipal authorities in Jerusalem have publicly

---

1. Interview with Teddy Kollek, former Mayor of Jerusalem, in *Israeli Daily
Ma'ariv* (Oct. 10, 1990), *quoted in* DOCUMENTS ON JERUSALEM, at 115 (Palestin-
ian Academic Society for the Study of International Affairs) (1996) [hereinafter
DOCUMENTS ON JERUSALEM].

2. IRA SHARKANSKY, GOVERNING JERUSALEM: AGAIN ON THE WORLD'S
AGENDA 36 (1996) (noting Kollek was the most prominent actor in Jerusalem).

3. *See id.* at 142, 144 (explaining Kollek employed a network of contacts to
keep him informed about Palestinian concerns and to provide individual Palestinians with personal contacts that could assist them with the local or national bu-
reaucracies); *see also* DOCUMENTS ON JERUSALEM, *supra* note 1, at 115.

called for equality in treatment of the city's Jewish and Palestinian inhabitants, since 1967, they have outwardly pursued policies that have catered only to the former group. In turn, this has only served to further exacerbate the deep divide that exists between the two communities.[4] As noted by Israeli Professor Ira Sharkansky, "[t]he city's Jews are significantly better off than the Palestinians, and the [municipal] policies for Jerusalem favor Jews over non-Jews."[5] If this is in fact the case, than it behooves one to examine the factors which have allowed the situation to develop.

Without any doubt, the principle determinant behind the disparity in treatment between Arabs and Jews in Jerusalem lies in the Israeli government's long-held official policy that the city, "whole and united," is the exclusive capital of the Jewish State and must "remain forever under Israel's sovereignty."[6] This assertion would not be extraordinary were it not for the fact that before Israel's armed forces conquered East Jerusalem in 1967 that sector of the city was exclusively populated by indigenous Palestinians,[7] many of whom were part of the wave of approximately 60,000 Palestinians forced to flea West Jerusalem in 1948.[8] To this day, Jerusalem remains central to the collective narrative and identity of the Palestinian people—colonized, dispossessed, occupied—who have, for their part, always regarded the city as the natural capital of a future Palestinian State, and

---

4. *See, e.g., The Status of Jerusalem*, U.N. Committee on the Exercise of the Inalienable Rights of the Palestinian People, at 25 (1997) (explaining that while the current Guidelines of the Government of the State of Israel stipulate that the government will allocate special resources to build and improve municipal services for Jewish and Arab residents, since 1967 the State has "constructed dwelling space for 70,000 Jewish families" in East Jerusalem "and only 555 dwelling units for its Palestinian residents"); *see also The Likud Party: Guidelines of the Government of Israel* (visited Nov. 20, 1998) <http://www.likud.org.il/policy/govguide.html> [hereinafter *Guidelines*].

5. *See* SHARKANSKY, *supra* note 2, at 17 (noting the economic element to the conflict between Jerusalem's communities).

6. *See Guidelines, supra* note 4, at pt. II, arts. 1, 3 (noting that the government will prevent any actions that counter Israel's exclusive sovereignty over Jerusalem).

7. *See The Status of Jerusalem, supra* note 4, at 25 (explaining that in 1967 there were no Jews in the eastern part of Jerusalem and in July 1993 there were 160,000 Jews to 155,000 Palestinians).

8. *See The Status of Jerusalem, supra* note 4, at 6.

have therefore refused to recognize Israeli sovereignty over it. In support of the Palestinian position, the international community has overwhelmingly and unequivocally stated that East Jerusalem is Occupied Territory and, as such, any assertion of Israeli sovereignty, in or over it, is contrary to well-established principles of international law.[9]

Despite this fact, however, the State of Israel has remained wedded to its conviction that all of Jerusalem—both the predominately Arab eastern sector and the largely Jewish western sector—must remain under its exclusive control.[10] To further this national policy, the Israeli Municipality of Jerusalem has waged an extensive campaign to entrench the Jewish State's hold on East Jerusalem through the promulgation of a number of municipal policies and land use planning laws carefully designed to alter the demographic and geographic character of the city.

This Essay will attempt to illustrate the efficacy with which these laws and policies have been employed by Israeli municipal authorities to create a situation in East Jerusalem that will not be reversed in the future.[11] To this end, a brief examination of the history of Israel's control over East Jerusalem will be undertaken, followed by a broader analysis of Israeli municipal policy and activity in the city. Among other things, it is the intent of this Essay to serve as a reminder of the enormous impact Israeli municipal and land use planning laws and policies have had on the natural development of local Palestinian space in East Jerusalem. This point should also be considered in light of the fact that Israel and the Palestine Liberation Organization ("PLO") have committed themselves in good-faith to negotiate the "final status" of Jerusalem under the framework of the current Oslo peace process.[12]

---

9. *See id.* at 29-41; *see also The Question of the Observance of the Fourth Geneva Convention of 1949 in Gaza and the West Bank Including Jerusalem Occupied by Israel in June 1967,* U.N. Committee on the Exercise of the Inalienable Rights of the Palestinian People, at 1 (1979).

10. *See Guidelines, supra* note 4, at pt. II, art. 3 (stating the government will thwart any attempt to undermine the unity of Jerusalem).

11. *See* John Quigley, *Sovereignty in Jerusalem,* 45 CATH. U. L. REV. 765, 780 (1996).

12. *See* Israel-Palestine Liberation Organization: Declaration of Principles on

I. BACKGROUND

A. ISRAELI LAW, INTERNATIONAL LAW AND EAST JERUSALEM SINCE 1967

East Jerusalem was captured by the Israeli armed forces when they conquered the West Bank and Gaza Strip in the Arab-Israeli war of June 1967 (See Map I).[13] Immediately following the hostilities, Moshe Dayan, then Israeli Defense Minister, proclaimed that "[t]he Israeli Defense Forces have liberated Jerusalem. We have reunited the torn city, the capital of Israel . . . never to part from it again."[14]

Thereafter, on June 27, 1967, the Israeli government passed the Law and Administration Ordinance (Amendment No. 11) Law, which provided for the extension of its law, jurisdiction, and admini-

---

Interim Self-Government Arrangements, Sept. 13, 1993, 32 I.L.M. 1525 (entered into force Oct. 13, 1993) [hereinafter DOP]. The Oslo Peace Process emerged out of the "historic" pronouncement of the DOP, concluded on Sept. 13, 1993, between Israel and the PLO, in Washington, D.C. *See id.* Under the DOP, Israel and the PLO agreed to bring the conflict between their peoples to an end through a series of 'interim negotiations' and 'agreements' in preparation for a permanent settlement of the conflict that was to be reached no later than five years after the signing of the Gaza-Jericho Agreement. *Id.* Although permanent status negotiations were initially opened on May 4, 1996, they were almost immediately thereafter brought to a standstill by the Israeli government. *Id.* On September 13, 1999, six years to the day after the signing of the DOP, the permanent status negotiations were re-opened by the parties, but have yet to produce any concrete results. *Id.* To date, several interim agreements have been concluded. *See, e.g.,* Protocol on Economic Relations, Israel-Palestine Liberation Organization Agreement on the Gaza Strip and the Jericho Area, Apr. 29, 1994, 33 I.L.M. 696 (forming Annex IV of the Gaza-Jericho agreement); Israel Palestine Liberation Organization: Agreement on the Gaza Strip and the Jericho Area, May 4, 1994, 33 I.L.M. 622; Israel-Palestine Liberation Organization: Agreement on Preparatory Powers and Responsibilities, Aug. 29, 1994, 34 I.L.M. 455; Israel-Palestine Liberation Organization: Interim Agreement on the West Bank and Gaza Strip, Sept. 28, 1995, 36 I.L.M. 551; Israel-Palestine Liberation Organization: Agreement on the Temporary International Presence in the City of Hebron, Jan. 21, 1997, 36 I.L.M. 547; Israel-Palestine Liberation Organization: Protocol Concerning the Redeployment in Hebron, Jan. 17, 1997, 36 I.L.M. 650; Israel-Palestine Liberation Organization: Wye River Memorandum, Oct. 23, 1998, 37 I.L.M. 1251; *Israel-Palestine Liberation Organization: Sharm El-Sheikh Memorandum,* 38 I.L.M. 1465.

13. *See* Quigley, *supra* note 11, at 772-74 (discussing Israel's taking of the West Bank from Jordan and the Gaza Strip from Egypt).

14. *See The Status of Jerusalem, supra* note 4, at 14.

stration to newly captured Arab East Jerusalem.[15] The next day the Israeli government enacted the Municipalities Ordinance (Amendment No. 6) Law, which authorized the Interior Minster to unilaterally enlarge the municipal boundaries of East Jerusalem "at his discretion and without an inquiry" into any impact it may have on the indigenous Palestinian populace.[16] Armed with this broad power, the minister proceeded to enlarge East Jerusalem's 6.5 square kilometer land area to encompass 71 square kilometers of expropriated Palestinian land (See Map II).[17] Subsequently, the Israeli government amalgamated the newly expanded East Jerusalem with West Jerusalem,[18] and, on June 29, 1967, the Assistant Israeli Commander of Jerusalem, Yaacov Salman, issued an order dissolving the twelve-member elected Arab Municipal Council of East Jerusalem, including its duly elected mayor, Mr. Rawhi al-Khatib.[19]

In the years that followed, both the General Assembly and Security Council of the United Nations ("U.N.") issued numerous resolutions declaring Israel's annexation of East Jerusalem to be contrary to international law, specifically the Fourth Geneva Convention Relative to the Protection of Civilian Persons in Time of War.[20] For instance, in Resolution 2253 (ES–V) of July 4, 1967, the General Assembly declared all "measures taken by Israel to change the status of

---

15. 21 L.S.I. 75 (1967).

16. 21 L.S.I. 75 (1967).

17. *See* ALLISON B. HODGKINS, THE JUDAIZATION OF JERUSALEM 6 (Palestinian Academic Society for the Study of International Affairs) (1996) (stating that the purpose of this exception of municipal Jerusalem was to include the maximum contiguous territory with the minimum non-Jewish population into Jerusalem's boundaries).

18. *See* Quigley, *supra* note 11, at 775.

19. *See* DOCUMENTS ON JERUSALEM, *supra* note 1, at 100 (setting forth the order dissolving the Jerusalem municipality).

20. *See* Aug. 12, 1949, 75 U.N.T.S. 287 (ratified by Israel, 6 July 1981). *See generally* S.C. Res. 267, U.N. SCOR, 24th Sess., U.N. Doc. S/INF/24/Rev.1 (1969); S.C. Res. 298, U.N. SCOR, 34th Sess., U.N. Doc. S/10338/Rev.1 (1971); S.C. Res. 478, U.N. SCOR, 35th Sess., U.N. Doc. S/14113 (1980); G.A. Res. 35/169E, U.N. GAOR, 35th Sess., U.N. Doc. A/35/L.42/Rev.1 (1980); G.A. Res. 41/162C, U.N. GAOR, 41st Sess., U.N. Doc. A/41/L.45, addendum pt. 1 (1986); G.A. Res. 49/36B, U.N. GAOR, 49th Sess., U.N. Doc. A/49/49 (1995); G.A. Res. ES-10, U.N. GAOR, 10th Emer. Sess., U.N. Doc. A/ES–10/L.5/Rev.1 (1999).

the City" to be "invalid,"[21] and in Resolution 252 of May 21, 1968, the Security Council proclaimed that "all legislative and administrative measures and actions taken by Israel ... which tend to change the legal status of Jerusalem are invalid and cannot change that status."[22] Notwithstanding these clear expressions of international opposition, however, Israeli authorities continued to implement policies designed to integrate Arab East Jerusalem with Jewish West Jerusalem, remaining unequivocally of the opinion that this process "was irreversible and not negotiable."[23]

The high-water mark of Israeli legislative attempts to consolidate this "unification" policy came with the passing of the so-called "Basic Law" on Jerusalem on July 30, 1980.[24] According to this law, "united" Jerusalem was declared to be the eternal capital of the State of Israel. Much like its reaction following the passing of the Law and Administration Ordinance (Amendment No. 11) Law and the Municipalities Ordinance (Amendment No. 6) Law in 1967, the international community reacted quickly to condemn the State of Israel through Resolution 478.[25]

In this Resolution, the U.N. Security Council affirmed the principle of the inadmissibility of the acquisition of territory by war and the continued applicability of the Fourth Geneva Convention[26] to "Palestinian and other Arab territories occupied since June 1967, *including Jerusalem*" [emphasis added]. It further declared that "the enactment of the 'basic law' by Israel" constituted "a violation of international law" and was "null and void and must be rescinded forthwith."[27] Again, the State of Israel chose to ignore this clear

---

21. *See* G.A. Res. 2253 (ES–V), U.N. GAOR, 22d Sess., Supp. No. 1, U.N. Doc. A/6789 (1967).

22. *See* S.C. Res. 252, U.N. SCOR, 23d Sess., U.N. Doc. S/8590/Rev.2 (1968) (calling upon Israel to rescind measures already taken and to desist from taking any further action that would change Jerusalem's status).

23. *See The Status of Jerusalem, supra* note 4, at 15.

24. *See Basic Law: Jerusalem, Capital of Israel* 34 L.S.I. 209 (1980).

25. *See* S.C. Res. 478, U.N. SCOR, 35th Sess., U.N. Doc. S/14113 (1980) (censuring Israel's enactment of its "basic law" on Jerusalem and the refusal to comply with relevant security council resolutions).

26. *See* Aug. 12, 1949, 75 U.N.T.S. 287.

27. *See* S.C. Res. 478, U.N. SCOR, 35th Sess., U.N. Doc. S/14113 (Aug. 19,

demonstration of international resolve and continued to pursue policies aimed at annexing occupied East Jerusalem to its larger Jerusalem Municipality. Contrary to what many hoped, the signing of the
Oslo peace accords did not dampen Israel's insistence on maintaining its program of forced demographic and geographic re-
engineering of the city. On the contrary, despite its agreement to refrain from initiating "any step that will change the status of the West
Bank and Gaza Strip" during the interim phase of negotiations with
the PLO,[28] since 1993, Israeli policies aimed at altering the status of
Jerusalem have been pursued at an unprecedented pace and scope,
resulting in even further displacement and dispossession of the city's
Palestinian inhabitants. This situation has impelled the General Assembly to continue its condemnation of Israel's annexation policies
in Jerusalem as "illegal," "null and void," and having "no validity
whatsoever."[29]

As will be illustrated below, "the strategies for ensuring" the Jewish State's national/political objectives in Jerusalem were, and have
continued to be, "developed and enacted on the municipal level."[30]
For this reason, it is important to examine Israeli municipal govern-

---

1980) (expressing concern over the enactment of a "basic law" in the Knesset declaring a change in the character and statute of Jerusalem).

28. *See Israel-Palestine Liberation Organization: Interim Agreement on the
West Bank and Gaza Strip*, Sept. 28, 1995, 36 I.L.M. 551, at art. 31(7) (stating that
the two sides view the West Bank and Gaza Strip as a single territorial unit, and its
integrity and status will be preserved during the interim period).

29. *See, e.g.,* G.A. Res. 49/87A, U.N. GAOR, 49th Sess., U.N. Doc. A/49/49
(1995); G.A. Res. 50/22A, U.N. GAOR, 50th Sess., U.N. Doc. A/50/L.37, addendum pt.1 (1995); G.A. Res. 51/27, U.N. GAOR, 51st Sess., U.N. Doc. A/51/49
(1996); G.A. Res. ES-10/2, U.N. GAOR, 10th Emer. Sess., U.N. Doc. A/RES/ES-
10/2 (1997) (discussing illegal Israeli actions in occupied East Jerusalem and the
rest of the occupied Palestinian territory); G.A. Res. ES-10/3, U.N. GAOR, 10th
Emergency Special Sess., U.N. Doc. A/RES/ES-10/3 (1997); G.A. Res. ES-10/4,
U.N. GAOR, 10th Emer. Sess., U.N. Doc. A/RES/ES-10/4 (1997) (reiterating the
demands made in resolutions ES-10/2 and ES-10/3); G.A. Res. 52/53, U.N.
GAOR, 52d Sess., U.N. Doc. A/RES/52/53 (1997); G.A. Res. ES-10/5, U.N.
GAOR, 10th Emer. Sess., U.N. Doc. A/RES/ES-10/5 (1998) (reaffirming its reso-
lutions ES-10/2, ES-10/3, and ES-10/4); G.A. Res. ES-10, U.N. GAOR, 10th
Emer. Sess., U.N. Doc. A/ES-10/L.5/Rev.1 (1999) (reiterating its condemnation of
the failure of the Israeli government to comply with the provisions of resolutions
ES-10/2, ES-10/3, and ES-10/4, and ES-10/5).

30. *See* HODGKINS, *supra* note 17, at 15 (asserting that the municipality is the
"engine driving the incorporation of East Jerusalem into Israel proper").

ment policies in East Jerusalem.

B. ISRAELI MUNICIPAL POLICY IN EAST JERUSALEM

Since 1967, Israeli municipal policy in East Jerusalem "has been dominated by one overriding purpose: to secure and maintain exclusive Israeli sovereignty over all parts of the city."[31] To this end, municipal governance is primarily concerned with the dual policy goals of achieving a decisive demographic superiority of Jews over Palestinians in the city[32]—historically, a central tenet of Zionist colonial policy for the whole of Palestine—and maintaining its geographic integrity as one single and indivisible administrative unit."

During his twenty-six year tenure as mayor, Kollek emerged as the chief architect of the Jewish State's municipal policy in Jerusalem. According to Allison Hodgkins ("Hodgkins"), "the Kollek municipality pursued planning policies intended to cut Greater Jerusalem [i.e. expanded East Jerusalem] off from the West Bank and facilitate its easy annexation into Israel proper."[34] It was under his administration that the long-held Israeli policies of Jewish settlement and land expropriation were cemented to transform Palestinian East Jerusalem into "a city that would largely be[come] Jewish."[35] Because "demography was a key element in the perceived imbalance between Jewish and 'non-Jewish' residents of the city," Kollek continually insisted that "making the city more conducive to Jewish settlement" would be the only effective policy course if the broader national goal of entrenching exclusive Israeli sovereignty was to be realized.[36] With this policy in mind, "Kollek era planners set [out] to fill" expanded East Jerusalem "with Jewish facts" in the form of exclusively Jewish settlements built, in the main, on illegally expropriated Palestinian land."[37] Invariably, "Kollek's municipality" pursued this policy so that

---

31. *See id.* at 20 (explaining Israel's policy goals for Jerusalem).

32. *See* SHARKANSKY, *supra* note 2, at 21.

33. *See* HODGKINS, *supra* note 17, at 19.

34. *See id.* at 15.

35. *See* SHARKANSKY, *supra* note 2, at 21.

36. *See* HODGKINS, *supra* note 17, at 17.

37. *See id.* at 17-18.

"united" Jerusalem would "be difficult to take apart" in the future.[18]

For the most part, throughout Kollek's term, he was concerned with publicizing his municipal policies as "benevolent and democratic."[39] As part of this strategy, it was Kollek who coined the idea that Jerusalem was an "ethnic and cultural mosaic" belonging equally to all of its inhabitants, both Jews and Arabs.[40] As noted earlier, this image of Jerusalem was designed to present the Israeli municipality as being truly concerned with the well being of the city's Palestinian inhabitants. Nevertheless, as pointed out by former Israeli municipal planner Sara Kaminker—and as betrayed by Kollek's very own words quoted at the outset of this Essay—the "mosaic" epithet was little more than "a beautiful marketing ploy for selling segregation."[41]

The current Israeli mayor of Jerusalem, Ehud Olmert ("Olmert"), ousted Kollek from office in 1993 but continued to effectuate the policies developed over the course of Kollek's long career. Thus, from the very outset of his administration, Olmert declared his intent to "make things happen on the ground to ensure the city will remain under Israeli sovereignty for eternity."[42] Supported unconditionally by the national governments of the late Prime Minister Yitzhak Rabin, former Prime Ministers Shimon Peres and Benjamin Netanyahu, and the current Prime Minister Ehud Barak, Olmert has unabashedly pursued the same dual policy objectives in East Jerusalem that were established by his predecessor: namely, achieving demographic superiority and maintaining geographic integrity. As noted by former Israeli municipal planner Yisrael Kimchi, "there is no tangible difference between Kollek and Olmert" with respect to their policies on East Jerusalem.[43] Both desired to sever the city from its natural West Bank hinterland, and at the same time infuse it with

---

38. *See* SHARKANSKY, *supra* note 2, at 142.

39. *See* HODGKINS, *supra* note 17, at 18.

40. *See* KHADER ABUSWAY ET AL., SIGNED, SEALED, DELIVERED: ISRAELI SETTLEMENT AND THE PEACE PROCESS 25 (1997) (analyzing Kollek's municipal policies).

41. *See* HODGKINS, *supra* note 17, at 18.

42. *See* KAREN ARMSTRONG, JERUSALEM: ONE CITY, THREE FAITHS 418 (1996) (noting that Olmert has no need to woo Israeli liberals).

43. *See* HODGKINS, *supra* note 17, at 20.

Israeli-Jewish settlers to manipulate its demographic character in a manner favorable to the Jewish State.

In sum, it must be understood that since taking control of East Jerusalem in 1967, successive Israeli municipal administrations in Jerusalem have sought to entrench their hold on the city through the promulgation of a "broad series of policy initiatives" designed "to create irreversible facts on the ground."[44] With respect to the Israeli government's current commitment to negotiate the final status of Jerusalem under the framework of the Oslo peace process, the Israeli Deputy Defense Minister recently expressed his opinion that the "consolidation of the existing territorial continuity [of the city] through [the] expansion of settlements as well as [the] construction of roads, tunnels and bridges and further land acquisition" must all "be presented in the future negotiations as a geographic fact" if Israel is to retain exclusive control over the city.[45] Although briefly alluded to above, the following section will explore in greater detail the principle methods by which Israeli municipal authorities in Jerusalem have pursued this policy of creating a *fait accompli* in the city.

II. FACTS ON THE GROUND: ISRAELI MUNICIPAL ACTIVITY IN EAST JERUSALEM

Since 1967, Israeli municipal planners in East Jerusalem have devised and implemented a host of mechanisms designed to manipulate land use and demography to ensure that the city remains under exclusive Israeli control in the future. As previously noted, the international community has declared Israel's use of these mechanisms to be illegal under international law.[46] The following is a brief examination of just six of these methods, and the practical impact they have had on the indigenous Palestinian residents of occupied East Jerusalem.

---

44. *See id.* at 21.

45. *See The Status of Jerusalem, supra* note 4, at 23.

46. *See* S.C. Res. 252, U.N. SCOR, 23d Sess., U.N. Doc. S/8590/Rev. 2 (1968); S.C. Res. 478, U.N. SCOR, 35th Sess., U.N. Doc. S/14113 (1980) (demonstrating that the U.N. and the international community have consistently condemned Israel's efforts to retain control of East Jerusalem).

A. EXPROPRIATION OF PALESTINIAN LAND

It will be recalled that immediately following the conquest of East Jerusalem in 1967, Israeli authorities unilaterally expanded the municipal boundaries of the occupied city from 6.5 square kilometers to 71 square kilometers—an increase of approximately eleven times the city's original size (See Map II).[47] "[T]hese new boundaries became the framework within which the Israeli government would alter the existing layout of the city . . . in an attempt to physically secure their control over" it.[48] As early as 1968, Israeli municipal authorities recognized that if expanded Arab East Jerusalem was to be converted into a Jewish city, the expropriation of Palestinian land would be imperative. According to the Jerusalem Master Plan of 1968:

> The majority of the [expanded] municipal land reserves that are amenable to [Israeli-Jewish] development are in private [Palestinian] hands. The effective development of the city will require the expropriation of substantial areas [emphasis added].[49]

With this strategic principle in mind, Israeli municipal planning committees set out to develop and effectuate a mass expropriation policy aimed at divesting Palestinian owners of vast tracts of land in expanded East Jerusalem for exclusive Jewish use.[50] Over the course of Israel's thirty-two year occupation of the city, this policy has taken shape in five separate stages and accounted for the expropriation of over 60,000 dunums of Palestinian land without compensation.[51] Altogether, this amounts to approximately 86.5 percent of the land area of East Jerusalem as defined by the city's expanded mu-

---

47. *See* HODGKINS, *supra* note 17, at 6 (documenting the expansion of Jerusalem's municipal boundaries in 1967).

48. *See id.* at 22.

49. *See* ETAN FELNER, A POLICY OF DISCRIMINATION: LAND EXPROPRIATION, PLANNING, AND BUILDING IN EAST JERUSALEM 30 (1995), *quoting* 1 JERUSALEM MASTER PLAN (1968).

50. *See* HODGKINS, *supra* note 17, at 22-23 (documenting the strategic zoning and planning practices of Israel to block Palestinian development).

51. *See The Status of Jerusalem, supra* note 4, at 22-23 (recounting the history of Israel's expropriation of Palestinian land; one dunum is approximately equal to one thousand square meters or 0.274 acres).

nicipal boundaries.[52]

Because Israel emerged the victor in the June 1967 war, it could have conceivably acquired all of East Jerusalem's land through force of arms. However, as pointed out by Hodgkins, "the desire to foster international legitimacy for their claims prompted [the Israelis] to use what they defined as legal methods of transferring Arab lands to Jewish ownership."[53] Although the majority of these "legal" methods were orders issued by local military commanders, Israeli municipal authorities in East Jerusalem relied quite heavily on these methods to acquire Palestinian land for exclusive Jewish use. For example, Military Order No. 70 (1967) allows the authorities to declare any portion of East Jerusalem land a "closed military area," thereby prohibiting anyone other than state authorities from making use of it.[54] Likewise, Military Order No. 150 (1968) allows a body known as the Israeli Custodian of Absentee Property to expropriate land belonging to Palestinians who were not recorded in the official East Jerusalem census conducted by Israel following the 1967 war.[55] Under this military order, once land is declared as belonging to an "absentee," it is reverted to the Custodian of Absentee Property (i.e. the state). Similarly, Military Order 321 (1968) affords authorities the right to expropriate any tract of land required for "public" use,[56] which is "almost always synonymous with exclusive Jewish use" in the context of land expropriation.[57] Again, it is important to emphasize that although in most cases the expropriating authority is usually a state actor (as opposed to a municipal one), the Israeli municipality of Jerusalem is regularly given the power to dispose of expropriated Palestinian property as it wishes. This implied authority is consistent with the general Israeli policy that once the state acquires land it automatically becomes the "inalienable property of the Jewish peo-

---

52. *See id.*

53. *See* HODGKINS, *supra* note 17, at 25.

54. *See id.* at 79 (discussing the Israeli method of confiscating and expropriating Palestinian land).

55. *See id.*

56. *See id.*

57. *See id.* at 23.

ple" and cannot be owned or leased by a non-Jew.[58]

On June 11, 1998, in conjunction with national authorities, the Israeli municipality of Jerusalem approved a proposal to formalize what it calls the "Greater Jerusalem Plan."[59] Under this plan, the current municipal boundaries of the city are to be expanded to include "approximately 10 percent of the land area of the West Bank" (See Map III).[60] Invariably, tens of thousands of dunums of more Palestinian land will be expropriated to impose more "facts on the ground" that will transform the demographic and geographic character of the area even further, thereby consolidating the Jewish State's exclusive "sovereignty" over the whole of the city.

B. THE IMPOSITION OF JEWISH SETTLEMENTS

Since the city's occupation began, "the key element" of Israeli municipal planning in East Jerusalem "has been the construction of more than 15 [Jewish] settlements in and around the boundaries ille-

---

58. *See* Atef Kubrusi, *An Economic Assessment of Total Palestinian Losses,* in SAMI HADAWI, PALESTINIAN RIGHTS AND LOSSES IN 1948: A COMPREHENSIVE STUDY 117-188 (1998) (documenting a consistent pattern of Zionist policies by Israel preventing the owning and leasing of land by non-Jews). Article 3 of the Constitution of the Jewish Agency provides that:

> (d) [l]and is to be acquired *as Jewish property* and subject to the provisions of Article 10 of this Agreement, the title to the lands acquired is to be taken in the name of the Jewish National Fund, to the end that the same shall be held as the *inalienable property of the Jewish people.*

Id. (emphasis added).

Likewise, Article 23 of the lease provisions of the Jewish National Fund provide, in part that:

> [T]he lessee undertakes [that]. . .*the holding shall never be held by any but a Jew.* If the holder, being a Jew, leaves as his heir a non-Jew, the Fund shall obtain the right of restitution. Prior to the enforcement of the right of restitution, the Fund must give the heir three months notice, within which period the heir shall transfer his rights to a Jew, otherwise the Fund may enforce the right of restitution and the heir may not oppose such enforcement.

Id. (emphasis added).

59. *See generally* MUNA HAMZEH-MUHAISEN, *Preempting Jerusalem,* 3 JERUSALEM QUARTERLY FILE (1999) (visited Jan. 18, 1999) <http://www.jqf-jerusalem.org/journal/1999/jqf3/muhaisen.html>.

60. *See The Status of Jerusalem, supra* note 4, at 23.

gally established in 1967."[61] Driven by the desire to maintain the geographic integrity of Jerusalem as a "united" city under exclusive Israeli control, these settlements are strategically arranged in locations around the northern, eastern, and southern outskirts of East Jerusalem to dismember it from its surrounding West Bank hinterland (See Map III). Benignly referred to by Israeli municipal planners as "neighborhoods," these exclusively Jewish settlements were constructed on expropriated Palestinian land, "completely alter[ing] the [geographic and demographic] landscape of East Jerusalem."[62]

Similar to the method used to expropriate Palestinian land, the construction of Jewish settlements by Israeli municipal authorities was largely accomplished in five distinct stages.[63] Today, major settlements exist at Ramat Eshkol, French Hill, Ma'aleh Dafna, Mount Scopus, Ramot, East Talpiot, Gilo, Neve Ya'acov, and Pisgat Ze'ev.[64] Together, these and other smaller settlements account for approximately 180,000 Jewish settlers[65] and comprise what is known as the "inner-ring" settlements encircling Arab East Jerusalem.[66] With the Israeli municipality's recent decision to begin construction of massive new settlements at Har Homa (indigenously known as Jabal Abu-Ghneim) and Ramat Shu'fat, the number of Jewish settlers in expanded East Jerusalem is projected to reach approximately 220,000 by the end of this year.[67] The Har Homa settlement is of particular significance because it represents the final "southern link" in the chain of inner-ring settlements surrounding the city (See Map

---

61. *See* HODGKINS, *supra* note 17, at 22.

62. *See id.* at 37.

63. *See The Status of Jerusalem, supra* note 4, at 22-23 (documenting the strategic construction of Jewish settlements).

64. *See id.* (discussing a report indicating that a majority of the Palestinian property in East Jerusalem and its surroundings were seized in five stages).

65. *See id.* at 23 (stating the number of Jewish settlers expected by the end of 1995).

66. *See* HODGKINS, *supra* note 17, at 39 (stating that the number of Jewish settlers was expected to expand by the end of the century after the status negotiations were completed).

67. *See The Status of Jerusalem, supra* note 4, at 23 (stating that the number of Jewish settlers was expected to expand by the end of the century).

III).[68]

The imposition of Jewish settlements in East Jerusalem has had a tremendous impact on the demographic composition of the city.[69] "Whereas in 1967 there were no Jews in East Jerusalem, in July 1993, the Government announced that it had achieved a Jewish majority there (160,000 Jews to 155,000 Palestinians)".[70] Since the establishment of Israel's Inter-ministerial Committee to Examine the Rate of Development in Jerusalem in 1973,[71] it has been a policy objective of successive Israeli municipal planners to maintain the population ratio in Jerusalem at approximately 78 percent Jews to 22 percent Palestinians.[72] Moreover, the recent approval of the Greater Jerusalem Plan will only serve to increase Jewish numbers in the expanded city, as the scheme calls for the absorption of four of the largest settlements in the Jerusalem area—Giv'at Ze'ev in the north, Ma'ale Adumim in the east, and Betar and Efrat in the south, collectively known as the "outer-ring" settlements (See Map III).[73]

To make rapid occupancy of the settlements possible, Israeli municipal planners and other governmental authorities have devised a number of substantial economic incentives aimed at attracting Jewish citizens to establish roots in East Jerusalem.[74] For example, new Jewish settlers are exempt from paying the amona, the principal municipal tax, for a period of five years from the date of settlement, after which time they are assessed at a reduced rate.[75] Furthermore,

---

68. *See id.* (discussing the United Nations' inability to stop the construction of Har Homa settlement, which created great concern over the future of Arab East Jerusalem).

69. *See id.* (arguing that the increasing number of Jewish settlers in Arab neighborhoods has disturbed Palestinian residents of East Jerusalem).

70. *See id.* at 25.

71. *See* HODGKINS, *supra* note 17, at 46 (stating that the committee determined that it was important for Jerusalem's future to ensure "the relative proportion of Jews and Arabs [in Jerusalem] as it was at the end of 1972").

72. *See The Status of Jerusalem, supra* note 4, at 25 (stating that after 1967, there was an increase of Jewish settlers in East Jerusalem).

73. *See* HAMZEH-MUHAISEN, *supra* note 59 (discussing the Israeli government's plan of settlement expansion and land confiscation).

74. *See* ABUSWAY ET AL., *supra* note 40, at 38 (discussing Israeli settlement strategies to attract Jewish settlers to East Jerusalem).

75. S. Kaminker, "Housing and Community Development Through Land Rec-

since 1967, over 70,000 Jewish settler families in the city have been provided with subsidized housing by the national government.[75] Similarly, in 1990, under the title of "On the Way to a Jewish Majority in Jerusalem," the government approved a plan that offered a 100 percent guarantee against losses incurred by contractors willing to construct settlements for new Jewish immigrants from the former Soviet Union.[77]

In what has been described as a "classic example of racial gerrymandering,"[78] the highly efficient manner in which Israeli municipal planners have constructed and populated illegal Jewish settlements in occupied East Jerusalem has been the single most important factor in the realization of the broader policy goal of ensuring that the city remains under exclusive Israeli control in the future.

C. ZONING PALESTINIAN LANDS AS "GREEN AREAS"

In addition to the expropriation methods outlined above, Israeli municipal officials are also exercising their planning authority to impose severe restrictions on Palestinian land use to eventually transfer such land to Jewish ownership.[79] Since 1967, one of the most popular forms of this type of land use restriction has been the so-called "green area" zoning designation.[80] Under this planning scheme, Israeli municipal authorities may zone any unexpropriated tract of Palestinian land as a "green area," effectively restricting it to agricul-

---

lamation" in M. Kothari and J. Abu-Shakrah, *Planned Dispossession: Palestinians, East Jerusalem and the Right to a Place to Live* (Geneva: COHRE, Occasional Paper No. 4, 1995) at 8.

76. *See id.* at 9.

77. *See* HODGKINS, *supra* note 17, at 48 (stating that in 1990, the Ministerial Immigration Committee objected to plans to provide housing for Soviet Union immigrants in Jerusalem).

78. *See id.* at 6.

79. *See* R. SHEHADEH, OCCUPIERS LAW: ISRAEL AND THE WEST BANK 217 (Institute for Palestine Studies, 1985) (discussing how the Antiquities Department has extensive powers to impose severe restrictions on land use based on archeological considerations).

80. *See* HODGKINS, *supra* note 17, at 26 (discussing Israel's tools for blocking Palestinian land development).

tural and other forms of agrarian use.[81] Although these zoned areas are theoretically "to be planted and to serve as public open spaces . . . in reality this designation is used to block Palestinian development" of lands desired by the municipality for future Jewish settlement.[82] The idea is to ensure that such lands remain free and clear of any physical impediments, such as Arab homes or buildings, which would make Jewish settlement construction difficult if and when expropriation decisions are finally made. In this manner, Israeli municipal planners have stunted the natural growth and development of East Jerusalem's Palestinian community to acquire more land to build future Jewish settlements.

The following two examples serve as good illustrations of how this process actually takes shape on the ground. In 1968, approximately 2000 dunums of Palestinian owned land in the East Jerusalem village of Shu'fat were designated as a "green area." Under this designation, the land was sowed with cypress seedlings and left undisturbed for twenty-six years. In 1994, the restrictive zoning was "suddenly changed" by the municipal government, which subsequently issued expropriation orders for it and proceeded to authorize the construction of Reches Shufaat, a new settlement for religious Jews.[83] Similarly, in 1968, a further 2000 dunums of Palestinian land at Jabal Abu-Ghneim on the southern outskirts of East Jerusalem were zoned as a "green area" by the Israeli municipality. Like the lands in Shu'fat, these tracts were left undeveloped for over two decades. Subsequently, in 1991, Israeli municipal authorities informed the Palestinian owners of the lifted "green area" designation and that the land would be expropriated to begin construction of the Jewish settlement of Har Homa (See Map III).[84]

---

81. *See id.* (defining "green areas" as Palestinian land where any development other than agriculture is strictly prohibited).

82. *See id.* at 27.

83. *See id.* (discussing how zoning laws changed and how, as a result, a new neighborhood for religious Jews was built).

84. *See id.* (stating that some tracts of land between Bethlehem and Jerusalem were zoned as green areas but were later made available for municipality construction).

D. TOWN PLANNING SCHEMES

The Town Planning Scheme ("TPS") is another effective tool utilized by Israeli municipal authorities to restrict Palestinian development in East Jerusalem.[85] As in most urban centers, TPSs (or documents similar to them) are required by the municipality in order to "supervise the development of an area in accordance with its zoning designation, expected population growth, housing needs, and infrastructure requirements."[86] In Jerusalem, it is impossible to acquire a development permit for an area that does not have a TPS approved by the Israeli municipal authorities.[87] The municipality's overarching desire to cement Israel's exclusive control over the occupied city dominates the TPS procedure in East Jerusalem because the main purpose of the process is to ensure that areas are developed in accordance with "the overall planning goals of the municipality."[88] As such, the needs of its Palestinian residents are simply not figured into planning considerations.[89]

For instance, because the TPS is an expensive ten-step process that "requires a high level of coordination and cooperation with the municipal authorities,"[90] (See Appendix) the Israeli government regularly provides Jewish settlers in East Jerusalem with substantial resources to put TPSs together, including the allocation of funds and the contracting of urban planners and architects.[91] With respect to development proposals for East Jerusalem's Arab neighborhoods, however, "all costs and resources needed to draw up a TPS fall on the

---

85. *See* Y. Stein, *The Quiet Deportation: Revocation of Residency of East Jerusalem Palestinians* (Jerusalem: The Israeli Information Center for Human Rights in the Occupied Territories, 1997) at 8 (discussing how planning schemes restrict the development of Palestinian neighborhoods).

86. *See* HODGKINS, *supra* note 17, at 29.

87. *See id.* (discussing how the TPS is used as a means of restricting development in Palestinian areas).

88. *See id.* at 30.

89. *See* Stein, *supra* note 85, at 8 (stating that planning schemes are primarily based on national and political considerations rather than on Palestinian needs).

90. *See* HODGKINS, *supra* note 17, at 29.

91. *See id.* at 30 (discussing how the Israeli government has the responsibility for re-parceling land).

Palestinians themselves."[92] As a result, the TPS process has proved to be an economic and bureaucratic obstacle for Palestinians, while at the same time "an efficient and successful exercise in urban planning" for Jewish settlers.[93] This is highlighted by the fact that over the past twenty-one years, Palestinian neighborhoods in East Jerusalem have received approval for only thirteen TPSs.[94]

Even where approved, the Israeli municipality has "invariably delayed and/or dramatically minimized TPSs for Palestinian neighborhoods."[95] For instance, although municipal authorities are legally required to issue a decision on TPSs within three years of an application, it took thirteen years for the Palestinian town of Shu'fat to be approved in 1996. Additionally, the plan called for the construction of 17,000 housing units, however, under the directive of Israeli Interior Minster Eli Suissa, the plan was eventually pared down to a mere 500 units.[96] Likewise, "[p]lanning procedures which began in Beit Safafa in 1977 also took 13 years to reach approval in 1990," plans "in Abu Tor took 12 years and a plan submitted in 1987 for Ras al-Amud has not [yet] received final approval."[97]

Not surprisingly, the TPS process profoundly impacts Palestinian growth and development in East Jerusalem, most notably with respect to housing shortages. As noted by a U.N. report, "since 1967 Israel has constructed dwelling space for 70,000 Jewish families on expropriated Arab land in East Jerusalem, and only 555 dwelling units for its Palestinian residents."[98] The same report noted that onerous municipal policies "and land use restrictions resulted in a situation in which at least 21,000 Palestinian families were practically homeless and had to live in tents and hovels, or share with other

---

92. *See id.*

93. *See id.*

94. *See id.*, at 31 (stating that since 1978, only 13 plans "have been approved which have any bearing on Palestinian neighborhoods").

95. *See id.*

96. *See id.* (noting the decrease in Palestinian housing units from 17,000 to 500 units).

97. *See id.* at 31-32.

98. *See The Status of Jerusalem, supra* note 4, at 25.

families."[99] When confronted with statistics similar to these during an examination of a TPS for the Palestinian villages of Um Tuba and Sur Baher, Israeli municipal sub-committee member, Elinor Barazaki, summed up the opinion of the municipality succinctly:

> There is a government decision to maintain the proportion between the Arab [minority] and Jewish [majority] populations in the city. . . The only way to cope with that ratio is through the housing potential. The growth potential is defined on this basis and the [housing] capacity is a function of that here as well.[100]

E. DEMOLITION OF PALESTINIAN HOMES

Because of the Israeli municipality's massive expropriation campaigns, onerous land use restrictions, and discriminatory planning schemes, many Palestinian landowners are forced to build houses without permits only to later face demolition orders.[101] Knowing that its policies have directly caused the overcrowding and severe housing shortages in Palestinian neighborhoods, Israeli municipal authorities in East Jerusalem have observed a policy of demolishing Palestinian homes constructed without the required building permit or built on land not zoned for residential use (i.e. "green areas").[102]

What makes this practice most unpalatable, aside from its obvious human rights implications, is the fact that the Israeli municipality publicizes its activity as redressing the consequences of "illegal" Palestinian construction, despite the fact that it is an agent of a state that is illegally occupying Arab East Jerusalem.[103] This political whitewash is what has allowed municipal officials to destroy an average of fifty East Jerusalem Palestinian homes per year between

---

99. *See id.*

100. *See* HODGKINS, *supra* note 17, at 34 (alterations added) (quoting Minutes of the Subcommittee Meeting for Planning and Building, Feb. 22, 1993).

101. *See* HAMZEH-MUHAISEN, *supra* note 59 (discussing the effects of restrictive zoning laws on the Palestinian population).

102. *See* HODGKINS, *supra* note 17, at 35 (reporting on the frequency of housing demolitions in East Jerusalem).

103. *See* M. Klein "Only Jewish Homes Destroy Peace" JERUSALEM POST [NORTH AMERICAN EDITION] (Apr. 16, 1999) at 11; *see also* SHARKANSKY, *supra* note 2, at 104 (citing issues surrounding Palestinian construction).

1986 and 1996.[104] Moreover, the Oslo peace process has not put an end to this practice. In fact, between 1993 and 1995, the Israeli municipality destroyed ninety-seven Palestinian homes,[105] and recently Olmert launched a massive campaign to demolish the homes of 2,600 East Jerusalem Palestinians who, according to his records, have built "illegally."[106]

F. REVOCATION OF PALESTINIAN RESIDENCY RIGHTS

Along with mechanisms designed to alter the geo-physical status of Jerusalem, since 1967, the Israeli Interior Ministry has actively sought to reduce the number of Palestinians in Jerusalem by employing "a series of discriminatory bureaucratic methods" that effectively operate to deport them from the city.[107]

Following Israel's conquest and annexation of the city, "Palestinians living within the municipal boundaries, as subsequently expanded, were classified as permanent residents of the State"[108]—not as Israeli citizens—under the Law of Entry into Israel (1952).[109] Thus, although it was the Jewish State that "entered" the city through military conquest, Israeli law treats Palestinian Jerusalemites as though they are "immigrants residing in their homes pursuant to the beneficence of Israel and not by right."[110] According to Regulation 11(c) of the Entry into Israel Regulations, "a permanent residency permit expires if the holder leaves Israel and settles in another country."[111] Regulation 11A of the same regulations, provides that "a person will be considered to have settled in a foreign country if he or she: (1) lived for more than seven years in a foreign country; (2) re-

---

104. *See* HODGKINS, *supra* note 17, at 35 (highlighting the number of housing demolitions in East Jerusalem).

105. *See id.* (reporting housing demolition statistics).

106. *See* HAMZEH-MUHAISEN, *supra* note 59 (emphasizing the Palestinian housing dilemma in Jerusalem).

107. *See* HODGKINS, *supra* note 17, at 51 (explaining measures taken by Israel in order to maintain the desired demographic ratio); *see also* Stein, *supra* note 85.

108. *See The Status of Jerusalem, supra* note 4, at 26.

109. *See* HODGKINS, *supra* note 17, at 52 (examining Israeli policy on Palestinian residency).

110. *See* Stein, *supra* note 85, at 7.

111. *See id.* at 6.

city.[119] Moreover, because Israeli authorities routinely apply an excessively high threshold with respect to the "center of life" standard, more often than not, Palestinian Jerusalemites are unable to prove to the Interior Minister that they in fact live in Jerusalem, and are, therefore, stripped of their right to remain there.[120]

Finally, because permanent residency rights do not automatically extend to the family of permanent residents, "Palestinian Jerusalemites marrying spouses from the rest of the Occupied Territories [or elsewhere] must apply for Family Reunification to legally reside together in Jerusalem."[121] Much like the process of gaining approval on a TPS for a Palestinian neighborhood, applications for family reunification notoriously take several years to process before a decision is reached.[122] As a result, Palestinian families are usually left with two alternatives: they may either live separately with the unrealistic hope that their application will be accepted swiftly or they may leave the city to live together. Obviously, if they choose to leave, the family will loose its residency rights in Jerusalem by virtue of Israel's "center of life" policy.[123]

Since its conquest of East Jerusalem in 1967, Israeli authorities have revoked the residency rights of over 4,000 Palestinian families.[124] Because of the severe housing shortage affecting Palestinians in Jerusalem—itself a consequence of Israeli settlement and discriminatory land use policies—nearly 12,000 Palestinian Jerusalemites currently live outside of the municipal boundaries of the city, and are, therefore, subject to having their residency rights revoked.[125] As with Israel's policies on land confiscation, Jewish settlement, and Palestinian development, its systematic campaign of revoking Palestinian residency rights in Jerusalem has been carefully designed to

---

119. *See id.* at 20.

120. *See id..*

121. HODGKINS, *supra* note 17, at 52-53 (alteration added).

122. *See* Stein, *supra* note 85, at 9.

123. *See id.* at 10.

124. *See* BADIL, *Confiscation of Palestinian Jerusalem I.D. Cards* (visited Feb. 24, 1999) <http://www.badil.org/resident/resstats.htm>.

125. *See* HODGKINS, *supra* note 17, at 54 (discussing the "center of life" requirement).

city.[119] Moreover, because Israeli authorities routinely apply an excessively high threshold with respect to the "center of life" standard, more often than not, Palestinian Jerusalemites are unable to prove to the Interior Minister that they in fact live in Jerusalem, and are, therefore, stripped of their right to remain there.[120]

Finally, because permanent residency rights do not automatically extend to the family of permanent residents, "Palestinian Jerusalemites marrying spouses from the rest of the Occupied Territories [or elsewhere] must apply for Family Reunification to legally reside together in Jerusalem."[121] Much like the process of gaining approval on a TPS for a Palestinian neighborhood, applications for family reunification notoriously take several years to process before a decision is reached.[122] As a result, Palestinian families are usually left with two alternatives: they may either live separately with the unrealistic hope that their application will be accepted swiftly or they may leave the city to live together. Obviously, if they choose to leave, the family will loose its residency rights in Jerusalem by virtue of Israel's "center of life" policy.[123]

Since its conquest of East Jerusalem in 1967, Israeli authorities have revoked the residency rights of over 4,000 Palestinian families.[124] Because of the severe housing shortage affecting Palestinians in Jerusalem—itself a consequence of Israeli settlement and discriminatory land use policies—nearly 12,000 Palestinian Jerusalemites currently live outside of the municipal boundaries of the city, and are, therefore, subject to having their residency rights revoked.[125] As with Israel's policies on land confiscation, Jewish settlement, and Palestinian development, its systematic campaign of revoking Palestinian residency rights in Jerusalem has been carefully designed to

---

119. *See id.* at 20.

120. *See id.*.

121. HODGKINS, *supra* note 17, at 52-53 (alteration added).

122. *See* Stein, *supra* note 85, at 9.

123. *See id.* at 10.

124. *See* BADIL, *Confiscation of Palestinian Jerusalem I.D. Cards* (visited Feb. 24, 1999) <http://www.badil.org/resident/resstats.htm>.

125. *See* HODGKINS, *supra* note 17, at 54 (discussing the "center of life" requirement).

alter the demographic composition of the city in an attempt to present a Jewish majority there as a *fait accompli* in any future final status negotiation with the PLO.

CONCLUSION

Since its "annexation of East Jerusalem in 1967, the Israeli government has adopted a policy of systematic and deliberate discrimination against the Palestinian population in [East] Jerusalem."[126] Driven by the overarching national policy of securing and maintaining exclusive Israeli control over the occupied city, Israeli municipal authorities have implemented a process designed to impose exclusively Jewish "facts on the ground" to re-engineer the city's demographic and geographic character in the Jewish State's favor. For the better part of a quarter-century, these policies were forged under the watchful eye of Kollek who viewed his role as "seeing to the Jewish majority" in the city.[127] Today, Omert, who has perfected these policies, repeatedly insists that Jerusalem must remain "the eternal" and "united" capital of Israel.[128]

Despite the fact that the international community has in no uncertain terms condemned Israeli actions in the city as constituting egregious violations of international law, municipal authorities continue to pursue planning policies designed to transform the city into the Jewish State's "undivided" capital. Some of the principal tools utilized by municipal authorities in this regard have been the wholesale expropriation of vast tracts of Palestinian land, the imposition of illegal Jewish settlements on that land, discriminatory zoning and planning processes, the demolition of "illegally" built Palestinian homes, and the revocation of Palestinian residency rights in the city.

Through its control over expropriated Palestinian lands in a grossly expanded East Jerusalem, Israeli municipal authorities have been able to impose a barrage of illegal Jewish settlements in the

---

126. *See* Stein, *supra* note 85, at 8.

127. *See* HODGKINS, *supra* note 17, at 16 (noting that in a meeting of the Jerusalem Municipality Council on January 25, 1988, Kollek made the following revealing statement about his job as mayor of the city: "I am seeing to the Jewish majority . . . that is why we are here, to see to [the Jewish majority].").

128. *See* DOCUMENTS ON JERUSALEM, *supra* note 1, at 130 (quoting Olmert's opening address to the "Jerusalem 3000" celebration).

area that have served national goals on two key levels. First, by inserting hundreds of thousands of Jewish citizens of Israel into occupied East Jerusalem, the demographic facts on the ground have been altered to the point that the city has in fact become numerically, politically, and economically dominated by a 77 percent Jewish settler majority. Second, through the strategic placement of these settlements in the form of two rings encircling East Jerusalem's northern, eastern, and southern outskirts, the city has been geographically severed from its natural West Bank hinterland, thereby helping to facilitate its physical annexation into Jewish West Jerusalem.

The onerous "green area" zoning designation and the discriminatory TPS procedure complement the foregoing. Since 1967, these restrictive land-use planning mechanisms have proved very helpful in curtailing the development of unexpropriated Palestinian lands desired by the Israeli municipality for future Jewish settlement. Because these mechanisms keep Palestinian lands undeveloped until the time is "ripe" for municipal expropriation,[129] Palestinian residents of East Jerusalem suffer from a severe overpopulation and housing crisis. In an effort to cope, Palestinians have been forced to develop their lands without proper municipal permits, and are thereby subject to the possibility of having their "illegally" built homes demolished by municipal authorities.

Finally, in yet another scheme concocted to alter the indigenous Palestinian character of East Jerusalem, Israeli municipal planners have launched a bureaucratic campaign to strip Palestinian inhabitants of the city of their rights to live there. Since 1967, thousands of Palestinian Jerusalemites have had their residency rights revoked through the use of obscure and onerous administrative laws that, needless to say, do not apply to Jews.

In essence, Israeli municipal planners in East Jerusalem, over the course of the past thirty-two years, have engaged in a concerted effort to establish a *fait accompli* in the city such that any future question as to its actual status as the "capital" of the Jewish State would be rendered completely academic. For a variety of political reasons, a discussion of which lies beyond the scope of this Essay, these mu-

---

129. *See* HODGKINS, *supra* note 17, at 26 (identifying land expropriation as a tool used by Israel to prevent Palestinians from settling in East Jerusalem).

nicipal planners have been extremely successful in achieving their goal. With the Oslo peace process recently put back on track after months of postponement and delay, it remains to be seen how Israel and the PLO intend to approach the question of negotiating the "final status" of Jerusalem. If anything is for certain, the facts on the ground in the city illustrate quite clearly that the question may have been settled long before the parties ever chose to meet at the negotiating table.

MAP I. PALESTINIAN TERRITORIES OCCUPIED IN 1967, INCLUDING JERUSALEM[130]

130. All copyrights reserved by the United Nations Cartographic Section. *See Map 3. Palestinian territories occupied in 1967, including Jerusalem*, Map No. 3243 Rev. 4, United Nations (June 1997) *in The Status of Jerusalem, supra* note 4.

MAP II. JERUSALEM OCCUPIED AND EXPANDED BY ISRAEL IN JUNE 1967[131]

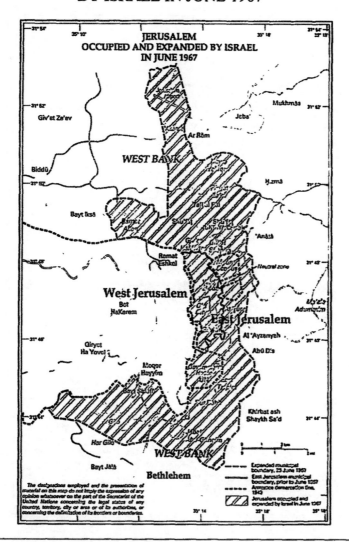

131. All copyrights reserved by the United Nations Cartographic Section. *See Map 4. Jerusalem occupied and expanded by Israel in June 1967*, Map No. 3640 Rev. 3, United Nations (June 1997) *in The Status of Jerusalem, supra* note 4.

MAP III. ISRAELI SETTLEMENTS IN AND AROUND JERUSALEM[132]

"GREATER" JERUSALEM AREA

---

132. All copyrights reserved by the United Nations Cartographic Section. *See Map 5. Israeli settlements in and around Jerusalem*, Map No. 3996, United Nations (June 1997) *in The Status of Jerusalem, supra* note 4.

APPENDIX A

THE TEN STEP PROCEDURE OF TOWN PLANNING SCHEMES (TPS)[133]

The local TPS goes through the following stages before its final approval:

1. The Local Planning and Building Committee decides that a TPS is required for a certain area and entrusts its preparation to experts;

2. The plan is conveyed to the Local Planning and Building Committee, which either recommends or rejects its deposition;

3. The plan, if approved by the Local Planning and Building Committee, goes to the District Planning and Building Committee for deposition;

4. Publication of the plan in the Official Gazette, in three daily newspapers and on the public bulletin boards in the particular neighborhoods. A two-month window is allowed for submission of objections to the District Committee;

5. Hearing of objections by the Local Committee;

6. First discussion of the objections by the District Committee;

7. Second discussion of the objections by the District Committee;

8. Approval of the plan by the Local Committee and the District Committee;

9. The TPS is approved by the Minister of the Interior;

10. Publication of notice of the approval and granting of legal validity to the plan. Upon final approval the TPS will be published in local newspapers, the Official Gazette and posted on neighborhood bulletin boards.

---

133. Adapted from HODGKINS, *supra* note 17, at 81.

Part VI

UN SECURITY COUNCIL
RESOLUTION 242

RESOLUTION 242: A LEGAL REAPPRAISAL OF THE RIGHT-WING ISRAELI INTERPRETATION OF THE WITHDRAWAL PHRASE WITH REFERENCE TO THE CONFLICT BETWEEN ISRAEL AND THE PALESTINIANS

JOHN McHUGO*

I. INTRODUCTION: THE 'RIGHT-WING ARGUMENT'

In the Six Day War in June 1967, East Jerusalem, the West Bank and the Gaza Strip came under Israeli military occupation, as well as the Sinai Peninsula and the Golan Heights. On 22 November that year, the UN Security Council unanimously passed Resolution 242, which it was hoped would provide a route to a permanent peace. It seems clear that Resolution 242 now has binding force[1] and that it is accepted by all parties today that Resolution 242 sets out the principles which must be applied in order to reach a settlement. The Resolution is recited in the preambles to the Oslo Accords.[2] This means that, in addition, it is binding on Israel and the PLO by agreement.[3]

Although Resolution 242 may now be accepted as the basis for peace, there remains a major issue of interpretation. The Palestinians maintain that Resolution 242 requires an Israeli withdrawal from all the occupied territories as part of any final settlement. Although areas within those territories might be transferred to Israel as part of that settlement, in the Palestinian view this may only come about through an agreement which has been freely reached by the parties, and under which the likelihood of Israel transferring territory which it occupied in 1948–9 to the Palestinians is just as great. It would appear that Israel disputes this, at least in public. Israeli Government web-sites,[4] articles in the media by writers favourable to right-wing Israeli stances, and letters written to the press frequently assert that a withdrawal from 'some' but not

---

* The author is a partner in Trowers & Hamlins and a Visiting Fellow at the Scottish Centre for International Law at Edinburgh University. He has written this Article in his personal capacity and the views expressed are his alone

[1] Security Council Resolution 338 'calls upon' the parties to implement Resolution 242 using language generally considered to have a mandatory character. See also VIII below.

[2] See in particular letter from Chairman Arafat to Prime Minister Rabin, 9 Sept 1993; Declaration of Principles on Interim Self-Government Agreements, 9 Sept 1993, Art 1; Preamble to Israeli–Palestinian Interim Agreement on the West Bank and the Gaza Strip of 28 Sept 1995.

[3] For a succinct discussion of this question, see Watson, 'The Oslo Accords: International Law and the Israeli-Palestinian Peace Agreements' (Oxford: Oxford University Press, 2000), at 31–4.

[4] See the website of the Israeli Ministry of Foreign Affairs, where material is deliberately posted with the intention of convincing the reader that Resolution 242 was never intended to lead to a return of 'all' the territories: <http://www.israel.mfa.gov>.

[*ICLQ* vol 51, October 2002 pp 851–882]

'all' of the territories was intended by Resolution 242.[5] This implies that Israel has a right to select areas of the territories it will retain, and presupposes that territorial adjustments will be in Israel's favour. For convenience, we will refer to this viewpoint as 'the Right-wing Interpretation' although it would seem to be official Israeli government policy. Supporters of the view include Eugene Rostow, who was US under-secretary of state for political affairs at the time the Resolution was debated. Rostow seems to have become a cheerleader for the Right-wing interpretation and the colonisation of the occupied territories by Israeli citizens, to boot.[6] An apparently sympathetic British Foreign Secretary has also made a statement on the floor of the House of Commons which has been taken to support the same position.[7] Mr Dore Gold, a former Israeli ambassador to the United Nations and currently a spokesman for the Israeli prime minister, has recently argued that the territories should be referred to as the 'Disputed Territories' rather than the 'Occupied territories'. He has gone so far as to write as follows:

> Under UN Security Council Resolution 242 from November 22, 1967—that has served as the basis of the 1991 Madrid conference and the 1993 Declaration of Principles—Israel is only expected to withdraw 'from territories' to 'secure and recognised boundaries' and not from 'the territories' or 'all the territories' captured in the Six-Day War. This deliberate language resulted from months of painstaking diplomacy. For example, the Soviet Union attempted to introduce the word 'all' before the word 'territories' in the British draft resolution that became Resolution 242. Lord Caradon, the British UN ambassador resisted these efforts. Since the Soviets tried to add the language of full withdrawal but failed, there is no ambiguity about the meaning of the withdrawal clause contained in Resolution 242, which was unanimously adopted by the UN Security Council.[8]

The implication is clear. Israel has a right to acquire parts of the occupied terri-

---

[5] For just two examples, see letter from Oliver Kamm to the London *The Times*, 28 Oct 2000 and letter from Milton Polton to the *International Herald Tribune* of 7 Dec 2000.

[6] See Rostow's address 'The Intent of UNSC Resolution 242: The View of Non-regional actors' in 'UN Security Council Resolution 242 The Building Block of Peacemaking', at 4-20 and in particular at p17: 'Since UNSC 242 calls on Israel to withdraw only from territories occupied in the course of the Six Day War—that is, not from *all* the territories or even from *the* territories it occupied in the course of the war—and since most of the boundaries in question are no more than armistice lines specifically designated as *not* being political boundaries, it is hard to believe that professional diplomats can seriously claim in 1992 that UNSC 242 requires Israel to return to the 1967 Armistice Lines. This Arab position is particularly bizarre applied to the West Bank and the Gaza Strip where, under the Mandate and Article 80 of the UN Charter, the Jewish people still have an incontestably valid claim to make close settlements on the land.'

[7] Mr Michael Stewart, Secretary of State for Foreign and Commonwealth Affairs, in reply to a question in Parliament, 9 Dec, 1969: 'As I have explained before, there is a reference, in the vital United Nations Security Council Resolution, both to withdrawal from territories and to secure and recognised boundaries. As I have told the House previously, we believe that these two things should be read concurrently and that the omission of the word 'all' before the word 'territories' is deliberate.' Hansard, Fifth Series, Vol 793, p 261.

[8] See Dore Gold, 'From "Occupied Territories" to "Disputed Territories" ', in *Jerusalem Viewpoints*, no 470, 3 *Shvat* 5762/ 16 Jan 2002.

tories. With the Israeli–Palestinian conflict currently at a critical and bloody stage, it is essential that such assertions are examined carefully. It will be the purpose of this Article to do just that. This writer believes that the Right-wing Interpretation is not only untenable as a construction of the wording of the Resolution, but also it is unsustainable as a good faith interpretation for the purposes of international law.

The English text of Resolution 242 is as follows:

The Security Council,

Expressing its continuing concern with the grave situation in the Middle East,

Emphasising the inadmissibility of the acquisition of territory by war and the need to work for a just and lasting peace in which every state in the area can live in security,

Emphasising further that all Member States in their acceptance of the Charter of the United Nations have undertaken a commitment to act in accordance with Article 2 of the Charter,

1. *Affirms* that the fulfilment of Charter principles requires the establishment of a just and lasting peace in the Middle East which should include the application of both the following principles: (i) Withdrawal of Israel armed forces from territories occupied in the recent conflict; (ii) Termination of all claims or states of belligerency and respect for and acknowledgement of the sovereignty, territorial integrity and political independence of every state in the area and the right to live in peace within secure and recognised boundaries free from threats or acts of force;

2. *Affirms further* the necessity (a) For guaranteeing the freedom of navigation through international waterways in the area; (b) For achieving a just settlement of the refugee problem; (c) For guaranteeing the territorial inviolability and political independence of every State in the area, through measures including the establishment of demilitarised zones;

3. *Requests* the Secretary-General to designate a Special Representative to proceed to the Middle East to establish and maintain contacts with the states concerned in order to promote agreement and assist efforts to achieve a peaceful and accepted settlement in accordance with the provisions and principles in this Resolution;

4. *Requests* the Secretary-General to report to the Security Council on the progress of the efforts of the Special Representative as soon as possible.[9]

Before analysing the text, it will be helpful to attempt to set out the twin arguments that are frequently used to support the Right-wing Interpretation. Both of them are encapsulated in the quotation from Mr Dore Gold above and, as we shall see, each of them is often repeated (frequently unchallenged) by reputable, independent scholars.

The first argument is linguistic. It is that the plain meaning of the wording in paragraph 2(i), 'Withdrawal from territories occupied in the recent conflict'

---

[9] S/8247.

can or should be construed to mean that Israel is only obliged to withdraw from 'some' of the territories, not 'all' the territories. The other argument is that the intention of the drafters of the Resolution in the Security Council was that Israel might retain some of the territories. The two arguments are also set out in a statement by Gerson in *Israel, the West Bank and International Law*:

> [Resolution 242] unanimously called for withdrawal from 'territories' rather than withdrawal from 'all the territories'. Its choice of words was deliberate and the product of much debate. They signify that withdrawal is required from some but not all the territories.[10]

He also states in a footnote:

> This becomes clear upon an examination of Security Council deliberations prior to reaching consensus on the text of Resolution 242. Several states made repeated attempts to require 'withdrawal from all *the* territories', which they interpreted to mean that only withdrawal from all of the territories would do. The defeat of these efforts makes it, therefore, incorrect to assert that withdrawal from *all* the territories is required.[11]

Gerson would seem to have in mind the oblique words of the Israeli Foreign Minister, Abba Eban, during the Security Council debate:

> For us, the resolution says what it says. It does not say that which it has specifically and consciously avoided saying. . . .
>
> [T]he crucial specifications . . . were discussed at length in consultations and deliberately and not accidentally excluded in order to be non-prejudicial to the negotiating position of all parties. The important words in most languages are short words, and every word, long or short, which is not in the text, is not there because it was deliberately concluded that it should not be there.[12]

This is a reference to the absence of 'all' and 'the' before 'territories'. Mr Eban invited his audience to draw their own conclusions, and gave notice to the world of the freedom of action that his government intended to allow itself.

II. THE PROCESS OF INTERPRETATION

Articles 31 and 32 of the Vienna Convention on the Law of Treaties have been used to interpret Resolution 242 before.[13] A strict construction of Article 32

---

[10] Gerson, *Israel, the West Bank and International Law* (London, Frank Cass, 1978), 76.

[11] Ibid, 104 n 179.

[12] United Nations Security Council Official Record ('UNSCOR'), 1382nd Meeting, paras 93–4.

[13] Arts 31 and 32 have been used by previous interpreters of the resolution, such as Professor Quincy Wright in 'The Middle East problem', 64 *American Journal of International Law* (1970), at 270 et seq. The text of Arts 31 and 32 is as follows:
Article 31:

> 1. A treaty shall be interpreted in good faith in accordance with the ordinary meaning to be given to the terms of the treaty in their context and in the light of its object and purpose.

would limit recourse to the use of supplementary means of interpretation to confirmation of the meaning arrived at by interpretation under Article 31 or as an aid to interpretation in the event that interpretation according to Article 31 '(a) leaves the meaning ambiguous or obscure; or (b) leads to a result which is manifestly absurd or unreasonable'. We do not, however, wish to exclude from consideration the argument based on the intention of the drafters of the Resolution. We will therefore agree with Schwebel that good faith requires that it should be possible to invoke preparatory work 'to correct the ordinary meaning otherwise deduced (if not to inform and influence the interpretation of the treaty from the outset).'[14] Our analysis will therefore attempt to interpret the Resolution in good faith by examining the ordinary meaning of the text and construing it in context and in the light of the object and purpose of the Resolution. Even though we believe we will have established a clear meaning for the text of the Resolution at that point, we will follow this by considering the most relevant material which provides supplementary means of interpretation, namely the record of the debate in the Security Council and the text of the other draft resolutions that were placed before the Council but not put to the vote.

A note of caution must, however, be sounded about the degree of reliance which may be placed on statements and documentation which form part of the less immediate context of the resolution, and the extent to which they may be used as aids to interpretation. The Official Records of the organs of the United Nations and the documentation referred to therein are publicly available, and contain official statements of the positions adopted by the member states. Yet if a researcher attempts to go beyond these courses, problems as to completeness

2. The context for the purpose of the interpretation of a treaty shall comprise in addition to the text, including its preamble and annexes: (a) any agreement relating to the treaty which was made between all the parties in connexion with the conclusion of the treaty; (b) any instrument which was made by one or more parties in connexion with the conclusion of the treaty and accepted by the other parties as an instrument related to the treaty.

3. There shall be taken into account, together with the context: (a) any subsequent agreement between the parties regarding the interpretation of the treaty or the application of its provisions;(b) any subsequent practice in the application of the treaty which establishes the agreement of the parties regarding its interpretation; (c) any relevant rules of international law applicable in the relationship between the parties.

4. A special meaning shall be given to a term if it is established that the parties so intended.

Article 32:

Recourse may be had to supplementary means of interpretation, including the preparatory work of the treaty and the circumstances of its conclusion, in order to confirm the meaning resulting from the application of Article 31, or to determine the meaning when the interpretation according to Article 31: (a) leaves the meaning ambiguous or obscure; or (b) leads to a result which is manifestly absurd or unreasonable.

[14] See Schwebel, 'May preparatory work be used to correct rather than to "confirm" the meaning of a treaty provision?', in *Theory of International Law on the threshold of the 21st Century, Essays in Honour of Krzustof Skubiszewski*, ed. J. Makarczyk (Kluwer Law, The Hague, 1996), at 546.

and availability creep in, to say nothing of objectivity. The relevant records of the chancelleries of the fifteen members of the Security Council and the four powers which were invited to attend but not to vote at its sessions are unlikely to be complete or available in their entirety. The files which are available for inspection are unlikely to have been produced specifically with research into the Resolution in mind, and may unintentionally omit important information, or such information may be permanently lost[15]. Statements by actors in the drama which were made after the event (such as those by Goldberg and Rostow referred to above, and those by Abba Eban to which reference is made below) may have been made with a particular and undisclosed purpose in mind, while statements such as that by Michael Stewart in the House of Commons are liable to have been honed and polished in order to support the policies of a particular government of the day. Secondary sources, such as the studies by Lall and Bailey rely (particularly in the case of Bailey) in large part on the memoirs of retired diplomats and interviews and correspondence between the author and individuals who once acted in an official capacity. Such sources should not be disregarded, but note should be taken of the caveat with which they should be used. The Official Records of the Security Council debate should be the evidence of the most immediate context for all pactical purposes. Other sources should be considered as more remote, regard being had in each case to the purpose of each document (or recollection of the writer or speaker), and the extent to which it can be shown to reflect objective facts about the meaning and status of the resolution.

It would appear that remarkably little attention has been paid by international lawyers to the interpretation of UN Security Council resolutions. However, the process of interpretation which we have outlined above is surely a reasonable initial approach to be adopted when attempting to establish the meaning of almost any text. When the process of analysis set out above has been completed, we will consider the work of Michael Wood on the interpretation of Security Council resolutions to see if it affects our conclusions. Wood also takes Articles 31 and 32 of the Vienna Convention as his starting point, and points out that the good faith requirement is buttressed by the obligation on Member States in Article 2(2) of the Charter to fulfil in good faith the obligations assumed by them in accordance with the Charter.[16]

Before concluding, we shall consider an unwelcome consequence for the state of Israel itself which flows from the adoption of the position we have

---

[15] It will be noted below that we have inspected the file of the British Mission to the UN now catalogued as FO 961/24 and made available under the Thirty Year Rule. This contains much valuable information about the evolution of Lord Caradon's draft. However, the file (and the series in which it is located) stop tantalisingly on the eve of the introduction of the Resolution into the Council. We do not claim that our search into the available British Archives is comprehensive, or that an entirely comprehensive search is possible Much relevant material will have inevitiably been lost.

[16] Michael C Wood, 'The Interpretation of Security Council Resolution 242', *Max Planck Yearbook of United Nations Law* [1998],.89.

called the Right-wing Interpretation, and will suggest that Israel would be well advised to repudiate it.

III. AN ANALYSIS OF THE ORDINARY MEANING OF THE TEXT

The Resolution is cast as one sentence, which emphasises the intention that it is to be construed as a single, integral whole and that no part of the Resolution is to be considered in isolation from the others. Subject to this, it will be seen that it divides into three distinct sections. The first section consists of the three preambular paragraphs that begin with the words 'Expressing' and 'Emphasising'. They set out common ground on which the Resolution is based. They are the most immediate context within which the meaning (and the object and purpose) of the provisions that follow must be determined.

The second section consists of numbered paragraphs 1 and 2, which each begin with the word 'Affirms'. In this analysis we will be particularly concerned with the two limbs of paragraph 1. For brevity, we will refer to paragraph 1 (i) as 'the Withdrawal Phrase' and to paragraph 1 (ii) as 'the Secure and Recognised Boundaries Phrase'.

The third section contains numbered paragraphs 3 and 4 which each begin with the word 'Requests'. Paragraph 3 shows that the purpose of the Resolution is 'to promote agreement and assist efforts to achieve a peaceful and accepted settlement in accordance with the provisions and principles in this Resolution'.

The structure of the Resolution is logical and ought therefore to be reasonably clear and uncontroversial. It is aimed at achieving the purpose set out in paragraph 3. This purpose should be achieved in accordance with the 'provisions and principles' in the Resolution. The Withdrawal Phrase and the Secure and Recognised Boundaries Phrase are specifically described as 'principles', but it can be assumed that the phrase 'provisions and principles' also covers the three subparagraphs in paragraph 2 and those principles contained in the preambular paragraphs.

Let us now consider the meaning of those parts of the wording of the Resolution which need some elaboration and which are most relevant to our analysis. We are concerned first and foremost with the ordinary meaning of the wording, the natural and probable meaning. Let us begin by looking at the second preambular paragraph: 'The Security Council. . . . Emphasising the inadmissibility of the acquisition of territory by war and the need to work for a just and lasting peace in which every state in the area can live in security.'

It used to be permissible for a state to acquire sovereignty over territory by right of conquest on the termination of a state of war. The right was abolished when the League of Nations was established in the aftermath of the First World War. The abolition of conquest extends to a prohibition of the acquisition of any territory by a state in actions of self-defence.[17] The vexed

---

[17] See Jennings and Watts, 'Oppenheim's International Law', 9th edn (Harlow, Longman,

question of who attacked whom in the various Arab–Israeli conflicts is therefore irrelevant to the analysis contained in this Article. What should be noted is the strength of the word 'inadmissibility' which was chosen by the drafters of the Resolution. It suggests that the prohibition of the acquisition of territory by war is a foundation on which the Resolution is predicated, and that 'the need to work for a just and lasting peace in which every state can live in security' is to be built upon this foundation.

IV. THE WITHDRAWAL PHRASE

We now come to the Withdrawal Phrase. We have already drawn attention to the way in which Israel appears to wish to read it and to the support which the Right-wing interpretation has received. That interpretation would now seem to be accepted as tenable among much academic opinion. Consider the following statement in Geoffrey Watson's book, *The Oslo Accords.*

> ·[Resolution 242] points in different directions at once. On the one hand, its preamble speaks of 'the inadmissibility of the acquisition of territory by war', implying that Israel should return all the territories obtained in the 1967 War. On the other hand, the English text of the resolution provides that peace 'should' (not 'must')[18] include withdrawal of Israeli forces 'from territories occupied in the recent conflict', not from 'the territories occupied' in that conflict.[19]

Watson's interpretation presupposes that the Resolution is ambiguous. But are Watson, Gerson and others right in assuming that the wording of the Withdrawal Phrase can be taken to mean what Dore Gold and others assert? This writer disagrees with them, and believes it is high time it was pointed out that this particular emperor has no clothes.

In the first place, the wording of the Withdrawal Phrase refers to a category of territories, namely those territories 'occupied in the recent conflict'. It treats these territories as a unity. If a withdrawal takes place from some, but not all, of these territories, can it be said that the principle contained in the Withdrawal Phrase has been complied with in full? A partial withdrawal would surely only be partial compliance with the principle. The absence of the word 'all' does not imply that 'some' was intended. Consider the following imaginary notice at the entrance to a park:

1992), 699 where Brownlie's *International Law and the Use of Force by States* is quoted with approval on this point. The prohibition extends to any unilateral attempt to acquire sovereignty over territory occupied in a war of self-defence. On this point, see Oppenheim, op cit, at 703–5 and nn 7 and 8. See also Korman, *The Right of Conquest: The Acquisition of Territory by Force in International Law and Practice* (Oxford: Oxford University Press, 1996), 203–14.

[18] A glance at the text of the Resolution as a whole will show that Watson's point about 'should' is a non-point. 'Should' governs the various components of the Secure and Recognised Boundaries Phrase in exactly the same way. Would Watson suggest that 'termination of all states of belligerency' 'should' be (but need not necessarily be) an ingredient of a final settlement?

[19] G Watson, *The Oslo Accords: International Law and the Israeli–Palestinian Peace Agreement'* (Oxford: Oxford University Press, 2000), 31.

'Dogs may swim in ponds in the park'.

Does this notice apply to 'all' dogs, or only to 'some' dogs? If the reader of the notice unleashes his dog so that it can have a swim, can the park keeper legitimately point to the notice and tell him that it does indeed apply to 'some' dogs, but not to the dog that the walker has just let off the lead? Let us assume that there are three ponds in the park. Does the notice refer to 'all ponds' which fall into the category of being 'in the park' or only to 'some' of the ponds, and if so which? The answer in each case must surely be 'all'.

If it is objected that there is some element of permissibility inherent in the existence of the word 'may' in the above example, let us consider an alternative example which has mandatory wording:

Dogs must be kept on the lead near ponds in the park.

It does not require more than common sense to realise that, once again, 'all dogs' and 'all ponds' are intended.

Moreover, wording can be found in other phrases in Resolution 242 where 'all' or a similar word is absent but where it is clear in context that 'all' is meant and there are no grounds to assume that only 'some' was intended. Consider paragraph 2 (a) which confirms the necessity of guaranteeing freedom of navigation 'through international waterways in the area', not 'all international waterways in the area'. There are a number of international waterways in the area: the Suez Canal, the Straits of Tiran at the entrance to the Gulf of Aqaba, and the Bab al-mandab at the entrance to the Red Sea. 'Area' is undefined. Does it cover some or all of these waterways? Does it extend further afield to include, say, the Straits of Hormuz, the Bosphorus or even the narrowing of the Mediterranean between Sicily and Tunisia, and the Straits of Gibraltar? If 'all' waterways are not intended to be covered by the phrase a major lack of clarity emerges. This cannot have been the intention. Good faith and the natural and only meaning require that the sense 'all international waterways' be implied.

A similar question arises over 'the right to live in peace within secure and recognised boundaries' in the Secure and Recognised Boundaries Phrase. Does the word 'within' imply that 'all' boundaries must be secure and recognised? Israel now has secure and recognised boundaries with Egypt and Jordan.[20] Yet no one would seriously suggest that this aspect of the Secure and Recognised Boundaries Phrase has been fully complied with and that there is therefore no requirement in Resolution 242 for a secure and recognised boundary to exist between, say, Israel and Syria as part of the final settlement between those two countries.

If 'all' is to be implied in these two examples, surely it should also be implied in the Withdrawal Phrase.

---

[20] Peace Treaty between Israel and Egypt, 26 Mar 1979; Treaty of Peace between the State of Israel and the Hashemite Kingdom of Jordan, 26 Oct 1994.

There are other objections to the Israeli Interpretation. In the first place, good faith requires that a text be construed in order to give it a clear meaning if this is possible. If the Israeli view that withdrawal applies only to 'some' and not 'all' of the territories were sustainable, it would lead to an unclear text and major uncertainties: which territories must Israel withdraw from, and which territories may it retain? Who should decide which these territories should be? Such uncertainties would be a recipe for conflict, and subsequent history shows that it is indeed arguable that the Right-wing Interpretation has led to conflict and substantial loss of life. Can it seriously be suggested that an unclear text would have been the deliberate intention of the Security Council? The Right-wing Interpretation starts from the premise that the text must be assumed to be ambiguous. This cannot be right if a clear meaning can be extracted from it.

We have also drawn attention to the abolition of the right of conquest in international law. Any suggestion that Israel could retain some of the territories would have been illegal. Can it be seriously suggested that the Security Council would have attempted to overturn this principle? The Right-wing Interpretation would imply that it did.

V. THE SECURE AND RECOGNISED BOUNDARIES PHRASE

We now turn to the Secure and Recognised Boundaries Phrase. This is that 'all claims or states of belligerency' should be terminated, that the sovereignty, territorial integrity, and independence of every state in the area should be respected and acknowledged, and that every state in the area should have 'the right to live in peace within secure and recognised boundaries free from threats or acts of force'. Is there another limb to the argument for the Right-wing interpretation? Can it be said that the boundaries should be adjusted in order to achieve 'secure and recognised borders', and that Israel consequently has a unilateral right to retain some of the territory occupied in 1967 in order to have such boundaries? As shown above, Gerson, for instance, has accepted the Right-wing Interpretation. Nevertheless, he limits it 'to territorial adjustments mandated by "security considerations" '. He suggests that these should be of a minor nature, and hints that this had been Israel's position before the 1967 War.[21]

This view is developed by Sharon Korman who reads the Withdrawal Phrase as not requiring a withdrawal from all the territories and believes the Resolution allows for minor territorial adjustments in favour of Israel for security considerations. She compromises this view, however, since she also maintains that these can only come about through a freely negotiated settlement, reached in terms of the provisions and principles contained in the Resolution. She continues, somewhat hesitantly:

[21] Gerson, op cit, 76.

Since such a settlement would not be a settlement imposed or dictated under threats or acts of force, it follows that [the Secure and Recognised Boundaries Phrase] is not to deny the inadmissibility of acquiring territory by force, but is rather to assert or suggest the following: (1) that a state which has been a victim of attack may be recognised as having a legitimate claim to border adjustments on the grounds of military security; (2) that the Security Council would, in this case, approve of border modifications to the extent deemed necessary for security; but (3) such changes could not be *enforced* by the state whose claim is admitted, but could only be effected in the context of a freely negotiated settlement, and only to the extent compatible with 'a just and lasting peace'—the essential point being that a peace treaty incorporating frontier changes must have some prospect of *permanence*: that is, it must not impose or dictate territorial arrangements which the party dictated to would seek to reverse as soon as the next opportunity offered.[22]

There are a number of inconsistencies in this proposition, even if one lets pass her statement that Israel was 'a victim of attack' without comment. In the first place, the maintenance of the Israeli occupation is only possible through 'threats or acts of force'. If her words are taken at face value, Korman would seem to imply that the occupation should have ended before negotiations began, and that its very continuation is itself a breach of Resolution 242. It is surely difficult to see how the Right-wing Interpretation is not intended to force the Palestinians (and the Egyptians and Syrians) to negotiate under the duress inherent in the occupation of their land. This threatens the 'prospect of *permanence*' which she envisages in the territorial arrangements she advocates, unless the negotiations lead to a total withdrawal (such as the withdrawal which Israel carried out from Egyptian territory when peace was made). The use of force to maintain an occupation inevitably hinders or destroys the possibility of the necessary basis of equality for negotiations to agree reciprocal territorial swaps. Moreover, we have already noted how the concept of acquisition of territory in a war of self-defence has been rejected by scholars. This is also Korman's view. She continues the passage quoted above by pointing this out:

Thus Security Council Resolution 242, while it does not deny the validity of territorial changes which it has itself acknowledged on grounds of security, does not support the right of the victim of attack to annex conquered territories or to impose a treaty of cession on the defeated state. As such, it provides strong evidence for the existence of the rule that all acquisitions of territory obtained by force, without qualification as to lawfulness, are inadmissible.[23]

Korman's inconsistency ultimately stems from her subscription to the view that the Withdrawal Phrase does not demand a total withdrawal from the occupied territories.

The main objection to an argument based on the Secure and Recognised

---

[22] Korman, op cit, 211–12.   [23] Ibid, 212.

Boundaries Phrase is that the wording does not state that boundary adjustments will necessarily occur. If peace comes, then the boundaries—wherever they lie—should automatically be 'secure and recognised', as Nabil Elaraby has pointed out.[24] Conversely, no adjustments can ever make a boundary secure in the absence of peace. By definition, such a boundary will not be recognised except as an armistice line. This being the case, unilateral adjustments to change the frontier in Israel's favour cannot be justified on the basis of the Secure and Recognised Boundaries Phrase.

Another problem with the argument is that Resolution 242 states that this principle applies to every state in the area, and not just Israel. It will be noted that the Withdrawal Phrase is the only principle in the Resolution that places an obligation on one party alone or refers directly to the 1967 War. All other principles and provisions are intended to be of general application and to apply to all parties. Just as Israel has a right to live in peace and security within secure and recognised boundaries without threats of force by its neighbours, each of Israel's Arab neighbours has exactly the same right to live in peace and security free of threats of force by Israel or any other state. Common sense demands that this should also apply to any state that comes into being at a later date—such as an independent Palestinian state. Resolution 242 was intended to provide a framework for negotiations. This implies that the parties should be on an equal footing and that each should respect the entitlement of the others under international law. This is difficult so long as Israel remains an occupying power with a record of abusing its position.

Our initial analysis of the text of Resolution 242 suggests that any territorial adjustments must be freely negotiated on a basis of reciprocity by parties treating each other as equals. This interpretation is free from ambiguity and obscurity and has not led to a result that is manifestly absurd or unreasonable. Many of the political statements made within the first few years after Resolution 242 which are today used to support the Right-wing Interpretation may equally well be taken to support the position which we are advocating here. Thus, when Michael Stewart, as British Foreign Secretary, told the House of Commons that the references in Resolution 242 to 'withdrawal from territories' and 'secure and recognised boundaries' should be read concurrently and 'that the omission of the word 'all' before the word 'territories' is deliberate',[25] he was not necessarily supporting the Right-wing Interpretation.

---

[24] See Nabil Elaraby in *UN Security Council Resolution 242: The Building Block of Peacemaking* (Washington DC: Washington Institute, 1993), at 42: 'With respect to UNSC's reference to "secure and recognised boundaries", I would like to stress that the withdrawal clause is clear. It does not mean "new" secure and recognised borders, but secure and recognised "existing" borders. The second part in the resolution refers to "termination of the state of belligerency", and that is addressed to every single party—both to Israel and the Arab countries. They can all live within secure and recognised boundaries. It has nothing to do with withdrawal; if it did, the resolution would have said so.' He also added, referring to the Withdrawal Phrase: 'The myth created on the flimsy and fallacious argument of the so-called definite article should really be dismissed by now.' Ibid., p.44

[25] Hansard. Fifth Series. vol. 793. 261.

He was speaking only two years after the passing of the Resolution. If negotiations had led to a comprehensive peace within a reasonable time shortly thereafter, it is perfectly possible that agreed and mutually compensating territorial swaps would have occurred at the same time as an Israeli withdrawal. Israel might indeed never have withdrawn from the areas which it gained in such swaps. It is a very different thing to imply, a third of a century later, that words such as those uttered by Michael Stewart were in support of an Israeli 'right' to retain areas it selected on a permanent basis.

We will now turn to the extrinsic evidence: the record of the debate in the Security Council and the other draft resolutions to see if they confirm (or correct) our initial analysis.

VI. SUPPLEMENTARY MEANS OF INTERPRETATION:
(1) THE SECURITY COUNCIL DEBATE

A number of draft resolutions were proposed and discussed to a greater or lesser extent, and the draft which was adopted as Resolution 242 was prepared after the Security Council members had had an opportunity to sound out each other's views as well as the views of the states which were party to the dispute. Once the new draft had been presented, no amendments were made to the text and it was debated and accepted unanimously. Two general statements were made about it in the debates in the Council which bear repetition here. The first was by Lord Caradon, the British representative who had initiated the draft and presented it to the Council:

> [T]he draft resolution which we have prepared is not a British text. It is the result of close and prolonged consultation with both sides and with all members of this Council. As I have respectfully said, every member of this Council has made a contribution in the search for common ground on which we can go forward. . . . I would say that the draft resolution is a balanced whole. To add to it or to detract from it would destroy the balance and also destroy the wide measure of agreement we have achieved together. It must be considered as a whole and as it stands. I suggest that we have reached the stage when most, if not all, of us want the resolution, the whole resolution and nothing but the resolution.
>
> . . . I would say that every delegation has a right, of course, and a duty to state its own views. As I said on Monday: 'Every delegation is entitled, indeed is expected, to state the separate and distinct policy of the Government it represents.'
>
> But the draft resolution does not belong to one side or the other or to any one delegation; it belongs to us all. I am sure that it will be recognised by us all that it is only the resolution that will bind us, and we regard its wording as clear. All of us, no doubt, have our own views and interpretations and understandings. I explained my own when I spoke on Monday last. On these matters each delegation rightly speaks only for itself.[26]

---

[26] UNSCOR, 1382nd Meeting, paras 58–61

The other general statement was by the US representative, Mr Goldberg:

> As Lord Caradon pointed out both on Monday and today, various members of the
> Council have views of their own for supporting the United Kingdom text. The
> voting of course takes place not on the individual or discrete views and policies
> of various members but on the draft resolution.[27]

A number of states did use the debate to state their 'individual or discrete
views' as to what the Resolution meant and we will now turn to these.
However, the views of Lord Caradon and Mr Goldberg support the approach
we have adopted to the analysis of the Resolution: it is the meaning of the text
which counts and it should be assumed that the text is clear unless shown
otherwise. Furthermore, Lord Caradon's reference to the way in which all
delegations had played their part in the production of the text indicates that the
'individual or discrete views' of each of the fifteen members of the Security
Council should be considered of more or less equal weight when cited in
support of a particular interpretation. His statement should also lead us to
anticipate a considerable degree of congruence in the views expressed by the
delegates on the interpretation of the Resolution.

What, then, were the 'individual or discrete views' of the various delegations, and do they show that more than one interpretation is possible?

Lord Caradon, for the United Kingdom, had, as he indicated, already
expressed his views. In the previous meeting of the Security Council, he had
quoted from a speech by George Brown, the British Foreign Secretary, to the
General Assembly as a statement of the British Government's policy:

> Britain does not accept war as a means of accepting disputes, nor that a state
> should be allowed to extend its frontiers as a result of war. This means that Israel
> must withdraw. But equally, Israel's neighbours must recognise its right to exist,
> and it must enjoy security within its frontiers. What we must work for in this area
> is a durable peace, the renunciation of all aggressive designs, and an end to poli-
> cies which are inconsistent with peace.[28]

Although this does not state in so many words that Israel must withdraw from
all the territories, the need for a total withdrawal is surely implicit provided
that it is accepted at the same time that Israel has a right to exist and must
'enjoy security within its frontiers'. It will be noted that Lord Caradon did not
suggest that those frontiers should necessarily be revised.

Lord Caradon's speech continued with praise for the initiative that Latin
American states had taken in the Security Council. He stated 'They have
insisted on fairness, on the basic principle of equal obligation.'[29] This is
significant, because the Latin American draft resolution for the General
Assembly was still before the Security Council and had carried very clear

---

[27] UNSCOR, 1382nd Meeting, para 64.
[28] UNSCOR, 1381st Meeting, para 20, quoting from the Official Records of the General
Assembly, Plenary Meetings, 1567th meeting, para 91.
[29] UNSCOR, 1381st Meeting, para 21.

wording on the question of Israeli withdrawal: 'The General Assembly ... urgently requests Israel to withdraw all of its forces from all the territories occupied by it as a result of the recent conflict.' Lord Caradon's praise for the Latin American initiative surely implied approval for this desire for a total withdrawal. If he did not intend there to be a total withdrawal, it is hard to see why he spoke these precise words. A total withdrawal is part of the 'equal obligation' which he implied that the Latin American text had achieved for Israel and the Arab states. To say otherwise would be to misread that text.

Lord Caradon also commented specifically on the relationship between the preambular paragraph concerning the inadmissibility of force and the Withdrawal Phrase:

> In our resolution we stated the principle of the 'withdrawal of Israel armed forces from territories occupied in the recent conflict' and in the preamble we empha-sised 'the inadmissibility of the acquisition of territory by war'. In our view, the wording of those provisions is clear ... In the long discussions with the repre-sentatives of the Arab countries they have made it clear that they seek no more than justice. The central issue of the recovery and the restoration of their territo-ries is naturally uppermost in their minds. The issue of withdrawal is all impor-tant to them, and of course they seek a just settlement to end the long suffering of the refugees.
>
> The Israelis, on the other hand, tell us that withdrawal must never be to insecu-rity and hostility. The action to be taken must be within the framework of a permanent peace, and withdrawal must be to secure boundaries. There must be an end to the use and threat and fear of violence and hostility.
>
> I have said before that those aims do not conflict; they are equal; they are both essential; they are interdependent. There must be adequate provision in any reso-lution to meet them both, since to pursue one without the other would be futile.[30]

Lord Caradon's words were obviously chosen with great care. His intention was that the Resolution should achieve a balance. A permanent peace would involve Arab recognition of Israel and Israel's territorial integrity: major concessions by the Arab states. An Israeli withdrawal to secure boundaries was to be balanced by the logical consequence of the inadmissibility of the acquisition of territory by war: Israel could not gain any territory as a result of the recent conflict. These were the principles on which the parties were to negotiate their settlement. In order to negotiate secure boundaries, Israel had to recognise its obligation to withdraw from the occupied territories. There was no implication that this would necessarily require territorial adjustments at all, let alone any which were purely for the benefit of Israel. If he had intended Israel to have the discretion to make such adjustments, he could not have stated that he regarded the wording of the Withdrawal Phrase as clear.

If the British delegate only stated this by implication, the Indian delegate's gloss on the British view adds additional force to the interpretation of that

---

[30] Ibid 1381st meeting, paras 31–7. Cf. 1379th Meeting, paras 11 and 12.

view which we have just set out. Mr Parthasarathi, the Indian delegate, repeated the statement by George Brown, the British Foreign Secretary, which Lord Caradon had already quoted at the previous meeting and which is contained in the quotation set out above. But he quoted more extensively from George Brown than Lord Caradon, including the following words:

> 'All members shall refrain in their international relations from the threat or use of force against the territorial integrity or political independence of any State ...' Here the words 'territorial integrity' have a direct bearing on the question of withdrawal, on which much has been said in previous speeches. I see no two ways about this; and I can state our position very clearly. In my view, it follows from the words in the Charter that war should not lead to territorial aggrandizement.[31]

George Brown's quotation from Article 2(4) of the United Nations Charter and reference to territorial integrity are particularly significant, since at that time Britain recognised Jordanian sovereignty over the West Bank. It implied that Mr Brown believed that Israel should withdraw from the entire West Bank as well as the other occupied territories. Both Mr Parthasarati, Lord Caradon and everyone else present would have read Mr Brown's words on that basis.

Mr Parthasarathi commented:

> My delegation has studied the United Kingdom draft resolution in the light of these two policy statements of the British Foreign Secretary. It is our understanding that the draft resolution, if approved by the Council, will commit it to the principle of total withdrawal of Israel forces from all the territories—I repeat, all, the territories—occupied by Israel as a result of the conflict which began on 5 June 1967 ...
>
> This being so, Israel cannot use the words 'secure and recognised boundaries' contained in operative paragraph 1 of the United kingdom draft resolution, to retain any territory occupied in the recent conflict. Of course, mutual territorial adjustments are not ruled out, as indeed they are not in the three-Power draft resolution co-sponsored by India.[32]

Lord Caradon welcomed this, in language which makes it hard to believe that he disagreed with the Indian delegate's interpretation of Britain's own interpretation of it:

> We must now all strain every effort for harmony and unity, and it is in this spirit that I warmly welcome the decision that has just been communicated to us by the distinguished Ambassador of India, speaking on behalf of himself and the other co-sponsors of the draft resolution which they presented to us. It marks a turning point; I feel that it opens the way to agreement and to action.[33]

Mr Kante, the representative of Mali, confirmed his agreement with the Indian

---

[31] UNSCOR, 1382nd Meeting, para 50, quoting from the Official Records of the General Assembly, 1529th Meeting, para 15.
[32] UNSCOR, 1382nd meeting, paras 52–3.
[33] Ibid, para 56.

interpretation of the requirement for Israeli withdrawal, using language that was as explicit as Mr Parthasathi's:

> Ma délégation confère donc à sa vote d'aujourd'hui le sens de l'interprétation claire et sans équivoque que le représentant de l'Inde a bien voulu donner des dispositions du texte britannique, à savoir: premièrement que le retrait des troupes de toutes les forces-armées d'Israël de tous les territoires arabes occupés à partir du 6 juin ne saurait être lié a aucune condition quelle qu'elle soit . . .[34]

Likewise, Mr Adebo, the representative of Nigeria, stated:

> We, for our part, feel that the resolution we have adopted does provide for what we believe are the essential factors to the peaceful and just settlement of the Middle East situation. One of these factors, as we have reiterated more than once, is the recognition of the inadmissibility of territorial aggrandizement by military conquest and, as a consequence, the withdrawal of Israel forces from all the territories that they occupied as a result of the recent conflict. But one of the essential factors also is that this withdrawal should take place in a context in which all the countries in the area, including Israel and all the Arab states, can feel and enjoy a sense of security. We therefore subscribe very heartily to what Lord Caradon said when he stated that the resolution must be taken as a whole.[35]

Nor were the three delegates who had submitted the non-aligned three power draft alone in being so explicit that the text of the Resolution required withdrawal from all the territories. Mr Tarabanov, the Bulgarian delegate stated:

> Nous pouvons constater avec satisfaction que, dans la résolution adoptée, l'inadmissibilité de l'acquisition de territoire par la force, proclamée dans le préambule en tant que principe général, est confirmée dans le premier point du dispositif de la résolution d'une façon claire et explicite par la demande de 'retrait des forces armées israeliénnes des territoires occupés lors du récent conflit'. Il s'agit d'une disposition précise, qui exige que les troupes d'Israël se retirent de tous les territoires occupés après le 4 juin 1967. C'est une application concrète du principe de l'inadmissibilité de l'acquisition de territoire par la guerre souligné dans la préambule de la résolution.

> Sous cette lumière se place également la question de la reconnaissance 'de l'intégrité territoriale et de l'indépendance politique de chaque Etat de la région et de leur droit de vivre en paix a l'intérieur de frontiérés sûres et reconnues'. C'est justement la paix et la sécurité de tous les Etats qui exigent avant tout l'interdiction de toute acquisition territoriale de la part d'un Etat aux dépens d'un autre par la guerre.

> La disposition concernant le retrait des troupes d'Israël de tous les territoires occupés est une condition importante pour mettre en oeuvre les autres principes enonces au paragraphe 1, alinéa ii, et au paragraphe 2 du dispositif de la résolution.[36]

Mr Makonnen, the Ethiopian delegate was explicit on the requirements for whichever draft was to go forward:

---

[34] Ibid, para 189.   [35] Ibid, para 76.   [36] Ibid, paras 139–41.

> With regard to the principles that need to be affirmed, we deem it most essential that due emphasis be put on the inadmissibility of acquisition of territory by war and hence on the imperative requirement that all Israel armed forces be withdrawn from the territories occupied as a result of military conflict. . . .[37]

He then stated that he would vote for a proposal that included these elements:

> I can only repeat that in the light of the statements that I have just made, our final position on any proposals will depend on whether or not they go a reasonable way to meet our test of balance and equity and on the extent to which they accommodate the basic elements that we consider to be essential for any Security Council decision at this crucial stage.[38]

Mr Makonnen's vote in favour of the Resolution thus implies that he was satisfied that it required an Israeli withdrawal of all its forces from the territories occupied in the recent conflict.

The French delegate, M. Berard, stated that the wording of the Withdrawal Phrase was clear and meant a withdrawal from the occupied territories, implying that a partial withdrawal would not be adequate. He contrasts this with the existence of other parts of the Resolution that he did not believe carried the same degree of clarity:

> On ne s'étonnera donc pas si j'indique que nous aurions souhaité que ce texte fût plus net sur certains points, y compris le mandat du représentant special.
>
> Mais nous devons admettre qu'en ce qui concerne le point que la délégation française a toujours présenté comme essentiel, celui du retrait des forces d'occupation, la résolution adoptée, si l'on se réfère au texte français qui fait foi au meme titre que le texte anglais, ne laisse place a aucune amphibologie puisqu'il parle de l'évacuation des territoires occupés, ce qui donne une interprétation indiscutable des termes *'occupied territories'*.[39]

If M Berard had intended 'l'évacuation des territoires occupés' to mean only withdrawal from some of the occupied territories, there would have been an ambiguity in what he said and he would have contradicted himself when he stated that the French text was clear on this point. His statement that the wording in the official French text was 'une interprétation indiscutable' of withdrawal from 'occupied territories' [ie 'territories occupied in the recent conflict'] indicates that he also believed the English wording to be clear and to refer to a total withdrawal. This has led Shabtai Rosenne to come close to admitting that both the English and the French texts are incompatible with a partial withdrawal.[40]

---

[37] Ibid, para 33.   [38] Ibid, para 37.   [39] Ibid, paras 110–11.

[40] Shabtai Rosenne, in an article which is trumpeted from the Israeli Government's website, draws attention to the French delegate's view that the meanings of the French and English texts were identical on the question of withdrawal. What Rosenne chooses to ignore is the possibility that the phrase 'withdrawal from territories occupied in the recent conflict' might be interpreted in the manner set out by us in this Article. He assumes that the words indicate a requirement for

Mr Kuznetzov, the Soviet delegate, was explicit both on the question of withdrawal and on the relationship between the Withdrawal Phrase and the Preamble:

> [W]e voted for the United Kingdom draft resolution, as interpreted by the representative of India, whose views we share. Thus, in the resolution adopted by the Security Council, the 'withdrawal of Israel armed forces from territories occupied in the recent conflict' becomes the first necessary principle for the establishment of a just and lasting peace in the Middle East. We understand the decision to mean the withdrawal of Israel forces from all, and we repeat, all territories belonging to Arab states and seized by Israel following its attack on those states on 5 June 1967. This is borne out by the preamble to the United kingdom draft resolution that stresses the 'inadmissibility of the acquisition of territory by war'. It follows that the provision contained in that draft relating to the right of all States in the Near East 'to live in peace within secure and recognised boundaries' cannot serve as a pretext for the maintenance of Israel forces on any part of the Arab territories seized by them as a result of war.[41]

On the other hand, Mr Ruda, the Argentinian representative, and possibly Mr De Carvalho Silos, the Brazilian representative, expressed reservations about the clarity of the wording of the Withdrawal Phrase. Although he did not refer to the Withdrawal Phrase explicitly, the Brazilian representative may well have had it in mind when he stated: 'The text does not give full satisfaction to my delegation.'[42] But he nevertheless implied that the general principles of international law prevented Israel acquiring land it had occupied, and that he therefore had no problem voting for the Resolution:

> I should like to restate, on behalf of my delegation, the general principle that no stable international order can be based on the threat or use of force, and that the occupation or acquisition of territories brought about by such means should not be recognised. The validity of this rule cannot be contested and is not being challenged by anyone around this table. Its acceptance does not imply that border-

---

a partial withdrawal, but makes no attempt to justify this view. The contradiction inherent in his position is plain from the unsatisfactory gymnastics into which he is forced in a vain attempt to give coherence to it. He is led to speculate as to why there is no word equivalent to 'some' in the French text, and comes within a whisker of admitting that both the English and the French texts are incompatible with an interpretation that only a partial withdrawal is intended: '[I]t is said that the indefinite quality of the English and Russian versions [of the Withdrawal Phrase]—which was a matter of political determinism—ought to be met by the introduction of a word such as 'certains' into the French version (and its equivalent in the Spanish). But in such a context, 'certains' would need some equivalent in English, for instance some, a word which does not appear in the English text and which, moreover, it is unlikely that a draftsman with any command of the English language from either side of the Atlantic would have willingly or wittingly inserted.' See Shabtai Rosenne, 'On Multi-lingual Interpretation', *Israel Law Review*, vol 6, 1971 at p 361. There are, of course, forms of wording which would have achieved his objective: 'partial withdrawal', 'selected withdrawals' or 'withdrawals appropriate to establish secure and recognised boundaries' would have been possibilities. But the whole point is that they would never have been accepted by the Security Council.

[41] UNSCOR, 1382nd Meeting, paras 118–19. Translated from the Russian.
[42] Ibid, para 128.

lines cannot be rectified as a result of an agreement freely concluded among the interested states.[43]

Thus, although he may not have been fully satisfied with the wording, he would clearly not accept an interpretation of the Resolution that would have conflicted with the rule that, as he put it, 'is not being challenged by anyone around this table'. Otherwise, he would not have voted for the Resolution. The attention that he drew to the possibility of rectifying boundaries by agreement likewise implies that he excluded the redrawing of boundaries in any unilateral way.

The Argentinian representative stated that 'we cannot, however, help but observe that we would have liked to see some improvements made in the drafting' and made a suggestion to add references in the Preamble to the UN Charter as a whole and in particular Articles 1 and 33 thereof. Then he added:

> With regard to the formula for the withdrawal of troops, which reads: 'withdrawal of Israel armed forces from territories occupied in the recent conflict', this does not, in our view, reflect a fully rounded-off notion; and although my delegation voted for paragraph 1 (i) of the draft, we would have preferred a clearer text, such as that submitted to the General Assembly by the Latin American countries in July, which provided for the withdrawal of Israel armed forces from all the territories occupied as a result of the recent conflict.

> We trust that the implementation of the formula adopted will achieve these ends; it is the only solution. We have always contended and still contend that, as the Brazilian representative pointed out, no international order be based on the threat or use of force, and that no recognition should be given to any territorial arrangement which has not been arrived at by peaceful means, nor to the validity of any occupation or acquisition of territories accomplished by force of arms.

> The second point is that of the right 'to live in peace within secure and recognised boundaries'. We take this expression as really meaning to live in security within agreed boundaries. . . .[44]

Like his Brazilian colleague, he excluded any unilateral move by Israel to adjust its frontiers at the expense of its neighbours or the annexation of occupied territory.

Even if the Brazilian and Argentinian delegates did not agree that the Withdrawal Phrase was clear in itself, what they said implied that they accepted that it was clear in the context of the Resolution taken as a whole against the background of international law.

It can thus be seen that the representatives of ten of the fifteen voting members made a point of stating on the record that they considered that the Resolution provided that Israel had no right to acquire any of the territories occupied in the Six Days War, and that it followed from this that the requirement to withdraw extended to all these territories. They can be divided into

[43] UNSCROR, 1382nd Meeting, para 127.
[44] *Israel Law Review*, vol 6, 1971, paras 161–4. Translated from the Spanish.

those who expressly stated that the Withdrawal Phrase was clear in requiring a total withdrawal: India, Mali, Nigeria, Bulgaria, the USSR, and France, and those who implied it was clear in the context of the Resolution as a whole: Britain, Ethiopia, Argentina, and Brazil. Britain would seem to straddle the two categories since, as we have seen, Caradon stated that the Withdrawal Phrase was clear and implied that it meant a total withdrawal.

None of the representatives of the five remaining members made a statement on the meaning of the Withdrawal Phrase or stated that it supported the Right-wing interpretation.[45] Gerson and others are thus wrong in asserting that the debate in the Security Council reveals that the intention of the drafters of the Resolution did not envisage total withdrawal. In the face of so many broadly congruent statements as to the effect of the Withdrawal Phrase when interpreted in the context of the Resolution as a whole, an inference that silence implied consent on the part of the states which did not take the opportunity to interpret the Withdrawal Phrase is not entirely unreasonable. Mr Goldberg was to write in 1973 that he considered the Resolution to be ambiguous and that it ' "tilts" in favour of adjustments to ensure secure boundaries for Israel without endorsing the complete redrawing of the map of the Middle-East'.[46] Whatever he may have meant by this in 1973, he did not say it at the time from the floor of the Security Council, although he did add towards the end of the debate that he 'had voted for the resolution and not for each and every speech that has been made'.[47]

The following will also be noted from the delegates' words quoted above: the British, Indian, Nigerian, Bulgarian, Ethiopian, Soviet, Brazilian, and Argentinian delegates all made a clear reference to the wording concerning the inadmissibility of the use of force in the preamble and used it to construe the

---

[45] It might be noted that Mr Borch, the Danish delegate stated that the Resolution 'does take into account all the essential interests of the parties involved' (UNSCOR, 1382nd Meeting, para 178). Mr Ignatieff, the Canadian delegate, stated that the 'resolution just adopted does, in our view, meet the essential positions of both sides, taking into account the various ideas which emerged from consultation among non-permanent members of the Council, as well as with the States in the area.' Ibid, para 132. These statements are surely incompatible with a belief that the Resolution entitles Israel to retain parts of the territories unilaterally. The Japanese delegation prepared its own draft, which never reached the floor of the Council, but which used the words 'withdrawal of Israel's armed force from the territories occupied as a result of the recent conflict and determination of the permanent national borders between Israel and the state concerned'. This is similarly incompatible with such a belief.

[46] See Goldberg, 'United Nations Security Council Resolution 242 and the prospects for peace in the Middle East', Columbia Journal of Transnational Law, Vol. 12, No. 2, 1973, p 191.

[47] 1382nd Meeting, para. 186. We consider below the relevant passage in the draft American resolution and note that this did not propose a licence for Israel to acquire territory taken during the fighting in 1967. Eban writes 'The United States ... had made clear through President Johnson that changes in the previous lines should not "reflect the weight of military conquests." (It was only later under the Nixon administration that the U.S. became accustomed to recommending the formula "minor changes")'. (Eban, Personal Witness, p 458.) As is the case with the statements of the Canadian, Danish, and Japanese, the absence of specific comment by Goldberg on the text of the Withdrawal Phrase cannot be taken as a tacit disagreement with the broadly congruent views of the delegates who interpreted the wording from the floor of the Council.

Withdrawal Phrase. The French delegate made a similar reference[48] and the Japanese delegate emphasised the principle of the inadmissibility of the acquisition of territory by war although he did not specifically link it to the Withdrawal Phrase.[49]

VII. SUPPLEMENTARY MEANS OF INTERPRETATION (2): THE ABSENCE OF 'ALL' AND ITS IRRELEVANCE

There is one final argument in support of the Right-wing Interpretation. The word 'all' that had been contained in the Latin American[50], Non-Aligned[51] and Soviet[52] drafts before the word 'territories' was absent from the British draft. This was scarcely an accident. Before Lord Caradon introduced the text at the 1379th Meeting of the Security Council, it would have been reasonable to suppose that he would have discussed it with the different delegations in private meetings, and it is quite clear that he actually did this.

Wording frequently evolves as part of the negotiation process, and no argument can be mounted purely on the basis of a change in wording if this would destroy or render unclear the meaning of a text that contains the common intention of the parties and is clear in context. Good faith surely requires this. The advice by the British and American representatives at the Security Council on the need for delegates to vote on the text of the Resolution, not on their individual or discrete views, was thus good advice.

Two writers, Arthur Lall and Sydney Bailey, have made studies of the proceedings at the Security Council during the crisis that led to the Six day War and the diplomatic moves in its aftermath that led to Resolution 242. They both discuss the question of the interpretation of the Withdrawal Phrase.

Lall's discussion of the deliberations in the days immediately before the vote draws attention to the situation arising from the introduction of the Soviet draft on 20 November, four days after Lord Caradon had produced the British text. The Arab states would have preferred the Soviet text, but Lall's view is that 'they did not regard it as significantly different, on the basic issues of principle, from the British proposal'.[53] On the question of the Withdrawal Phrase, Lall contrasts the two as follows: '[The Soviet draft] . . . clearly called for withdrawal of all forces to positions held before June 5, 1967, whereas the British text only implied full-scale withdrawal.' [54] In other words, Lall found the text sufficiently clear even without the word 'all' in the Withdrawal Phrase for the difference in wording not to matter.

Bailey draws attention to the period before the vote when Lord Caradon and his colleagues engaged 'in a forceful campaign in the English language to

---

[48] Ibid, para 112.   [49] Ibid, para 173
[50] S/8235.   [51] S/8227.   [52] S/8253.
[53] Lall, *The UN and the Middle East Crisis, 1967* (New York and London: Columbia University Press), 1968), 260.
[54] Ibid, 257.

commend the English version of the text and, in order to commend, they also had to expound, interpret, clarify, explain, elucidate'. According to Rafael, the Israeli ambassador to the UN, Caradon tried to have 'the' inserted before 'territories', but was forced to back down under pressure from the USA and Israel. If Israeli sources are to be believed, President Johnson of the USA also rebuffed approaches from the Soviet prime minister to agree to the insertion of the word 'all' before territories, and there can be little doubt that Israel fought hard to exclude the word. On the other hand, in discussions with Arab diplomats, Caradon reassured them that the expression 'territories occupied in the recent conflict' referred to all such territories. Caradon was right in his interpretation of the meaning, and thus the absence of 'all' or 'the' is irrelevant.[55]

A point which writers favourable to the Right-wing Interpretation frequently fail to mention is that the Latin American, Non-Aligned and Soviet drafts all contained wording which corresponded to the recital 'Emphasising the inadmissibility of the acquisition of territory by war ...'[56] which Lord Caradon inserted in his text, which was based on the American draft.[57] The American draft was the only draft that did not contain an express reference to the principle that the acquisition of territory by war is inadmissible. If writers favourable to the Right-wing Interpretation are to make assumptions as to the meaning of the wording on the basis of the evolution of the text, they ought, in all intellectual honesty, to draw attention to Lord Caradon's insertion of the preamble concerning the inadmissibility of the acquisition of territory by war as at least an equally significant development in its evolution.

Furthermore, and even more importantly, the relevant paragraph in the American draft resolution concerning withdrawal does not aid their argument in any way, even though it does not contain 'all' or 'the' before territories. This paragraph runs as follows:

> The Security Council ... *Affirms* that the fulfilment of the above Charter principles requires the achievement of a state of just and lasting peace in the Middle East embracing withdrawal of armed forces from occupied territories, termination of claims or states of belligerence, mutual recognition and respect of the right of every state in the area to sovereign existence, territorial integrity political independence, secure and recognised boundaries, and freedom from the threat or use of force.[58]

Withdrawal of armed forces from occupied territories' is one of a list of items

---

[55] See Bailey, *The Making of Resolution* 242 (Dordrecht/Boston Lancaster: Martinus Nijhoff, 1985), 153–4.

[56] Thus, the Latin American text contained the wording: 'The General Assembly ... declares that the validity of the occupation or acquisition of territories brought about by such means should not be recognised', The Afro-Asian text contained: 'Occupation or acquisition of territory by military conquest is inadmissible under the Charter of the United Nations.' The Soviet text contained: 'the principle that the seizure of territories as a result of war is inadmissible.'

[57] Telegram No 3078, UK Mission in New York to Foreign Office, 7 Nov 1967. FO 961/24.

[58] S/8229.

governed by the participle 'embracing'. Another item in the same list is 'secure and recognised boundaries'. Both items have identical places in the grammar and syntax of the sentence, and should be treated equally with every other item on the list. As was argued above when discussing the context of the wording of Resolution 242 itself, it cannot be assumed that only 'some' of the boundaries should be secure and recognised. In the American wording, if the boundaries are 'all' to be secure, then by the same token 'withdrawal of armed forces from occupied territories' should apply to 'all' occupied territories; and 'termination of claims or states of belligerence' should be taken to mean 'all' claims or states of belligerence. All three are on exactly the same footing.[59]

The International Court of Justice has held that the modification of a text as a draft evolves does not necessarily imply a change in meaning.[60]

When Abba Eban emphasised that 'the important words in most languages are short words, and every word, long or short, which is not in the text, is not there because it was deliberately concluded that it should not be there', he refrained from mentioning two very significant points. The first is that a text stands or falls on the basis of its own wording, and it is only when its meaning is still unclear that further interpretation is necessary. The second point is that, just like 'all' and 'the', 'some' is a short, single syllable word.

Records released from the archives of the British Mission to the United Nations add a further gloss on the evolution of the wording. Eban may have succeeded in securing the absence of 'all' or 'the' before territories, but in the negotiations over the wording he also suffered two significant defeats. When Caradon started from the bland American text, he knew the Arab states were concerned specifically that it would not require a full Israeli withdrawal. Aware that he would need to reassure them, Caradon added two things to his draft.

The first was the words 'in the recent conflict' after the reference to occupied territories.[61] By this addition, it became clear that a specific category of territories was meant. As pointed out above, the wording of the Withdrawal Phrase implies that these territories are to be treated as a unity, and a partial withdrawal would only be a partial compliance with the principle. Eban sensed this. In a diplomatic note he stated:

---

[59] This was also the view of Goldberg. When he elaborated the text to the Security Council, he stated that withdrawal was 'on a par with the other essentials listed in the same paragraph.' See UNSCOR, 1377th Meeting, para 63.

[60] See the judgment of the ICJ in the 'Case concerning Maritime Delimitation and Territorial Questions between Qatar and Bahrain (*Qatar v Bahrain*)', *Jurisdiction and Admissibility Phase, ICJ Reports* (1995) at para 41 where the Court held that the change of wording between an earlier draft for some minutes ('the Doha Minutes') and the final agreed and signed text did not necessarily imply a change in the meaning of the wording: 'The Court is unable to see why the abandonment of a form of wording corresponding to the interpretation given by Qatar to the Doha Minutes should imply that they must be interpreted in accordance with Bahrain's thesis.'

[61] Telegram No 3078, UK Mission in New York to Foreign Office, 7 November 1967. FO 961/24.

The words 'in the recent conflict' convert the principle of eliminating occupation into a mathematically precise formula for restoring the June 4 Map.[62]

The other insertion was the preambular 'Emphasising the inadmissibility of the acquisition of territory by war', which we have already discussed. This insertion was made a couple of days later. Eban fought hard to persuade Caradon to delete this phrase as well. He may have enlisted the support of the American, Canadian and Danish delegates in support of both deletions. All three delegates saw Caradon jointly and tried to persuade him to delete both phrases.[63] But Eban was unsuccessful in achieving this goal as well. His attempt to have both phrases deleted shows that he appreciated the significance of the wording, and how it would make the Right-wing Interpretation untenable. The deletion of 'all' (or, rather, the failure to add 'all' to the text) was not quite the triumph for Israeli diplomacy that it is often alleged to be.[64]

VIII. ADDITIONAL POINTS ON INTERPRETATION

We must now consider whether there are any additional rules of interpretation which are relevant to our view of Resolution 242. A Security Council resolution is not a treaty. As Thirlway has pointed out:

> In one sense, a resolution represents, like a treaty, a meeting of wills, a coming-together of the (possibly opposing) aspirations of the States whose representatives have negotiated its drafting. In another sense, it is a unilateral act, an

---

[62] He added, 'Israel will not reconstruct that map at any time or in any circumstances.' See 'Comment by Foreign Minister of Israel' and Telegram 3164, UK Mission in New York to Foreign Office, 12 Nov 1967. FO 961/24.

[63] See 'Comments on the U.K. draft resolution made by US, Canadian, and Danish representatives on 14 November', FO 961/24.

[64] Eban took a major part in the discussions of the evolving text of Resolution 242 and contributed substantially to its development, most notably with regard to the wording of the Secure and Recognised Boundaries Phrase as well as the 'deletion' of 'all' and 'the'. In his 'Abba Eban: An Autobiography' (London: Weidenfeld & Nicholson, 1977) and 'Personal Witness: Israel through my eyes' (New York: Putnam, 1992), he gives accounts of his recollections of the negotiations in and around the Security Council debates. He makes no mention whatsoever of his unsuccessful attempt to delete 'in the recent conflict'. Whether this was a deliberate decision not to bring it to the reader's attention or through a lapse of memory must be a matter for speculation. He does, however, mention the addition of the preambular reference to 'the principle that there should be no acquisition of territory by war', and suggests in his autobiography that it had to be inserted 'to get a majority' (Autobiography: 451). In 'Personal Witness', he states that the wording was inserted 'in deference to Latin American pressure' and that 'Since Argentina and Brazil were necessary for the vote, they had to be accommodated'. He also adds that Caradon had 'his own reasons' for strengthening the language. The Latin Americans would, of course, have had in mind the principle of colonial *uti possidetis* which was adopted in Latin America on independence in the nineteenth Century and which abolished the doctrine of title by conquest in the region. This may have been mentioned to Eban by Caradon, but Eban does not inform his readers that the abolition of the principle of title by conquest had spread beyond Latin America to the rest of the World. He betrays what seems to be a cynical attitude to this particular part of the wording: 'Since the territories of most states have been decisively influenced by war, [the inadmissibility of the acquisition of territory by war] seems a somewhat insincere proposition' (Personal Witness, 457).

assertion of the will of the organ adopting it, or a statement of its collective view of a situation.[65]

Although Michael Wood draws attention to this dictum in his article 'The Interpretation of Security Council Resolutions' which appears to be one of the very few attempts to consider this topic, Thirlway's words do not affect Wood's view (which we share) that the starting point for the process of interpretation should be Articles 31 and 32 of the Vienna Convention. In the tentative conclusions which he draws at the end of his article, Wood first adapts Lord McNair's words on treaties to state that 'the aim of interpretation should be ... to give effect to the intention of the Council as expressed by the words used by the Council in the light of the surrounding circumstances'. He then states that the interpreter will seek to apply the principles of the Vienna Convention 'even if this is not expressly stated' Yet he concludes with a word of warning:

> But caution is required. SCRs are not treaties: indeed the differences are very great. Nor are SCRs necessarily all of the same nature. SCRs must be interpreted in the context of the United Nations Charter. It becomes highly artificial, and indeed to some extent is simply not possible, to seek to apply all the Vienna Convention rules *mutatis mutandis* to SCRs.
>
> In the case of SCRs, given their essentially political nature and the way they are drafted, the circumstances of the adoption of the resolution and such preparatory work as exists may often be of greater significance than in the case of treaties. The Vienna Convention distinction between the general rule and supplementary means has even less significance than in the case of treaties. In general, less importance should be attached to the minutiae of language. And there is considerable scope for authentic interpretation by the Council itself.[66]

He elaborated on some of these points earlier in his article:

> [g]iven the way SCRs are drafted, and the fact that for the most part they are intended to have political and not legal effect, it would be a mistake to approach the text as if it were drawn up with the care and legal input of a treaty. ....
> Inconsistencies in the use of terms and ungrammatical constructions are not uncommon, and it is misleading to pay undue attention to such matters, to analyse them under a microscope as one might English legislation or a treaty. On the other hand one cannot deliberately ignore such matters; they may be deliberate and important. But how does an outsider know? Or even an insider some time later?[67]

He also advised prudence when considering preambles to SCRs:

> The preambles to SCRs may assist in interpretation, by giving guidance to their object and purpose, but they need to be treated with caution since they tend to be

---

[65] Thirlway, 'The Law and Procedure of the International Court of Justice 1960–89', *BYIL* (1996), pp.29 et seq. Quoted in Wood, op cit, 85–6.

[66]. Wood, op. cit., 95.

[67] Ibid. 89.

used as a dumping ground for proposals that are not acceptable in the operative paragraphs. And there is no conscious effort to ensure that the object and purpose of each operative provision is reflected in the preamble.[68]

Where does all this leave us? What Wood suggests is essentially that every Security Council Resolution should be considered separately in its own context. Resolution 242 was, from the outset, intended to provide a pathway to peace and to lay down principles which would achieve it. The mission of the Secretary-General's representative envisaged in paragraphs 3 and 4 of the Resolution may now be long forgotten but, as we have pointed out above, the object and purpose of the Resolution as set out in these paragraphs are clear. The principles contained in the preamble and the first two paragraphs have remained those which the international community envisages as the requirements for the establishment of comprehensive peace, and Israel and the PLO have agreed to implement them.

Nevertheless, the question must be addressed: is it right to put the wording of Resolution 242 under the microscope in the way that we have done? Was it meant to be no more than a diplomatic and political document, possibly even one intended by Perfidious Albion to be susceptible of different and conflicting interpretations? Security Council resolutions which are intended to be of binding force are generally introduced under Chapter VII of the Charter. Resolution 242 would appear to have been introduced under Chapter VI. As such, it would appear to have constituted a 'recommendation' as to how the parties might settle their disputes by peaceful means, although the view that it was binding from the time of its adoption was taken by the Soviet Union and the Arab countries.[69] The intention was to formalise the principles contained in the Resolution on a higher level than that of a mere diplomatic document, so that they could provide the framework for the settlement of the entire Arab–Israeli dispute. We have seen in what minute detail the members of the Security Council analysed the wording before them. It was they who chose to put the wording under the microscope. They did this advisedly because they realised both the need to reach agreement as a goal in itself, and the need for that agreement to contain a workable set of principles which were compatible with international law. We have already referred to the later crystallisation of Resolution 242 into a text having binding force.[70] It is hard to believe that the delegates who debated the text did not expect this to happen.

It is thus scarcely surprising that, in the particular case of Resolution 242, importance happens to have been attached to 'the minutiae of language' from the outset, as we have seen from the discussion contained in the minutes of the Security Council meetings and the different drafts. Wood's conclusions

---

[68] Ibid, 86–7.

[69] Bailey and Daws, *The Procedure of the UN Security Council* (Oxford: Oxford University Press?, 1998), 270–1. The authors also draw attention to some interesting shifts in the views of some members of the United Nations as to whether resolutions under Chapter VI are binding.

[70] See nn 1 and 2 above.

confirm us in our view that more importance should, perhaps, be given to the available supplementary means of interpretation than would always be the case with regard to a treaty. We have found that the use of such means of interpretation support us in our view. The fact that so many of the delegates made a point of going on the record in the Security Council debate to indicate that they interpreted the Withdrawal Phrase in the light of the preamble concerning the inadmissibility of the acquisition of territory by war shows that in this particular case the delegates considered the preamble an integral part of the Resolution, and certainly not 'a dumping ground for proposals which are not acceptable in the operative paragraphs'. The record of the debate shows that the delegates acted as if they were construing a legal document in which precise wording was important.

Wood also draws attention to the 'considerable scope for authentic interpretation by the Council itself.[71] In a sense, the Council interpreted Resolution 242 when it passed Resolution 338, using mandatory language which brings it within Article 25 of the Charter. Whether this interpretation was an 'amendment' is not a question which need trouble us today. Moreover, earlier this year the Council adopted the language of 'secure and recognised boundaries' from Resolution 242 in the preamble to Resolution 1397.[72] By doing so, it reiterated the significance which it attached to the Secure and Recognised Boundaries Phrase and stressed its reciprocal nature, as it is applicable both to Israel and the Palestinian state.

IX. THE UNWELCOME CONSEQUENCE OF THE RIGHT-WING INTERPRETATION

What effect does Resolution 242 have on the territories which lay on the Israeli side of the 1949 Cease-fire lines with Egypt and Jordan? Some writers draw attention to the fact that the Withdrawal Phrase did not call for an Israeli withdrawal from territories occupied by Israel in 1948-9, and imply that this omission consolidated Israeli title over all such territory. Thus, Watson[73] states:

> Resolution 242 . . . implicitly superseded the territorial formula in the Partition Resolution, since it called only for an Israeli withdrawal from territories occupied in the 1967 War, not withdrawal to the borders envisaged by the Partition Resolution.

With respect, we would suggest that this interpretation is correct as regards withdrawal of armed forces, but should not be deemed to perfect any Israeli title to territory which was imperfect when Resolution 242 was passed. There is a confusion between the law of title to territory and the law of armed conflict which is a fudge at the heart of the Right-wing Interpretation. It is the 'inad-

---

[71] Wood, op cit, 95.
[72] The preamble also recites Resolutions 242 and 338.
[73] Watson, op cit, 24.

missibility of the acquisition of territory by war' in the preamble which recites the law on territorial sovereignty and imports it directly into the Resolution, not the Withdrawal Phrase. Resolution 242 does not 'supersede the territorial formula in the Partition Resolution'.

This brings us inevitably to the question of what constitutes the sovereign territory of Israel. Although, as a sovereign state, Israel must certainly possess sovereign territory, there is uncertainty as to its extent. Since the signing of the peace treaties between Israel and Egypt and Israel and Jordan, the borders laid down in those treaties provide the borders between Israel and these two particular neighbours. However, these treaties are without prejudice to the status of the West Bank, East Jerusalem, and the Gaza Strip.[74]

Moreover, doubts have been expressed by scholars over the question of whether the territorial framework envisaged by the Partition Plan ever came into effect in a manner which would *ipso jure* grant Israel sovereignty over the territory allocated to the Jewish State by that plan. Sir Elihu Lauterpacht has argued that the disorder in Palestine at the end of the Mandate which was caused by the British withdrawal, the Arab rejection of the Partition resolution, the creation of Israel and the entry of Arab armies with the intention of crushing Israel 'all led to a situation of such juridical confusion as to exclude any tracing of an orderly devolution of sovereignty'. He continues:

> But if there was, upon the termination of the mandate, a sovereignty vacuum in Palestine, the large question arises of how it could validly be filled. The suggestion that there was a vacuum of sovereignty does not imply that Palestine became at the end of the mandate a *terra nullius*, a land owned by no-one in which anyone was free to stake a claim by simply combining physical presence with an assertion of title. Slight though the legal effect of the Partition Resolution might be, it is difficult to conceive of it as having opened Palestine to the law of the jungle, to be carved up on the basis of first come first served.[75]

We will not attempt on this occasion to analyse the status of those portions of the territory allocated to the Arab State under the UN Partition Plan which had been seized by Israel by the time of the 1949 Armistices or to examine the status of the territory allocated to the Jewish state under that plan. However, as we have seen, the emphasis on the inadmissibility of the acquisition of territory by war in Resolution 242 is of general application and, in sharp contrast to the Withdrawal Phrase, is not limited to territories occupied in 'the recent conflict'. Resolution 242 can thus be interpreted as preventing Israel from consolidating title over all territory taken by force at any time in the absence of a final peace settlement.[76] Certainly there should be no assumption that

---

[74] See 'Peace Treaty between Israel and Egypt', 26 Mar 1979, Art 2; 'Treaty of Peace between the State of Israel and the Hashemite Kingdom of Jordan', 26 Oct 1994, Art 3.

[75] E Lauterpacht, 'Jerusalem and the Holy Places', Anglo-Israel Pamphlet No19, London 1968, 41–2.

[76] On this point, see Quincy Wright, 'The Middle East Problem', 64 *American Journal of International Law* (1970), at 271: 'The extension of Israel's occupation beyond the original UN

Israel may have a claim to parts of the territories occupied in 1967, although this is implied in the current Israeli predilection for referring to the territories occupied in 1967 as 'disputed'.[77] The Armistice Agreements were without prejudice to territorial sovereignty, and therefore Israel was barred by its own action in signing them from consolidating its title up to the armistice lines so long as those agreements remained in force.[78] It is inconceivable that Israel could have perfected that title in the period of less than six months between the Six Days War and the passing of Resolution 242, a period during which armed conflict continued. However, if any validity is to be attributed to the designation of the territories occupied in 1967 as 'disputed territories', Israel should be aware that the territory on the Israeli side of the 1949 Armistice Lines must *ipso jure* be treated as 'disputed'. Israeli title can only be perfected through the final peace settlement envisaged by Resolution 242 and subsequent resolutions, which alone can establish 'secure and recognised boundaries'. Failing this, Israel will always be exposed to a risk that claims may be brought for the territories which Israel took in 1948–9.

X. CONCLUSION

This analysis has attempted to apply the rules of interpretation contained in Articles 31 and 32 of the Vienna Convention to the text of Resolution 242 in order to establish the meaning of the Withdrawal Phrase. We have seen that a clear meaning is given to the Withdrawal Phrase if it is read as requiring an Israeli withdrawal from all the territories occupied in 1967. Such a reading is not only linguistically possible, but accords with the letter and the spirit of the Resolution when read as a whole.

Through the application of Schwebel's proposition that good faith requires that extrinsic evidence, in this case the records of the Security Council debate and the discarded Latin American, Non-aligned, Soviet and US drafts, should be invoked in order to confirm or correct the meaning which the drafters intended the wording to carry, any possibility of a gap between the wording and the intention disappears. It is impossible to see how an independent scholar can examine the records of the Security Council debate and claim that they support a contention that Israel had the right to retain areas of the territories occupied in 1967 save through a freely negotiated agreement. The possi-

---

grant as a result of the Arab-Israeli hostilities of 1948–9 and the armistices negotiated in 1949 are justified as temporary measures to end the hostilities. The principle of no acquisition of territory by war should, if strictly applied, require the cease fire lines to be at the frontiers before hostilities began, thus preventing military occupations as well as acquisitions by force, but the overriding responsibility of the United Nations to stop hostilities justified the acceptance of the armistices as temporary cease fire lines to be soon superseded by permanent boundaries established by peaceful means.'

[77] See, eg, Dore Gold, op cit.

[78] See Egypt–Israel Armistice Agreement, 24 Feb 1949, Art.4; General Armistice Agreement between Israel and Jordan, 3 Apr 1949, Art 6.

bility of such agreement is impeded by the maintenance of the occupation for over a third of a century. Indeed, it must be submited that the continuation of the occupation is itself a breach of Resolution 242, since it depends on 'threats or acts of force' and implies a victor's right to extract concessions by duress, in breach of the rule that title to territory may not be acquired by war. The territories occupied in 1967 may only be described as 'disputed' if the territories on the other side of the 1949 Armistice lines are described in the same way.

A very serious question mark is also raised over whether the Right-wing interpretation is sustainable as a good faith interpretation for the purposes of international law. We believe that it is not. Good faith surely requires internal consistency and a lack of contradiction, as well as compliance with the law. The scholars who read Resolution 242 as only requiring a withdrawal from 'some' of the territories fail to surmount these hurdles. They either fail to consider them or view the text as contradictory: but how can the text be contradictory when a clear and internally consistent meaning can be extracted from it?

Part VII

SELF-DETERMINATION AND BELLIGERENT OCCUPATION

Journal of Refugee Studies Vol. 2 No 1 1989

The Palestinians, the Uprising, and International Law

ADAM ROBERTS*

Professor Roberts is Montague Burton Professor of International Relations and Fellow of Balliol College, Oxford. He co-edited Documents on the Laws of War (OUP 1982) and was joint author of Academic Freedom under Israeli Military Occupation (WUS 1984). His most recent book is United Nations, Divided World: The UN's Roles in International Relations (OUP 1988).

Can international law, and especially that part of it which relates to the conduct of military occupations, have any part to play in the long-standing, deep, and tragic conflict between Israel and the Arabs? Can it in any way have a bearing on the issues raised by the Palestinian uprising in the Occupied Territories, an uprising which reflects among other things the frustration of the inhabitants (of whom a very high proportion are refugees) in face of the repeated failures to achieve a diplomatic settlement of that conflict?

These questions are bound to be answered with a degree of scepticism. The Arab-Israeli conflict, of which the Palestinian uprising is the latest manifestation, is peculiarly bitter. At its heart are two peoples who have much in common including the experience of suffering discrimination, expulsion, and invasion. Tragically these peoples are locked in a conflict which involves religion, ethnic identity, rival claims to the same land, the use of violent and terroristic methods, and mutual fears of extermination.

It is not self-evident that international law, which is so often flawed in its regulation of conflicts which are much less deep-seated and bitter, can either help resolve significant aspects of the Arab-Israeli conflict, or place some restraints on the methods used in that conflict. Indeed, law itself easily gets conscripted into the service of one side or another: all too often existing international agreements and legal principles are seen, not as a means of mediating the conflict, but as instruments which can be rolled up and used as truncheons with which to hit the other side.

Yet the Palestinian uprising in the West Bank and Gaza, which began on 9 December 1987, has raised, or re-raised, a number of international legal questions in very sharp form. These questions include:

1) What body of international law regulates the situation in the Occupied Territories?

2) What is Israel entitled, and not entitled, to do to preserve public order in these territories?
3) Is Israel entitled to bring settlers into the territories?
4) Is Israel entitled to deport the inhabitants?
5) What is the status of Palestinian refugees in the Territories?
6) Can the international community do anything to assist implementation of the applicable rules of international law?

Since the uprising began, questions such as these have received rather less public attention from the international community than have questions to do with a possible peace settlement. The powers with an interest in the Middle East, especially the USA, reacted at first to the uprising by engaging in exploratory talks on the subject of a possible peace settlement. Various ideas for a political solution were discussed — some of them little more than dusted-down versions of older schemes, known to be unacceptable to one party or another. It appears that the amount of occupied land Israel was prepared to consider giving up was less than any of the Arab parties could contemplate accepting. The Shultz initiative effectively ended on 6 April 1988 when the US Secretary of State, after a long round of shuttle diplomacy, departed from Jerusalem with the brave words: 'I depart Israel but not the initiative.'

The extensive round of international diplomacy in early June 1988 did not open up any immediate prospect of a breakthrough on the question of a Middle East peace settlement. At the Reagan-Gorbachev summit in Moscow on 29 May – 2 June there was discussion of the Arab-Israeli problem, but there are grounds for scepticism as to whether there was sufficient progress to bring a diplomatic settlement any closer. The subsequent attempt by George Shultz to revive the US initiative, in his visit to the Middle East immediately after the Moscow summit, appeared to yield no results. The emergency summit of the Arab League in Algiers on 7–9 June marked a high point in Arab unity and declarations of support for the PLO, and as such was a highly significant event; but it did not produce a formula for peace talks that had a better chance of acceptance than any of its predecessors.

As George Shultz knows, having burnt his fingers in the Middle East before, any efforts to get a peace between the intensely suspicious and insecure parties to the Arab-Israeli dispute face almost insuperable difficulties. In recent years, although the Palestine Liberation Organization has embarked upon some very significant policy changes (both as regards its ultimate aims, and as regards methods of struggle), it has not yet gone far enough to reassure Israel (nor, perhaps, its Arab neighbours) that a future Palestinian state would be a good neighbour and a factor of stability in the region. Meanwhile, Israel's position has become both more confused and more obdurate, with the Likud gaining popular support at the expense of its Labour coalition partner, and Labour distancing itself from some of its members, most notably Abba Eban MK, who had expressed criticisms of the methods used in the attempt to suppress the Palestinian uprising.[1]

28   *Adam Roberts*

Despite these developments, a· political-cum-territorial solution acceptable to all parties remains very hard to envisage. It is a terrible tragedy that, at the time when the uprising broke out, the various political leaderships involved did not have negotiating positions which had any chance at all of acceptance; and that they have moved so slowly and hesitantly, if at all, to remedy this dismal situation. As a result, peace talks, though urgently needed, are not likely to be successful in the short term. They cannot be a substitute for other approaches.

The response of the international community to the uprising in the Occupied Territories has had another, less publicized, aspect — one related more to the conduct of the occupation than its termination. Many governments have made strong representations to Israel about the need to observe in full the provisions of the 1949 Geneva Civilians Convention. Does this approach have any prospect of affecting events for the better? It is first necessary to look briefly at the tangled question of the status of the West Bank and Gaza.[2]

International Rules Applicable in the West Bank and Gaza

States are bound to observe a wide range of international rules not only within their own territory, but also in any territory they occupy or administer. Such rules are not limited to laws-of-war agreements specifically covering military occupations (such as the 1907 Hague Regulations and 1949 Geneva Convention IV), but include also commitments of various types on a wide range of other matters, from the safety of civil aviation to the control of narcotics — and, indeed, the status of refugees.

It is best to begin by looking at a major body of law — namely the laws of war — which affects all inhabitants of the Territories: not only the refugees, but also the indigenous population. It is laws-of-war agreements which contain the most succinct and relevant rules so far as the position of the inhabitants of occupied territory is concerned: although, as will be seen below, these rules are not entirely free of problems so far as they relate to the position of refugees.

The whole idea that an area of inhabited territory can be viewed as merely 'occupied', rather than conquered, is itself a triumph of international legal thinking. In earlier times, if a state had military control of an area, it was often assumed to have the right to administer it as it pleased. The idea that an occupant has a provisional status only, and must observe certain agreed rules of restraint pending a peace settlement, emerged only slowly. The concept of 'military occupation' is now widely accepted by states, and indeed forms a necessary complement to the fundamental principle of international law, reflected in the UN Charter, prohibiting forcible acquisition of territory. It is partly because the international community has never deviated from its view of Israel's role in the lands it took over in 1967 as being provisional that these territories have been the subject of such continuous diplomatic attention. Therefore, international law, even if it is observed very imperfectly by the parties, influences the way that the entire problem of the future of the West

Bank and Gaza is perceived — not just in foreign offices, but in the areas most directly concerned.

However, the proposition that Israel is an occupying power, with all the rights and duties attaching to that status, is not completely uncontested. It is accepted by the overwhelming majority of states. But the two parties most directly involved — Israel on the one hand, and the PLO on the other — have both expressed certain doubts about this proposition. If these two antagonists agree on nothing else, they appear to be in accord on one point: that the status of these territories is so special that the normal rules of military occupation are not fully applicable. A brief look at these viewpoints is a necessary preliminary to considering the application of international law in the West Bank and Gaza.

Israel deserves some credit for by and large accepting in principle that the rules relating to military occupations are applicable. However, there have been some important qualifications to this position: qualifications of real substance, not of cosmetics. Frequently commentators worry about mere questions of nomenclature, and suggest that because, for example, Israel has called its system of military government one of 'civil administration', it is therefore denying that it is an occupant. This is incorrect. Occupation regimes can be called any of a hundred names, and the key question remains whether the occupier, however he calls himself, is willing to observe the relevant international rules. It is on this point that there are two major grounds for concern.

First, ever since 1967 Israel has said that it does not view the 1949 Geneva Convention IV (which is the major international agreement relating to the conduct of occupations) as formally applicable on a *de jure* basis: it is, however, willing to apply the 'humanitarian provisions' of the Convention on a *de facto* basis.[3] Israel says that it takes this view because neither the West Bank nor Gaza was, in the words of the Convention's Article 2, 'the territory of a High Contracting Party' before Israel occupied it in 1967. This is true enough, but it is very doubtful whether it is a valid reason for viewing the Convention as not formally applicable. Moreover, there is bound to be concern that Israel has never defined what it means when it says it will apply the Convention's 'humanitarian provisions': does it mean all, or merely some, articles of the Convention?

Second, there has been an increasingly strong political tendency in Israel to deny that Israel's role in the West Bank and Gaza is that of an occupant at all. Especially from the late 1970s onwards, with the advent to power of the Likud, the West Bank and Gaza were officially viewed as part of 'Eretz Israel'. Maps were published which showed absolutely no distinction between Israel's pre-1967 frontiers and the lands occupied since then. Flats in new settlements were advertised in both Israeli and American papers with no reference to the fact that they were in the Occupied Territories. Clearly this attitude, of viewing the West Bank and Gaza as part of the national territory, was bound to have a corrosive effect on Israel's observance of the body of international law relating to military occupations. However, this attitude did not completely change the situation. Even if Israel had its own idiosyncratic view of the status of the

Occupied Territories, it did not openly challenge the status of the inhabitants as people entitled to protection under the relevant rules of international law. Moreover, the Israel Defence Forces, like any large department of government charged with a complex task, has to operate in the Territories in accord with certain clear principles and guidelines: and the best ones available, even if they were not perfectly observed, were those derived from the law on military occupations.

The tendency in Israel to view the West Bank and Gaza as part of the national territory had many causes, ranging from religious fundamentalism to a simpler, secular belief that holding on to these territories was necessary if Israel was to be secure from attack. One further cause was a perception that it was very unsatisfactory to have the status of an occupying power indefinitely, when there was no serious prospect of a peace settlement to end the occupation in a manner which would reflect the needs of Israel, its neighbours, and the inhabitants of the Territories. Thus Israeli impatience with the lack of progress in negotiations in the 1970s, and especially with the Arab refusal to accept the 1978 Camp David autonomy proposals, was harnessed by the Likud in its efforts in the 1980s to colonize the Territories and alter their status.

The PLO, too, was reluctant to accept that the law on occupations applied fully in the West Bank and Gaza. It did accept that there was an occupation, but then insisted that it was of such a special character that some of the normal rules relating to occupations could not apply. In a number of statements and publications, the PLO appeared to take the line that Israel was an aggressor-occupant, and as such was not entitled to the extensive rights which interional law recognizes an occupant to have.[4] This position was certainly understandable, for no one likes to accept that an adversary has extensive rights to control the lives of his compatriots or allies, even on a provisional and limited basis. However, in legal terms it was, and remains, incorrect. It is a simple and elementary principle of the laws of war that those laws (including the ones relating to occupations) must apply fully, irrespective of how the war or military occupation actually began.

The Israeli and PLO positions deserve attention, not because they are legally impressive or internationally persuasive, but rather because they show just how serious the obstacles are to any reliance on international law as a means of mitigating the conflict between Israelis and Palestinians. These positions have not been found at all persuasive by the international community, either at the regional or the global level. UN General Assembly resolutions urging the full *de jure* applicability of the 1949 Geneva Civilians Convention have regularly attracted near-unanimous support.

In short, there is no serious room for doubt about the fact that the Israeli occupations of these Territories are bound to be conducted in accord with the provisions laid down in the 1970 Hague Regulations and the 1949 Geneva Convention IV. Israel is also bound, like any other state, by international customary law, and by the relevant provisions of the human rights conventions to which it is a party. Some of the various rules contained in all these instruments need careful interpretation to fit with the complex facts of the case — especially in a prolonged occupation, which inevitably throws up problems rather different in character from those envisaged at the Hague and Geneva.

Israel and the Right to Maintain Public Order

Israel, as an occupying power, has a right in international law to maintain public order. There is no room for doubt on this point. It is a right implicit in the 1907 Hague Regulations, Article 43:

> The authority of the legitimate power having in fact passed into the hands of the occupant, the latter shall take all the measures in his power to restore, and ensure, as far as possible, public order and safety, while respecting, unless absolutely prevented, the laws in force in the country.

However, there are limits beyond which an occupant may not go in its efforts to maintain public order. For example, collective punishments are prohibited not only in the 1907 Hague Regulations, Article 50, but also in the 1949 Geneva Convention IV, Article 33.

Inhabitants who oppose the occupying power may be punished, but any trial and punishment — normally by the occupier's military courts sitting in the occupied territory — must conform with certain elementary requirements. In the 1949 Geneva Convention IV, Article 5 deals with the case of a person 'detained as a spy or saboteur, or as a person under definite suspicion of activity hostile to the security of the occupying power'. Such a person can, in cases where absolute military security so requires, lose the right of communication. Article 68 deals with the case of persons 'who commit an offence which is solely intended to harm the Occupying Power, but which does not constitute an attempt on the life or limb of members of the occupying forces, nor a grave collective danger . . .' Such persons can be interned or imprisoned. Internment is governed by very extensive and detailed provisions in the 1949 Geneva Convention IV.

Can such provisions be reconciled with the Israeli responses to the Palestinian uprising? There is no doubt at all that uprisings in occupied territories create a risk of total collapse of all constraints, legal or otherwise. There is an element of contractual thinking in some of the law on occupations, and some writers have even gone so far as to assert that the population, in return for protection, owes the occupant a duty of obedience. Even if that view is questioned, resistance does still, as a matter of fact, create risks of a breakdown of civilized constraints. Such a risk of breakdown is especially severe in cases where violent acts are carried out clandestinely by guerrilla or terrorist groups, or when they assume extreme forms, such as the alleged use of forest fires by Palestinians.[5] There is bound to be pressure on an occupant to engage in collective punishments in response to such acts, questionable as such a response undoubtedly is in both legal and practical terms.

The Palestinian uprising involves very serious risks of this kind. However, a special feature of the uprising should be noted. It has achieved much of its effect precisely because it has involved mass participation in actions which are very different from earlier guerrilla or terrorist attacks. The stone-throwing Palestinians have been widely perceived as underdogs. Not counting guerrilla infiltrations, the death toll in the first six months of the uprising was three Israelis and at least 213 Palestinians.[6] As so often in history, the most effective methods of struggle have not been the most offensive or aggressive ones.

Making all allowances for the difficulties they face, some Israeli actions in response to the uprising do appear very questionable. There has, rightly, been much comment on particular episodes. One notable example concerns the events at the village of Beita, near Nablus, following incidents on 6 April in which two Palestinians and a 15-year-old Jewish girl from the settlement of Elon Moreh died. Houses of several villagers were blown up before anything like a full picture had emerged of the incident which had occasioned this punishment. The girl who died turned out to have been killed, not by Palestinian stoning as at first alleged, but by the bullet of an Israeli security guard.

Much of the Israeli response to the uprising was shaped by the policy of 'force, power, and beatings' which was enunciated by Defence Minister Rabin on 20 January 1988. This policy led, unintentionally but inevitably, to numerous excesses. Interviews with victims from the West Bank and Gaza in late January 1988 convinced me that beatings had been carried out arbitrarily, the crime of some victims being what they were — Palestinians — rather than what they had done. Many such cases have become the subject of Israeli Army internal inquiries and, in some instances, disciplinary proceedings. The spectacle of Israeli forces beating up more or less defenceless Arabs has done immense harm to Israel's standing in the world. The stone-throwing inhabitants gained much more sympathy for their cause than did any number of guerrilla or terrorist acts organized from outside.

There are many other aspects of the Israeli response to the uprising that are doubtful in international legal terms. It seems probable, on the basis of published reports, that the killing in Tunis on 16 April of Khalil al-Wazir (Abu Jihad), the number two leader of the PLO, was carried out by an Israeli hit squad.[7] Israeli sources indicated that this was in retaliation for an attack on an Israeli bus in the Negev on 7 March, for which Mr Wazir's military organization, Fatah, had claimed responsibility. Perhaps the best legal justification Israel could have produced for this assassination, if it had accepted public responsibility for it, would have been that it was a reprisal — an act which, itself illegal, is a response to an illegal act by the adversary and is conducted with the explicit purpose of making the adversary conform with international law. However, this justification is hardly open to Israel, as it did not formally accept responsibility for this act, and so could not make its purpose explicit. Quite apart from the question of the legality of this action, there are bound to be questions about its prudence: it raised questions, in the USA and elsewhere, about whether Israel was not itself engaging in a form of terrorism; and it contributed to a partial reconciliation between different factions of the Palestinian liberation movement when Yasser Arafat visited Syria later in the same month.

Israel does have a real problem in responding to the uprising. Its part-time forces are small in number, ill-trained for arduous public order duties, and caught between the wrath of stone-throwing Palestinians and the zealotry of armed Israeli settlers. Israel has a right to maintain public order, and to use forceful measures to do so if they are necessary. Moreover, Israelis may legitimately ask why their soldiers should be expected to observe every article laid down in The Hague and Geneva when the PLO has a record of involvement in terrorist acts which by their very nature, being conducted clandestinely and aimed against civilians, are a violation of the most basic principles of the laws of war. To the extent that such considerations and arguments have any validity, they confirm the already-noted difficulty of bringing international law to bear on this particular conflict. Yet it remains true that Israel, like the states it adjoins, is bound to observe the provisions of international law, and must be willing to accept criticism, and remedy faults, if it fails to do so.

The Question of Settlers in the Occupied Territories

In the West Bank and Gaza there are now some 60,000 Israeli settlers — a doubling of numbers in the past five years which has contributed powerfully to Palestinian frustration. Their very presence creates numerous points of friction with the inhabitants. In the course of the uprising there have been numerous clashes with settlers, including the shootings at the village of Beita. The high risk that the uprising will degenerate into inter-communal violence is at least partly due to the presence of settlements.

The 1949 Geneva Convention IV, Article 49, paragraph 6, is widely viewed as completely prohibiting the establishment of settlements:

> The Occupying Power shall not deport or transfer parts of its own civilian population into the territory it occupies.

This provision was put into the Convention as a reaction to the extensive changes of population which the Axis occupation powers in the Second World War brought about in many of the countries which they occupied. The provision can also be defended on the grounds that the introduction of settlements often makes peace harder to achieve, and sows the seeds of future conflicts — as the British have discovered in Northern Ireland, where a three-centuries-old conflict between Protestant settlers and Catholic inhabitants continues to this day.

Israelis sometimes defend the settlements as legal, on either of two grounds. The first is to assert that some settlements are not civilian in character, and are hence not subject to the prohibition in Article 49. It is undoubtedly true that there are settlements, especially some of the earlier ones, which did have a largely military purpose and character: to the extent that this is true, and especially if they were clearly temporary, such settlements might be justifiable in international legal terms. But this simply does not apply to the great majority of Israeli settlements in the West.Bank and Gaza, many of which were set up as permanent commuter suburbs of Jerusalem and Tel Aviv, not as bastions to protect Israel from invasion.

The second ground for defending the legality of the settlements depends on a claim that the settlements represent nothing other than voluntary population movements — the exercise, as it were, of a presumed fundamental human right to move house. In this view, the settlements are not the result of the occupying power deciding to 'transfer parts of its own civilian population into the territory it occupies', to quote the words of Article 49. Therefore, the argument goes, the prohibition in the Geneva Convention does not apply. This argument is not at all convincing. It has been amply documented that the ambitious settlements programme of the 1980s was planned, encouraged, and financed at government level.[8]

The massive Israeli settlements programme is quite simply contrary to international law. However, it is now so far advanced, and so plainly in violation of the 1949 Geneva Convention, that it actually creates a powerful reason for Israel's continuing refusal to accept that the Convention is fully applicable in the Occupied Territories on a *de jure* basis. By causing friction with the Palestinian inhabitants of the territories, the programme may even have added to the work of the Israel Defence Forces — hardly the intention of the early settlers. In short, the settlements programme is a disaster.

However, the momentum of the settlements programme may be declining. Not only have the ambitious Israeli targets for the number of settlers not been met (there were supposed to be 100,000 in the West Bank by the end of 1986), but also it seems likely that one of the effects of the uprising will be to discourage the 'fair-weather' settlers — those searching for a nice flat and a cheap mortgage — from moving to such controversial surroundings. In this sense at least, the Palestinian uprising may positively assist the observance of at least one provision of international law — the prohibition on settlements.

Israel and Deportations from Occupied Territory

Within the Occupied Territories there has always been a fear that Israel would try to deport large numbers of people to neighbouring Arab states. Granted the population movements associated with an earlier phase of the Arab-Israeli conflict, this fear was not surprising, and it revived in the 1980s mainly because the presence of one and a half million Palestinians in the Territories is obviously in conflict with ambitious schemes for Eretz Israel. From an Israeli perspective the demographic question became extremely serious in the second half of the 1980s, as evidence mounted of rapid population growth among the Palestinians. Indeed, projections were published suggesting that, all other things being equal, by the year 2010 the Jewish and Arab populations in all of Mandatory Palestine would reach parity.[9]

In actual fact the Israeli authorities have so far only sought to use deportations in a limited way — to rid themselves of particular named opponents of their rule. Some subtle legal justifications for this have been produced. However, the 1949 Geneva Convention IV, Article 49, paragraph 1, is unambiguous:

> Individual or mass forcible transfers, as well as deportations of protected persons from occupied territory to the territory of the Occupying Power or to that of any other country, occupied or not, are prohibited, regardless of their motive.

This provision might not cover all cases, and especially not cases of individuals who are not residents of the territories but have, for example, entered them illegally or remained there beyond the duration of a permit.[10] However, its meaning so far as the mass of the inhabitants of the West Bank and Gaza are concerned is clear.

The rule against deportations may be openly challenged in coming months and years. One disturbing aspect of the Israeli swing to the right as a result of the uprising has been an apparent increase in the number of Israelis favouring deportations. According to a survey conducted for Tel Aviv University, four Israelis in every ten support the idea of 'transferring' the Arab populations out of the West Bank and Gaza Strip.[11]

Since the prohibition on deportations is an important principle which many states wish to see upheld, the international community would be likely to oppose strenuously any large-scale deportation moves which looked like expulsion of the population. Even though the precise actions that would be taken may not be clear, this is an important constraint on Israeli policy, and it is due to the requirements of international law.

The Status of the Refugees in the West Bank and Gaza

Of the approximately 1.4 million inhabitants of the West Bank and Gaza, a remarkably high proportion — approaching 50 per cent — are classified as refugees, at least by the definitions used by the UN Relief and Works Agency for Palestine Refugees in the Near East (UNRWA). The competence of UNRWA extends to those who left their homes in Palestine as a result of the 1948 conflict and are now living in one of the countries where UNRWA operates, and also to their offspring. It has also had some competence in respect of those displaced and in serious need of assistance as a result of the June 1967 war.[12] Because of these special arrangements in respect of Palestinian refugees, the UN High Commissioner for Refugees is not involved.[13]

Are there any special rules, forms of protection, or international agreements which apply particularly to the refugees in the West Bank and Gaza, and suggest that they have a different legal status from the other inhabitants of the Occupied Territories? To answer this question comprehensively it would be necessary to look in detail at many legal provisions of several different types, including:

> Those provisions of laws-of-war agreements (such as the 1949 Geneva Convention IV) which relate specifically to refugees;

The various agreements associated with the creation and continuing operations of UNRWA;

Various mandatory UN Security Council resolutions referring to the refugee problem;[14]

Some (but not all) general international agreements on refugee matters.

As far as the fundamental rights of the refugees *vis-à-vis* the occupying power are concerned, it is probably the first of these categories — i.e. the laws-of-war one — which is most important. However, its application is not entirely free from elements of doubt. The 1949 Geneva Convention IV, Article 4, paragraph 1, says:

> Persons protected by the Convention are those who, at a given moment and in any manner whatsoever, find themselves, in case of a conflict or occupation, in the hands of a party to the conflict or Occupying Power of which they are not nationals.

So far as the refugees in the West Bank and Gaza are concerned, this paragraph might seem to pose some problems. If a refugee from Israel, having settled in the West Bank or Gaza before 1967, could in any way be viewed as still a national of Israel, then it might be argued that he or she was not protected by the Convention. This view might seem to be reinforced by the terms of Article 70, paragraph 2. This specifies that nationals of the occupying power who before the outbreak of hostilities sought refuge in the territory of the occupied state are the subject of some minimal guarantees, and goes on to imply that it might be permissible for the occupant to deport such people for certain offences.

However, any argument that the refugees in the West Bank and Gaza are not entitled to enjoy the full benefit of the Convention would be extremely artificial, and would be open to criticism on several grounds. The most important is the most obvious: since the refugees in fact left in 1948, they were not nationals of Israel in any case. Moreover, the 1977 Geneva Protocol I additional to the 1949 Geneva Conventions and Relating to the Protection of Victims of International Armed Conflicts, Article 73, states clearly:

> Persons who, before the beginning of hostilities, were considered as stateless persons or refugees under the relevant international instruments accepted by the Parties concerned or under the national legislation of the State of refuge or State of residence shall be protected persons within the meaning of Parts I and III of the Fourth Convention, in all circumstances and without any distinction.[15]

Although Israel is not a party to the 1977 Geneva Protocol I, this particular provision may well be accepted as a reasonable modification of the law.[16] At all events, in actual practice Israel does not appear to have drawn a legal distinction, so far as the application of the 1949 Geneva Convention IV is concerned, between the refugees in the West Bank and Gaza and the other inhabitants.

The second paragraph of the 1949 Geneva Convention IV, Article 4, should also be cited:

> Nationals of a State which is not bound by the Convention are not protected by it. Nationals of a neutral State who find themselves in the territory of a belligerent State, and nationals of a co-belligerent State, shall not be regarded as protected persons while the State of which they are nationals has normal diplomatic representation in the State in whose hands they are.

This paragraph does not appear to pose any problems: none of the refugees in the West Bank and Gaza are nationals of a state not bound by the Convention, as all the countries in the region are parties to all four 1949 Geneva Conventions; and none of the refugees are nationals of a neutral state or a co-belligerent of Israel.

The International Community and the Observance of Rules

Is there any prospect that Israel can be induced to observe fully the key provisions of international law which bear on the current situation, including the prohibitions on civilian settlements, on expulsions of the inhabitants, and on indiscriminate punishment of the inhabitants?

The first point to bear in mind is that some outside pressure in this direction may be counter-productive. If Israelis feel that they are being pressed to observe international norms purely in order to undermine their position, or if they suspect that admonitions are coming from states which do not care for Israel's security, they may well not listen to what they are told. Likewise, if recommendations to observe international law have a mechanical character, and are not based on a serious attempt to understand the actual situation in Israel and the Occupied Territories, they may fall on barren ground. The past efforts of the international community in respect of the Arab-Israel problem, including those organized under United Nations auspices, have not been free of such faults.

However, in the past some outside pressure has had an effect. Israel is vulnerable to persuasion and pressure from other states, and especially from its main ally, the USA. During the Reagan years, since 1981, the USA government has soft-pedalled its traditionally strong commitment to international law, and President Reagan even went on record at one point in his first term as saying that the Israeli settlements in the West Bank were acceptable. However, the Reagan years are now at an end. In future, US governments are likely to put more emphasis on the observance of international rules — especially so as far as the Middle East is concerned. There are signs that the uprising has begun to change at least some American minds towards a more critical attitude to Israel, at least on the matter of its occupation policies. This important change could well be reversed if Israel's very existence was seen to be once again threatened, or if the Palestinian uprising degenerated into terrorism. However, assuming such disasters do not materialize, then a period of stronger US pressure on Israel can be anticipated.

38   *Adam Roberts*

Other states may also have an important role to play, including the states in the region. The parties most directly interested (Jordan and Egypt) could, if they so wished, take the important initiative of trying to get the UN to request from the International Court of Justice an advisory opinion on certain key legal questions. These could include: whether the 1949 Geneva Convention IV is applicable in the Occupied Territories on a *de jure* basis; whether international human rights law is applicable; whether the settlements established by Israel are in accord with international law; and various other questions arising from the many problems which have arisen in this prolonged occupation.

At the end of the day, political realism suggests that the question of Israel's observance of international norms cannot be completely separated from the no less tangled question of the PLO's observance of the same norms. Likewise, pressure on Israel to accept that its role is that of occupant is much more likely to be effective if Israel's adversaries, especially the PLO, can develop a negotiating position that is unambiguously clear on the emotionally and politically difficult matter of accepting that the Israelis, as well as the Palestinian Arabs, have a right of self-determination. For only if there is a persuasive Palestinian position on this matter — a position convincing to third parties such as the EEC countries — will it be possible in the long haul to get Israel to revert to the position that it is only an occupant in the territories, not a sovereign.

Formidable as the difficulties are, the action of many governments in pressing Israel to observe in full, and on a *de jure* basis, the provisions of the 1949 Geneva Convention IV makes both legal and political sense. The Convention cannot itself provide a solution to the problems of the area. But pressure for its full implementation can serve as a reminder to Israel that there is an international interest in seeing to it that Israel exercises restraint in its conduct there pending negotiations. Indeed, observance of the convention is a necessary if not a sufficient condition for a future peace.

1   Abba Eban, a former Israeli foreign minister, was left off a list of the Labour Party's election candidates in early June 1988. He was quoted as saying that the main reason was that: 'I asked questions about such controversial issues as the policy of beatings adopted by the Army in the Administered Territories and also whether any such policy decisions should be left to one man or taken collectively.' *The Observer*, London, 19 June 1988.

2.   I have explored the question of the status of West Bank and Gaza more fully in 'Decline of Illusions: The Status of the Israeli-occupied Territories Over Twenty-One Years', *International Affairs*, Royal Institute of International Affairs, London, vol. 64, no. 3, Summer 1988.

3.   For a thorough exposition of this Israeli view, see Meir Shamgar (ed.), *Military Government in the Territories Administered by Israel: The Legal Aspects*, vol. 1, Hebrew University, Faculty of Law, Jerusalem, 1982.

4   See, for example, F Yahia, *The Palestine Question and International Law*, PLO Research Center, Beirut, 1970, p. 184; Ezzeldin Foda, *Israeli Belligerent Occupation and Palestinian Armed Resistance in International Law*, PLO Research Center, Beirut, 1970; and a 1981 PLO document submitted to UNESCO, the text of which is contained in UNESCO document 22 C/18 of 30 August 1983.

5.   Report from Tel Aviv by Howard Goller, Reuters, in *The Independent*, London, 13 June 1988.

6.   *Ibid.*

The Palestinians, the Uprising, and International Law   39

7. The fullest account of the killing of Khalil al-Wazir was by Glenn Frankel, 'Wazir's Killing: A First Account', *International Herald Tribune*, Paris, 22 April 1988.

8. See, for example, Meron Benvenisti, *The West Bank Data Base Project, 1987 Report: Demographic, Economic, Legal, Social and Political Developments in the West Bank*, The Jerusalem Post, Jerusalem, 1987, pp. 51–65.

9. Benvenisti, *1987 Report*, p. 5.

10. The latter issue, of overstaying a visa, was stressed in the Supreme Court ruling of June 1988 upholding the deportation order against Dr Mubarak Awad, head of the Palestinian Center for the Study of Nonviolence. Dr Awad was accused of fanning the flames of the Palestinian uprising. He had been an Arab resident of East Jerusalem when Israel took it over in 1967, but had also acquired US citizenship. It was this factor which led the Supreme Court to view his expulsion as legitimate. He was put on a plane to New York on 13 June 1988.

11. Report from Arie Haskel in Jerusalem, *The Observer*, London, 12 June 1988.

12. The key sources of UNRWA's authority are UN General Assembly Resolutions 302 (IV) of 8 December 1949, establishing UNRWA; and 2252 (ES-V) of 4 July 1967. For further details see Guy S Goodwin-Gill, *The Refugee in International Law*, Oxford University Press, 1985 edition, p 57; and Atle Grahl-Madsen, *The Status of Refugees in International Law*, vol. 1, Sijthoff, Leyden, 1966, p. 3.

13. The Statute of the Office of the UNHCR, adopted by the UN General Assembly on 14 December 1950, Paragraph 7(c), prescribes 'that the competence of the High Commissioner . . . shall not extend to a person . . . who continues to receive from other organs or agencies of the UN protection or assistance.' There is a counterpart of this provision in the 1951 Convention Relating to the Status of Refugees, Article 1D, which specifies that the Convention does not apply to such persons. This is not altered by the 1967 Protocol Relating to the Status of Refugees.

14. For example, UN Security Council Resolution 242 of 22 November 1967 affirmed *inter alia* the necessity 'for achieving a just settlement of the refugee problem'.

15. This Article avoids any reference to Parts II and IV of the 1949 Geneva Convention IV for simple reasons Part IV is solely about execution of the Convention, and Part II is applicable to refugees anyway. As the first Article of Part II (i.e. Article 13) states: 'The provisions of Part II cover the whole of the populations of the countries in conflict, without any adverse distinction based, in particular, on race, nationality, religion or political opinion, and are intended to alleviate the sufferings caused by war '

16. On this point see particularly Yoram Dinstein's fine article 'Refugees and the Law of Armed Conflict', *Israel Yearbook on Human Rights*, vol. 12, 1982, pp. 94–109.

* This paper was presented at the Symposium at Queen Elizabeth House, Oxford, on 'The West Bank and Gaza Strip: The problems of the Palestinian Refugees and Non-Refugees', 8–10 July, 1988. It is a revised and enlarged version of an article which appeared in *Arab Affairs*, no. 6, London, Spring 1988 © Adam Roberts, 1988, 1989

NOTE, THE WEST BANK AQUIFER AND CONVENTIONS REGARDING LAWS OF BELLIGERENT OCCUPATION

Jamal L. El-Hindi*

Although the recent unrest in Israel and the West Bank[1] periodically captures the world's attention, the underlying reasons for the conflict rarely receive enough attention. While there has been a renewed emphasis on understanding the history of the Arab-Israeli dispute, coverage of certain aspects is still lacking. One of these areas involves the question of Palestinian and Israeli natural resources, most of which are inextricably linked and which may serve either as obstacles or pathways to peace. Water is the most crucial of these resources and the West Bank aquifer has become the last and most important viable water source in the region. While settlement of the conflict will bring a day in which both parties realize that mutual respect and cooperation are the surest roots to stability, the issues surrounding Israel's present use of the West Bank aquifer must be addressed to prepare for that occasion. As a belligerent occupier of the region, Israel has certain concerns and rights regarding the exploitation of the aquifer. These rights and concerns, however, are limited by the presently accepted international rules of belligerent occupation.

This Note will provide an introductory analysis of the conventions on belligerent occupation as they apply to the West Bank aquifer. Part I provides a brief analysis of the current situation in the region. Part II provides an overview of the relevant conventions on belligerent occupation and then focuses on how these laws apply to underground water resources in the West Bank. Finally, Part III outlines potential developments for the maintenance of complicity with the developing law of belligerent occupation, taking into account developments in international water law.

I. The Current Situation

Israel and the West Bank lie within a semi-arid region bordering

---

* University of Michigan Law School, Class of 1990.

1. The topic of this note is the West Bank aquifer. By focusing on this region the author does not intend to imply that similar issues addressed here do not arise in other Israeli occupied territories, such as Gaza and the Golan Heights.

the Eastern Mediterranean Sea. The climate in the region ranges from semi-arid to arid. The greatest average rainfall of 750 to 500 millimeters per year (30-20 inches per year) falls on the coastal plains and western highlands while other regions receive considerably less precipitation.[2] By comparison, the record mean annual rainfalls for Los Angeles and Detroit are 14.91 inches and 31.49 inches respectively.[3]

Population growth due to immigration into Israel and a high rate of birth in the West Bank continues to place the region's scarce water resources under tremendous pressure. Israel already uses roughly 95 percent of its available annual renewable water sources.[4] Through special domestic and agricultural conservation methods, the Israelis have efficiently maximized water utilization, but a major consequence of water scarcity in the region is the overuse of underground resources.[5]

Much of the water that Israel uses originates outside of its borders. A great portion of this extraterritorial water originates in the West Bank aquifer, a watershed straddling the border between Israel and the Occupied Territories. Israel and the West Bank constitute a single natural geological region for the exploitation of underground water.[6] Most of the recharging of the aquifer occurs under the West Bank proper as rainwater and groundwater collected by the Judean and Samarian highlands flows underground toward the Mediterranean coast.[7] Israeli legal scholars recognize the importance of the joint aquifer to the quality of life in Israel and the corresponding need to protect and preserve its viability when discussing Israeli policies in the West Bank:

> [T]he small number of subterranean catchment areas that exist are common to Israel and the Region [West Bank]. Any increase in the amount of water taken by one side reduces the amount available for the other, and can sometimes lead to permanent salination. To maintain the quan-

---

2. United Nations Natural Resources Council, Groundwater in the Eastern Mediterranean and Western Asia, 9 Natural Resources/Water Series at 73, U.N. Sales No. E.82.II.A.8 (1983) [hereinafter Resources Council Report]. The Resources Council Report provides substantial geographical data for Israel.

3. THE WEATHER ALMANAC 383, 527 (J. Ruffner & F. Bair eds. 1981).

4. T. NAFF & R. MATSON, WATER IN THE MIDDLE EAST: CONFLICT OR COOPERATION? 46 (1984); *see also* Report of the Secretary-General, *Permanent Sovereignty over national resources in the occupied Palestinian and other Arab territories,* at 7, U.N. Doc. No. A/39/326 (1984) [hereinafter Secretary-General Report 1984].

5. T. NAFF & R. MATSON, *supra* note 4, at 46.

6. Report of the Secretary-General, *Permanent sovereignty over national resources in the occupied Arab territories,* at 7, U.N. Doc. No. A/36/648 (1981) [hereinafter Secretary-General Report 1981].

7. Stauffer, *The Price of Peace: The Spoils of War,* AMERICAN-ARAB AFFAIRS, Summer 1982, at 43, 45.

tity and quality of water and avoid excessive use, restrictions have been placed on water-drilling, pumping and agricultural consumption in Israel, principally by imposing quotas. To balance the situation, a similar system of control was introduced in the Region.[8]

Various estimates place the contribution of the West Bank aquifer to annual Israeli consumption at between 25 and 40 percent of the State's needs.[9]

A. Consequences of Israeli occupation and development policies

Water development within Israel has benefitted from the occupation of the West Bank due to the Military Government's control over water development in the Territories. The ability to inhibit indigenous West Bank Palestinians from using the valuable water resources beneath them guarantees a steady flow of underground water into Israeli wells. Of the estimated 600 million cubic meters (mcm) available per year in the West Bank aquifer, 475 mcm flow westward toward the Israeli coast. Due to overpumping in Israel and restrictions on Palestinian pumping in the West Bank, Israel currently exploits 95.5 percent of the westward flow, while the West Bank inhabitants draw only 4.5 percent of the resource.[10] The flow, as noted earlier, also provides crucial water pressure to prevent Israeli coastal wells from being destroyed by the encroaching subsurface sea waters.

The Israeli gains, however, have led to Palestinian losses. There is little doubt that absent Israeli occupation, the local population in the West Bank would currently be using the aquifer at a much higher rate. Though technologically lacking before the occupation began in 1967, it is likely that the region would have begun to tap and utilize water resources in the same manner that neighboring Jordan has. The United Nations Secretary-General notes that not only have the Palestinians been prevented from advancing their agricultural economy, but they have been forced to retrogress:

> [A]s a result of Israeli actions already taken, the economic activity of a number of Arab inhabitants has already been reduced to a near subsistence level, as water which was available to them as of 1967 has been reallocated by the Israeli authorities for the use of new Jewish settlements or for Israel's own use.[11]

---

8. ISRAEL NATIONAL SECTION OF THE INTERNATIONAL COMMISSION OF JURISTS, THE RULE OF LAW IN THE AREAS ADMINISTERED BY ISRAEL 59-60 (1981).

9. T. NAFF & R. MATSON, *supra* note 4, at 46-47 (roughly 40 percent); D. PERETZ, THE WEST BANK: HISTORY, POLITICS, SOCIETY & ECONOMY 65 (1986) (roughly one third); M. BENVENISTI, 1986 REPORT: DEMOGRAPHIC, ECONOMIC, LEGAL, SOCIAL AND POLITICAL DEVELOPMENT IN THE WEST BANK 20 (1986) (roughly one quarter).

10. M. BENVENISTI, *supra* note 9, at 21.

11. Secretary-General Report 1981, *supra* note 6, at 7.

To ensure that West Bank residents do not increase their use of groundwater, the Israeli military government has placed tight restrictions on the drilling of Arab wells.[12] The Israeli policy of requiring government permits to drill new wells has been extended to the West Bank to the disadvantage of the indigenous population. While under former Jordanian water legislation drilling permits were automatically issued to replace wells that had become insufficient for their licensed purpose, including irrigation, Israeli authorities have refused permission, for reasons of water security, for the drilling of new Arab irrigation wells.[13] Despite the retrictions in the name of water security which the Israelis have imposed on Palestinians, Israel's direct use of the aquifer has increased due to pumping of water for Jewish settlements. Between 1967 and 1984, drilling of new wells was prohibited for Arab farmers (apart from two wells) while the Israeli water authority was permitted to drill at least 30 new wells.[14] The capacity of each of these wells dwarfs that of Arab wells which are rarely permitted to be improved. Average Israeli wells with deep bores pump much more water than average Arab wells.[15] One scholar has summarized the apparent inequities that Israel's water policies create in the Occupied Territories this way:

> In effect, Israel is helping itself (or more precisely, its settlements) to the generous use of Arab groundwater in the eastern drainage area of the Jordan Valley, while imposing manifold restrictions on Palestinian water usage, especially from the western aquifers, on the grounds that it threatens salination of supplies to Israel proper. Irrigation wells have been metered and stiff fines imposed on Palestinians who exceed posted limits. Settlements by contrast, are not restricted.[16]

Israeli officials emphasizing the importance of continued Israeli control over the West Bank aquifer corroborate such a description. Former Minister of Agriculture Ariel Sharon has warned of the dangers

---

12. The restrictive Israeli legislation relating to water resources allocation has been enforced in the Occupied Territories under the auspices of Military Order No. 92 of 1967, concerning "Powers for water concerns," and Military Order No. 158 of 1967, amending the Jordanian Law on Water Supervision of 1953 as regards the West Bank. Secretary-General Report 1984, *supra* note 4, at 9. *But see Letter dated 19 March 1985 from the Chargé d'Affaires a.i. of the Permanent Mission of Israel to the United Nations addressed to the Secretary-General*, at 19-21, U.N. Doc. A/40/188 (1985) (arguing that restrictions are for the benefit of local inhabitants).

13. Secretary-General Report 1984, *supra* note 4, at 9; *see also* Stork, *Water and Israel's Occupation Strategy*, Merip Reports, July-August 1983 at 19, 21.

14. Secretary-General Report 1984, *supra* note 4, at 14.

15. Thirty percent of all water extracted from the West Bank aquifer is pumped by Israeli wells. Dillman, *Water Rights in the Occupied Territories*, J. PALESTINE STUD., Autumn 1989, at 46, 57. Stork states that Israeli wells in the West Bank drew "about 40 percent as much as the 33 million cubic meters produced by all 314 Palestinian wells." Stork, *supra* note 13, at 22.

16. Stork, *supra* note 13, at 22.

of relinquishing control of the aquifer,[17] while Prime Minister Menachem Begin's administration insisted that full Israeli control of West Bank water resources must be a component of any proposal for Palestinian autonomy.[18]

The international legal status of the West Bank is currently the subject of much controversy but is not within the scope of this note. For the purpose of the present topic, it is important only to note that by occupying the West Bank at the end of the Six-Day War of 1967, Israel had gained control of the land above the West Bank aquifer and continues to have the status of a *de facto* occupier.

II. The Situation in Light of the Rules on Belligerent Occupation

The codified rules on belligerent occupation appear in two principal sources. The broad state acceptance of the Hague Regulations of 1907[19] places them within the scope of customary international law. The Geneva Conventions, promulgated in 1949[20] and accepted as law by 165 states, were intended as a supplement to the Hague Regulations. The Hague Regulations primarily addressed issues surrounding the actual conduct of war, but also dealt with protection of the rights of individuals.[21] The Geneva Conventions attempted to fill gaps in the humanitarian protections outlined in the Hague rules. Protocols to the Geneva Conventions have called for further restrictions on the powers of a belligerent occupier while at the same time including wars of national liberation within the scope of belligerent occupation law.[22] Both the Hague Regulations and the Geneva Conventions and Protocols represent relatively recent trends in modern rules of warfare to limit the absolute powers of states in battle.[23] They were the culmination of liberal theories designed to prevent occupying powers from ex-

---

17. Skutel, *Water in the Arab-Israel Conflict*, INTERNATIONAL PERSPECTIVES 22 (July/August 1986).

18. Stork, *supra* note 13, at 21.

19. Regulations appended to the Fourth Hague Convention of the Laws and Customs of War on Land, 32 Stat. 1803, II Malloy 2042, 1 Bevans 247 1907 [hereinafter Hague Regulations].

20. 75 U.N.T.S. 5 (1949). Of particular importance to the present issue is the Fourth Geneva Convention Relative to the Protection of Civilian Persons in Time of War of August 12, 1949, 6 U.S.T. 3516, T.I.A.S. No. 3365, 75 U.N.T.S. 287 [hereinafter Fourth Geneva Convention].

21. Roberts, *The New Rules for Waging War: The Case Against Ratification of Additional Protocol I*, 26 VA. J. INT'L L. 109, 114 (1985).

22. *Id.* at 124.

23. Report of the Secretary General, *Implications, under international law, of the United Nations resolutions on permanent sovereignty over natural resources, on the occupied Palestinian and other Arab territories and on the obligations of Israel concerning its conduct in these territories*, at 13-14, U.N. Doc. A/38/265 (1983) [hereinafter Secretary-General A/38/265].

erting undue interference with the sovereign of an occupied territory and the civilian interests within it.[24]

A. *Application of Norms of Belligerent Occupation to the West Bank*

The applicability of international norms to the West Bank and other territories occupied by Israel is the subject of some controversy. While Israel declares that it abides *de facto* by the rules of the Fourth Geneva Convention which it ratified in 1951, it refuses to acknowledge the Convention's mandatory application to the Arab territories it occupied after the Six-Day War of 1967. Simply put, the official Israeli position is based on the assertion that only territory from which a legitimate sovereign has been ousted is within the scope of the Geneva norms.[25] The questionable legitimacy of Jordanian sovereignty over the West Bank from 1949 to 1967, Israel argues, disqualifies the territory from the above definition and thus precludes mandatory application of the Fourth Geneva Convention.[26]

The official Israeli stance has been criticized by a number of commentators[27] and the applicability of the Fourth Geneva Convention to the occupied territories has been asserted by the International Committee of the Red Cross, various United Nations bodies including the Security Council and the General Assembly, and most governments including the United States.[28] For the purposes of their application, the *de facto* implementation of the rules of the Fourth Geneva Convention moots the technical refusal by Israel of *de jure* invocation. Furthermore, Israel readily accepts the application of the Hague Regulations to the Occupied Territories.[29] Thus, while questions of the

---

24. E. FEILCHENFELD, THE INTERNATIONAL ECONOMIC LAW OF BELLIGERENT OCCUPATION 10 (1942).

25. Shamgar, *The Observance of International Law in the Administered Territories*, 1 ISRAEL Y.B. HUM. RTS. 262, 263 (1971). Meir Shamgar was Attorney General of Israel when he adopted the above argument.

26. *Id.* at 265; E. COHEN, HUMAN RIGHTS IN THE ISRAELI-OCCUPIED TERRITORIES 1967—1982 44 (1985). Cohen states that Israel's primary concern in denying applicability of the Convention involved a reluctance to recognize in any manner the legitimacy of Jordanian sovereignty over the region. *Id.* at 45.

27. E. COHEN, *supra* note 26, at 51; Boyd, *The Applicability of International Law to the Occupied Territories*, 1 ISRAEL Y.B. HUM. RTS. 258 (1971); W. MALLISON & S. MALLISON, THE PALESTINE PROBLEM IN INTERNATIONAL LAW AND WORLD ORDER (1986). For a criticism of Israeli arguments regarding other territories, see Note, *The Law of Belligerent Occupation and the Legal Status of the Gaza Strip*, 9 MICH. Y.B. INT'L LEGAL STUD. 385, 389 (1988). For a synopsis of the arguments for and against applicability of the Fourth Geneva Convention to the Occupied Territories, see Recent Developments, *Recent Israeli Security Measures under the Fourth Geneva Convention*, 3 CONN. J. INT'L L. 485 (1988).

28. Boyd, *supra* note 27, at 259.

29. E. COHEN, *supra* note 26, at 43.

jurisdiction of the rules governing occupation may have extra-political ramifications, they are of little importance to a discussion of their actual implementation in the case of the West Bank aquifer.

Any application of these rules to the type of issues surrounding the West Bank aquifer, however, is qualified in part by the reluctance of States to eschew broad economic rights within the territories they may come to occupy. Both the Hague Regulations and the Geneva Conventions are relatively silent on the broader economic rights of the citizenries they are intended to protect. Von Glahn states that while the Geneva Conventions provided beneficial elaborations of the positive principles appearing in the Hague Regulations, the absence of explicit references that would limit the economic rights of occupying powers was clearly intentional:

> [C]ertain vital areas of belligerent occupation have been left untouched by the [1949 Conventions] and are thus not regulated specifically by conventional international law, such as many aspects of economic exploitation of occupied enemy areas. This omission is not very surprising, inasmuch as the contents of both the Hague Regulations and the Fourth Geneva Convention represent compromises between sharply opposing national points of view and denote in many instances the current maximum concessions which major military powers are willing to grant in favor of the inhabitants of occupied territory. No one need wonder excessively at the hesitation of military men and of politicians to sacrifice all economic benefits possibly accruing from belligerent occupation in an age when technological warfare depends on a steady supply of raw materials and manufactured goods of almost infinite variety.[30]

Underlying von Glahn's statement is the notion that the broad economic exploitation of occupied territory becomes an irresistible asset to support the militarily mobilized societies of today's conflicts which have replaced the pillaging private armies of yesterday. The danger of inexplicit rules regarding economic exploitation comes in the form of occupiers who employ harsh economic measures "which remain within the letter of the law even if they run counter to its original spirit" of protecting a territory's inhabitants.[31]

One body of law which sought to fill in the economic gaps of occupation law has yet to receive broad acceptance. Protocol I of the Geneva Conventions of 1949[32] aims to "reaffirm and develop the

---

30. G. VON GLAHN, THE OCCUPATION OF ENEMY TERRITORY. . . A COMMENTARY ON THE LAW AND PRACTICE OF BELLIGERENT OCCUPATION 20-21 (1957).

31. E. FEILCHENFELD, *supra* note 24, at 25.

32. Protocol Additional to the Geneva Conventions of 12 August 1949, and Relating to the Protection of Victims of International Armed Conflicts (Protocol I), *opened for signature* Dec. 12, 1977, U.N. Doc. A/32/144, Annex I, *reprinted in* 16 I.L.M. 1391 (1978), and INTERNATIONAL COMMITTEE OF THE RED CROSS, PROTOCOLS ADDITIONAL TO THE GENEVA CONVENTIONS OF 12 AUGUST 1949, at 3 (1977) [hereinafter Protocol I].

provisions protecting the victims of armed conflicts and to supplement measures intended to reinforce their application."[33] The protocol is marked by its sweeping protection of occupied people's rights and its tighter restrictions on occupying powers. In particular, Protocol I addresses the protection of objects indispensable to the survival of a civilian population.[34] Water resources are explicitly included within the language of article 54[35] and article 55 states that "care shall be taken in warfare to protect the natural environment against widespread, long-term and severe damage."[36]

While the language of article 54 appears directly applicable to the question at hand, as of December 1986, only 66 countries had ratified or acceded to it.[37] Although Jordan has ratified the protocol, Israel has neither signed nor ratified it. The United States, the Soviet Union and other dominant actors in international affairs also have not ratified the document.[38] Given the lack of Israel's adherence to Protocol I, it is not directly applicable to the situation regarding the West Bank aq-

---

33. *Id.*, preamble.

34. Protocol I, article 54, paragraph 2 reads:

It is prohibited to attack, destroy, remove or render useless objects indispensable to the survival of the civilian population, such as foodstuffs, agricultural areas for the production of foodstuffs, crops, livestock, drinking water installations and supplies and irrigation works, for the specific purpose of denying them for their sustenance value to the civilian population or to the adverse Party, whatever the motive, whether in order to starve out civilians, to cause them to move away, or for any other motive.

The above language is qualified by that found in the third and fifth paragraphs of the same article:

3. The provisions in paragraph 2 shall not apply to such of the objects covered by it as used by an adverse Party:

(a) as sustenance solely for the members of its armed forces; or

(b) if not as sustenance, then in direct support of military action, provided, however, that in no event shall actions against these objects be taken which may be expected to leave the civilian population with such inadequate food or water as to cause its starvation or force its movement.

5. In recognition of the vital requirements of any Party to the conflict in the defence of its national territory against invasion, derogation from the prohibitions contained in paragraph 2 may be made by a Party to the conflict within such territory under its own control where required by imperative military necessity.

Id.

35. *Id.*

36. *Id.* at art. 55. While the language of article 55 arguably might apply to the protection of water aquifers as a part of the environment, further language in article 55 implies that it applies to only those actions of warfare "intended. . . or expected to cause such damage to the natural environment and thereby to prejudice the health or survival of the population." *Id.*

37. International Committee for the Red Cross, *Status of Four Geneva Conventions and Additional Protocols I and II*, 26 I.L.M. 553 (1987).

38. In 1987, U.S. President Reagan recommended Senate ratification of Protocol II Relating to the Victims of Non-International Armed Conflicts, *reprinted in* 16 I.L.M. 1442 (1977), but did not submit Protocol I for ratification, describing it as "fundamentally and irreconcilably flawed." Message from the President transmitting Protocol II Additional to the 1949 Geneva Conventions, Relating to the Protection of the Victims of Non-International Armed Conflicts, 26 I.L.M. 561, 562 (1987).

uifer; while the protocol is championed by the United Nations as a new development in substantive international law,[39] its cold reception by other international actors precludes it from consideration as a source of customary law.[40] Protocol I's directly relevant language can serve only as a persuasive model of how Israel might behave regarding the West Bank aquifer, not how it must behave to be in accord with international law. Further discussion of the relevant non-obligatory norms of Protocol I will appear in the final section of this note dealing with potential developments.

B. *Application of the Hague Regulations and the Fourth Geneva Convention*

Despite the absence of explicit provisions dealing with the protection of economic resources in the Hague Regulations and the Fourth Geneva Convention, both documents codify principles applicable to such protection. The case of the West Bank aquifer is particularly complex in this regard because of the many ways in which water and water usage can be categorized for the purposes of both bodies of law. For example, water may or may not be considered an immovable property under the terms protecting such properties in the Hague Regulations. Similarly, water may or may not fall within the scope of those provisions dealing with foodstuffs and medical supplies in the Fourth Geneva Convention. Furthermore, water from wells may qualify as private property, public property or a hybrid between the two in the form of municipal property; the different ownership categories determine which principles to apply in both the Hague and Geneva instruments. Finally, water may even be categorized as a weapon integral to the conflict between the parties. The ubiquity of water in the above theoretical paradigms is a direct result of its scarcity in the actual situation. The geological linking of crucial water supplies in the region guarantees the preeminence of water considerations in all aspects of occupation. The relative abundance of water in Europe during the periods of conflict which gave rise to the Hague and Geneva instruments likely explains the oversight of its potential importance in other regions.

In light of the above, water potentially applies to many portions of

---

39. Secretary General A/38/265, *supra* note 23, at 12.

40. The diverging opinions apparent among scholars after the presentation of Protocol I also weakens any assertions that it has become customary. *See generally* Roberts, *supra* note 21; Bagley, *Ratification of Protocol I to the Geneva Conventions of 1949 by the United States: Discussion and Suggestions for the American Lawyer-Citizen*, 11 LOY. L.A. INT'L & COMP. L. J. 439 (1989); Aldrich, *Commentary: Progressive Development of the Laws of War: A Reply to Criticisms of the 1977 Geneva Protocol I*, 26 VA. J. INT'L L. 693 (1986).

the conventional laws on occupation. The most obvious of these is the concept of usufruct embodied in article 55 of the Hague Regulations of 1907.[41] Article 55 reads:

> The occupying State shall be regarded only as an administrator and usufructuary of public buildings, real estate, forests, and agricultural estates belonging to the hostile State, and situated in the occupied country. It must safeguard the capital of these properties, and administer them in accordance with the rules of usufruct.[42]

While the Hague Regulations offer no specific definition of the term usufruct, it is apparent that the drafters realized its use as a legal term of art and intended that it inculcate general principles associated with it at the time.[43] Generally defined, usufruct is "the right of using and enjoying the property of other people, without detriment to the substance of the property."[44] A common understanding is that usufruct permits the exploitation of the fruits of a property without a broader right of ownership.[45] Included within the common definition of usufruct and the "safeguard" language used in article 55 is the notion that the powers of the occupant are limited by a concern for the future value of the property. Von Glahn states that while article 55 grants an occupying power the right to profit, it prohibits it from exploiting the property "beyond normal use."[46]

The scope of article 55 encompassing state-owned public buildings, real estate, forests and agricultural estates also distinguishes these items from movable state-owned chattels subject to appropriation under article 53.[47] Article 53, paragraph 1, of the Hague regulations reads:

> An army of occupation can only take possession of cash, funds, and realizable securities which are strictly the property of the State, depots of arms, means of transport, stores and supplies, and, generally, all *movable* property belonging to the State which may be used for operations of war.[48]

While the movable-immovable properties distinction is not explicitly spelled out in the Regulations, the necessary interpretations of articles

---

41. Secretary-General A/38/265, *supra* note 23, at 13-14.

42. Hague Regulations, *supra* note 19, art. 55.

43. Clagett & Johnson, *May Israel as a Belligerent Occupant Lawfully Exploit Previously Unexploited Resources on the Gulf of Suez?*, 72 AM. J. INT'L L. 558, 566 (1978).

44. *Id.* at 567, *citing* THE INSTITUTES OF JUSTINIAN 2.4 (J Abdy & B. Walker trans. 1876). For an analysis of the difference between usufruct and title, see Goldie, *Title and Use (and Usufruct)—An Ancient Distinction Too Oft Forgot*, 79 AM. J. INT'L L. 689 (1985).

45. United States Dept. of State Legal Adviser, Memorandum of Law, Oct. 1 1976, *reprinted in* 16 I.L.M. 733, 736 (1977) [hereinafter U.S. Memorandum].

46. G. VON GLAHN, *supra* note 30, at 177.

47. *See* E. FEILCHENFELD, *supra* note 24, at 52-54.

48. Hague Regulations, *supra* note 19, art. 53 (emphasis added).

53 and 55 have led most scholars to accept the distinction.[49] The distinction becomes critical regarding items for which a classification is not readily apparent. Under article 53, the occupying power's right to possess state-owned movable properties is much broader than in the case of immovable state-owned property.[50] In addition to state-owned financial resources, military equipment, transport systems and stockpiles, the occupying power can legitimately appropriate any other movable property of the enemy state if it can serve a military purpose.[51] Once a resource classifies as a munition, nothing bars an occupying power from exhausting it under article 53. Conversely, article 55 limits an occupying power's ability to exhaust resources, but, on its face, the article does not restrict usufructuary rights only to those resources adaptable to military purposes. Article 55 has no explicit limitations on the nature of the occupier's use of the resources, but scholars have suggested that such limitations exist. The post-World War II notion that the economy of an occupied region could only be required to bear the expenses of the occupation itself restricts an article 55 usufructuary from disposing of property for purposes other than the maintenance of public order.[52] Thus, article 55 further protects properties integrally associated with the territory occupied from the exhaustion of supply implicitly accepted for movable properties in article 53.

The situation most analogous to that of the West Bank aquifer and the source of the most recent discussion of usufruct as it relates to belligerent occupancy involves the extraction of oil.[53] The Israeli practice of exploiting oil fields previously developed by Egypt began shortly after Israel occupied the Sinai territory in the Six-Day war of 1967. When these fields were returned to Egypt under the phased Israeli-Egyptian disengagement agreements in the 1970s, Israel began to develop Egypt's previously unexploited oil reserves in the eastern Gulf of Suez.[54] The activities ran counter to the interests of a U.S. oil company and the United States and Israel exchanged legal memoranda expressing their respective theories on the validity of Israel's actions under the Hague Regulations.[55] The United States took the position

---

49. *See, e.g.,* E. FEILCHENFELD, *supra* note 24, at 52; G. VON GLAHN, *supra* note 30, at 176.

50. G. VON GLAHN, *supra* note 30, at 180.

51. *Id.* at 181. Von Glahn adds that in modern practice, few state-owned articles escape confiscation by an occupying power because of broad interpretations regarding the adaptability of most raw materials into arguably military purposes. *Id.*

52. Secretary General A/38/265, *supra* note 23, at 15.

53. *Id.* at 14.

54. *See* Clagett & Johnson, *supra* note 43, at 558.

55. U.S. Memorandum, *supra* note 45; Government of Israel, Memorandum of Law, *re-*

that the exploitation of previously unexploited immovable property was a violation of article 55 of the Hague Regulations in that it violated generally accepted principles regarding usufruct.[56] Israel contended that the applicability of the Hague Regulations in the Sinai was questionable,[57] but that, even within the Regulations' limits, the Israeli practice was legitimate.

Both parties referred to a decision by the Singapore Court of Appeal[58] which dealt with privately owned oil deposits exploited by Japanese forces during the World War II occupation of the Dutch East Indies. The Chief Justice's ruling that the oil deposits were immovable[59] supports the United States argument. A concurring opinion provides some support to the Israeli argument that such reserves may classified as munitions subject to legitimate confiscation by an occupying force under article 53 of the Hague Regulations.[60] Some commentators have provided different views as to whether oil deposits may be classified as munitions, but none conclusively state that such property is not immovable.[61]

While underground water sources and oil deposits differ in many respects, the similarities between them in determining whether subsurface water resources are immovable for article 55 purposes cannot be ignored. Both oil and subsurface water require subterranean extraction through varying levels of collective effort. Both are integrally linked to the properties beneath which they are located. Both may

---

printed in 17 I.L.M. 432 (1978) [hereinafter Israel Memorandum]. *See* Clagett & Johnson, *supra* note 43, at 566.

56. "The civil law tradition generally recognizes a usufructuary's right to continue, at the previous rate of exploitation, to work mines that had that had been already opened by the owner at the time the usufruct began. The usufructuary may not open new mines and exploit them even at a reasonable rate." U.S. Memorandum, *supra* note 45, at 737 (basing their argument on French civil law and common law as representative norms). The State Department noted that German rules regarding usufruct were more liberal than those outlined above, but added that article 55's separate emphasis on an occupying power's duty to safeguard the capital of the property precludes any rule which even less protection for that capital than the French or common law interpretations." *Id.* at 740.

57. Israel Memorandum, *supra* note 55, at 432, 442. The Israeli argument cites Feilchenfeld for the proposition that the Hague Regulations on belligerent occupation apply to only the type of belligerent occupation involving armies "still fighting in the field." *Id.* at 433.

58. N.V. de Bataafsche Petroleum Maatschappij v. The War Damage Commission, 23 I.L.R. 810 (1956).

59. *Id.* at 824.

60. The concurrence of Justice Whitton indicates that "changes in the nature of warfare necessarily make it difficult to determine whether crude oil is a '*munition de guerre*'." Whitton does not refute the majority opinion's determination that oil deposits are immovable, but suggests that article 53 is more applicable to the situation than article 55 because of oil's increasingly strategic value. *Id.* at 846-47. He eventually agrees with the court's outcome because of the wrong inflicted upon the private owners who were not recompensed by the Japanese as required under other Hague Regulations regarding requisition of private property. *Id.* at 849.

61. Clagett & Johnson, *supra* note 43, at 563 n.27.

straddle international boundaries. Though underground water sources are renewable and oil deposits are essentially non-renewable, overdrafting of water aquifers may lead to permanent damage and consequent non-renewability.[62] Instances of such abuse classify as "mining" because of the essential inability of an aquifer to renew itself when the overdraft has been too severe.[63] Hence, oil deposits and certain underground water supplies would seem to deserve similar treatment in international law.

The traditional line of demarcation between movable and immovable items is drawn by prevailing notions of the economic significance of the item.[64] Yiannopoulos describes the traditional reasons for providing extra property protections to immovable items and contrasts them with modern trends:

> Since ancient times and up to the era of the industrial revolution, landed property was regarded as the most important species of wealth from the viewpoints of both social and individual interests. Hence, particular rules were developed to safeguard interests connected with the use and enjoyment of landed property. In modern times, economic emphasis has shifted to values other than landed property and the law has been slowly developing in new directions. In medieval civil law, the criteria for the distinction between movables and immovables were durability and the utility of the thing as a source of income. In contemporary civil law the distinction rests, in principle, on physical notions and on "inherent" characteristics of things.[65]

Given the essential nature of underground water in the West Bank and Israel, and water's importance to societal wealth generally, underground water resources would appear to qualify for the special protection protection provided for immovable properties under the Yiannopoulos description. The United Nations Secretary General has underscored the fact that "the economic value of land in this region is directly dependent on the availability of water supplies."[66]

Assuming that the West Bank aquifer falls within a pattern of state

---

62. The potential for this in Israel is outlined in Davis, Maks, & Richardson, *Israel's Water Policies*, J. PALESTINE STUD., 3, 16 (Winter 1980) (outlining an Israeli author's concerns that previously static salinity belts surrounding Israel's main fresh water aquifer might irreversibly spoil sweet waters due to excessive pumping from the aquifer). Overextraction has already been associated with irreversible salinity damage to some West Bank wells in the vicinity of Jericho where two new wells were sunk by the Israeli government near an existing well. Dillman, *supra* note 15, at 56. *See also* D. PERETZ, *supra* note 9, at 65.

63. J. SAX & R. ABRAMS, LEGAL CONTROL OF WATER RESOURCES 831 (1986); *but see id.* at 822-24 (discussion of the general differences between overdraft and mining).

64. Yiannopoulos, *Movables and Immovables in Louisiana and Comparative Law*, 22 LA. L. REV. 517, 518 (1962).

65. *Id.* Yiannopoulos goes on to state that policy developments may lead to classifications of movable and immovable properties contrary to lay notions. *Id.*

66. Secretary-General Report 1984, *supra* note 4, at 6.

ownership, under article 55 of the Hague Regulations, Israel assumes a usufructuary power over it. While the power to control the aquifer is complete, it's use by Israel is limited to that which "safeguards" the value of the property and does not exceed normal use.[67] The nature of Israel's use is also confined to that which maintains public order and safety in the West Bank. Israel's present activities regarding the aquifer may exceed these limitations.

Water resources for the West Bank are under the authority of *Mekorot*, the Israeli Water Company, which is owned jointly by the Israeli government, the Jewish Agency, the Jewish National Fund and Histadrut, an Israeli workers union.[68] Much of the activity of *Mekorot* involves the establishment and maintenance of a water distribution system that meets the needs of the country's inhabitants. Since the beginning of its occupation in 1967, Israel has settled civilians within the West Bank, both around Jerusalem and in outlying regions.[69] *Mekorot* has increasingly permitted and overseen the tapping of the West Bank aquifer to meet the domestic and irrigation needs of Israeli settlers.[70] Simultaneously, *Mekorot*, along with the Israeli government, has severely restricted the ability of Palestinian inhabitants to use the aquifer themselves.[71]

The result of *Mekorot* and goverment policies has been disproportionately high levels of consumption by a relatively small number of Israeli settlers. Such consumption may exceed the twin constraints of "normal use" and "maintanence of public order." Excluding the entire population of East Jerusalem, Israeli settlers amount to only three percent of the West Bank population, yet they account for 20 percent of its total water consumption with 96 percent of that consumption assigned to irrigation.[72] Thus, three percent of the West Bank population outside of Jerusalem is using roughly 20 percent of the area's consumable water for non-domestic purposes. This high level of agricultural use combined with restrictions on the indigenous population's water accessibility arguably constitutes an abnormal use contrary to the spirit of article 55 which is intended to safeguard resources for the occupied populace.

There are substantive and theoretical abnormalities in the Israel's

---

67. *See supra* notes 45-47 and accompanying text.

68. Dillman, *supra* note 15, at 54.

69. The legal or illegal status of these settlements in light of international law is not within the scope of this note.

70. Dillman, *supra* note 15, at 54-59.

71. Secretary-General Report 1984, *supra* note 4, at 11-12.

72. D. PERETZ, *supra* note 9, at 65.

present use. The use is abnormal in practice because it far exceeds the traditional per capita consumption of the Palestinian residents;[73] it is also abnormal in principle because Israel, through its restrictive policies, has turned the West Bank aquifer into an Israeli reservoir. An assumedly "normal" use of the aquifer would entail independent, but responsible tapping of the resource by the indigenous population. Under the present "abnormal" use, Palestinians are prevented from satisfying their own water needs to satisfy Israel's evergrowing needs.

Abnormalities also exist in the legal and institutional framework for water administration imposed by the Israeli government. Present Israeli policies and practices differ fundamentally from those in effect in the West Bank before 1967.[74] One example of this is Israel's implementation of a "water sharing" system whereby it freely moves water from one water basin or aquifer to another.[75] Under formerly implemented Jordanian laws, such transfers were forbidden.[76] Such shifting can affect use patterns and established water rights in the region. To the extent "water sharing" results in a net water loss to the Occupied Territories, it raises the issue of direct water transfer from the Occupied Territory to the occupying power's own territory.[77]

Arguably the Israelis are using the aquifer in a manner which the Palestinians would soon adopt if left to their own devices; it might follow that such irrigation projects do not constitute abnormal use. However, the normal use of water should be defined by the indigenous Palestinians rather than the occupying force. If they decide to change water consumption patterns on their own, they will obviously change the standard for normal use. This change is their own prerogative and

---

73. In 1982, the West Bank Palestinian consumption per capita approached 35 cubic meters per year in towns and 15 cubic meters per year in villages. While this consumption is predicted to gradually increase to 60 cubic meters in towns and 35 cubic meters in villages per annum by the year 2010, planned consumption per capita for Israeli settlements is 90 cubic meters per annum. M. BENVENISTI, *supra* note 9, at 22. "The total amount of water planned for allocation to the Arab sector (agricultural and domestic consumption) [in 1990] is 137 million cubic meters per year (for about one million people) and for the Jewish Population, approximately 100 million cubic meters (for about 100,000 people)." *Id.*

74. Secretary-General Report 1984, *supra* note 4, at 15.

75. *Id.* at 15 (citing STATE OF ISRAEL, MINISTRY OF DEFENSE, JUDEA-SAMARIA AND THE GAZA DISTRICT: A SIXTEEN-YEAR SURVEY (1967-83)).

76. *Id.*

77. *Id.* Concerns related to "water sharing" have recently reached a new level. Israeli water officials have authorized an ambitious drilling project near Bethlehem into part of the eastward running aquifer. The well, at a proposed depth of 1,000 meters with horizontal branches, may threaten shallow Arab wells. Fifty percent of the outflow would be directed to West Jerusalem and West Bank settlements. *See Letter dated July 1987 from the Permanent Representative of Jordan to the United Nations addressed to the Secretary-General,* U.N. DOC. A/42/385 (1987); *Plan to Drill for Water on West Bank Stirs Dispute,* The Washington Post, Oct. 1, 1987, at A31, col. 1.

a sovereign right. As an occupying power, however, Israel cannot foist these changes upon an occupied people without overstepping the bounds of normal use. To hold that an occupying power can unilaterally redefine normal use patterns, would negate any meaning that the doctrine would have regarding proper limits to an occupying power's actions.

The water that remained within the aquifer due to relatively low levels of irrigation in the area before the Israeli occupation is arguably similar to the unexploited oil fields in the Sinai prior to the Israeli occupation there. The United States argument that new oil wells were violative of article 55's principle of usufruct implies that new water wells would be equally prohibited. While, as has been stated, water is a more readily renewable resource than oil, commentators have expressed a concern over potentially permanent damage to the aquifer as a result of overextraction.[78]

The above arguments assume the correct application of the concept of usufruct and article 55 of the Hague regulations. As noted earlier, it is sometimes questionable whether article 53 of the Hague Regulations, governing the requisition a state's movable property adaptable to the operations of war, should apply instead.[79] While von Glahn argues that most state-owned articles can be construed to involve a military function,[80] the use of water as a weapon at first appears counter intuitive. Greenspan is one theorist who has classified water as a potential instrument of war: "Enemy forces may be deprived of food and water in order to compel them to surrender. For this purpose springs may be dried up and rivers and aqueducts diverted."[81] As crucial as water supply is in the Middle East, it is more likely to become a useful weapon than in other regions. Most of the direct conflicts in the Arab-Israeli disputes can be linked with aggressive and defensive water policies on both sides.[82] In this "water as a weapon analysis," however, it is important to keep in mind the distinction that Greenspan makes regarding enemy "forces." His statement implies that civilians in a conflict should not be subject to the same

---

78. *See supra* note 8 and accompanying text.

79. *See supra* note 61 and accompanying text.

80. G. VON GLAHN, *supra* note 30, at 181.

81. M. GREENSPAN, THE MODERN LAW OF WARFARE 316-17 (1959). Greenspan goes on to state, however, that it is forbidden to deliberately contaminate water intended to be used by the enemy. *Id.*

82. *Report of the Security Council Commission Established Under Resolution 446 (1979)*, at 36, U.N. Doc. S/14268 (1980) [hereinafter Security Council Report 1980]; *see also* Skutel, *supra* note 17, at 22. Israel, Syria and Jordan have each engaged in water diversion projects with presumably negative effects on other parties in the region. *See* T. NAFF & R. MATSON, *supra* note 4, at 36-37.

measures. This implication is backed by the primary purposes of the laws of belligerent occupation which are to protect civilians during time of war. Thus, water is a legitimate weapon only against "forces," an isolated group of troops, for instance, and not against civilians. It follows that while Israel may be able to seize control of the West Bank aquifer because of its potential uses as a weapon against Israel, it must not deprive Palestinian civilians of the resource. Uncoordinated activitites of civilians, unlike those of governments or military forces, do not amount to use of water as a munition. In seizing the resource, Israel must acknowledge that, vis-à-vis Palestinian civilians, water is not a weapon. Therefore, even if Israel decides to control the resource, it cannot justifiably deprive Palestinian civilians from using it under Israeli dominion.

The above analysis indicates a gap in Greenspan's perception of water as a weapon. Greenspan only views water as a direct military weapon and does not consider its general security value. Regardless of a state of conflict or peace between Israel and the Palestinians, water security in Israel depends on maintaining a certain underground flow from the West Bank. Water security for Palestinians entails maintaining an increasing flow to the surface. Given the apparent value of water as a security asset and its value as a vital natural resource, the best rule to adapt in such a circumstance would consider water as both a vital natural resource and a strategic asset. This result seems to call for the joint and simultaneous application of articles 53 and 55 of the Hague Regulations. While water may be requisitioned as a potential instrument of war under article 53, it should also be subject to article 55's conditions of usufruct outlined earlier. This combination of rules takes into account the security of the occupying power and the well-being of the occupied civilian populace. Under such an analysis, the occupied regions's resources are protected from exhaustion by the principles of usufruct, while the occupying power can requisition the water it needs for legitimate security purposes only. While the combined powers of article 53 and article 55 appear to be less than those of each regulation taken separately,[83] such a result reinforces the principles behind the rules despite the technical ambiguities in their language. Thus, the economic inadequacies of the rules as noted by Feilchenfeld and von Glahn[84] can be overcome in the crucial concern

---

83. Put simply, in the combination of the two regulations, article 53 limits the application of article 55 to military purposes and article 55 places usufructuary conditions on the requisitions of article 53. It must be noted that the combined approach need only be taken with properties such as water, which while potentially of strategic value, are crucial to the well being of the civilian populace.

84. *See supra* notes 30-31 and accompanying text.

for water resources.

Thus far, the analyses of both article 55's concept of usufruct and article 53's application to properties adaptable for military purposes have assumed that water in the West Bank has always been a state-owned resource. This assumption is a broad one, but is not without arguable validity. Under Jordanian law, contrary to present Israeli law, private water ownership rights were recognized.[85] However, groundwaters, before being brought to the surface, were not subject to private ownership.[86] Water in an aquifer was thus implicitly subject to the state's jurisdiction. Underground Water Control Regulation, No. 88 of 1966 provided the state with the authority to regulate the flow of underground water prior to the 1967 War.[87] The limits to the actual ownership of underground waters and the state's subsequent control act qualify the resource as state property for the purposes of the laws of belligerent occupation.[88] Still, issues of mixed public/private property may arise in the form of state-owned resources subject to municipal or proprietary rights.[89] In such a case, the right itself to pump water may be considered a private property.

If any underground water or the right to pump it is determined to be of a private nature, it would be subject to stronger protections against the occupier's use. Article 52 of the Hague Regulations provides that:

> Requisitions in kind and services shall not be demanded from municipalities or inhabitants except for the need of army occupation. They shall be in proportion to the resources of the country, and of such nature as to not involve the population in the obligation of taking part in the operations of the war against their country.[90]

Thus if any underground waters or the use thereof are of a private or municipal nature, they are only subject to requisition for use by army forces. The proportionality language of the regulation requires that care be taken that such use does not exhaust the local supply.

Though articles 55 and 53 of the Hague Regulations are the most generally applicable rules of belligerent occupation regarding the West Bank aquifer, the Fourth Geneva Convention provides more specific language. The Fourth Geneva Convention supplements the general rules of the Hague Regulations with an increased emphasis on the

---

85. D. CAPONERA, WATER LAWS IN MOSLEM COUNTRIES 99 (1973).

86. *Id.*

87. *Id.*

88. *See* E. FEILCHENFELD, *supra* note 24, at 52 (discussing the tests by which to determine questionably state-owned properties for the purposes of the Hague Regulations).

89. *See* Secretary-General Report 1984, *supra* note 4, at 9.

90. Hague Regulations, *supra* note 19, art. 52.

rights of individual citizens during a time of occupation. While rules to protect the entire citizenry are less clear than those applying specifically to individuals and institutions, the convention does include provisions that elaborate on the Hague Regulations protection of group rights. Article 55 of the Fourth Geneva Convention is particularly relevant to the question of the West Bank aquifer. The second paragraph of the article reads:

> The Occupying Power may not requisition foodstuffs, articles or medical supplies available in the occupied territory, except for use by the occupation forces and administration personnel, and then only if the requirements of the civilian population have been taken into account. Subject to the provisions of other international Conventions, the Occupying Power shall make arrangements to ensure that fair value is paid for any requisitioned goods.[91]

While water resources are not specifically mentioned as they are in the later Protocol I,[92] they are likely to fall under the scope of "foodstuffs" or "articles." The general language of the provision implies a high level of protection of the occupied people's rights to use any resources, private or public, existing in the territory with minimal interference from the requisitioning of the occupying power. Unlike articles 55 and 53 of the Hague Regulations, article 55 of the Fourth Geneva Convention makes no distinction between state-owned and privately owned goods.[93]

While Israeli courts have accepted government arguments that settlements, and presumably the water that they draw from the West Bank aquifer, are justified by Israel's security needs,[94] it is questionable whether such a notion of general security needs falls within the scope of "use by the occupation forces and administration personnel" outlined in the provision. In any regard, the Israeli well-drilling operations in the region have rarely taken into account the needs of the occupied populace. One example of Israeli indifference to the needs of the occupied populace is seen in the drilling of Israeli wells in close

---

91. Fourth Geneva Convention, *supra* note 20, art. 55.

92. *See supra* note 34 and accompanying text.

93. In fact, another article in the convention with potential application to natural resources specifically negates the difference between publicly and privately held property. Article 53 of the Fourth Geneva Convention deals with destruction of property and reads:

> Any destruction by the Occupying Power of real or personal property belonging to individually or collectively to private persons, or to the State, or to other public authorities, or to social or cooperative organizations, is prohibited, except where such destruction is rendered absolutely necessary by military operations.

In addition to highlighting the lack of differentiation between public and private property, article 53 may also be specifically applicable to the West Bank aquifer. High levels of Israeli water extraction from the aquifer may lead to its destruction. Deep bore wells placed near more shallow Arab wells have arguably led to the individual destruction of Arab water facilities.

94. E. COHEN, *supra* note 26, at 156-59.

proximity to Palestinian wells. New wells dug for Israeli settlements within a few hundred meters of existing Arab wells or springs have drastically diminished the water supply of certain villages.[95] Thus while the Israeli government has claimed *de facto* compliance with the Fourth Geneva Convention, it does not appear to meet its high standards.

III. POTENTIAL DEVELOPMENTS

So far this note has analyzed the application of existing conventions on belligerent occupation to the situation of the West Bank aquifer. In each case, the analysis has been an exercise in tailoring relatively ill-fitting rules to meet a situation which the drafters of the conventions did not anticipate. The necessary exploitation of the same crucial groundwater resources by both the occupied and the occupier in an arid region appears to be a scenario in which the needs of both parties are mutually exclusive. The water security needs of Israel require some form of guarantee that a certain amount of water continue to flow from the West Bank aquifer, not only to supply usable water but also to provide the necessary water pressure to prevent Mediterranean salination of Israeli wells. The sovereignty and development of Palestinians, however, is equally dependent upon self-control of the water resources beneath them.

The only international rule that begins to approach an accommodation of both parties interests, article 54 of Protocol I of the Geneva Conventions of 1949, has been discussed briefly in the previous section. Though Protocol I in its entirety has not been ratified by Israel, there are strong arguments for the implementation of article 54 alone in the case of the West Bank aquifer. The concepts of article 54 when combined with developing principles of international groundwater law can create a mutually beneficial situation rather than the mutually exclusive outcome discussed above.

Article 54 states quite boldly that "[i]t is prohibited to . . . . remove [or] . . . render useless objects indispensable to the survival of the civilian population, such as . . . drinking water installations and supplies and irrigation works, for the specific purpose of denying them for their sustenance value to the civilian population . . . whatever the motive . . . ."[96] The official commentary on the Protocol emphasizes that the

---

95. Security Council Report 1980, *supra* note 82, at 41-42 (listing six villages by name and recounting incident where one Israeli well was approved despite a warning from the water authority of adverse affects to nearby Arab wells).

96. Protocol I, *supra* note 34, art. 54, para. 2.

rule was intended to cover "all possibilities"[97] of an occupier's actions. The current Israeli practices of decisively limiting the Palestinian use of indigenous water supplies would apparently fall under the prohibiting scope of the provision. The Israeli actions essentially "remove" the aquifer from the use of the occupied civilians; certain Palestinian wells have arguably been "rendered useless" by wells drilled for Israeli settlements.

Thus article 54 of Protocol I is the first international norm that can directly curtail the activities of an occupying power in the case of groundwater. Built into the rule, however, is a qualifying provision that takes into consideration the security needs of the occupying power. Paragraph 5 of the provision recognizes the "vital requirements of any Party to the Conflict in the defence of its national territory against invasion. . . ."[98] While the rule explicitly allows derogation from article 54's principles to defend only against an invasion, implicit within the rule is the notion that an occupying state may derogate from article 54 in a legitimate case of general self-defense. The water needs of any country in an arid land are obviously a matter of national security on a par with that of national defense. Thus, while article 54 would severely limit current Israeli water policies regarding the West Bank aquifer, there is an implicit escape clause within the rule that takes Israeli water security into consideration.

Such a result parallels the developments of international water law as it applies to shared resources. While the sovereignty of individual states, including occupied states, is respected, the notion of mutual cooperation in the development and equitable use of shared water resources is also fostered. Such water law rules developed first through the necessary cooperation of nonconflicting states, but they can also be applied to the situation in West Bank despite the present hostilities between occupier and occupied.

International water law in general has traditionally been divided into separate categories depending on the use of the water in question. The distinction between international agreements concerning the navigability of waterways and those concerning international water consumption is just one example of the former specialization of international water law. However, the discovery of the hydrological connections between surface water and groundwater has led to the concept of the "International Water Basin" in the discussion of non-

---

97. INT'L COMMITTEE OF THE RED CROSS, COMMENTARY ON THE ADDITIONAL PROTOCOLS OF JUNE 1977 TO THE GENEVA CONVENTIONS OF 12 AUGUST 1949, at 655 (Y. Sandoz, C. Swinarski & B. Zimmerman eds. 1987).

98. Protocol I, *supra* note 34, art. 54, para. 5.

transportation related water issues. The basin concept melds notions of surface water and groundwater law together, while emphasizing that parties using the same water resources should respect each other's needs. The United Nations Natural Resources Council has stated:

> Whenever there is a hydrological interconnexion, surface or underground, and more than one state's territory is involved, the water resources so occurring and connected must be treated as international, which is to say that their development and utilization are to be undertaken in accordance with the pertinent conventional and customary international law principles and rules.[99]

Among the principles that the United Nations has espoused concerning water is the notion of equitable utilization.[100] In defining "equitable use" commentators consider the factors of ownership, present use, seniority, reasonability and overall optimal use potential.[101] In addition to equitable utilization, the United Nations has called for: 1) review of existing techniques for managing shared water resources, 2) cooperation and establishment of institutions and programs, and 3) exchange of information.[102] The international water law principles which have begun to develop between non-conflicting countries are easily adaptable to the rules of belligerent occupation. Both bodies of law have the similar goal of protecting the sovereign and individual interests of countries in conflict. Both bodies of law deal with national security and well-being. In the case of the West Bank aquifer, it is only natural that the laws of belligerent occupation should mirror the principles behind international water law.

Applying the principles of article 54 of Protocol I in light of international water law norms can lead to a situation in which both Palestinian and Israeli interests are maximized. Under article 54, the Israelis would be required to curtail their present practice of limiting water supplies to the indigenous Palestinians. They would also be forced to change their policies regarding use of the West Bank aquifer for Israeli settlements. These changes do not mean that Palestinians

---

99. *Management of International Water Resources: Institutional and Legal Aspects*, UN Nat. Resources Council, Water series No.1, at 9 (1975).

100. At the Mar Del Plata Conference on water use in 1977, the committee included the following among their proposals:

> In relation to the use, management and development of shared water resources, national policies should take into consideration the right of each state sharing the resources to equitably utilize such resources to equitably utilize such resources as the means to promote bonds of solidarity and cooperation.

U.N. WATER CONFERENCE, MAR DEL PLATA at 53, U.N. Doc. E/CONF.70/29, U.N. Sales No. E.77.II.A.12 (1977) [hereinafter Mar Del Plata Conference].

101. Caponera & Alhéritière, *Principles for Internationl Groundwater Law*, INTERNATIONAL GROUNDWATER LAW 39 (L. Teclaff & A. Utton eds. 1981).

102. Mar Del Plata Conference, *supra* note 100, at 53-58.

would have carte blanche power over the aquifer. Under the twin constraints of article 54 and international water laws, Palestinians would have to consider Israeli water security needs when exploiting the resource for their own purposes. They may even be required under the equitable use theories, which take into account present use of water resources, to sell water to Israeli institutions. Such a result takes away the economic advantages the Israelis have maintained in their occupation of the West Bank, but it does not threaten their security, the primary goal of the occupation. A forced sale of water resources is a partial invasion of Palestinian sovereignty or autonomy, but it at least presents them with fair compensation for Israeli use of the aquifer. Both sides would end up compromising toward a jointly optimal solution rather than an individually optimal situation which would deny the other's water security.

The dovetailing of international groundwater laws and laws of belligerent occupation may also necessitate joint administration of the West Bank aquifer by the conflicting parties. Joint administration, with equal participation by Israeli and Palestinian institutions, better reflects the spirit of the rules of belligerent occupation to protect the occupied region's sovereign integrity while ensuring the occupier's security interests. Joint administration also furthers the equitable utilization doctrine outlined in the principles of international water law.

In a jointly administered system, both sides would gain. Each side currently enjoys a geographical or geological advantage over the other in some form of water resource. The position of the Palestinians over portions of the West Bank aquifer which feed Israeli wells has been discussed extensively. Outside the scope of this note so far has been the advantageous position Israeli holds over the Occupied Territories in terms of the surface waters of the Jordan River system.[103] Offsetting advantages increase the likelihood that each side will seek to respect the other's concerns. Each side could obtain fair benefits from the water resource over which the other side enjoys a natural advantage.

Whether the parties choose independent, but cooperative measures or joint administration in order to equitably distribute crucial resources, either method would comply with the conventions on belligerent occupation and international water law far better than the present Israeli practice. Though Israel will undoubtedly lose certain economic and security advantages that it now possesses, those short-

---

103. Israel borders the southward flowing Jordan River at a point north of the river's contact with the West Bank.

term advantages are less palatable in the long run. Quenching the thirst of the conqueror at the complete expense of the Palestinians only raises resentment and acts of desperation in the occupied region. Implementing a system today that fairly accounts for Israeli security and Palestinian needs will strengthen mutually beneficial water sharing between the two regions in the future.

IV. Conclusion

The water issue is one of the most crucial in the Israeli-Palestinian conflict. While territorial disputes may be solved by guaranteed borders, shared water resources, particularly those underground, do not acknowledge lines on a map. The issue is exacerbated by the present Israeli occupation of Palestinian territory. Though currently accepted conventions regarding the laws of belligerent occupation only address the issue of shared water resources tangentially, they do imply certain standards which Israel apparently fails to meet regarding the West Bank aquifer. At the very least, Israel has violated the spirit of the conventions which serve to protect occupied inhabitants from undue interference by the occupying power.

The direct address of water concerns in Protocol I to the Fourth Geneva Convention provides a positive rule within which the needs of both parties may be met. Additionally, general principles of international water sharing could be implemented in a system whereby Israeli and Palestinian interests are equally matched. Such cooperation is necessary to prevent either party from benefitting from the thirst of the other.

ON THE ROAD TO APARTHEID: THE BYPASS ROAD NETWORK IN THE WEST BANK

by Samira Shah[*]

TABLE OF CONTENTS

*   B.A., University of Chicago (1992); M.A., University of Chicago (1993); J.D.,
Columbia University School of Law (expected 1998); Executive Editor, *Columbia Human
Rights Law Review* (1997-98). This Article draws upon research conducted during the
summer of 1996 while the author was an intern at Al-Haq, a Palestinian non-
governmental human rights organization affiliated with the International Commission
of Jurists. The author would like to express her gratitude to the researchers and staff of
Al-Haq and to Khalil Tufakji for their help in the research necessary for this Article.
Special thanks to Alexis Demopoulos, Terence Dougherty, Nicole Erb, Bryan Sells,
Rashmi Airan, and Samantha Schreiber for their assistance in the preparation of this
Article. The author welcomes all comments on this Article, which may be directed to
Samira Shah c/o Columbia University School of Law, 435 West 116th Street, New York,
NY 10027.

INTRODUCTION

In the past four years the Israeli government has built an unprecedented number of roads in the West Bank. These roads form part of the bypass road network planned for the West Bank which links Israeli settlements in the West Bank to each other and to Israel, bypassing Palestinian urban centers. Of the original 650 kilometers of roads planned for the network, approximately 230 kilometers had been constructed by April 1996.[1] Bypass roads in the West Bank are not

---

1.   Alon Pinkas, *Tsomet MK: IDF Pullout from Gaza to Start Next Month—Ministry Submits NIS 2B. Plan for Road Building in Areas,* Jerusalem Post, Jan. 9, 1994. In January 1994, the Israeli Ministry of Housing, in coordination with the Israeli Defense Forces (IDF), presented to the Israeli Treasury a NIS 2 billion (approximately U.S. $700 million) plan to build and pave 650 kilometers of bypass roads in the West Bank. This plan will hereinafter be referred to as the IDF road plan. *See also* Assaf Adiv, *Avoid the Arabs,* Challenge, July–Aug. 1994, at 22. Interview with Khalil Tufakji, a Palestinian geographer at the Arab Studies Society in Jerusalem (June 25, 1996) (stating that approximately 230 kilometers of bypass roads had been constructed by April 1996).

designed to serve the infrastructural needs of the local Palestinian population. They are built for Israeli settlers and military at the expense of the Palestinian population. While Palestinians are denied access to these roads, their land is routinely seized to construct them.

Although the term "bypass road" has come into vogue only recently, the idea behind the roads is not new. The design of the current bypass road plan is strikingly similar to an early plan for Israeli settlement of the West Bank proposed by Gush Emmunim, a radical settler organization, in 1978. This settlement plan—as well as settlement plans developed in the 1980s—aimed at developing West Bank settlements into Jewish communities that would be an integral part of Israel. Along with the settlement plans came further road plans to develop the infrastructure of the settlements. This infrastructure was to be linked with that of Israel, tying together Jewish communities in the West Bank and Israel through an integrated road network.

In its justification for imposing the bypass road network on the West Bank, the Israeli government referred to the sections of the Oslo Agreements mandating redeployment—withdrawal from certain areas and relocation to others—of the Israeli Defense Forces (the IDF).[2] The IDF argued that if they were to redeploy from areas of Palestinian authority in the West Bank, they could not guarantee the security of the Israeli settlers in the West Bank. Thus, the settlers needed roads which would enable them to travel within the West Bank and to Israel without passing through any areas under Palestinian authority. With this rationale, the IDF maintains that the roads are being built for security purposes (to ensure the security of the settlers). However, as the high incidence of Israeli settler killings on the bypass roads attests, the network not only fails to ensure their security, but actually places settlers at greater risk.

In addition to connecting Israeli settlements to each other and the rest of Israel, the bypass road network serves to separate Palestinian communities. The road network is a military grid in the West Bank, dividing and surrounding the Palestinian regions with militarily-controlled roads. Since the military closed the roads to Palestinians, the grid enables the military to seal off the Palestinian

---

2.   The Declaration of Principles on Interim Self-Government Arrangements, Sept. 13, 1993, Isr.-PLO, art. I, 32 I.L.M. 1525 (1993) [hereinafter Oslo I]; Israeli-Palestinian Interim Agreement on the West Bank and the Gaza Strip, Sept. 28, 1995, Isr.-PLO, Ch. 5, art. XXXI, ¶ 5, 36 I.L.M. 551 (1997) [hereinafter Oslo II].

regions and maintain control over them. Thus, the network furthers Israel's policy of *de facto* annexation of the West Bank.

Another purpose of the bypass road network is to allow Israel to confiscate Palestinian land while it is still under Israeli authority. The IDF has seized or expropriated an estimated 23,000 dunums (5681 acres) of Palestinian land specifically for the purpose of constructing bypass roads.[3] Most of the land that has been confiscated has been agricultural land, which is usually the sole source of livelihood for its owners. Thousands of olive and almond orchards and vineyards have been uprooted from the confiscated land and from the areas of prohibited building on either side of the roads.[4] Dozens of houses have been demolished because they were in the path of the bypass road or simply within the security area on either side of the roads.[5] The land confiscation and property destruction have also caused harm to the environment and to rich archaeological sites.

The bypass road network has devastating effects on Palestinian statehood, sovereignty, and self-determination. The roads carve up the West Bank, creating enclaves of Palestinian authority with definite boundaries. The roads prevent the expansion of these enclaves and ensure that there will be no territorial contiguity in the West Bank. To

---

3.   One dunum equals 0.247 acres or 1,000 square meters. Interview with Khalil Tufakji, *supra* note 1. As the construction of the roads progresses, more land will be confiscated. *Cf. Israel Denies Reports of Land Confiscation for Settlements, Quarries* (BBC television broadcast, Dec. 10, 1996) (reporting that in a Voice of Israel broadcast on December 9, 1996, a senior Israeli security source said that only 15,000 dunums of land have been confiscated for the construction of security fences and settlement roads).

4.   *See* Al-Haq's field report numbers 94/122, 94/134, 94/159, 95/198, and 96/148 (on file with author); Meron Benvenisti & Shlomo Khayat, The West Bank and Gaza Atlas 60 (1988). Building and agricultural activities are prohibited in the designated margins of the road—anywhere from 100 to 200 meters along both sides of the road.

5.   *See* Allegra Pacheco & Yifat Susskind, *Paving the Way to the Final Status*, Challenge, Jan.–Feb. 1996, at 9 (noting that six houses were demolished in Hebron to facilitate construction of Road 60); Joel Greenberg, *Caught in Crackdown, Arabs' Hopes Lie in Ruins*, N.Y. Times, Aug. 6, 1997, at A3 (stating that a house was demolished because it was built near a bypass road close to Hebron); *Settlers Not Using Bypass Roads*, Palestine Rep., Jan. 12, 1996, at 16 (stating that at the end of December 1995, six Palestinian homes were destroyed because they were "too close" to the bypass road around Bethlehem); LAW—The Palestinian Society for the Protection of Human Rights and the Environment, *Palestinian Homes Under Attack While Jewish Settlements Strengthened* (Aug. 14, 1996) (press release) <http://www.birzeit.edu/lawe/press/1996/aug _14.html> [hereinafter LAW] (stating that two houses in 'Anata and Jaba' were demolished to clear the path for a bypass road from Ramallah to the settlement of Pisgat Ze'ev).

this end, there is a network of roads encircling every major Palestinian city. There are heavy concentrations of these roads between Ramallah and Jerusalem, and between Jerusalem, Bethlehem, and Hebron. These areas are densely populated, and without the roads, could be contiguous areas of Palestinian inhabitation. The bypass roads and the land confiscation ensure that even after the peace process is complete, there will be no such contiguity.

The construction of the bypass road network violates international humanitarian law and the Oslo Agreements. Since Israel is still occupying the West Bank and Gaza Strip,[6] the international humanitarian laws codified in the Regulations attached to the 1907 Hague Convention IV[7] and the Fourth Geneva Convention[8] apply. As such, confiscation of land for the purpose of building bypass roads violates the Hague Regulations. Furthermore, bypass roads further Israel's settlement policies in the West Bank and thereby violate the Fourth Geneva Convention.

The Israelis have demonstrated their commitment to the bypass road network by spending U.S. $600 million on bypass roads in 1995 alone.[9] The roads send a clear message that they, and the settlements which they serve, are here to stay. The bypass roads prejudice the outcome of the permanent status negotiations because they create a permanent reality on the ground, linking together the settlements and facilitating their expansion and construction. Furthermore, many of the

---

6.   While Oslo II transfers a limited amount of authority over the West Bank and Gaza Strip from Israel to the Palestinian Council, it does not remove Israel from its position as occupier of the West Bank and Gaza Strip. Oslo II divides the West Bank into Areas A, B, and C which respectively constitute approximately 3%, 24%, and 73% of the West Bank. The agreement transfers "all civil powers and duties" in Areas A and B to the Palestinian Council during the first phase of redeployment. In addition, Oslo II transfers police powers from the Israeli military to the Palestinian Authority in Area A. Since Israel retains the responsibility for the security of settlers and Israelis in all areas of the West Bank, it does not abdicate full authority over Area A. In Area B, Israel still maintains police and security responsibilities. Israel retains its full civil, police, and security authority over Area C. *See infra* Part I.B; *see also* Oslo II, *supra* note 2.

7.   Convention Respecting the Laws and Customs of War on Land (1907 Hague Convention IV), Oct. 18, 1907, Annex, art. 55, 36 Stat. 2277, T.S. No. 539, 1 Bevans 631 [hereinafter Hague Regulations].

8.   Geneva Convention Relative to the Protection of Civilian Persons in Times of War, Aug. 12, 1949, 6 U.S.T. 3516, 75 U.N.T.S. 287 [hereinafter Geneva Convention IV].

9.   *Settlers Propose Massive Settlement Program After Elections*, Report on Israeli Settlement in the Occupied Territories (Found. for Middle East Peace, Wash., D.C.), May 1996, at 3.

roads are being built along the Green Line (Israel's borders established before 1967) and around Jerusalem, effectively extending Israel's borders beyond the Green Line and extending the boundaries of Jerusalem. The bypass roads further Israel's *de facto* annexation of Jerusalem and allow Israel to increase the number of Israeli inhabitants of the area it calls Jerusalem, thus prejudicing the permanent status of Jerusalem. The bypass roads are permanent facts on the ground which alter the status quo of the West Bank, including East Jerusalem, existing before the 1967 Israeli occupation, in violation of both the letter and the spirit of the Oslo Agreements.

This Article will demonstrate that the bypass road network destroys the economy of the West Bank, undermines the peace process, and violates international law.[10] In Part I, the Article will briefly recount the history of the Palestinian-Israeli conflict and the international agreements and laws relevant to it. In Part II, the Article will describe the strategic importance of road planning to the Israeli occupation of the West Bank. In Part III, the Article will address current impacts of the road network itself, emphasizing its effects on the Palestinian economy. In Part IV, the Article will argue that the road network violates the Oslo Agreements already signed by the Palestine Liberation Organization (PLO) and the Israeli government and that it prejudices the outcome of the upcoming Permanent Status Negotiations. Finally, in Part V, the Article will demonstrate that the bypass road network contravenes Israel's rights and responsibilities as an occupying nation under the international laws governing belligerent occupations.

I. BACKGROUND

A.   Historical Background

1.   1916-1948

Prior to World War I, the area now known as Israel was known as Palestine and was part of the Ottoman Empire. During World War I, as the fall of the Ottoman Empire became imminent, the governments

---

10.   This Article deals only with the bypass road network in the West Bank. Although the IDF has constructed bypass roads in the Gaza Strip as well, it has constructed a much larger network of roads in the West Bank. Also, due to the restrictions on movement between the West Bank and the Gaza Strip, I was unable to collect much data on the bypass roads in the Gaza Strip.

of France and Great Britain signed the Sykes-Picot Agreement on May 16, 1916.[11] France and Great Britain agreed "to recognize and protect an independent Arab State or a Confederation of Arab States" upon the disintegration of the Ottoman Empire.[12] In December 1917, Palestine was occupied by the Allied Forces under General Allenby of Britain.[13]

After World War I, the Allied Powers divided the former Ottoman Empire into mandates, and Great Britain was given a mandate from the League of Nations to govern Palestine.[14] Article 22 of the Covenant of the League of Nations established the Mandates System, which was based on the concept that these territories needed the tutelage of "advanced nations" in order to develop.[15] The degree of tutelage was to depend on the extent of political maturity of the territory concerned.[16] Palestine, like the other Arab territories of the former Ottoman Empire, was to be treated as a highly-developed territory with little need of tutelage.[17] Palestine's existence as an independent nation was to be "provisionally recognized subject to the rendering of administrative advice and assistance by a Mandatory until such time as [it was] able to stand alone."[18]

All of the Mandates over Arab territories, with the exception of Palestine, led to the independence recognized in the Covenant.[19] Predominant among the reasons that the Mandate did not lead to the independence of Palestine were the contradictions inherent in the Mandate described below.[20] Although the wishes of the community were to be a principal consideration in the selection of the Mandatory and in

---

11.   United Nations, The Origins and Evolution of the Palestine Problem: 1917–1988, 81 (1990) [hereinafter Origins].

12.   *Id.*

13.   Palestinian Academic Society for the Study of International Affairs, PASSIA Diary, 1996, at 239 [hereinafter PASSIA Diary].

14.   Origins, *supra* note 11, at 18.

15.   League of Nations Covenant art. 22.

16.   Origins, *supra* note 11, at 19.

17.   The most developed territories were classified as "A" Mandates, the less developed as "B," and the least developed as "C." The Arab lands of the former Ottoman Empire were classified as "A" Mandates. Origins, *supra* note 11, at 20; League of Nations Covenant art. 22.

18.   League of Nations Covenant art. 22.

19.   Origins, *supra* note 11, at 20.

20.   *See infra* notes 22–25 and accompanying text.

the eventual self-government of the territory, the British had their own wishes with regard to Palestine.[21]

In November 1917, the British Foreign Secretary, Sir Arthur James Balfour, expressed the British Government's intentions with regard to Palestine in what has come to be known as the Balfour Declaration.[22] Balfour stated that, "His Majesty's Government views with favour the establishment in Palestine of a national home for the Jewish people, and will use their best endeavours to facilitate the achievement of this object . . . ."[23] The Balfour Declaration was incorporated into the British Mandate, and the "pivotal role of the Balfour Declaration in virtually every phase of the Palestinian issue cannot be exaggerated."[24] The Covenant of the League of Nations envisioned the Mandate as the best method to ensure the well being and development of the peoples inhabiting the Mandated Territories.[25] Contrary to the rights and wishes of the Palestinians, the Mandate sought the establishment in Palestine of a national home for another people.

The British governed Palestine under their mandate from 1922 to 1947, and during that time, the Jewish population in Palestine increased by approximately 725%.[26] In 1917, before the British Mandate, the native Arab population constituted 90% of the total population of Palestine, and the Jewish population accounted for approximately 9% of the total population.[27] By the end of the British Mandate, the Arab population constituted approximately 67% of the total population, and the Jewish population accounted for 33% of the total population.[28]

---

21.   League of Nations Covenant art. 22 (stating that the wishes of the communities classified as "A" Mandates "must be a principal consideration in the selection of the Mandatory").

22.   Origins, *supra* note 11, at 8.

23.   *Id.*

24.   *Id.*

25.   *Id.* at 32. *See also* League of Nations Covenant art. 22.

26.   Origins, *supra* note 11, at 71.

27.   Origins, *supra* note 11, at 162; *see also* PASSIA Diary, *supra* note 13, at 187; David McDowall, Palestine and Israel: The Uprising and Beyond 17 (1989). The first Zionist settlers began to arrive in Palestine in the 1880s, and "[b]y 1914 85,000 such settlers had arrived in Palestine, amounting to 9 per cent of the population." *Id.*

28.   Origins, *supra* note 11, at 71-72, 162; *see also* PASSIA Diary, *supra* note 13, at 190; Eyal Benvenisti & Eyal Zamir, *Private Claims to Property Rights in the Future Israeli-Palestinian Settlement*, 89 Am. J. Int'l L. 295, 297 n.8 (1995).

During the twenty-year British Mandate in Palestine, violence continually erupted between the Palestinian Arabs and the Zionists. The Palestinians were frustrated with the large-scale Jewish immigration into Palestine and the refusal of the British to recognize their right to self-government.[29] The Zionists resorted to violence "to hold the ground they had gained and to press towards their ultimate aspirations of a Jewish State in Palestine."[30] Britain tried without success to bring independence to Palestine and to resolve the conflicting aspirations of the Palestinians and the Zionists, and in February 1947, Great Britain presented the problem of Palestine to the United Nations.[31]

On November 29, 1947, the United Nations issued Resolution 181, recommending the partition of Palestine into a Jewish and an Arab state with Jerusalem and Bethlehem as a separate entity under a special international regime.[32] The partition plan granted the Jewish population in Palestine just over 56% of the area at a time when they owned 6.2% of the land and constituted one-third of the total population.[33] After the partition plan was announced, violence erupted in Palestine and within three months, 869 people died and 1,909 people were injured in Palestinian-Jewish clashes.[34] Jewish paramilitary attacks on Palestinian villages led to the mass exodus of Palestinian Arabs to other areas of Palestine as well as to other countries.[35] The violence escalated as the neighboring Arab states (Egypt, Iraq, Syria, Lebanon, and Transjordan) joined in the hostilities and fought what came to be known as the 1948 Arab-Israeli or Middle East War.[36]

---

29.   Origins, *supra* note 11, at 63.
30.   *Id.*
31.   *Id.* at 98.
32.   *See* G.A. Res. 181, U.N. GAOR, 2d Sess., U.N. Doc. A/519, at 131 (1947); *see also* Maps 1 and 2 *infra* pp. 285-86.
33.   *See* G.A. Res. 181, *supra* note 32; *see also* Origins, *supra* note 11, at 162; PASSIA Diary, *supra* note 13, at 190.
34.   Origins, *supra* note 11, at 132.
35.   *Id.* at 132-35.
36.   *Id.* at 138.

2.   1948-1967

On May 14, 1948, Israel declared its independence as a state, and on the following day, the British Mandate officially ended.[37] The Israeli forces were well-armed and well-trained and quickly overpowered the forces of the intervening Arab states.[38] By the end of the war, Israel occupied most of the territory of Palestine, with the exception of the area along the West Bank of the Jordan River (known since as "the West Bank") and a strip of land along the Mediterranean Sea (known since as "the Gaza Strip").[39]

The 1948 Arab-Israeli War ended with the signing of bilateral armistice agreements between Israel and Egypt (February 24, 1949), Israel and Lebanon (March 23, 1949), Israel and Jordan (April 3, 1949), and Israel and Syria (July 20, 1949).[40] These armistice agreements divided Palestine into three territorial units. Israel held most of the territory (77%), Jordan occupied the West Bank, including the eastern part of Jerusalem, and Egypt occupied the Gaza Strip.[41] The agreements specified that they did not prejudice the political positions of any of the parties with regard to the ultimate settlement of the dispute over Palestine.[42] Specifically, the agreements gave Israel no legal right to the territories occupied during the 1948 hostilities beyond those areas specified in U.N. Resolution 181.[43] The West Bank and the Gaza Strip combined constituted 23% of Palestine.[44] Thus, the area seized by Israel in the 1948 war was 37.5% greater than the territory proposed for the state of Israel by U.N. Resolution 181.

Between the issuance of U.N. Resolution 181 and September 1949, over one-half of the indigenous Palestinian population left their homes.[45] The United Nations estimates that approximately 726,000 Palestinians fled or were expelled from their homes in the territory in which the state of Israel was established.[46] Four hundred and eighteen Palestinian villages and settlements had been depopulated and erased

---

37.   *Id.* at 137.
38.   *Id.* at 138-39.
39.   *Id.* at 139. *See* Map 1 *infra* p. 285.
40.   PASSIA Diary, *supra* note 13, at 190.
41.   *See* Origins, *supra* note 11, at 162.
42.   *Id.* at 141.
43.   *Id.*
44.   PASSIA Diary, *supra* note 13, at 190.
45.   Origins, *supra* note 11, at 162.
46.   *Id.* at 135, 162.

from the map as a result of Israeli military activities, expulsion orders, and the exodus of Palestinian civilians.[47]

On May 11, 1949, Israel was admitted as a member of the United Nations.[48] The preamble of the resolution admitting Israel to the United Nations specifically referred to Israel's commitment to implement U.N. Resolutions 181 and 194.[49] U.N. Resolution 194 established a right of peaceful return of the Palestinians to their homes in the territory occupied by Israel in 1948.[50] The resolution also called for the establishment of a "permanent international regime for the Jerusalem area which will provide for the maximum local autonomy for distinctive groups consistent with the special international status of the Jerusalem area."[51]

In April 1950, Jordan unilaterally annexed the West Bank, including East Jerusalem, by a decree declaring the two banks of the Jordan River to be the Hashemite Kingdom of Jordan.[52] However, this annexation was never recognized by any Arab country, by the Arab League, or by any other state (except Pakistan and Britain).[53] Nonetheless, after this annexation, Jordanian legislation was applied to the West Bank.[54] Egypt administered the Gaza Strip as an occupied territory "whose inhabitants were not Egyptian citizens but, rather, citizens of Palestine."[55] Both the West Bank and the Gaza Strip

---

47.   PASSIA Diary, *supra* note 13, at 190. From 1948 to 1953, the U.N. Relief and Works Agency for Palestine Refugees in the Near East established 18 refugee camps in the West Bank and eight camps in Gaza to accommodate a portion of the refugees from the 1948 war. *Id.* at 202.

48.   G.A. Res. 273, U.N. GAOR, 3d Sess., U.N. Doc. A/855 (1949).

49.   *Id.*

50.   G.A. Res. 194, U.N. GAOR, 3d Sess., 186th mtg. at 21, U.N. Doc. A/810 (1948). In relevant part, the Resolution

> [r]esolves that the refugees wishing to return to their homes and live at peace with their neighbours should be permitted to do so at the earliest practicable date, and that compensation should be paid for the property of those choosing not to return and for loss of or damage to property which, under principles of international law or in equity, should be made good by the Governments or authorities responsible.

Id.

51.   *Id.*

52.   Origins, *supra* note 11, at 145; PASSIA Diary, *supra* note 13, at 190.

53.   Benvenisti & Zamir, *supra* note 28, at 301–02.

54.   *Id.* at 302.

55.   *Id.* at 304.

remained under Jordanian and Egyptian rule respectively, until the June 1967 war between Israel and neighboring Arab states.

3.   1967-1991

After two decades of tense and troubled relations, on June 5, 1967, Israel attacked Egypt.[56] Pursuant to their defense agreements with Egypt, Jordan and Syria joined in the fighting.[57] On June 11, 1967, the Six Day War was over, and Israel had captured and occupied the Sinai peninsula, a portion of the Golan Heights, and the remaining territory of Palestine: the West Bank, including East Jerusalem, and the Gaza Strip.[58] On June 28, 1967, Israel unilaterally annexed East Jerusalem, applying Israeli "law, jurisdiction and administration" to that part of the city.[59] Thereafter, Israel applied the same laws to East Jerusalem as it did to Israel, and it administered the West Bank, excluding Jerusalem, and the Gaza Strip through a military government.

The United Nations criticized Israel's occupation of the West Bank, including East Jerusalem and the Gaza Strip, and its attempt to annex East Jerusalem unilaterally. The Security Council declared that Israel's annexation of East Jerusalem was invalid and that East Jerusalem remained an occupied territory like the West Bank and the Gaza Strip.[60] On November 22, 1967, the Security Council unanimously

---

56.   McDowall, *supra* note 27, at 29.

57.   *Id.* at 29-30.

58.   Origins, *supra* note 11, at 145. The West Bank, including East Jerusalem, and the Gaza Strip will be referred to collectively as the Occupied Territories. The 1967 war, like the 1948 war, resulted in a mass exodus of Palestinians. Approximately 500,000 Palestinians were displaced during the 1967 war. *Id.* at 162.

59.   Benvenisti & Zamir, *supra* note 28, at 299; *see* Law and Administration Order (No. 1), 5727-1967 (June 28, 1967); *see also* Map 2 *infra* p. 286.

60.   *See* S.C. Res. 252, U.N. SCOR, 23d Sess., 1426th mtg. at 9, U.N. Doc. S/INF/23/Rev.1 (1968); *see also* G.A. Res. 33/113, U.N. GAOR, 33d Sess., Supp. No. 45, at 70, U.N. Doc. A/33/45 (1978); G.A. Res. 31/106A, U.N. GAOR, 31st Sess., Supp. No. 39, at 50, U.N. Doc. A/31/39 (1976); G.A. Res. 2254, U.N. GAOR, 5th Sess., Supp. No. 1, at 4, U.N. Doc. A/6798 (1967); G.A. Res. 2253, U.N. GAOR, 5th Sess., Supp. No. 1, at 4, U.N. Doc. A/6798 (1967); S.C. Res. 476, U.N. SCOR, 35th Sess., 2242d mtg. at 13, U.N. Doc. S/INF/36 (1980); S.C. Res. 446, U.N. SCOR, 34th Sess., 2134th mtg. at 4, U.N. Doc. S/INF/35 (1979); S.C. Res. 298, U.N. SCOR, 26th Sess., 1582d mtg. at 6, U.N. Doc. S/INF/27 (1971); S.C. Res. 267, U.N. SCOR, 24th Sess., 1485th mtg. at 4, U.N. Doc. S/INF/27 (1971).

adopted Resolution 242[61] which called on Israel to withdraw from the territories it occupied during the 1967 war.[62] Implicitly, the resolution recognized Israel's pre-1967 borders, known as the "Green Line," including the territory it occupied in the 1948 war beyond the areas delineated by U.N. Resolution 181.[63] Security Council Resolution 242 has been the basis for all subsequent discussions of a peaceful settlement to the Israeli-Palestinian conflict.

Israel has occupied the West Bank, including East Jerusalem, and the Gaza Strip since 1967. During the past thirty years, the United Nations unsuccessfully attempted to resolve the Israeli-Palestinian conflict through a number of resolutions and peace conferences.[64] The United Nations called on Israel to withdraw from the Occupied Territories and condemned Israeli policies within the Occupied Territories. In the course of its efforts, the United Nations catalogued a number of Israeli policies and practices that exacerbated the conflict. General Assembly Resolution 32/91C lists many of these policies and practices:

    (a) The annexation of parts of the occupied territories;
    (b) The establishment of Israeli settlements therein and the transfer of an alien population thereto;
    (c) The evacuation, deportation, expulsion, displacement and transfer of Arab inhabitants of the occupied territories, and the denial of their right of return;
    (d) The confiscation and expropriation of Arab property in the occupied territories and all other transactions for the

---

61.   S.C. Res. 242, U.N. SCOR, 22d Sess., 132d mtg. at 8, U.N. Doc. S/INF.Rev.2 (1967).

62.   *Id.*

63.   Origins, *supra* note 11, at 148.

64.   Although the United Nations recognized the Palestine Liberation Organization (PLO) as the legitimate representative of the Palestinian people in 1974, the PLO and the Israeli government did not recognize each other. Because the PLO and the Israeli government refused to enter into direct negotiations with each other, the United Nations operated as a mediator between the two and conducted conferences with each separately. In 1969, the United Nations explicitly and formally recognized the Palestinian people in G.A. Res. 2535 B, U.N. GAOR, 24th Sess., Supp. No. 30, at 25, U.N. Doc. A/7630 (1969). In 1970, the United Nations recognized the right of the Palestinian people to self-determination in G.A. Res. 2672C, U.N. GAOR, 25th Sess., Supp. No. 28, at 36, U.N. Doc. A/8028 (1970). In 1974, the United Nations invited the PLO to participate in deliberations of the General Assembly on the question of Palestine and granted the PLO the status of observer in the General Assembly and in international conferences held under U.N. auspices.

acquisition of land involving the Israeli authorities, institutions or nationals on the one hand, and the inhabitants or institutions of the occupied territories on the other;
(e)   The destruction and demolition of Arab houses;
(f)   Mass arrests, administrative detention and ill-treatment of the Arab population;
(g)   The ill-treatment and torture of persons under detention;
(h)   The pillaging of archaeological and cultural property;
(i)   The interference with religious freedoms and practices as well as family rights and customs;
(j)   The illegal exploitation of the natural wealth, resources and population of the occupied territories.[65]

During the 1970s and early 1980s, the Palestinians engaged in protests against Israeli occupation with sporadic violent attacks, stone-throwing, demonstrations, boycotts, and commercial shutdowns. After twenty years of unsuccessful peace conferences and unheeded U.N. resolutions condemning Israeli practices, the Palestinians initiated the massive uprising known as the intifada in December 1987. During the next three years, the Palestinians held numerous protest demonstrations to which the IDF, special forces, police, and Jewish settlers responded with "live ammunition, indiscriminate beatings of Palestinians, as well as other means of repression."[66]

B.   The Oslo Agreements

In October 1991, a Palestinian delegation entered into negotiations with the Israeli government in the first successful peace conference since the beginning of the conflict. Ultimately, the negotiations led to the Oslo Agreements between the PLO and the Israeli government. The first Oslo Agreement (Oslo I) set up a framework for eventual Palestinian self-rule based on U.N. Security

---

65.   G.A. Res. 32/91, U.N. GAOR, 32d Sess., Supp. No. 45, at 69, U.N. Doc. A/32/45 (1977). The United Nations passed similar resolutions in previous years as well. *See, e.g.,* G.A. Res. 31/106C, U.N. GAOR, 31st Sess., Supp. No. 39, at 50, U.N. Doc. A/31/39 (1976); G.A. Res. 3525A, U.N. GAOR, 30th Sess., Supp. No. 34, at 41, U.N. Doc. A/10034 (1975); G.A. Res. 3240A, U.N. GAOR, 29th Sess., Supp. No. 31, at 34, U.N. Doc. A/9631 (1974).
66.   Origins, *supra* note 11, at 251.

Council Resolutions 242 and 338.[67] That framework includes a series of further negotiations and agreements, culminating with the Permanent Status Negotiations. The Permanent Status Negotiations are designed to bring an end to the Israeli occupation of the West Bank and Gaza Strip and to decide the fate of Jerusalem, Palestinian refugees, settlements, borders, and security arrangements.[68] These negotiations must yield a permanent agreement by May 4, 1999.[69] In the interim period, the West Bank on the whole remains occupied although fragments of the West Bank enjoy limited Palestinian self-rule.

On May 4, 1994, Israel and the PLO signed another agreement pursuant to the framework established by Oslo I. This was the Agreement on the Gaza Strip and the Jericho Area known as the "Cairo Agreement."[70] Pursuant to this agreement, the IDF redeployed in the Gaza Strip.[71] The IDF withdrew from approximately 60% of the Gaza Strip and from the West Bank town of Jericho.[72] Thereafter, Israel transferred its authority over Jericho and 60% of the Gaza Strip to the PLO.[73]

On September 28, 1995, the PLO and Israel entered into the Israeli-Palestinian Interim Agreement on the West Bank and Gaza Strip, known as Oslo II.[74] Oslo II set up a complicated geographical framework for limited Palestinian self-rule. It divided the West Bank into Areas A, B, and C, corresponding to Palestinian cities, Palestinian

---

67.   Oslo I, *supra* note 2. After the Middle East War of October 1973, the U.N. Security Council issued Resolution 338 on October 22, 1973. S.C. Res. 338, U.N. SCOR, 28th Sess., 1747th mtg. at 10, U.N. Doc. S/INF/29 (1973). This resolution calls for a cease fire, the implementation of Security Council Resolution 242, and negotiations "between the parties concerned under appropriate auspices aimed at establishing a just and durable peace in the Middle East." *Id.*

68.   Oslo II, *supra* note 2.

69.   Agreement on the Gaza Strip and the Jericho Area, May 4, 1994, Isr.-PLO, art. XXIII, 33 I.L.M. 622 (signed at Cairo). In this agreement, Israel and the PLO set May 4, 1999 as the date by which they must enter into a permanent agreement.

70.   *Id.*

71.   *Id.* at art. II.

72.   Abigail E. Abrash, Statement on behalf of the Palestinian Centre for Human Rights, Gaza City, and the Robert F. Kennedy Memorial Center for Human Rights before the House Committee on International Relations Subcommittee on International Operations and Human Rights on Human Rights Under the Palestinian Authority, Federal Document Clearing House Congressional Testimony, July 23, 1996.

73.   Serge Schmemann, *Israel-P.L.O. Deal Reported on 1998 West Bank Pullout, Easing Way to Hebron Pact,* N.Y. Times, Jan. 13, 1997, at A1, A8. On May 13, 1994, Israel handed over Jericho to Palestinian rule.

74.   Oslo II, *supra* note 2.

villages, and Israeli settlements and military installations, respectively.[75] Area A encompasses seven major Palestinian centers— Jenin, Tulkarem, Nablus, Qalqilya, Ramallah, Bethlehem, and Hebron— and constitutes approximately 3% of the West Bank.[76] Area B makes up roughly 24% of the West Bank and consists of designated Palestinian towns, villages, refugee camps, and hamlets scattered throughout the West Bank.[77] The remaining 73% of the West Bank is designated as Area C and contains Palestinian villages, Israeli military installations, Israeli settlements, and Israeli roads.[78]

Oslo II sets up a schedule for the IDF to redeploy in the West Bank.[79] During the first phase of redeployment, the IDF was to redeploy from the seven cities in Area A and from the territory surrounding those cities in Area B. The IDF was to carry out this redeployment in seven stages during the seven weeks between February 11 and March 30, 1996.[80] The last scheduled redeployment was from Hebron, which was to end on March 30, 1996.[81] Redeployment of the IDF from specified locations in Area C was to take place after the inauguration of the Palestinian Council in three intervals of six months each.[82]

According to Oslo II, the Palestinian Council assumed all civil powers and responsibilities, including planning and zoning, in Areas A and B during this first phase of redeployment.[83] It also assumed limited

---

75.   *Id.* at ch. 2, art. XI. *See* Maps 3 and 4 *infra* pp. 287–88.

76.   David Millikin, *The Israeli Government Decided Overnight That Its Troops Would Withdraw from Nine Percent of the West Bank Under a Redeployment Agreement Signed with the Palestinians, Israeli Radio Announced,* Agence France Presse, Mar. 6, 1997, *available in* LEXIS, News Library, Curnws File.

77.   For a list of the areas included in Area B, see Oslo II, *supra* note 2, at annex I, app. 6; Millikin, *supra* note 76 (Area B constitutes 24% of the West Bank). *See also Knesset Debates Oslo B Agreement; Prime Minister Presents Agreement with Palestinians to Knesset for Approval* (BBC Summary of World Broadcasts, Oct. 7, 1995), *available in* LEXIS, News Library, Curnws File (Address of Prime Minister Yitzhaq Rabin to the Knesset in which he stated: "Areas A and B constitute some 27 percent of the West Bank's territory. Area C, which is under our [Israeli] control, constitutes more than 70 percent of the West Bank.").

78.   Millikin, *supra* note 76 ("Israel maintains full control over the remaining 73 percent, known as area C, where 144 Jewish settlements and Israeli military installations are located.").

79.   Oslo II, *supra* note 2, at annex I, app. 1.

80.   *Id.*

81.   *Id.*

82.   *Id.*

83.   *Id.* at art. XI, ¶ 2.

"civil powers and responsibilities not relating to territory" in Area C.[84] Oslo II also scheduled the deployment of the Palestinian Police in certain numbers to specified locations within Areas A and B.[85] The Palestinian Council also assumed the powers and responsibilities for internal security and public order in Area A.[86] In Area B, the Palestinian Council assumed responsibility for public order, but Israel retained overriding responsibility for internal security.[87] Israel maintained all security and public order responsibilities in Area C.[88] However, as the Israeli military redeployed in Area C, responsibility for internal security was to be transferred to the Palestinian police in Areas B and C.[89] During the interim period, the Israeli military retained responsibility for the security of settlers and other Israelis throughout the West Bank, for borders, and for external security.[90]

The IDF redeployments have not been carried out along the timeline specified by Oslo II. Although the IDF withdrew from the first six Palestinian cities and redeployed in the surrounding areas as scheduled, its withdrawal from Hebron was delayed. In the meantime, Israeli Prime Minister Shimon Peres was voted out of office, and Benjamin Netanyahu, an opponent of the Oslo Agreements, was elected as the new Prime Minister.[91] Although Prime Minister Netanyahu agreed to honor the Oslo Agreements, he delayed negotiating the terms of the IDF withdrawal from Hebron for several months.[92]

On January 15, 1997, Israel and the Palestinian National Authority agreed that the IDF would withdraw from 80% of Hebron on January 17 and that Israeli troops would remain in the other 20% of the city to guard the 400 Jewish settlers who refused to leave.[93] They also agreed that the IDF would withdraw from an unspecified portion of rural areas, the size of which Israel would determine on its own, in the West Bank in three phases—the first by March 7, 1997, the second by

---

84.   *Id.*
85.   *Id.* at annex I, app. 2.
86.   *Id.* at annex I, art. V, ¶ 2.
87.   *Id.*
88.   *Id.* at arts. XII, XIII.
89.   *Id.* at art. XIII.
90.   *Id.* at art. X.
91.   Schmemann, *supra* note 73, at A8.
92.   *Id.*
93.   *Israeli Army Demolishes Three Homes in Hebron*, Agence France Presse, Feb. 12, 1997, *available in* LEXIS, News Library, Curnws File.

September 1997, and the third by August 1998.[94] Israel later announced that the total area from which it would withdraw in the first phase would constitute 9% of the West Bank—7% located in Area B, and 2% located in Area C.[95] Significantly, these areas were not territorially contiguous with any of the isolated towns already under Palestinian self-rule.[96]

The Oslo Agreements have brought Palestinian self-rule to limited areas of the West Bank. Nonetheless, the overwhelming majority of the West Bank remains under Israeli occupation. While the legal status of the West Bank is currently in flux, the West Bank is still occupied within the meaning of the international laws governing belligerent occupations. As such, these international laws, codified in the Hague Regulations[97] and the Fourth Geneva Convention,[98] still apply to the West Bank.

C.   Legal Background: International Laws Governing Belligerent Occupations

The initial international codification of the laws of war focused on the treatment of combatants in war rather than on the treatment of civilians. The first international conventions to address the treatment of civilians in time of war were the 1864 Geneva Convention on the wounded[99] and the Regulations annexed to the 1899 Hague Convention II[100] and 1907 Hague Convention IV.[101] The First and Second World Wars demonstrated the inadequacy of these conventions in protecting civilians in times of war. Thus, after World War II, the International Committee of the Red Cross (ICRC) prepared four draft conventions that revised three previous conventions and established a fourth for the protection of civilian persons in times of war. During the Diplomatic

---

94.   Millikin, *supra* note 76.
95.   *Id.*
96.   *Id.*
97.   Hague Regulations, *supra* note 7.
98.   Geneva Convention IV, *supra* note 8.
99.   Convention for the Amelioration of the Condition of the Wounded in Armies in the Field, Aug. 22, 1864, *reprinted in* The Laws of Armed Conflicts: A Collection of Conventions, Resolutions and Other Documents 279 (Dietrich Schindler & Jiri Toman eds., 3d ed. 1988).
100.   Hague Convention II with Respect to the Laws and Customs of War on Land, July 29, 1899, 32 Stat. 1803, 1811, T.S. No. 403, 1 Bevans 247.
101.   Hague Regulations, *supra* note 7.

Conference for the Establishment of International Conventions for the Protection of Victims of War, sixty-four states discussed the ICRC draft conventions and the conference resulted in the four 1949 Geneva Conventions.

The Regulations attached to the 1907 Hague Convention IV (Hague Regulations) and the 1949 Geneva Convention IV Relative to the Protection of Civilian Persons in Time of War (Fourth Geneva Convention) include provisions relating to belligerent occupation. These provisions constitute the law governing an occupying power's rights and responsibilities in the territory under its occupation. Neither the Hague Regulations nor the Fourth Geneva Convention specifically addresses the economic development of occupied territories. Nonetheless, these Conventions provide the framework for evaluating a state's rights and duties to develop the territory under its occupation.

The laws of belligerent occupation attempt to balance the military needs of the occupant with the protection of the occupied population. As the fundamental premise of a military occupation is that it is temporary in nature, the laws governing belligerent occupation also attempt to protect the reversionary interests of the legitimate sovereign. During an especially prolonged occupation the needs of both the occupied population and of the occupier will necessitate relatively permanent changes, such as road construction, in the occupied territory. However, because of the temporary nature of an occupation, the legality of any permanent change made by the occupier in the occupied territory is questionable. Moreover, the needs and interests of the occupying power may be fundamentally opposed to those of the occupied population. The occupying power's concern for the interests of the occupied population may not be genuine, and any changes the occupying power effects in the occupied territory on the basis of this professed interest must be suspect.

1.   Applicability of the Hague Regulations and the Fourth Geneva Convention

a.   Hague Regulations

Since Israel, Jordan, and Egypt did not exist as sovereign states at the time of the 1899 and 1907 Hague Conventions, they were not signatories to these conventions. None has subsequently ratified or acceded to the Hague Convention of 1907 and its attached regulations. Nonetheless, the Regulations annexed to the Hague Conventions are declaratory of customary international law[102] and are thus binding on all states, including those that are not parties to the conventions and regulations.[103] Moreover, after the 1948 War of Independence, the "Israeli Supreme Court specifically recognized the declaratory nature of the Fourth Hague Convention."[104] Thus, as customary international law, the Hague Regulations are binding upon Israel in the West Bank, East Jerusalem, and the Gaza Strip.

The official Israeli government position with regard to the applicability of the Hague Regulations has been somewhat ambiguous.[105] Nonetheless, the Israeli Supreme Court, sitting as the High Court of Justice, has held that the Hague Regulations are a part of customary international law.[106] The Court has also held that, as customary international law, the Hague Regulations are binding upon the Israeli military administration in "Judea and Samaria."[107]

---

102. *See* Trial of the Major War Criminals before the International Military Tribunal, 1: 253-4, 6 F.R.D. 69, 130 (1946); 41 Am. J. Int'l L. 172, 248–49 (1947) (in which the International Military Tribunal at Nuremberg held that the rules in the Hague Convention IV and its Regulations were "recognized by all civilized nations" and were "regarded as being declaratory of the laws and customs of war"); Yoram Dinstein, *The International Law of Belligerent Occupation and Human Rights*, 8 Isr. Y.B. on Hum. Rts. 104, 107 (1978); Gerhard von Glahn, Taxation under Belligerent Occupation, *in* International Law and the Administration of Occupied Territories 341, 344 (Emma Playfair ed., 1992); *see also* Judgment of the International Military Tribunal of the Far East, 1948, United Nations War Crimes Commission, 15 L. Rep. of Trials of War Criminals 13 (Tokyo 1949) (in which the International Military Tribunal at Tokyo also expressed this view).

103. Dinstein, *supra* note 102, at 104–05; *see also* Thomas S. Kuttner, *Israel and the West Bank: Aspects of the Law of Belligerent Occupation*, 7 Isr. Y.B. on Hum. Rts. 166, 172 (1977); von Glahn, *supra* note 102, at 344.

104. Kuttner, *supra* note 103, at 171.

105. *See* Adam Roberts, *Prolonged Military Occupation: The Israeli-Occupied Territories Since 1967*, 84 A.J.I.L. 44, 63; *see also* von Glahn, *supra* note 102, at 345–46.

106. H.C. 606/78, H.C. 610/78, Ayyoub v. Minister of Defence (Beth-El case), 33(2) P.D. 113, *summarized in* 9 Isr. Y.B. on Hum. Rts. 337 (1979).

107. H.C. 390/79, Dweikat v. Israel (the *Elon Moreh* case), 40(2) P.D. 617, *summarized in* 9 Isr. Y.B. on Hum. Rts. 345 (1979). "Judea and Samaria" refer to the West Bank.

On December 17, 1967, the Israeli military government issued an order stating that "the term 'the Judea and Samaria Region' shall be identical in meaning for all purposes . . . to the term 'the West Bank Region.'" This change in terminology, which has been followed in Israeli official statements since that time, reflected a historic attachment to these areas and rejection of a name that was seen as

b.   Fourth Geneva Convention

Unlike the Hague Regulations, the Fourth Geneva Convention has not been regarded as solely representative of customary international law. Thus, it is legally binding only on those states who are parties to it. Israel, Jordan, and Egypt are all parties to the Fourth Geneva Convention. Israel signed the Convention on December 8, 1949 and ratified it on July 6, 1951. The only reservation Israel made to the Convention was with respect to the use of the Red Shield of David as a distinctive sign of medical services.[108]

Article 2 of the Fourth Geneva Convention lists the situations in which the Convention is applicable:

> [Paragraph 1] In addition to the provisions which shall be implemented in peacetime, the present Convention shall apply to all cases of declared war or of any other armed conflict which may arise between two or more of the High Contracting Parties, even if the state of war is not recognized by one of them.
> [Paragraph 2] The Convention shall also apply to all cases of partial or total occupation of the territory of a High Contracting party, even if the said occupation meets with no armed resistance.
> [Paragraph 3] Although one of the Powers in conflict may not be a party to the present Convention, the powers who are parties thereto shall remain bound by it in their mutual relations. They shall furthermore be bound by the Convention in relation to the said Power, if the latter accepts and applies the provisions thereof.[109]

According to the ICRC Commentary on the Fourth Geneva Convention, this article attempted to remove any question of the applicability of the Convention in times of war, other armed conflict, or partial or total

---

implying Jordanian sovereignty over them.

Roberts, *supra* note 105, at 231.

108.   Reservations and Declarations Concerning the Four Geneva Conventions of 12 August 1949, *reprinted in* The Laws of Armed Conflicts: A Collection of Conventions, Resolutions and Other Documents 506 (Dietrich Schindler & Jiri Toman eds., 1981).

109.   Geneva Convention IV, *supra* note 8, at art. 2.

occupation.[110] The article was meant to address situations in which a state refuses to recognize the existence of a state of war or refuses to observe humanitarian conventions, because it "contest[s] the legitimacy of the enemy Government" or because the enemy sovereign temporarily disappears as a result of annexation or capitulation.[111] Thus, the ICRC's intent in drafting Article 2 was to remove any doubt that the Convention is applicable and binding on a High Contracting Party even if that party contests the legitimacy of the enemy government or if the enemy sovereign state has temporarily disappeared.

Article 4 includes inhabitants of occupied territories in the list of persons protected by the Convention: "Persons protected by the Convention are those who, at a given moment and in any manner whatsoever, find themselves, in case of a conflict or occupation, in the hands of a Party to the conflict or Occupying Power of which they are not nationals."[112] According to the ICRC Commentary, the phrase "in the hands of" is used in a very general sense, and the "mere fact of being in the territory of a Party to the conflict or in occupied territory implies that one is in the power or 'hands' of the Occupying Power."[113] Thus, Article 4 extends protection to all civilian inhabitants of the occupied territory who are not nationals of the occupying power.[114]

Article 47 safeguards the rights of protected persons in the occupied territories, irrespective of the laws of the occupying power:

> Protected persons who are in occupied territory shall not be deprived, in any case or in any manner whatsoever, of the benefits of the present Convention by any change introduced, as the result of the occupation of a territory, into the institutions or government of the said territory, nor by any agreement concluded between the authorities of the occupied territories and the Occupying Power, nor by any annexation by the latter of the whole or part of the occupied territory.[115]

---

110. International Committee of the Red Cross, Commentary on the Geneva Conventions of 12 August 1949: Geneva Convention IV Relative to the Protection of Civilian Persons in Times of War 17–18 (Jean S. Pictet ed., 1958) [hereinafter ICRC Commentary].

111. *Id.* at 18.

112. Geneva Convention IV, *supra* note 8, at art. 4.

113. ICRC Commentary, *supra* note 110, at 47.

114. *Id.* at 46–47. This protection includes people in the occupied territories who have no nationality.

115. Geneva Convention IV, *supra* note 8, at art. 47.

In general, this article provides that the laws of the occupying power may not deny protected persons in the occupied territories the protection of the Convention. According to the ICRC Commentary, Article 47 was intended to address the situation which occurred during the Second World War in which occupying powers interfered with the fundamental institutions of the occupied territory.[116] Article 47 does not absolutely prohibit the occupying power from modifying the institutions or government of the occupied territory. Rather, its purpose is to ensure that any changes made in the organization of the state do not deprive protected persons from the rights and safeguards normally provided to them.[117]

Article 47 also highlights the distinction between occupation and annexation. "The most basic tenet of the law of belligerent occupation is that occupation as such does not transfer title to the territory."[118] Occupation is a temporary, *de facto*, rather than *de jure*, situation that interferes with the territory's power to exercise its rights.[119] It does not deprive the occupied territory of its statehood or its sovereignty.[120] By contrast, in annexation, the annexing state acquires all or part of the occupied territory, incorporates it into its own territory, and obtains all of the sovereign rights in the annexed territory.[121] Because of the temporary and *de facto* nature of an occupation, the occupying power does not have a right to dispose of the territory and cannot annex it.[122] This provision in Article 47 addresses the situation in which an occupying power claims to have annexed the occupied territory and denies the residents in the territory the protections afforded to civilians in an occupied territory. Thus, under Article 47, an "Occupying Power continues to be bound to apply the Convention as a whole even when, in disregard of the rules of international law, it claims during a conflict to have annexed all or part of an occupied territory."[123] Article 47 prevents an occupying power from engaging in certain activities "as a basis for contending that the protected persons in

---

116. ICRC Commentary, *supra* note 110, at 273. The occupying powers changed constitutional forms or the forms of government in the occupied territory, established new military or political organizations, dissolved the state, or formed new political entities.

117. *Id.* at 274.

118. Dinstein, *supra* note 102, at 105.

119. ICRC Commentary, *supra* note 110, at 275.

120. *Id.*

121. *Id.*

122. *Id.*

123. *Id.* at 276.

occupied territory were no longer entitled to the benefits of the protections accorded to them" by the Convention.[124]

The Fourth Geneva Convention applies, by its terms, to "all cases of partial or total occupation of the territory of a High Contracting Party, even if the said occupation meets with no armed resistance."[125] Occupation is defined in Articles 42 and 43 of the Hague Regulations. Article 42 states that a "[t]erritory is considered occupied when it is actually placed under the authority of the hostile army. The occupation extends only to the territory where such authority has been established and can be exercised."[126]

Since the authority over the West Bank, Gaza Strip, and East Jerusalem has in fact passed into the hands of Israel and the Israeli military actually exercises its authority in these territories, the territories can be considered occupied within the meaning of the Hague Regulations and the Fourth Geneva Convention. Since Israel, Jordan, and Egypt are all parties to the 1949 Geneva Convention IV, the Convention applies to the territories occupied by Israel. In the opinion of the U.N. General Assembly and Security Council, the 1949 Geneva Convention IV applies to all Arab territories—including Jerusalem,[127] the West Bank, and Gaza Strip—occupied by Israel since 1967.[128] Similarly, the ICRC maintains that the Fourth Geneva Convention applies to all of the territories Israel occupied in 1967, because the "conditions specified for the application of the Fourth Geneva

---

124. 2 Howard S. Levie, The Code of International Armed Conflict 717 (1986).

125. Geneva Convention IV, *supra* note 8, at art. 2.

126. Hague Regulations, *supra* note 7, at art. 42.

127. Under Article 47 of the Fourth Geneva Convention, Israel's annexation of East Jerusalem does not relieve Israel of its obligation to apply the Convention. Geneva Convention IV, *supra* note 8, at art. 47.

128. *See, e.g.,* G.A. Res. 47/64E, U.N. GAOR, 47th Sess., Supp. No. 49, at 28, U.N. Doc. A/47/49 (1993); G.A. Res. 44/48B, U.N. GAOR, 44th Sess., Supp. No. 49, at 107, U.N. Doc. A/44/49 (1989); G.A. Res. 3005, U.N. GAOR, 27th Sess., Supp. No. 30, at 30, U.N. Doc. A/8730 (1972); G.A. Res. 2727, U.N. GAOR, 25th Sess., Supp. No. 28, at 36, U.N. Doc. A/8028 (1970); G.A. Res. 2443, U.N. GAOR, 23d Sess., Supp. No. 18, at 50, U.N. Doc. A/7218 (1968); G.A. Res. 2252, U.N. GAOR, ES-V, Supp. No. 1, at 3, U.N. Doc. A/6798 (1967); S.C. Res. 681, U.N. SCOR, 45th Sess., 2970th mtg. at 8, U.N. Doc. S/INF/46 (1990); S.C. Res. 607, U.N. SCOR, 43d Sess., 2780th mtg. at 1, U.N. Doc. S/INF/44 (1988); S.C. Res. 605, U.N. SCOR, 42d Sess., 2777th mtg. at 4, U.N. Doc. S/INF/43 (1987); S.C. Res. 465, U.N. SCOR, 35th Sess., 2203d mtg. at 5, U.N. Doc. S/INF/36 (1980); S.C. Res. 446, U.N. SCOR, 34th Sess., 2134th mtg. at 4, U.N. Doc. S/INF/35 (1979).

Convention exist in the conflict between Israel and the Arab countries . . . ."[129]

Israel's official position is that it is not an occupying power within the meaning of the Fourth Geneva Convention because, as Benvenisti describes, it "ha[s] not ousted any legitimate sovereign, and therefore a condition precedent to the application of the Convention d[oes] not exist."[130] Israel never recognized the legitimacy of the Jordanian and Egyptian military governments in the West Bank, East Jerusalem, and the Gaza Strip because it could not unilaterally change the international status of these territories.[131] Thus, Israel argued that the "circumstances envisioned by the Fourth Geneva Red Cross convention do not exist because the situation here is not one in which a legitimate sovereign and an occupying power are confronting one another."[132]

This position overemphasizes the Convention's concern for the legitimate sovereign of the occupied territory. It rests on the assumption that the purpose of the Fourth Geneva Convention is to protect the rights of the sovereign from the occupant.[133] While the purpose of the laws of belligerent occupation, in general, is to balance military necessity with the protection of the inhabitants of the occupied territory and the interests of the legitimate sovereign,[134] the primary purpose of the 1949 Geneva Convention IV Relative to the Protection of Civilian Persons in Time of War is, as its title and the ICRC Commentary suggest, the protection of civilians, not their sovereigns.[135]

Furthermore, the Fourth Geneva Convention does not condition its applicability on the recognition of titles to territory.[136] The ICRC

---

129. 1984 ICRC Ann. Rep. (1985). The ICRC has maintained this position in all of its annual reports.

130. Eyal Benvenisti, The West Bank Data Base Project, Legal Dualism: The Absorption of the Occupied Territories into Israel 51 (1989).

131. Paul J.I.M. de Waart, Dynamics of Self-Determination in Palestine 91 n.153 (1994). For a more involved discussion on this point, see Esther R. Cohen, Human Rights in the Israeli-Occupied Territories, 1967–1982, at 35–64 (1985).

132. de Waart, *supra* note 131, at 92 (quoting the testimony of Y.Z. Blum, professor of international law at Hebrew University, at the October 1977 hearings before the Immigration and Naturalization Subcommittee of the Committee on the Judiciary on the question of the West Bank settlements and the treatment of Arabs in the Israeli-occupied territories).

133. de Waart, *supra* note 131, at 92.

134. Kuttner, *supra* note 103, at 169.

135. ICRC Commentary, *supra* note 110, at 10–11.

136. Dinstein, *supra* note 102, at 107.

Commentary on the Fourth Geneva Convention expresses the view that the recognition of a state's sovereignty over an area is not a precondition to the applicability of the Convention.[137] The drafters of Article 2 intended the provision to apply regardless of disputes over sovereignty.[138] Moreover, according to the ICRC Commentary, the second paragraph of Article 2 refers only to situations in which the "occupation has taken place without a declaration of war and without hostilities, and makes provision for the entry into force of the Convention in those particular circumstances."[139] Whenever a territory is occupied during hostilities, paragraph 1 is the relevant provision, because the Convention will have been in force since the outbreak of hostilities or the declaration of war and remains in force thereafter throughout any ensuing hostilities or occupation.[140] The parties to the Convention must respect and apply it even if a party to the conflict is not a party to the Convention. Thus, if a High Contracting Party occupies the territory of its enemy during hostilities, paragraph 1 of Article 2 applies to the situation even if the legitimate sovereign of the occupied territory is not a High Contracting Party.

In 1971, without passing judgment on the *de jure* applicability of the Fourth Geneva Convention, the Attorney General of Israel announced that the Israeli Government had decided to act *de facto* in accordance with the humanitarian provisions of the Convention.[141] This *de facto* application of the humanitarian provisions of the Convention has at least three major shortcomings. First, the term "humanitarian provisions" is ambiguous, and Israel has never definitively identified to which Convention provisions the term refers, if not all provisions.[142] Second, since the Convention does not have the force of law in Israel, the Israeli courts have been reluctant to "base their decisions fairly and squarely on the Fourth Geneva Convention."[143] Finally, the "hint of *ex gratia* about Israel's application of the Convention could be construed

---

137. ICRC Commentary, *supra* note 110, at 17-18.

138. *Id.*

139. *Id.* at 21-22.

140. *Id.*

141. Meir Shamgar, The Observance of International Law in the Administered Territories, 1 Isr. Y.B. on Hum. Rts. 262, 263 (1971).

142. Adam Roberts, Prolonged Military Occupation: The Israeli-Occupied Territories 1967-1988, *in* International Law and the Administration of Occupied Territories 25, 48 (Emma Playfair ed., 1992).

143. *Id.* at 48.

as carrying an implication that it might unilaterally interpret, or eventually abrogate, its terms."[144]

In summary, the Israeli Supreme Court accepts the Hague Regulations as law. The Israeli Government accepts, in somewhat ambiguous terms, the "humanitarian" provisions of the Fourth Geneva Convention. Moreover, considerations of Articles 2 (describing the states to which the Convention is applicable), 4 (defining which people are covered by the Convention), and 47 (distinguishing between annexation and occupation) support the applicability of the Fourth Geneva Convention in Israel as law.

II. ROAD PLANNING IN THE WEST BANK UNDER ISRAELI OCCUPATION

Throughout the occupation, land has been a central issue in the Israeli-Palestinian conflict. Since 1967, Israel has seized approximately 73% of the land in the West Bank and the Gaza Strip.[145] Israel has used this land for military purposes, for settlements, and for roads in the West Bank.

Palestinians have objected to many of the Israeli road plans for the West Bank because of the political motivations behind the road construction, the land expropriation it entails, and the limited benefits of the roads for the Palestinian population. The bypass roads, by definition, are designed for the exclusive use of Israelis. Palestinians may not travel on or across these roads. Despite this, the land expropriated to build the roads invariably belongs to Palestinians.

Road construction in the West Bank under Israeli occupation has impeded Palestinian economic development. Beginning with the "Trans-Samaria" highway, road-planning became an increasingly attractive means of expanding and developing Israeli settlements in the West Bank. Prior to Israeli occupation, the road system in the West Bank consisted of a series of north-south roads in the center with lateral access roads branching off to either side.[146] The "Trans-Samaria" highway, built between 1976 and 1980, was the first major east-west

---

144. *Id.* at 48–49.
145. PASSIA Diary, *supra* note 13, at 221.
146. Aziz Shehadeh et al., Al-Haq, Israeli Proposed Road Plan for the West Bank: A Question for the International Court of Justice 2 (1984).

link to Israel.[147] Designed to integrate the West Bank road system into the Israeli system, it led to the proliferation of settlements along the road and to a rise in the number of settlers living in the areas served by the road.[148] The highway also led to a decline in Palestinian land use along the road, and limited the expansion of Palestinian towns in the area.[149]

Even before the completion of the "Trans-Samaria" highway, Gush Emunim, a radical settler organization, realized the expansionist potential a strategic road network in the West Bank would have for Jewish settlement.[150] In 1978, Gush Emunim presented the Likud government with a detailed settlement and road plan. The proposed plan would "divide Arab population centers into isolated blocs."[151]

The World Zionist Organization (WZO) incorporated the Gush Emunim plan into the settlement plan it published in 1983.[152] The WZO plan called for the construction of 346.5 kilometers of roads in the West Bank.[153] Apart from improving existing roads, the highest priority was given to building roads to bypass the Arab population centers.[154] According to the scholars Benvenisti and Khayat, the goal of the WZO plan was to establish Jewish settlement blocks throughout the West Bank and ensure that Arab areas "would be isolated and their growth would be hindered by [a] massive road network and non settler Israeli presence."[155]

The Israeli government also put forward road plans resembling those of Gush Emunim and the WZO. Shortly after the WZO published its plan, the Israeli government published Road Plan Number 50 in February 1984.[156] Road Plan Number 50 hindered the economic development of the Palestinian population in the West Bank by

---

147. David Grossman & Amiram Derman, The West Bank Data Base Project, The Impact of Regional Road Construction in the West Bank 10 (1989); Shehadeh, *supra* note 146, at 2.

148. Grossman & Derman, *supra* note 147, at 10–11; *see also* Shehadeh, *supra* note 146, at 2.

149. Shehadeh, *supra* note 146, at 2.

150. Benvenisti & Khayat, *supra* note 4, at 64.

151. *Id.*

152. *Id.*

153. Grossman & Derman, *supra* note 147, at 11. Of the proposed roads, 88 kilometers were built by 1986.

154. *Id.*

155. Benvenisti & Khayat, *supra* note 4, at 59.

156. Shehadeh, *supra* note 146, at 1-2.

preventing Palestinians from "using their agricultural land, existing installations and resources such as wells and irrigation schemes, and from expanding their towns and villages . . . ."[157] While settlers played a central role in designing the plan, not only were the Palestinian landholders excluded from the planning phase, but they were also not given the right to voice objections to the implementation of the plan.[158] During the intifada, the government of Yitzhak Shamir used Road Plan Number 50 in planning a series of "'intifada bypass' roads and roads connecting settlements with Israel . . . ."[159] Bypass roads appeared once again among the 400 kilometers of roads called for in Shamir's "Great Roads Plan" in April 1992.[160]

The current IDF bypass road plan consists of settlement roads bypassing Palestinian population centers and four "trans-Judea and Samaria" "strategic highways" closed to Palestinian traffic.[161] Since the stated purpose of this road plan was to ensure the security of settlers in the West Bank as the Israeli military redeployed, the IDF presented the plan as a "peace plan because it facilitates Israeli redeployment."[162] However, as Meron Benvenisti noted, the plan is strikingly similar to the settlement plan proposed more than fifteen years earlier by Gush Emunim.[163]

The major difference between the Gush Emunim plan and the current IDF bypass road plan is that the latter calls for more roads passing close to the major Palestinian cities. The other difference is that the bypass road plan is being implemented by the Israeli government,

---

157. *Id.* at 1.

158. *Id.* at 2; *see also New Roads Create an Asphalt Revolution,* Report on Israeli Settlement in the Occupied Territories (Found. for Middle East Peace, Wash., D.C.), May 1995, at 7 [hereinafter *New Roads*].

159. *New Roads, supra* note 158 at 7.

160. *Id.*

161. *See* Michael Schwartz, *Hole-y Land,* Challenge, Jan.-Feb. 1995, at 6; Pinkas, *supra* note 1. (IDF Road Plan); *Settlement Time Line,* Report on Israeli Settlement in the Occupied Territories, Sept.-Oct. 1997 (Found. For Middle East Peace, Wash., D.C.) (On April 30, 1997, the IDF announced another plan to construct additional bypass roads at the cost of U.S. $330 million.); *Israeli Army Drafts "Secret" Plan for Bypass Roads in West Bank* (BBC Broadcast, Aug. 16, 1996) (an IDF brochure describing the roads estimated that the construction of 1 kilometer would cost $1 million); *see also* Map 5 *infra* p. 289.

162. Schwartz, *supra* note 161, at 7.

163. *Id.* (referring to Meron Benvenisti's statement in Ha'aretz, Nov. 24, 1995). The major difference between the two plans is that the IDF plan calls for more roads passing close to the major Palestinian cities.

ostensibly as part of the peace plan. The Gush Emunim plan was seen as a radical settlement plan while the IDF plan has "attained the status of an instrument for Israel-Palestinian reconciliation."[164] Linked with redeployment, the bypass road network was transformed from a settlement plan into a peace plan, quelling opposition to it and hastening its implementation.

In his book, *A Place Among the Nations*, Netanyahu offers a plan for the West Bank in which Israel would "retain the powers and prerogatives of the sovereign, including such matters as military defense, foreign affairs, and control of the currency and foreign trade, while the Arab population could manage many of the areas of daily life."[165] Specifically, Netanyahu proposes that the West Bank be divided up into four counties, centered around four cities: Jenin, Nablus, Ramallah, and Hebron.[166] Each county would be comprised of one of these cities and the towns and villages surrounding it.[167] Israeli citizens would continue living in the settlements in the West Bank, and they, along with the Israeli forces, would have free access to the roads dividing the Arab counties.[168] The Israeli forces would continue to have access to every part of the West Bank, including the Arab counties.[169] Under this plan, East Jerusalem would remain unquestionably in the hands of Israel.[170] Indeed, Dore Gold, a chief political advisor to Netanyahu wrote in a 1995 study that "the assertion of such territorial control would produce an Arab sector in East Jerusalem that was isolated from the West Bank and could not effectively serve as a national capital."[171]

Critics of the bypass road plan argue that it divides the West Bank into South African style bantustans.[172] The *Washington Quarterly*

---

164. *New Roads, supra* note 158, at 7.
165. Benjamin Netanyahu, A Place Among the Nations 351 (1993).
166. *Id.*
167. *Id.*
168. *Id.* at 352. *See* Map 6 *infra* p. 290.
169. *Id.*
170. *Id.* at 346.
171. Dore Gold, *Jerusalem* (1995), *quoted in* David Gardner, *Eternal Divide in the Thrice Holy City*, Fin. Times (London), Sept. 28, 1996, at 11.
172. *See* David Makovsky, *Beyond Hebron . . . The Future is Now*, Jerusalem Post, Dec. 13, 1996, at 8; Trudy Rubin, *Netanyahu's Leopard-Skin Solution Won't Work*, Baltimore Sun, Mar. 21, 1997, at 17A; Robert Mahoney, *Arafat Critic "Cautious" About Return*, Reuters North American Wire, Nov. 12, 1996, *available in* LEXIS, News Library, Curnws File.

described the plan as "a land-eating, road-building program in the West Bank clearly aimed at segmenting the land into enclaves."[173] Netanyahu's Infrastructure Minister, Ariel Sharon, an avid proponent of the plan, refers to the enclaves as cantons.[174] This notion of cantons is consistent with Prime Minister Benjamin Netanyahu's vision for the future of the West Bank. Regardless of the term, the idea is the same—the roads "ensure the Palestinians have no territorial contiguity between their cities, so they could never form a state. Instead, settlements and roads would essentially box in Palestinian urban areas. According to this approach, these areas would not only be boxed in, but the IDF could enter these areas at will."[175]

Although Netanyahu, in an interview with the *Jerusalem Post*, rejected the idea of dividing the West Bank up into cantons, his actions belie his words.[176] While the previous Israeli administration may have begun construction on the bypass road network, Netanyahu greatly enhanced the scope and scale of the network once he assumed office. Netanyahu pledged that his government "w[ould] continue to expand settlements and w[ould] make sure that [Israelis] stay in them forever."[177] Netanyahu has given his support to the expansion of settlements not only along the borders of the West Bank but also to the expansion of settlements such as Nahliel, alongside densely populated Palestinian areas in the heart of the West Bank.[178] The *Jerusalem Post* found that "it would be hard to understand the logic of plans to expand places such as Nahliel, which is just northeast of Ramallah, if Netanyahu did not accept the idea of cantons."[179]

---

173. Adam Garfinkle, *Israel and Palestine: A Precarious Partnership*, Wash. Q., Summer 1997, at 3.

174. Makovsky, *supra* note 172.

175. *Id.*

176. *Id.*

177. *Netanyahu: Israel to Stay in West Bank Settlements "Forever,"* Deutsche Presse-Agentur, Nov. 26, 1996, *available in* LEXIS, News Library, Curnws File.

178. *See, e.g.*, Barton Gellman, *From Settlement to City on West Bank; Planned Expansion Would Put Jewish Metropolis in Prime Arab-Inhabited Area*, Wash. Post, Dec. 9, 1996, at A10.

179. Makovsky, *supra* note 172.

III. IMPACT OF THE BYPASS ROAD NETWORK ON ECONOMIC DEVELOPMENT IN THE WEST BANK

A.   Overview of Israel's Economic Policies in the West Bank under Occupation

Israeli economic policies during occupation severely restrict the expansion and diversification of the economies of the West Bank and Gaza Strip, keeping the two areas as largely non-communicating entities, while fragmenting and segmenting each of them internally.[180] These occupation policies restructure the West Bank and Gaza Strip economies such that they are at once complementary to the Israeli economy and heavily dependent upon it.[181] Moreover, these policies ensure that the West Bank economy will never compete with the Israeli economy.[182] In the end, the West Bank economy is integrated with the Israeli economy only insofar as the West Bank is a captive market for Israeli goods and provides exploitable resources such as water, raw materials, and cheap labor.[183] Ironically, Israel's successful economic development depends heavily upon the underdevelopment of the Occupied Territories.[184]

Israel has pursued this interventionist economic policy since 1967. It has resulted in major changes in the structure and performance of the Palestinian economy.[185] These changes took the form of a decline in agriculture, industrial stagnation, persistent trade and payments deficits, marketing bottlenecks, increased unemployment, and large-scale labor migration.[186] Labor from the territories was recruited to work in the Israeli economy.[187] Legally, 60,000 Palestinians work in Israel, while an estimated 40,000 work there illegally.[188] Since Palestinian natural resources are no longer under the control of

---

180.   UNCTAD, Developments in the Services Sector in the West Bank and the Gaza Strip 23-24 (1995).

181.   *Id.*

182.   *Id.*

183.   *Id.*

184.   *Id.*

185.   *Id.*

186.   *Id.*

187.   Fawzi A. Gharaibeh, The Economies of the West Bank and Gaza Strip 133 (1985).

188.   *Netanyahu's Advisor to meet Mahmoud Abbas*, Agence France Presse, Aug. 21, 1996, *available in* LEXIS, News Library, Curnws File.

Palestinians, the financial sector is incapable of mobilizing resources, and private consumption is fueled mainly by non-domestic sources of income.[189] The Palestinian economy was thus restrained in its scope, scale and rate of growth, and its structure was fragmented by these external economic pressures.[190]

Factors that contributed to this situation include unregulated access of Israeli goods to the market of the occupied territory, minimal infrastructure development, impediments to industrial development, and access to cultivated areas.[191] Accordingly, the Palestinian economy grew increasingly dependent on the expanding Israeli economy in numerous spheres.[192] For example, the West Bank and Gaza Strip became the second-largest export market for Israel after the United States.[193] In 1987, imports to the Palestinian territory from Israel were valued at over $580 million.[194] During that same year, the GDP of the occupied territory totaled under $1,750 million.[195]

B.   Economic Impact of the Bypass Roads

The bypass road network has negative repercussions for all sectors of the Palestinian economy in the West Bank. While facilitating movement between the settlements and Israel, the network restricts Palestinian movement and breaks up Palestinian territorial contiguity, impeding the flow of commerce and workers from area to area. Furthermore, the construction of the roads involved the seizure of agricultural land, the closure of stone quarries, and the destruction of houses, leaving many Palestinians in the West Bank without capital, without jobs, and without homes.

---

189.   *Id. See also* UNCTAD, *supra* note 180, at 23-24.
190.   UNCTAD, *supra* note 180, at 23-24.
191.   *Id.*
192.   *Id.*
193.   *Id.*
194.   *Id.*
195.   *Id.* at 24.

1.   Agricultural Sector

The agricultural sector has borne much of the economic hardship resulting from the bypass roads.[196] Most of the lands seized or expropriated for the bypass roads were owned by small land owners with only a few dunums of farming land, which constituted their primary source of income.[197] In the Bethlehem area alone, some 280 families lost their primary source of income (olive trees) when their land was seized on March 26, 1996, for a bypass road north of the city.[198]

The construction of each bypass road has entailed the uprooting of thousands of fruit-bearing trees and the seizure or expropriation of at least 23,000 dunums (5,681 acres) of land specifically for the purpose of building bypass roads.[199] For example, the Israeli military uprooted 5,000 almond trees, olive trees, and grape vines in order to build a bypass road extending west from Road 60 to the settlements of Hadar Beitar Ilit Beitar close to Husan and Nahalin.[200] The road from Gilo to Mount Abu Ghneim has led to the seizure of 1,500 dunums (390.5 acres) of land and the uprooting of thousands of fruit-bearing olive and almond trees.[201]

In addition, the Israeli military has taken Palestinian land indirectly to be used in building bypass roads. In June of 1996, the Israeli military declared 70,000 dunums (17,290 acres) of land in the village of Al-Samou' a closed military area.[202] Although the land was not explicitly expropriated to build a road, there are plans for a bypass road within the closed area.[203]

---

196.   *Id.*

197.   Taqrīr mūjaz 'an al-turuq al-iltifāfiyah wa al-mustautinat wa al-musādarat fi baitalahm (Summary Report on Bypass Roads, Settlements, and Land Confiscation in Bethlehem), Al-Haq, 1996 [hereinafter Summary Report]; *see also* Samira Shah, Al-Haq, The Bypass Road Network in the West Bank 25 (1997).

198.   Shah, *supra* note 197, at 51.

199.   For Al-Haq's statistics on trees uprooted in Hebron, see Shah, *supra* note 197, at 64–72. For information on trees uprooted in other areas, see Al-Haq's field report number 95/198 (on file with author). Interview with Khalil Tufakji, *supra* note 1 (providing the statistics on the amount of land seized or expropriated for the purpose of constructing bypass roads).

200.   Summary Report, *supra* note 197.

201.   Shah, *supra* note 197, at 51.

202.   *Id.* at 25.

203.   *Id.*

2.   Restrictions on Movement

In addition to the immediate economic repercussions for those whose lands have been taken, the restrictions the roads impose on movement within the West Bank have also led to financial losses. Israeli road blocks and checkpoints along the bypass roads prevent Palestinians from using the roads. Although enforcement of the prohibition is erratic, the possibility of enforcement significantly restricts Palestinian movement within the West Bank.[204] In addition to the fixed checkpoints, moving checkpoints spring up along the roads, and military patrols and settler guard vehicles patrol the roads to ensure that no Palestinians are traveling on them.[205]

In some cases the bypass roads act as barriers, rendering certain lands inaccessible. The patrols—the Israeli military guards and the settlement guards—forbid residents from crossing the road and tending to their farms or caring for their livestock (sheep and goats).[206] The bypass road north of Ramallah between the settlements of Talmon B and C and Na'lah blocks residents in the Silwad region (whose lands have not been seized) from using their lands.[207] In order to build the road, the Israeli military also blasted part of a hill, leaving a sheer cliff between the road and the land on top of the hill. The farmers who own the land on top of the hill can no longer get to it.[208]

Road 60 isolates the Arab villages in the area by separating them from one another.[209] The road lies between Al-Khader, Beit Jala, and Bethlehem and between the villages of Nahalin, Wadi Fukin, Husan, and Batir.[210] The Israeli military has restricted movement between these villages by putting up semi-permanent road blocks on the intersections of the main roads close to Al-Khader.[211] After the Palestinian Authority entered Bethlehem, the Israeli army began closing off Road 60, thereby closing off Area A (Bethlehem) and prohibiting the residents of Area B (the rest of the villages in the

---

204. Summary Report, *supra* note 197.
205. *Id.* The license plates issued to Palestinians in the West Bank are a different color than those issued to Israelis. Thus, it is easy for the patrols to spot a car issued to a Palestinian resident of the West Bank.
206. Summary Report, *supra* note 197.
207. Shah, *supra* note 197, at 26.
208. *Id.*
209. Summary Report, *supra* note 197.
210. *Id.*
211. *Id.*

Bethlehem area) from entering Bethlehem, Beit Jala, and Al-Khader.[212] Generally, the area suffered from massive unemployment because the villagers were prohibited from going to their jobs in Bethlehem.[213] The closure was especially detrimental to teachers, nurses, and day laborers.[214]

When Road 60 was built, the pre-existing dirt roads in the area used to transport agricultural products were destroyed.[215] Qabatiya, Wadi Fukin, and Batir produce crops throughout the year.[216] The farmers in these areas need to transport their crops daily to the markets in Bethlehem, Beit Jala, Beit Sahour, and Jerusalem.[217] Their farms produce vegetables such as zucchini, eggplant, parsley, and cabbage, which cannot be stored for long periods of time.[218] The closure in February 1996 led a large part of the crop to perish.[219] The farmers were able to salvage part of the crop and sell it locally for a fraction of its cost. Batir's eggplant crop was especially hard hit.[220] In fact, in constructing the bypass roads, the Israeli military authority has closed or destroyed numerous existing local roads in the Hebron, Bethlehem, and Ramallah areas.[221] These roads were used primarily for transporting agricultural produce. Once they were destroyed, the farmers had no means of transporting their produce to markets.

---

212. *Id.*

213. *Id.*

214. *Id.* Closing off Area A from Area B by closing the roads between the two areas also caused other, noneconomic problems. For example, the cemetery for the village of Al-Khader (in Area B) lies beyond the road block. A number of funeral processions were prohibited from entering the cemetery on the pretext that Area A was closed. Thus, the residents were forced either to carry the body to the cemetery, walking around the checkpoint through the eastern mountainous region, or to return with the body to the village and prepare a tomb for the dead in the village. *Id.*

215. *Id.*

216. *Id.*

217. *Id.*

218. *Id.*

219. *Id.*

220. *Id.*

221. On the destruction of dirt roads in the Bethlehem region, see Summary Report, *supra* note 197. On the destruction of a dirt road in the Ramallah region, see Al-Haq's field report number 94/159 (on file with author).

3.   Stone Quarries

Al-Haq, a Palestinian human rights organization located in the West Bank, documented some of the effects of the bypass roads on the stone quarry industry and on the agricultural sector since 1994. In the past two years, the IDF has raided and shut down fifteen stone factories and twenty-five stone quarries in the Bethlehem region and twenty stone quarries in the Nablus region.[222] In the Bethlehem region, the Israeli government closed the stone factories and quarries because they were located in the area of a proposed bypass road.[223] The road, now built, extends from the east of the Efrat settlement (close to the village of Al-Ma'sara) south to the entrance of the Ashqar settlement (east of the village Al-Sheiyukh).

At the beginning of 1994, the Israeli government began constructing a settlement bypass road around the city of Nablus, extending from the village of Dir Sharaf and passing through the villages of Tel, Madama, and 'Asira al-Qibliya.[224] Most of the stone quarries in this region had been in operation since 1989 and had only recently begun to yield a significant amount of stone.[225] The quarries were operating under Israeli licenses that were renewed annually.[226] When construction began on the road, members of the Israeli civil administration and of the construction-licensing authority started raiding the stone quarries and threatening to punish the owners if they did not close their quarries.[227] They raided the quarries and confiscated work equipment and forced the owners to pay fines and sign statements promising not to go back to work.[228]

Since the quarries had only recently begun to produce a significant amount of stone, they had been operating at a loss, and their closures amounted to huge financial losses for their owners.[229] Moreover, the hundreds of workers employed by these quarries lost their means of livelihood.[230] In addition to the owners and workers of

---

222. Summary Report, *supra* note 197; *see* Al-Haq's field report number 95/62 (on file with author).
223. Summary Report, *supra* note 197.
224. Al-Haq's field report number 95/62 (on file with author).
225. *Id.*
226. *Id.*
227. *Id.*
228. *Id.*
229. *Id.*
230. *Id.*

the stone quarries, the construction industry, which relied on the stone from these quarries for building, suffered financial losses when the quarries were closed.[231]

4.   Destruction of Homes and Other Property

In addition to the acquisition and destruction of agricultural lands, the construction of bypass roads has led to the destruction of structures in their path. The bypass road north of Ramallah, connecting the settlements of Talmon B and C with Na'lah, destroyed a warehouse for agricultural products, plastic pipes, and an electricity network.[232] The Israeli military has ordered a number of houses to be demolished in order to build bypass roads. In the Bethlehem region, two houses belonging to the family of Mustafa Shushah were demolished during the construction of the bypass road extending west from Road 60 to the settlements of Hadar Beitar and Beitar Ilit close to Husan and Nahalin.[233] In Al-Walja, two houses were demolished because they fell in the region of prohibited building alongside road 60 between Al-Walja and Batir.[234] A family cemetery was also destroyed because it was located in the path of the road.[235] In the Hebron area, two houses were also destroyed for the construction of a bypass road.[236] Another house in 'Anata and one in Jaba' were demolished to clear the path for a bypass road from Ramallah to the settlement of Pisgat Ze'ev.[237] Similarly, six houses in the ancient casbah quarter of Hebron were demolished to facilitate the construction of Road 60.[238]

By no means a comprehensive list, these fourteen homes in widespread areas underscore the personal costs of the bypass roads on a people who can neither use the roads nor obtain building permits to

---

231. *Id.*
232. Şaqq tarīq al-iltifāfiya wa tajrīf arādin fī mintaqa Ras Karkar [Building a Bypass Road and Bulldozing Land in the Ras Karkar Area], Al-Quds (Jerusalem), Apr. 26, 1996, at 3.
233. Summary Report, *supra* note 197.
234. *Id.*
235. *Id. See also* Palestine Report, *supra* note 5.
236. *See* Greenberg, *supra* note 5 (stating that the house of Fayad Jadarat was demolished because it was built near a bypass road close to Hebron); *Israeli Army Demolished Palestinian Homes Near Hebron*, Agence France Presse, Aug. 18, 1997, *available in* LEXIS, News Library, Curnws File.
237. *See* LAW, *supra* note 5.
238. *See* Pacheco & Susskind, *supra* note 5.

build new homes. In 1996, the IDF demolished 140 homes in the West Bank.[239] In the first eight months of 1997 alone, the IDF demolished ninety Palestinian homes, and another 500 are scheduled for destruction in the near future.[240] While many of these homes were built without permits, most of the homes were destroyed because they were built near bypass roads, Israeli settlements, or Israeli military bases.[241]

5.   Archaeological Sites

The construction of the roads led to the destruction of a number of historical and archaeological sites. These sites fell in the path of the roads or in the prohibited building area on either side of the roads.[242] There were a number of such sites in the Bethlehem area.[243] The IDF also ordered the destruction of other archeological sites in the region of Abu Gheneim and Bethlehem because they fall in the trajectory of proposed bypass roads.[244]

Other archaeological sites were rendered inaccessible because the roads put them in Area C Israeli settlement areas.[245] This is the fate of the ruins of Abu Dawir, close to Sa'ir, a Byzantine and Islamic

---

239.   Arieh O'Sullivan & Margot Dudkevitch, *Indyk: Oslo 'Broken Down,'* Jerusalem Post, May 19, 1997, at 1.

240.   Greenberg, *supra* note 5, at A3.

241.   O'Sullivan & Dudkevitch, *supra* note 239. Allegra Pacheco, an Israeli lawyer with LAW—The Palestinian Society for the Protection of Human Rights and the Environment, stated:

> [It is] nearly impossible for a Palestinian to get a building permit [in Area C]. . . . Most of Area C is zoned as agricultural land, where building is almost banned, under a 1942 zoning plan drawn up by the British Mandate authorities which Israel relies on in issuing permits to construct homes. This plan has not been altered since 1942 and does not reflect the increase of the Palestinian population since . . . Jewish settlements are built on the same land zoned for agriculture. But for them, the authorities change the zoning plans for residential building.

Israeli Army Destroys Arab Home Near Hebron, Agence France Presse, Sept. 3, 1997, *available in* LEXIS, News Library, Curnws File.

242.   Summary Report, *supra* note 197.

243.   *Id.*

244.   *Id.*

245.   *Id.*

archaeological site.[246] The archaeological sites of both Maqir Khalifa (the seat of the Caliph), an Islamic archaeological site in Al-Sheiyukh, and Al-Deir in the region of Al-Musafir south of Al-Nuquh are now inaccessible to Palestinians because they fall inside bypass Road 35.[247] Similarly, since the ruins of Ma'ale Adumin are now part of the settlement Ma'ale Adumin, Palestinians may view the ruins only with a special permit.[248]

>   6.   Tourism

Since 1967, the Israeli occupation of the West Bank and annexation of East Jerusalem have been especially detrimental to tourism as a source of income for Palestinians.[249] Tourism was particularly hard hit by the occupation in large part because the flow of Arab tourists to the West Bank completely stopped.[250] Since approximately 60% of all the tourists visiting the West Bank before the occupation came from Arab countries, income from tourism dropped dramatically during the occupation.[251] Furthermore, once Israel annexed East Jerusalem, it restricted Palestinians from building in the city, leading to the deterioration of existing tourist facilities and the lack of new ones. Thus, most foreign tourists coming to visit the holy sites in East Jerusalem and the West Bank preferred to use the Israeli tourist service.[252]

The bypass road network is also detrimental to tourism in the West Bank. Since the bypass roads restrict movement within the West Bank, they make destinations in the West Bank more difficult to access and less attractive to tourists. Furthermore, the destruction of a number of the archaeological and historical sites[253] in the area has resulted in fewer attractions for tourists to visit.

---

246.   *Id.*
247.   *Id.*
248.   *Id.*
249.   Gharaibeh, *supra* note 187, at 98.
250.   *Id.*
251.   *Id.*
252.   *Id.* at 98–99.
253.   Summary Report, *supra* note 197.

IV. IMPEDIMENTS TO THE PEACE PROCESS

In addition to the economic effects of the bypass road network, the roads have negative implications for the Oslo Agreements and for the likelihood of the Agreements to bring about Palestinian self-rule and an end to Israeli occupation in the West Bank. First, the bypass roads violate several provisions in Oslo I and Oslo II. Second, the roads prejudice the outcome of the Permanent Status Negotiations because they create facts on the ground which alter the status of settlements, Jerusalem, and borders in the interim period.

A.   Violations of the Oslo I and Oslo II

Neither Oslo I nor Oslo II mentions bypass roads specifically. Although they both mandate redeployment of Israeli troops in the West Bank and give the Israeli military the responsibility for the security of settlers in the interim period, bypass roads were not included in the security arrangements of the Agreements.[254] Furthermore, although settlements are recognized in the interim period, their fate will be determined in the Permanent Status Negotiations and nothing in the interim period is allowed to prejudice the outcome of their fate.[255]

The bypass road network has been described as necessary for the redeployment of the IDF. According to this argument, since Israel retains the responsibility of the security of settlers even after the Israeli military has withdrawn from certain areas, the roads were needed so that the settlers could move within the West Bank and from the West

---

254. Oslo I, *supra* note 2, at arts. XIII, XIV. Oslo I mandates a withdrawal of Israeli forces from the Gaza Strip and Jericho area and a redeployment of Israeli forces from populated areas. *See also* Oslo II, *supra* note 2, at ch. 2, art. X, ¶ 1 (requiring redeployment of Israeli troops from "populated areas in the West Bank—cities, towns, villages, refugee camps and hamlets" before Palestinian elections); Oslo II, *supra* note 2, at ch. 2, art. XII, ¶ 1 (stating that Israel maintains the "responsibility for overall security of Israelis and Settlements, for the purpose of safeguarding their internal security and public order, and will have all the powers to take the steps necessary to meet this responsibility"). The Agreed Minutes to the Declaration of Principles have a similar provision: "Israel will continue to be responsible for external security, and for internal security and public in order [sic] of settlements and Israelis." Oslo I, *supra* note 2, at annex II.

255. Oslo I, *supra* note 2, at art. V, ¶ 3. ("It is understood that these [permanent status] negotiations shall cover remaining issues, including: Jerusalem, refugees, settlements, security arrangements, borders, relations and cooperation with other neighbors, and other issues of common interest.").

Bank to Israel without passing through areas under Palestinian authority. The roads would therefore fall within the realm of activities permitted by Oslo II under a security rationale. However, the roads may not have been needed to ensure the security of the settlers, nor is it clear that bypass roads actually safeguard settlers.[256] To the contrary, some settlers refuse to use the roads because they feel they leave themselves open to attack if they travel on roads used only by settlers.[257] The roads actually decrease the security of the settlers by rendering anyone on the road an easy target, and they have already resulted in the deaths of several settlers.[258]

The construction of bypass roads violates Articles 2, 27, and 40 of Oslo II's Protocol Concerning Civil Affairs.[259] These articles refer to archaeological sites, planning and zoning, and water rights, respectively. The bypass roads also violate Articles VIII, IX, and X of Oslo II's Protocol on Economic Relations, which deal with agriculture, industry, and tourism, respectively.

Under Article 2, paragraph 9, "[e]ach side undertakes upon itself to respect sites in the West Bank and the Gaza Strip which are regarded as holy, or which hold archaeological value."[260] However, in order to build the bypass roads, Israel has destroyed numerous archaeological sites in the Bethlehem area,[261] in violation of this provision of the Agreement.

Since the roads restrict Palestinian land use, they limit planning and zoning. Under Article 27 of Annex III, the "[p]owers and responsibilities in the sphere of Planning and Zoning in the West Bank and the Gaza Strip shall be transferred from the military government and its Civil Administration to the Palestinian side."[262] Since building is prohibited on either side of the roads, the road network constitutes a

---

256. Pacheco & Susskind, *supra* note 5.

257. *See* Palestine Rep., *supra* note 5; *see also* Daoud Kuttab, *Apartheid Stalks the Palestinians*, L.A. Times, Dec. 25, 1996, at B9 (noting that two settlers were killed while driving along a bypass road in the West Bank in early December); *Four Wounded in West Bank Shooting*, Reuters Financial Service, Dec. 11, 1996, *available in* LEXIS, News Library, Curnws File [hereinafter *Four Wounded*] (citing an Israeli army radio report that four people were wounded, one critically, in a shooting on a bypass road near Ramallah).

258. *See* Palestine Rep., *supra* note 5; *see also* Kuttab, *supra* note 257; *Four Wounded, supra* note 257.

259. Oslo II, *supra* note 2, at annex III, app. 1.

260. *Id.* at annex III, app 1, art. 2, ¶ 9.

261. Summary Report, *supra* note 197.

262. Oslo II, *supra* note 2, at annex III, app. 1, art. 27, ¶ 1.

de facto zoning system, delimiting areas in which there can be no building. Furthermore, the roads encircling cities such as Bethlehem and Ramallah create a boundary around the cities beyond which they cannot expand. The roads preempt any Palestinian attempts to plan and zone in the West Bank because they create a zoning system within which Palestinian planning and zoning must operate. Thus, the roads prevent the full transfer of authority in the area of planning and zoning to the Palestinian side from the military government, violating Article 27.

The construction of bypass roads on water reservoirs violates Oslo II. Under Article 40, paragraph 21, "[e]ach side shall take all necessary measures to prevent any harm, pollution, or deterioration of water quality of the water resources."[263] Military order number 5/3/96 specifically expropriates land located in a water reservoir for the purpose of building a road. Similarly, military order number t/34/96 seizes land in a water reservoir. Building a road on a water reservoir could harm, pollute, or deteriorate the water in the reservoir, thus violating Israel's agreement to prevent such harm to water resources.

As stated above, the bypass roads violate Articles VIII, IX, and X of the Protocol on Economic Relations.[264] Article VIII guarantees the free movement of agricultural produce between the two sides.[265] Rather than promoting the free movement of agricultural produce between the two sides, the bypass roads have prevented it. Both in the Bethlehem and the Ramallah area, local roads used for the transportation of agricultural products were torn up in order to construct bypass roads. Since the bypass roads were closed to farmers, they were left with no means of transporting their produce. The produce rotted and the people expecting the arrival of the produce did not receive it.

Article IX of the Protocol on Economic Relations states that, "[e]ach side will do its best to avoid damage to the industry of the other side and will take into consideration the concerns of the other side in its industrial policy."[266] In conjunction with the construction of a settlement bypass road around Nablus, Israel raided and closed down twenty

---

263. *Id.* at annex III, app. 1, art. 40, ¶ 21.
264. *Id.* at annex V.
265. *Id.* at annex IV, art. VIII, ¶ 1 ("There will be free movement of agricultural produce, free of customs and import taxes between the two sides, subject to the following exceptions and arrangements."). None of the exceptions applies to the construction of bypass roads or closing of bypass roads to Palestinian traffic.
266. *Id.* at annex IV, art. IX, ¶ 3.

Palestinian stone quarries in the region.[267] Contrary to Israel's agreement to avoid damage to Palestinian industry, it has severely damaged the Palestinian stone quarry industry.

Finally, the construction of the bypass roads violates the terms of Article X of the Protocol on Economic Relations on Tourism. Article X states that both the Palestinian and Israeli sides shall "protect, guard and ensure the maintenance and good upkeep of historical, archaeological, cultural and religious sites and all other tourist sites" under their respective jurisdictions.[268] Contrary to the terms of this article, Israel has destroyed numerous historical and archaeological sites, particularly in the Bethlehem region, for the construction of bypass roads.[269]

1.   Prejudicing the Permanent Status Negotiations

Oslo II's recognition of settlements in the interim period does not authorize the construction of bypass roads. Furthermore, Article XXXI of Oslo II explicitly states that "[n]either party shall initiate or take any step that will change the status of the West Bank and the Gaza Strip pending the outcome of the permanent status negotiations."[270] The bypass roads prejudice the outcome of the Permanent Status Negotiations because they structurally divide the Palestinian areas and connect the Israeli settlements, ensuring the permanence of the settlements. The roads also extend Israel's borders beyond the Green Line and around Jerusalem. This *de facto* annexation of Jerusalem and the area within the Green Line prejudices the permanent status of these areas.

2.   Expanding and solidifying settlements

Not only do the roads disconnect and isolate the Palestinian population areas in the West Bank, but they also connect the Israeli settlements to each other and to Israel, bringing Israeli territorial

---

267.   Al-Haq's field report number 95/62 (on file with author).

268.   Oslo II, *supra* note 2, at annex V, art. X, ¶ 2, ("Each side shall, under its respective jurisdiction, protect, guard and ensure the maintenance and good upkeep of historical, archaeological, cultural and religious sites and all other tourist sites, to fit their status as well as their purpose as a destination for visitors.").

269.   Summary Report, *supra* note 197.

270.   Oslo II, *supra* note 2, at ch. 5, art. XXXI,¶ 7.

contiguity to the West Bank for the first time in modern history. Bypass roads guarantee the presence and expansion of settlements in the West Bank. The roads simultaneously reduce Palestinian areas by seizing Palestinian land while they expand Israeli areas in the West Bank by providing new land for the expansion of settlements.

Recently, Israeli Prime Minister Benjamin Netanyahu expressed his support of building more bypass roads as well as building settlements alongside the bypass roads.[271] Ze'ev Hever, the leader of Amana, the settlement arm of the Council of Jewish Settlements in Judea, Samaria, and the Gaza Strip, applauded the bypass road plan for giving "settlement in Judea and Samaria a big boost."[272] In the words of settler leader Yoel Bin Nun, "[t]he most reasonable way to preserve Jewish settlements is by increasing their daily security, creating settlement blocs and joining them with roads."[273]

3.   Erasing the Green Line

Road Number 6 and bypass roads connecting settlements on either side of the Green Line have the effect of erasing it.[274] Road Number 6, the Trans-Israel Highway, has a projected trajectory weaving in and out of the Green Line, establishing a new border.[275] Road Number 3, connecting the West Bank settlements between the Modi'in settlement (the largest of the Seven Stars) inside the Green Line to East Jerusalem, also employs this concept of a mobile Green Line.[276] West of Ramallah, 32,500 dunums (8,027.5 acres) of land were confiscated from the villages of Aboud and Luban.[277] Tufakji suspects that some of this land will be used in building a road between the Shoham settlement inside the Green Line and the West Bank

---

271. Netanyahu yu'yid al-binā' al-istītānī 'alā tūl al-šawāri' al-iltifāfīya li-kalq tawāsul iqlīmī [Supports Building Settlements Alongside Bypass Roads to Create Territorial Continuity], Al-Quds (Jerusalem), July 26, 1996, at 1, 8.

272. *Settlers Propose Massive Settlement Program After Elections, supra* note 9, at 3.

273. Pacheco & Susskind, *supra* note 5 (quoting Yoel Bin Nun's statement in Ha'Aretz, Sept. 9, 1994).

274. Michael Schwartz, *The Road to Amman Passes through Rosh Ha'ayin*, Challenge, Nov.-Dec., 1994, at 24.

275. *Id.*

276. Michael Schwartz, *The Green Line Train to Jerusalem*, Challenge, Sept.-Oct., 1995, at 16.

277. Dalia Habash, *Closed for Military Purposes*, Challenge, May–June, 1994, at 29.

settlement of Ofarim.[278] Another bypass road extends from Taibe inside the Green Line to the settlement of Shavei Shamron southeast of Tulkarem. The roads and settlements along the Green Line have rendered it "as fluid as a river changing course."[279]

4.   Annexation of Jerusalem

The bypass roads around Jerusalem serve to expand the annexed area of "Greater Jerusalem." In addition to the ring road around Jerusalem (connecting the Israeli settlements to the south of East Jerusalem with those to the north), there are three planned bypass roads with a total length of 36.5 kilometers that lie within the Jerusalem district itself.[280] One will be an extension of a bypass road extending from the southern part of the West Bank. It will connect the settlements of Qedar, Site, A'lmon, Mishor Adumum, Pisgat Ze'ev, Adam, and A'tarot Industrial Zone and then continue northwest into the Ramallah district towards Israel.[281] The second road branches off from the first, extending from the east of A'tarot Industrial Zone south towards Ramot Alon and Rekhes Shua'fat.[282] The last road will link the Nabi Samuwil area to the settlement of Giva'at Haradar, passing through the lands of the Palestinian village Beit Iksa.[283] These three roads will form a semicircle around Jerusalem from Qedar, southeast of Jerusalem to Giva'at Haradar, northwest of Jerusalem on the Green Line.

To complete the circle of roads cutting Jerusalem off from the West Bank, the bypass road plan calls for additional roads extending from the Green Line southwest of Jerusalem to the hills southeast of Jerusalem. Road 375, originating inside of the Green Line, travels eastward to connect the settlement of Beitar to Highway 60, cutting off Jerusalem from the southwestern part of the West Bank.[284] A new military road extending eastward from the Gilo settlement to the

---

278. *Id.*

279. Schwartz, *supra* note 276.

280. 6 Applied Research Institute—Jerusalem (ARIJ), Environmental Profile for the West Bank, District of Jerusalem, at ch. 6 (1996).

281. *Id.*

282. *Id.*

283. *Id.*

284. Michael Schwartz, *Beitar Expands, Batir Shrinks*, Challenge, March–April, 1995, at 15.

proposed Har Homa settlement on Mount Abu Ghneim will cut Jerusalem off from Bethlehem and the rest of the southern West Bank.

The military road that extends from the settlement of Gilo east to Mount Abu Ghneim, the site of the proposed Har Homa settlement, is the most well-known bypass road in the West Bank.[285] The military bulldozers began clearing the land, although the case was still pending in an Israeli court.[286] This road has serious repercussions for the future of Jerusalem and Bethlehem.[287] It cuts off Jerusalem from the West Bank to the south and cuts off Bethlehem from Jerusalem and the West Bank to the north.[288] Thus, it furthers Israel's *de facto* annexation of Jerusalem and extends the annexed area.[289]

5.   Fragmentation of Palestinian Areas

The roads form a militarily-controlled grid in the West Bank, creating cantons in the West Bank that are based on Oslo II's division of the West Bank into Areas A, B, and C. The roads allow the Israeli military to close off areas within the West Bank. The Israeli government currently can close off the West Bank as a whole or it can close off specific areas within the West Bank. Without territorial contiguity, Palestinian statehood, sovereignty, and self-determination become not only politically uncertain, but also physically impracticable. Thus, "the political value of the roads lies in their capacity to fragment Palestinian areas, enabling Israel to continue to dominate the West Bank, even with reduced military presence."[290]

The bypass roads allow for separation within the West Bank by surrounding and containing Palestinian areas. Highway 60, extending from the Israeli town of Arad south of the West Bank to Afula north of the West Bank, forms the backbone of the plan. It cuts the West Bank in half, zigzagging past the major Palestinian cities.[291] Thus, it passes by the east of Hebron, the west of Bethlehem, the east of Ramallah, the west of Nablus, the east of Tulkarem (with a branch cutting off Tulkarem from the south), and the west of Jenin. Auxiliary bypass

---

285. Summary Report, *supra* note 197.
286. *Id.*
287. *Id.*
288. *Id.*
289. *Id.*
290. Pacheco & Susskind, *supra* note 5.
291. *New Roads, supra* note 158.

roads will connect Highway 60 to the settlements surrounding the Palestinian cities.[292]

The roads create artificial boundaries beyond which Palestinians may not build, prohibiting the expansion of the towns. In some cases, a road may cut a village in half. The placement of the roads renders effective municipal planning impossible. Thus, the bypass road network constitutes a *de facto* system of zoning, establishing where a town ends and where Palestinians may and may not build.

The bypass roads, like the settlements, are spread out throughout the West Bank. Extending across the West Bank, this reticular road network simultaneously allows for separation and annexation. The bypass road network creates a separate space for Israeli settlers in the West Bank, allowing them to "travel alongside Palestinian communities as if they weren't there."[293] Since the bypass road grid creates a potentially-permanent Israeli space in the West Bank, it constitutes a *de facto* annexation of the West Bank. Furthermore, the roads further Israeli annexation of Palestinian lands by erasing the Green Line and extending the boundaries of Jerusalem.

In annexing Jerusalem, erasing the Green Line, isolating Palestinian towns, and increasing Israeli settlement in the West Bank, the bypass road network achieves four of the most sought-after goals of "right-wing" Israeli politicians. Ironically, these achievements were accomplished in the name of peace by the Labor government.[294] Under the guise of promoting the security of Israeli settlers in the West Bank, the roads create permanent facts on the ground that assume, and therefore prejudice, the outcome of the Permanent Status Negotiations.

---

292. *Id.*

293. Adiv, *supra* note 1.

294. In the words of the current Likud party Finance Minister Dan Meridor:

> In this regard, we have to praise Yitzhak Rabin, may he rest in peace, and Shimon Peres, who during the last four years raised the number of Jews in Judea and Samaria by 40 percent. . . . We should also praise the Israeli left, which didn't utter a word about this for four years and the American government, which knew but didn't care. And also we should give thanks to the Palestinian Authority which saw that we were building but did not permit this to disrupt the peace process.

Stephen Siegel, *Reaping What You Sow*, In These Times, Oct. 14, 1996, at 6.

V. DISCUSSION: ISRAEL'S RIGHTS AND RESPONSIBILITIES UNDER THE
HAGUE REGULATIONS AND THE FOURTH GENEVA CONVENTION WITH
REGARD TO THE BYPASS ROAD NETWORK

The bypass road network raises a number of problems relating to the rights and responsibilities of an occupying power in the territory under its occupation. First, does an occupying power have the right to build a road system in occupied territory exclusively for the use of its own nationals? Second, insofar as the land used for the roads is the property of the occupied population, may the occupying power expropriate, seize, or confiscate it and/or destroy the structures or crops attached to that land? Finally, the bypass road plan brings the legality of the settlements and the roads serving them into question.

A.   Hague Regulations

The Hague Regulations limit a state's powers within the territory under its occupation. Articles 42 through 56 of the Hague Regulations protect both the inhabitants of an occupied territory and the legitimate sovereign of the territory. Article 42 states that "[t]erritory is considered occupied when it is actually placed under the authority of the hostile army. The occupation extends only to the territory where such authority has been established and can be exercised."[295] Because 40% of the Gaza Strip and 73% of the West Bank are still under the authority of the Israeli military, both the Gaza Strip and the West Bank are defined as occupied territories.

Article 43 of the Hague Regulations is relevant to the first question concerning the occupier's right to construct a road system in the occupied territory for the exclusive use of its own population. Article 43 attempts to limit the legislative power of the occupying State in the territories under its occupation:[296]

> The authority of the legitimate power having in fact passed into the hands of the occupant, the latter shall take all the measures in his power to restore, and ensure, as far as

---

295. Hague Regulations, *supra* note 7, at art. 42.
296. *See* Edmund H. Schwenk, *Legislative Power of the Military Occupant under Article 43, Hague Regulations*, 54 Yale L.J. 393 (1945).

> possible, public order and safety, while respecting, unless .
> absolutely prevented, the laws in force in the country.[297]

While this article restricts the situations in which the occupying power may circumscribe the laws of the legitimate sovereign and introduce its own legislation, the efficacy of this limitation is questionable at best.

There is a well-noted discrepancy between the original French text of Article 43 and the above-quoted, semi-official English translation of the article. The phrase "public order and safety" was translated from the French, "*l'ordre et la vie publics.*" The English translation does not represent the exact meaning of this phrase, which refers to the entire social and commercial life of the community.[298] Some commentators have suggested that the term "civil life" would more adequately represent the meaning of the French "*la vie publique.*"[299] Thus, the occupant's obligation would be to "take all the measures in his power to restore and ensure, as far as possible, public order and civil life, while respecting, unless absolutely prevented, the laws in force in the country."[300]

Since the phrase "public order and civil life" is more comprehensive than the phrase "public order and safety," this interpretation affords a state greater legislative authority in the territories under its occupation. Under this provision, the occupying power's responsibility is to restore and ensure public order and civil life. It may do so through its own legislation only if it is "absolutely prevented" from respecting the laws in force in the country.

Taken literally, the phrase "unless absolutely prevented" could be construed as an impossible condition, and Article 43 could be read as an absolute prohibition against derogating from the usual laws of the occupied country.[301] However, the phrase has not been interpreted in such a manner. Rather, Article 43 has been interpreted as a requirement that the occupant, in restoring public order and civil life, respect the laws in force in the occupied territory unless prevented from doing so by "absolute necessity."[302]

---

297.   Hague Regulations, *supra* note 7, at art. 43.
298.   2 Henry Wheaton, Wheaton's Elements of International Law 783 (Arthur Barriedale Keith ed., 6th Eng. ed. 1929); *see also* Schwenk, *supra* note 296.
299.   Wheaton, *supra* note 298, at 783; *see also* Schwenk, *supra* note 296.
300.   Schwenk, *supra* note 296.
301.   *Id.* at 399–400.
302.   *Id.* at 400–01.

The type of necessity required to justify a change in the law of the occupied country is also open to interpretation. Some commentators confine the legislative departures to cases of military necessity.[303] Dinstein and Schwenk suggest that such an interpretation is too narrow.[304] They argue the legislative power of an occupying power under Article 43 is broad. Thus, in addition to the military or security needs of the occupying power, the needs of the civilian population under occupation would justify a departure from the requirement of respecting the laws in force in the occupied territory.[305] Since the occupying power itself may determine whether a case of necessity exists and its decision is not subject to review, Article 43 relies on the occupying power to exercise self-restraint.[306]

In *The Christian Society for the Holy Places v. Minister of Defence*, the Israeli Supreme Court, sitting as the High Court of Justice, addressed the Military Government's authority to legislate in the West Bank under Article 43 of the Hague Regulations.[307] The court held that the Military Government's action in that case was within its authority under Article 43. The critical factor for the court was the motivation of the Military Government.[308] The court held that the proposed law upheld Article 43, because the Military Government was passing a law for the welfare of the occupied inhabitants (the Palestinians). The court opined that a "legislative act which has nothing to do with concern for the welfare of the inhabitants is *ultra vires* the authority of the Occupying Power."[309] In other words, the court speculated that laws might be proposed that had nothing to do with the concern for the occupied inhabitants, and it recognized that such laws would violate Article 43. Assuming that the term "inhabitants" refers to the inhabitants of the West Bank protected by the Hague Regulations (the Palestinian population) and not to the Israeli settlers, the Military

---

303. *Id.*
304. Yoram Dinstein, *The Israel Supreme Court and the Law of Belligerent Occupation: Article 43 of the Hague Regulations,* 25 Isr. Y.B. on Hum. Rts. 1, 8-9 (1995). Schwenk, *supra* note 296, at 400-01.
305. *Id.* Schwenk, *supra* note 296, at 400-01.
306. Meurer, Die Voelkerrechtliche Stellung der vom Feind Besetzten Gebiete 22 (1915), *translated in* Schwenk, *supra* note 296, at 412.
307. H.C. 337/71, Christian Society for the Holy Places v. Minister of Defence, 26(1) P.D. 574, *summarized in* 2 Isr. Y.B. on Hum. Rts. 354 (1972).
308. *Id.* at 355; Dinstein, *supra* note 304, at 5.
309. Dinstein, *supra* note 304, at 5.

Government would not havé the authority to promulgate a road plan which did not serve the Palestinian population.

The court's interpretation of the Military Government's authority to legislate under Article 43 has been criticized as too narrow and untenable.[310] In subsequent decisions, the court has not confined itself to this interpretation and it has upheld, as consistent with Article 43, legislation enacted by the Military Government on the basis of military necessity and security concerns.[311] The general consensus among legal scholars is that under Article 43 an occupant has, "as a matter of course, the right to issue such regulations as may be required for legitimate military ends."[312] Since the bypass road plan could be justified as a security need or as a military necessity, it would not be inconsistent with Israel's legislative authority under Article 43.[313] In *Tabib v. Minister of Defence*, the court held that Road Plan Number 50 was consistent with the Military Government's legislative authority under Article 43 because the plan was required for security reasons.[314]

Articles 43, 46, and 52 of the Hague Regulations are relevant to the discussion of whether Israel may confiscate, seize, expropriate, or requisition privately-owned land and destroy the structures or crops attached to that land for the purpose of building the bypass road network. Article 46 of the Hague Regulations prohibits the confiscation of private property.[315] This prohibition applies only to outright

---

310. *Id.* at 6.

311. H.C. 507/85, Tamimi v. Minister of Defence, 41(4) P.D. 57, 62, *summarized in* 18 Isr. Y.B. on Hum. Rts. 248 (1988); H.C. 87/85, Arjov v. Commander of IDF Forces in the Judea and Samaria Region, 42(1) P.D. 353, 365, *summarized in* 18 Isr. Y.B. on Hum. Rts. 255 (1988).

312. Ernst H. Feilchenfeld, The International Economic Law of Belligerent Occupation 86 (1942).

313. Although the efficacy of the bypass road network in addressing security needs of the settlers is debatable, Israel is entitled to determine its own military needs and how best to address those needs. *See* ICRC Commentary, *supra* note 110, at 302.

314. H.C. 202/81, Tabib v. Minister of Defence, 36(2) P.D. 622, 635, *summarized in* 13 Isr. Y.B. on Hum. Rts. 364 (1983). The Court found that there was a military and strategic interest in the construction of high-speed highways facilitating the swift movement of troops across the territories in the event of war. *See* Emma Playfair, *Playing on Principle? Israel's Justification for Its Administrative Acts in the Occupied West Bank, in* International Law and the Administration of Occupied Territories 205, 218–19 (Emma Playfair ed., 1992).

315. Article 46 states that "private property cannot be confiscated," and requires that private property be respected. Hague Regulations, *supra* note 7, at art. 46.

confiscation but not to lawful seizures, expropriations, or requisitions of land.[316]

According to the legal scholar Ernst Feilchenfeld, "during an occupation the occupant's right and duty to maintain public order and safety may involve expropriation. . . . If the occupant engages in expropriations, the 'laws in force in the country' will normally have to be observed, under Article 43."[317] Under the Jordanian law which was in force in the West Bank in 1967, land may be expropriated only for the public benefit.[318] Thus, if the Israeli Military Government were to adhere to the Jordanian law, it would not have the authority to expropriate land for bypass roads that serve Israeli settlements in the West Bank but do not benefit the Palestinian population.

Military Order 321 authorizes the expropriation of land in "Judea and Samaria" for public purposes. Although this order seems to comply with the Jordanian law on expropriations, the "public" to which it refers is not always the Palestinian population of the West Bank.[319] As discussed above, Israel has the authority to modify the laws in force or to enact new laws. It is doubtful that this authority includes the power to redefine the public to exclude the occupied population. Moreover, as a general rule, an occupant may not expropriate private property without paying compensation to the property holder.[320] However, between March 1994 and April 1996, at least eleven of the Israeli military regulations expropriating land for the purpose of building roads in the West Bank offered no form of compensation.[321] Arguably, these expropriations are unlawful and tantamount to

---

316. Feilchenfeld, *supra* note 312, at 51.

317. *Id.* at 50. Feilchenfeld assumes that the projects necessitating expropriations would be for the benefit of the sovereign of the occupied territory, not for the occupant: "[A]n occupant may provide for expropriation in connection with civil legislation passed for the maintenance of law and order. But in this case the expropriations would be for the benefit of the sovereign, not for that of the occupant." *Id.* at 38.

318. Benvenisti & Khayat, *supra* note 4, at 62.

319. *See* Al-Haq, *Israeli Land Acquisition and Settlement in the Occupied Territories,* Hum. Rts. Focus, Aug. 20, 1991, at 3–4. Military Order 321 is usually used to expropriate land for the purposes of building settlements or settlement roads. For the proposition that settlements and settlement roads are "diametrically opposed to the interests" of the public, see Raja Shehadeh, The Law of the Land: Settlements and Land Issues Under Israeli Military Occupation 30 (1993).

320. Feilchenfeld, *supra* note 312, at 50–51.

321. Israel Military Regulations numbers 5/3/94, 5/4/94, 5/5/94, 5/1/95, 5/2/95, 5/4/95, 5/1/96, 5/3/96, 20/5/96, 5/4/96, and 21/4/96 issued in accordance with Israel Military Government Order 321, issued Mar. 28, 1969 (on file with author).

confiscation, which is prohibited under Article 46. However, the issue has not yet been adjudicated.

Under Article 52 of the Hague Regulations, an occupier may requisition private property only "for the needs of the army of occupation."[322] According to Feilchenfeld, this article applies to real estate as well as other tangible and intangible property.[323] Although the occupier may acquire the title to movable property, it does not acquire the title to real estate.[324] However, the "regulations on the requisitioning of real estate do not answer the question of the extent to which an occupant may provide for expropriation in connection with civil legislation passed for the maintenance of law and order."[325] Feilchenfeld assumes that such expropriations would be for the benefit of the legitimate sovereign of the occupied territory, not for the occupant.[326]

In *Dweikat v. Government of Israel* (the *Elon Moreh* case), the Israeli Supreme Court held that the requisition of private property in order to build a civilian settlement could not be justified on the basis of military necessity within the meaning of Article 52.[327] The court did not base its holding on the proposition that civilian settlements, by their nature, could never serve military needs; rather it found that the Elon Moreh settlement, in particular, was not built for military needs because

---

322.   Hague Regulations, *supra* note 7, at art. 52. Article 52 provides that:

> [R]equisitions in kind and services shall not be demanded from municipalities or inhabitants except for the needs of the army of occupation. They shall be in proportion to the resources of the country, and of such a nature as not to involve the population in the obligation of taking part in military operations against their own country. Such requisitions and services shall only be demanded on the authority of the commander in the locality occupied.

Id.

323.   *Id.* at 37–38.

324.   *Id.* ("In the case of movable property the occupant usually takes title, and, if the requisition is lawful, valid title. Real estate, however, cannot be consumed or used up; the needs of the occupant, therefore do not require a change in title . . . .").

325.   Feilchenfeld, *supra* note 312, at 38.

326.   *Id.*

327.   H.C. 390/79, Dweikat v. Israel (the *Elon Moreh* case), 40(2) P.D. 617, *summarized in* 9 Isr. Y.B. on Hum. Rts. 345 (1979).

> the decision to establish a permanent settlement intended
> from the outset to remain in its place forever—even beyond the
> duration of the military government which was established in
> Judea and Samaria—encounters a legal obstacle which is
> insurmountable, because the military government cannot
> create in its area facts for its military needs which are
> designed *ab initio* to exist even after the end of the military
> rule in that area, when the fate of the area after the
> termination of military rule is still not known.[328]

The Israeli Supreme Court has not maintained a similar stance with
regard to the requisition of property for other potentially-permanent
settlements when the Israeli Government has argued that these
settlements serve military needs.[329]

The court's reasoning in the *Elon Moreh* case cuts to the heart
of the problem posed by permanent structures built by Israel in the
territories under its occupation. Israel and the PLO have entered into
agreements contemplating the end of the Israeli occupation of the West
Bank and Gaza Strip. Yet, Israel is building roads which will exist even
after the end of its military rule in the area. The military necessity of
the roads in this instance is questionable, because the roads are being
built for the security needs of the settlers, although the fate of the
settlements in the West Bank has yet to be decided. Following the
reasoning of the *Elon Moreh* court, the bypass road network also
"encounters a legal obstacle which is insurmountable."[330] To build roads
for settlements while the fate of settlements is as yet undecided is to
assume their fate and plan for their continued existence.

Redeployment revived the practice of seizing private property
for "military purposes." The Israeli military is confident that building
bypass roads to facilitate redeployment constitutes an appropriate
military purpose for which land may be seized. Between December 1994
and April 1996, the IDF issued at least twenty-nine military orders to
seize land in the West Bank for "military purposes."[331] Although these

---

328. *Id.* at 350.

329. *See* H.C. 302/72, Sheikh Suleiman Hussein Odeh Abu Hilu v. Government of
Israel, 27(2) P.D. 169, *summarized in* 5 Isr. Y.B. on Hum. Rts. 384 (1975); H.C. 610/78,
H.C. 606/78, Ayyoub v. Minister of Defence, 33(2) P.D. 113, *summarized in* 9 Isr. Y.B. on
Hum. Rts. 337 (1979).

330. H.C. 390/79, *Dweikat*, *summarized in* 9 Isr. Y.B. on Hum. Rts. at 350.

331. Israel Military Orders entitled "Order Concerning Seizure of Land": t/25/94,
t/25/94 (extension), t/26/94, t/8/95, t/9/95, t/11/95, t/12/95, t/12/95 (addition), t/13/95,
t/15/95 (extension), t/16/95, t/23/95, t/25/95, t/26/95, t/29/95, t/35/95, t/37/95, t/6/96, t/10/96,

orders seize the land for five years,[332] building a road on the land indicates that the land will not be returned to its owner after five years.

The orders state that the owners of the land and/or the provincial governors may apply to receive rent for the use of the land and/or compensation for the land.[333] However, on principle, the owners do not apply for the rent or the compensation. Thus, it is unclear whether or not the owners would receive the compensation were they to apply for it. Finally, these orders are not distributed directly to the owners of the land seized. Rather, they are placed in the District Coordination Offices, the Civil Administration Offices, the office of the Custodian of Government and Absentee Property, *inter alia.*[334] The orders themselves do not incorporate a procedure by which to object to the seizure of land.[335]

The Israeli Supreme Court has sanctioned the requisition of property for the construction of roads based on its interpretation of the Military Government's legislative authority under Article 43. In *Jamait Askan v. Commander of IDF Forces in the Judea and Samaria Region,* the petitioner challenged the legitimacy of Road Plan Number 50 on the grounds that the requisition of land for the road did not serve the interests of the civilian population of the West Bank.[336] The IDF argued that the road plan simultaneously furthered the interests of the

---

t/11/96, t/17/96, t/18/96, t/19/96, t/24/96, t/30/96, t/31/96, t/32/96, t/34/96, and t/35/96 (on file with author).

332.   Two of the orders listed, t/8/95 and t/29/95, seize the land for four and three years respectively.

333.   *See* Israel Military Orders entitled "Order Concerning Seizure of Land": t/25/94, t/25/94 (extension), t/26/94, t/8/95, t/9/95, t/11/95, t/12/95, t/12/95 (addition), t/13/95, t/15/95 (extension), t/16/95, t/23/95, t/25/95, t/26/95, t/29/95, t/35/95, t/37/95, t/6/96, t/10/96, t/11/96, t/17/96, t/18/96, t/19/96, t/24/96, t/30/96, t/31/96, t/32/96, t/34/96, and t/35/96 (on file with author).

334.   *See* Israel Military Orders entitled "Order Concerning Seizure of Land": t/25/94, t/25/94 (extension), t/26/94, t/8/95, t/9/95, t/11/95, t/12/95, t/12/95(addition), t/13/95, t/15/95 (extension), t/16/95, t/23/95, t/25/95, t/26/95, t/29/95, t/35/95, t/37/95, t/6/96, t/10/96, t/11/96, t/17/96, t/18/96, t/19/96, t/24/96, t/30/96, t/31/96, t/32/96, t/34/96, and t/35/96 (on file with author).

335.   *See* Israel Military Orders entitled "Order Concerning Seizure of Land": t/25/94, t/25/94 (extension), t/26/94, t/8/95, t/9/95, t/11/95, t/12/95, t/12/95 (addition), t/15/95 (extension), t/16/95, t/23/95, t/25/95, t/29/95, t/35/95, t/37/95, t/6/96, t/10/96, t/11/96, t/17/96, t/18/96, t/19/96, t/24/96, t/30/96, t/31/96, t/32/96, t/34/96, and t/35/96 (on file with author).

336.   H.C. 393/82, Jamait Askan v. Commander of IDF Forces in the Judea and Samaria Region, 37(4) P.D. 785, *summarized in* 14 Isr. Y.B. on Hum. Rts. 301 (1984).

military and the interests of the civilian population of the West Bank.[337] The court upheld the military's authority to enact Road Plan Number 50 and to requisition land for the road construction.[338] The court stated that the Military Government is entitled to take the measures it deems necessary to ensure growth and development in the territories and to invest in infrastructure.[339] Since the court held that the road plan served the interests of the civilian population of the West Bank, it did not give its opinion on the military's authority to requisition land for a road plan which does not serve the interests of the civilian population of the West Bank.

Article 55 limits the occupant's use of immovable public property in the occupied territory. It states that "the occupying State shall be regarded only as administrator and usufructuary of public buildings, real estate, forests, and agricultural estates belonging to the hostile State, and situated in the occupied country. It must safeguard the capital of these properties, and administer them in accordance with the rules of usufruct."[340] Generally, usufruct is defined as the "right to enjoy the benefits of the use of something owned by another so long as the property is not damaged or altered in any way."[341] Although the occupant may use or even lease public lands, the lease or contract may not extend beyond the conclusion of the war.[342] Similarly, the occupant may cut and sell timber and crops and work the mines in the occupied territory.[343] There has been no authoritative decision on the extent to which the occupant may use resources such as minerals, oil, and water in the occupied territory.[344]

B.   Fourth Geneva Convention

Articles 52, 53, and 147 of the Fourth Geneva Convention pertain to the acquisition and destruction of property for the purpose of building bypass roads. Article 49 addresses the legality of settlements and the construction of roads serving them. Since Israel does not accept

---

337. *Id.*
338. *Id.*
339. *Id.* at 804–05. *See* Dinstein, *supra* note 304, at 14. In arriving at its holding, the court stressed the prolonged nature of the occupation.
340. Hague Regulations, *supra* note 7, at art. 55.
341. Levie, *supra* note 124, at 767.
342. Feilchenfeld, *supra* note 312, at 55.
343. *Id.*
344. Levie, *supra* note 124, at 767.

the *de jure* applicability of the Fourth Geneva Convention, the Convention does not have the force of law in Israel. Thus, we do not have the benefit of the Israeli Supreme Court's interpretation of the provisions of the Fourth Geneva Convention.

The requisition and expropriation of large amounts of agricultural land in the West Bank may be seen as a violation of Article 52 of the Fourth Geneva Convention. Article 52 concerns the protection of workers and forbids the occupying power from engaging in "[a]ll measures aiming at creating unemployment or at restricting the opportunities offered to workers in an occupied territory, in order to induce them to work for the Occupying Power."[345] This article prohibits practices that artificially create unemployment or diminish the possibility of finding employment. During the Second World War, the occupying powers intentionally created unemployment in the occupied territories "in order to create a labor pool available to work elsewhere."[346] Among these practices were the "setting up of employment monopolies, the closing down of industries, [and] the creation of a shortage of raw materials necessary for production."[347] Article 52 attempts to put an end to such practices.

In constructing the bypass road network, the Israeli Military Government has requisitioned and expropriated over 20,000 dunums (4,940 acres) of agricultural land in the West Bank.[348] With fewer employment opportunities in the West Bank, Palestinians are compelled to look for work elsewhere. Many former agricultural laborers work as migrant laborers in Israel.[349] Similarly, construction of the bypass roads has created a shortage of raw materials necessary for production. The Israeli military has raided and shut down numerous stone quarries in the West Bank.[350] They have also uprooted thousands of olive trees, creating a shortage in the olives used to produce olive oil.[351]

---

345. Geneva Convention IV, *supra* note 8, at art. 52.

346. Levie, *supra* note 124, at 729.

347. ICRC Commentary, *supra* note 110, at 300.

348. Interview with Khalil Tufakji, *supra* note 1.

349. Erica Lang, *The Occupied Territories: Destruction or Development? A Study of the Problems and Prospects for Economic, Social, and Political Development, in* A Context of Colonialism 16 (1990) (quoting statistics from the ILO).

350. *See* Al-Haq's field report number 95/62 (on file with author).

351. For information on trees uprooted, see Al-Haq's field report number 95/198 (on file with author).

Articles 53 and 147 provide further limitations on a state's use of land in the territory under its occupation. Article 53 limits the extent to which an occupying power may destroy the property of those in an occupied territory: "Any destruction by the Occupying Power of real or personal property belonging individually or collectively to private persons, or to the State, or to other public authorities, or to social or co-operative organizations, is prohibited, except where such destruction is rendered absolutely necessary by military operations."[352] This provision applies to property that is both personal and real property, including private property of protected persons, state property, that of the public authorities (districts, municipalities, provinces, etc.) or of cooperative organizations.[353] The prohibition applies only to the destruction of this property. Under international law, the occupying power has the right to dispose of property in the occupied territory under certain circumstances.[354] These include the "right to requisition private property, the right to confiscate any movable property belonging to the State which may be used for military operations and the right to administer and enjoy the use of real property belonging to the occupying state."[355]

With regard to the destruction of property, the protection afforded by this provision is strong, but the exception—absolute necessity for military operations—is broad. The occupying power may engage in the destruction of property in the occupied territory if required by military operations. Moreover, the occupying power is the judge of the importance of the military necessity for such operations.[356] However, the occupying power must implement this provision in good faith—it should not construe the exception so broadly as to make a nullity of the protections afforded by the article.[357] Thus, when considering the destruction of property, the occupying power should reasonably balance the damage caused by the destruction with the military advantages gained through it.

---

352. Geneva Convention IV, *supra* note 8, at art. 53.
353. ICRC Commentary, *supra* note 110, at 301.
354. *Id.*
355. *Id.*
356. *Id.*
357. *Id.* ("The Occupying Power must therefore try to interpret the clause in a reasonable manner: whenever it is felt essential to resort to destruction, the occupying authorities must try to keep a sense of proportion in comparing the military advantages to be gained with the damage done.").

Under Article 147, the "extensive destruction and appropriation of property, not justified by military necessity and carried out unlawfully and wantonly" constitute a grave breach of the Convention, rendering the occupying power liable to penal sanction under Article 146.[358] This article prohibits not only the destruction of property in occupied territory, but also its extensive appropriation. However, this article does not prohibit an isolated incident of destruction and appropriation of property. In order to constitute a grave breach of the Convention, the destruction and appropriation of property must be extensive.[359]

In the course of building the bypass roads, the Israeli military demolished several houses and other structures in the path of or within the proscribed building area on either side of the roads.[360] Whether these destructions were avoidable or whether they were absolutely necessary is questionable. The ICRC Commentary suggests that an occupier should balance the military advantages gained by the destruction of property with the damage done.[361] Nonetheless, the occupier is entitled to judge reasonably the military necessity of its operations.[362] Thus, the Israeli military may, without violating Articles 53 and 147, destroy houses and other structures if it determines that there is a reasonable military necessity for doing so.

Finally, the bypass road network, like the settlements it serves, violates Article 49 of the Fourth Geneva Convention. Article 49 addresses transfers and deportations of both the residents of the occupied territory and the civilian population of the occupying power. The last paragraph of Article 49 states that the "Occupying Power shall not deport or transfer parts of its own civilian population into the territory it occupies."[363] The purpose of this provision was to prevent the transfer of portions of the population of an occupying power to the occupied territory for political and racial reasons or for purposes of

---

358. Geneva Convention IV, *supra* note 8, at art. 146.
359. ICRC Commentary, *supra* note 110, at 601.
360. *See* Pacheco & Susskind, *supra* note 5 (noting that six houses were demolished in Hebron to facilitate construction of Road 60); Greenberg, *supra* note 5; Palestine Report, *supra* note 5 (stating that at the end of December 1995, six Palestinian homes were destroyed because they were "too close" to the bypass road around Bethlehem); LAW, *supra* note 5 (stating that two houses in 'Anata and Jaba' were demolished to clear the path for a bypass road from Ramallah to the settlement of Pisgat Ze'ev).
361. ICRC Commentary, *supra* note 110, at 302.
362. *Id.*
363. Geneva Convention IV, *supra* note 8, at art. 49.

colonization.[364] During World War II, such practices had negative repercussions for the economic condition of the occupied population and "endangered their separate existence as a race."[365]

Such transfers are also contrary to the temporary nature of an occupation. Colonization threatens the temporary nature of an occupation in that it gives the occupying population an attachment to the territories under occupation. As the occupying power builds up the occupied territory for the transferred population, its attachment to the occupied territory grows. This attachment may predispose the occupying population to a permanent settlement in the occupied territory.

Legal scholars have drawn a distinction between "the transfer of people—which is forbidden under Article 49—and the voluntary settlement of nationals of the occupant, on an individual basis, in the occupied territory."[366] Roberts argues that such a distinction is of little relevance in the case of Israeli settlements in the West Bank in light of the "ambitious settlements program of the 1980s, which was planned, encouraged and financed at the governmental level . . . ."[367] When the government has so actively pursued settlement in the West Bank, there "can be no question but that such settlement . . . violates the final paragraph of Article 49 of the Fourth Geneva Convention."[368]

The United Nations General Assembly and Security Council have also been highly critical of Israeli settlements, and Security Council Resolution 465 called settlements "a flagrant violation of the Geneva Convention."[369] Such willful violations of Article 49 of the Geneva Convention became "regarded as grave breaches of [the 1977] Protocol."[370] In the opinion of the ICRC, both the settlements and settlement roads are contrary to Article 49's prohibition against

---

364.   ICRC Commentary, *supra* note 110, at 283.

365.   *Id.*

366.   Dinstein, *supra* note 304, at 124.

367.   Roberts, *supra* note 105, at 85; *see also* Meron Benvenisti, The West Bank Data Base Project 1987, Report 5, at 51-65 (1987).

368.   Kuttner, *supra* note 103, at 218.

369.   S.C. Res. 465, U.N. SCOR, 35th Sess., 2203d mtg. at 5, U.N. Doc. S/INF/36 (1980); *see also* G.A. Res. 43/58C, U.N. GAOR, 43d Sess., Supp. No. 49, at 121, U.N. Doc. A/43/49 (1988); G.A. Res. 39/95C, U.N. GAOR, 39th Sess., 100th mtg. at 2, U.N. Doc. A/RES/39/95 (1984); G.A. Res. 35/122B, U.N. GAOR, 35th Sess., Supp. No. 48, at 90, U.N. Doc. A/35/48 (1980); G.A. Res. 31/106A, U.N. GAOR, 31st Sess., Supp. No. 39, at 50, U.N. Doc. A/31/39 (1976).

370.   Protocol Additional to the Geneva Conventions of 12 August 1949, and Relating to the Protection of Victims of International Armed Conflicts (Protocol 1), adopted by the Conference June 8, 1977, art. 85, 1125 U.N.T.S. 3, 16 I.L.M. 1392 (1977).

transfers of the civilian population of an occupying power into occupied territory.[371] The bypass road network exists to serve the Israeli settlements in the West Bank, and the settlements violate Article 49 of the Fourth Geneva Convention. Thus, combining these two statements leads to the conclusion that the bypass road network also violates Article 49.

CONCLUSION

The bypass road network perpetuates Israel's occupation of the West Bank through a racially-segregated, militarily-controlled road system. The network imposes a military grid on the West Bank, dividing the Palestinian areas into cantons separated and surrounded by militarily-controlled roads. Thus, the road system allows the Israeli military to control the West Bank with fewer military personnel.

The bypass road plan allows the Israeli military literally to occupy Palestinian land with roads. The network has served as the vehicle for continued land confiscation, allowing the Israeli military to redefine Palestinian land as land needed for military purposes or public purposes (utilizing its own definition of "public" which excludes Palestinians). By seizing and expropriating Palestinian land, the Israeli military decreases the amount of Palestinian-held land and increases Israeli land holdings in the West Bank.

Furthermore, the road system facilitates the growth and development of the Israeli settlements, perpetuating Israel's colonization of the West Bank. In keeping with previous settlement plans, the bypass roads link Israeli settlements in the West Bank to each other and to Israel, thus encouraging further settlement. This scheme allows the settlements to expand along the bypass roads and makes the settlements more attractive because of their easy access to Israel. By creating territorial contiguity between the settlements on either side of the Green Line, the roads effectively erase the Green Line, lifting the psychological barrier it created for many Israelis against settling in the West Bank.

The bypass road network serves simultaneously to impede the economy of the Palestinians in the West Bank and to boost the economy of the Israeli settlers in the West Bank. While facilitating movement

---

371.   1984 ICRC Ann. Rep., *supra* note 129, at 66. The ICRC has maintained this position in all of its annual reports in which it discusses settlements.

between the settlements and Israel, the network restricts Palestinian movement and breaks up Palestinian territorial contiguity, impeding the flow of commerce and workers from area to area, with negative repercussions in all sectors of the West Bank economy. Moreover, the seizure of agricultural land, raiding and closing of stone quarries, and destruction of houses have impoverished many Palestinians in the West Bank.

As the Israeli settlements flourish, the Palestinian communities languish. Like the apartheid system in South Africa, the bypass road system promotes the advantage of one racial group over another. Israeli settlers benefit from a modern road system while the Palestinians are relegated to a deteriorating one. As with other systems of racial segregation and discrimination, the bypass road network cannot hope to promote peace but rather will cause further tension and conflict.

The bypass road network serves as a structural impediment to Palestinian self-determination, sovereignty, and statehood. As the network preempts any Palestinian land-use planning, it prevents the Palestinians from determining how best to use their land and natural resources. Since the roads are barriers rather than links between Palestinian areas, they prevent expansion, promote overcrowding, and prevent Palestinian territorial contiguity. Without territorial contiguity, Palestinian self-determination, sovereignty, and statehood are not only politically uncertain but also practically impossible.

The detrimental effects of the bypass road network have been condemned by international humanitarian laws as well as the Interim Israeli-Palestinian Agreements. The construction of bypass roads violates Articles 43, 46, 52, and 55 of the Hague Regulations of 1907, and Articles 49, 52, 53, and 147 of the Fourth Geneva Convention. In addition, the bypass road network violates Articles 2, 27, and 40 of Oslo II's Protocol Concerning Civil Affairs and Articles VIII, IX, and X of Oslo II's Protocol on Economic Relations.

Most importantly, the bypass road network violates Article XXXI of Oslo II by prejudicing the Permanent Status Negotiations, ensuring that the negotiations will not result in a viable solution that recognizes the right of the Palestinian people to self-determination. The bypass roads prejudice the outcome of the Permanent Status Negotiations because they permanently divide the Palestinian areas while linking together the settlements, facilitating their expansion and construction. The roads themselves alter the status quo existing before the 1967 Israeli occupation. Furthermore, the roads built along the Green Line and around Jerusalem extend Israel's borders beyond the

Green Line and around an expanded Jerusalem. In this way, the network furthers Israel's *de facto* annexation of Jerusalem.

The bypass road network alters the status quo of the West Bank not by agreement, but in spite of the Oslo agreements. The network is not the necessary outgrowth of Israeli military redeployment in the West Bank; rather, it is the fruition of a settlement plan proposed almost twenty years ago. It imposes an old, condemned unilateral political solution on the West Bank under the guise of a bilateral agreement. Rather than promoting peace, the bypass road network spurs conflict by perpetuating Israel's occupation and colonization of the West Bank. Altering the geography and demography of the West Bank, the network preempts and assumes the results of the Permanent Status Negotiations, foreclosing the possibility that the negotiations will end the occupation and recognize the right of the Palestinian people to self-determination.

MAPS

Map 1. The Partition of Palestine[372]

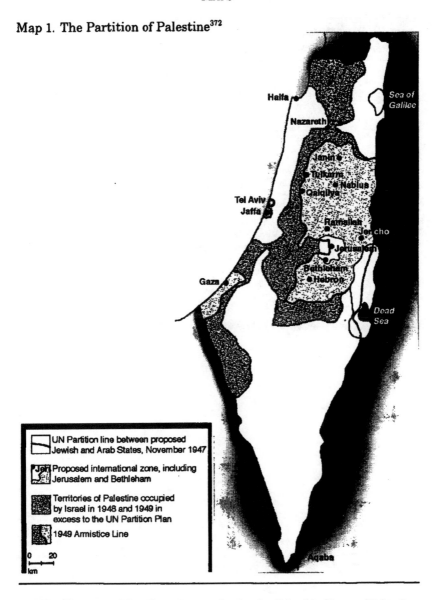

UN Partition line between proposed
Jewish and Arab States, November 1947

Proposed international zone, including
Jerusalem and Bethlehem

Territories of Palestine occupied
by Israel in 1948 and 1949 in
excess to the UN Partition Plan

1949 Armistice Line

0   20
km

372. Map created by Alexis Demopoulos for the *Columbia Human Rights Law Review.*

Map 2. U.N. Proposed Boundaries for Jerusalem—Nov. 1947[373]

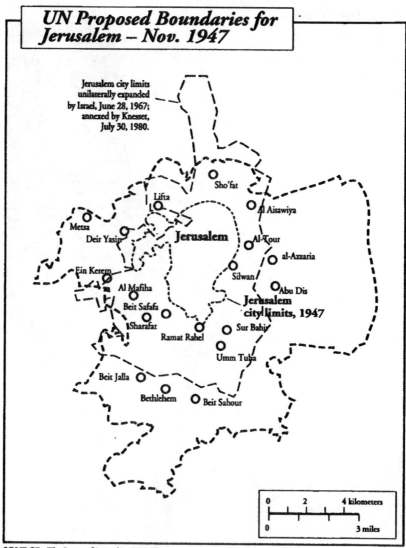

SOURCE: *The Status of Jerusalem,* United Nations, New York, 1979.

---

373.   Reprinted with the permission of the Foundation for Middle East Peace.

Map 3. Oslo II Map Outlining Areas A, B, and C[374]

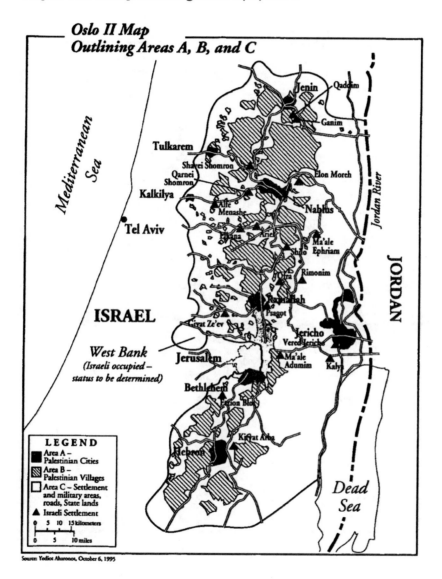

Oslo II Map
Outlining Areas A, B, and C

Source: Yediot Aharonot, October 6, 1995

---

374.   Reprinted with the permission of the Foundation for Middle East Peace.

Map 4. West Bank[375]

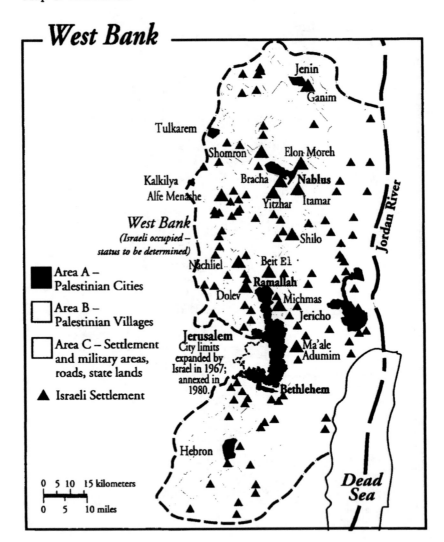

375.   Reprinted with the permission of the Foundation for Middle East Peace.

Map 5. Road Map for IDF Redeployment[376]

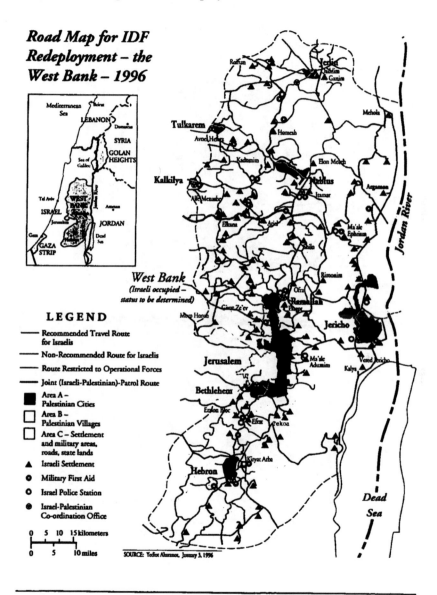

Road Map for IDF Redeployment – the West Bank – 1996

LEGEND

⸻ Recommended Travel Route for Israelis

- - - Non-Recommended Route for Israelis

⸻ Route Restricted to Operational Forces

⸻ Joint (Israeli-Palestinian)-Patrol Route

■ Area A – Palestinian Cities

□ Area B – Palestinian Villages

□ Area C – Settlement and military areas, roads, state lands

▲ Israeli Settlement

◉ Military First Aid

○ Israel Police Station

● Israel-Palestinian Co-ordination Office

SOURCE: *Yediot Aharanot*, January 3, 1996

---

376.   Reprinted with the permission of the Foundation for Middle East Peace.

Map 6. Netanyahu's "Allon Plus" Final Status Map[377]

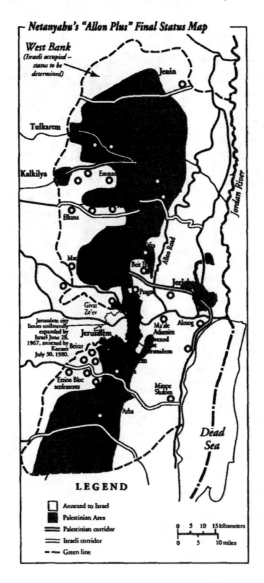

---

377.   Reprinted with the permission of the Foundation for Middle East Peace.

VOLUME 44, NUMBER 1, WINTER 2003

On the Fourth Geneva Convention and the Occupied Palestinian Territory

Ardi Imseis*

I. INTRODUCTION

Since the Peace of Westphalia in 1648, the international system has witnessed countless armed conflicts, all of which have had devastating impacts on the societies enmeshed in them.[1] As the European state system evolved over the course of the seventeenth, eighteenth, and nineteenth centuries, recourse to war was widely considered a legitimate tool of statecraft. As Karl von Clausewitz put it, war was "merely the continuation of policy by other means."[2] In the course of pursuing such policy, numerous territories were overrun and scores were left at the mercy of conquering armies that, more often than not, terrorized civilian populations under their control. It is with civilian populations subject to foreign military occupation that this Article is chiefly concerned.

The atrocities perpetrated against the populations of occupied Europe during World War II accounted for the high civilian casualty rate in that war. In the territories occupied by Nazi Germany "millions of human beings were torn from their homes, separated from their families and deported" to death and slave labor camps, while their unguarded property was either looted or destroyed.[3] Similar gross violations of human rights, though narrower in scope and character, were carried out by Japanese and Russian occupation forces during the course of the war.[4] In the wake of what emerged as one of the most horrific episodes in human history, "representatives of almost every established State met in Geneva in 1949 to sign revised conventions intended to cope with the effects of the new phenomenon of 'total

---

* B.A., University of Toronto, 1991; LL.B., Dalhousie University, 1999; LL.M., Columbia University, 2002. This Article was written while in residence as a fellow of the Human Rights Institute, Columbia University School of Law, 2001–02. I should like to express my gratitude to John Quigley, George Bisharat, Lori F. Damrosch, Rema Jamous Imseis, and Diana Buttu for providing valuable commentary on an earlier draft.

1. *See generally* PAUL KENNEDY, THE RISE AND FALL OF THE GREAT POWERS (1988).

2. KARL VON CLAUSEWITZ, ON WAR 87 (Michael Howard & Peter Paret eds. & trans., Princeton University Press 1984) (1832).

3. JEAN PICTET, HUMANITARIAN LAW AND THE PROTECTION OF WAR VICTIMS 129–30 (1975).

4. GERHARD VON GLAHN, LAW AMONG NATIONS: AN INTRODUCTION TO PUBLIC INTERNATIONAL LAW 663–64 (7th ed. 1996).

war' on civilian populations as well as on military personnel."[5] The result was the promulgation of the Geneva Conventions of 1949 (Geneva Conventions),[6] one of which is focused on protecting civilians from the effects of war and armed conflict.

The Geneva Convention Relative to the Protection of Civilian Persons in Time of War, generally known as the Fourth Geneva Convention, is widely regarded as a codification of customary international law.[7] It supplements the earlier 1907 Hague Convention IV Respecting the Laws and Customs of War on Land (1907 Hague Convention), along with its annexed Regulations (1907 Hague Regulations).[8] To a large extent, the Fourth Geneva Convention and the 1907 Hague Regulations govern the law of belligerent occupation—that branch of international humanitarian law that regulates "the occupation of enemy territory in time of war,"[9] as well as "after a cease-fire or truce, when civilians could be subjected to military occupation in the absence of a final political settlement."[10] The Fourth Geneva Convention outlines the rights and duties of the occupying power (or belligerent occupant) and sets out the law of how civilian populations are to be treated while the occupying power maintains effective control in the occupied territory.[11] Although the Fourth Geneva Convention attempts to strike a balance between the rights of the occupier and the occupied, its "overriding aim ... is to ensure that claims of military exigency do not result in the violation of basic political and human rights of the civilians under military occupation."[12] To ensure this end, the convention not only provides a fairly thorough restate-

---

5. United Nations, Comm. on the Exercise of the Inalienable Rights of the Palestinian People (UNCEIRPP), The Question of the Observance of the Fourth Geneva Convention of 1949 in Gaza and the West Bank Including Jerusalem Occupied by Israel in June 1967, at 4 (1979). It should be noted that the 1949 Geneva Conventions, *infra* note 6, were not the exclusive product of post-war developments. As noted by Adam Roberts and Richard Guelff, they "were the outgrowth of efforts undertaken before the Second World War to draft new conventions; and they were also the product of the experience of the war itself." *Prefatory Note: The Four 1949 Geneva Conventions,* Documents on the Laws of War 195, 195 (Adam Roberts & Richard Guelff eds., 3d ed. 2000).

6. Geneva Convention for the Amelioration of the Condition of the Wounded and Sick in Armed Forces in the Field, Aug. 12, 1949, 6 U.S.T. 3114, 75 U.N.T.S. 31 *(entered into force* Oct. 21, 1950); Geneva Convention for the Amelioration of the Condition of the Wounded, Sick and Shipwrecked Members of Armed Forces at Sea, Aug. 12, 1949, 6 U.S.T. 3217, 75 U.N.T.S. 85 *(entered into force* Oct. 21, 1950); Geneva Convention Relative to the Treatment of Prisoners of War, Aug. 12, 1949, 6 U.S.T. 3316, 75 U.N.T.S. 135 *(entered into force* Oct. 21, 1950); Geneva Convention Relative to the Protection of Civilian Persons in Time of War, Aug. 12, 1949, 6 U.S.T. 3516, 75 U.N.T.S. 287 *(entered into force* Oct. 21, 1950) [hereinafter Fourth Geneva Convention].

7. Documents on the Laws of War, *supra* note 5, at 196.

8. Convention Respecting the Laws and Customs of War on Land, Oct. 18, 1907, 36 Stat. 2277, 1 Bevans 631 *(entered into force* Jan. 26, 1910) [hereinafter 1907 Hague Convention].

9. von Glahn, *supra* note 4, at 662.

10. UNCEIRPP, *supra* note 5, at 1.

11. *See* Antonio Cassese, *Powers and Duties of an Occupant in Relation to Land and Natural Resources, in* International Law and the Administration of Occupied Territories: Two Decades of Israeli Occupation of the West Bank and Gaza Strip 419, 420 (Emma Playfair ed., 1992) [hereinafter International Law and Administration].

12. UNCEIRPP, *supra* note 5, at 1.

ment of the substantive positive law on belligerent occupation, but it also furnishes a number of internal procedural "mechanisms . . . available to ensure the effective implementation" of its provisions.[13] The latter are exemplified by the obligation expressed in article 1 of the convention by which the High Contracting Parties undertake not only to respect, but also to *ensure respect* for its provisions "in all circumstances."[14]

"An important, but implicit, assumption of much of the law on occupations is that military occupation is a provisional state of affairs."[15] That is to say that states of occupation are regarded as temporary in nature.[16] Nevertheless, the post–World War II era has witnessed a number of prolonged military occupations, including the Allied occupation of Germany and Japan,[17] South Africa's occupation of Namibia,[18] and Indonesia's occupation of East Timor.[19] Of all prolonged military occupations, however, no other has been the subject of as much international attention as the State of Israel's military occupation of the West Bank, including East Jerusalem, and the Gaza Strip, collectively known as the Occupied Palestinian Territory (OPT).[20]

This year will mark the thirty-sixth year of Israel's control of the OPT, making it the longest military occupation in modern history.[21] During this

---

13. Statement of Miranda Joubert, Advocate, Legal Affairs Division, Department of Foreign Affairs, South Africa, to the United Nations International Meeting on the Convening of the Conference on Measures to Enforce the Fourth Geneva Convention in the Occupied Palestinian Territory, including Jerusalem, 43, 44, Cairo (June 14–15, 1999) (on file with the Harvard International Law Journal) [hereinafter United Nations International Meeting].

14. FOURTH GENEVA CONVENTION, *supra* note 6, art. 1 (emphasis added).

15. Adam Roberts, *Prolonged Military Occupation: The Israeli-Occupied Territories 1967–1988*, *in* INTERNATIONAL LAW AND ADMINISTRATION, *supra* note 11, at 25, 28.

16. Statement of David Delparaz, head of ICRC delegation in Cairo, to the United Nations International Meeting, *supra* note 13, at 47, 48.

17. Roberts, *supra* note 15, at 29.

18. *See id.* at 31.

19. *See* SHARON KORMAN, THE RIGHT OF CONQUEST: THE ACQUISITION OF TERRITORY BY FORCE IN INTERNATIONAL LAW AND PRACTICE 281–92 (1996).

20. A word about terminology is in order. Since 1967 the West Bank, Gaza Strip, and East Jerusalem have been referred to by a number of different names, a matter usually dependent on who is framing the terms of reference. Official Israel, for instance, refers to those areas as either "Judea, Samaria, and Gaza" or the "administered territories" (neither of which include East Jerusalem, illegally annexed by Israel in 1967). On the other hand, the Palestine Liberation Organization (PLO) and the international community, through such bodies as the U.N. Security Council, the U.N. General Assembly, and the International Committee of the Red Cross, have referred to those areas as the "Occupied Territories," the "West Bank, Gaza Strip, and East Jerusalem," and the "Occupied Palestinian Territories," reflecting what seems to be an intention to regard these areas as the territory where the Palestinian people are legitimately entitled to exercise their right to self-determination. Most recently, the United Nations has begun to refer to the areas collectively as the "Occupied Palestinian *Territory*," a deliberate usage of the singular form of the term, apparently for the purpose of underscoring the contiguous nature of what is regarded as the self-determination unit of the Palestinian people. *See, e.g.*, G.A. Res. ES-10/6, U.N. GAOR, 54th Sess., Supp. No. 49, U.N. Doc. A/ES-10/6 (1999). In keeping with this practice, the West Bank, including East Jerusalem, and the Gaza Strip, will be referred to collectively as the Occupied Palestinian Territory (OPT) throughout this Article.

21. *See* Edward W. Said, *Emerging Alternatives in Palestine*, AL-AHRAM WKLY. (Egypt), Jan. 10–16, 2002, http://www.ahram.org.eg/weekly/2002/568/op2.htm. *See also* Emadeddin J. Fraitekh, *Palestinians*

period, the policy of successive Israeli governments toward the OPT has made Israel the focus of intense domestic and international criticism. As put by attorney Allegra Pacheco:

> Since 1967, the Israeli military has consistently violated nearly every provision of the Fourth Geneva Convention. Human rights organizations worldwide, from Amnesty International to Israel's own B'Tselem, as well as the United States government, have issued hundreds of statements and reports criticizing Israel's violations. Among the lists are: torture of over 50,000 Palestinians; over 1,500 Palestinians deported; annexation of East Jerusalem; construction of over 150 Jewish settlements [i.e., colonies]; illegal transfer of over 400,000 Israeli civilians into the occupied territories; repeated collective punishment . . . demolition of over 8,000 homes and villages in East Jerusalem and the West Bank and Gaza; pillage of Palestinian natural resources, including water, quarries, and trees; and the illegal appropriation of over 70 percent of the occupied territories.[22]

For its part, Israel officially denies that the Fourth Geneva Convention applies de jure to the OPT,[23] and strenuously resists the accusation that its military authorities have been the source of any systematic violations of international law in the territory.[24] The Palestinian point of view, on the other hand, holds that the Fourth Geneva Convention is de jure applicable to the OPT[25] (a position, as will be seen, that enjoys the unqualified support of the international community), and that Israel's failure to abide by its provisions, as well as the international community's failure to ensure that Israel respect those provisions, has allowed for the wholesale violation of the human rights of the civilians living under Israeli military rule.[26] In September 2000, a renewed uprising (dubbed the "al-Aqsa intifada") erupted in the OPT in response to the lack of progress in ending the military occupation through the Israel-Palestine Liberation Organization (PLO) peace process[27]—a process, it is important to note, that has been accompanied by an increase in

---

Must Take the Moral Ground, HA'ARETZ (Tel Aviv), Dec. 11, 2002, at 5.

22. Allegra Pacheco, *Flouting Convention: the Oslo Agreements, in* THE NEW INTIFADA: RESISTING ISRAEL'S APARTHEID 181, 184–85 (Roane Carey ed., 2001).

23. Although Israel has never recognized the *de jure* applicability of the Fourth Geneva Convention to the OPT, it has always claimed to abide by its "humanitarian" provisions *de facto*. This position was first outlined in Yehuda Blum, *The Missing Reversioner: Reflections on the Status of Judea and Samaria*, 3 ISR. L. REV. 279, 293–94 (1968), and Meir Shamgar, *The Observance of International Law in the Administered Territories*, 1 ISR. Y.B. HUM. RTS. 262, 265–66 (1971). For further comment, see *infra* text accompanying notes 248–297.

24. *See, e.g.*, Israel Defense Force Spokesperson's Unit, *Palestinian Lies as an Integral Part of the Struggle against Israel*, http://www.idf.il/english/news/lies.stm.

25. Statement of Nabil Shaath, Minister for Planning and International Cooperation, Palestinian Authority, to the United Nations International Meeting, *supra* note 13, at 9.

26. *See generally* Pacheco, *supra* note 22.

27. *See infra* text accompanying notes 173–190.

gross violations of international humanitarian law in the OPT.[28] Like the previous intifada of 1987 to 1993, the al-Aqsa intifada has highlighted the importance of both reaffirming and reexamining the role international humanitarian law must play in protecting civilian populations living under foreign military occupation.[29]

This Article will examine the state of international humanitarian law in the OPT and provide fresh insight into the role it has in governing relations between Israel and the millions who continue to live subject to its military rule. Specifically, it will argue for the indispensability of the Fourth Geneva Convention and discuss various ways it may be used to protect the interests of all concerned. To that end, the body of the Article will be divided into three parts. Part II will outline the historical development of the conflict in Israel/Palestine in order to provide the reader with a contextual framework within which to approach the subject. Part III will examine the law of belligerent occupation in relation to the OPT, with particular attention devoted to the development and nature of that body of law, the theoretical debate regarding the applicability of the Fourth Geneva Convention to the OPT, and Israel's record of observance of the Fourth Geneva Convention. Finally, Part IV will explore the question of the enforcement of the Fourth Geneva Convention in the OPT, examining the wide array of municipal and international means available, including a brief assessment of the role the Israel-PLO peace accords have in this respect.

II. Historical Background

Although Israel's occupation of the OPT is the result of the June 1967 Arab-Israeli war, a tracing of the historical development of the conflict in Israel/Palestine is imperative to fully appreciate the broader legal and political context which has allowed the occupation to endure.[30] In the pages that follow, an abridged account of that history will be offered, covering the rise of political Zionism in the late nineteenth century to the al-Aqsa intifada. But first, a note on historiography is in order.

Few political conflicts of the twentieth century have engendered more debate among contemporary historians than the conflict over Israel/Palestine. Though scholarship on the question is voluminous, it is as deeply divided as the protagonists themselves. To a certain degree, the traditional historical narratives of each of the parties to the conflict have been designed more to serve political interests than the purpose of authentic scholarly inquiry. While "political invention of history is common to both Israel and the Arab

---

28. Pacheco, *supra* note 22, at 185. *See also* B'TSELEM, OSLO: BEFORE AND AFTER: THE STATUS OF HUMAN RIGHTS IN THE OCCUPIED TERRITORIES (1999) (*prepared by* Naemi Carmi).

29. For a comparison between the Intifada of 1987–1993 and the Intifada that broke out in September 2000, see Ghassan Andoni, *A Comparative Study of Intifada 1987 and Intifada 2000, in* THE NEW INTIFADA, *supra* note 22, at 209.

30. Cassese, *supra* note 11, at 3.

States," this is so "for markedly different reasons."[31] To a large extent, "Arab official histories seek to advance state interests by mobilizing citizens disillusioned by the defeat of national armies and the loss of Arab Palestine, while Israeli official histories seek to reaffirm a sort of Zionist manifest destiny while diminishing responsibility for the negative consequences of the [1948] war."[32]

In the early 1980s, the Israeli side of the historical ledger changed with the opening up of repositories of official governmental papers by the Israel State Archives and Central Zionist Archives.[33] Among the materials were records of events that have long stood at the center of the dispute, namely the 1948 Arab-Israeli war and the creation of the Palestine refugee problem.[34] This primary archival material formed the basis of the scholarship of a cadre of Israeli-Jewish historians that "challenged the traditional [Zionist] historiography of the birth of the State of Israel," which, according to one of them, had hitherto "remained largely unchallenged outside the Arab world."[35] The New Historians—as the group has become known—include Simha Flapan,[36] Benny Morris,[37] Ilan Pappé,[38] Avi Shlaim,[39] and Tom Segev.[40] Their critical scholarship has "exposed as mere myths a large number of long accepted truisms" underlying the traditional Israeli historical narrative.[41] Among these are the assertions that the Palestine refugees had voluntarily left their homes in 1948 on the orders of Arab leaders who promised a return "with the conquering Arab armies,"[42] and "that a defenseless Israel faced destruction by" a numerically and militarily superior "Arab Goliath."[43] Other such myths include claims that in 1967 the Arab states, led by Egyptian President Gamal 'Abd al-Nasser, were bent on waging aggressive war against Israel,[44] and that post-war Israeli policy was

---

31. THE WAR FOR PALESTINE: REWRITING THE HISTORY OF 1948, at 2 (Eugene L. Rogan & Avi Shlaim eds., 2001) [hereinafter THE WAR FOR PALESTINE].

32. *Id.*

33. LAURENCE J. SILBERSTEIN, THE POSTZIONISM DEBATES: KNOWLEDGE AND POWER IN ISRAELI CULTURE 96–102 (1999).

34. *Id.*

35. AVI SHLAIM, THE IRON WALL: ISRAEL AND THE ARAB WORLD, at xi (2000).

36. *See* SIMHA FLAPAN, THE BIRTH OF ISRAEL: MYTHS AND REALITIES (1987).

37. *See* BENNY MORRIS, 1948 AND AFTER: ISRAEL AND THE PALESTINIANS (1994); BENNY MORRIS, THE BIRTH OF THE PALESTINIAN REFUGEE PROBLEM, 1947–1949 (1987) [hereinafter MORRIS, THE BIRTH]; BENNY MORRIS, ISRAEL'S BORDER WARS, 1949–1956: ARAB INFILTRATION, ISRAELI RETALIATION AND THE COUNTDOWN TO THE SUEZ WAR (1993).

38. *See* ILAN PAPPÉ, BRITAIN AND THE ARAB-ISRAELI CONFLICT, 1948–1951 (1988); ILAN PAPPÉ, THE MAKING OF THE ARAB-ISRAELI CONFLICT, 1947–1951 (1992).

39. *See* THE WAR FOR PALESTINE, *supra* note 31; AVI SHLAIM, COLLUSION ACROSS THE JORDAN: KING ABDULLAH, THE ZIONIST MOVEMENT, AND THE PARTITION OF PALESTINE (1988) [hereinafter SHLAIM, COLLUSION ACROSS THE JORDAN]; SHLAIM, *supra* note 35.

40. *See* TOM SEGEV, 1949: THE FIRST ISRAELIS (1986).

41. SILBERSTEIN, *supra* note 33, at 97.

42. *Id.*

43. THE WAR FOR PALESTINE, *supra* note 31, at 3.

44. SHLAIM, *supra* note 35, at 237.

guided by an intention to return the West Bank to Arab hands upon the conclusion of a peace agreement with Jordan.[45]

Although "there is certainly scope for new Arab histories of the Palestine war" as well as other post-1948 developments in the conflict, "Arab intellectuals lack the material for the task."[46] This is largely due to the fact that Egypt, Jordan, Iraq, Syria, and Lebanon have not declassified their governmental archives as Israel has.[47] Although the extent to which any opening up of the official Arab archives will offer a refutation of the findings of Israel's New Historians is uncertain, any such development would be unlikely to offer new insight into the strictly Zionist/Israeli policies documented by the New Historians concerning the issues most central to the conflict (such as Israel's policies regarding the expulsion/flight of the Palestinians or its retention of the OPT).[48] That said, the government of Israel must be given full credit for its commitment to a relatively liberal archival policy.[49] Israel's new historiography has confirmed much, though by no means all, of the Palestinian historical narrative, partially bridging the historical gap between Israeli and Palestinian scholars. Additionally, for one of today's most profound Palestinian historians, Nur Masalha, access to Israel's declassified records has proved invaluable in helping him provide fresh insight into many of the questions a number of his predecessors, most notably Constantine Zurayq[50] and Walid al-Khalidi,[51] grappled with in the 1950s, 1960s, and 1970s.[52] It is for these reasons that no reliable discussion of the history of the Israel/Palestine conflict can now be undertaken without reference to Israel's new historiography, or to other scholarship based on Israel's recently declassified archival materials. To the extent to which it is practical then, this seminal body of work will be used as the basis of the brief historical survey that follows.

---

45. *Id.* at 255.

46. THE WAR FOR PALESTINE, *supra* note 31, at 6.

47. While some scholars have had access to official Arab archival materials, "Arab governments only open their records for research, if they open them at all, in a haphazard and arbitrary manner." *See id.* at 6.

48. *See infra* text accompanying notes 95–105, 141–151.

49. According to Morris, however, "there is still a severe problem of access to documents" in relation to "1967 and its aftermath." Benny Morris, *Looking Back: A Personal Assessment of the Zionist Experience,* TIKKUN, Mar.-Apr. 1998, at 40, 49.

50. *See* CONSTANTINE ZURAYQ, THE MEANING OF THE DISASTER (R. Bayley Winder trans., 1956).

51. *See* WALID AL-KHALIDI, FROM HAVEN TO CONQUEST: READINGS IN ZIONISM AND THE PALESTINE PROBLEM UNTIL 1948 (1971). For more recent work by al-Khalidi, see ALL THAT REMAINS: THE PALESTINIAN VILLAGES OCCUPIED AND DEPOPULATED BY ISRAEL IN 1948 (Walid Khalid ed. 1992) [hereinafter ALL THAT REMAINS], and Walid al-Khalidi, *Plan Dalet: Master Plan for the Conquest of Palestine,* 18 J. PALESTINE STUD. 4 (1988).

52. *See* NUR MASALHA, EXPULSION OF THE PALESTINIANS: THE CONCEPT OF "TRANSFER" IN ZIONIST POLITICAL THOUGHT, 1882–1948 (1992) [hereinafter MASALHA, EXPULSION OF THE PALESTINIANS]; NUR MASALHA, IMPERIAL ISRAEL AND THE PALESTINIANS: THE POLITICS OF EXPANSION (2000) [hereinafter MASALHA, IMPERIAL ISRAEL]; NUR MASALHA, A LAND WITHOUT A PEOPLE: ISRAEL, TRANSFER AND THE PALESTINIANS 1949–1996 (1997).

A. 1882–1948

The conflict over Israel/Palestine finds its origins in the development of political Zionism in late nineteenth-century Europe.[53] In answer to centuries of persecution suffered by Jews "in Western and especially Eastern Europe," political Zionism called for the establishment of "an independent Jewish existence in Palestine, the ancient land of Israel, which the Jews had last governed nineteen hundred years before."[54] Zionism embodied a rejection of assimilation into European society as the solution to the so-called "Jewish Question," and postulated in its place the creation of a modern nation-state in Palestine in which Jewish self-determination could develop and flourish.[55] In contrast to forms of revisionist Zionism that would later develop in Israel in the post-1967 era,[56] early political Zionism was largely secular in outlook,[57] and highly influenced by the dominant socio-political mores of imperial Europe. Accordingly, in the words of Zionism's founding father, Theodor Herzl, the transformation of Palestine into a Jewish State was not only conceived as an emancipatory concept for European Jewry, but was in essence a "colonial idea,"[58] a sort of *mission civilisatrice* that would enable the Jewish people to "form a portion of the rampart of Europe against Asia, an outpost of civilization against barbarism."[59]

Of course, in the late nineteenth century Palestine was inhabited by well over 500,000 indigenous Palestinians,[60] who had themselves been settled in that land for well over two millennia.[61] Of these, over eighty percent were Muslim, approximately ten percent were Christian, and about five to seven percent were Jews.[62] Theirs was a traditional, largely agrarian society that, despite religious difference, "enjoyed much in common linguistically and culturally."[63] Politically, Palestine was administered as a portion of the Ottoman Empire, with local authority "in the hands of notables or chiefs, heads of prominent families who became the tax collectors of their regions."[64] Although the emergence of Arab nationalism would soon give rise to calls for

---

53. Benny Morris, *Revisiting the Palestinian Exodus of 1948*, *in* THE WAR FOR PALESTINE, *supra* note 31, at 37, 39. *See also* CHARLES D. SMITH, PALESTINE AND THE ARAB-ISRAELI CONFLICT 23–24 (4th ed. 2001).

54. SMITH, *supra* note 53, at 33.

55. *See* THEODOR HERZL, THE JEWISH STATE 85–97 (Sylvie d'Avigdor trans., Dover Publ'ns 1998) (1896).

56. *See* SHLAIM, *supra* note 35, at 549. *See also* MASALHA, IMPERIAL ISRAEL, *supra* note 52.

57. *See* SMITH, *supra* note 53, at 25.

58. ABDULLAH SCHLIEFER, THE FALL OF JERUSALEM 23 (1972).

59. HERZL, *supra* note 55, at 96.

60. *See* Janet Abu Lughod, *The Demographic Transformation of Palestine*, *in* THE TRANSFORMATION OF PALESTINE: ESSAYS ON THE ORIGIN AND DEVELOPMENT OF THE ARAB-ISRAELI CONFLICT 140 (Ibrahim Abu Lughod ed., 1987) [hereinafter THE TRANSFORMATION OF PALESTINE].

61. *See* SAMI HADAWI, BITTER HARVEST: A MODERN HISTORY OF PALESTINE 30–31 (1989).

62. *Id.*

63. *Id.*

64. SMITH, *supra* note 53, at 21.

Palestinian Arab independence,[65] the Palestinians in the late nineteenth century lacked the political maturity of their European-Jewish counterparts in the Zionist movement.

For the Zionists, it was the presence of an indigenous Arab people in Palestine that posed their most vexing dilemma—their "demographic problem," as it was termed.[66] As noted by Benny Morris, this dilemma formed the very "root of the Zionist-Arab conflict" itself.[67] How would it be possible to colonize Palestine and transform it into a Jewish state when it was already inhabited by an indigenous Arab people? How would it be possible, in the words of Morris, for "a round peg to fit into a square hole?"[68]

The initial solution put forth by the Zionists was to establish an organized program of mass Jewish immigration and colonization.[69] According to Morris, this was undertaken with the philosophy that "[g]radually the [Jewish] minority would demographically overwhelm the native majority, despite the Arabs' higher birth rates; once the Jews were in a majority, a Jewish state would naturally ensue."[70] In the three and one-half decades between the establishment of the first Zionist colony in Palestine in 1882 and the end of World War I,[71] however, Zionist immigration and colonization continued at a pace insufficient to substantially alter the balance of demography in the country.[72] By 1918 the percentage of Jewish inhabitants, both native and settler, stood at approximately eight percent.[73] The defeat of the Ottoman Empire in World War I, and the subsequent transfer of authority over Palestine to Britain by way of a League of Nations Mandate, held out the possibility that Jewish numbers would still be afforded ample opportunity to increase. In the Balfour Declaration of 1917, Britain committed itself to "the establishment in Palestine of a national home for the Jewish people."[74] At that time, the Palestine Arabs numbered some ninety-two per-

---

65. *See* Richard P. Stevens, *Zionism as a Phase of Western Imperialism*, *in* THE TRANSFORMATION OF PALESTINE, *supra* note 60, at 57–58.

66. Morris, *supra* note 53, at 40.

67. *Id.* at 39.

68. *Id.*

69. *Id.*

70. *Id.*

71. The colony was named Rishon Letzion, Hebrew for "First in Zion." *See* GERSHON SHAFIR, LAND, LABOUR, AND THE ORIGINS OF THE ISRAELI-PALESTINIAN CONFLICT, 1882–1914, at 51 (1989).

72. Morris, *supra* note 53, at 39–40.

73. *See* HADAWI, *supra* note 61, at 48–49.

74. The Balfour Declaration was issued on November 2, 1917, by Lord Arthur Balfour, British Foreign Secretary, to Lord Rothschild on behalf of the World Zionist Organization. The full text of the declaration reads as follows:

His Majesty's Government view with favour the establishment in Palestine of a national home for the Jewish people and will use their best endeavours to facilitate the achievement of this object, it being clearly understood that nothing shall be done which may prejudice the civil and religious rights of existing non-Jewish communities in Palestine or the rights and political status enjoyed by Jews in any other country.

The Balfour Declaration was incorporated into the terms of the Palestine mandate in 1922. W. THOMAS MALLISON & SALLY V. MALLISON, THE PALESTINE PROBLEM IN INTERNATIONAL LAW AND WORLD ORDER 47 (1986).

cent of the population[75] and had developed an indigenous national movement calling for the establishment of a government deriving its authority
from the will of the people.[76] For them, the Balfour Declaration represented
a violation of the "sacred trust of civilization" contained in article 22(1) of
the League of Nations Covenant,[77] under which Britain was legally obliged
as the mandatory power to secure the "well-being and development" of the
people of Palestine whose political independence had been "provisionally
recognized" under article 22(4) of the Covenant.[78] The British paid no heed
to this objection, and Jewish immigration and colonization was allowed to
continue in varying degrees throughout the period of the mandate, which
ran from 1922 to 1948.[79]

As the Yishuv, or pre-state Zionist community in Palestine, grew during
the mandate, clashes with the Arab population became increasingly common. "From the Zionist perspective," Arab objection to their program was
to be expected and was largely considered "a problem for the British."[80]
"From the Arab perspective, the expansion of the Yishuv posed a recognized
threat that they should try to resist" if "the progressive loss" of their country
was to be forestalled.[81] Nationwide Palestinian riots in 1920, 1921, and
1929 had little relative effect on continued Zionist immigration,[82] and a
full-scale rebellion between 1936 and 1939 was brutally put down by the
British.[83] Growing in size though the Yishuv was, "[b]y the 1930s many of
the Zionist leaders understood that the pace of Jewish immigration was insufficient to lead within the foreseeable future to a Jewish majority."[84] "By

---

75. SAMI HADAWI, PALESTINIAN RIGHTS AND LOSSES IN 1948: A COMPREHENSIVE STUDY 15–16
(1988).

76. *See* David Waines, *The Failure of the Nationalist Resistance, in* THE TRANSFORMATION OF PALES-
TINE, *supra* note 60, at 217–24. *See also* JOHN QUIGLEY, PALESTINE AND ISRAEL: A CHALLENGE TO
JUSTICE 18 (1990).

77. MALLISON & MALLISON, *supra* note 74, at 63.

78. *Id.* at 64. There is a fairly detailed literature dealing both with the legality and morality of the
Balfour Declaration and British Mandate that falls outside of the scope of the present study. For those
interested in examining the topic at further length see MALLISON & MALLISON, *supra* note 74, at 18–78;
and LEONARD STEIN, THE BALFOUR DECLARATION (1961).

79. The extent of British indifference to Palestinian concerns was attested to by Lord Arthur Balfour
himself in a memorandum to the British government dated August 11, 1919. In discussing the conflict
between the "Jewish national home" policy of the Balfour Declaration and the "sacred trust of civilization" embedded in the League of Nations Covenant, the British Foreign Secretary stated:

> The contradiction between the letter of the [League of Nations] Covenant and the policy of the Al-
> lies is even more flagrant in the case of the "independent nation" of Palestine than in that of the
> "independent nation" of Syria. For in Palestine we do not propose even to go through the form of
> consulting the wishes of the present inhabitants of the country . . . . The four Great Powers are
> committed to Zionism. And Zionism, be it right or wrong, good or bad, is rooted in age-long tradi-
> tions, in present needs, in future hopes, of far profounder import than the desires and prejudices of
> the 700,000 Arabs who now inhabit that ancient land.

MALLISON & MALLISON, *supra* note 74, at 77–78.

80. SMITH, *supra* note 53, at 121.

81. *Id.* at 123.

82. *Id.* at 124–28. '

83. *Id.* at 134–44.

84. Morris, *supra* note 53, at 40.

the end of 1936, Jews constituted" a mere "28 percent of the total population."[85] Accordingly, a second solution to their 'demographic' problem had
to be devised.

As documented by Nur Masalha and a number of Israel's New Historians,
the solution developed by the Zionists was the concept of "transfer"—"a
euphemism denoting the organized removal of the indigenous population of
Palestine to neighboring countries."[86] Although traditional Zionist historiography denies the existence of any such phenomenon,[87] Israel's declassified
archives have proved that throughout the 1930s and 1940s, "consensus or
near-consensus in support of transfer" had emerged at the highest levels of
the Yishuv leadership.[88] According to Benny Morris:

> The last and, let me say obvious and most logical, solution to the Zion-
> ists' demographic problem lay the way of transfer: you could create a
> homogenous Jewish state or at least a state with an overwhelming Jew-
> ish majority by moving or transferring all or most of the Arabs out of
> its prospective territory. And this, in fact, is what happened in 1948.[89]

By the late 1940s, tensions between the Jewish and Arab communities in
Palestine had so escalated that Britain, still recovering from World War II,
decided to end its mandate and hand the problem over to the United Nations. With the Nazi holocaust of European Jewry still fresh in the minds of
the international community, the U.N. General Assembly voted to partition
Palestine into a Jewish State and an Arab State by way of Resolution 181 on
November 29, 1947.[90] The Palestinians viewed partition as an attempt to
solve Europe's Jewish Question at their expense, and was therefore rejected
out of hand.[91] The Zionists, on the other hand, widely accepted partition as

---

85. Abu Lughod, supra note 60, at 151.
86. MASALHA, EXPULSION OF THE PALESTINIANS, supra note 52, at 1.
87. Shabtai Teveth, Charging Israel with Original Sin, COMMENTARY, Sept. 1989, at 24, 24.
88. Morris, supra note 53, at 44. As pointed out by Morris, this consensus included eminent figures
such as David Ben Gurion, who "had come out strongly in favor of transfer," id. at 43; Menahem Ussish-
kin, who found "nothing immoral about transferring 60,000 Arab families," id. at 44; and Moshe Shertok (Sharett), who considered transfer to "be the archstone, the final stage in the political development"
of the Jewish state, id. at 46. Further, Nur Masalha observes:

> It should not be imagined that the concept of transfer was held only by maximalists or extremists
> within the Zionist movement. On the contrary, it was embraced by almost all shades of opinion,
> from the Revisionist right to the Labour left. Virtually every member of the Zionist pantheon of
> founding fathers and important leaders supported it and advocated it in one form or another, from
> Chaim Weizmann and Vladimir Jabotinsky to David Ben-Gurion and Menahem Ussishkin. Sup-
> porters of transfer included such moderates as the "Arab appeaser" Moshe Shertok and the socialist
> Arthur Ruppin, founder of Brit Shalom, a movement advocating equal rights for Arabs and Jews.
> More importantly, transfer proposals were put forward by the Jewish Agency itself, in effect the
> government of the Yishuv.

MASALHA, THE EXPULSION OF THE PALESTINIANS, supra note 52, at 2.
89. Morris, supra note 53, at 40.
90. G.A. Res. 181, U.N. Doc. A/310 (1947). For a thorough discussion of the legality of the partition
resolution, see MALLISON & MALLISON, supra note 74, at 166–73.
91. For the Palestinian position on partition, see HENRY CATTAN, PALESTINE AND INTERNATIONAL

the culmination of over five decades of significant colonizing effort.[92] Yet, it brought their demographic problem into sharp relief. For the population of their prospective state under the U.N. partition was roughly fifty-five percent Jewish to forty-five percent Arab, thereby rendering the formation of an exclusively Jewish state impossible without the massive ethnic cleansing of the native Arabs.[93]

The war that followed partition lasted from December 1947 to July 1949, and involved both local and inter-state conflict.[94] The first six months of fighting was completely local in nature, fought between the Yishuv and the indigenous Arabs and resulting in the forced expulsion and flight of over 300,000 Palestinians from within the borders of the proposed Jewish State.[95] The remainder of the war was fought on an inter-state basis following the Arab states' invasion of Israel on May 15, 1948, with the latter expanding its borders to control some seventy-eight percent of mandatory Palestine by war's end.[96] During this phase of the war, an additional 400,000 Palestinians fled or were forcibly expelled, thereby bringing the total number of Palestinian refugees in the 1948 war to approximately 700,000.[97] In response to this humanitarian catastrophe, the U.N. General Assembly passed Resolution 194 of December 11, 1948 calling on Israel to repatriate the refugees "at the earliest practicable date."[98] Repatriation was barred, however, by a special war-time decision of the Israeli Cabinet in June 1948,[99] and by the Zionists' deliberate destruction of between 369 and 418 of the villages whence the refugees were expelled or had fled.[100] Today, the Palestinian refugees, including their descendants, number between 3.9 and 5 million persons,[101] and continue to remain in forced exile predominately, but not exclusively, in the OPT, Lebanon, Syria, Jordan, and Egypt. It is

---

LAW: THE LEGAL ASPECTS OF THE ARAB-ISRAELI CONFLICT (1973).

92. There was a significant portion of the Yishuv that objected to the partition on the ground that the whole of Palestine should have been allotted to the Jewish State. *See generally* FLAPAN, *supra* note 36, at 15–53.

93. Morris, *supra* note 53, at 40.

94. *See generally* MORRIS, THE BIRTH, *supra* note 37.

95. SMITH, *supra* note 53, at 199.

96. HADAWI, *supra* note 75, at 81.

97. Morris, *supra* note 53, at 37. It is important to note that actual number of Palestinian refugees from the 1948 war is disputed to this day. Arab officials have traditionally estimated it to be as high as 900,000, while Israeli officials have usually cited 520,000. In 1949, the United Nations Relief and Works Agency for Palestine Refugees in the Near East (UNRWA) recorded numbers as high as 960,000. *See* LEX TAKKENBERG, THE STATUS OF PALESTINIAN REFUGEES IN INTERNATIONAL LAW 18–19 (1998).

98. G.A. Res. 194, ¶ 11, U.N. Doc. A/810 (1948).

99. Morris, *supra* note 53, at 38.

100. The figure of 369 is given in MORRIS, THE BIRTH, *supra* note 37, at xiv–xviii. The figure of 418 is offered by Khalidi in ALL THAT REMAINS, *supra* note 51, at 585.

101. UNRWA reports that, as of June 30, 2002, there are 3,973,360 registered Palestine refugees. UNRWA Public Information Office, *UNRWA in Figures—30 June 2002*, http://www.un.org/unrwa/pr/pdf/uif-june02.pdf. Salman Abu Sitta, a Palestinian academic, asserts that the number of Palestinian refugees (defined more broadly than UNRWA's categorization) is approximately 5 million. Salman Abu Sitta, *The Implementation of the Right of Return*, *in* THE NEW INTIFADA, *supra* note 22, at 299, 303.

their plight that forms the central question in the conflict over Is-
rael/Palestine.

There are still considerable differences of opinion regarding the extent to
which the expulsion and flight of the Palestinians in 1948 was preordained
or merely a product of military exigency. Masalha, for instance, asserts that
the expulsion and flight was long-planned by the Zionists, and for proof
points to the seriousness with which the Yishuv leadership studied the policy of transfer in the decades prior to 1948 as well as the existence and implementation in 1948 of military plans "anchored in the . . . concept of
transfer."[102] On the other hand, Morris asserts that despite the prevalence of
transfer in pre-state Zionist political thought and the execution of military
plans that necessitated forced expulsion, it was, to be sure, "born of war, not
by design, Jewish or Arab."[103] Thus, it is no longer disputed that the refugees were expelled and/or forced to flee during the 1948 war. The only matter now in dispute concerns the animus behind the expulsion/exodus. In the
words of Morris, "above all . . . the refugee problem was caused by attacks
by Jewish forces on Arab villages and towns and by the inhabitants' fear of
such attacks, compounded by expulsions, atrocities, and rumors of atrocities."[104] Again, this stands in sharp contrast to the traditional Zionist assertion that the Palestinians left their homes on the orders of their own leaders,
who promised a safe return once the Jewish state was destroyed.[105]

B. 1949–1966

Following the 1948 war, the remaining twenty-two percent of Palestine
territory that had not been conquered by Israel—the West Bank, including
East Jerusalem, and the Gaza Strip—was effectively taken over by Jordan
and Egypt, respectively. Jordan's King Abdullah had long coveted the
Haram al-Sharif compound in East Jerusalem enclosing the Dome of the
Rock and the al-Aqsa Mosque, Islam's third holiest shrine.[106] As noted by

---

102. MASALHA, THE EXPULSION OF THE PALESTINIANS, *supra* note 52, at 178. The principal military
plan in question was officially known as *Tochnit Dalet*, or "Plan D." According to Shlaim,

[t]he aim of Plan D was to secure all the areas allocated to the Jewish state under the U.N. partition
resolution as well as Jewish settlements outside these areas and corridors leading to them, so as to
provide a solid and continuous basis for Jewish sovereignty. The novelty and audacity of the plan lay
in the orders to capture Arab villages and cities, something the Haganah [Israeli armed forces] had
never attempted before. Although the wording of Plan D was vague, its objective was to clear the
interior of hostile and potentially hostile Arab elements, and in this sense it provided a warrant for
expelling civilians. By implementing Plan D in April and May [1948], the Haganah thus directly
and decisively contributed to the birth of the Palestinian refugee problem.

SHLAIM, *supra* note 35, at 31.

103. MORRIS, THE BIRTH, *supra* note 37, at 286.

104. Morris, *supra* note 53, at 38.

105. SILBERSTEIN, *supra* note 33, at 100. It is important to note that, from a legal standpoint, the
animus behind the expulsion of the Palestinians in 1948 bears no relevance to the fact that under international refugee, humanitarian, and human rights law, the refugees enjoy the right to return to their
homes.

106. *See generally* SHLAIM, COLLUSION ACROSS THE JORDAN, *supra* note 39.

Avi Shlaim, "[h]aving gained military control over the West Bank, Abdullah set in motion a process of creeping annexation that culminated in the Act of Union in April 1950," whereby the West Bank was officially annexed to Jordan.[107] Although the Act of Union contained a clause stating that it was without prejudice to "the final settlement of Palestine's just cause,"[108] Jordan's annexation was "unanimously denounced" by the Arab League as being contrary to its policy regarding Palestine, adopted on April 12, 1948, which stated that:

> The Arab armies shall enter Palestine to rescue it. His Majesty [King Farouk, representing the League] would like to make it clearly understood that such measures should be looked upon as temporary and devoid of any character of the occupation or partition of Palestine, and that after completion of its liberation, that country would be handed over to its owners to rule in the way they like.[109]

With the exception of Britain and Pakistan, the Jordanian annexation was not recognized by any member of the international community.[110] With respect to the Gaza Strip, Egypt harbored neither political designs nor the inclination to annex; it administered the Gaza Strip in accordance with Arab League policy until 1967.[111]

During this period, Israel faced a steady flow of Palestinian refugees attempting to return to their homes and, to a lesser extent, lightly armed irregular bands intent on doing so through force of arms.[112] In order to consolidate both its internal and external security, Israel maintained its wartime state of emergency, declared on May 19, 1948 under the Defence (Emergency) Regulations (1945)—an amended version of the regulations used by the British to quell the Palestinian rebellion of 1936–1939.[113] In addition to allowing its armed forces wide latitude in dealing with cross-border Palestinian "infiltrators,"[114] these regulations allowed for the imposition of a system of military rule aimed at "the fragmentation and division of the [Palestinian] Arab population" that had remained inside what became the state of Israel following the 1948 war.[115] Under this regime, local Israeli military commanders were empowered to "exercise legislative, judicial and executive powers over extensive spheres of life" of the roughly 170,000 Palestinian

---

107. SHLAIM, *supra* note 35, at 43.

108. Territory and Sovereignty of States, 2 WHITEMAN DIGEST § 8, at 1166, *quoted in* Allan Gerson, *Trustee-Occupant: The Legal Status of Israel's Presence in the West Bank*, 14 HARV. INT'L L.J. 1, 38 (1973).

109. *Id.*

110. Gerson, *supra* note 108, at 38.

111. Emma Playfair, *Introduction* to INTERNATIONAL LAW AND ADMINISTRATION, *supra* note 11, at 4.

112. SHLAIM, *supra* note 35, at 82.

113. *See* URI DAVIS, ISRAEL: AN APARTHEID STATE 72 n.1 (1987).

114. According to Shlaim, "[a]ltogether between 2,700 and 5,000 infiltrators were killed in the period 1949–1956, the great majority of them unarmed." SHLAIM, *supra* note 35, at 82.

115. MENACHEM HOFNUNG, DEMOCRACY, LAW AND NATIONAL SECURITY IN ISRAEL 95 (1996).

citizens of Israel, including the demolition of homes, imposition of curfews, collective punishment, deportation, and arbitrary arrest, search, and detention.[116] This military regime, which did not apply to Jewish citizens of the state, remained in place until 1966. By this time, relations between Israel and its Arab neighbors had deteriorated even further, due in no small part to the increasing influence of Cold War politics,[117] and a second regional war in 1956.[118]

During this period, the Palestine Liberation Organization (PLO) emerged as the political representative of the Palestinian people.[119] Established on June 1, 1964, it was charged with leading the "struggle to liberate their land and return to it to practice their right to self-determination."[120] In order to accomplish this, "an elaborate bureaucratic structure" was developed to administer the regional and international affairs of the Palestinian people and to provide them with "a variety of social services . . . in [the] diaspora."[121] Inspired by the "success of the Algerian revolt against the French,"[122] as well as by the general momentum of the decolonization period of the 1960s, the PLO adopted a policy of armed struggle as a means of liberating Palestine.[123] As will be seen below, although the political contours of the Palestinian homeland have varied over time—from the whole of mandatory Palestine at the time of the PLO's founding, to merely the OPT in the late 1980s—the "overriding goal" of the PLO has remained "securing for the Palestinian people the opportunity to return to their homeland under circumstances that will enable them to exercise self-determination."[124]

C. 1967–1992

The Six-Day War of 1967 witnessed the most wide-ranging political transformation in the Middle East since 1948. In this third Arab-Israeli war, Israel conquered the West Bank and East Jerusalem from Jordan, the Gaza Strip and Sinai peninsula from Egypt, and the Golan Heights from Syria, in blitzkrieg fashion between June 5 and 10, 1967.[125] There has traditionally been great controversy over who was to blame for the war; more specifically, whether Israel's launching of the war "with a surprise air strike on enemy

---

116. *Id.* at 50. *See also* QUIGLEY, *supra* note 76, at 102–04.

117. *See* SMITH, *supra* note 53, at 278–81.

118. SHLAIM, *supra* note 35, at 178–85.

119. *See id.* at 187.

120. Omar M. Dajani, *Stalled Between Seasons: The International Legal Status of Palestine During the Interim Period*, 26 DENV. J. INT'L L. & POL'Y 27, 50 (1997) (paraphrasing THE PALESTINIAN NATIONAL CHARTER, art. 26, *in* BASIC POLITICAL DOCUMENTS OF THE ARMED PALESTINIAN RESISTANCE MOVEMENT (Leila S. Kadi trans., 1969)).

121. Dajani, *supra* note 120.

122. SMITH, *supra* note 53, at 273.

123. YEZID SAYIGH, ARMED STRUGGLE AND THE SEARCH FOR STATE: THE PALESTINIAN NATIONAL MOVEMENT: 1949–1993, at 100–06 (1997).

124. Dajani, *supra* note 120, at 50.

125. *See* SHLAIM, *supra* note 35, at 241–50.

airfields" constituted aggression or a legitimate exercise of self-defense under article 51 of the Charter of the United Nations.[126] Article 51 allows a state to use a proportionate measure of force in self-defense if it is the object of an "armed attack."[127] Where there is no armed attack, as was the case in the Six-Day War, "it is not clear" whether "a preemptive strike is lawful."[128] While "most authorities agree" that "preemptive self-defense is not permitted under international law,"[129] some say it may be allowed in cases where "the imminence of an attack is so clear and the danger so great that defensive action is essential for self-preservation."[130] Adopting this reasoning, traditional Israeli historiography asserts that the aerial bombardment of Egypt on June 5, 1967, was a legitimate act of preemptive self-defense in response to an imminent Egyptian attack.[131] Proponents of this theory point to, inter alia, Egypt's closure of the straits of Tiran to Israeli shipping, its positioning of troops in the Sinai desert, and various verbal threats issued by President Gamal 'Abd al-Nasser.[132] Traditional Arab historiography, on the other hand, asserts that Israel's preemptive strike was unlawful and constituted an act of armed aggression deliberately embarked upon "in order to fulfill its long-standing territorial ambitions."[133] Proponents of this theory invoke, inter alia, Israel's pre-attack troop build-up and talk of overthrowing the Syrian government,[134] as well as its ex post facto admission on the third day of hostilities that it authored the initial strike notwithstanding its report to the U.N. Security Council on the first two days of hostilities that the launching of its attack was in response to an Egyptian first strike.[135]

As is the case with the Palestine refugee question, Israel's new historiography has helped bridge the gap between these two divergent historical narratives. According to Avi Shlaim, "the June 1967 war was the only one that neither side wanted."[136] The archival materials illustrate that "[t]he war resulted from a crisis slide that neither Israel nor her enemies were able to control."[137] To be sure, Shlaim notes that Egypt's "Nasser neither wanted nor planned to go to war with Israel,"[138] as evidenced by former Israeli Prime Minister and elder statesman David Ben Gurion's admission that "I very much doubt whether Nasser wanted to go to war, and now we are in serious

---

126. *Id.* at 241. *See* U.N. CHARTER art. 51. *See also* QUIGLEY, *supra* note 76, at 163–64.

127. U.N. CHARTER art. 51.

128. QUIGLEY, *supra* note 76, at 165.

129. *Id.*

130. Oscar Schachter, *The Right of States to Use Armed Force,* 82 MICH. L. REV. 1620, 1634 (1984), *quoted in* LORI F. DAMROSCH ET AL., INTERNATIONAL LAW: CASES AND MATERIALS 969 (4th ed. 2001).

131. *See, e.g.,* JULIUS STONE, ISRAEL AND PALESTINE: ASSAULT ON THE LAW OF NATIONS 46 (1981).

132. QUIGLEY, *supra* note 76, at 164.

133. SHLAIM, *supra* note 35, at 241–42.

134. *Id.* at 236–39. *See also* QUIGLEY, *supra* note 69, at 158.

135. *See* QUIGLEY, *supra* note 76, at 163.

136. SHLAIM, *supra* note 35, at 236.

137. *Id.*

138. *Id.* at 237.

trouble."[139] This was consistent with statements of other leading Israelis, including Yitzhak Rabin, then an Israeli General and Chief of Staff in charge of reporting on Egyptian military capabilities to the Israeli cabinet, who admitted that "I do not believe that Nasser wanted war. The two divisions he sent into the Sinai on May 14 would not have been enough to unleash an offensive against Israel. He knew it and we knew it."[140] While Shlaim's work does not fully reconcile the Israeli and Arab narratives, it elucidates the subjective intentions of the parties on the eve of the war. As will be seen in the coming section, these intentions have figured prominently in Israeli arguments regarding the applicability of the Fourth Geneva Convention to the OPT.

As a result of Israel's capture of the West Bank, East Jerusalem, and the Gaza Strip, the Jewish state had established full control over the whole of what was once mandatory Palestine. Military success, however, was accompanied by a serious dilemma for Israel: the 'demographic' problem that was thought laid to rest in 1948 suddenly resurfaced.[141] In addition to the approximately 440,000 Palestinian refugees that had been created by the war,[142] roughly 1.3 million Palestinians remained in the OPT.[143] As noted by Shlaim, while the Israeli government was intent on holding on to the conquered territory, it "was reluctant to incorporate a substantial Palestinian population into the Jewish state . . . . The problem was how to keep the West Bank without turning Israel into a binational state."[144] Ultimately, the answer lay in imposing military rule over the OPT and its Palestinian Arab inhabitants.

With the exception of a unilaterally expanded East Jerusalem illegally annexed, Israel extended its Defence (Emergency) Regulations (1945) to the West Bank and Gaza Strip, thereby imposing martial law on the Palestinian inhabitants of the OPT.[145] On November 22, 1967, the U.N. Security Council passed Resolution 242 reaffirming "the inadmissibility of the acquisition of territory by war," and calling upon Israel to withdraw its "armed forces from territories occupied in the recent conflict."[146] With respect to East Jerusalem, the Security Council asserted in Resolution 252 on May 21, 1968 that "all legislative and administrative measures and actions taken by Israel . . . which tend to change the legal status of Jerusalem are invalid and cannot change that status."[147]

---

139. *Id.* at 239.
140. QUIGLEY, *supra* note 76, at 164.
141. *See* MASALHA, IMPERIAL ISRAEL, *supra* note 52, at 22.
142. This number includes approximately 200,000 second-time refugees from the 1948 war. *See* TAK-ENBERG, *supra* note 97, at 17.
143. MASALHA, IMPERIAL ISRAEL, *supra* note 52, at 22.
144. SHLAIM, *supra* note 35, at 255.
145. Playfair, *supra* note 111, at 8.
146. S.C. Res. 242, U.N. SCOR, 22d Sess., 1382d mtg., U.N. Doc. S/INF (1967).
147. S.C. Res. 252, U.N. SCOR, 23d Sess., 1421st mtg., U.N. Doc. S/8590 (1968).

For its part, Israel set out to fortify its control over the OPT through the promulgation of hundreds of military orders—"occupiers laws," as one authority has put it [148]—effectively vesting in the Israeli military governor absolute power to legislate in the OPT. "Until 1982, this significant body of law" was unpublished and therefore "remained unavailable both to the general public and to practicing lawyers."[149] Among other things, these military orders have enabled the Israeli military authorities to expropriate Palestinian land, and construct exclusively Jewish colonies (settlements) on that land; demolish Palestinian homes; deport Palestinians; arrest, search, and detain Palestinians for indefinite periods without warrant, charge, or trial; mistreat—including torture—Palestinian political detainees; usurp Palestinian natural resources; and impose curfews and other forms of collective punishment on hundreds of thousands of Palestinians at a time.[150] Although more will be said about Israel's record in the OPT in the coming section, suffice it to say that much of it has contravened the law of belligerent occupation in general, and the provisions of the Fourth Geneva Convention in particular.[151]

It was Israel's sustained record of abuse and denial of Palestinian collective and human rights—most notably the right to self-determination—that led to the intifada of 1987–1993, a spontaneous grassroots uprising in which "tens of thousands of ordinary civilians, including women and children," daily demonstrated against the military occupation and its excesses.[152] Characterized by "popular street demonstrations and commercial strikes," the weapons of choice in this popular revolt were stones and molotov cocktails, and the target was the then 20 year-old military occupation and its matrix of colonial domination in the OPT.[153] Not since the rebellion of 1936–1939 had the Palestinian people expressed such an overwhelming collective desire for freedom from foreign rule. As noted by Avi Shlaim, "[t]he standard of revolt against Israeli rule had been raised" with the intifada, and the rallying cry "was self-determination and the establishment of an independent Palestinian state" in the OPT.[154]

---

148. *See* RAJA SHEHADEH, OCCUPIER'S LAW: ISRAEL AND THE WEST BANK (1988).

149. Raja Shehadeh, *The Legislative Stages of the Israeli Military Occupation, in* INTERNATIONAL LAW AND ADMINISTRATION, *supra* note 11, at 151.

150. *See* Richard A. Falk & Burns H. Weston, *The Relevance of International Law to Israeli and Palestinian Rights in the West Bank and Gaza, in* INTERNATIONAL LAW AND ADMINISTRATION, *supra* note 11, at 125.

151. *Id.* at 127–29.

152. SHLAIM, *supra* note 35, at 451. For one of the most authoritative political and historical accounts of the intifada 1987–1993, see F. ROBERT HUNTER, THE PALESTINIAN UPRISING: A WAR BY OTHER MEANS (1991). *See also* GEOFFREY ARONSON, ISRAEL, PALESTINIANS AND THE INTIFADA: CREATING FACTS ON THE WEST BANK (1987); DON PERETZ, INTIFADA: THE PALESTINIAN UPRISING (1990); ZE'EV SCHIFF & EHUD YA'ARI, INTIFADA (Ina Friedman ed. & trans., 1990).

153. SHLAIM, *supra* note 35, at 451–54.

154. *Id.* at 451.

The brutality of Israel's response to the intifada—embodied in its "Iron Fist" policy of "might, force and beatings" to quell the unrest[155]—made it the object of intense domestic and international criticism.[156] This criticism, in turn, contributed to a fundamental Israeli rethinking of its position vis-à-vis the OPT.[157] In July 1988, eight months into the uprising, King Hussein "announced that Jordan was cutting its legal and administrative ties with the West Bank," thereby rescinding the 1950 Act of Union.[158] This disengagement strengthened the political position of the PLO in the OPT,[159] and forced Israel to confront the reality of the PLO as the sole legitimate representative of the Palestinian people—long the ultimate taboo for the Jewish state, given its policy "to never recognize the PLO, enter into any negotiations with the PLO, or agree to the establishment of a Palestinian state."[160] For its part, the PLO used the intifada "to bolster the international legitimacy of the Palestinian national liberation movement,"[161] and to moderate its political program to suit the goals of the uprising.[162] When, in November 1988, the Palestine National Council[163] issued the largely symbolic Palestinian Declaration of Independence proclaiming "the establishment of the State of Palestine on our Palestinian territory with its capital Holy Jerusalem,"[164] it did so with express reference to U.N. partition Resolution 181 and *only* with respect to the pre-1967 "territorial boundaries of the West Bank (including East Jerusalem) and the Gaza Strip."[165] This ultimately created the possibility of a negotiated settlement based on the principle of a two-state solution as outlined in U.N. Security Council Resolution 242, the principle which eventually formed the basis of peace negotiations between Israel and the PLO.

D. 1993–2002

The Israel-PLO peace process—also known as the Oslo peace process[166]— was inaugurated on September 13, 1993 with the signing of the Declaration of Principles on Interim Self-Government Arrangements (DOP).[167] The

---

155. *See id.*

156. Falk & Weston, *supra* note 150, at 126–27.

157. *See* SHLAIM, *supra* note 35, at 453–54.

158. *Id.* at 457.

159. *Id.* at 459.

160. *Id.* at 330.

161. Dajani, *supra* note 120, at 59.

162. *See* SHLAIM, *supra* note 35, at 465–66.

163. The Palestinian parliament-in-exile.

164. *Palestinian Declaration of Independence*, ¶ 10, U.N. GAOR, 43d Sess., Annex 3, Agenda Item 37, U.N. Doc. A/43/827 (1988), *quoted in* Dajani, *supra* note 120, at 57.

165. *Id.* at 58.

166. The process was so named in reference to the city in which the parties met secretly to frame the terms of the first of their accords. *See* GEOFFREY WATSON, THE OSLO ACCORDS: INTERNATIONAL LAW AND THE ISRAELI-PALESTINIAN PEACE AGREEMENTS 41 (2000).

167. DECLARATION OF PRINCIPLES ON INTERIM SELF-GOVERNMENT ARRANGEMENTS, Isr.-P.L.O., Sept. 13, 1993, 32 I.L.M. 1525 [hereinafter DOP].

foundation for the Oslo process was an exchange of letters in which the PLO recognized "the right of the State of Israel to exist in peace and security," and Israel recognized "the PLO as the representative of the Palestinian people."[168] Under the DOP, Israel and the PLO undertook to conclude a number of interim agreements leading to a final settlement of their conflict based on the "land-for-peace" formula outlined in U.N. Security Council Resolutions 242 and 338.[169] The interim phase was to last no longer than five years, and was intended to lead the parties into direct negotiations on the "permanent status" of the OPT, to commence "no later than the beginning of the third year of the interim period."[170] Although the parties have concluded a number of interim agreements,[171] "the peace process has repeatedly broken down" and permanent status negotiations—delayed for nearly four years—have failed to produce any major breakthroughs.[172]

In the meantime, the interim period (1994–1999) was characterized by a continuation of gross human rights violations by Israel in the OPT,[173] including, but not limited to, extra-judicial killing,[174] administrative detention and torture,[175] expansion of Jewish colonial settlements,[176] and demolition of Palestinian homes.[177] All of this was exacerbated by the imposition in March 1993 of a prolonged Israeli military blockade (commonly referred to as "closure") of Palestinian areas following a series of bomb attacks in Israel.[178] This blockade—prohibited under international humanitarian law as

---

168. Watson, *supra* note 166, at 315–16.

169. In addition to emphasizing "the inadmissibility of the acquisition of territory by war" and calling upon Israel to withdraw its armed forces "from territories occupied" in the 1967 war, U.N. Security Council Resolution 242 affirmed that "the establishment of a just and lasting peace in the Middle East" required "[t]ermination of all claims or states of belligerency and respect for and acknowledgement of the sovereignty, territorial integrity and political independence of every State in the area and their right to live in peace within secure and recognized boundaries free from threats or acts of force." S.C. Res. 242, U.N. SCOR, 22d Sess., 132d Mtg., U.N. Doc. S/INF.Rev.2 (1967). U.N. Security Council Resolution 338 was adopted during the October 1973 Arab-Israeli war and called upon all parties to implement "Security Council Resolution 242 (1967) in all its parts." S.C. Res. 338, U.N. SCOR, 28th Sess., U.N. Doc. S/11036 (1973).

170. DOP, *supra* note 167, art. V, ¶ 2.

171. To date, the following interim agreements have been concluded: Protocol on Economic Relations, forming annex IV of the Gaza-Jericho Agreement, Isr.-P.L.O., Apr. 29, 1994, 33 I.L.M. 696; Agreement on the Gaza Strip and the Jericho Area, Isr.-P.L.O., May 4, 1994, 33 I.L.M. 622; Agreement on Prepatory Powers and Responsibilities, Isr.-P.L.O., Aug. 29, 1994, 34 I.L.M. 455; Interim Agreement on the West Bank and Gaza Strip, Isr.-P.L.O., Sept. 28, 1995, 36 I.L.M. 551; Agreement on the Temporary International Presence in the City of Hebron, Isr.-P.L.O., Jan. 21, 1997, 36 I.L.M. 547; Protocol Concerning the Redeployment in Hebron and Note for the Record, Isr.-P.L.O., Jan. 17, 1997, 36 I.L.M. 650; Wye River Memorandum, Isr.-P.L.O., Oct. 23, 1998, 37 I.L.M. 1251; Sharm El-Sheikh Memorandum, Isr.-P.L.O., Sept. 4, 1999, 38 I.L.M. 1465.

172. Watson, *supra* note 166, at 310.

173. *See* B'Tselem, *supra* note 28, at 2.

174. *Id.* at 7–8.

175. *Id.* at 13–15.

176. *Id.* at 4–5. *See also* Pacheco, *supra* note 22, at 191.

177. *See* B'Tselem, *supra* note 28, at 8–11.

178. *See* Sara Roy, *Decline and Disfigurement: The Palestinian Economy After Oslo, in* The New Intifada, *supra* note 22, at 91, 98.

a form of collective punishment[179]—had a devastating economic impact on the OPT.[180] Palestinian unemployment reached seventy percent in the Gaza Strip and fifty percent in the West Bank,[181] gross domestic product in the OPT declined by 18.4% between 1992 and 1996,[182] and the Palestinian economy suffered a total loss of $2.8 billion between 1993 and 1996.[183] Combined with the lack of progress in ending the occupation through the repeatedly stalled peace negotiations, this "steady impoverishment" of the Palestinians led to the outbreak of the al-Aqsa intifada in September 2000 which continues as of the time of writing.[184]

Although there are many similarities between the al-Aqsa intifada and the intifada of 1987–1993, two principal differences are manifestly apparent. First, from a conceptual standpoint, whereas the earlier intifada was directed solely at resisting and finally ending the Israeli military occupation, the al-Aqsa intifada seems additionally directed toward protesting the current Palestinian leadership—widely perceived as corrupt and incompetent for having engaged in a political process that has allowed Israel to consolidate its hold over the OPT, while continuing to infringe on inalienable Palestinian rights, most notably the right of the 1948 refugees to return to their homes and the right of the Palestinian people to self-determination.[185] Second, relative to its predecessor, the al-Aqsa intifada has been exponentially more violent in its cycles of resistance and repression, with the result that the rate of casualties on both sides has far surpassed anything experienced in the period between 1987 and 1993. According to Amnesty International, between September 2000 and December 2002 approximately 1800 Palestinians and 600 Israelis were killed,[186] the vast majority of them civilians.[187] This is largely due to the expansion of tactics to include "limited, localized armed struggle" against Israeli military targets in the OPT,[188] interspersed with sporadic suicide bomb attacks against Israeli civilians.[189] Israel, on the other hand, has intensified its occupation and unleashed "large-scale military operations" on Palestinian "civilian areas and refugee

---

179. See FOURTH GENEVA CONVENTION, supra note 6, art. 33.

180. See Roy, supra note 178, at 100–01, 103.

181. B'TSELEM, supra note 28, at 23.

182. Id. at 19.

183. Id.

184. Roy, supra note 178, at 101.

185. Pacheco, supra note 22, at 185–91. For a thorough discussion of the point of view that the Oslo accords amount to little more than an alternate means by which Israel can maintain its control over the OPT, see EDWARD W. SAID, PEACE AND ITS DISCONTENTS: ESSAYS ON PALESTINE IN THE MIDDLE EAST PEACE PROCESS (1995); EDWARD W. SAID, THE END OF THE PEACE PROCESS: OSLO AND AFTER (2000); RAJA SHEHADEH, FROM OCCUPATION TO INTERIM ACCORDS: ISRAEL AND THE PALESTINIAN TERRITORIES (1997).

186. Amnesty Int'l, Israel and the Occupied Territories: An Ongoing Human Rights Crisis (Dec. 2002), http://web.amnesty.org/web/web.nsf/pages/IOT_home.

187. See B'Tselem, Total Casualties Since Dec. 1987 (Jan. 2002), http://www.btselem.org/English/Statistics/Total_Casualties.asp.

188. Andoni, supra note 29, at 209.

189. AMNESTY INT'L, BROKEN LIVES: A YEAR OF INTIFADA 41–44 (2001).

camps," including the disproportionate and indiscriminate use of live fire by thousands of ground troops, and shelling from Merkava tanks, Apache helicopter gun-ships, and F-16 fighter jets.[190]

Of course, at the heart of the problem lies Israel's 35 year military occupation of the OPT and the policies it has pursued there since 1967. In light of the current crisis, a discussion of the role international humanitarian law has in protecting the civilian population in the OPT is especially imperative.

III. The Law of Belligerent Occupation and the Occupied Palestinian Territory

A. *The Development and Nature of the Law of Belligerent Occupation*

The modern law of belligerent occupation was an outgrowth of the traditional international law and practice concerning the right to acquire territory by force, or the right of conquest. The right of conquest is defined simply "as the right of the victor, in virtue of military victory or conquest, to sovereignty over the conquered territory and its inhabitants."[191] Throughout most of recorded history the right of conquest was treated as a self-evident proposition of force and statecraft, a corollary of the right of the sovereign to exercise absolute dominion over everything coming under his control. As noted by Graber, according to this right the conquering sovereign "could do what he liked" with conquered lands "and their inhabitants":

> He could devastate the country, appropriate all public and private property, kill the people, or take them prisoners, or make them swear allegiance to himself and force them to fight in his army against their old sovereign. He could even before the war was decided dispose of the territory by annexing it or ceding it to a third state.[192]

As early as the seventeenth century, Grotius counseled the need for conquering sovereigns to use "more humane practices" in their disposition of conquered territories and their civilian populations.[193] It was not until the middle of the eighteenth century, however, that the "modern concept of belligerent occupation" was articulated by Vattel.[194] He asserted "that possession acquired under occupation was not definite until the treaty of peace," thereby introducing the notion that occupation is best understood "as a provisional condition, vastly different in its legal consequences from con-

---

190. The Secretary General, *Secretary General Tells Security Council Middle East Crisis 'Worst in Ten Years'; Calls on Palestinians, Israelis to 'Lead Your Peoples Away from Disaster,'* Mar. 12, 2002, at 1, U.N. Doc. SG/SM/8159 SC/7325 (2002). *See also* Edward W. Said, *What Price Oslo?*, AL-AHRAM WKLY. (Egypt), Mar. 14–20, 2002, at 13, http://www.ahram.org.eg/weekly/2002/577/op2.htm.

191. KORMAN, *supra* note 19, at 8.

192. DORIS A. GRABER, THE DEVELOPMENT OF THE LAW OF BELLIGERENT OCCUPATION 1863–1914: A HISTORICAL SURVEY 13 (1949).

193. *Id.*

194. *Id.* at 14.

quest."[195] Whereas conquest implied the right to assume sovereignty, belligerent occupation only vested the conqueror with temporary rights of administration pending a political settlement. Through this formulation, an important theoretical distinction between the concepts of *belligerent occupation* and *subjugation* emerged—the former being "a defined legal position which falls far short of sovereignty [and] which comes into operation as soon as enemy territory is occupied," and the latter being a signification "that the war has come to a close, . . . a state of affairs which alone qualifies the victor to substitute itself for the pre-existing sovereign in the conquered territory."[196] Although these jurisprudential developments helped set the stage for the emergence of the modern law of belligerent occupation, its process of maturation was relatively slow. As a result, the modern conception of belligerent occupation did not become a prevailing international legal norm until the middle of the nineteenth century.[197]

The first codification of the law of belligerent occupation was prepared by Dr. Francis Lieber of Columbia University in 1863.[198] His *Instructions for the Government of the Armies of the United States in the Field*, also known as the Lieber Code, was issued on April 24, 1863 as General Order No. 100 to Union forces in the American Civil War at President Abraham Lincoln's request.[199] The Lieber Code expounded upon the laws of war in general, covering "very traditional and practical subjects like guerrilla warfare, captured enemy property, and the treatment of prisoners."[200] Significantly, however, approximately one-third of the code was devoted to the law of belligerent occupation,[201] and it articulated the modern principle that belligerent occupation is in essence a temporary condition in which the powers of the belligerent occupant are not without limit.[202] The fact that the Lieber Code was a national legal development did not detract from its law-making value on the international plane.[203] Not long after it was issued, "[i]t became the model for many other national manuals (for example, those of the Netherlands in 1871, France in 1877, Serbia in 1879, Spain in 1882, Portugal in 1890, and

195. *Id.*

196. KORMAN, *supra* note 19, at 110.

197. *Id.* An expression of an earlier acceptance of the norm is found in the position adopted by the United States Supreme Court in *American Insurance Co. v. Bales of Cotton*, 26 U.S. 511 (1828), where Chief Justice Marshall stated that "the usage of the world is, if a nation be not entirely subdued, to consider the holding of a conquered territory as a mere military occupation, until its fate shall be determined at the treaty of peace." *Id.* at 542.

198. GRABER, *supra* note 192, at 14.

199. *Id.*

200. PETER MAGUIRE, LAW AND WAR: AN AMERICAN STORY 36 (2000).

201. GRABER, *supra* note 192, at 15.

202. *Id.* at 37–39.

203. In fact, as noted by Roberts and Guelff, "[n]ational manuals of military law and rules of engagement can serve as perhaps the closest links between the laws of war and belligerent armed forces in the field." DOCUMENTS ON THE LAWS OF WAR, *supra* note 5, at 12.

Italy in 1896), and it prepared the way for" further international developments in the area.[204]

The first international effort to codify the law of belligerent occupation took place as part of a general intergovernmental conference on the laws of war in 1874 at Brussels.[205] Attended by delegates from 16 European states,[206] the Brussels conference developed a code, the Brussels Declaration, that built upon many of the principles laid down by Lieber in 1863.[207] As noted by Graber, however, the Brussels Declaration was "more humane and respect[ed] the rights of the peaceful population to a greater degree than the Lieber code."[208] Although the Brussels Declaration did not result in the conclusion of an international treaty, "its influence was far-reaching because subsequent codes on the laws and customs of war . . . were patterned according to it."[209] Shortly after it was promulgated, the Institute of International Law endorsed the Brussels Code and "decided to sponsor a draft code" of its own with the view to convincing each member of the international community to incorporate it into its national military manual.[210] The result was the adoption in 1880 of the Oxford Code, named for the venue at which the Institute met to complete the project. Because "the framers of the Oxford code had tried to specify and codify existing laws, rather than formulate new rules . . . there is very little substantial difference between the rules promulgated in the Brussels code and those set out in the Oxford code."[211] Furthermore, because the Oxford Manual was intended "a basis for national legislation," no international treaty followed its dissemination.[212]

That changed in 1899, when representatives of 26 states met at the Hague Peace Conference to conclude a number of treaties on the laws of war, among them the 1899 Hague Convention II Respecting the Laws and Customs of War on Land (1899 Hague Convention).[213] The 1899 Hague Convention "represented the first successful effort of the international community to codify a relatively comprehensive regime governing the laws of land warfare."[214] However, because the "convention merely bound the contracting parties to issue instructions to their armies in accordance with" its provisions, many states either adopted it in a diluted form or not at all.[215] Accordingly, the international community reconvened at the Hague in 1907 to

---

204. *Id.* at 12–13.
205. GRABER, *supra* note 192, at 20.
206. *Id.* at 21–22.
207. *Id.* at 20.
208. *Id.* at 28.
209. *Id.* at 26.
210. *Id.* at 28.
211. *Id.* at 29.
212. DOCUMENTS ON THE LAWS OF WAR, *supra* note 5, at 68.
213. HAGUE CONVENTION II RESPECTING THE LAWS AND CUSTOMS OF WAR ON LAND, July 29, 1899, 32 Stat. 1803, 187 Consol. T.S. 429 [hereinafter 1899 HAGUE CONVENTION].
214. DOCUMENTS ON THE LAWS OF WAR, *supra* note 5, at 68.
215. GRABER, *supra* note 192, at 33–34.

make appropriate revisions to the 1899 convention, the result of which was the 1907 Hague Convention, along with its annexed regulations.[216] Of the fifty-six articles in the 1907 Hague Regulations, fourteen addressed the law of belligerent occupation. These articles did not constitute a complete overhaul of the 1899 effort, but one of their innovations was to provide that "[a] belligerent party which violates the provisions of the said Regulations shall, if the case demands, be liable to pay compensation," thereby giving rise to international civil liability for actions arising out of the conduct of war.[217] It would take nearly forty more years for the international community to assert, in convention form at least, that criminal liability could also flow in similar circumstances.[218]

It was the ravages committed against civilian populations during the world wars that demonstrated the need for the international community to develop a more comprehensive body of law aimed specifically at the protection of civilians in time of war. Up to that point, the law of belligerent occupation was concerned predominantly with the rights of political elites in occupied territories, with the rights of ousted sovereigns vis-à-vis belligerent occupants.[219] As a result, the 1907 Hague Regulations—which were the governing "treaty[-]based rules in force" in this period—proved hopelessly inadequate in protecting against the internment, deportation, enslavement, and murder of millions of civilians in occupied Europe during the wars.[220] From the interwar period to the end of World War II, the International Committee of the Red Cross (ICRC) was charged with the task of fashioning a revised codification of the law of belligerent occupation to address this major deficiency in the law.[221] The result was the promulgation of the Fourth Geneva Convention on August 12, 1949,[222] which, along with the 1977 Geneva Protocol I Additional to the Geneva Conventions of 12 August 1949, Relating to the Protection of Victims of International Armed Conflicts,[223] has emerged as the principal international convention on the law of belligerent occupation.

The Fourth Geneva Convention was not intended to supercede the 1899 and 1907 Hague conventions or regulations, but was rather designed to supplement them.[224] Therefore, the Hague law continues to apply to all

---

216. 1907 HAGUE CONVENTION, *supra* note 8.

217. *Id.* art. 3. *See also* GRABER, *supra* note 192, at 33–34.

218. CHARTER OF THE INTERNATIONAL MILITARY TRIBUNAL, AGREEMENT FOR THE PROSECUTION AND PUNISHMENT OF THE MAJOR WAR CRIMINALS OF THE EUROPEAN AXIS, annex, Aug. 8 1945, 59 Stat. 154, 82 U.N.T.S. 279.

219. EYAL BENVENISTI, THE INTERNATIONAL LAW OF OCCUPATION 105–06 (1993).

220. DOCUMENTS ON THE LAWS OF WAR, *supra* note 5, at 300.

221. *Id.* at 195–96, 299–300.

222. *See id.* at 300.

223. GENEVA PROTOCOL I ADDITIONAL TO THE GENEVA CONVENTIONS OF 12 AUGUST 1949, RELATING TO THE PROTECTION OF VICTIMS OF INTERNATIONAL ARMED CONFLICTS, June 8, 1977, 1125 U.N.T.S. 3.

224. FOURTH GENEVA CONVENTION, *supra* note 6, art. 154. *See also* DOCUMENTS ON THE LAWS OF WAR, *supra* note 5, at 300.

cases of belligerent occupation. Moreover, the rules codified in both the Hague law and the Fourth Geneva Convention are understood by the international community to form part of the customary international law of war.[225] The *erga omnes* character of the provisions contained in the Fourth Geneva Convention in particular is evidenced by the fact that there are at present 189 High Contracting Parties to the instrument, the same number of States Members of the United Nations.[226] The Fourth Geneva Convention is not *completely* declarative of customary international law principles on the law of war, however. The framers of the convention, recognizing that much of international humanitarian law continued to exist in the form of unwritten customary principles, inserted an important provision stipulating that even where the High Contracting Parties denounced the convention,[227] such denunciation:

> shall in no way impair the obligations which the Parties to the conflict shall remain bound to fulfil by virtue of the principles of the law of nations, as they result from the usages established among civilized peoples, from the laws of humanity and the dictates of the public conscience.[228]

It is significant to note that this proviso was modeled after the so-called "Martens Clause" of the 1899 Hague Convention,[229] included in that treaty because of the serious disagreement that arose among the treaty's drafters over the issue of whether the inhabitants of occupied territory possessed the right to resist under international law.[230] By virtue of its inclusion, all states continue to be bound by the customary international law of war even if they denounce the Fourth Geneva Convention.[231]

---

225. On the customary nature of the Hague law, see BENVENISTI, *supra* note 219, at 98. *See also* DOCUMENTS ON THE LAWS OF WAR, *supra* note 5, at 68. On the customary nature of the Fourth Geneva Convention, see Statement of Jordan Paust to the United Nations International Meeting, *supra* note 13, at 20, 21. *See also* DOCUMENTS ON THE LAWS OF WAR, *supra* note 5, at 196.

226. Int'l Comm. of the Red Cross, *Geneva Conventions of 12 August 1949 and Additional Protocols of 8 June 1977: Ratifications, Accessions and Successions*, http://www.icrc.org/eng/party_gc.

227. Under article 158 of the convention, the High Contracting Parties are at liberty to denounce the convention upon one year's notice to the Swiss Federal Council so long as the denouncing power is not at the time of denunciation involved in a conflict to which the convention applies. *See* FOURTH GENEVA CONVENTION, *supra* note 6, art. 158.

228. *Id.*

229. The Martens Clause is found in the preamble to the 1899 Hague Convention and states that:
[u]ntil a more complete code of the laws of war is issued, the high contracting Parties think it right to declare that in cases not included in the Regulations adopted by them, populations and belligerents remain under the protection and empire of the principles of international law, as they result from the usages established between civilized nations, from the laws of humanity, and the requirements of the public conscience.
1899 HAGUE CONVENTION, *supra* note 213, pmbl.

230. DOCUMENTS ON THE LAWS OF WAR, *supra* note 5, at 8–9.

231. With the exception of those States who unequivocally and consistently express their intention not to accept a custom that is in the process of formation.

As its proper style suggests, the Fourth Geneva Convention is chiefly concerned with protecting the rights of civilians in time of war. This concern for individuals lies at the heart of the Convention's main contributions to the law of belligerent occupation, which, according to Benvenisti, are twofold. First, the convention "delineates a bill of rights for the occupied population,"[232] who are afforded the legal status of "protected persons" under Article 4.[233] Taking its cue from the principles established at Nuremberg, the convention affirms the right of civilian persons to be protected against, inter alia, willful killing,[234] torture or inhuman treatment,[235] deportation,[236] collective punishment,[237] and extensive destruction and appropriation of property,[238] and classifies these acts as "grave breaches," which are considered war crimes under international law.[239] Second, the convention shifts attention from the rights of the ousted sovereign to the rights of the civilian population under occupation—an important departure from the state-centric philosophy underpinning the traditional law and a signification of the "growing awareness in international law of the idea that peoples are not merely the resources of states, but rather that they are worthy of being the subjects of international norms."[240]

Of course, the two most important substantive principles of the traditional law of belligerent occupation continue to figure prominently in the Fourth Geneva Convention regime. The first of these is the principle that belligerent occupation represents a temporary condition during which the role of the belligerent occupant is limited merely to that of the de facto administrative authority. Accordingly, the belligerent occupant is prohibited from altering the status of the occupied territory, and is allowed to "amend the laws and regulations in force in the territory only to the extent needed to enable it to meet its obligations under the . . . Convention," which include ensuring both the well-being of the protected population and the security of its armed forces.[241] As the case of the OPT illustrates, the phenomenon of prolonged occupation "has produced particular problems" for this principle

---

232. BENVENISTI, *supra* note 219, at 105.
233. Article 4 of the Fourth Geneva Convention defines protected persons as "those who, at a given moment and in any manner whatsoever, find themselves, in case of a conflict or occupation, in the hands of a Party to the conflict or Occupying Power of which they are not nationals." FOURTH GENEVA CONVENTION, *supra* note 6, art. 4.
234. *Id.* arts. 3(1)(a), 32, 147.
235. *Id.*
236. *Id.* arts. 49(1), 49(6), 147.
237. *Id.* art. 33.
238. *Id.* arts. 33, 53, 147.
239. ROME STATUTE OF THE INTERNATIONAL CRIMINAL COURT, art. 8, July 17, 1998, U.N. Doc. 32/A/CONF. 183/9, 37 I.L.M. 999 (*entered into force* July 1, 2002) [hereinafter ROME STATUTE]. *See also* STATUTE FOR THE INTERNATIONAL CRIMINAL TRIBUNAL FOR THE FORMER YUGOSLAVIA, art. 2, May 25, 1993, 32 I.L.M. 1159, 1192 (1993) [hereinafter ICTY STATUTE]; STATUTE FOR THE INTERNATIONAL CRIMINAL TRIBUNAL FOR RWANDA, arts. 3, 4, Nov. 8, 1994, 33 I.L.M. 1598 (1994) [hereinafter ICTR STATUTE].
240. BENVENISTI, *supra* note 219, at 106.
241. Delparaz, *supra* note 16, at 48.

of law, given the fact that "the longer an occupation continues, the more difficult it is to ensure effective compliance with the Fourth Geneva Convention."[242] In this respect, Benvenisti has noted that because "the Fourth Geneva Convention stop[s] short of requiring the occupant to develop (not just maintain) the economic, social, and educational infrastructures[,] . . . a protracted occupation . . . might lead to stagnation, and consequently to the impoverishment and backwardness of the occupied community."[243]

The second of the important traditional principles was summarized best by Oppenheim when he noted that belligerent occupation does not yield so much as "an atom of sovereignty in the authority of the occupant."[244] This is an affirmation of the *jus cogens* rule of international law prohibiting the acquisition of territory through the threat or use of force, a pillar upon which the law of belligerent occupation rests.[245] In instances where the ousted sovereign may not have possessed full legal title to the occupied territory, as is the case in the OPT, this gives rise to the question "in whom does sovereignty in the territory lie?" Benvenisti rightly observes that a contemporary reading of the law of belligerent occupation much ackowledge the principle of "self-determination of peoples and the complementary idea that sovereignty lies in the people and not its government."[246] Accordingly, "the modern occupant needs to heed the political interests of this people," who are "the sovereign."[247] However, in an age where questioning the sovereignty of the ousted power has been used by belligerent occupants as a means to refuse to recognize the applicability of the Fourth Geneva Convention, thereby denying the occupied population the protections affirmed therein, it is important to guard against becoming too focused on questions of sovereignty, critical though they may be. Rather, of foremost importance is ensuring that so long as the belligerent occupant maintains effective control over the occupied territory, the civilian population must be accorded the benefit of the protections set forth in the convention.

B. *The Applicability of the Fourth Geneva Convention to the OPT*

In the period since the Fourth Geneva Convention was promulgated in 1949, occupying powers have routinely failed "to recognize the applicability of the law of [belligerent] occupation to their actions in foreign countries

---

242. *Id.*

243. BENVENISTI, *supra* note 219, at 105.

244. L. Oppenheim, *The Legal Relations Between an Occupying Power and the Inhabitants*, 33 L.Q. REV. 363, 364 (1917), *quoted in* Yoram Dinstein, *The International Law of Belligerent Occupation and Human Rights*, 8 ISR. Y.B. ON H.R. 104, 106 (1978).

245. *See* Declaration on Principles of International Law concerning Friendly Relations and Cooperation among States in accordance with the Charter of the United Nations, G.A. Res. 2625, U.N. GAOR, 25th Sess., Supp. No. 28, at 121 (1970). *See also* S.C. Res. 242, *supra* note 146.

246. BENVENISTI, *supra* note 219, at 29.

247. *Id.* at 183.

under their control."[248] Examples include the Indonesian occupation of East Timor,[249] the Soviet occupation of Afghanistan,[250] and the Iraqi occupation of Kuwait.[251] The Fourth Geneva Convention has been signed and ratified by all states directly involved in the Arab-Israeli conflict, including Israel.[252] Although Israel initially expressed an intention to apply the Fourth Geneva Convention to the OPT following the June 1967 war,[253] since October 1967 it has consistently taken the position that the convention is not de jure applicable to the West Bank and the Gaza Strip.[254] Instead, it has only declared an intention to act de facto in accordance with the "humanitarian provisions" of the Fourth Geneva Convention with respect to the OPT (excluding annexed East Jerusalem),[255] an official enumeration of which has never been offered by Israel and in any event, a curious notion given the complete humanitarian object and purpose of the convention. The upshot of this official position is that Israel views its presence in the OPT not as an "occupation," but rather as an "administration," completely "unaccountable to the Fourth Geneva Convention and the law of belligerent occupation," and mitigated only by a vague undertaking to apply in good faith those protections it deems suitable for the Palestinian civilian population.[256] Later, the question of Israel's observance of the Fourth Geneva Convention in the OPT will be examined in some detail. The following pages will be devoted

---

248. *Id.* at 149.

249. *Id.* at 153–59.

250. *Id.* at 160–63.

251. *Id.* at 150–51.

252. UNCEIRPP, *supra* note 5, at 3. With respect to the State of Palestine, a note appended to all four 1949 Geneva Conventions states the following:

> Palestine. On 21 June 1989 the Depositary received a letter from the Permanent Mission of Palestine to the UN Office at Geneva stating "that the Executive Committee of the Palestine Liberation Organization, entrusted with the functions of the Government of the State of Palestine by decision of the Palestine National Council, decided on 4 May 1989, to adhere to the four Geneva Conventions of 12 August 1949 and the two Protocols additional thereto . . . ." On 13 September 1989 the Depositary circulated a note stating: "Due to the uncertainty within the international community as to the existence or the non-existence of a State of Palestine . . . the Swiss Government . . . is not in a position to decide whether this communication can be considered as an instrument of accession . . . ." The note also stated: "The unilateral declaration of application of the four Geneva Conventions and of the additional Protocol I made on 7 June 1982 by the Palestine Liberation Organization remains valid."

DOCUMENTS ON THE LAWS OF WAR, *supra* note 5, at 362.

253. This intention was codified by the Israeli military through the promulgation of Military Proclamation Number 3 on June 7, 1967. Pursuant to Article 35 of this military order, all Israeli military courts and officers were made legally bound to "apply the provisions of the Geneva Conventions of 13 August 1949 [sic] regarding the protection of civilians during war as to all which pertains to legal proceedings. If there should be any contradiction between the provisions of the order and the Geneva Conventions, the provisions of the Conventions should apply." SHEHADEH, *supra* note 148, at xi. As noted by Raja Shehadeh, "Article 35 of Proclamation No. 3 was quietly deleted by Military Order 144" four months later in October 1967. *Id.*

254. UNCEIRPP, *supra* note 5, at 4.

255. Blum, *supra* note 23, at 293–94. *See also* Shamgar, *supra* note 23, at 266.

256. Falk & Weston, *supra* note 150, at 131.

to an analysis of the legal debate regarding the Convention's applicability to the OPT, and the international community's position on the matter.

In asserting its position, the Israeli government has relied upon the so-called "missing reversioner" theory first advanced in 1968 by Professor Yehuda Blum of the Hebrew University[257] and subsequently elaborated upon by a handful of pro-Israeli legal scholars.[258] The missing reversioner theory is based upon two separate but related arguments. The first of these turns on a unique interpretation of common article 2 of the Geneva Conventions, which states, in part, that "[t]he Convention shall . . . apply to all cases of partial or total occupation of the *territory of a High Contracting Party* . . . ."[259] Asserting that the object and purpose of the law of belligerent occupation is to protect the rights of the ousted sovereign holding valid legal title,[260] it is argued that because Jordan and Egypt were not the legitimate sovereigns in the OPT prior to 1967 owing to their alleged unlawful aggression against Israel in 1948,[261] that territory cannot be said to constitute the "territory of a High Contracting Party" under common article 2, thereby rendering the Fourth Geneva Convention totally inapplicable. In Professor Blum's words:

> [T]he concurrent existence, in respect of the same territory, of both an ousted legitimate sovereign and a belligerent occupant lies at the root of all those rules of international law, which, while recognising and sanctioning the occupant's rights to administer the occupied territory, aim at the same time to safeguard the reversionary rights of the ousted sovereign. It would seem to follow that, in a case like the present where the ousted State never was the legitimate sovereign, those rules of belligerent occupation directed to safeguarding that sovereign's reversionary rights have no application.[262]

The second argument of the missing reversioner theory holds that Israel possesses better title to the OPT than does Jordan or Egypt, based on a notion of "defensive conquest."[263] The claim maintains that because Israel came into control of the OPT in 1967 through a defensive war against Jordan and Egypt, neither of whom held valid legal title to that territory, its control of the OPT is tantamount to perfect legal title. Again, according to Professor Blum, because

---

257. Blum, *supra* note 23. Professor Blum was later Israel's Permanent Representative to the United Nations.

258. *See* Shamgar, *supra* note 23, at 265–66. *See also* STONE, *supra* note 131, at 177–78, 209 n.2.

259. *E.g.*, FOURTH GENEVA CONVENTION, *supra* note 6, art. 2 (emphasis added). The article is common to all four conventions.

260. Blum, *supra* note 23, at 293.

261. Falk & Weston, *supra* note 150, at 131.

262. Blum, *supra* note 23, at 293.

263. UNCEIRPP, *supra* note 5, at 4–6.

no state can make a legal claim to Judea and Samaria [*viz.* the OPT] that is equal to that of Israel, this relative superiority of Israel may be sufficient under international law to make Israel's possession of those territories virtually undistinguishable from an absolute title to be valid *erga omnes*; . . . I would, therefore, conclude by saying that Israel cannot be considered as an occupying power within the meaning given to this term in international law in any part of the former Palestine mandate, including Judea and Samaria.[264]

Israel's legal position on the applicability of the Fourth Geneva Convention to the OPT has enjoyed very limited support. As noted by Professor Richard Falk, the missing reversioner argument is "strained and artificial in character, and [has] commanded little to no respect among 'highly qualified publicists' or within the organized international community."[265] Yoram Dinstein, an Israeli professor of law at Tel Aviv University, has dismissed the theory as being "based on dubious legal grounds."[266] One of its most vociferous detractors was Professor W. Thomas Mallison of George Washington University. In the late 1970s and early 1980s, Professor Mallison set out a number of arguments effectively countering the Blum theory,[267] a brief account of which follows.

With respect to the claim postulating the necessity that the "legitimate sovereign" be displaced by the belligerent occupant, Professor Mallison noted that there is no evidence to support the interpretation of the words "territory of a High Contracting Party" as used in common article 2 of the Geneva Conventions to refer only to full legal title as the "legitimate sovereign." It is well accepted that the word "territory" was intended by the framers of the Fourth Geneva Convention to connote, "in addition to *de jure* title, a mere *de facto* title to the territory."[268] If the case were otherwise, any belligerent occupant would be able to evade the obligations imposed by the Fourth Geneva Convention by contesting the validity of the title of the ousted power to the territory—a notion, according to Professor Mallison, that "finds no support in either the text of the Convention or its negotiating history."[269] Similarly, the unilateral assertion that the Fourth Geneva Convention cannot apply because of the fact that the ousted power's control over

264. *The Colonization of the West Bank Territories by Israel: Hearing Before the Subcomm. on Immigration and Naturalization of the Senate Comm. on the Judiciary*, 95th Cong. 35 (1978) [hereinafter *Senate Judiciary Hearings*] (statement of Yehuda Blum).

265. Falk & Weston, *supra* note 150, at 132. *See also* MALLISON & MALLISON, *supra* note 74, at 252–62; Roberts, *supra* note 15, at 25; SHEHADEH, *supra* note 148, at xi–xiii; Türkkaya Ataöv, *The Status of Jerusalem as a Question of International Law*, *in* THE LEGAL ASPECTS OF THE PALESTINE PROBLEM WITH SPECIAL REGARD TO THE QUESTION OF JERUSALEM 139–40 (Hans Köchler ed., 1981); T. A. Van Baarda, *Is it Expedient to Let the World Court Clarify, in an Advisory Opinion, the Applicability of the Fourth Geneva Convention in the Occupied Territories?*, 10 NETH. Q. HUM. RTS. 4 (1992).

266. Dinstein, *supra* note 244, at 107.

267. *Senate Judiciary Hearings*, *supra* note 264, at 46–71 (statement of W. T. Mallison).

268. MALLISON & MALLISON, *supra* note 74, at 254.

269. *Id.* at 255.

the territory was the result of unlawful aggression in the first instance leads to an absurd result, namely that although "the inhabitants of the West Bank were the victims of Jordanian aggression in 1948," it is because of this aggression that "these civilians must be victimized further by being denied the humanitarian protections of the [Geneva] Civilians Convention under Israeli occupation."[270] As stated by Professor Mallison, if "humanitarian law were to be interpreted so that its application were made contingent upon acceptance by the belligerent occupant of the justness and the non-aggressive character of the war aims of its opponent, it is clear that this law would never be applied."[271] In essence, this branch of the Blum theory is regarded as unpersuasive because it places too much discretion in the hands of the would-be belligerent occupant, and "it frustrates the entire humanitarian purpose" of the Fourth Geneva Convention, which is to protect the interests of *civilian persons* in time of war, not governments.[272]

With respect to the claim of title to the occupied territory on the basis of "defensive conquest," Israel's position runs into a factual impediment: its actions in the 1967 war may not in fact have been defensive at all. As illustrated above, Israel's new historiography has laid serious challenge to this idea through the use of primary Israeli archival materials that illustrate that its leadership possessed subjective knowledge that Israel did not face an imminent threat of an armed attack justifying its purported preemptive strike against Egypt.[273] In any event, even if one were to concede arguendo that Israel's actions in 1967 were defensive, as did Professor Mallison, the Blum thesis must fail on the ground that it offends the *jus cogens* principle of the inadmissibility of the acquisition of territory through the threat or use of force.[274] This is consistent with the demise in international law and practice of the right of conquest, "defensive" or otherwise,[275] and the contemporaneous emergence of the law of belligerent occupation, being provisional in nature and carrying "an implicit duty to withdraw once hostilities have been brought to an end."[276] Furthermore, the relevant international law on the use of force in self-defense does not permit the defending state to acquire territory through such use of force. As noted by Professor Mallison, "[a] state exercising national defense may go beyond its national boundaries to repel an attack, but it may not go beyond its national boundaries to acquire territory .... If international law provided for an exception to this basic rule under the heading of 'defensive conquest,' it would prove to be an irresisti-

---

270. *Id.* at 256–57.
271. *Id.* at 257.
272. *Id.*
273. *See supra* text accompanying notes 136–140.
274. *See* MALLISON & MALLISON, *supra* note 74, at 259.
275. Falk & Weston, *supra* note 150, at 133.
276. *Id.* at 134.

ble attraction for a militaristic and expansionist state."[277] In essence, the concept of defensive conquest is unknown in modern international law.

Another challenge to the missing reversioner thesis, not raised by Professor Mallison, is that it fails to take into account the effect of the international law on self-determination of peoples. As noted above, any contemporary reading of the law of belligerent occupation must necessarily take into account a core principle underlying the right to self-determination, that sovereignty lies in the people of a state and not in its governing elites.[278] Some jurists have asserted that the principle of self-determination may be *jus cogens*.[279] Thus, Professor Blum's omission of any discussion of the political rights of the Palestinian people in the OPT—his failure to entertain the possibility that *they* might constitute the lawful reversioner in that territory—renders his thesis and Israel's reliance on it problematic. This is especially so given that the right of the Palestinian people to exercise self-determination within the borders of mandatory Palestine has long been recognized by the international community,[280] and since 1967 the territorial unit within which that right is expected to one day be fulfilled has widely been taken to be the OPT.[281]

This conclusion is bolstered by the fact that the whole of the international community—except Israel—is of the opinion that the West Bank, including East Jerusalem, and the Gaza Strip are incontrovertibly subject to the provisions of the Fourth Geneva Convention.[282] Since 1967 the U.N. Security Council has issued scores of resolutions affirming the applicability of the Fourth Geneva Convention to the OPT, and calling upon Israel to abide by its terms as the occupying power.[283] For example, following Israel's decision

---

277. MALLISON & MALLISON, *supra* note 74, at 259.

278. *See supra* text accompanying notes 244–247.

279. *See* DAMROSCH ET AL., *supra* note 130, at 269.

280. This recognition goes back to article 22 of the League of Nations Covenant and the recognition by the U.N. General Assembly in the 1947 Partition of an Arab State in Palestine. *See supra* text accompanying notes 75–78, 90. *See also* Dajani, *supra* note 120, at 33–35, 40. Two notable exceptions to this historical near consensus are Israel and the United States, who have only relatively recently acknowledged the existence of the Palestinian people as such, with the accompanying right to self-determination.

281. For a discussion of international law and opinion on the question of Palestinian self-determination, see Dajani, *supra* note 120, at 33–48.

282. Falk & Weston, *supra* note 150, at 135.

283. *See, e.g.,* S.C. Res. 1322, U.N. SCOR, 55th Sess., 4205th mtg., U.N. Doc. S/RES/56 (2000); S.C. Res. 904, U.N. SCOR, 49th Sess., 3351st mtg. at 108, U.N. Doc. S/RES/50 (1994); S.C. Res. 799, U.N. SCOR, 47th Sess., 3151st mtg. at 6, U.N. Doc. S/RES/48 (1992); S.C. Res. 726, U.N. SCOR, 47th Sess., 3026th mtg. at 5, U.N. Doc. S/RES/48 (1992); S.C. Res. 694, U.N. SCOR, 46th Sess., 2989th mtg. at 2, U.N. Doc. S/RES/47 (1991); S.C. Res. 681, U.N. SCOR, 45th Sess., 2970th mtg. at 8–9, U.N. Doc. S/RES/46 (1990); S.C. Res. 673, U.N. SCOR, 45th Sess., 2949th mtg. at 7, U.N. Doc. S/RES/46 (1990); S.C. Res. 672, U.N. SCOR, 45th Sess., 2948th mtg. at 7, U.N. Doc. S/RES/46 (1990); S.C. Res. 641, U.N. SCOR, 44th Sess., 2883d mtg. at 14, U.N. Doc. S/RES/45 (1989); S.C. Res. 636, U.N. SCOR, 44th Sess., 2870th mtg. at 14, U.N. Doc. S/RES/45 (1989); S.C. Res. 608, U.N. SCOR, 43d Sess., 2781st mtg. at 2, U.N. Doc. S/RES/44 (1988); S.C. Res. 607, U.N. SCOR, 43d Sess., 2780th mtg. at 1, U.N. Doc. S/RES/44 (1988); S.C. Res. 605, U.N. SCOR, 42d mtg. at 4, U.N. Doc. S/RES/43 (1987); S.C. Res. 592, U.N. SCOR, 42d Sess., 2727th mtg. at 7, U.N. Doc. S/RES/42 (1986); S.C. Res. 484, U.N. SCOR, 35th Sess., 2260th mtg. at 16, U.N. Doc. S/RES/36 (1980); S.C. Res. 478, U.N.

to deport "hundreds of Palestinian civilians" from the OPT in 1992, the Security Council passed Resolution 799 on December 18, 1992, reaffirming "the applicability of the Fourth Geneva Convention of 12 August 1949 to all the Palestinian territories occupied by Israel since 1967, including Jerusalem, and affirm[ing] that deportation of civilians constitutes a contravention of its obligations under the Convention."[284] Similarly, since 1967 the General Assembly has issued hundreds of similar resolutions, though usually in much harsher language than that adopted by the Security Council.[285] For instance, in Resolution 42/60 of December 8, 1987 the General Assembly reiterated that the Fourth Geneva Convention "is applicable to all Arab territories occupied since June 1967, including Jerusalem,"[286] and condemned Israel's "continued and persistent violation" of the convention, "in particular those violations which the Convention designates as 'grave breaches' thereof," which "are war crimes and an affront to humanity."[287] Significantly, most of these General Assembly resolutions were (and continue to be) passed by an overwhelming majority, usually with only one or two states—Israel and, frequently, the United States—voting against them, and are therefore sound evidence of international opinion on the matter.[288]

To this international consensus on the applicability of the Fourth Geneva Convention to the OPT has been added the opinions of a number of other

SCOR, 35th Sess., 2245th mtg. at 14, U.N. Doc. S/RES/36 (1980); S.C. Res. 476, U.N. SCOR, 35th Sess., 2242d mtg. at 13, U.N. Doc. S/RES/36 (1980); S.C. Res. 471, U.N. SCOR, 35th Sess., 2226th mtg. at 10–11, U.N. Doc. S/RES/36 (1980); S.C. Res. 469, U.N. SCOR, 35th Sess., 2223d mtg. at 9–10, U.N. Doc. S/RES/36 (1980); S.C. Res. 468, U.N. SCOR, 35th Sess., 2221st mtg. at 9, U.N. Doc. S/RES/36 (1980); S.C. Res. 465, U.N. SCOR, 35th Sess., 2203d mtg. at 5, U.N. Doc. S/RES/36 (1980); S.C. Res. 452, U.N. SCOR, 34th Sess., 2159th mtg. at 8, U.N. Doc. S/RES/35 (1979); S.C. Res. 446, U.N. SCOR, 34th Sess., 2134th mtg. at 4, U.N. Doc. S/RES/35 (1979); S.C. Res. 271, U.N. SCOR, 24th Sess., 1512th mtg. at 5, U.N. Doc. S/RES/24/Rev.1 (1969).

284. S.C. Res. 799, supra note 283, at 6.

285. See, e.g., G.A. Res. 56/204, U.N. GAOR, 56th Sess., Supp. No. 49, 90th plen. mtg., U.N. Doc. A/56/49 (2001); G.A. Res. ES-10/8, U.N. GAOR, 56th Sess., 15th plen. mtg., U.N. Doc. A/ES-10/8 (2001); G.A. Res. 56/60, U.N. GAOR, 56th Sess., Supp. No. 49, 82d plen. mtg., U.N. Doc. A/56/49 (2001); G.A. Res. 55/131, U.N. GAOR, 55th Sess., Supp. No. 49, at 211, U.N. Doc. A/55/49 (2000); G.A. Res. 54/77, U.N. GAOR, 54th Sess., Supp. No. 49, 71st plen. mtg. at 143, U.N. Doc. A/54/49 (1999); G.A. Res. 53/54, U.N. GAOR, 53d Sess., Supp. No. 49, 78th plen. mtg. at 133, U.N. Doc. A/53/49 (1998); G.A. Res. 52/65, U.N. GAOR, 52d Sess., Supp. No. 49, 69th plen. mtg. at 129, U.N. Doc. A/53/49 (1997); G.A. Res. 42/160 C, U.N. GAOR, 42d Sess., Supp. No. 49, 95th plen. mtg. at 114, U.N. Doc. A/42/49 (1987); G.A. Res. 32/91 A, U.N. GAOR, 32d Sess., Supp. No. 45, 101st plen. mtg. at 69, U.N. Doc. A/32/49 (1977); G.A. Res. 2252 (ES-V), U.N. GAOR, Supp. No. 1, 1548th plen. mtg. at 3, U.N. Doc. A/6798 (1967).

286. G.A. Res. 42/160 C, U.N. GAOR, 42nd Sess., Supp. No. 49, at 114, U.N. Doc. A/42/49 (1987).

287. G.A. Res. 42/160 D, U.N. GAOR, 42nd Sess., Supp. No. 49, at 114, U.N. Doc. A/42/49 (1987).

288. See, e.g., G.A. Res. 47/70 B, U.N. GAOR, 47th Sess., Supp. No. 49, at 98, U.N. Doc. A/46/49 (1992) (vote: 141 for, 1 against, 4 abstaining); G.A. Res. 45/69, U.N. GAOR, 45th Sess., Supp. No. 49, at 32, U.N. Doc. A/45/49 (1990) (vote: 141 for, 2 against, 3 abstaining); G.A. Res. 44/2, U.N. GAOR, 44th Sess., Supp. No. 49, at 12, U.N. Doc. A/44/49 (1989) (vote: 140 for, 2 against, 6 abstaining); G.A. Res. 43/21, U.N. GAOR, 43rd Sess., Supp. No. 49, at 26, U.N. Doc. A/43/49 (1988) (vote: 130 for, 2 against, 16 abstaining); G.A. Res. 42/160 C, U.N. GAOR, 42nd Sess., Supp. No. 49, at 114, U.N. Doc. A/42/49 (1987) (vote: 143 for, 1 against, 8 abstaining).

intergovernmental and non-governmental organizations such as the United Nations Commission on Human Rights, the International Commission of Jurists, and the ICRC.[289] The ICRC is of particular importance because it was the body that originally drafted the Fourth Geneva Convention in 1949, and it is vested with a special status under articles 30 and 143 of the convention as a third-party monitor in occupied territories.[290] As noted by a U.N. study, "[t]his impartial body is usually extremely reticent in comment, normally dealing in confidence with the authorities concerned."[291] It is in this capacity that the ICRC has consistently declared that the Fourth Geneva Convention "is applicable *in toto*" to the OPT, and that it is unacceptable "that a duly ratified international treaty may be suspended at the wish of one of the parties" (i.e., Israel).[292]

For its part, although the Supreme Court of Israel has held since 1988 that the relatively terse 1907 Hague Regulations apply to the OPT because they form a part of international customary law, to this day it has maintained that the far more expansive Fourth Geneva Convention is not justiciable in Israeli courts because it "constitutes treaty law as opposed to customary law," which has not been formally incorporated into municipal law by an act of the Israeli legislature—i.e., the Fourth Geneva Convention is non-self-executing.[293] There are two problems with this judicial approach to the question of the applicability of the Fourth Geneva Convention. First, as discussed above, it is not the case that the Fourth Geneva Convention does not constitute customary international law. On the contrary, "[a] report of the U.N. Secretary-General to the Security Council in May 1993 concerning the establishment of the" International Criminal Tribunal for the Former Yugoslavia (ICTY) "affirmed that the law embodied in the four 1949 Geneva Conventions had become part of customary international law."[294] Likewise, countless experts on the law of belligerent occupation have asserted that Israel is bound by the Fourth Geneva Convention because the convention "reflects customary humanitarian law."[295] Second, under article 27 of the

---

289. UNCEIRPP, *supra* note 5, at 11–12.

290. For instance, article 143 of the Fourth Geneva Convention provides, in part, that representatives of the ICRC:

[S]hall have permission to go to all places where protected persons are, particularly to places of internment, detention and work. They shall have access to all premises occupied by protected persons and shall be able to interview the latter without witnesses, personally or through an interpreter. Such visits may not be prohibited except for reasons of imperative military necessity, and then only as an exceptional and temporary measure. Their duration and frequency shall not be restricted. Such representatives and delegates shall have full liberty to select the places they wish to visit. The Detaining or Occupying Power . . . may agree that compatriots of the internees shall be permitted to participate in the visits.

FOURTH GENEVA CONVENTION, *supra* note 6, art. 143.

291. UNCEIRPP, *supra* note 5, at 11.

292. INT'L COMM. OF THE RED CROSS, *Unsolved Problems Covered by the Fourth Convention*, 1975 ANNUAL REPORT 22.

293. BENVENISTI, *supra* note 219, at 112.

294. DOCUMENTS ON THE LAWS OF WAR, *supra* note 5, at 196.

295. Final Document of the United Nations International Meeting, *supra* note 13, at 87.

Vienna Convention on the Law of Treaties—which is itself widely regarded as declarative of customary international law and to which Israel is a signatory[296]—a party to a treaty "may not invoke the provisions of its internal law as justification for its failure to perform a treaty."[297] Thus, as a matter of international law, Israel is bound as a High Contracting Party to the Fourth Geneva Convention to apply the convention's provisions to the OPT notwithstanding the fact that its domestic law considers it to be a non-self-executing treaty. Having concluded that the Fourth Geneva Convention is indeed applicable to the OPT, the following section will be devoted to a discussion of Israel's record of observance of the convention over the course of its 35-year military occupation.

C. *Israeli Violations of the Fourth Geneva Convention in the OPT*

As noted at the outset, since 1967 "the Israeli military has consistently violated nearly every provision of the Fourth Geneva Convention" in its capacity as the occupying power in the OPT.[298] Under article 4 of the Fourth Geneva Convention, the approximately 3.1 million Palestinian civilian inhabitants of the OPT have the status of "protected persons."[299] This status entitles them to the human rights protections enshrined therein, which the occupying power itself has a legal duty to safeguard. For reasons of economy, it is impossible to completely catalogue all of Israel's violations of the Fourth Geneva Convention here. For that purpose, a great many studies have been produced by such groups as Amnesty International,[300] Human Rights Watch,[301] B'Tselem,[302] al-Haq,[303] and the International Commission of Ju-

---

296. DAMROSCH ET AL., *supra* note 130, at 453–54.

297. VIENNA CONVENTION ON THE LAW OF TREATIES, art. 27, May 23, 1969, 1155 U.N.T.S. 331 (1969) [hereinafter VIENNA CONVENTION].

298. Pacheco, *supra* note 22, at 184.

299. FOURTH GENEVA CONVENTION, *supra* note 6, art. 4.

300. *See* AMNESTY INT'L, REPORT AND RECOMMENDATION OF AN AMNESTY INTERNATIONAL MISSION TO THE GOVERNMENT OF THE STATE OF ISRAEL, 3–7 JUNE 1979 (1980) [hereinafter AMNESTY INT'L, REPORT OF MISSION TO ISRAEL]. *See also* AMNESTY INT'L, *supra* note 189.

301. *See generally* HUMAN RIGHTS WATCH, TORTURE AND ILL-TREATMENT: ISRAEL'S INTERROGATION OF PALESTINIANS FROM THE OCCUPIED TERRITORIES (1994).

302. *See generally* RON DUDAI, FREE REIN: VIGILANTE SETTLERS AND ISRAEL'S NON-ENFORCEMENT OF THE LAW (2001); RON DUDAI, NO WAY OUT: MEDICAL IMPLICATIONS OF ISRAEL'S SIEGE POLICY (2001); RON DUDAI, TACIT CONSENT: ISRAELI LAW ENFORCEMENT ON SETTLERS IN THE OCCUPIED TERRITORIES (2001) [hereinafter DUDAI, TACIT CONSENT]; YEHEZKEL LEIN, NOT EVEN A DROP: THE WATER CRISIS IN PALESTINIAN VILLAGES WITHOUT A WATER NETWORK (2001); YAEL STEIN, STANDARD ROUTINE: BEATINGS AND ABUSE OF PALESTINIANS BY ISRAELI SECURITY FORCES DURING THE AL-AQSA INTIFADA (2001).

303. *See* AL-HAQ, A NATION UNDER SIEGE: AL-HAQ ANNUAL REPORT ON HUMAN RIGHTS IN THE OCCUPIED PALESTINIAN TERRITORIES, 1989 (1990); AL-HAQ, ISRAEL'S WAR ON EDUCATION IN THE WEST BANK: A PENALTY FOR THE FUTURE (1988); AL-HAQ, PUNISHING A NATION: HUMAN RIGHTS VIOLATIONS DURING THE PALESTINIAN UPRISING, DECEMBER 1978–DECEMBER 1988 (1988); AL-HAQ, BRIEFING PAPERS ON TWENTY YEARS OF ISRAELI OCCUPATION OF THE WEST BANK AND GAZA (1987); AL-HAQ, IN THEIR OWN WORDS: HUMAN RIGHTS VIOLATIONS IN THE WEST BANK (1983); Jonathan Kuttab, *Avenues Open for the Defence of Human Rights in the Israeli-Occupied Territories*, *in* INTERNATIONAL LAW AND ADMINISTRATION, *supra* note 11, at 489.

rists.[304] Suffice it to say, the al-Aqsa intifada in the OPT has been accompanied by a drastic increase in serious violations of international humanitarian law, many of which constitute grave breaches of the Fourth Geneva Convention and thus war crimes under international law. This Section will discuss a number of these violations, with a focus on Israel's more long-term grave breaches.

1. Annexation and Illegal Expropriation of Palestinian Land

Annexation of occupied territory is absolutely prohibited under the law of belligerent occupation.[305] Article 47 of the Fourth Geneva Convention stipulates that the convention shall continue to apply to occupied territory notwithstanding any attempt by the occupying power to annex the territory in whole or in part.[306] Similarly, article 147 of the Fourth Geneva Convention identifies as a "grave breach" the "extensive . . . appropriation of property, not justified by military necessity and carried out unlawfully and wantonly."[307] Under article 8, section 2(a)(iv) of the Rome Statute this act is considered a war crime.[308]

Since the turn of the twentieth century, the issue of land has remained at the heart of the Israel/Palestine conflict.[309] In many respects, the objectives of modern Zionist policy respecting the OPT closely mirror those of the Zionist settlers in the pre-1948 period.[310] Since 1967, Israel has engaged in a systematic campaign of usurpation of Palestinian land in the OPT for the purpose of establishing exclusively Jewish colonies.[311] By and large, this campaign has manifested itself through two distinct methods. The first is annexation and describes Israel's land policy in and around occupied East Jerusalem. The second is expropriation and embodies its policy respecting the remainder of the OPT. Each of these phenomena will be dealt with in turn.

Immediately following the close of hostilities in June 1967, the Israeli government passed a number of acts which extended its municipal law and jurisdiction to occupied East Jerusalem, effectively annexing the city in violation of international law. Among other things, Israel unilaterally expanded the city's "6.5 square kilometer land area to encompass 71 square kilometers of expropriated Palestinian land" in the surrounding areas of the West

304. Jordan J. Paust et al., *Report of the ICJ Mission of Inquiry into the Israeli Military Court System in the Occupied West Bank and Gaza*, 14 HASTINGS INT'L & COMP. L. REV. 1 (1990) [hereinafter *ICJ Mission of Inquiry*].

305. BENVENISTI, *supra*, note 219, at 3.

306. FOURTH GENEVA CONVENTION, *supra* note 6, art. 47.

307. *Id.* art. 147.

308. ROME STATUTE, *supra* note 239, art. 8, § 2(a)(iv).

309. Ibrahim Matar, *Exploitation of Land and Water Resources for Jewish Colonies in the Occupied Territories*, in INTERNATIONAL LAW AND ADMINISTRATION, *supra* note 11, at 443, 444.

310. *Id.*

311. See *infra* text accompanying notes 329–356 for a discussion of Jewish colonies in the OPT.

Bank,[312] and set out to develop and effectuate a mass expropriation policy aimed at divesting Palestinian owners of vast tracts of land.[313] Over the course of the 35-year occupation, Israel has expropriated—without compensation—over 60,000 dunums of Palestinian land in occupied East Jerusalem, all of which has been converted to exclusive Jewish use.[314] This amounts to roughly 86.5% of the total land area of occupied East Jerusalem as expanded by Israel.[315] Among the ostensibly legal methods used to justify this illegal annexation and expropriation have been: Military Order Number 70 (1967), allowing Israeli authorities to arbitrarily declare any locale a "closed military area," transferring all use to the state;[316] Military Order Number 150 (1968), enabling the state to expropriate land belonging to "absentee" Palestinian owners, or individuals who were not accounted for in an Israeli census following the 1967 war;[317] and Military Order Number 321 (1968), authorizing the state to unilaterally expropriate Palestinian land for "public" purposes, which is "almost always synonymous with exclusive Jewish use."[318] In July 1980, Israel attempted to further consolidate its annexation of occupied East Jerusalem through the passing of its "Basic Law: Jerusalem," under which the city was declared the eternal capital of the state.[319] In response, the United Nations Security Council passed Resolution 478, affirming, inter alia, "that the enactment of the 'basic law' by Israel constitutes a violation of international law and does not affect the continued application of the" Fourth Geneva Convention to the OPT, "including Jerusalem," and "that all legislative and administrative measures and actions taken by Israel, the occupying Power, which have altered or purport to alter the character and status of" the city "are null and void and must be rescinded forthwith."[320]

Israeli law and policy respecting the remainder of the OPT is highly similar to that governing its control over occupied East Jerusalem, with the exception that it has not formally annexed the territory. Instead, it has utilized a host of near identical military orders to expropriate a massive expanse of Palestinian land, resulting in the de facto annexation of the vast majority of the OPT, without having to absorb its large Palestinian population through the extension of its citizenship.[321] Since 1967, the hundreds of military orders that have been used as a pretext for this policy include: Military

---

312. ALLISON B. HODGKINS, THE JUDAIZATION OF JERUSALEM 6 (1996). The laws in question are the Law and Administration Ordinance (Amendment No. 11) Law, 21 L.S.I. 75 (1967), and the Municipalities Ordinance (Amendment No. 6) Law, 21 L.S.I. 75 (1967).

313. HODGKINS, *supra* note 312, at 22–23.

314. UNITED NATIONS, COMM. ON THE EXERCISE OF THE INALIENABLE RIGHTS OF THE PALESTINIAN PEOPLE, THE STATUS OF JERUSALEM 22–23 (1997). Note: one dunum is approximately equal to 1,000 square meters or 0.247 acres.

315. *Id.*

316. HODGKINS, *supra* note 312, at 79.

317. *Id.*

318. *Id.* at 23.

319. Basic Law: Jerusalem, Capital of Israel, 34 L.S.I. 209 (1980).

320. S.C. Res. 478, *supra* note 283, at 14.

321. *See* SHEHADEH, *supra* note 185, at 3.

Order Number 59 (1967), permitting the Israeli military government to declare all lands not registered with them as "state lands," thereby restricting their use to Israeli authorities;[322] Military Order Number 58 (1967), enabling Israeli authorities to confiscate lands of those "absent" during the 1967 census;[323] Military Order Number S/1/96, allowing Israeli authorities to unilaterally declare Palestinian land a "closed military area," thereby preventing its use from all but the state";[324] and Military Order Number T/27/96, permitting Israeli authorities to expropriate Palestinian land for "public" purposes.[325]

Importantly, notwithstanding its express agreement in article XXXI(7) of the 1995 Interim Agreement on the West Bank and Gaza Strip to refrain from initiating or taking "any step that will change the status of the West Bank and Gaza Strip pending the outcome of the permanent status negotiations,"[326] Israel has continued to expropriate Palestinian land in the OPT.[327] As stated above, the purpose of this expropriation has been to continue its colonization of the OPT. There is little doubt that under article 147 of the Fourth Geneva Convention, Israel's extensive annexation—itself invalid under article 47—and expropriation of Palestinian land in the OPT constitutes a "grave breach" of international humanitarian law.[328]

2. Jewish Colonial Settlement

Article 49 of the Fourth Geneva Convention provides that "[t]he Occupying Power shall not deport or transfer parts of its own civilian population into the territory it occupies."[329] Under article 8, section 2(b)(viii) of the Rome Statute, this act is defined as a "serious violation of the laws and customs applicable in international armed conflict" and may give rise to individual criminal responsibility thereunder.[330] According to the official ICRC commentary on the Fourth Geneva Convention, the intent of article 49 was to "prevent a practice adopted during the Second World War by certain Powers, which transferred portions of their own population to occupied territory for political and racial reasons or in order, as they claimed, to colonize those territories."[331]

---

322. SHEHADEH, *supra* note 148, at 27.

323. *Id.* at 35.

324. U.N. Econ. & Soc. Council, *Report on the Economic and Social Repercussions of the Israeli Settlements on the Palestinian People in the Palestinian Territory, Including Jerusalem, Occupied Since 1967, and on the Arab Population of the Syrian Golan Heights*, U.N. ESCOR, 52d Sess., ¶ 15, U.N. Doc. A/52/172/E/1997/71 (1997).

325. *Id.* ¶ 14.

326. INTERIM AGREEMENT ON THE WEST BANK AND GAZA STRIP, art. XXXI(7), Isr.-P.L.O., Sept. 28, 1995 [hereinafter INTERIM AGREEMENT].

327. *See* Geoffrey Aronson, *Settlement Monitor*, J. PALESTINE STUD., Autumn 1996, at 128.

328. For United Nations pronouncements on this issue, see S.C. Res. 465, *supra* note 283, at 5; G.A. Res. 47/70 C, *supra* note 288, at 98.

329. FOURTH GENEVA CONVENTION, *supra* note 6, art. 49.

330. ROME STATUTE, *supra* note 239, art. 8, § 2(b)(viii).

331. OSCAR M. UHLER ET AL., THE GENEVA CONVENTIONS OF 12 AUGUST 1949: COMMENTARY

For its part, Israel has never concealed the colonial intent underlying its 35-year program of annexation and expropriation of Palestinian land in the OPT. In similar fashion to Yishuv policy in the pre-1948 period, since 1967, Israeli state planners have colonized the OPT with exclusively Jewish settlements intended to impose a *fait accompli*, rendering any future withdrawal by the occupying power—whose international legal status is merely that of a provisional administrator with limited powers and no sovereign rights—all but impossible. According to a 1980 plan prepared by Mattiyahu Drobles of the Settlement Department of the World Zionist Organization (the so-called "Drobles Plan"):[332]

> The best and most effective way of removing every shadow of doubt about our intention to hold on to Judea and Samaria [i.e., the West Bank] forever is by speeding up the [Jewish colonial] settlement momentum in these territories. The purpose of settling the areas between and around the centers occupied by the minorities [that is, the Palestinian majority in the West Bank] is to reduce to the minimum the danger of an additional Arab state being established in these territories. Being cut off by Jewish settlements, the minority population will find it difficult to form a territorial and political continuity.[333]

Over the course of the occupation, Israel's colonial settlement policy in the OPT has largely developed along the lines articulated in the Drobles Plan. Palestinian city centers have been surrounded by ever-expanding Jewish colonies and bypass roads.[334] According to the United Nations Special Rapporteur to the Commission on Human Rights, this has had the effect of dividing the West Bank "into some 60 discontiguous zones" and "segmenting the Gaza Strip into four parts."[335] Palestinian freedom of movement to and from these areas is severely restricted by an intricate network of Israeli military checkpoints that may only be traversed by those possessing special travel permits from the Israeli military authorities. The construction of

---

283 (Jean S. Pictet ed., Ronald Griffin & C.W. Dumbleton trans., 1958).

332. The World Zionist Organization was constituted by Theodor Herzl at the First Zionist Congress in Basel, Switzerland in 1897. MALLISON & MALLISON, *supra* note 74, at 19. "Since the 1922 League of Nations Mandate for Palestine, the term 'Zionist Organization' has been equivalent to the term 'Jewish Agency.'" *Id.* at 8. Today it operates as a quasi-governmental body of the government of the state of Israel, existing both within the state and extraterritorially, "to achieve the political objectives of Zionism." *Id.*

333. MATTIYAHU DROBLES, MASTER PLAN FOR THE DEVELOPMENT OF SETTLEMENT IN JUDEA AND SAMARIA (1980), *as quoted in* Matar, *supra* note 309, at 446.

334. For a discussion of Israel's network of bypass roads intended to service its system of colonies in the West Bank, see Samira Shah, *On the Road to Apartheid: The Bypass Road Network in the West Bank,* 29 COLUM. HUM. RTS. L. REV. 221 (1997).

335. U.N. Comm'n on Human Rights, *Question of the Violation of Human Rights in the Occupied Arab Territories, Including Palestine—Update to the Mission Report on Israel's Violations of Human Rights in the Palestinian Territories Occupied Since 1967, Submitted by Giorgio Giacomelli, Special Rapporteur, to the Commission on Human Rights at its Fifth Special Session,* U.N. ESCOR, 57th Sess., ¶ 26, U.N. Doc. E/CN.4/2001/30 (2001) [hereinafter *Human Rights Commission Update*].

Jewish colonies in and around occupied East Jerusalem has had a particularly devastating impact, altering the demography of the city in the Jewish state's favor, and geographically severing it from its natural West Bank hinterland.

Over the course of Israel's occupation, the number of Jewish settlers in the OPT has steadily increased, with colonial settlement construction fluctuating "between 2,000 and 5,000 housing units each year."[336] Whereas in 1972 there were 8,400 Jewish settlers in the OPT, by 1992 that number reached 250,784.[337] Again, notwithstanding its commitment in the Interim Agreement to refrain from altering the status of the OPT pending the outcome of permanent status negotiations with the PLO, since the onset of the peace process in 1993, the number of Jewish settlers has increased at an unprecedented rate. As of February 2002, the population of Jewish settlers in the OPT stood at appoximately 384,000, with no sign of the settlement process receding.[338] Since his election in January 2001, Israeli Prime Minister Ariel Sharon has authorized construction of more than fifty new colonies on expropriated Palestinian land.[339] In the West Bank, including East Jerusalem, there are 376,000 Jewish settlers living in 141 colonies among approximately 2 million Palestinians.[340] Nevertheless, the lands upon which the colonies are built (in addition to "adjacent confiscated land, settlement [bypass] roads and other land controlled by the" Israeli military authorities) amount to fifty-nine percent of the total land area of the West Bank.[341] In the Gaza Strip—an area only 140 square miles in size—7000 Jewish settlers live on twenty percent of the land, with the remainder left for the approximately 1.1 million Palestinian inhabitants, the vast majority of them impoverished refugees, making it one of the most densely populated places on earth.[342]

In addition to severely limiting the amount of land resources available to the indigenous Palestinian population in the OPT, Israel's Jewish colonies have been the cause of an acute water shortage for Palestinians.[343] With many of the colonies "strategically located to command access to the main aquifer underlying the West Bank,"[344] Israel has maintained a "patently unfair" distribution of water since 1967.[345] For instance, Jewish "settlers con-

---

336. Found. for Middle East Peace, *Israeli Settlements in the Occupied Territories: A Guide* (Mar. 2002), http://www.fmep.org/reports/2002/sr0203.html.

337. *Id.*

338. *Id.*

339. Geoffrey Aronson, *New "Outposts" Lead Settlement Expansion*, REPORT ON ISRAELI SETTLEMENT IN THE OCCUPIED TERRITORIES, Sept.-Oct. 2002, http://www.fmep.org/reports/2002/v12n5.html

340. Found. for Middle East Peace, *supra* note 336.

341. *Id.*

342. *Id.*

343. *See* LEIN, *supra* note 302.

344. Found. for Middle East Peace, *supra* note 336.

345. LEIN, *supra* note 302, at 3.

sume six times more water per capita than Palestinians,"[346] while "218 Palestinian communities are not connected to a water network."[347]

Even more problematic than the water problem, is the security problem. Since 1967, the Israeli military has furnished Jewish settlers with arms that have frequently been used to terrorize Palestinians in the OPT.[348] In the period between December 1987 and March 2001, "119 Palestinians, among them 23 minors, [were] killed by Jewish settlers."[349] As documented by the Israeli human rights organization, B'Tselem, this settler violence occurs with the "tacit consent" of Israeli military authorities who rarely, if ever, punish the perpetrators with the same severity exacted against Palestinians[350]—not an insignificant matter given "Israel's legal duty, as an occupying power, to protect the well-being and security of the Palestinian population under its control."[351] This difference in treatment is no doubt the result of the fact that since 1967 Israel has imposed two different systems of law in the OPT, in what Allegra Pacheco has called "an apartheid-like legal and rights structure."[352] Under this structure, separate Israeli civilian and military legal systems operate concurrently in the OPT, the applicability of which is determined solely by the nationality of the individual concerned, effectively dividing the population along racial lines. As such, Jewish colonial settlers are extra-territorially subject to Israeli civilian laws as Israeli-Jewish citizens, while the Palestinian inhabitants of the OPT are strictly subject to the much more repressive Israeli military laws.[353] Thus, in addition to violating article

---

346. Found. for Middle East Peace, *supra* note 336.

347. LEIN, *supra* note 302, at 6.

348. *See generally* DUDAI, TACIT CONSENT, *supra* note 302.

349. *Id.* at 3.

350. *Id.* at 36. As noted by Dudai,

> [settler] violence occurs against the background of leniency and prolonged impotence of the Israeli law-enforcement authorities. These factors received much media coverage following two recent decisions of Israeli courts. The first was the Supreme Court's ruling to accept the Parole Board's decision to release Yoram Skolnick, convicted of killing a Palestinian who was tied up, after serving only eight years in jail. . . . The second decision was the Jerusalem District Court's sentence, following a plea bargain, of Nahum Korman to six months' public service for his manslaughter conviction in the killing of an 11-year-old Palestinian boy.

Id. at 3.

351. *Id.* Israel's colonial settlement policy in the OPT has been roundly condemned by the international community as being in clear violation of article 49 of the Fourth Geneva Convention. For instance, following three assassination attempts by Jewish settlers on the Palestinian mayors of Nablus, Ramallah, and al-Bireh in 1980, the U.N. Security Council passed Resolution 471 of June 5, 1980, expressing its deep concern "that the Jewish settlers in the occupied Arab territories are allowed to carry arms, thus enabling them to perpetrate crimes against the civilian Arab population," and "that Israel, as the occupying Power, has failed to provide adequate protection to the civilian population in the occupied territories in conformity with the provisions of the [Fourth] Geneva Convention." S.C. Res. 471, *supra* note 283, at 10–11. Likewise, following the massacre of twenty-nine Palestinian Muslim worshipers in the Ibrahimi Mosque in al-Khalil (Hebron) by a Jewish settler in 1994, the U.N. Security Council passed Resolution 904 of March 18, 1994, calling "upon Israel, the occupying Power, to continue to take and implement measures, including inter alia, confiscation of arms, with the aim of preventing illegal acts of violence by Israeli settlers." S.C. Res. 904, *supra* note 283, at 108.

352. Pacheco, *supra* note 22, at 191.

353. As noted by Dudai,

49 of the Fourth Geneva Convention, Israel's Jewish colonial settlements in the OPT potentially represent very serious transgressions of other international human rights and criminal law conventions, including the International Convention on the Elimination of all forms of Racial Discrimination,[354] the Rome Statute,[355] and the International Convention on the Suppression and Punishment of the Crime of Apartheid.[356]

3. Wilful and Extrajudicial Killing or Execution

Just as all municipal legal systems prohibit the crime of murder, article 147 of the Fourth Geneva Convention outlaws the "wilful killing" of protected persons and categorizes such acts as "grave breaches" of the convention.[357] Similarly, article 8, section 2(a)(i) of the Rome Statute defines the "wilful killing" of protected persons in occupied territory as a war crime.[358]

Since 1967, Israel has employed a policy authorizing the wilful killing of Palestinian civilians engaged in mass protests and popular marches against the occupation. This policy initially came to the fore during the intifada of 1987–1993, in which hundreds of civilian protesters were killed by Israeli military authorities, and tens of thousands were maimed and permanently injured through the use of live fire and rubber-coated metal bullets.[359] As discussed previously, the Israeli response to the al-Aqsa intifada has been exponentially more violent than its predecessor, with the result that, between its outbreak in September 2000 and December 2002, approximately 1800 Palestinians have been killed,[360] the "vast majority" of them by live gunfire.[361] According to B'Tselem, "[t]he principal reason for these deaths is

---

[t]he Israeli [civilian] legal system grants [Jewish] settlers a number of legal rights that are absent from the military-justice system applying to Palestinians. The period of detention of a suspect before being brought before a judge, the right to meet with an attorney, the defenses available to a defendant at trial, maximum sentences set by law, release of prisoners before serving a full sentence—all of these differ in the two systems of law, with the Israeli [civilian] system granting more extensive rights and defenses.

DUDAI, TACIT CONSENT, *supra* note 302, at 5.

354. INTERNATIONAL CONVENTION ON THE ELIMINATION OF ALL FORMS OF RACIAL DISCRIMINATION, art. 1, Mar. 7, 1966, 660 U.N.T.S. 195 (1966).

355. ROME STATUTE, *supra* note 239, art. 7, § 1(j).

356. INTERNATIONAL CONVENTION ON THE SUPPRESSION AND PUNISHMENT OF THE CRIME OF APARTHEID, G.A. Res. 3068, U.N. GAOR, 28th Sess., Supp. No. 30, at 75, U.N. Doc. A/9030 (1973).

357. FOURTH GENEVA CONVENTION, *supra* note 6, art. 147.

358. ROME STATUTE, *supra* note 239, art. 8, § 2(a)(i).

359. *See* B'Tselem, *Palestinians Killed in the Occupied Territories (including East Jerusalem), since the Beginning of the Intifada (Dec. 9, 1987) until the end of January 2002*, http://www.btselem.org/English/Statistics/Total_Casualties.asp.

360. Amnesty Int'l, *supra* note 186.

361. B'Tselem, *The Open Fire Regulations*, http://www.btselem.org/english/Open_Fire_Regulations/index.asp. According to LAW: The Palestinian Society for the Protection of Human Rights and the Environment (LAW), a non-governmental organization operating in Jerusalem, between September 2000 and March 22, 2002, 1200 Palestinians were killed, and 18,485 were injured. According to their statistics, "[a]bout 81.07% of those killed and 97.02% of those injured are civilians not serving in the PA [Palestinian Authority] civilian police or security forces." LAW, *Updated Overview of Israeli War Crimes and Crimes Against Humanity*, Apr. 2, 2002 (*prepared by* Dianne Luping), http://www.lawsociety.org/Reports/

the deliberate policy of allowing lethal gunfire in situations where [Israeli] soldiers are not in danger" or in "life-threatening situations."[362] Under its internal "open fire regulations," the Israeli military authorizes its troops to use live fire only in "life-threatening" situations, but includes in its definition of "life-threatening" the act of stone-throwing—the most widely used tactic among Palestinian civilian protesters in the OPT.[363] Particularly disturbing is the evidence found by the U.N. Commission on Human Rights in its report on the first seven months of the al-Aqsa intifada "that many of the deaths and injuries inflicted were the result of head wounds and wounds to the upper body, which suggests an intention to cause serious bodily injury rather than to restrain demonstrations/confrontations."[364]

Quite apart from its practice of using live fire on unarmed civilian protesters, since 1967 Israel has engaged in the practice of "extrajudicial executions or targeted political assassinations" of members or leaders of Palestinian resistance groups in the OPT.[365] According to a recent Amnesty International report:

> Israel has for years pursued a policy of assassinating its political opponents. Because extrajudicial executions are universally condemned, most governments who practice assassinations surround such actions in secrecy and deny carrying out the killings they may have ordered. Although the Israeli government prefers to talk about "targeted killings" and "preventative actions" (or "pinpointed preventative actions") rather than "extrajudicial executions," members of the Israeli government have confirmed that such killings are a deliberate government policy carried out under government orders.[366]

Over the course of the occupation, the methods employed by Israel in its commission of these acts have included sniper fire, undercover death squads, and—especially in the current uprising—heavy weapons, such as rocket fire from Apache helicopter gunships or F-16 jet fighters.[367] Since September 2000, "at least 72 Palestinian activists have been assassinated" using these methods.[368] In addition, "at least 20 bystanders (including 5 children)" have

---

362. B'Tselem, *supra* note 361.

363. *Id.*

364. U.N. Comm'n on Human Rights, *Question of the Violation of Human Rights in the Occupied Arab Territories, Including Palestine—Report of the Human Rights Commission Established Pursuant to Commission Resolution S-5/1 of 19 October 2000*, U.N. ESCOR, 57th Sess., ¶ 47, U.N. Doc. E/CN.4/2001/121 (2001) [hereinafter *Human Rights Commission Report*].

365. *Id.* ¶ 54.

366. AMNESTY INT'L, *supra* note 189, at 32–33.

367. *See Human Rights Commission Update, supra* note 335, ¶ 11. *See also Human Rights Commission Report, supra* note 364, ¶ 57. For statistical information on the number of extrajudicial killings committed by Israeli death squads, see B'Tselem, *Casualties by the Undercover Units in the Occupied Territories (including East Jerusalem) since the Beginning of the Intifada (Dec. 9, 1987), until the End of April 2001*, http://www.btselem.org/English/Open_Fire_Regulations/Undercover_Units_Statistics.asp.

368. LAW, *supra* note 361.

been killed as a result.[369] Although the Israeli military authorities claim that those who are killed extrajudicially are legitimate military targets due to their alleged involvement in the killing of Israelis, no evidence or proof of guilt is ever offered, nor is the right to make full answer and defense afforded.[370] As noted by the U.N. Commission on Human Rights, in the absence of any proof to the contrary, the civilian character of those targeted remains intact and they continue to enjoy the status and rights of protected persons under the Fourth Geneva Convention.[371] In any event, "there is no legal foundation" in the law of belligerent occupation "for killing protected persons on the basis of suspicion or even on the basis of evidence of their supposedly menacing activities or possible future undertakings."[372] In essence, such extrajudicial executions amount to "wilful killings" under article 147 of the Fourth Geneva Convention and, by extension, are war crimes at international law.

Even more unsettling has been Israel's practice of targeting ambulances, medical relief workers, and journalists in the OPT during the al-Aqsa intifada. According to a B'Tselem report, between February 28 and March 13, 2002, "intentional [Israeli] attacks on medical teams and the prevention of medical teams from treating the sick and wounded [were] almost unprecedented."[373] In that period alone, a total of five Palestinian medical personnel were killed while on duty,[374] including the head of the Palestinian Red Crescent Society (PRCS) in Jenin,[375] with many more seriously wounded. Inves-

---

369. *Id.* One such case was the extrajudicial killing of Jamal Mansur and Jamal Salim on July 31, 2001. The event was reported in AMNESTY INT'L, *supra* note 189, at 37–38, as follows:

On 31 July 2001 the Israeli Air Force killed eight people, among them two children and two journalists, and wounded 15 others, including a human rights defender, as they shot two missiles from an Apache helicopter at the Nablus-based Palestinian Centre for Information, run by a Hamas leader, Jamal Mansur. The two Hamas leaders killed, Jamal Mansur and Jamal Salim, had both been held in the past in administrative detention by Israel. Jamal Mansur had later spent more than three years in detention without charge or trial under the PA [Palestinian Authority] between 1997 and 2000. The two journalists killed, Muhammad Beshawi and 'Uthman Qatanani, were apparently interviewing Jamal Mansur at the time of the attack. Two children, Ashraf Khader, aged six, and Bilal Khader, aged 11, were killed as they played outside, while their mother visited a clinic in the same building. Ahmad Abu Shallal, a human rights defender, who was critically injured, works for the International Solidarity organization, based in Washington, USA. He was reportedly visiting the office of the Palestinian Centre for Information to collect material for a report he was preparing on refugees.

370. AMNESTY INT'L, *supra* note 189, at 34. *See also Human Rights Commission Report, supra* note 364, ¶ 62.

371. *Human Rights Commission Report, supra* note 364, ¶ 62.

372. *Id.* ¶ 63. *See, e.g.,* FOURTH GENEVA CONVENTION, *supra* note 6, art. 27 (providing that "[p]rotected persons are entitled, in all circumstances, to respect for their persons, . . . especially against all acts of violence"). *See also id.* art. 32 (providing that "[t]he High Contracting Parties specifically agree that each of them is prohibited from taking any measure of such a character as to cause the physical suffering or extermination of protected persons in their hands"); *id.* art. 68 (limiting the application of the death penalty by an occupying power and, in any event, requiring a judicial trial prior to such punishment).

373. Press Release, B'Tselem, *Stop Shooting at Ambulances and Allow Medical Treatment,* Mar. 14, 2002, http://www.btselem.org/English/Press_Releases/2002/020314.asp.

374. *Id.*

375. Press Release, Human Rights Watch, *Israel: Cease Attacking Medical Personnel,* Mar. 9, 2002,

tigations by B'Tselem, Human Rights Watch, and the ICRC demonstrate that this targeting has become "an integral part of Israeli policy" in the OPT.[376] According to Amnesty International, between March 29 and April 5, 2002 "more than 350 ambulances had been denied access" to the sick and wounded, "and 185 ambulances had been hit by [Israeli] gunfire."[377] As a result, on April 5, 2002 the ICRC announced its decision "to limit its movements in the West Bank to a strict minimum" owing to Israeli military "attacks on its vehicles and premises."[378]

Members of the international media cannot be said to enjoy much better treatment. The International Federation of Journalists has repeatedly protested Israeli targeting of media personnel and outlets in the OPT, in what it considers "a vicious attempt to prevent journalists from reporting on a story that affects millions of people around the world."[379] Over the course of the al-Aqsa intifada, at least three journalists have been killed by Israeli fire, and many more have been wounded, prompting the Committee to Protect Journalists to declare "the West Bank as the world's worst place to be a journalist."[380] Israel's policy of attacking medical relief workers and journalists—all "protected persons" under article 4 of the Fourth Geneva Convention—gives cause for serious concern not only because the killings of those directly targeted amount to grave breaches under the convention,[381] but more generally because it impedes the provision of emergency medical relief and interna-

http://hrw.org/press/2002/03/medics030902.htm.

376. Press Release, B'Tselem, *supra* note 373. *See also* Press Release, Int'l Comm. of the Red Cross, *Israel and the Occupied and Autonomous Territories: ICRC Appeals for Protection of Medical Staff*, Mar. 8, 2002, Press Release 02/19, http://www.icrc.org/Web/eng/siteeng0.nsf/iwpList74/F34CD17608954CACC125 6B98004B0DCB. Human Rights Watch reported the following incident:

Ibrahim Assad, a PRCS driver, and Kamal Salem, of the United Nations Relief and Works Agency for Palestine Refugees (UNRWA) were killed by Israeli fire on March 7 while en route to provide emergency assistance to wounded in the West Bank town of Tulkarem. Medical personnel have informed Human Rights Watch that Ibrahim Assad had received permission to move forward from the Israeli authorities. He drove some 750 meters, and was shot in the hand from the machine gun of an Israeli tank. He exited the ambulance, and was then shot in the head. The International Committee of the Red Cross and PRCS have publicly stated that all ambulances were clearly marked and were coordinating their movements closely with the Israeli authorities.

Human Rights Watch, *supra* note 375.

377. *See* AMNESTY INT'L, ISRAEL AND THE OCCUPIED TERRITORIES: THE HEAVY PRICE OF ISRAELI INCURSIONS 12 (2002). In the words of Peter Hansen, Commissioner-General of UNRWA, "I would strongly suggest that when 185 ambulances have been hit, including 75 percent of UNRWA's ambulances . . . this is not the result of stray bullets by mistake hitting an ambulance, this can only be by targeting ambulances."

378. Press Release, Int'l Comm. of the Red Cross, *Israel and the Occupied/Autonomous Territories: ICRC Restricts it Movements in the West Bank*, Apr. 5, 2002, http://www.icrc.org/Web/eng/siteeng0.nsf/ iwpList74/BC00D2113B04DA2EC1256B9800471FBC.

379. Press Release, Int'l Fed'n of Journalists, *Journalists Say Israel Should be Punished for "Reckless War on Media,"* Apr. 9, 2002, http://www.ifj.org/publications/press/pr/327.html. *See also* Calin Neacsu, *Israeli Army Also Targets Reporters in Ramallah*, AGENCE FRANCE PRESSE, Apr. 5, 2002.

380. *Israel's News Blackout Criticized*, BBC NEWS, May 3, 2002, http://news.bbc.co.uk/hi/english/ world/middle_east/newsid_1966000/1966094.stm. *See also* Press Release, Int'l Fed'n of Journalists, *Journalists Accuse Israel of "Failure of Discipline" After Italian Journalist is Killed in Hail of Bullets*, Mar. 13, 2002, http://www.ifj.org/publications/press/pr/311.html.

381. FOURTH GENEVA CONVENTION, *supra* note 6, art. 147. *See also id.* arts. 16–23.

tional reporting crucial to protecting the interests of the civilian population in the OPT.

4. Torture or Inhuman Treatment

International law imposes an absolute prohibition on the use of torture or inhuman treatment.[382] This means that the right to be free from such abuse is non-derogable, no matter the circumstances. It is in this context that "torture or inhuman treatment" is defined as a "grave breach" under article 147 of the Fourth Geneva Convention.[383] Likewise, article 8, section 2(a)(ii) of the Rome Statute defines the "torture or inhuman treatment" of protected persons in occupied territory as a war crime.[384]

Although it has historically denied it, since 1967 Israel has systematically engaged in the torture and inhuman treatment of thousands of Palestinian political detainees in the OPT. In 1987, an Israeli judicial commission of inquiry (the "Landau Commission") was charged with the task of investigating the truth of various allegations that its General Security Service (GSS) was engaged in such practices. The Landau Commission "revealed that between 1971 and 1986 the GSS systematically employed the use of physical pressure on Palestinian suspects under interrogation to procure 'confessions'" that would subsequently form the basis of convictions in military courts.[385] Although it did not publicly specify what methods the GSS had used in this period,[386] the Landau Commission noted that they regularly involved "cases of criminal assault."[387] Notwithstanding these findings, the Landau Commission took the position that the Israeli "government should acknowledge that some measure of coercion is permissible, and then codify and carefully monitor the allowable techniques."[388] Accordingly, the commission recommended that the Israeli authorities use a "moderate measure of physical pressure" in the interrogation of Palestinian political detainees.[389] In November 1987, the Israeli government endorsed the Landau Commission recommendations.[390]

---

382. MELISSA PHILLIPS, TORTURE FOR SECURITY: THE SYSTEMATIC TORTURE AND ILL-TREATMENT OF PALESTINIANS IN ISRAEL 25 (1995).

383. FOURTH GENEVA CONVENTION, supra note 6, art. 147.

384. ROME STATUTE, supra note 239, art. 8, § 2(a)(ii).

385. HUMAN RIGHTS WATCH, supra note 301, at 49.

386. That information is still classified. Id. at 48.

387. COMMISSION OF INQUIRY INTO THE METHODS OF INVESTIGATION OF THE GENERAL SECURITY SERVICE REGARDING HOSTILE TERRORIST ACTIVITIES, LANDAU COMMISSION REPORT, ¶ 4.20, quoted in HUMAN RIGHTS WATCH, supra note 301, at 48 [hereinafter LANDAU COMMISSION REPORT]. Despite these findings, the commission asserted that because Israel regularly faced "hostile terrorist acts" the interrogation methods employed by the GSS were "largely to be defended, both morally and legally." LANDAU COMMISSION REPORT, supra, ¶ 1.8.

388. HUMAN RIGHTS WATCH, supra note 301, at 50.

389. See LANDAU COMMISSION REPORT, supra note 387, ¶ 1.8.

390. PHILLIPS, supra note 382, at 53.

The effect of the Landau Commission recommendations exposed itself immediately following the outbreak of the Intifada of 1987–1993. Because the recommendations authorized the use of "physical pressure" on persons suspected of "political subversion,"[391] thousands of Palestinians in the OPT were arbitrarily arrested and tortured for engaging in what would otherwise fall within the "spectrum of indigenous and permissible activity."[392] These acts "included, *inter alia*, participating in marches consisting of ten or more persons for political purposes, displaying flags or emblems of any political significance, possessing banned books or any publication deemed adverse by the military authorities, and expressing any support or sympathy for the activities or aims of any 'hostile organization.'"[393] According to a number of independent studies conducted by groups such as Amnesty International, Human Rights Watch, B'Tselem, and al-Haq, the methods of torture utilized by Israel in its interrogation of Palestinians included electric shock;[394] violent beatings (often with implements such as truncheons and rifle butts) to all areas of the body including bottoms of feet, the torso, and genitals;[395] sexual assault, including sodomy;[396] application of burning cigarettes;[397] violent shaking;[398] partial suffocation;[399] prolonged abusive body positioning;[400] prolonged exposure to temperature extremes, including the use of refrigerator units;[401] prolonged sleep, space, and toilet deprivation;[402] and death threats and threats of rape of the detainee or female relatives in its interrogation of Palestinians.[403] According to Human Rights Watch, an average of 4000 to 6000 Palestinians have been subjected to interrogation by Israel every year since 1987.[404] Many of these individuals "have died during, or as a result of, the interrogation process."[405]

In addition to the express support torture and inhuman treatment has received at the governmental level, in a series of 1996 cases, the Supreme Court of Israel effectively authorized "the use of physical force against [Pal-

---

391. *ICJ Mission of Inquiry, supra* note 304, at 13.

392. PHILLIPS, *supra* note 382, at 60.

393. *Id.* at 60–61.

394. *Id.* at 23. *See also* STANLEY COHEN & DAPHNA GOLAN, THE INTERROGATION OF PALESTINIANS DURING THE INTIFADA: ILL-TREATMENT, "MODERATE PHYSICAL PRESSURE," OR TORTURE? 32, 35 (1991).

395. *See* HUMAN RIGHTS WATCH, *supra* note 301, at 187–98. *See also* COHEN & GOLAN, *supra* note 394, at 34, 87, 90.

396. AMNESTY INT'L, REPORT OF MISSION TO ISRAEL, *supra* note 300, at 18.

397. COHEN & GOLAN, *supra* note 394, at 34.

398. HUMAN RIGHTS WATCH, *supra* note 301, at 187–98.

399. COHEN & GOLAN, *supra* note 394, at 35.

400. HUMAN RIGHTS WATCH, *supra* note 301, at 111–46.

401. *Id.* at 147–54.

402. *Id.* at 156–86.

403. *Id.* at 199–204.

404. *Id.* at x.

405. Ardi Imseis, *"Moderate" Torture on Trial: Critical Reflections on the Israeli Supreme Court Judgment Concerning the Legality of General Security Service Interrogation Methods,* 19 BERKELEY J. INT'L L. 328, 337 (2001).

estinian] detainees."[406] Following an intense international campaign criti-cizing this policy, a case was brought before the Court in 1999 in which it was asked to rule on the legality of the GSS's use of "moderate physical and psychological pressure."[407] In its ruling, the Court purported to outlaw the use of torture by the GSS.[408] Nevertheless, Israel's treatment of Palestinian detainees during the al-Aqsa intifada has cast serious doubt on this ruling.

According to Amnesty International, "an increasing number of cases of alleged torture [have been] recorded" since September 2000.[409] Between March 29 and April 11, 2002, "more than 4,000 Palestinians were arrested," hundreds en masse, and the arrests were "almost invariably accompanied by cruel and degrading treatment."[410] In November 2001, the United Nations Committee Against Torture reported "that there were numerous allegations of torture and ill-treatment by [Israeli] law-enforcement personnel"—in-cluding the use of methods purportedly outlawed by the Supreme Court in 1999—and "called for Israel to take steps to prevent [such] abuses."[411] For

---

406. AMNESTY INT'L, REPORT 1997, at 193 (1997).

407. *See generally* Imseis, *supra* note 405

408. In a consolidated application brought in late 1999 against the GSS and other governmental bodies and figures, the Court was requested to rule on the legality in Israeli law of the use by the GSS of certain methods of "psychological pressure" and "a moderate degree of physical pressure" on Palestinian detainees in the OPT pursuant to the Landau Commission recommendations. *Supreme Court of Israel: Judgement Concerning the Legality of the General Security Service's Interrogation Methods*, 38 I.L.M. 1471, 1477 (1999). The only "interrogation methods" in issue were the use of violent shaking, a number of pro-longed abusive body positioning techniques, excessive tightening of handcuffs, and prolonged sleep deprivation. *Id.* at 1474–76. The Court held that under Israeli law, as at the time of judgment, the GSS lacked the legal authority to make use of these methods in its interrogation of Palestinians. *Id.* at 1489. Although the judgment was generally lauded as bringing an end to Israel's use of torture in the OPT, this conclusion is tenuous at best. In addition to being plagued by a number of serious legal lacunae—in-cluding a failure even to discuss whether the interrogation methods reviewed amounted to torture under international law—the Court instructed the legislature that if it wanted to authorize the GSS to use such measures of moderate physical and psychological pressure it would have to do so via an express govern-mental enactment. *Id.* at 1487.

409. AMNESTY INT'L, *supra* note 189, at 62.

410. According to Amnesty International, such arrests have followed

[t]he typical pattern [of] a summons by the IDF [i.e., Israeli military] by loudspeaker for all male Palestinians between certain ages (usually 15 to 45) to report at a designated assembly point. [In a number of cases] the loudspeaker had warned that anyone who failed to report might be killed . . . . Once there they were sorted, usually by being asked basic details such as name and age, some were immediately released. However, the majority were blindfolded and handcuffed with plastic hand-cuffs (which can tighten and be extremely painful). Some were numbered on their wrists. However, after protests in the Knesset (Israeli Parliament) and in many sectors of Israeli society, this practice, which was not general, was stopped. The vast majority of those arrested said they were not given any food for the first 24 hours and were not allowed even to go to the toilet; they had to relieve themselves on the ground where they sat. During a season when nights remain extremely cold, no blankets were given to detainees during the first night of their detention. Those arrested and de-tained included many children reportedly as young as 14 or 15.

AMNESTY INT'L, *supra* note 377, at 22.

411. In its final report concerning Israel, the U.N. Commission on Human Rights's Committee Against Torture expressed concern, inter alia,

that the 1999 Supreme Court decision did not contain a definite prohibition of torture; that there were continuing allegations of use of interrogation methods by the Israel Security Agency [i.e., GSS] against Palestinian detainees that were prohibited by the ruling; that there were allegations of torture and ill-treatment of Palestinian minors; that there was continued use of incommunicado deits part, Israel has issued a number of fresh military orders granting it extremely wide powers of arrest and detention,[412] including an order issued on April 5, 2002 retroactively determining that any Palestinian "detained on or after March 29, 2001, can be held for 18 days before being brought before a judge," and "that during the eighteen days of detention, the detainee does not have a right to see a lawyer."[413] In response, B'Tselem filed a petition before the Supreme Court demanding that the "detainees be allowed to meet with lawyers and that the court forbid the use of physical force against the detainees during interrogation."[414] Following a brief hearing on April 7, 2002, a three-judge panel of the Court rejected the petition and upheld the State's argument that under the current circumstances in the OPT "it is impossible to allow" Palestinian detainees "to see lawyers."[415] As for the question of the allegations of torture, the Court "refused to discuss the matter" altogether.[416]

5. *Wilfully Causing Great Suffering or Serious Injury to Body or Health*

Article 147 of the Fourth Geneva Convention outlaws the act of "wilfully causing great suffering or serious injury to body or health" of protected persons, and classifies this as a "grave breach" of the Convention.[417] Similarly, article 8, section 2(a)(iii) of the Rome Statute defines the act of "wilfully causing great suffering or serious injury to body or health" of protected persons in occupied territory as a war crime.[418]

It is evident that this particular crime can encompass virtually all of the grave breaches canvassed thus far. There is little doubt that the cumulative effect of Israel's prolonged military occupation of the OPT has "caused great suffering" and "serious injury to body or health" of the millions of Palestinians subject to its rule. Among other things, the Palestinians' rights to life, liberty, housing, property, food, adequate health care, and education, have all

---

tention, even of children; that there had been very few prosecutions undertaken against alleged perpetrators of torture and ill-treatment, and that there were reported instances of 'extra-judicial killings.'

Press Release, United Nations, *Committee Against Torture Concludes Twenty-seventh Session*, Nov. 23, 2001, http://www.unog.ch/news2/documents/newsen/cat0139e.html.

412. One particular order is directed specifically toward Palestinian children. As noted by the United Nations Special Rapporteur to the Commission on Human Rights,

Israeli Military Order 132 allows for the arrest and detention of Palestinian children aged from 12 to 14 years. At the beginning of the current intifada [i.e., the al-Aqsa intifada], some 70 Palestinian minors were reportedly detained in Israeli prisons. Since then, this number has increased to more than 250. These children range in age from 14 to 17 years, of whom at least 105 are from Jerusalem.

Human Rights Commission Update, *supra* note 335, ¶ 17.

413. B'Tselem, *Torture and Total Communication Ban in Ofer Detention Camp*, http://www.btselem.org/English/Special/Ofer_Detention_Camp.asp.

414. *Id.*

415. *Id.*

416. *Id.*

417. FOURTH GENEVA CONVENTION, *supra* note 6, art. 147.

418. ROME STATUTE, *supra* note 239, art. 8, § 2(a)(iii).

been violated without let since 1967.[419] Of particular concern have been the numerous policies wilfully pursued by Israel aimed at collectively punishing the Palestinians.[420] Some of the most notorious examples of this have been Israel's use of city- or region-wide shoot-to-kill curfews for extended periods of time,[421] the imposition of strict limitations on freedom of movement within the OPT, requiring all Palestinians to possess special travel permits from the Israeli military authorities to traverse the 130 to 150 military checkpoints separating Palestinian villages and towns,[422] and the bulldozing of Palestinian homes—"usually . . . without notice and at night"—belonging to the families of youth suspected of "throwing rocks at Israeli soldiers" in popular demonstrations against the occupation.[423]

The al-Aqsa intifada has been met with a drastic increase in Israeli collective punishment policies that have caused "great suffering or serious injury to body or health" of the Palestinians in the OPT. These policies have included:

> deliberate attacks on medical staff, ambulances, fieldclinics [sic] and hospitals, preventing or restricting access to medical aid and assistance, resulting in deaths, and denial of primary/secondary health care[;] . . . regular and targeted bombardments, shelling and shootings at civilians in civilian areas; regularly flying [over] civilian areas with helicopter gunships and F-16 warplanes; incursions with tanks, armoured personnel carriers and troops; taking over homes and schools as military posts to launch further attacks on civilians—with attacks on residents/destruction of their property/looting and pillage; [and] killings, injuries and various cruel [and] degrading treatment of civilians by Israeli forces at checkpoints.[424]

In addition, and as noted by the United Nations Special Rapporteur to the Commission on Human Rights, "Israeli officials have openly admitted a strategy of restricting the Palestinian economy with the intent and purpose of effecting social control" in the OPT.[425] The effect of this policy—which is rooted in the imposition of a comprehensive military blockade of Palestinian towns and villages—has been to increase the already acute poverty rate in the OPT "from 21.1 per cent. in September 2000, to 31.8 per cent. at the end of 2001."[426] As a result, between September 2000 and March 2001, "the number of Palestinians living on less than U.S.$2 per day [increased] from

---

419. *See Human Rights Commission Update, supra* note 335. *See also* INTERNATIONAL LAW AND ADMINISTRATION, *supra* note 11.

420. Collective punishment is prohibited under article 33 of the FOURTH GENEVA CONVENTION, *supra* note 6.

421. *See* LAW, *supra* note 361.

422. *Id.*

423. UNCEIRPP, *supra* note 5, at 25.

424. Luping, *supra* note 421. *See also Human Rights Commission Update, supra* note 335.

425. *Human Rights Commission Update, supra* note 335, ¶ 20.

426. *Id.* ¶ 21.

650,000 to 1 million."[427] According to a September 2002 report issued by the U.N. Special Coordinator for the Middle East Peace Process, this figure has increased to at least sixty percent of the Palestinian population in the OPT, approximately two million persons.[428] In an attempt to alleviate this humanitarian disaster, "the World Food Programme" has drawn "on its emergency food reserves" in order "to distribute wheat flour to 13,000 [newly impoverished] families," not including the substantial Palestinian refugee population in the OPT.[429] As for them, UNRWA has reported that it is "struggling to provide basic food supplies" to the refugee camps in the OPT.[430] Israeli lawmakers have on more than one occasion declared this policy of economic siege as central to a purported "war of attrition" against the Palestinians, pursued with the aim to "starve them out."[431]

6. *Unlawful Deportation or Transfer*

Article 49 of the Fourth Geneva Convention provides that "[i]ndividual or mass forcible transfers, as well as deportations of protected persons from occupied territory . . . are prohibited, regardless of their motive."[432] Likewise, article 147 of the Fourth Geneva Convention prohibits the "unlawful deportation or transfer" of protected persons from occupied territory, and classifies this as a "grave breach" of the convention.[433] Similarly article 8, section 2(a)(vii) of the Rome Statute defines the "unlawful deportation or transfer" of protected persons from occupied territory as a war crime.[434]

More than any other provision of the Fourth Geneva Convention, the prohibition on the deportation or transfer of protected persons is perhaps the most directly linked to the horrors of World War II. As noted earlier, it was in Nazi-occupied Europe that "millions of human beings were torn from their homes, separated from their families and deported" to death and slave labor camps.[435] Bearing this in mind, the framers of the convention set out in articles 49 and 147 to ensure that future occupying powers would be absolutely barred from deporting or transferring protected persons for any purpose. According to the official ICRC commentary on the Fourth Geneva Convention, "the prohibition [on forcible transfers] is absolute and allows of no exceptions, apart from those stipulated in paragraph 2."[436] Paragraph 2 of

---

427. *Id.* ¶ 14.
428. Office of the U.N. Special Coordinator in the Occupied Territories, *The Impact of Closure and Other Mobility Restrictions on Palestinian Productive Activities, 1 January 2002–30 June 2002*, at 2 (Oct. 2002), http://www.un.org/News/dh/mideast/econ-report-final.pdf.
429. *Id.*
430. *Id. See also* UNRWA, *Emergency Appeal 2002—Progress Report* (Feb. 2002), http://www.un.org/unrwa/emergency/pdf/report14.pdf.
431. LAW, *supra* note 361.
432. FOURTH GENEVA CONVENTION, *supra* note 6, art. 49.
433. *Id.* art. 147.
434. ROME STATUTE, *supra* note 239, art. 8, § 2(a)(vii).
435. PICTET, *supra* note 3, at 129–30.
436. UHLER ET AL., *supra* note 331, at 279.

article 49 allows the occupying power *to evacuate* an area "if the security of the population or imperative military reasons so demand," but it is clear from the language of the provision that such evacuation is not to be understood as deportation or transfer, and in any event is intended to be temporary.[437] According to the ICRC commentary, "protected persons who have been evacuated are to be brought back to their homes as soon as hostilities in the area have ended."[438]

Since 1967, deportation and transfer has been "one of the harshest punishments Israel has used against Palestinians from the" OPT.[439] As a matter of policy, Israeli deportation orders have always been completely summary in nature, offering no opportunity of appeal, and deemed to be absolutely final by the issuing authorities.[440] According to Roberts, Palestinians deported from the OPT have tended to "fall into two broad categories: political leaders and those alleged to be involved directly in hostile activities."[441] Without any doubt, the former group has been most affected by Israel's deportation policy.[442] Covering a wide spectrum of Palestinian intelligentsia, this group has included, inter alia, lawyers, professors, teachers, doctors, trade unionists, religious leaders, and human rights activists. Although there are currently no comprehensive studies detailing the exact number of Palestinians that have been deported by Israel up to the present date, one American source places the figure at just over 1100 for the period between 1967 and 1979,[443] and an authoritative Israeli source states that at least 2000 Palestinians had been deported from the West Bank alone between 1967 and 1986.[444] In its attempt "[t]o thwart resistance" to the occupation, the Israeli "government expelled hundreds of persons" during the course of the intifada of 1987–1993, "primarily those it considered potential leaders" of the popular revolt.[445] The most egregious instance of this occurred on December 17, 1992, when over four hundred Palestinians (among them professors, lawyers, teachers, and clerics) were deported en masse to Lebanon.[446]

---

437. FOURTH GENEVA CONVENTION, *supra* note 6, art. 49. The relevant part of the article reads as follows:

> Nevertheless, the Occupying Power may undertake total or partial evacuation of a given area if the security of the population or imperative military reasons so demand. Such evacuations may not involve the displacement of protected persons outside the bounds of the occupied territory except when for material reasons it is impossible to avoid such displacement. Persons thus evacuated shall be transferred back to their homes as soon as hostilities in the area in question have ceased.

Id.

438. UHLER ET AL., *supra* note 331, at 280–81.

439. B'TSELEM, *supra* note 28, at 22.

440. *Id. See also* UNCEIRPP, *supra* note 5, at 30.

441. Roberts, *supra* note 15, at 65–66.

442. *Id.* at 66.

443. Ann Lesch, *Israeli Deportation of Palestinians From the West Bank and Gaza Strip, 1967–1978*, J. PALESTINE STUD., Winter 1979, at 101, 102.

444. MERON BENVENISTI, THE WEST BANK HANDBOOK: A POLITICAL LEXICON 87 (1986).

445. QUIGLEY, *supra* note 76, at 201.

446. *See* S.C. Res. 799, *supra* note 283, at 6. *See also* B'TSELEM, *supra* note 28, at 22.

The international community—through such bodies as the United Nations Security Council and the United Nations General Assembly—has in no uncertain terms expressed its reprobation with Israel's deportation policy, deeming it to be in clear violation of the law of belligerent occupation in general, and the Fourth Geneva Convention in particular.[447] Both the Israeli government and the Israeli Supreme Court, on the other hand, have defended the policy on a number of grounds, including the argument that deportations from the OPT are "different in character and intent from those that took place in World War II," and that Palestinian deportees are not "protected persons" under the Fourth Geneva Convention.[448]

B'Tselem reports that since the signing of the DOP in 1993, Israel has not used the "draconian measure" of deportation or transfer.[449] Nevertheless, as documented by Masalha, the notion that the Palestinians should *altogether* be transferred from the OPT to other Arab countries has gained increased political currency in Israeli governmental circles in recent years, spearheaded by the official political platforms of the right-wing Moledet, Tehya, and Tzomet parties, as well as by various independent calls for such a mass transfer from members of the Israeli Knesset.[450] The fact that these and other rationales for the unlawful deportation and transfer of Palestinians have been advanced by both the legislative and judicial branches in Israel has only served to contribute to "the deep fears among the Palestinian population [in the OPT] that the deportations carried out" since 1967 represent "the thin end of the wedge, to be followed by larger expulsions" of the sort that occurred during the 1948 and 1967 wars.[451]

7. *Wilful Deprivation of the Rights of Fair and Regular Trial*

One of the most fundamental principles of criminal justice in any legal system is the timely right to make full answer and defense before a compe-

---

447. For Security Council resolutions, see, for example, S.C. Res. 799, *supra* note 283, at 6; S.C. Res. 726, *supra* note 283, at 5; S.C. Res. 694, *supra* note 283, at 4; S.C. Res. 681, *supra* note 283, at 8–9; S.C. Res. 641, *supra* note 283, at 14; S.C. Res. 636, *supra* note 283, at 14; S.C. Res. 608, *supra* note 283, at 2; S.C. Res. 607, *supra* note 283, at 1; S.C. Res. 484, *supra* note 283, at 16; S.C. Res. 469, *supra* note 283, at 9–10; and S.C. Res. 468, *supra* note 283, at 9. For General Assembly resolutions, see, for example, G.A. Res. 48/41 C, U.N. GAOR, 48th Sess., Supp. No. 49, 75th plen. mtg., U.N. Doc. A/48/49 (1993); G.A. Res. 47/70 E, U.N. GAOR, 47th Sess., Supp. No. 49, 85th plen. mtg., U.N. Doc. A/47/49 (1992); G.A. Res. 46/76, U.N. GAOR, 46th Sess., Supp. No. 49, 69th plen. mtg., U.N. Doc. A/46/49 (1991); G.A. Res. 45/69, *supra* note 288, at 32; G.A. Res. 44/2, *supra* note 288, at 12; G.A. Res. 42/160 D, *supra* note 287, at 114; G.A. Res. 41/63 D, U.N. GAOR, 41st Sess., Supp. No. 53, 95th plen. mtg., U.N. Doc. A/41/53 (1986); G.A. Res. 40/161 E, U.N. GAOR, 40th Sess., Supp. No. 53, 118th plen. mtg., U.N. Doc. A/40/53 (1985); G.A. Res. 39/95 D, U.N. GAOR, 39th Sess., Supp. No. 51, 100th plen. mtg., U.N. Doc. A/39/51 (1984); G.A. Res. 38/79 D, U.N. GAOR, 38th Sess., Supp. No. 47, 98th plen. mtg., U.N. Doc. A/38/47 (1983); and G.A. Res. 37/88 D, U.N. GAOR, 37th Sess., Supp. No. 51, 100th plen. mtg., U.N. Doc. A/37/51 (1982).

448. Roberts, *supra* note 15, at 66. *See also* UNCEIRPP, *supra* note 5, at 29; Kuttab, *supra* note 303.

449. B'TSELEM, *supra* note 28, at 22. *But see* H.C. 7015/02, Ajuri v. IDF Commander, [2002] I.L.R. 45 (Israel) (arising out of claims of illegal transfer).

450. *See* MASALHA, IMPERIAL ISRAEL, *supra* note 52, at 163–95.

451. Roberts, *supra* note 15, at 66.

tent and impartial judicial tribunal. Articles 71 to 74 of the Fourth Geneva Convention provide for these and other fundamental penal rights, including the right to "be promptly informed, in writing, [and] in a language" understood by accused persons, "of the particulars of the charges preferred against them";[452] the right to "be assisted by a qualified advocate or counsel of their own choice, who shall be able to visit them freely";[453] and the right to an appeal from a conviction.[454] Likewise, article 147 of the Fourth Geneva Convention prohibits the occupying power from "wilfully depriving a protected person of the rights of fair and regular trial," and classifies such deprivation as a "grave breach" of the convention.[455] Similarly article 8, section 2(a)(vi) of the Rome Statute states that "wilfully depriving a . . . protected person of the rights of fair and regular trial" constitutes a war crime.[456]

Since 1967, Israel has continually violated these penal provisions of the Fourth Geneva Convention in its treatment of Palestinian detainees in the OPT. By far, the most egregious form of this violation has been Israel's practice of administrative detention, which is "detention without charge or trial, authorized by administrative order rather than judicial decree."[457] Under regulations 108 and 111 of Israel's Defence (Emergency) Regulations (1945), local military commanders are authorized to unilaterally order the administrative detention of protected persons in the OPT.[458] Successive Israeli governments have insisted that "[a]dministrative detention is resorted to only in cases where there is corroborating evidence that an individual is engaged in illegal acts which [involve a] danger to state security."[459] Yet, as noted by B'Tselem, Israeli "authorities do not inform detainees or their attorneys of the material on which the detention is based, so it is impossible to question the accuracy of the charges and the justification for the detention."[460] Moreover, "detention order[s] may be renewed indefinitely, for periods of up to six months each time,"[461] and done so by Israeli military commanders "without a judicial hearing."[462] As noted by Amnesty International, since 1967, a great many of Israel's administrative detainees have been prisoners of conscience, held for the "non-violent exercise of [their] right to freedom of expression and association."[463] During the intifada of 1987–1993, "the overall number of Palestinians who were administratively

---

452. FOURTH GENEVA CONVENTION, *supra* note 6, art. 71.

453. *Id.* art. 72.

454. *Id.* art. 73.

455. *Id.* art. 147.

456. ROME STATUTE, *supra* note 239, art. 8, § 2(a)(vi).

457. B'TSELEM, *supra* note 28, at 13.

458. Amnesty Int'l, *Administrative Detention: Despair, Uncertainty and Lack of Due Process*, 2 n.1, Apr. 30, 1997, Report MDE 15/03/1997, http://web.amnesty.org/aidoc/aidoc_pdf.nsf/index/MDE150031997ENGLISH/$File/MDE1500397.pdf.

459. *Id.* at 2.

460. B'TSELEM, *supra* note 28, at 13.

461. *Id.*

462. Amnesty Int'l, *supra* note 458, at 1.

463. *Id.* at 2.

detained was well over 5,000. These included students, labourers, human rights workers, journalists, trade unionists, and teachers."[464] Since the signing of the DOP in 1993, Israel's practice of administrative detention in the OPT has continued unabated.[465] According to B'Tselem, between 1993 and 1999, Israel "detained some one thousand Palestinians for periods ranging from two months to five and a half years."[466] Not surprisingly, the al-Aqsa intifada has been accompanied by a considerable increase in the number of Palestinian administrative detainees imprisoned by Israel. On May 5, 2002, Israel authorities informed the High Court of Justice that close to 1000 such individuals were being held[467]—among them 'Abd al-Rahman al-Ahmar, a local human rights activist and "former B'Tselem fieldworker" who was eventually released on May 23, 2002 after having been imprisoned by Israel without charge or trial for 325 days.[468]

For those Palestinians in the OPT who are afforded a trial by Israel, circumstances are scarcely better. Because their affairs are strictly governed by Israeli military law, trials of Palestinian detainees are conducted before Israeli military courts.[469] According to Amnesty International, the justice meted out by these courts is "seriously flawed."[470] For example:

> [j]udges and prosecutors are officers serving in the IDF [Israeli military] or the reserves. Judges are appointed by the IDF Regional Commander upon the recommendation of the Military Advocate General who is advised by a special committee. They are promoted almost exclusively from the ranks of prosecutors. Once appointed, judges have no right of tenure and can be removed by the Regional Commander. As a result of this lack of tenure and the close links between military judges and prosecutors, serious doubts have been expressed about their impartiality.[471]

In addition, because of Israel's intricate system of military checkpoints used to enforce its blockade of Palestinian areas in the OPT, Palestinian lawyers are frequently unable to meet with their clients or attend important hearings.[472] Because Israeli military courts are located "in military camps or attached to [Jewish] settlements, Palestinian lawyers need authorization to

---

464. *Id.*

465. B'Tselem, *supra* note 28, at 13.

466. *Id.* at 13–14.

467. B'Tselem, *Administrative Detention—Statistics*, http://www.btselem.org/english/Administrative_Detention/Statistics.asp.

468. B'Tselem, *Human Rights Activists in Administrative Detention*, http://www.btselem.org/English/Administrative_Detention/Human_Rights_Activists.asp.

469. AMNESTY INT'L, *supra* note 189, at 64. Again, this is to be distinguished from Israeli-Jewish settlers in the OPT who enjoy the benefits of the Israeli civilian legal system. *See supra* text accompanying notes 352–353.

470. AMNESTY INT'L, *supra* note 189, at 64.

471. *Id.*

472. *Id.*

enter these areas, and often, even with this permission, they may be forbidden to pass through."[473]

Putting aside the fact that a great number of Palestinian detainees are convicted and sentenced to imprisonment for acts that are permissible under the law of belligerent occupation and pose no direct threat to Israel's national survival,[474] other more substantive problems with Israel's system of military justice in the OPT persist. One such problem is that military "[t]rials are usually based on confessions and plea bargains" procured through highly questionable means.[475] The fact that Israeli authorities have for years been known to use torture to elicit confessions, that then form the basis of convictions against their Palestinian deponents, casts doubt on the fairness of the military trial process in the OPT.[476] Furthermore, the fact that "[b]ail is almost invariably refused" and "the time spent waiting for a trial might be roughly equivalent to the time that a person convicted of [an] offence would spend in prison as their sentence"—which is particularly the case respecting the common offences of throwing stones or molotov cocktails—a "not guilty" plea usually guarantees a longer period of detention.[477] Finally, one of the most glaring problems with Israel's military trials of Palestinians in the OPT is the inordinately harsh sentences handed down by its judges. It is not uncommon for Palestinian youth who partake in stone throwing or tire burning in popular demonstrations against the occupation to be sentenced to more than one year's imprisonment.[478] Likewise, Palestinians convicted of serious crimes are dealt with in a much harsher manner than their Israeli-Jewish counterparts in the OPT. According to a recent B'Tselem study, "[w]hereas a Palestinian who kills an Israeli is punished to the full extent of the law, and sometimes his family as well, it is extremely likely that an Israeli who kills a Palestinian will not be punished or will receive only a light sentence."[479]

---

473. *Id.*

474. *See supra* text accompanying notes 391–393. *See also* COHEN & GOLAN, *supra* note 394, at 28.

475. AMNESTY INT'L, *supra* note 189, at 64.

476. *See supra* text accompanying notes 385–416.

477. AMNESTY INT'L, *supra* note 189, at 65.

478. Defence for Children Int'l/Palestine Section, *Violations of Palestinian Children's Rights Stemming from the Israeli Occupation—Fact Sheet* (Mar. 2002), http://www.dci-pal.org/english/reports/factviol.html.

479. DUDAI, TACIT CONSENT, *supra* note 302, at 37. One example of this disparity in sentencing can be seen in the manner in which the cases of Nahum Korman, a Jewish settler, *see supra* note 350, and Sana' 'Amer, a fourteen-year-old Palestinian girl, were dealt with by Israeli authorities. After being convicted of the manslaughter of an eleven-year-old Palestinian boy, Korman was sentenced following a plea bargain to six months of public service. *See* DUDAI, TACIT CONSENT, *supra* note 302, at 3. On the other hand, Sana' 'Amer was charged with planning to stab a Jewish settler after she watched her sister 'Abir attempt to do so. Sana', who had a knife in her pocket when she was arrested, refused an offered plea bargain to serve a three-year prison sentence. "Although she was a minor and had been found . . . without committing any offence, she was sentenced to one year's imprisonment with an additional four-year sentence suspended for five years." *See* AMNESTY INT'L, *supra* note 189, at 65–66.

IV. ENFORCEMENT OF THE FOURTH GENEVA CONVENTION IN THE OCCUPIED PALESTINIAN TERRITORY

Enforcement "is an important but ultimately secondary office in any system of law."[480] This is so "because the question of enforcement can only arise where there has already been a failure" to secure the "primary purpose of law in maintaining defined normative standards of behaviour."[481] In the context of the law of belligerent occupation, the primary purpose "is the effective and impartial protection of victims of armed conflict rather than the punishment of war crimes and other violations after they have been committed."[482] Nevertheless, in cases where there has been an abject failure to ensure compliance with normative standards through proactive implementation of legal obligations *before* breaches take place—as with Israel's violations of the Fourth Geneva Convention—it becomes imperative as a practical matter to shift the focus of analysis to a consideration of the means available to enforce such obligations ex post facto.

The concept of enforcement is typically associated with notions of coercion and retribution. Depending on the context and contours in which enforcement in this sense plays itself out, the result can be either positive or negative.[483] In recent years, a number of scholars have attempted to introduce new theories of compliance with legal obligations at the international level, postulating a move from an "enforcement model" which is necessarily based on coercion, to a "managerial model" that relies primarily on cooperation and problem-solving.[484] Again, for reasons of economy a debate over the relative advantages and disadvantages of these competing theoretical approaches is not here possible. Suffice to say, however, that the extent to which these new theories tend to restrict themselves to situations where violations are not absolutely "premeditated and deliberate,"[485] but are rather the result of an unintended "lack of capability or clarity or priority" to comply, they would seem ill-suited to deal with the case of the enforcement of the Fourth Geneva Convention in the OPT.[486] For Israel has furnished the international community with little reason to believe that its consistent violation of this important body of law has been the result of anything other

---

480. Statement of Hilaire McCoubrey to the United Nations International Meeting [hereinafter McCoubrey Statement], *supra* note 13, at 66.

481. *Id.*

482. *Id.*

483. The Allies' treatment of Germany after World War I and World War II exemplifies the difference in possible outcomes. Whereas the post-World War I settlement at Versailles was seen as unduly punitive in nature and possibly contributing to the growth of Nazi Fascism in the 1930s, the post-World War II settlement and the Marshall Plan were widely regarded as successful in transforming Germany into a thriving democracy.

484. ABRAM CHAYES & ANTONIA HANDLER CHAYES, THE NEW SOVEREIGNTY: COMPLIANCE WITH INTERNATIONAL REGULATORY AGREEMENTS 3 (1995). *See also* DAVID CORTRIGHT & GEORGE A. LOPEZ, THE SANCTIONS DECADE: ASSESSING UN STRATEGIES IN THE 1990s (2d ed. 2000).

485. CHAYES & CHAYES, *supra* note 484, at 9.

486. *Id.* at 22.

than a premeditated and deliberate policy course, limited only by considerations of realpolitik and protected externally by its special relationship with the United States.[487]

That said, this section will attempt to canvass a number of the available methods of bringing Israel as the occupying power in the OPT into a state of compliance with the terms of the Fourth Geneva Convention, particularly in relation to its "grave breaches" regime. These methods can be said to fall into two distinct categories: municipal enforcement measures and international enforcement measures. For reasons that will become apparent, emphasis will be placed on the latter category. It should be kept in mind, however, that all of the measures here examined find their common legal genus in the obligation in article 1 of the Fourth Geneva Convention of all High Contracting Parties "to respect and to ensure respect for the present Convention in all circumstances,"[488] and in the principle of *pacta sunt servanda*—that "every treaty in force is binding upon the parties to it and must be performed by them in good faith."[489]

A. Municipal Enforcement Measures

This category is meant to cover those enforcement measures that are local in nature and which contemplate the active involvement of the two parties most directly affected by the state of affairs in the OPT, namely Israel and the 3.1 million Palestinian inhabitants of the OPT. Generally, these methods of enforcement fall into two separate spheres: unilateral enforcement and bilateral enforcement.

As discussed earlier, "in all cases of hostile occupation of territory the primary duty of enforcement falls upon the occupying Power itself."[490] In this sense, it can be said that the Fourth Geneva Convention may be enforced by Israel unilaterally. This flows from article 146, which states in part that:

> The High Contracting Parties undertake to enact any legislation necessary to provide effective penal sanctions for persons committing, or ordering to be committed, any of the grave breaches of the present Convention defined in the following Article.
>
> Each High Contracting Party shall be under the obligation to search for persons alleged to have committed, or to have ordered to be committed, such grave breaches, and shall bring such persons, regardless of their nationality, before its own courts. It may also, if it prefers, and in accor-

---

487. *See supra* text accompanying note 288. *See also* NOAM CHOMSKY, THE FATEFUL TRIANGLE: THE UNITED STATES, ISRAEL AND THE PALESTINIANS (1999); CAMILLE MANSOUR, BEYOND ALLIANCE: ISRAEL IN U.S. FOREIGN POLICY (1994).

488. FOURTH GENEVA CONVENTION, *supra* note 6, art. 1.

489. VIENNA CONVENTION, *supra* note 297, art. 26.

490. McCoubrey Statement, *supra* note 480, at 70.

dance with the provisions of its own legislation, hand such persons over for trial to another High Contracting Party concerned, provided such High Contracting Party has made out a prima facie case.

Each High Contracting Party shall take measures necessary for the suppression of all acts contrary to the provisions of the present Convention other than the grave breaches defined in the following Article.[491]

Although this provision has been understood by some to embody the principle *aut dedere aut judicare*—that is, the legal obligation of a High Contracting Party to prosecute or extradite any person suspected of committing war crimes or ordering such crimes to be committed—some, including a recent judge ad hoc of the International Court of Justice (ICJ), have suggested that it actually goes one step further in codifying the principle *promo prosequi, secundo dedere*—the idea that domestic prosecution of suspected war criminals is to be resorted to before extradition.[492] In any event, it is clear that this provision places Israel under a legal obligation to "enact legislation penalizing the commission of grave breaches . . . and also to track down and bring to trial persons suspected of having committed or ordering the commission of such offences."[493] Israel is also obliged to protect against the commission of violations of the Fourth Geneva Convention that do not amount to "grave breaches" under article 147.

Clearly, "the most immediate forum for the enforcement" of the Fourth Geneva Convention in the OPT is through the "Israeli judicial system itself."[494] As noted by Jonathan Kuttab, co-founder of al-Haq, "[m]uch has been made by the Israeli authorities of the fact that they have allowed the residents of the Occupied Territories access to their highest court," which is often lauded as an effective "watch-dog [that] provides judicial oversight of activities of the military government."[495] Although "Palestinians have had mixed views about going to the High Court"—their concerns have ranged from the political implications of attorning to the jurisdiction of a foreign colonial power's court, to the practical difficulties of obtaining competent, willing, and reasonably priced Israeli lawyers who are more likely to be familiar with the court's procedure and case law than local Palestinian practitioners—a relatively small number have brought cases before it in an attempt to seek remedies for Israel's excesses in the OPT.[496] Unfortunately, as noted by Kuttab, "there have been an insignificant number of [cases] where Palestinians obtained . . . the recourse that they sought in matters pertain-

---

491. FOURTH GENEVA CONVENTION, *supra* note 6, art. 146.
492. Arrest Warrant of 11 April 2000 (Congo v. Belg.), 2002 I.C.J. (Feb. 14) (dissenting opinion of Judge ad hoc Van den Wyngaert, at 32), http://www.icj-cij.org/icjwww/idocket/iCOBE/iCOBEframe.htm.
493. McCoubrey Statement, *supra* note 480, at 70.
494. *Id.*
495. Kuttab, *supra* note 303, at 493. *See also* Benvenisti, *supra* note 219, at 123.
496. *Id.*

ing to the military government or its agents."[497] This should come as no surprise, given the fact that over the years the Israeli Supreme Court, sitting as the High Court of Justice, has upheld such practices as unlawful deportations and transfers,[498] and torture and inhumane treatment.[499] In any event, in none of these cases has the Court applied the terms of the Fourth Geneva Convention, because of its declaration that the convention is non-self-executing (rejecting the convention's status as a codification of customary international law) and therefore requiring of specific legislation incorporating it into Israeli domestic law before the Court can regard itself as competent to apply its provisions.[500] Of course, the reason no such legislation has been passed is the Israeli government's long-held position that the Fourth Geneva Convention is not de jure applicable to the OPT. As a result, Israel has never taken any of the "enforcement" steps required of it as a High Contracting Party in article 146 to enact legislation penalizing the commission of grave breaches, to search for and prosecute or extradite any individuals suspected of committing or ordering the commission of such breaches, or to penalize those suspected of committing other violations of the convention not amounting to grave breaches. From a practical standpoint, this is particularly troubling given that Israel, as the occupying power, is by far the most capable and best positioned of all of the High Contracting Parties to undertake the task of bringing those responsible for war crimes and other transgressions of the Fourth Geneva Convention in the OPT to justice.

Another manner in which the Fourth Geneva Convention may be enforced municipally is by agreement of the parties—that is to say, through bilateral enforcement. It is sometimes overlooked that if Israel and the PLO were to conclude a final peace treaty putting a complete end to the military occupation of the OPT, there would be no need for anyone to even discuss the Fourth Geneva Convention. In this way, it has been noted that "[t]he best means of securing the primary endeavour of the Fourth Geneva Convention is, paradoxically, to ensure that it is not applicable."[501] The most obvious point of reference in this respect is the Oslo Accords. Unfortunately, though, the accords omit any reference to the Fourth Geneva Convention or the law of belligerent occupation,[502] so they are not a viable bilateral enforcement mechanism. As a result, they do not expressly recognize the West Bank, including East Jerusalem, and the Gaza Strip as occupied territory, nor do they recognize Israel's status as a belligerent occupant. These major lacunae were no doubt the product of the imbalance of negotiating power between Israel and the PLO, among other things. Nevertheless, the Oslo

---

497. *Id.*
498. *See supra* text accompanying notes 439–448.
499. *See supra* text accompanying notes 385–416.
500. *See supra* text accompanying note 293.
501. McCoubrey Statement, *supra* note 480, at 72.
502. John Quigley, *The Israel-PLO Agreements Versus the Geneva Civilians Convention,* 7 PALESTINE Y.B. INT'L L. 45, 57 (1992/1994).

Accords raise an important issue related to the enforcement of the Fourth
Geneva Convention in these types of political situations: namely, to what
extent may the purported representatives of the occupied population derogate from the terms of the convention in its agreements, interim or otherwise, with the occupying power?

A number of the provisions of the Oslo Accords conflict with the terms of
the Fourth Geneva Convention. For instance, under article 5 of the DOP,
negotiations over the final status of Jerusalem were postponed during most
of the interim period.[503] As noted by Quigley, although Israel's annexation
of East Jerusalem is clearly illegal under the law of belligerent occupation,
this provision may "appear to be a condonation by the PLO of Israel's tenure
there, at least on a temporary basis."[504] Similarly, under article 5 of the DOP,
negotiations over the final status of Jewish colonies in the OPT were also
postponed for most of the interim period, and under article 8 Israeli jurisdiction was effectively extended over the colonies and settlers.[505] Although
such colonies are strictly prohibited under article 49 of the Fourth Geneva
Convention, these provisions can also be construed as an acquiescence by the
PLO to Israel's sovereign jurisdiction over these areas and persons. Nevertheless, there are two very important provisions of the Fourth Geneva Convention that effectively render these and other aspects of the Oslo Accords "a
nullity."[506]

First, article 7 of the Fourth Geneva Convention provides, in part, that although agreements may be made between the purported political representatives of the occupied population and the occupying power, no such
"agreement shall adversely affect the situation of protected persons, as
defined by the present Convention, nor restrict the rights which it confers
upon them."[507] Second, article 47 of the Fourth Geneva Convention states
that:

> Protected persons who are in occupied territory shall not be deprived,
> in any case or in any manner whatsoever, of the benefits of the present
> Convention by any change introduced, as the result of the occupation of
> a territory, into the institutions or government of the said territory, *nor
> by any agreement concluded between the authorities of the occupied territories and
> the Occupying Power*, nor by any annexation by the latter of the whole or
> part of the occupied territory.[508]

---

503. DOP, *supra* note 167, art. V(3).
504. Quigley, *supra* note 502, at 52.
505. DOP, *supra* note 167, arts. V(3), VIII. *See also* The Agreement on the Gaza Strip and the Jericho
Area, *supra* note 171, art. 5.
506. Quigley, *supra* note 502, at 46.
507. FOURTH GENEVA CONVENTION, *supra* note 6, art. 7.
508. *Id.* art. 47 (emphasis added).

Consistent with the Fourth Geneva Convention's overriding aim of protecting the interests of civilian persons in time of war, the purpose behind these two provisions was to forestall the possibility of "pressure being exerted by belligerent occupants on local authorities."[509] As noted by Pacheco, "[t]he harsh experience of the Vichy regime after the Nazi conquest of France provided all-too-familiar reasons for the Convention's drafters to prevent the recurrence of such a situation."[510] Thus, the ICRC commentary on the convention notes that:

> Agreements concluded with the authorities of the occupied territory represent a more subtle means by which the Occupying Power may try to free itself from the obligations incumbent on it under occupation law; the possibility of concluding such agreements is therefore strictly limited by Article 7 ... and the general rule expressed there is reaffirmed by [Article 47].[511]

Accordingly, to the extent that the Oslo Accords conflict with the requirements of the Fourth Geneva Convention, the latter shall prevail as a matter of international law.[512]

B. International Enforcement Measures

International enforcement measures include both independent and collective state activity. These methods of enforcement can be said to fall into two separate spheres: those internal to the Fourth Geneva Convention and those external to it.

One of the principal internal mechanisms is the obligation contained in article 146 of all High Contracting Parties to enact legislation penalizing the commission of grave breaches, to search for and prosecute or extradite any individuals suspected of committing or ordering the commission of such breaches, and to penalize those suspected of committing other violations of the convention not amounting to grave breaches. It has been demonstrated how this provision forms the basis of considerable legal duties on Israel as both a High Contracting Party and the occupying power in the OPT. In addition, however, it also "implicitly authorizes the exercise of universal jurisdiction" by the national courts of every other High Contracting Party to the Fourth Geneva Convention.[513]

Universal jurisdiction "refers to the authority of domestic courts and international tribunals to prosecute certain crimes, regardless of where the offense occurred, the nationality of the perpetrator, or the nationality of the

---

509. Quigley, *supra* note 502, at 47.
510. Pacheco, *supra* note 22, at 199.
511. Uhler, *supra* note 331, at 274.
512. Quigley, *supra* note 502, at 46–47.
513. Statement of William A. Schabas to the United Nations International Meeting, *supra* note 13, at 73, 76.

victim."[514] The concept rests upon the rationale that some crimes—such as war crimes—are so universally condemned, they warrant the exercise by any competent national or international judicial authority of criminal jurisdiction over those alleged to have perpetrated them, without regard to the traditional factors upon which such jurisdiction is usually based.[515] It is well to recall that the principle of universal jurisdiction "received its most significant judicial affirmation" by the Supreme Court of Israel "in litigation involving [its] right to prosecute" Nazi war criminal Adolf Eichmann.[516] Today, a growing number of states have begun to enact domestic legislation empowering their courts to invoke universal jurisdiction in accordance with their obligations under article 146.[517] Accordingly, universal jurisdiction exercised at the national level would seem to hold out one possibility of enforcing the Fourth Geneva Convention in the OPT.

Another enforcement mechanism internal to the Fourth Geneva Convention is its provision for the appointment of Protecting Powers. Under article 9, Protecting Powers have the duty "to safeguard the [humanitarian] interests of the Parties to the conflict."[518] It is implied that such Protecting Powers are appointed by agreement of the parties.[519] In the absence of agreement, the ICRC may substitute for the Protecting Powers under article 11. Among other things, Protecting Powers must "lend their good offices" in order to settle disagreements "between the Parties to the conflict as to the application or interpretation of the provisions of" the convention;[520] they

---

514. Michael P. Scharf & Thomas C. Fischer, *Forward to* Symposium, *Universal Jurisdiction: Myths, Realities, and Prospects,* 35 NEW ENG. L. REV. 227, 227 (2001).

515. These traditional factors include the principles of (1) territoriality (where the state assumes jurisdiction over crimes committed in its territory); (2) protection (where the state assumes jurisdiction over crimes prejudicial to its national security, even if committed by non-nationals extra-territorially); (3) active personality (where the state assumes jurisdiction over crimes committed by its nationals, even if committed extra-territorially); and (4) passive personality (where the state assumes jurisdiction over extra-territorial crimes committed by non-nationals against its nationals). *See* Research in International Law of Harvard Law School, *Jurisdiction with Respect to Crime,* 29 AM. J. INT'L L. 435 (Supp. 1935).

516. Schabas, *supra* note 513, at 76. Adolf Eichmann headed the Nazi Gestapo during World War II. Israeli secret service agents forcibly abducted him from Argentina and transferred him to Israel to stand trial for the genocide of millions of Jews in Nazi Germany and Nazi-occupied Europe during World War II. The defense argued that the court did not have jurisdiction because Eichmann had been abducted in a foreign state in violation of international law. The court relied, in part, on the doctrine of universal jurisdiction to dismiss the defense argument. It stated:

> Not only do all the crimes attributed to the appellant bear an international character, but their harmful and murderous effects were so embracing and widespread as to shake the international community to its foundations. The State of Israel therefore was entitled, *pursuant to the principle of universal jurisdiction and in the capacity of a guardian of international law and an agent for its enforcement,* to try the appellant.

Attorney General of Israel v. Eichmann, 36 I.L.R. 277, 304 (S. Ct. 1962) (Isr.) (emphasis added).

517. For a survey of state practice, see generally AMNESTY INT'L, UNIVERSAL JURISDICTION: THE DUTY OF STATES TO ENACT AND IMPLEMENT LEGISLATION, ch. 6 (2001) ("Crimes Against Humanity: State Practice at the National Level"), http://web.amnesty.org/aidoc/aidoc_pdf.nsf/index/IOR530092001 ENGLISH/$File/IOR5300901.pdf.

518. FOURTH GENEVA CONVENTION, *supra* note 6, art. 9.

519. Delparaz, *supra* note 16, at 50.

520. FOURTH GENEVA CONVENTION, *supra* note 6, art. 12.

must "be informed of any transfers and evacuations" of protected persons by the occupying power "as soon as they have taken place";[521] they "are at liberty to verify the state of the food and medical supplies in the occupied territories";[522] they must be informed by the occupying power of all judicial proceedings taken against protected persons and, with few exceptions, have the right to attend such proceedings;[523] and they are entitled "to go to all places where protected persons are, particularly to places of internment, detention and work," and to privately interview them without limit as to duration and frequency.[524]

Notwithstanding the extensive enforcement role envisioned for Protecting Powers by the framers of the Fourth Geneva Convention, the mechanism itself "has virtually remained a dead letter."[525] At no point over the course of Israel's thirty-five-year occupation has any Protecting Power been appointed. Although the ICRC has maintained a permanent presence in the OPT since 1967,[526] its attempts to substitute as the Protecting Power pursuant to article 11 have never materialized.[527] While the ICRC has rendered "valuable humanitarian services" by visiting detainees and providing medical assistance,[528] its efforts have ultimately proved inadequate to meet the tremendous needs of the protected persons in the OPT. To ensure the safety of all parties, the PLO has repeatedly requested the international community to send some form of multi-national peacekeeping or observer force to the OPT. These efforts have been particularly intensive since the outbreak of the al-Aqsa intifada, but Israel and the United States have consistently rejected them.[529] In light of the current crisis unfolding in the OPT, the revival of the institution of Protecting Powers is one further enforcement mechanism that the international community should develop, either by seeing to the appointment of certain High Contracting Parties to the position, or by providing the ICRC with the necessary diplomatic, economic, and political support to accomplish this task.

Among the mechanisms of enforcement that are external to the Fourth Geneva Convention is the newly established International Criminal Court (ICC). The ICC was formed by an international conference that met at Rome in 1998, and represents "a milestone in the development of international

---

521. *Id.* art. 49.

522. *Id.* art. 55.

523. *Id.* arts. 71, 74, 75.

524. *Id.* art. 143.

525. Statement of Hussein A. Hassouna, Permanent Observer for the League of Arab States, to the United Nations International Meeting, *supra* note 13, at 57, 59.

526. Delparaz, *supra* note 16, at 50.

527. UNCEIRPP, *supra* note 5, at 11. *See also* G.A. Res. 2851, U.N. GAOR, 26th Sess., Supp. No. 29, 2027th plen. mtg. at 48, U.N. Doc. A/8429 (1971).

528. UNCEIRPP, *supra* note 5, at 11. *See also* Delparaz, *supra* note 16, at 50.

529. In March 2001 (seven months following the outbreak of the al-Aqsa intifada), the United States vetoed a draft Security Council resolution, tabled by Ireland, Britain, Norway, and France, to establish an international observer force for the OPT. *See* Noam Chomsky, *Foreward* to THE NEW INTIFADA, *supra* note 22, at 6, 18.

law."[530] It was designed with the aim of providing the international community with a permanent judicial forum in which those accused of the most serious international crimes (i.e., war crimes, crimes against humanity, genocide) could be brought to justice. Thus, article 8 of the Rome Statute "contains an extensive list of acts constituting war crimes"[531] that includes those acts defined as "grave breaches" in article 146 of the Fourth Geneva Convention, as well as "[o]ther serious violations of the laws and customs applicable in international armed conflict."[532] Although the ICC obtained the sixty ratifications required for its entry into force on April 11, 2002,[533] 28 states have "either voted against" it "or abstained" from the adoption process altogether.[534] Among those states who voted against was Israel, "stating specifically that the drafters had gone beyond the customary enumeration of war crimes by including the issues of transfer of populations to occupied territories."[535]

Accordingly, Israel is not a State Party to the Rome Statue, making it difficult, though not impossible, for any of its nationals to be brought to justice before the ICC for war crimes. Under article 13(b) of the Rome Statute, the ICC may exercise jurisdiction over crimes committed by, or in the territory of, non-parties if the U.N. Security Council, acting under chapter VII of the U.N. Charter, refers a case to the Prosecutor.[536] The position of the United States on the council makes such a referral unlikely, but this option is theoretically open to the world community and is worthy of exploration at least at the diplomatic level.[537] The ICC's temporal jurisdiction may present another difficulty, though not a fatal one. Under article 11, the court "has jurisdiction only with respect to crimes committed after the entry into force of [the] Statute."[538] Because the Rome Statute entered into force on July 1, 2002, it is possible that an adjudication before the ICC of any war crimes committed by Israeli nationals between 1967 and that date will be barred *ratione temporis*. One way around this potential impediment, would be to argue that Israel's war crimes amount to "continuing offences" at law, because, although they "may consist of separate acts or a course of conduct," such conduct can be said to arise from a "singleness of thought, purpose or action which may be deemed a single impulse."[539] Given Israel's ongoing

530. DOCUMENTS ON THE LAWS OF WAR, *supra* note 5, at 668.

531. *Id.*

532. ROME STATUTE, *supra* note 239, art. 8, § 2(b).

533. The ICC officially entered into force on July 1, 2002. Leila Nadya Sadat, *ASIL Insights: The International Criminal Court Treaty Enters into Force* (Apr. 2002), http://www.asil.org/insights/insigh86.htm.

534. DOCUMENTS ON THE LAWS OF WAR, *supra* note 5, at 668.

535. Schabas, *supra* note 513, at 74.

536. ROME STATUTE, *supra* note 239, art. 13(b). *See also 1998 Rome Statute of the International Criminal Court: Extracts: Prefatory Note*, DOCUMENTS ON THE LAWS OF WAR, *supra* note 5, at 668, 669.

537. *But see infra* text accompanying notes 569–573.

538. ROME STATUTE, *supra* note 239, art. 11, § 1.

539. BLACK'S LAW DICTIONARY 321–22 (6th ed. 1990).

record and stated policies concerning torture, deportation, land confiscation, and settlement construction, this argument would seem plausible.

A related external mechanism for enforcing the Fourth Geneva Convention in the OPT is to have resort to the ICJ. The ICJ was established in 1945 by the U.N. Charter "as the principal judicial organ of the United Nations."[540] Accordingly, all members of the United Nations, including Israel, are parties to the ICJ Statute and may therefore make use of the court.[541] The jurisdiction of the ICJ is limited to adjudicating "contentious" cases between states, and issuing "advisory opinions."[542] The court's contentious jurisdiction derives from article 36(1) of the ICJ Statute, which provides that it may hear "all cases which the parties refer to it and all matters specially provided for in the Charter of the United Nations or in treaties and conventions in force."[543] Although the Fourth Geneva Convention contains no specific clause referring potential disputes to the ICJ, the Geneva Diplomatic Conference of 1949 expressly recommended "that, in the case of a dispute relating to the interpretation or application of the present Conventions which cannot be settled by other means, the High Contracting Parties concerned endeavour to agree between themselves to refer such dispute to the ICJ."[544]

Nevertheless, the contentious jurisdiction of the ICJ is confronted with two considerable obstacles. First, because Palestine is not yet a full Member of the United Nations (and by extension the ICJ Statute), nor a High Contracting Party to the Fourth Geneva Convention,[545] it cannot agree with Israel to refer a case to the ICJ pursuant to either the ICJ Statute or the recommendation of the Geneva Diplomatic Conference. Second, and in any event, Israel has "specifically stipulated that it will not admit the jurisdiction of the Court in relation to matters pertaining to belligerent occupation."[546] Thus, it would seem unlikely that the contentious jurisdiction of the ICJ could be invoked to consider the enforcement of the Fourth Geneva Convention in the OPT.

The same is not so with respect to the ICJs advisory jurisdiction, however. Under article 65(1) of the ICJ Statute "[t]he Court may give an advisory opinion on any legal question at the request of whatever body may be authorized by or in accordance with the Charter of the United Nations to make such a request."[547] Under article 96(1) of the U.N. Charter, both the Security Council and the General Assembly are authorized to request an ad-

---

540. STATUTE OF THE INTERNATIONAL COURT OF JUSTICE, June 26, 1945, 59 Stat. 1055 [hereinafter ICJ STATUTE].

541. DAMROSCH ET AL., supra note 130, at 854.

542. McCoubrey Statement, supra note 480, at 71.

543. ICJ STATUTE, supra note 539, art. 36(1).

544. Resolution 1 of the Geneva Diplomatic Conference of 1949, quoted in McCoubrey Statement, supra note 480, at 71.

545. But see supra note 252.

546. McCoubrey Statement, supra note 480, at 71.

547. ICJ STATUTE, supra note 539, art. 65(1).

visory opinion.[548] Likewise, under article 96(2), the General Assembly may authorize any other U.N. organ or specialized agency to request an advisory opinion, provided the subject matter of the request falls "within the scope of their activities."[549] Thus, an advisory opinion may be sought from the ICJ on any number of matters, including the questions of the applicability of the Fourth Geneva Convention to the OPT and international responsibility regarding its enforcement.[550] Although the ICJ has shown a reluctance to render advisory opinions on "matters which are in reality contentious cases," its recent judgment in the *1996 Advisory Opinion on the Threat or Use of Nuclear Weapons* may be indicative of a shift in policy.[551] The greatest strength of the Advisory Opinion option is that the General Assembly may act independently of the Security Council, which is so often unable to act given the United States' policy on the issue.[552] Therefore, this option should "be studied carefully,"[553] if not for the possibility that it may provide a final answer to the question of the enforcement of the Fourth Geneva Convention in the OPT, than for the prospect that it might provide the international community with a step in the right direction.[554]

Another enforcement mechanism external to the Fourth Geneva Convention is the creation of an ad hoc international criminal tribunal. Criminal tribunals of this sort first appeared in 1945 with the establishment of the International Military Tribunals at Nuremberg and Tokyo by the Allied Powers.[555] Thereafter, no similar tribunals were created to prosecute violations of the laws and customs of war for nearly half a century. In 1993, the United Nations Security Council established the ICTY to try individuals alleged to have committed war crimes and crimes against humanity during the wars associated with the dissolution of that country in the early 1990s.[556] The following year, the International Criminal Tribunal for Rwanda (ICTR) was created to prosecute those responsible for the genocide of "an estimated half a million to one million people" in Rwanda in 1994.[557] Because both the ICTY and ICTR possess specialized temporal and subject-matter jurisdiction, it is not possible for them to preside over the prosecution of war crimes committed in the OPT. Nevertheless, they provide models for the creation of a similar ad hoc tribunal for the OPT, which would be in keeping with current trends in international criminal law and the global struggle against impunity. In January 2002, the United Nations and the

---

548. U.N. CHARTER art. 96(1).

549. *Id.* art. 96(2).

550. *See, e.g.*, Van Baarda, *supra* note 265.

551. McCoubrey Statement, *supra* note 480, at 71.

552. *But see infra* text accompanying notes 569–573.

553. Statement of Paul Tavernier, Director, Research and Studies Centre for Human Rights and Humanitarian Law, to the United Nations International Meeting, *supra* note 13, at 61, 62.

554. *Id.* at 71.

555. DOCUMENTS ON THE LAWS OF WAR, *supra* note 5, at 565.

556. *Id.* at 565–66. *See* ICTY STATUTE, *supra* note 239.

557. *Id.* at 615. *See* ICTR STATUTE, *supra* note 239.

government of Sierra Leone agreed to establish a specialized criminal tribunal for war crimes committed during its ten-year civil war,[558] and calls for the establishment of an ad hoc court to try war crimes stemming from Indonesia's prolonged military occupation of East Timor have been circulating for well over a year.[559] Of course, given the unlikely prospect of agreement by Israel to the creation of an ad hoc criminal tribunal, the establishment of such a court would likely only be possible with the active participation of the Security Council. Thus, although the prospect is theoretically possible and should be given serious consideration, it must "be thought vanishingly small" in the present political climate.[560]

Yet another external mechanism that may be employed to enforce the Fourth Geneva Convention in the OPT is the use of various "forms of economic pressure," such as restrictions on trade, foreign investment, and foreign aid.[561] Israel currently enjoys preferential trade agreements with a number of states and regional entities, including Canada, the European Union, and the United States.[562] Even more importantly, Israel has been "the largest cumulative recipient of U.S. aid since World War II."[563] According to conservative estimates, Israel currently receives over $3.2 billion per year, and, since 1949 it has received a total of over $91 billion.[564] There is little question that much of this money directly underwrites Israeli's military occupation, not to mention the construction of colonies, bypass roads, and the like.[565]

Among other approaches, the exertion of economic pressure on Israel can take place at both the national level by individual states, as well as at the regional level, by bodies such as the European Union, where states can act in concert to deprive Israel of the benefits of an open trade policy so long as it continues to violate the Fourth Geneva Convention in the OPT. Similarly, such pressure may be exerted internationally by the United Nations. Under chapter VII of the U.N. Charter, if the Security Council determines that a conflict constitutes a threat to international "peace and security" it may require all Member States to apply measures short of the use of force to rem-

---

558. Chris McGreal, *Unique Court to Try Killers of Sierra Leone*, GUARDIAN (London), Jan. 17, 2002, at 15.

559. Mark Devenport, *Proposal for Timor Tribunal*, BBC NEWS, Dec. 22, 1999, http://news.bbc.co.uk/1/hi/world/americas/574490.stm. *See also* Human Rights Watch, *World Report 2001: East Timor: Human Rights Developments* (2001), http://www.hrw.org/wr2k1/asia/etimor.html.

560. McCoubrey Statement, *supra* note 480, at 71.

561. Tavernier, *supra* note 553, at 62.

562. *See* FREE TRADE AGREEMENT, CAN.-ISR., July 31, 1996, http://www.dfait-maeci.gc.ca/tna-nac/cifta-en.asp; EURO-MEDITERRANEAN AGREEMENT ESTABLISHING AN ASSOCIATION BETWEEN THE EUROPEAN COMMUNITIES AND THEIR MEMBER STATES AND THE STATE OF ISRAEL, Nov. 20, 1995, http://www.moit.gov.il/root/sachar_hutz/heskermin_ben/eumedagr.htm; AGREEMENT ON THE ESTABLISHMENT OF A FREE TRADE AREA, ISR.-U.S., Apr.22, 1985, 24 I.L.M. 653.

563. Shirl McArthur, *A Conservative Total for U.S. Aid to Israel: $91 Billion—and Counting*, WASHINGTON REPORT ON MIDDLE EAST AFFAIRS, Jan.-Feb. 2001, at 15, 15.

564. *Id.*

565. *Id.*

edy the matter, including the use of economic sanctions.[566] Although the Security Council has historically been reluctant to resort to chapter VII powers in this manner, recent years have witnessed the emergence of a changing trend. Thus,

> [w]hereas the Council had only imposed sanctions twice in the first forty-five years of its existence, against Rhodesia in 1966 and South Africa in 1977, during the 1990s, the Security Council imposed comprehensive or partial sanctions against Iraq (1990), the former Yugoslavia (1991, 1992, and 1998), Libya (1992), Liberia (1992), Somalia (1992), parts of Cambodia (1992), Haiti (1993), parts of Angola (1993, 1997, and 1998), Rwanda (1994), Sudan (1996), Sierra Leone (1997), and Afghanistan (1999).[567]

The sanctions regimes recently imposed have not been perfect. As the cases of Iraq and Haiti demonstrate, the effect of sanctions can sometimes go beyond the intended political objective to create humanitarian disasters far beyond anything imagined.[568] For this reason, any sanctions regime imposed on Israel must be limited in scope and directed toward the single objective of bringing it into a state of full compliance with the terms of the Fourth Geneva Convention in the OPT. Economic sanctions focused on Israel's military or colonial settlement development may be a good first step. Because the mechanism of international sanctions must conventionally pass through the Security Council, the United States' veto power presents a considerable political obstacle. Although the option of economic sanctions is therefore theoretically available, the current political climate in the Security Council would not seem to lend itself favorably to the possibility of it coming to fruition any time soon.

One possible solution would be to invoke the General Assembly's deemed residual responsibility over the maintenance of international peace and security in accordance with its "Uniting for Peace" resolution of November 3, 1950.[569] Article 24 of the U.N. Charter provides that the Security Council shall have "*primary* responsibility for the maintenance of international peace and security."[570] Against the backdrop of the Cold War conflict in Korea, the General Assembly argued "that this did not preclude [it] from exercising a secondary or residual responsibility."[571] Accordingly, it passed the Uniting for Peace resolution in which it "asserted authority to act in matters relating to international peace and security if the Security Council could not dis-

---

566. U.N. CHARTER art. 41.

567. CORTRIGHT & LOPEZ, *supra* note 484, at 1–2.

568. *Id.* at 2. *See also* GEOFF SIMONS, THE SCOURGING OF IRAQ (1998); George E. Bisharat, *Sanctions as Genocide*, 11 TRANSNAT'L L. & CONTEMP. PROBS. 379 (2001).

569. G.A. Res. 377, U.N. GAOR, 5th Sess., Supp. No. 20, at 10, U.N. Doc. A/1775 (1950).

570. U.N. CHARTER art. 24(1) (emphasis added).

571. MICHAEL AKEHURST, A MODERN INTRODUCTION TO INTERNATIONAL LAW 224–25 (6th ed. 1991).

charge its 'primary' responsibility because of lack of unanimity among the permanent members."[572] Although the extent of the General Assembly's power to act is merely recommendatory, since Korea "the resolution has had limited but significant application, notably with respect to the creation of the United Nations Emergency Force in the wake of the Suez crisis of 1956."[573]

In point of fact, the Uniting for Peace formula was used by the General Assembly in Resolution ES-10/6 of February 9, 1999 at its tenth emergency special session to call for the convening of an international conference on measures to enforce the Fourth Geneva Convention in the OPT.[574] The Conference of High Contracting Parties to the Fourth Geneva Convention, as it was officially called, was convened at Geneva by the government of Switzerland in its capacity as the depositary of the convention on July 15, 1999.[575] Aside from its immediate importance to protecting the civilian population of the OPT, the conference was significant as the first time in the Fourth Geneva Convention's history that the High Contracting Parties met to discuss matters of enforcement.[576] The conference thus held out the possibility of having "historical precedence" not only for the OPT, but also "for the direction of international humanitarian law and the future success of the convention in protecting civilians under future occupations."[577] Unfortunately, however, the convening of the meeting was accompanied by tremendous political pressure levied by the United States and Israel, both of whom boycotted the event arguing that the meeting "would interfere with the peace process."[578] By the eve of the meeting, international political support had waned to the point that the PLO decided to "request" the High Contracting Parties to adjourn the conference *sine die*.[579]

The international human rights community reacted swiftly. Amnesty International issued a press release in which it expressed absolute consternation for what transpired:

> Amnesty International is appalled by a 10 minute meeting of the High Contracting Parties to the Geneva Conventions, convened today in Geneva, which failed to consider enforcement measures to ensure that Israel respect its obligations under the Fourth Geneva Convention.

---

572. DAMROSCH ET AL., *supra* note 130, at 1012.

573. *Id.* at 1013.

574. *Introduction* to United Nations International Meeting, *supra* note 13, at 1.

575. Amnesty Int'l, *Israel: Fourth Geneva Convention Meeting: An Abdication of Responsibility* (July 15, 1999), http://www.amnesty-usa.org/news/1999/51504799.htm.

576. Pacheco, *supra* note 22, at 200.

577. *Id.*

578. *Id.*

579. *Id.* at 201. Pacheco notes that the PLO actually presented its decision to request an adjournment as "a good will gesture to Israel's new government" under Ehud Barak, who had just then defeated Benyamin Netanyahu for the premiership of Israel. *Id.*

The High Contracting Parties have only met to decide to defer their responsibilities. It is a supreme irony that, on the 50th anniversary of the
Geneva Conventions, a conference that was set up to bring back to the
limelight the plight of the protected population in the Occupied Territories lasts only 10 minutes. Today marks a scandalously missed opportunity to reaffirm international humanitarian law. . . .

Israel, as a High Contracting Party, has been violating the Fourth Geneva Convention for more than 30 years, when it carries out wilful
killings extrajudicially, when it tortures or when it indiscriminately
uses force . . . . The High Contracting Parties themselves however have
violated their obligation enshrined in Article 1 of the Convention, to
ensure respect for the Fourth Geneva Convention.[580]

The High Contracting Parties were afforded an opportunity to redeem
themselves following the outbreak of the al-Aqsa intifada, when the General
Assembly confirmed the Swiss government's request to re-convene the conference in Resolution ES-10/7 of October 20, 2000, again adopted pursuant
to the Uniting for Peace formula.[581] Accordingly, the High Contracting Parties met once more at Geneva on December 5, 2002 for the resumption of
the earlier meeting. The resumed conference was successful in so far as it
provided the High Contracting Parties an opportunity to reaffirm the de
jure applicability of the Fourth Geneva Convention to the OPT, as well as to
"call upon all parties, directly involved in the conflict or not, to respect and
to ensure respect for the Geneva Conventions in all circumstances, [and] to
disseminate and take measures necessary for the prevention and suppression
of breaches of the Conventions."[582] The conference did not, however, "agree
on concrete measures" to enforce the convention.[583] To be sure, the closing
statement of the Chair of the meeting reminded those in attendance that
"[t]he real follow-up to this Conference must be the implementation of humanitarian law. Nothing more or less."[584] Until the High Contracting Parties take substantive action to implement, not merely re-state, the Fourth
Geneva Convention, they will remain in breach of their duty under article 1

---

580. Amnesty Int'l, *supra* note 575.

581. Opening Statement of Ambassador Peter Maurer of Switzerland to the Conference of High Contracting Parties to the Fourth Geneva Convention, Geneva, Switzerland (Dec. 5, 2001), http://www.
eda.admin.ch/eda/e/home/foreign/hupol/4gc/docum2.Par.0004.UpFile.pdf/mg_011205_4gcclopstm2_e.
pdf.

582. Declaration of the Conference of High Contracting Parties to the Fourth Geneva Convention,
Geneva, Switzerland (Dec. 5, 2001), http://www.eda.admin.ch/eda/e/home/foreign/hupol/4gc/docum2.
Par.0006.UpFile.pdf/mg_011205_4gcdeclarn_e.pdf.

583. Press Release, Amnesty Int'l, *Israel: Respect for the Fourth Geneva Convention Must be Ensured by
High Contracting Parties Meeting in Geneva* (Dec. 4, 1999), http://www.amnesty-usa.org/news/2001/ is-
rael12042001.html.

584. Closing Statement of Ambassador Peter Maurer (Switz.) to Conference of High Contracting Parties to the Fourth Geneva Convention, Geneva, Switzerland (Dec. 5, 2001), http://www.eda.admin.ch/
eda/e/home/foreign/hupol/4gc/docum2.Par.0004.UpFile.pdf/mg_011205_4gcclopstm2_e.pdf.

to "ensure respect" for the convention. In this regard, it is well to note the ICRC commentary regarding the object and purpose of article 1:

> [t]he use . . . of the words "and to ensure respect for" was, however, deliberate; they were intended to emphasize the responsibility of the Contracting Parties . . . . It follows, therefore, that in the event of a Power failing to fulfill its obligations, the other Contracting Parties (neutral, allied or enemy) may, and should, endeavour to bring it back to an attitude of respect for the Convention. The proper working of the system of protection provided by the Convention demands in fact that the Contracting Parties should not be content merely to apply its provisions themselves, but should do everything in their power to ensure that the humanitarian principles underlying the Conventions are applied universally . . . .
>
> It is clear that Article 1 is no mere empty form of words, but has been deliberately invested with imperative force. It must be taken in its literal meaning.[585]

V. CONCLUSION

This Article has attempted both to reaffirm and reexamine the role international humanitarian law must play in protecting civilian populations subject to foreign military occupation. To this end, it has focused on Israel's thirty-five-year military occupation of the OPT, and the paramount function of the Fourth Geneva Convention in accomplishing this task. Promulgated in response to the atrocities of World War II, the primary purpose of the Fourth Geneva Convention is to ameliorate the effects of war on civilian populations. In many respects, the Convention "may be considered as the expression of the international community's sense of revulsion at the treatment accorded to Jews who came under the Nazi regime" in occupied Europe.[586] It is not without irony, therefore, that Israel has refused to recognize its responsibilities as an occupying power under the Fourth Geneva Convention, or even that the Convention applies de jure to the OPT. Since 1967, Israel "has flagrantly and defiantly contravened both the letter and spirit of" the Fourth Geneva Convention without hindrance or let[587] including the systematic commission of very serious war crimes.

Equally significant, however, has been the international community's inadequate response to Israel's behavior. Israel's occupation of the OPT provided "the first occasion on which the value of the [Fourth Geneva] Conven-

---

585. ICRC COMMENTARY TO THE IV GENEVA CONVENTION 16–17 (Jean S. Pictet ed., 1958), *quoted in* Pacheco, *supra* note 22, at 200.

586. *Report of the Special Committee to Investigate Israeli Practices Affecting the Human Rights of the Population of the Occupied Territories*, ¶ 41, U.N. Doc. A/18089 (Oct. 5, 1970) [hereinafter *Report of the Special Committee*].

587. Falk & Weston, *supra* note 150, at 135.

tion itself and the genuineness of individual nations' adherence to it could be put to the test."[588] By all accounts, the High Contracting Parties to the Convention have failed to meet this test. Apart from the consistent reaffirmation of the de jure applicability of the Fourth Geneva Convention to the OPT, as well as Israel's responsibilities thereunder, the international community has done very little to ensure its respect in the manner that was intended by its framers. This Article has canvassed some, though not all, of the available enforcement mechanisms for realizing this goal. At this critical juncture, the international community's "failure to act effectively will strike a blow at the Convention norms and at the entire scheme of international humanitarian law."[589] In the final analysis, if the letter and spirit of the Convention are to be salvaged in any meaningful way, the international community must see to its immediate enforcement in the OPT.

---

588. *Report of the Special Committee, supra* note 586, ¶ 42.
589. Schabas, *supra* note 513, at 77.

Illegal Occupation: Framing the Occupied Palestinian Terrority

By

Orna Ben-Naftali, Aeyal M. Gross & Keren Michaeli[*]

> ... If all time is eternally present
> All time is unredeemable.
> What might have been is an abstraction
> Remaining a perpetual possibility
> Only in a world of speculation.
> T.S. Eliot, Burnt Norton

I.
INTRODUCTION

A. The Missing Question of the Legality of an Occupation

Is the continued Israeli occupation of the Palestinian territory conquered in 1967 legal or illegal?[1] We explore this question in this Article. Curiously, amongst the wealth of legal writings on various aspects of this occupation, most concern Israel's compliance or noncompliance with its obligations as an occupy-

[*] Orna Ben-Naftali is a senior lecturer at the Law School, The College of Management, Academic Studies in Tel-Aviv; Aeyal Gross is a senior lecturer at Tel-Aviv University Law Faculty; and Keren Michaeli is a senior research fellow at the Law School, The College of Management, Academic Studies in Tel-Aviv. Earlier versions of this paper were presented in the following conferences, and the authors wish to thank their participants for their helpful comments: the Inaugural Conference of the European Society of International Law (International Humanitarian Law Agora) (Florence, 13-15 May 2004); the Heinrich Boll Foundation, Annual Foreign Policy Conference on the Role of International Law and the United Nations (Berlin, 24-25 May 2004); and the Conference on Democracy and Occupation, held at the Concord Center for the Interplay Between International Law and National Law, the Law School, The College of Management Academic Studies in Tel-Aviv (6-8 June 2004). The authors are grateful to Yuval Shany for his comments on an earlier draft of this article. The authors also wish to thank the editors of the Berkeley Journal of International Law, and in particular Robert da Silva Ashley, Thomas W. Walsh, Alessandra Pelliccia, and Andrea Lindemann, for their helpful work on this article.

1. In August 2005, Israel pulled out its settlements and military forces from the Gaza Strip. The question whether this amounts to the end of the occupation in this area remains open and its determination depends on factual and legal considerations relating to the notion of "effective control," which are beyond the scope of this article. Even if one assumes that Gaza is no longer occupied, our discussion applies to the rest of the Palestinian territory, which Israel continues to occupy, i.e. the West Bank including East Jerusalem, which constitutes a far more substantial area both in terms of territory and the extent of Jewish settlements.

ing power; virtually no attention has been paid to the question of the legality of the occupation itself.[2]

Indeed, when the Secretary-General of the United Nations, in a statement to the Security Council on March 12, 2002, called on Israel to "end the illegal occupation,"[3] critics accused him of engaging in a "redefinition of the Middle East conflict . . . . A new and provocative label of 'illegality' is now out of the chute and running loose."[4] This genie, however, was soon put back in the bottle, when the spokesman for the Secretary-General clarified that the word "illegal" referred to Israel's refusal to accept the legal obligations that the status of an occupying power entails and to its actions running contrary to these obligations, actions that both the Security Council and the General Assembly have declared illegal.[5] The discourse thus appeared to resume its habitual focus on *specific actions undertaken within* the occupation, as distinct from *the nature of* the occupation as a normative regime. Even the recent advisory opinion rendered by the International Court of Justice (ICJ), *Legal Consequences of the Construction of a Wall in the Occupied Palestinian Territory*,[6] while critical of both this construction and the related settlement enterprise, and decreeing their illegality, still focused on specific actions by Israel without questioning the legality of the occupation regime as such.

The virtual immunity from critical discussion conferred on the regime of this occupation cannot be explained away on political grounds. Indeed, the Israeli occupation has been subject to a widespread political and moral critique, both internationally and domestically. The reason lies in the perception of the occupation as a factual, rather than a normative, phenomenon. Thus posited, the fact of occupation generates normative results—the application of the international laws of occupation—but in itself does not seem to be part of that, or any other, normative order.

One might understand this practically axiomatic perception in three ways. First would be to conceive of the phenomenon of occupation as a fact of power,

---

2. A search in Lexis-Nexis on the Israeli occupation of the occupied Palestinian territory generated 171 entries concerned with various Israeli actions and positions as an occupying power, and no entry relative to the legality of the very occupation itself. Similar results were obtained from Westlaw. Note further that, since 1999, the term "occupied Palestinian territory" (hereinafter "OPT"), is gradually substituting the terms "the West Bank, Gaza Strip and East Jerusalem" and "Palestinian occupied territories" in the terminology of the United Nations referring to the areas occupied by Israel since 1967, to connote the contiguous nature of the area where the Palestinians are entitled to exercise their right to self-determination. *See, e.g.*, G.A. Res. ES-10/6, U.N. GAOR, 52d Sess., Supp. No. 494, U.N. Doc. A/ES-10/6 (1999).

3. Press Release, Security Council, Secretary-General Tells Security Council Middle East Crisis 'Worst in Ten Years'; Calls on Palestinians, Israelis to 'Lead Your Peoples Away From Disaster,' U.N. Doc. SC/7325 (March 12, 2002).

4. George P. Fletcher, *Annan's Careless Language*, NY TIMES, March 21, 2002, at A37.

5. Frederic Eckhard, Letter to the Editor, *A Delicate Word in the Mideast*, NY TIMES, March 23, 2002, at A16.

6. 2004 I.C.J. 131 (Jul. 9), *at* http://www.icj-cij.org/icjwww/idocket/imwp/imwpframe.htm [hereinafter *Construction of a Wall*]. There are various terms used to describe this construction, for example *fence* and *separation barrier*. We use the term "Wall" in accordance with the ICJ's language in this advisory opinion.

a kind of *Grundnorm*, which itself is grounded in an extra-legal domain.[7] A second alternative is to situate the phenomenon as legally permissible absent a norm prohibiting occupation.[8] A third option is to identify a norm that governs the phenomenon, differentiating between a legal and an illegal occupation. This identification involves a legal construction relating to both the normative order an occupation generates and to the normative order that generates the legal regime of occupation.

The first two perspectives presuppose an answer to the question this article seeks to answer, but each is problematic. The barren beauty of Kelsian formalism, underlying the first option, offers a vision of law far too narrow to account for the substantive interaction of form with function, structure with substance, fact with norm, and power with law.[9] The splendid "majesty of law,"[10] implicit in the second option, is equally deceptive by purporting to subject power to law in a manner that may well disregard the many other ways and means of their interaction.[11] Both perspectives thus generate the same troubling results: international law becomes an apology for power,[12] and the very phenomenon of occupation is excluded from a critical legal review. Such exclusion is an invitation for excessive power.

This article posits the third approach. This approach locates the occupation within a normative framework that differentiates between legality and illegality and may both resolve the specific question of the legality of the Israeli occupation and redefine the contours of the legal discourse on occupation.

B. The Thesis and Structure of the Article

The underlying principle of the international legal order rests on a pre-

---

7. HANS KELSEN, GENERAL THEORY OF LAW AND STATE 116 (1945). The text above does not suggest that Kelsen would have regarded occupation as a basic norm, which is therefore not subject to the test of validity. On the contrary, under Kelsen's theory, occupation would be considered a legal norm within a normative system the basic norm of which authorizes the creation by States of customary and conventional international law.

8. The Case of the S.S. Lotus (Fr. v. Turk.), 1927 P.C.I.J. (Ser. A) No. 10, at 18 (Sep. 7).

9. For a critique of Kelsen's pure theory of law, see, for example, J. W. HARRIS, LEGAL PHILOSOPHIES 59-75 (1980); Ronald Dworkin, *Comments on the Unity of Law Doctrine (A Response)*, in ETHICS AND SOCIAL JUSTICE 200 (Howard E. Kiefer & Milton K. Munitz eds., 1970); Herbert L.A. Hart, *Kelsen's Doctrine of the Unity of Law*, in Kiefer & Munitz 171-99; JOSEPH RAZ, THE CONCEPT OF A LEGAL SYSTEM: AN INTRODUCTION TO THE THEORY OF THE LEGAL SYSTEM 93-120 (1980 ed.) (1970).

10. Justice Oliver Wendell Holmes coined this term in an address reprinted in *The Path of Law*, 10 HARV. L. REV. 457 (1897). The conception of law implied in this alternative is majestic, or reflective of imperialistic positivism, inasmuch as it conceives of the law as governing all human actions, either forbidding—or authorizing—each and every action, thereby rejecting the theoretical possibility of legal lacunae.

11. Such interaction is one of the major elements comprising the Critical Legal Studies (CLS) critique of legal liberalism. *See, e.g.*, DUNCAN KENNEDY, A CRITIC OF ADJUDICATION: FIN DE SIECLE (1997). In the context of international law, see MARTTI KOSKENNIEMI, FROM APOLOGY TO UTOPIA: THE STRUCTURE OF INTERNATIONAL LEGAL ARGUMENT (1989).

12. In reference to Koskenniemi's terms, see *id. See also* Martti Koskenniemi, *The Politics of International Law*, 1 EUR. J. INT'L. L. 4 (1990).

sumption of sovereign equality between states.[13] Current international law understands sovereignty to be vested in the people, giving expression to the right to self-determination.[14] Analytically, the phenomenon of occupation challenges this standard order by severing the link between sovereignty and effective control in the occupied territory.[15] This exceptional situation is thus not merely factual, it is also normative because it exists only by virtue of the norm's suspension.[16]

The international law of occupation enters the picture signifying both the need to distinguish between order and chaos and the need to distinguish between orders: between the rule and the exception. In distinguishing between order and chaos, the function of international law is to manage the situation; to eliminate chaos through control of the exceptional situation. In distinguishing between orders, its function is to create an orderly space which is defined by its exceptionality—by its suspension of the rule.

We argue that the legality of the phenomenon of occupation, as it relates to the function of managing the situation, is to be measured in relation to three fundamental legal principles:

(a) Sovereignty and title in an occupied territory are not vested in the occupying power. The roots of this principle emanate from the principle of the inalienability of sovereignty through actual or threatened use of force. Under contemporary international law, and in view of the principle of self-determination, sovereignty is vested in the population under occupation.[17]

---

13. Enshrined in Article 2(1) of the Charter of the United Nations, June 26, 1945, 59 Stat. 1031, T.S. No. 993, 3 Bevans 1153 (1945).

14. *See* Eyal Benvenisti, *The Security Council and the Law of Occupation: Resolution 1483 on Iraq in Historical Perspective,* 1 IDF L. REV. 19, 28 (2003) [hereinafter Benvenisti, *Resolution 1483*]. On the right to self-determination, *see infra* notes 17, 76-86 and accompanying text.

15. This notion of suspension was already recognized in the first attempt to codify the international law of occupation, in the *Final Protocol and Project of an International Declaration Concerning the Laws and Customs of War,* Aug. 27, 1874, *reprinted in* THE LAWS OF ARMED CONFLICT: A COLLECTION OF CONVENTIONS, RESOLUTIONS AND OTHER DOCUMENTS 26-34 (Dietrich Schindler & Jiri Toman eds., 3d ed. 1988) [hereinafter Brussels Declaration]. *See infra* notes 237-43 and accompanying text.

16. The tension between the rule and the exception formed one of the basic tenets of Carl Schmitt's critique of the liberal state and, indeed, of the very rule of law. *See* CARL SCHMITT, POLITICAL THEOLOGY: FOUR CHAPTERS ON THE CONCEPT OF SOVEREIGNTY (George Schwab trans., 1988)[hereinafter SCHMITT, POLITICAL THEOLOGY]. A critical discussion of Schmitt's concept of "the exception" is offered in Section II.B *infra.*

17. Traditionally, sovereignty was attached to the state that held title to the territory prior to the occupation. Currently, the focus has shifted to the rights of the population under occupation. *See generally* Benvenisti, *Resolution 1483, supra* note 14. Note that a potential tension may be generated by this shift in focus between the state which held the territory prior to occupation and the population under occupation. Under current international law, this tension may be solved either generally by recognizing the primacy of the right to self-determination of the people or, in a more constricted fashion, by a determination whether the latter are entitled to an external or merely to an internal self-determination. On the differences between external and internal self-determination, see James Crawford, *The Right to Self-Determination in International Law: Its Development and Future, in* PEOPLES RIGHTS 7-67 (Philip Alston ed., 2001). In the case at hand, given both Jordan's dissociation from the West Bank and the widespread recognition of the Palestinian right to self-determination, it is clear that the sovereignty lies with the Palestinian people. For a review of the

(b) The occupying power is entrusted with the management of public order and civil life in the territory under control. In view of the principle of self-determination, the people under occupation are the beneficiaries of this trust. The dispossession and subjugation of these people violate this trust.[18]

(c) Occupation is temporary.[19] It may be neither permanent nor indefinite.

These principles, as we will show, interrelate: the substantive constraints on the managerial discretion of the occupant elucidated in principles "(a)" and "(b)" generate the conclusion in "(c)" that occupation must necessarily be temporary. Violating the temporal constraints expressed in principle "(c)" cannot but violate principles "(a)" and "(b)," thereby corrupting the normative regime of occupation in the sense that an occupation that cannot be regarded as temporary defies both the principle of trust and of self-determination. The violation of any one of these principles, therefore, unlike the violation of a specific norm that reflects them,[20] renders an occupation illegal *per se*. This is the nature of the Israeli oc-

---

U.N.'s recognition of the Palestinian right to self-determination, *see* ANTONIO CASSESE, SELF-DETERMINATION OF PEOPLES: A LEGAL REPRISAL 238-39 (1995) [hereinafter CASSESE, SELF-DETERMINATION]. As Cassese notes, "practically all states (and inter-governmental organizations) except Israel, take the view that the Palestinians are entitled to self-determination." *Id.* at 240. *See also* Frances Raday, *Self-Determination and Minority Rights*, 26 FORDHAM INT'L. L. J. 453 (2003) (discussing the right to self-determination of both Jews within Israel's 1948 Armistice Line and Palestinians in the West Bank and Gaza). Raday distinguishes the right to self-determination from the minority rights of Israeli-Palestinians and of Jews living in the West Bank and Gaza. It is important to note that Israel itself seems to have recognized this right, albeit implicitly, at least since the Oslo Accords of 1993, as can be inferred from both the text and the context of the Declaration of Principles signed between Israel and the PLO in 1993. CASSESE, SELF-DETERMINATION, at 243-45; Is-raeli-Palestine Liberation Organization: Declaration of Principles on Interim Self-Government Arrangements, Sept. 13, 1993, 32 I.L.M. 1525 (1993). Article 3(1) stipulated that elections for the Palestinian Interim Self-Government Authority will be held "[i]n order that the Palestinian people in the West Bank and the Gaza Strip may govern themselves according to democratic principles." Article 3(3) states, "[t]hese elections will constitute a significant interim preparatory step toward the realization of the legitimate rights of the Palestinian people and their just requirements." *Id.* at art. 3(2); *see also* U.S. Department of State, A Performance-Based Roadmap to a Permanent Two-State Solution to the Israeli-Palestinian Conflict, Apr. 30, 2003, *available at* http://www.state.gov/r/pa/prs/ps/2003/20062.htm (acknowledging Israel's acceptance of the idea of "an independent, democratic, and viable Palestinian state" as part of the Middle East Roadmap); Statement by Prime Minister Ariel Sharon After the Aqaba Summit Meeting, June 4, 2003, Israeli Ministry of Foreign Affairs, *at* http://www.mfa.gov.il/MFA/Government/Speeches+by+Israeli+leaders/2003/ ("Israel . . . has lent its strong support for President's Bush's vision . . . of two states—Israel and a Palestinian state—living side by side in peace and security . . . . It is in Israel's interest . . . for the Palestinians to govern themselves in their own state."). In the *Construction of a Wall* Advisory Opinion, the Palestinian right to self-determination was explicitly recognized, the Court opining that "the existence of a 'Palestinian people' is no longer in issue," and noting that Israel itself has recognized this right. *Construction of a Wall, supra* note 6, ¶ 118. It is significant in this context to note that the Court further discussed Israel's right to exist peacefully, side by side with a Palestinian state. *Id.* ¶¶ 71, 162.

18. A discussion of the principle of trust as embedded in the normative regime of occupation is offered in Section II.A.3 *infra*.

19. *See Construction of a Wall, supra* note 6, Separate Opinion of Judge Elaraby, ¶ 3.1; Separate Opinion of Judge Koroma, ¶ 2. A discussion of the temporal constraints of the normative regime of occupation is offered in Section II.A.4 *infra*.

20. Article 53 of the Fourth Geneva Convention, for example, prohibits the destruction by

cupation of the Occupied Palestinian Territory (OPT). Section II.A: Intrinsic Dimensions of the Israeli Occupation of the OPT, substantiates this argument.

We further argue that the legality of occupation, in its function to create an orderly space that is nevertheless distinct from the normal political order of sovereign equality between states, is to be measured by its exceptionality: once the boundaries between the normal order (i.e., sovereign equality between states) and the exception (i.e., occupation) are blurred, an occupation becomes illegal. The nexus between the two functions is clear: an occupation that is illegal from the perspective of managing an otherwise chaotic situation is also illegal in that it obfuscates the distinction between the rule and its exception. Yet, the distinction between these two forms of illegality is important; the former is grounded in the intrinsic principles of the law of occupation, while the latter is extrinsic to this law and delineates its limits. The Israeli occupation of the OPT is illegal both intrinsically and extrinsically. Section II.B: Extrinsic Dimensions of the Israeli Occupation of the OPT, substantiates this argument.

The concluding section (III) of this article focuses on the indeterminacies of this occupation as reflecting both its essential feature and its legitimizing mechanism, and proceeds to consider the normative consequences of an illegal occupation.

It is worthwhile to recall that the ICJ has already determined the illegality of one historic occupation: the presence of South Africa in Namibia following the revocation of the mandate by the General Assembly.[21] The Court started with the historical fact of South Africa's presence in Namibia (then called South

---

the occupying power of "real or personal property belonging individually or collectively to private persons, or to the State, or to other public authorities, or to social or cooperative organizations . . . , except where such destruction is rendered absolutely necessary by military operations." This provision is a specific norm: it specifies an element of the occupant's responsibility as a trustee in the occupied territories. A destruction of a house may thus be in violation of this norm, but such a violation in and of itself does not undermine the underlying principle of trust.

21.   This was followed by a decision of the Security Council that declared the continued presence of South Africa in Namibia to be illegal. *See* S.C. Res. 276, U.N. SCOR, 25th Sess., Res. & Dec. at 1, 2, U.N. Doc. S/INF/25 (1970). *See also Legal Consequences for States of the Continued Presence of South Africa in Namibia (South-West Africa) Notwithstanding Security Council Resolution 276 (1970)*, 1971 I.C.J. 16 (June 21) [hereinafter *Continued Presence of South Africa in Namibia* Advisory Opinion]. Note that the Court's reasoning emanated from the revocation of the Mandate. The separate opinion of Vice President Ammoun, however, emphasized that the Court's reasoning was not limited to the violations of the stipulations of the Mandate and gave due consideration to the right of peoples to self-determination as well as to violations of human rights of the people of Namibia by the South African authorities. *See* Separate Opinion of Vice President Ammoun, *id.* at 71-72. Note further that in the *Construction of a Wall* Advisory Opinion, *supra* note 6, the ICJ's historical narrative of the events leading to the construction of the Wall emphasized that the territory used to be a mandate and the Opinion contains several references to, and draws analogies from the *Continued Presence of South Africa in Namibia* Advisory Opinion. *See id.* at ¶¶ 70, 88. Several of the judges who appended separate opinions took exception to this analogy. *See* Separate opinion of Judge Higgins, *id.* at ¶ 2; Separate opinion of Judge Kooijmans, *id.* at ¶ 33. The merits of the analogy notwithstanding, it should be noted that whereas in the case of South Africa's presence in Namibia the Court was asked to opine on the nature of the presence itself, the question relative to the Palestinian territory did not focus on the nature of the Israeli presence therein, that is, on the occupation, but rather on the legality of a specific action undertaken in its context.

West Africa) and then proceeded to deduce the illegality of that continuing presence from various pertinent components that had characterized this fact.[22]

Our inquiry proposes to complement this type of historical approach with an analytical perspective that focuses on the legal and political structure of the phenomenon of occupation. We hope that this discussion will advance the current discourse on the legality of occupation regimes.

C. Current Discourse on the Legality of Occupation Regimes

The current discourse on the legality of occupation regimes is in dire need of development and articulation. The occupation of Iraq indicates that the phenomenon of occupation, far from becoming obsolete, is revived. It now claims legitimacy on the basis of purposes inherently at odds with belligerent occupations; that is, the liberation of a people from an abusive regime.[23] At the same time, the little discussion the issue has generated thus far seems both polarized and lacking specificity. Thus, the inherent tension between the right to self-determination and the legality of occupation has led Antonio Cassese to conclude that "self-determination is violated whenever there is a military invasion or belligerent occupation of a foreign country, except where the occupation—*although unlawful*—is of a minimal duration or is solely intended as a measure of repelling, under Article 1 of the UN Charter, an armed attack initiated by the vanquished Power and consequently is not protracted."[24] This view, then, regards all occupations as inherently unlawful, but admits that the legitimacy of the initial act—the use of force in self-defense—may provide a legal justification for an occupation's existence, subject to a strict, albeit unspecified, temporal limitation.[25]

---

22. *See infra* notes 152-60 and accompanying text.

23. Since occupation is perceived as a fact rather than as a norm, the discourse surrounding the invasion and occupation of Iraq focused primarily on the legality and legitimacy of the *use of force* by the U.S. and not on that of the *occupation*. Underlying these arguments, however, is the implicit presumption that the legitimacy accorded to the U.S. action extends to the occupation itself. Thus, writes Anne-Marie Slaughter, "the United States and its allies can justify their *intervention* if the Iraqi people welcome their coming and if they turn immediately back to the United Nations to help rebuild the country." Anne-Marie Slaughter, *Good Reasons for Going Around the UN*, N.Y. TIMES, MAR. 18, 2003, at A33 (emphasis added). For criticism, see Richard A. Falk, *Future Implication of the Iraq Conflict: What Future for the UN Charter System of War Prevention?*, 97 AM. J. INT'L. L. 590, 596-97 (2003). Falk criticizes claims that a regime change constitutes a legal basis for humanitarian intervention. *See also* David J. Scheffer, *Future Implication of the Iraq Conflict: Beyond Occupation Law*, 97 AM. J. INT'L. L. 842, 851 (2003) (indicating that because the law of occupation is ill-suited for the purposes of changing a regime or rebuilding a country, a nation-building policy by the U.N. rather than a U.S. occupation is required).

24. CASSESE, SELF-DETERMINATION, *supra* note 17, at 99 (emphasis added).

25. *Cf.* Judge Elaraby, *Construction of a Wall, supra* note 6, Separate Opinion of Judge Elaraby, ¶ 3.1. Judge Elaraby cites with approval an article authored by Professors Richard Falk and Burns Weston, which argues that "[o]ccupation, as an illegal and temporary situation, is at the heart of the whole problem." Judge Elaraby does not explain why an occupation is illegal and does not make a connection between its temporary duration and illegality. His reliance on Falk and Weston suggests that the illegality stems from the original act of force that generated the occupation. For a more detailed discussion of this argument, see Richard A. Falk & Burns H. Weston, *The Relevance*

A different position, recently advanced by Eyal Benvenisti, posits that the notion of "illegal occupation" could amount to "major qualifications if not a revolution in the law of occupation."[26] This notion, observes Benvenisti, has its roots in various international documents, wherein an occupation was grouped together with unlawful modalities of governance such as colonialism and apartheid.[27] The latter, however, should not be read as advocating the outlawing of the modality of occupation in its entirety. Rather, only an occupant who uses this modality as an indefinite grant of power and refuses to negotiate its withdrawal "abuses its power and might taint its continuing presence in the occupied territory with illegality."[28] An occupation that has not been thus abused retains its legal validity. Support for this limited notion of illegality, says Benvenisti, is found in Security Council Resolution 1483 of May 22, 2003, which recognized the authorities, responsibilities, and obligations under applicable international law of the "occupying powers" in Iraq, and called upon "all concerned to comply fully with their obligations under international law including in particular the Geneva Conventions of 1949 and the Hague Regulations of 1907,"[29] thereby reviving the neutral connotation of the doctrine of belligerent occupation and relieving it of its derogatory undertone.[30]

Practice has echoed, to a large extent, this scholarly debate. Thus, the inherent tension between the full enjoyment of human rights and the situation of occupation has led the Special Rapporteur of the United Nations Commission of Human Rights, John Dugard, to conclude in one of his Reports on the Violation of Human Rights in the Occupied Arab Territories that "violations of human rights are a necessary consequence of military occupation."[31] Israel understood this conclusion to imply that, "while military occupation may not itself be inherently illegal, it necessarily leads to violations of human rights, and so presumably must be illegal, if not directly then at least indirectly. This remarkable legal thesis contravenes the entire body of humanitarian law dealing with belligerent

---

of *International Law to Israeli and Palestinian Rights in the West Bank and Gaza, in* INTERNATIONAL LAW AND THE ADMINISTRATION OF OCCUPIED TERRITORIES 125, 146-47 (Emma Playfair ed., 1992).

26.   Eyal Benvenisti, *Resolution 1483, supra* note 14, at 33.

27.   Benvenisti lists the following documents: The Charter of Economic Rights and Duties of States of Dec. 12, 1974, G.A. Res. 3281, 29 U.N. GAOR, 29th Sess., Supp. No. 31, art. 16(1), at 52, U.N. Doc. A/9631 (1974)); GA Res. 3171, section 2, U.N. GAOR, 28th Sess., Supp. No. 30, at 52, U.N. Doc. A/9030 (1973); Protocol Additional to the Geneva Conventions of 12 August 1949, and Relating to the Protection of Victims of International Armed Conflicts (Protocol I), June 8, 1977, art. 1(4), 1125 U.N.T.S. 3 [hereinafter Protocol I]; International Convention Against the Taking of Hostages, Dec. 18, 1979, art. 12(12), U.N. Doc. A/C.6/34/L.23, *reprinted* in 18 I.L.M. 1456 (1979). Benvenisti, *Resolution 1483, supra* note 14, at 32-33.

28.   *Id.* at 34.

29.   U.N. S/RES/1483 (2003), ¶ 5.

30.   *See* Benvenisti, *Resolution 1483, supra* note 14, at 36-38.

31.   *See* Question of the Violation of Human Rights in the Occupied Arab Territories, Including Palestine, Report of the Special Rapporteur of the Commission on Human Rights on the Situation of Human Rights in the Palestinian Territories Occupied By Israel Since 1967 (A/57/366), Aug. 29, 2002, ¶ 21 [hereinafter 2002 REPORT ON THE VIOLATIONS OF HUMAN RIGHTS IN THE OCCUPIED ARAB TERRITORIES].

occupation."[32]

The polarization evinced by the above positions underscores the need to clarify and develop the legal discourse and to refine the criteria by which we measure the legality of an occupation. Torn between the position that all occupations are inherently illegal and the position that an occupation is a neutral fact that defies any such characterization, the criteria that have been advanced in this context seem to focus on either the legitimacy of the initial act of occupation or on the legality of specific actions undertaken during the course of an occupation. The discussion further seems to refer to the duration of occupation but fails to specify or otherwise qualify this reference.

We propose to advance the discussion by positing that an occupation, while neither initially nor inherently illegal, is not neutral. Occasioned by, and extending the use of force—regardless of its initial justification and notwithstanding the prohibition on this use[33]—it is to be viewed and monitored critically, lest the much necessary law of occupation becomes a shield for the violation of its own extrinsic purpose and intrinsic principles. The specification of this purpose and these principles provide adequate criteria for determining the legality or illegality of any specific occupation. Lack of such criteria may well generate a legitimizing effect allowing this precarious, albeit not necessarily illegal, situation to indeed become illegal.

II.

THE LEGAL MATRIX OF OCCUPATION

A. *Intrinsic Dimensions of the Israeli Occupation of the OPT: the Norms of Occupation*

The Israeli occupation of the OPT violates the three basic tenets of the normative regime of occupation and is, therefore, intrinsically illegal. This section discusses the basic principles informing this normative regime and then applies them to the Israeli occupation. Sub-section (1), *The Evolving Concept of*

---

32. Question of the Violation of Human Rights in the Occupied Arab Territories, Including Palestine, Note Verbale Dated 16 December 2002 from the Permanent Representative of Israel to the United Nations Office at Geneva Addressed to the Secretariat of the Commission of Human Rights, Commission of Human Rights, 59th Sess., E/CN.4/2003.G/21, ¶ 9, (Dec. 23, 2002) [hereinafter *Note From Israel to the U.N.*].

33. See in this context, Roberts' discussion of a possible grounding of an argument made by the Palestinians on the illegality of the Israeli occupation, in the presumed fact that Israel was an aggressor in 1967. Adam Roberts, *Prolonged Military Occupation: The Israeli Occupied Territories Since 1967*, 84 AM. J. INT'L. L. 44, 49-51 (1990) [hereinafter Roberts, *Prolonged Military Occupation*]. In his list of seventeen types of occupations, Roberts includes "illegal occupation" as a category, but puts this term within quotation marks, and raises a doubt about its validity, based on the ground that this term is used to refer to an occupation which is perceived as being the outcome of aggression. Adam Roberts, *What is a Military Occupation?*, 55 Brit. Y.B. INT'L. L. 249, 293-94 (1984) [hereinafter Roberts, *Military Occupation*]. Our argument about the illegality of occupation does not rest upon facts relating to the question of initial aggression. Such a position, as Roberts argues, is not tenable, given that the law of war, including the law of occupation, equally applies to all states, whether aggressors or victims of aggression.

Occupation, discusses the major cornerstones in the development of this normative regime and the extent of their applicability to the occupation at hand. Subsection (2), *Occupation Suspends Sovereignty*, focuses on the first basic tenet of this regime, that is, that occupation does not confer title. Sub-section (3), *Trust Matters*, discusses the second basic principle of the normative regime of occupation, according to which an occupation regime is a form of trust under which the occupant, without forsaking its own security interests, is nevertheless obligated to act as a trustee on behalf of the occupied population. Sub-section (4), *Right on Time*, is concerned with the last basic principle of the normative regime of occupation, which decrees that an occupation must be temporary, as distinct from indefinite. In each sub-section, the normative conclusions generated by the discussion are then applied to the Israeli occupation of the OPT.

1. The Evolving Concept of Occupation

(a) Defining the Phenomenon of Occupation

The phenomenon of occupation is currently defined as "the effective control of a power (be it one or more states or an international organization, such as the United Nations) over a territory to which that power has no sovereign title, without the volition of the sovereign of that territory."[34]

This widely accepted definition contains three notable features. First, it is expansive so as to cover varied types of occupation. The rationale behind this expansiveness is clear: the moment an occupation exists, the normative regime of occupation—which comprises a host of humanitarian rules—applies. This broad definition curbs the defiance of occupying powers who are reluctant to abide by those rules and deny that the specific situation qualifies as an occupation.[35] Israel's rejection of the applicability of the Fourth Geneva Convention to the OPT, discussed below, underscores this point.[36]

Secondly, the definition incorporates the principle of the inalienability of sovereignty. This principle is the most fundamental tenet of the law of occupation in three senses. First, it indicates that occupation does not confer title.[37] Second, it recognizes that the situation of occupation is exceptional, as it deviates from the normal order of sovereign states insofar as it reflects the suspension of the link between sovereignty and effective control. It is this exceptionality, in turn, that defines both the substantive and the temporal nature of the relationship between the occupying power and the sovereign.[38] Taken together, these principles demarcate the boundaries of the phenomenon in relation to the

---

34. EYAL BENVENISTI, THE INTERNATIONAL LAW OF OCCUPATION 4 (1993) [hereinafter BENVENISTI, LAW OF OCCUPATION].

35. Richard R. Baxter, *Some Existing Problems of Humanitarian Law*, 14 REVUE DE DROIT PENAL MILITAIRE ET DE DROIT DE LA GUERRE 297, 298 (1975).

36. *See infra* notes 87-109 and accompanying text.

37. This principle is discussed in Section II.A.2 *infra*.

38. *See infra* sections II.A.3 (the trust principle) and II.A.4 (the temporal principle).

normal order of the international state system. Finally, the definition notably signifies that the phenomenon of occupation is currently understood in a manner quite distinct from its original conception. The remaining part of this sub-section describes briefly the legal evolution of the concept of occupation and the changing circumstances that have shaped and re-shaped it.

(b) Historical Development of the Law of Occupation

The evolution of the concept of occupation and the rules attached to it, like the development of the laws of war in general, reflects the general shift in international law away from a state-centric system toward the recognition and promotion of the role and rights of individuals. Indeed, the tension between rights of states and rights of individuals is the hallmark of the laws of war. It is thus unsurprising that early efforts to codify the law of belligerent occupation primarily concerned the rights and interests of states, often at the expense of individuals. The normative reflection of this concern found expression in the subjection of principles of humanity to those of military necessity.[39]

The Lieber Code,[40] commissioned by President Lincoln for training Union forces during the U.S. Civil War, is generally credited as the first milestone in the genesis of the law of belligerent occupation.[41] The Code clearly prioritizes military over humanitarian considerations: while it recognized minimum protection of the civilian population,[42] it also sanctioned starvation and bombardment of civilians without warning, when military necessity so required.[43]

The first international attempt to codify the law of belligerent occupation took place in Brussels in 1874, where delegates of seventeen European states convened to draft comprehensive regulations on warfare.[44] This effort generated a final declaration that was never ratified: the great powers viewed it as "too 'humanitarian,'"[45] while the small nations considered the articles on occupation as detrimental to their interests in calling on their populations for aid in resisting

---

39. Chris Jochnick & Roger Normand, *The Legitimation of Violence: A Critical History of the Laws of War*, 35 HARV. INT'L. L. J. 49 (1994).

40. Instructions for the Government of Armies of the United States in the Field, General Orders No. 100, Apr. 24, 1863, *reprinted in* Schindler & Toman, *supra* note 15, at 3 [hereinafter Lieber Code].

41. About one-third of the Code's provisions relate to belligerent occupation. *See generally,* DORIS A. GRABER, THE DEVELOPMENT OF THE LAW OF BELLIGERENT OCCUPATION 1863-1914—A HISTORICAL SURVEY 15 (1949).

42. Lieber Code, *supra* note 40, arts. 22-23, 34-38.

43. *Id.* at arts. 14, 15, 17, 19. Although the Code was issued during the Civil War, it was designed to cover international conflicts, as evidenced by the fact that the Union viewed the Confederate forces as *de facto* belligerent. *See* GRABER, *supra* note 41, at 18-19. Furthermore, between the years 1870 and 1893, other countries— including Prussia, the Netherlands, France, Russia, Serbia, Argentina, Great Britain and Spain—adopted similar manuals or codes. *See* LESLIE C. GREEN, THE CONTEMPORARY LAW OF ARMED CONFLICT 30 (2d ed. 2000).

44. Christopher Greenwood, *Historical Development and Legal Basis, in* THE HANDBOOK OF HUMANITARIAN LAW IN ARMED CONFLICTS 1, 10 (Dieter Fleck ed., 1995) [hereinafter Greenwood, *Historical Development*].

45. Jochnick & Normand, *supra* note 39, at 67.

invasions by larger armies.[46]

There was, however, some agreement on the definition of occupation. Article 1 of the Brussels Declaration defined occupation as a territory actually placed under the authority of a hostile army bounded by the territories around which it could establish and exercise authority.[47] There was no agreement as to the exact meaning of the term "actually placed under the authority." Article 2 read, "[t]he authority of the legitimate Power being suspended and having in fact passed into the hands of the occupant, the latter shall take all the measures in his power to restore and ensure, as far as possible, public order and safety."[48] Thus defined, the concept of occupation mirrored nineteenth century European political consciousness: war was waged between sovereign states and the protected interests belonged to them.[49] Thus, the rights of the population took a back seat to the interests of the sovereign. As between states, however, the Brussels Declaration is notable for recognizing that the situation of occupation is one of *suspension*: the normal order of the international society wherein the legitimate sovereign exercises effective authority is suspended in relation to the occupied territory and population. It is not, however, terminated. The occupying power assumes responsibility for managing the occupied territory to prevent chaos for the duration of the occupation. This assumption does not, however, confer sovereignty on the occupier.

The definition of belligerent occupation survived the two subsequent codification projects of the laws of war in The Hague Conventions and their annexed Regulations. The Conventions were the products of two conferences held at The Hague in 1899 and 1907, and constituted a comprehensive, albeit incomplete,[50] codex of the laws of war.

The most relevant convention for this discussion is the 1907 Fourth Hague Convention and annexed Regulations,[51] which by WWII had attained customary status.[52] Article 42 of the 1907 Hague Regulations reiterated verbatim the definition of belligerent occupation expressed in Article 1 of the Brussels Declara-

---

46.   GRABER, *supra* note 41, at 24-25. Today, however, that section of the declaration that concerns occupation, which was not revised by later conventions, is regarded as customary and applicable to the Israeli occupation. *See* Greenwood, *Historical Development, supra* note 44, at 10.

47.   Brussels Declaration, *supra* note 15, at 3.

48.   *Id.*

49.   David Goodman, *The Need for Fundamental Change in the Law of Belligerent Occupation*, 37 STAN. L. REV. 1573, 1591 (1985).

50.   The preamble of Convention (IV) respecting the Laws and Customs of War on Land and its annex: Regulations concerning the Laws and Customs of War on Land, Oct. 18, 1907, Reg. 42, 36 Stat. 2277, 1 Bevans 631, states that: "It has not, however, been found possible at present to concert regulations covering all the circumstances which arise in practice." [hereinafter: 1907 Hague Regulations].

51.   *Id.*

52.   *Judgment of the Nuremberg International Military Tribunal* (30 Sept. 1946), *in* 22 TRIAL OF THE MAJOR WAR CRIMINALS BEFORE THE INTERNATIONAL MILITARY TRIBUNAL: NUREMBERG, 14 NOVEMBER 1945 – 1 OCTOBER 1946 411, 497 (1948). *See also Legality of the Threat or Use of Nuclear Weapons*, 1996 I.C.J. 226, 257-58 (July 8) [hereinafter *Nuclear Weapons* Advisory Opinion]. This was the basis of the Israeli High Court of Justice decision to apply the Regulations to the Palestinian Occupied Territories. *See* H.C. 610/78, Oiev v. Minister of Defense, 33(2) P.D. 113.

tion.[53] Article 43 of the 1907 Hague Regulations stipulated that "the authority of the legitimate power having in fact passed into the hands of the occupant, the latter shall take all the measures in his power to restore, and ensure, as far as possible, public order and safety/civil life, while respecting, unless absolutely prevented, the laws in force in the country."[54] This provision became the cornerstone for the determination of the nature and scope of the occupant's responsibility. That duty is of a temporary duration and the occupying power is to manage the territory in a manner that protects civil life, exercising its authority as a trustee of the sovereign.[55] Further protection of the occupied population was provided by the Regulations in respect of family honor and the rights to life, private property, and religious convictions and practices.[56] Pillage[57] and collective sanctions[58] were forbidden.[59]

Thus, modern occupation law traditionally recognized and regulated only belligerent occupation characterized by four main features: (a) the occupation is undertaken by a belligerent state; (b) it is over a territory of an enemy belligerent state; (c) it occurs during the course of war or armed conflict; and, (d) before any armistice agreement is concluded.[60] Also, the occupation extends only to those areas over which the occupant exercises effective control.[61] The assumption underlying this approach is that no other authority exists in the occupied area.[62] Further, control is measured by the authority's ability to assume the primary responsibility that attaches to an occupying power: the ability to issue and enforce directives to the inhabitants of the territory,[63] or, in other words, the oc-

53. *See also* regulation 42 of the Convention (II) with Respect to the Laws and Customs of War on Land and its annex: Regulations concerning the Laws and Customs of War on Land, July 29, 1899, 32 Stat. 1803, 1 Bevans 247.

54. Note that the language of the official French version refers to "l'ordre et la vie publique" and that the term "civil life" is more accurate and appropriate than the term "safety," used in the English version. The term "civil life" is far broader than the term "safety" inasmuch as the former encompasses the entire commercial and social life of a country. *See* JOHN WESTLAKE, II INTERNATIONAL LAW: WAR 95 (2d ed. 1913). According to the preparatory work on the Brussels Declaration, which produced the original French term, the correct translation is "civil life" and not "safety" as the semi-official English translation put it. *See* Edmund H. Schwenk, *Legislative Power of the Military Occupant under Article 43, Hague Regulations*, 54 YALE L. J. 393, 393 n.1 (1945).

55. Arnold Wilson, *The Laws of War in Occupied Territories*, 18 TRANSACTIONS GROTIOUS SOC'Y 17, 38 (1933); Roberts, *Military Occupation*, *supra* note 33, at 295. For a discussion of the principle of trust, see *infra* Section II.A.3 *infra*.

56. 1907 Hague Regulations, *supra* note 50, at art. 46.

57. *Id.* at art. 50.

58. *Id.*

59. For additional reference, see the preface to the 1899 Convention (II), *supra* note 53, which stated that the parties agree to "diminish the evils of war, as far as military requirements permit."

60. The fact that the Conventions did not alter the definition of occupation is hardly surprising. According to Jochnick and Normand, while considered by many an important achievement in the effort to humanize war, the Conventions did not challenge the subjection of humanitarian concerns to military necessity. *See* Jochnick & Normand, *supra* note 39, at 68-77.

61. Roberts, *Military Occupation*, *supra* note 33, at 261.

62. *See* 1907 Hague Regulations, *supra* note 50, at art. 43.

63. Hans-Peter Gasser, *Protection of the Civilian Population*, *in* Fleck, *supra* note 44, at 209, 243.

cupant's ability to have its will prevail everywhere in the territory.[64]

This traditional definition of occupation proved unsatisfactory during WWII. For example, in cases where the occupied states encountered little, if any, armed resistance, or where the territories were not necessarily administered by the armed forces of the occupant, as was the case with Denmark and Czechoslovakia, the traditional definition of occupation was inadequate.[65] Furthermore, inadequate protection afforded to the occupied population was painfully evident throughout the war and highlighted the need for occupation law reforms.[66]

The four 1949 Geneva Conventions, of which the fourth Convention is the most relevant for the purposes of this discussion, were concluded in the light of lessons learned from WWII.[67] The second paragraph of Common Article 2 of the four Geneva Conventions expanded the applicability range of the laws of occupation by including therein that occupation has taken place even without a declaration of war and without hostilities.[68] Article 4 of the Fourth Geneva Convention then applies the Convention's provisions to "protected persons" who, either during an armed conflict or during an occupation, find themselves in the hands of a party to the Convention of which they are not nationals. The term "in the hands of" applies to persons who are not necessarily in the physical custody of the occupant. Instead, it pertains to all people present in the territory under the control of the occupant other than its own nationals or the nationals of its allies.[69] The Fourth Geneva Convention expanded not only the application of the rules of belligerent occupation, but also the duties incumbent on the occupant with respect to the civilian population, thus constituting a new and far broader bill of rights when compared to the previous Hague Conventions.[70] Thus, it is the protection of the occupied civilian population, rather than the facilitation of

---

64. GERHARD VON GLAHN, THE OCCUPATION OF ENEMY TERRITORY 29 (1957) [hereinafter VON GLAHN, OCCUPATION].

65. Roberts, *Military Occupation, supra* note 33, at 252.

66. VON GLAHN, OCCUPATION, *supra* note 64, at 16.

67. Convention for the Amelioration of the Condition of the Wounded and Sick in Armed Forces in the Field, Aug. 12, 1949, 75 U.N.T.S. 31; Geneva Convention for the Amelioration of the Condition of the Wounded, Sick and Shipwrecked Members of Armed Forces at Sea, Aug. 12, 1949, 75 U.N.T.S. 85; Geneva Convention Relative to the Treatment of Prisoners of War, Aug. 12, 1949, 75 U.N.T.S. 135; Geneva Convention Relative to the Protection of Civilian Persons in Time of War, Aug. 12, 1949, 75 U.N.T.S. 287 [hereinafter Fourth Geneva Convention].

68. *See* JEAN S. PICTET, COMMENTARY—THE GENEVA CONVENTION RELATIVE TO THE PROTECTION OF CIVILIAN PERSONS IN THE OF WAR 21 (1958). Article 2 reads as follows:

In addition to the provisions which shall be implemented in peacetime, the present Convention shall apply to all cases of declared war or of any other armed conflict which may arise between two or more of the High Contracting Parties, even if the state of war is not recognized   by   one   of   them.
The Convention shall also apply to all cases of partial or total occupation of the territory of a High Contracting Party, even if the said occupation meets with no armed resistance. Although one of the Powers in conflict may not be a party to the present Convention, the Powers who are parties thereto shall remain bound by it in their mutual relations. They shall furthermore be bound by the Convention in relation to the said Power, if the latter accepts and applies the provisions thereof. *Id.*

69. *Id.* at 46.

70. BENVENISTI, LAW OF OCCUPATION, *supra* note 34, at 105.

cilitation of governmental interests, which informs the Fourth Geneva Convention.[71] This is a clear shift of concern from governments to people.[72]

Still, under the Fourth Geneva Convention, the qualifications of situations which constitute occupation require some nexus to an armed conflict. Further, the Convention seemed to stipulate that the occupied territory should form part of the territory of another High Contracting Party.[73] Consequently, the rules enumerated in the four Conventions did not apply to any form of occupation other than belligerent occupation.[74] This also proved unsatisfactory. As the twentieth century drew to a close, other types of occupation surfaced, and the ever-heightened interest in protecting the civilian populations required that these new types of occupations also be subject to the provisions of the Fourth Geneva Convention. [75]

(c) The Transition into the Contemporary Law of Occupation: the Growing Significance of Self-Determination

The growing concern for the plight of civilians reflects two paradoxical yet interrelated facets of the latter half of the last century: the development of the international human rights discourse, and the undeniable recognition of the fact that wars are being waged against civilians rather than soldiers.[76] The growing significance of the right to self-determination reflects, to a large extent, an attempt by the international community to take account of both these developments. Already recognized in the UN Charter,[77] the two International Covenants on human rights,[78] several General Assembly resolutions,[79] and opinions rendered by the ICJ,[80] the right to self-determination produced a wave of interna-

---

71. PICTET, *supra* note 68, at 614.

72. BENVENISTI, LAW OF OCCUPATION, *supra* note 34, at 99-100.

73. The second paragraph of article 2 of the Fourth Geneva Convention refers to a territory of a High Contracting Party. Israel relied on this clause in support of its position that the Fourth Geneva Convention is inapplicable to the OPT. For more on this argument and a critique of its use, see *infra* notes 87-109 and accompanying text.

74. *See* VON GLAHN, OCCUPATION, *supra* note 64, at 27.

75. For a typology of occupations, see Roberts, *Military Occupation, supra* note 33, at 260-95.

76. World War II, Vietnam, Kosovo, Bosnia, and Rwanda, are but a few notable examples of this observation. *See generally* CHRIS HEDGER, WAR IS A FORCE THAT GIVES US MEANING 28 (2002).

77. United Nations Charter, *supra* note 13, at arts. 1, 55

78. International Covenant on Civil and Political Rights, Dec. 19, 1966, art. 1(1), 999 U.N.T.S. 175, G.A. Res. 2200 (XXI), 21 U.N. GAOR, Supp. (No. 16) 49, U.N. Doc. A/6316 (1967) [hereinafter ICCPR]; International Covenant on Economic, Social and Cultural Rights, Dec. 16, 1966, art. 1(1), 993 U.N.T.S. 3, G.A. Res. 2200A(XXI), 21 U.N. GAOR, art. 11(1), U.N. Doc. A/6316 (1976) [hereinafter ICESCR].

79. *See, e. g.,* Declaration on the Granting of Independence to Colonial Countries and Peoples, G.A. Res. 1514, 15 U.N. GAOR Supp. (No. 16) at 66, U.N. Doc. A/4684 (1960). *See also infra* note 81.

80. *See Continued Presence of South Africa in Namibia* Advisory Opinion, *supra* note 21, Separate Opinion of Vice Presdient Ammoun, *supra* note 21; Western Sahara, 1975 I.C.J. 12, 31-33 (Oct. 16).

tional approval for the lawful struggle for self-determination of peoples subject to foreign domination—including occupation.[81]

It is against this backdrop that the development in occupation law as articulated in Article 1(4) of the First Additional Protocol of the Geneva Conventions should be read:

> The situations referred to in the preceding paragraph include armed conflicts in which peoples are fighting against colonial domination and alien occupation and against racist régimes in the exercise of their right of self-determination, as enshrined in the Charter of the United Nations and the Declaration on Principles of International Law concerning Friendly Relations and Co-operation among States in accordance with the Charter of the United Nations.[82]

Article 1(4) was designed to cover occupied territories severed either from a nonparty state or otherwise lacking clear international status.[83] The drafters of this First Additional Protocol ("Protocol") had, *inter alia*, the OPT in mind. Israel and a few other states—most notably, the United States—refused to join the Protocol.[84]

The controversy generated by Article 1(4) questioned the customary status of many of the Protocol's provisions[85] and blurred the contours of their application. This was detrimental to the ongoing development of international humanitarian norms, since the Protocol promoted humanitarian concerns over military necessity.[86] One must not, however, ignore the influence Article 1(4) has had on the law of occupation. As the Israeli example itself clearly demonstrates, inter-

---

81.   *See* Declaration on Principles of International Law Concerning Friendly Relations and Co-operation Among States in Accordance with the Charter of the United Nations, G.A. Res. 2625, U.N. GAOR, 25th Sess., Supp. No. 28, at 121, U.N. Doc. A/8028 (1970) ("every state has the duty to refrain from any forcible action which deprives peoples . . . of their right to self-determination and freedom and independence. In their actions against, and resistance to, such forcible action in pursuit of the exercise of their right to self-determination, such peoples are entitled to seek and to receive support in accordance with the purpose and principles of the Charter." *See also* G.A. Res. 3281, *supra* note 27, at art. 16(1); Permanent Sovereignty over Natural Resources, GA Res. 3171, *supra* note 27. *See also Construction of a Wall* Separate Opinion of Judge Elaraby, *supra* note 6, ¶ 3.1 (expressing his approval of Falk and Weston's conclusion that "[i]n effect, the illegality of the Israeli occupation regime itself set off an escalatory spiral of resistance and repression, and under these conditions all considerations of morality and reason establish a right of resistance inherent in the population. This right of resistance is an implicit legal corollary of the fundamental legal rights associated with the primacy of sovereign identity."). Falk & Weston, *supra* note 25, at 146-47. On the different readings of these documents, see the positions of Cassese and Benvenisti, *supra* text accompanying notes 23-30.

82.   Protocol I, *supra* note 27 (emphasis added).

83.   MICHAEL BOTHE ET AL., NEW RULES FOR VICTIMS OF ARMED CONFLICTS 51, 52 (1982).

84.   Theodor Meron, *The Time Has Come for the United States to Ratify Geneva Protocol I*, 88 AM. J. INT'L L. 678, 683 (1994).

85.   Christopher Greenwood, *Customary Law Status of the 1977 Geneva Protocols*, in HUMANITARIAN LAW OF ARMED CONFLICT: CHALLENGES AHEAD 93 (Astrid J.M. Delissen & Gerard J. Tanja eds., 1991); Georges Abi-Saab, *The 1977 Additional Protocols and General International Law: Some Preliminary Reflections*, in Delissen & Tanja, *supra* at 115, 119; THEODOR MERON, HUMAN RIGHTS AND HUMANITARIAN NORMS AS CUSTOMARY LAW 62-70 (1989).

86.   *See* Protocol I, *supra* note 27, at art. 51(5)(6) (considering an attack which "may be expected to cause incidental loss of civilian life, injury to civilians, damage to civilian objects, or a combination thereof, which would be excessive in relation to the concrete and direct military advantage anticipated," as a prohibited indiscriminate attack).

national recognition of the need to apply occupation laws to situations outside traditional belligerent occupation has taken root in contemporary international law.

(d) Application of the Law of Occupation to the OPT

Israel has long maintained that the Fourth Geneva Convention is not applicable to the occupied territories.[87] This contention relies on the second paragraph of Article 2 of the Fourth Geneva Convention, according to which, since the territories did not form part of the territory of a High Contracting Party upon their occupation, the Convention does not apply.[88] Israel based this argument on Jordan's annexation of the West Bank in 1950, which was recognized by only Britain and Pakistan.[89] Israel also based this argument on the fact that Egypt never claimed the Gaza Strip as part of its territory.[90]

Israel's position exemplifies the inadequacy of the traditional definition of occupation. The narrow definition allows exploitation by states attempting to refrain from providing minimal protection to occupied civilian populations. The Israeli position is also quite telling because it has been so widely rejected, even within Israel itself.[91]

The first legal response to the Israeli position is formalistic. First, there is no evidence that the term "territory of a High Contracting Party," as used in Common Article 2, refers solely to full legal title. Rather, it pertains to a *de facto* title of territory.[92] The rationale underlying this argument is that the Convention's drafters did not intend to provide occupants with discretion to ascertain the validity of title the ousted power had with respect to the territory.[93] Second,

---

87. It is interesting to note that the Security Provisions Order issued by the Israeli military commander on the day the IDF took over the West Bank contained a reference to the Fourth Geneva Convention as well as a determination that, in legal proceedings in established military tribunals, the Convention will have precedence over the Order. This Order, however, was revoked soon thereafter. *See* DAVID KRETZMER, THE OCCUPATION OF JUSTICE 32, 33 (2002).

88. Meir Shamgar, *Legal Concepts and Problems of the Israeli Military Government—The Initial Stage, in* MILITARY GOVERNMENT IN THE TERRITORIES ADMINISTRATED BY ISRAEL 1967-1980 13, 33-34 (Meir Shamgar ed., 1982) [hereinafter Shamgar, *Legal Concepts*].

89. Yehuda Z. Blum, *The Missing Reversioner: Reflections on the Status of Judea and Samaria,* 3 ISR. L. REV. 279 (1968).

90. Meir Shamgar, *The Observance of International Law in the Administered Territories,* 1 ISR. Y.B. HUM. RTS. 262, 263 (1971) [herinafter Shamgar, *Observance*]; Stacy Howlett, *Palestinian Private Property Rights in Israel and the Occupied Territories,* 34 VAND. J. TRANSNAT'L L. 117, 153 (2001). Both Jordan and Egypt are parties to the Fourth Geneva Convention.

91. *See, e.g.,* Yoram Dinstein, *The International Law of Belligerent Occupation and Human Rights,* 8 ISR. Y.B. HUM. RTS. 104, 107 (1978); ESTHER R. COHEN, HUMAN RIGHTS IN THE ISRAELI-OCCUPIED TERRITORIES 1967-1982, 51-56 (1985). For a concise summary of the arguments and counter-arguments, see Orna Ben-Naftali & Keren R. Michaeli, *'We Must Not Make a Scarecrow of the Law': A Legal Analysis of the Israeli Policy of Targeted Killings,* 36 CORNELL INT'L. L. J. 233, 260-61 (2003) [hereinafter Ben-Naftali & Michaeli, *Targeted Killings*]; Benham Dayanim, *The Isreali Supreme Court and the Deportation of Palestinians: The Interaction of Law and Legitimacy,* 30 STAN. J. INT'L L. 115, 143-150 (1994); KRETZMER, *supra* note 87, at 31-35.

92. W. THOMAS MALLISON & SALLY V. MALLISON, THE PALESTINIAN PROBLEM IN INTERNATIONAL LAW AND WORLD ORDER 254 (1986).

93. *Id.* at 255. Indeed, the disputed status does not prevent the applicability of the laws of

the first paragraph of Article 2 is the relevant paragraph to apply when an occupation begins during a war, as in the present case.[94] This is supported by the ICRC's Commentary on Common Article 2 of the Convention.[95]

A second line of reasoning is based on the Palestinian right to self-determination. Accordingly, sovereignty lies in the people, not in a government. The Israeli position is thus untenable because it ignores the possibility that the Palestinian people constitute the lawful *reversioner* of the territories.[96] A related argument assumes that title cannot exist in a vacuum. Whether or not the 1948 Jordanian occupation and subsequent annexation were legal, Palestinians ultimately allowed the annexation, combining their sovereignty with that of Jordan's, resulting in the territories being taken from a High Contracting Party.[97]

Lastly, the third line of reasoning is teleological and focuses on the rights of the occupied population: the rationale underlying the Fourth Geneva Convention is to ensure protection of the civilian population from a foreign occupying power. Indeed, for all intent and purposes, Israel is a foreign occupying power of the Palestinian population. The Convention is part of international humanitarian law, the main purpose of which is protection of local populations regardless of whether a legitimate sovereign state exists.[98] Therefore, there is no justification for denying a local population the protections afforded by the Fourth Geneva Convention.[99]

---

occupation. Throughout the 20th century, territorial disputes have often preceded or accompanied military occupations: the long standing dispute between Argentina and England over the Falkland Islands; Indonesia's invasion into east Timor; the Moroccan intervention in western Sahara. So was the South African occupation of Namibia.

94. Roberts, *Prolonged Military Occupation*, *supra* note 33, at 64; BENVENISTI, LAW OF OCCUPATION, *supra* note 34, at 109-10; COHEN, *supra* note 91, at 53.

95. PICTET, *supra* note 68, at 20-22.

96. Ardi Imseis, *On the Fourth Geneva Convention and the Occupied Palestinian Territory*, 44 HARV. INT'L. L. J. 65, 97 (2003).

97. Joseph H. H. Weiler, *Israel, the Territories and International Law: When Doves are Hawks*, *in* ISRAEL AMONG THE NATIONS 381, 386-87 (Alfred E. Kellermann et al. eds., 1998).

98. It is interesting to note in this context that pursuant to the Israeli High Court of Justice's (HCJ) ruling of April 18, 2002, H.C.J. 769/02, *The Public Committee Against Torture v. Government of Israel* (the legality of targeted killings case), which requested the parties, inter alia, to state their positions on what system of law applies to the issue, the Respondent's brief (Supplementary Statement by the State's Attorney's Office) argued not only that International Human Rights Law is inapplicable, but that the Respondent will use the term "Law of Armed Conflicts" rather than "International Humanitarian Law": "Without going into a profound discussion on the logic inherent in the new term ('international humanitarian law'), it is important to emphasize that one of its disadvantages, in the Respondent's way of thought, is the risk of confusing this term, which includes the 'laws of war' and the term 'international human rights law', which is another area altogether and separate from international law, which deals with the protection of the fundamental rights of individuals within state." H.C.J. 769/02, The Public Committee Against Torture v. Government of Israel, Supplementary Statement by the State's Attorney's Office of 2 Feb. 2003, Para. 40 (unofficial translation) (on file with authors). On the co-application of humanitarian and human rights law in occupied territories, see Orna Ben-Naftali and Yuval Shany, *Living in Denial: The Application of Human Rights in the Occupied Territories*, 37 ISR. L. REV., 17 (2003-04) [hereinafter *Living in Denial*].

99. Gasser, *supra* note 63, at 244; GEOFFRY R. WATSON, THE OSLO ACCORD: INTERNATIONAL LAW AND THE ISRAELI-PALESTINIAN PEACE AGREEMENTS 138 (2000). For a discussion on the effect Israel's occupation has had on the Palestinian population, see *infra* section

The international community widely embraced the concept of a Palestinian right to self-determination, as evidenced in the resolutions of the General Assembly[100] and the Security Council.[101] Accordingly, the international community demanded that Israel apply the Fourth Geneva Convention to the OPT. Israel declared that it would apply the "humanitarian provisions" of the Convention to the Palestinian territories,[102] a declaration relied upon by the Israeli High Court of Justice (HCJ) in petitions pertaining to various measures undertaken by Israel in the OPT.[103]

Finally, the ICJ had the opportunity to rule on this issue in its recent *Construction of a Wall* Advisory Opinion. In it, the ICJ endorsed the first and third reasoning.[104] Having first opined that, as of 1967, "all these territories (includ-

---

II.A.3. The position that the Fourth Geneva Convention should be interpreted based on the substance of the relations, given that its purpose is to protect individuals, was taken by the International Criminal Tribunal for the Former Republic of Yugoslavia in the Tadic judgment. Prosecutor v. Tadic (Case IT-94-1-A) (1999) ¶ 168, *at* http://www.un.org/icty/tadic/appeal/judgement/tad-aj990715e.pdf. For a discussion of this judgment as representing the transformations in humanitarian law from being state centered to being individuals-centered, see Eyal Benvenisti, THE INTERNATIONAL LAW OF BELLIGERENT OCCUPATION, preface (2004) [hereinafter *Preface*]. See also, Partial Award, Central Front, Ethiopia Claim No. 2, April 28, 2004, ¶¶ 28-29, at http://www.pca-cpa.org/ENGLISH/RPC/EECC/ET%20Partial%20Award.pdf., where the Eritrea-Ethiopia Claims Commission rejected the link between the disputed status of certain territories and the protection of individuals present in these territories. The protections of international humanitarian law, held the Commission, "should not be cast into doubt because the belligerents dispute the status of the territory." *Id.* The Commission rejected the idea that only territory to which title is clear can be occupied territory. *Id.*

100. *See, e.g.,* G.A. Res. 32/91, U.N. GAOR, 32d Sess., 101st plen. mtg. at 69, U.N. Doc. A/RES/32/91 (1977); G.A. Res. 33/113, U.N. GAOR, 33rd Sess., 87st plen. mtg. at 70, U.N. Doc. A/RES/33/113 (1978); G.A. Res. 44/48, U.N. GAOR, 44th Sess., 78st plen. mtg. U.N. Doc. A/RES/144/48 (1989).

101. *See, e.g.,* S.C. Res. 237, U.N. SCOR, 1361st mtg. at 5 (1967); S.C. Res. 446, U.N. SCOR, 2134th mtg. at 4 (1979); S.C. Res. 605, U.N. SCOR, 2777th mtg. at 4 (1987); *see also* Roberts, *Prolonged Military Occupation, supra* note 33, at 69-70.

102. Shamgar, *Observance, supra* note 90, at 266.

103. *See, e.g.,* H.C. 2977/02, Adallah v. Commander of the IDF in the West Bank, 56(3) P.D. 6; H.C. 3451/02, Almadani v. Minister of Defense, 56(3) P.D. 30, 35-36; H.C. 4363/02, Zindah v. Commander of the IDF Forces in the Gaza Strip Judgment of May 28, 2002 (unpublished); H.C. 7015/02, Ajuri v. Commander of the IDF in the Judea and Samaria, 56(6) P.D. 352; H.C. 2056/04, The Village Council of Beit Surik et al. v. the Government of Israel and the Military Commander of the West Bank, 58(5) P.D. 807; H.C. 7957/04, Mara'abe v. The Prime Minister of Israel (unpublished), *available at* www.court.gov.il. Prior to the breakdown of the Oslo Accord, Israel had transferred most administrative functions in some of the territories to the Palestinian authority. This prompted it to declare that the transfer of control indicates that Israel was no longer an occupant. *See* WATSON, *supra* note 99, at 176. This position seems dubious, given both the relatively small percentage of the OPT that was transferred to the civilian administration of the Palestinian authority and the discontinuity of the territories. In effect, Israel continued to exercise effective control over the OPT. In any case, Israel's re-occupation of Gaza Strip and the West Bank during the second *Intifada* has rendered the argument irrelevant. The recent withdrawal from the Gaza Strip is likely to resurrect that argument with respect to this area. *See supra* note 1.

104. The Court stated that the "[t]he object of the second paragraph of Article 2 is not to restrict the scope of application of the Convention, as defined by the first paragraph ... the drafters of the Fourth Geneva Convention sought to guarantee the protection of civilians in time of war regardless of the status of the occupied territories." *Construction of a Wall, supra* note 6, ¶ 95.

ing East Jerusalem) remain occupied territories,"[105] it proceeded to conclude that:

> [T]he Fourth Geneva Convention is applicable in any occupied territory in the event of an armed conflict arising between two or more High Contracting Parties. Israel and Jordan were parties to that Convention when the 1967 armed conflict broke out. The Court accordingly finds that the Convention is applicable in the Palestinian territories which before the conflict lay to the east of the Green line and which, during the conflict were occupied by Israel, there being no need for any further enquiry into the precise prior status of those territories.[106]

The ICJ discussion in this advisory opinion underscores the rationale for a wider definition of occupation to ensure that the law of occupation is applied to a broader range of situations.[107] This clearly lends significant legal weight to the compelling underlying logic in favor of applying the Geneva regime to the occupation in the OPT.

Having determined the relevance of the normative regime of occupation to the issue at hand, we can now proceed to discuss its essential foundations. "The foundation upon which the entire law of occupation is based," writes Benvenisti, "is the principle of inalienability of sovereignty through the actual or threatened use of force. Effective control by foreign military force can never bring about by itself a valid transfer of sovereignty."[108] The rule of non-recognition, forbidding states to recognize title thus acquired, is the normative consequence of this principle.[109] The following sub-section details this fundamental principle.

2. Suspension of Sovereignty: Occupation Does Not Confer Title

(a) Acquisition of Territory by Force is Impermissible Even If the Force is Used Legally

This basic tenet of the law of occupation rests on and reflects the well-established general international legal principle that the acquisition of territory by force does not confer a valid title to that territory.[110] This principle holds even if force is used legally—for example in self-defense—and even if the status of the territory under consideration is disputed.[111] The rationale behind this

---

105. *Construction of a Wall, supra* note 6, ¶ 78. This conclusion follows a discussion pertaining to the status of the OPT, *id.* at ¶¶ 70-77, dating back to the Mandate. The Court notes specifically that various events subsequent to 1967 "have done nothing to alter this situation" (of occupation). *Id.* at ¶ 78.

106. *Id.* at ¶ 101. Before reaching its conclusion the Court discussed some of the arguments for and against the application of the Fourth Geneva Convention discussed above, placing a special emphasis on the subsequent interpretation of the Convention by the UN Security Council and General Assembly, the State Parties to the Convention, the Red-Cross and the Israeli Supreme Court. *Id.* at ¶¶ 90-100.

107. The question, whether all rules of occupation are relevant to all types of occupations in all circumstances, is interesting but as it is incidental to this paper, shall not be discussed here.

108. BENVENISTI, LAW OF OCCUPATION, *supra* note 34, at 5.

109. SURYA P. SHARMA, TERRITORIAL ACQUISITION, DISPUTES AND INTERNATIONAL LAW 148 (1997).

110. BENVENISTI, LAW OF OCCUPATION, *supra* note 34, at 5.

111. *See* Partial Award, Central Front, Ethiopia Claim No. 2, *supra* note 99.

principle is an obvious manifestation of two fundamental norms of the international legal order: the prohibition on the use of force and the right to self-determination.[112]

It is instructive to note in this context that the rule of non-recognition for the acquisition of title, as distinct from its prohibition, is not a novel idea. Rather, it was well established when the laws of occupation began to take form,[113] in an era preceding the prohibition on the use of force.

Thus, up until the late eighteenth century, international law recognized the right of conquest, "the right of the victor, in virtue of military victory or conquest, to sovereignty over the conquered territory and its inhabitants."[114] The occupant was considered the absolute owner of the occupied territory and therefore could dispose of it in any way it saw fit, including by annexation.[115] The premise upon which the laws of war were drafted, however, is that of the territorial integrity of states. All that was being sought by the laws of belligerent occupation was the maintenance of a status quo until a final resolution of the dispute was reached between the occupant and the ousted sovereign. It is for this reason that Article 43 of the Fourth Hague Conventions did not confer sovereign powers on the occupant, but rather limited its authority to maintain public order and civil life, while "respecting, unless absolutely prevented, the laws in force in the country."[116] This proviso precluded the annexation of the territory by the occupant.[117] This preclusion was further clarified in Article 47 of the Fourth Geneva Convention, which emphasized that annexation of an occupied territory during wartime, before the conclusion of any peace treaty, does not deprive protected persons of the rights guaranteed by the Convention.[118] Consequently, annexation does not alter the status of the territory or its population.[119] The latest affirmation of this principle is found in Article 4 of the Protocol, restating that neither occupation of a territory nor the application of the Protocol's provisions shall affect the legal status of the territory under dispute.[120]

The non-recognition rule, however, did not in itself render the acquisition

---

112. As discussed in the text accompanying *supra* notes 74-81, the right to self determination has supplanted, in this context, the right of states to sovereign equality and territorial integrity. See *Construction of a Wall*, *supra* note 6, ¶¶ 87-88.

113. *See, e.g.*, L. Oppenheim, *The Legal Relations Between an Occupying Power and the Inhabitants*, 33 L. Q. Rev. 363, 364 (1917). *Cf.* Lieber Code, *supra* note 40, at art. 33 (implicitly authorizing annexation prior to the conclusion of a peace treaty).

114. SHARON KORMAN, THE RIGHT OF CONQUEST; THE ACQUISITION OF TERRITORY BY FORCE IN INTERNATIONAL LAW AND PRACTICE 9 (1996).

115. GRABER, *supra* note 41, at 13.

116. *See supra* notes 49-55 and accompanying text.

117. GEORG SCHWARZENBERGER, INTERNATIONAL LAW AS APPLIED BY INTERNATIONAL COURTS AND TRIBUNALS 166-67 (3d ed. 1957).

118. *See* Fourth Geneva Convention, *supra* note 67, at art. 47.

119. PICTET, *supra* note 68, at 275-76. Pictet emphasizes the fact that the reference to annexation in the article cannot be considered as implying recognition of it as a means to acquire territory and that the contrary is true. *Id.*

120. COMMENTARY ON THE ADDITIONAL PROTOCOLS OF 8 JULY 1977 TO THE GENEVA CONVENTIONS OF 12 AUGUST 1949 73, 74 (Yves Sandoz et al. eds., 1987) [hereinafter COMMENTARY ON THE ADDITIONAL PROTOCOLS].

of territory completely illegal. Rather, acquisition has become illegal as a result of gradual renunciation by the international community of the use of force as an acceptable policy.[121] The principle, enshrined in Article 2(4) of the UN Charter, that "all members shall refrain in their international relations from the threat or use of force against the territorial integrity or political independence of any state, or in any other manner inconsistent with the purposes of the United Nations,"[122] reflects one of the most basic principles of international law today.

The unacceptability of territorial acquisition through the use, or threat, of force is thus viewed as a corollary of the prohibition on the use of force.[123] The rationale behind this derives from the principle of *ex injuria jus non oritur*[124] and was succinctly articulated by Robert Jennings: "To brand as illegal the use of force against the 'territorial integrity' of a state, and yet at the same time to recognize a rape of another's territory by illegal force as being itself a root of legal title to the sovereignty over it, is surely to risk bringing the law into contempt."[125]

This formulation leaves open the possibility that a territory occupied through the use of legal force (that is, force not in violation of Article 2(4) of the UN Charter) may confer title.[126] However, a main feature of Article 2(4) is the elimination of any potential benefit emanating from the use of force, rendering it an unattractive policy to pursue, and consequently, the rejection of any type of force utilized as a means of achieving territorial change.[127] Furthermore, the argument that acquisition of territory by force used in self-defense pursuant to Article 51 of the UN Charter can confer legal title rests on the dangerous assumption that any extension of a legal use of force is legal.[128] This is inconsistent with the limits attached to the right of self-defense, namely, that the force used is proportionate to the threat of immediate danger. As a result, when the threat has diminished, it no longer sustains the right to self-defense. Therefore, the right to have recourse to self-defense does not include the right to permanently seize the territory of the attacked.[129] Indeed, Article 51 is an exception to the rule prohibiting the use of force and should be narrowly construed to limit the right to self-

---

121. For a detailed description of the evolution of the prohibition on the use of force, see YORAM DINSTEIN, WAR, AGGRESSION AND SELF-DEFENSE 78, 79-98 (2001).

122. U.N. Charter, *supra* note 13, at art. 2(4).

123. *See Construction of a Wall, supra* note 6, ¶ 87. *See also* KORMAN, *supra* note 114, at 200-18.

124. Hersch Lauterpacht, *The Limits of the Operation of the Law of War*, 30 BRIT. Y.B. INT'L. L. 206, 233-37 (1953); Felice Morgenstern, *The Validity of the Acts of the Belligerent Occupant*, 28 BRIT. Y.B. INT'L. L. 291, 321 (1951).

125. ROBERT Y. JENNINGS, THE ACQUISITION OF TERRITORY IN INTERNATIONAL LAW 54 (1963).

126. *See, e.g.*, SCHWARZENBERGER, *supra* note 117, at 297; Rudolf L. Bindschedler, *Annexation*, 3 Encyclopedia Pub. Int'l. L. 19 (1982); Rosalyn Higgins, *The June War: The United Nations and Legal Background*, 3 J. CONTEMP. HIS. 253, 270 (1968).

127. KORMAN, *supra* note 114, at 201.

128. JENNINGS, *supra* note 125, at 55.

129. *Id. See also* Derek W. Bowett, *International Law Relating to Occupied Territory: A Rejoinder*, 87 L. Q. REV. 473, 475 (1971).

defense only as a means to restore the status quo.[130]

Finally, the most convincing basis for the rejection of the argument that legitimizes the acquisition of territory through use of force in self-defense is the frequent inability to distinguish between the aggressor and the victim in a particular conflict. Wars, and memories of grievances, tend to rest on competing narratives that often defy aggressor/victim determinations. The Security Council, a political body entrusted with this determination,[131] is hardly a satisfactory arbitrator of history and of collective consciousness. Thus, differentiation with respect to the legality of title between one achieved through illegal use of force, and one achieved through a legal use of force rests on shaky ground, and ultimately undermines the coherence of the rule.[132]

The conclusion that no use of force can confer legal title finds support in the UN Declaration on Principles of International Law Concerning Friendly Relations and Co-operation among States. That document does not distinguish between legal and illegal uses of force when it states that *"no* territorial acquisition resulting from the threat or use of force shall be recognized as legal."[133] Despite Israel's adamant claim that the 1967 war was pursued in self-defense, the same rationale underlies the UN Security Council's Middle East Resolution 242, which reiterated the inadmissibility of the acquisition of territory by war.[134]

In sum, the legality of occupation, or lack thereof, cannot be grounded in the determination that an occupation was occasioned as a result of self-defense. Thus, the debate about the legality of Israel's original action in occupying the OPT during the 1967 war—a debate reflected in the different narratives which shape the conflict—is irrelevant to the question with which this paper is concerned.[135] Indeed, even if the Israeli narrative of a war fought in self-defense was accepted as the shared assumption of the conflict, it is irrelevant to both the determination of the legality of the continued occupation and to the principle of the inalienability of sovereignty.

Another important conclusion is that the Israeli annexation of East Jerusalem—expanding gradually its boundaries from 6.5 to 71 square kilometers—is

---

130. Brun-Otto Bryde, *Self-Defense,* 4 Encyclopedia Pub. Int'l. L. 212, 213-14 (1982); KORMAN, *supra* note 114, at 205. Korman indicates that the narrow ambit of Article 51 prohibits even the annexation of a territory of an aggressor that repeatedly uses the territory as a base for attacks and can therefore might still be considered proportionate. *Id.* at 204-05.

131. Article 39 of the United Nations Charter, *supra* note 13.

132. JENNINGS, *supra* note 125, at 55-56.

133. G.A. Res. 2625, *supra* note 81.

134. For the different views on the subject, see Amos Shapira, *The Six-Day War and the Right to Self Defence,* 6 ISR. L. REV. 65 (1971); Ibrahim F. I. Shihata, *Destination Embargo of Arab Oil: Its Legality Under International Law,* 68 AM. J. INT'L. L. 591, 598-601 (1974); Eugene V. Rostow, *The Illegality of the Arab Attack on Israel of October 6, 1973,* 96 AM. J. INT'L. L. 272, 274-82 (1975).

135. Criticizing the Secretary-General's reference to the Israeli occupation as "illegal," George Fletcher argued, *inter-alia,* that: "[F]ew seem to care anymore that the 1967 war was a war of self-defense for Israel." Fletcher, *supra* note 4. Responding to this criticism, the spokesman for the Secretary-General noted that "[i]n using the word illegal . . . Secretary General Kofi Annan had no intention of entering the debate about the legality of Israel's original action." *See supra* note 5.

illegal.[136] This illegality was affirmed by both the Security Council and the General Assembly, with the consequence that under international law the area is still considered occupied.[137] The ICJ's *Construction of the Wall* Advisory Opinion confirms this conclusion.[138]

(b) Occupation Does Not Confer Title In Light of the Principle of Self-Determination

The principle of self-determination complements the principle that use of force cannot confer legal title to territory. Self-determination informs not only United Nations decisions regarding Israel's annexation of occupied East Jerusalem and its settlements in the OPT, [139] but also the Security Council's vision of "a region where two states, Israel and Palestine, live side by side within secure and recognized borders."[140] Underlying this determination is the rationale that if people, according to Common Article 1(1) of the International Covenants on Human Rights, have the right to "freely determine their political status,"[141] then sovereignty belongs to the people, and no valid title can be transferred in disregard of the will of the population of the territory.[142] This point was wholeheartedly approved by the *Construction of a Wall* Advisory Opinion regarding the *de facto* annexation of the vast Palestinian territories by way of settlement establishments and the construction of the Wall by Israel.[143]

An occupation, thus, suspends sovereignty insofar as it severs its ordinary link with effective control; but it does not, indeed it cannot, alter sovereignty. Effective control must be exercised in a manner that accords with the obligations of the occupying power as a trustee. The meaning of this form of trust is detailed

---

136. Israel extended its law to East Jerusalem on 26 June 1967. *See* The Law and Administration Ordinance (Amendment No. 11) Law, 21 L.S.I. 75 (1967); The Municipalities Ordinance (Amendment No. 6) Law, 21 L.S.I. 75 (1967). It formally annexed that area on 30 June 1980. *See* The Basic Law: Jerusalem, Capital of Israel, 34 L.S.I. 209 (1980).

137. *See* S.C. Res. 478, U.N. SCOR, 35th Sess., 2245th mtg. at 14, U.N. Doc. S/INF/36 (1980); G.A. Res. 35/169E, U.N. GAOR, 35th Sess., Supp. No. 48, at 208-2209, U.N. Doc. A/35/48 (1981); S.C. Res. 673, U.N. SCOR, 46th Sess., 2949 mtg. at Res. & Dec. 7, U.N. Doc. S/INF/46 (1991). Israel based its claim to sovereignty over East Jerusalem essentially on its right to fill the sovereignty vacuum which existed since the termination of the mandate, an argument which generated a debate among Israeli international lawyers and failed to gain the support of the international community. On the debate within Israel, see for example, Yehudah Blum, *The Redemption of Zion in International Law*, 3 ISR. L. REV. 279 (1968); Yoram Dinstein, *The Future Redemption of Zion in International Law*, 27 HAPRAKLIT 5 (1971). For a discussion on the legal status of Jerusalem, see John Quigley, *The Future of Jerusalem: A Symposium: Sovereignty in Jerusalem*, 45 CATH. U. L. REV. 765 (1996). Similar reactions followed Israel's annexation of the Golan Heights, a Syrian territory occupied by Israel during the Six-Day war of 1967. *See* Golan Heights Law, 36 L.S.I. 7 (5742-1981/2); S.C. Res. 497 (1981); G.A. Res. 36/226A (1981); G.A. Res. 39/146A (1984).

138. *Construction of a Wall, supra* note 6, ¶¶ 74-75, 120-22.

139. G.A. Res. 37/88C, U.N. GAOR, 37th Sess., Supp. No. 51, at 93, U.N. Doc. A/37/51 (1982-83); S.C. Res. 465, U.N. SCOR, 35th Sess., 2203d mtg. at 5, U.N. Doc S/INF/36 (1980).

140. S.C. Res. 1397, U.N. SCOR, 4489th mtg., U.N. Doc. S/RES/1397 (2002).

141. *See also* G.A. Res. 1514 (XV), *supra* note 79.

142. Imseis, *supra* note 96, at 97; BENVENISTI, LAW OF OCCUPATION, *supra* note 34, at 183; KORMAN, *supra* note 114, at 228.

143. *Construction of a Wall, supra* note 6, ¶¶ 118-22. *See infra* section II.A.4.d.iii.

in the following sub-section.

3. Trust Matters: Occupation As a Form of Trust

(a) The Framework of this Trust

Implicit in the principle that occupation does not confer title and that the occupant is vested with the authority, in the words of Article 43 of the 1907 Fourth Hague Convention, "to take all the measures in his power to restore, and ensure, as far as possible, public order and safety/civil life, while respecting, unless absolutely prevented, the laws in force in the country," is the notion of trusteeship. Occupied territories "constitute . . . a sacred trust, which must be administered as a whole in the interests both of the inhabitants and the legitimate sovereign or the duly constituted successor in title."[144]

The framework of the trust consists of two features: the security needs of the occupying power on the one hand and the maintenance of civil life on the other hand. The trust thus carries with it a potential conflict of interests between those of the population and those of the occupant. In the nineteenth century's context, where governmental involvement in the life of the population was minimal, this framework produced two primary rules: the occupant bore the negative duty of refraining from infringing on the most basic rights of the inhabitants, while the latter possessed the duty of obedience to the occupant.[145]

With the continued evolution of the law of occupation, the scale began to tip to the side of the inhabitants. The Fourth Geneva Convention seems to reject the idea that the occupied population was under any international legal obligation to obey the occupant.[146] In parallel, the Convention considerably expands the protection of the inhabitants, setting obligations to respect their persons, honor, family life, religious convictions, and customs; to ensure humane treatment and freedom from discrimination; and, in particular, the protection of women.[147] The Convention also prohibits the infliction of physical suffering, corporal punishment, medical experiments, collective punishment, pillage, reprisals, the taking of hostages, deportations, and retroactive criminal legislation and

---

144. *Construction of a Wall, supra* note 6, Separate Opinion of Judge Koroma, ¶ 2; Wilson, *supra* note 55, at 38.

145. The duty of obedience stemmed from three possible sources: municipal law (i.e., the population was to follow the laws of the land as they were the laws of the legitimate sovereign); international law (i.e., the duties incumbent upon the sovereign gave rise to corollary rights); and the physical ability of the occupant to enforce such obedience. *See generally* Oppenheim, *supra* note 113, at 365-69; Richard R. Baxter, *The Duty of Obedience to the Belligerent Occupant*, 27 BRIT. Y.B. INT'L L. 235 (1950) [hereinafter Baxter, *Obedience*].

146. For example, the terms "war rebellion" and "war treason" were not incorporated in the Convention. *See generally* Fourth Geneva Convention, *supra* note 67. Furthermore, while providing the occupant with the right to take measures against protected persons who carry out acts detrimental to the security of the occupant, it nevertheless preserves most of their rights under the Convention. *Compare id.* at arts. 27, 64 *with id.* at arts. 5, 68; *see also* Baxter, *Obedience, supra* note 145, at 261, 264.

147. Fourth Geneva Convention, *supra* note 67, at arts. 27, 75.

punishment. The right of the occupant to compel the inhabitants to work is restricted. The Convention further imposes positive duties on the occupant with regard to protecting children, ensuring food and medical supplies, maintaining hospitals, providing certain due process rights, and providing certain rights of imprisoned persons.[148] The Convention also restricts the right of the occupant to detain protected persons and stipulates substantial protection for detainees.[149]

The expanded protection of the inhabitants culminates with the currently prevailing view that international human rights law applies concurrently with international humanitarian law to occupied territories: the latter is the *lex specialis*, but the former applies either in cases of lacunae or for interpenetrative purposes.[150] Indeed, the longer the occupation, the heavier the weight to be accorded to the human rights of the occupied population.[151] The inseparability of human rights guarantees from the concept of trust rests at the heart of the ICJ advisory opinion concerning the *Legal Consequences of the Continued Presence of South Africa in Namibia*. The Court construed the relationship between South Africa and Namibia as a "sacred trust"[152] and found South Africa's continued infringement of the rights and well-being of the inhabitants of Namibia to de-

---

148. *Id.* at arts. 32, 33, 34, 49, 65, 67, 51, 52, 50, 55, 59-62, 56, 57, 66, 69, 71-73, 76, 77, respectively.

149. *Id.* at arts. 79-135.

150. *See Construction of a Wall, supra* note 6, ¶¶ 105-13; *Nuclear Weapons* Advisory Opinion, *supra* note 52, at 249. For similar views, see Cyprus v. Turkey, App. No. 8007/77, Eur. Comm'n H.R. Dec. & Rep. 85, 149-50 (1979); Loizidou v. Turkey, 310 Eur. Ct. H.R. (Ser. A) at 24 (1995); Abella v. Argentina, Case 11.137, Inter-Am. C.H.R., Report No. 55/97, OEA/Ser.L./V./II.95, doc. 7 rev. 271, ¶¶ 161, 166 (1997). Israel rejects this confluence of legal regimes, but its position has been widely rejected by both international bodies and scholars. For the Israeli stand, see STATE OF ISRAEL, IMPLEMENTATION OF THE INTERNATIONAL COVENANT ON ECONOMIC, SOCIAL AND CULTURAL RIGHTS – SECOND PERIODIC REPORT, Aug. 3, 2001, ¶¶ 5-8, U.N. Doc. E/1990/6/Add.32 (2001); STATE OF ISRAEL, IMPLEMENTATION OF THE INTERNATIONAL COVENANT ON CIVIL AND POLITICAL RIGHTS – SECOND PERIODIC REPORT, Nov. 20, 2001, ¶ 8, U.N. Doc. CCPR/C/ISR/2001/2 (2001); STATE OF ISRAEL, IMPLEMENTATION OF THE INTERNATIONAL COVENANT ON CIVIL AND POLITICAL RIGHTS – ADDITIONAL INFORMATION, April 20, 2001, ¶¶ 2-5, U.N. Doc. E/1989/5/Add.14 (2001). This was also the position taken by the Israeli delegation before the International Committee on the Rights of the Child and the International Committee on the Elimination of Racial Discrimination. *See* Summary Record of the 829th meeting: Israel, Oct. 10, 2002, ¶¶ 39-42, U.N. Doc. CRC/C/SR.829 (2002); Note Verbale dated 8 August 1994 from the Permanent Representative of Israel to the United Nations Office at Geneva, U.N. Doc. CERD/C/282 (1995). For the position of relevant international bodies, see CONCLUDING OBSERVATIONS OF THE COMMITTEE ON ECONOMIC, SOCIAL AND CULTURAL RIGHTS: ISRAEL, May 23, 2003, ¶ 15, U.N. Doc. E/C.12/1/Add.90 (2003); CONCLUDING OBSERVATIONS OF THE HUMAN RIGHTS COMMITTEE: ISRAEL, Aug. 5, 2003, ¶ 11, U.N. Doc CCPR/CO/78/ISR (2003). For a legal analysis of the respective positions, as well as a summary and a critical review of the *Construction of a Wall* advisory opinion in this respect, see Ben-Naftali & Shany, *supra* note 98.

151. COHEN, *supra* note 91, at 29; Roberts, *supra* note 33, at 97.

152. Roberts, *supra* note 33, at 28-32. While the relationship between South Africa and Namibia represents a unique case (i.e., the mandate system established by the League of Nations), the reasoning of the Court nevertheless seems to apply generally given the Court's interpretation of the traditional concept of trust, found in the mandate system, in light of recent legal developments, namely, self-determination and independence of the people and basic human rights. Furthermore, the Court construed South Africa's presence in Namibia following the revocation of the mandate as an occupation.

stroy "the very object and purpose of that relationship."[153] Therefore, the Court held the UN General Assembly's termination of the mandate to be valid and the continuing presence of South Africa in Namibia—a presence which thereafter was a foreign occupation[154]—to be illegal.[155]

It is interesting to note in this context that the Court reiterated this position in its recent *Construction of a Wall* Advisory Opinion. In the part of the opinion dealing with the status of the OPT, the Court narrates the history of the conflict, the roots of which are described as follows: "Palestine was part of the Ottoman Empire. At the end of the First World War, a class "A" Mandate for Palestine was entrusted to Great Britain by the League of Nations."[156] The Court recalled that, in its 1950 opinion on the *International Status of South West Africa*,[157] it held that "two principles were considered to be of paramount importance" with respect to territories that were placed under the Mandate system: "the principle of non-annexation and the principle that the well-being and development of . . . peoples [not yet able to govern themselves] form[ed] 'a sacred trust of civilization.'"[158]

The Court returned to this point in a later part of the opinion concerned with determining the relevant international legal rules applicable to the issue at hand. Recalling its 1971 opinion on the *Continued Presence of South Africa in Namibia*, the Court stated that "current developments in international law in regard to non-self governing territories . . . made the principle of self-determination applicable to all [such territories] . . . . [T]hese developments leave little doubt that the ultimate objective of the sacred trust . . . was the self-determination of the people concerned."[159] What the Court seemed to be doing, then, was to construct the concept of a "sacred trust," the origins of which were rooted in the Mandate system, as the common denominator of all situations where people are not self-governing, occupation included. That construction is facilitated by the historical fact that Palestine was a Mandate territory, and that the roots of the Israeli-Palestinian conflict rested in the dissolution of the Mandate. This construction enabled the Court to emphasize not only the principle of self-determination, but also the related notion of a "sacred trust" as applicable to the OPT.[160]

The trust, especially one emanating from a belligerent type of occupation

---

153. *Continued Presence of South Africa in Namibia* Advisory Opinion, *supra* note 21, at 47.

154. Roberts, *supra* note 33, at 293-94.

155. *Continued Presence of South Africa in Namibia* Advisory Opinion, *supra* note 21, at 54.

156. *Construction of a Wall*, *supra* note 6, ¶ 70.

157. *International Status of South-West Africa*, 1950 I.C.J. 128 (July 11).

158. *Id.* at 131; *Construction of a Wall*, *supra* note 6, ¶ 70.

159. *Continued Presence of South Africa in Namibia* Advisory Opinion, *supra* note 21, at 52-54; *Construction of a Wall*, *supra* note 6, ¶ 88.

160. Note that some of the judges who appended separate opinions took issue with this analogy. *See Construction of a Wall*, *supra* note 6, Separate Opinion of Judge Higgins, ¶ 2; Separate opinion of Judge Kooijmans, ¶ 33.

rather than from a mandate, does not abrogate the security interests of the occupying power.[161] The Convention explicitly provides exceptions to some of the guarantees afforded to the population, based on military necessity and conditions.[162] Furthermore, the occupant is allowed to take measures against protected persons in the form of promulgating penal laws[163] and assigning residence[164] and internment.[165] That being said, such authority seems to have fallen out of favor in recent years in light of pronouncements by the international community endorsing the right of an occupied population to rise against the occupant in its pursuit of self-determination.[166] Security measures are thus subject to careful scrutiny.

The balance between humanitarian and human rights concerns—pouring content into the notion of trust, on the one hand, and military necessity, delimiting but never substituting this trust on the other hand—is thus a hallmark of the current law of occupation. The working assumption behind this arrangement is that an occupation is of a relatively short duration.[167] The restriction on the occupant's authority to amend the laws of the country so as to make necessary reforms, which might be called for throughout the years, underscores this point. In long-term occupations, the result may well be the stagnation of all aspects of life: economic, political, cultural, and social existence, with harsh consequences for the population. It is, in fact, hard to reconcile such an outcome with the occupant's general duty to ensure civil life in the occupied territory.[168] Furthermore, the longer the occupation lasts, the higher the likelihood of an uprising by the population, acting in pursuit of its right to self-determination. This, in turn, is likely to generate stricter security measures by the occupant, to the detriment of the population. The net result would thus be less, rather than more, weight given to the humanitarian and human rights concerns of the population, especially in the event of an unsuccessful uprising. The trust then would be sacrificed at the

---

161. It is interesting to note that Allan Gerson referred to the Israeli occupation as a "trustee occupation." He argues that this type of occupation occurs when the legal status of the territory prior to the occupation was short of full sovereignty, the occupation was not generated by a war of aggression, and the occupant was seeking to positively develop the area. The occupant should be seen as a trustee responsible for promoting the population's right of self-determination and should, therefore, not be constrained by the law requiring the preservation of the status quo. *See* Allan Gerson, *Trustee Occupant: The Legal Status of Israel's Presence in the West Bank*, 14 HARV. INT'L L. J. 1 (1973). This typology, however, is problematic from the perspective of law and fact alike. From a legal perspective, as discussed in the text above, the concept of trust underlies the law of occupation in general; from a factual perspective, it is unclear whether Israel's occupation stemmed from a war of self-defense, and even if it did, it is clear that it has not assumed the role of a trustee fostering the Palestinian right to self-determination, as acknowledged by Gerson himself already in 1978. *See* ALLAN GERSON, ISRAEL, THE WEST BANK AND INTERNATIONAL LAW 78-82 (1978).

162. *See, e.g.*, Fourth Geneva Convention, *supra* note 67, at arts. 27, 49, 51, 53.

163. *Id.* at art. 64.

164. *Id.* at art. 78.

165. *Id.* at art. 42.

166. *See supra* section II.A.1.c.

167. *See infra* section II.A.4.a.

168. BENVENISTI, LAW OF OCCUPATION, *supra* note 34, at 147; Roberts, *supra* note 33, at 52; Goodman, *supra* note 49.

altar of the interests of the occupying power in maintaining its hold over the occupied territory. Such indeed is the sorry story of the Israeli occupation of the OPT.[169]

(b) Application of the Framework to the OPT

The story of the occupation is inseparable from the settlement enterprise. The latter generates both the dispossession of and the discrimination against the Palestinians and signifies Israel's breach of the trust contemplated by the normative regime of occupation. In order to substantiate this argument, the remaining part of this section discusses the genesis of the settlements and the debate concerning their legality. We then focus on various consequences of the settlements' construction and maintenance, including the confiscation of land, the existence of two separate legal systems in the area, operating along ethnic lines, and the effects of such actions on the daily life of the occupied population. While the Devil may well be in the details, for the purposes of this discussion, we are less concerned with specific violations of the law of occupation occasioned by any particular action—violations that have attracted attention elsewhere in the relevant literature—but, rather, with identifying the basic structure and nature of this occupation regime.

(i) The Settlements

Immediately following the 1967 war, the Labor government then in power initiated the settlement project based ostensibly on security considerations.[170] When the Likud Party formed a government in 1977, the security motive gave way to an ideological claim to the entire OPT, based on historical and religious grounds. The settlements enterprise thus became a "holy work" which Prime Minister Shamir, who took office after Begin in 1983, vowed to pursue.[171] That year, the Ministry of Agriculture and the World Zionist Organization, a quasi-governmental organization entrusted with furthering the political objectives of Zionism, jointly prepared a master plan for the development of the settlements designed "to achieve the incorporation (of the West Bank) into the (Israeli) national system."[172] A comparison between its details and current realities indicate a high degree of geographical, if not demographical, materialization.[173] This has been achieved by a dual Israeli policy of land expropriation from the

---

169. *Construction of a Wall, supra* note 6, Separate Opinion of Judge Elaraby, ¶ 3.1. *See also supra* note 81.

170. *See* MERON BENVENISTI, THE WEST BANK DATA PROJECT: A SURVEY OF ISRAEL'S POLICIES 30-36 (1984); RAJA SHEHADEH, OCCUPIER'S LAW: THE WEST BANK AND THE RULE OF LAW 15-49 (1985) [hereinafter SHEHADEH, OCCUPIER'S LAW].

171. Cited in John Quigley, *Living in Legal Limbo*, 10 PACE INT'L. L.R. 1, 6 (1998).

172. *Id.* The first settlement plan prepared by the World Zionist Organization stated clearly that the objectives of the settlements were to fragment the Palestinian population and prevent it from forming "a territorial continuity and political unity." *See* KRETZMER, *supra* note 87, at 76.

173. BENVENISTI, *supra* note 170, at 19-28.

Palestinians and economic incentives to the settlers.[174] As a result of this policy, there are at present some 120 settlements in the West Bank with over 230,000 settlers. The much ado about the recent withdrawal from the Gaza Strip involved the dismantlement of a mere 16 settlements and the evacuation of less than 10,000 settlers. About 180,000 settlers live in the neighbourhoods of the expanded area of East Jerusalem.[175] The population growth in the settlements is three times that of Israel.[176]

The land upon which the settlements are built in the West Bank, in addition to adjacent confiscated land, settlement bypass roads, and other land controlled by the military, amount to 59% of the West Bank. The settlements and the bypass roads connecting them to each other as well as to Israel have divided the West Bank into some 60 non-contiguous zones. East Jerusalem is severed from the rest of the West Bank.[177]

---

174. B'TSELEM, The Israeli Information Center for Human Rights in the Occupied Territories, LAND GRAB: ISRAEL'S SETTLEMENT POLICY IN THE WEST BANK, *available at* http://www.btselem.org/english/Publications/Summaries/Land_Grab_2002.asp [hereinafter LAND GRAB]. The settlers and other Israeli citizens working or investing in the settlements are entitled to significant financial benefits, such as generous loans for the purchase of apartments, part of which is converted to a grant, significant price reductions in leasing land, incentives for teachers, exemption from tuition fees in kindergartens, free transportation to school, grants for investors, infrastructure for industrial zones, incentives for social workers, and reductions in income tax for individuals and companies. The Ministry of the Interior provides increased grants for the local authorities in the territories relative to those provided for communities within Israel. In the year 2000, the average per capita grant in the Jewish local councils in the West Bank was approximately sixty-five percent higher than the average per capita grant in local councils inside Israel. The discrepancy in the grants for the regional councils is even greater: the average per capita grant in 2000 in the regional councils in the West Bank was 165 percent of that for a resident of a regional council inside Israel. *Id.*

175. *See* Foundation for Middle East Peace, Statistics, *at* http://www.fmep.org/settlement_info/statistics.html; *see also* B'TSELEM, Settlements Population By Year, the West Bank, *at* http://www.btselem.org/English/Settlements/Settlement_population.xls. Prior to the recent withdrawal from the Gaza Strip, which totals 140 square miles, less than 10,000 Jews lived on 20% of the land, and 1.1 million Palestinians in the remaining area. *See* Foundation for Middle East Peace, ISRAELI SETTLEMENTS IN THE OCCUPIED TERRITORIES: A GUIDE - A SPECIAL REPORT OF THE FOUNDATION FOR MIDDLE EAST PEACE, *available at* http://www.fmep.org/reports/special_reports/no11-march2002/index.html. In tandem with the pull-out from Gaza, Israel dismantled 4 settlements in Northern Samaria in the West Bank, where some 580 settlers lived. Some of these settlers relocated to Israel while others relocated to other settlements in the West Bank. The area was not handed over to the Palestinians.

176. *See* QUESTION OF THE VIOLATION OF HUMAN RIGHTS IN THE OCCUPIED ARAB TERRITORIES, INCLUDING PALESTINE, Report of the Special Rapporteur of the Commission on Human Rights, John Dugard, on the Situation of Human Rights in the Palestinian Territories Occupied by Israel since 1967. Res. 1993/2 A, 14, U.N. Doc. E/CN.4/2004/6, Sep. 8, 2003 [hereinafter 2003 REPORT ON THE SITUATION OF HUMAN RIGHTS IN THE PALESTINIAN TERRITORIES].

177. *See* QUESTION OF THE VIOLATION OF HUMAN RIGHTS IN THE OCCUPIED ARAB TERRITORIES, INCLUDING PALESTINE, Update to the Mission Report on Israel's Violations of Human Rights in the Palestinian Territories Occupied Since 1967, Submitted by Giorgio Giacomelli, Special Rapporteur, to the Commission on Human Rights at its Fifth Special Session. U.N. Doc. E/CN.4/2001/30, Mar. 21, 2001 at ¶ 26. For a discussion of the politics of the geography and planning of the settlements, see Rafi Segal and Eyal Weizman, *The Mountain Principle of Building in Heights, in* A CIVILIAN OCCUPATION: THE POLITICS OF ISRAELI AGRICULTURE 79 (Rafi Segal and Eyal Weizman eds., 2003).

*(ii) Dispossession: Violations of the Law of Occupation
Generated as a Result of the Settlements*

The legal debate concerning the Israeli settlements has focused primarily on Article 49 paragraph 6 of the Fourth Geneva Convention, which prohibits the occupant from transferring parts of its own civilian population into the territory it occupies.[178] The Israeli government has always maintained that the prohibition does not include voluntary transfer by citizens to occupied territories because it was informed by, and should be interpreted in light of, the policies practiced by Germany during WWII, to which the Israeli policy cannot be compared.[179] This position is not entirely consistent with the ICRC commentary on the Fourth Convention, according to which the intent of this provision was to maintain a general demographic status quo in occupied territories.[180] Further pronouncements by the Parties to the Convention rejected the Israeli interpretation by declaring the settlements as a breach of Article 49 paragraph 6.[181] This situation prompted the adoption of a different version of this prohibition in Article 8(2)(b)(viii) of the Rome Statute, which criminalizes such transfers whether they are undertaken directly or indirectly.[182] This provision might well render Israel's incentive policy as an "indirect transfer," and largely explains Israel's decision not to ratify the Statute.[183] Further, given that the Israeli government built the settlements and provided financial incentives to settlers, the correct conclusion seems to be that the settlement project is a "direct transfer" and thus falls within the scope of the original prohibition of Article 49 paragraph 6.[184]

---

178.   Such transfer further constitutes a grave breach of Protocol I. *See* Protocol I, *supra* note 27, at art. 85(4)(a). As already noted, Israel is not a party to the Protocol. *See supra* note 82-84 and accompanying text.
179.   For the Israeli position, see Israeli Settlements and International Law, at http:// www.mfa.gov.il/mfa/go.asp?MFAH0jyz0]; Ayelet Levy, *Israel Rejects Its Own Offspring: The International Criminal Court*, 22 Loy. L.A. Int'l & Comp. L. Rev. 207, 230-31 (1999); Jean-Marie Henckaerts, *Deportation and Transfer of Civilians in Time of War*, 26 Vand. J. Transnat'l L. 469, 472 (1993).
180.   PICTET, *supra* note 68, at 283.
181.   *See* DECLARATION OF THE CONFERENCE OF THE PARTIES TO THE FOURTH GENEVA CONVENTION, Dec. 5, 2001, *available at* http://www.eda.admin.ch/eda/e/home/foreign/hupol/4gc /docum2.Par.0006.UpFile.pdf/mg0112054gcdeclarne.pdf]; GERHARD VON GLAHN, LAW AMONG NATIONS: AN INTRODUCTION TO PUBLIC INTERNATIONAL LAW 675-76 (7th ed. 1996).
182.   Rome Statute of the International Criminal Court, art. 8(2)(b)(viii), July 17, 1998, U.N. Doc. A/CONF. 183/9; 37 I.L.M. 1002 (1998); 2187 U.N.T.S. 90.
183.   *See* Statement by Israeli Foreign Ministry Legal Advisor, Allen Baker, Jan. 3, 2001, *available at* http://www.mfa.gov.il/MFA/MFAArchive/2000_2009/2001/1/International+Criminal+ Court+-+Press+Briefing+by+I.htm. Israel signed the Statute on Dec. 31, 2001, attaching a declaration conveying its disappointment in the "politicization" of the Statute by the insertion of "formulations tailored to meet the political agenda of certain states." *Id.* On Aug. 28, 2002, Israel informed the U.N. Secretary-General of its intention not to ratify the Statute. For the status of ratifications of the Rome Statute, including declarations made by Israel, see http://untreaty.un.org/ENGLISH/bible/englishinternetbible/partI/chapterXVIII/treaty10.asp#N3.
184.   *See* Catriona Drew, *Self-determination, Population Transfer and the Middle East Peace Accords*, in HUMAN RIGHTS, SELF-DETERMINATION AND POLITICAL CHANGE IN THE OCCUPIED PALESTINIAN TERRITORIES 119, 144-46 (Stephen Bowen ed., 1997). A recent official report presented to the Prime Minister's Office by an attorney especially hired for this purpose (Ta-

The ICJ had an opportunity to opine on this matter in its advisory opinion on the *Construction of a Wall*, as the "wall's sinuous route has been traced in such a way as to include within that area the great majority of the Israeli settlements in the occupied Palestinian Territory (including East Jerusalem)."[185] Noting that "since 1977, Israel has conducted a policy and developed practices involving the establishment of settlements in the Occupied Palestinian Territory, contrary to the terms of Article 49 paragraph 6," the Court concluded that "the Israeli settlements in the Occupied Palestinian Territory (including east Jerusalem) have been established in breach of international law."[186]

Israel's extensive confiscation of Palestinian land, carried out to satisfy the needs of the continuing expansion of the settlements,[187] might also amount to a grave breach of Article 147. Article 147 prohibits "extensive appropriation of property, not justified by military necessity and carried out unlawfully and wantonly."[188] Such action is criminalized by Article 8(2)(a)(iv) of the Rome Statute.

The method and effect of this expropriation merit attention. Following a determination by the Israeli High Court of Justice (HCJ) that private land could not be confiscated for the establishment of civilian settlements,[189] the Israeli government moved quickly to define ever greater portions of the occupied territories as "state land." The lack of a comprehensive land ownership registration in the OPT, which made it quite difficult for individuals to prove their land ownership, as well as a governmental decision to designate all uncultivated rural land as "state land," facilitated the expansion of the definition of "state land."[190] The effect of these practices has been two-fold: first, the *de facto* dispossession of individual Palestinians; second, the dispossession of the Palestinian population of land reserves that should have primarily served its interests. Instead, these lands are administered by the Israel Land Administration, a body set up under Israeli Law to administer state land in Israel proper, and now being used for set-

---

lya Sasson) observed that there are at least 105 unauthorized "outposts," some of them construed on private Palestinian land, and there is evidence that governmental authorities were involved in the establishment of many of those. The clear implication is that the rest of the settlements were indeed "authorized." *See Opinion on Unauthorized Outposts, Prime Minister's Office Communication Department* (March 2005), *available at* http://www.pmo.gov.il/NR/rdonlyres/0A0FBE3C-C741-46A6-8CB5-F6CDC042465D/0/sason2.pdf.

185.   *Construction of a Wall, supra* note 6, ¶ 119.

186.   *Id.* at ¶ 120. The Court reached this conclusion based inter alia on U.N. Security Council Resolution 446, *supra* note 101.

187.   Such expropriation has continued during and after the Oslo process. For a discussion on the expropriation methods, see generally RAJA SHEHADEH, FROM OCCUPATION TO INTERIM ACCORDS: ISRAEL AND THE PALESTINIAN TERRITORIES 4-35 (1997); Imseis, *supra* note 96, at 102.

188.   The *Construction of a Wall* Advisory Opinion does not cite Article 147 of the Fourth Geneva Convention as relevant to the case at hand. This is due to the Court's interpretation of Article 6 as precluding the applicability of all but 43 of the Convention's 159 articles, including Article 147. We take issue with this interpretation, as is discussed at *infra* section II.A.4.b.

189.   H.C. 390/79, Dewikat v. Government of Israel, 34(1) P.D.1; *see also* KRETZMER, *supra* note 87, at 85-89.

190.   For a detailed account of these practices and the complex set of legal mechanisms that enable them, see LAND GRAB, *supra* note 174; SHEHADEH, OCCUPIER'S LAW, *supra* note 170, at 22-41; KRETZMER, *supra* note 87, at 89-94.

tlements.[191]

Israel has also used control over planning to restrict the growth of Palestinian towns and villages while expanding the settlements.[192] This control has been exercised by omission—that is, by refraining from "preparing updated regional outline plans for the West Bank. As a result, until the transfer of authority to the Palestinian Authority (and, to this day, in area 'C'), two regional plans prepared in the 1940's by the British Mandate continue to apply."[193] Subsequent "special partial outline plans" for some four hundred villages, far from alleviating the problem of inadequate planning schemes, underscored its rationale as they constituted demarcation plans which prohibited construction outside existing lines. This administrative and legal structure has then been used both to justify the rejection of Palestinians' applications for building permits on private land, and to issue demolition orders for houses that were constructed without a permit.[194] Thus, the law that vested the occupant with the power to ensure the welfare of the occupied population has been used by the former to advance its own interests to the detriment of the latter.

Indeed, while different phenomena are associated with the settlements—such as unequal allocation of water resources coupled with acute water shortage in the Palestinians villages[195] and acts of violence committed by settlers against the Palestinian population which receive no proper response from the Israeli security forces[196]—it is the legal terrain wrought by the occupation which is of

---

191. KRETZMER, *supra* note 87, at 95.

192. Israel transferred the planning authority from the Jordanian Ministry of the Interior to the Commander of the IDF Forces in the region. Following the Oslo Accords, Israel retained this authority over area C, comprising some 60% of the West Bank territory and some 600,000 Palestinians. *See generally* LAND GRAB, *supra* note 174.

193. *Id.*

194. *Id.*; Amnesty International, Demolition and Dispossession: The Destruction of Palestinian Homes, MDE 15/059/1999 (Dec. 1999), *at* http://web.amnesty.org.library.index/ENGMDE 150591999?open&of=ENG-ISR.

195. The average Palestinian in the West Bank residing in communities connected to a water network consumes sixty liters of water per day. The consumption of water by people not thus connected, while unknown, is certainly lower. The average consumption per capita in Israel as well as in the settlements is almost six times higher, that is, 350 liters a day. In practical terms this discrepancy means that settlements enjoy an unlimited supply of running water which allows for swimming pools and green lawns, while their neighboring Palestinians often lack drinking and bathing water. *See* YEHEZKEL LEIN, NOT EVEN A DROP: THE WATER CRISIS IN PALESTINIAN VILLAGES WITHOUT A WATER NETWORK (2001); Yehezkel Lein, *Thirsty for a Solution: The Water Crisis in the Occupied Territories and Its Resolution in the Final Status Agreement* (2002), *at* http://www.btselem.org/Download/engwater.doc; Yehezkel Lein, *Disputed Waters: Israel's Responsibility for the Water Shortage in the Occupied Territories* (1998), *at* http://www.btselem.org/Download/Disputed_Waters_Eng.doc.

196. *See* S.C. Res. 471, 5 June 1980, U.N. SCOR 35th Sess., 2226th mtg., U.N. Doc. S/RES/36 (1980); S.C. Res. 904, 18 March 1994, U.N. SCOR 49th Sess., 3351th mtg., U.N. Doc. S/RES/50 (1994) (calling on Israel to assume its obligation to protect the civilian population and to take measures, including the confiscation of arms, to prevent illegal acts of violence by Israeli settlers). According to B'TSELEM, Israeli civilians killed 145 Palestinians in the OPT: among them, 25 children. Other activities against the Palestinian inhabitants include setting up roadblocks to disrupt normal Palestinian life, shooting at roof-top water heaters, burning cars, smashing windows, destroying crops and uprooting trees, and harassing merchants and owners of stalls in the market. *See*

special relevance to our analysis. There are separate legal systems operating concurrently in the West Bank, effectively dividing the population along ethnic lines. Jewish settlers are extra-territorially subject to Israeli civilian law, whereas the Palestinians are subject to the Israeli military law and to local law.[197] Two methods are used to generate this situation: first, the application of Israeli law *in personam* to Israeli citizens and Jews in the OPT; second, the partial application of Israeli law, on a supposedly territorial basis, to the Jewish settlements in the OPT. Each of these arrangements merits our brief attention.

The personal application of Israeli law works in a myriad of ways. For example, Emergency Regulations issued by the Israeli government, and renewed regularly through legislation,[198] determine that Israeli courts will have jurisdiction over criminal offences committed by Israeli citizens (and, in general, by people who are present in Israel) in the OPT, even if the offence took part in areas under the control of the Palestinian Authority.[199] Further, the law extending the Emergency Regulations determines that, for certain statutes, people who live in the OPT will be considered residents of Israel if they are Israeli citizens *or* are "entitled to immigrate to Israel under the Law of Return" (i.e., Jews and family members of Jews).[200] These statutes, seventeen in total, include the Income Tax Ordinance, the Social Security Law of 1968, and the National Health Care Law of 1994.[201] The net result is a different set of rights and duties applying to different groups in the OPT along ethnic lines. Finally, in this context, we should note the extension, on a personal basis, of Israel's Election Law, which determines that Israelis who reside in territories held by the Israeli Defense Forces

---

B'TSELEM, VIOLENCE OF SETTLERS AGAINST PALESTINIANS, *available at* http://www.btselem.org/english/Settlers_Violence/Settlers_Violence.asp; Ron Dudai, *Free Rein: Vigilant Settlers and Israel's Non-Enforcement of the Law* (2001), *at* http://www.btselem.org/Download/Free_Rein_Eng.doc; Yhezkel Lein, *The Performance of Law Enforcement Authorities in Responding to Settler Attacks on Olive Harvesters, at* http://www/bstelem.org/Download/2002_Olive_Harvest_Eng.doc. This violence is particularly prevalent in Hebron, a city where 180,000 Palestinians live, and where a population of approximately 450 Jewish settlers is effectively allowed to humiliate, threaten, and exercise violence against Palestinian property and people. *See* Shlomo Swissa, *Hebron, Area H2: Settlements Cause Mass Departure of Palestinians, at* http://www.btselem.org/Download/2003_Hebron_Eng.doc.; Breaking the Silence: Soldiers Speak Out about their Service in Hebron (5 Nov. 2004), *available at* http://www.breakingthesilence.org.il/what_we_did_en.asp. In May 2005, the HCJ rejected a petition by Palestinian residents of Hebron asking for the enforcement of criminal law against the Jewish settlers of Hebron. *See* H.C.J. 454/03, Halabi v. Prime Minister, *available at* http://www.court.gov.il.

197. Imseis, *supra* note 96, at 106.

198. Law for the Extension of Emergency Regulations (Judea, Samaria and the Gaza Strip—Judging for Offences and Legal Aid) 1971.

199. Other regulations allow Israeli courts in civil suits to engage with matters relating to residents of the OPT. Civil Procedure Regulations (Issuing of Documents to the Occupied Territories) 1969.

200. The Law of Return of 1950 gives, in Article 1, the right to immigrate to Israel to Jews (defined in Article 4B as a person who is the offspring of a Jewish mother, or converted to Judaism, and is not a member of another religion); and also to children, grandchildren, and spouses of Jews; and to spouses of children and grandchildren of Jews, unless they were born Jews and willingly converted to another religion (Article 4A). Law of Return, 1950, 4 L.S.I. 114 (1950).

201. This law does not apply in areas under the control of the Palestinian Authority, a fact that has no practical effect as Israelis and Jews do not reside in these areas.

(IDF) will be able to vote in their place of residence.[202] This provision is significant, especially considering Israel's lack of absentee ballot voting.[203] Its effect is to allow Israeli settlers in the OPT to take part in choosing the government which rules these territories as an occupying power, whereas the Palestinian residents of the very same territories, who are also subject to the actions of this very same government, do not partake in choosing it.[204]

Whereas the personal application of Israeli law to Israelis—and in some cases, to non-Israeli Jews—in the OPT is effected through Emergency Regulations issued by the Israeli government and extended by the Israeli legislature, territorial application occurs through Orders issued by the Israeli Military Commander in the territories.[205] These Orders give special status to Jewish settlements in the OPT by applying certain aspects of Israeli law in various spheres, such as education, to those territorial units, giving them the privileges enjoyed by localities within Israel. The same mechanism further prohibits Palestinians from entry into the settlements unless they possess a special permit. Israelis are exempt from the need for a special permit to enter the settlements. Israelis are defined for this purpose as (1) residents of Israel; (2) residents of the territories who are Israeli citizens, or who are allowed to immigrate to Israel under the Law of Return; or, (3) people who are not residents of the territories, but who have a valid visa to Israel. This definition extends the privilege of entering the settlements beyond Israeli citizens and Jews to tourists who are neither Israeli nor Jewish.[206] Given this last qualification, the supposedly territorial application of these laws may also be seen as personal. The net result is the creation of two separate legal regimes, including rules restricting freedom of movement, based on a combination of ethnic and territorial factors.

It should finally be noted that in a recent decision concerning the rights of Israeli settlers evacuated from the Gaza strip, the HCJ decided that the Israeli Basic Laws (which comprise the nascent constitution of Israel), including the Basic Law: Human Liberty and Dignity, apply *in personam* to Israelis in the occupied territories. In the same decision, the Court left open the question of the application of these laws to non-Israeli residents (i.e. the Palestinians) of the same territories.[207]

202. Election Law (Consolidated Version) 1969, at art. 147.

203. Israeli law does not allow Israeli citizens, with the exception of diplomats and similar official groups of people, to vote outside the geographic boundaries of Israel. *See id.* at art. 6.

204. For an analysis of the Israeli legislation applying Israeli law on a personal basis to Israelis in the territories, see Amnon Rubinstein, *The Changing Status of the "Territories" (West Bank and Gaza): From Escrow to Legal Mongrel,* 8 TEL AVIV UNIVERSITY STUDIES IN LAW 59, 68-72 (1988). For a discussion of the significance of the difference in suffrage, see Oren Yiftachel, *'Ethnocracy': The Politics of Judaizing Israel/Palestine,* 6 Constellations 364, 377 (1999).

205. Order Regarding Management of Regional Councils (No. 783) and Order Regarding Management of Local Council (No. 892), *in* LAND GRAB, *supra* note 174.

206. Order Concerning Security Instructions (Judea and Sameria) (No. 378) 1970—Announcement on a Closed Area (Israeli settlements), *in* LAND GRAB, *supra* note 174. For a discussion of the military legislation applying Israeli law on the settlements on a territorial basis, see Rubinstein, *supra* note 204, at 72-79.

207. H.C.J. 1661/05, Regional Council Gaza Beach v. The Knesset, at ¶¶ 78-80 (unpub-

The partial application of Israeli law to the OPT, observed leading Israeli constitutional law scholar Amnon Rubinstein in his 1988 article *The Changing Status of the "Territories"(West Bank and Gaza): From Escrow to Legal Mongrel*, blurred the boundaries between Israel and the territories.[208] This partial application also propelled the drastic change in the status of the territories from "escrow" to "legal mongrel." Once perceived as an "'escrow' under the rules of international law—that is as a trust—they have gradually been incorporated in practice into the realm of Israel's rule."[209] The substitution of the "legal mongrel" for the "escrow" clearly signifies the breach of trust by the occupier and, *prima facie*, appears to have generated the veiled annexation of the territories. Given that the violation of trust and the veiled annexation violate the two basic tenets of the normative regime of occupation, it would be more appropriate to conclude that the transition effected was from an "escrow" to an "illegal" mongrel. Indeed, a "legal mongrel," at least in this context, seems to be an oxymoron: the "mongrel" is illegal.

Furthermore, closer scrutiny reveals that, from a legal perspective, the Israeli government's actions actually constitute a greater violation of international law than that which would have been created by a straight-forward annexation, as they confer the benefits of annexation to the occupier without requiring it to incorporate the people under occupation to its polity, with its ensuing rights and privileges. When combined with the different treatment and rights accorded to settlers,[210] often at the expense of the Palestinians, the occupation appears to resemble a form of colonial regime—the hallmark of which is the exploitation of the resources of the territory for the benefits of the home country and its citizens—rather than a belligerent occupation.[211] Indeed, it may well amount to prohibited discrimination as defined by Article 1 of the Convention on the Elimination of All Forms of Racial Discrimination[212] and under the Interna-

---

lished), *available at* www.court.gov.il. The question of the applicability of the Basic Law to the rights of Palestinians was also left open by the HCJ in an earlier decision that dealt with the detention conditions of Palestinians in the OPT. H.C.J. 3278/02, The Center for the Defense of the Individual v. Commander of the IDF Forces in the West Bank, 57(1) PD 385.

208. Rubinstein, *supra* note 204, at 59.

209. *Id.* at 67.

210. The different treatment is evident in numerous situations, primarily in relation to land, water, planning, protection from violence and the rule of law. Note that the HCJ recently acknowledged that "the Israeli settlements (in Judea and Samaria) received special benefits, and the State invested in their construction and expansion many resources, a treatment that was not accorded to the local population." *See* H.C.J. 548/04, Amna v. IDF Commander in Judea and Samaria (Feb 26, 2004) (unpublished) (on file with authors).

211. KRETZMER, *supra* note 87, at 75, 197. Kretzmer notes the significance, in this context, of Israel's invocation of the law of occupation in order to thus justify the limitations on the rights of the Palestinians. For a discussion of this position, see Yaffa Zilbershatz, *The Control of the IDF in the Judea, Samaria and Gaza: Belligerent Occupation or Colonial Take-Over*, 20 BAR-ILAN STUD. 547 (2004).

212. International Convention on the Elimination of All Forms of Racial Discrimination, *opened for signature* Mar. 7, 1966, 660 U.N.T.S. 195 [hereinafter CERD]. Article 1 defines the term "racial discrimination" as "any distinction, exclusion, restriction or preference based on race, color, descent, or national or ethnic origin which has the purpose or effect of nullifying or impairing the

tional Convention on the Suppression and Punishment of the Crime of Apartheid.[213] In its extreme form, that is, if practiced as a widespread or systematic policy, apartheid is criminalized in Article 7(1)(j) of the Rome Statute as a crime against humanity.[214]

---

recognition, enjoyment or exercise, on an equal footing, of human rights and fundamental freedoms in the political, economic, social, cultural or any other field of public life." *Id.* at art. 1. It is interesting to mention in this context that in the *Construction of a Wall* Advisory Opinion, *supra* note 6, the Court noted that the construction of the Wall was accompanied by the creation of a new administrative regime and that under this regime, the part of the West Bank lying between the Green Line and the Wall had been designated as a "Closed Area": "Residents of this area may no longer remain in it, nor may non residents enter it, unless holding a permit or identity card issued by the Israeli authorities . . . . Israeli citizens, Israeli permanent residents and those eligible to immigrate to Israel in accordance with the Law of Return may remain in, or move freely to, from and within the Closed Area without a permit." *Construction of a Wall Advisory Opinion*, *supra* note 6, ¶ 85. The Court returned to this point in the application part of the Opinion, when it determined that "that construction, the establishment of a closed area . . . and the creation of enclaves have moreover imposed substantial restrictions on the freedom of movement of the inhabitants of the Occupied Palestinian Territory (with the exception of Israeli citizens and those assimilated thereto)." *Id.* at ¶ 133. These references to a regime which operates on the basis of ethnic distinctions seem to suggest the prima facie relevance of the CERD, and it is therefore surprising that the Court failed to refer to it when it enumerated the human right treaties to which Israel is a party and which are, at least potentially, applicable to the issue at hand. *See* Ben-Naftali & Shany, *Living in Denial*, *supra* note 98.

    213. Convention on the Suppression and Punishment of the Crime of Apartheid, Nov. 30, 1973, 1015 U.N.T.S. 243. Article II(a)(3) defines Apartheid, *inter alia*, as "[A]ny legislative measures and other measures calculated to prevent a racial group or groups from participation in the political, social, economic and cultural life of the country and the deliberate creation of conditions preventing the full development of such a group or groups, in particular by denying to members of a racial group or groups basic human rights and freedoms, including the right to work, the right to form recognized trade unions, the right to education, the right to leave and to return to their country, the right to a nationality, the right to freedom of movement and residence, the right to freedom of opinion and expression, and the right to freedom of peaceful assembly and association." *Id.* at art. II(a)(3). Article II(a)(4) also incorporates into the definition "[A]ny measures, including legislative measures, designed to divide the population along racial lines by the creation of separate reserves and ghettos for the members of a racial group or group . . . the expropriation of landed property belonging to a racial group or groups or to members thereof." *See also* Samira Shah, *On the Road to Apartheid: The Bypass Road Network in the West Bank*, 29 COLUM. HUM. RTS. L. REV. 221, 283 (1997). While there are many differences between the former regime of Apartheid in South Africa and the occupation regime of the OPT, it is interesting to note here that a prevailing discourse regarding the Israeli-Palestinian peace process in Israel is one of "separation." The question arises whether this "separation" may not resemble the separation entailed in the regime of "apartheid." This discussion brings up complex questions about the possible solutions to the Israeli-Palestinian conflict and the viability of the "separation" thesis that does not amount to apartheid. The problem of resemblance to apartheid, thus, did not go away but to some extent extenuated during the years of the Oslo process. *See* Aeyal M. Gross, *The Constitution, Reconciliation, and Transitional Justice: Lessons from South Africa and Israel*, 40 STAN. J. INT'L. L. 47 (2004). In this sense, it is interesting to compare the peace processes in Israel/Palestine and in South-Africa. Both processes probably continued traditional approaches toward the solution of these conflicts: incorporation in South Africa and partition in the Israeli-Palestinian context. The question for the Israeli-Palestinian situation is how to create partition that does not entail apartheid. For a perspective on why these two conflicts took such different turns despite their similar roots, see generally RAN GREENSTEIN, GENEALOGIES OF CONFLICT: CLASS, IDENTITY AND STATE IN PALESTINE/ISRAEL AND SOUTH AFRICA (1995).

    214. Article 7(2)(h) defines the crime of apartheid as "inhumane acts of a character similar to those referred to in paragraph 1, committed in the context of an institutionalized regime of systematic oppression and domination by one racial group over any other racial group or groups and committed with the intention of maintaining that regime." *Supra* note 182. For a discussion of the customary status of the crime of apartheid, see ANTONIO CASSESE, INTERNATIONAL CRIMINAL LAW

For the purposes of the argument advanced in this section, however, it is not necessary to determine whether or not the occupation of the OPT has become a form of colonialism or resembles an apartheid regime. Rather, it is sufficient to conclude that, inasmuch as the legal structure of the occupation regime is *designed* to—and in fact *does*—serve the interests of the settlers at the expense of the interests of the occupied population, it breaches the obligations of the occupant under Article 43 of the 1907 Fourth Hague Convention, thus violating the basic tenet of trust inherent in the law of occupation.[215] Inasmuch as the justness of an occupation is determined, as recently suggested by Michael Walzer in the context of the American occupation of Iraq, by its political direction and the distribution of benefits it provides,[216] the occupation of the OPT appears to be neither legal nor just.

(iii) Disrupting the Fabric of Life of the Occupied Population

The unjustness of the political geography created by the above-described complex legal system of the occupation is most poignant in its effect on the daily life of the occupied population, particularly as it severely restricts Palestinian freedom of movement. An intricate network of some 300 checkpoints and roadblocks divides the OPT internally into a patchwork of cantons. Permits are required to travel from one canton to the other; Gaza is completely isolated from the rest of the Palestinian territory.[217] These multitudinous divisions and barriers constitute an enormous constraint on the ability of Palestinians to get to work, schools, hospitals, friends, and family.[218] Assessing this situation, the Special Rapporteur of the Human Rights Commission concluded that "settlements are linked to each other and to Israel by a vast system of bypass roads that have a 50- to 75-meter buffer zone on each side in which no building is permitted. These settlements and roads, which separate Palestinian communities and deprive Palestinians of agricultural land, have fragmented both land and people. In effect, they foreclose the possibility of a Palestinian State as they destroy the

---

25 (2003), suggesting that while apartheid constitutes a state delinquency under customary international law, it does not yet entail individual criminal responsibility under that law. For an extensive discussion of the illegality of apartheid, see also Separate Opinion of Vice President Ammoun in *Continued Presence of South Africa in Namibia* Advisory Opinion, *supra* note 21, at 77-88.

215. It is worthwhile to note here that the Israeli Supreme Court contributed to the undermining of Article 43 when it allowed large scale changes in local law and included the settlers as part of the local population for the purposes of Article 43. *See* KRETZMER, *supra* note 87, at 187.

216. *See* MICHAEL WALZER, ARGUING ABOUT WAR, 162-65 (2004). Walzer posits that the political direction of the occupation is to steadily "empower the locals," and the benefits are to be "widely distributed," for the occupation to be just. Such empowerment may necessitate changes in local law, especially in cases where the occupation purports to serve as a transitional regime from a dictatorial to a democratic form of government. Such changes, while ostensibly conflicting with the language of various provisions of the law of occupation, may nevertheless be permissible if they promote its overall purposes in a manner that advances, rather than violates, its basic tenets. *See* Benvenisti, *Preface*, *supra* note 99.

217. 2003 REPORT ON THE SITUATION OF HUMAN RIGHTS IN THE PALESTINIAN TERRITORIES, *supra* note 176, at 9-10.

218. *Id.* at 9.

territorial integrity of the Palestinian Territory."[219]

Further measures affecting movement and, indeed, any resemblance of a normal life are closures that prohibit Palestinian movement without special permits and curfews that compel inhabitants to stay in their homes.[220] Curfews and closures constitute the primary cause for Palestinian economic losses.[221] The cumulative effect of checkpoints and curfews is a sharp decline in access to health care,[222] in health standards generally (due to shortages of food, clean water, access to hospitals), and rising rates of unemployment and poverty.[223]

It is clear that these, and other measures,[224] not only violate fundamental

---

219. 2002 REPORT ON THE VIOLATIONS OF HUMAN RIGHTS IN THE OCCUPIED ARAB TERRITORIES, *supra* note 31, at 8. *See also* Drew, *supra* note 184, at 146-54 (providing a detailed argument on the ways the settlements violate the Palestinian right to self determination).

220. B'TSELEM, FREEDOM OF MOVEMENT, *available at* http://www.btselem.org/english/Freedom_of_Movement/index.asp; 2003 REPORT ON THE SITUATION OF HUMAN RIGHTS IN THE PALESTINIAN TERRITORIES, *supra* note 176, at 9 (noting the slight decrease in the number of Palestinians thus affected by curfews from approximately 520,000 in 2002 to 390,000 in 2003).

221. THE WORLD BANK (WEST BANK AND GAZA OFFICE, JERUSALEM), TWENTY-SEVEN MONTHS – INTIFADA, CLOSURES, AND PALESTINIAN ECONOMIC CRISIS: AN ASSESSMENT, ch. 2, ¶ 2.5. (May, 2003) [hereinafter WORLD BANK REPORT].

222. *See* Combined Report of B'TSELEM and PHYSICIANS FOR HUMAN RIGHTS-ISRAEL, HARM TO MEDICAL PERSONNEL (Dec. 2003), *available at* http://www.phr.org.il/Phr/Pages/PhrArticles_index.asp?Cat=13.

223. 2003 REPORT ON THE SITUATION OF HUMAN RIGHTS IN THE PALESTINIAN TERRITORIES, *supra* note 176, at 10.

224. Such other measures include, for example, targeted killings. Out of 2,305 Palestinians killed by Israel's security forces during the *Al-Aqsa* Intifada, 181 were specifically targeted by Israel and 111 bystanders were killed in the course of these operations. B'TSELEM, FATALITIES IN THE AL-AQSA INTIFADA: 29 SEPTEMBER 2000-20 APRIL 2005, *available at* http://www.btselem.org/English/Statistics/Casualties.asp. 377 Israeli citizens were killed by Palestinians within Israel and another 198 were killed in the OPT. *See generally* AMNESTY INTERNATIONAL, ISRAEL AND THE OCCUPIED TERRITORIES: STATE ASSASSINATIONS AND OTHER UNLAWFUL KILLINGS 9 (2001), *available at* http://web.amnesty.org/library/Index/eng MDE150052001. For a comprehensive analysis of the legality of the policy, see Ben-Naftali & Michaeli, *Targeted Killings*, *supra* note 91. The execution of the policy has been suspended since the Feb. 2005 cease-fire agreement. Another measure of dubious legality is administrative detention. In the beginning of March 2003, Israel held more than one thousand Palestinians in administrative detention, i.e. detention without charge or trial, authorized by administrative order rather than by judicial decree. *See* B'TSELEM, ADMINISTRATIVE DETENTION, *available at* http://www.btselem.org/english/Administrative_Detention/index.asp. Throughout the years, this measure was exercised against Palestinian voicing their opposition against the Israeli occupation and as a substitute for criminal trials in cases where the evidence could not substantiate criminal charges. *See* AMNESTY INTERNATIONAL, ISRAEL AND THE OCCUPIED TERRITORIES: DESPAIR, UNCERTAINTY AND LACK OF DUE PROCESS (1997), *available at* http://web.amnesty.org/library/index/engmde150031997; B'TSELEM, ADMINISTRATIVE DETENTION IN THE OCCUPIED TERRITORIES, *available at* http://www.btselem.org/english/Administrative_Detention/Occupied_Territories.asp. Detainees are further deprived of due process rights. *See* Imseis, *supra* note 96, at 119-20. In addition to all the above, Israel has been carrying out, until recently, a policy of house demolition, destroying close to 1,000 houses since 1987. *See* B'TSELEM, HOUSE DEMOLITIONS-STATISTICS, *available at* http://www.btselem.org/english/HouseDemolitions/Statistics.asp. This means is justified by Israel as necessary to prevent the houses from becoming a haven for militants against the IDF and the settlement and as a punishment against those who committed crimes against Israel as well as for deterrence purposes. *See* 2003 REPORT ON THE SITUATION OF HUMAN RIGHTS IN THE PALESTINIAN

norms of both humanitarian and human rights law,[225] but render the very conduct of civil life in the OPT practically impossible. It is, indeed, "a human tragedy that is unfolding in Palestine."[226] The construction of the Wall signifies the culmination of these policies, their devastating effect on life in the territories, and the violation of the very notion of trust which underlies an occupying power's responsibilities *vis-à-vis* the occupied population. The ICJ's reading of this situation is quite pertinent:

> the route chosen for the wall gives expression *in loco* to the illegal measures taken by Israel with regard to Jerusalem and the settlements, as deplored by the Security Council . . . . There is also a risk of further alterations to the demographic composition of the Occupied Palestinian Territory . . . . inasmuch as it is contributing . . . to the departure of Palestinian population from certain areas . . . . That construction, along with the measures taken previously, thus severely impedes the exercise by the Palestinian people of its right to self-determination.[227]

(iv) The (Im)balance of Security

The destruction of the fabric of life of the Palestinian residents of the OPT is evident. It is equally clear, however, that an occupying power, while required to maintain civil life in the territories under its effective control, is not required to forsake its own security interests. Indeed, Israel contends that the Palestinians, having responded to Israel's offer to end the conflict with the *al-Aqsa intifada* comprising indiscriminate terrorist attacks—attacks constituting crimes against humanity[228]—against Israeli citizens, are to be held responsible for their situation.[229] Israel argues further that "many of the Palestinian terrorist groups per-

---

TERRITORIES, *supra* note 176, at 13-14. As far as this means is exercised for deterrence purposes and for the punishment of families of suicide bombers, it might amount to prohibited reprisals and collective punishment and extensive property damage unwarranted by military necessity by Articles 33 and 53 of the Fourth Geneva Convention, respectively. *See* Fourth Geneva Convention, *supra* note 67, at arts. 33, 53.

225. *The Construction of a Wall* Advisory Opinion, *supra* note 6, ¶¶ 123-37. The Court held that the consequences for the occupied population amount to breaches of their rights to privacy and freedom of movement, as guaranteed by Articles 17 and 12 respectively of the ICCPR, *supra* note 78; the right of access to holy places enshrined in G.A. Resolution 181 (II), the Armistice Agreement as well as the subsequent peace treaty between Israel and Jordan; the rights to work, to an adequate standard of living, to health and to education under Articles 6, 7, 11, 12, 13 respectively of the ICESCR, *supra* note 78, as well as Articles 16, 24, 27 and 28 of the Convention on the Rights of the Child. G.A. Res. 44/25, annex 44, U.N. GAOR Supp. (No. 49) at 167, U.N. Doc. A/44/49 (1989).

226. *See* Question of the Violation of Human Rights in the Occupied Arab Territories, Including Palestine, Report of the Special Rapporteur of the Commission of Human Rights on the Situation of Human Rights in the Palestinian Territories Occupied By Israel Since 1967, Addendum: Note by the Secretary-General (A/57/366/Add.1), ¶ 2 (Sep. 16, 2003).

227. *Construction of a Wall*, *supra* note 6, ¶ 122.

228. *See* AMNESTY INTERNATIONAL, WITHOUT DISTINCTION—ATTACKS ON CIVILIANS BY PALESTINIAN ARMED GROUPS (July, 2002), *available at* http://www.amnesty.org.

229. *See, e.g.*, Israel's Response to the Report Submitted by the Special Rapporteur on the Right to Food, submitted to the Commission on Human Rights, 60th Sess., E/CN.4/2004/G/14, ¶¶ 5, 6 (Nov. 26, 2003) (indicating the Rapporteur's failure to take account of the Palestinians' responsibility for the encouragement of terror attacks against Israel, which form the basis of Israel's actions taken in self defense).

petrate their atrocities not to put an end to Israel's presence, but rather to frustrate any political progress that may do just that."[230]

Israel's thesis thus rests on an attempt to sever the nexus between the occupation and the *intifada* and, indeed, between its obligations as an occupying power and its right and duty to protect its own citizens and security. In doing so, it challenges, *inter alia*, the observation of the Special Rapporteur of the United Nations Commission of Human Rights that "violations of human rights are a necessary consequence of military occupation."[231] As was noted above, Israel regards this observation as "an attempt to rewrite international law" and as a "remarkable legal thesis" which "contravenes the entire body of humanitarian law dealing with belligerent occupation, which establishes standards to be maintained by States that find themselves in a situation of occupying territory."[232]

Israel is right in maintaining that the international law of occupation establishes such standards and that, therefore, an occupation does not *ipso facto* entail a violation of either human rights or its own governing regime; such a construction would have rendered the normative regime which governs the situation not only redundant, but illegal *ab initio*. It does not follow, however, that the violations of human rights and of humanitarian law in the OPT are not a necessary consequence of this specific occupation; that is, that they are generated by Israel's breach of the basic tenets of the law of occupation rather than by the mere fact of occupation.

This breach is evident in the following position taken by Israel and approved by the HCJ. According to this position, the security concerns of the occupying power (within Article 43 of the Hague Regulations)—against which the rights of the Palestinians should be balanced—include protection of the lives and safety of Israeli settlers, and therefore, of the settlements themselves. Thus, the balancing act between the security needs of the occupying power on the one hand, and the maintenance of civil life on the other hand, is imbalanced in a way detrimental to the rights of the Palestinian population, when the added burden of protecting the illegal settlements is used as a security concern to justify the impairment of the Palestinian rights.[233]

---

230. Note From Israel to the U.N., *supra* note 32, at sec. 2.

231. 2002 REPORT ON THE VIOLATIONS OF HUMAN RIGHTS IN THE OCCUPIED ARAB TERRITORIES, *supra* note 31, at 4.

232. Note From Israel to the U.N., *supra* note 32, at sec. 3.

233. See H.C.J. 10356/02, Hess v. Commander of the IDF Forces in the West Bank, 58 (3) P.D. 443; H.C.J. 7957/04 *Mara'abe case*, *supra* note 103. In the first of these cases, the rationale stated in the text was accepted by the HCJ as a basis for authorizing the Israeli army to seize land owned by Palestinians and destroy structures in Hebron for the purpose of allowing the settlers safe access to the Cave of the Patriarchs. In the latter case, the Court determined that the military commander is authorized to construct the separation barrier in the occupied area for the purpose of defending the lives and safety of the Israeli settlers. While the HCJ held that the injury to the rights of the Palestinians in the specific segment of the barrier before it in this case was disproportionate, its principled position illustrates how the settlements and their incorporation into the military commander's security considerations act in a way that upsets the balancing act as envisaged in international law, are part of the breach of trust discussed in this section. *See* Aeyal Gross, *The* Construction of a Wall *Between the Hague and Jerusalem: The Enforcement and Limits of Humanitarian Law and the*

In order to assess the issue of the (im)balance of security and to evaluate the respective positions articulated above, it is necessary to inquire into the last tenet of the normative regime: its temporal dimension. The following subsection undertakes this inquiry.

4. Right on Time: An Occupation Is Temporary

(a) The Normative Provisions Indicating the Temporary Nature of Occupation

The two basic principles discussed above—the inalienability of sovereignty vested in the people and its management as a form of trust—generate the third principle of occupation: its temporality. Indeed, the very essence of occupation is founded on this idea. Thus, writes Graber:

> The modern law of belligerent occupation is anchored in the concept that occupation differs in its nature and legal consequences from conquest. It is therefore not surprising that the early definitions of the modern concept of occupation are chiefly concerned with the main aspects of this difference, namely the *temporary nature* of belligerent occupation as contrasted with the permanency of conquest, and *the limited, rather than the full powers* which belligerent occupation entails for the occupant.[234]

It is in this light that one should understand the various provisions in the documents detailing the law of occupation that have, *ab initio*, imposed constraints on the managerial powers of the occupant, evidencing the temporary nature of its control. The Lieber Code already provided, in Article 3, that martial law imposed by the occupant only *suspends* criminal and civil law as well as domestic administration and government during the period of occupation.[235] Article 32 of that Code spoke of suspension or termination of certain individual relationships, but emphasized that only a peace treaty may settle such changes.[236] In the same vein, Article 2 of the Brussels Declaration defined the ousted authority as *suspended*; Article 3 complemented this characterization by stating that "with this object he shall maintain the laws which were in force in the country in time of peace, and shall not modify, suspend or replace them unless necessary."[237]

Article 43 of the 1899 and 1907 Hague Conventions corresponded to Articles 2 and 3 of the Brussels Declaration by imposing a duty on the occupant to respect, unless "absolutely prevented," the laws in force in the country.[238] Although not expressly defining the authority of the former sovereign as "suspended," the Hague Convention neither altered the temporary concept of occupation nor its underlying rationale that the occupant does not acquire sovereignty, but merely exercises a temporary right of administration until the

---

Structure of Occupation (forthcoming).

234. GRABER, *supra* note 41, at 37 (emphasis added).
235. Lieber Code, *supra* note 40.
236. *Id.* at art. 31.
237. Brussels Declaration, *supra* note 15.
238. 1907 Hague Convention of 1907, *supra* note 51, at art. 43.

status of the territory is finally determined.[239] Indeed, Article 43 prevents the occupant from creating laws, an unquestionable attribute of sovereignty,[240] which are not absolutely necessary for the specific temporary context of occupation, such as for the maintenance of order, the safety of the occupier's forces, and the realization of the legitimate purpose of the occupation.[241] The enactment of laws and regulations that have no reasonable relation to the purposes of occupation are illegitimate.[242] This understanding of the provisional, non-sovereign status of the occupant is reaffirmed by Article 55 of the 1907 Fourth Hague Convention, stating that the occupant is merely to administer and safeguard public buildings, real estate, and the agricultural estates belonging to the state.[243]

This idea of occupation as a temporary form of control underlies the provisions of the Fourth Geneva Convention.[244] Due, however, to the shift in emphasis of the Convention from the rights of the ousted sovereign to the welfare of the occupied population,[245] the temporal restrictions on the occupying authority are more implicit than explicit when compared to earlier codes. Thus, for instance, the non-recognition of annexation stipulated in Article 47 of the Fourth Convention is informed by, but does not explicitly state, the temporary nature of occupation.[246] This may also be said with regard to paragraph 6 of Article 49, which prohibits the settlement of the occupant's nationals in the occupied territory. In addition to the WWII experience with the mass transportation of population, which informed Article 49 paragraph 6, the provision was also designed to ensure that the sociological and demographic structure of the territory be left unchanged.[247]

Further indication of the temporary nature of occupation and its limitation to the preservation of the status quo is found in Article 54 of the Convention, which stipulates that the status of judges and public officials in the territory shall

---

239. Everett P. Wheeler, *Government de facto*, 5 AM. J. INT'L. L. 66, 70 (1911); Oppenheim, *supra* note 113, at 437; GRABER, *supra* note 41, at 68-69; VON GLAHN, OCCUPATION, *supra* note 64, at 31.

240. Gasser, *supra* note 63, at 254.

241. Arnold D. McNair, *Municipal Effects of Belligerent Occupation*, 57 L. Q. REV. 33, 35 (1941). According to Benvenisti, the drafters of Article 43 viewed military necessity as the sole ground preventing the occupant from maintaining the old order. BENVENISTI, LAW OF OCCUPATION, *supra* note 33, at 14. This has changed over the course of the twentieth century and scholars began to ponder other legitimate grounds for legislation as the safeguarding of the welfare of the occupied population. VON GLAHN, OCCUPATION, *supra* note 64, at 97.

242. THE JUDGE ADVOCATE GENERAL SCHOOL, LAW OF BELLIGERENT OCCUPATION: TEXT No. 11, 35-37 (1944).

243. Gasser, *supra* note 63, at 246.

244. Fourth Geneva Convention, *supra* note 67.

245. *See supra* notes 67-83 and accompanying text.

246. PICTET, *supra* note 68, at 274; BENVENISTI, LAW OF OCCUPATION, *supra* note 34, at 99.

247. Gasser, *supra* note 63, at 246; PICTET, *supra* note 68, at 283. This prohibition could also be understood as designed to prevent a situation wherein citizens of the occupying power reside in the occupied area and are subject to a different legal regime. *See* discussion accompanying notes 195-214.

not be altered.[248] This proscription reaffirms the maintenance of the country's judicial and administrative structure, which is expected to go on functioning without hindrance,[249] and enhances the conclusion that the occupant authority is temporal and non-sovereign.

Article 64 contains a similar provision with respect to the laws in place. Its first paragraph states that "the penal law of the occupied territory shall remain in force, with the exception that they may be repealed or suspended by the occupying power in cases where they constitute a threat to its security or an obstacle to the application of the present Convention." The second paragraph of the article, however, is more telling:

> The Occupying Power may, however, subject the population of the occupied territory to provisions that are essential to enable the Occupying Power to fulfill its obligations under the present Convention, to maintain the orderly government of the territory, and to ensure the security of the Occupying Power, of the members and property of the occupying force or administration, and likewise of the establishments and lines of communication used by them.[250]

Unlike the first paragraph that speaks of only "penal law," the second paragraph refers to "provisions." In light of the drafting history of the Article and the issues dealt with in the Convention, this provision applies to all types of laws.[251] Indeed, the Convention's Commentary suggests that Article 64 "expresses, in a more precise and detailed form, the terms of Article 43 of the Hague regulations, which lays down that the Occupying Power is to respect the laws in force in the country 'unless absolutely prevented.'"[252] The reason for the more permissive language of Article 64 lies, according to Benvenisti, in the need to provide the occupant with the proscriptive means to fulfill its obligation under the Convention, the extent of which reaches far beyond that stipulated in earlier codes.[253] This, indeed, expresses the growing concern for the welfare of the occupied population that characterizes the Geneva Convention.[254]

(b) Article 6 of the Fourth Geneva Convention

Article 6 of the Fourth Geneva Convention relates most directly to the temporal limits of occupation and thus merits special attention. It provides in paragraph 3:

---

248. Fourth Geneva Convention, *supra* note 67, at art. 54.
249. Gasser, *supra* note 63, at 257.
250. Fourth Geneva Convention, *supra* note 67, at art. 64.
251. BENVENISTI, LAW OF OCCUPATION, *supra* note 34, at 101-02.
252. PICTET, *supra* note 68, at 335.
253. BENVENISTI, LAW OF OCCUPATION, *supra* note 34, at 104.
254. Benvenisti has recently argued that "Article 64 retains little of Hague's Article 43's strong bias against modifying local law," as the occupant under the Geneva Convention "is no longer the disinterested watch guard, but instead a very involved regulator and provider," granted with "wide legislative powers under Article 64." This change in the role of the occupant, says Benvenisti, is due to the focus of the Geneva regime on the population under occupation. *See* Benvenisti, *Resolution 1483, supra* note 14, at 28-30. The legislative powers of the occupying power are thus designed to advance only its legitimate functions.

> In the case of occupied territory, the application of the present Convention shall cease one year after the general close of military operations; however, the Occupying Power shall be bound, for the duration of the occupation, to the extent that such Power exercises the functions of government in such territory, by the provisions of the following Articles 1 to 12, 27, 29 to 34, 47, 49, 51, 52, 53, 59, 61 to 77, 143.

The ICJ considered this provision in the *Construction of a Wall* Advisory Opinion. The Court opined that:

> A distinction is also made in the Fourth Geneva Convention between provisions applying during military operations leading to the occupation and those that remain applicable throughout the entire period of occupation .... Since the military operations leading to the occupation of the West Bank in 1967 ended a long time ago, only those Articles of the Fourth Geneva Convention referred to in Article 6, paragraph 3, remain applicable in that occupied territory.[255]

We submit that this textual interpretation, leading to the conclusion that long-term occupations reduce the responsibilities of occupying powers *vis-à-vis* the occupied civilian population, is an absurd conclusion; it is unwarranted by the text and is further incongruent with the purpose and legal practice of the normative regime of occupation, confusing a problem with a solution.[256]

Textually, Article 6 refers to a "general close of military operations." It does not, however, refer to military operations "leading to the occupation."[257] The latter is a judicial insertion. The realities of the occupation in general, and in particular the circumstances surrounding the construction of the wall (itself a military operation), attest to the fact of on-going military operations. Even a literal reading of the text of Article 6 should have revealed its inapplicability on its own terms. Indeed, Article 6 lends itself to an entirely different reading.

According to the language of Article 6, in an occupation that lasts longer than one year after the close of military operations, only 23 of the 32 articles comprising Section III of the Convention, which deals with occupied territories, would continue to apply.[258] The nine articles that would cease to apply include, for instance, the obligation incumbent on the occupying power to "facilitate the proper working of all institutions devoted to the care and education of chil-

---

255. *Construction of a Wall*, *supra* note 6, ¶ 125. In para. 126, the Court proceeded to identify Articles 47, 49, 52, 53, and 59 of the Fourth Geneva Convention as relevant to the question at hand. For a similar interpretation, see Yoram Dinstein, *The International Legal Status of the West Bank and the Gaza Strip—1998*, 28 ISR. Y.B. HUM. RTS. 37, 42-44 (1998) [hereinafter Dinstein, *Legal Status*].

256. For a critical review of this aspect of the Advisory Opinion, see Orna Ben-Naftali, *'A La Recherche du Temps Perdu': Rethinking Article 6 of the Fourth Geneva Convention in the Light of the Legal Consequences of the Construction of a Wall in the Occupied Palestinian Territory Advisory Opinion*, 38(1-2) ISR. L. REV. 211 (2005) [hereinafter Ben-Naftali, *Temps Perdu*].

257. *Construction of a Wall*, *supra* note 6, ¶ 125. Note paragraph 135, where, in the context of addressing the term "military operations" in Article 53 in order to determine the existence of military exigencies, the Court said that such exigencies "may be invoked in occupied territories even after the general close of military operations that *led to their occupation*." Id. at ¶ 135 (emphasis added).

258. While 43 of the 159 Articles of the Conventions continue to apply, the emphasis is on Articles 47-78 comprising the relevant Section III.

dren"[259] and "the duty of ensuring the food and medical supplies of the population."[260] It is unreasonable to assume that the drafters of the Convention intended for children to be deprived of proper schooling or for the population to be deprived of medical supplies and food in long-term occupations; such an intention would defy the Convention's main objective. The only reasonable conclusion, therefore, is that the working assumption behind Article 6 was that the situation of an occupation is bound to be relatively short and that responsibilities of this kind would be transferred to local authorities in a process leading to the end of the exceptional situation of occupation. The *travaux préparatoires* and the Commentary confirm this assumption.[261] Once reality defies the assumption, however, the rationale informing Article 6 disappears and, insofar as law is to make sense, it should no longer apply.

Subsequent developments in both law and legal practice lend support to our proposed reading of the provision. Once it became clear that the drafters' assumption regarding the short duration of occupations was not supported by reality, and that this provision may be construed by occupying powers as limiting their responsibilities under the Convention precisely in situations where the those responsibilities should be expanded, the provision was abrogated: Article 3(b) of Additional Protocol I provides for the application of the Protocol's provisions until the termination of the occupation.[262]

The argument that Article 6 of the Fourth Geneva Convention limits the Convention's scope of applicability was never raised before Israeli Courts. Indeed, the Israeli High Court of Justice had applied provisions that would have otherwise become inapplicable in light of the language of Article 6.[263] This practice characterizes other prolonged occupations,[264] thereby lending support to the proposition that Article 3(b) of Protocol I enjoys customary status.[265]

---

259. Fourth Geneva Convention, *supra* note 67, at art. 50.

260. *Id.* at art. 55.

261. *See* 2A FINAL RECORD OF THE DIPLOMATIC CONFERENCE OF GENEVA 1949, 623-25; PICTET, *supra* note 68, at 63; GREEN, *supra* note 43, at 258 (2d ed., 2000); Roberts, *Prolonged Military Occupation, supra* note 33, at 56 (advancing four arguments for the inapplicability of Article 6).

262. Protocol I, *supra* note 27. *See also* COMMENTARY ON THE ADDITIONAL PROTOCOLS, *supra* note 120, at 66; Roberts, *Prolonged Military Occupation, supra* note 33, at 56. Admittedly, the language of Article 3(b) is unclear and could be construed as suggesting that it applies the Fourth Geneva Convention subject to its own terms. For this construction, see Dinstein, *Legal Status, supra* note 255. Such reading, however, defies both the drafters' intention and the teleological test of international humanitarian law.

263. For example, Article 78 of the Fourth Geneva Convention was recently applied by the HCJ in *Ajuri, supra* note 103. For reviews of this judgment, see Daphne Barak-Erez, *Assigned Residence in Israel's Administered Territories: The Judicial Review of Security Measures,* 33 ISR. Y.B. HUM. RTS. 303 (2003); Eyal Benvenisti, *Ajuri et al.—Israel High Court of Justice, 3 September 2002,* 9 EUR. PUB. L. 481 (2003) [hereinafter Benvenisti, *Ajuri*]; Orna Ben-Naftali & Keren Michaeli, *The Call of Abraham: Between Man and 'Makom': Following HCJ 7015/02* Ajuri v. IDF Commander in the West Bank, 15 HAMISHPAT 56 (2003) (Hebrew). Note that while Article 78 provides less for the obligations and more for the rights of the Occupying Power, endowing it with the power to subject protected persons to assigned residence and to internment, the fact remains that the Court applied this provision, regardless of Article 6.

264. Roberts, *Prolonged Military Occupation, supra* note 33, at 55.

265. On the customary status of most of the Protocol I provisions, see *supra* note 85.

Further, the Court's determination regarding the limited scope of applicability of the Fourth Geneva Convention is incongruent with—and defies the rationale behind—its determination regarding the applicability of various human rights instruments together with humanitarian law in occupied territories. This co-application is designed to offer greater protection to the civilian population. It is this incongruence which explains the odd conclusion of the Court that Israel had violated some of its human rights obligations, but not those very same obligations as they appear in the Fourth Geneva Convention.[266] The implication is that human rights law came into play to fill a lacuna in the Geneva Convention, despite the fact that the Convention contains relevant provisions. The lacuna, therefore, is constructed only to be filled by another, and less suitable normative source (in so far as humanitarian law, as distinct from human rights law, is the *lex specialis* in situations of occupation).[267] This does not make sense.

It follows from the above that a proper reading of Article 6 should have generated the conclusion that this provision has, as Roberts suggested, "correctly identified [the] problem" of prolonged occupation, but failed to offer a proper solution.[268] It is regrettable that the Court confused the solution with the problem. Had it engaged in a discussion of the temporal assumption informing the Fourth Geneva Convention, it could have not merely produced a better reading of Article 6, but further shed light on the temporal limitations of an occupation. The remaining part of this Section offers such a discussion.

(c) The Temporary/Indefinite Indeterminacy and the Construction of "Reasonable Time"

There is thus overwhelming evidence for the proposition that the normative regime of occupation requires that it be temporary.[269] There are, however, no exact time limits set for its duration. This absence has been explained, indeed explained away, by Justice Shamgar of the Israeli Supreme Court as being reflective of "a factual situation," generating the conclusion that, "pending an alternative political or military solution this system of government could, from a

---

266. For instance, Article 50, protecting children's right to education, does not apply, but this very same right as it appears in Article 28 of the Convention on the Rights of the Child and Articles 10, 13, and 14 of the ICESCR, *supra* note 78, does apply. Similarly, Articles 55 and 56, which stipulate the duty of the occupant to ensure the population's health through provision of food and medical supplies and the maintenance of medical and hospital establishments, have no applicability while similar duties, far less specific, clear, and legally binding, enshrined in Articles 11 and 12 of the ICESCR (the right to an adequate standard of living and the right to health respectively) and Articles 24 and 27 of the CRC (the rights to health and adequate standard of living and development respectively) do apply.

267. The ICJ itself determined that, while international human rights law is applicable to situations of armed conflicts, international humanitarian law is the *lex specialis*. *See Construction of a Wall, supra* note 6, ¶¶ 104-06. A similar determination was made by the ICJ in its *Nuclear Weapons* Advisory Opinion, *supra* note 52, ¶ 25. On the co-application of human rights law and humanitarian law to occupied territories, see Ben-Naftali & Shany, *Living in Denial, supra* note 98.

268. Roberts, *Prolonged Military Occupation, supra* note 33, at 57.

269. *See Construction of a Wall, supra* note 6, Separate Opinion of Judge Elaraby, ¶ 3.1; Separate Opinion of Judge Koroma, ¶ 2.

legal point of view, continue indefinitely."[270] This argument is not persuasive.

A legal point of view is not merely reflective of a factual situation, nor does it sanction the substitution of "indefinite" for "temporary." A temporary situation has a definite end. An indefinite situation may, or may not, have an end. The two situations are very different. In order to appreciate the point, it is useful to reflect momentarily on the human condition, which is largely controlled by our awareness that our existence is temporary. Were we to conceive of our existence as indefinite, it is quite likely that the human condition would be altered significantly. "Under the heaven," we may hopefully presume, there is "a time for every purpose," but on earth, we humbly acknowledge, time is a limited resource.[271] Time thus affects us individually and socially and it is our awareness of the temporary nature of the human existence which shapes our social institutions, including our law.

Far from reflecting time as naturally indefinite, law allocates, distributes, and mediates time as a "commodity, the supply of which is not inexhaustible."[272] Law shapes our perceptions of the realities of time as a historical, social, cultural, and political construct.[273] Law thus defines not only the supposedly natural time of birth and death, of childhood and adulthood, but it also incorporates certain assumptions about individual and collective time to delineate rights and duties.[274] Indeed, the very principle of legality, as well as foundational legal presumptions, contain embedded conceptions of demarcated time, without which they, and law itself, would be meaningless.[275]

Law, then, is preoccupied with time. Given that the distribution of limited resources is a major legal function, the construction of time as a limited resource implies that law is interested in the distribution of time. Time, however, unlike other natural commodities, is *construed* as limited. As such, it cannot be distributed *in abstracto*, but only in relation to a concrete action. Indeed, it is the very conception of time as a limited resource that endows the concrete action with meaning and requires time allocation relative to competing interests.

---

270. Shamgar, *Legal Concepts, supra* note 88, at 43. Justice Shamgar served as a judge in the Israeli Supreme Court since 1975 and as its Chief Justice since 1983.

271. *Ecclesiastes* 3:1.

272. William H. Rehnquist, *Successful Lawyers Pay the Price*, 82 A.B.A. J. 100 (1996).

273. On the ways time is conceived by law, see generally Carol J. Greenhouse, *Just in Time: Temporality and the Cultural Legitimation of Law*, 98 YALE L. J. 1631 (1989); David M. Engel, *Time and Community*, 21 L. & SOC'Y REV. 605 (1987); Rebbeca R. French, *Time in the Law*, 72 U. COL. L. REV. 663 (2001); TODD RAKOFF, THE LAW OF SOCIAL TIME: A TIME FOR EVERY PURPOSE: LAW AND THE BALANCE OF LIFE (2002); JED RUBENFELD, FREEDOM AND TIME: A THEORY OF CONSTITUTIONAL SELF-GOVERNMENT (2001).

274. Statutes of limitations; jurisdictional time limits; civil and criminal procedure laws; the laws of evidence, intellectual property protections; the rule against perpetuities; and sentencing are but examples that immediately come to mind and all embody legal assumptions about human interaction with time.

275. For example, the principle of *nullum crimen sine lege*, that is, of non-retroactivity, is meaningful only due to the centrality of the concept of time. Similarly, any legal presumption would have been rendered meaningless were it not for the temporal dimension which allows for its refutation.

An example may illustrate this point. Administrative detention is a concrete action which involves two competing interests: the public safety on the one hand, and the human right to liberty on the other hand. As time is understood as a limited resource, the individual cannot be detained indefinitely and it is for this reason that a reasonable time limit is set on the action.[276] Clearly, if temporality was not of the essence in administrative detention, the competing interests would be meaningless. In this sense, it is time, then, that delineates liberty and renders it meaningful; if administrative detention were permitted indefinitely, liberty would have lost its meaning.

It is equally unreasonable to place the concrete situation of occupation within an indefinite time frame. If occupation "could, from a legal point of view, continue indefinitely," the interests it is designed to protect—the interest of the occupied people to reach the point in time when they regain control over their lives and exercise their right to self-determination, and the interest of the international system in resuming its normal order of sovereign equality between states—would be rendered meaningless. Thus, the core assumptions of the normative regime of occupation would be defied if an occupation can be stymied indefinitely. The temporary, as distinct from the indefinite, nature of occupation is thus the most necessary element of the normative regime of occupation, as it gives meaning and effect—both factual and legal—to the concepts of liberty, freedom, and the right to self-determination.

The notion of "reasonable time" underlies any concrete limits set by law on the duration of an action. The very same rationale holds for setting limits on the duration of actions which are not defined in concrete temporal terms; the conclusion that actions not defined in concrete temporal terms somehow transform the temporary into the indefinite is unreasonable. Indeed, in such situations, the concrete time limit is determined by the legal construct of "reasonable time," deriving from the legal principle of "reasonableness."[277] What is a reasonable time for an action depends on the nature, purpose, and circumstances of the action.[278]

---

276. Even the Israeli Military Order Number 1229 provides that a period of detention shall not exceed six months, although it may be extended in light of security considerations. While Order No. 1229 does not mandate that the detainee be brought before a judge prior to his detention, it does allow detainees to appeal their detention or extension of detention before a military judge. *See* B'TSELEM, *available at* http://www.btselem.org/english/Administrative_Detention/Israeli_Law.asp.

277. The principle of reasonableness is a general principle of international law. Its application has generated the conclusion that a right cannot be exercised in a wholly unreasonable manner causing harm disproportionate to the right holder's interests. *See* BIN CHENG, GENERAL PRINCIPLES OF LAW: AS APPLIED BY INTERNATIONAL COURTS AND TRIBUNALS 121-23 (1987); *See also* WTO, REPORT OF THE APPELLATE BODY IN UNITED STATES - STANDARD FOR REFORMULATED AND CONCENTRATED GASOLINE AND LIKE PRODUCTS OF NATIONAL ORIGIN, *reprinted in* 35 I.L.M. 603, 626 (1996).

278. For example, the Uniform Negotiable Instruments Law sets standards for the measurement of "reasonable time." *See* RICHARD SPEIDEL & STEVE H. NICKS, NEGOTIABLE INSTRUMENTS AND CHECK COLLECTIONS (THE NEW LAW) IN A NUTSHELL 60, 61, 148, 149, 152 (4th ed. 1993). Similarly, the "reasonable time" for taking an action is contemplated in the Uniform Commercial Code (Colorado) as depending "on the nature, purpose and circumstances of such action." *See*

(d) Applying the Construction of "Reasonable Time" to the OPT: The Purpose, Nature, and Circumstances of the Occupation

(i) The Purpose of the Occupation

Given the preceding discussion regarding the inalienability of sovereignty, the nature of the relationship between the occupied population and the occupying power as a form of trust, and the related rationale for the temporary nature of an occupation, it is clear that the purpose of the regime of occupation is to manage the situation in a manner designed to bring about political change and to generate a resumption of the normal order of international society. Relevant international norms further decree that this change should come about by peaceful means[279] and realize the principle of self-determination.[280] The positions taken by the ICJ, the General Assembly, and the Security Council with respect to the illegality of South Africa's post-mandate presence in Namibia all serve to underscore the point.[281] Israel's indefinite occupation frustrates the purpose of this regime.

(ii) The Nature of the Occupation

Indeed, it is not only the purpose of the regime of occupation, but also its essential nature, that may well be defied if the occupation is allowed to continue indefinitely. The occupied population under foreign control does not enjoy the full range of human rights, in the very least insofar as it is deprived of citizenship and the rights attached to that status. The prolongation of such a situation may well be in the interests of an occupying power who may rely on the provisions of the law relative to the maintenance of the status quo, as well as to its security concerns, to the detriment of the population. Given that the occupant is likely to treat its own citizens in a manner vastly different from the manner with which it treats the occupied population, the result may well be the *de facto* institutionalization of Apartheid of some sort.[282] Such a scenario, while ostensibly legal in terms of a "rule-book" conception of the rule of law, is manifestly illegal in terms of a "right" conception of the rule of law.[283] Indeed, in making the

---

http://www.law.du.edu/russell/contracts/ucc/4-1-204.htm. The Israeli Supreme Court has itself resorted to the principle of reasonable time in order to determine the time limits of a judicial institutionalization order. *See* C.A. 3845/02, Anonymous v. The District Adult Psychiatric Committee (unpublished). This determination relied on a similar decision by the U.S. Supreme Court, *Jackson v. Indiana*, 406 U.S. 715, 738 (1972).

279.   U.N. Charter, *supra* note 13, at art. 2(3).

280.   *See supra* section II.A.2.b. The fact that current international law legitimizes an armed struggle by occupied people attempting to realize their right to self-determination and emerge as a new sovereign state attests to the importance attached to the realization of this right.

281.   *See supra* notes 152-55 and accompanying text.

282.   Roberts, *Prolonged Military Occupation, supra* note 33, at 52. *See also supra* note 213 and accompanying text.

283.   To use Dworkin's reference to a formal and a substantive conception of the rule of law: the former is interested in the enforceability of law regardless of its content, that is, in order; the latter is interested in the substance, nature and justification of the order, determined by the balance

very rule of law a casualty of an indefinite occupation, it corrupts the law.[284]

(iii) The Circumstances of the Occupation

The achievement of the purpose of a peaceful political change leading to a new sovereign state is a major policy issue. Matters of policy necessitate planning designed to achieve the desired result. Such planning, especially in respect of complicated and bitterly contested political issues that are not within the absolute control of one party, as is the Israeli-Palestinian conflict, is neither a trivial nor an immediate matter. It is a long-term process; it may be incremental; and it may, indeed, fail. It is possible, however, to evaluate whether such a policy was in the making *ex ante*. This evaluation requires the examination of the circumstances of the specific occupation.

The most relevant circumstances to be examined in this respect are whether the occupying power has annexed the occupied territory or has otherwise indicated an intention to retain its presence there indefinitely. The examination of Israel's annexation of East Jerusalem, the expropriation of vast portions of Palestinians land to establish settlements in the OPT, to construct the bypass roads,[285] and, most recently, to erect the Wall, all suggest such an intention. The Wall, especially, merits our brief attention.

As noted in the preceding subsection,[286] the Wall's route does not follow the 1967 border. While its final path is yet unclear and, indeed, changes regularly in response to internal[287] and external[288] pressures, it is clearly designed to incorporate major settlements and many settlers into the Israeli side of it. In some areas it creates a barrier that encircles Palestinian villages; in others, it isolates them from the rest of the West Bank.[289] The Special Rapporteur of the UN

---

thereby achieved between the individual and society; between liberty and security. *See generally* RONALD DWORKIN, A MATTER OF PRINCIPLE 11 (1985).

284.　*See* 2002 REPORT ON THE VIOLATIONS OF HUMAN RIGHTS IN THE OCCUPIED ARAB TERRITORIES, *supra* note 31, at 12 ("the rule of law is one casualty of the conflict in the occupied Palestinian Territory, but the main casualties are the people of both Palestine and Israel").

285.　*See supra* notes 173-77; 187-95; 217-27 and accompanying text.

286.　*See supra* note 185, 227 and accompanying text.

287.　Internal pressures emanate from the settlers who are represented in the Government, on the one hand, and from the Israeli High Court of Justice, on the other hand. The Court, having determined that the current route in sections of the Wall that were the subject of the appeal fails to meet the proportionality test of both international humanitarian law and Israeli administrative law, ordered the re-routing of a 20-mile section of what is termed in Israel the "separation fence." *See* H.C. 2056/04, *Beit Surik case*, *supra* note 103. The same rationale, generating similar results, was applied in H.C. 7957/04, *Mara'abe case*, *supra* note 103. Similar appeals pertaining to other segments of the wall are currently pending before the HCJ.

288.　The most notable external pressure stems from the *Construction of a Wall*, *supra* note 6. The opinion, which was rendered pursuant to a request submitted by the U.N. General Assembly, G.A. Res. A/RES/ES-10/14, U.N. GAOR, 10th Emer. Sess. 23d Plen. Mtg. (Dec. 8, 2003), held that the construction of the Wall in any part of the OPT is illegal and specified the legal consequences emanating from said illegality. The Opinion was adopted by the General Assembly in GA Res. A/ES-10/L.18/Rev. 1 (July 20, 2004) (150 votes in favor, 6 against and 10 absentees).

289.　It should, however, be noted that this kind of effect on Palestinian villages is taken into consideration by the HCJ in determining whether the route of the wall meets the standard of propor-

Commission on Human Rights concluded that "the construction of the Wall within the West Bank and the continued expansion of settlements, which, on the face of it, have more to do with territorial expansion, de facto annexation or conquest, raise serious doubts about the good faith of Israel's justifications in the name of security."[290] The ICJ's conclusion on this issue is quite pertinent:

> Whilst the Court notes the assurance given by Israel that the construction of the wall does not amount to annexation and that the wall is of a temporary nature . . . it nevertheless cannot remain indifferent to certain fears expressed to it that the route of the wall will prejudge the future frontier between Israel and Palestine, and the fear that Israel may integrate the settlements and their means of access. The Court considers that the construction of the wall and its associated regime create a "fait accompli" on the ground that could well become permanent, in which case, and notwithstanding the formal characterization of the wall by Israel, it would be tantamount to *de facto* annexation.[291]

Had the Court entertained the notion that the space between the "temporary" and the "permanent" is inhabited by the "indefinite," its conclusion would have—and should have—been that the construction of the Wall is indicative less of a *de facto* annexation that may happen in the (permanent) future, and more of such an annexation that has been effected in the (indefinite) present.

When one considers the huge investment of Israeli resources to build the Wall,[292] and the territorial expansion the Wall achieves,[293] the only reasonable conclusion is that Israel, far from treating the OPT as a negotiation card to be returned in exchange for peace, has already effected a *de facto* annexation of[294]

---

tionality and accounts for the recent decision ordering the state to change its course. *See* H.C. 7957/04, *Mara'abe case, supra* note 103.

290.   *See* 2003 REPORT ON THE SITUATION OF HUMAN RIGHTS IN THE PALESTINIAN TERRITORIES, *supra* note 176, at 15.

291.   *Construction of a Wall, supra* note 6, ¶ 121.

292.   While it is virtually impossible to calculate the total investment, as it runs the whole gamut from military expenditure to monetary incentives to settlers, some figures are sufficiently telling for the present discussion: during the last decade, the Israeli Government invested $2.5 billion in constructing new houses in the OPT, 50% of which was public, compared with 25% public financing inside the green line. During the same period, the Government allocated to municipalities an average of NIS 5,428 per settler, a year, compared to 3,807 per citizen in Israel. *See* SHLOMO SVIRSKI ET AL., GOVERNMENTAL FUNDING OF ISRAELI SETTLEMENT IN JUDEA AND SAMARIA AND THE GOLAN HEIGHTS IN THE NINETIES: MUNICIPALITIES, HOUSING AND ROADS CONSTRUCTION (Jan. 2002) (Hebrew), *available at* http://www.adva.org/ivrit/diur.html. Just the cost of constructing the by-pass roads in the OPT since Oslo has been estimated at more than $265 million. *See* Ze'ev Schiff, *The March of Folly of the By-Pass Roads*, HA'ARETZ, Feb. 15, 2002, at B1. The projected cost of the Wall is $1.4 billion. 2003 REPORT ON THE SITUATION OF HUMAN RIGHTS IN THE PALESTINIAN TERRITORIES, *supra* note 176, at 8.

293.   *See supra* notes 185, 287-91 and accompanying text.

294.   Unlike the *de jure* annexation of East Jerusalem, the actions described in the text lack the official act of annexation, but nevertheless amount to a *de facto* annexation, effected without giving the Palestinians the rights of citizenship, made visibly and materially clear by the planned path of the Wall. As noted by the Special Rapporteur of the UN Commission on Human Rights, John Dugard, "Language is a powerful instrument. This explains why words that accurately describe a particular situation are often avoided." Focusing merely on the Wall, the Special Rapporteur observed that "[T]he Wall that Israel is presently constructing within the territory of the West Bank . . . goes by the name of 'Seam Zone,' 'Security Fence' or 'Separation Wall'. The word 'annexation' is avoided as it is too accurate a description and too unconcerned about the need to obfuscate the

a substantial part of the OPT.[295] The resulting political geography of the OPT, having been thus divided into a multitude of non-contiguous cantons, would not allow the Palestinians to exercise their right to self-determination in a viable sovereign State,[296] frustrating the desired political change clearly articulated by the Security Council.[297] The question remains whether Israel's security concerns justify the settlements and the chain of actions following their establishment.

(iv) The (Im)balance of Security Revisited

Israel claims that its actions are justified by legitimate security concerns, especially in the light of suicide bombing, and that they are simply temporary measures evidencing no intention to alter political boundaries.[298] This argument, however, is untenable on the basis of both substantive law and the facts on the ground.

It is clear that the substantive law of occupation recognizes the legitimate security concerns of the occupying power. However, such recognition does not extend to all means and methods used to arguably further this security.[299] Indeed, it does not extend to settlements: paragraph six of Article 49 of the Fourth Geneva Convention contains no exception to its prohibition of settlements on the grounds of such security considerations; security concerns cannot, therefore,

---

truth .... The fact must be faced that what we are presently witnessing in the West Bank is a visible and clear act of territorial annexation under the guise of security .... Annexation of this kind goes by another name in international law—conquest." 2003 REPORT ON THE SITUATION OF HUMAN RIGHTS IN THE PALESTINIAN TERRITORIES, *supra* note 176, at 6, 8.

    295. Ze'ev Schiff, a leading commentator in Ha'Aretz newspaper, contemplating merely the cost of the by-pass roads, concluded that:

> three explanations stand behind this reality. The first is that these expenditures express an intention never to give up the territories and all the rest is an illusion. The second is that we have decided to build, step-by-step, the road system of the Palestinian State that will be established in the territories, at the expense of the Israeli taxpayer. The third possible explanation is that the governmental systems of Israel have been dragged into this as if forced by a demon and without anyone being able to stop the March of Folly.

Schiff, *supra* note 292. Given that governments are not presumed to be possessed by demons, the obvious cynicism of the second explanation, and the broader context and raison d'etre of the by-pass roads, that is, the settlements' enterprise, the first explanation is clearly the only reasonable conclusion. *See also* Ran HaCohen, *Letter from Israel*, Mar. 1, 2002, *available at* http://antiwar.com/hacohen/pf/p-h030102.html. The concern that the Wall is tantamount to annexation was the focus of the debate held during the 4841th Security Council meeting on October 14, 2003. *See* U.N. Press Release SC/7895, In Day-Long Security Council Meeting, Palestine Observer Says Israeli Seecurity Wall Involves De Facto Annexation of Occupied Land (Oct. 14, 2003), *available at* http://www.un.org/News/Press/docs/2003/sc7895.doc.htm.

    296. *See* 2003 REPORT ON THE SITUATION OF HUMAN RIGHTS IN THE PALESTINIAN TERRITORIES, *supra* note 176, at 14. The ICJ reiterated this position in *Construction of a Wall*, *supra* note 6, ¶ 122.

    297. S.C. Res. 1397, *supra* note 140 (envisioning "a region where two states, Israel and Palestine, live side by side within secure and recognized borders").

    298. *Construction of a Wall*, *supra* note 6, ¶ 116.

    299. *See supra* notes 161-69 and accompanying text.

render the settlements a valid security measure.[300] Even if, for the sake of argument, one dissociates the construction of the Wall from the settlements and examines the legality of this one measure in isolation, it would be hard to legally sustain the security claim in view of the fact that a significant portion of the Wall does not actually separate Palestinians from Israelis; rather, it separates them from other Palestinians. This separation of Palestinian from Palestinian renders Israeli security claims vacuous and bolsters the argument that the Wall disproportionately hurts Palestinians. Given that the Wall, much like the bypass roads and the settlements themselves, are as inseparable in reality as they are in applicable law, the legal grounds for the Israeli position are tenuous at best.

Further, the credibility of the "temporary" label Israel attaches to these alleged security measures is seriously questionable given the relevant legal history. It is through allegedly temporary "requisition for military needs" orders that Palestinian lands were seized. These lands were never returned.[301] It is quite instructive, in this context, to ponder the Israeli State Attorney's response to the Israeli High Court of Justice in the context of an appeal against the construction of the Wall:

> The State is not prevented from seizing land by means of temporary seizure orders even for the purpose of erecting structures that are not necessarily temporary in nature. By way of illustration: in Judea and Samaria, temporary seizure orders have been used to erect permanent structures of many kinds, such as bypass roads and Israeli communities.[302]

This language game between the "temporary" and the "permanent" functions to legitimize actions that would have been otherwise prohibited, and is, in fact, made possible once an occupation has ceased to be, and to be conceived as, temporary. Such an occupation, as the discussion pertaining to its purpose, nature, and circumstances demonstrates, has exceeded its reasonable duration. Such an occupation, in substituting an indefinite for a temporary control, violates the basic principle of temporariness underlying the normative regime of occupation.

The above does not suggest that the occupation is permanent. The recent withdrawal of Israel from the Gaza Strip shows that a political decision can effect the dismantling of settlements and, perhaps, lead to the end of occupation. The discussion does suggest, however, that in substituting an "indefinite" for a "temporary" occupation, Israel has violated the normative regime of occupation. It is instructive to note in this context that following the political decision to

---

300.   *Construction of a Wall, supra* note 6, ¶ 135.
301.   LAND GRAB, *supra* note 174.
302.   Comm. App./2597, Kafr 'Aqeb Development Committee et al. v. Ministry of Defense et al., Response of the State, at sec. 33/c, *reproduced in* BEHIND THE BARRIER, B'TSELEM HUMAN RIGHTS VIOLATION AS A RESULT OF ISRAEL'S WALL: POSITION PAPER (APRIL, 2003) [hereinafter *Kafr 'Aqeb Development Committee*], *available at* http://www.diak.org/Roadmap/2003_ Behind_The_Barrier_Eng.htm#_ftnref84. The HCJ itself had, in the past, accepted this logic when it contemplated, and authorized, the *temporary* seizure of Palestinian land for the building of *permanent* settlements. *See* H.C. 610/78, Ayun v. Minister of Defense, 33(2) P.D. 113, 131 (Opinion of Judge Landau); *Id.* at 134 (Opinion of Judge Ben-Porat).

withdraw from, and dismantle the settlements in, the Gaza Strip, the Israeli High Court of Justice emphasized the temporary—as distinct from the indefinite—nature of occupation to deny the settlers' claim to remain in the settlements.[303] This decision is normatively sound. The fact that it was never made in order to question the legality of the settlements enterprise in the preceding decades demonstrates that the temporary/indefinite indeterminacy is being used to legitimize power, not to contain it: the temporary nature of occupation was resurrected to replace its "indefinite" construction only when a political decision to pull-out was reached.

In conclusion, the very same actions which indicate that the occupation can no longer be regarded as temporary also disclose the violation of the substantive constraints imposed by the law of occupation on the managerial discretion of the occupying power; they amount to a *de facto* annexation of large portions of the occupied territory and entail gross violations of humanitarian and human rights norms and defy both the principle of the inalienability of sovereignty and the principle of trust. The violation of the temporal constraints cannot but violate the two other basic tenets of the law of occupation; the latter necessarily generate the conclusion that an occupation must be temporary. The Israeli occupation, having thus violated the three basic principles underlying the normative regime of occupation, is a conquest in disguise. It is, therefore, intrinsically illegal. The examination of its legality from an extrinsic perspective is undertaken in Section II.B below.

B. Extrinsic Dimensions of the Israeli Occupation of the OPT: The Nomos[304] of Occupation

The above discussion of the intrinsic dimensions of the Israeli occupation of the OPT concentrates on the way Israel has managed the occupation in the light of the foundational normative standards set by the law of occupation. Its focus, thus, is the *substance* of the normative regime of occupation; it serves as a measuring-rod for assessing various actions undertaken by the Occupant. In this section, the focus shifts to the normative and political *structure* of the occupation as a situation distinct from the regular order of the international society; we

---

303. H.C.J. 1661/05, *Regional Council Gaza Beach case*, *supra* note 207, ¶¶ 8-9, 115, 126.

304. The use of the term "*nomos*" in the section's title encompasses its varied meanings for Cover, for Schmitt and for Agamben. For Cover, it indicates a normative universe, comprising both rules and the narratives that give them meaning. *See* Robert Cover, *Nomos and Narrative*, 97 HARV. L. REV. 4 (1983). For Schmitt, it meant that right as original violence, as difference, rather than universalistic rationality being the foundation of law. *See* CARL SCHMITT, DER NOMOS DER ERDE (1974), *discussed in* Carlo Galli, *The Critic of Liberalism: Carl Schmitt's Antiliberalism: Its Theoretical and Historical Sources and Its Philosophical and Political Meaning*, 21 CARDOZO L. REV. 1597, 1601 (2000). Giorgio Agamben's analysis brings Schmitt's theory of the exception, explicated in this section, to its logical conclusion by stating that the concentration camp—as a paradigmatic structure—has become the modern political nomos: the space where the exception and the rule, the fact and the norm, are indistinguishable and law becomes meaningless. *See* GIORGIO AGAMBEN, HOMO SACER: SOVEREIGN POWER AND BARE LIFE 166, 167-80 (Daniel Heller-Roazen trans., 1988).

focus on its exceptionality.

Structurally, the law of occupation bears strong resemblance to an emergency regime. This regime, with roots dating back to the Roman-Commissarial model, rests on three precepts: exceptionality, limited scope of powers, and temporary duration.[305] In this discourse, then, a situation of emergency is separated and distinguished from the ordinary state of affairs as it signifies an occurrence which does not conform to the rule. Because the emergency situation is the exception, its duration must be limited and it must generate no permanent effects; it merely suspends the rule.[306] This is also why the norm is regarded as superior to the exception: the existing legal order defines the terms under which it is suspended, and the powers granted in such a situation are to be used for the purpose of an expeditious re-establishment of the status quo, that is, of a return to normalcy.[307]

The basic tenets of the normative regime of occupation in the international arena largely conform to this constitutional model. The normal order of affairs is based on the principle of sovereign equality between states that are, at least to some extent, presumed to be founded on the ideas of self-government and self-determination. The severance of the link between sovereignty and effective control, and life under foreign rule, constitute an exceptional state of affairs and the law of occupation recognizes it as an exception; it is to be managed so as to ensure return to normalcy. This is why the occupant has only limited powers in terms of both scope and time, and is not permitted to act in a manner designed to yield permanent results.[308]

Indeed, modern studies of emergency situations concerned with the derogation from human rights law thereby occasioned have concluded that: "[a]bove and beyond the rules . . . one principle, namely, the principle of provisional status, dominates all others. The right of derogation (of human rights) can be justified solely by the concern to return to normalcy."[309] This conclusion holds true and applies equally to occupation.

A reversal of the relationship between the norm and the exception gener-

---

305. *See* THEODOR E. MOMMSEN, THE HISTORY OF ROME 325, 326 (1908). For later references to this classical model, see, for example, NICOLO MACHIAVELLI, THE DISCOURSES 194, 198 (Bernard Crick ed. & Leslie Walker trans., 1970); JEAN JACQUES ROUSSEAU, THE SOCIAL CONTRACT AND DISCOURSES 293, 294-96 (G.D.H. Cole trans., Alfred A. Knopf 1993).

306. For the essential features of the traditional model of emergency powers, see Oren Gross, *Exception and Emergency Powers: The Normless and Exceptionless Exception: Carl Schmitt's Theory of Emergency Powers and the "Norm-Exception" Dichotomy*, 21 CARDOZO L. REV. 1825, 1836-39 (2000) [hereinafter *Exception and Emergency Powers*].

307. *Id.*

308. *See supra* section II.A.1-4.

309. STUDY OF THE IMPLICATIONS FOR HUMAN RIGHTS OF RECENT DEVELOPMENT CONCERNING SITUATIONS KNOWN AS STATE OF SIEGE OR EMERGENCY, U.N. ESCOR, 35th Sess., Agenda Item 10, 69 U.N. Doc. E/CN.4/Sub.2/1982/15 (1982) (N. Questiaux). *See also* Oren Gross & Fionnuala Ni Aolain, *To Know Where We Are We Need To Know Where We Are: Revisiting States of Emergency*, in HUMAN RIGHTS: AN AGENDA FOR THE 21ST CENTURY 79 (Angela Hegarty & Siobhan Leonard eds., 1999).

ates, as of necessity, the terminus of every normative system.[310] Carl Schmitt's political theology, wherein the norm becomes subservient to the exception, is both a precedent and a warning. "The rule," said Schmitt, "proves nothing; the exception proves everything: it confirms not only the rule but also its existence, which derives only from the exception."[311] The state of emergency, which in German is called a "state of exception" (*Ausnahmezeustand*), is one where the rule of man prevails over the rule of law[312] and where the Leviathan reigns supreme.[313] The result is a Hobbesian state of war—indeed the clearest case of an exception—where, bereft of any rights, the only meaningful distinction for a person to make is between the reified constructs of 'friend' and 'foe'.[314] This situation signifies the destruction of both the normative regime of the exception, and of the general rule. From a normative perspective, it is thus as meaningless as it is indefensible.[315]

One lesson to be drawn from the above is the importance of retaining a clear distinction between fact and norm; between the rule and the exception, lest the exception becomes a new rule, and generates a new conception of reality. This is important because in this new conception of reality, one's security habitually overrides one's enemy's human rights.[316] Indeed, the reversal of the relationship between the rule and the exception operates as a legitimizing device allowing for a discussion of various specific violations of human rights carried out in the name of security as if they are the exception to the normal order of things, thereby obfuscating the fact that the violations have become the rule, not

---

310. Giacomo Marramo, *Schmitt and the Categories of the Political: The Exile of the Nomos: For a Critical Profile of Carl Schmitt*, 27 CARDOZO L. REV. 1567 (2000).

311. SCHMITT, POLITICAL THEOLOGY, *supra* note 16, at 15.

312. Heiner Bielefeld, *Carl Schmitt's Critique of Liberalism: Systemic Reconstruction and Countercriticism*, 10 CAN. J. L. & JURIS. 65, 68 (1997).

313. Schmitt was fascinated with Hobbes and regarded himself as his heir, ending his commentary on Hobbes' Leviathan with the words: "You shall no longer teach in vain, Thomas Hobbes." *See* CARL SCHMITT, THE LEVIATHAN IN THE STATE THEORY OF THOMAS HOBBS: MEANING AND FAILURE OF A POLITICAL SYMBOL (George Schwab & Erna Hilfstein trans., 1996). On the affinity between Schmitt and Hobbes, see David Dyzenhous, *Now the Machine Runs Itself: Carl Schmitt on Hobbes and Kelsen*, 16 CARDOZO L. REV. 1 (1994); John P. McCormick, *Fear, Technology and the State: Carl Schmitt, Leo Strauss and the Revival of Hobbes in Weimar and National Socialist Germany*, 22 POL. THEORY 619 (1994).

314. For Schmitt's 'friend'/'enemy' distinction, see CARL SCHMITT, THE CONCEPT OF THE POLITICAL, 25-37 (J. Harvey Lomax trans., 3rd ed. 1996). For an analysis, see Andrew Norris, *Carl Schmitt on Friends, Enemies and the Political*, TELOS 68 (Summer 1998). On the odd history of Schmitt's reception in the Anglo-American academia, see Emanuel Richter, *The Critic of Liberalism: Carl Schmitt: The Defective Guidance for the Critique of Political Liberalism*, 21 CARDOZO L. REV. 1619 (2000).

315. This was the political theology of the Third Reich. On Schmitt's defense of the President's action in July 1932 in *Prussia v. Reich*, which was based on his construction of emergency, see DAVID DYZENHAUS, LEGALITY AND LEGITIMACY: CARL SCHMITT, HANS KELSEN AND HERMANN HELLER IN WEIMAR 70-85 (1997).

316. Harold Lasswell noted that "[a]n insidious outcome of continuing crisis is the tendency to slide into a new conception of normality that takes vastly extended control for granted, and thinks of freedom in smaller and smaller dimensions." HAROLD D. LASSWELL, NATIONAL SECURITY AND INDIVIDUAL FREEDOM 29 (1950), *quoted in* Gross, *Exception and Emergency Powers*, *supra* note 306, at n.155.

the exception.

The Schmittian exception, reflects Giorgio Agamben in his book *Homo Sacer*, has generated the conditions of possibility for the concentration camp, a space created once the exception—the temporary suspension of the rule— becomes the rule.[317] This space, where the extraordinary and the provisional condition becomes ordinary and permanent, says Agamben, is not limited to Nazi concentration camps. It is paradigmatic to every situation where the political machinery of the modern nation state finds itself in a continuous crisis and decides to take it upon itself to defend the biological life of the nation, collapsing human rights into citizens' rights,[318] subsuming humanity into citizenry, and making the former the "exceptionless exception."[319] In such a situation, the enemy, stripped of human rights, is stripped of his humanity. Having been excluded from the body-politic, he has only his own body as a political tool and it is through this political body that he interacts with the body-politic that has thus reified him.[320] This may well be the typology of the suicide bomber. It does not justify his actions which may amount to war crimes and, when directed against civilians, may amount to crimes against humanity,[321] but it does contextualize them.

In order to contain the eruption of a Schmittian friend/enemy politic, the international rule of law recognized the situation of occupation as an exception. It created a normative regime designed to ensure that the effective control of the occupying power is exercised in a manner that is temporary, respectful of the humanitarian needs and human rights of the occupied population, and leads to an expeditious return to normalcy based on sovereign equality. An occupation that fails to do this is substantively and intrinsically illegal (in terms of the law of occupation), as well as structurally and extrinsically illegal (in terms of the international legal order which provides the normative framework within which the law of occupation operates). The Israeli occupation of the OPT has thus failed.

---

317. AGAMBEN, *supra* note 304, at 166-68.

318. *Id.* at 126-31, 174-76. Agamben, noting the very ambiguity of the title "*Declaration des droits de l'Homme et du Citoyen*" refers in this context to Arendt's discussion of the paradox wherein "[T]he Conception of human rights, based upon the assumed existence of a human being as such, broke down at the very moment when those who professed to believe in it were for the first time confronted with people who had indeed lost all other qualities and specific relationships— except that they were still human." *See* HANNAH ARENDT, THE ORIGINS OF TOTALITARIANISM 299 (1979). Thus, in the nation-state system, human rights that are considered inalienable have become meaningless once they cannot be attached to the citizens of a nation-state. The refugee, the person who was supposed to be the "human rights" person *par excellence* has thus become the paradigm of 'bare life.'

319. A term coined by Gross in his analysis of Schmitt's theory of the exception. *See* Gross, *Exception and Emergency Powers, supra* note 306.

320. AGAMBEN, *supra* note 304, at 187-88.

321. WITHOUT DISTINCTION, *supra* note 228.

III.

CONCLUDING OBSERVATIONS: THE MATRIX OF AN ILLEGAL OCCUPATION AND ITS NORMATIVE CONSEQUENCES

In light of the above conclusion, one should revisit Israel's arguments regarding its security concerns and the measures taken to ensure that they are met.[322] It is beyond dispute that terrorist attacks present a major challenge to the conduct of normal life. This has become painfully evident in many parts of the world following 9/11. What should, however, be disputed is the equation Israel has drawn between the Palestinians and al-Qaeda, and indeed between the former and worldwide Islamic fanaticism. The Palestinians engage in a struggle for freedom by an occupied people; the latter is an amorphous and transnational group intent on destroying the democratic way of life. The Israeli equation lends support to the Israeli argument, discussed above, that the Palestinian response to Israel's most generous peace offerings at Camp David evidences Palestinian's lack of good faith engagement in the peace process and exposes their true motivation: the destruction of the only democratic state in the Middle-East, Israel. What is missing from the equation, however, is the occupation. The equation is thus self-serving as it allows for the obfuscation of the cause and effect relations which exist between this occupation and Palestinian violence. These relations do not justify terrorist attacks against civilians—there is no justification for such attacks—but they do contextualize them and refocus the attention on the nature of the Israeli occupation of the OPT.[323]

Furthermore, our argument regarding the illegality of the continued Israeli occupation of the OPT rests on the violation by Israel of the basic tenets of the normative regime of occupation. The various arguments advanced in support of Israeli actions in the territory in the name of security thus fail to overcome our argument. The question of whether a particular action by the IDF undertaken to advance Israel's security has violated certain rights of the protected population is distinct from the question of the illegality of the regime of occupation.

Focusing on the nature of this regime—as distinct from analyzing specific actions undertaken within it—reveals that obfuscation and the blurring of boundaries is the defining feature of the Israeli occupation. Its indeterminacy has operated to legitimize that which would have otherwise been determined illegal.

---

322. This issue has been discussed *supra* in section II.4.d.iv.

323. The essential features of the occupation regime of the OPT date back to at least 1977, thus preceding both the second and the first *intifadas*, and making the assignment of blame for the failure of the peace process to the Palestinians, its accuracy notwithstanding, irrelevant to the present discussion. Note further that the period of the occupation consists of four segments: (1) 1967-1987 (first period); 1987-1993 (first *Intifada*); 1993-2000 (the Oslo peace process); 2000-present (the collapse of the peace process and the second *Intifada*). The establishment of the Palestinian Authority did not alter the fact of occupation, not least because Israel neither ceased to exercise effective control over the territories nor to allow the expansion, or "natural growth," of the settlements. *See Construction of a Wall*, *supra* note 6, ¶ 78. These facts have led some observes to compare the creation of the Palestinian Authority to the creation of Bantustans in Apartheid South Africa. *See, e.g.,* CHRISTINE BELL, PEACE AGREEMENTS AND HUMAN RIGHTS 189, 190 (2000).

Thus, while Israel has consistently argued that the West Bank and the Gaza Strip are not occupied territories, the State's attorneys have sought to justify Israel's actions in the territories which restrict the rights of Palestinians on the basis of the law of occupation.[324] Similarly, the HCJ, while never confirming the applicability of the Fourth Geneva Convention to the territories, has nevertheless decided to apply its humanitarian provisions in a manner that has allowed the IDF to exercise the powers of a belligerent occupant but which rejected the vast majority of Palestinian petitions.[325] In this manner, Israel has been able to enjoy the credit for applying international humanitarian law while at the same time violating its essential tenets.[326] This occupation/non-occupation indeterminacy is complemented by its twin annexation/non-annexation indeterminacy: Israel acts in the territory as a sovereign insofar as it settles its citizens there and extends to them its laws on a personal and on a mixed personal/territorial bases, yet insofar as the territory has not been formally annexed and insofar as this exercise of sovereignty falls short of giving the Palestinian residents citizenship

---

324. On the state's resort to the Geneva Conventions as a basis for exercising its powers, see generally the arguments advanced by KRETZMER, *supra* note 87, at 197.

325. On the jurisprudence of the HCJ, see KRETZMER, *supra* note 87, at 38. Two major issues where the court rejected Palestinian petitions and allowed the army to act in ways that *de facto* negated protections that the Geneva Convention sought to give, are deportations, and home demolitions. *Id.* at 49-52, 165-86, 145-63. In the context of both issues, the HCJ interpreted the Geneva Convention in a way that allowed the Israeli army to use these measures notwithstanding the specific prohibitions on them in the text of the Convention. This interpretation has been highly controversial. On the legitimizing function of the HCJ in rejecting over 99% of Palestinians petitions but accepting some which thereby become symbolic "Landmark cases," which legitimizes the authority of the HCJ without significantly affecting the rights of the Palestinians, see Ronen Shamir, *Landmark Cases and the Reproduction of Legitimacy: the Case of Israel's High Court of Justice*, 24 L. & SOC'Y REV. 781 (1990). A recent change in the direction of this jurisprudence should however be noted as it may well indicate a trend towards greater recognition of the humanitarian and human rights plight of the Palestinians, as is evidenced in the HCJ's analysis of the proportionality requirement in connection with the construction of the Wall. *See* H.C. 2056/04, *Beit Surik* case, *supra* note 103; H.C. 7957/04, *Mara'abe* case, *supra* note 103; H.C. 3239/02, Mar'ab. v. The IDF Commander in Judea and Samaria (not yet published) (applying human rights instruments to the occupied territories).

326. A credit noted particularly for its rarity, insofar as it has been the practice of occupying powers to deny the very applicability of the law of occupation. *See* Baxter, *Some Existing Problems*, *supra* note 35, at 288; Roberts, *Prolonged Military Occupation*, *supra* note 33, at 46. There is a difference, however, between admitting the relevance of and referring to international humanitarian law and applying it in a manner consistent with its purpose. While the HCJ does apply this law in a manner that occasionally has favored a Palestinian petition directly (and especially recently in the context of petitions against specific segments of the Wall) and, perhaps more significantly, indirectly, by exercising its "shadow" function to encourage the state to retreat from a contested action before a decision is rendered, it has not, in the main, applied this law in a manner that advances its main purpose. For an analysis of the "shadow function" of the court in this context, see Yoav Dotan, *Judicial Rhetoric, Government Lawyers and Human Rights: the Case of the Israeli High Court of Justice During the Intifada*, 33 L. & SOC'Y REV. 319 (1999); KRETZMER, *supra* note 87, at 189-91. For an example of a recent decision wherein the HCJ relied on the Geneva Convention in order to determine that Article 78 of the Fourth Geneva Convention authorizes the Military Commander to assign the residence of Palestinians from the West Bank to the Gaza Strip and that such assignment is distinct from the prohibition on deportation contained in Article 49 of the same Convention, see *Ajuri*, *supra* note 103. For reviews of this judgment, see Barak-Erez, *supra* note 263; Benvensiti, *Ajuri*, *supra* note 263; Ben-Naftali & Michaeli, *The Call of Abraham*, *supra* note 263.

rights, Israel is not acting as a sovereign.[327] In this manner, Israel enjoys both the powers of an occupant and a sovereign in the OPT, while Palestinians enjoy neither the rights of an occupied people nor the rights of citizenship. This indeterminacy allows Israel to avoid accountability in the international community for having illegally annexed the territories, while pursuing the policies of "greater Israel"[328] in the West Bank without jeopardizing its Jewish majority.[329] It is, finally, the blurring of the boundaries between the temporary and the indefinite,[330] and between the rule and the exception,[331] which has donned a

---

327. *See supra* section II.A.3. Indeed, Roberts notes that "Israel may see some advantage in the continuation of the status of occupied territory, because this arrangement provides a legal basis for treating the Arab inhabitants of the territories entirely separately from the citizens of Israel: such a view suggests that the law of occupation could potentially pave the way for a kind of *apartheid*." Roberts, *Military Occupation, supra* note 33, at 272-73. For a description of a similar concern, see Roberts, *Prolonged Military Occupation, supra* note 33, at 79-80. The law of occupation may indeed pave the way for a kind of *apartheid*, but only to the extent that it will be interpreted as excluding the notion of illegal occupation. Indeed, in the context of the OPT, Joseph Weiler noted that the construction of Israel's control of the territories as a belligerent occupation helped digest and perhaps prolong "a reality of de facto annexation, of occupation *ad infinitum* coupled with the luxury of not having to integrate the local population into the democratic processes of the occupying nation." Weiler explains this by the fact that the law of occupation was created with short occupation in mind, and thus the present rules are not fit for an occupation which has lasted for over thirty years. Weiler, *supra* note 97, at 390. The legitimization Weiler points to is the consequence of a law of occupation which does not incorporate a notion of an occupation becoming illegal when it turns into a de facto annexation.

328. On the "Greater Israel" (*Eretz Isreal*/Land of Israel) ideology and its implications, see Baruch Kimmerling, *Between the Primordial and the Civil Definitions of the Collective Identity: Eretz Israel or the State of Israel?, in* COMPARATIVE SOCIAL DYNAMICS: ESSAYS IN HONOR OF S. N. EISENSTADT 262-83 (Eric Cohen et al. eds., 1985). The settlement project cannot be understood outside of this context as there is an overlap between the occupied territories and the historical and religious "Greater Israel." *See* Baruch Kimmerling, *Boundaries and Frontiers of the Israeli Control System: Analytical Conclusions, in* THE ISRAELI STATE AND SOCIETY: BOUNDRIES AND FRONTIERS 265, 277 (Baruch Kimmrling ed., 1989).

329. It is interesting to note in this context that demography plays a significant role within Israel proper, especially with respect to its Palestinian minority. The latter, while enjoying the myriad of rights associated with citizenship, are nevertheless discriminated against, most notably with respect to land rights as they most directly pertain to the "judaization" process of the land of Israel. This process has led to the characterization of the Israeli regime as an "ethnic democracy"—a concept which appears to be an oxymoron—or as an "ethnocracy." Placed in this context, the occupation regime attempts to replicate the same process by extending the ethnic regime which exists within Israel's recognized borders. The result is an Israeli state whose existence as a democracy is put in doubt. On discrimination of Palestinians citizens of Israel with respect to land rights, see Alexander Kedar, *The Legal Transformation of Ethnic Geography: Israeli Law and the Palestinian Landholder 1948-1967,* 33 N.Y.U. J. INT'L. L. & POL. 923 (2001); Aeyal Gross, *The Dilemma of Constitutional Property Rights in Ethnic Land Regimes: Israel and South Africa Compared,* 121 S. AFRICAN L. J. (2004). On the concept of an "ethnic democracy," see Sammy Smooha, *Minority Status in an Ethnic Democracy: The Status of the Arab Minority in Israel,* 13 ETHNIC & RACIAL STUD. 389-413 (1990). On the critique of this concept, see As'ad Ghanem et al., *Questioning "Ethnic Democracy": A Response to Sammy Smooha,* 3 ISR. STUD. 253 (1998). On the alternative concept of "Ethnocracy," see Oren Yiftachel, *'Ethnocracy': The Politics of Judaizing Israel/Palestine,* 6 CONSTELLATIONS 364 (1999). For a detailed discussion of this debate, see Aeyal Gross, *Democracy, Ethnicity and Constitutionalism in Israel: Between the "Jewish State" and the "Democratic State",* 2 SOTSYOLOGIA ISRAELIT 647 (2000).

330. *See supra* section II.A.4.

331. *See supra* section II.B.

mantle of legitimacy on this occupation and has made possible the continuous interplay of occupation/non-occupation and annexation/non-annexation. This mantle, however, much like the Emperor's New Clothes, should not obfuscate our vision of the naked illegality of this regime.

"[T]he qualification of a situation as illegal," observed the ICJ, "does not itself put an end to it. It can only be the first necessary step in an endeavour to bring the illegal occupation to an end."[332] While law, in itself, is surely no substitute for statesmanship and cannot therefore "bring the illegal occupation to an end," there are normative results which do follow from illegality. A state "whose conduct constitutes an internationally wrongful act having a continuing character is under an obligation to cease that conduct, without prejudice to the responsibility it has already incurred."[333]

Further, the qualification of the occupation as "illegal," while it does not affect the continued application of both humanitarian and human rights law (so as to avoid a legal vacuum and to offer protection to the occupied population so long as the illegal situation persists), does affect the legality of the security measures taken in its defense—as distinct from measures undertaken to protect Israel itself—as such measures are thereby illegal themselves.[334] This consequence is relevant both to the legal assessment of various security measures undertaken by Israel, including but not limited to the Wall, and to the legal validity of the arguments raised within Israel by soldiers who refuse to partake in the defense of the occupation. Indeed, the perception of the Israeli occupation as illegal and illegitimate might well have been the main factor which informed the ICJ's perception of the Wall in the *Construction of a Wall* Advisory Opinion. While refraining from commenting on the occupation regime itself, the Court was well aware of the "greater whole" of which the Wall is but one aspect.[335] This might explain, for example, its off-hand rejection of Israel's self-defense argument, based on Article 51 of the UN Charter, on the ground that Israel was not reacting in response to force used by another state but rather to force emanating from within its territory in light of the control it is exercising in the OPT.[336]

It may, however, be possible to construe additional normative consequences emanating from an indefinite occupation which, as discussed above,

---

332. *Continued Presence of South Africa in Namibia* Advisory Opinion, *supra* note 21, at 52.

333. DRAFT ARTICLES ON STATE RESPONSIBILITY, art. 43, Report of the ILC on the Work of its 48th session, U.N. GAOR, 51th Sess., Supp. No. 10 at 142, U.N. Doc. A/51/10 (1996).

334. The argument does not propose that actions taken in an armed conflict are to be measured in relation to the question of whether the original use of force was legal or not. Indeed, such an argument would have blurred the important distinction between *jus ad bellum* and *jus in bello*. It merely argues that actions undertaken in defense of an illegal occupation are illegal themselves.

335. *Construction of a Wall*, *supra* note 6, ¶ 54.

336. *Id.* at ¶ 139. It is this assumption that raised the objection of several judges who felt the Court did not take fair notice of the illegal acts performed by the Palestinians and thus disregarded the context of the question at hand. *See id.* Separate Opinion of Judge Higgins, ¶¶ 15-18; Declaration of Judge Burgenthal, ¶¶ 3-6; Separate Opinion of Judge Owada, ¶¶ 26-29, 31.

necessarily constitutes an assault on both sovereign integrity and fundamental human rights. Such an occupation defies the basic tenets of both the laws of occupation and the normal order of the international society. The time has come for the international community to promulgate clear time limitations for the duration of an occupation, thereby offering a solution to the problem identified in, but not resolved by, Article 6 of the Fourth Geneva Convention.[337] The international community may wish to entertain the thought that, in cases of occupations lasting longer than a year, and pending a comprehensive political solution, the effective control over the occupied territory be transferred from the occupying power to an appropriate international authority.[338] It may further wish to consider the possibility that a refusal by an occupying power to thus transfer control be construed as a form of aggression.[339] Indeed, the rationale underlying the criminalization of aggression, that is, that it is a framework for an entire body of international crimes, as explained by the Nuremberg International Military Tribunal, seems to apply here as well.[340] This notion is, perhaps, somewhat baffling and difficult to accept, given the nearly axiomatic conception of occupation as a fact of life.[341] But, then, was not aggression, too, before WWII, perceived as an acceptable albeit regrettable fact of life regulated by the Covenant of the League of Nations?[342]

Whether or not the international community decides to deter similar in-

---

337. *See* section II.A.4.b.

338. See Ben-Naftali, *Temps Perdu, supra* note 256.

339. The International law definition of aggression is yet undecided. While criminalized in Article X of the Nuremberg Charter as a 'crime against peace,' see Charter of the International Military Tribunal and Protocol of 6 October 1945, Aug. 8, 1945, 59 Stat. 1544, 82 U.N.T.S. 279, it was not properly defined therein. Since then, the international community has struggled to define the phenomenon. *See* G.A. Res. 3314, U.N. GAOR, 29th Sess., Definition of Aggression, Annex, Definition of Aggression, U.N. Doc. A/Res./3314 (XXIX) (1974). Under Resolution 3314, "aggression is the use of armed force by a State against the sovereignty, territorial integrity or political independence of another State, or in any other manner inconsistent with the Charter of the United Nations." *Id.* This definition, however, applies only as far as state responsibility goes. No consensus exists as to the definition of aggression as a crime. For this reason, while enumerated as one of the crimes under the jurisdiction of the ICC, as stipulated in Article 5(1)(d) of the Rome Statute, Article 5(2) provides for the suspension of such jurisdiction until a definition is agreed upon by state parties. *See generally* Grant M. Dawson, *Defining Substantive Crimes Within the Subject Matter Jurisdiction of the International Criminal Court: What Is the Crime of Aggression?*, 19 N.Y.L. SCH. J. INT'L & COMP. L. 413 (2000).

340. An aggressive war is "essentially an evil thing . . . . To initiate a war of aggression . . . is not only an international crime; it is the supreme international crime differing only from other war crimes in that it *contains within itself the accumulated evil of the whole.*" *See* OFFICE OF THE UNITED STATES CHIEF OF COUNCIL FOR PROSECUTIONS OF AXIS CRIMINALITY, 1 NAZI CONSPIRACY AND AGGRESSION 16 (1946) (emphasis added).

341. Support for this position is found in Separate Opinion of Vice-President Ammoun, *Continued Presence of South Africa in Namibia* Advisory Opinion, *supra* note 22, at 89-92.

342. *See* PETER MALANCZUK, AKEHURST'S MODERN INTRODUCTION TO INTERNATIONAL LAW 306, 307-09 (7th ed. 1997). Article 12(1) of the Covenant established a procedure by which parties to a dispute should settle their differences before resorting to war. They had to submit the dispute to arbitration or judicial settlement or to inquiry by the Council and "agree in no case to resort to war until three months after the award by the arbitrators or the judicial decision, or the report by the Council."

stances where the boundaries between the rule and the exception become blurred, leading to the *nomos* of occupation by taking any of the measures recommended above, remains "a perpetual possibility only in a world of speculation."[343] Such speculation is clearly outside the scope of the present paper. It suffices to note that the materialization of such a possibility, much like the carrying out of the normative consequences which currently do follow from the illegality of the occupation or the construction of the Wall, cannot on their own eliminate the Israeli-Palestinian conflict. When coupled with wise and decent statesmanship, however, they may well assist in its resolution.

---

343. In reference to T.S. Eliot's poem which is cited at the beginning of the paper.

An Intimate Disengagement:
Israel's withdrawal from Gaza,
the Law of Occupation and of
Self-Determination

*Iain Scobbie**

1 INTRODUCTION

As the final text of this article was being prepared, Israel launched Operation Summer Rain on 28 June 2006 in response to the taking of Corporal Gilad Shalit by Palestinian militants following an attack on Israel Defence Forces on 25 June 2006. At the time of writing (July 2006), Israel's military operations in Gaza are continuing, and the final outcome cannot yet be discerned. This is not the appropriate place to discuss the legality of these actions – whether those of Israel or those of armed Palestinian groups. As matters are still in a state of flux, it is premature to reach a definitive legal conclusion. Nevertheless, the deployment of Israel Defence Forces in Gaza has an obvious pertinence to the issue examined in this article, the international status of Gaza following Israel's apparent withdrawal in August 2005. Consequently, where necessary and relevant, a provisional and tentative legal assessment of the implications of Operation Summer Rain will be attempted.

2 THE ISSUE IN QUESTION

In August 2005, Israel evacuated its settlements and withdrew its land forces from Gaza. This was in accordance with its Revised Disengagement Plan of 6 June 2004,[1] the implementation of which was intended to ensure that:

> In any future permanent status arrangement, there will be no Israeli towns and villages in the Gaza Strip. On the other hand, it is clear that in the West Bank, there

---

* Sir Joseph Hotung Research Professor in Law, Human Rights and Peace Building in the Middle East, School of Oriental and African Studies, University of London.
1 Available at: <www.mfa.gov.il/MFA/Peace+Process/Reference+Documents/Revised+Disengagement+Plan+6-June-2004.htm>.

are areas which will be part of the State of Israel, including major Israeli population centers, cities, towns and villages, security areas and other places of special interest to Israel.[2]

To this end, Israel claimed that its evacuation of Gaza had the consequence that there was no longer any permanent presence of Israeli security forces within Gaza.[3] Sub-section 1 of Section 3 (*Security Situation following the Relocation*), however, provides:

1. The State of Israel will guard and monitor the external land perimeter of the Gaza Strip, will continue to maintain exclusive authority in Gaza air space, and will continue to exercise security activity in the sea off the coast of the Gaza Strip.
2. The Gaza Strip shall be demilitarized and shall be devoid of weaponry, the presence of which does not accord with the Israeli-Palestinian agreements.
3. The State of Israel reserves its fundamental rights of self-defense, both preventive and reactive, including where necessary the use of force, in respect of threats emanating from the Gaza Strip.

The primary implication of the Disengagement Plan was set out in Principle Six (Political and Security Implications) of the Revised Disengagement Plan. This provides:

The completion of the plan will serve to dispel the claims regarding Israel's responsibility for the Palestinians within the Gaza Strip.

The meaning of Principle Six is intentionally ambiguous: it refers to the termination of Israel's responsibility for the population of Gaza, but says nothing about the status of the territory itself. Before the implementation of the Revised Disengagement Plan, Gaza was territory occupied by Israel: did the implementation of the plan entail a change in the international status of Gaza? In particular, once Israeli troops and settlers were withdrawn, was Gaza no longer occupied?

3 GAZA – OCCUPIED OR NOT OCCUPIED?

In anticipation of the implementation of the Revised Disengagement Plan, the Canadian Government's International Development Research Centre commissioned a report – the Aronson Report[4] – to examine the implications of disengagement. This noted that when then-Prime Minister Sharon initially announced the unilateral withdrawal plan in April 2004, one of the declared objectives was to end Israel's role and responsibility as the occupying power in Gaza. In particular, Article 2 of the 18 April 2004 Disengagement Plan provided that, the completion of withdrawal would mean that there would be "no permanent Israeli civilian or military presence" in the evacuated areas, and

---

2 Revised Disengagement Plan, Section 1 (*Political and Security Implications*), Principle Three.
3 Revised Disengagement Plan, Section 2.A (*Main Elements: The Process*), Article 3.1, *The Gaza Strip.*
4 A "lightly edited version" of this report has been published as Aronson, G., *Issues arising from the implementation of Israel's disengagement from the Gaza Strip*, 34 Journal of Palestine Studies 49 (2005).

therefore there would "be no basis for the claim that the Gaza Strip is occupied territory".[5] This express reference to Gaza as "occupied territory" was deleted in the 6 June 2004 Revised Disengagement Plan which was approved by the Cabinet.

The Aronson Report argues that one of the reasons for this deletion was that the Israeli Cabinet had received legal advice to the effect that any claim regarding the end of occupation could not be maintained while Israel remained in control of the Philadelphi corridor (the Salah al Din border road), essentially a buffer zone along the Egypt/Gaza border, and arguably also ports and airports. Retaining control of these areas was seen as enough to give Israel *de facto* control over the territory and thus maintain the occupation.[6] In the event, Israel reached an agreement with Egypt which took over security functions in the Philadephi Corridor,[7] but Israel remains in effective control of Gaza's airspace and maritime zones. Further, passage through the Rafah crossing between Gaza and Egypt is regulated by an agreement concluded between Israel and the Palestinian Authority, subject to an annexed statement of principles, and under the supervision of the European Union Border Assistance Mission.[8] Nevertheless, in a *Ha'aretz* article pubished in December 2004, Shavit Matias, the deputy to Israel's Attorney-General for international law was quoted as saying:

> When we quit Philadelphi, even if the Palestinians don't yet have a port or airport, the responsibility will no longer be ours. The area will not be considered occupied territory. When the Palestinians have a crossing to Egypt and additional options for transferring merchandise, even if there is no port yet, we have no responsibility.[9]

The question under consideration in this article is quite simple: is this view correct?

---

5   Available at: <http://electronicintifada.net/bytopic/historicaldocuments/264.shtml>; and also: <www.mfa.gov.il/MFA/Peace+Process/Reference+Documents/Disengagement+Plan+ +General+Outline.htm>.

6   Aronson, above n. 4, pp. 49-50: see also Roy, S., *Praying with their eyes closed: reflections on the disengagement from Gaza*, 34 Journal of Palestine Studies 64 (2005), p. 70.

7   For an account of the basic principles of the Israel-Egypt "military arrangement" on the deployment of Egyptian border guards on the Egyptian side of the corridor, see the Israeli Cabinet Communique of 28 August 2005, available at: <www.mfa.gov.il/MFA/Government/ Communiques/2005/Cabinet+Communique+28-Aug-2005.htm>.

8   The instruments dealing with the Rafah crossing – the 15 November 2005 Israel-PA Agreement on Movement and Access and annexed Agreed Principles for Rafah Crossing, and 23 November 2005 Agreed Arrangement on the European Union Border Assistance Mission at the Rafah Crossing Point on the Gaza-Egyptian Border (concluded at the invitation of Israel and the Palestinian Authority) may be found at: <www.nad-plo.org/listing.php?view=palisraeli_ roadagree>; and at: <www.mfa.gov.il/MFA/Peace+Process/Reference+Documents/Agreed+ documents+on+movement+and+access+from+and+to+Gaza+15-Nov-2005.htm>. See also, the EU Council press release 15011/05 (Presse 322) which gives an account of the mission of the Border Assistance Mission, available at: <http://register.consilium.eu.int/pdf/en/05/st15/ st15011.en05.pdf>.

   The crossing was closed by Israel following the capture of Cpl. Shalit. Israel claimed this was done to prevent him being smuggled into Egypt.

9   See Aronson, above n. 4, p. 51.

Commentators are divided on this. Some, such as Aronson, argue that because Israel retains a "security envelope" around Gaza, controlling who and what goes in and out of the territory, disengagement did not terminate occupation.[10] In contrast stand the revised views of Bruderlein on the nature of effective military control.[11] Bruderlein states that effective military control is essentially a question of fact, and is not dependent on the size and distribution of the occupying forces within a territory. He cites the *Tsemel* case before the Israel Supreme Court which held that occupation forces do not need to be in actual control of all the territory and population, but simply have the potential capability to do so.[12] This ruling is in accordance with the decision in the *List* case by the U.S. Military Tribunal at Nuremberg,[13] and also with the *Naletili and Martinovi* case before the International Criminal Tribunal for the Former Yugoslavia. In the latter, the Trial Chamber referred to an occupant having "a sufficient force present, or the capacity to send troops within a reasonable time to make the authority of the occupying power felt".[14] Nevertheless, Bruderlein continues, and this is the change introduced into the revised version, that,

> some form of military presence on land remains a necessary condition for an occupation, i.e. a military occupation cannot be solely imposed by the control of the national airspace by a foreign air force...or of the national seashore by a foreign navy. The law of occupation belongs historically to the law of land warfare which requires, at its core, a land-based security presence.[15]

Again the question arises: which view is correct? Is the question wider than one that is dependent simply on the law of land warfare? Bruderlein's positioning of occupation questions solely within this context may be seen as rather formalistic. It is important to bear in mind that the situation is not one of creating an occupation, which as a practical matter would appear to require

---

10 Aronson, above n. 4, p. 51; see pp. 51-53.

11 See Bruderlein, C., *Legal aspects of Israel's disengagement plan under international humanitarian law*. <http://www.ihlresearch.org/opt/pdfs/briefing3466.pdf>. This paper was initially issued in, and is dated, November 2004 but at some later point it was revised, modifying the original analysis of "effective military control". The paper does not indicate that it has been amended and, moreover, it retains its original date. I am grateful to Anne Massagee for drawing this to my attention.

12 See Bruderlein, above n. 11, p. 9, n.14. *Tsemel v. Minister of Defence*, HCJ 102/82, 37(3) Piskei Din 365; also cited employing a more extended quotation in Lein, Y., *One big prison: freedom of movement to and from the Gaza Strip on the eve of the Disengagement Plan* (B'Tselem/HaMoked: Jerusalem: 2005; and <www.hamoked.org.il/items/12800_eng.pdf>) pp. 73-74. *Tsemel* is summarised in 13 *Israel Yearbook on Human Rights* 360 (1983), see pp. 362-363 in particular. This and the following cases dealing with "effective occupation" are discussed in more detail below.

13 See *Trial of Wilhelm List and others* (the *Hostages* trial), VIII Law Reports of Trials of War Criminals 34 (1949), pp. 55-56.

14 *Prosecutor v. Naletili and Martinovi*, Case No.IT-98-34-T (trial judgment, 31 March 2003), available at: <www.un.org/icty/naletilic/trialc/judgement/nal-tj030331-e.pdf>, p. 74, para. 217. In support of this ruling, the Trial Chamber cited as authority the United Kingdom's *Manual of military law of war on land*, Part III, paras. 502 and 506 (1958); the United States' *The law of land warfare: Field manual No.27-10*, Chapter 6, para. 356 (1956); and the New Zealand Defence Force's *Interim law of armed conflict manual*, paras. 1302.2, 1302.3 and 1302.5 (1992).

15 Bruderlein, above n. 11, p. 9.

the use of ground forces to create and maintain control,[16] but rather is whether an existing occupation has been terminated or maintained. Termination could well involve different considerations: the conditions required to end an occupation are not as clearly delineated in the governing instruments as those which determine whether and when an occupation has been established. As von Glahn comments, "most books on international law make little mention of the intricate and numerous problems arising at the end of...military occupation".[17]

4 IS THE END OF OCCUPATION PURELY A FACTUAL QUESTION?

Occupation has been described as "a transitional period following invasion and preceding the cessation of hostilities" which "imposes more onerous duties on an occupying power than on a party to an international armed conflict".[18] The term is not defined in 1949 Geneva Convention IV relative to the Protection of Civilian Persons in Time of War: on the whole it relies on the definition contained in the Regulations annexed to 1907 Hague Convention IV respecting the Laws and Customs of War on Land which have the status of customary international law.[19]

It is settled that the test which determines the start of an occupation is essentially a question of fact,[20] albeit one which must be distinguished from invasion pure and simple:

> Invasion is the marching or riding of troops – or the flying of military aircraft – into enemy country. Occupation is invasion plus taking possession of enemy country for the purpose of holding it, at any rate temporarily. The difference between mere

---

16 von Glahn raises the hypothesis of an occupation being created through control of a territory's airspace: "Since international law does not contain a rule prescribing the military arm through which an effective belligerent occupation is to be exercised, it might be theoretically possible to maintain necessary control through the occupant's air force alone". Nevertheless he comments that the practical problems which would arise in this type of occupation "would seem to rule out such an experiment". See von Glahn, G., *The occupation of enemy territory: a commentary on the law and practice of belligerent occupation* (University of Minnesota Press: Minneapolis: 1957), pp. 28-29.

17 von Glahn, above n.16, p. 257.

18 *Prosecutor v Naletili and Martinovi*: <www.un.org/icty/naletilic/trialc/judgement/nal-tj030331-e.pdf>, p. 73, para. 214.

19 See *Prosecutor v Naletili and Martinovi*: <www.un.org/icty/naletilic/trialc/judgement/nal-tj030331-e.pdf>, p. 73, para. 215. The customary nature of the Hague Regulations was declared by the International Criminal Tribunal at Nuremberg in the *Trial of German major war criminals*, Cmd. 6964 (1946) p. 65. The customary status of the Regulations has since been affirmed by various other courts, see, e.g. *In re Krupp* (U.S. Military Tribunal at Nuremberg), 15 Annual Digest 620, p. 622; *R. v Finta* (Canadian High Court of Justice), 82 ILR 425, p. 439; *Affo v. IDF Commander in the West Bank* (Israel High Court), 83 ILR 122, p. 163; *Polyukhovich v. Commonwealth of Australia* (Australian High Court), 91 ILR 1, p. 123. See also Meron, T., *Human Rights and Humanitarian Norms as Customary Law* (Clarendon Press: Oxford: 1989), pp. 38-40.

20 See McNair, A. and Watts, A.D., *The Legal Effects of War* (Cambridge UP: Cambridge: 1966, 4th Edn.), pp. 377-378; and Schwarzenberger, G., *International Law as applied by International Courts and Tribunals. Vol.II: The Law of Armed Conflict* (Stevens: London: 1968), p. 324.

invasion and occupation becomes apparent from the fact that an occupant sets up some kind of administration, whereas the mere invader does not.[21]

This distinction flows clearly from the terms of Articles 42 and 43 of the Hague Regulations, which provide:

42. Territory is considered occupied when it is actually placed under the authority of the hostile army.

The occupation extends only to the territory where such authority has been established and can be exercised.[22]

43. The authority of the legitimate power having in fact passed into the hands of the occupant, the latter shall take all the measures in his power to restore, and ensure, as far as possible, public order and safety, while respecting, unless absolutely prevented, the laws in force in the country.

Thus, in the *List* case, the U.S. Military Tribunal ruled that

an occupation indicates the exercise of governmental authority to the exclusion of the established government. This presupposes the destruction of organised resistance and the establishment of an administration to preserve law and order. To the extent that the occupant's control is maintained and that of the civil government eliminated, the area will be said to be occupied.[23]

Traditionally, the test for the termination of an occupation was seen as a simple corollary of this, and likewise a question of fact – "Occupation comes to an end when an occupant withdraws from a territory, or is driven out of it":[24]

---

21 Oppenheim, L., *International Law: a Treatise. Vol.II: Disputes, War and Neutrality* (Longman: London: 1952, 7th Edn. by Lauterpacht, H.) (hereinafter Oppenheim-Lauterpacht), p. 434: see also, *Re Lepore*, 13 Annual Digest of Public International Law Cases 354 (Supreme Military Tribunal, Italy: 1946) at p. 355; *Disability pension case*, 90 International Law Reports 400 (Federal Social Court, F.R. Germany: 1985) at p. 403; and von Glahn, above, n.16, pp. 28-29. See also below on the notion of effective control of occupied territory.

22 Given *Operation Summer Rain*, it is worth emphasising that Geneva Convention IV comes into operation in relation to the civilian population earlier than the provisions of Section III of the Hague Regulations which deal with belligerent occupation. Article 6 of Geneva Convention IV provides that it applies "from the outset of any conflict or occupation mentioned in Article 2". The International Committee of the Red Cross' commentary to Article 6 states that this language was employed to indicate that the Convention "became applicable as soon as the first acts of violence were committed...Mere frontier incidents may make the Convention applicable, for they may be the beginning of a more widespread conflict. The Convention should be applied as soon as troops are in foreign territory and in contact with the civilian population." Accordingly, the term "occupation" in Article 6 bears a wider meaning than in Article 42 of the Hague regulations: "So far as individuals are concerned, the application of the Fourth Geneva Convention does not depend upon the existence of a state of occupation within the meaning of Article 42...The relations between the civilian population of a territory and troops advancing into that territory, whether fighting or not, are governed by the present Convention. There is no intermediate period between what might be termed the invasion phase and the inauguration of a stable regime of occupation. Even a patrol which penetrates into enemy territory without any intention of staying there must respect the Convention in its dealings with the civilians it meets." Pictet, J. (ed), *Commentary to Geneva Convention IV relative to the protection of civilian persons in time of war* (ICRC: Geneva: 1958) pp. 59-60. See also Mettraux, G., *International Crimes and the Ad Hoc Tribunals* (Oxford U.P.: Oxford: 2005) pp. 64-71; and *Prosecutor v. Naletili and Martinovi*: <www.un.org/icty/naletilic/trialc/judgement/nal-tj030331-e.pdf>, pp. 74-75, paras. 219-221.

23 VIII Law Reports of Trials of War Criminals 34 (1949), pp. 55-56.

the moment the invader voluntarily evacuates [occupied] territory, or is driven away by a *levée en masse*, or by troops of the other belligerent, or of his ally, the former condition of things *ipso facto* revives. The territory and individuals affected are at once, so far as International Law is concerned, considered again to be under the sway of their legitimate sovereign. For all events of international importance taking place on such territory the legitimate sovereign is again responsible towards third States, whereas during the period of occupation the occupant was responsible.[25]

This traditional test depends entirely upon factual criteria to the exclusion of normative considerations. This approach now appears inadequate – for instance, it fails to take into account the possibility, far less the legitimacy, of the termination of an occupation under the auspices of the Security Council, as occurred in Iraq.[26] Also, during the drafting of the Geneva Conventions, the view was expressed that in prolonged occupations there could be a gradual transfer of powers to the administrative departments of the occupied power, but that this would not alter the fact of occupation.[27]

Facts are undoubtedly important to determine when an occupation ends – "Who effectively exercises the authority? Is it the new government? Or is it still the former occupying power? International recognition by states and the United Nations is likely to play an important role"[28] – but is a test which is essentially dependent on an instrument a century old still fitted for contemporary conditions?[29]

At the Diplomatic Conference which culminated in the adoption of the 1977 Additional Protocols to the 1949 Geneva Conventions, the majority of participating States emphasised that, in order to maintain the unity of international law, international humanitarian law could not be isolated and self-contained but had to take into account the rules of general international

---

24 Oppenheim-Lauterpacht, above, n. 21, p. 436: see also Heintschel von Heinegg, W., *Factors in war to peace transitions*, 27 Harvard Journal of Law and Public Policy 843 (2003-2004), at p. 845: "The end of an occupation is a question of fact. It will be brought about by any loss of authority over the territory in question".

25 Oppenheim-Lauterpacht, above n. 21, p. 618.

26 See Security Council resolution 1546 (8 June 2004), reproduced 43 *International Legal Materials* 1459 (2004); and also Carcano, A., *End of occupation in 2004? The status of the multinational force in Iraq after the transfer of sovereignty to the interim Iraqi government*, 11 Journal of Conflict and Security Law 41 (2006); McCarthy, C., *The paradox of the international law of military operations: sovereignty and the reformation of Iraq*, 10 ibid 43 (2005); and Roberts, A., *The end of occupation: Iraq 2004*, 54 International and Comparative Law Quarterly 27 (2005). For critical accounts of the conduct of the occupation of Iraq, see, Afsha, E., *Limits and limitations of power: the continued relevance of occupation law*, 7 German Law Journal 563 (2006) available at: <www.germanlawjournal.com>; and Fox, G.H., *The occupation of Iraq*, 36 Georgetown Journal of International Law 195 (2005).

27 See Pictet, above n. 22, pp. 62-63: for the *travaux*, see *Final Record of the Diplomatic Conference of Geneva of 1949* (Federal Political Department: Berne: 1949), Vol. IIA, pp. 623-625, 775-776 and 815-816, and Vol. IIB, pp. 386-388. Compare Dinstein, Y., *The international legal status of the West Bank and the Gaza Strip–1998*, 28 Israel Yearbook on Human Rights 37 (1998).

28 Lavoyer, J.P., *Jus in bello: occupation law and the war in Iraq*, 98 ASIL Proc 121 (2004), p. 123. On the importance of the recognition of the termination of occupation, see Pictet, above n. 22, p.63; and also Aronson, above n. 4, pp. 59-61.

29 Article 6 of 1949 Geneva Convention IV does not deal with the end of occupation *per se*, but with the conditions under which the Convention ceases to apply, whether in whole or in part: see, Pictet, above n. 22, pp. 58-64.

law. In this connection, emphasis was placed on the need to adapt international humanitarian law to conform with the principle expounded by the International Court of Justice in the *Namibia Advisory Opinion*,[30] namely that "an international instrument must be interpreted and applied within the overall framework of the juridical system in force at the time of the interpretation".[31] Accordingly, can it be argued that developments in international law since 1907 have amended the traditional test used to determine the end of occupation by introducing normative factors?

The assumption embedded in the traditional test is that occupation terminates when authority passes back into the hands of the displaced sovereign. This must be a genuine transfer and not simply a pretence which masks a retention of authority by the occupant. To employ Roberts' phrase, "it is the reality not the label that counts",[32] as:

> the withdrawal of occupying forces is not the sole criterion of the ending of an occupation; and the occupant has not necessarily withdrawn at the end of all occupations.[33]

The nature of the authority that must be exercised by a post-occupation government in order to establish that the occupation has effectively ended can only be sovereignty, the classic formulation of which is that of Judge Huber in the *Island of Palmas* case:

> Sovereignty in the relations between States signifies independence. Independence in relation to a portion of the globe is the right to exercise therein, to the exclusion of any other State, the functions of a State.[34]

The determination whether a post-occupation entity is truly sovereign, able to exercise actual independence over the territory in question, is not a simple matter of fact but introduces normative factors into the issue.[35]

Further, self-determination, which has been termed "one of the essential principles of contemporary international law",[36] may also be relevant. It should be recalled that in the *Legal Consequences of the Construction of a Wall in the Occupied Palestinian Territory* advisory opinion,[37] the International Court of Justice authoritatively affirmed the entitlement of the Palestinian people to

---

30 See Sandoz Y *et al.* (eds), *Commentary on the Additional Protocols of 8 June 1977 to the Geneva Conventions of 12 August 1949* (ICRC: Geneva: 1987), pp. 51-52.

31 *Legal consequences for States of the continued presence of South Africa in Namibia (South West Africa), notwithstanding Security Council resolution 276 (1970) advisory opinion*, ICJ Rep, 1971, 16 at p. 31, para. 53.

32 Roberts, above, n. 26, p. 47.

33 Roberts, above n. 26, p. 28.

34 *Island of Palmas case* (United States/Netherlands, 1928), 2 Reports of International Arbitral Awards 829, p. 838. The "classic" judicial definition of independence is that of Judge Anzilotti in the *Austro-German Customs Union advisory opinion*, PCIJ, Ser.A/B, No.41, pp. 57-58 (1931).

35 On the disjunction between formal and actual independence in the context of Statehood, see Crawford, J., *The Creation of States in International Law* (Clarendon Press: Oxford: 2006, 2nd Edn.), pp. 62-89.

36 *East Timor case* (Portugal v. Australia), ICJ Rep, 1995, 90 at p. 102, para. 29.

37 *Legal consequences of the construction of a wall in the occupied Palestinian territory advisory opinion*, 9 July 2004: text available on the website of the International Court of Justice: <www.icj-cij.org>, and also as UN Doc.A/ES-10/273 (13 July 2004), and at 43 International Legal Materials 1009 (2004).

the right of self-determination, ruling that this had also been recognised by Israel.[38] The Court further held that self-determination was a right *erga omnes*, whose realisation all U.N. Member States, by virtue of General Assembly resolution 2625 (XXV) (24 October 1970),[39] as well as all States parties to the U.N. Covenants on Human Rights by virtue of common Article 1 of these Covenants, had the duty to promote.[40] Further, as Roberts notes, the "essential feature of the ending of an occupation is often, though not always, an act of self-determination", although he cautions that this cannot be "the sole decisive criterion for determining when an occupation ends".[41]

Self-determination has had a direct influence on specific treaty provisions that unequivocally form part of international humanitarian law *per se*. This is particularly true of 1977 Additional Protocol I:[42] self-determination provided an important part of the substantive normative backdrop to the negotiation of this instrument. Before the convening of the Diplomatic Conference that led to the conclusion of Additional Protocol I, the General Assembly adopted resolution 3103 (XXVIII) (12 December 1973), which was entitled *Basic principles of the legal status of the combatants struggling against colonial and alien domination and racist régimes*. This recalled in its penultimate preambular paragraph that there was a "need for the elaboration of additional international instruments and norms envisaging, *inter alia*, the increase of the protection of persons struggling for freedom against colonial and alien domination and racist régimes". The fourth preambular paragraph reaffirmed that such struggles were undertaken in exercise of the right of self-determination.

A consequence of the influence of self-determination on Additional Protocol I was the adoption of Article 1.4 which extended the definition of international armed conflict to encompass "armed conflicts in which peoples are fighting against colonial domination and alien occupation[43] and against racist régimes in the exercise of their right of self-determination". Wilson notes that this provision demonstrated widespread support for self-determination as an established legal right.[44] Governments which opposed or abstained in the vote

---

38 *Legal consequences of a wall* Advisory Opinion, 43 International Legal Materials (2004), pp. 1041-1042, para.118.

39 In the *Nicaragua* case, the International Court ruled that resolution 2625 expressed rules of customary international law – see *Military and paramilitary activities in and against Nicaragua case: merits judgment (Nicaragua v. United States)*, ICJ Rep. 1986, 14 at pp. 99-100, para.188: see also *Legal consequences of a wall* Advisory Opinion, 43 International Legal Materials (2004), p. 1034, para.87.

40 *Legal consequences of a wall* Advisory Opinion, 43 International Legal Materials (2004) 1034, para. 88: see also, p. 1053, paras. 155-156.

41 Roberts, above n. 26, p. 8.

42 1977 Protocol I Additional to the Geneva Conventions of 12 August 1949: Israel is not a party to this treaty, although a number of its provisions express customary international law.

43 Sandoz, above n. 30, p. 54 notes: "The expression 'alien occupation' in the sense of this paragraph – as distinct from belligerent occupation in the traditional sense of all or part of the territory of one State being occupied by another State – covers cases of partial or total occupation of a territory which has not yet been fully formed as a State." Notes omitted: see also Cassese, A., *Self-determination of Peoples: a Legal Reappraisal* (Cambridge U.P.: Cambridge: 1995), 90 *et seq.*

44 Wilson, H., *International Law and the Use of Force by National Liberation Movements* (Clarendon Press: Oxford: 1988), pp. 77-78.

on Article 1.4[45] did so because they thought that the criteria it employed were arbitrary and subjective, and feared that it would lead to an unequal and partial application of international humanitarian law. No delegation argued that the use of force in pursuit of self-determination was, in itself, illegitimate.[46]

Accordingly, self-determination has been recognised as a relevant factor in international humanitarian law, but its constituent treaties do not determine its consequences, if any, in the termination of an occupation. This is a matter which must be determined by examining the import, contours and inter-relationship of the doctrines in issue:

> The law of war is to be found not only in treaties, but in the customs and practices of states which gradually obtained universal recognition, and from the general principles of justice applied by jurists and practised by military courts. The law is not static, but by continual adaptation follows the needs of a changing world. Indeed, in many cases treaties do no more than express and define for more accurate reference the principles of law already existing.[47]

5 EFFECTIVE CONTROL – THE TRADITIONAL DOCTRINE

Article 42 of the Hague Regulations provides that territory is occupied when it is actually under the authority of the adversary, but that occupation extends only to the territory where that authority "has been established and can be exercised". As Oppenheim-Lauterpacht observes, this definition "is not at all precise" but that when an occupant is able to assert authority over territory "it matters not with what means, and in what ways, his authority is exercised".[48] The test is one of effective control, but the conditions by which this is established varies with the nature of the territory. An occupant need only deploy troops strategically to occupy a larger area:[49]

> for occupation of an area it is not necessary to keep troops permanently stationed throughout that area. It is sufficient that the national forces have withdrawn, that the inhabitants have been disarmed, that measures have been taken to protect life and property and to secure order, and that troops are available, if necessary to enforce authority in the area.[50]

---

45 Article 1.4 was adopted by 87 votes to 1, with 11 abstentions – only Israel cast a negative vote: the abstaining States were Canada, Federal Republic of Germany, France, Guatemala, Ireland, Italy, Japan, Monaco, Spain, the United Kingdom, and the United States – see Wilson, above n. 44, p. 165.

46 Wilson, above, n. 44, p. 128.

47 *List* trial, VIII Law Reports of Trials of War Criminals 34 (1949), p. 54.

48 Oppenheim-Lauterpacht, above, n. 21, p. 435.

49 See, e.g. Lein, above, n. 12, p. 74; Oppenheim-Lauterpacht, above, n. 21, p. 435; and also the separate opinion of Judge Kooijmans in the *Armed activities on the territory of the Congo* case, *Democratic Republic of the Congo v. Uganda*, 19 December 2005, available on the International Court's website: <www.icj-cij.org>, and at 45 International Legal Materials 353 (2006), p. 360, paras.42-49: compare the judgment of the Court, *ibid*, pp. 310-311, paras.172-179.

50 U.K. Ministry of Defence, *The Manual of the Law of Armed Conflict* (Oxford U.P.: Oxford: 2004), p. 276, para. 11.3.2.

Israel's withdrawal from Gaza, the Law of Occupation and of Self-Determination 13

As Benvenisti notes, however, although an occupant has the legal duty to establish an administration of territory it occupies, today this "is the rare exception rather than the rule".[51] Thus, in the *Armed activities on the territory of the Congo* case, Judge Kooijmans noted in his separate opinion:

> Occupants feel more and more inclined to make use of arrangements where authority is said to be exercised by transitional governments or rebel movements or where the occupant simply refrains from establishing an administrative system.[52]

Further, as the U.S. Military Tribunal held in the *List* case, when considering the effect of resistance to occupation:

> While it is true that the partisans were able to control sections of these countries [Greece, Yugoslavia and Norway] at various times, it is established that the Germans could at any time they desired assume physical control of any part of the country. The control of the resistance forces was temporary only and did not deprive the German Armed Forces of its status of an occupant.[53]

Similarly, in the *Tselem* case, which was heard before the Israel High Court and dealt with the internment of individuals by the IDF in Southern Lebanon in 1982, Justice Shamgar ruled that the application of the laws of war, including Geneva Convention IV, to an occupied area was not dependent on the existence of a durable belligerent occupation or the creation of a military administration in the area,[54] but rather:

> One of the tests is whether the military forces are capable of entering into the shoes of the previous governing bodies, and not just that they did so in practice...Applicability of the third chapter of the Hague Regulations and applicability of the comparable provisions of the Fourth [Geneva] Convention are not dependent on the existence of a special organized system that takes the form of a military government. The duties and powers of the military forces, resulting from effective occupation of a particular territory, arise and are created as a result of military control of the territory, that is, even if the military forces maintain control only by means of regular combat units, without having a special military framework for the [military] government's needs.[55]

This ruling is supported by the judgment of the International Court in the *Armed activities in the Congo (D.R.C. v. Uganda)* case. The Court ruled that a Ugandan occupation of Congolese territory would be established if its forces "had substituted their own authority for that of the Congolese Government", and it would be irrelevant "whether or not Uganda had established a structured military administration of the territory occupied".[56]

---

51 Benvenisti, E., *The International Law of Occupation* (Princeton U.P.: Princeton: 1993) pp. 4-5: see also, *U.K.* Manual, above, n. 50, p. 276, para. 11.3.1; *Prosecutor v. Tadi?*, Case No. IT-94-1-T (trial judgment, 7 May 1997): <www.un.org/icty/tadic/trialc2/judgement/tad-tsj70507JT2-e.pdf> pp. 204-205, para.584; and *Prosecutor v. Blaski*, Case No. IT-95-14-T (trial judgment 3 March 2000): <www.un.org/icty/blaskic/trialc1/judgement/bla-tj000303e.pdf> p. 51, para. 149.

52 45 *International Legal Materials* 271 (2006), 353 at p. 359, para. 41.

53 VIII *Law Reports of Trials of War Crimes Trials* 34 (1949), p. 56.

54 13 *Israel Yearbook on Human Rights* 318 (1983), p. 363.

55 *Tselem* judgment, as translated and quoted in Lein, above, n. 12, pp. 73-74.

56 45 *International Legal Materials* 271 (2006), p. 310, para.173.

The view that effective occupation could lie in the capacity to assert control was also affirmed by the Yugoslav Tribunal in *Prosecutor v Naletili and Martinovi* where it ruled that one of the guidelines to determine whether an occupation was established was whether "the occupying power has a sufficient force present, or the capacity to send troops within a reasonable time to make the authority of the occupying power felt".[57] Indeed, there is arguably even some authority that occupation can arise when a threat of force is followed by capitulation:

> It is not necessary to discuss here the question whether Germany was technically a belligerent power at all in relation to Czechoslovakia when control was assumed by the former country without any armed resistance on the part of the latter. If submission by the victim to a threat of immediate invasion relieves the other party of the character of a belligerent, the case for the application in our Courts of the same rules as to the consequences of control would appear to be an *a fortiori* one.[58]

Probably little weight should now be placed on this ruling, as the situation it envisages was subsequently expressly regulated by Article 2.2 of Geneva Convention IV, which provides that the Convention applies to all instances of the partial or total occupation of the territory of a High Contracting Party, even if this "meets with no armed resistance".[59] Nevertheless, the authorities are agreed that occupation can be established and maintained when the occupant has the capacity to exert control over territory. Once established, does this require a physical presence on the ground, or can an occupation be maintained by other means?

6 EFFECTIVE CONTROL AND THE CHANGED NATURE OF WARFARE

When the Hague Regulations were adopted in 1907, aerial warfare was (at most) rudimentary, although Article 25 prohibited the attack or bombardment of undefended towns, villages, dwellings and buildings "by whatever means". This phrase was intended to encompass aerial warfare. On the same day the Conference adopted its various Conventions, 18 October 1907,[60] it also adopted Declaration XIV prohibiting the Discharge of Projectiles and Explosives from Balloons. This prohibited "the discharge of projectiles and explosives from balloons or by other new methods of a similar nature". Although technically still in force, this Declaration has few parties and has been rendered obsolete by subsequent practice.

---

57 *Prosecutor v. Naletili and Martinovi:* <www.un.org/icty/naletilic/trialc/judgement/nal-tj030331-e.pdf>, p. 74, para. 217.
58 *Anglo-Czechoslovak and Prague Credit Bank v. Janssen* (Australia: Supreme Court of Victoria, 1943), 1943-45 Annual Digest 43, p. 47.
59 On the interpretation of this provision, see Pictet, above, n. 22, pp. 21-22.
60 The Wright brothers' first flight of 39 metres, which lasted 12 seconds at an altitude of just over 3 metres, took place on 17 December 1907.

Oppenheim-Lauterpacht indicates that international law is indifferent as to the manner by which authority is exercised over occupied territory,[61] and von Glahn thinks it at least theoretically possible that an occupation may be maintained through the control of the adversary's airspace.[62] Bruderlein, on the other hand, argues that land-based forces are indispensable for an occupation, which cannot be created by an adversary's control of airspace or maritime zones.[63] There is some virtue in Bruderlein's claim; he correctly notes that the no-fly zone over southern Iraq[64] did not amount to belligerent occupation, but should there not be a difference between the creation of an occupation and its subsequent maintenance? If, once an occupation is established, effective control lies in the capacity to make the authority of the occupying power felt within a reasonable time or, in the words of Israel's High Court, to "maintain control only by means of regular combat units", then is there any reason why this should not be done through aerial warfare? Indeed, the importance of air power was stressed by Major General Amos Yadlin in 2004 after he became head of Israeli military intelligence. An Israeli air force officer, he stated:

> Our vision of air control zeroes in on the notion of control. We're looking at how you control a city or a territory from the air when it's no longer legitimate to hold or occupy that territory on the ground.[65]

Further, at least in the circumstances of Gaza, only to consider Israel's withdrawal of ground troops and continued control of its airspace in isolation is to ignore the wider context.

7 EFFECTIVE CONTROL AND GAZA – THE WIDER CONTEXT

Apart from the military method by which effective control may be exercised and Israel's enforcement of its "security envelope" around Gaza – its control of terrestrial borders, whether as principal or through the agency of Egypt and the E.U.'s Border Assistance Mission, and of Gaza's maritime zones and airspace – other issues are relevant to determine whether Gaza remained occupied after implementation of the Disengagement Plan.

An assessment of these issues must proceed at two distinct normative levels. General international law is relevant to the analysis of the situation not simply for Israel and Palestine but, importantly, also for third States. Equally pertinent, however, are the specific bilateral obligations assumed by Israel and Palestine

---

61 Oppenheim-Lauterpacht, above, n. 21, p. 35.

62 von Glahn, above, n. 16, pp. 28-29.

63 Bruderlein, above, n. 11, p. 9.

64 For an account, see Malone, D.M., *The International Struggle over Iraq: Politics in the U.N. Security Council 1980-2005* (Oxford U.P.: Oxford: 2006) 97-101; and also Schmitt, M.N., *Clipped wings: effective and legal no-fly zone rules of engagement*, 20 Loyola LA *International and Comparative Law Journal* 727 (1997-98).

65 Quoted in Li, D., *The Gaza Strip as laboratory: notes in the wake of disengagement*, 35 Journal of Palestine Studies 38 (2006), p. 48.

as a result of the instruments adopted during the Oslo process.[66] The 1969 Vienna Convention on the Law of Treaties does not govern the Oslo instruments because one of the parties, the Palestine Liberation Organisation, is not a State. The Vienna Convention consciously adopted a restricted definition of treaties for its purposes, reflected in Article 1 which expressly provides: "The present Convention applies to treaties between States."[67] Further, Article 2.1.a defines a treaty as "an international agreement concluded between States in written form and governed by international law, whether embodied in a single instrument or in two or more related instruments and whatever its particular designation". Article 3 of the Vienna Convention, however, provides that the Convention does not prejudice the legal force of "international agreements concluded between States and other subjects of international law", nor the application to them of rules contained in the Convention which have customary status.[68] On the basis of customary law, Watson convincingly argues that the Oslo instruments are binding bilateral treaties.[69]

Further, neither Israel nor Palestine has claimed that the 1995 Israel-Palestine Liberation Organisation Interim Agreement, in particular, has terminated as the result of the operation of the customary law of treaties following alleged material breach or by the operation of the *clasula rebus sic stantibus*.[70] Indeed, Section 1 (*Political and Security Implications*) Principle Seven of the Disengagement Plan expressly contemplates the continued applicability of these instruments:

> The process set forth in the plan is without prejudice to the relevant agreements between the State of Israel and the Palestinians. Relevant arrangements shall continue to apply.

---

66 Principally, the 1993 Israel-Palestine Liberation Organisation Declaration of Principles on Interim Self-Government Arrangements, 32 International Legal Materials 1525 (1993); 1994 Israel-Palestine Liberation Organisation Agreement on the Gaza Strip and Jericho Area, 33 *ibid* 622 (1994); 1995 Israel-Palestine Liberation Organisation Interim Agreement on Implementation of the Declaration of Principles, 36 *ibid* 551 (1997); 1997 Israel-Palestine Liberation Organisation Protocol concerning the Redeployment in Hebron, 36 *ibid* 650 (1997); 1998 Israel-Palestine Liberation Organisation Wye River Memorandum, 37 *ibid* 1251 (1998); and 1999 Israel-Palestine Liberation Organisation Sharm el-Sheikh Memorandum on Implementation Timeline of Outstanding Commitments Signed and the Resumption of Permanent Status Negotiations, 38 *ibid* 1465 (1999).

67 See the Final Draft Articles and Commentary on the Law of Treaties adopted by the International Law Commission in 1966, reproduced Watts, A., *The International Law Commission 1949-1998* (Oxford U.P.: Oxford: 1999), Volume II, p. 619, *Commentary to draft Article 1*, para. 2.

68 See *Commentary to draft Article 3*, Watts, above, n. 67, pp. 626-627.

69 See Watson, G.R., *The Oslo Accords: International Law and the Israeli-Palestinian Peace Agreements* (Oxford U.P.: Oxford: 2000) pp. 57-102, and his *The "wall" decisions in legal and political context*, 99 American Journal of International Law 6 (2005), pp. 22-24: see also Benvenisti, E., *The Israeli-Palestinian Declaration of Principles: a framework for future settlement*, 4 European Journal of International Law 542 (1993); but compare Sabel, R., *Review of Watson's "The Oslo Accords"*, 95 American Journal of International Law 248 (2001), pp. 249-251.

70 See, e.g. Watson, above, n. 69 (*Wall decisions*), p. 23.

Israel's withdrawal from Gaza, the Law of Occupation and of Self-Determination 17

Nevertheless, the implementation of the Disengagement Plan expressly contemplates a unilateral change by Israel of the legal status of Gaza – "the State of Israel is required to initiate moves not dependent on Palestinian cooperation"[71] – which, as Principle Six states, aims to "dispel the claims regarding Israel's responsibility for the Palestinians within the Gaza Strip".

A belligerent occupant bears duties in relation to the territory and its people; for instance, under Article 43 of the Hague Regulations, the duty to maintain public order within the territory, and under Articles 55 and 56 of 1949 Geneva Convention IV, the duties of ensuring that food and medical supplies are available to the population and of ensuring and maintaining public health and hygiene within the territory "to the fullest extent of the means available to it". As implementation of the Revised Disengagement Plan aimed to divest Israel of these and its other responsibilities, Principles Six and Seven are surely contradictory. For instance, Article XXXI.7 of the 1995 Israel-Palestine Liberation Organisation Interim Agreement on the West Bank and the Gaza Strip, which was re-affirmed in Article V of the Wye River Memorandum,[72] provides:

> Neither side shall initiate or take any step that will change the status of the West Bank and the Gaza Strip pending the outcome of the permanent status negotiations.

If Principle Six envisages a unilateral change effected by Israel in the status of Gaza, then this entails a breach of Article XXXI.7. It is difficult to see what guarantee against prejudice Principle Seven may afford in this eventuality.[73]

Crawford comments that the Oslo instruments "are remarkably unforthcoming on issues of status, no doubt because of fundamental disagreements between the parties".[74] That Israel did not relinquish authority within the Occupied Territories is clear from the provisions of the 1995 Interim Agreement which established and yet simultaneously circumscribed the powers of the Palestinian Interim Self-Government Authority (styled "the Council" in the Agreement). Pending its creation, these powers are to be exercised by the

---

71 Revised Disengagement Plan, Section 1 (*Political and Security Implications*), Principle One.

72 The Israeli Cabinet approved the Wye River Memorandum on 11 November 1998. This decision is available at: <www.mfa.gov.il/MFA/Peace+Process/Guide+to+the+Peace+Process/Government+Decision+on+the+Wye+River+Memorandum+N.htm>. It is worth noting that paragraph 8 of this decision provided: "The government asserts that a unilateral declaration by the Palestinian Authority on the establishment of a Palestinian state, prior to the achievement of a Final Status Agreement, would constitute a substantive and fundamental violation of the Interim Agreement. In the event of such a violation, the government would consider itself entitled to take all necessary steps, including the application of Israeli rule, law and administration to settlement areas and security areas in Judea, Samaria and Gaza as it sees fit. Israel reiterates its position, in accordance with the Agreement with the Palestinian Authority, that the final status must be the result of free negotiations between the parties without the implementation of unilateral steps which will change the status of the area." For commentary on this, see Crawford, above, n. 35, p. 445.

73 It should also be recalled that Section 1 (*Political and Security Implications*), Principle Three envisages the maintenance of settlements in the West Bank and thus contradicts, e.g. Interim Agreement Article XXXI.5 which expressly reserves the question of settlements for the permanent status negotiations.

74 Crawford, above, n.35, p. 433.

Palestinian Authority.[75] In implementing the 1993 Declaration of Principles, the 1995 Interim Agreement did not transfer sovereignty to the PLO but simply created a temporary régime until the outcome of the final status negotiations.[76] This is clear at the outset of the Interim Agreement, as Article I.1 provides:

> Israel shall transfer powers and responsibilities as specified in this Agreement from the Israeli military government and its Civil Administration to the Council in accordance with this Agreement. Israel shall continue to exercise powers and responsibilities not so transferred.

Article III.6 restricts the jurisdiction of the Council to those matters specified in Article XVII. In principle, the Council's jurisdiction is specified in Article XVII.1:

> In accordance with the [Declaration of Principles], the jurisdiction of the Council will cover West Bank and Gaza Strip territory as a single territorial unit, except for:
> (a) issues that will be negotiated in the permanent status negotiations: Jerusalem, settlements, specified military locations, Palestinian refugees, borders, foreign relations and Israelis: and
> (b) powers and responsibilities not transferred to the Council.

In relation to paragraph (a), Crawford points out that although this ostensibly defines the jurisdiction of the Palestinian Authority in "normal territorial terms", in practical effect its competence is restricted to "jurisdiction over Palestinians (and visitors)".[77] Further, Article XVIII.2 restricts the legislative power of the Council to matters over which it has jurisdiction, subject to the exigencies of paragraph 4.a:

> Legislation, including legislation which amends or abrogates existing laws or military orders, which exceeds the jurisdiction of the Council or which is otherwise inconsistent with the provisions of the [Declaration of Principles], this Agreement, or of any other agreement that may be reached between the two sides during the interim period, shall have no effect and shall be void *ab initio*.

These provisions clearly demonstrate that the Palestinian Authority does not possess the exclusive governmental powers which are characteristic of sovereignty. One can only concur with the opinion of a former Legal Adviser to the Israeli Ministry of Foreign Affairs that, under the Declaration of Principles and thus throughout the interim period, "the Palestinian Council will not be independent or sovereign in nature". Moreover:

---

75 1995 Interim Agreement, Article I.2 provides: "Pending the inauguration of the Council, the powers and responsibilities transferred to the Council shall be exercised by the Palestinian Authority established in accordance with the Gaza-Jericho Agreement, which shall also have all the rights, liabilities and obligations to be assumed by the Council in this regard. Accordingly, the term 'Council' throughout this Agreement shall, pending the inauguration of the Council, be construed as meaning the Palestinian Authority."

76 On the status and powers of the Palestinian Authority under the Interim Agreement, see Dajani, O.M., *Stalled between seasons: the international legal status of Palestine during the interim period*, 26 *Denver Journal of International Law and Policy* 27 (1997), pp. 60-74.

77 Crawford, above, n. 35, p. 444.

the military government will continue to be the source of authority for the Palestinian Council and the powers and responsibilities exercised by it in the West Bank and Gaza Strip.[78]

Of particular note is the retention by Israel of competence over foreign relations by virtue of Articles IX.5 and XVII.1.a. Singer argued that this was crucial in denying Statehood to the Palestinian entity pending the outcome of the final status negotiations.[79]

Consequently, the Palestinian Authority – "an interim local government body with restricted powers"[80] – may best be seen as an administration to which the occupant has devolved competence. The drafters of Geneva Convention IV had envisaged that this could occur during a prolonged occupation, without terminating that occupation.[81] As Bruderlein notes, the end of occupation requires the termination of the military control of the Occupying Power over the governmental affairs of the occupied population that limits that people's right to self-determination.[82] This resonates with Judge Huber's definition of independence in the *Island of Palmas case*, namely "the right to exercise therein, to the exclusion of any other State, the functions of a State".[83] Obviously occupation turns this on its head, as occupation lies in the exclusion of the right of the territorial sovereign to exercise power on its territory. Thus, for instance, in his separate opinion in the *Armed activities on the territory of the Congo* case, Judge Kooijmans quoted with approval from the United States' *Manual on the Law of Land Warfare*:

> occupation presupposes a hostile invasion, resisted or un-resisted, as a result of which the invader has rendered the invaded government incapable of exercising its authority, and [secondly] that the invader is in a position to substitute its own authority for that of the former government.[84]

Given the restrictions on the powers of the Palestinian Authority in the Interim Agreement, if Principle Seven of the Disengagement Plan is to be taken at face value in its avowal that "the plan is without prejudice to the relevant

---

78 Singer, J., *The Declaration of Principles on Interim Self-Government Arrangements: some legal aspects*: <gopher://israel-info.gov.il:70/00/mad/dop/ 940201s.dop>, on file with author. This article was also published by the International Association of Jewish Lawyers and Jurists in 1 Justice 4 (1994).

79 See Singer, J., *Aspects of foreign relations under the Israeli-Palestinian Agreements on interim self-government arrangements for the West Bank and Gaza*, 26 Israel Law Review 268 (1994), pp. 269-273.

80 Crawford, above, n. 35, p. 444.

81 See Pictet, above, n. 22, pp. 62-63, and pp. 272-276. As Dajani notes, above, n.76, pp. 77-78, there is a presumption against the creation of a new State on a territory under belligerent occupation. These are generally seen as puppet States which lack independence. See also Crawford, above, n. 35, pp. 78-83 and pp. 156-157; and Marek, K., *Identity and Continuity of States in Public International Law* (Droz: Geneva: 1968, 2nd Edn.), pp. 110-120. Dajani (at pp. 90-91) argues that separation between the PLO and Palestinian Authority preserves Palestinian negotiators' independence from Israel, and thus avoids the application of this presumption.

82 Bruderlein, above, n. 11, p. 1.

83 *Island of Palmas case* (United States/Netherlands, 1928), 2 Reports of International Arbitral Awards 829, p. 838.

84 Separate opinion of Judge Kooijmans, 45 International Legal Materials (2006) p. 360, para. 45.

agreements", then the Plan contains an intractable contradiction. It cannot both efface Israel's responsibilities for Gaza and yet maintain the legal integrity of the Oslo instruments.

If, however, implementation of the Disengagement Plan were to amount to a unilateral termination of occupation, all other things being equal, breach of treaty probably would not be fatal to an Israeli claim that it had successfully divested itself of responsibility for Gaza's population, even although this had been effected unlawfully in a manner which engaged Israel's responsibility. The legal consequences of breach of the Interim Agreement would, however, in principle only be relevant in the bilateral relations between Israel and Palestine. Palestine could choose either to pursue remedies available under Article XXI of the Interim Agreement,[85] or simply disregard the breach. For third States (and international organisations), breach of a bilateral agreement is a *res inter alios acta* in which they have no legal interest, and which entails no mandatory legal consequences for them.

8 TERMINATION OF OCCUPATION – A NEW NORMATIVITY?

Israel's obligations towards Gaza are not delimited solely by the law of occupation and the bilateral Olso instruments, but also by general international law.[86] It may be recalled that in the *Legal consequences of a wall* Advisory Opinion, the International Court of Justice authoritatively affirmed the entitlement of the Palestinian people to the right of self-determination, ruling that this had been recognised by Israel,[87] and moreover was a right *erga omnes* whose realisation all U.N. Member States had the duty to promote.[88] Disengagement concerns a possible change in the international status of territory. Given its status as an "essential principle" of contemporary international law, the principle of self-determination must play a significant role in the legal appraisal of disengagement, particularly in evaluating the implications for third States and international organisations.

---

85 Article XXI (Settlement of differences and disputes) provides: "Any difference relating to the application of this Agreement shall be referred to the appropriate coordination and cooperation mechanism established under this Agreement. The provisions of Article XV of the [Declaration of Principles] shall apply to any such difference which is not settled through the appropriate coordination and cooperation mechanism, namely:
  1. Disputes arising out of the application or interpretation of this Agreement or any related agreements pertaining to the interim period shall be settled through the Liaison Committee;
  2. Disputes which cannot be settled by negotiations may be settled by a mechanism of conciliation to be agreed between the Parties.
  3. The Parties may agree to submit to arbitration disputes relating to the interim period, which cannot be settled through conciliation. To this end, upon the agreement of both Parties, the Parties will establish an Arbitration Committee."
86 See Crawford, above, n. 35, pp. 448, n. 286.
87 43 *International Legal Materials* (2004), pp. 1041-1042, para. 118.
88 43 *International Legal Materials* (2004), pp. 1034, para. 88: see also, p. 1053, paras.155-156.

The International Law Commission's exegesis of the Court's jurisprudence argues that self-determination is not simply an obligation *erga omnes* which all States must respect, but also that it has *ius cogens* status. In other words, that it is peremptory – States cannot derogate from its exigencies in their international relations.[89] Doctrine affirms that there is a conceptual connection between the two categories of obligations *erga omnes* and *ius cogens* norms, but does not conclusively affirm their coincidence.[90] De Hoogh underlines that obligations *erga omnes* are essentially connected with remedies available to States following a breach of international law, whereas the notion of *ius cogens* norms places emphasis on their substantive content.[91] When considering the impact of self-determination on the law of occupation, the issue is that of the influence of its substantive content – in particular all States' duty to promote respect for and realisation of this right – rather than the remedies to which they may have recourse following a denial of self-determination.

Termination of occupation, to be legally effective, must be in conformity with the requirements of self-determination. This is a matter of concern to all States. If the exigencies of self-determination are disregarded, then this breach of self-determination can only entail a duty for States of non-recognition of the illegal situation thus created, as well as a duty not to render aid or assistance in maintaining that illegal situation.[92] Nor would States be absolved of their duty to promote, through joint and separate action, the actual realisation of the right of the people entitled to self-determination.[93]

In the *Legal consequences of a wall* Advisory Opinion, the Court's elucidation of the implications of the Palestinian people's right to self-determination is rather terse and couched abstractly. This attracted criticism from within the Court itself. For instance, while endorsing the Court's affirmation of the Palestinian people's right to self-determination, Judge Higgins thought it "quite detached from reality for the Court to find that it is the wall that presents a 'serious impediment' to the exercise of this right".[94] Nevertheless, elsewhere

---

89 International Law Commission, *Report of the work of the 53rd session*, U.N. Doc.A/56/10, *Commentary to Article 40* of its *2001 Articles on Responsibility of States for Internationally Wrongful Acts, ibid* 282 at p. 284, para. 5: reproduced at: <http://www.un.org/law/ilc/reports/2001/english/chp4.pdf>, and also, Crawford, J, *The International Law Commission's Articles on State Responsibility: Introduction, Text and Commentaries* (Cambridge U.P.: Cambridge: 2002), pp. 246-247.

90 See, for instance, de Hoogh, A.. *Obligations Erga Omnes and International Crimes* (Kluwer: The Hague: 1996), pp. 53-56, p. 91; and Ragazzi, M., *The Concept of International Obligations Erga Omnes* (Clarendon Press: Oxford: 1997), Chapter Three, p. 182 and p. 190. See also, Scobbie, I., *Unchart(er)ed waters?: consequences of the advisory opinion on the legal consequences of the construction of a wall in the Occupied Palestinian Territory for the responsibility of the UN for Palestine*, 16 European Journal of International Law 941 (2005), pp. 949-952.

91 de Hoogh, above, n. 90, p. 53: compare Ragazzi, above, n. 90, p. 203 et seq.

92 Compare *Legal consequences of a wall* Advisory Opinion, 43 International Legal Materials (2004) p. 1053, para. 159.

93 Compare *Legal consequences of a wall* Advisory Opinion, 43 International Legal Materials (2004), p. 1034, para.88 and p. 1053, para. 156.

94 *Legal consequences of a wall* Advisory Opinion, separate opinion of Judge Higgins, 43 *International Legal Materials* 1058 (2004), pp. 1062-1063, para. 30: see pp. 1062-1063, paras. 28-31.

and also in the context of an argument on self-determination, Judge Higgins cautioned against:

> the pursuance of a policy of legal deconstructionism – the systematic attempt to empty everything of all substance and meaning. Resolutions must be shown to say nothing. Findings must be shown not to have been made. The substantive rights of others must be shown to amount to nothing more than United Nations procedures that may or may not be invoked, but which have no objective existence of their own.[95]

The question is therefore that of identifying the content of self-determination – the aspects of the "objective existence" of this right – relevant to the termination of occupation.

Like many legal concepts, self-determination designates a core content and an associated, yet integral, bundle of rights and duties. The core content is clear:

> all peoples have the right freely to determine, without external interference, their political status and to pursue their economic, social and cultural development, and every State has the duty to respect this right in accordance with the provisions of the Charter.[96]

Further:

> The establishment of a sovereign and independent State, the free association or integration with an independent State or the emergence into any other political status freely determined by a people constitute modes of implementing the right of self-determination by that people.[97]

Following Drew's analysis,[98] self-determination has two distinct vectors. The classic formulation of its core content emphasises self-determination as process – the right freely to determine a political status – but this entails that self-determination must have a substantive content:

> the right to a process does not exhaust the content of the right of self-determination under international law. To confer on a people the right of "free choice" in the absence of more substantive entitlements – to territory, natural resources, etc – would simply be meaningless. Clearly, the right of self-determination cannot be exercised in a substantive vacuum. This is both explicit and implicit in the law. For example, implicit in any recognition of a people's right to self-determination is recognition of the legitimacy of that people's claim to a particular territory and/or set of resources...[T]he following can be deduced as a non-exhaustive list of the substantive entitlements conferred on a people by virtue of the law of self-determination...: (a) the right to exist – demographically and territorially – as a

---

95 Professor Higgins, advocate for Portugal, *East Timor case* (*Portugal v. Australia*), Pleadings, CR.1995/13 (13 February 1995), p. 8, para. 1.

96 General Assembly resolution 2625 (XXV) (24 October 1970), *Declaration on principles of international law concerning friendly relations and co-operation among States in accordance with the Charter of the United Nations:* affirmed *Legal consequences of a wall* Advisory Opinion, 43 International Legal Materials (2004), pp. 1034-1035, paras. 88-89.

97 General Assembly resolution 2625.

98 Drew C, *The East Timor story: international law on trial*, 12 European Journal of International Law 651 (2001).

Israel's withdrawal from Gaza, the Law of Occupation and of Self-Determination 23

people; (b) the right to territorial integrity; (c) the right to permanent sovereignty over natural resources; (d) the right to cultural integrity and development; and (e) the right to economic and social development.[99]

In connection with the Israeli planned withdrawal from Gaza, two aspects of self-determination take on particular importance: the exercise of the process, of the free determination by the Palestinian people of its political status; and the substantive issue of the integrity of the self-determination unit.

Drew notes that:

> Despite its text book characterization as part of human rights law, the law of self-determination has always been bound up more with notions of sovereignty and title to territory that what we traditionally consider to be "human rights".[100]

This uncontroversial view also found expression in Palestine's written statement to the International Court during the *Legal consequences of a wall* Advisory Opinion proceedings. Palestine repeatedly spoke of "the territorial sphere over which the Palestinian people are entitled to exercise their right of self-determination".[101]

Similarly, in the *East Timor case* proceedings, Portugal underlined that self-determination has a territorial basis, and that its exercise simultaneously decides both the destination of the people and of the territory. Portugal described the relationship between the people and the territory as a "principle of individuality". This entails that the territory which is the basis of the right is legally distinct from any other territory and, moreover, is entitled to territorial integrity. It forms a single unit which must not be dismembered. Further:

> un territoire qui constitue l'assise du droit d'un peuple á disposer de lui même...ne peut changer de statut juridique que par un acte d'autodétermination de ce peuple. La Résolution 1541 du 17 décembre 1960 de l'Assémblée générale précise bien cette norme.[102]

Leaving to one side East Jerusalem, which Israel has purported to annex despite the protests of other States and the United Nations that this is illegal,[103] Israel and the Palestine Liberation Organisation have agreed that the West Bank

---

99 Drew, above, n. 98, p. 663: paragraph break suppressed and notes omitted: for a similar affirmation of a substantive core content of self-determination, see Orakhelashvili, A., *The impact of peremptory norms on the interpretation and application of United Nations Security Council resolutions*, 16 European Journal of International Law 59 (2005), p. 64.

100 Drew, above, n. 98, p. 663.

101 See, e.g. *Legal consequences of a wall* Advisory Opinion Pleadings, Palestine Written Statement, p. 239, para. 548 and p. 240, para. 549.

102 *East Timor* Pleadings, Portuguese Memorial (18 November 1991), p. 195, para. 7.01: emphasis suppressed in quotation. See also *Legal consequences of a wall* Advisory Opinion Pleadings, League of Arab States Written Statement, p. 62, para. 8.2 and p. 76, para. 8.28.

103 For instance, for the views of the European Union, see, e.g. Marston, G. (ed.), *United Kingdom materials on international law*, 61 British Yearbook of International Law 463 (1990) p. 624; *ibid*, 62 British Yearbook 535 (1991), pp. 696, 697; and *ibid*, 64 British Yearbook 615 (1993), p. 724; for the United States' view, see 1976 *United States practice in international law*, p. 634, and for a consensus statement issued by the Security Council on 12 November 1976, see *ibid*, 711 at p. 712; see also, in particular, Security Council resolutions 476 (30 June 1980) and 478 (20 August 1980), and the review of Security Council action at *Legal consequences of a wall* Advisory Opinion, 43 International Legal Materials (2004), p. 1031, para. 75.

and Gaza form "a single territorial unit" whose integrity is to be preserved pending the conclusion of permanent status negotiations.[104] Consonant with the International Court's finding that the Interim Agreement affirmed the Palestinian people's right to self-determination,[105] this simply records the status and integrity of the West Bank and Gaza as a single self-determination unit, upon which the Palestinian people are entitled to exercise that right. Further, relying on the Interim Agreement, the Israel High Court has affirmed Israel's recognition of the unity of the West Bank and Gaza as a single territorial unit.[106]

In the case of withdrawal from Gaza, two aspects of self-determination assume fundamental importance: the substantive aspect of the territorial integrity of the self-determination unit; and the process aspect of the free expression of the will of the Palestinian people.

As Portugal declared in the *East Timor case* proceedings, the fundamental idea that dominates the exercise of the right of self-determination is that of freedom of choice:

> au sens où le choix accompli par la population concernée doit s'être effectué en l'absence de toute contrainte extérieure, notamment militaire.[107]

A situation imposed unilaterally by an occupant involves no choice on the part of the population entitled to self-determination, and thus cannot under any circumstances be considered as an exercise of that right. This does not observe – indeed it brazenly disregards – the process aspect of self-determination, and consequently cannot change the status of the territory in question. As Australia affirmed during the *East Timor case* proceedings, a State will:

> breach the obligation to respect the right of a people to self-determination if its conduct prevents or hinders the exercise by the people of a non-self-governing territory of their right freely to determine their future political status.[108]

Consequently, any claim that the international status of Gaza may be changed by virtue of unilateral action undertaken by Israel which does not take into account the free choice of the indigenous population is manifestly a breach of self-determination, in addition to a breach of the provisions of the Interim Agreement.

---

104 See the 1993 Declaration of Principles on Interim Self-Government Arrangements, Article IV; and the 1995 Washington Israeli-Palestinian Interim Agreement on the West Bank and the Gaza Strip, Article XI.1: for commentary, see Shehadeh, R., *From occupation to Interim Accords: Israel and the Palestinian Territories* (Kluwer: London: 1997), pp. 35-37.
 The question of Jerusalem is, of course, a matter reserved for the permanent status negotiations, see the *Agreed minutes* to the Declaration of Principles on Interim Self-Government Arrangements, *Understanding in relation to Article IV*; and 1995 Interim Agreement, Articles XVII.1 and XXXI.5.

105 *Legal consequences of a wall* Advisory Opinion, 43 International Legal Materials (2004), pp. 1041-1042, para.118.

106 *Ajuri v. IDF Commander, HCJ 7015/02* (3 September 2002), [2002] IsrLR 1, opinion of President Barak, pp. 17-18, para. 22. See also Lein, above n. 12, pp. 20-21, who notes, *inter alia*, that Israel incorporated the Interim Agreement in its entirety into its military legislation in both the West Bank and Gaza, and that this legislation has not been revoked.

107 *East Timor* Pleadings, Portuguese Memorial, p. 91, para. 4.22.

108 *East Timor* Pleadings, Australian Counter-Memorial (1 June 1992), p. 167, para. 375.

To evaluate the self-determination issues that might be implicated in Israel's withdrawal by concentrating solely on Gaza is, however, to adopt too narrow a focus. To note that no self-determination process has taken place in Gaza is to consider only the procedural aspect of the right: it fails to consider its substantive content. One substantive aspect is decisive in evaluating the disengagement plan: the population of Gaza alone cannot exercise a right of self-determination. It possesses no such right: in the case of Palestine, that right belongs to the population of the territorial self-determination unit as a whole which comprises the West Bank (including occupied East Jerusalem) as well as Gaza. The territorial integrity of a self-determination unit[109] cannot be disrupted, particularly by a belligerent occupant:

> If an occupant controlled only part of a state and that part was not considered to be a distinct unit entitled to self-determination, the occupant would not be entitled to effect the secession of the occupied area (as in Northern Cyprus). Similar considerations imply that the occupant would not be entitled to establish a new government in such a region even if its inhabitants supported such an act.[110]

Whether one considers either the process aspect of self-determination, or the substantive aspect of the occupant's duty to maintain the integrity of the territory, Israel's unilateral withdrawal – insofar as this aims to change the international status of Gaza – either fails to observe the requirements of the former, or threatens to breach the latter, or both.[111] Accordingly, Israel's withdrawal does not respect the right of the Palestinian people to self-determination and thus is in breach of international law, whether respect for self-determination is conceived of as an obligation *erga omnes* incumbent upon all States or as a peremptory norm. Within the compass of the law of self-determination, what consequences flow for the international legal status of Gaza after Israel's withdrawal?

9 THE NORMATIVE CONSEQUENCES OF SELF-DETERMINATION

If it is correct to conclude that Israel's unilateral attempt to change the international status of Gaza is in breach of the Palestinian people's right to self-determination, then other States have a duty not to endorse the result Israel seeks to achieve. Even if self-determination is regarded only as an obligation *erga omnes*, as opposed to a *ius cogens* norm, then its breach entails a

---

109 On the territorial integrity of self-determination units, albeit within the context of decolonisation, see, e.g. Cassese, above n. 43, p. 72 and pp. 78-79.

110 Benvenisti, above, n. 51, 183: see also, Roberts, above, n. 26, pp.28-29; and Sassòli, M., *Article 43 of the Hague Regulations and peace operations in the twenty-first century*. <http://www.ihlresearch.org/ihl/pdfs/sassoli.pdf>, 14. In the separate opinion he appended to the *Legal consequences of a wall* Advisory Opinion, Judge Koroma expressed this point more bluntly: "Under the régime of occupation, the division or partition of an occupied territory by the occupying Power is illegal", 43 International Legal Materials 1056 (2004), p. 1057, para. 4.

111 As noted above, it will also be in breach of the obligation Israel assumed under Article XXXI.7 of the 1995 Interim Agreement.

duty of non-recognition for third States.[112] Further, in its commentary on Article 6 of Geneva Convention IV regarding the conditions under which the Convention ceases to apply, the ICRC indicated that where a termination of occupation involves a change in the international status of the occupied territory:

> The Convention could only cease to apply as the result of a political act, such as the annexation of the territory or its incorporation in a federation, and then only if the political act in question had been recognized and accepted by the community of States; if it were not so recognized and accepted, the provisions of the Convention must continue to be applied.[113]

Non-recognition of any change in Gaza's status is thus doubly mandated.

This, however, is based on the assumption that Israel has withdrawn from Gaza and no longer exerts effective control over the discharge of governmental functions. If this is so, then at least an initial supposition must be that the exercise of sovereignty resides with the Palestinian Authority—that it has gained "the right to exercise...to the exclusion of any other State, the functions of a State".[114] As von Glahn observes, in all cases of the termination of belligerent occupation of enemy territory "it can be assumed that the legitimate sovereign will be in control of the territory in question as soon as the occupation ends".[115]

Aronson saw this as a further complication in the post-withdrawal puzzle of Gaza's status which he raised with "a senior member of Israel's national security establishment". Aronson thought that there were three possible solutions: Palestinian sovereignty; Egyptian rule; or some third-party administration. He was informed that there was a fourth option, "None of the above":

> In other words, an acceptable scenario for Israel would be the continuation of the control and authority exercised by Palestinian institutions created by Israel and the PLO under the Oslo accords, but now expanded de facto by an end to occupation. Without the creation of a sovereign successor in the wake of Israel's withdrawal, the Gaza Strip under this scenario would belong to no state (*terra nullius*). This is an extraordinary proposition.[116]

This indeed would be anomalous: international law prefers sovereignty over territory to rest somewhere or other, and preferably with a State. The principal contemporary exception of territory unclaimed by any State or putative State is Antarctica, but that is regulated by treaty, as indeed are the West Bank and Gaza by virtue of the Oslo instruments whose force and legal validity the Disengagement Plan avowedly preserves.

Neither Egypt nor any third party have claimed rights of sovereignty or administration over Gaza following disengagement. It therefore must be considered whether withdrawal constitutes a devolution of authority to the

---

112 *Legal consequences of a wall* Advisory Opinion, 34 International Legal Materials (2004), p. 1053, para. 159.

113 Pictet, above, n. 22, p. 63.

114 Judge Huber, *Island of Palmas* case (1928), 2 Reports of International Arbitral Awards 829, p. 838.

115 von Glahn, above, n. 16, p. 257.

116 Aronson, above, n. 4, p. 54.

Palestinian Authority, causing it to become the presumptive government of an independent Gaza, which is perceived as the initial, if partial, emergence of Palestine as a State. Accordingly, simply by unilaterally removing its presence from Gaza, has Israel propelled Gaza into the world of States? The validity of this assumption depends on whether Gaza fulfils the internationally recognised requirements for Statehood.

The classic account of the basic criteria for Statehood is that contained in Article 1 of the 1933 Montevideo Convention on the Rights and Duties of States. This provides:

> The State as a person of international law should possess the following qualifications: (a) a permanent population; (b) a defined territory; (c) government; and (d) capacity to enter into relations with other States.[117]

These criteria constitute the minimum elements of Statehood[118] and, as Crawford notes, they are based on the principle of effectiveness of territorial units,[119] which is essentially a factual test. Manifestly, a permanent population inhabits Gaza, and its borders are reasonably well-defined. The requirement of territory for the purposes of the criteria of Statehood does not entail that the territory in question has exactly defined or undisputed borders. If this were the case, then Israel itself would not be a State. As the International Court of Justice observed in the *North Sea continental shelf* cases, there is:

> no rule that the land frontiers of a State must be fully delimited and defined, and often in various places and for long periods they are not, as is shown by the case of the entry of Albania into the League of Nations (*Monastery of Saint Naoum, Advisory Opinion, 1924, PCIJ, Series B, No.9*, at p.10).[120]

In broad terms, the requirement of government entails that there is an authority which is "in general control of its territory, to the exclusion of other entities not claiming through or under it".[121] This formulation is obviously influenced by Judge Huber's definition of independence in the *Island of Palmas* case. Indeed Crawford, like other doctrinal writers, substitutes independence

---

117 Reproduced, 29 American Journal of International Law: Document supplement 75 (1934).

118 See, for instance, Brownlie, I., *Principles of Public International Law* (Oxford U.P.: Oxford: 2003, 6th Edn.), pp. 70-72; Crawford, above, n. 35, pp. 45-62; Higgins, R., *The Development of International Law through the Political Organs of the United Nations* (Oxford U.P.: London: 1963), pp. 17-42; Jennings, R.Y. and Watts, A., *Oppenheim's International Law: Volume One, Peace* (Longmans: London: 1992, 9th Edn.), pp. 120-123; Lauterpacht, H., *Recognition in International Law* (Cambridge U.P.: Cambridge: 1947), pp. 26-32; and Okeke, C.N., *Controversial Subjects of Contemporary International Law* (Rotterdam U.P.: Groningen: 1974), p. 87. On Palestine and Statehood, see Boyle, F.A., *The creation of the State of Palestine*, 1 European Journal of International Law 301 (1990): the better view is expressed by Crawford and Watson – see Crawford, J., *The creation of the State of Palestine: too much too soon?*, 1 European Journal of International Law 307 (1990), his *Israel (1948-1949) and Palestine (1998-1999): two studies in the creation of States*, in Goodwin-Gill, G. and Talmon, S. (eds.), *The Reality of International Law: Essays in Honour of Ian Brownlie* (Clarendon Press: Oxford: 1999), p. 95, and above, n. 35, pp.421-448; and Watson, above, n. 69 (*Oslo Accords*), pp. 60-63.

119 Crawford, above, n. 35, p. 6.

120 *North Sea continental shelf cases (Federal Republic of Germany v. Denmark; Federal Republic of Germany v. the Netherlands)*, ICJ Rep, 1969, 3 at p. 32, para. 46.

121 Crawford, above, n. 35, p. 59; see pp. 55-62.

for the traditional criterion of the capacity to enter into relations with other States. As he correctly observes, this capacity is not confined to States and is better seen as a consequence of, rather than a criterion, for Statehood.[122] Independence is the central requirement of Statehood, which is dependent on the existence of an effective government.[123]

A distinction must, however, be drawn between formal and actual independence.[124] Formal independence denotes the situation when an entity apparently possesses the outward signs of Statehood: actual independence describes the factual ability of the relevant authorities to exercise governmental powers – in other words, whether the government in fact fulfils Judge Huber's definition of independence. Formal independence can mask a relationship of dependence, where an ostensibly independent government acts under the direction of another State. This relationship is frequently associated with some form of occupation, such as Japan's creation of Manchukuo in occupied Manchuria in the early 1930s.[125] If, for the purposes of argument, we assume that disengagement has terminated occupation in terms of the (traditional) law of armed conflict, and an effective and independent government emerges, may that government legitimately be able to claim that Gaza is a State?

The traditional criteria for Statehood – population, territory, government and independence – are based on the notion of (factual) effectiveness, but in contemporary international law Statehood is tempered by normative considerations. If an entity, ostensibly qualified to be a State according to the traditional criteria, emerges into the international arena in breach of a normative component of Statehood, then its existence is tainted by illegal creation. Consequently it cannot claim to be a State. A clear example of the denial of Statehood to an entity that apparently fulfilled the traditional descriptive requirements was Rhodesia, which emerged as a result of the Unilateral Declaration of Independence promulgated by its minority racial government in 1965. This was seen as the creation of an entity in violation of the right to self-determination which thus could not be recognised as a State.[126] Breach of self-determination has also been adduced as a reason for the non-recognition of the "homeland-States" or bantustans created by the South

---

122 Crawford, above, n. 35, pp. 61-62: see also, Brownlie, above n. 118, pp. 71-72; and Jennings and Watts, above, n. 118, p. 122. In relation to Palestine's ability to conduct foreign relations under the Oslo instruments, see Singer, above, n. 79 (*Aspects of foreign relations*).

123 See, e.g. Crawford, above, n. 35, p. 62; Higgins, above, n. 118, p. 25; Lauterpacht, above, n. 118, pp. 27-28; and Marek, above, n. 81, p. 162.

124 See, for instance, Brownlie, above, n. 118, pp. 71-72; Crawford, above, n. 35, pp. 67-89: Higgins, above, n. 118, pp. 26-27; Lauterpacht, above, n. 118, pp. 26-30; and Marek, above, n. 81, pp. 165-180.

125 See, e.g. Crawford, above, n. 35, pp. 74-76, pp. 78-83; Dugard, J., *Recognition and the United Nations* (Grotius: Cambridge: 1987), pp. 27-35; Lauterpacht, above, n. 118, pp. 46-47; and Marek, above, n. 81, pp. 110-122, and pp. 173-179. Article 47 of Geneva Convention IV attempts to guard against the formation of ostensibly independent, but nonetheless puppet, authorities in occupied territory, see the materials cited above, n. 81.

126 See, for instance, Crawford, above, n. 35, pp. 128-131; Dugard, above, n. 125, pp. 90-98; Okeke, above, n. 118, p. 81 *et seq*; and Wilson, above, n. 44, p. 69.

African government during the *apartheid* period.[127] This consequence follows logically from the status of self-determination as a peremptory norm of international law which cannot be disregarded in international relations. Entities which purport to be States but which have been created in violation of self-determination are legal nullities:

> they are without legal effect as States, not because they fail to meet the essential requirements of statehood but because their existence violates a peremptory rule of international law.[128]

Accordingly, even if we assume that Israeli disengagement terminated its occupation and that Gaza fulfils the traditional descriptive requirements of Statehood, it cannot claim to be nor can it be regarded as a State by other international actors. Israel's Disengagement Plan violated the process aspect of the Palestinian people's right to self-determination because of the absence of popular consultation. Further, were the claim to be made that Gaza alone had emerged as the putative State of Palestine, this would breach the substantive aspect of self-determination which prohibits the dismemberment of the self-determination unit. Consequently, any claim that Gaza can achieve Statehood as a result of the disengagement is the assertion of a legal nullity:

> An act offending against *jus cogens* cannot be voidable or relatively invalid but only void. All acts and transactions, such as treaties, unilateral acts and actions of states that offend again *jus cogens* are void and not voidable.[129]

Any consideration of the factual effectiveness of the territorial entity is over-ridden by the circumstance of illegal creation arising from the breach of the peremptory norm of self-determination. Whether seen as a norm with *ius cogens* status or as an obligation *erga omnes*, third States are under a duty not to recognise Gaza as a State.

This argument is, however, redundant because it is clear that Gaza is not formally or actually independent. A State's sovereignty extends over its territorial sea, and to the airspace above its territorial sea and land territory.[130] The Disengagement Plan expressly states that Israel will continue to exercise control of Gaza's maritime zones and airspace. If a State claims to possess a discretionary authority to intervene in the internal affairs of a putative State, whether or not this claim is based in consent, this is inconsistent with the

---

127 See Crawford, above, n. 35, pp. 338-348; Dugard, above, n. 125, pp. 98-108: and also, more generally, deKieffer, D. and Hartquist, D., *Transkei: a legitimate birth*, 13 New England Law Review 428 (1978); Dugard, J., *South Africa's "independent" homelands: an exercise in denationalization*, 10 Denver Journal of International Law and Policy 11 (1980); Heydt, D., *Nonrecognition of the independence of Transkei*, 10 Case Western Reserve Journal of International Law 167 (1978); Norman, G., *The Transkei: South Africa's illegitimate child*, 12 New England Law Review 585 (1977), and his *The Transkei revisited*, 13 New England Law Review 792 (1978); Richardson, H., *Self-determination, international law and the South African bantustan policy*, 17 Columbia Journal of Transnational Law 185 (1978); and Rogers, B., *Divide and rule: South Africa's bantustans* (International Defence and Aid Fund: London: 1980, 2nd Edn.).

128 Dugard, above, n. 125, p. 131, see pp. 127-131; and also Crawford, above, n. 35, pp. 97-107.

129 Orakhelashvili, above, n. 99, p. 83.

130 See, e.g. Jennings and Watts, above, n. 118, p. 479, p. 573, pp. 600-601 and pp. 650-655.

latter's formal independence.[131] While Article XXXI.13 of the Interim Agreement contained arrangements for effective Israeli control of the maritime areas off Gaza, which one can only assume are maintained in the Disengagement Plan, the usurpation of authority over airspace appears to be unilateral. Either way, Gaza is unable to exercise "to the exclusion of any other State, the functions of a State" in these areas, which is fatal to any claim to independence. As Israel continues to exercise governmental functions in Gaza, how can it be claimed that occupation has ended?

It is impossible to accept at face value and in good faith the provisions of the Revised Disengagement Plan because of the contradictions it contains. It is at once a claim both to divest Israel of responsibilities for Gaza's population while retaining powers over the territory that would otherwise fall to be exercised by the legitimate government. Principle Six, that completion of the plan will dispel claims regarding Israel's responsibility for the Palestinians within Gaza, clearly contemplates that Israel will either divest itself of responsibility for Gaza completely, or that it will remain as occupant of the territory, but without the concomitant obligations, mandated by international law, owed to its inhabitants. The latter is a legal impossibility: a State cannot unilaterally absolve itself from the performance of its duties under international law. It can, of course, act as if these obligations did not exist and thus breach them, but a State cannot unilaterally cancel its obligations and declare that they no longer exist. The former option, that disengagement has terminated occupation, is not borne out by an analysis of the terms and implications of the Disengagement Plan. The Plan is a disingenuous manifesto whereby Israel seeks to foist onto the Palestinian Authority the dual status of sovereign government in Gaza while maintaining it as a local administration in the West Bank whose authority is ultimately derived from the military government. It is a classic example of an occupant "inclined to make use of arrangements where authority is said to be exercised by [a] transitional government"[132] in an attempt to disguise the truth in the hope of evading responsibility.

10 THE REALITIES OF EFFECTIVE CONTROL – OPERATION SUMMER RAIN

This assessment of the post-disengagement status of Gaza is only reinforced by Operation Summer Rain which was launched on 28 June 2006 in response to the seizure of IDF Corporal Gilad Shalit on 25 June 2006 by Palestinian militants. The IDF stated that the purpose of its military intervention in Gaza was:

---

131 See Crawford, above, n. 35, pp. 71-72.
132 Separate opinion of Judge Kooijmans, *Armed activities on the territory of the Congo* case, 45 International Legal Materials (2006), p. 359, para. 41.

to prevent the kidnappers from transferring the soldier within or out of the Gaza Strip and otherwise disrupt their activity, and to send a clear message to the terror organizations holding the soldier captive that if he is not released safely and quickly, further operational means remain available to the IDF.[133]

This communique also noted that, *inter alia*, that armoured forces had entered into the Dahaniya area which "represents a strategic control and observation point over the area of Rafah and the Southern Gaza Strip".

This is not the place to examine the legality of the capture of Corporal Shalit, the military response by Israel, or the conformity of the conduct of the hostilities with international humanitarian law. It is enough to note that the re-entry of Israeli ground forces demonstrates that the Disengagement Plan did not end the occupation, even if one applies the traditional doctrine of effective control. The ease with which the IDF re-established a physical presence on the ground in Gaza clearly fulfils the ruling in *Prosecutor v Naletili and Martinovi* that a guideline to determine whether an occupation exists is whether "the occupying power has...the capacity to send troops within a reasonable time to make the authority of the occupying power felt".[134] This test was not a legal innovation created by the Yugoslav Tribunal but simply re-stated established law, following the U.S. Military Tribunal at Nuremberg in the *List* case. An occupation subsists when the military forces of the adversary can "at any time they desired assume physical control of any part of the country",[135] as the IDF did during Operation Summer Rain in Gaza.

---

133 IDF communication, *Operation Summer Rain: IDF enters southern Gaza Strip to secure release of abducted soldier*, 28 June 2006: <www.mfa.gov.il/MFA/Government/Communiques/2006/ IDF%20enters%20southern%20Gaza%20Strip%20to%20secure%20release%20of%20 abducted%20soldier%2028-Jun-2006>: see also the *Political-security Cabinet communique*, 5 July 2006, <www.mfa.gov.il/MFA/Government/Communiques/2006/Political-Security%20 Cabinet%20Communique%205-Jul-2006>.
134 *Naletili and Martinovi:* <www.un.org/icty/naletilic/trialc/judgement/nal-tj030331-e.pdf>, p. 74, para.217.
135 VIII Law Reports of Trials of War Crimes Trials 34 (1949), p. 56.

Part VIII

PALESTINIAN STATEHOOD

Forum: The Algiers Declaration on Palestine

The Creation of the State of Palestine

Francis A. Boyle *

The Elements of Palestinian Statehood

The Intifadah has been a time of terrible tragedy and great suffering for the Palestinian people. And yet, paradoxically, it has also proven to be the time of their greatest glory, an affirmation of their essential dignity as an independent people. As a result of these elemental processes, the Unified Leadership of the Intifadah requested the Palestine Liberation Organization (PLO) to proclaim the existence of a new state of Palestine in recognition of the courage, suffering, and bravery of the Palestinian people living under Israeli occupation. On 31 July 1988 the creation of the Palestinian state became an inevitability when King Hussein of Jordan announced that he was terminating all forms of administrative and legal ties with what he called the West Bank. And on 15 November 1988 the independent state of Palestine was proclaimed by the Palestine National Council meeting in Algiers, by a vote of 253 to 46, as well as in front of Al-Aksa Mosque in Jerusalem, the capital of the new state, after the close of prayers.

I will not bother to discuss at great length the legal basis for the Palestinian people to proclaim their own state. This matter has already been analyzed in detail by me in a position paper that was requested by the PLO in 1987 and later published in the summer 1988 issue of *American-Arab Affairs* entitled *"Create the State of Palestine!"* Generally put, however, there are four elements constituent of a state: territory, population, government and the capacity to enter into relations with other states. As I argued in my position paper, all four characteristics have been satisfied by the newly proclaimed independent state of Palestine.

Indeed, as long ago as 1919 the Palestinian people were provisionally recognized as an independent nation by the League of Nations in League Covenant Article 22(4) as well as by the 1922 Mandate for Palestine that was awarded to Great Britain. This provisional recognition continues into effect today because of the conservatory clause found in Arti-

---

* University of Illinois.

cle 80(1) of the United Nations Charter. Pursuant to the basic right of self-determination of peoples as recognized by U.N. Charter Article 1(2) and by the International Court of Justice in its *Namibia* and *Western Sahara* Advisory Opinions, the Palestinian people have proceeded to proclaim their own independent state in the land they have continuously occupied for thousands of years.

1. Territory

The territory of a state does not have to be fixed and determinate. For example, Israel does not have fixed and permanent borders (except most recently with respect to Egypt) and yet it is generally considered to be a state. Thus, the state of Palestine does not have to have declared borders either. Rather, borders will be negotiated between the government of Israel and the government of Palestine. This is the same way peace negotiations would be carried out between any other two states/governments in dispute over the existence of their respective borders. To be sure, however, it is quite clear from reading the Palestinian Declaration of Independence and the attached Political Communiqué that the PLO contemplates that the new state of Palestine will consist essentially of what has been called the West Bank and Gaza Strip, with its capital being East Jerusalem.

2. Population

In occupied Palestine there lives the population of the Palestinian people; they have lived there forever, since time immemorial. They are the original inhabitants and occupants of this territory. They are fixed and determinate, and so they definitely constitute a distinguishable population. They have always been in possession of their land and therefore are entitled to create a state therein.

3. Government

During the course of his various public pronouncements in Europe during December 1988, Yasir Arafat, Chairman of the Executive Committee of the Palestine Liberation Organization, stated that the PLO is currently serving as the Provisional Government of the state of Palestine. Acting in conjunction with the Unified Leadership of the Intifadah, this Provisional Government already controls substantial sections of occupied Palestine as well as the entire populace of occupied Palestine. It is thus already exercising effective control over large amounts of territory and people and is providing basic administrative functions and social services to the Palestinian people living in occupied Palestine and abroad. This is all that is required for there to be a fulfillment of this criterion for statehood under international law.

4. The capacity to enter into international relations.

Over 114 states have already recognized the newly proclaimed state of Palestine, which is more than the 93 that maintain some form of diplomatic relations with Israel. Furthermore, on 15 December 1988 the United Nations General Assembly adopted Resolution 43/177, essentially recognizing the new state of Palestine and according it observer-state status throughout the United Nations Organization. That resolution was adopted by a vote of 104 in favor, the United States and Israel opposed, and 44 states abstaining. For reasons fully explained in my position paper, the General Assembly's recognition of the new state of Palestine is constitutive, definitive, and universally determinative.

The Framework for Negotiating a Comprehensive Middle East Peace

The Intifadah will continue until the Israeli government is willing to sit down and negotiate an overall peace settlement with the PLO. In this regard the Palestine National Council (PNC) has taken several steps in the Palestinian Declaration of Independence and in the Political Communiqué attached thereto in order to establish the framework necessary for negotiating a comprehensive peace settlement with Israel. In addition, Yasir Arafat has made several public pronouncements in his official capacity as Chairman of the Executive Committee of the PLO, which is functioning as the Provisional Government of the state of Palestine. As such, Arafat's statements constitute Unilateral Declarations of Intention that are binding upon the PLO and the state of Palestine as a matter of customary international law. Indeed, Arafat has just become the first President of the state of Palestine.

First, the Declaration of Independence explicitly accepts the General Assembly's Partition Resolution 181(II) of 1947. The significance of this cannot be overemphasized. Prior thereto, from the perspective of the Palestinian people, the Partition Resolution was deemed to be a criminal act perpetrated upon them by the United Nations. The acceptance of the Partition Resolution in their actual Declaration of Independence itself signals a genuine desire by the Palestinian people to transcend the past forty years of history and to reach an historic accommodation with Israel on the basis of a two-state solution. The Declaration of Independence is the foundational document for the state of Palestine. It is definitive, determinative, and irreversible.

Second, in the Declaration of Independence the Palestine National Council declared its commitment to the purposes and principles of the United Nations Charter, to the Universal Declaration of Human Rights and to the policy and principles of non-alignment. This last commitment indicates quite clearly that the state of Palestine would be prepared to forswear any type of security treaty arrangements with the Soviet Union along the lines of the one currently in existence between Syria and the U.S.S.R. This is clearly intended to be a confidence building measure for the benefit of Israel.

Third, in the Declaration of Independence the Palestinian National Council declared that without prejudice to its natural right to defend the state of Palestine, the PNC rejected "the threat or use of force, violence and intimidation against its territorial integrity and political independence or those of any other state." This latter commitment clearly applies to Israel.

Fourth, in the Political Communiqué attached to the Declaration of Independence the Palestine National Council indicated its willingness to accept United Nations supervision over occupied Palestine on an interim basis in order to terminate Israeli occupation. The Palestinian plan for U.N. supervision could be implemented by means of a U.N. trusteeship imposed upon Palestine in accordance with Chapter XII of the United Nations Charter. The PNC's expressed willingness to accept temporary U.N. supervision (or even temporary supervision by U.S. troops) over their state is clearly intended to serve as another confidence building measure for the benefit of Israel.

Fifth, in the Political Communiqué the Palestine National Council has called for the convocation of an International Peace Conference on the Middle East on the basis of U.N. Security Council Resolution 242 (1967) and 338 (1973) that shall guarantee the legitimate national rights of the Palestinian people, first and foremost among which is their right to self-determination. In other words, the Palestine National Council has now explicitly accepted Resolutions 242 and 338. The PNC's solemn acceptance of Resolutions 242 and 338 represents a significant concession by the Palestinians. The 1947 U.N. Partition Plan called for the Palestinian people to have a much larger section of historic Palestine for their state than do the 1967 boundaries set forth in Resolutions 242/338. In this regard, I should point out that Israel officially accepted the Partition Resolution in its own Declaration of Independence and as a condition for its admission to membership in the United Nations. By comparison, today the PLO would be prepared to accept boundaries for the state of Palestine that would consist essentially of the West Bank, Gaza Strip and East Jerusalem.

Sixth, in the Political Communiqué the PNC indicated its willingness to establish a voluntary confederation between the states of Jordan and Palestine if necessary in an attempt to accommodate the United States and Israeli governments' wishes that Palestine somehow be linked to Jordan, a wish expressed in the Allon Plan of 1976, the Camp David Accords of 1978 and more recently in the so-called Reagan Peace Plan of 1982. Despite their strident opposition to the latter two approaches when initiated by the United States government, the Palestinian people are now prepared to accommodate the objective of establishing some type of confederal link between Jordan and Palestine. The PNC's acceptance of confederation with Jordan is intended to be yet another confidence building measure for the benefit of Israel.

Seventh, in the Political Communiqué the PNC "once again states its rejection of terrorism in all its forms, including state terrorism..." In this regard, on 6 December 1988 Yasir Arafat stated that he renounced all forms of terrorism and was ready to start negotiations that would eventually lead to peace in the Middle East. Furthermore, at his Geneva press conference on 14 December 1988, Arafat accepted Resolutions 242 and 338 without directly coupling them with demands for Palestinian independence; he specifically stated that Israel has the right to exist in peace and security, and declared: "We totally and absolutely renounce all forms of terrorism including individual, group and state terrorism." With that statement Arafat technically fulfilled all the conditions set forth by the United States government in order for it to commence negotiations with the PLO.

Therefore, on 14 December 1988 President Ronald Reagan authorized the start of a diplomatic dialogue between the United States and the PLO. In his Statement on American relations with the PLO of that date, President Reagan called for "the beginning of direct negotiations between the parties, which alone can lead to such a peace." The implication was quite clear that the "parties" to which Reagan was referring meant the PLO and Israel. Thus it now appears to be the implicit position of the United States government that the next stage in the development of the Middle East peace process must be direct negotiations between Israel and the PLO.

To the same effect have been several recent statements by President Bush's Secretary of State James Baker that the Israeli government will probably have to begin negotiating a peace settlement directly with the PLO because all the Palestinian people living in occupied Palestine accept the PLO as their sole and legitimate representative. The long-standing hope of the United States government and the Israeli government that there could be found quislings among the people living in occupied Palestine who could negotiate a so-called peace settlement with Israel that would allow for the outright return of this territory to Jordanian rule has now been effectively repudiated by America. In this regard, on 3 April 1988 President George Bush bluntly stated that Israel should end its occupation of Arab lands and that the Palestinians must be given their political rights by means of an international peace conference.

The Creation of the State of Palestine

Jerusalem

Various individuals and organizations have given an ominous interpretation to the fact that the Palestinians proclaimed Jerusalem to be their capital. Although I am not authorized to speak for the PLO, I know that they are certainly prepared to be flexible with respect to negotiating over the ultimate status of Jerusalem. In all fairness, however, I should point out that neither Israel nor Palestine nor both together have the basic right under international law to dispose of Jerusalem. Rather, the 1947 Partition Resolution called for the creation of an international trusteeship for the city of Jerusalem that was to administered as a *corpus separatum* apart from both the Jewish state and the Arab state contemplated therein.

Yet I do not believe it would be necessary to go so far as to establish a separate United Nations trusteeship for the city of Jerusalem under Chapter XII of the U.N. Charter. Rather, all that would need to be done is for the Israeli army to withdraw from the city of Jerusalem and a special United Nations Middle East Peace Supervision Force (UNMEPS) to be substituted in its place. UNMEPS would maintain security within the city of Jerusalem while the provision of basic services to the inhabitants would continue much as before.

The simple substitution of a U.N. peacekeeping force for the Israeli army would have the virtue of allowing both Israel and Palestine to continue making whatever claims to sovereignty they want with respect to the city of Jerusalem. Thus, Israel could continue to maintain that Jerusalem is the sovereign territory of Israel, its united capital, and shall remain as such, one and undivided forever. The Israeli Knesset would remain where it is as a capital district and the Israeli flag could be flown anywhere throughout the city of Jerusalem.

Likewise, the state of Palestine could maintain that Jerusalem is its sovereign territory and capital. Palestine would be entitled to construct a parliament building and capital district within East Jerusalem, perhaps on the Mount of Olives near where there is a community center today. The Palestinian flag could also be flown anywhere within the territorial domain of the city of Jerusalem. Both Israel and Palestine would be entitled to maintain ceremonial honor guards, perhaps armed with revolvers, at their respective capital districts. But no armed troops from either Israel or Palestine would be permitted within Jerusalem.

The current residents of Jerusalem would be citizens of either Israel, or Palestine, or both, depending upon the respective nationality laws of the two states involved. Current residents of Jerusalem would be issued a United Nations identity card to that effect, which would give them and only them the right to live within the city of Jerusalem. Nevertheless, all citizens of the state of Palestine would be entitled to enter Jerusalem through U.N. checkpoints at the eastern limits of the city. Likewise, all citizens of the state of Israel would be entitled to enter Jerusalem at U.N. checkpoints located at the western limits of the city. Yet mutual rights of access for their respective citizens to the two states through Jerusalem would be subject to whatever arrangements could be negotiated between the government of Israel and the government of Palestine as part of an overall peace settlement.

In addition, both Israel and Palestine would have to provide assurances to the United Nations that foreign tourists and visitors would be allowed unimpeded access through their respective territories in order to visit the Holy Sites in the city of Jerusalem. Some type of U.N. transit visa issued by UNMEPS should be deemed to be sufficient for this purpose by both governments. Of course this right of transit could not be exercised in a manner deleterious to the security interests of the two territorial sovereigns.

Francis A. Boyle

The Next Step Toward Peace

Quite obviously opportunity for peace has been created by the Palestinian Declaration of Independence, its attached Political Communiqué, and subsequent public statements made by Yasir Arafat acting in his official capacity. What is needed now from the Bush administration is the same type of dynamic leadership and will for peace that was demonstrated by the Carter administration at Camp David over a decade ago. Failure by the governments of the United States and Israel to seize this moment for peace will only make another general war in the Middle East an inevitability.

The Creation of the State of Palestine:
Too Much Too Soon?

*James Crawford**

I. Introduction

It seems to be difficult for international lawyers to write in an impartial and balanced way about the Palestine issue. Most of the literature, some of it by respected figures, is violently partisan. It is true that this only reflects much of the political and personal debate about Palestine. Still, such a level of partisanship in legal discourse is disturbing. Perhaps the sceptics are right in claiming that "impartiality" is a facade and a pretence, in which case Boyle at least has the merit of honesty and lack of hypocrisy in his pleading. But the problem is that, if they are right, we should not merely give up the pretence but the game itself. And the obstinate fact remains that the actors, most of the time, continue to use the language of law in making and assessing claims. (International law scholars are not like critics in an empty theatre). That the language of law is used implies that these claims *can* be assessed, on the basis of values which extend beyond allegiance to a particular party, country, bloc or religion.

It may be conceded that Boyle's evident and – if his work is to be read as stating a legal claim rather than as a disguised oath of allegiance – regrettable partisanship has illustrious antecedents, on both sides of the dispute. Even so, an unusually high proportion of what Boyle has to say is directed at issues of strategy and is concerned to advocate a certain position within the overall spectrum of the Palestinian cause. However, those views are supported by legal arguments of various kinds, which call for separate examination. To the extent that it involves propositions of international law, Boyle's thesis, as outlined in "The Creation of the State of Palestine"[1] and stated in more detail elsewhere,[2] involves three basic propositions:

(1) Having regard to the classical "four elements constituent of a state", Palestine, under the provisional government of the Palestine Liberation Organization, is already a state in international law: "all four characteristics have been satisfied by the newly proclaimed independent state of Palestine."

*   Challis Professor of International Law, Dean, Faculty of Law, University of Sydney; Associé, Institut de Droit International.
1   Boyle, 'The Creation of the State of Palestine', *EJIL* (1990) 301.
2   See Boyle, 'Create the State of Palestine!' (1988) 7 *Scandinavian Journal of Development Alternatives* 25.

James Crawford

(2) The General Assembly, whether as the successor of the League of Nations with respect to the mandate system or by virtue of the authority to recognize the new state, and in its Resolution 43/177 has "essentially" done so, such recognition "being constitutive, definitive, and universally determinative." (Boyle has however already stated that the Palestine National Council's Declaration of Independence was "definitive, determinative and irreversible").

(3) To add yet a third level of determinacy (to make assurance trebly sure), he adds that other states, and in particular Israel and the United States, are bound to accept the new state, either because the international status of the Palestinian people had already been "provisionally recognized" in Article 22 of the League of Nations Covenant, a position preserved by Article 80 of the Charter, or (in the case of Israel) because its acceptance of the Partition Resolution was a "condition for its admission" to the United Nations.

Other questions which he discusses include the present legal status of Jerusalem, and the partly related issue of the modalities for terminating the Israeli occupation of the occupied territories. Boyle's "solution" for the Jerusalem problem would involve a demilitarized *"corpus separatum"*, under United Nations auspices, with neither side relinquishing its claim to sovereignty over the Old City. His suggestion for an orderly termination of Israeli occupation seems to be involve the imposition of a trusteeship with the United Nations itself, apparently, as administering authority. Both suggestions raise complex legal issues: for example, are the occupied territories "now held under mandate" within the meaning of Article 77(1)(a) of the United Nations Charter, and if not, which state or states are currently "responsible for their administration"? But they raise even more formidable difficulties at the levels of policy, practicality and finance, and there seems no need to discuss them in detail here. But it is necessary to say at least something about the other three arguments.

II. The Status of Palestine under the Traditional Criteria for Statehood

It is a curious feature of modern discussions of territorial status that the "traditional definition" of a state, as expressed in the four criteria referred to in the Montevideo Convention on the Rights and Duties of States of 1933,[3] continues to exercise so strong a hold. It is even more curious when the Montevideo definition, which looks to the ostensibly separate elements of territory, permanent population, government and the capacity to enter into relations with other states, is then minutely examined – in some cases one would say tortured – in order to be able to argue that a particular entity fits within those criteria.

Even applying the Montevideo Convention, in a relatively superficial way, in accordance with its terms, it is difficult to see how Palestine could constitute a state. Its whole territory is occupied by Israel, which functions as a government in the territory. The Palestine Liberation Organization has never functioned as a government in respect of the occupied territories. But the Montevideo Convention treats statehood essentially as an existing state of affairs, as a matter of fact as much as a matter of law.[4] And as a matter of fact, notwithstanding that allegiance, neither the PLO nor the Palestine National Council

---

[3]　165 *LNTS* 19.

[4]　See J. Crawford, *The Creation of States in International Law* (1979) 36-48 for an examination and critique of the Montevideo formula.

The Creation of the State of Palestine

has been in a position to exercise the whole range of governmental powers within the territory concerned. That they may have a right to do so – or, more accurately, that the Palestinian people may have a right to choose a representative authority to govern themselves – is beside the point, from the perspective of the Montevideo formula. That formula is concerned with the existence of secure governing authority rather than with any right to exercise that authority in future. It should be recalled that the Montevideo Convention was drafted at a time when the principle of self-determination was not generally recognized in international law, and when the implications of the nascent rule prohibiting the use of force between states in this context had not been worked out. It may be that the idea of statehood, imperfectly expressed in the Montevideo Convention, has been modified by these developments. But it is curious that the debate about the statehood of entities such as Palestine is still conducted in terms of that Convention. Boyle's essay is a good example of this.

Rather than examining separately the four apparently discrete criteria listed in the Montevideo formula, it is preferable to focus on the notion of state independence as a prerequisite for statehood. Essentially that notion embodies two elements – the existence of an organized community on a particular territory, exclusively or substantially exercising self-governing power, and secondly, the absence of the exercise of another state, and of the right of another state to exercise, self-governing powers over the whole of that territory.[5]

From this perspective, the often stated proposition that the absence of clearly delimited boundaries is not a prerequisite to statehood is axiomatic. Boundaries are the consequence of territory. But territory, in the context of statehood, is not "something owned." It is the basis in space for the organized community which is the state. No doubt the PLO directly and indirectly exercises considerable influence within the occupied territories, and commands the allegiance of a significant part of the population of those territories. But this falls far short of what is required in terms of the first element, the existence of an organized self-governing community. Moreover, that Israel's governmental power and authority over those territories does not amount, for the most part, to a claim of sovereignty, that it would be unlawful if it did amount to a consensus that the Palestinian people are entitled to form a state – none of this could affect the point that they do not currently do so, if the generally-accepted principle of state independence is applied. In this respect Boyle fails to face up either to the law or the facts.

Of course there are other conceptions of statehood under which different results might be reached. The first and most obvious alternative – though Boyle does not rely upon it – is the constitutive theory of statehood. According to this view an entity is a state if, and only if, it is recognized as such by other states. But the difficulty is that the constitutive theory inevitably leads to extreme subjectivity in the notion of the state. There is no rule that majority recognition is binding on third states in international law. At present Palestine has been recognized as a state by over 100 states, but it does not yet command anything like the level of quasi-unanimous support as such which would be required to establish a particular rule of international law to the effect that Palestine is a state. In the absence of such a "particular" rule, the constitutive theory leads inevitably to the proposition that another state is not bound to treat an entity as a state if it has not recognized it. Since the crucial actors here are the United States and Israel, which vehemently do not recognize Palestine as a state, the theory leads nowhere. In any event, there are compelling reasons for rejecting the constitutive theory, and most modern authorities do so.[6]

---

5   *Id.,* 48-71.
6   *Id.,* 15-24, with references to other authorities.

James Crawford

The second alternative would be to seek to take advantage of developments in international law since 1945 which have arguably modified the conception of statehood from that implied by the Montevideo formula. There has been a certain departure from the notion of a state as an effective territorial community independent of other states. Instead, notions of entitlement or disentitlement to be regarded as a state have been influential, at least in some situations. Thus entities which would have otherwise qualified as a state may not do so because their creation is in some significant sense illegitimate (Rhodesia, the Bantustans, the Turkish Federated States of Cyprus). Palestine involves the converse problem, that of an entity which is not sufficiently effective to be regarded as independent in fact, but which is thought entitled to be a state.

It should be stressed that we are not dealing with the situation of the extinction of states which were once, incontestably, established as such. The situation here involves the establishment of a new state on territory over which other states have claims of one kind or another. On this issue the practice is limited, though it is not non-existent. In the case of a number of former Portuguese territories in Africa (Guinea-Bissau being the best example[7]) the view was taken that the National Liberation Organization's extensive *de facto* control over large parts of the territory in question, and the apparent inevitability of its success, combined with the principle of self-determination, meant that the entity became a state in circumstances in which the recognition of its statehood would otherwise have been premature. Although the arguments in favour of premature statehood were often not set out or were poorly articulated, the importance of the principle of self-determination in such cases seems to have been that it disentitled the former sovereign to rely on its authority over the territory. On the other hand it is significant that in each of these cases the liberation organization did have a significant degree of control in the territory, such that its victory could reasonably be said to be imminent. Moreover the issue presented was one of a simple yes/no kind -- independence for the territory in question or the continuation of colonial rule. There was no question of any subsisting claim by the colonial power, or indeed by any other state, to significant parts of the territory in question.

The situation in Namibia provides an instructive contrast. There, notwithstanding the undoubted entitlement of the people of Namibia to self-determination, as declared by the International Court in the *Namibia* case,[8] and despite the fact that the relevant liberation organization, SWAPO, did have a high degree of allegiance, and a fluctuating degree of control, in Namibia, there was no attempt to treat Namibia as being already legally a state. Instead action was taken to bring about its independence, and in the meantime to seek to protect the rights of the people of Namibia through other means (e.g. the Resolution of the United Nations Committee for Namibia on Permanent Sovereignty over its Natural Resources). In this situation the modalities of achieving independence were of great importance, and were undoubtedly an important factor in leading states to maintain the distinction between the rights of the people of Namibia and their present status. Much the same thing could be said of the Western Sahara, especially having regard to the presence of a relatively powerful neighbouring state with claims over the territory.

Thus although a majority of states have taken the view that the next logical step beyond the Guinea Bissau situation should be taken in the case of Palestine, a significant minority of states opposes that step. There is certainly not the level of support in state practice, nor in the other sources of international law, to support that additional development.

7	*Id.*, 260-1.
8	ICJ Rep (1971) 16.

The Creation of the State of Palestine

practice, nor in the other sources of international law, to support that additional development.

This is not to say that the territory now designated as the territory of Palestine lacks a special legal status, or that appropriate representatives of the people of that territory do not share that status for various international purposes. But the continuing reservations held about the status of Palestine are reflected, both in the practice of international organizations and in the actions of individual states. For example, on 12 May 1989 the 42nd World Health Assembly deferred consideration of the application of Palestine for admission as a member of the World Health Organization. The preamble of the relevant resolution (A42/VR/10) states, in part:

> Recognizing in this context that the legal and other issues related to the application of Palestine for membership of the World Health Organization require further detailed study...

Similarly the Executive Board of UNESCO deferred consideration of a Palestinian application for membership of UNESCO, while adopting measures to ensure that Palestine had the fullest possible opportunity (short of membership) of participation in the work of UNESCO.[9]

Another expression of doubt as to the status of Palestine is contained in the Note of Information which Switzerland, as the depository of the 1949 Geneva Conventions on the Laws of War and the 1977 Protocols, addressed to States Parties. In that Note Switzerland reported that it had declined to accept a "communication" from the permanent observer of Palestine to the United Nations office in Geneva, acceding to the Conventions and Protocols, on the grounds that

> Due to the uncertainty within the international community as to the existence or the non-existence of a State of Palestine and as long as the issue has not been settled in an appropriate framework, the Swiss Government, in its capacity as depository ... is not in a position to decide whether this communication can be considered as an instrument of accession in the sense of the relevant provisions of the Conventions and their additional Protocols... The unilateral declaration of application of the four Geneva Conventions and of the additional Protocol I made on 7 June 1982 by the Palestine Liberation Organization remains valid.[10]

Against this general background some brief comments should be made about two other arguments used by Boyle to support the case for the statehood of Palestine.

III. The Authority of the General Assembly to Recognize Palestinian Statehood

Boyle takes a very extensive view of the General Assembly's authority to recognize Palestinian statehood, specifically by its Resolution 43/177. These seem to be three main bases for this authority. The first involves the "provisional recognition" given to

---

[9] See UNESCO 132 EX/31, 29 September 1989, and the associated *Consultation* by Professor Alain Pelet, 7 September 1989.

[10] Embassy of Switzerland, Note of Information sent to States Parties to the Convention and Protocol, 13 September 1989.

James Crawford

the sovereignty of the nations subject to "A" class mandates pursuant to Article 22 of the League of Nations Covenant. That provisional recognition would be a right of peoples saved or reserved by Article 80 of the United Nations Charter. But the fact is that, with the exception of Iraq, the "provisional recognition" given by Article 22 did not amount to much.[11] In practice the "A" class mandates were subject to the normal mandatory regime, and it was not argued that the status of the territories concerned was that of independent states. In this context the distinction between "state" and "nation", rejected by Boyle, is crucial: certain "peoples" or "nations" were recognized by Article 22 as having rights of a relatively immediate kind, but these did not as yet amount to statehood.

The second element supporting General Assembly Authority, according to Boyle, arises from his assertion that the General Assembly was the successor to the League of Nations with respect to the mandate system. But there was no direct succession between the League of Nations and the United Nations in this or in other respects, and this lack of succession was wholly deliberate. Instead, the International Court in 1950[12] and again in 1971[13] supported the exercise by the United Nations of authority with respect to mandates on the basis of arguments which did not depend on a rule of succession. Moreover, although the General Assembly acquired power through these means to revoke the mandate for South West Africa, that power was not of a general discretionary or governing kind, but was more in the nature of a declaratory power exercised on behalf of the international community in a situation where no state had sovereignty over the territory concerned. The binding character of that decision, and in particular the legal consequences for states as set out in the *Namibia Opinion*, were in a substantial part due to the operation of Security Council resolutions pursuant to Article 25 of the Charter. No doubt there are important implications for the status of Palestine in these arguments. But they stop far short of the proposition that the General Assembly can recognize Palestine as a state, and not merely for such "internal" purposes of the United Nations as observer status, with an effect which is "constitutive, definitive, and universall' determinative." What the position would be if Palestine was actually admitted to United Nations membership is, of course, another question.

IV. The Position of Dissenting or Opposing States

Finally I should briefly note Boyle's arguments to the effect that both the United States and Israel are bound to accept the status of Palestine as a new state, notwithstanding their consistent opposition. So far as the United States is concerned, the principal ground for the argument is based upon the "provisional recognition" by Article 22 of the League of Nations Covenant of the status of the nations under "A" class mandates, a position preserved in Article 80 of the Charter. This argument has already been dealt with. It is only necessary to add, to the extent that it may be relevant, that the United States was not a party to the Covenant. It could be argued that Article 80 cannot have the effect of preserving treaty rights as against states which were not parties to the relevant treaties. Perhaps the better view, however, is that Article 80 is a mere savings clause of an essentially declaratory and limited kind.

So far as Israel is concerned, Boyle's argument is principally based upon the proposition that Israel's acceptance of the Partition Resolution (General Assembly Resolution

---

11 Crawford, *supra* note 337-40.
12 *Status of South West Africa Opinion*, ICJ Rep (1950) 128.
13 *Namibia Opinion*, ICJ Rep 1071, p. 16.

The Creation of the State of Palestine

181(II) of 29 November 1947) was "a condition for its admission" to the United Nations. The essential point here is that, although the relevant Jewish organization did accept the Partition Resolution when it was first adopted, the Resolution was not accepted by the Arab states involved. Instead war broke out, leading to a cease-fire on quite different boundaries. Israel was not admitted to the United Nations on the basis of a division of territory which in any way reflected the partition resolution. Moreover the Charter makes no provision for "conditional admission."

V. Conclusion

It has to be said that the case for Palestinian statehood presented by Boyle is weak and unconvincing. Indeed it is weaker and more unconvincing than it need have been, having regard to some of the post-1945 developments, and in particular to the case of Guinea Bissau. But if that case is to be justified on the premise "*nasciturus pro jam natus habetur*",[14] the fact remains that a real State of Palestine is by no means yet assured. For a Palestinian State to be properly described as "*nasciturus*", what is needed is statesmanship on all sides, and respect for the rights of the peoples and states of the region. The manipulation of legal categories is unlikely to advance matters.

[14]   See Crawford, *supra* note 391-2.

Stalled Between Seasons: The International Legal Status of Palestine During the Interim Period

What god shall resurrect us

in his flesh?

After all, the iron cage is shrinking.

The hangman will not wait

though we wail from birth

in the name of these happy ruins.

What narrow yesterdays,

what stale and shriveled years . .

Even storms come begging

when the sky matches the gray

of the sand,

leaving us stalled between seasons

barricaded by what we see.[†]

Palestine first appeared on the United Nations' agenda as a question.[1] To a great extent, it remains one. The Palestinian people have sought for much of this century to achieve national independence, striving for international recognition of their right to determine freely their political status in the territory they claim as their own. In the 1960s, the Palestine Liberation Organization (PLO) emerged as the international representative of the Palestinian people and, since then, has played a central role in defining and pursuing their national aspirations. In 1993, the PLO and the government of Israel agreed to a Dec-

* Law clerk to Judge Dorothy W. Nelson, United States Court of Appeals for the Ninth Circuit. J.D., Yale Law School, February 1997; B.A. Northwestern University, 1991. The author would like to thank Professor Michael Reisman for his thoughtful comments on earlier drafts of this paper. The author also appreciates the support of the Schell Center for International Human Rights and the Coca-Cola World Fund, which funded my preliminary research at the United Nations Centre for Human Rights. Finally, I gratefully acknowledge the limitless patience and support of M.T. and Ninon Dajani.

† Ali Ahmed Said (Adonis), *Elegy for the Time at Hand*, in THE BLOOD OF ADONIS: SELECTED POEMS (Samuel Hazo trans.,1971).

1. One of the United Nations General Assembly's first items of business was to create a Special Committee to examine "the question of Palestine." *See* G.A. Res. 104 (S-1), U.N. Doc. A/310, at 6-7 (1947). For a thoughtful analysis of the origins and implications of the phrase, see EDWARD SAID, THE QUESTION OF PALESTINE 3-9 (1979).

laration of Principles on Interim Self-Governing Arrangements (DOP)[2]
that established a framework for limited Palestinian self-government
during an interim period, pending resolution of the permanent status of
the territory occupied by Israel since 1967. Pursuant to the DOP, they
have concluded a series of agreements elaborating upon and implementing transitional arrangements. The parties, however, have yet to
agree on either from what or to what they are making a transition.
Upon taking power, the Likud Government of Israeli Prime Minister
Benjamin Netanyahu issued guidelines declaring that it "would oppose
the establishment of a Palestinian state or any foreign sovereignty west
of the Jordan River."[3] In contrast, a member of the Palestinian leadership has asserted that "[t]here will be neither peace nor security without an independent Palestinian state . . . ."[4]

This disagreement regarding what Palestine will be prompts consideration of what Palestine is. In one of its few references to the future, the DOP states that elections for the Palestinian Council established to administer portions of the Occupied Palestinian Territories
(OPT) during the interim period are to constitute ". . . a significant interim preparatory step toward the realization of the legitimate rights of
the Palestinian people and their just requirements."[5] This declaration
raises a number of important questions; foremost, what is the nature of
"the legitimate rights of the Palestinian people"? Is the right to self-
determination among them? If so, to what extent are the interim arrangements a "significant . . . preparatory step" toward their realization? And how do the interim arrangements — particularly the establishment of the Palestinian Interim Self-Governing Authority (PA) —
affect the status of existing Palestinian public bodies in the international system?

In this essay, I undertake to answer these questions. I begin in
Part One by reviewing the Palestinian claim to self-determination, out-
lining international legal treatment of the principle, and evaluating its
applicability to the people and territory of Palestine. Next, in Part Two,
I examine the Palestinian public bodies established in pursuit of Pales-
tinian national rights by analyzing the structure and legal status of the
PLO, the "State" of Palestine established by the Palestine National
Council in 1988, and the PA created by the DOP and subsequent
agreements. Finally, in Part Three, I try to define the legal status of
Palestine as it is presently constituted, and to evaluate the extent to

2. Israel-Palestine Liberation Organization: Declaration of Principles on Interim
Self-Government Arrangements, Sept. 13, 1993, Isr.-PLO, 32 I.L.M. 1528 (1993) [herein-
after Declaration of Principles].
3. *The New Government's Guidelines*, JERUSALEM POST, June 18, 1996, at 3.
4. Adviser to Yasser Arafat rejects Puerto Rico-like Palestine, AGENCE FRANCE-
PRESSE, Nov. 9, 1996, available in 1996 WL 12177831.
5. Declaration of Principles, *supra* note 2, art. 3, para. 3. The same language appears in the Interim Agreement concluded by the parties in 1995. *See also* The Israeli-
Palestinian Interim Agreement on the West Bank and the Gaza Strip, art. 2, para. 2,
(September 28, 1995) <http://www.israel-mfa.gov.il/peace/interim.html> [hereinafter Interim Agreement].

which it fulfills the legal requirements for the exercise of self-determination.

I. THE PALESTINIAN CLAIM TO SELF-DETERMINATION

The principle of self-determination is the legal foundation on which the Palestinian people's struggle for national independence is based. In international practice, however, the principle of self-determination becomes a right only when invoked under certain circumstances, with the status of both the population and the territory concerned determining the viability of the exercise of self-determination. As will be seen, the Palestinians have attained broad international recognition of their right to self-determination in the OPT. Moreover, as I argue below, the territory they claim constitutes a viable self-determination unit.

A. *The Principle of Self-Determination*

Self-determination has come to elicit broad recognition as an international human right.[6] The United Nations Charter states explicitly that "respect for the principle of equal rights and self-determination" should form the basis for relations among nations in the world system[7] and provides implicitly for its vindication in its provisions regarding the disposition of trusteeships and non-self-governing territories.[8] The 1970 Declaration on Principles of International Law Concerning Friendly Relations and Co-operation Among States (hereinafter Declaration on Friendly Relations), moreover, characterizes the principle as a right, proclaiming that "by virtue of the principle of ... self-determination of peoples all peoples have the right freely to determine, without external interference, their political status."[9] Similarly, both

---

6. For a thorough analysis of the historical development of the principle of self-determination, *See* Goyora Binder, *The Kaplan Lecture on Human Rights: The Case for Self-Determination*, 29 STAN. J. INT'L L. 223, 223-48 (1993); John Collins, Note, *Self-Determination in International Law: The Palestinians*, 12 CASE W. RES. J. INT'L L. 137, 138-143 (1980); Rupert Emerson, *Self-Determination*, 65 AM. J. INT'L L. 459 (1971).

7. U.N. CHARTER art. 1, para. 2; *See also* art. 55.

8. *See* M.C. Baussiouni, *"Self-Determination" and the Palestinians*, 65 AM. SOC'Y INT'L L. PROC. 31, 32 (1971) (arguing that Chapters XI, XII, and XIII of the U.N. Charter embody the principle of self-determination "in spirit"); JAMES CRAWFORD, THE CREATION OF STATES IN INTERNATIONAL LAW 356 (1979) (stating that Chapter XI of the U.N. Charter is an attempt to apply "somewhat similar ideas to those embodied in Article 22 of the [League of Nations] Covenant to a far broader category of territory.").

9. G.A. Res. 2625, U.N. GAOR, 25th Sess., Supp. No. 28, at 124, U.N. Doc. A/8028 (1970). The Resolution was passed unanimously by the General Assembly and "is generally viewed as an authoritative interpretation of the U.N. Charter." Binder, *supra* note 6, at 236. Binder argues:
The Declaration was the culmination of a lengthy effort to legitimate the U.N. Charter for its newer signatories in the developing world who took no part in its drafting. The Declaration was drafted by a committee appointed to develop an official interpretation on which the new as well as the old members could agree.
The internal evidence of the Declaration's authoritative character includes:
    (a) the resolution's self-description as a 'Declaration' in its title; (b) the resolution's 'declaration' that 'the principles of the Charter which are embodied

the International Covenant on Civil and Political Rights and the Covenant on Economic, Social, and Cultural Rights affirm that "all peoples" have a right to self-determination, and that "[b]y virtue of that right they freely determine their political status and freely pursue their economic, social, and cultural development."[10] By the express terms of these international instruments, self-determination has been elevated to the status of a right.

The scope and legal force of the right, however, have varied in application. As Professor Cherif Bassiouni has suggested:

> 'Self-determination' is a catch-all concept which exists as a principle, develops into a right under certain circumstances, unfolds as a process and results in a remedy. As an abstract principle it can be enunciated without reference to a specific context; as a right it is operative only in a relative context, and as a remedy, its equitable application is limited by the rights of others and the potential injuries it may inflict as weighed against the potential benefits it may generate.[11]

Central among the equitable concerns to which Professor Bassiouni alludes has been regard for the sovereignty of states. Because "peoples" can be defined broadly or narrowly, the right of self-determination can be construed to bestow national rights upon almost any minority group, with potentially destructive consequences for the internal stability and territorial integrity of States. Perhaps unsurprisingly then, States generally have proven hesitant to interpret the right to self-determination

---

in this Declaration constitute basic principles of international law[;] (c) the reference in the resolution's title to U.N. Charter article 1 ('Friendly Relations') and in its first paragraph to the 'Principles' of the United Nations listed in U.N. Charter article 2; (d) the observation in the Declaration's pmbl. that 'progressive development and codification' of those principles would 'promote the realization of the purposes of the United Nations[;]' and (e) the implicit reference to U.N. Charter article 13, conferring on the General Assembly authority to 'encourage the progressive development of international law and its codification.'
The external evidence for the authority of the Declaration would include the Declaration's adoption by consensus, combined with two customary canons of construction. The first is that in treaty interpretation, 'There shall be taken into account, together with the context any subsequent agreement between the parties regarding the interpretation of the treaty or the application of its provisions,' and 'any subsequent practice in the application of the treaty which establishes the agreement of the parties regarding its interpretation.'
The second is the custom of reading constitutional texts as necessarily conferring on the institutions they establish authority to 'interpret their own constitutional powers and the specific provisions of the text so constituting them.

Id. at 236 n.52 (citations omitted).

    10. International Covenant on Economic, Social, and Cultural Rights, *came into force on* January 3, 1976, part I, art.1, para. 1, 993 U.N.T.S. 3, 5; International Covenant on Civil and Political Rights, *came into force on* March 23, 1976, part I, art. 1, para. 1, 999 U.N.T.S. 171, 173.

    11. Baussiouni, *supra* note 8, at 33.

as conveying the right to secession from a sovereign State.[12] Accordingly, the Declaration on Friendly Relations makes clear that it does not "authoriz[e] or encourag[e] any action which would dismember or impair the territorial integrity or political unity of sovereign and independent States conducting themselves in compliance with the principle of self-determination of peoples."[13] Self-determination, therefore, has not been accepted to be the unqualified right of all peoples.

Indeed, notwithstanding Judge's Dillard's assertion in the *Western Sahara Case* that "[i]t is for the people to determine the destiny of the territory and not the territory the destiny of the people,"[14] the status of a territory has proven significant in determining whether and how a given people will exercise self-determination. As noted above, States generally have been unwilling to recognize that a right of self-determination extends to peoples residing within the borders of an existing State if the exercise of that right would compromise the sovereignty or territorial integrity of that State. In these situations, State practice has been to regard self-determination as a principle, rather than as a right. As Crawford concludes, "[Self-determination] is not a right applicable directly to any group of people desiring political independence or self-government. Like sovereignty, it is a legal principle. It applies as a matter of right only after the unit of self-determination has been determined by the application of appropriate rules."[15] The question, then, is how to determine what constitutes a "self-determination unit."

The archetypal self-determination units are former mandated territories and colonies. The U.N. Charter places dependent territories into two categories: trusteeships and non-self-governing territories.[16] The principle of self-determination was a basic premise of the Charter's provisions regarding the disposition of trusteeships,[17] and it was gradually accepted to be relevant to the administration and disposition of other non-self-governing territories as well. In its 1971 *Namibia Opinion*, the International Court of Justice (I.C.J.) determined that State practice, as

---

12. CRAWFORD, *supra* note 8, at 265 (describing broad non-recognition of Biafra after secession from Nigeria); Emerson, *supra* note 6, at 464-65 (citing the United Nations unwillingness to support Katanga's secession from the Congo). *See also* G.A. Res. 1514 (XV), U.N. GAOR, 15th Sess., Supp. No. 16, at 67, U.N. Doc. A/4684 (1960) ("Any attempt aimed at the partial or total disruption of the national unity and the territorial integrity of a country is incompatible with the purposes and principles of the Charter of the United Nations.").

13. Declaration on Friendly Relations, *supra* note 9.

14. Advisory Opinion on Western Sahara, 1975 I.C.J. 12, 122 (Oct. 16, 1975) (separate opinion of J. Dillard).

15. CRAWFORD, *supra* note 8, at 101.

16. *See* U.N. CHARTER, chs. 11-13.

17. Article 76 of the Charter states that one of the purposes of the trusteeship system is the "progressive development [of the inhabitants of trust territories] towards self-government or independence as may be appropriate to the particular circumstances of each territory and its peoples and the freely expressed wishes of the peoples concerned ..." U.N CHARTER, art. 76; *see also* CRAWFORD, *supra* note 8, at 92 (referring to mandated and trust territories as "the primary type of self-determination territory).

reflected in the General Assembly's adoption of the Declaration on the Granting of Independence to Colonial Countries and Peoples, and in "the political history of mandated territories in general," indicated that international law had come to require application of the principle of self-determination to all non-self-governing territories that had been under colonial regimes.[18] This view was affirmed by the I.C.J. in the *Western Sahara Case*.[19]

The history of decolonization consequently provides some basis for identifying non-self-governing territories whose peoples are entitled to self-determination. Chapter XI of the U.N. Charter offers only vague guidance for determining which territories and or peoples qualify, refer- ring simply to "territories whose peoples have not yet attained a full measure of self-government."[20] As Crawford states, "[t]he meaning of these terms is not self-evident and has not been entirely settled by sub- sequent practice."[21] He notes that Article 74 of the Charter makes a distinction between non-self-governing territories and the "metropolitan areas" of existing States, suggesting that "the problem of minorities not inhabiting a clearly defined territory but scattered throughout a State" therefore falls outside of the scope of Chapter XI.[22] The result is that one must consequently determine how to distinguish between non-self- governing territories within and outside a metropolitan State.

In 1959, the General Assembly established a committee to examine the obligations imposed by Chapter XI upon administering States.[23] On the basis of its report, the Assembly passed Resolution 1541 (XV), which sets out "principles which should guide members in determining whether or not an obligation exists to transmit the information called for under Article 73(e) of the Charter."[24] Principle IV of the Resolution states, "*[p]rima facie* there is an obligation to transmit information in respect of a territory which is geographically separate and is distinct ethnically and/or culturally from the country administering it."[25] Once this *prima facie* case is established, other factors could then inform the evaluation of whether a territory is non-self-governing under Chapter XI of the Charter; the central issue being whether those factors "affect the relationship between the metropolitan State and the territory con- cerned in a manner which arbitrarily places the latter in a position or status of subordination."[26] A territory therefore falls under the ambit of the Charter's provisions regarding non-self-governing territories if it is separate from, distinct from, and subordinate to a metropolitan State.

In sum, the principle of self-determination becomes a legal right

---

18. 1971 I.C.J. 6, 31.

19. 1975 I.C.J. 12, 31-3.

20. U.N. Charter, art. 73.

21. CRAWFORD, *supra* note 8, at 359.

22. *Id.* (discussing the U.N. CHARTER art. 74).

23. *See* GOODRICH, HAMBRO, & SIMONS, CHARTER OF THE UNITED NATIONS: COMMENTARY AND DOCUMENTS 461-62 (1969).

24. G.A. Res. 1541, *supra* note 12.

25. *Id.* Annex, Principle 4.

26. *Id.* Annex, Principle 5.

only when it is invoked by a group recognized to constitute a people and with regard to a territory that can serve as a self-determination unit. As I will show, Palestine meets both of these criteria.

B. The Palestinian People

Juridical recognition of the Palestinian people by the international community has expanded in accordance with the development of more inclusive conceptions of participation in the international process and with the Palestinians' evolving conception of national identity. The Palestinians, initially, were defined by what they were not: in 1922, a nascent League of Nations identified them simply as the "existing non-Jewish communities in Palestine." By the end of the 1960s, however, the United Nations General Assembly recognized the Palestinians to be a people and attributed to them the attendant rights to self-determination and sovereignty. This section traces international recognition of the Palestinian people as it has developed over the course of this century.

1. 1919-1947: The Arab Inhabitants of Palestine

The states that structured the international order at the conclusion of the first World War provisionally recognized Palestine to be an independent nation. The League of Nations Covenant [hereinafter Covenant], signed in 1919 in conjunction with the Treaty of Versailles,[27] marked an initial, though perhaps reluctant, departure from the state-focused vision of the international community that prevailed during the nineteenth century. [28] Reflecting the Great Powers' acquiescence to President Woodrow Wilson's advocacy in favor of the principle of self-determination,[29] the Covenant acknowledged the existence of "peoples not yet able to stand by themselves under the strenuous conditions of the modern world" and declared that their "well-being and develop-

---

27. One historian has suggested that "neither the Europeans nor the Americans could have the peace treaty without the League or the League without the peace treaty; both would stand or fall together. . . ." F.S. NORTHEDGE, THE LEAGUE OF NATIONS: ITS LIFE AND TIMES, 1920-1946, at 39 (1986).

28. During the nineteenth century, the European Concert maintained a state-focused vision of international participation, recognizing the legal status only of nations that had been incorporated into recognized states. The "society of nations," as then defined, might more accurately have been characterized as a society of states. Binder, *supra* note 6, at 227.

29. Binder, *supra* note 6, at 228, Scholars disagree about the extent to which the Covenant implies or incorporates the principle of self-determination. *Cf.* L.C. Green, *Self-Determination and Settlement of the Arab-Israeli Conflict,* 65 AM. SOC'Y INT'L L. PROC. 40, 42, 56 (1971) (arguing that Article 22 of the League of Nations is not a recognition of the right to self determination); John A. Collins, Note, *Self-Deter-mination in International Law: The Palestinians,* 12 CASE W. RES. J. INT'L L. 137, 158 (1981) (arguing that the Covenant implicitly recognizes the right to self-determination); Rupert Emerson, *Self-Determination,* 65 AM. J. INT'L L. 459, 463 (1971) (making no reference to the Covenant, but stating that the right of self-determination advocated by Wilson applied to peoples of the Middle East).

ment" formed "a sacred trust of civilization."[30] In accordance with this vision, the Covenant delegated responsibility for carrying out this trust to certain "advanced nations" under whose tutelage the designated Mandates presumably could progress.[31] Palestine, along with the other communities formerly under the sovereignty of the Turkish (Ottoman) Empire, was categorized as developed enough to warrant "provisional" recognition, "subject to the rendering of administrative advice and assistance by a Mandatory until such time as [it was] able to stand alone." [32] The Covenant, therefore, bestowed a level of international recognition upon the "nation" of Palestine with the expectation that it shortly would achieve statehood.

Article 22 of the Covenant, which established the framework for the mandates system, appears to define this "nation" in primarily communal terms. Its provision regarding the "A" Mandates, as Palestine and the other former Turkish provinces would later be known, states that "[c]ertain *communities* . . . have reached a stage of development where their existence as independent nations can be provisionally recognized . . . ."[33] The Covenant committed, moreover, to giving prime consideration to the wishes of these "communities" in the selection of the Mandatory.[34] These provisions seem to reflect an acknowledgment that the peoples in this category were more than simply the inhabitants of defined territories, that they were coherent communities that were politically organized enough to articulate preferences regarding their national development. The communal focus of the "A" Mandates provision becomes even more apparent when contrasted with the more territorial definitions of the "B" and "C" Mandates. The "B" Mandates provision makes reference to "peoples," rather than "communities," and makes "the administration of the territory" — not the rendering of administrative advice — the Mandatory's prime responsibility.[35] Moreover, while the "A" Mandates provision makes no reference at all to territory, the Covenant defines the "C" Mandates in entirely territorial terms, making only incidental reference to their "population."[36] The Covenant appears, therefore, to do more than recognize Palestine as a territory; it recognizes the Palestinians as a nation.[37]

The terms of the Mandate for Palestine, which was approved by the League of Nations Council on July 24, 1922, departed in a number of respects from Article 22(4) of the Covenant, shifting significantly away from recognition of a Palestinian national community. As an initial matter, the League of Nations Council ignored the Covenant's requirement that the wishes of the indigenous community be a prime criterion

---

30. LEAGUE OF NATIONS COVENANT, art. 22, para. 1.

31. *Id.* art. 22, para. 2.

32. *Id.* art. 22, para. 4 (emphasis added).

33. *Id.*

34. *Id.*

35. *Id.* art. 22, para. 5.

36. *Id.* art. 22, para. 6.

37. *See* W. THOMAS MALLISON & SALLY V. MALLISON, THE PALESTINE PROBLEM IN INTERNATIONAL LAW AND WORLD ORDER (1986) 189-90.

in the selection of the Mandatory, assigning the Mandate to Great Britain without the consent of Palestine's population.[38]   The Mandate, moreover, entrusted to Great Britain "the administration of the territory of Palestine,"[39] words more reminiscent of the role assigned to "B" Mandatories than of the "A" Mandatories. Most significantly, in contrast to its numerous explicit commitments to the establishment of a "Jewish national home" in Palestine,[40] the Mandate referred to the indigenous Arab population of the country, which in 1922 represented almost 90% of Palestine's total population,[41] primarily in contradistinction to the Jewish population.[42] The Mandate, therefore, transformed the "independent nation" provisionally recognized by the Covenant into an assortment of "non-Jewish communities" that happened to reside within the borders of the territory of Palestine.

Some have argued that this conception of the Palestinians simply conforms to the historical record — that the Arabs in Palestine in 1917 were an undifferentiated segment of the larger Arab nation that stretched from Syria to Morocco and that they possessed no independent communal identity that could form the basis for nationhood.[43] According to this view, the national aspirations of Arabs in Palestine were given adequate means of fulfillment by the allocation to "the Arabs" of the vast tracts of land that presently comprise the Arab states.[44] Moreover, it has been suggested that the kingdom of Transjordan, which in 1922 was established as an independent principality, was, itself, a "Palestinian Arab State" and consequently fulfilled whatever interests in self-determination Palestinians legitimately could claim.[45]

---

38. NORTHEDGE, *supra* note 26, at 205.

39. Mandate for Palestine, Pmbl., *in* 44 Stat. 2184 (1924).

40. *Id.* (incorporating Balfour Declaration, expressing support for ". . .establishment in Palestine of a national home for the Jewish people,. . ."; recognizing Jewish grounds for "reconstituting their national home in" Palestine); *Id.* at art.2, 2185 ("The Mandatory shall be responsible for placing the country under such political, administrative and economic conditions as will secure the establishment of the Jewish national home . . . ."); *Id.* at art.4 (setting terms for creation of Jewish agency ". . .to assist and take part in the development of the country" and recognizing the Zionist organization in that capacity); *Id.* at art.6 (committing to facilitation of Jewish immigration to Palestine); *Id.* at art.7, 2186 (committing to acquisition of Palestinian citizenship by Jews).

41. *See* WALID KHALIDI, BEFORE THEIR DIASPORA 86 (1984).

42. Mandate for Palestine, *supra* note 38, at 2184, (committing not to take steps that "might prejudice the civil and religious rights of existing non-Jewish communities. . . ."); *Id.* at art.2 ("The Mandatory shall be responsible for . . . [helping to establish the Jewish national home] . . . and the development of self-governing institutions, and also for safeguarding the civil and religious rights of all the inhabitants of Palestine, irrespective of race and religion."); *Id.* art. 3 (qualifying commitment to Jewish immigration to ensure "that the rights and position of other sections of the population are not prejudiced"); *Id.* at art.9 (guaranteeing "[r]espect for the personal status of the various peoples and communities and for their religious interests . . .").

43. *See, e.g.,* JULIUS STONE, ISRAEL AND PALESTINE 10-15 (1981).

44. *Id.* at 15-16.

45. *Id.* at 22-25. Stone's position rests on the following premises: (1) that the designation "Palestine" referred historically to the territory on both sides of the Jordan River, *id.* at 22; (2) that the division of the territory into the mandates of Palestine and Transjordan represented "a last-minute encroachment on the already small allocation to

While it seems clear that Palestinian national identity at the beginning of the century was intertwined to a significant extent with a more general Arab identity,[46] it does not follow that the establishment of other Arab states negates the Palestinians' right to self-determination in Palestine. Had a different chain of events placed the entire territory of Palestine under, for instance, the rule of Jordan's King Abdallah, Palestinians may have had some difficulty establishing that the principle of self-determination mandated their independence from Jordan, since the Palestinians and Jordanians, as Arab peoples, have long been connected by history and culture and were not always clearly separated by national borders. The notion that the self-determination rights of the people of Jaffa or Ramallah or Jerusalem were amply satisfied by the establishment of an independent state fifty or one hundred miles away and that their cities and land consequently could be "allocated" to a largely foreign[47] population is, however, difficult to square with authoritative interpretations of the principle of self-determination.[48]

Moreover, as indifferent to the political rights of the indigenous Palestinians as the Mandate for Palestine appears to have been, it was

---

the Jewish nation in the self-determination distribution. . . ." *id.* at 23; (3) that the population of Jordan is, at present, comprised largely of Palestinians, most of whom possess Jordanian citizenship; and (4) that Jordanians and Palestinians share a historical and cultural "affinity," *id.* at 24.
The historical accuracy of Stone's assertions is worthy of some skepticism. *See, e.g.* ALBERT HOURANI, A HISTORY OF THE ARAB PEOPLES 318 (1991) (referring to Transjordan as land east of Palestine and noting that Britain acknowledged no Jewish claim to it); KHALDI, *supra* note 42, at 27-29 (reviewing historical references to Palestine as land west of the Jordan River); Ibrahim Abu-Lughod, *Palestinian Culture and Israel's Policy*, ARAB STUDIES Q., Spring/Summer 1985, at 95, 97-99 (discussing distinguishing characteristics of Palestinian culture).

46. To concede this point is not to suggest that the Arabs in Palestine were culturally indistinguishable from other Arab peoples at the beginning of the twentieth century. The urban and agricultural lifestyles and traditions of Palestinians made them very different from the predominantly Bedouin population of Transjordan. *See* ARTHUR GOLDSHMIDT, A CONCISE HISTORY OF THE MIDDLE EAST 272-73 (3d ed. 1988); *See generally* Abu-Lughod, *supra* note 66, at 95,97-99 (discussing distinguishing characteristics of Palestinian culture).

47. Ninety percent of the Jewish population of Palestine in 1946 had immigrated to the country in the previous four decades. *See* HENRY CATTAN, PALESTINE AND INTERNATIONAL LAW 88 (1977). Most Jewish immigrants came from Central Europe, Poland, and the Soviet Union. *Id.*

48. The 1970 Declaration on Principles of International Law Concerning Friendly Relations and Co-operation Among States, which is generally seen as an authoritative interpretation of the U.N. Charter's self-determination provisions, *see supra* note 10, and accompanying text, states that "by virtue of the principle of . . . self-determination of peoples . . . all peoples have the right freely to determine, without external interference, their political status," Declaration on Friendly Relations, *supra* note 9, at 123. Even if one assumes, *arguendo*, that the people of Palestine were merely a part of the larger "Arab people" in 1922, it is difficult not to see the "allocation" of their territory by foreign powers to a foreign population as "external interference."

not designed to facilitate placing the indigenous Arab[49] population of Palestine under the sovereignty of a "Jewish State." The Mandate, like the Balfour Declaration from which its language is drawn, commits to the establishment only of a Jewish national home in Palestine.[50] The Balfour Declaration was adopted by the British War Cabinet only after it received Zionist assurances that they did not seek to establish a "Jewish Republic or other form of State in Palestine or any part of Palestine."[51] Moreover, Great Britain refused to interpret the language of the Balfour Declaration as contemplating the transformation of Palestine into a Jewish State.[52]

The framers of the Mandate seem to have envisioned the eventual establishment of a single state in Palestine. For instance, although the Mandate committed in several capacities to helping to secure the establishment of a Jewish national home, it provided for the enactment of a single nationality law for the country, stating that the law should include "provisions framed so as to facilitate the acquisition of Palestinian citizenship by Jews who take up their permanent residence in Palestine."[53] This provision acknowledged the concept of Palestinian nationality and framed it in non-communal (i.e. not Jewish or Arab) terms. Similarly, the Mandate stated that "[t]he Administration of Palestine shall take all necessary measures to safeguard the interests of the community in connection with the development of the country"[54] and expressed Britain's commitment to support "the development of self-governing institutions" in Palestine.[55] The broad non-exclusive language of these provisions suggests that the framers of the Mandate conceived of Palestine as a single country whose inhabitants would possess a single nationality and would govern themselves with a single administration. Although inter-communal strife prompted Britain to reconsider this approach, it seems clear that the eventual establishment of a single state of Palestine was Britain's original intention. [56]

Despite these apparent intentions, Britain's policies over the course of the Mandate contributed to the development of severe inter-communal tension in Palestine. The British Mandatory Government's commitment to the creation of a Jewish national home in Palestine, and its initially liberal Jewish immigration policies, aroused the resentment

---

49. The term "Arab" is used loosely here to include the entire indigenous population of the country, including Muslims, Christians, and Jews.

50. Mandate for Palestine, *supra* note 39, at 2184; *See* John A. Collins, *Self-Determination in International Law; The Palestinians*, 12 CASE W. RES. J. INT'L L. 137, 157 (1980).

51. MALLISON & MALLISON, *supra* note 37, at 38.

52 CATTAN, *supra* note 47.

53. Mandate for Palestine, *supra* note 39, art. 7, at 2186 (emphasis added).

54. *Id.* art. 11, at 2186 (emphasis added).

55. *Id.* art. 2, at 2185.

56. This textual analysis is supported by the expressed statements of British officials at several points during the Mandate. *See* BERNARD WASSERSTEIN, THE BRITISH IN PALESTINE: THE MANDATORY GOVERNMENT AND THE ARAB-JEWISH CONFLICT, 1917-1929, at 109 (1978); NORTHEDGE, *supra* note 27, at 214. *See generally* W. THOMAS MALLISON, THE BALFOUR DECLARATION: AN APPRAISAL IN INTERNATIONAL LAW (1973).

of indigenous Palestinians who identified themselves as part of a broader Arab nation and feared being placed under the rule of European immigrants.[57] These tensions generated increasingly violent inter-communal strife in Palestine and led the British Peel Commission to conclude in 1937 that "[a]n irrepressible conflict has arisen between two national communities within the bounds of one small country."[58] Based on these observations, the Commission recommended the partition of Palestine into Jewish and Arab states, the latter to be incorporated into Transjordan. The proposal raised the ire of both the Zionists, who felt that the territory allocated to them was too small, and the Arab Palestinians, who challenged Britain's right to partition their territory at all.[59] Although Britain eventually abandoned this proposal declaring its goal to be "the establishment within ten years of an independent Palestine State,"[60] Arab-Jewish relations continued to deteriorate.

In February 1947, Great Britain formally acknowledged that it lacked the power to impose a settlement in Palestine and returned the Mandate to the United Nations, which assumed responsibility for League of Nations trusteeships. After accepting the return of the Mandate in May, the United Nations established a committee composed of delegates from eleven United Nations member states to evaluate the situation in Palestine and make recommendations regarding the future of the territory. In August, a majority of the Committee recommended a partition plan that divided Palestine into three territories — an Arab state, a Jewish state, and an internationally administered enclave around Jerusalem — in a contorted geographical arrangement that one British scholar has described as "two fighting serpents entwined in an inimical embrace."[61] The Partition Plan stated that "[i]ndependent Arab and Jewish States . . . shall come into existence in Palestine two

---

57. Christians and Muslims in Palestine began to unite during the early part of the 1900's in opposition to Zionist national aspirations. For instance, after Zionists held a procession in Jerusalem in November 1918 to celebrate the first anniversary of the Balfour Declaration, a deputation of Christian and Muslim sects, headed by the mayor of Jerusalem, submitted a written protest to the British Military Governor of Palestine articulating its concern that the Zionists would be given sovereignty over them. Responding to Zionist assertions that Palestine had become their national home, the deputation stated:

> If it is meant that they should obtain national liberty in the country, why should this be confined to the Jews and not to others? . . . We Arabs, Muslim and Christian, have always sympathized profoundly with the persecuted Jews in their misfortunes in other countries. . . . We hoped for their deliverance and prosperity. But there is a wide difference between this sympathy and the acceptance of such a nation in our country, to be made by them a national home, ruling over us and disposing of our affairs.

WASSERSTEIN, *supra* note 56, at 32. *See also* JAMAL R. NASSAR, THE PALESTINE LIBERATION ORGANIZATION: FROM ARMED STRUGGLE TO THE DECLARATION OF INDEPENDENCE 9 (1991) (quoting an editorial from the Jerusalem daily demanding "self-rule," "unity of territory" and "rejection of a Zionist immigration" in Palestine).

58. MARK TESSLER, A HISTORY OF THE ISRAELI-PALESTINIAN CONFLICT 241-42 (1994).

59. *Id.* at 242.

60. *Id.* at 245 (quoting a White Paper issued by Malcolm MacDonald in May 1939).

61. *Id.* at 259 (quoting George Kirk).

months after the evacuation of the armed forces of the mandatory Power has been completed but in any case not later than 1 October 1948."[62] It then set forth an outline for a multi-phased transition period during which each of the States was to develop provisional governmental institutions,[63] and conditioned international recognition of each State upon its establishment of effective independence and its declared commitment to guarantee the protection of religious sites and minority rights.[64]

The Plan, however, never came into effect. Although, after some initial hesitation, the Zionists declared their willingness to accept the recommendations, the Palestinian Arabs rejected them out of hand, arguing that the United Nations had no right to allocate the majority of their territory to the Zionists (who, in March 1947, claimed possession of less than seven percent of the land in Palestine and ownership of only 5.66%[65] and represented less than a third of the territory's population).[66] The United Nations General Assembly nevertheless endorsed the partition resolution on November 29, 1947 by a vote of thirty-three to thirteen, with ten abstentions.[67] Almost immediately thereafter, full-scale war broke out between the Arabs and the Zionists. On May 14, 1948, after establishing control over all of the territory allocated to the Jewish state (and over some allocated to the Arab state),[68] a provisional Zionist national council announced the establishment of the State of Israel on the portion of Palestine allocated by the Partition Plan to form the Jewish State. Israel captured more territory allocated to the Arab state in fighting after its independence. By the time armistice agreements were concluded in 1949, its official boundaries encompassed almost 80% of the territory of Palestine.[69]

In light of these circumstances, the effect of United Nations Resolution 181 (which recommended implementation of the Partition Plan) on the international legal status of Palestine's indigenous inhabitants remains unclear.[70] Although the Partition Plan required each of the proposed States to make a declaration that included a commitment to guarantee the political[71] and religious[72] rights of all Palestinians (Arab

---

62. *Plan of Participation with Economic Union*, G.A. Res. 181 (II), part 1, sec. A, para. 3, U.N. Doc. A/519, at 133 (1947).

63. *Id.* part 1, sec. B., at 133.

64. *Id.* part 1, sec. F., at 142.

65. CATTAN, *supra* note 47, at 88 (citing United Nations statistics); KHALIDI, *supra* note 41, at 236.

66. *See* ABU LUGHOD, THE DEMOGRAPHIC TRANSFORMATION OF PALESTINE 155 (1973).

67. TESSLER , *supra* note 58, at 261.

68. *Id.* at 263.

69. CATTAN, *supra* note 47, at 24.

70. A discussion of the legitimacy of the United Nations' decision to endorse the Partition Plan falls beyond the scope of this essay. For a critical evaluation of the legal dimensions of this issue, *see* CATTAN, *supra* note 47, at 75-89.

71. G.A. Res. 181 (II), *supra* note 62, part 1, sec. C, ch. 3, para. 1 ("Palestinian citizens shall, upon the recognition of independence, become citizens of the State in which they are resident and enjoy full civil and political rights.").

72. *Id.* at part 1, sec. C, ch. 2 (defining religious and minority rights).

and Jewish), it defined the two states in clearly communal terms. For instance, it provided for voluntary population transfers between the two states and prohibited Arabs and Jews residing within the proposed territory of their own respective states from seeking citizenship in the other state.[73] These provisions show that the United Nations acknowledged the existence of two national communities in Palestine, each on the verge of achieving the status of statehood. Accordingly, they reflect a tacit recognition by the United Nations of the Palestinian Arab nation.

Over the course of the Mandate, therefore, the indigenous inhabitants of Palestine received implicit international recognition as a people entitled to statehood. This recognition is apparent from the terms of the League of Nations Covenant, which granted provisional recognition of the independent nationhood of the communities designated as "A" Mandates. While the terms of the Mandate for Palestine departed significantly from this conception of the Palestinian Arabs, defining Palestine in primarily territorial terms, U.N. Resolution 181 and the Partition Plan affirmed that the Palestinian Arabs were entitled to a State of their own.

2. 1948-1969: From Inhabitants to Refugees

Following the establishment of the State of Israel, the international community began to regard Palestinians in individual rather than communal terms.[74] Although the Partition Plan had provided for voluntary population transfers between the proposed Jewish and Arab states,[75] United Nations resolutions following the creation of the State of Israel maintained a territorial focus. The U.N. sought to restore the former inhabitants of Palestine to their homes, whether they were located within the newly-created State of Israel or in what remained of the lands allocated by the Partition Plan to the Arab state.[76] The Palestine Arabs, therefore, were viewed simply as individual refugees, the former inhabitants of the territory of Palestine.[77] This approach continued beyond the June 1967 War.[78]

This shift away from international recognition of Palestinian Arab nationhood likely resulted, at least in part, from changes in the conception of self-determination. One writer has suggested recently that the West's reaction against nationalism after World War II — driven both

---

73. *Id.* at part 1, sec. C, ch. 3, para. 1.
74. MALLISON & MALLISON, *supra* note 37, at 189-90.
75. G.A. Res. 181 (II), *supra* note 62, part 1, sec. C, ch. 3, para. 1.
76. G.A. Res. 194 (III), para. 11, U.N. Doc. A/810, at 21, 24 (1948). Similarly, the U.N. created in 1948 a relief agency—UNRWA—to provide assistance to "Palestine Refugees," not Palestinian refugees, reflecting a view of them as the inhabitants of the territory of Palestine rather than as an independent people.
77. S.C. Res. 89, U.N. SCOR, 5th Sess., at 9, U.N. Doc. S/1907 (1950).
78. Security Council Resolution 259 refers to "the inhabitants of the Arab territories under military occupation by Israel." U.N. SCOR, 23d Sess., at 11, U.N. Doc. S/INF/23/Rev.1 (1968).

by horror at Nazi atrocities and by increasing economic and political internationalization — translated into a renunciation by Western nations of the Wilsonian concept of self-determination and a reaffirmation of the principle of state sovereignty.[79] Although the United Nations Charter commits the United Nations to the development of "friendly relations among nations based on respect for the principle of equal rights and self-determination of peoples,"[80] to the postwar framers of the United Nations Charter, "[s]elf-determination was [still] . . . only . . . a means of furthering the development of friendly relations among states and . . . strengthen[ing] universal peace . . . with the obvious consequence that it might and indeed should be set aside when its fulfillment would give rise to tension and conflict among states."[81] Support for Palestinian nationhood was not easily reconciled with this new vision of self-determination. The Palestinian Arabs, as individuals, were entitled either to repatriation or to compensation for their lost possessions. They could seek vindication of their individual rights within existing state structures. Their claims to nationhood and to the right to establish an independent state, however, were subordinated to the maintenance of the political order established in the Middle East following the Arab-Israeli War.[82]

3. 1969-Present: Peoplehood, Participation, & Self-Determination

In the late 1960s, however, a culmination of factors[83] brought the United Nations General Assembly to reaffirm the recognition of Palestinian nationhood articulated in the League of Nations Covenant and the 1947 Partition Plan. Beginning in 1969, the General Assembly passed a series of resolutions recognizing: (1) the Palestinians' status as a people; (2) the centrality of their participation to the achievement of a just resolution of the Palestine question; and (3) their right to self-determination. This recognition, however, was not extended by all Member States. Until 1993, Israel and the United States refused to recognize the Palestinians' peoplehood or their right to participation in the Middle East peace process, and both countries continue to refrain from expressly acknowledging the Palestinians' right to self-

---

79. Binder, *supra* note 6, at 230-31.
80. UNITED NATIONS CHARTER, art. 1, para. 2.
81. Binder, *supra* note 6, at 230-31 (quoting Antonio Cassese, *The Helsinki Declaration and Self-Determination, in* HUMAN RIGHTS, INTERNATIONAL LAW, AND THE HELSINKI ACCORD 83, 94 (Thomas Buergenthal ed., 1977)); *Cf.* GOODRICH, ET. AL, *supra* note 23, at 30-31 (discussing U.N. Charter framers' varying interpretations of right to self-determination).
82. *See* TESSLER, *supra* note 58, at 275-279 (discussing subordination of Palestinian national aspirations to Israeli, Jordanian, and Egyptian political concerns); William J. O'Brien, *The PLO in International Law,* 2 B.U. INT'L L.J. 349, 352 (1984) (identifying the Arab States' failure to take Palestinians seriously as a factor motivating the establishment of the PLO in 1964).
83. Among these factors were the recent independence and participation of former colonial territories in the General Assembly; Israel's occupation of the remaining territory of Palestine following the June 1967 War; and the wresting of control over the PLO from the Arab States by Palestinian *fedayeen.*

determination. As discussed below, however, the actions of Israel and the United States, in this regard, have been at odds with the broad recognition of Palestinian national aspirations by other members of the international community.

The General Assembly departed from its previous focus on the individual rights to repatriation and compensation of refugees from Palestine in 1969, recognizing the Palestinians' status as a people. In resolution 2535, the General Assembly reaffirmed "the inalienable rights of the people of Palestine,"[84] stating that the Palestinian refugee problem had arisen from a denial of the Palestine Arabs' rights under the United Nations Charter and the Universal Declaration of Human Rights.[85] It, thereby, acknowledged that the Palestinians were more than stateless individuals and that their statelessness had resulted from a denial of their right to constitute themselves as a national community. This recognition of Palestinian peoplehood has been reaffirmed by all subsequent General Assembly resolutions dealing with the subject.[86] Accordingly, during its 1970 session, the General Assembly began to use the designation "the Palestinians,"[87] instead of referring to them as the Palestine Arabs, the Palestine refugees, or the (former) inhabitants of Palestine.

In addition to extending international recognition to the Palestinian people, the General Assembly began, during this period, to regard them as primary participants in the settlement of the Palestine question. Previously, U.N. resolutions acknowledged no role at all for the Palestinians. Security Council Resolution 242, for instance, made no specific reference to the Palestinians except insofar as it affirmed the necessity of "achieving a just settlement of the refugee problem."[88] While Resolution 242 emphasized "the need to work for a just and lasting peace," it defined this peace as being one in which "every State in the area can live in security."[89] Maintaining the focus on the inviolability of state sovereignty apparent in the U.N. resolutions following the 1947 Arab-Israeli War, it made no reference to a Palestinian role in the peace process or to Palestinian national rights. In contrast, General Assembly Resolution 2628 (XXV), passed during the 1970 session, recognized the vindication of Palestinian rights to be "an indispensable

---

84. G.A. Res. 2535 (XXIV), U.N. GAOR, 24th Sess., Supp. No. 30, at 25, U.N. Doc. A/7630 (1969).

85. *Id.* sec. B, pmbl..

86. MALLISON & MALLISON, *supra* note 37, at 190.

87. G.A. Res. 2628 (XXV), U.N. GAOR, 25th Sess., Supp. No. 28, at 5, U.N. Doc. A/8028 (1970).

88. S.C. Res. 242 U.N. SCOR, 22d Sess., at 8, U.N. Doc. S/INF/22/Rev. 2 (1967). U.N. Resolution 242 deals with the Palestinians in two ways: (1) it states that the U.N. Charter requires "the establishment of a just and lasting peace" based in part on "[w]ithdrawal of Israel armed forces from territories occupied in the recent conflict"; and (2) it affirms the necessity of "achieving a just settlement of the refugee problem." *Id.* In light of resolutions throughout the 1960s, the phrase "just settlement of the refugee problem" likely alludes to General Assembly Resolution 194(III), U.N. Doc. A/810, at 24 (1948), which demanded the repatriation or compensation of refugees.

89. S.C. Res. 242, *supra* note 88.

element for the establishment of a just and lasting peace in the Middle East."[90] Building upon that premise, the General Assembly resolved in 1974 that "the Palestinian people is a principal party to the question of Palestine" and invited the Palestine Liberation Organization to participate in plenary meetings of the General Assembly concerning Palestine.[91] In a subsequent resolution, moreover, the General Assembly requested that the Secretary General "establish contacts with the Palestine Liberation Organization on all matters concerning the question of Palestine."[92] The General Assembly, therefore, affirmed that the vindication of the rights of the Palestinian people was a central component of any just resolution of the Palestine question and that, accordingly, the Palestinian people had a right to participate in the settlement of that question.

In a series of resolutions during the same period, the General Assembly made explicit that this right to participation emerged from the Palestinians' right to self-determination. General Assembly Resolution 2649 — entitled Universal Realization of the Right of Peoples to Self-determination and Speedy Granting of Independence to Colonial Countries and Peoples — condemned "those Governments that deny the right to self-determination of peoples recognized as being entitled to it, especially of the peoples of southern Africa and Palestine."[93] Through this and subsequent resolutions,[94] the General Assembly recognized the legitimacy of the Palestinian national liberation movement and analogized it to other efforts to eradicate the vestiges of colonialism.

This recognition, however, has not been unanimous. While the existence of a Palestinian people and their right to participate in the resolution of the Palestine question appear no longer to be in contention, their right to self-determination has not been fully recognized by the two States, Israel and the United States, that are most able to prevent its realization. In September 1993, in anticipation of the signing of the DOP, Israel Prime Minister Yitzhak Rabin wrote to PLO Chairman

---

90. G.A. Res. 2628 (XXV), *supra* note 87.

91. G.A. Res. 3210 (XXIX), U.N. GAOR, 29th Sess., Supp. No. 31, at 3, U.N. Doc. A/9631 (1974).

92. G.A. Res. 3236, U.N. GAOR, 29th Sess., Supp. No. 31, at 4, U.N. Doc. A/9631 (1974) (emphasis added). The international role and status of the Palestine Liberation Organization is discussed in greater depth below. *See infra* Section II(A).

93. G.A. Res. 2649 (XXV), U.N. GAOR, 25th Sess., Supp. No. 28, at 73-74, U.N. Doc. A/8028 (1970).

94. *See* G.A. Res. 2672 (XXV), U.N. GAOR, 25th Sess., at 35-36, U.N. Doc. A/8028 (1970) (recognizing "that the people of Palestine are entitled to equal rights and self-determination, in accordance with the Charter of the United Nations"); G.A. Res. 2787 (XXVI), U.N. GAOR, 26th Sess., Supp. No. 29, at 82, U.N. Doc. 8429 (1971) (entitled "Importance of the universal realization of the right of peoples to self-determination and of the speedy granting of independence to colonial countries and peoples for the effective guarantee and observance of human rights;" "Reaffirming the inalienable rights of all peoples, and in particular those of the Palestinian people, to freedom, equality, and self-determination, and the legitimacy of their struggles to restore those rights."); G.A. Res. 2949 (XXVII) (8 Dec. 1972), U.N. GAOR, 26th Sess., Supp. No. 29, at 82, U.N. Doc. 8429 (1971).

Yasser Arafat stating that, in light of the PLO's acceptance of U.N. resolutions 242 and 338, its recognition of Israel's right to exist, and its commitment to renounce terrorism, Israel recognized the PLO "as the representative of the Palestinian people."[95] Further, in the DOP itself, the Government of Israel and the PLO, as representative of the Palestinian people, agreed to "recognize their mutual, legitimate and political rights,"[96] words the two parties reaffirm in their subsequent agreements.[97] Although these commitments by Israel fall short of the PLO's recognition of Israel's right "to exist in peace and security,"[98] they represent formal recognition that the Palestinians possess "legitimate and political rights" as a people. The scope of the rights recognized by Israel is, however, difficult to assess.

The agreements concluded between the PLO and Israel pursuant to the DOP are silent with regard to Palestinian self-determination. The U.N. Security Council resolutions to which the agreements refer make no direct reference to the issue of self-determination or even name the Palestinian people, Resolution 242 affirming only the need for "a just settlement of the refugee problem."[99] The U.N. General Assembly recently has made some effort to link Palestinian self-determination to Resolution 242. Following the conclusion of the DOP, the Assembly passed a resolution reaffirming that final status negotiations between Israel and the PLO should be based, *inter alia*, upon:

> (a) [t]he realization of the legitimate national rights of the Palestinian people, *primarily the right to self-determination*, (b) [t]he withdrawal of Israel from the Palestinian territory occupied since 1967, including Jerusalem, and from the other occupied Arab territories, [and] (c) guaranteeing arrangements for peace and security for all States in the region, *including those named in resolution 181(II) of 29 November 1947, within secure and internationally recognized boundaries.*[100]

The resolution, therefore, not only expresses the Assembly's sense that Palestinian self-determination should be a basis of permanent status negotiations, but also incorporates the principle into Resolution 242 by including the states named by Resolution 181 (and therefore, the Arab State envisaged by the 1947 Partition Plan) among the States whose borders should be respected. Israel and the United States both voted against the resolution, however, with Israel asserting that it predetermined the outcome of permanent status negotiations and the United States seeking to avoid focusing on "divisive and polarizing

---

95. Letter from Yitzkah Rabin to Yasser Arafat, THE PALESTINIAN-ISRAELI PEACE AGREEMENT: A DOCUMENTARY RECORD 128-29 (Inst. For Palestinian Studies, ed. 1993) [hereinafter THE PALESTINIAN ISRAELI PEACE AGREEMENT].

96. Declaration of Principles, *supra* note 2, at 1527.

97. *See* Interim Agreement, *supra* note 5, pmbl.; Gaza-Jericho Agreement, pmbl.

98. THE PALESTINIAN-ISRAELI PEACE AGREEMENT, *supra* note 95, at 128.

99. *See* S.C. Res. 242, *supra* note 87; S.C. Res. 338, U.N. SCOR, 28th Sess., at 10, U.N. Doc. S/INF/29 (1973); Bassiouni, *supra* note 8, at 35.

100. G.A. Res. 48/158D, U.N. GAOR, 48th Sess. (1993) (emphasis added).

statements."[101]

It is, therefore, uncertain whether the governments of Israel and the United States recognize the Palestinian right to self-determination. In view of Israel's acknowledgment that the Palestinians are a people and possess the "legitimate rights" attendant to that status, Israel's unwillingness to support the General Assembly Resolution may arise from the view that, even if the Palestinians do possess a right to self-determination, as the vast majority of the international community has recognized, the ultimate status of the territory that they claim is not theirs alone to decide. That is, that the OPT do not constitute a viable self-determination unit. As discussed below, however, that position is difficult to reconcile with international practice regarding the disposition of non-self-governing territories.

C. The Territory of Palestine

A people's right to exercise self-determination is constrained by the status of the territory to which they lay claim. As Professor Bassiouni suggests, "[i]n the abstract, people determine their goals regardless of geographic limitations; however, realistically, [self-determination] is exercisable only when it can be actuated within a given territory susceptible of acquiring the characteristics of sovereignty . . . ."[102] Thus, while authoritative international instruments recognize self-determination to be a right of all peoples, the full exercise of that right, in practice, has been restricted to the populations of certain classes of territory. Owing perhaps, to the fact that the law of self-determination has developed largely within the context of decolonization, the territories most universally recognized to be "self-determination units" have been mandate territories and the former colonial holdings of metropolitan States.

In order to assess the scope of the Palestinian right to self-determination, it is necessary to evaluate the extent to which the OPT themselves comprise a self-determination unit. The provisional recognition of Palestine's independence in the League of Nations Covenant and in U.N. Resolution 181(II) arguably confers this status upon Palestine.[103] As argued below, however, this status can also be seen to emerge from the U.N. Charter's provisions regarding the disposition of non-self-governing territories. While the OPT may not be a former colonial territory *per se*, and Israel's role in the OPT has been one of a belligerent occupant rather than an administering authority, the OPT otherwise conform to the Charter's definition of a non-self-governing

---

101. 1993 U.N.Y.B. 530, U.N. Sales No. E.94.I.1.

102. Bassiouni, *supra* note 8, at 34.

103. With the exception of the U.S. administered Pacific Islands, all "A" , "B" and "C" Mandates have achieved independence. *See* CRAWFORD, *supra* note 8, at 426-28. *See also* Allen Gerson, *Trustee-Occupant: The Legal Status of Israel's Presence in the West Bank,* 14 HARV. INT'L L.J. 1, 24-27 (1973) (arguing that sovereignty in mandated territories resides ultimately in their populations, who have the right eventually to exercise that sovereignty through independence).

territory. Since international law has evolved to recognize the right of the populations of all non-self-governing territories to self-determination, so too must Israel recognize the Palestinians' right to self-determination on their territory.

Based on the framework established by the U.N. Charter for the definition and disposition of non-self-governing territories, the OPT constitute a self-determination unit. Although the U.N. General Assembly has interpreted Chapter XI of the Charter primarily to apply to territories that were colonies in 1945,[104] the Charter, itself, requires U.N. Members "which have *or assume* responsibilities for the administration"[105] of non-self-governing territories to abide by its provisions.[106] This suggests that it is applicable to territories acquired by metropolitan States after 1945.[107] The General Assembly's subsequent resolutions analogizing the Palestinian liberation movement to other anti-colonial movements imply, moreover, that the OPT possess characteristics similar to the colonial territories to which Chapter XI has been recognized to apply. Further, as discussed below, the OPT conform to Chapter XI's definition of non-self-governing territories in that they are separate from, distinct from, and subordinate to Israel, the State presently administering them.

Under U.N. General Assembly Resolution 1541, there is a *prima facie* obligation to transmit information "in respect of a territory which is geographically separate and is distinct ethnically and/or culturally from the country administering it."[108] The OPT meet all three criteria. The OPT's geographic separateness from Israel is apparent from a number of factors. First, the international community — including both the U.N. Security Council and the General Assembly — consistently has regarded Israel's presence in the OPT as an occupation of foreign territory and has demanded the withdrawal of Israeli forces. [109] Second, while members of the Israeli polity have laid claims to the OPT on the basis of religious, political, security, and other interests, the Government of Israel has not annexed the OPT.[110] Accordingly, Israel has

---

104. *See* G.A. Res. 1541 (XV), *supra* note 24, at Annex, Principle 1.

105. U.N. CHARTER, art. 73 (emphasis added).

106. *See* CRAWFORD, *supra* note 8, at 359-60.

107. *Id.*

108. G.A. Res. 1541 (XV), *supra* note 24, at Annex, Principle IV.

109. *See, e.g.*, G.A. Res. 49/62D, U.N. GAOR, 49th Sess. (1994); G.A. Res. 2443(XXIII), U.N. GAOR, 23d Sess. (1968). The fact that the U.N. Security Council and the General Assembly have demanded that Israel recognize the *de jure* applicability of the Fourth Geneva Convention to the OPT confirms its view that the OPT are not seen as part of the State of Israel. *See The Situation in the Arab Territories Occupied by Israel*, S.C. Res. 446, U.N. SCOR, 34th Sess., at 4, U.N. Doc. S/INF/35 (1979); G.A. Res. 48/41 B, U.N. GAOR, 48th Sess., Supp. No. 49, at 114, U.N. Doc. A/48/49 (1993) (demanding that Israel accept *de jure* applicability of Fourth Geneva Convention to OPT).

110. Although the Knesset extended Israeli law over East Jerusalem shortly after its occupation in 1967 and made "unified Jerusalem" the capital of Israel in 1980, its Annexation has been condemned by the U.N. General Assembly and Security Council. G.A. Res. 49/87A, U.N. GAOR, 49th Sess. (1994) (citing past resolutions); S.C. Res. 252, U.N. SCOR, 23d Sess., at 9, U.N. Doc. S/INF/23/Rev.1 (1968).

imposed a separate legal regime upon the OPT than that prevailing in Israel, and Palestinian residents of the territories have been granted no right to citizenship in Israel. Finally, the express terms of the Interim Agreement concluded between Israel and the PLO affirm that both parties see the West Bank and the Gaza Strip "as a single territorial unit, the integrity and status of which will be preserved during the interim period."[111] While the Interim Agreement does not indicate precisely what "status" will be preserved, it does affirm that the OPT constitute a distinct, coherent territorial unit.

The population of the OPT, moreover, is to a great extent ethnically and culturally distinct from the population of Israel. [112] The distinctions between the two populations were explicitly recognized in the United Nations 1947 Partition Plan and are the implicit basis for the international community's recognition of Palestinian peoplehood. The differences in the predominant languages and religions of the two populations also attest to this distinction. While almost two hundred thousand Israeli citizens presently reside in the OPT, their presence in the Territories has repeatedly been condemned by the international community as an illegal contravention of humanitarian law.[113] They constitute, moreover, only a small percentage of the Territories' total population. The OPT, therefore, are geographically, ethnically, and culturally distinct from the State of Israel. On that basis, there exists a presumption under Principle IV that the OPT is a non-self-governing territory under Chapter XI of the U.N. Charter.

Once the *prima facie* case described in Principle IV has been met, Principle V provides for scrutiny of other elements of the relationship between the concerned territory and the metropolitan State in order to assess the extent to which the territory has been placed "in a position or status of subordination."[114] As discussed in Part II(C), below, the OPT remain almost entirely under Israeli authority and control, even though portions of the Territories have been administered by the PA since June 1994.

The OPT, therefore, possess the attributes, though not the formal

---

111. Interim Agreement, *supra* note 5, at ch. 2, art. 11, para. 1.

112. I must admit that I speak of ethnic and cultural distinctions with some hesitation. Ethnicity and culture are dynamic, largely imagined concepts that, like the communities they are used to describe, resist rigid delineation. It is, after all, only an accident of history that we do not now speak of "Jewish Palestinians" with lack of irony with which we speak of "Christian Palestinians." Many writers have reflected thoughtfully on these issues. *See, e.g.*, BENEDICT R. O'G. ANDERSON, IMAGINED COMMUNITIES: REFLECTIONS ON THE ORIGIN AND SPREAD OF NATIONALISM (1983); JAMES CLIFFORD, THE PREDICAMENT OF CULTURE: TWENTIETH-CENTURY ETHNOGRAPHY, LITERATURE, AND ART (1988); CLIFFORD GEERTZ, THE INTERPRETATION OF CULTURES: SELECTED ESSAYS (1973); FRANTZ FANON, THE WRETCHED OF THE EARTH (Constance Farrington trans., 1968); FRANCOISE LIONNET, AUTOBIOGRAPHICAL VOICES: RACE, GENDER, SELF-PORTRAITURE (1989); EDWARD W. SAID, ORIENTALISM (1978).

113. *See* Adam Roberts, *Prolonged Military Occupation: The Israeli-Occupied Territories Since 1967*, 84 AM. J. INT'L L. 44, 85-86 & nn. 152-53 (1990) (citing U.N. General Assembly and Security Council Resolutions condemning Israeli settlement activity).

114. G.A. Res. 1541 (XV), *supra* note 24, Annex, Principle V.

48   DENV. J. INT'L L. & POL'Y   VOL. 26:1

status, of a non-self-governing territory under the terms of Chapter XI of the U.N. Charter. It would be naive, if not cynical, however, to characterize Israel's occupation of the West Bank and Gaza as a form of trusteeship, although at least one writer has suggested that Israel assume the role of "trustee-occupant."[115] Since Israel is an occupying power with significant economic and political interests in the OPT and a relationship of extreme enmity with its population, it is unlikely that its acceptance of "the obligation to promote to the utmost . . . the well-being of the inhabitants" [116] of the West Bank and Gaza would be received with great confidence by the Palestinian population. The point of demonstrating the OPT's functional status as a non-self-governing territory is not, therefore, in order to recommend a shift in Israel's status from occupant to trustee but, rather, to show that the OPT possess the requisite characteristics for the exercise of self-determination. The OPT are a coherent and distinct territorial unit that is separate, both legally and practically, from Israel. In light of the fact that the populations of other non-self-governing territories that meet these criteria have been seen to possess the right to self-determination, the OPT should be recognized to constitute a legitimate self-determination unit.

II. PALESTINIAN PUBLIC BODIES

The international community, therefore, has recognized the Palestinians' status as a people, the centrality of their participation to equitable resolution of the Palestine question, and, by and large, their inalienable right under the United Nations Charter and other international instruments to self-determination. This recognition of Palestinian peoplehood — and the international participation it has facilitated — has resulted, to a great extent, from the establishment of Palestinian public bodies, which have served both as constitutive expressions of Palestinian nationhood and as vehicles for the pursuit of self-determination. The Palestine Liberation Organization (PLO) has, for many years, represented — in the myriad senses of the word — the Palestinian people. Through the PLO, the Palestinians have established a symbolic State and a very real administrative authority. This section examines the functions and international status of each of these bodies.

A. The Palestine Liberation Organization

Over the last thirty years, the PLO has emerged as the international representative of the Palestinian people and has played an instrumental role in defining and pursuing Palestinian national aspirations. This section analyzes the PLO's legitimacy as representative of the Palestinian people and its international status, as it has developed since its establishment in 1964.

---

115. Gerson, *supra* note 103, at 45-47.
116. U.N. CHARTER, art. 73.

1. Representation of the Palestinian People

In January 1964, Egyptian president Gamal abd-el-Nasser convened the first Arab Summit Conference in an attempt to formulate responses to Israel's plan to divert the waters of the Jordan River for its own use. Although the Conference proved unable to develop a viable strategy to counteract Israel's plans, it did recommend the establishment of "a sound basis for organizing the Palestinian people in order to enable them to assume their duties in liberating their homeland and determining their destiny."[117] Accordingly, a council selected by committees composed of Palestinians in various Arab countries met that spring and on June 1, 1964 established the PLO and adopted the Palestine National Covenant. Although the Covenant is occasionally referred to as the "PLO Covenant," it is more than an organizational charter. By its own terms, at least, it represents a constitutive expression of Palestinian nationhood; defining the Palestinian people and articulating their national character and aspirations, as well as establishing the PLO to act as their international representative and to work toward vindication of their national rights.

The Covenant defines the Palestinian people in ethnic, temporal, and territorial terms. Perhaps reflecting the emphasis at the time of its enactment on the principle of Arab unity, the Covenant's first article proclaims, "Palestine is the homeland of the Palestinian people. It is an inseparable part of the bigger Arab nation, and its people are an integral part of the Arab people."[118] The Covenant, therefore, situates both the territory of Palestine and the Palestinian people within the Arab nation. Although this provision arguably is designed more to emphasize the incongruity of the "Zionist-imperialist"[119] presence in the region than to define an ethnic or cultural criterion for Palestinian nationality. More substantively, the Covenant defines the Palestinian people in temporal and territorial terms. Article Five states, "[t]he Palestinians are those Arab citizens who under normal conditions used to live in Palestine[120] until 1947; they include those who remained there as well as those who were evicted. The offsprings [sic] of an Arab Palestinian parent, since that date, whether born in Palestine or outside, are regarded as Palestinians."[121] The Covenant also states that "Jews who

---

117. NASSAR, *supra* note 57, at 20. President Nasser initially proposed creating a "Palestinian entity." *Id.* at 19. During discussion of the issue, the leaders of the Arab states represented at the conference, suggested a variety of forms, ranging from the creation of a Palestinian state in the West Bank and Gaza Strip (which at the time were occupied by Jordan and Egypt, respectively) to the formation of a national liberation front. *See* LEILA KADI, ARAB SUMMIT CONFERENCES AND THE PALESTINE PROBLEM 99 (1966).

118. Palestine National Covenant, art. 1, *reprinted in* NASSAR, *supra* note 57, app. 2 at 219.

119. Palestine National Covenant, art. 15, *reprinted in* NASSAR, *supra* note 57, app. 2 at 220.

120. *See generally* Palestine National Covenant, art. 2, *reprinted in* NASSAR, *supra* note 57, app. 2 at 219 (defining Palestine in terms of "the borders that existed during the British Mandate").

121. Palestine National Covenant, art. 5, *reprinted in* NASSAR, *supra* note 57, app. 2 at

used to live under normal conditions in Palestine until the Zionist invasion of the country are to be considered Palestinians."[122] The Covenant, therefore, defines the Palestinians as the people who resided in the territory of Palestine, as delimited by the British Mandate, before 1947 (or, for Jewish Palestinians, before 1923) and their descendants.

Having thus defined the Palestinian people, the Covenant assigns to the PLO the role of facilitating the liberation of their homeland. This role is apparent not only from its name — the Palestine *Liberation* Organization — but also from article 26 of the Covenant:

The Palestine Liberation Organization, which represents all the forces of the Palestinian revolution, is responsible for the activities of the Arab Palestinian people *in their struggle to liberate their land and return to it to practice their right to self-determination.* This applies to all military, political, and financial matters, as well as anything related to the Palestinian problem on the Arab and international levels.[123]

The Covenant makes clear that, whatever functions the PLO might assume in relation to the Palestinian people and the international community, its overriding goal is securing for the Palestinian people the opportunity to return to their homeland under circumstances that will enable them to exercise self-determination. Since its creation, the PLO has developed an elaborate bureaucratic structure and administers a variety of social services to Palestinians in diaspora. Nevertheless, its focus has not been the amelioration of conditions in exile, but rather the termination of the condition of exile. While it has on occasion played a significant role in the national politics of other countries in the region (despite the Covenant's commitment to the contrary),[124] it has not sought to represent the interests of Palestinians as members of the national communities of the States in which they reside. Rather, its political activities have focused on those States' policies regarding Israel and the question of Palestine. It is in this capacity that the PLO characterizes itself as the sole legitimate representative of the Palestinian people.[125]

The internal legitimacy of this claim among the Palestinian people

---

219.

122. Palestine National Covenant, art. 6, *reprinted in* NASSAR, *supra* note 57, app. 2 at 219. The PLO selected 1923 as the year when the "Zionist invasion" began. As Cherif Bassiouni has pointed out, however, "That cut-off date is debatable since Palestinian Arab representatives agreed in the ensuing years to an immigration quota which allowed for the lawful entry of many European Jews." Baussiouni, *supra* note 8, at 38.

123. Palestine National Covenant, art. 26, *reprinted in* NASSAR, *supra* note 57, app. 2 at 222 (emphasis added).

124. *See* Palestine National Covenant, art. 27, *reprinted in* NASSAR, *supra* note 57, app. 2 at 222 ("The Palestine Liberation Organization cooperates with all Arab States, each according to its potentials, and it adheres to a neutral policy in its relations with these States in the light of the requirements of the liberation battle. On the basis of this, it does not interfere in the internal affairs of any Arab State").

125. As discussed in the next section, the international community roundly accepts the PLO's claim to represent the Palestinian people.

has been consistently affirmed. As a liberation organization representing the sometimes disparate interests of a dispersed population, the
PLO has not functioned democratically at all times.[126] Nevertheless,
Palestinians continually have identified the PLO as their international
representative since its founding in 1964. Palestinian labor unions and
women's and students' groups pledged their support for the organization promptly after it was created, and they have continued to regard it
as the sole legitimate representative of the Palestinian people.[127] Other
Palestinian institutions, including newspapers, political parties, and
guerrilla groups, also have acknowledged the legitimacy of the PLO's
representative status.[128] Perhaps most indicative of the internal legitimacy of the PLO, however, has been the consistent failure of other
States to circumvent it in their dealings with the Palestinians. Israel,
for instance, was unable to establish an alternative Palestinian leadership structure in the Occupied Territories in the 1970s, when the
elected mayors in the West Bank agreed to confine their dealings with
the Israelis to municipal matters on the grounds that the PLO was the
"political representative" of all of the Palestinian people.[129] Similarly,
even though the PLO did not participate directly in the 1991 Madrid
Conference, the Palestinian delegation affirmed in its response to the
invitation to participate that "[t]he fact that the PLO has agreed not to
be directly or overtly involved in the process at present, does not in any
way prejudice its role as the sole legitimate representative of the Palestinian people everywhere, and the only body empowered to negotiate or
conclude agreements on behalf of the Palestinian people."[130] The PLO,
therefore, has firmly established its status among Palestinians as their
sole international representative.

A brief review of the organization's institutions of internal governance reveals some of the contours of this representation. Although the
PLO has not sought recognition as a government in exile,[131] its institutions are modeled after governmental structures and provide Palestinians worldwide with an array of social services. [132] The PLO has two
primary policymaking organs: the Palestine National Council (PNC), a
300 to 400 member body that functions as the PLO's legislative branch;
and the Executive Committee, a fifteen member council apparently
based in form on the British cabinet system.[133] The PNC, alone, is empowered to make or change basic PLO policy positions.[134] Its members,

126. *See* NASSAR, *supra* note 57, at 74-76 (discussing democratic and autocratic strains
apparent in PLO politics).
   127. *Id.* at 30-31.
   128. *Id.* at 31-36.
   129. *Id.* at 35. *See generally* 7 J. PALESTINE STUD. 132-36 (1978) (presenting Israeli
press coverage regarding Palestinian municipal elections and PLO).
   130. Palestinian Response to Madrid Invitation, Oct. 22, 1991. THE PALESTINIAN-
ISRAELI PEACE AGREEMENT, *supra* note 95, at 14.
   131. *See* notes 140-41, *infra* and accompanying text.
   132. *See* NASSAR, *supra* note 37, at 68-73.
   133. *Id.* at 50.
   134. William V. O'Brien, *The PLO in International Law*, 2 B.U. INT'L L. J. 349, 355
(1984).

who serve three-year terms, assemble annually to consider the report of the Executive Committee, the Organization's budget, proposals by various committees, and other policy matters.[135] PNC members originally were elected based upon a geographic scheme, under which members of the PLO assembled quarterly on the local level to elect representatives.[136] Following the 1967 War, however, the PLO adopted an occupational electoral scheme, in order to make mobilization possible under Israeli occupation, since Israel permitted the organization of professional and labor unions.[137] Presently, the various Palestinian resistance organizations (e.g. *Fatah* and the Popular Front for the Liberation of Palestine) and mass unions and syndicates (e.g. the General Union of Palestinian Women and the General Union of Palestinian Students) hold seats on the Council in much the same way as would political parties in a national legislature.[138]

The PLO Executive Committee has the mandate of establishing and supervising the organization's bureaucratic institutions and of ensuring that PNC policies are implemented.[139] Originally, the Chairman of the Committee, who is appointed by the National Council, selected the members of the Executive Committee, but the system was altered later to require their election by the Council.[140] Yasser Arafat has been Chairman of the Executive Committee since his election to the position at the fifth session of the PNC in February 1969.[141]

The PLO's institutional structure to a great extent reflects its mandate. It was conceived as and remains a liberation organization. It has never characterized itself as a government-in-exile. According to Anis Kassim, "authoritative officials of the PLO" have taken the position that the establishment of a government-in-exile would "create problems of dual loyalty for Palestinians living in different countries" and possibly "invite conflicts with host governments."[142] Kassim suggests that, while the PLO might seek to establish such a government at some point in the future, the Palestinians remain — or remained (Kassim wrote in 1980) — too "far way from realizing their objectives" to make it a prudent enterprise.[143] Moreover, it is unclear whether the PLO has the power to

---

135. NASSAR, *supra* note 57, at 50.

136. *Id.* at 73.

137. *Id.* at 73-74.

138. *See generally id.* at 60-61. Fateh has been the largest movement in the PLO since 1969. *See generally id.* at 80-86. It should be noted that the various unions with representatives in the PLO are not occupational in the traditional sense — they do not represent the interests of workers as workers, for instance. As Nassar explains, "[t]hese unions are formed around political and social issues rather than work-related questions. These unions do not concern themselves with worker-management matters, but function mainly to mobilize their members behind the Palestinian cause." *Id.* at 74.

139. *Id.* at 51.

140. *Id.*

141. *Id.* at 60-61.

142. Anis Kassim, *The Palestinian Liberation Organization's Claim to Status: A Juridicial Analysis Under International Law*, 9 DENV. J. INT'L L. & POL'Y 1, 31-32 (1980).

143. *Id.* Although there was some expectation that the PLO might move to establish itself as a government body following the issuance of the Palestinian Declaration of Inde-

reconstitute itself in that way. As noted above, the Palestine National Covenant assigns the PLO the role of facilitating circumstances through which Palestinians can exercise their right to self-determination on their territory. The PLO's role ends, therefore, when the exercise of self-determination begins. [144] Under the Covenant, the PLO does not have the power to determine, itself, how to constitute the Palestinian nation; whether, for example, it should take the form of an independent State or should enter into an association with another State. Since the PLO's international legitimacy emerges from its role as representative of the Palestinian people, the power ultimately to ratify or decline agreements regarding the final status of Palestine remains with the Palestinian people.

2. International Status

a. Recognition

The Palestine Liberation Organization's legitimacy as the international representative of the Palestinian people has been affirmed consistently by the United Nations General Assembly, Security Council, and other constituent organs, as well as by most States in the international system, including, since 1993, Israel and the United States. However, few States or organizations outside of the Arab World have recognized the PLO as a government.

United Nations

The United Nations General Assembly has extended recognition to the PLO as the international representative of the Palestinian people and, accordingly, has facilitated its participation in United Nations activities. As discussed above, the General Assembly recognized, in the early 1970s, the rights of the Palestinian people to participate in the settlement of the Palestine question and, more broadly, to self-determination. Pursuant to this recognition, in October 1974, it invited the PLO, which one month earlier had been affirmed by the Arab League to be "the sole legitimate representative of the Palestinian people,"[145] to participate during plenary sessions in its deliberations re-

---

pendence, it has not taken steps formally to alter its status. NASSER, *supra* note 57, at 43.

144. Testimony introduced on behalf of the PLO in litigation related to the *Achille Lauro* incident conforms to this conception of the PLO's role: "The PLO describes itself as 'the internationally recognized representative of a sovereign people *who are seeking* to exercise their rights to self-determination, national independence, and territorial integrity. The PLO is the internationally recognized embodiment of the nationhood and sovereignty of the Palestinian people *while they await the restoration of their rights through the establishment of a comprehensive [sic], just and lasting peace in the Middle East.'"* Klinghoffer v. Achille Lauro, 739 F. Supp. 854, 857 (S.D.N.Y. 1990) (quoting Ramsey Clark Aff., Apr. 27, 1987) (emphasis added).

145. THE PALESTINIAN-ISRAELI PEACE AGREEMENT, *supra* note 95, at 210-11. The Rabat Summit marked Jordan's acquiescence to the PLO's claim to represent the Palestin-

garding the question of Palestine.[146] Shortly thereafter, the General Assembly approved even broader participation by the Palestinian people in United Nations activities, requesting the Secretary General "to establish contacts with the Palestine Liberation Organization on *all matters* concerning the question of Palestine."[147] Finally, during the same session, the General Assembly granted the PLO the status of observer, inviting it to participate in the work of the General Assembly and of all international conferences convened either by the General Assembly or under the auspices of other United Nations organs.[148] Accordingly, a number of United Nations organs and independent agencies have extended observer status to the PLO or have cooperated with it to provide services to the Palestinian people.[149]

The observer status granted to the PLO gives it broader access to General Assembly activities than that granted to any other non-state entity. For instance, while the PLO has access to both the plenary and Main Committees of the General Assembly,[150] the other national liberation movements (excepting the South West Africa People's Organization (SWAPO)) have been accorded access only to the Main Committees,[151] and their participation in General Assembly activities has been limited to deliberations regarding the territories that they claim to represent.[152] The other liberation movements, moreover, have been invited to participate only in United Nations conferences, meetings, and other seminars that concern their countries, while the PLO and SWAPO — before Namibia's independence — have been invited to participate in the sessions and work of all such conferences.[153] Non-governmental organizations, similarly, are entitled to attend only public meetings of the General Assembly and committee meetings on items relevant to their work.[154] Even intergovernmental organizations generally have access

---

ian people after having previously claimed that role for itself. Kassim, *supra* note 141, at 18 n.99.

146. G.A. Res. 3210 (XXIX), *supra* note 91, at 3.

147. U.N. GAOR, 29th Sess., Supp. No. 31, at 4, U.N. doc. A/9631 (1974). The vote on this resolution was 89 in favor, 8 against, and 37 abstentions. Israel and the United States were among the states voting against the resolution. Patrick J. Travers, *The Legal Effect of United Nations Action In Support of the Palestinian Liberation Organization and the National Liberation Movements if Africa,* 17 HARV. INT'L L. J. 561, 570-71 (1976). In its 1975 session, the General Assembly emphasized that Palestinian participation in U.N. deliberations regarding the Middle East would be on "equal footing" with all other parties. U.N. GAOR, 30th Sess., Supp. No 34, at 3, U.N. Doc. A/10034 (1975).

148. G.A. Res. 3237 (XXIV), U.N. GAOR, 30th Sess., Supp. No. 31, at 5, U.N. Doc. A/9631 (1974). This resolution reflected the General Assembly's broader objective of shifting the role of observers from simple observation to active participation. *See* Erik Suy, *The Status of Observers in International Organizations,* 160 ACADEMIE DE DROIT INTERNATIONALE 75,130-31 (1978).

149. Travers, *supra* note 147, at 569-75.

150. Suy, *supra* note 148, at 107 (citing G.A. Res. 3237 (XXIX) (1974)).

151. *Id.*

152. Travers, *supra* note 147, at 570.

153. Suy, *supra* note 148, at 111-12.

154. *Id.* at 106.

only to international conferences that deal with matters of direct interest to them.[155] Erik Suy, the former Legal Counsel to the United Nations, suggests that the breadth of access afforded the PLO emerges from the assumption that it is "strongly connected with [the] future state[] of the people [it] represents" and therefore has "a much wider interest in the works undertaken by the United Nations than regional intergovernmental organizations, the work and interest of which are expected to be more limited."[156] The General Assembly, therefore, has established a unique status for the PLO; while it has not been granted the full access to U.N. activities accorded Member States, its recognized connection to the land and people of Palestine has facilitated broader participation than other non-State entities.

The Security Council has proven less sympathetic to Palestinian participation than the General Assembly, due in large part to the United States' traditional rejection of attempts to establish direct links with the PLO.[157] The Security Council has, however, acknowledged the PLO's representative status. In 1975, and again in 1976 and 1978, it invited the PLO to take part in the debate over a resolution that would have condemned Israel for its repeated air attacks on Lebanon. What is notable about the invitation is that it extended to the PLO "the same rights conferred upon a member State invited to participate under rule 37,"[158] rather than relying upon rule 39, under which the African movements appeared before the Council. [159] Although the legal validity and implications of the invitation have been hotly disputed,[160] it appears beyond contention that the Council's decision to structure PLO participation in this way was calculated to reaffirm the PLO's status as representative of a people with recognized national rights. Since then, however, the Security Council has done little to facilitate the expansion of the PLO's international participation. Other International Organizations

The PLO has also been recognized by and permitted to participate in the activities of other international organizations, but this recognition largely has been limited to organizations with members sympathetic to the Palestinian cause. Arab regional organizations and Islamic organizations have granted the PLO the broadest recognition and participation, giving it the status and privileges of a State member.

---

155. *Id.* at 112.

156. *Id.*

157. *See* Travers, *supra* note 147, at 573.

158. U.N. Monthly Chronicle, No. 1, at 14-15 (1976). "Rule 37 applies to '[a]ny Member of the United Nations which is not a member of the Security Council;' rule 39 applies to 'persons.'" Kassim, *supra* note 142, at 20.

159. Travers, *supra* note 147, at 573.

160. *See, eg.,* Kassim, *supra* note 142, at 20-21, 31 (suggesting that invitation and implicit recognition of the PLO by the Security Council constituted authoritative legal precedent); Evyatar Levine, *A Landmark on the Road to Legal Chaos: Recognition of the PLO as a Menace to World Public Order,* 10 DENV. J. INT'L L. & POL'Y 259, 259-61 (1981); Leo Gross, *Voting in the Security Council and the PLO,* 70 AM. J. INT'L L. 470, 476-91 (1976).

Among these organizations are the League of Arab States and its specialized agencies (e.g. the Arab Fund for Economic and Social Development), the Organization of the Islamic Conference, the Arab Monetary Fund, the Council of Arab Economic Unity, and the Islamic Development Bank.[161] The nonaligned nations conference also has invited the participation of the PLO as a full member.[162] States

The governments of more than one hundred states have extended recognition to the PLO, generally in its capacity as the representative of the Palestinian people.[163] Among these States are most of the countries in the developing world and former Soviet bloc, as well as China, Japan and a number of European countries, including France, Belgium, Italy, Sweden, and Austria.[164] In 1993, moreover, Israeli Prime Minister Yitzhak Rabin wrote a letter to PLO Chairman Yasser Arafat stating that "the Government of Israel has decided to recognize the PLO as representative of the Palestinian people."[165] More than half of these countries have accorded the PLO full diplomatic status and have authorized the establishment of PLO embassies within their borders. A number of others have permitted the PLO to establish offices under the auspices of the Arab League.[166] With a few exceptions, however, the embassies have played more of a symbolic role than a practical one.[167]

b. International Status

The international status of the PLO has been a point of some contention among legal scholars. One commentator, Anis Kassim, characterized the PLO as a "territorial public body," which he defined to include "territorial units the elites of which are in the process of consolidating their respective nation state units."[168] He argued that, by virtue of its broad recognition as the international representative of the Palestinian people, [169] its exercise of typical governmental functions,[170] and its role as successor to the Arab Higher Committee, which, Kassim suggested, had elicited *de facto* recognition as a public body by Great Britain and Arab governments,[171] the PLO was legally entitled to participate in the international process as representative of the Palestinian people.[172]

---

161. *See generally* YEARBOOK OF INTERNATIONAL ORGANIZATIONS (33d ed. 1996).

162. Kassim, *supra* note 142, at 3 n.3.

163. O'Brien, *supra* note 134, at 379.

164. NASSAR, *supra* note 57, 163.

165. Letter from Yasser Arafat to Yitzkah Rabin (Sept. 9, 1993), THE PALESTINIAN-ISRAELI PEACE AGREEMENT, *supra* note 95, at 129.

166. O'Brien, *supra* note 134, at 379.

167. *Id.* at 380.

168. Kassim, *supra* note 142, at 9.

169. *Id.* at 19-22.

170. *Id.* at 22-26, 32.

171. *Id.* at 18.

172. *Id.* at 33. In support of his position, Kassim cited numerous precedents acknowledging that governments in exile, anti-colonial movements, and fledgling revolutionary governments are subjects of international law and extending to them recognition com-

In a critique of Kassim's analysis, Israeli Military Judge Evyatar Levine suggested that the PLO, as a non-state entity, could claim no right to international recognition as representative of a people[173] and that the PLO's lack of control over any portion of the territory it claimed differentiated it from other revolutionary movements that had received international recognition.[174] Another critic, Professor William O'Brien, argued in 1984 that internal divisions prevented the PLO from effectively representing the Palestinian people at the international level: "[i]n its present disarray, the PLO can apparently not perform the most essential of all functions of an organization purporting to represent a people, namely, negotiating diplomatically on their behalf."[175] O'Brien suggested, moreover, that the PLO's broad recognition by international organizations and States had little functional significance since the PLO had not (in 1984) been recognized by Israel or the United States, the two States most capable of effecting or stifling Palestinian national aspirations.[176]

Much has changed since these commentators debated the PLO's status in the early 1980s. The PLO has renounced terrorism and has established diplomatic connections with Israel and the United States, both of whom recognize it as the legitimate representative of the Palestinian people and as a "partner" in the ongoing Middle East peace negotiations. Also, the PLO is substantially connected to the Palestinian administration governing sections of the OPT under the DOP and its progeny. In view of these developments, the objections cited above to Kassim's characterization of the PLO as a "territorial public body," and, more broadly, to the PLO's participation in the international process lack currency. While, as discussed below, neither the establishment of the "State of Palestine" in 1988 or the PA in 1994 has altered the PLO's international role and status, both have helped to facilitate universal recognition of the PLO as international representative of the Palestinian people.

B. The "State" of Palestine

1. The Palestinian Declaration of Independence

During its nineteenth session, in November 1988, the PNC voted to adopt the Palestinian Declaration of Independence, proclaiming "the establishment of the State of Palestine on our Palestinian territory with its capital Holy Jerusalem."[177] The Declaration clearly was conceived,

---

mensurate with that granted to nascent states. *Id.* at 9-13.

173. Levine, *supra* note 160, at 247-48.

174. *Id.* at 248-49.

175. O'Brien, *supra* note 134, at 392.

176. *Id.* at 392-95.

177. *Palestinian Declaration of Independence*, 19ᵗʰ Sess., para. 10, U.N. Doc. A/43/827 (1988) [hereinafter Declaration of Independence].

in part, as a symbolic gesture in support of the Palestinian *intifada*, which at that time had been in progress for eleven months.[178] The terms of the Declaration, however, suggest that the PNC intended for the Declaration to have broader consequences. Following its expulsion from Lebanon in 1982, the PLO leadership began to focus more resolutely on achieving a negotiated settlement with Israel within an internationally-mediated framework. To that end, it heightened its efforts to fortify its international legitimacy, pursuing the establishment of diplomatic relations with the United States and engaging in an informal dialogue with leaders of the Israeli peace movement. The Declaration of Independence appears designed to legitimate the PLO's political agenda by reconciling it with the already-existing legal framework established by the United Nations for resolution of the Palestine question.

The Declaration of Independence bases its proclamation of Palestine's independence on two specific international commitments to the Palestinian people and, more generally, on the principles enshrined in the United Nations Charter. First, it makes reference to the League of Nations' recognition of Palestine as a provisionally independent nation in Article 22 of the League of Nations Covenant and in the Treaty of Lausanne,[179] arguing that those authorities confirm the falsehood of the notion that Palestine was ever a "land without a people." Secondly, it characterizes the 1947 partition plan endorsed in U.N. General Assembly Resolution 181 as bestowing "international legitimacy" upon the Palestinian Arab people's claim to self-determination and sovereignty.[180] Since the PNC voted, after its adoption of the Declaration, to declare the territorial boundaries of the state of Palestine to be the West Bank (including East Jerusalem) and the Gaza Strip, the Declaration's evocation of Resolution 181 appears to represent a retroactive acceptance of the principle of dividing Palestine into two states, the idea being that nothing has occurred since 1947 that would nullify the Palestinian right to sovereignty recognized in Resolution 181.

Finally, the Declaration states that the occupation of Palestinian land has subverted the Charter and subsequent resolutions of the United Nations, which guarantee "the right of Return, the right of independence, [and] the right to sovereignty over territory and homeland."[181] Although it does not make reference to a specific provision of the U.N. Charter, several clauses of the Charter could be construed as bestowing these rights on the Palestinians. The Charter states, for instance, that one of the purposes of the United Nations is the development of "friendly relations among nations based on respect for the prin-

---

178. *Id.* para. 9 (speaking of the *intifada* as having been the decisive change prompting Palestinian independence). *See also* Youssef M. Ibrahim, *P.L.O. Proclaims Palestine to be an Independent State; Hints at Recognizing Israel*, N.Y. TIMES, Nov. 15, 1988, at A1 ("The announcement by the Palestinian council had been expected for months. Leaders of the Palestinian uprising in the West Bank and Gaza have demanded the gesture in recognition of their 11-month-long insurrection . . .").

179. Declaration of Independence, *supra* note 177, para. 4.

180. *Id.* para. 5.

181. *Id.* para. 6.

ciple of equal rights and *self-determination of peoples* . . . ."[182] Article 55 of the Charter uses a similar formula to express the United Nations' goals in the fields of social and economic development and human rights. Further, Article 73 compels U.N. members assuming responsibility for non-self-governing territories "to develop self-government, to take due account of the political aspirations of the peoples, and to assist them in the progressive development of their free political institutions, according to the particular circumstances of each territory and its peoples and their varying stages of advancement."[183] Finally, the U.N. General Assembly has interpreted the Charter's requirement that States refrain from the use of force in international relations as a prohibition of action that "deprives peoples under foreign domination of their right to self-determination and freedom and independence and of their right to determine freely their political status and pursue their economic, social, and cultural development."[184] These provisions of the Charter can all be seen to legitimize the Palestinians' claims to self-determination and the pursuit of sovereignty.

Beyond demonstrating the legitimacy of Palestinian national aspirations within the established international legal framework, however, it is unclear precisely what purpose the Declaration is intended to serve. Despite its retroactive acceptance of Resolution 181 and, shortly thereafter, its acceptance of U.N. Resolutions 242 and 338, the PNC made no effort following the Declaration to reconstitute itself as a government-in-exile and, thereby, to formalize Palestine's status as a State under occupation. Similarly, the PNC Central Council's election of Yasser Arafat to the position of President of the State appears to have been little more than honorific, there having been no apparent distinction between his responsibilities as President and as Chairman of the PLO. As suggested by the Declaration's call to other Arab peoples "to consolidate and enhance the emergence *in reality* of our state,"[185] the PNC's decision to proclaim the independence of Palestine appears to have been a largely symbolic gesture, an attempt to affirm the reasonableness and international legal legitimacy of the Palestinian cause.

2. International Recognition

To the extent that the Declaration was conceived as an effort to bolster the international legitimacy of the Palestinian national liberation movement, it met with considerable success. Perhaps unsurprisingly, Israel's Likud-dominated coalition government refused to recognize the legitimacy of any unilateral action taken by the PLO, which it continued to regard as a terrorist organization.[186] A number of other

182. U.N. CHARTER, art. 1 ¶ 2 (emphasis added).
183. *Id.* art. 73(b).
184. G.A. Res. 2160 (XXI), U.N. GAOR, 21st Sess., Supp. No. 16, at 4, U.N. Doc. A/6316 (1966) (apparently basing prohibition of denial of self-determination on Charter art. 2(4)); *see also* CRAWFORD, *supra* note 8, at 89-90.
185. Declaration of Independence, *supra* note 177, para. 12 (emphasis added).
186. 1988 U.N.Y.B. 208, U.N. Sales No. E.93.I.100.

nations welcomed the move, however, at least thirteen of them immediately recognizing the newly-declared state.[187] By April 1989, 114 nations had extended some form of recognition to the Palestinian state,[188] but the majority of these countries appear to have recognized the State to be a legitimate aspiration, not an existing reality.[189]

The U.N. General Assembly took a similar approach. In Resolution 43/177, the General Assembly voted to replace the designation "Palestine Liberation Organization" with "Palestine" within the United Nations system, but it did so "without prejudice to the observer status and functions of the Palestine Liberation Organization within the United Nations system."[190] Thus, while the General Assembly (on a vote of 104-2-36, the United States and Israel voting against the resolution) explicitly affirmed the Palestinians' right to exercise their sovereignty over the West Bank and Gaza, it stopped short of altering the status of the PLO. Significantly, however, the General Assembly ratified the Declaration's interpretation of Resolution 181 as legitimating the establishment in the Occupied Territories of a Palestinian state.[191] In subsequent resolutions, moreover, the General Assembly began to interpret U.N. Security Council Resolution 242 to require that the territorial integrity of the States created by Resolution 181 be respected, appearing, thereby, to recognize the PNC's retroactive acceptance of the 1947 Partition Plan and affirming that the terms of the Plan continue to legitimate the Palestinians' claim to self-determination.

C. *The Palestinian Interim Self-Government Authority (PA)*

Over the course of several months in 1993, while formal peace negotiations within the framework established by the 1991 Madrid Peace Conference proceeded separately (and largely without progress), representatives of the Israeli government and the PLO engaged in at least fourteen rounds of secret meetings in Oslo, the process mediated by the late Johann Jorgen Holst, former foreign minister of Norway. This process led to formal mutual recognition between the State of Israel and the PLO, as the representative of the Palestinian people, and to the formulation of the DOP, which was signed on September 13, 1993 by Is-

---

187. *13 Countries Back Palestinian Move*, N.Y. TIMES, Nov. 16, 1988, at A10.

188. Arafat is Elected President of State He Hopes to Form, N.Y. TIMES, Apr. 3, 1989, at A3.

189. The U.S.S.R., for instance, recognized "the proclamation of the Palestinian state," but noted that its "practical" creation would result from a "comprehensive settlement" in the region. Phillip Taubman, *Moscow Lauds P.L.O. State But Is Vague on Recognition*, N.Y. TIMES, Nov. 19, 1988, § 1, at 4. Similarly, Egypt, Norway, and Spain expressed support for the PNC move, although they did not bestow formal recognition on the State of Palestine. *13 Countries Back Palestinian Move, supra* note 185.

190. G.A. Res. 43/177, U.N. GAOR, 43rd Sess., Supp. No. 49, at 62, U.N. Doc. A/43/49 (1988).

191. The General Assembly acknowledged its awareness "of the proclamation of the State of Palestine by the Palestine National Council *in line with General Assembly resolution 181 (II)* and in exercise of the inalienable rights of the Palestinian people." *Id.* (emphasis added).

raeli Foreign Minister Shimon Peres and Mahmoud 'Abbas, head of the PLO's Political Department. The DOP created a framework for long-term negotiations regarding the final status of the OPT and the establishment in the interim period of a Palestinian self-governing authority. Subsequent agreements concluded between the Government of Israel and the PLO further defined the functions and jurisdiction of this PA, which began to administer portions of the OPT in May 1994.

This section analyzes the PA's jurisdiction and claim to legitimacy with a view toward evaluating its legal status in relation to Israel, the PLO, the Palestinian people, and the international community.

1. Jurisdiction

The powers, structure, and jurisdiction of the PA are defined by the Israeli-Palestinian Interim Agreement on the West Bank and the Gaza Strip (IA), which was concluded in Washington, D.C. on September 28, 1995, pursuant to Article VII of the DOP.[192] The Interim Agreement, as its name suggests, is a self-consciously temporary arrangement. While it governs the administration of portions of the OPT during "the transitional period," the Agreement is purposefully vague about both to what and from what the parties are making a transition.[193] It makes no fundamental changes to the legal status of the OPT[194] and, indeed, explicitly limits its effect to the interim period.[195] The OPT, therefore, remain under Israeli occupation, even if Palestinians are now afforded a broader role in their administration. Accordingly, the authority of the Palestinian governing institutions established by the DOP is entirely local in character.

The central components of the Palestinian Interim Self-Government Authority (PA) are a Council with limited legislative authority, a President, and an executive authority. The Interim Agreement fixes the size of the Council at eighty-two members[196] and provides for the democratic election of its members by registered Palestinian voters residing in the OPT, including (parts of) Jerusalem.[197]

---

192. Because the IA supersedes earlier agreements between the PLO and Israel, such as the Agreement on the Gaza Strip and Jericho Area, Interim Agreement, pmbl., cl. 10, this essay does not address the terms of the other agreements. Interim Agreement, 36 I.L.M. 551, 558.

193. The only constraint on final status negotiations acknowledged by the Interim Agreement is that the permanent settlement must be "based on Security Council Resolutions 242 and 338." Id. pmbl., at 558.

194. Article 31 of the Interim Agreement states, "Neither side shall initiate or take any step that will change the status of the West Bank and the Gaza Strip pending the outcome of the permanent status negotiations." Id. ch. 5, art. 31, cl. 7, at 567.

195. Article 31 of the Interim Agreement states, "Nothing in this Agreement shall prejudice or preempt the outcome of the negotiations on the permanent status to be conducted pursuant to the DOP. Neither Party shall be deemed, by virtue of having entered into this Agreement, to have renounced or waived any of its existing rights, claims, or positions." Id. art. 31, cl. 6, at 567.

196. Id. ch. 1, art. 4, at 559.

197. See generally id. Annex 3. The IA disqualifies from election candidates who are

The President of the PA is also democratically-elected.[198] Both the President and the Council members are to serve throughout the transitional period, which is to have ended by May 4, 1999.[199] While the Council technically possesses both legislative and executive authority, the IA provides for the delegation of its executive authority to a committee comprised of the President of the PA and other persons appointed by the President and approved by the Council.[200]

The IA strictly enumerates the powers of all three components of the PA, limiting their authority and jurisdiction to Palestinian affairs at the local level. Article One of the IA, which sets the basic terms for the transfer of authority, states that "Israel shall transfer powers and responsibilities as specified in this Agreement from the Israeli military government and its Civil Administration to the Council in accordance with this Agreement. Israel shall continue to exercise powers and responsibilities not so transferred."[201] The terms of this provision make three things clear: first, that the limited authority transferred to the PA flows from the Israeli military government, not from the Palestinian people; second, that Israel possesses all residual authority over the OPT; and, third, that the transfer of authority is defined by agreement of both sides, not unilaterally by Israel. The first two points are reflected throughout the IA's provisions regarding the PA's territorial, functional, and personal jurisdiction, each of which is reviewed in turn below. The apparent implications of the third point, particularly with regard to the PA's legitimacy, are discussed later in this essay.

·a. Territorial Jurisdiction

The IA provides for a phased transfer of territorial jurisdiction[202] from the Israeli Civil Administration and Military Government to the PA. Although the Agreement affirms that both sides regard the West Bank and Gaza Strip as "a single territorial unit, the integrity and status of which will be preserved during the interim period,"[203] it divides that "unit" into a patchwork of smaller districts, each classified into one of three categories: Area "A," Area "B," and Area "C."[204] The IA

---

members of groups that advocate "racism" or pursue their aims "by unlawful or non-democratic means." *Id.* Annex 2, art. 3, para. 2.

198. *Id.* ch. 1, art. 3, para. 3, at 559.

199. *Id.* ch. 1, art. 3, para. 4, at 559.

200. *Id.* ch. 1, art. 5, para. 4. At least 80% of the members of the Executive Authority must be elected members of the Council. *Id.* at ch. 1, art. 5, para. 4, cl. (c), at 559.

201. *Id.* ch. 1, art. 1, para. 1, at 558

202. Territorial jurisdiction is defined in the Interim Agreement as including "land, subsoil, and territorial waters, in accordance with the provisions of this Agreement." *Id.* ch. 3, art. 17, para. 2(a), at 564. As discussed below in the functional jurisdiction section, the Interim Agreement places significant restraints on the exercise of Palestinian territorial jurisdiction in all spheres of authority.

203. *Id.* ch. 2, art.11, para. 1, at 561.

204. The Gaza Strip is not subject to the same territorial classifications. Gaza effectively is divided into two territories, one under Palestinian authority (as in Areas A and B

assigns the PA varying degrees of territorial jurisdiction over the areas in each of these categories.

Area "A" includes portions of major Palestinian population centers in the OPT and represents, in total, three percent of the West Bank.[205] Pursuant to the IA, the Israeli military redeployed its forces away from these areas prior to the elections for the Council, which took place on January 20, 1996. The PA's functional and personal jurisdiction, as defined by the IA, have full force in Area A. The PA also has authority over "internal security and public order in Area A."[206]

Area "B", which represents twenty-seven percent of the West Bank,[207] consists of other Palestinian-populated regions of the OPT, including a number of small towns, villages, and hamlets. Area B, like Area A, falls entirely within the PA's functional and personal jurisdiction. The "B" areas differ from the "A" areas, however, in two significant respects: first, Israeli redeployment out of these areas is to take place over a more extended period of time; and, second, while the Council is to assume "responsibility for public order for Palestinians," Israel maintains "overriding responsibility for security for the purpose of protecting Israelis and confronting the threat of terrorism."[208]

Area "C" covers all remaining territory in the West Bank and Gaza Strip. Included in this category are all Jewish settlements, areas that Israel considers to be of strategic importance, and unpopulated areas. Area C encompasses the vast majority of the OPT: thirty-five to forty percent of the Gaza Strip and approximately seventy percent of the West Bank. The PA is to assume limited functional and personal jurisdiction (over Palestinians only) in Area C during the first phases of Israeli redeployment.[209] During these initial phases, Israel will retain complete territorial jurisdiction over Area C, [210] but it is to transfer gradually "powers and responsibilities relating to territory" to the PA over an eighteen month period.[211] Settlements and Israeli military installations, however, will remain entirely under Israeli control since they are considered to be among the "issues that will be negotiated in

---

of the West Bank) and one under Israeli authority, the latter comprised of the Israeli military installations and settlements in Gaza. *Id.* ch. 2, art.11, para. 1, at 561.

205. Al Haq, Draft Analysis of Basic Law sec. 1.2.1.

206. Interim Agreement, ch. 2, art. 13, para. 1, 36 I.L.M. 551, 561. During the 1996 session of the Commission on Human Rights, the representative of the Permanent Observer from Palestine criticized Israel for violating this provision of the IA, citing the Israeli assassination in Gaza of Hamas operative Yehia Ayyash.

207. Haq, *supra* note 205.

208. Interim Agreement, ch. 2, art. 13, para. 2, 36 I.L.M. 551, 562.

209. As of late November 1996, even this limited jurisdiction has not yet been transferred. *Id.* ch. 2, art. 17, para. 2 (c) (d), at 564.

210. "In Area C, during the first phase of redeployment Israel will transfer to the Council civil powers and responsibilities not relating to territory . . . ." *Id.* ch. 2, art. 11, para. 2(c), at 561.

211. *Id.* ch. 2, art. 11, para. 2(e), at 562.

the permanent status negotiations."[212]   Israel, moreover, will retain "authority to exercise its powers and responsibilities with regard to internal security and public order."[213]   The Israeli deployment of combat forces throughout Area C and into Areas A and B in response to mass demonstrations by Palestinians following the opening of a tunnel beneath the Dome of the Rock in Jerusalem suggests that Israel is likely to continue to interpret this provision as broad authority for pursuing whatever security measures it deems prudent.

Two additional facets of the Interim Agreement's (IA) territorial jurisdiction provisions bear mention. First, although East Jerusalem legally remains part of the Occupied West Bank, and despite its illegal annexation by Israel, the IA does not give the PA any form of jurisdiction over the city and its residents, although a small number of Palestinian residents of Jerusalem (5,000) were permitted to register to vote in Palestinian Council elections. Secondly, although the West Bank city of al-Khalil (Hebron) has 120,000 Palestinian residents, the IA applies special arrangements to it for the interim period as a result of the continued presence of 120 Israeli settlers. As Al-Haq summarizes:

The Oslo B Agreement divides al-Khalil into two areas of administration, designated as H-1 and H-2. The Council will assume all civilian powers and responsibilities throughout al-Khalil in relation to Palestinian residents, as in other West Bank cities. In Area H-2 the IDF will not redeploy and will retain all powers and responsibilities for internal security and public order.[214]

Thus, under the IA, al-Khalil/Hebron is to be split into two sectors: one treated essentially as an Area-B territory, with partial PA jurisdiction; the other treated as an Israeli settlement, over which the PA can exercise no jurisdiction at all. Israel's new Likud administration led by Prime Minister Benjamin Netanyahu has expressed dissatisfaction with this arrangement, however, and negotiations to revise the provision have continued for several months without final resolution.[215]

During the interim period, therefore, the PA will assume limited authority over a limited portion of the OPT. The division of the OPT into these categories and the maintenance of Israeli control over Israeli settlements, which, particularly in the West Bank, are scattered between Palestinian population centers, ensure that the different areas under the territorial jurisdiction of the PA are largely non-contiguous. Palestinians residing within them consequently remain subject to Israeli controls on movement between towns and cities in the West Bank, as well as between the West Bank and Gaza Strip. In these respects, the IA appears to define the PA's authority in largely popular — as opposed to territorial — terms. This emphasis is also apparent in the IA's

---

212. *Id.*

213. *Id.* Annex 3, art. 4, para. 4.

214. Haq, *supra* note 205.

215. *See* Christopher Walker, *West Bank Disputes Delay Plan for Summit*, THE TIMES OF LONDON, Dec. 7, 1996.

provisions concerning the PA's functional and personal jurisdiction.

b. Functional Jurisdiction

The Interim Agreement defines the PA's functional jurisdiction in specific terms and makes clear that all powers beyond the scope of that sphere reside with Israel.[216] Accordingly, the IA requires the Palestinian Council to confine its legislative and executive acts to the areas within its jurisdiction. Legislation that exceeds the scope of the Palestinian Council's authority "or that is otherwise inconsistent with the provisions of the DOP, [the Interim] Agreement, or of any other agreement that may be reached between the two sides during the interim period" is to be considered *void ab initio*.[217] In order to facilitate the evaluation of disputed legislation, the IA establishes a Legal Committee comprised of an equal number of Israelis and Palestinians and requires the "communication" of all Palestinian legislation to the Israeli side of the Committee.

Substantively, the functional jurisdiction assigned to the PA is confined to the internal affairs of the Palestinian population in the OPT. The IA appears to place governmental functions into three primary categories: (1) functions to be transferred entirely to the Council; (2) functions to be coordinated between the Council and the Israeli authorities in the OPT; and (3) functions remaining entirely under Israeli authority. Governmental functions that fall primarily within the province of Palestinian internal affairs — e.g. health, education, culture, etc. — are placed into the first category; functions that implicate Israeli concerns in the Territories — primarily infrastructure issues — fall into the second; and functions related to external affairs, including external security, fall into the third. In this respect, the Council's functional jurisdiction closely parallels — and, to a great extent, works in tandem with — its multi-tiered territorial jurisdiction.

The first tier of functional jurisdiction — generally designated "transfer of authority" by the IA — is characterized by transfer to the PA of primary authority over issues that concern the Palestinian population exclusively and by required cooperation in any related areas that conceivably implicate Israeli concerns. For most issues falling into this category, the IA assigns the PA full authority in Areas A and B and

---

216. Article 17 of the Interim Agreement states, *inter alia:*
　　(3) The Council has, within its authority, legislative, executive, and judicial powers and responsibilities as provided for in this Agreement.
　　(4) (a) Israel, through its military government, has the authority over areas that are not under the territorial jurisdiction of the Council, powers and responsibilities not transferred to the Council and Israelis.
　　(b) To this end, the Israeli military government shall retain the necessary legislative, judicial, and executive powers and responsibilities, in accordance with international law. This provision shall not derogate from Israel's applicable legislation over Israelis in personam.
Interim Agreement, ch. 3, art. 17, paras. 3-4, 36 I.L.M 551, 564.
　217. *Id.*

provides for a gradual transition of authority in Area C (certain areas, such as Israeli settlements, remaining permanently outside of PA). For instance, while the IA provides for the transfer to the PA of "[p]owers and responsibilities in the sphere of archaeology" in Areas A and B, authority in area C is to be "transferred gradually;" additionally, the IA establishes a Joint Committee of experts "to deal with archaeological issues of common interest" and requires each side to inform the other of the discovery of any new sites in the sections of the OPT under its jurisdiction.[218] Similarly, while the IA transfers authority to the PA over social welfare services, it requires the Palestinians, upon request, to provide Israel with reports regarding juvenile offenders,[219] presumably to serve Israel's security interests. The IA establishes similar frameworks for the transfer of authority in the following areas: agriculture[220] and forests;[221] direct taxation;[222] education and culture;[223] gas, fuel, and petroleum facilities;[224] health;[225] insurance;[226] interior affairs;[227] labor;[228] land registration;[229] legal administration;[230] local government;[231] parks;[232] planning and zoning;[233] population registry and documentation;[234] postal services;[235] telecommunications;[236] tourism;

---

218. *Id.* Annex 3, app. 1, art. 2, para. 4, at 605.

219. *Id.* Annex 3, app. 1, art. 33, para. 3(b), at 619.

220. *Id.* Annex 3, app. 1, art. 1, at 604.

221. *Id.* Annex 3, app. 1, art. 14, at 609.

222. *Id.* Annex 3, app. 1, art. 8, at 606.

223. *Id.* Annex 3, app. 1, art. 9, at 607.

224. *Id.* Annex 3, app. 1, art. 15. The PA must inform Israel of any oil exploration or production that it undertakes. *Id.* para. 4(a), at 610.

225. *Id.* Annex 3, app. 1, art. 17, at 611.

226. *Id.* Annex 3, app. 1, art. 19, at 612.

227. *Id.* Annex 3, app. 1, art. 20. "Interior affairs" is defined by the IA as including, *inter alia*, "licensing of newspapers and publications and censorship of films and plays." *Id.* para. 1, at 613.

228. *Id.* Annex 3, app. 1, art. 21, at 613.

229. *Id.* Annex 3, app. 1, art. 22, at 613.

230. *Id.* Annex 3, app. 1, art. 23, at 614.

231. *Id.* Annex 3, app. 1, art. 24, at 615. In addition to giving the PA a wide degree of latitude in defining and managing local government institutions, the IA transfers to the Palestinian local governments the authority to issue building permits for various purposes. *Id.* at para. 5.

232. *Id.* Annex 3, app. 1, art. 26, at 615.

233. *Id.* Annex 3, app. 1, art. 27, at 616.

234. *Id.* Annex 3, app. 1, art. 28, at 616-17. Under the IA, the administrative dimensions — e.g. the issuance of identity cards, the maintenance of birth and death records, etc. — are to be handled by Palestinians, but Israel is to be informed of "Every change in its population registry, including, inter alia, any change in the place of residence of any resident." *Id.* para. 4.

235. *Id.* Annex 3, app. 1, art. 29, at 617. Emphasizing the local nature of the PA, as defined in the IA, Palestinian postage stamps are to contain only the terms "Palestinian Council" or "Palestinian Authority." *Id.* para. 2(a), at 618. The PLO is to arrange for sending and receiving postal items between the Palestinian side and foreign countries through commercial agreements with Postal Authorities of Jordan, Egypt, and Israel. *Id.* para. 6(a). The PLO's status at the Universal Postal Union, however, is not to change *Id.* para. 6(b).

236. *Id.* Annex 3, app. 1, art. 36, at 620. Under the IA, the PA may construct its own telecommunications network, although, in the interim, it will enter into a commercial

transportation;[237] public works and housing;[238] and holy sites.[239] The spheres of authority transferred to the PA, therefore, are primarily municipal functions. To the extent that they move beyond being local concerns — implicating regional resource allocation, infrastructure development, or international relations — the IA requires coordination with Israel.

Accordingly, the IA places into the second category of functional jurisdiction — partial authority — those spheres involving the OPT as a whole, as opposed to the local affairs of municipalities. For these functions, the IA requires cooperation between the PA and Israeli authorities in the OPT, establishing a Civil Affairs Coordination and Cooperation Committee (CAC) composed of an equal number of Palestinians and Israelis and charged with addressing "matters arising with regard to infrastructures, such as roads, water, and sewage systems, power lines and telecommunications infrastructure, which require coordination according to [the] Agreement."[240] Like the territorial jurisdiction provisions described above, the IA's assignment of partial functional jurisdiction to the PA in spheres related to general infrastructure prevents the Palestinians from establishing effective authority over the OPT as a whole, limiting their power to the affairs of individual municipalities in the Territories. Indeed, since any significant construction in Area C for any purpose can proceed only with Israeli approval, the Palestinians' capacity to construct an independent infrastructure is severely constrained by the IA.

The IA's provisions concerning electricity reflect these tensions well. The Agreement provides for the establishment of a Palestinian Energy Authority (PEA), to which it assigns the authority "to issue licenses and to set rules, tariffs, and regulations in order to develop electricity systems."[241] It also establishes a Joint Electricity Subcommittee to deal with "issues of mutual interest concerning electricity."[242] The Palestinians, therefore, have jurisdiction over the administrative dimensions of electricity provision and have a forum within which to coordinate broader functions with the Israelis. The remaining details regarding the assignment of powers and responsibilities over electricity, however, remain unresolved. Israeli and Palestinian negotiators have yet to agree on the scope of the Palestinian authority over electricity. Indeed, the two sides have precisely opposite positions: the Palestinians seek primary authority over the electrical grid in the entire West Bank and construction rights throughout that territory but would agree to Is-

---

agreement with the Israeli telephone company (Bezeq). As in other spheres, however, the PA must seek Israeli approval for any construction in Area C. *Id.* para. a(2).

237. *Id.* Annex 3, app. 1, art. 37-38, at 622-23.
238. *Id.* Annex 3, app. 1, art. 30, at 618.
239. *Id.* Annex 3, app. 1, art. 32, at 619.
240. *Id.* Annex 3, art. 1, para. 1(c)(2), at 603.
241. *Id.* Annex 3, app. 1, art. 10, para. 2 (merged version), at 607.
242. *Id.* Annex 3, app. 1, art. 10, para. 8 (merged version), at 608.

raeli operation and maintenance of electricity supply systems within the Israeli settlements and military installations; the Israelis, conversely, seek to retain control over the OPT's electricity infrastructure but would cede local, administrative authority to the Palestinians.[243] In the absence of agreement, "the existing status quo in the sphere of electricity in the West Bank and Gaza Strip shall remain unchanged."[244] Since the status quo and the Israeli position are virtually indistinguishable, the prospects for expanded Palestinian authority in this sphere appear limited. Thus, the infrastructure issues that strike closest to defining the future of the OPT generally and Palestinian self-rule specifically remain largely unresolved, resulting in the perpetuation of the *status quo ante*, i.e. Israeli occupation and control.

The Interim Agreement, moreover, prohibits the PA from assuming any jurisdiction at all over functions that involve external relations. Article 17 of the IA states, "[i]n accordance with the DOP, the jurisdiction of the [Palestinian] Council will cover West Bank and Gaza Strip territory as a single territorial unit, except for: (a) issues that will be negotiated in the permanent status negotiations: Jerusalem, settlements, specified military locations, Palestinian refugees, borders, foreign relations and Israelis."[245] Although the Agreement acknowledges the PLO's role as international representative of the Palestinian people and permits it to "conduct negotiations and sign agreements with states or international organizations for the benefit of the Council" in certain spheres, including economic, cultural, scientific, and educational agreements,[246] the Council itself is denied "powers and responsibilities in the sphere of foreign relations." [247] It cannot establish embassies, consulates or other types of foreign missions abroad or facilitate their establishment in the West Bank or Gaza Strip.[248] It also cannot contribute to the defense of the OPT's against "external threats."[249] Furthermore, under the IA, any involvement between the Council and representatives of foreign states and international organizations — even for the approved purpose of carrying out cultural, scientific, or educational agreements — is not to be considered "foreign relations."[250] Through these provisions, the IA expressly disallows the PA from participating in the international process in any way that could influence its international status.

The functional jurisdiction of the PA, therefore, is limited to an array of municipal powers and responsibilities. The IA explicitly prohibits the PA from engaging in external relations, except in relation to the provision of basic services to the local population and the economic de-

---

243. These positions are represented in the "merged version" of Annex 3, Appendix 1, Article 10 of the IA. *Id.* at 607-608.
244. *Id.* Annex 3, app. 1, art. 10 (merged version), at 608.
245. *Id.* ch. 3, art. 17, para. 1(a), at 564.
246. *Id.* ch. 1, art. 9, para. 5(b), at 561.
247. *Id.* para. 5(a).
248. *Id.*
249. *Id.* ch. 1, art. 12, para. 1, at 562.
250. *Id.* ch. 1, art. 9, para. 5(c), at 561.

velopment of the OPT. It also severely circumscribes the PA's role in the management of OPT-wide infrastructures, establishing a system of required coordination with the Israelis that leaves ultimate authority over these issues to Israel.[251] Thus, although the IA makes repeated reference to maintaining the territorial integrity of the OPT, the agreement ultimately has more to do with local governance of the Palestinian population than with the development of Palestinian territorial autonomy.

c. Personal Jurisdiction

The fact that the PA governs a population, rather than a territory, is also apparent from its limited personal jurisdiction. Article 17 of the IA states, "[t]he territorial and functional jurisdiction of the Council will apply to all persons, except for Israelis, unless otherwise provided in this Agreement."[252] According to the Agreement, Israel maintains exclusive personal jurisdiction over Israelis in all criminal matters, even for offenses committed in areas under PA (i.e. Areas A and B).[253] Israelis, moreover, will only come under the jurisdiction of Palestinian judicial authorities in civil matters when they explicitly consent in writing to that jurisdiction, when they maintain ongoing businesses in territory under Palestinian authority, or when the subject matter of the action is real property located in Palestinian territory.[254] The PA's powers, therefore, extend only over the Palestinian population and other non-Israelis within Palestinian jurisdiction.

2. Legitimacy

The Interim Agreement provides for the transfer of authority over the Palestinian population in the West Bank and Gaza Strip from Israel to the PA. As noted above, the terms of this transfer were determined through a process of negotiation between Israel and the PLO. The DOP and the IA consequently are neither unilateral enactments by the State of Israel nor agreements between Israel and the Palestinian population currently residing in the OPT. Rather, they are international agreements between the Government of Israel and the PLO, acting on behalf of all Palestinian people. Thus, while the PA derives its authority in the OPT from Israel, it derives its legitimacy, at least during the interim period, from its relationship to the PLO in its capacity as international representative of the Palestinian people. The legal and func-

---

251. While the Interim Agreement (IA) provides a three-tier process for the settlement of disputes including, ultimately, their submission to arbitration, IA, ch. 3, art. 21, the IA's arbitration clause is arguably pathological. Id. at 566. There is no indication regarding the arbitral forum or the applicable law. Submission to arbitration is entirely voluntary. The uselessness of the clause is demonstrated by the recent unsuccessful attempt by Palestinian negotiators to have the dispute regarding the electricity infrastructure submitted to international arbitration.

252. *Id.* ch. 3, art. 17, para. 2(c), at 564.

253. *Id.* Annex 4, art. 1, para. 2, at 635.

254. *Id.* Annex 4, art. 3, para. 2, at 638.

tional relationship between the PLO and the PA consequently bears some review.

As discussed earlier in this essay, the international community unanimously recognizes the Palestinians' status as a people and their right to participate in the resolution of the question of Palestine. Most States also recognize the Palestinians' right to national self-determination. To give substance to this recognition the international community, including, since 1993, Israel and the United States, has consented to the PLO's participation in the international process as the representative of the Palestinian people. Because the PLO is recognized only as agent for the Palestinian people, its international legitimacy hinges upon international confidence that it represents the interests of the Palestinian people, in whom the rights to participation and self-determination reside. The PLO, consequently, is bound to act in accordance with the wishes of the Palestinian people, as a whole, not simply that portion that resides in the OPT.

The decisions of the Palestine National Council (PNC) and the Central Committee, its subsidiary, provide the best indication of the extent to which the agreements concluded between the PLO and the Government of Israel have elicited the approval of the Palestinian people. In 1974, the PNC "called for the establishment of an independent national authority over any part of Palestine that may be liberated."[255] The Arab League ratified this approach during its Summit Conference in Rabat in 1974, and that ratification was later cited as precedent supporting the establishment of the PA.[256] More recently, the Central Committee of the PNC voted on October 11, 1993 to ratify the DOP,[257] which was signed one month earlier by Yasser Arafat, acting on the authority of the Executive Committee of the PLO.[258] Since the DOP established the framework within which the ongoing PLO-Israel negotiations have proceeded, the PNC, by ratifying it, authorized the Executive Committee of the PLO to conclude further agreements consistent with its terms.[259] The PA, therefore, was established with the authorization of the PLO and, by extension, of the Palestinian people.

The establishment of the PA, however, does not alter the relationship between the PLO and the Palestinian people — either those living within the OPT or those residing in other States. Although the PLO Executive Committee played a significant role in governing the sections

---

255. NASSAR, *supra* note 57, at 63.

256. *Id.*

257. Israelis, Palestinians Laud PLO Ratification of Peace Accord, UPI, Oct. 12, 1993, available in LEXIS, Nexis Library, UPI file.

258. *See generally*, Executive Committee, Statement on the Declaration of Principles, Tunis, Sept. 12, 1993, THE PALESTINIAN-ISRAELI PEACE AGREEMENT, *supra* note 95, at 143.

259. One PLO official in the United States suggests that these measures constitute a delegation of authority to conduct negotiations from the PNC, where ultimate authority in the PLO resides, to the Executive Committee and Chairman Arafat. Interview with Khalis A. Foutah, Deputy Chief Representative, Palestine Liberation Organization, Palestine National Authority, Washington, D.C. (Feb. 9, 1996).

of the OPT under Palestinian administration during the transitional period before the election of the Palestinian Council in January 1996, it did so purely in a caretaker capacity until the Council was in a position to assume the functions assigned to it by the DOP and IA.[260] Otherwise, the PLO and the PA have very different functions vis-à-vis the Palestinian people. The PA, as discussed above, has largely municipal authority over the affairs of Palestinians in the OPT. It lacks the legal competence to make any broader decisions regarding the Palestinian people living outside the OPT or even regarding the ultimate status of Palestinians in the OPT. These functions remain the province of the PLO, which, as discussed in the next section, continues to serve as the representative of the Palestinian people in negotiations with Israel and in other international contexts.

Conversely, the PLO does not have legal authority over decisions of the PA that relate to local governance of the Palestinians in the OPT. The Interim Agreement, in its provisions regarding Palestinian Council elections, states, "[i]n order that the Palestinian people of the West Bank and the Gaza Strip may govern themselves according to democratic principles, direct, free, and general elections will be held for the Council and (the President) of the Executive Authority of the Council . . . ."[261] This provision emphasizes that the Council is to represent the interests of the "Palestinian people in the West Bank and Gaza Strip," who, through the Council, will "govern *themselves*." Thus, only their elected leaders in the OPT have the authority to make decisions included in the Council's functional jurisdiction.

This interpretation is supported by the Palestinian Election Law, which was issued by the PA in early December 1995. Article 12 of the Election Law requires members of the Palestine National Council (the PLO's legislative organ) who are seeking office in the PA Palestinian Council not only to reside within the OPT, but also to transfer their registration with any external constituencies to one of the interior constituencies in the OPT, thereby preventing any one person from serving both interior and exterior constituencies.[262] The Election Law thereby formalizes the distinction between the interests of Palestinians residing in the OPT and those who remain in diaspora and emphasizes the local

---

260. During the transitional period before the Council's election, the territories under Palestinian self-rule (the Gaza Strip, excluding Israeli settlements and military installations, and beginning with Jericho, several of the population centers in the West Bank) were governed by a Palestinian Council of National Authority, which was established pursuant to a Basic Law approved by the Central Committee of the PNC. Draft Basic Law for the National Authority During the Transitional Period, art. 58(1) (June 1994). The Council acted in a caretaker capacity during the transitional period and was "generally . . . responsible for the government and administration of the affairs of the country." *Id.* art. 59. The Basic Law made the Chairman of the Executive Committee of the PLO the "President" of the Council, *id.* art. 50, and provided for the appointment of other Council members by the PLO Executive Committee, *id.* art. 58(1). The Council's term ended upon the election of the Palestinian Council provided for by the Interim Agreement.

261. Interim Agreement, ch. 1, art. 2, para. 1, 36 I.L.M. 551, 559.

262. The Palestine National Authority, Palestinian Election Law, art. 12, para. 7 *in* Palestine Report, Special Supplement, Jan. 12, 1996.

character of representation in the Palestinian Council.

It is worth mentioning, however, that although the PLO and the PA are legally and functionally divided, they are intrinsically intertwined: the PLO negotiated the creation of the PA; the two bodies share a leader (President/Chairman Arafat) and are dominated by the same political party (*Fatah*);[263] and at least six of the elected members of the Palestinian Council also hold positions in the Palestine National Council.[264] A PLO official in the United States has suggested that this overlap helps to ensure consistency between PLO and PA positions and more fluid coordination of their activities.[265] This arrangement has, however, elicited severe criticism with many Palestinians arguing that the administration of Yasser Arafat has become unresponsive to the needs of Palestinians in diaspora.[266] Critics also have expressed concern that the establishment of the PA has marginalized the PLO's political bodies and has relegated the PLO to the role of international "wheeler-dealer" on behalf of the PA.[267]

In view of these concerns, it is important to emphasize that while the PA's authority over the affairs of Palestinians in the OPT is based upon the transfer of powers and responsibilities from the Government of Israel, its legitimacy emerges from the Palestinian people. Its external legitimacy derives from the role that the PLO, as international representative of the Palestinian people, played in negotiating and approving its establishment, and its internal legitimacy arises from the participation of the Palestinian population in the OPT in the election of the Palestinian Council.[268]

3. International Participation

The PA can participate in the international process only through the PLO. As discussed above, the Interim Agreement expressly prohibits the PA itself, from assuming powers and responsibilities in the

---

263. Candidates affiliated with *Fatah* won 76% of the votes in the January elections for the Palestinian Council. Ghada Karmi, *What Role for the Palestinian Diaspora After Oslo?*, in PALESTINIAN ELECTION AND THE FUTURE OF PALESTINE: A SPECIAL REPORT 98 (The Center for Policy Analysis in Palestine, ed. 1996).

264. The following Palestinian Council members are PNC members: Hakam Bal'awi (Tulkarem District); Dawood El-Zeir (Bethlehem District); Sharif Ali Hussein Mash'al'Abbas Zaki (Hebron District); Nabil ' Amr (Hebron District); Abdul Jawad Saleh (Ramallah District); Azmi El-Shuai'bi (Ramallah District).

265. Foutah Interview, *supra* note 259. Interestingly, Mr. Foutah's business card identifies him as the Chief Representative in the United States of both the PLO and PA, an arrangement that would seem to be precluded by the terms of the Interim Agreement.

266. *See* Karmi, *supra* note 263, at 11 (citing Arabic press report that eighty thousand Palestinian refugees signed petition denouncing Palestinian Council elections because Palestinians outside of OPT were excluded from voting).

267. *Id.* at 12-13.

268. The elections for Palestinian Council members yielded an extremely high overall turnout rate of 79% of registered voters, despite the attempted boycott of the elections by opposition parties. Salma A. Shawa, *The Palestinian Elections: A Strong Start Into an Uncertain Future*, WASH. RPT. ON MIDDLE EAST, Apr. 1996, at 23.

sphere of foreign relations. It does, however, permit the PLO to "conduct negotiations and sign agreements with states or international organizations for the benefit of the Council" in the spheres of economic, social, and technical development.[269] As discussed earlier in this essay, the PLO has established relationships with and participated in the proceedings of a variety of international organizations. Under the terms of the IA, the PLO may work with these organizations to address the specific problems and needs of the Palestinians in the OPT. In this respect, the PLO can participate more substantively in the international process than it could before its link to the Palestinian population in the OPT was formalized by the DOP.

The IA appears, however, to limit the extent to which the PLO may use this broadened participation as a basis for altering its international status during the interim period. This issue emerges in the IA's terms regarding the provision of postal services to the OPT's population. The Agreement states, "[w]ithout derogating from the generality of paragraph 5 of Article IX of this Agreement (Foreign Relations), the status of the Palestinian side to this Agreement in the Universal Postal Union (UPU) will remain as it is at present, and the Palestinian side will not be party to any action to alter or change its status."[270] In the context of the Agreement, the "Palestinian side" refers to the PLO, which is not a member of the UPU. The provision, therefore, precludes the PLO from seeking membership in the UPU as a "sovereign state,"[271] despite the UPU's traditionally liberal membership policy.[272] Although the Interim Agreement does not address this issue with regard to other organizations, it is indicative of the likely reaction from Israel to PLO attempts to alter its status in other international organizations. Since Israel will continue to control the admission of foreign visitors to the OPT throughout the Interim Period,[273] it will be in a position to stifle PLO efforts that it views as possibly prejudicing the outcome of final status negotiations.

4. Conclusion

The majority of the States in the international system have recognized that the Palestinian people form a nation and are entitled freely to determine their political status. In order to facilitate vindication of that right, the international community has consented to the participa-

---

269. Interim Agreement, ch. 1, art. 9, para. 5(b), 36 I.L.M. 551, 561.

270. *Id.* Annex 3, app. 1, art. 29, para. 6(b), at 618.

271. "Article 3(1) of the Constitution of the UPU prescribes that 'any sovereign state may apply for admission as a member.'" W. MICHAEL REISMAN, PUERTO RICO AND THE INTERNATIONAL PROCESS: NEW ROLES IN ASSOCIATION 79 (1975).

272. According to Michael Reisman, the gates to membership in the UPU have been "opened wide," with little discussion of the be attributes of sovereignty. As he notes, "Membership in the UPU] includes the Netherland Antilles wazzu and Surinam, Portuguese provinces in West Africa, East Africa, Asia, and Oceania, Liechtenstein, Monaco, the Vatican, San Marino, and so on. With such a liberal membership policy, there has been no need for the development of associate status." *Id.*

273. Interim Agreement, Annex 1, 36 I.L.M. 551, 569.

tion of the Palestinian people in the international process through their international representative, the Palestine Liberation Organization. The PLO, however, does not govern the Palestinian people; rather, it exists to secure for them the opportunity to govern themselves, and its legitimacy and international status arise from that role. Neither the establishment of the symbolic State in 1988 nor the creation of the PA in 1994 legally altered the relationship between the PLO and the Palestinian people: the 1988 Declaration of Independence simply marked an official redefinition of Palestinian national aspirations — a retroactive acceptance of the two-state solution embodied in the 1947 U.N. Partition Plan; and the PA was established as a government of limited authority to serve the local needs of the Palestinians residing in the OPT during the interim period and to create a practical foundation for some broader form of self-government.

III. THE INTERNATIONAL LEGAL STATUS OF PALESTINE UNDER INTERIM SELF-GOVERNMENT ARRANGEMENTS

Thus, Palestine at present is a people, a territory, a liberation organization with a legal status as something more than a liberation organization, a State with a legal status as something less than a State, and an Interim Authority of rather limited authority. But is Palestine more than the sum of its parts? Can the public bodies established to represent and liberate the people and territory of Palestine be fused into an entity with a legal status of its own? In this section, I undertake to situate Palestinian public bodies within the normative framework governing the exercise of self-determination. Ultimately, I will argue that, while the legal and functional separation of the PLO and the PA has precluded Palestine from acquiring an international legal status independent of those bodies, that separation also has served to preserve the independence of the PLO as the international representative of the Palestinian people, which is a necessary precondition for its role in facilitating the legal exercise of Palestinian self-determination.

A. *The Exercise of Self-Determination*

Modern international law has developed relatively defined standards to govern the legal exercise of self-determination. As Crawford notes, "[i]t is a peculiarity of this area of practice that it is possible to be more certain about the 'consequences' of self-determination than about the criteria for the territories to which the principle is regarded as applying."[274] The goal articulated by the U.N. Charter for non-self-governing territories is the eventual attainment of "a full measure of self-government."[275] The General Assembly has interpreted the Charter to permit three alternatives:

A Non-Self-Governing Territory can be said to have reached a full

---

274. CRAWFORD, *supra* note 8, at 91-92.
275. U.N. Charter, art. 73.

measure of self-government by[:]

(a) Emergence as a sovereign independent State;

(b) Free association with an independent State; or

(c) Integration with an independent State.[276]

Thus, although self-government most frequently has taken the form of full independence from the administering State,[277] "[m]any federations, real unions, personal unions and associations are treated with equanimity by the international decision process."[278] Indeed, for entities too small or underdeveloped to be economically or politically viable as independent States, association or integration with another State can provide the self-determining population with heightened security and broader access to other markets, while at the same time permitting the associate to maintain a discrete political identity and to participate in potentially significant ways in the international process.[279]

Association and integration have taken a variety of forms in the international system, providing populations with different levels of independence from metropolitan States. The formal status of association maintains both parties' legal status of statehood but involves "the significant subordination of and delegations of competence by one of the parties (the associate) to the other (the principal)."[280] Thus, to cite one example, although Puerto Rico maintains a relationship of association with the United States — it has delegated significant foreign affairs powers to the United States, and its citizens hold United States passports — it remains a sovereign State and legally may terminate the association if its population so desires. Even integration within another State need not entirely extinguish the autonomy and international personality of the subordinate political entity. For instance, although Greenland was integrated within the realm of Denmark in 1952, the territory retains a significant degree of autonomy under Home Rule arrangements,[281] and it maintains a limited international personality.[282]

---

276. G.A. Res. 1541 (XV), *supra* note 24, at Annex, Principle VI; Declaration on Friendly Relations, *supra* note 9, at 124. The International Court of Justice endorsed the General Assembly's interpretation in the *Western Sahara Case*. *Western Sahara Case*, 1975 I.C.J. 12, 32.

277. As Crawford notes, "[o]f approximately 100 Chapter XI territories in the period 1945-78, 59 achieved joint or separate independence (this includes Grenada, Surinam, and Singapore, which had a previous status of self government)." CRAWFORD, *supra* note 8, at 369 n.60.

278. REISMAN, *supra* note 271, at 11.

279. *See generally id.* at 19-20, 51-103; *see also* CRAWFORD, *supra* note 8, at 370-77.

280. REISMAN, *supra* note 271, at 10. Neither the delegation of its foreign affairs competence nor the existence of common trade agreements, common currency, or common citizenship have deemed to extinguish the international personality of an associate. *Id.* at 17.

281. Under the Greenland Home Rule Act, Greenland is defined as a "distinct community within the Kingdom of Denmark." NII LANTE WALLACE-BRUCE, CLAIMS TO STATEHOOD IN INTERNATIONAL LAW 191 (1994) (quoting the Greenland Home Rule Act art. 1). Accordingly, Greenland has a legislature and executive with authority in the areas of "taxation, education, culture, church affairs, production and export, supplies and

Similarly, while China resumed its sovereignty over Hong Kong in 1997, the Joint Declaration concluded between China and the United Kingdom assures that Hong Kong will enjoy "a high degree of autonomy, except in foreign and defense affairs."[283] These and many other precedents show that a territory may preserve limited international personality and autonomy even in the context of association or integration with another State.

Where the right of self-determination is involved, however, the legal inquiry in such cases does not end with a declaration that a self-determining population has opted for association or integration. As Professor Michael Reisman notes, "[t]he lawfulness of particular associations is determined by content and not by form."[284] Article One of the International Covenants on Civil and Political and Economic, Social, and Cultural Rights declares, "[a]ll peoples have the right to self-determination. By virtue of that right they *freely* determine their political status and *freely* pursue their economic, social, and cultural development."[285] Apparent from the Covenants' definition of self-determination is that the right, if nothing else, revolves around freedom — the freedom of a people to define their own political status and to determine for themselves the nature of their relationships with other members of the international system. That is not to say, of course, that that freedom is absolute. In a world system characterized by both interdependency and at least *de facto* inequality, the freedom of every community is constrained by myriad political and economic factors. Nevertheless, the right to self-determination would be rendered an empty promise if the choice among types of self-government were imposed upon, rather than selected by, the concerned population. Interna-

---

transport, technology, telecommunications and housing." *Id.* at 191-92. The areas excluded from Greenland's home rule authority are external relations, financial, monetary and currency policy, defense, the administration of justice and police, and constitutional, contract, inheritance, and family law. *Id.* at 192.

282. Greenland is affiliated with the European Community as an Overseas Territory; it also sends its own delegation to the Nordic Council, where it is treated as an independent nation, and it is a member of the Inuit Circumpolar Conference, which has observer status at the United Nations. *Id.* at 192-93. Moreover, the Greenland Home Rule Act requires that treaties affecting the interests of Greenland be referred to home rule authorities before they are concluded by Denmark. *Id.* at 193.

283. *Id.* at 203-04. Hong Kong nevertheless will continue to participate, albeit to a limited degree, in the international arena. The Basic Law of the Hong Kong Special Administrative Region of the People's Republic of China stipulates that, under the name Hong Kong, China, the territory may establish and maintain diplomatic relations and conclude agreements in the fields of economics, trade, financial, monetary, shipping, communications, tourism, culture, and sports. *Id.* at 204-05. Since Hong Kong has not been regarded as a self-determination unit, however, its disposition is not directly relevant to the question of Palestine.

284. REISMAN, *supra* note 271, at 11.

285. International Covenant on Economic, Social, and Cultural Rights, *opened for signature* Dec. 16, 1966, art. 1, para. 1, 993 U.N.T.S. 5; International Covenant on Civil and Political Rights, *opened for signature* Dec. 19, 1966, art. 1, para. 1, 999 U.N.T.S. 173 (emphasis added).

tional practice, accordingly, has been to strive to assure that self-government has been achieved through the free choice of the self-determining people.

One way in which the international community has evaluated the integrity of an exercise of self-determination is by examining popular support for the decision. A choice of association or integration has elicited particular scrutiny, since there is a greater possibility that these forms of self-determination resulted from coercion by a metropolitan State, rather than from the free choice of the concerned population.[286] Principle VII(a) of the Annex to U.N. General Assembly Resolution 1541 (XV) states, "[f]ree association should be the result of a free and voluntary choice by the peoples of the territory concerned expressed through informed and democratic processes."[287] As Professor Reisman points out, the consent of the elite or effective leader no longer suffices to ratify the association: "[i]n contemporary practice, the demand for plebiscite or some other reliable consultation of popular will indicates that dispositions of territorial communities can be effected lawfully only with the free and informed consent of the members of that community."[288] Resolution 1541 is even more explicit in its provisions regarding integration, requiring that integration be "the result of the freely expressed wishes of the territory's peoples acting with full knowledge of the change in their status, their wishes having been expressed through informed and democratic processes, impartially conducted and based on universal adult suffrage."[289] Thus, the international community has come to require objective evidence of popular support among a self-determining population for a decision to associate with or be incorporated within another State.

This principle has also been applied, at least on one occasion, in the context of independence. The principle of self-determination requires not only that a territory be self-governing, but also that the people of that territory be self-governing. The international community consequently has been unwilling to recognize the independence of territories whose population effectively has been denied the opportunity to exercise self-determination by the transfer of power to an unsupported or unrepresentative government.[290] While, as Crawford points out, "self-determination does not necessarily involve the establishment of a democracy based on the principle of 'one vote, one value,' and the administering authority has a measure of discretion in determining the persons in the territory to whom the grant of authority will be made,"[291] the international community has required that authority be transferred to a government possessing the support of a territory's general popula-

---

286. *See* CRAWFORD, *supra* note 8, at 370, 373.

287. G.A. Res. 1541 (XV), *supra* note 12, at Annex, Principle VII(a).

288. Reisman, *supra* note 271, at 12, *quoting* STEPHANSKY, PUERTO RICO IN THE UNITED STATES AND THE CARIBBEAN 95 (T. Szulc. ed. 1971).

289. G.A. Res. 1514 (XV), *supra* note 12, at Annex, Principle IX(b).

290. *See* DUGARD, RECOGNITION AND THE UNITED NATIONS 97-98 (1987) (discussing non-recognition of white minority government of Rhodesia).

291. CRAWFORD, *supra* note 8, at 219.

tion.[292]

The United Nations also has sought to confirm the voluntary consent of a population to an association by scrutinizing the terms of the agreement between the metropolitan and associated States. It has required for instance that there be procedures in place that permit the Associate to terminate the association as easily as the metropolitan State and that demonstrate that the association is "a continued expression of the right of self-determination of the people of the Associated State."[293]

Because of concern about the voluntariness of putative exercises of self-determination, international law requires special scrutiny when a territory's status changes while it is under belligerent occupation. The Fourth Geneva Convention provides:

> Protected persons who are in occupied territory shall not be deprived, in any case or in any matter whatsoever, of the benefits of the present Convention by any change introduces, as the result of the occupation of a territory, into the institutions or government of the said territory, nor by any agreement concluded between the authorities of the occupied territories and the Occupying Power, nor by any annexation by the latter of the whole or part of the occupied territory.[294]

There is a presumption that a State that comes into being under belligerent occupation is a puppet State, and, as a result, it should not be recognized as independent by other States.[295] The international norm against the recognition of puppet states traditionally has been defined in terms of state sovereignty: a puppet state is an organ of the occupant State and, therefore, is subordinate to its legal order; since a sovereign State is subordinate only to international law, a puppet state cannot be recognized as sovereign.[296] While this argument need not be framed with reference to self-determination, the norm against recognition of puppet States suggests that the creation of a puppet State is not a valid exercise of self-determination since Principle VI of General Assembly Resolution 1541 permits only "[e]mergence as a *sovereign* independent State." An occupant State, therefore, may not avoid its legal obligations to the population of an occupied territory simply by obscuring its control through the creation of a puppet State. Indeed, Marek suggests that the presumption that a State or government established during a belligerent occupation is of a puppet character can "only be re-

---

292. *Id.* at 220 (citing the U.N. Security Council and General Assembly's insistence that the United Kingdom not transfer power to the white minority government of Rhodesia and, rather, "promote the country's attainment of independence in accordance with the aspirations of the majority of the population.").

293. *Id.* at 376.

294. Geneva Convention Relative to the Protection of Civilian Persons in Time of War, Aug. 12, 1949, art. 47, 6 U.S.T. 3548, 75 U.N.T.S. 318.

295. *See* KRYSTYNA MAREK, AND CONTINUITY OF STATES IN PUBLIC INTERNATIONAL LAW 113 (1968).

296. *See id.* at 113-14.

butted after the liberation of the territory."[297]

In sum, therefore, international law requires that self-determination be exercised with regard for the free will of the self-determining population. The establishment of statehood is not the only legitimate outcome: the international community has shown tolerance for decisions by self-determining populations to associate with or integrate within another State, rather than to establish complete independence. These alternative outcomes have, however, elicited greater scrutiny by the international community, particularly when, as in cases of military occupation, there is great potential that an ostensible exercise of self-determination resulted from coercion rather than free choice.

B. The Legal Status of Palestine

International law recognizes the participation of a variety of types of actors in the international process. Under traditional doctrine, states were the only recognized international participants.[298]Over the course of the twentieth century, however, international law has come to recognize the participation of other, non-state entities.[299] McDougal, Laswell, and Reisman define a participant in the international constitutive process as "an individual or an entity which has at least minimum access to the process of authority in the sense that it can make claims or be subjected to claims."[300] As their definition suggests, different types of international actors participate in different capacities, the breadth of their participation determined by their relations with other actors in the international system. Accordingly, "an international person need not possess all the international rights, duties, and powers normally possessed by states. Some states only possess some of those rights and duties; they are therefore only in those limited respects subjects of international law and thus only possess limited international personality."[301] Thus, although States remain preeminent within the international process, it is no longer their exclusive province.

Under prevailing international legal standards, Palestine is not a State. Although the PLO and the PA each fulfill aspects of the objective criteria for statehood at least as well as some recognized States, the two bodies do not, together, form a unit independent and unified enough to constitute a State. The PLO remains the independent voice and international representative of the Palestinian people, but it lacks direct authority over the population and territory of Palestine. Conversely, while the PA directly governs segments of the OPT, its authority is subordinated to Israel's, and it is prohibited by the DOP and subsequent

---

297. *Id.*

298. *See* Myres McDougal et al., *The World Constitutive Process of Authoritative Decision*, 19 J. LEGAL EDUC. 253, 262 & n.8 (1967); J.D. van der Vyver, *Statehood In International Law*, 5 EMORY INT'L L. REV. 9, 12 (1991).

299. *See* Suy, *supra* note 148 , at 84, 100-01.

300. McDougal, *supra* note 298, at 262.

301. LASSA OPPENHEIM, INTERNATIONAL LAW ch.2, sec. 33 (H. Lauterpacht ed., 8th ed. 1955).

80 DENV. J. INT'L L. & POL'Y VOL. 26:1

agreements from independently participating in international affairs. The relationship between the PA and the PLO consequently may best be characterized as a variation on association, although neither entity is a sovereign State. Ultimately, while this arrangement does not itself represent a fulfillment of the Palestinian right to self-determination, it leaves open the possibility for the free exercise of self-determination in the future.

1. Statehood

The creation of States is a matter appraised by international law. Indeed, the idea that an entity's international legal status could be subject to definition by another State's municipal law repudiates one of the central premises of modern international law: the sovereign equality of States. Since no one State legally may impose its municipal order upon another, some higher order must prevail over interstate relations. As Marek explains, "[s]ince they break the framework of municipal law, the birth, extinction, and transformation of States can be made subject of a legal inquiry only by reference to a legal order which is both higher than State law and yet belongs to the same system of norms . . . ." [302] Thus, while "[i]nternational law does not 'create' States, just as a State does not 'create' individuals . . . [i]t is international law and international law alone which provides the legal evaluation of the process, determines whether the entity is in fact a State, delimits its competences and decides when it ceases to exist."[303] Since an entity's participation in the international system is defined by its perceived status among other international actors, however, there has been some controversy regarding the role that recognition plays in conferring the legal status of Statehood on aspirant communities.

Two predominant views have emerged regarding this issue: the declaratory approach and the constitutive approach. The orthodox constitutive approach holds, generally, that an entity legally becomes a State when other international actors recognize it to be one, the act of recognition being constitutive of a new State's legal status. According to Lauterpacht, this view is based upon a Hegelian vision of international law "as a loose 'law of co-ordination' based on agreement as distinguished from the overriding command of a superior rule of law." [304] States, within this perspective, exist only in relation to one another, their status emerging from their relationships, not on the basis of objective legal criteria. Proponents of the declaratory view argue that this relativist dimension of the constitutive approach is "destructive of the very notion of an international community."[305] They maintain that an entity becomes a State when it fulfills the legal criteria for statehood and that,

302. MAREK, *supra* note 295, at 2.

303. *Id.*

304. HERSCH LAUTERPACHT, RECOGNITION IN INTERNATIONAL LAW 38 (1947).

305. MAREK, *supra* note 295, at 132, *quoting* TI-CHIANG CHEN, THE INTERNATIONAL LAW OF RECOGNITION 42 (L.C. Green ed., 1951).

therefore, recognition by other states is simply declaratory of an existing fact. As Chen summarizes:

> The fact that States cannot have the same faculty for appreciating the fact of the fulfillment of [the] requirements [for statehood] is no reason for denying that there is an objective point of time at which such fulfillment takes place. Third States may be unable or unwilling to acknowledge this fact, but they certainly cannot alter it to suit their ignorance, caprice, or self-interest.[306]

Lauterpacht attempts to reconcile the declaratory and constitutive approaches by suggesting that while recognition is "declaratory of facts," it is "constitutive of rights." He reasons, "[a] State may exist as a physical fact. But it is a physical fact which is of no relevance for the commencement of particular international rights and duties until by recognition — and nothing else — it has been lifted into the sphere of law, until by recognition it has become a juridical fact."[307]

An evaluation of the relative merits of each of these approaches is beyond the scope of this essay. It suffices to note that an entity's claim to Statehood may be evaluated either on the basis of objective legal criteria or in light of the degree of recognition it has received by the international community. As discussed below, Palestine has yet to achieve statehood within either framework.

2. The Declaratory Approach and the Montevideo Convention Criteria for Statehood

The declaratory view of recognition, as noted above, holds that an entity becomes a State when it fulfills the internationally accepted criteria for statehood.[308] The Montevideo Convention of 1933 established four criteria for evaluating an entity's claim to statehood. The entity is required to possess: "(a) permanent population; (b) a defined territory; (c) government; and (d) capacity to enter into relations with other states."[309] The requirement of independence is also frequently appended to the Montevideo criteria.[310] Although the Montevideo Convention technically binds only the parties to it, its criteria for statehood, with minor variations, have been widely accepted as authoritative by international jurists.[311]

Although the analysis below addresses each of the criteria indi-

---

306. CHEN, *supra* note 305, at 44-45.

307. LAUTERPACHT, *supra* note 303, at 75.

308. These criteria are also relevant to Lauterpacht's view of recognition insofar as he recommends that States base their decisions about whether to recognize a nascent State on the applicable legal criteria, rather than political concerns. *Id.* at 55.

309. Convention on Rights and Duties of States, Dec. 26, 1933, art. 1, 165 U.N.T.S. 19 [hereinafter Montevideo Convention].

310. *See generally* MAREK, *supra* note 295 at 162-68.

311. *See, e.g.,* CRAWFORD, *supra* note 8, at 31-34; WALLACE-BRUCE, *supra* note 281, at 51. *Cf.* OPPENHEIM, *supra* note 301, § 34 (replacing the requirement of capacity to enter into foreign relations with the requirement of sovereignty).

vidually, it is important to note, as an initial matter, that they cannot be applied piecemeal. Marek summarizes prevailing opinion as follows: "[t]here is a State in the international law sense, when there is an independent legal order, effectively *valid throughout* a defined territory *with regard to* a defined population."[312] Similarly, Oppenheim states, "[a] state proper is in existence when a people is settled *in* a territory *under its own* sovereign government."[313] As these jurists' opinions suggest, the Montevideo criteria relate to and find definition in one another. A putative state, therefore, must possess a government that, itself, governs a population within a specified territory and that, itself, has the capacity to enter into foreign relations. While Palestine fulfills aspects of each of the Montevideo criteria, it continues to lack a full measure of independence, which synthesizes and gives substance to the other criteria for statehood.

a. Defined Territory

The international community has adopted an exceptionally flexible construction of the "defined territory" criterion for statehood. In order to qualify for statehood, an entity's territory need not exceed a minimum size.[314] It also need not be "coherent . . . or conform to any particular form." [315] Finally, the entity seeking statehood need not have perfectly-delimited territorial boundaries. This standard was articulated in a well-known decision of the Polish-German Mixed Arbitral Tribunal:

> Whatever may be the importance of the delimitation of boundaries, one cannot go so far as to maintain that as long as this delimitation has not been legally effected, the state in question cannot be considered as having any territory whatsoever . . . In order to say that a state exists . . . it is enough that this territory has a sufficient consistency, even

---

312. MAREK, *supra* note 295, at 162 (emphasis added). The following statement by U.S. President Grant, cited by Marek as indicative of state practice regarding the conditions for statehood, also draws attention to the relationship between the criteria:

> [T]here must be a people occupying a *known* territory, united under some known and defined form of government, acknowledged by those subject thereto, in which the functions of government are administered by usual methods, competent to mete out justice to citizens and strangers, to afford remedies for public and for private wrongs, and able to assume the correlative international obligations and capable of performing the corresponding international duties *resulting from its acquisition of the rights of sovereignty*. A power should exist complete in its organization, ready to take and able to maintain its place among the nations of the earth.

Marek, *supra* note 295, at 165, *quoting* J.B. MOORE, A DIGEST OF INTERNATIONAL LAW 107-08 (1906).

313. OPPENHEIM, *supra* note 301, § 34 (emphasis added).

314. CRAWFORD, *supra* note 8, at 36 (stating that Tuvala, Malta, Nauru, Liechtenstein and Seychelles —ranging in size from 26 sq. km. to 170 sq. km.—have been all recognized as meeting the defined territory requirement). WALLACE-BRUCE, *supra* note 281, at 51.

315. WALLACE-BRUCE, *supra* note 281, at 38 (noting that the international community recognizes states, such as the United States and Tanzania, comprised of non-contiguous territory).

though its boundaries have not yet been accurately delimited, and that the state actually exercises independent public authority over that territory.[316]

As the Tribunal made clear, the defined-territory criterion does not require the legal demarcation of a state's boundaries. Indeed, the international community has on several occasions extended recognition to states whose territorial borders remained in dispute.[317] What appears central, instead, is the putative state's exercise of independent governmental authority over a territory.[318]

It is in that last respect that Palestine, as presently constituted, fails to meet the defined territory criterion. One commentator has suggested that Palestine is not a defined territory because "[w]hat territory is Palestine remains the source of bitter conflict."[319] However, that analysis seems to ignore the traditionally flexible interpretation of the defined territory criterion. What territory is Palestine, after all, is no greater a source of conflict than what territory is Israel.[320] Moreover, the PLO has defined very specific territorial goals for a State of Palestine — the West Bank and Gaza Strip[321] — and a substantial portion of

---

316. CRAWFORD, *supra* note 8, at 52 (quoting *Deutsche Continental Gas-Gesellschaft v. Polish State*, (1929) 5 A.D. No. 5, 14-15). *See also* MAREK, *supra* note 295, at 163 ("It may happen that, in special circumstances, international law will provisionally accept, as its subject, a community with only a rough delimitation of its territorial and personal spheres ."); RESTATEMENT (THIRD) FOREIGN RELATIONS LAW OF THE U.S. 201 cmt. b ("An entity may satisfy the territorial requirement for statehood even if its boundaries have not been finally settled, if one or more of its boundaries are disputed, or if some of its territory is claimed by another state.").

317. *See, e.g., Monastery of St. Naoum Case*, 1924 P.C.I.J. (ser. B) No. 9, at 10 (granting Albania international recognition and induction into League of Nations despite dispute over Serbo-Albanian); *North Sea Continental Shelf Cases*, 1969 I.C.J. 3, 32 (Feb. 20).

318. *See* CRAWFORD, *supra* note 8, at 40 ("The only requirement is that the State must consist of a certain coherent territory effectively governed—a formula which demonstrates that the requirement of territory is rather a constituent of government and independence than a separate criterion of its own.").

319. Kathryn M. McKinney, Comment, *The Legal Effects of the Israeli-PLO Declaration of Principles: Steps Toward Statehood for Palestine*, 18 SEATLE U. L. REV. 93, 95 (1994).

320. Indeed, recognition of Israel was urged by the United States *despite* the controversy regarding its borders. WALLACE-BRUCE, *supra* note 281, at 53 (quoting Jessup, U.S. Representative to the Security Council, advocating admission of Israel to the U.N., U.N. SCOR, 383rd Mtg, Supp. No. 128, at 9-12, (1948):

> One does not find in the general classic treatment of this subject [definition of a state in international law] any insistence that the territory of a state must be exactly fixed by definite frontiers. . . The formulae in the classic treatises somewhat vary, one from the others, but both reason and history demonstrate that the concept of territory does not necessarily include precise delimitations of the boundaries of that territory. The reason for the rule that one of the necessary attributes of a state is that it shall possess territory is that one cannot contemplate a state as a kind of disembodied spirit. Historically, the concept is one of insistence that there must be some position of the earth's surface which its people inhabit and over which its government exercises authority.'

321. *See supra* text accompanying notes 179-180 (discussing Palestinian Declaration of Independence).

the international community recognizes the legitimacy of those territorial aspirations.[322]   Although the precise boundaries of such a state have yet to be precisely delimited, that fact, as noted above, has never been regarded as a barrier to meeting the "defined territory" requirement.   Thus, ongoing controversy regarding the proper boundaries of Palestine is not an impediment to the Palestinian claim to statehood.

What *is* an impediment is the fact that a Palestinian government does not yet exercise independent authority over a defined territory.   As discussed above, agreements between Israel and the PLO severely limit the territorial, functional, and personal jurisdiction of the PA.   While the PA has significant municipal authority over areas of the OPT, it does not possess sovereignty over them in any practical sense.   Israel retains authority to review all legislation governing the administration of the territories, it has personal jurisdiction over all Israelis in the territories, it exercises control over most aspects of economic development and security in the territories, and it continues to regulate movement between the Palestinian administrative enclaves.   As a result, it cannot be said that a Palestinian government exercises independent authority over any territory at all.

b. Permanent Population

International jurists also have construed broadly the Convention's permanent population requirement.   According to Wallace-Bruce, the criterion "simply requires that there must be people identifying themselves with the territory no matter how small or large the population might be."[323] Oppenheim provides a somewhat different interpretation, defining a "people" as "an aggregate of individuals *who live together as a community*, though they may belong to different races or creeds or cultures, or be of different colour."[324] His definition suggests that a putative state's population not only must form a national community, but also must live together as one.   Combining these two interpretations, a state's population should (1) identify themselves with a territory and (2) live together as a community.

The Palestinian population meets both criteria.   Palestinians not only identify with the territory of Palestine, they define themselves in terms of it.[325] Although a large segment of the Palestinian population, as defined by the PLO Covenant, is dispersed across the globe, the existence of Palestinian refugees does not, as some have suggested,[326] defeat their claim to constitute a permanent population.   Palestinians live together as a community in the West Bank and Gaza Strip, where they form the vast majority of the population.   The fact that members of

---

322. *See* G.A. Res. 48/158D, *supra* note 100.
323. WALLACE-BRUCE, *supra* note 281, at 53. In 1984, thirty-six United Nations member States had populations of less than one million. DUGARD, *supra* note 290 at 71.
324. OPPENHEIM, *supra* note 301, at sec. 34 (emphasis added).
325. *See supra* text accompanying notes 117-124.
326. McKinney, *supra* note 319, at 96.

their national community reside elsewhere and may, if circumstances permit, return to Palestine at a later date is irrelevant to Palestine's viability as a State.   No doubt millions of people in the world may claim citizenship in countries in which they do not presently reside; their residence elsewhere does not, however, extinguish those states' claims to possessing a permanent population.   The Palestinian population in the OPT, therefore, constitute Palestine's permanent population.

c. Government

Although there has been some movement toward making respect for the rights of citizens a requirement for statehood,[327] the government criterion does not require that a state adhere to a particular form of government.   The international community has recognized states with myriad forms of government, from people's republics to constitutional monarchies to theocracies.[328]   Rather, the government[329] criterion can be reduced to the elements of effectiveness and legal title.   As Crawford observes, "[t]he point about 'government' is that it has two aspects: the actual exercise of authority, and the right or title to exercise that authority."[330]   A government's effectiveness — or "actual exercise of authority" — refers to its structural coherence and its general capacity to maintain law and order within a territory.   An examination of state practice with regard to this element, however, reveals little in the way of standards.   States have recognized governments, such as the former Belgian Congo (Zaire), that possessed only the most tenuous grasp of authority.[331]   The second element, legal title, refers to the government's exclusive legal right under international law to govern a territory.[332] This right may have been granted by the former sovereign of the territory[333] or recognized in accordance with the principle of self-determination.   Therefore, the government criterion possesses both factual and legal dimensions.

---

327. *See* DUGARD, *supra* note 290, at 97-98 (discussing developing norm of non-recognition of regimes based upon systematic denial of population's civil and political rights); van der Vyver, *supra* note 298, at 14.

328. WALLACE-BRUCE, *supra* note 281, at 54.

329. MAREK, *supra* note 295, at 162. Marek uses the term "legal order" instead of government.

330. CRAWFORD, *supra* note 8, at 44.

331. Crawford describes the situation in the Belgian Congo when recognition was granted to it in 1960 as follows:

> No effective preparations had been made; the new government was bankrupt, divided, and in practice hardly able to control even the capital. Belgian and other troops intervened, shortly after independence, under claim of humanitarian intervention; and extensive Unites States financial and military assistance became necessary almost immediately. Among the tasks of the United nations force was, or came to be, the suppression of secession in Katanga, the richest Congolese province. Anything less like effective government it would be hard to imagine.

Id. at 43.

332. *Id.* at 44.

333. *Id.*

State practice appears to indicate, however, that a strong legal title can compensate for a lack of effectiveness and, conversely, that a weak legal title requires more complete effectiveness.[334] According to Crawford, it is this inverse relationship that explains the international community's willingness to grant early recognition to the Belgian Congo despite its government's relative lack of control over the country.[335] It similarly explains the almost universal non-recognition of the government of Rhodesia, which assumed power in contravention of the principle of self-determination, even though the Rhodesian government maintained effective control over the country.[336]

The long-standing dispute over the legal title to the West Bank and Gaza Strip has been the focus of a large body of scholarly literature. An appraisal of that debate is beyond the scope of this essay. Regardless of the strength of the Palestinians' general claim of right to self-government, however, the interim character and extraordinarily limited powers of the PA make it impossible to characterize that body as the "effective government" of the OPT. The PA's authority, after all, is conferred on it by the agreements reached between Israel and the PLO, not by international law. While an independently constituted Palestinian government conceivably could assert a legitimate claim to being the "effective government" of Palestine without having established full control over the territory it claims, the PA is not such a government. Since the PLO at present exercises authority in the OPT only through its relationship to the PA, its effectiveness is similarly limited. Palestine therefore lacks an effective government.

d. Capacity to enter into foreign relations.

A state's capacity to enter into foreign relations is evaluated in terms of its legal competence to participate in the international process and to carry its international obligations into effect on the domestic level. The economic[337] and political[338] factors that define the breadth of its international activity are not relevant to the determination. As Crawford explains, the foreign relations requirement is essentially a synthesis of the government and independence criteria: "[c]apacity or competence ... depends partly on the power of internal government of a territory, without which international obligations may not be carried into effect, and partly on the entity concerned being separate for the purpose of such relations so that no other entity carries out and accepts

---

334. MAREK, *supra* note 295, at 102.

335. CRAWFORD, *supra* note 8, at 44.

336. *See* DUGARD, *supra* note 290, at 97-98.

337. "Capacity" here refers to a state's legal competence, not its economic or monetary situation. WALLACE-BRUCE, *supra* note 281, at 56-57 (discussing a significant number of countries that lack economic capacity to participate fully in the international system but are nevertheless recognized as states).

338. *See id.* at 55-56 ("'Capacity' in this context refers to legal competency. Once that competency exists, it is left to the discretion of the entity to choose which international persons it desires to engage in relations with.").

responsibility for them."[339] The international recognition of Liechtenstein's statehood[340] illustrates the centrality of independence to the foreign relations criterion: while Liechtenstein has delegated the conduct of its foreign relations to Switzerland, it remains politically independent, its foreign relations "carried out by Switzerland only from case to case and inasmuch as they are the subject of a special instruction of the Government of the Principality."[341] Thus, the actual capacity to participate in the international process is subordinate to independence, which is itself the legal basis for a state's foreign relations activity. Accordingly, while independent states participate more fully than other types of entities, their participation is "not a criterion, but rather a consequence, of statehood, and one which depends on the status and situation of particular states."[342]

Although the PLO has demonstrated its capacity to enter into foreign relations on behalf of the Palestinian people, the legal and functional separation of the PLO and the PA prevent the PLO from independently implementing international obligations in the territory and with regard to the population of Palestine. Under the terms of the DOP and the subsequent agreements concluded pursuant to it, Israel maintains authority over most aspects of the PA's external relations; the PLO is empowered to represent it only in international negotiations regarding economic, social, and technical development. It cannot regulate the flow of goods and persons into and out of Palestinian territory; it cannot facilitate the establishment of diplomatic missions from foreign countries in its territory; and it cannot translate international commitments affecting the territory or population of Palestine into PA policies without first obtaining Israel's consent. Thus, while the PLO engages in international relations, its activities are one step removed from the territory and population of Palestine.[343] Under these circumstances, Palestine, as a national and territorial unit, does not have the capacity to engage independently in international relations.

e. Independence

A requirement generally appended to — and implicit in[344] — the

---

339. CRAWFORD, *supra* note 8, at 47.

340. Liechtenstein is a party to the Statute of the International Court of Justice, a privilege reserved to states. U.N. Charter, art. 93. DUGARD, *supra* note 290, at 77.

341. CRAWFORD, *supra* note 8, at 190 (quoting Note of June 18, 1973: SCOR 29th yr., Sp. Supp. No. 2, 120).

342. *Id.* at 47.

343. *See* McKinney, supra note 319, at 112-13; James L. Prince, *The International Legal Implications of the November 1988 Palestinian Declaration of Statehood*, 25 STAN. J. INT'L L. 681, 696 (1989).

344. Wallace-Bruce suggests that the independence requirement is implicit in the capacity to enter into foreign relations. WALLACE-BRUCE, *supra* note 281, at 57. *See also* CRAWFORD, *supra* note 8, at 47 ("[E]ach State is an original foundation predicated on a certain basic independence. This was represented in the Montevideo formula by 'capacity to enter into relations with other States.'").

Montevideo criteria is independence.[345] Indeed, some international jurists see independence as the central criterion for statehood, all other requirements subordinate to and emerging from it.[346] The classic formulation of the independence criterion appears in Judge Anzilotti's opinion in the *Austro-German Customs Union Case:*

> [T]he independence of Austria within the meaning of Article 88 is nothing else but the existence of Austria, within the frontiers laid down by the Treaty of Saint Germain, *as a separate state not subject to the authority of any other State or group of States.* Independence as thus understood is really no more than the normal condition of States according to international law; it may also be described as sovereignty (*suprema potestas*), or external sovereignty, by which is meant that the State has over it no authority other than that of international law.[347]

Independence in this context means, therefore, that a State must be separate and sovereign, that is, that it possess a legal order that is both distinct from another State's and subordinate only to international law.[348]

The separateness requirement is logically grounded in the very concept of international law. As Marek explains, independence is a criterion for statehood because "international law, above all, is a legal order governing relations between independent States, that is to say, between separate and distinct entities. No international law would be either possible or necessary, without a clear delimitation of its subjects, which together form the international community."[349] The existence of an international community, therefore, presupposes the existence of defined individual members. It is perhaps in vindication of this principle that international law requires that a putative State govern a defined territory and population. Definition, after all, presupposes differentiation.

The independence requirement is not, however, satisfied by separateness alone. The additional element of sovereignty ensures that a State has the legal capacity to effect the commitments into which it has entered on behalf of its population and territory. As Judge Huber stated in the *Island of Palmas Case:* "[s]overeignty in the relations between states signifies independence. Independence in regard to a portion of the globe is the right to exercise therein, to the exclusion of any other state, the functions of a state."[350] Sovereignty, therefore, is framed in exclusive terms. An independent State, in the international context, cannot be subordinate to another State's legal order.

---

345. *See generally* MAREK, *supra* note 295, at 162-68.
346. CRAWFORD, *supra* note 8, at 48 (citing a number of international legal scholars) (emphasis added).
347. 1931 P.C.I.J. (ser. A/B), at 57 (Anzilotti, J., concurring).
348. *See* CRAWFORD, *supra* note 8, at 51-52.
349. MAREK, *supra* note 295, at 162-63.
350. CRAWFORD, *supra* note 8, at 48 (quoting *Island of Palmas Arbitration*, 2 R.I.A.A. 829, 838 (1928) (Huber, J.)).

Palestine arguably fulfills the requirement of separateness, but not of sovereignty. The West Bank and Gaza Strip are territorially distinct from the State of Israel and are governed by a separate legal order.[351] Palestinian residents of the OPT are not represented in the Israeli Government, they are subject to separate laws and a separate judicial system, and they may not claim the legal rights guaranteed to residents of Israel. The international community, moreover, has consistently regarded the OPT as legally separate from Israel and has decried Israel's attempts to impose its legal order on the Territories.

As discussed at length in Section II(C), however, the PA has established, at best, only limited sovereignty over the territories under its administration. Israel continues to exercise many state functions in the OPT, including the maintenance of overriding control over the Territories' infrastructure, borders, and security; and it is empowered by the agreements concluded pursuant to the DOP to veto any of the PA's legislative enactments that it deems objectionable. In view of these arrangements, it would be difficult to characterize the PA as an independent entity. While the PLO's independence is not compromised by the DOP and subsequent agreements, the PLO does not, itself, possess legal authority over the OPT; under the DOP, that authority resides in the PA and in Israel. Thus, the government of the population and territory of Palestine, the PA, lacks the independence necessary to consolidate Palestine's legal status as a State.

3. The Constitutive Approach

In order for an entity's statehood to be "constituted" by recognition, it must first be recognized to be a State. The establishment of the PA has not, however, brought about international recognition of Palestinian statehood. Indeed, while the United Nations General Assembly and several individual States have expressed the hope that the current peace process will culminate in the establishment of a State of Palestine, no State or international body has recognized the PA as an independent State, and the PLO has not urged such recognition. Palestine consequently is no more a State under the constitutive approach than under the declaratory approach.

4. Transitional Association

As presently constituted, Palestine does not fit easily into defined

---

351. The recent agreements between the PLO and Israel affirm the legal and territorial distinctness of the OPT. *See, e.g.,* Interim Agreement, ch. 2, art. 11, para. 1, 36 I.L.M. 551 (stating that both sides regard the West Bank and Gaza Strip as "a single territorial unit, the integrity and status of which will be preserved during the interim period"). Although Israeli citizens residing in the OPT may claim the protection of Israeli law, those rights flow from their Israeli citizenship, not from their residence in the OPT. In much the same way, the United States Constitution protects American citizens abroad from invasions of their rights by the U.S. Government. *See generally,* Gerald L. Neuman, *Whose Constitution?,* 100 YALE L.J. 909 (1991).

categories of international status. Under the interim arrangements established by the DOP, Palestine may best be described as a transitional association between the PA and the PLO. The PLO, which has been recognized to possess an independent international personality as representative of the Palestinian people, has been delegated the power to act on behalf of the PA in the international arena with regard to specific substantive areas. Nevertheless, the PA's constituent organs (the President and Legislative Council) are elected by and serve the interests of the population of the OPT. They form a local government with largely municipal functions and, with regard to those functions, they are independent of the PLO. In this limited respect, the relationship between the two public bodies approximates an association between states.

That noted, however, several factors distinguish the PA-PLO relationship from the traditional legal status of association. Foremost, of course, neither entity is a State. While each, as seen above, possesses certain attributes of statehood, neither meets the objective or subjective criteria requisite for that status. Moreover, the powers withheld from the PLO by the DOP — i.e. the authority to conclude international agreements (with parties other than Israel) that affect the status or security of the OPT — are held by Israel, not by the PA. The PA is consequently in a position of subordination to both the PLO and Israel. Further, the current arrangements have elicited the support of the Palestinian population only insofar as they are transitional. The terms of the DOP, as approved by the PNC, characterize the PA as an interim measure pending the conclusion of permanent status negotiations. The idiosyncratic association between the PA, the PLO, and Israel therefore cannot be seen as an exercise of the free choice of the Palestinian people, who cannot alter the international status of their territory at will.

The relationship between the existing Palestinian public bodies does, however, have an important function with regard to the exercise of Palestinian self-determination. As discussed in Section III(A), above, international law requires heightened scrutiny of changes to a territory's status while it is under belligerent occupation in order to ensure that the changes meet the approval of the territory's population. Agreements concluded between the authorities of an occupied territory and the Occupying Power are especially suspect, raising concerns about the authorities' capacity for independent action. Although the potential for coercion in negotiations between Israel and the Palestinians remains great so long as the OPT remain under Israeli occupation, the relationship between the PLO and the PA helps to preserve Palestinian negotiators' independence from Israel and to avoid the presumption that the PA is merely a puppet of the Government of Israel. Perhaps ironically, the separation between the two public bodies serves these interests as much as the connections between them. While the fact that the PLO sanctioned and negotiated the transitional arrangements provides them with international legitimacy,[352] its legal and functional separation from the PA ensures that the entity conducting permanent status negotiations with Israel is not subordinate to Israeli authority. Since independence is a prerequisite for freedom, the continuing independence of the international representative of the Palestinian people is essential to the free exercise of Palestinian self-determination.

IV. CONCLUSION

In the words of the Syrian poet Adonis, Palestine remains "stalled between seasons." The international community has afforded universal recognition to the Palestinians' peoplehood, and most States support their right to self-determination in the territory defined in the 1988 Palestinian Declaration of Independence. Moreover, all States recognize the special status of the PLO as international representative of the Palestinian people. Through the establishment of the PA, the PLO now has the opportunity to translate its efforts on the international front into more concrete benefits for the Palestinian population in the OPT. The creation of the PA has not, however, altered the international status of the PLO or, more broadly, of Palestine. It does not itself represent a fulfillment of the national aspirations articulated in the Palestinian Declaration of Independence or of the internationally-recognized legal rights that it invoked. The legal and functional separation of the PLO and the PA erected by the DOP and subsequent agreements maintains the independence of the PLO, despite Israeli control of the OPT. It also serves, however, as a barricade against changes in the status of either public body: it denies the PLO effective authority over the territory it claims for the Palestinians, and it denies the PA independence and access to the international decision-making process.

The Government of Israel and the PLO have allocated the permanent status of the OPT to the final stage of negotiations within the framework established by the DOP. The PLO has consistently articulated its commitment to the establishment of an independent Palestinian state in the OPT and has emphasized the inadequacy of any proposed solutions that fall short of that goal.[353] Although Israel's Labor Party adopted a platform omitting the once-standard clause rejecting the establishment of a Palestinian state before Israeli elections last June,[354] the Likud government of Benjamin Netanyahu has stated unequivocally that it opposes Palestinian statehood.[355] While a majority of

352. *See infra* Section II(C)(1).

353. The establishment of an independent Palestinian state remains the PLO's chief negotiating goal, according to the Organization's Chief Representative in the United States. Interview with Khalil A. Foutah, *supra* note 259; *see also Advisor to Yasser Arafat Rejects Puerto-Rico-like Palestine*, AGENCE FRANCE-PRESSE, Nov. 9, 1996, *available in* 1996 WL 12177831.

354. *See* Stephen McFarland, *Foes Soften on Palestine: Israel Party Platform Vote*, DAILY NEWS (New York), Apr. 26, 1996, at 2.

355. Government Guidelines for the Israeli Government Elected on 29 May 1996, JERUSALEM POST, June 18, 1996, at 3.

the States represented in the U.N. General Assembly regard Palestinian statehood to be a legitimate aspiration, the United States traditionally has opposed the idea, supporting instead association of Palestine with Jordan.[356] An evaluation of the status most beneficial to the Palestinian people and most likely to ensure the maintenance of long-term minimum order in the Middle East will require a thorough assessment of the political conditions and economic relationships in the region, an undertaking beyond the scope of this essay (and, regrettably, the capacities of its author). It is important to make clear at the outset, however, that the process of evaluating these alternatives should be informed, indeed governed, by certain core legal principles. Perhaps above all, while the Palestinians' exercise of self-determination may manifest itself in any one of a number of forms of self-government, international law requires that the outcome ultimately be the freely-expressed choice of the Palestinian people.

---

356. *See, e.g.*, Letter from President Ronald Reagan to Prime Minister Menachem Begin (Sept.1,1982), THE PALESTINIAN-ISRAELI PEACE AGREEMENT, *supra* note 95, at 253-56. ("In the Middle East context, the term self-determination has been identified exclusively with the formation of a Palestinian state. We will not support this definition of self-determination.") The United States government has not articulated its present official position on the issue. *See, Remarks of Former Secretary of State James A. Baker III at the Center for Middle East Peace and Economic Cooperation Conference*, FED. NEWS SERV., *available in* 1996 WL 5796086.

Part IX

THE WALL

REVUE BELGE DE DROIT INTERNATIONAL
2004/1 — Éditions BRUYLANT, Bruxelles

LEGAL CONSEQUENCES OF THE CONSTRUCTION OF A WALL IN THE OCCUPIED PALESTINIAN TERRITORY : A COMMENTARY

BY

Roger O'KEEFE

UNIVERSITY LECTURER IN LAW, UNIVERSITY OF CAMBRIDGE
& FELLOW, MAGDALENE COLLEGE, CAMBRIDGE

On 9 July 2004, the International Court of Justice delivered one of its most eagerly awaited advisory opinions since its establishment in 1945. Those hoping for drama could not have been disappointed. The sweeping and categorical nature of the Court's opinion in *Legal Consequences of the Construction of a Wall in the Occupied Palestinian Territory* (1) stunned most observers, to the delight of some and the distress of others. The Court, finding that it had jurisdiction and deciding to comply with the General Assembly's request for an opinion, held that the construction of the wall currently being built by Israel in the occupied territory of the West Bank, including in and around East Jerusalem, along with « *its associated régime* », which includes the Israeli settlements, are contrary to international law. It further held that, in addition to terminating its breaches of international law, to ceasing construction of and dismantling the existing structure immediately, and to repealing or rendering ineffective all related legislation and regulations, Israel is under an obligation to make reparation for all damage caused by the construction of the wall. The Court declared, moreover, that all states are obliged neither to recognize the illegal situation resulting from the wall's construction nor to render aid or assistance in maintaining the situation created by it, and that the High Contracting Parties to the Fourth Geneva Convention are further obliged, within the bounds of the Charter and international law, to ensure Israel's compliance with that Convention. Finally, the Court took the view that the United Nations should consider what further action is required to bring the illegal

---

(1) *Legal Consequences of the Construction of a Wall in the Occupied Palestinian Territory*, General List No. 131, Advisory Opinion, 9 July 2004, http://www.icj-cij.org/icj.www/idocket/imwp/imwpframe.htm (« *Wall in the Occupied Palestinian Territory* »).

situation to an end, « *taking due account of the present Advisory Opinion* » (2).

The following commentary fills in the factual background to *Legal Consequences of the Construction of a Wall in the Occupied Palestinian Territory*, before moving to an extended summary of the opinion and a discussion of it. It concludes with a brief account of reactions to the Court's findings.

I. — BACKGROUND

A. — *The wall* (3)

In 2002, in avowed pursuance of a plan to curb infiltration into Israel by Palestinian suicide bombers from the centre and north of the area known as the West Bank (4), the Israeli Cabinet approved in several stages the construction of what it terms a « security fence » and what the General Assembly, the I.C.J. and the following commentary refer to as a « wall » (5). Construction of what was claimed to be a temporary measure duly commenced. Subsequently, on 1 October 2003, the Israeli Cabinet approved the full proposed route of the wall, which was to run for 720 kilometres along the West Bank. Construction work was well under way by the time the General Assembly requested the advisory opinion on 8 December 2003.

According to a report prepared by the U.N. Secretary-General, the wall consisted, and was further to consist, of a fence with electronic sensors; a ditch, up to 4 metres deep in places; a two-lane asphalt patrol road; a trace road, *viz.* a strip of sand smoothed to detect footprints, running alongside the fence; and six coils of barbed wire stacked on top of each other to mark the perimeter of the complex, which had a total width of 50 to 70 metres, increasing to 100 metres at some points (6). Of the roughly 180 kilometres completed or under construction by 24 November 2003, around 8.5 kilometres — « *generally found where Palestinian population centres are close to or abut Israel* » (7) — featured a concrete wall.

---

(2) The foregoing is a more or less verbatim restatement of the Court's *dispositif* : see *ibid.*, § 163.

(3) See *ibid.*, §§ 79-85 and Report of the Secretary-General prepared pursuant to General Assembly resolution ES-10/13, A/ES-10/248, 24 November 2003.

(4) The reference is to the west bank of the River Jordan.

(5) See, in this regard, *Wall in the Occupied Palestinian Territory*, *loc. cit.*, § 67 : « *[T]he 'wall' in question is a complex construction, so that the term cannot be understood in a limited physical sense. However, the other terms used, either by Israel ('fence') or by the Secretary-General ('barrier'), are no more accurate if understood in the physical sense. In this Opinion, the Court has therefore chosen to use the terminology employed by the General Assembly.* » The same goes for this commentary.

(6) See *ibid.*, § 82.

(7) *Ibid.*

For the greater part of its northernmost course, the wall, both finished and foreshadowed, lies within the territories occupied by Israel since the « Six-Day War » of 1967 (« the Occupied Palestinian Territory » or « the occupied territories ») : in some parts, it runs just inside the so-called « Green Line », the dividing line between Israel and the Occupied Palestinian Territory (8); in others, it deviates more than 7.5 kilometres from the Green Line to include, on the Israeli side, settlements constructed by Israel in the occupied territories, encircling in the process Palestinian population centres; and for 1 to 2 kilometres it lies on the Israeli side of the Green Line (9). Moving south, the planned route penetrates the Occupied Palestinian Territory by up to 22 kilometres. When it comes to Jerusalem, the wall as built and planned lies « *well beyond the Green Line and even in some cases beyond the eastern municipal boundary of Jerusalem as fixed by Israel* » (10). On the basis of this route, both constructed and projected, approximately 975 square kilometres (or 16.6 per cent of the West Bank) would lie between the Green Line and the wall, an area where 237,000 Palestinians and 320,000 Israeli settlers (including 178,000 in East Jerusalem) are reported to live (11). A further 160,000 Palestinians « *would live in almost completely encircled communities, described as enclaves in the [Secretary-General's] report* » (12).

The construction of the wall has brought with it a new administrative régime. The stretch of the West Bank between the Green Line and the wall was designated a « Closed Area » by the Israel Defence Forces in October 2003, which makes the continued presence of residents and the entry of non-residents subject to the possession of a permit or identity card issued by the Israeli authorities, with most residents having been issued such permits for a limited period. Israeli citizens, permanent residents of Israel and persons entitled to immigrate to Israel in accordance with its Law of Return are allowed to « *remain in, or move freely to, from and within* » the Closed Area without a permit (13). « *Access to and exit from the Closed Area can only be made through access gates, which are opened infrequently and for short periods* » (14).

---

(8) This line corresponds to the armistice demarcation line agreed between Israel and Jordan on 3 April 1949, after the first Arab-Israeli war : see *ibid.*, § 72.

(9) See, in this regard, *ibid.*, § 67 : « *The Court notes [...] that the request of the General Assembly concerns the legal consequences of the wall being built 'in the Occupied Palestinian Territory, including in and around East Jerusalem'. [...] [S]ome parts of the complex are being built, or are planned to be built, on the territory of Israel itself; the Court does not consider that it is called upon to examine the legal consequences arising from the construction of those parts of the wall.* »

(10) *Ibid.*, § 83.

(11) *Ibid.*, § 84.

(12) *Ibid.*

(13) *Ibid.*, § 85.

(14) *Ibid.*

Information on the wall and its associated régime submitted to and relied on by the Court (15) described substantial restrictions on the freedom of movement of Palestinian inhabitants of the West Bank, particularly in urban areas like Jerusalem and its environs, and, with this, increasing difficulties in access to health services, educational establishments and water; serious repercussions for agricultural production linked to the destruction and confiscation of agricultural land, olive trees, citrus groves, greenhouses and wells, as well as to the cutting-off of Palestinian farmers from fertile agricultural land and important wells; similarly serious repercussions for Palestinian shops and businesses; and, as a consequence of all of this, the continuing departure, in certain areas, of significant numbers of Palestinians from their residences.

B. — *The request* (16) *and the proceedings*

After the veto by the U.S. of two draft Security Council resolutions of 1997 on certain Israeli settlements in the Occupied Palestinian Territory, the General Assembly, acting pursuant to G.A. resolution 377 A (V) (« Uniting for Peace »), convened its Tenth Emergency Special Session, under the rubric « Occupied East Jerusalem and the rest of the Occupied Palestinian Territory ». Subsequently adjourned, the Tenth Emergency Special Session was reconvened eleven times between 15 July 1997 and 8 December 2003. On 9 October 2003, the Chairman of the Arab Group of U.N. Member States requested a meeting of the Security Council to consider « *grave and ongoing Israeli violations of international law [...]* », including with this request a draft Security Council resolution condemning as illegal Israel's construction of the wall. The Council accordingly convened its 4841st and 4842nd meetings on 14 October 2003, by which time it had before it a second draft resolution condemning the wall. This latter draft resolution was debated by the Council and eventually put to a vote. It was not adopted on account of the negative vote of the U.S.

The Tenth Emergency Special Session of the General Assembly was subsequently reconvened and, by G.A. resolution ES-10/13 of 27 October 2003, the Assembly demanded that Israel stop and reverse the construction of the wall, and requested the Secretary-General to report within a month on Israel's compliance with this demand. The Session then temporarily adjourned. On 19 November 2003, the Security Council adopted S.C. resolution 1515 (2003), in which it endorsed « the Quartet Performance-based Roadmap to a Permanent Two-State Solution to the Israeli-Palestinian Conflict » (17) (« the Roadmap ») and « *[c]alled on the parties to fulfil their obliga-*

---

(15) See *ibid.*, § 133.
(16) See *ibid.*, §§ 18-23.
(17) S/2003/529.

tions under the Roadmap in cooperation with the Quartet [...] » (18). The con-struction of the wall was not discussed at the meeting, and neither the Roadmap nor S.C. resolution 1515 (2003) made specific reference to it.

Finally, with the Secretary-General's report pursuant to G.A. resolution ES-10/13 having been issued on 24 November (19), the Tenth Emergency Special Session of the General Assembly met again on 8 December 2003, and at this meeting adopted G.A. resolution ES-10/14 (20), entitled « Illegal Israeli Actions in Occupied East Jerusalem and the rest of the Occupied Palestinian Territory », in which it requested an advisory opinion from the I.C.J. on the following question :

> « What are the legal consequences arising from the construction of the wall being built by Israel, the occupying Power, in the Occupied Palestinian Territory, including in and around East Jerusalem, as described in the report of the Secretary-General, considering the rules and principles of international law, including the Fourth Geneva Convention of 1949, and relevant Security Council and General Assembly resolutions ? »

General Assembly resolution ES-10/14 was adopted by 90 votes in favour to 8 against, with 74 states abstaining.

The Court invited written and oral statements (21) from the U.N. and Member States, as well as from Palestine, in light of the observer status granted it by the General Assembly and its co-sponsorship of the draft resolution requesting the opinion. It also permitted written statements from the League of Arab States and the Organization of the Islamic Con-ference. In accordance with Article 65 (2) of the I.C.J. Statute, the U.N. Secretary-General submitted to the Court a dossier of documents likely to throw light on the question. The oral hearings took place over three days, from 23 to 25 January 2004. Israel declined to take part in the oral proceedings and restricted its Written Statement to jurisdictional objec-tions.

C. — *The political sensitivities*

The proceedings, both written and oral, and the Court's deliberation took place in an atmosphere of intense public interest and against an incendiary political backdrop perhaps unprecedented in that body's history. Few past proceedings can have achieved front-page newspaper coverage worldwide or witnessed opposing groups of protesters outside the Peace Palace, some of them bearing the remains of a bombed-out bus. Even fewer can have seen

---

(18) The « Quartet » comprises representatives of the U.S., the E.U., the Russian Federation and the U.N. itself.

(19) Report of the Secretary-General prepared pursuant to General Assembly resolution ES-10/13, *loc. cit.*

(20) See Annex 1 to this article for the full text of G.A. res. ES-10/14, 8 December 2003.

(21) See Statute of the I.C.J., Art. 66 (2) and (4).

a feature on opposing counsel in *The Jerusalem Post* (22). For the first time, the Court authorized live internet video coverage of the hearings and the reading of the opinion. For the first time, the Court felt compelled to warn journalists, given the well-publicised leaking of the text the day before, that the official version of the opinion would only be available at the conclusion of the Court's public reading.

In Israel and the occupied territories, the cycle of suicide bombings (albeit considerably curtailed) by Palestinian militant factions and the assassination of Palestinian political and paramilitary figures by the Israel Defence Forces continued throughout the written and oral phases, and this in the context of over fifty-six years of Arab-Israeli enmity, with its attendant geopolitical polarization and destabilization. Arguments over the right of a state to protect its people against indiscriminate attacks were invoked in the febrile climate of the « global war on terror » and of the increasingly bloody resistance to the occupation of Iraq.

The Court must have been uncomfortably conscious of the undoubted but unknowable impact that any opinion, or refusal to give an opinion, would have on the ground. To decline to give an opinion or to give an opinion favourable to Israel might encourage the politics of despair in the occupied territories, triggering an upsurge in violent attacks against Israeli civilians, recruiting more to the cause, fatally isolating the Palestinian moderates and setting alight the much-vaunted « Arab street » across the whole of the Middle East (and the « Muslim street » from Iran to Indonesia). But to render an opinion favourable to Palestine might equally legitimate suicide bombings in the eyes of Palestinian militants and supporters, while at the same time fuelling Zionist extremism, leading to an increase in attacks against Palestinian civilians and perilously deepening the divisions within Israeli society. On the other hand, although the Israeli Government had promised to ignore any adverse findings by the Court, an I.C.J. opinion ruling the wall unlawful might have an influence on legal challenges to its construction pending before the Supreme Court of Israel, a judicial body whose rulings no Israeli government could dismiss. In the final analysis, there was simply no way for the Court to predict whether any opinion it rendered would prove a watershed in the peaceful resolution of one of the world's most volatile, acrimonious and long-running conflicts, an aggravation of it, or a cry in the wilderness.

There were also implications for the future of the Court itself and maybe, more broadly, for the judicial settlement of international disputes. A refusal to render an opinion, or the rendering of an opinion favourable to Israel, might discredit the Court and international judicial process generally in the eyes of the Third World, whose confidence had been hard

(22) KATZ, Yaakov, « PA hires 'world's best' counsel for fence case », *Jerusalem Post*, 8 February 2004.

won after the *South-West Africa Cases* (23). Conversely, an opinion favourable to Palestine would be a boon to the Court's universal legitimacy and prestige, and might even encourage sceptical states to submit contentious cases to adjudication.

In addition, there was a range of delicate issues relating to the composition of the Court. The presence of Judge Elaraby was a bone of contention. In letters to the Court dated 31 December 2003 and 15 January 2004, Israel had alleged that Judge Elaraby's previous participation, in a diplomatic capacity, in the General Assembly's Tenth Emergency Special Session, his prior involvement, in varying official roles, in negotiations between Egypt and Israel, and an interview given to an Egyptian newspaper in August 2001 all precluded him from participation in the case, a submission rejected by the Court in an Order of 30 January 2004 (24). There were confessional and national complications too. The U.S. and U.K. judges, both Jewish, were said to have been distressingly aware that any vote by them to decline to give an opinion or to do anything less than condemn Israel would play into the hands of antisemitic conspiracy theorists in the Middle East and elsewhere, a consideration said to have been a factor in dissuading Judge Higgins from siding in dissent with Judge Buergenthal in the Court's Order of 30 January 2004. Their respective positions were further complicated by their countries' invasion and occupation of Iraq, popularly thought in the Arab world to have been motivated in part by the desire of U.S. neoconservatives to maintain Israel's regional military supremacy. On the other hand, Judges Koroma, Elaraby and Al-Khasawneh are Muslims, the last two from countries which fought four wars with Israel between 1948 and 1973, even if both (Egypt, in the case of Judge Elaraby, and Jordan, as regards Judge Al-Khasawneh) have now made peace with the Jewish State. The position of Judge Simma, a German, was also sensitive, in light of the Holocaust (of which Judge Buergenthal is a survivor). Even Judge Guillaume, a Frenchman, was in an awkward spot, given the publicised recrudescence of antisemitism in France and the worsening strains in that state's relationship with Israel.

To add to this volatile mix, on 30 June 2004, nine days before the I.C.J. was due to deliver its opinion and too late for it to take into account, the Supreme Court of Israel, sitting as the High Court of Justice in respect of cases originating in the occupied West Bank, held that the wall — or « security fence », as it was termed — was legitimately motivated by security concerns and not by the political desire to annex territory, but

---

(23) *South-West Africa Cases (Ethiopia v South Africa; Liberia v South Africa)*, Second Phase, 18 July 1966, *I.C.J. Rep.*, 1966, 6.

(24) *Legal Consequences of the Construction of a Wall in the Occupied Palestinian Territories (Request for Advisory Opinion)*, Order, 30 January 2004, http://www.icj-cij.org/icj.www/idocket/imwp/imwpframe.htm. Judge Elaraby makes brief reference to this Order in the introduction to his separate opinion appended to the Opinion of 9 July 2004.

that the protections afforded the inhabitants of occupied territory by international humanitarian law had to be observed, the outcome in each given instance being determined by the application of the principle of proportionality (25). The Supreme Court approached the question not by attempting to assess the proportionality of the fence as a whole, since « *[i]ts proportionality varie[d] according to local conditions* », but rather « *according to the various orders that were issued for the construction of different parts of the fence* » (26). The upshot of its proportionality calculus was that the Supreme Court held seven sections of an approximately forty-kilometre stretch of the wall to be illegal.

In the event, the I.C.J. achieved a remarkable and welcome degree of consensus, from the unanimous finding that the Court had jurisdiction to the 13:2 split (Judges Kooijmans and Buergenthal dissenting) on the legal consequences of the construction of the wall for third states, with every other element of the *dispositif* being decided by 14 votes to 1 (Judge Buergenthal dissenting). Six judges (Judges Koroma, Higgins, Kooijmans, Al-Khasawneh, Elaraby and Owada) appended separate opinions and one (Judge Buergenthal) a declaration.

II. — DETAILED SUMMARY OF THE JUDGMENT

A. — *Jurisdiction*

§ 1. *The existence of jurisdiction*

Israel was alone in challenging *in limine* the Court's jurisdiction to render the advisory opinion. Every other state and the various international organizations which participated in the proceedings implicitly or explicitly accepted that the Court enjoyed jurisdiction to give the opinion requested by the General Assembly. In the event, the Court concluded that it did indeed have jurisdiction (27).

The Court prefaced its examination of the question by recalling its competence under Article 65 (1) of its Statute to « *give an advisory opinion on any legal question at the request of whatever body may be authorized by or in accordance with the Charter of the United Nations to make such a request* ». In turn, it pointed to the authority conferred on the General Assembly by Article 96 (1) of the U.N. Charter to request an advisory opinion « *on any*

(25) *Beit Sourik Village Council v The Government of Israel*, Supreme Court of Israel sitting as the High Court of Justice, 30 June 2004, H.C.J. 2056/04.

(26) *Ibid.*, § 49.

(27) See *Wall in the Occupied Palestinian Territory, loc. cit.*, § 42.

legal question » (28). While noting the gratuity of its doing so (29), it went on to observe that the subject-matter of the request fell squarely within the competence of the General Assembly as delineated in Article 10 of the Charter and elaborated on in Article 11 (2). Article 10 states that the General Assembly « *may discuss any questions or any matters within the scope of the present Charter [...]* », while Article 11 (2) provides that the Assembly « *may discuss any questions relating to the maintenance of international peace and security brought before it by any Member of the United Nations [...]* ». As specifically regards Article 11 (2), the Court outlined how the question of the construction of the wall had been brought before the General Assembly by Member States during the Assembly's Tenth Emergency Special Session, which had been convened to examine what the Assembly deemed to constitute a threat to international peace and security, namely « *the repeated violation by Israel [...] of international law and its failure to comply with relevant Security Council and General Assembly resolutions and the agreements reached between the parties [...]* » (30).

In reaching its unanimous conclusion that it enjoyed jurisdiction to give the opinion, the Court was called upon to address the validity of General Assembly resolution ES-10/14, the resolution which contained the Assembly's request, and the concept of a « *legal question* » within the meaning of Article 65 (1) of the Statute of the I.C.J. and Article 96 (1) of the Charter.

a) *The validity of G.A. resolution ES-10/14*

Challenging the Court's jurisdiction, Israel had contended that, even if the General Assembly had been meeting in regular session when it requested the opinion, it would have acted *ultra vires* the Charter (31). Basing its argument on Article 12 (1) of the Charter, which states that the Assembly « *shall not make any recommendation* » (32) with regard to a dispute or situation « *[w]hile the Security Council is exercising in respect of [that] dispute or situation the functions assigned to it in the present Charter* »

---

(28) See *ibid.*, §§ 14-15. Article 96 (1) of the Charter states : « *The General Assembly or the Security Council may request the International Court of Justice to give an advisory opinion on any legal question.* »

(29) See *ibid.*, § 16. The power to request an opinion on « *any legal question* » distinguishes the authority conferred on the General Assembly and Security Council respectively by Art. 96 (1) from that bestowed on other organs of the United Nations and specialized agencies by Art. 96 (2). The latter are only competent to request advisory opinions on « *legal questions arising within the scope of their activities* ». Contrast, in this regard, *Legality of the Threat or Use of Nuclear Weapons*, Adv. Op., 8 July 1996, *I.C.J. Rep.*, 1996 (I), 226 (the General Assembly request) with *Legality of the Use by a State of Nuclear Weapons in Armed Conflict*, Adv. Op., 8 July 1996, *I.C.J. Rep.*, 1996 (I), 66 (the W.H.O. request).

(30) See *ibid.*, §§ 17-23, quoting G.A. res. ES-10/2, 25 April 1997.

(31) See Written Statement by the Government of Israel on Jurisdiction and Propriety, 30 January 2004, http://www.icj-cij.org/icj.www/idocket/imwp/imwpframe.htm, pp. 77-81, §§ 4.46-4.58.

(32) The provision continues : « *... unless the Security Council so requests.* »

(its first and foremost function being « *primary responsibility for the main-tenance of international peace and security* » (33), Israel had highlighted the fact that resolution ES-10/14 was adopted while the Security Council was actively engaged with the situation in the Middle East, including the Palestinian question.

The Court, remarking in passing that a request for an advisory opinion « *is not in itself a 'recommendation' by the General Assembly 'with regard to [a] dispute or situation'* » (34), examined the evolution of U.N. practice in the interpretation and application of Article 12 (1), from its initial position that the Assembly could not make a recommendation on a question concer-ning the maintenance of international peace and security while the matter remained on the Council's agenda to the contemporary adoption of recom-mendations on matters which still appeared on the Council's agenda as long as the Council had not « *adopted any recent resolution concerning them* » (35). It drew attention to the view expressed by the U.N.'s Legal Counsel during the twenty-third session of the General Assembly « *that the Assembly inter-preted the words 'is exercising the functions' in Article 12 of the Charter as meaning 'is exercising the functions at this moment'* » and noted « *that there has been an increasing tendency over time for the General Assembly and the Security Council to deal in parallel with the same matter concerning the main-tenance of international peace and security* » (36). It concluded — without elaboration — that « *the accepted practice of the General Assembly, as it has evolved* », and therefore G.A. resolution ES-10/14, was consistent with Article 12 (1) and that, as such, the Assembly had not exceeded its com-petence by submitting the request contained in that resolution (37).

The Court then turned its attention to Israel's main and more specific contention that the necessary preconditions laid down in G.A. resolution 377 A (V) (« Uniting for Peace ») — pursuant to which the Assembly's Tenth Emergency Special Session had been convened, had continued to act and had requested the advisory opinion — for consideration by the General Assembly of questions of international peace and security had not been met. Resolution 377 A (V) provides that « *if the Security Council, because of lack of unanimity of the permanent members, fails to exercise its primary responsibility for the maintenance of international peace and security in any case where there appears to be a threat to the peace, breach of the peace, or act of aggression, the General Assembly shall consider the matter with a view to making appropriate recommendations to Members for collective measures* ». Israel had submitted that the General Assembly was not entitled to justify

---

(33) U.N. Charter, Art. 24.
(34) *Wall in the Occupied Palestinian Territory, loc. cit.*, § 25.
(35) *Ibid.*, § 27.
(36) *Ibid.* The Court cites as examples « *the matters involving Cyprus, South Africa, Angola, Southern Rhodesia and more recently Bosnia and Herzegovina and Somalia* ».
(37) *Ibid.*, § 28.

its request to the Court by reference to the Security Council's inaction since the latter had never been seised of a draft resolution proposing that it should itself request an opinion from the Court on the legal consequences of the wall : « *there [had] been no lack of unanimity of the permanent members or failure by the Council to act on the matter which the co-sponsors of the advisory opinion request brought before the Emergency Special Session* » since « *[t]he matter was simply never brought before the Security Council* » (38). As it was, Israel further argued, the Security Council — prior to the General Assembly's request — had adopted S.C. resolution 1515 (2003), endorsing the Roadmap, and thus continued at the time to exercise its primary responsibility for the maintenance of international peace and security (39).

The Court proceeded to ascertain whether the two requirements for General Assembly action specified in « Uniting for Peace » — namely, that the Security Council has failed to exercise its primary responsibility as a result of a negative vote of one or more of the permanent members and that the situation represents a threat to the peace, breach of the peace or act of aggression — had been fulfilled at the time the General Assembly convened its Tenth Emergency Special Session, in particular when the Assembly adopted G.A. resolution ES-10/14, requesting the advisory opinion. It pointed out that when the Tenth Emergency Special Session was initially convened in 1997 the Security Council had been prevented, by the use by one of the permanent members of its veto, from taking a decision in relation to certain Israeli settlements in the Occupied Palestinian Territory, at a time when there existed (as indicated in G.A. resolution ES-10/2) a threat to international peace and security. It noted, moreover, that the Tenth Emergency Special Session was reconvened on 20 October 2003 on the same basis as in 1997, after the veto on 14 October 2003 of a draft Security Council resolution on the construction of the wall, which the Court characterised again as the Council's failure to act as envisaged in « Uniting for Peace »; and it observed that the Council did nothing by way of reconsidering its position, neither adopting any resolution on the wall nor indeed discussing the matter, between 14 October 2003 and 8 December 2003, the date on which the General Assembly requested the advisory opinion (40). As such, the Assembly's Tenth Emergency Special Session « *was duly reconvened and could properly be seised, under resolution 377 A (V), of the matter now before the Court* » (41). The Court « *also emphasize[d] that, in the course of this Emergency Special Session, the General Assembly could adopt any resolution falling within the subject-matter for which the Session had been convened, and otherwise within its powers, including a resolution seeking the*

(38) Written Statement by the Government of Israel, *loc. cit.*, pp. 75-76, § 4.40, emphasis omitted.

(39) *Ibid.*, p. 77, § 4.45.

(40) *Wall in the Occupied Palestinian Territory, loc. cit.*, § 31.

(41) *Ibid.*

Court's opinion », and it was « *irrelevant in that regard that no proposal had been made to the Security Council to request such an opinion* » (42). Nor did the Court think that what had been called the « rolling » character of the Tenth Emergency Special Session, queried by Israel, was relevant to the validity of the General Assembly's request; (43) and it could not identify any U.N. rule which might have been violated by the fact that the meeting of the Tenth Emergency Special Session of 8 December 2003, at which the request for an advisory opinion was adopted, had been convened while the Assembly was meeting in regular session (44).

« *Finally* », the Court stated,

> « the Tenth Emergency Special Session appears to have been convened in accordance with Rule 9 (*b*) of the Rules of Procedure of the General Assembly, and the relevant meetings have been convened in pursuance of [*sic*] the applicable rules. As the Court stated in its Advisory Opinion of 21 June 1971 concerning the *Legal Consequences for States of the Continued Presence of South Africa in Namibia (South West Africa) notwithstanding Security Council Resolution 276 (1970)*, a 'resolution of a properly constituted organ of the United Nations which is passed in accordance with that organ's rules of procedure, and is declared by its President to have been so passed, must be presumed to have been validly adopted' (*I.C.J. Reports 1971*, p. 22, para. 20). » (45)

In this light, the Court could not see any reason why the presumption was to be rebutted in the circumstances before it (46).

b) « *legal question* »

The Court was also called upon to deal with the familiar contention that the question asked was not a « *legal question* » within the meaning of Article 96 (1) of the Charter and Article 65 (1) of the Statute of the Court, so that the Court had no jurisdiction to render the opinion requested. Israel's objection was that the question was « *uncertain in its terms with the result that it [was] not amenable to a response by the Court* » (47) — that it was « *not possible to decipher with reasonable certainty the legal meaning of the question* » (48). First, the reference to the wall's « legal consequences » was

---

(42) *Ibid.*, § 32.
(43) *Ibid.*, § 33.
(44) *Ibid.*, § 34.
(45) *Ibid.*, § 35.
(46) *Ibid.*
(47) Written Statement of the Government of Israel, *loc. cit.*, p. 83, § 5.2.
(48) *Ibid.*, p. 84, § 5.3.

capable of two interpretations (49). Secondly, the legal consequences for whom had not been specified, and « *[l]egal consequences [did] not exist in the abstract* » (50). Israel also alluded to the « *highly political and partisan [...] character* » of the question, although, in the jurisdictional context, it formally eschewed the argument that the question was political, as opposed to legal (51).

The Court had no trouble in dismissing Israel's objections by reference to its well-established case-law. The question was of a legal character :

> « [The] question is directed to the legal consequences arising from a given factual situation considering the rules and principles of international law, including the Geneva Convention relative to the Protection of Civilian Persons in Time of War of 12 August 1949 [...] and relevant Security Council and General Assembly resolutions. The question submitted by the General Assembly has thus, to use the Court's phrase in its Advisory Opinion on *Western Sahara*, 'been framed in terms of law and raise[s] problems of international law'; it is by its very nature susceptible of a reply based on law; indeed, it is scarcely susceptible of a reply otherwise than on the basis of law. In the view of the Court, it is indeed a question of a legal character (see *Western Sahara, Advisory Opinion, I.C.J. Reports 1975*, p. 18, para. 15). » (52)

As to the alleged lack of clarity, it was pointed out that the unclear drafting of a question does not deny the Court jurisdiction but simply calls for clarification in the course of interpretation, something the Court « *has often done in the past* » (53). As it was, what the Court was being asked to do was sufficiently clear :

> « In the present instance, if the General Assembly requests the Court to state the 'legal consequences' arising from the construction of the wall, the use of these terms necessarily encompasses an assessment of whether that construction is or is not in breach of certain rules and principles of international law. Thus, the Court is first called upon to determine whether such rules and principles have been and are still being breached by the construction of the wall along the planned route. » (54)

Nor did the Court consider the allegedly abstract nature of the question an issue going to jurisdiction; even if it were, a *jurisprudence constante* of the Court in answer to abstractness as an issue of propriety made it plain « *that 'the Court may give an advisory opinion on any legal question, abstract*

---

(49) « *The question asked could first be interpreted as a request for the Court to find that the construction of the wall is illegal, and then to give its opinion on the consequences of that illegality. [...] A second possible interpretation of the request, it is said, is that the Court should assume that the construction of the wall is illegal, and then give its opinion on the legal consequences of that assumed illegality.* » : *Wall in the Occupied Palestinian Territory, loc. cit.*, § 36. Israel further objected to each of these possible courses of action, for different reasons.

(50) Written Statement of the Government of Israel, *loc. cit.*, p. 88, § 5.15.

(51) *Ibid.*, p. 83, § 5.2.

(52) *Wall in the Occupied Palestinian Territory, loc. cit.*, § 37.

(53) *Ibid.*, § 38. The Court cites numerous such instances in this paragraph.

(54) *Ibid.*, § 39.

or otherwise' (55). Anyway, the question before the Court was not an abstract one and it was for the Court to determine for whom the consequences referred to would arise (56). As for the alleged political character of the question, the Court brushed aside the objection by citing well-worn authority to the effect that the political aspects of a question are not sufficient to deprive it of its character as a « legal question » and that neither the political nature of the motivation for a request nor the political implications of any opinion to be given are relevant to establishing the Court's jurisdiction (57).

§ 2. *The propriety of exercising jurisdiction*

Any refusal by the Court to accede to the General Assembly's request was always going to hinge more on the propriety of its exercise of a jurisdiction it enjoyed than on the lack of jurisdiction to begin with. It was to this sole point that several of the Written Statements of participant states were directed (58). So it was that the Court was called upon to answer the contention that it should invoke its discretionary power to decline to render an opinion, as acknowledged in Article 65 (1) of its Statute (« *The Court* may *give an advisory opinion [...]* » (59), since the exercise of its jurisdiction in the present circumstances would be improper and inconsistent with its judicial function.

First, the request was said to concern a contentious matter between Israel and Palestine to the adjudication of which Israel had not consented and which the Court should therefore not entertain, following the authority of the Permanent Court of International Justice in *Status of Eastern Carelia* (60). (The gist of *Eastern Carelia* was that the proceedings before

(55) *Ibid.*, § 40, quoting *Legality of the Threat or Use of Nuclear Weapons, loc. cit.*, 236, § 15, referring in turn to *Conditions of Admission of a State to Membership of the United Nations (Article 4 of the Charter)*, Adv. Op., 28 May 1948, *I.C.J. Rep.*, 1947-1948, 61, *Effect of Awards of Compensation Made by the United Nations Administrative Tribunal*, Adv. Op., 13 July 1954, *I.C.J. Rep.*, 1954, 51 and *Legal Consequences for States of the Continued Presence of South Africa in Namibia (South West Africa) notwithstanding Security Council Resolution 276 (1970)*, Adv. Op., 21 June 1971, *I.C.J. Rep.*, 1971, 27, § 40.

(56) *Ibid.*

(57) *Ibid.*, § 41, citing *Application for Review of Judgment No. 158 of the United Nations Administrative Tribunal*, Adv. Op., 12 July 1973, *I.C.J. Rep.*, 1973, 172, § 14, *Conditions of Admission, loc. cit.*, 61-62, *Competence of the General Assembly for the Admission of a State to the United Nations*, Adv. Op., 3 March 1950, *I.C.J. Rep.*, 1950, 6-7, *Certain Expenses of the United Nations (Article 17, paragraph 2 of the Charter)*, Adv. Op., 20 July 1962, *I.C.J. Rep.*, 1962, 155, *Legality of the Threat or Use of Nuclear Weapons, loc. cit.*, 234, § 13 and *Interpretation of the Agreement of 25 March 1951 between the WHO and Egypt*, Adv. Op., 20 December 1980, *I.C.J. Rep.*, 1980, 87, § 33.

(58) See the respective Written Statements of Australia, Belgium, Cameroon, Canada, the Czech Republic, the Federated States of Micronesia, Germany, Greece, Italy, the Marshall Islands, the Netherlands, Palau, the United Kingdom and the United States, http://www.icj-cij.org/icj.www/idocket/imwp/imwpframe.htm.

(59) Emphasis added.

(60) *Status of Eastern Carelia*, Adv. Op., 23 July 1923, *P.C.I.J. Ser. B*, No. 5.

the Court, while formally advisory, were for all intents and purposes contentious, and the Court's jurisdiction in contentious proceedings depended
on the consent of the parties, in accordance with Article 36 of the Statute
of the P.C.I.J., now Article 36 of the Statute of the I.C.J.) Secondly, it was
argued that an advisory opinion from the Court on the legal consequences
of the construction of the wall could impede a negotiated political solution
to the Israel-Palestine conflict, undermining more specifically the process
set out in the Roadmap. Next, especially in light of Israel's decision not to
address the merits in its Written Statement and not to take part in the oral
proceedings, it was submitted, drawing on *Interpretation of Peace Treaties
with Bulgaria, Hungary and Romania* (61), that the Court did not have at
its disposal the evidence necessary for it to come to a conclusion : it would
be confronted with factual issues impossible to clarify. Israel had asserted
in particular that any consideration by the Court of the legal consequences
of the construction of the wall would have to take into account, *inter alia*,
the nature and scope of the security threat to which the wall was intended
to respond, as well as the effectiveness of that response, and the impact of
the wall on Palestinians, which « *would require extensive documentary, witness and expert evidence from all the parties involved* » (62). A further objection was that the opinion requested would serve no useful purpose. The
point of an advisory opinion was to clarify the law for the requesting U.N.
organ or agency with a view to that body's future action. In the present
circumstances, however, the General Assembly did not need the Court's
opinion since it had already declared the wall illegal and had already determined the legal consequences of this by demanding that Israel halt its construction and dismantle what had been built. Nor had the General
Assembly ever made clear the use to which it would put the Court's
opinion. Finally, calling in aid the maxim *nullus commodum capere potest de
sua injuria propria*, Israel claimed that the principle of good faith and a
requirement of « clean hands » compelled the Court to decline to render an
opinion, since Palestine was responsible for the violent acts against Israel
and its population that the wall was aimed at addressing.

The Court prefaced its discussion of the propriety of acceding to the
General Assembly's request by reaffirming its longstanding and often-
repeated conviction that, bearing in mind its responsibilities as « *the principal judicial organ of the United Nations* » (Charter, Article 92), only « com-

---

(61) *Interpretation of Peace Treaties with Bulgaria, Hungary and Romania*, Adv. Op., First
Phase, 30 March 1950, *I.C.J. Rep.*, 1950, 65. While the Court cites no page, the reference is to
ibid., 72. See also, in this light, *Eastern Carelia, loc. cit.*, 28.
(62) Written Statement of the Government of Israel, *loc. cit.*, p. 109, § 8.5, reference and
emphasis omitted.

pelling reasons » should lead it to decline to render an advisory opinion (63). Its answer to a request from a U.N. organ or agency « *represents its participation in the activities of the Organization, and, in principle, should not be refused* » (64). The Court drew attention to the fact that the I.C.J. « *has never, in the exercise of [its] discretionary power, declined to respond to a request for an advisory opinion* » (65) and emphasized that the sole occasion on which the P.C.I.J. had done so, namely in *Eastern Carelia* itself, was a function of

> « 'the very particular circumstances of the case, among which were that the question directly concerned an already existing dispute, one of the States parties to which was neither a party to the Statute of the Permanent Court nor a Member of the League of Nations, objected to the proceedings, and refused to take part in any way' (*Legality of the Threat or Use of Nuclear Weapons, I.C.J. Reports 1996 (I)*, pp. 235-236, para. 14). » (66)

Nonetheless, the Court made it clear that the discretionary refusal of an advisory opinion on the grounds of judicial property was still a course of action open to it :

> « These considerations do not release the Court from the duty to satisfy itself, each time it is seised of a request for an opinion, as to the propriety of the exercise of its judicial function, by reference to the criterion of 'compelling reasons' [...] » (67).

In this light, the Court proceeded to respond in detail to the various objections to its exercise of jurisdiction.

Addressing, first, Israel's lack of consent to the Court's jurisdiction over the relevant subject-matter, the Court recalled what it had said in *Western Sahara* (affirming, in principle, *Eastern Carelia*), namely that the lack of an interested state's consent « *might constitute a ground for declining to give the opinion requested [...] when the circumstances disclose that to give a reply would have the effect of circumventing the principle that a State is not obliged to allow its disputes to be submitted to judicial settlement without its consent* » (68). It also recalled that the Court in *Western Sahara* had found that, while the matter before it did evidence a legal controversy (and hence a dis-

---

(63) *Wall in the Occupied Palestinian Territory, loc. cit.*, § 44, citing *Certain Expenses, loc. cit.*, 155 and, as one possible example among many, *Difference Relating to Immunity from Legal Process of a Special Rapporteur of the Commission of Human Rights*, Adv. Op., 29 April 1999, *I.C.J. Rep.*, 1999 (I), 78-79, § 29.

(64) *Ibid.*, citing *Interpretation of Peace Treaties, loc. cit.*, 71 and, by way of further example, *Difference Relating to Immunity, loc. cit.*, 78-79, § 29.

(65) *Ibid.* The Court pointed out, for the apparent avoidance of doubt, that its refusal to give the opinion asked of it by the W.H.O. in *Legality of the Use by a State of Nuclear Weapons in Armed Conflict, loc. cit.*, had nothing to do with considerations of judicial propriety but stemmed from its lack of jurisdiction *in limine*.

(66) *Ibid.*

(67) *Ibid.*, § 45.

(68) *Ibid.*, § 47, quoting *Western Sahara*, Adv. Op., 16 October 1975, *I.C.J. Rep.*, 1975, 25, §§ 32-33.

pelling reasons » should lead it to decline to render an advisory opinion (63). Its answer to a request from a U.N. organ or agency « *represents its participation in the activities of the Organization, and, in principle, should not be refused* » (64). The Court drew attention to the fact that the I.C.J. « *has never, in the exercise of [its] discretionary power, declined to respond to a request for an advisory opinion* » (65) and emphasized that the sole occasion on which the P.C.I.J. had done so, namely in *Eastern Carelia* itself, was a function of

> « 'the very particular circumstances of the case, among which were that the question directly concerned an already existing dispute, one of the States parties to which was neither a party to the Statute of the Permanent Court nor a Member of the League of Nations, objected to the proceedings, and refused to take part in any way' (*Legality of the Threat or Use of Nuclear Weapons, I.C.J. Reports 1996 (I)*, pp. 235-236, para. 14). » (66)

Nonetheless, the Court made it clear that the discretionary refusal of an advisory opinion on the grounds of judicial property was still a course of action open to it :

> « These considerations do not release the Court from the duty to satisfy itself, each time it is seised of a request for an opinion, as to the propriety of the exercise of its judicial function, by reference to the criterion of 'compelling reasons' [...] » (67).

In this light, the Court proceeded to respond in detail to the various objections to its exercise of jurisdiction.

Addressing, first, Israel's lack of consent to the Court's jurisdiction over the relevant subject-matter, the Court recalled what it had said in *Western Sahara* (affirming, in principle, *Eastern Carelia*), namely that the lack of an interested state's consent « *might constitute a ground for declining to give the opinion requested [...] when the circumstances disclose that to give a reply would have the effect of circumventing the principle that a State is not obliged to allow its disputes to be submitted to judicial settlement without its consent* » (68). It also recalled that the Court in *Western Sahara* had found that, while the matter before it did evidence a legal controversy (and hence a dis-

---

(63) *Wall in the Occupied Palestinian Territory, loc. cit.*, § 44, citing *Certain Expenses, loc. cit.*, 155 and, as one possible example among many, *Difference Relating to Immunity from Legal Process of a Special Rapporteur of the Commission of Human Rights*, Adv. Op., 29 April 1999, *I.C.J. Rep.*, 1999 (I), 78-79, § 29.

(64) *Ibid.*, citing *Interpretation of Peace Treaties, loc. cit.*, 71 and, by way of further example, *Difference Relating to Immunity, loc. cit.*, 78-79, § 29.

(65) *Ibid.* The Court pointed out, for the apparent avoidance of doubt, that its refusal to give the opinion asked of it by the W.H.O. in *Legality of the Use by a State of Nuclear Weapons in Armed Conflict, loc. cit.*, had nothing to do with considerations of judicial propriety but stemmed from its lack of jurisdiction *in limine*.

(66) *Ibid.*

(67) *Ibid.*, § 45.

(68) *Ibid.*, § 47, quoting *Western Sahara*, Adv. Op., 16 October 1975, *I.C.J. Rep.*, 1975, 25, §§ 32-33.

in this regard. The Court cannot regard this factor as a compelling reason to decline to exercise its jurisdiction. » (77)

It also dismissed the objection that the construction of the wall was only one aspect of the Israel-Palestine conflict, the totality of which could not be properly addressed in the proceedings before the Court. While it acknowledged that the wall was only one part of a wider problem, it emphasized that « *the question that the General Assembly ha[d] chosen to ask [...] [was] confined to the legal consequences of the construction of the wall* » and that it « *would only examine other issues to the extent that they might be necessary to [sic] its consideration of the question put to it* » (78).

Considering, next, the alleged lack of essential evidence, this was something to be determined in each case (79). In the present instance, the Court had been presented with sufficient information by the U.N. and by participants, including in Israel's Written Statement (limited though it formally was to questions of jurisdiction and judicial propriety), and many other relevant documents of the Israeli government were in the public domain (80). Nor was the objection that « *others may evaluate and interpret these facts in a subjective or political manner* » any reason « *for a court of law to abdicate its judicial task* » (81).

With respect to the requested opinion's putative lack of any useful purpose, the Court drew on familiar authority to the effect that the purpose of this and any advisory opinion was to guide the relevant U.N. organ or agency in respect of its own action (82). As for the General Assembly's failure to make clear what such action might be (that is, what use it would make of an opinion), the Court reiterated what it had said in *Legality of the Threat or Use of Nuclear Weapons*, namely that the General Assembly « *has the right to decide [on this] for itself [...]* » (83). It was not for the Court to « *substitute its assessment of the usefulness of the opinion requested for that of the organ that seeks such opinion, namely the General Assembly* » (84), and, as it was, it appeared that the General Assembly had not yet determined all the possible consequences of its own resolution (85). In this light, « *[t]he Court's task would be to determine in a comprehensive manner the legal consequences of the construction of the wall, while the General Assembly — and*

---

(77) *Ibid.*, § 53.
(78) *Ibid.*, § 54.
(79) *Ibid.*, § 56.
(80) *Ibid.*, § 57.
(81) *Ibid.*, § 58.
(82) *Ibid.*, § 60, citing *Reservations to the Convention on the Prevention and Punishment of the Crime of Genocide*, Adv. Op., 28 May 1951, *I.C.J. Rep.*, 1951, 19, *Namibia, loc. cit.*, 24, § 32 and *Western Sahara, loc. cit.*, 37, § 72.
(83) *Ibid.*, § 61, quoting *Legality of the Threat or Use of Nuclear Weapons, loc. cit.*, 237, § 16.
(84) *Ibid.*, § 62.
(85) *Ibid.*

110   ROGER O'KEEFE

*the Security Council — may then draw conclusions from the Court's
findings* » (86).

Finally, the Court gave Israel's « clean hands » argument short shift, considering it irrelevant. « *[I]t was the General Assembly which requested the
advisory opinion, and the advisory opinion [was] to be given to the General
Assembly, and not to a specific State or entity* » (87).

Having thus dismissed every objection raised to the propriety of its rendering the opinion, the Court concluded that there was « *no compelling
reason for it to use its discretionary power not to give that opinion* » (88).

B. — *Merits*

§ 1. *The legality of the construction of the wall*

The Court prefaced its treatment of the merits by explaining that in
order to indicate the legal consequences of the construction of the wall in
the Occupied Palestinian Territory, as requested by the General Assembly,
it had first to determine whether or not this construction violated international law (89). It had made the same point earlier in reply to Israel's
jurisdictional objection that the question was ambiguous (90). In coming to
this determination, the Court was obliged — given Israel's decision not to
address the merits in its Written Statement — to glean the Israeli legal
position on the issues in contention from an annex to the Secretary-
General's report prepared pursuant to G.A. resolution ES-10/13, entitled
« Summary legal position of the Government of Israel » (91).

a) *The status of the Palestinian Occupied Territory, including East
Jerusalem*

The Court first undertook a brief analysis of the status of the territory
in question, beginning with a potted history of Palestine from the end of
the Ottoman Empire and the creation of the League of Nations « A » Class
Mandate, through the U.N. Partition Plan of 1947, the independence of the
State of Israel and the Arab-Israeli war of 1948, to the Six-Day War of
1967 and Security Council resolutions 242 (1967), 298 (1971) and 478
(1980), arriving finally at the 1994 treaty of peace between Israel and Jordan and the « Oslo agreement » and other agreements between Israel and

---

(86) *Ibid.*
(87) *Ibid.*, § 64.
(88) *Ibid.*, § 65.
(89) *Ibid.*, § 68.
(90) *Ibid.*, § 39.
(91) A/ES-10/248, Annex I.

the Palestine Liberation Organization (P.L.O.) (92). The Court observed that, in accordance with customary international law, as reflected in Article 42 of the Hague Regulations of 1907 (93), territory is characterized as occupied « *when it is actually placed under the authority of the hostile army* » and that this occupation « *extends only to the territory where such authority has been established and can be exercised* » (94). Recalling that the territories lying between the Green Line and the eastern boundary of Palestine as it existed under the Mandate were occupied by Israel in 1967 in the course of armed conflict between it and Jordan (the latter's own occupation since 1949 thereby being displaced, a fact never expressly noted), the Court held that these territories were thus occupied territories in which Israel had the status of occupying Power under customary international law (95). Subsequent events having done nothing to alter the situation, the Court found that « *[a]ll these territories (including East Jerusalem) remain occupied territories and Israel has continued to have the status of occupying Power* » (96).

b) *The relevant law*

After briefly describing the wall itself, the Court proceeded to outline the law relevant to assessing the legality of Israel's conduct. It began by pointing to the rule reflected in G.A. resolution 2625 (XXV) of 24 October 1970 (« Declaration on Principles of International Law concerning Friendly Relations and Co-operation among States in accordance with the Charter of the United Nations ») that « *[n]o territorial acquisition resulting from the threat or use of force shall be recognized as legal* », a corollary of the prohibition on the threat or use of force embodied in Article 2 (4) of the Charter and recognized by the Court as customary, in the same way that the Charter's rules on the use of force were recognized as customary in *Nicaragua* (97). The Court also highlighted a people's right to self-determination, as proclaimed in the Charter, reaffirmed in G.A. resolution 2625 (XXV) and embodied in Article 1 common to the International Covenant on Civil and Political Rights (I.C.C.P.R.) and the International Covenant on Economic, Social and Cultural Rights (I.C.E.S.C.R.) (98), pursuant to which every

---

(92) See *Wall in the Occupied Palestinian Territory, loc. cit.*, §§ 70-77.

(93) Regulations Respecting the Laws and Customs of War on Land annexed to the Convention (IV) Respecting the Laws and Customs of War on Land, 18 October 1907, *U.K.T.S.*, 1910, No. 9.

(94) *Wall in the Occupied Palestinian Territory, loc. cit.*, § 78.

(95) *Ibid.*

(96) *Ibid.*

(97) *Ibid.*, § 87, citing *Military and Paramilitary Activities in and Against Nicaragua (Nicaragua v United States of America)*, Merits, 27 June 1986, *I.C.J. Rep.*, 1986, 98-101, §§ 187-190.

(98) 16 December 1966, *U.N.T.S.*, vol. 999, p. 171 and 16 December 1966, *U.N.T.S.*, vol. 993, p. 3 respectively.

state has the duty to refrain from any forcible action which deprives peoples of that right (99). In this light, it recalled that the right to self-determination applies to all non-self-governing territories, that the ultimate objective of « *the sacred trust of civilization* » enshrined in the League of Nations mandate system was the self-determination of the peoples in question, and that the right of peoples to self-determination is a right *erga omnes* (100). The Court then reiterated that the provisions of the Hague Regulations (to which Israel is not party) are consonant with customary international law (101).

Next, the Court examined whether the Fourth Geneva Convention of 1949 (« Convention (IV) relative to the Protection of Civilian Persons in Time of War ») (102), to which both Israel and Jordan are parties, applies to the Occupied Palestinian Territory, including East Jerusalem. Israel, « *contrary to the great majority of the other participants* » (103) in the proceedings, has always disputed the Convention's applicability *de jure* to the West Bank, arguing that the fact that it was not sovereign Jordanian territory when occupied by Israel in 1967 (104) means that it was not « *the territory of a High Contracting Party* » within the meaning of Article 2 of the Convention, which governs the instrument's scope of application (105). The Court, applying the customary rule of treaty interpretation reflected in Article 31 of the Vienna Convention on the Law of Treaties, noted that, as provided in the first paragraph of Article 2 of the Fourth Geneva Convention, the Convention applies when there exists an armed conflict between two or more parties to the Convention — and applies, in this event, to any territory occupied in the course of the conflict by one of the High Contract-

---

(99) *Wall in the Occupied Palestinian Territory*, *loc. cit.*, § 88.

(100) *Ibid.*, citing *Namibia*, *loc. cit.*, 31, §§ 52-53, *Western Sahara*, *loc. cit.*, 68, § 162 and *East Timor (Portugal v Australia)*, 30 June 1995, *I.C.J. Rep.*, 1995, 102, § 29. The phrase « *the sacred trust of civilization* » derives from Art. 22 (1) of the Covenant of the League of Nations, which established the mandate system.

(101) *Ibid.*, § 89, citing the Judgment of the International Military Tribunal at Nuremberg, 30 September and 1 October 1946, 65 and *Legality of the Threat or Use of Nuclear Weapons*, *loc. cit.*, 256, § 75.

(102) 12 August 1949, *U.N.T.S.*, vol. 75, p. 287.

(103) *Wall in the Occupied Palestinian Territory*, *loc. cit.*, § 90.

(104) Although the Court never makes this explicit, Jordan had occupied the territory, which comprised the greater part of the proposed Palestinian state envisaged by the rejected U.N. Plan of Partition for mandated Palestine, in the Arab-Israeli war of 1948.

(105) Article 2 states :

« In addition to the provisions which shall be implemented in peace-time, the present Convention shall apply to all cases of declared war or of any other armed conflict which may arise between two or more of the High Contracting Parties, even if the state of war is not recognized by one of them.

The Convention shall also apply to all cases of partial or total occupation of the territory of a High Contracting Party, even if the said occupation meets with no armed resistance.

Although one of the Powers in conflict may not be a party to the present Convention, the Powers who are parties thereto shall remain bound by it in their mutual relations. They shall furthermore be bound by the Convention in relation to the said Power, if the latter accepts and applies the provisions thereof. »

ing Parties — and that it is not the object of the second paragraph of Article 2 to exclude from this application territories not under the sovereignty of one of these parties. Such an interpretation « *reflects the intention of the drafters of the Fourth Geneva Convention to protect civilians who find themselves, in whatever way, in the hands of the occupying Power [...] regardless of the status of the occupied territories* », an intention made manifest in Article 47 of the Convention (106). This interpretation was confirmed, applying Article 32 of the Vienna Convention on the Law of Treaties (107), by the *travaux préparatoires* (108), and accorded with the position taken by the High Contracting Parties to the Fourth Geneva Convention (109), the International Committee of the Red Cross (I.C.R.C.) (110), the General Assembly (111) and the Security Council (112), all of which affirmed the *de jure* applicability of the Fourth Geneva Convention to the Occupied Palestinian Territory. The Court noted, furthermore, a judgment of 30 May 2004 of the Supreme Court of Israel which held that the Israeli military operations in Rafah were governed by the Convention (113). « *In view of the foregoing* », it concluded :

> « [T]he Court considers that the Fourth Geneva Convention is applicable in any occupied territory in the event of an armed conflict arising between two or more High Contracting Parties. Israel and Jordan were parties to that Convention when the 1967 armed conflict broke out. The Court accordingly finds that that Convention is applicable in the Palestinian territories which before the conflict lay to the east of the Green Line and which, during that conflict, were occupied by Israel [...] » (114).

In this light, « *there [was] no need for any enquiry into the precise prior status of those territories* » (115).

The Court then examined whether the international human rights conventions to which Israel is party are applicable in the Occupied Palestinian

---

(106) *Wall in the Occupied Palestinian Territory, loc. cit.*, § 95. For the text of Art. 47, see *infra*.

(107) See *ibid.*, § 94, citing *Oil Platforms (Iran v United States of America)*, Preliminary Objections, 12 December 1996, *I.C.J. Rep.*, 1996 (II), 812, § 23, *Kasikili/Sedudu Island (Botswana/Namibia)*, 13 December 1999, *I.C.J. Rep.*, 1999 (II), 1059, § 18 and *Sovereignty over Pulau Ligitan and Pulau Sipadan (Indonesia/Malaysia)*, Merits, 17 December 2002, *I.C.J. Rep.*, 2002, 645, § 37.

(108) *Ibid.*, § 95.

(109) *Ibid.*, § 96.

(110) *Ibid.*, § 97.

(111) *Ibid.*, § 98.

(112) *Ibid.*, § 99.

(113) *Ibid.*, § 100. The I.C.J. does not give the name of the case. Note that although Rafah is in the Gaza Strip, not the West Bank, the same considerations apply *mutatis mutandis*, although the Israeli courts are bound by Israeli law to recognize East Jerusalem as part of Israel. The Gaza Strip, part of mandated Palestine, was occupied by Egypt in the Arab-Israeli war of 1948 but was not recognised as its sovereign territory.

(114) *Ibid.*, § 101. Judge Buergenthal agreed with this conclusion : see *ibid.*, dec. BUERGENTHAL, § 2.

(115) *Ibid.*

Territory. Israel, contrary to those other participants which addressed the issue, denies this, taking the view that it is international humanitarian law which applies to situations of armed conflict, such as in the West Bank and Gaza Strip, and that human rights treaties are designed to protect individuals from their own government in peacetime (116). The Court recalled first what it had said on the relationship between international humanitarian law and international human rights law in *Legality of the Threat or Use of Nuclear Weapons*, when it rejected the contention that questions relating to the unlawful loss of life in hostilities were governed by the laws of armed conflict to the exclusion of the International Covenant on Civil and Political Rights (I.C.C.P.R.) :

> « [T]he protection of the International Covenant on Civil and Political Rights does not cease in times of war, except by operation of Article 4 of the Covenant whereby certain provisions may be derogated from in a time of national emergency. Respect for the right to life is not, however, such a provision. In principle, the right not arbitrarily to be deprived of one's life applies also in hostilities. The test of what is an arbitrary deprivation of life, however, then falls to be determined by the applicable *lex specialis*, namely, the law applicable in armed conflict which is designed to regulate the conduct of hostilities. » (117)

The Court continued in its own words :

> « More generally, the Court considers that the protection offered by human rights conventions does not cease in case of armed conflict, save through the effect of provisions for derogation of the kind to be found in Article 4 of the International Covenant on Civil and Political Rights. As regards the relationship between international humanitarian law and human rights law, there are thus three possible situations : some rights may be exclusively matters of international humanitarian law; others may be exclusively matters of human rights law; yet others may be matters of both these branches of international law [...] » (118).

As a consequence, in order to answer the question put to it, the Court would « *have to take into consideration both these branches of international law, namely human rights law and, as* lex specialis, *international humanitarian law* » (119). Turning then to the second legal question raised by Israel's position, the Court considered whether the two international Covenants on human rights and the Convention on the Rights of the Child (120) are applicable outside the respective territories of the States Parties and, if so, in what circumstances. It observed that Article 2 (1) of the I.C.C.P.R., in which each State Party undertakes to respect and to ensure the rights recognized in the Covenant « *to all individuals within its territory and subject*

---

(116) Summary legal position of the Government of Israel, *loc. cit.*, § 4.

(117) *Wall in the Occupied Palestinian Territory, loc. cit.*, § 105, quoting *Legality of the Threat or Use of Nuclear Weapons, loc. cit.*, 240, § 25.

(118) *Ibid.*, § 106.

(119) *Ibid.*

(120) 20 November 1989, *U.N.T.S.*, vol. 1577, p. 43.

to its jurisdiction », could be interpreted either conjunctively or disjunctively : that is, it could cover only individuals who are both present within a State's territory and subject to that State's jurisdiction or it could encompass both individuals present within a State's territory and those outside that territory but subject to that State's jurisdiction (121). As for which was the correct interpretation, the Court observed that, « *while the jurisdiction of States is primarily territorial, it may sometimes be exercised outside the national territory* » and remarked that « *it would seem natural* », given the object and purpose of the I.C.C.P.R., that States Parties should be bound by its provisions even in the event of the latter (122). It noted that « *[t]he constant practice of the Human Rights Committee [...] has found the Covenant applicable where the State exercises its jurisdiction on foreign territory* », a stance endorsed by the Covenant's *travaux préparatoires* (123). It also drew attention to the Committee's conclusion of 2003 that the Covenant applies to the Occupied Palestinian Territory (124), before stating :

> « In conclusion, the Court considers that the International Covenant on Civil and Political Rights is applicable in respect of acts done by a State in the exercise of its jurisdiction outside its own territory. » (125)

As regards the International Covenant on Economic, Social and Cultural Rights (I.C.E.S.C.R.), the Court, after reflecting that the absence of any provision governing its scope of application *ratione loci* « *may be explicable by the fact that this Covenant guarantees rights which are essentially territorial* », considered it « *not to be excluded that it applies both to territories over which a State party has sovereignty and to those over which that State exercises territorial jurisdiction* »; (126) recalled, in this light, the view of the Committee on Economic, Social and Cultural Rights that Israel's obligations under the Covenant apply to all territories and populations under its effective control; (127) and concluded by rejecting Israel's position on the applicability of the Covenant to the occupied territories, adding :

> « [The Court] would also observe that the territories occupied by Israel have for over 37 years been subject to its territorial jurisdiction as the occupying

---

(121) *Ibid.*, § 108.

(122) *Ibid.*, § 109.

(123) *Ibid.* Of the Human Rights Committee's practice, the Court cites *López Burgos v Uruguay*, Case No. 52/79, *Lilian Celiberti de Casariego v Uruguay*, Case No. 56/79 and *Montero v Uruguay*, Case No. 106/81.

(124) *Ibid.*, § 110, quoting CCPR/CO/78/ISR, § 11 : « *in the current circumstances, the provisions of the Covenant apply to the benefit of the population of the Occupied Territories, for all conduct by the State party's authorities or agents in those territories that affect the enjoyment of the rights enshrined in the Covenant and fall within the ambit of State responsibility of Israel under the principles of public international law* »

(125) *Ibid.*, § 111.

(126) *Ibid.*, § 112. « *Thus* », the Court remarks, « *Article 14 makes provision for transitional measures in the case of any State which 'at the time of becoming a Party, has not been able to secure in its metropolitan territory or other territories under its jurisdiction compulsory primary education, free of charge'.* »

(127) *Ibid.*, quoting E/C.12/1/Add.90, §§ 15 and 31.

Power. In the exercise of the powers available to it on this basis, Israel is bound by the provisions of the International Covenant on Economic, Social and Cultural Rights. Furthermore, it is under an obligation not to raise any obstacle to the exercise of such rights in those fields where competence has been transferred to Palestinian authorities. » (128)

Finally, the Court held that the Convention on the Rights of the Child applies in the occupied territories too, given the explicit statement in Article 2 that « *States Parties shall respect and ensure the rights set forth in the [...] Convention to each child within their jurisdiction* » (129).

c) *Application of the law to the construction of the wall and its associated régime*

The Palestinians and other participants in the proceedings had alleged that the construction of the wall was an attempt by Israel at the *de facto* annexation of parts of the Occupied Palestinian Territory, including East Jerusalem, in violation of the prohibition on the acquisition of territory by force and, consequently, in violation of the right of the Palestinian people to self-determination. They emphasized, in particular, what they alleged to be the intended change that the wall would make to the demographic composition of the territories by reinforcing Israeli settlements illegally built there. Israel's position, on the other hand, is that the sole purpose of the wall, which it claims to be temporary, is to counter terrorist attacks emanating from the West Bank (130). For its part, the Court recalled references by the General Assembly and the Security Council, in the specific context of Palestine, to the customary rule on the inadmissibility of the acquisition of territory by armed force, drawing particular attention to S.C. resolution 242 (1967) and the Council's condemnation of measures to change the legal status of Jerusalem (131). The Court also observed, in the context of the right of a people to self-determination, that the existence of a « Palestinian people » was no longer contested, not even by Israel (132). It further noted that the wall's proposed route was not only such as to include within the Closed Area (*viz.* the land between the Green Line and the wall) around 80 per cent of the Israeli settlers in the Occupied Palestinian Territory but seemed also to have been drawn in such a way as to include the great majority of the Israeli settlements themselves (133). In this regard, the Court highlighted Article 49 (6) of the Fourth Geneva

---

(128) *Ibid.*
(129) *Ibid.*, § 113. Judge Buergenthal agreed that international human rights law was applicable to the Occupied Palestinian Territory : see *ibid.*, dec. BUERGENTHAL, § 2.
(130) See *ibid.*, § 116.
(131) *Ibid.*, § 117.
(132) *Ibid.*, § 118.
(133) *Ibid.*, § 119.

Convention (134), which it held to prohibit « *any measures taken by an occupying Power in order to organize or encourage transfers of parts of its own population into [...] occupied territory* », before stating :

> « In this respect, the information provided to the Court shows that, since 1977, Israel has conducted a policy and developed practices involving the establishment of settlements in the Occupied Palestinian Territory, contrary to the terms of Article 49, paragraph 6 [of the Fourth Geneva Convention] [...] » (135)

Recalling the Security Council's view as to the « *flagrant* » illegality of this policy and these practices (136), the Court itself concluded :

> « [T]he Israeli settlements in the Occupied Palestinian Territory (including East Jerusalem) have been established in breach of international law. » (137)

It then continued :

> « Whilst the Court notes the assurance given by Israel that the construction of the wall does not amount to annexation and that the wall is of a temporary nature [...], it nevertheless cannot remain indifferent to certain fears expressed to it that the route of the wall will prejudge the future frontier between Israel and Palestine, and the fear that Israel may integrate the settlements and their means of access. The Court considers that the construction of the wall and its associated régime create a 'fait accompli' on the ground that could well become permanent, in which case, and notwithstanding the formal characterization of the wall by Israel, it would be tantamount to *de facto* annexation. » (138)

The Court finally recalled, in addition to the 80 per cent of the Israeli settlers who would reside there, the 16 per cent of the West Bank that would be included in the Closed Area and the 160,000 Palestinians who would, as a result of the wall, « *reside in almost completely encircled communities* » :

> « In other terms, the route chosen for the wall gives expression *in loco* to the illegal measures taken by Israel with regard to Jerusalem and the settlements, as deplored by the Security Council [...] There is also a risk of further alterations to the demographic composition of the Occupied Palestinian Territory resulting from the construction of the wall inasmuch as it is contributing [...] to the departure of Palestinian populations from certain areas. That construction, along with measures taken previously, thus severely impedes the exercise by the Palestinian people of its right to self-determination, and is therefore a breach of Israel's obligation to respect that right. » (139)

With this, the Court turned to issues of international humanitarian and human rights law.

---

(134) The sixth unnumbered paragraph of Art. 49 reads : « *The Occupying Power shall not deport or transfer parts of its own civilian population into the territory it occupies.* ».

(135) *Wall in the Occupied Palestinian Territory, loc. cit.*, § 120.

(136) *Ibid.*, citing S.C. resolutions 446 (1979), 452 (1979) and 465 (1980), and quoting the last.

(137) *Ibid.* Judge Buergenthal concurred on this point : see *ibid.*, dec. BUERGENTHAL, § 9.

(138) *Ibid.*, § 121.

(139) *Ibid.*, § 122.

The Court first distinguished Section II of the 1907 Hague Regulations (including Article 23 (g), on the destruction of enemy property), which deals with hostilities and is thus not currently applicable to the West Bank, from Section III of the Regulations, which deals with military authority in occupied territories and therefore applies, drawing attention in the latter regard to the obligations imposed by Articles 43, 46 and 52 (140). It also noted the distinction drawn in Article 6 of the Fourth Geneva Convention between those provisions applicable during hostilities and those which remain applicable within occupied territory after the general close of military operations, before highlighting, as part of this second group, Articles 47, 49, 52, 53 and 59 (141). After summarising the relevant information submitted to it on the wall and its associated régime, it stated :

> « [I]t appears that the construction of the wall has led to the destruction or requisition of properties under conditions which contravene the requirements of Articles 46 and 52 of the Hague Regulations of 1907 and Article 53 of the Fourth Geneva Convention. » (142)

(140) *Ibid.*, § 124. Article 43 obliges the Occupying Power to « *take all measures within his power to restore, and, as far as possible, insure public order and life, respecting the laws in force in the country* ». Article 46 provides, in relevant part, that private property « *must be respected* » and « *cannot be confiscated* ». Article 52 states :

« Requisitions in kind and services shall not be demanded from municipalities or inhabitants except for the needs of the army of occupation. They shall be in proportion to the resources of the country, and of such a nature as not to involve the inhabitants in the obligation of taking part in military operations against their own country.

Such requisitions and services shall only be demanded on the authority of the commander in the locality occupied.

Contributions in kind shall as far as possible be paid for in cash; if not, a receipt shall be given and the payment of the amount due shall be made as soon as possible. »

(141) *Ibid.*, §§ 125-126. As stipulated in Art. 6, the provisions applicable to occupied territory comprise Arts 1-12, 27, 29-34, 47, 49, 51, 52, 53, 59, 61-77 and 143.

(142) *Ibid.*, § 132. Article 47 reads : « *Protected persons who are in occupied territory shall not be deprived, in any case or in any manner whatsoever, of the benefits of the present Convention by any change introduced, as the result of the occupation of a territory, into the institutions or government of the said territory, nor by any agreement concluded between the authorities of the occupied territories and the Occupying Power, nor by any annexation by the latter of the whole or part of the occupied territory.* ». Article 49 states in relevant part :

« Individual or mass forcible transfers, as well as deportations of protected persons from occupied territory to the territory of the Occupying Power or to that of any other country, occupied or not, are prohibited, regardless of their motive.

Nevertheless, the Occupying Power may undertake total or partial evacuation of a given area if the security of the population or imperative military reasons so demand. Such evacuations may not involve the displacement of protected persons outside the bounds of the occupied territory except when for material reasons it is impossible to avoid such displacement. Persons thus evacuated shall be transferred back to their homes as soon as hostilities in the area in question have ceased.

[...]

[Sixth paragraph] The Occupying Power shall not deport or transfer parts of its own civilian population into the territory it occupies. »

Article 52 provides in relevant part : « *All measures aiming at creating unemployment or at restricting the opportunities offered to workers in an occupied territory, in order to induce them to work for the Occupying Power, are prohibited.* ». Article 53 reads : « *Any destruction by the Occupying Power of real or personal property belonging individually or collectively to private persons, or to*

As regards the relevant human rights law, the Court noted that, while Israel has entered a derogation to the I.C.C.P.R. as permitted by Article 4, this applies only to Article 9, the right to liberty and security of the person, with the result that the other provisions of the Covenant « *remain applicable not only on Israeli territory, but also on the Occupied Palestinian Territory* » (143). In this light, it declared :

> « [T]he construction of the wall and its associated régime impede the liberty of movement of the inhabitants of the Occupied Palestinian Territory (with the exception of Israeli citizens and those assimilated thereto) as guaranteed under Article 12, paragraph 1, of the International Covenant on Civil and Political Rights. They also impede the exercise by the persons concerned of the right to work, to health, to education and to an adequate standard of living as proclaimed in the International Covenant on Economic, Social and Cultural Rights and in the United Nations Convention on the Rights of the Child. Lastly, the construction of the wall and its associated régime, by contributing to the demographic changes referred to [previously], contravene Article 49, paragraph 6, of the Fourth Geneva Convention and the Security Council resolutions cited [previously]. » (144)

The Court added that « *account must also be taken* » of specific guarantees of freedom of access to the Holy Places, in particular Israel and Jordan's mutual undertaking via the General Armistice Agreement of 1949, which remained binding on Israel for the Holy Places which fell under its control

---

the State, or to other public authorities, or to social or cooperative organizations, is prohibited, except where such destruction is rendered absolutely necessary by military operations. ». Finally, Article 59 states :

« If the whole or part of the population of an occupied territory is inadequately supplied, the Occupying Power shall agree to relief schemes on behalf of the said population, and shall facilitate them by all the means at its disposal.

Such schemes, which may be undertaken either by States or by impartial humanitarian organizations such as the International Committee of the Red Cross, shall consist, in particular, of the provision of consignments of foodstuffs, medical supplies and clothing.

All Contracting Parties shall permit the free passage of these consignments and shall guarantee their protection.

A Power granting free passage to consignments on their way to territory occupied by an adverse Party to the conflict shall, however, have the right to search the consignments, to regulate their passage according to prescribed times and routes, and to be reasonably satisfied through the Protecting Power that these consignments are to be used for the relief of the needy population and are not to be used for the benefit of the Occupying Power. »

(143) *Ibid.*, § 127.

(144) *Ibid.*, § 134. Article 12 (1) of the I.C.C.P.R. states : « *Everyone lawfully within the territory of a State shall, within that territory, have the right to liberty of movement and freedom to choose his residence.* ». As regards the I.C.E.S.C.R., while the Court itself makes no mention of specific provisions, the right to work is guaranteed by Art. 6, the right to health by Art. 12, the right to education by Art. 13 and the right to an adequate standard of living by Art. 11. For its part, the Convention on the Rights of the Child guarantees the right to health in Art. 24, the right to an adequate standard of living in Art. 27 and the right to education in Art. 28. Finally, the sixth unnumbered paragraph of Art. 49 of the Fourth Geneva Convention provides that « *[t]he Occupying Power shall not deport or transfer parts of its own civilian population into the territory it occupies* ». The Security Council resolutions referred to are S.C. resolutions 446 (1979), 452 (1979) and 465 (1980).

in 1967 and which had been confirmed in Article 9 (1) of the 1994 Israel-Jordan peace treaty (145).

The Court went on to observe that some of the relevant provisions of international humanitarian law contain clauses permitting considerations of military necessity to be taken into account in their application, although, out of the provisions of which Israel stood in breach, only Article 53 of the Fourth Geneva Convention makes such allowance, forbidding as it does the destruction of both real and personal property « *except where such destruction is rendered absolutely necessary by military operations* ». In this context, while the Court held that the military exigencies contemplated by such provisions may be invoked in occupied territories even after the general close of hostilities,

> « it [was] not convinced that the destructions carried out contrary to the prohibition in Article 53 of the Fourth Geneva Convention were rendered absolutely necessary by military operations. » (146)

Similarly, the Court noted that some of the human rights guarantees to which it had drawn attention contain clauses which allow states to restrict these rights subject to certain conditions, one of these being the right to freedom of movement embodied in Article 12 of the I.C.C.P.R., paragraph 3 of which admits restrictions « *which are provided by law, are necessary to protect national security, public order (*ordre public*), public health or morals or the rights and freedoms of others, and are consistent with the other rights recognized in the [...] Covenant* ». That said, the Court continued :

> « [I]t is not sufficient that such restrictions be directed to the ends authorized; they must also be necessary for the attainment of those ends. As the Human Rights Committee put it, they 'must conform to the principle of proportionality' and 'must be the least intrusive instrument amongst those which might achieve the desired result' (CCPR/C/21/Rev.1/Add.9, General Comment N° 27, para 14). On the basis of the information available to it, the Court finds that these conditions are not met in the present instance. » (147)

As for the rights secured by the I.C.E.S.C.R., the Court pointed out that their enjoyment is subject to a clause of general application in Article 4 allowing « *such limitations as are determined by law only in so far as this may be compatible with the nature of these rights and solely for the purpose of promoting the general welfare in a democratic society* ». But it added :

> « The Court would further observe that the restrictions on the enjoyment by the Palestinians living in the territory occupied by Israel of their economic, social and cultural rights, resulting from Israel's construction of the wall, fail to meet a condition laid down by Article 4 of the International Covenant on

---

(145) *Ibid.*, § 129. See Treaty of Peace Between The State of Israel and The Hashemite Kingdom of Jordan, 26 October 1994, *U.N.T.S.*, vol. 2042, p. 395.

(146) *Ibid.*, § 135.

(147) *Ibid.*, § 136.

Economic, Social and Cultural Rights, that is to say that their implementation must be 'solely for the purpose of promoting the general welfare in a democratic society'. » (148)

In conclusion, the Court recapitulated its findings as to the conformity of Israel's conduct with the relevant international humanitarian and human rights law :

« To sum up, the Court, from the material available to it, is not convinced that the specific course Israel has chosen for the wall was necessary to attain its security objectives. The wall, along the route chosen, and its associated régime gravely infringe a number of rights of Palestinians residing in the territory occupied by Israel, and the infringements resulting from that route cannot be justified by military exigencies or by the requirements of national security or public order. The construction of such a wall accordingly constitutes breaches by Israel of various of its obligations under the applicable international humanitarian law and human rights instruments. » (149)

With this the Court turned to possible circumstances precluding the wrongfulness of Israel's actions.

d) *Circumstances precluding wrongfulness*

Israel's legal position is that the construction of the wall is a non-forcible measure undertaken in the exercise of, and consistent with, its inherent right to self-defence, as recognized in Article 51 of the Charter and S.C. resolutions 1368 (2001) and 1373 (2001) (150). The Court remarked, however, that Article 51 of the Charter recognizes a right of self-defence « *in the case of armed attack by one State against another State* » and that « *Israel does not claim that the attacks against it are imputable to a foreign State* » (151). It also noted « *that Israel exercises control in the Occupied Palestinian Territory and that, as Israel itself states, the threat which it regards as justifying the wall originates within, and not outside, that territory* », making the situation different from that envisaged in S.C. resolutions 1368

---

(148) *Ibid.*

(149) *Ibid.*, § 137.

(150) In the preamble to S.C. res. 1368 (2001), adopted on 12 September 2001 in the immediate aftermath of the terrorist attacks on the World Trade Centre and the Pentagon, the Security Council « *[r]ecognize[s] the inherent right of [...] self-defence in accordance with the Charter* »; and in § 1, it « *regards such acts, like any act of international terrorism, as a threat to international peace and security* ». In the preamble to S.C. res. 1373 (2001), 28 September 2001, the Council reaffirms both these elements of S.C. res. 1368 (2001). In this light, Israel's position seems to be that terrorist attacks engage Art. 51 of the Charter. Although the precise legal basis for this reliance on self-defence is not clear, it seems predicated — given Israel's explicit recognition of the non-forcible nature of its acts — on self-defence as a circumstance precluding the wrongfulness of the construction of the wall and its associated régime. See, in this regard, Articles on Responsibility of States for Internationally Wrongful Acts, A/RES/56/83, Annex, 12 December 2001, Art. 21.

(151) Wall in the Occupied Palestinian Territory, *loc. cit.*, § 139.

(2001) and 1373 (2001) (152). The right to self-defence in accordance with Article 51 of the Charter was thus irrelevant.

Finally, the Court — *proprio motu*, it appears — considered whether Israel could rely on a state of necessity as a circumstance precluding the wrongfulness of its conduct. But first it felt « *bound to note that some of the conventions at issue in the present instance include qualifying clauses of the rights guaranteed or provisions for derogation* » and thought « *it might be asked whether a state of necessity as recognized in customary international law could be invoked with regard to those treaties as a ground for precluding the wrongfulness of the measures or decisions being challenged* », « *[s]ince those treaties already address considerations of this kind within their own provisions* » (153). It was not, however, required to rule on this question. Rather, the Court recalled what it had said in *Gabčíkovo-Nagymaros Project*, namely that the state of necessity as recognized by customary international law « *can only be invoked under certain strictly defined conditions* », that « *the State concerned is not the sole judge of whether those conditions have been met* », and that one of these conditions (as « *stated by the Court in terms used by the International Law Commission* ») was that the conduct under challenge be « *the only way for the State to safeguard an essential interest against a grave and imminent peril* » (154). It then stated :

> « In the light of the material before it, the Court is not convinced that the construction of the wall along the route chosen was the only means to safeguard the interests of Israel against the peril which it has invoked as justification for that construction. » (155)

It added :

> « The fact remains that Israel has to face numerous indiscriminate and deadly acts of violence against its civilian population. It has the right, and indeed the duty, to respond in order to protect the life of its citizens. The measures taken are bound nonetheless to remain in conformity with applicable international law. » (156)

It concluded :

> « [T]he Court considers that Israel cannot rely on a right of self-defence or on a state of necessity in order to preclude the wrongfulness of the construction of the wall [...] The Court accordingly finds that the construction of the wall, and its associated régime, are contrary to international law. » (157)

---

(152) *Ibid.*
(153) *Ibid.*, § 140. See, in this light, Articles on Responsibility of States, *loc. cit.*, Art. 55 (« *Lex specialis* »).
(154) *Ibid.*, quoting *Gabčíkovo-Nagymaros Project (Hungary/Slovakia)*, 25 September 1997, *I.C.J. Rep.*, 1997, 40, § 51 and Articles on Responsibility of States, *loc. cit.*, Art. 25.
(155) *Ibid.*
(156) *Ibid.*, § 141.
(157) *Ibid.*, § 142.

In this way, the Court wrapped up its discussion of the legality of the wall and its associated régime.

§ 2. — *The legal consequences of Israel's unlawful conduct*

It followed from the Court's conclusion as to the unlawfulness of the construction of the wall in the Occupied Palestinian Territory and its associated régime that Israel's responsibility was engaged (158). By way of resulting secondary obligation, Israel was under a duty « *to comply with the international obligations it ha[d] breached* », namely « *its obligation to respect the right of the Palestinian people to self-determination and its obligations under international humanitarian law and international human rights law* » (159). It was furthermore « *[to] ensure freedom of access to the Holy Places that came under its control during the 1967 War* » (160). Next, Israel was under an obligation « *to put an end to the violation of its international obligations flowing from the construction of the wall [...]* », an obligation well established in general international law which the Court had often confirmed (161). The Court elaborated :

> « 151. Israel accordingly has the obligation to cease forthwith the works of construction of the wall being built by it in the Occupied Palestinian Territory, including in and around East Jerusalem. Moreover, in view of the Court's finding [...] that Israel's violations of its international obligations stem from the construction of the wall and from its associated régime, cessation of those violations entails the dismantling forthwith of those parts of that structure situated within the Occupied Palestinian Territory, including in and around East Jerusalem. All legislative and regulatory acts adopted with a view to its construction, and to the establishment of its associated régime, must forthwith be repealed or rendered ineffective, except in so far as such acts, by providing for compensation or other forms of reparation for the Palestinian population, may continue to be relevant for compliance by Israel with [its further] obligations [...]
>
> 152. Moreover, given that the construction of the wall in the Occupied Palestinian Territory has, *inter alia*, entailed the requisition and destruction of homes, businesses and agricultural holdings, the Court finds further that Israel has the obligation to make reparation for the damage caused to all the natural or legal persons concerned. [...] »

The Court recalled in this light the « *essential forms of reparation in customary law* » laid down in *Factory at Chorzów*, namely restitution in kind (*restitutio in integrum*) or, if this is impossible, payment of a sum corres-

---

(158) *Ibid.*, § 147.
(159) *Ibid.*, § 149.
(160) *Ibid.*
(161) *Ibid.*, § 150, citing *Nicaragua, loc. cit.*, 149, § 292, *United States Diplomatic and Consular Staff in Tehran (United States of America v Iran)*, Merits, 24 May 1980, *I.C.J. Rep.*, 1980, 44, § 95 and *Haya de la Torre (Colombia v Peru)*, Merits, 13 June 1951, *I.C.J. Rep.*, 1951, 82.

ponding to the value which a restitution in kind would bear, as well as the award of damages for loss sustained (162), specifying :

> « Israel is accordingly under an obligation to return the land, orchards, olive groves and other immovable property seized from any natural or legal person for purposes of construction of the wall in the Occupied Palestinian Territory. In the event that such restitution should prove to be materially impossible, Israel has an obligation to compensate the persons in question for the damage suffered. The Court considers that Israel also has an obligation to compensate, in accordance with the applicable rules of international law, all natural or legal persons having suffered any form of material damage as a result of the wall's construction. » (163)

It was not just Israel, however, which bore the legal consequences of its unlawful construction of the wall and its associated régime.

The Court went on to consider the legal consequences for other states. It observed that « *the obligations violated by Israel include certain obligations erga omnes* », *viz.* obligations which, in the words of *Barcelona Traction*, « *are by their very nature 'the concern of all States', [so that] 'all States can be held to have a legal interest in their protection'* » (164). The first of these was the right of the Palestinian people to self-determination, which the Court in *East Timor* observed to have an *erga omnes* character and which, in accordance with G.A. resolution 2625 (XXV), « *[e]very State has the duty to promote, through joint and separate action [...]* » (165). The second were certain of Israel's obligations under international humanitarian law, which, recalling its dictum in *Legality of the Threat or Use of Nuclear Weapons*, the Court considered « *essentially of an* erga omnes *character* » (166). It also drew attention to Article 1 of the Fourth Geneva Convention (common to all four Geneva Conventions), by which the High Contracting Parties « *undertake to respect and to ensure respect for the [...] Convention in all circumstances* » and from which it followed « *that every State party to that Convention, whether or not it is a party to a specific conflict, is under an obligation to ensure that the requirements of the instruments in question are complied with* » (167). The Court then stated :

> « Given the character and the importance of the rights and obligations involved, the Court is of the view that all States are under an obligation not to recognize the illegal situation resulting from the construction of the wall in the Occupied Palestinian Territory, including in and around East Jerusalem. They are also under an obligation not to render aid or assistance in maintaining the situation created by such construction. It is also for all States, while

---

(162) *Ibid.*, § 152, quoting *Factory at Chorzów (Germany v Poland)*, Merits, 13 September 1928, *P.C.I.J. Rep. Ser. A*, No. 17, 47.

(163) *Ibid.*, § 153.

(164) *Ibid.*, § 155, quoting *Barcelona Traction, Light and Power Company, Limited (Belgium v Spain)*, Second Phase, 5 February 1970, *I.C.J. Rep.*, 32, § 33.

(165) *Ibid.*, § 156, quoting *East Timor, loc. cit.*, 102, § 29 and G.A. res. 2625 (XXV).

(166) *Ibid.*, § 157, quoting *Legality of the Threat or Use of Nuclear Weapons, loc. cit.*, 257, § 79.

(167) *Ibid.*, § 158.

respecting the United Nations Charter and international law, to see to it that any impediment, resulting from the construction of the wall, to the exercise by the Palestinian people of its right to self-determination is brought to an end. In addition, all the States parties to the Geneva Convention relative to the Protection of Civilian Persons in Time of War of 12 August 1949 are under an obligation, while respecting the United Nations Charter and international law, to ensure compliance by Israel with international humanitarian law as embodied in that Convention. » (168)

Finally, the Court spoke of the legal consequences for the U.N., taking the view « *that the United Nations, and especially the General Assembly and the Security Council, should consider what further action is required to bring to an end the illegal situation resulting from the construction of the wall and the associated régime, taking due account of the present Advisory Opinion* » (169).

§ 3. *Epilogue*

The Court inserted two final paragraphs by way of epilogue. Inspired by an avowed concern to lend its support to the purposes and principles enshrined in the Charter, especially the maintenance of international peace and security and the peaceful settlement of disputes, it « *emphasize[d] the urgent necessity for the United Nations as a whole to redouble its efforts to bring the Israeli-Palestinian conflict [...] to a speedy conclusion, thereby establishing a just and lasting peace in the region* » (170), before continuing :

> « The Court would emphasize that both Israel and Palestine are under an obligation scrupulously to observe the rules of international humanitarian law, one of the paramount purposes of which is to protect civilian life. Illegal actions and unilateral decisions have been taken on all sides, whereas, in the Court's view, this tragic situation can be brought to an end only through implementation in good faith of all relevant Security Council resolutions, in particular resolutions 242 (1967) and 338 (1973). The 'Roadmap' approved by Security Council resolution 1515 (2003) represents the most recent of efforts to initiate negotiations to this end. The Court considers that it has a duty to draw the attention of the General Assembly, to which the present Opinion is addressed, to the need for these efforts to be encouraged with a view to achieving as soon as possible, on the basis of international law, a negotiated solution to the outstanding problems and the establishment of a Palestinian State, existing side by side with Israel and its other neighbours, with peace and security for all in the region. » (171)

On this note, the Court proceeded to the *dispositif*.

(168) *Ibid.*, § 159.
(169) *Ibid.*, § 160.
(170) *Ibid.*, § 161.
(171) *Ibid.*, § 162.

ROGER O'KEEFE

III. — DISCUSSION

The Court's views as to the law, as far as they can be ascertained and as far as they go, are correct on all major counts. Where not based on existing authority, they are rational readings of the relevant rules and principles. There is no conclusive legal finding which even those disappointed by the outcome could seriously contest. As for the Court's application of this law to the facts, which is obviously a matter of appreciation in any judicial proceedings, it is — from the distant and mediated vantage point of this commentator — difficult to tell how accurate this is, although it does seem more plausible than not.

But while the Court's conclusions are sound, its exposition of them leaves something to be desired. The opinion is often unsatisfying in methodological and stylistic terms. It is too prone to bald, *ex cathedra* pronouncements of law and fact, which give little indication of the Court's reasoning (172). It demands a good deal of reading between the lines, which can only foster ambiguity. Of course, it almost goes without saying that a degree of ambiguity can be constructive in diplomacy, and the principle judicial organ of the United Nations can hardly be unaware of the need for diplomatic nuance (173), especially when exercising its non-binding advisory jurisdiction and when the most crucial interested state objects to the proceedings. A certain delphic quality also allows the Court to hint at and to seek to influence legal and political controversies beyond its present remit without formally exceeding its mandate and risking its legitimacy. But a court's central function is, as one might expect, judicial, and its legitimacy as a judicial organ, indeed its *raison d'être*, stems largely from the clarity, cogency and, as the sum of these, persuasiveness of its reasoning and the guidance it can provide for future conduct. This is all the more

---

(172) To cite just three examples mentioned by Judge Higgins in her separate opinion, « the 'history' as recounted by the Court in paragraphs 71-76 » is unsatisfactory (*ibid.*, sep. op. HIGGINS, § 16); the Court's treatment of international humanitarian law is « somewhat light » (*ibid.*, § 25) and its « findings of law are notably general in character, saying remarkably little as concerns the application of specific provisions of the Hague Rules or the Fourth Geneva Convention along particular sections of the route of the wall » (*ibid.*, § 40); and, as regards Israel's compliance with the I.C.E.S.C.R., the Court was « able to do no more than observe, in a single phrase, that the wall and its associated régime 'impede the exercise by the persons concerned of the right to work, to health, to education and to an adequate standard of living as proclaimed in the [Covenant]...' (para 134) » (*ibid.*, § 27). The « rather two-dimensional » historical résumé given by the Court is also cogently criticized by Judge Kooijmans (*ibid.*, sep. op. KOOIJMANS, §§ 7-10), who regrets too « that the summary of the Court's findings in paragraph 137 does not contain a list of treaty provisions which have been breached » (*ibid.*, § 29).

(173) « The Court [...] does not function in a void. It is the principal judicial organ of the United Nations and has to carry out its function and responsibility within the wider political context. » : *ibid.*, sep. op. KOOIJMANS, § 12.

so when that court is exercising an advisory function (174). And it is doubly so in the international legal system, where judicial decisions, being subsidiary sources of law (175), are only as useful as the light they shed on the primary sources, and where allegations of geopolitical bias are easy to make but hard to dispel. Both these factors call for transparency of judicial logic.

Perhaps some of the Court's resistance to spelling out its reasoning is the result of the strenuous and very welcome effort it made to achieve near-unanimity, which tends to necessitate the finessing of the possibly different routes by which the different judges come to their respective conclusions. But that is not so obviously the case here, where the separate opinions reveal no serious divergences on the main points in issue. Nor does it explain the Court's highly impressionistic approach to the facts. Rather, the opacity of certain aspects of the opinion is a further manifestation of the « civilianization » of the Court's judgments — that is, their growing assimilation to the characteristic style of judgment of the Civil Law tradition, with its terse, formulaic sequence of recitation of opposing arguments, blank statement of relevant law and implicitly deductive conclusion. (Indeed, it is no coincidence that the present opinion, while officially drafted in both French and English, was clearly drafted first in French, which is also the language of the authoritative text : several tell-tale signs give this away (176)). It might be asked whether this exceedingly spare style of judicial pronouncement is well-suited to an uncodified and often unwritten body of law like public international law, in which, whether one admits it or not, the I.C.J. plays an enormously influential role in shaping the rules. It might also be questioned whether such judicial minimalism is appropriate when pronouncing upon violations of individual human rights, which the Court was effectively doing here, for the first time in its history, and where it is acting as much as a tribunal of fact as of law. By not

(174) In the words of Judge Higgins in her separate opinion,

« [i]t might have been expected that an advisory opinion would have contained a detailed analysis, by reference to the texts, the voluminous academic literature and the facts at the Court's disposal [...] Such an approach would have followed the tradition of using advisory opinions as an opportunity to elaborate and develop international law. »

Ibid., sep. op. Higgins, § 23.

(175) See Statute of the I.C.J., Art. 38 (1)(d).

(176) Take the followings examples (emphasis added). At *Wall in the Occupied Palestinian Territory, loc. cit.*, § 35, the English states that « *the relevant meetings have been convened* in pursuance of *the applicable rules* », whereas comparison with the French (« *les séances pertinentes ont été convoquées* selon *les règles en vigueur* ») makes it clear that what is meant is « pursuant to ». At *ibid.*, § 84, the French construction « *près de 320 000 colons israéliens* (dont *178 000 environ à Jérusalem-Est)* » is rendered unsyntactically as « *nearly 320,000 Israeli settlers* (of whom *178,000 in East Jerusalem)* », rather than « of whom... are... » or, more simply, « including ». At *ibid.*, § 106, the French « *la Cour estime que la protection offerte par les conventions régissant les droits de l'homme ne cesse pas* en cas de *conflit armé* » becomes « *the Court considers that the protection offered by human rights conventions does not cease* in case of *armed conflict* », rather than « in the event of ». Finally, at *ibid.*, § 122, « *En d'autres termes* » is translated as « *In other terms* », rather than the idiomatic « In other words ».

proceeding on paper in a more adequately forensic manner, the Court has left itself open to the unfair accusation that it paid no attention to the reality on the ground.

A. — *Jurisdiction*

The Court's finding on the existence of jurisdiction was the only unanimous aspect of its judgment and is relatively uncontroversial. There is nothing surprising in its treatment of the notion of a « legal question »; indeed, its findings reiterate everything it has said before on the issue, even if sometimes in response to arguments not, strictly speaking, advanced by Israel (177). As for the challenge to the validity of G.A. resolution ES-10/ 14, it was optimistic of Israel — and, tellingly, Israel alone — to allege that the General Assembly's practice since at least the early 1960s of considering and taking action on a question of international peace and security while the question remains on the Security Council's agenda represents an incorrect interpretation and application of the words « *is exercising* », as found in Article 12 (1) of the Charter (178). The Court has always accorded conclusive weight to the established practice of U.N. organs in the interpretation and application of their Charter powers (179), and although the Assembly's current practice represents an about-face from its earlier stance, it is now of considerable longstanding and has not, as such, been contested

---

(177) Consider the Court's addressing « *what [was] contended to be the abstract nature of the question* » (*ibid.*, § 40), even though Israel insisted that « *[t]he issue of legal certainty is not to be confused with the issue that has arisen in previous advisory opinions as to whether a question is unduly abstract, ie, where the meaning of the question is certain but where it is said that it fails to relate to a specific factual situation* » (Written Statement of the Government of Israel, *loc. cit.*, pp. 83-84, § 5.3, reference omitted). Consider, too, the Court's dismissal of « *the view, which has also been advanced in the present proceedings, that it has no jurisdiction because of the 'political' character of the question posed* » (*Wall in the Occupied Palestinian Territory, loc. cit.*, § 41), despite the unambiguous statement that « *Israel's objection, so far as jurisdiction is concerned, is not that the question is 'political' [...]* » (Written Statement of the Government of Israel, *loc. cit.*, p. 83, § 5.2).

(178) On this practice, see SIMMA, Bruno *et al.* (eds), *The Charter of the United Nations. A Commentary*, 2nd ed., Oxford, O.U.P., 2002, vol. I, 290; GRAY, Christine, *International Law and the Use of Force*, Oxford, O.U.P., 2000, 150.

(179) See *Competence of the General Assembly, loc. cit.*, 9; *Certain Expenses, loc. cit.*, 159-161, 165, 170-179; *Namibia, loc. cit.*, 22, § 22. See also, in this light, Art. 31 (3)(b) of the Vienna Convention on the Law of Treaties, 1155 U.N.T.S. 331, which states that, when interpreting a treaty provision, « *[t]here shall be taken into account [...] any subsequent practice in the application of the treaty which establishes the agreement of the parties regarding its interpretation [...]* ». The Court has recognised the rules of treaty interpretation contained in Art. 31 of the Vienna Convention as consonant with customary international law : see *Territorial Dispute (Libya/Chad)*, 13 February 1994, *I.C.J. Rep.*, 1994, 21-22, § 41 and *Kasikili/Sedudu Island, loc. cit.*, § 18. Note too, in this regard, Art. 5 of the Vienna Convention (« *The present Convention applies to any treaty which is the constituent instrument of an international organization [...]* »), which chimes with the Court's approach to the interpretation of the Charter. As stated in *Certain Expenses, loc. cit.*, 157, « *[o]n the previous occasions when the Court has had to interpret the Charter of the United Nations, it has followed the principles and rules applicable in general to the interpretation of treaties, since it has recognized that the Charter is a multilateral treaty, albeit a treaty having certain special characteristics* ».

for decades (180). That said, the Court's treatment of the question is remarkably breezy. The more intriguing contention on Israel's part was that the meeting of the Tenth Emergency Special Session of the General Assembly on 8 December 2003 at which G.A. resolution ES-10/14 was adopted constituted an invalid invocation of « Uniting for Peace », *viz.* G.A. resolution 477 A (V) — and, therefore, an invalid application of Article 12 (1) of the Charter, on which « Uniting for Peace » is essentially a gloss (181). Even so, the Court's finding on this point is eminently reasonable, especially given *Namibia*'s presumption of validity (182). It may also have the welcome effect of giving permanent members of the Security Council pause before they veto resolutions on threats to the peace which defy the international legal order.

Far more interesting is that the Court was drawn at all on the *ultra vires* issue since, on closer analysis, it was unnecessary for the determination of its jurisdiction. The gist of both Israeli objections was that the General Assembly, in applying Article 12 (1) of the Charter in an invalid manner to (re)convene the Tenth Emergency Special Session and ultimately to request the advisory opinion at the meeting of the Session on 8 December 2003, ended up exceeding its competence under Article 11 (2) of the Charter in questions relating to the maintenance of international peace and security. But it is not at all clear how this would have affected the Court's jurisdiction to give the opinion. Article 65 of the Statute of the I.C.J. states that « *[t]he Court may give an advisory opinion on any legal question at the request of whatever body may be authorized by or in accordance with the Charter of the United Nations to make such a request* ». In turn, Article 96 (1) authorizes the General Assembly to request the I.C.J. to give an advisory opinion « *on any legal question* », and there is no obvious reason why this should not be characterized as a free-standing competence, albeit it one inserted in Chapter XIV of the Charter (« The International Court of Justice ») without cross-reference to or from Chapter IV (« The General Assembly ») and, in

---

(180) SIMMA *et al.* (eds), *loc. cit.*, 290.

(181) « Uniting for Peace » is best seen as a sort of practice statement on Art. 12 (1) by which the General Assembly has announced that the vetoing of a Security Council resolution on a given question of international peace and security will be taken by the Assembly to mean, for the purposes of Art. 12 (1), that the Council is not « *exercising in respect of [that] dispute or situation the functions assigned to it* », thereby engaging the Assembly's powers under Art. 11 (2) in relation to the same question. See, to similar effect, *Wall in the Occupied Palestinian Territory, loc. cit.*, sep. op. KOOIJMANS, §§ 15-16. In Dinstein's words, « *[t]he central concern of 'Uniting for Peace' is often presented as one of defining a failure on the part of the Security Council to exercise its responsibility or, at least, ascertaining which UN organ is to decide that such a failure has occurred* » : DINSTEIN, Yoram, *War, Aggression and Self-Defence*, 3rd ed., Cambridge, C.U.P., 2001, 274. See also, *e.g.*, ANDRASSY, Juraj, « Uniting for Peace », *A.J.I.L.*, 1956, vol. 50, 572; SIMMA *et al.* (eds), *loc. cit.*, 291. The I.C.J. implicitly upheld the validity under the Charter of G.A. res. 377 A (V) in *Certain Expenses, loc. cit.*, but did not address the provision directly. No state challenged the resolution's constitutionality in the present proceedings.

(182) See *Namibia, loc. cit.*, 22, § 20, quoted and relied on by the Court at *Wall in the Occupied Palestinian Territory, loc. cit.*, § 35.

particular, its provisions on the Assembly's functions and powers. The elaboration of the Assembly's functions and powers in Chapter IV « *is not exhaustive, since many additional functions and powers are attributed to the G.A. in Chapters IX, X, XII, XIII, and XV* » (183). Nor is it irrelevant in this light that a request for an advisory opinion is not a « recommendation », within the meaning of Articles 10, 11 and 12 of the Charter, a point made by the Court (184). In short, the fact that the meeting of the General Assembly's Tenth Emergency Special Session on 8 December 2003 was allegedly *ultra vires* the Assembly's authority under Article 11 (2) should not have made it *ultra vires* the Assembly's authority under Article 96 (1) to request an opinion from the I.C.J. on any legal question. As such, the Assembly would still have been « *authorized by or in accordance with the Charter of the United Nations to make such a request* », in the words of Article 65 (1) of the Statute of the I.C.J., and — provided that the question was a legal one — the Court would still have had jurisdiction to give the opinion. The Assembly's alleged excesses of competence would have amounted to no more than « *procedural irregularities* », in the words of the Court itself (185).

No doubt the Court was eager to be seen to be taking Israel's arguments seriously, in the knowledge that its stark conclusions on the merits would inevitably provoke unfounded charges of bias. Perhaps it was also not averse to sending a message to the General Assembly and other U.N. organs about the importance of adherence to their respective Charter competences and the value of procedural regularity. And lacking, as it does, formal powers of judicial review of the acts of U.N. organs (186), the only permissible way for the Court to scrutinise the validity of the conduct of the General Assembly in the present circumstances was in the purported exercise of its inherent competence to determine its own jurisdiction (187).

As to the propriety of exercising jurisdiction, the Court's findings are again — at least in formal legal terms — comparatively unproblematic. Even those states which abstained on or voted against the General Assembly's request could not have been shocked by the Court's decision to accede

---

(183) Simma *et al.* (eds), *loc. cit.*, 258.

(184) *Wall in the Occupied Palestinian Territory*, *loc. cit.*, § 25.

(185) *Ibid.*, § 33.

(186) « *In the legal systems of States, there is often some procedure for determining the validity of even a legislative or governmental act, but no analogous procedure is to be found in the structure of the United Nations. Proposals made during the drafting of the Charter to place the ultimate authority to interpret the Charter in the International Court of Justice were not accepted; the opinion which the Court is in the process of rendering is an advisory opinion. As anticipated in 1945, therefore, each organ must, in the first place at least, determine its own [competence].* » : *Certain Expenses*, *loc. cit.*, 168 (original emphasis).

(187) It is in much the same way that the Appeals Chamber of the International Criminal Tribunal for the former Yugoslavia in *Prosecutor v Tadic*, IT-94-1, Appeals Chamber, Decision on jurisdiction, 2 October 1995, *I.L.R.*, vol. 105, 419, examined, in the exercise of its *compétence de la compétence*, the validity of the actions of the Security Council.

to it. The I.C.J. has fended off virtually identical challenges to the propriety of giving an advisory opinion on numerous occasions in the past and the principles on which it has relied are very familiar. Indeed, in many ways, this aspect of the request was a rerun of *Western Sahara* (188) and, before it, albeit involving the Security Council, *Namibia* (the question triggering which the drafters of the present request clearly sought to imitate (189)). And if ever a legal controversy were not just bilateral (190) but of direct and intimate concern to a U.N. organ, it is the question of Palestine to the General Assembly. It was, after all, the Assembly which recommended to U.N. Members on 29 November 1947 the adoption and implementation of the Plan of Partition for the Palestine Mandate set forth in G.A. resolution 181 (II). Literally hundreds of resolutions since attest to that organ's abiding interest in the question. As for the availability of sufficient evidence, while it is true that the Court did not have before it a detailed documentary statement from Israel's point of view (191), the 126-megabyte dossier compiled and presented to it by the U.N. Secretariat (192), which included reports by the U.N. Secretary-General, by two U.N. Special Committees and by two Special Rapporteurs of the U.N. Commission on Human Rights, formed a sufficiently comprehensive and impartial evidentiary basis for the opinion.

Moreover, the principles reiterated by the Court on the significance of an interested state's lack of consent to advisory proceedings are sensible and arguably desirable. Whatever the merits of the Court's solicitous approach

---

(188) Note, however, the distinction highlighted by Judge Higgins (*Wall in the Occupied Palestinian Territory*, loc. cit., sep. op. HIGGINS, §§ 12-13) and Judge Owada (*ibid.*, sep. op. OWADA, § 12).

(189) As Judge Higgins observes, « *[i]t is apparent (not least from the wording of the request to the Court) that an attempt has been made by those seeking the Opinion to assimilate the Opinion on the wall to that obtained from the Court regarding Namibia* » : *ibid.*, sep. op. HIGGINS, § 2. Judge Kooijmans refers to « *the clear analogy in wording with the request in the* Namibia *case* » : *ibid.*, sep. op. KOOIJMANS, § 39. Judge Owada speaks of « *the similarity in language in the formulation of the request* » : *ibid.*, sep. op. OWADA, § 11. Judge Higgins'criticisms of the analogy with *Namibia* in the specific context of the propriety of the Court's exercise of jurisdiction are thought-provoking : see *ibid.*, sep. op. HIGGINS, §§ 2-13. See, similarly, *ibid.*, sep. op. OWADA, §§ 10-11.

(190) See *ibid.*, sep. op. KOOIJMANS, § 27 :

« [T]he Court's finding that the subject-matter of the General Assembly [*sic*] cannot be regarded as being 'only a bilateral matter between Israel and Palestine' (para 49), is in my view worded in a felicitous way since, in regard to the issue of the existence of a bilateral dispute, it avoids the dilemma of 'either/or'. A situation which is of legitimate concern to the organized international community and a bilateral dispute with regard to that same situation may exist simultaneously. The existence of the latter cannot deprive the organs of the organized community of the competence which has been assigned to them by the constitutive instruments. »

See also, similarly, *ibid.*, sep. op. HIGGINS, §§ 6-9 and *ibid.*, sep. op. OWADA, §§ 9-10 and 14. It is noteworthy that Art. 102 (3) of the Court's Rules recognizes that advisory proceedings might deal with « *a legal question actually pending between two states* ».

(191) See *ibid.*, sep. op. HIGGINS, § 40 and *ibid.*, dec. BUERGENTHAL, generally.

(192) The dossier is available at http://www.icj-cij.org/icj.www/idocket/imwp/imwpframe.htm.

to third-party « consent » to contentious proceedings (193), a too-easy
extrapolation of the *Monetary Gold* principle to its advisory jurisdiction —
where there are no parties, as such, to a dispute, as such — would be an
over-accommodation of the voluntarist basis of the Court's dispute-settle-
ment function at the expense of its advisory function and, through it, the
Court's responsibility towards the international rule of law. While there
may have been cogent enough grounds for refusing the request in the
idiosyncratic *Eastern Carelia*, it would be hard to justify a refusal today
when, unlike the P.C.I.J., the I.C.J. is itself an organ of the U.N. and is
mandated by the Charter to perform an advisory function for the Organization; and when, unlike Russia *vis à vis* the League, every state in the world
bar the Vatican City is a Member of the U.N. and, as such, *has* consented — at least in formal terms — to the Court's exercise of its Charter-
based advisory jurisdiction by signing up to Article 96, a point made by the
Court itself in *Namibia* and *Western Sahara* (194).

B. — *Merits*

§ 1. *Israel's breaches*

Two points are worth highlighting at the outset regarding the scope of
the Court's findings as to Israel's various breaches of international law.

First, the Court lays emphasis on the route of the wall as built and
presently planned (195). At the same time, automatic conclusions *a contrario* should be cautioned against. The Court is very careful not to prejudice future political negotiations on so-called « final status » issues by
suggesting that the territorial extent of the right of the Palestinian people
to self-determination (or, putting it another way, the territorial extent of
the Palestinian people as a self-determination unit) is restricted to the
Occupied Palestinian Territory; (196) as such, given that the frontiers of
the Arab (*viz.* Palestinian) state proposed by the U.N. Partition Plan of
1947 lie to the west of the Green Line (which, in formal terms, is no more
than the General Armistice Line agreed in 1949 between Israel and Jordan), it cannot be a foregone conclusion that the construction of an identical wall along a route adhering scrupulously to the Green Line would not
equally interfere with this right and amount too to the creation of a *fait
accompli* in violation of the prohibition on the acquisition of territory by

---

(193) See *Monetary Gold Removed from Rome in 1943 (Italy v France, United Kingdom and
United States of America)*, Preliminary Question, 15 June 1954, *I.C.J. Rep.*, 1954, 19; *East
Timor, loc. cit.* But *cf. Certain Phosphate Lands in Nauru (Nauru v Australia)*, Preliminary
Objections, 26 June 1992, *I.C.J. Rep.*, 1992, 240.

(194) See *Namibia, loc. cit.*, 23, § 31; *Western Sahara, loc. cit.*, 24, § 30.

(195) See *Wall in the Occupied Palestinian Territory, loc. cit.*, §§ 121, 122, 137 and 140.

(196) Recall that the Occupied Palestinian Territory comprises not just the West Bank
(including East Jerusalem) but also the Gaza Strip.

force. The same applies *mutatis mutandis* to individual human rights like freedom of movement.

Secondly, it was not just the construction of the wall that the Court found to be illegal and that Israel is under an obligation to terminate. Section (3) A of the *dispositif* states that « *[t]he construction of the wall being built by Israel, the Occupying Power, in the Occupied Palestinian Territory, including in and around East Jerusalem, and its associated régime, are contrary to international law* »; (197) and at paragraph 143, the Court summarizes its findings on the legality of Israel's conduct as follows :

> « The Court having concluded that, by the construction of the wall in the Occupied Palestinian Territory, including in and around East Jerusalem, *and by adopting its associated régime*, Israel has violated various international obligations incumbent upon it (see paragraphs 114-137 above) [...] » (198)

What is meant, therefore, by « *its associated régime* » is to be found among paragraphs 114 to 137. One aspect of this régime is obviously the range of legislative and regulatory measures associated with the wall, from the requisitions of land to the restrictions imposed on the Palestinian populace by the declaration of the Closed Area. A second aspect, however, is the Israeli settlements in the Occupied Palestinian Territory, including East Jerusalem, discussed at paragraphs 119 to 122, and at paragraph 120 the Court holds « *that the Israeli settlements in the Occupied Palestinian Territory (including East Jerusalem) have been established in breach of international law* ». In short, the opinion finds not only the construction of the wall to be illegal but with it the policy and practice of Israeli settlements in the occupied territories, considered as part of its « *associated régime* ». Moreover, Section (3) B of the *dispositif* provides in a general manner that « *Israel is under an obligation to terminate its breaches of international law* », which must include an obligation to put a stop to Israeli settlement in the territories, including in and around East Jerusalem.

At the same time, Section (3) B of the *dispositif* goes on specifically to mention only the cessation of the construction of the wall, its dismantling, and the repeal or rendering ineffective of all related legislative and regulatory acts. Similarly, Section (3) C speaks only of Israel's obligation « *to make reparation for all damage caused by the construction of the wall [...]* », as do the relevant paragraphs (152 and 153) of the preceding text. As for other states, Section (3) D of the *dispositif* refers solely to their obligation « *not to recognize the illegal situation resulting from the construction of the wall and not to render aid or assistance in maintaining the situation created by such construction* ». Section (3) D, however, refers also to the additional obligation incumbent upon High Contracting Parties to the Fourth Geneva Convention « *to ensure compliance by Israel with international*

---

(197) *Wall in the Occupied Palestinian Territory, loc. cit.*, § 163 (emphasis added).
(198) Emphasis added.

humanitarian law as embodied in that Convention », and it is the sixth unnumbered paragraph of Article 49 of the Convention that the Israeli settlements are held in paragraph 120 to breach. Moreover, Section (3) E of the *dispositif*, mirroring paragraph 160 of the preceding text, speaks of further action by the U.N. « *to bring an end to the illegal situation resulting from the construction of the wall and the associated régime* ».

The Court's decision not to back up its finding that the settlements are unlawful with an explicit statement of Israel's obligation to dismantle them, to repeal or render ineffective all related legislative and regulatory acts, and to make reparation for all damage caused by their construction possibly reflects discomfort among some of the judges (although a discomfort not revealed in any of the separate opinions or in the lone declaration) at the way the Court shoe-horned the issue of the settlements and a determination of their illegality into an advisory opinion on the construction of the wall (199). There is, indeed, something a little gratuitous about this. After all, the policy and practice of Israeli settlements in the West Bank, beginning in 1977, long predates the construction of the wall. Moreover, the question asked by the General Assembly makes no mention of the wall's « associated régime », let alone the settlements specifically. That said, the preamble to GA resolution ES-10/14 does include the following recital :

> « *Recalling in particular* relevant United Nations resolutions affirming that Israeli settlements in the Occupied Palestinian Territory, including East Jerusalem, are illegal and an obstacle to peace and to economic and social development as well as those demanding the complete cessation of settlement activities [...] »

In this light, the Court's consideration of the legality of the settlements within its consideration of the legality of the wall is not grossly illegitimate. Nonetheless, while there is no doubt that the settlements are in plain contravention of Article 49 of the Fourth Geneva Convention, Israel is perhaps entitled to feel a little aggrieved that the Court declared them so in the present opinion (200).

§ 2. *The prohibition on the acquisition of territory by force*

The Court's condemnation of attempts at *de facto* conquest through the creation of *faits accomplis* reflects a sensibly realistic approach to the legal characterization of fact, with its emphasis on substance over form. But its perfunctory single-paragraph account of the prohibition on the acquisition of territory by force would have benefited from elaboration. It would have

---

(199) See *Wall in the Occupied Palestinian Territory, loc. cit.*, §§ 119-122.

(200) Interestingly, Judge Buergenthal, who took the view that the settlements violate the sixth paragraph of Article 49 of the Fourth Geneva Convention, thought that « *[i]t follows that the segments of the wall being built by Israel to protect the settlements are* ipso facto *in violation of international law* » : *ibid.*, dec. BUERGENTHAL, § 9.

been helpful for the Court to state explicitly that the prohibition applies
even to territory of indeterminate sovereignty and even to uses of force in
self-defence, especially in light of Israel's past assertions (201) and the
temptation analogous claims may pose to other states. Obviously the Court
implies both these things, and without doubt correctly so, when it restates
the signally unqualified declaration in G.A. resolution 2625 (XXV) that
« *[n]o territorial acquisition resulting from the threat or use of force shall be
recognized as legal* », when it recalls S.C. resolution 242 (1967), and when it
applies the prohibition to that part of the territory of former mandated
Palestine originally intended for the Arab state proposed in the U.N. Partition Plan and occupied by Israel in 1967. It is also telling that the Court
never refers in this regard to « the unlawful use of force » or to « the use of
force not in accordance with the Charter of the United Nations » or the like.
But it is difficult to see why these important points could not have been
made expressly. It is hard to imagine how this might prejudice final status
negotiations.

§ 3. *The relationship between international humanitarian and human rights
law*

The Court could similarly have been more expansive and precise as to the
relationship between international humanitarian law and international
human rights law, especially in the specific context of belligerent occupation. Simply restating its brief and ambiguous dictum from *Legality of the
Threat or Use of Nuclear Weapons* does not take us very far (202). Nor, for
that matter, does the almost comically uninformative statement that

« [a]s regards the relationship between international humanitarian law and
human rights law, there are thus three possible situations : some rights may
be exclusively matters of international humanitarian law; others may be
exclusively matters of human rights law; yet others may be matters of both
these branches of international law. » (203)

That the Court's treatment of the question is so uninstructive is all the
more disappointing in light of the questions increasingly raised, implicitly
or explicitly, about the relationship between the two bodies of law before
the European Court of Human Rights (204), the Inter-American Commis-

---

(201) Israel has argued, *inter alia*, that it acted in self-defence in the Six-Day War.
(202) See *Wall in the Occupied Palestinian Territory, loc. cit.*, § 105.
(203) *Ibid.*, § 106.
(204) See *Loizidou v Turkey (Preliminary Objections)*, 23 February 1995, *I.L.R.*, vol. 103,
622 and *Loizidou v Turkey (Merits)*, 18 December 1996, *I.L.R*, vol. 108, 443; *Ergi v Turkey*,
28 July 1998, *E.H.R.R.*, 1998-IV, No. 81; *Cyprus v Turkey*, 10 May 2001, *I.L.R.*, vol. 120, 11;
Bankovic v Belgium and others (Admissibility), 12 December 2001, *I.L.R.*, vol. 123, 94.

sion on Human Rights (205) and the Inter-American Court of Human Rights (206), as well as by recent events in Guantánamo Bay (207), Afghanistan and Iraq.

But it is not simply that the Court's statements on the interaction of international humanitarian and international human rights law are unhelpful. Perhaps more significant is that what the Court has to say about reparation has startling implications for the relationship between the two fields. It states :

> « [G]iven that the construction of the wall in the Occupied Palestinian Territory has, *inter alia*, entailed the requisition and destruction of homes, businesses and agricultural holdings, the Court finds [...] that Israel has the obligation to make reparation for the damage caused to all the natural or legal persons concerned. » (208)

It goes on to elaborate :

> « Israel is accordingly under an obligation to return the land, orchards, olive groves and other immovable property seized from any natural or legal person for purposes of construction of the wall in the Occupied Palestinian Territory. » (209)

Up to this point, this is all fairly orthodox. But the Court then adds :

---

(205) See *Salas v United States of America*, 14 October 1993, *I.L.R.*, vol. 123, 117; *Abella v Argentina*, 18 November 1997, Report No. 55/97, Annual Report of the Inter-American Commission on Human Rights 1997, OEA/Ser.L/V/II.98, Doc. 6.rev, 13 April 1998; *Coard v United States of America*, 29 September 1999, *I.L.R.*, vol. 123, 156; *Decision on Request for Precautionary Measures (Detainees at Guantanamo Bay, Cuba)*, 12 March 2002, *I.L.M.*, 2002, vol. 41, 532. All relate to the American Declaration on the Rights and Duties of Man, rather than to the American Convention on Human Rights.

(206) *Bámaca Velásquez v Guatemala*, 25 November 2000, *Inter-Am. Ct H.R. (Ser. C)*, N – 70 (2000).

(207) Indeed, the U.S.'s international legal argument in relation to the detainees at Guantánamo centres on the relationship between international humanitarian and international human rights law, as follows : (i) The Third Geneva Convention (to which the U.S. is party), applicable in the event of international armed conflict (such as that in Afghanistan) to persons who have « fall[en] into the power of the enemy », represents *lex specialis* to the *lex generalis* of the I.C.C.P.R. and customary human rights guarantees. (ii) As such, the human right not to be arbitrarily detained is inapplicable during armed conflict to hostile combatants captured by U.S. military forces. (iii) Insofar as such persons qualify as prisoners of war, their detention is governed by the Third Geneva Convention, which does not afford them the right to a court or to counsel unless and until they are charged with an offence. (iv) Insofar as such persons do not qualify as prisoners of war, their detention is governed neither by the Third Geneva Convention nor by human rights law, and hence they again have no right to a court or counsel. (v) Those detainees captured fighting against U.S. forces in Afghanistan do not qualify as prisoners of war within the meaning of Art. 4 of the Third Geneva Convention. (vi) The second limb of Art. 5 of the Third Geneva Convention is inapplicable, since there is no doubt as to whether such persons qualify as prisoners of war, their status having been authoritatively determined by the U.S. executive. See Response of the United States to *Request for Precautionary Measures — Detainees in Guantanamo Bay, Cuba*, 15 April 2002, *I.L.M.*, 2002, vol. 41, 1015, especially 1017-8 and 1021-5.

(208) *Wall in the Occupied Palestinian Territory*, loc. cit., § 152.

(209) *Ibid.*, § 153.

« In the event that such restitution should prove to be materially impossible, Israel has an obligation to compensate the persons in question for the damage suffered. » (210)

In other words, Israel is obliged to compensate these persons *directly*. Now, there would be nothing particularly striking about this statement if what we were talking about was Israel's violation of international human rights law : the relevant persons, being the bearers of the rights violated, would constitute the injured parties and would be entitled to reparation in their own right. The Court's finding would represent the first time that it has recognized a customary international law of human rights remedies, and would be welcome; but it would not be revolutionary. The point is, however, that we are not talking here about international human rights law but about international humanitarian law. The violations cited are characterized by the Court as follows :

« [I]t appears that the construction of the wall has led to the destruction or requisition of properties under conditions which contravene the requirements of Articles 46 and 52 of the Hague Regulations of 1907 and of Article 53 of the Fourth Geneva Convention. » (211)

In other words, the persons in question are to be compensated directly for violations of international humanitarian law. This is a controversial proposition, litigated without success to date in the Japanese (212) and German (213) courts. If it were generalized, it would approximate to the abolition of the juridical distinction between international humanitarian law and international human rights law. Prohibitions laid down in the former would generate, in effect, individual rights.

It is difficult to imagine that this is what the Court intended, and there is good reason to see the Court's statement not as a general proposition of law but as an anomaly necessitated by the peculiar fact that there is no Palestinian state such as could be considered injured by Israel's breaches of international humanitarian law and to which the compensation in question could be paid (214). It is telling in this regard that the Court's statement of Israel's « *obligation to compensate the persons in question for the damage suffered* » is followed by its statement, seemingly in relation to Israel's violations of international human rights law, of an « *obligation to compensate, in accordance with the applicable rules of international law, all*

---

(210) *Ibid.*

(211) *Ibid.*, § 132.

(212) See *X et al v State of Japan*, Tokyo District Court, 30 November 1998, reproduced and translated at *Japanese Annual I.L.*, 1999, vol. 42, 143. See also *Japanese Annual I.L.*, 1996, vol. 39, 265.

(213) See Case 1 O 361/02, Civil Court of Bonn (1. Zivilkammer des Landgerichts Bonn), 10 December 2003, reproduced at http://www.uni-kassel.de/fb10/frieden/themen/NATO-Krieg/varvarin-urteil.html.

(214) Query whether the Court is also implying that neither the Palestinian Authority nor the Palestine Liberation Organization as such could be trusted with the monies.

natural or legal persons having suffered any form of material damage as a result of the wall's construction » (215). The implication *a contrario* is that whereas damages for violations of human rights are payable to the relevant persons as a matter of principle, the payment of damages directly to natural and legal persons for violations of humanitarian law, though indicated in the present circumstances, is not otherwise « *in accordance with the applicable principles of international law* ».

That said, the indication of damages payable directly to the persons harmed by Israel's breaches of international humanitarian law would be consonant with one reading of the Court's view of international humanitarian law as *lex specialis* to international human rights law (216). It will be recalled in this regard that the Court restates its dictum from *Legality of the Threat or Use of Nuclear Weapons* :

> « '[T]he protection of the International Covenant on Civil and Political Rights does not cease in times of war, except by operation of Article 4 of the Covenant whereby certain provisions may be derogated from in a time of national emergency. Respect for the right to life is not, however, such a provision. In principle, the right not arbitrarily to be deprived of one's life applies also in hostilities. The test of what is an arbitrary deprivation of life, however, then falls to be determined by the applicable *lex specialis*, namely, the law applicable in armed conflict which is designated to regulate the conduct of hostilities.'[...] » (217)

What the Court might mean by this is simply that, while human rights law does not cease to apply by mere virtue of the existence of a state of armed conflict, the conduct of hostilities is regulated by the laws of armed conflict and, for these specific purposes, the laws of armed conflict apply instead of human rights law. In other words, derogation aside, there is nothing to stop human rights law applying in armed conflict but the conduct of hostilities, as a specific aspect of armed conflict, is governed exclusively by humanitarian law. Presumably this would also be the case *mutatis mutandis* for belligerent occupation : in short, where there is applicable humanitarian law, it effectively ousts any applicable human rights law to the extent of any overlap. Alternatively, the Court's final sentence (« *The test of what is an arbitrary deprivation of life [...] then falls to be determined by [...] the law applicable in armed conflict [...]* ») gives rise to a second possibility, namely that human rights law does continue to apply even to the conduct of hostilities but that a tribunal charged with determining whether, in this context, a state has adequately secured the relevant right must assess that state's conduct by reference to the standard embodied in the laws of armed conflict. A violation of the relevant rule of humanitarian law will, in this context, afford conclusive evidence of the

---

(215) *Wall in the Occupied Palestinian Territory, loc. cit.*, § 153 (emphasis added).
(216) See *ibid.*, §§ 105 and 106.
(217) *Ibid.*, § 105, quoting *Legality of the Threat or Use of Nuclear Weapons, loc. cit.*, § 25.

violation of the applicable human rights guarantee. That is, both humanitarian law and human rights law can apply to the conduct of hostilities : if a tribunal is charged with determining whether a violation of humanitarian law has occurred, it simply looks to the applicable rule of humanitarian law; if a tribunal is charged with determining whether a violation of human rights law has occurred, it looks to the relevant rule of humanitarian law as the standard for assessing whether the applicable rule of human rights law has been breached. For what it is worth, this second construction of the Court's dictum in *Legality of the Threat or Use of Nuclear Weapons* is the one placed on it by the Inter-American Commission on Human Rights (218). More to the point, that this second construction was the one intended by the Court in that case is made clearer by the last sentence of the quoted paragraph, which was omitted by the Court in the present opinion and which reads :

> « Thus whether a particular loss of life, through the use of a certain weapon in warfare, is to be considered an arbitrary deprivation of life contrary to Article 6 of the Covenant, can only be decided by reference to the law applicable in armed conflict and not deduced from the terms of the Covenant itself. » (219)

If the second construction is indeed what the Court meant in *Nuclear Weapons*, and hence in the present opinion, what goes for the conduct of hostilities would again presumably go *mutatis mutandis* for belligerent occupation : in short, the applicable rules of humanitarian law can be used to determine whether any applicable rules of human rights law have been breached. In this light, the Court's finding that Israel is under an obligation to compensate directly those persons, natural and legal, harmed by its breaches of international humanitarian law could be explained as a more or less orthodox « award » of compensation to persons who have suffered injury as a consequence of Israel's violation of their human rights, as evidenced by its violation of those rules of humanitarian law relevant to belligerent occupation.

---

(218) See *Coard, loc. cit.*, 170-1, § 42 :

« [I]n a situation of armed conflict, the test for assessing the observance of a particular right, such as the right to liberty, may, under given circumstances, be distinct from that applicable in a time of peace. For that reason, the standard to be applied must be deduced by reference to the applicable lex specialis. [Footnote : 'See *Advisory Opinion on the Legality of the Threat or Use of Nuclear Weapons* [1996] I.C.J. Rep (para 25).'] [...] As will be seen in the analysis which follows, the Commission determined that the analysis of the petitioners' claims under the [American] Declaration [on the Rights and Duties of Man] within their factual and legal context requires reference to international humanitarian law, which is a source of authoritative guidance and provides the specific normative standards which apply to conflict situations. In the present case, the standards of humanitarian law help to define whether the detention of the petitioners was 'arbitrary' or not under the terms of Arts I and XXV of the Declaration. [...] »

See also *Detainees at Guantanamo Bay, Cuba., loc. cit.*

(219) *Legality of the Threat or Use of Nuclear Weapons, loc. cit.*, 240, § 25.

As it is, however, the way the Court in the present opinion states its conclusions in relation to international humanitarian law strongly suggests that this is not what it had in mind when it held that Israel must directly compensate persons harmed by its violations of international humanitarian law. It is fairly clear that it was referring to Israel's violations of international humanitarian law *quâ* international humanitarian law. But its reluctance to elaborate in the first place on the relationship between this corpus of law and international human rights law promotes ambiguity and speculation, and represents a frustrating disservice to international human rights tribunals, which must continue to struggle with this problem (220).

§ 4. *The extraterritorial application of international human rights law*

In contrast to its handling of the relationship between international humanitarian and human rights law, the Court examined at some length the question of the extraterritorial application of the relevant international human rights instruments, and its conclusions as to the applicability of these treaties to Israel's actions in the Occupied Palestinian Territory are sound. Its more general finding that the I.C.C.P.R. and I.C.E.S.C.R. apply extraterritorially to areas under the effective territorial control of a State Party involves a rational and solidly supported construction of Article 2 (1) of the former (as seemingly read into the latter), and — leaving aside the distinct interpretative issue posed by Article 2 (1) of the I.C.C.P.R.'s conjunctive phrase « within its territory and *subject to its jurisdiction* » (221) — it accords with the approach taken by both the European Court of Human Rights (222) and the Inter-American Commission on Human Rights (223). Unfortunately, however, the Court's statements leave it unclear whether the Covenants are capable of extraterritorial application *only* in those situations where the respondent state exercises control over the territory in which the putative violations occur, as is the case (with a few customary exceptions) under the European Convention on Human Rights (224). As regards the I.C.E.S.C.R., the question is perhaps academic, given that all the rights it guarantees, if violated extraterritorially, could only realisti-

---

(220) To co-opt the words of Judge Higgins, « *the structure of the Opinion, in which humanitarian and human rights law are not dealt with separately, makes it [...] extremely difficult to see what exactly has been decided by the Court* » : *Wall in the Occupied Palestinian Territory, loc. cit.*, sep. op. HIGGINS, § 24.

(221) Emphasis added.

(222) See *Loizidou (Preliminary Objections), loc. cit.*, 641-3, §§ 59-64; *Loizidou (Merits), loc. cit.*, 465, § 52; *Bankovic, loc. cit.*, 108-113, §§ 54-71.

(223) See *Saldaño v Argentina*, 11 March 1999, Report No. 38/99, Annual Report of the Inter-American Commission on Human Rights 1998, OEA/Ser.L/V/II.102, Doc. 6.rev, 16 April 1999, §§ 17-20 (American Declaration and Convention); *Coard, loc. cit.*, 168, § 37 (American Declaration).

(224) See *Bankovic, loc. cit.*, 109-116, §§ 59-82. The position under the American Declaration on the Rights and Duties of Man and the American Convention on Human Rights remains ambiguous : see *Saldaño, loc. cit.*, §§ 17-20; *Coard, loc. cit.*, 168, § 37.

cally be violated in the context of a degree of territorial control (225) or in the *sui generis* circumstances pertaining to diplomatic or consular agents and other embassy or consulate staff. When it comes to the I.C.C.P.R., the Court's position is ambiguous. On the one hand, it relies on two communications before the Human Rights Committee arising out of arrests carried out extraterritorially by government agents, and as such not involving effective territorial control (226). On the other hand, it quotes, with apparent approval, a statement by the Human Rights Committee in its 1998 state report on Israel that emphasizes « *the long-standing presence of Israel* » in the occupied territories and « *the exercise of effective jurisdiction by Israeli security forces therein* » (227). Its conclusion — that « *the Court considers that the [I.C.C.P.R.] is applicable in respect of acts done by a State in the exercise of its jurisdiction outside its own territory* » (228) — merely begs the question (229). It might have been hoped that the Court would make this point plain. At the same time, if the point was that the I.C.C.P.R. applies extraterritorially only where the State Party exercises effective territorial control, it is understandable that it did not, conscious as it must have been that an unambiguous statement to this effect could be opportunistically abused to excuse the extraterritorial abductions and denials of due process apparently occurring in pursuit of the « war on terror ». It might also have had in mind a possible continuation of « targeted killings » from the air by the Israel Defence Forces after the proposed Israeli withdrawal from the Gaza Strip, as well as similar strikes, past and potentially future, against individuals in neighbouring states.

§ 5. *Self-defence as a circumstance precluding wrongfulness*

The Court could also have been more forthcoming on self-defence as a circumstance potentially precluding the wrongfulness of Israel's construction of the wall, within the meaning of Article 21 of the International Law Commission's Articles on Responsibility of States for Internationally Wrongful Acts — if this is indeed what Israel is arguing when it seeks to justify the wall by reference to self-defence. For a start, it could have addressed Judge Higgins's doubt as to whether « *non-forcible measures (such as the building of a wall) fall within self-defence under Article 51 of the Charter* » (230). With respect, Judge Higgins's question seems to miss the point.

---

(225) The Court itself refers to the rights guaranteed by the I.C.E.S.C.R. as being « *essentially territorial* » : *Wall in the Occupied Palestinian Territory, loc. cit.*, § 112.

(226) See *ibid.*, § 109.

(227) *Ibid.*, § 110, quoting CCPR/C/79/Add.93, § 10.

(228) *Ibid.*, § 111.

(229) The same can be said of the Court's brisk conclusion that the Convention on the Rights of the Child applies extraterritorially, premised as it is simply on Art. 2 (1)'s stipulation that « *States Parties shall respect and ensure the rights set forth in the present Convention to each child within their jurisdiction* » : see *ibid.*, § 113.

(230) *Ibid.*, sep. op. HIGGINS, § 35.

The question is not whether the construction of an anti-terrorism wall falls within Article 51 of the Charter. Article 51, as such, is an exception to the prohibition on the use of force laid down in Article 2 (4) of the Charter (231) and thus encompasses only forcible measures. The point of self-defence as a circumstance precluding wrongfulness is, in the words of the ILC's commentary to Article 21, that « *[s]elf-defence may justify non-performance of certain obligations* other than that under Article 2 (4) of the Charter *provided that such non-performance is related to the breach of that provision* » (232). In other words, the question in the present case was whether the various breaches of international humanitarian and human rights law occasioned by Israel's construction of the wall, and by its associated régime, could be justified as measures taken alongside and related to a use of force by Israel in response to an armed attack against it. It is not clear, however, whether the Court fully grasped this itself. If it did, it could have performed a valuable service by pointing out, as the ILC commentary does, that self-defence does not preclude the wrongfulness of conduct « *in all cases or with respect to all obligations* » : (233)

> « Examples [where self-defence does not preclude the wrongfulness of conduct] relate to international humanitarian law and human rights obligations. The Geneva Conventions of 1949 and Protocol I of 1977 apply equally to all the parties in an international armed conflict, and the same is true of customary international humanitarian law. Human rights treaties contain derogation provisions for times of public emergency, including actions taken in self-defence. As to obligations under international humanitarian law and in relation to non-derogable human rights provisions, self-defence does not preclude the wrongfulness of conduct. » (234)

Borrowing the words of the Court in *Legality of the Threat or Use of Nuclear Weapons*, the ILC explains that « *[a] State acting in self-defence is 'totally restrained' by an international obligation if that obligation is expressed or intended to apply as a definitive constraint even on States in armed conflict* » (235). The Court missed a golden opportunity to reiterate this vital point.

§ 6. *Obligations for all states and implications for the U.N.*

The Court's finding that « *all States are under an obligation not to recognize the illegal situation resulting from the construction of the wall and not to render*

---

(231) Commentary to Article 21, para. (1), *International Law Commission : Report on the work of its fifty-third session (23 April — 1 June and 2 July — 10 August 2001)*, A/56/10, 177. Note that the ILC's Articles are without prejudice to the Charter : Articles on Responsibility of States, *loc. cit.*, Art. 59.

(232) Commentary to Article 21, para. (2), *International Law Commission : Report on the work of its fifty-third session, loc. cit.*, 178 (emphasis added).

(233) Commentary to Article 21, para. (3), *ibid.*

(234) Commentary to Article 21, para. (3), *ibid.* (footnote omitted).

(235) Commentary to Article 21, para. (4), *ibid.*, 179 (footnote omitted).

cally be violated in the context of a degree of territorial control (225) or in the *sui generis* circumstances pertaining to diplomatic or consular agents and other embassy or consulate staff. When it comes to the I.C.C.P.R., the Court's position is ambiguous. On the one hand, it relies on two communications before the Human Rights Committee arising out of arrests carried out extraterritorially by government agents, and as such not involving effective territorial control (226). On the other hand, it quotes, with apparent approval, a statement by the Human Rights Committee in its 1998 state report on Israel that emphasizes « *the long-standing presence of Israel* » in the occupied territories and « *the exercise of effective jurisdiction by Israeli security forces therein* » (227). Its conclusion — that « *the Court considers that the [I.C.C.P.R.] is applicable in respect of acts done by a State in the exercise of its jurisdiction outside its own territory* » (228) — merely begs the question (229). It might have been hoped that the Court would make this point plain. At the same time, if the point was that the I.C.C.P.R. applies extraterritorially only where the State Party exercises effective territorial control, it is understandable that it did not, conscious as it must have been that an unambiguous statement to this effect could be opportunistically abused to excuse the extraterritorial abductions and denials of due process apparently occurring in pursuit of the « war on terror ». It might also have had in mind a possible continuation of « targeted killings » from the air by the Israel Defence Forces after the proposed Israeli withdrawal from the Gaza Strip, as well as similar strikes, past and potentially future, against individuals in neighbouring states.

§ 5. *Self-defence as a circumstance precluding wrongfulness*

The Court could also have been more forthcoming on self-defence as a circumstance potentially precluding the wrongfulness of Israel's construction of the wall, within the meaning of Article 21 of the International Law Commission's Articles on Responsibility of States for Internationally Wrongful Acts — if this is indeed what Israel is arguing when it seeks to justify the wall by reference to self-defence. For a start, it could have addressed Judge Higgins's doubt as to whether « *non-forcible measures (such as the building of a wall) fall within self-defence under Article 51 of the Charter* » (230). With respect, Judge Higgins's question seems to miss the point.

---

(225) The Court itself refers to the rights guaranteed by the I.C.E.S.C.R. as being « *essentially territorial* » : *Wall in the Occupied Palestinian Territory, loc. cit.*, § 112.

(226) See *ibid.*, § 109.

(227) *Ibid.*, § 110, quoting CCPR/C/79/Add.93, § 10.

(228) *Ibid.*, § 111.

(229) The same can be said of the Court's brisk conclusion that the Convention on the Rights of the Child applies extraterritorially, premised as it is simply on Art. 2 (1)'s stipulation that « *States Parties shall respect and ensure the rights set forth in the present Convention to each child within their jurisdiction* » : see *ibid.*, § 113.

(230) *Ibid.*, sep. op. HIGGINS, § 35.

The question is not whether the construction of an anti-terrorism wall falls within Article 51 of the Charter. Article 51, as such, is an exception to the prohibition on the use of force laid down in Article 2 (4) of the Charter (231) and thus encompasses only forcible measures. The point of self-defence as a circumstance precluding wrongfulness is, in the words of the ILC's commentary to Article 21, that « *[s]elf-defence may justify non-performance of certain obligations* other than that under Article 2 (4) of the Charter *provided that such non-performance is related to the breach of that provision* » (232). In other words, the question in the present case was whether the various breaches of international humanitarian and human rights law occasioned by Israel's construction of the wall, and by its associated régime, could be justified as measures taken alongside and related to a use of force by Israel in response to an armed attack against it. It is not clear, however, whether the Court fully grasped this itself. If it did, it could have performed a valuable service by pointing out, as the ILC commentary does, that self-defence does not preclude the wrongfulness of conduct « *in all cases or with respect to all obligations* » : (233)

> « Examples [where self-defence does not preclude the wrongfulness of conduct] relate to international humanitarian law and human rights obligations. The Geneva Conventions of 1949 and Protocol I of 1977 apply equally to all the parties in an international armed conflict, and the same is true of customary international humanitarian law. Human rights treaties contain derogation provisions for times of public emergency, including actions taken in self-defence. As to obligations under international humanitarian law and in relation to non-derogable human rights provisions, self-defence does not preclude the wrongfulness of conduct. » (234)

Borrowing the words of the Court in *Legality of the Threat or Use of Nuclear Weapons*, the ILC explains that « *[a] State acting in self-defence is 'totally restrained' by an international obligation if that obligation is expressed or intended to apply as a definitive constraint even on States in armed conflict* » (235). The Court missed a golden opportunity to reiterate this vital point.

§ 6. *Obligations for all states and implications for the U.N.*

The Court's finding that « *all States are under an obligation not to recognize the illegal situation resulting from the construction of the wall and not to render*

---

(231) Commentary to Article 21, para. (1), *International Law Commission : Report on the work of its fifty-third session (23 April — 1 June and 2 July — 10 August 2001)*, A/56/10, 177. Note that the ILC's Articles are without prejudice to the Charter : Articles on Responsibility of States, *loc. cit.*, Art. 59.

(232) Commentary to Article 21, para. (2), *International Law Commission : Report on the work of its fifty-third session, loc. cit.*, 178 (emphasis added).

(233) Commentary to Article 21, para. (3), *ibid.*

(234) Commentary to Article 21, para. (3), *ibid.* (footnote omitted).

(235) Commentary to Article 21, para. (4), *ibid.*, 179 (footnote omitted).

aid or assistance in maintaining the situation created by such construction »
represents its first practical implementation of the concept of rights and
obligations *erga omnes* since *Namibia* (236), and constitutes a significant
further step in its unannounced (and unmourned) interment of the *South-
West Africa Cases* (237). The same can be said of its view that « *[t]he
United Nations, and especially the General Assembly and Security Council,
should consider what further action is required to bring to an end the illegal
situation resulting from the construction of the wall and the associated régime
[...]* ». Both of these statements also represent the Court's actualization of
Part Two, Chapter Three (Articles 40 and 41) of the ILC's Articles on
Responsibility of States, dealing with « Serious Breaches of Obligations
under Peremptory Norms of General International Law » (238) — that is,
serious breaches of *jus cogens*. Article 41 (2) of the ILC's Articles reads :

> « No State shall recognize as lawful a situation created by a serious breach
> within the meaning of article 40, nor render aid or assistance in maintaining
> that situation. »

Article 41 (1) provides :

> « States shall cooperate to bring to an end through lawful means any serious
> breach within the meaning of article 40. »

The ILC's commentary to Article 41 (1) adds that such cooperation
« *could be organized in the framework of a competent international organization, in particular the United Nations* » (239). In this light, the Court's
statements imply that Israel's conduct « *involves a gross or systematic
failure* » by it to fulfil « *an obligation arising under a peremptory norm of
general international law* », to use the language of paragraphs 2 and 1
respectively of Article 40.

But while the realization of both ideas — rights and obligations *erga
omnes*, on the one hand, and *jus cogens*, on the other — is a welcome
progressive development, the Court does nothing in the present opinion to
clarify the relationship between what are, at some level of principle, two
distinct juridical concepts, the first to do with the opposability of certain
rules and, consequently, with the invocation of responsibility for their
breach, the second to do (at the very least) with the non-derogability of

---

(236) *Namibia, loc. cit.*, § 126. But *cf. Wall in the Occupied Palestinian Territory, loc. cit.*, sep.
op. HIGGINS, §§ 37-39.

(237) *South-West Africa Cases, loc. cit.*

(238) See, in this regard, Articles on Responsibility of States, *loc. cit.*, Art. 40 (« Application
of this Chapter »), which provides :

« 1. This Chapter applies to the international responsibility which is entailed by a serious
breach by a State of an obligation arising under a peremptory norm of general international law.

2. A breach of such an obligation is serious if it involves a gross or systematic failure by the
responsible State to fulfil the obligation. »

(239) Commentary to Article 41, para. (2), *International Law Commission : Report on the work
of its fifty-third session, loc. cit.*, 287.

certain rules (240). The Court merely affirms and adds to a curious dictum from *Legality of the Threat or Use of Nuclear Weapons* which seems to conflate three legal concepts, namely a norm's possible *erga omnes* character, its possible *jus cogens* character and, at a more basic level, its possible customary character :

> « 'a great many rules of humanitarian law applicable in armed conflict are so fundamental to the respect of the human person and 'elementary considerations of humanity' ...', that they are 'to be observed by all States whether or not they have ratified the conventions that contain them, because they constitute intransgressible principles of international customary law' (*I.C.J. Reports 1996 (I)*, p. 257, para. 79). In the Court's view, these rules incorporate obligations which are essentially of an *erga omnes* character. » (241)

All the same, it should not be suggested that the relationship between rights and obligations *erga omnes* and *jus cogens* is by any means worked out in the doctrine, or even static. The two qualities do, after all, seemingly adhere to the same norms and probably express different facets of an essentially common if darkly glimpsed insight. Indeed, it might be observed that Part Two, Chapter Three of the ILC's Articles itself attaches certain « horizontal » implications to the peremptory character of a norm, or at least to the gross or systematic breach of a peremptory norm; and the ILC's prefatory commentary to this chapter speaks of rights and obligations *erga omnes* and peremptory norms as being « *closely related development[s]* » (242), concluding that « *[w]hether or not peremptory norms of general international law and obligations to the international community as a whole are aspects of a single basic idea, there is at least very substantial overlap between them* » (243). « *But* », the commentary later adds, « *there is at least a difference in emphasis* » (244).

As for the Court's distinct finding that the primary obligation laid down in Article 1 common to the four Geneva Conventions — not only to respect

---

(240) Judge Kooijmans admits to having « *considerable difficulty in understanding why a violation of an obligation* erga omnes *by one State should necessarily lead to an obligation for third states* » (*Wall in the Occupied Palestinian Territory*, loc. cit., sep. op. Kooijmans, § 40) and he expressly declines to deal « *with the tricky question whether obligations* erga omnes *can be equated with obligations arising under a peremptory norm of general international law* » (*ibid.*, § 41).

(241) *Ibid.*, § 157. See, in this regard, Judge Higgins : « *[T]he invocation (para 157) of 'the* erga omnes' *nature of violations of humanitarian law seems [...] irrelevant. These intransgressible principles are generally binding because they are customary international law, no more and no less.* » (*ibid.*, sep. op. Higgins, § 39).

(242) Commentary to Part Two, Chapter Three, para. (4), *International Law Commission : Report on the work of its fifty-third session*, loc. cit., 279.

(243) Commentary to Part Two, Chapter Three, para. (7), *ibid.* The commentary continues : « *The examples which the International Court has given of obligations towards the international community as a whole all concern obligations which, it is generally accepted, arise under peremptory norms of general international law. Likewise the examples of peremptory norms given by the Commission in its commentary to what became article 53 of the Vienna Convention [on the Law of Treaties] involve obligations to the international community as a whole. [...]* » (*ibid.*, footnotes omitted).

(244) *Ibid.*

but also to « *ensure respect* » for the Conventions — imposes on High Contracting Parties to the Fourth Convention « *the obligation, while respecting the United Nations Charter and international law, to ensure compliance by Israel with international humanitarian law as embodied in that Convention* », this accords with the ICRC's commentaries on the provision (245). In short, the obligation imposed is one of lawful diplomatic and other measures in the event of another High Contracting Party's breach of the Convention. The phrase « *while respecting the United Nations Charter* » is a familiar term of art which states the relatively obvious, namely that common Article 1 does not authorize the use of armed force to secure a Party's compliance with the Convention. This and the further reference to « *international law* » would, however, admit of non-forcible countermeasures by the High Contracting Parties to the Convention.

Finally, in the context of the obligations incumbent upon the High Contracting Parties to the Fourth Geneva Convention, it is interesting that the Court, although holding that « *the construction of the wall has led to the destruction [...] of properties under conditions which contravene the requirements of [...] Article 53* », did not turn to examine whether some of this destruction might amount *prima facie* to the grave breach of « *extensive destruction [...] of property, not justified by military necessity and carried out unlawfully and wantonly* », within the meaning of Article 147 of the Convention. Article 146 imposes a range of obligations on High Contracting Parties in respect of grave breaches of the Convention (246). At the same time, the Court's reluctance was completely understandable, and it was wise to exercise discretion in this regard (247). Although there would have been no need to identify individuals, and its findings would not have been binding, let

---

(245) See PICTET, Jean, *The Geneva Conventions of 12 August 1949. Commentary. IV. Geneva Convention relative to the Protection of Civilian Persons in Time of War*, Geneva, I.C.R.C., 1958, 16; SANDOZ, Yves et al., *Commentary on the Additional Protocols of 8 June 1977 to the Geneva Conventions of 12 August 1949*, Geneva/The Hague, I.C.R.C./ Nijhoff, 1987, §§ 41-46. But *cf. Wall in the Occupied Palestinian Territory*, loc. cit., sep. op. KOOIJMANS, §§ 47-50, citing KALSHOVEN, Frits, « The Undertaking to Respect and Ensure Respect in all Circumstances : From Tiny Seed to Ripening Fruit », *Y.I.H.L.*, 1999, vol. 2, 28.

(246) Article 146 provides in relevant part :

« The High Contracting Parties undertake to enact any legislation necessary to provide effective penal sanctions for persons committing, or ordering to be committed, any of the grave breaches of the present Convention defined in the following Article.

Each High Contracting Party shall be under the obligation to search for persons alleged to have committed, or to have ordered to be committed, such grave breaches, and shall bring such persons, regardless of their nationality, before its own courts. It may also, if it prefers, and in accordance with the provisions of its own legislation, hand such persons over for trial to another High Contracting Party concerned, provided such High Contracting Party has made out a prima facie case.

Each High Contracting Party shall take measures necessary for the suppression of all acts contrary to the provisions of the present Convention other than the grave breaches defined in the following Article. [...] »

(247) But *cf.* the view of Judge Elabary : *Wall in the Occupied Palestinian Territory*, loc. cit., sep. op. ELARABY, § 3.3.

alone constitute a formal verdict, the plain constitutional fact is that the I.C.J. is not a criminal tribunal. Moreover, while it is one thing to decide on state responsibility in the absence of an interested party, it is quite another to imply the criminal responsibility of individuals on the basis of anything less than the fullest possible documentary and oral evidence and in the absence of the persons impugned (248). Furthermore, indicating the consequences for the other High Contracting Parties of any *prima facie* grave breaches would have necessitated an examination of whether Article 146 of the Convention imposes an obligation on such Parties to provide for universal jurisdiction over suspected offenders, a question which divided the Court in *Arrest Warrant* (249). That said, relevant Israeli ministers, military chiefs of staff and members of the armed forces will no doubt be even more wary now about where they travel.

IV. — REACTIONS

It almost goes without saying that the Palestinian Authority/Palestine Liberation Organization warmly welcomed the opinion (250). The Permanent Observer for Palestine hailed it in the General Assembly as « *a watershed event [with] the potential to elevate the situation in the Middle East to a new level [...] based on international law and the ideals of peace and reconciliation* » (251). Addressing the Assembly on behalf of the Arab Group, the representative of Jordan described it as « *the truth* » and declared that the Court had proved itself « *a legal refuge that can be resorted to when politics and military power try to supersede the rule of law* » (252). Speaking on behalf of the Non-Aligned Movement, the Malaysian delegate described the opinion as « *a significant milestone in international law* » (253), and the

---

(248) Consider, in this light, Art. 14 (3)(d) of the I.C.C.P.R., guaranteeing an accused's right « to be tried in his presence », as mirrored in Art. 21 (4)(d) of the Statute of the International Criminal Tribunal for the former Yugoslavia (S/25704, Annex, as amended), Art. 20 (4)(d) of the Statute of the International Criminal Tribunal for Rwanda (S/RES/955 (1994), Annex) and Arts 63 (1) and 67 (1)(d) of the Rome Statute of the International Criminal Court (A/CONF.183/9, English text as corrected).

(249) *Arrest Warrant of 11 April 2000 (Democratic Republic of the Congo v Belgium)*, General List No. 121, 14 February 2002, http://www.icj-cij.org/icj.www/idocket/iCOBE/iCOBEframe.htm. See *ibid.*, sep. op. GUILLAUME, § 17; *ibid.*, dec. RANJEVA, § 7; *ibid.*, sep. op. HIGGINS, KOOIJMANS & BUERGENTHAL, §§ 28-32. But others affirmed that the grave breaches provisions mandate universal jurisdiction : see *ibid.*, sep. op. REZEK, § 7; *ibid.*, sep. op. BULA-BULA, § 65; *ibid.*, diss. op. VAN DEN WYNGAERT, § 59.

(250) Militant groups, however, scorned its value. Sami Abu Zuhri, the Hamas spokesman in Gaza, was quoted as saying : « *The Jews tell us we are outlaws but look what happens when Palestinians win in court. [...] We already know what international law says : that we have the right of armed resistance against the occupation.* » : MCGREAL, Chris, « Barrier ruling shifts the debate », *Guardian*, 10 July 2004.

(251) A/ES-10/PV.24, 16 July 2004, p. 5.

(252) *Ibid.*, p. 10.

(253) *Ibid.*, p. 19.

fourteenth Ministerial Conference of the Non-Aligned Movement issued a
« Declaration on Palestine » welcoming the opinion and fully accepting its
findings and conclusions (254). Israel's Prime Minister Ariel Sharon, on the
other hand, « *totally reject[ed]* » the opinion, calling it « *one-sided* » and
« *based solely on political considerations* ». Characterizing it as « *immoral and
dangerous* », he claimed that it sent « *a deadly message that encourages
terrorism [...]* », and blamed it for the 11 July 2004 bomb attack in Tel
Aviv (255). He promised that Israel would push on with the construction
of the wall. Jonathon Peled, a foreign ministry official, spoke of Israel's
« *very close dialogue with the American administration and [its] European
friends to discuss the implications of [the] advisory opinion and to enlist their
assistance and their cooperation in preventing the Palestinians from exploiting
United Nations and international bodies for their political gain* » (256).

In the event, on 20 July 2004, the General Assembly's Tenth Emergency
Special Session — by a margin of 150 votes in favour to 6 against, with 10
abstentions — adopted G.A. resolution ES-10/15 (257), which acknowledged the advisory opinion, demanded that Israel comply with its obligations as identified by the Court, called on all Member States to comply with
their obligations, requested the Secretary-General to establish a register of
damage suffered by all natural and legal persons as a result of the wall's
construction, called on the High Contracting Parties to the Fourth Geneva
Convention to ensure Israel's respect for the Convention, and invited Switzerland, as the Convention's depositary, to conduct consultations and to
report to the General Assembly on the matter, including on the possibility
of resuming the Conference of High Contracting Parties to the Convention.
The resolution also called on both the Israeli Government and the
Palestinian Authority immediately to implement their respective obligations under the Roadmap. The U.S. delegate to the Assembly, voting
against the resolution, expressed his government's concern at « *some of the
apparent legal conclusions in the opinion* » (258). The representative of the
Netherlands, speaking on behalf of the European Union, made it clear that
although the Union had voted in favour of the resolution, it had reservations about certain paragraphs of the opinion (259). The Israeli delegate,
decrying resolution ES-10/15, acknowledged nonetheless that Israel was

---

(254) Declaration on Palestine, XIV Ministerial Conference of the Non-Aligned Movement,
Durban, South Africa, 17-19 August 2004, http://www.nam.gov.za/media/040820a.htm.

(255) « Sacred right to fight terror overrides the court, says Sharon », *Guardian*, 12 July 2004.

(256) McGREAL, *loc. cit.* As one might expect, media reaction around the world was varied,
some of it going beyond the bounds of civil discourse. For example, the *Washington Post's*
Charles Krauthammer wrote : « *It must be noted that one of the signatories of this attempt to force
Israel to tear down its most effective means of preventing the slaughter of innocent Jews was the judge
from Germany. The work continues.* » : KRAUTHAMMER, Charles, « Travesty at The Hague »,
Washington Post, 16 July 2004.

(257) See Annex 2 to this article for the full text of G.A. res. ES-10/15, 20 July 2004.

(258) A/ES-10/PV.27, 20 July 2004, p. 4.

(259) *Ibid.*, p. 8.

« *not above the law* » and would « *ensure that the route of the security fence complies fully with international law, as detailed by its Supreme Court* » (260).

As it turned out, in mid-August, the Supreme Court of Israel — sitting as the High Court of Justice in relation to petitions challenging the legality of sections of the wall near the West Bank villages of Shukba, Budrus and Beit Jala — ordered the Israeli Government to produce within 30 days a statement assessing the ramifications of the I.C.J.'s opinion (261). As a result, Attorney General Menachem Mazuz presented Prime Minister Sharon with a report produced by a specially appointed committee of lawyers, warning that « *[t]he decision creates a political reality for Israel on the international level* » which « *may result in sanctions* ». He warned that the I.C.J.'s opinion « *could reflect gradually on the decisions of the courts in Israel with regards to administering military authority in the West Bank and the building of the separation fence* ». He recommended that the government make a concerted effort to ensure that plans for the fence's route comply with the criteria for proportionality laid down by the Supreme Court of Israel in its judgment of 30 May (262).

With the adoption of G.A. resolution ES-10/15, there was apparently a feeling among some supporters of the Palestinian cause that the issue of the Court's opinion should now be put to rest and not pursued as a major subject for debate in the General Assembly, let alone the Security Council. The E.U., and reputedly some Arab states, were said to have advised the P.L.O. in private discussions that the U.N. route had been exhausted and that it was now up to Israel and the Palestinians to sort the matter out through negotiation (263).

*

* *

After the legal drama, politics resumes, but it cannot be politics as usual. The Court's findings will make it very hard for permanent members of the Security Council to veto resolutions on Palestine. The opinion also casts an uncomfortable light on aspects of foreign aid and arms sales to Israel, and

(260) *Ibid.*, p. 7.

(261) See ERLANGER, Steven, « High court in Israel revisits wall policy », *New York Times*, 20 August 2004, http://www.iht.com/articles/534890.html. The Supreme Court is bound, however, not to consider the I.C.J.'s opinion applicable to East Jerusalem, which Israeli law treats as part of the State of Israel.

(262) See YOAZ, Yuval, « AG : Hague fence ruling may lead to sanctions against Israel », *Haaretz*, 19 August 2004, http://www.haaretz.com/hasen/objects/pages/PrintArticleEn-.jhtml ?itemNo = 466870; IZENBERG, Dan, « A-G : Cabinet should approve each new fence section », *Jerusalem Post*, 19 August 2004, http://www.jpost.com/servlet/Satellite ?pagename-= JPost/JPArticle/ShowFull&cid = 1092884504193&p = 1006688055060. The Supreme Court case referred to is *Beit Sourik Village Council*, *loc. cit.*

(263) SHAMIR, Shlomo, « EU opposed to more talks on fence at UN », *Haaretz*, 15 September 2004, http://www.haaretz.com/hasen/objects/pages/PrintArticleEn.jhtml ?itemNo = 478090.

will result in increased political pressure on European governments to suspend at least certain aspects of the E.U.-Israel association agreement (264). In the end, it can only be hoped that the opinion has a constructive influence on a just and lasting settlement to the wider problem, even if, in relation to the wall itself, it is unlikely in the short term to emulate Joshua at Jericho.

Only time will tell too what impact the opinion will have on the future role of the Court. Fears that it will spark an explosion of speculative and politically ill-advised requests for advisory opinions designed to circumvent a lack of contentious jurisdiction are probably unfounded. If a unified and mobilised General Assembly was ever radically to reconceive the use to which the Court is put in promoting an international rule of law, it would probably have been in the wake of *Western Sahara*, an advisory opinion of comparable political significance, which came at the height of Non-Aligned activism and which, in legal terms, represented the culmination of the evolution of the principles on the propriety of advisory opinions. Since 1975, the rate-limiting step has remained the need to muster a majority in the General Assembly in favour of a request, and in the Security Council the veto remains as formidable an obstacle as ever. Moreover, advisory opinions remain non-binding, even if their political value is not be underestimated. If anything, the most likely upshot of the present opinion for the Court will be the participation of otherwise-unwilling interested states in all phases of future advisory proceedings : when the Court is going to render an opinion anyway, it makes little sense not to put your case.

On the day the Court's opinion was handed down, the spokesman for the Israeli Prime Minister ventured the prediction that it « *will find its place in the garbage can of history* » (265). Very few things can be certain about the impact of *Legal Consequences of the Construction of a Wall in the Occupied Palestinian Territory*. One of them is that it will be remembered for some time to come.

ANNEX 1

General Assembly resolution ES-10/14,
8 December 2003 (footnotes omitted)

Illegal Israeli actions in Occupied East Jerusalem and the rest of the Occupied Palestinian Territory

The General Assembly,

Reaffirming its resolution ES-10/13 of 21 October 2003,

---

(264) See Euro-Mediterranean Agreement establishing an association between the European Communities and their Member States, of the one part, and the State of Israel, of the other part, 20 November 1998, OJ L 147/18, 21.6.2000.

(265) « World court tells Israel to tear down illegal wall », *Guardian*, 10 July 2004.

Guided by the principles of the Charter of the United Nations,

Aware of the established principle of international law on the inadmissibility of the acquisition of territory by force,

Aware also that developing friendly relations among nations based on respect for the principle of equal rights and self-determination of peoples is among the purposes and principles of the Charter of the United Nations,

Recalling relevant General Assembly resolutions, including resolution 181 (II) of 29 November 1947, which partitioned mandated Palestine into two States, one Arab and one Jewish,

Recalling also the resolutions of the tenth emergency special session of the General Assembly,

Recalling further relevant Security Council resolutions, including resolutions 242 (1967) of 22 November 1967, 338 (1973) of 22 October 1973, 267 (1969) of 3 July 1969, 298 (1971) of 25 September 1971, 446 (1979) of 22 March 1979, 452 (1979) of 20 July 1979, 465 (1980) of 1 March 1980, 476 (1980) of 30 June 1980, 478 (1980) of 20 August 1980, 904 (1994) of 18 March 1994, 1073 (1996) of 28 September 1996, 1397 (2002) of 12 March 2002 and 1515 (2003) of 19 November 2003,

Reaffirming the applicability of the Fourth Geneva Convention as well as Additional Protocol I to the Geneva Conventions to the Occupied Palestinian Territory, including East Jerusalem,

Recalling the Regulations annexed to the Hague Convention Respecting the Laws and Customs of War on Land of 1907,

Welcoming the convening of the Conference of High Contracting Parties to the Fourth Geneva Convention on measures to enforce the Convention in the Occupied Palestinian Territory, including Jerusalem, at Geneva on 15 July 1999,

Expressing its support for the declaration adopted by the reconvened Conference of High Contracting Parties at Geneva on 5 December 2001,

Recalling in particular relevant United Nations resolutions affirming that Israeli settlements in the Occupied Palestinian Territory, including East Jerusalem, are illegal and an obstacle to peace and to economic and social development as well as those demanding the complete cessation of settlement activities,

Recalling relevant United Nations resolutions affirming that actions taken by Israel, the occupying Power, to change the status and demographic composition of Occupied East Jerusalem have no legal validity and are null and void,

Noting the agreements reached between the Government of Israel and the Palestine Liberation Organization in the context of the Middle East peace process,

Gravely concerned at the commencement and continuation of construction by Israel, the occupying Power, of a wall in the Occupied Palestinian Territory, including in and around East Jerusalem, which is in departure from the Armistice Line of 1949 (Green Line) and which has involved the confiscation and destruction of Palestinian land and resources, the disruption of the lives of thousands of protected civilians and the de facto annexation of large areas of territory, and underlining the unanimous opposition by the international community to the construction of that wall,

Gravely concerned also at the even more devastating impact of the projected parts of the wall on the Palestinian civilian population and on the prospects for solving the Palestinian-Israeli conflict and establishing peace in the region,

Welcoming the report of 8 September 2003 of the Special Rapporteur of the Commission on Human Rights on the situation of human rights in the Palestinian territories occupied by Israel since 1967, in particular the section regarding the wall,

Affirming the necessity of ending the conflict on the basis of the two-State solution of Israel and Palestine living side by side in peace and security based on the Armistice Line of 1949, in accordance with relevant Security Council and General Assembly resolutions,

Having received with appreciation the report of the Secretary-General, submitted in accordance with resolution ES-10/13,

Bearing in mind that the passage of time further compounds the difficulties on the ground, as Israel, the occupying Power, continues to refuse to comply with international law vis-à-vis its construction of the above-mentioned wall, with all its detrimental implications and consequences,

Decides, in accordance with Article 96 of the Charter of the United Nations, to request the International Court of Justice, pursuant to Article 65 of the Statute of the Court, to urgently render an advisory opinion on the following question :

> What are the legal consequences arising from the construction of the wall being built by Israel, the occupying Power, in the Occupied Palestinian Territory, including in and around East Jerusalem, as described in the report of the Secretary-General, considering the rules and principles of international law, including the Fourth Geneva Convention of 1949, and relevant Security Council and General Assembly resolutions ?

ANNEX 2

General Assembly resolution ES-10/15,
20 July 2004 (footnotes omitted)

Advisory opinion of the International Court of Justice on the *Legal Consequences of the Construction of a Wall in the Occupied Palestinian Territory*, including in and around East Jerusalem

The General Assembly,

Guided by the principles enshrined in the Charter of the United Nations,

Considering that the promotion of respect for the obligations arising from the Charter and other instruments and rules of international law is among the basic purposes and principles of the United Nations,

Recalling its resolution 2625 (XXV) of 24 October 1970, on the Declaration on Principles of International Law concerning Friendly Relations and Cooperation among States in accordance with the Charter of the United Nations,

Reaffirming the illegality of any territorial acquisition resulting from the threat or use of force,

Recalling the Regulations annexed to the Hague Convention Respecting the Laws and Customs of War on Land of 1907,

Recalling also the Geneva Convention relative to the Protection of Civilian Persons in Time of War of 12 August 1949, and relevant provisions of customary law, including those codified in Additional Protocol I to the Geneva Conventions,

Recalling further the International Covenant on Civil and Political Rights, the International Covenant on Economic, Social and Cultural Rights and the Convention on the Rights of the Child,

Reaffirming the permanent responsibility of the United Nations towards the question of Palestine until it is resolved in all aspects in a satisfactory manner on the basis of international legitimacy,

Recalling relevant Security Council resolutions, including resolutions 242 (1967) of 22 November 1967, 338 (1973) of 22 October 1973, 446 (1979) of 22 March 1979, 452 (1979) of 20 July 1979, 465 (1980) of 1 March 1980, 476 (1980) of 30 June 1980, 478 (1980) of 20 August 1980, 904 (1994) of 18 March 1994, 1073 (1996) of 28 September 1996, 1397 (2002) of 12 March 2002, 1515 (2003) of 19 November 2003 and 1544 (2004) of 19 May 2004,

Recalling also the resolutions of its tenth emergency special session on illegal Israeli actions in Occupied East Jerusalem and the rest of the Occupied Palestinian Territory,

Reaffirming the most recent resolution of the fifty-eighth session of the General Assembly on the status of the Occupied Palestinian Territory, including East Jerusalem, resolution 58/292 of 6 May 2004,

Reaffirming also the right of the Palestinian people to self-determination, including their right to their independent State of Palestine,

Reaffirming further the commitment to the two-State solution of Israel and Palestine, living side by side in peace and security within recognized borders, based on the pre-1967 borders,

Condemning all acts of violence, terrorism and destruction,

Calling upon both parties to fulfil their obligations under relevant provisions of the road map, the Palestinian Authority to undertake visible efforts on the ground to arrest, disrupt and restrain individuals and groups conducting and planning violent attacks, and the Government of Israel to take no actions undermining trust, including deportations and attacks on civilians and extrajudicial killings,

Reaffirming that all States have the right and the duty to take actions in conformity with international law and international humanitarian law to counter deadly acts of violence against their civilian population in order to protect the lives of their citizens,

Recalling its resolution ES-10/13 of 21 October 2003, in which it demanded that Israel stop and reverse the construction of the wall in the Occupied Palestinian Territory, including in and around East Jerusalem,

Recalling also its resolution ES-10/14 of 8 December 2003, in which it requested the International Court of Justice to urgently render an advisory opinion on the following question :

> « What are the legal consequences arising from the construction of the wall being built by Israel, the occupying Power, in the Occupied Palestinian Territory, including in and around East Jerusalem, as described in the report of the Secretary-General, considering the rules and principles of international law, including the Fourth Geneva Convention, of 1949, and relevant Security Council and General Assembly resolutions ? »,

Having received with respect the advisory opinion of the Court on the *Legal Consequences of the Construction of a Wall in the Occupied Palestinian Territory*, rendered on 9 July 2004,

Noting in particular that the Court replied to the question put forth by the General Assembly in resolution ES-10/14 as follows :

> « A. The construction of the wall being built by Israel, the occupying Power, in the Occupied Palestinian Territory, including in and around East Jerusalem, and its associated regime, are contrary to international law;

» B. Israel is under an obligation to terminate its breaches of international law; it is under an obligation to cease forthwith the works of construction of the wall being built in the Occupied Palestinian Territory, including in and around East Jerusalem, to dismantle forthwith the structure therein situated, and to repeal or render ineffective forthwith all legislative and regulatory acts relating thereto, in accordance with paragraph 151 of this Opinion;

» C. Israel is under an obligation to make reparation for all damage caused by the construction of the wall in the Occupied Palestinian Territory, including in and around East Jerusalem;

» D. All States are under an obligation not to recognize the illegal situation resulting from the construction of the wall and not to render aid or assistance in maintaining the situation created by such construction; all States Parties to the Fourth Geneva Convention relative to the Protection of Civilian Persons in Time of War of 12 August 1949 have in addition the obligation, while respecting the United Nations Charter and international law, to ensure compliance by Israel with international humanitarian law as embodied in that Convention;

» E. The United Nations, and especially the General Assembly and the Security Council, should consider what further action is required to bring to an end the illegal situation resulting from the construction of the wall and the associated regime, taking due account of the present Advisory Opinion. »,

Noting that the Court concluded that « the Israeli settlements in the Occupied Palestinian Territory (including East Jerusalem) have been established in breach of international law »,

Noting also the statement made by the Court that « Israel and Palestine are under an obligation scrupulously to observe the rules of international humanitarian law, one of the paramount purposes of which is to protect civilian life », and that « in the Court's view, this tragic situation can be brought to an end only through implementation in good faith of all relevant Security Council resolutions, in particular resolutions 242 (1967) and 338 (1973) »,

Considering that respect for the Court and its functions is essential to the rule of law and reason in international affairs,

1. *Acknowledges* the advisory opinion of the International Court of Justice of 9 July 2004 on the *Legal Consequences of the Construction of a Wall in the Occupied Palestinian Territory*, including in and around East Jerusalem;

2. *Demands* that Israel, the occupying Power, comply with its legal obligations as mentioned in the advisory opinion;

3. *Calls upon* all States Members of the United Nations to comply with their legal obligations as mentioned in the advisory opinion;

4. *Requests* the Secretary-General to establish a register of damage caused to all natural or legal persons concerned in connection with paragraphs 152 and 153 of the advisory opinion;

5. *Decides* to reconvene to assess the implementation of the present resolution, with the aim of ending the illegal situation resulting from the construction of the wall and its associated regime in the Occupied Palestinian Territory, including East Jerusalem;

6. *Calls upon* both the Government of Israel and the Palestinian Authority to immediately implement their obligations under the road map, in cooperation with the Quartet, as endorsed by Security Council resolution 1515 (2003), to achieve the

vision of two States living side by side in peace and security, and emphasizes that both Israel and the Palestinian Authority are under an obligation scrupulously to observe the rules of international humanitarian law;

7. *Calls upon* all States parties to the Fourth Geneva Convention to ensure respect by Israel for the Convention, and invites Switzerland, in its capacity as the depositary of the Geneva Conventions, to conduct consultations and to report to the General Assembly on the matter, including with regard to the possibility of resuming the Conference of High Contracting Parties to the Fourth Geneva Convention;

8. *Decides* to adjourn the tenth emergency special session temporarily and to authorize the President of the General Assembly at its most recent session to resume its meeting upon request from Member States.

The World Court's Ruling Regarding Israel's West Bank Barrier and the Primacy of International Law: An Insider's Perspective

Pieter H.F. Bekker†

Introduction

On July 9, 2004, the International Court of Justice ("ICJ" or "Court"), the principal judicial organ of the United Nations ("UN") seated at the Peace Palace in The Hague (The Netherlands), issued an Advisory Opinion in the case concerning the "Legal Consequences of the Construction of a Wall in the Occupied Palestinian Territory."[1] The ruling was in response

---

† LL.M. (Harvard); LL.B., Ph.D. (Int'l Law) (Leiden). The author, who was a staff lawyer in the ICJ Registry between 1992 and 1994, served as Senior Counsel to Palestine in the advisory proceeding before the ICJ while on unpaid leave from his law firm. The views expressed herein, which are based on a presentation given as part of a program organized by the Cornell Jewish Law Students Association and the National Lawyers Guild on November 22, 2004, are solely those of the author. Portions of this speech have been adapted from a talk given by the author at the United Nations International Meeting on the Question of Palestine, held at the UN Office in Geneva on March 9, 2005.

1. Advisory Opinion, Legal Consequences of the Construction of a Wall in the Occupied Palestinian Territory, 2004 I.C.J. 131 (July 9), 43 I.L.M. 1009 [hereinafter Wall Opinion], *available at* http://www.icj-cij.org/icjwww/idocket/imwp/imwpframe.htm (last visited Mar. 1, 2005). While the ICJ unanimously upheld its jurisdiction to give the requested Advisory Opinion, the vote on the substantive part was 14-1 (Buergenthal, J. (U.S.), dissenting). For a summary of the Wall Opinion, see Pieter H.F. Bekker, *The World Court Rules that Israel's West Bank Barrier Violates International Law*, American Society of International Law, *at* http://www.asil.org/insights/insigh141.htm (July 2004). For further scholarly commentary on the Wall Opinion see *Agora: ICJ Advisory*

to a 90-8 vote by the UN General Assembly in December 2003[2] that requested the Court's advice regarding the legal aspects of Israel's construction of a barrier separating part of the West Bank and East Jerusalem from Israel.[3]

The case before the ICJ represented my inaugural involvement with the Middle East crisis. Never before had I studied the problem closely, from either side. My conviction as a former United Nations official and ICJ staff lawyer that the primacy of international law must be upheld motivated me to serve on Palestine's legal team in the ICJ case.[4] There is nothing "anti-Israeli" or "pro-Palestinian" about supporting that fundamental principle. There also is nothing inconsistent about condemning suicide bombings and colonial settlements in occupied territory equally, as I do. My involvement with Palestine has remained limited to the ICJ proceeding, and these observations are made in my individual capacity as an ICJ specialist.[5]

Opinion on Construction of a Wall in the Occupied Palestinian Territory, 99 Am. J. Int'l L. 1 (2005).

2. *Yes to Israel Vote*, Calgary Sun, Dec. 9, 2003, at 26. Voting against the resolution were the United States, Israel, Australia, Ethiopia, Nauru, Marshall Islands, Micronesia, and Palau. *Id.*

3. The text of the General Assembly's request read as follows:

What are the legal consequences arising from the construction of the wall being built by Israel, the occupying Power, in the Occupied Palestinian Territory, including in and around East Jerusalem, as described in the report of the Secretary-General, considering the rules and principles of international law, including the Fourth Geneva Convention of 1949, and relevant Security Council and General Assembly resolutions?

Illegal Israeli Actions in Occupied East Jerusalem and the Rest of the Occupied Palestinian Territory (Israel's Apartheid Wall), G.A. Res. ES-10/14, 10th Emergency Special Sess., Agenda Item 5 (2003). For a background description of the Assembly's request, see Pieter H.F. Bekker, *The UN General Assembly Requests a World Court Advisory Opinion on Israel's Separation Barrier*, American Society of International Law, *at* http://www.asil.org/insights/insigh121.htm (Dec. 2003). It must be emphasized that this was not a contentious proceeding involving Palestine and Israel as "parties." There are no "parties" in advisory proceedings initiated by eligible UN organs. As the ICJ pointed out, "The Court's Opinion is given not to the States, but to the organ which is entitled to request it." Wall Opinion, 2004 I.C.J. 131, para. 47, *reprinted in* 43 I.L.M. at 1025 (quoting Interpretation of Peace Treaties with Bulgaria, Hungary and Romania, First Phase, Advisory Opinion, 1950 I.C.J. 65, 71); *see also id. at* para. 50, *reprinted in* 43 I.L.M. at 1025 ("The opinion is requested on a question which is of particularly acute concern to the United Nations, and one which is located in a much broader frame of reference than a bilateral dispute.").

4. *See* Advisory Opinion, Applicability of the Obligation to Arbitrate under Section 21 of the United Nations Headquarters Agreement of 26 June 1947, 1988 I.C.J. 12, 34, para. 57 (Apr. 26) [hereinafter PLO Mission Opinion]. In that case, the ICJ recalled "the fundamental principle of international law that international law prevails over domestic law," which it noted "was endorsed by judicial decision as long ago as the arbitral award of 14 September 1872 in the *Alabama* case between Great Britain and the United States, and has frequently been recalled since . . . ."

5. My dealings were limited to interactions with officials in Palestine's Permanent Observer Mission to the United Nations in New York. For an authoritative description of Palestine's status within the United Nations, see PLO Mission Opinion, 1988 I.C.J. at 15, para. 8. (defining PLO's status as an "organization[ ] which ha[s] received a standing invitation from the General Assembly to participate in the sessions and the work of the General Assembly as an observer").

To be clear, no cause is so just that it can justify targeting innocent civilians and noncombatants through suicide bombings or other violent attacks, and nobody questions Israel's right to protect its citizens against such attacks, so long as Israel complies with international law. Those suicide bombings rightly were condemned, in no uncertain terms, in not one but two long paragraphs in Palestine's written statement to the ICJ,[6] and again as part of Palestine's oral statement before the Court.[7] But the focus on suicide bombings is mistaken in this context.

As an officer of the Court, my duty in any case is to search for the truth and to apply the applicable law to the facts. What are the facts in this particular case? In stark contrast to what Israel has claimed and some media have reported, the ICJ case was not about Israel's right to protect itself (i.e., Israeli sovereign territory and its inhabitants) through the construction of a "fence" or "barrier" or "wall"—Israel, if it chooses, has both the right under international law to build a security fence and the practical possibility and ability to do so, as long as it does so on its own territory.[8] Rather, the case was about the actual course, or the route, of the West Bank barrier ("the Wall") as it extends past the "Green Line"—the line indicated in the 1949 Israel-Jordan Armistice Agreement that constitutes the recognized Israeli border pending the outcome of "final status" negotiations. For this reason, although it purportedly protects Israeli citizens against suicide bombings and other violent attacks, the Wall—or at least 99% of it that is situated to the east of the Green Line—is an illegal measure. In fact, as aerial photographs and other objective evidence submitted to the ICJ demonstrate, the Wall is designed to protect and perpetuate settlements in the West Bank and in East Jerusalem—measures repeatedly declared by the competent UN bodies to be illegal under international law.

The 64-page judicial opinion is a landmark ruling in more than one respect. It represents a historic development pertaining to the question of

---

6. *See* Legal Consequences of the Construction of a Wall in the Occupied Palestinian Territory (Request For An Advisory Opinion), Written Statement Submitted by Palestine, at 95, paras. 217, 226, Wall Opinion, 2004 I.C.J. 131 [hereinafter Palestinian Statement], *available at* http://www. icj-cij.org /icjwww/idocket/imwpstatements/WrittenStatement_08_Palestine.pdf (last visited Mar. 1, 2005).

7. Oral statement of Dr. Nasser Al-Kidwa, Ambassador and Permanent Observer of Palestine to the United Nations, in Public Sitting Held on Monday 23 February 2004, at 10 a.m., at the Peace Palace, President Shi Presiding, 2004 I.C.J. Pleadings, CR 2004/1, at 24, para. 21 ("We condemn any violence directed at civilians in this conflict, whether Israeli or Palestinian. We consider the suicide bombings to be unlawful."), *available at* http://www.minfo.gov.ps/statements/english/oral_statement_eng.pdf (last visited Mar. 6, 2005).

8. A recurring theme in Israel's ongoing opposition to the ICJ case has been the allegation that the Court from the outset showed bias by including the word "wall" in the official case title, as opposed to "barrier" or "fence." Opting for "wall"—the terminology employed by the UN General Assembly in its Request For An Advisory Opinion—the ICJ explained that "the other terms used, either by Israel ('fence') or by the [United Nations] Secretary-General ('barrier'), are no more accurate if understood in the physical sense." Wall Opinion, 2004 I.C.J. 131, para. 67, *reprinted in* 43 I.L.M. at 1029. The Court observed that "the 'wall' in question is a complex construction, so that that term cannot be understood in a limited physical sense." *Id.*

Palestine, as well as a unique opportunity for emphasizing the rule of international law in the efforts to resolve the Israeli-Palestinian problem. The ICJ's authoritative statements on the applicable international law should change the parameters for any negotiated solution to this problem. First, the ruling was the first-ever international judicial pronouncement on a current aspect of the crisis. Second, the ICJ authorized what it called "Palestine" to participate (over Israel's objection). Third, the Court concluded that the Palestinian territory concerned is "occupied" by Israel, and not "disputed," as Israel has claimed. Fourth, the ICJ found that the Israeli settlements, around which the Wall is built, violate international law. Fifth, the Court concluded that the Geneva Conventions are applicable to the Palestinian population and that international human rights law applies to Palestinians alongside international humanitarian law. The ICJ found that Israel's construction and operation of the Wall violates both. Finally, the ICJ rejected Israel's security arguments pertaining to the Wall on the basis of the applicable international law.

The sections that follow highlight some of the ICJ's principal pronouncements in this case.

1. Judicial Focus

First and foremost, it must be underscored that the ICJ case signaled the first time that an international *judicial* organ has ruled, based on facts documented in numerous United Nations reports, on a prominent aspect of the problem by applying rules of international law. In the past, only the General Assembly and the Security Council, which are the political organs of the United Nations, had dealt with the Israeli-Palestinian problem, with varying results.

While the ICJ acknowledged that the Security Council, by Resolution 1515 of November 19, 2003, had endorsed the so-called "Roadmap to a Permanent Two-State Solution to the Israeli-Palestinian Conflict" ("Roadmap"), it pointed out that neither the Roadmap nor Resolution 1515 contains any specific provisions concerning the construction of the Wall, so that these documents did not prevent the ICJ from ruling on the Wall's legality.[9]

In other words, the ICJ rejected Israel's argument that the Wall's existence is presumptively intertwined with the Roadmap process and that it cannot be treated as distinct from that process.[10] Instead, the ICJ con-

---

9. *See* Wall Opinion, 2004 I.C.J. 131, para. 22, *reprinted in* 43 I.L.M. at 1018.

10. Israel contended that "[t]he only way to resolve the differences between Israel and the Palestinians, including the dispute over the fence, is through direct negotiations, as stipulated by UN Security Council resolutions and the Roadmap." ICJ Advisory Opinion on Israel's Security Fence, 9 July 2004, Israeli Statement, Wall Opinion, 2004 I.C.J. 131 [hereinafter "Israeli Statement"] (text on file with author), *available at* http://www.mfa.gov.il/MFA/About™he+Ministry/MFA+Spokesman/2004/Statement+on+ICJ+Advisory+Opinion+9-July-2004.htm (last visited Mar. 5, 2005). This statement ignores that Israel actively opposed and delayed adoption of the Roadmap and has attached more than a dozen reservations to it. Moreover, Israel has violated many binding Secur-

cluded that the Wall is not part of any future "permanent status" issues (such as borders and refugees). Rather, it exists outside the negotiating framework for peace and outside the boundaries of international law; thus endangering the feasibility of a viable state for the Palestinian people and undermining future negotiations based on the "two-state" principle and international law.

II.   Palestine's Participation and Representation in the ICJ Proceeding

Another highlight of the case is the fact that the ICJ allowed Palestine to participate in the proceeding, despite its Observer status with the UN General Assembly.[11] Palestine did not waste this unique opportunity. Its legal team before the ICJ consisted of the leading international law and ICJ specialists from Oxford and Cambridge, Belgium, Egypt, Palestine, and myself from The Netherlands.[12] Palestine's team members were of Christian, Jewish, and Muslim faiths. We readily accepted this assignment because we were all convinced that the Wall, having regard to its location and the restrictive measures surrounding its construction and operation, constitutes a gross violation of international law.

Most important, Palestine's legal team did not receive any instructions whatsoever from the Palestinian authorities in Ramallah. Palestine let the specialists handle the case.

III.   "Occupied" Status of Palestinian Territory

Another major development represented by the ICJ ruling relates to the fact that it is the first time that an international court has ruled on the status of the Palestinian territory.

The ICJ noted that the territories situated between the line indicated in the 1949 Israel-Jordan Armistice Agreement, the so-called "Green Line," and the former eastern boundary of Palestine under the League of Nations Mandate of Palestine (including East Jerusalem) are *occupied* territories in which Israel has had the status of "occupying Power" since 1967.[13] The Court thus rejected Israel's position that these are "disputed" territories

---

ity Council resolutions relating to the Palestinian situation. *See Wall* Opinion, *supra* note 1, at para. 99.

11. *See supra* note 5. Palestine is neither a UN member state nor a party to the ICJ Statute. Israel's argument that the advisory proceeding in reality concerned a bilateral dispute between Israel and Palestine over which the ICJ lacks jurisdiction absent Israel's consent is problematic, given that Israel does not recognize Palestinian statehood. On non-state participation in ICJ proceedings, see Dinah Shelton, *The Participation of Non-governmental Organizations in International Judicial Proceedings*, 88 Am. J. Int'l L. 611 (1994).

12. Namely, James Crawford (University of Cambridge) (Australian); Vaughan Lowe (University of Oxford) (British); Georges Abi-Saab (Graduate Institute of International Studies, Geneva) (Egyptian); and Jean Salmon (Free University of Brussels) (Belgian), as Counsel and Advocate; and Anis Kassim (Amman) (Jordanian-Palestinian), Raja Aziz Shehadeh (Ramallah) (Palestinian), and this author (Dutch) as Senior Counsel.

13. Wall Opinion, 2004 I.C.J. 131, para. 78, *reprinted in* 43 I.L.M. at 1031.

whose legal status is subject to negotiation.[14]

This point alone should have a major impact on the Roadmap process. As of July 9, 2004, neither Israel nor its allies can claim in good faith[15] that the territory that is the subject of the Israeli-Palestinian crisis is "disputed," as opposed to "occupied." Important legal ramifications flow from this characterization, especially the illegality of the acquisition of territory resulting "from the threat or use of force against the territorial integrity or political independence of any State,"[16] and the prohibition on making changes to the status of the occupied territory, including the transfer of the Israeli population to occupied Palestinian territory, as Israel has done through settlements built since 1967.[17]

IV. Illegality of Israeli Settlements

Perhaps the most remarkable aspect of the ruling is the fact that the ICJ explicitly condemned the settlements that Israel has established in Palestinian territories occupied by it since 1967. Israel had initially justified the settlements as being only "temporary" structures when it began building them some 37 years ago and now there are nearly 400,000 Israeli settlers living in over 150 settlements—thus causing one to doubt the legitimacy of similar guarantees made in connection with the Wall.[18]

---

14. *See* Benjamin Netanyahu, *Why Israel Needs a Fence*, N.Y. TIMES, July 13, 2004, at A19 (asserting that the "fence is being built in disputed territories that Israel won in a defensive war in 1967").

15. U.N. CHARTER art. 2(2).

16. *See* Wall Opinion, 2004 I.C.J. 131, para. 87, *reprinted in* 43 I.L.M. at 1034 (quoting U.N. CHARTER art. 2, para. 4).

17. *See id.* at paras. 117, 120, *reprinted in* 43 I.L.M. at 1041-42 (noting that international humanitarian law "prohibits not only deportations or forced transfers of population such as those carried out during the Second World War, but also any measures taken by an occupying Power in order to organize or encourage transfers of parts of its own population into the occupied territory").

18. Israel's claim that the Wall is a "temporary" measure, Israeli Statement, *supra* note 10, is not credible given the multi-million-dollar investment Israel is making in connection with the Wall, as documented in UN reports and Israeli government sources. Furthermore, even if the Wall were temporary, much of the damage being done in connection with the construction of the Wall is permanent and irreversible (e.g., some 100,000 trees, including 83,000 olive trees, have been uprooted). Moreover, Israel's claim that the Wall is simply an inconvenience to the Palestinians affected by it trivializes the crippling and lasting effects of the Wall on the Palestinian people and the Palestinian economy, as documented in UN reports. Once the Wall is completed, Palestine estimates that 37.5% of the Palestinian population of the West Bank, or 865,300 people, either will be located on the Israeli side of the Wall or will have lost land to the other side of the Wall. *See* Palestinian Statement, *supra* note 6, at 121-22, para. 271. The ICJ considered that "the construction of the wall and its associated régime create a 'fait accompli' on the ground that could well become permanent, in which case, *and notwithstanding the formal characterization of the wall by Israel*, it would be tantamount to *de facto* annexation." Wall Opinion, 2004 I.C.J. 131, para. 121, *reprinted in* 43 I.L.M. at 1042 (emphasis added). *See also Report of the Special Rapporteur of the Commission on Human Rights, John Dugard, on the Situation of Human Rights in the Palestinian Territories Occupied by Israel Since 1967*, at 2, U.N. Doc. E/CN.4/2004/6 (Sept. 8, 2003), *available at* http://www.unhchr.ch/html/menu2/2/60chr/summaries/8_E.doc (last visited Mar.

While Palestine did not specifically ask the ICJ to declare the settlements illegal, the Court felt logically bound to come to this conclusion. Palestine had submitted a series of satellite images and other evidence showing what Palestine and other participants in the advisory proceeding argued was an unmistakable connection between the route of the Wall and the Israeli settlements in the West Bank and in East Jerusalem. Based on this evidence, the ICJ observed that, within the "Closed Area" between the Green Line and the Wall, the Wall's "sinuous route has been traced in such a way as to include within that area the great majority of Israeli settlements in the Occupied Palestinian Territory (including East Jerusalem)," involving around 80% of the Israeli settlers.[19] The ICJ concluded that "the Israeli settlements in the Occupied Palestinian Territory (including East Jerusalem) have been established in breach of international law."[20]

Even Judge Buergenthal (United States), the only ICJ judge who dissented on the grounds that the Court should have declined to render the advisory opinion, stated that "the segments of the wall being built by Israel to protect the settlements are ipso facto in violation of international humanitarian law."[21] Even he recognized that the Wall, or at least large segments of it, is built "to protect the settlements." This means that the ICJ was, in fact, unanimous on the question of the illegality of the settlements that the Wall obviously is designed to protect. The settlements being clearly illegal under international law, there can be no legal right to protect such settlements or related infrastructure by diverting the course of the Wall away from the Green Line. It really is a clear and shut case.

In light of the Court's holding regarding the Israeli settlements, no UN member state can declare in good faith that any Israeli settlement constitutes an acceptable reality on the ground that future negotiations on final status issues cannot upset. Israel cannot claim under international law that any land occupied by it since 1967 should be a part of the State of Israel, now or in the future, unless the Palestinians voluntarily give up their territorial rights. Prime Minister Sharon's "Disengagement Plan," which the Israeli Parliament accepted on October 26, 2004, violates international law to the extent it unilaterally perpetuates any illegal settlements in the West Bank or in East Jerusalem.

Faced with these statements of the UN's judicial body, Palestinians rightly wonder why they should negotiate with Israel over what 15 international judges have already declared illegal. This question is legitimate, because the ICJ referred to the need to achieve "as soon as possible, on the basis of international law, a negotiated solution."[22] As of July 9, 2004,

---

3, 2005) ("The evidence strongly suggests that Israel is determined to create facts on the ground amounting to de facto annexation.").

19. Wall Opinion, 2004 I.C.J. 131, paras. 119, 122, *reprinted in* 43 I.L.M. at 1042. The ICJ also stated that "the route chosen for the wall gives expression *in loco* to the illegal measures taken by Israel with regard to Jerusalem and the settlements, as deplored by the Security Council." *Id.* at para. 122, *reprinted in* 43 I.L.M. at 1043.

20. *Id.* at para. 120, *reprinted in* 43 I.L.M. at 1042.

21. *Id.* at para. 9, *reprinted in* 43 I.L.M. at 1081 (Buergenthal, J., dissenting).

22. *Id.* at para. 162, *reprinted in* 43 I.L.M. at 1054.

The Palestine Question in International Law

Israel no longer can claim in good faith that the settlements are legal, or at best "disputed," and that their fate should be negotiated. Why should illegalities be subject to negotiations, which according to the ICJ are to proceed "on the basis of international law?"

V.   "Geneva" and Human Rights Protections for Palestinians

The ICJ also found that both the 1949 Fourth Geneva Convention Relative to the Protection of Civilian Persons in Time of War,[23] to which Israel is a party, and the 1907 Hague Regulations Annex to the 1907 Hague Convention IV Respecting the Laws and Customs of War on Land,[24] a source that is binding on Israel as customary international law, are applicable to Israel's occupation of the Palestinian territories, and have been violated by Israel's construction of the Wall.[25] The ICJ thereby rejected Israel's position that, since Article 2 of the Fourth Geneva Convention says that the Convention applies only to "occupation of the territory of a High Contracting Party," and since the West Bank and East Jerusalem are not within the recognized territory of any such party, Israel is not legally bound to apply the Convention on those places.[26]

In a key ruling, the Court concluded that the Fourth Geneva Convention is applicable de jure in the Occupied Palestinian Territory given the existence of an armed conflict that had arisen between Israel and Jordan, two contracting parties, at the start of the June 1967 war.[27] It noted that numerous resolutions of the General Assembly and the Security Council have affirmed the de jure applicability of the Fourth Geneva Convention and that Israel's Supreme Court found in a May 30, 2004 judgment that the Convention applied in Rafah, which is situated in the Occupied Palestinian Territory.[28] Specifically, the ICJ concluded that the changes caused by Israel in the demographic composition of the Palestinian area affected by the Wall are in contravention of Article 49 of the Fourth Geneva Convention concerning the deportation or transfer of civilian population.[29]

---

23. Geneva Convention Relative to the Protection of Civilian Persons in Time of War, Aug. 12, 1949, 75 U.N.T.S. 287, 6 U.S.T. 3516. *See generally* Ardi Imseis, *On the Fourth Geneva Convention and the Occupied Palestinian Territory*, 44 Harv. Int'l L.J. 65 (2003) (arguing that the Fourth Geneva Convention is indispensable and discussing means of implementing it to protect the interests of Israelis and Palestinians alike).
24. Oct. 18, 1907, 36 Stat. 2277, T.S. No. 539.
25. Wall Opinion, 2004 I.C.J. 131, paras. 78, 98, *reprinted in* 43 I.L.M. at 1031, 1037.
26. *See Report of the Secretary-General Prepared Pursuant to General Assembly Resolution ES-10/13*, GAOR, 10th Emergency Special Sess., U.N. Doc. A/ES-10/248 (Nov. 24, 2003), Annex 1 (summarizing the legal position of the Government of Israel).
27. Wall Opinion, 2004 I.C.J. 131, para. 101, *reprinted in* 43 I.L.M. at 1037-38.
28. *Id.* at paras. 98-100, *reprinted in* 43 I.L.M. at 1037; *see also* SC Res. 1544 (May 19, 2004). More than two dozen Security Council resolutions adopted over a 30-year period and numerous General Assembly resolutions have confirmed that the Fourth Geneva Convention is applicable to the Occupied Palestinian Territory.
29. Wall Opinion, 2004 I.C.J. 131, paras. 126, 134-35, *reprinted in* 43 I.L.M. at 1044, 1048. Judge Buergenthal agreed. *Id.* at para. 9, *reprinted in* 43 I.L.M. at 1080-81 (Buergenthal, J., dissenting) ("I agree that [Article 49(6) of the Fourth Geneva Conven-

The ICJ also rejected Israel's claim that the International Covenant on Civil and Political Rights ("ICCPR"), the International Covenant on Economic, Social and Cultural Rights ("ICESCR"), and the UN Convention on the Rights of the Child, all human rights treaties that have been ratified by Israel, are not applicable to the Occupied Palestinian Territory. The Court pointed out that the protection offered by human rights conventions, which are applicable both to territories over which a state has sovereignty and to those over which that state exercises jurisdiction outside sovereign territory, does not cease in case of armed conflict, save through the effect of provisions for derogation included in those instruments—none of which were found to apply in the case of the Wall.[30]

VI. Israel's Security Defense Rejected

Israel has offered no adequate explanation of the justification for the actual route that the Wall follows to the east of the Green Line, beyond bald assertions of its security interest. In the aftermath of the ICJ's ruling, Israel stated that "[i]f there were no [Palestinian] terrorism, there would be no fence."[31] This statement ignores both the place of occurrence of the terror attacks on Israelis and the route of the Wall in the context of international law.

Under international law, Israel can defend only Israeli territory, which undeniably is situated to the *west* of the Green Line. In other words, Israel should build a security fence on its own territory along the Green Line if it wants to protect Israeli citizens against Palestinian terrorists entering Israel and stay within the bounds of the applicable international law. If the Wall truly were about Israel's security, it could be built on Israel's own territory, not on territory that the great majority of the world community considers to be occupied Palestinian land and where Israel has no proprietary rights. If Israel had built the entire Wall on its own territory along the Green Line, there in fact would have been no ICJ case.

Apart from the problem of the Wall's location, Israel's claim that "[t]he fence is a non-violent security measure and it saves lives"[32] is not supported by the facts or the law. In fact, the Wall has resulted in widespread property destruction and it has taken lives. Innocent Palestinian civilians have lost their lives as a consequence of the discriminatory permit and gate system administered by Israel in connection with the Wall. For example, the Israeli Defense Forces prevented an ambulance on its way to the nearest hospital with Lamis Taysser, a 26-year-old Palestinian woman who was in labor, from crossing a gate in the Wall on December 23, 2003. One of her

tion] applies to the Israeli settlements in the West Bank and that their existence violates Article 49, paragraph 6.").

30. *See id.* at paras. 102-13, 127-31, 136-37, *reprinted in* 43 I.L.M. at 1038-40, 1045-46, 1048-49.

31. Israeli Statement, *supra* note 10. In the ICJ proceeding, Israel chose not to submit its detailed arguments, together with any and all reports and other evidence, on the substantive aspects of the General Assembly's request.

32. *Id.*

twin babies died during birth in the ambulance, and the other succumbed the next day on Christmas Eve, all because of the Wall.[33]

The ICJ was not convinced that the specific course that Israel has chosen for the Wall was necessary to attain its security objectives. The Court recognized that the Wall is not just a linear phenomenon, but that it comes with a regime of restrictive measures affecting the Palestinian population.[34] In the Court's view, the Wall, along the route chosen, and its associated regime "gravely infringe a number of rights of Palestinians residing in the territory occupied by Israel."[35]

After weighing all the arguments, including arguments that Israel chose not to plead before the ICJ, the Court concluded that "the infringements resulting from that route cannot be justified by military exigencies or by the requirements of national security or public order."[36]

Thus, as of July 9, 2004, Israel's Supreme Court cannot conclude in good faith that the route of the Wall to the east of the Green Line that the ICJ rejected satisfies the necessity criterion that international law attaches to state actions that derogate from fundamental rules of humanitarian and human rights law. This argument was explicitly rejected by the ICJ.[37] And if the necessity criterion is not satisfied, the related criterion of proportionality, on which the Supreme Court rulings rely, becomes moot.[38] The ICJ's ruling calls for Israel "to dismantle forthwith the structure" of the Wall (i.e., 99% of it that extends past the Green Line into the West Bank)—it is not simply a matter of the "adjustment" within the West Bank of the Wall's route as it runs to the east of the Green Line, as the decisions of Israel's Supreme Court suggest.[39] The principle of the primacy of international law leaves no margin of appreciation for Israel's courts—they must recognize and enforce the ICJ's ruling on this point by rejecting any segment extending past the Green Line into the West Bank.

---

33. See Written Statement of Palestine, app. 3, at 86, *available at* http://www.palestine-un.org/icj/pdf/appendices.pdf (last visited Mar. 6, 2005).

34. Wall Opinion, 2004 I.C.J. 131, paras. 85, 133, 142, *reprinted in* 43 I.L.M. at 1033, 1047-48, 1050. Segments of the Wall involve "double-walled" areas in which a second wall extends from the principal wall and encircles and encloses a certain area.

35. *Id.* at para. 137, *reprinted in* 43 I.L.M. at 1049.

36. *Id.*

37. *Id.* para. 136, *reprinted in* 43 I.L.M. at 1048-49.

38. *See* Oil Platforms (Iran v. U.S.), 2003 I.C.J. 90, paras. 43, 73-77, *reprinted in* 42 I.L.M 1334, 1353, 1360-62; *see also id.* at para. 48, *reprinted in* 42 I.L.M. at 1387 (Higgins, J., separate opinion) (asserting that "in general international law, 'necessary' is understood also as incorporating a need for 'proportionality'"). The question of proportionality does not arise because the requirement that the Wall be a proportionate response to threats facing Israel would arise only if the initial necessity, which must arise from military operations (not merely military occupation), were demonstrated.

39. Wall Opinion, 2004 I.C.J. 131, para. 163(3)(B), *reprinted in* 43 I.L.M. at 1055; *cf.* H.C. 2056/04, Beit Sourik Village Council v. Israel, *reprinted in* 43 I.L.M. 1099 (2004) (holding that the route of the Wall was satisfied by military necessity but that some portions of the Wall did not meet the proportionality requirement). General Assembly Resolution ES-10/13 of October 21, 2003, which was sponsored by the European Union and adopted by a vote of 144-4, had already demanded that Israel stop and reverse its construction of the Wall. Israel's failure to comply with that resolution led to the Assembly's request for an advisory opinion.

Israel's complaint, voiced in the aftermath of the ICJ ruling, that "the Advisory Opinion fails to address the essence of the problem and the very reason for building the fence–Palestinian terror,"[40] is refuted by the very text of the Opinion.[41] One is reminded that Israel chose not to address the merits in the ICJ proceeding, focusing instead on making its case in the "court of public opinion."

Benjamin Netanyahu, Israel's Finance Minister and a former Prime Minister, nonetheless commented in a leading newspaper on July 13, 2004, that "the court's decision makes a mockery of Israel's right to defend itself."[42] The text of the ICJ's Opinion, which devotes at least five paragraphs (138–42) on several pages to the issue. again suggests the opposite. In this context, the ICJ recognized explicitly that Israel "has the right, and indeed the duty, to respond [to deadly acts of violence against its civilian population] in order to protect the life of its citizens."[43] But the Court emphasized at the same time that the "measures taken are bound nonetheless to remain in conformity with applicable international law."[44] These latter words routinely are ignored in reporting about the ICJ case, even though they constitute the very essence of the ICJ's ruling and its emphasis on the applicability of international law.

A state's right to self-defense does not extend to territory occupied illegally under international law and not forming part of a recognized state. The right to self-defense is premised upon the occurrence of "an armed attack" under Article 51 of the UN Charter and applies only "in the case of armed attack by one State against another State."[45] As the ICJ noted, "Israel does not claim that the attacks against it are imputable to a

---

40. Israeli Statement, *supra* note 10.

41. *See* Wall Opinion, 2004 I.C.J. 131, paras. 138–42, *reprinted in* 43 I.L.M. at 1049–50 (concluding that Israel could have prevented terror using less restrictive means); *see also id.* at para. 55, *reprinted in* 43 I.L.M. at 1027 (mentioning "the security threat to which the wall is intended to respond"); *id.* at para. 57, *reprinted in* 43 I.L.M. at 1027–28 (noting Israel's security concerns); *id.* at para. 80, *reprinted in* 43 I.L.M. at 1032 ("what Israel describes as a 'security fence'"); *id.* at para. 116, *reprinted in* 43 I.L.M. at 1041 ("Israel has argued that the wall's sole purpose is to enable it effectively to combat terrorist attacks launched from the West Bank"); *id.* at para. 137, *reprinted in* 43 I.L.M. at 1049 (mentioning Israel's "security objectives"); *id.* at para. 141, *reprinted in* 43 I.L.M. at 1050 ("The fact remains that Israel has to face numerous indiscriminate and deadly acts of violence against its civilian population.").

42. Benjamin Netanyahu, *supra* note 14. Mr. Netanyahu also complained that the ICJ's Opinion "mentions terrorism only twice." The issue is not, however, how many times the ICJ uses the specific words "terror" or "terrorism." Violence is referred to by different words in international law, which the Advisory Opinion employs in multiple forms. *See, e.g.*, Wall Opinion, 2004 I.C.J. 131, para. 141, *reprinted in* 43 I.L.M. at 1050. (referring to "deadly acts of violence"). Also, a state's right to protect its citizens in light of national security requirements must be distinguished from that state's right to self-defense under international law. *See infra* note 46.

43. Wall Opinion, 2004 I.C.J. 131, para. 141, *reprinted in* 43 I.L.M. at 1050.

44. *Id.* The ICJ concluded that "Israel cannot rely on a right of self-defence or on a state of necessity in order to preclude the wrongfulness of the construction of the wall resulting from the considerations mentioned in paragraphs 122 and 137 above." *Id.* at para. 142, *reprinted in* 43 I.L.M. at 1050.

45. *Id.* at para. 139, *reprinted in* 43 I.L.M. at 1049–50.

foreign State," so that "Article 51 of the Charter has no relevance in this case."[46] In any event, it is not a general right for a state to take forcible measures outside its sovereign territory in order to prevent the commission of crimes within the state.

VII.   To Bind or Not To Bind?

While it is true that Advisory Opinions of the ICJ formally are non-binding, it would be a mistake to claim that this nonbinding character means that such opinions are without legal effect: the legal reasoning embodied in them reflects the Court's authoritative views on important issues of international law and, in arriving at them, the ICJ follows essentially the same rules and procedures that govern its binding judgments delivered in contentious cases between sovereign states.[47] An Advisory Opinion derives its status and authority from the fact that it is the official pronouncement of the principal judicial organ of the United Nations.

Indeed, Judge Rosalyn Higgins, the British ICJ judge who was critical of large parts of the ICJ's opinion but ultimately voted in favor of all its operative paragraphs, stated that "the Court's position as the principal judicial organ of the United Nations suggests that the legal consequence for a finding that an act or situation is illegal is the same" as a binding decision of a UN organ acting under Articles 24 and 25 of the UN Charter.[48] The Court's Advisory Opinion includes clear findings that the construction of the Wall and its associated regime are contrary to international law and that the Israeli settlements established on the West Bank (including East Jerusalem) are in breach of international law.

The fact that the ICJ concluded that the obligations violated by Israel's construction of the Wall include certain obligations *erga omnes*, i.e., obligations that all states must observe and which constitute *intransgressible* principles or "super-rules" of international law, means that those obligations transcend, as it were, the nonbinding Opinion that refers to them.[49] In other words, these obligations can be said to apply to Israel and other

---

46. *Id.* As mentioned above, Israel does not recognize Palestinian statehood. In the case of military operations forming part of an armed conflict (including in occupied territory), the conditions of international humanitarian law apply, which include that of absolute military necessity under Article 53 of the Fourth Geneva Convention. *Id.* at para. 135, *reprinted in* 43 I.L.M. at 1048.

47. As a free handbook issued by the ICJ Registry explains, "the authority and prestige of the Court attach to its advisory opinions and . . . where the organ or agency concerned endorses that opinion, that decision is as it were sanctioned by international law." THE INTERNATIONAL COURT OF JUSTICE 87 (4th ed. 1996), *available at* http://www.icj-cij.org/icjwww/igeneralinformation/ibbook/Bbookchapter6.HTM (last visited Mar. 6, 2005).

48. Wall Opinion, 2004 I.C.J. 131, para. 38, *reprinted in* 43 I.L.M. at 1064 (Higgins, J. separate opinion). According to Article 25 of the UN Charter, "[t]he Members of the United Nations agree to accept and carry out the decisions of the Security Council in accordance with the present Charter." U.N. CHARTER art. 25.

49. *See* Wall Opinion, 2004 I.C.J. 131, paras. 88, 155-57, *reprinted in* 43 I.L.M. at 1034, 1053. In this context, the ICJ referred to the Palestinian people's right to self-determination and fundamental principles of international humanitarian law. *See id.*

states independently of the Court's Opinion. Israel may attack the ICJ as the messenger, but the message itself is indeed of an intransgressible nature.

VIII. Implementation

As a first step toward implementation of the ICJ's ruling, the UN General Assembly voted overwhelmingly (150-6) to acknowledge the Advisory Opinion and to demand Israel's compliance on July 20, 2004, while deciding "to reconvene to assess the implementation of the present resolution."[50] This represents only the third instance in which the Assembly has decided on follow-up action after receiving an advisory opinion, having received a dozen since 1945.[51]

This development means that we now know the legal position regarding core aspects of the Israeli-Palestinian problem, including the Wall and the settlements, as judicially determined by the ICJ in its Advisory Opinion and as acknowledged by the General Assembly, the UN organ endowed with primary responsibility for the question of Palestine. The Opinion thus represents what one of Israel's leading international law scholars has called the law at large recognized by the United Nations.[52] That law represents the will of the international community. As a UN member state, Israel is bound by that law, as are all the other member states.

The July 20, 2004 resolution specifically considered that "respect for the International Court of Justice and its functions is essential to the rule of law and reason in international affairs."[53] Yet Israel's Finance Minister

---

50. Advisory Opinion of the International Court of Justice on the Legal Consequences of the Construction of a Wall in the Occupied Palestinian Territory, Including in and Around East Jerusalem, U.N. GAOR, 10th Emergency Special Sess., U.N. Doc. A/RES/ES-10/15 (2004). The six UN member states voting against the resolution were Australia, Federated States of Micronesia, Israel, Marshall Islands, Palau, and the United States. General Assembly Emergency Session Overwhelmingly Demands Israel's Compliance With International Court of Justice Opinion, U.N. Doc. GA/10248 (July 20, 2004).

51. The UN Committee on the Exercise of the Inalienable Rights of the Palestinian People convened a "United Nations Meeting on the Question of Palestine" with the theme "Implementing the ICJ Advisory Opinion on the Legal Consequences of the Construction of a Wall in the Occupied Palestinian Territory—the role of Governments, intergovernmental organizations and civil society" at the United Nations Office in Geneva, Switzerland, on March 8-10, 2005. *See* UN Meeting on Question of Palestine Discusses Responsibility of Governments in Upholding International Law, U.N. Doc. GA/PAL/981 (Mar. 9, 2005).

52. SHABTAI ROSENNE, 3 THE LAW AND PRACTICE OF THE INTERNATIONAL COURT, 1920-1996, at 1756-57 (3d ed. 1997).

53. The importance of the rule of law rightly was stressed in the UN Secretary-General's address to the 59th Session of the General Assembly: "[T]oday the rule of law is at risk around the world. Again and again, we see fundamental laws shamelessly disregarded—those that ordain respect for innocent life, for civilians, for the vulnerable—especially children." Kofi Annan, Secretary-General's Address to the General Assembly (Sept. 21, 2004), *available at* http://www.un.org/apps/sg/sgstats.asp?nid=1088 (last visited Mar. 6, 2005). As examples, the Secretary-General referred to the destruction of homes and land seizure in Palestine and "needless civilian casualties caused by Israel's excessive use of force." *Id.* The ICJ concluded, inter alia, that the Wall violates funda-

wrote in the *New York Times*, in reaction to the ICJ's ruling, that "the government of Israel will ignore it."[54] The Sharon administration has kept true to this pledge not to comply with the obligations mentioned in the ICJ's ruling. This stance puts at risk Israel's claim that it is the only law-abiding democracy in the Middle East,[55] for Israel's Supreme Court has ruled that Israeli law consists of both domestic law and customary international law.[56] "Law" also means international law (including intransgressible principles) binding on Israel. Israel cannot claim immunity from international law.[57] Israel's administrative, legislative and judicial organs must respect the primacy of international law.

Conclusion

There would have been no ICJ case had Israel built the Wall entirely on its own territory along the Green Line, as opposed to constructing it around illegal settlements in occupied Palestinian land, including East Jerusalem. It cannot credibly be said that Israel was treated unfairly in the ICJ proceeding or that the ICJ's ruling is one-sided as Israel has claimed.

Israel had the opportunity to participate fully in the written and oral phases of the proceeding and to submit to the ICJ whatever evidence it deemed fit. It chose not to address the merits in the written phase and it elected not to participate at all in the oral phase.[58] The ICJ's ruling contains many paragraphs addressing arguments that Israel chose not to plead

mental rights proclaimed in the United Nations Convention on the Rights of the Child. Wall Opinion, 2004 I.C.J. 131, para. 134, *reprinted in* 43 I.L.M. at 1048.

54. *See* Benjamin Netanyahu, *supra* note 14.

55. On April 11, 2005, Israel's Prime Minister Ariel Sharon stated after an official meeting with U.S. President George W. Bush: "I wish to reiterate that Israel is a society governed by the rule of law." *Bush Urges Freeze on West Bank Settlement*, CNN.COM, Apr. 12, 2005, *available at* http://www.cnn.com/2005/WORLD/meast/04/11/bush.mideast/index.html (last visited Apr. 20, 2005).

56. *See* Rotem Giladi, *The Practice and Case Law of Israel in Matters Related to International Law*, 31 ISR. L. REV. 803 (1997).

57. Israel's contention that the Israeli Supreme Court "alone has the capacity to fully address all aspects of" the Wall matter underscores Israel's claim to such immunity. Israeli Statement, *supra* note 10. As Judge Schwebel (U.S.) stated in his separate opinion attached to the PLO Mission Opinion: "[o]n the international legal plane, national law cannot derogate from international law, . . . a State cannot avoid its international responsibility by the enactment of domestic legislation which conflicts with its international obligations." PLO Mission Opinion, 1988 I.C.J. 12, 42 (Apr. 26) (Schwebel, J., separate opinion). The same considerations apply to the decisions of a state's highest court that go against the state's international obligations. The ICJ held that "[a]ll legislative and regulatory acts adopted with a view to [the Wall's] construction, and to the establishment of its associated régime, must forthwith be repealed or rendered ineffective [by Israel]." Wall Opinion, 2004 I.C.J. 131, para. 151, *reprinted in* 43 I.L.M. at 1052. In addressing this point, there is no margin of appreciation left for Israel's Government or courts.

58. The United Nations, 44 of its member states (including Israel), Palestine, the League of Arab States, and the Organization of the Islamic Conference all filed written statements within the time limit fixed by the ICJ in an Order dated December 19, 2003. *See* ICJ Communiqué 2004/5 (Feb. 3, 2004). During February 23-25, 2004, the ICJ heard the oral statements of 12 UN member states representing four different regions (South Africa; Algeria; Saudi Arabia; Bangladesh; Belize; Cuba; Indonesia; Jordan; Mada-

during the oral phase.[59] The ICJ emphasized that "both Israel and Palestine are under an obligation scrupulously to observe the rules of international humanitarian law," and that "[i]llegal actions and unilateral decisions have been taken on all sides. . . ."[60]

Nobody questions Israel's right to protect its citizens against violent attacks that the Palestinian leadership unequivocally has condemned, so long as Israel complies with international law. Noting that "Israel has to face numerous indiscriminate and deadly acts of violence against its civilian population," the ICJ confirmed that Israel "has the right, and indeed the duty, to respond in order to protect the life of its citizens," but at the same time reminded Israel that any "measures taken are bound nonetheless to remain in conformity with applicable international law"—a requirement that the Wall, in its location and operation, fails to meet.[61]

The July 9, 2004 Opinion has become the yardstick for measuring Israel's compliance with international law. In evaluating how to respond to the adverse ruling, Israel and other states should consider that countries that are the target of ICJ rulings by and large comply with such rulings to avoid being considered an outlaw or "rogue" member of the community of nations, defying international law and undermining the authority of the principal judicial organ of the United Nations. No state is immune from international law, and the ICJ plays an essential "guardian" role in protecting the primacy of the intransgressible principles of international law identified by it.

The ICJ's findings in the Wall Opinion are rooted in international law and have the strength of that law. The ruling constitutes a most powerful reminder that the question of Palestine, in all its facets, is subject to inter-

---

gascar; Malaysia; Senegal; and Sudan), in addition to the League of Arab States, the Organization of the Islamic Conference, and Palestine.

59. The ICJ took the first 65 paragraphs of its 1635-paragraph ruling to analyze Israel's procedural objections (which the ICJ rejected unanimously), even though Israel chose not to participate in the hearings and plead those objections, and it devoted several pages to the merits of arguments that Israel did not even make in its written statement of January 30, 2004.

60. Wall Opinion, 2004 I.C.J. 131, para. 162, *reprinted in* 43 I.L.M. at 1054. Israel obtained knowledge of Palestine's legal arguments more than two weeks before January 30, 2004, the deadline for filing written statements with the ICJ, after the Israeli authorities at Ben Gurion International Airport in Tel Aviv temporarily confiscated (and presumably made copies of) all of the documents in the possession of three members of Palestine's ICJ team returning from a team meeting in Geneva, Switzerland, on January 12, 2004. This prompted Palestine's Permanent Observer to the United Nations to file an official complaint with the UN Secretary-General on January 14, 2004.

61. *Id.* at para. 141, *reprinted in* 43 I.L.M. at 1050. As aptly summarized by one scholar:

> It is important to appreciate that the Court is not objecting to the security wall as a means of insulating Israeli society against Palestinian terrorism, but to the construction of the wall on occupied Palestinian territory and the evident effort to incorporate almost 80 percent of the Israeli settlements (including 320,000 of about 400,000 settlers), which were established in violation of Article 49(6) of the Fourth Geneva Convention.

Richard A. Falk, *Toward Authoritativeness: The ICJ Ruling on Israel's Security Wall*, 99 Am. J. Int'l L. 42, 47 (2005).

national law. The General Assembly's acknowledging resolution demanded (1506) not that Israel and all UN member states comply with the nonbinding ruling of the ICJ, but that they comply with "the legal obligations as mentioned in the Advisory Opinion," thereby underscoring that the focus should not be on the ICJ as the messenger, but on those legal obligations.

Useful lessons can be learnt from history. Namibia, which once was occupied by South Africa against the will of the international community, gained independence in 1990, nineteen years after the ICJ issued its Advisory Opinion that paved the way for Namibian statehood. While there are important differences between the Namibian situation and the Israeli-Palestinian crisis, there is no reason why the ICJ's ruling of July 9, 2004 should not prove to be a similar catalyst for change in the situation between Israel and Palestine and will lead, in the shortest possible term, to what the principal judicial organ of the United Nations described as "the establishment of a Palestinian State, existing side by side with Israel and its other neighbors, with peace and security for all in the region."[62] In attaining that goal, all those involved must respect the primacy of international law. As stated by Richard Falk, "Anyone who believes in the rule of law in international affairs should be encouraged by the approach taken by the Court, so widely and impressively endorsed in this advisory opinion."[63]

---

62. Wall Opinion, 2004 I.C.J. 131, para. 162, *reprinted in* 43 I.L.M. at 1054.
63. Falk, *supra* note 61, at 46.

Leiden Journal of International Law, 19 (2006), pp. 393–440
© Foundation of the Leiden Journal of International Law   Printed in the United Kingdom   doi:10.1017/S0922156506003360

HAGUE INTERNATIONAL TRIBUNALS

The *Construction of a Wall* between The Hague and Jerusalem: The Enforcement and Limits of Humanitarian Law and the Structure of Occupation

AEYAL M. GROSS*

Abstract

The ICJ considered the Wall in terms of the structure of the Israeli occupation and the settlements, which is one of de facto annexation. By contrast, the Israeli HCJ uses proportionality to regulate within the occupation. This approach may be inherent in humanitarian law, but involves a misplaced transplantation of the proportionality doctrine and an imbalanced rights/security equation. Contrary to the HCJ's determination, which attributes the different conclusions of the two courts to the different factual backgrounds available to them, this article argues that they reflect the courts' variant attitudes towards the barrier and its place within the broader context of the occupation and its structure. The looming shadow of the ICJ affected the HCJ's decision. On critical questions of international law, however, a wall separates international law as articulated in The Hague and the decisions issued in Jerusalem, pointing to the need for a new articulation of existing theories on transnational legal processes.

Key words

Advisory Opinion on *Legal Consequences of the Construction of a Wall in the Occupied Palestinian Territory*; International Court of Justice; international humanitarian law; occupation; proportionality; transnational legal process

---

* Faculty of Law, Tel-Aviv University; agross@post.tau.ac.il. The author is grateful to Yaara Alon, Daphne Barak-Erez, Orna Ben-Naftali, Eyal Benvenisti, Sandy Kedar, Barak Medina, Keren Michaeli, Avner Pinchuk, Amnon Reichman, and Yuval Shany for their comments on a previous draft of this article. He also benefited from conversations with Hanoch Dagan and Karen Knop. Thanks to Nimrod Karin for his extensive and excellent research assistance. He is also grateful to Batya Stein for providing her excellent editing and language skills and her invaluable contribution to the article. Thanks are due to the Cegla Center for Interdisciplinary Research of the Law at Tel Aviv University for a grant that made the research for this article possible. Earlier versions of this article were presented in the Faculty Workshop of Tel-Aviv University Faculty of Law and in the Public Law Teachers Forum of the Israeli Association of Public Law; the author is grateful to the participants of both fora for their helpful comments. The author teaches international and constitutional law in the Faculty of Law of Tel-Aviv University. He is also a member of the board of the Association for Civil Rights in Israel (ACRI). ACRI's legal department represented and represents petitioners in some of the cases heard by the Israeli High Court of Justice discussed in this article. In the *Mara'abe* case, ACRI represented petitioners and also joined as one. The author participated in consultations concerning this and other cases involving the subject matter of this article. The opinions expressed in the article, however, are his own and should not be attributed to ACRI.

1. INTRODUCTION

The Advisory Opinion issued by the International Court of Justice (ICJ) on the *Legal Consequences of the Construction of a Wall in the Occupied Palestinian Territory*[1] in July 2004 has been the subject of extensive scholarly debate.[2] Some of the comments also addressed a parallel decision rendered nine days previously by the Israeli Supreme Court sitting as the High Court of Justice (HCJ) in the case of *Beit Sourik Village Council v. The Government of Israel*,[3] dealing with a section of the same separation barrier[4] examined by the ICJ.[5] The Advisory Opinion and the process in The Hague leading to it were also discussed at length in a second decision involving the barrier rendered by the HCJ 14 months later, in *Mara'abe v. The Prime Minister of Israel*.[6] In this judgment, the HCJ dealt with another section of the barrier and also discussed the status of the Advisory Opinion in domestic law, while addressing the differences between its own positions and those of the ICJ.

Many of the academic and non-academic analyses were extremely critical of the Advisory Opinion. Some opposed it altogether, either because they held that the Court should have refused the request to address this question or because they thought it had reached the wrong conclusion.[7] Others, who seemed to agree with the Court's decision to entertain the request and were at least partly supportive of its conclusions, argued that its legal and/or factual reasoning, or its procedural fairness, had been extremely flawed.[8]

---

1. *Legal Consequences of the Construction of a Wall in the Occupied Palestinian Territory* (Advisory Opinion), Judgment of 9 July 2004, (2004) 43 ILM 1999 (hereafter Advisory Opinion).
2. See especially the two symposia devoted to the Advisory Opinion: 'Agora: ICJ Advisory Opinion on *Construction of a Wall in the Occupied Palestinian Territory*', (2005) 99 AJIL 1; 'Special Double Issue: Domestic and International Judicial Review of the Construction of the Separation Barrier', (2005) 38 *Israel Law Review* 6.
3. HCJ 2056/04 *Beit Sourik Village Council v. The Government of Israel*, 58(5) P.D. 807 (2004), translated in (2005) 38 *Israel Law Review* 83 and (2005) 43 ILM 1099 (hereafter *Beit Sourik*).
4. The question of what to call the structure being built in the West Bank remains controversial. Although the title of this article cites the title of the ICJ Opinion, which used the term 'wall', others think the term 'fence' is more appropriate. Throughout the article, unless in a direct quote, I will use the term 'barrier' (or 'separation barrier'), which is perhaps the best description.
5. For articles that look at both cases together see G. Watson, 'The "Wall" Decision in Legal and Political Context', (2005) 99 AJIL 6; D. Kretzmer, 'The Advisory Opinion: The Light Treatment of International Humanitarian Law', (2005) 99 AJIL 88; D. Kretzmer, '"Introduction" to Special Double Issue: Domestic and International Judicial Review of the Construction of the Separation Barrier', (2005) 38 *Israel Law Review* 6; Y. Shany, 'Capacities and Inadequacies: A Look at the Two Separation Barrier Cases', (2005) 38 *Israel Law Review* 230; Y. Shany, 'Head against the Wall? Israel's Rejection of the Advisory Opinion on the *Legal Consequences of the Construction of a Wall in the Occupied Palestinian Territories*', in *Yearbook of International Humanitarian Law* 2004 (forthcoming); A. De Puy, 'Bringing Down the Barrier: A Comparative Analysis of the ICJ Advisory Opinion and the High Court of Justice of Israel's Ruling on Israel's Construction of a Barrier in the Occupied Territories', (2005) 13 *Tulsa Journal of International and Comparative Law* 275. Further elaborate discussion of the *Beit Sourik* decision is to be found in some of the articles in the *Israel Law Review* symposium issue, *supra* note 2.
6. HCJ 7957/04 *Mara'abe v. The Prime Minister of Israel* (not yet published) (hereafter *Mara'abe*), English translation available at http://elyon1.court.gov.il/files_eng/04/570/079/a14/04079570.a14.pdf.
7. See, e.g., M. Pomerance, 'The ICJ's Advisory Jurisdiction and the Crumbling Wall Between the Political and the Judicial', (2005) 99 AJIL 26; M. Pomerance, 'A Court of "UN" Law', (2005) 38 *Israel Law Review* 134; R. Wedgwood, 'The ICJ Advisory Opinion on the Israeli Security Fence and the Limits of Self-Defense', (2005) 99 AJIL 52; K. Calvo-Goller, 'More than a Huge Imbalance: The ICJ's Advisory Opinion on the Legal Consequences of the Construction of the Barrier', (2005) 38 *Israel Law Review* 165; R. Sabel, 'The International Court of Justice Decision on the Separation Barrier and the Green Line', (2005) 38 *Israel Law Review* 316.
8. See, e.g., I. Scobbie, 'Words My Mother Never Taught Me: "In Defense of the International Court"', (2005) 99 AJIL 76; A. Imseis, 'Critical Reflections on the International Humanitarian Law Aspects of the ICJ Wall

Critics favourably disposed to the ICJ's conclusions take a position resembling that of some of the ICJ's judges, who concurred with the result but added separate opinions criticizing the gaps in the ICJ's reasoning.[9] Some of them engage in attempts to understand why the ICJ's reasoning is lacking in many aspects,[10] while others fill in the 'missing pages'[11] in the Advisory Opinion and provide some of the reasoned and well-argued legal basis that they find to be missing.[12]

In this article I examine the Advisory Opinion and the HCJ rulings on the separation barrier (in, but not limited to, the *Beit Sourik* and *Mara'abe* judgments) as part of international law enforcement in general, focusing on International Humanitarian Law (IHL) regarding occupation and, specifically, on the Israeli occupation of the Occupied Palestinian Territory (OPT).

Throughout the article I consider the enforcement but also the limits of humanitarian law, pointing to conclusions that may be drawn from the legal proceedings conducted so far concerning the barrier. It is my argument that humanitarian law as applied by the HCJ uses the doctrine of proportionality to regulate a belligerent occupation. Although it may thereby alleviate some of the occupation's effects, the HCJ does not challenge this occupation's basic structure, which views the settlers' rights as security concerns that can justify placing restrictions on the rights of the local residents. I also argue that the HCJ's legal analysis involves a misplaced transplantation of doctrines of proportionality developed in international and domestic law to the context of occupation, leading to an imbalanced rights/security equation. Broader conclusions about the limits of the proportionality analysis and the validity of the separation between authority and proportionality are also suggested.

Unlike the HCJ, the ICJ did challenge the basic structure of Israeli occupation, which is one of a de facto annexation. I argue that, contrary to the HCJ's determination that attributed the differences between the conclusions reached by the two courts to the different factual backgrounds available to them, the different conclusions should mostly be attributed to the two courts' variant attitudes towards

---

Advisory Opinion', (2005) 99 AJIL 102; Kretzmer, 'The Light Treatment', *supra* note 5; Shany, 'Capacities and Inadequacies', *supra* note 5; O. Ben-Naftali, "*A la Recherche du Temps Perdu*": Rethinking Article 6 of the Fourth Geneva Convention in Light of the *Legal Consequences of the Construction of a Wall in the Occupied Palestinian Territory* Advisory Opinion', (2005) 38 *Israel Law Review* 211; T. Broude, 'The Legitimacy of the ICJ's Advisory Competence in the Shadow of the *Wall*', (2005) 38 *Israel Law Review* 189.

9. See especially the Separate Opinions of Judge Higgins, Judge Kooijmans, and Judge Owada. A critical view of the Court's reasoning was also taken by Judge Buergenthal, who dissented from the Court's decision to hear the case, and thus from the Advisory Opinion itself. In his Declaration, Judge Buergenthal also addressed the merits part of the Advisory Opinion, and pointedly criticized the gaps in the Court's reasoning.

10. See especially I. Scobbie, 'Smoke Mirrors and Killer Whales: The International Court's Opinion on the Israeli Barrier Wall', (2004) 5 *German Law Journal* 1107, available at http://www.germanlawjournal.com/print.php?id=495. Scobbie argues that the Court's drafting method sometimes makes its reasoning 'less candid than one might desire'. The Advisory Opinion, he suggests, seeks to convey only the 'lowest common denominator' of the various judicial opinions. For a similar explanation see L. Fisler Damrosch and B. Oxman, 'Agora: ICJ Advisory Opinion on *Construction of a Wall in the Occupied Palestinian Territory*: Editor's Introduction', (2005) 99 AJIL 1, at 1.

11. On 'missing pages' in a court's decisions in another context, see L. Baker, 'The Missing Pages of the Majority Opinion in *Romer v. Evans*', (1997) 68 *University of Colorado Law Review* 387; J. Halley, 'Gay Rights and the Courts – The Amendment 2 Controversy: *Romer v. Hardwick*', (1997) 68 *University of Colorado Law Review* 373.

12. See especially Imseis, *supra* note 8.

the questions of 'security' and of the barrier itself and its place within the broader context of the structure of the occupation.

I further argue that typical of the HCJ's discussion of these issues are artificial separations between security and politics, between authority and proportionality, and between different sections of the barrier. In its rulings, the HCJ accepted, but at the same time also rejected, Israel's security arguments regarding specific segments of the barrier and, in so doing, it took an unprecedented step by intervening in security arguments in the name of international law. I argue that the looming shadow of the Advisory Opinion issued in The Hague affected this HCJ decision. The story of the barrier, therefore, is an important case study for learning about the indirect influence of international law, which emerges here as limited: on critical questions of international law, a wall separates international law as articulated in The Hague and the HCJ's decisions given in Jerusalem. The two courts may thus be seen as talking *at* rather than *to* each other. Judicial proceedings surrounding the barrier, then, shed light on the need to rearticulate existing theories on transnational legal processes and on the dialogue between courts.

By the time the question of the barrier was referred to the ICJ in 2003, it had already been pending before the HCJ.[13] Both the *Beit Sourik* decision and the Advisory Opinion issued several days later held against the government of Israel, ruling, respectively, that the building of specific segments of the barrier, or of any parts of it built in the OPT, is illegal. Nevertheless, these decisions are also strikingly different: the ICJ Advisory Opinion looked at the building of the barrier as a whole, and the question the General Assembly asked the ICJ to address concerned the legal consequences 'arising from the construction of the wall being built by Israel, the occupying Power, in the Occupied Palestinian Territory, including in and around East Jerusalem'.[14] By contrast, the *Beit Sourik* case was limited to a section of the barrier located near Jerusalem. Note, however, that questions similar to the one addressed to the ICJ were at the same time pending before the HCJ too. The first of these more generalized petitions argued that building the barrier in the occupied territory is illegal under international law in general and the law of belligerent occupation in particular.[15] Of two others, one challenged the permits system associated with the barrier,[16] and another asked to change the arrangements concerning the gates in the barrier.[17] The petition concerning the permits system challenged the military orders declaring the area between the barrier and the Green Line[18] to be a closed military zone

---

13. The Israeli High Court of Justice enjoys original jurisdiction over petitions made against government agencies regarding their capacities as such. See Basic Law: The Judiciary, 38 L.S.I 181 (1984), Art. 15, available at http://www.mfa.gov.il/MFA/MFAArchive/1980_1989/Basic per cent20Law- per cent20The per cent20Judiciary.
14. UN Doc. A/RES/ ES-10/14, 10 Dec. 2003, quoted in Advisory Opinion, *supra* note 1, para. 1.
15. HCJ 9961/03 *Hamoked – The Center for the Defense of the Individual v. The Government of Israel* (pending).
16. HCJ 639/04 *The Association for Civil Rights in Israel v. The IDF Commander in Judea and Samaria* (pending).
17. HCJ 11344/03 *Faiz Salem v. The IDF Commander in Judea and Samaria* (pending). On 27 July 2005 the HCJ issued a decision within this petition, stating that it would hear it together with the petition in HCJ 639/04 challenging the permit regime.
18. The Green Line is the name given to the border that had existed between Israel and the West Bank, which was held by Jordan before the 1967 war, and thus currently marking the boundary between Israel and the occupied territories.

requiring its Palestinian residents to procure special permits to remain there. The other demanded that the gates in the barrier, through which Palestinians must pass in order to travel to work, school, and other services in the West Bank, remain open 24 hours a day rather than for limited periods, and that the army allow vehicles as well as agricultural and mechanical equipment to pass through. The first of these petitions would have allowed the HCJ to deal with the legality of building the barrier in the OPT as a whole, and in the two others the HCJ could have addressed several basic features of the barrier's functioning gravely impinging on the life of the Palestinian population. The HCJ chose to give preference to localized petitions, and the judgment it issued shortly before the ICJ gave its Advisory Opinion concerned one of the barrier's sections. In its second major decision concerning the barrier, in *Mara'abe*, the HCJ again dealt with a particular section. The effects of looking at the 'parts' rather than the 'whole' will be discussed throughout this article.

In section 2 of this article I analyse the Advisory Opinion and the basis for its holding that building the barrier in the OPT is illegal. This part discusses, *inter alia*, the ICJ's failure to distinguish, in its discussion of self-defence, between questions of *jus ad bellum* and questions of *jus in bello*. Section 3 deals with the major decisions of the HCJ on this issue. Section 4 considers how the HCJ engages the Advisory Opinion. Section 5 explores the effect that the decisions of both courts had on one another and on the barrier itself, and offers thoughts about the role and the limits of humanitarian law in this context. Finally, section 6 considers the place of the barrier within the structure of the occupation and the logic of separation. It looks at the barrier's role in the dissection of the occupied territory and the regulation of people's lives and bodies, based on ethnic criteria.

2. THE HAGUE: ONE OPINION, TWO ILLEGALITIES

The ICJ dealt with the barrier as a whole and found that building it in the OPT is illegal and that Israel is under an obligation to cease construction works, to dismantle the structure already built, to repeal or render ineffective all legislative and regulatory acts relating thereto, and to make reparations for all damages caused by the construction of the barrier.[19]

The ICJ relied on the Secretary-General's report, stating that, for most of its course, the barrier lies within the occupied territory 'and deviates from the Green Line to encompass settlements, while encircling Palestinian population areas'.[20] The ICJ further noted the large number of Palestinians who would be living in the area between the Green Line and the barrier and the administrative regime to which they would be subject; the area would be declared 'closed' and its residents would be unable to remain there unless they held a permit issued by the Israeli authorities. As reviewed by the ICJ, the regulations issued by the Israeli army determined that Israeli citizens, Israeli permanent residents, and those eligible to immigrate to Israel in accordance with the Law of Return (although the ICJ failed to say so explicitly,

---

19.   Advisory Opinion, *supra* note 1, paras. 149–53, 163.
20.   Ibid., para. 83.

this last is a synonym for Jews[21]) may remain in the closed area without a permit. The ICJ also noted that access to and exit from the closed area would be allowed only through gates to be opened infrequently and for short periods.[22]

The ICJ concluded that, in light of these circumstances, Israel had violated several binding international obligations when constructing the barrier and endorsing the associated regime.[23] The ICJ's determination of illegality rested on two arguments which constitute the main core of the decision.

2.1. The ICJ on the building of the barrier in the Occupied Territory

The first argument related to the 'big picture': the ICJ determined that it is apparent the barrier's route had been planned so as to include within Israel the great majority of Israeli settlements in the OPT; that these settlements are illegal pursuant to Article 49(6) of the Fourth Geneva Convention, which prohibits the transfer of population of an occupying power into the territory it occupies; that the route of the barrier may prejudge further negotiations between Israel and Palestine; and that Israel might use it to integrate the settlements and their means of access.[24] Thus the ICJ stated that it considered

> that the construction of the wall and its associated regime create a 'fait accompli' on the ground that could well become permanent, in which case, and notwithstanding the formal characterization of the wall by Israel as temporary, it would be tantamount to de facto annexation.[25]

---

21. The Law of Return, 5710-1950, 4 LSI 114 (1950), available at http://www.mfa.gov.il/MFA/MFAArchive/1950_1959/Law+of+Return+5710-1950.htm. The permit system was later changed in some aspects, including omission of the special status given specifically to non-Israeli Jews. However, for the most part the changes seem cosmetic only. See note 22, *infra*.

22. Advisory Opinion, *supra* note 1, paras. 84–5. A similar outline of the facts appears in the petitions brought to the HCJ mentioned above against the permits system and the gates' opening hours. See notes 16–17 and accompanying text, *supra*. In a brief to the HCJ submitted in *The Association for Civil Rights in Israel v. The IDF Commander in Judea and Samaria* (*supra* note 16), the Israeli army announced that it had identified problems affecting residents of the 'seam zone' in connection with the permit system and the location and opening times of the gates. The army recommended that the permits be replaced by permanent cards for residents of the 'seam zone' and also other changes, including extending the opening hours for gates serving agricultural purposes. Although the brief stated that these recommendations were already being implemented, it also indicated that residents of the 'seam zone' would still need a special card to be allowed to remain in the area where they live, valid for a period that will be determined by the Israeli army. Holders of this permanent resident card would be exempt from procuring a special permit to be in the 'seam zone', and the process for obtaining these cards would be simplified. The question remains whether the new permanent-resident cards system is not actually the same as the existing permits system, other than in name. Also, people not residing in the 'seam zone', but who need to enter it for work purposes, including farmers whose lands are located there, will still require special permits to enter it. Palestinians will be allowed to enter and exit the 'seam zone' only through the gates indicated in their permit. Meanwhile, new orders issued by the Israeli army changed the terms of the general permit allowing people to be present in the 'seam zone'. They now include Israeli citizens and residents, as well as visitors to Israel who hold a valid visa to Israel. The category of non-Israeli Jews was omitted, although those for the most part would fall under the category of visitors to Israel holding a valid visa. It seems, then, that the Palestinians, whether they reside in the 'seam zone' or need to enter it for any purpose, will de facto remain the only ones needing a special permit (or card) to be in this area. The changes are detailed in letters from the Legal Advisor's Office to the Judea and Samaria area in the Israeli Defense Forces to the Association of Civil Rights in Israel dated 20 Sept. 2005 and 20 Dec. 2005, and in military orders attached to the letters.

23. Advisory Opinion, *supra* note 1, para. 143. For an overview of the Advisory Opinion and its place within the Israeli–Palestinian conflict see P. J. I. M. De Waart, 'International Court of Justice Firmly Walled in the Law of Power in the Israeli–Palestinian Peace Process', (2005) 18 LJIL 467.

24. Advisory Opinion, *supra* note 1, paras. 119–20.

25. Ibid., para. 121.

The route of the barrier, said the ICJ, 'gives expression *in loco* to the illegal measures taken by Israel with regard to Jerusalem and the settlements'.[26] Based on the effect of the barrier on the Palestinian population, the large number of Palestinians who would live in encircled communities because of it, and the risk of further alterations to the demographic composition of the OPT, the ICJ also concluded that the construction of the barrier together with previous measures 'severely impedes the exercise by the Palestinian people of its right to self-determination, and is therefore a breach of Israel's obligation to respect this right'.[27]

2.2. The ICJ on violations of humanitarian and human rights norms resulting from the barrier

The second major pillar of the ICJ's decision concerning the illegality of the barrier touches on the violation of specific provisions of IHL and international human rights law. The ICJ examined Israel's actions and their effect on the lives of Palestinians in the OPT in the light of certain provisions in the Fourth Geneva Convention,[28] the Hague Regulations of 1907, the International Covenant on Civil and Political Rights, the International Covenant on Economic, Social, and Cultural Rights, and the Convention on the Rights of the Child. The rights said to be infringed through the violation of these provisions include liberty of movement and the rights to work, health, education, and an adequate standard of living, besides provisions concerning the protection of property.[29] Information that Palestinians living between the barrier and the Green Line would be cut off from their land, workplaces, schools, health clinics, and other social services was pertinent to the ICJ's determination on this matter.[30] In a succinct discussion, the ICJ determined that none of the exceptions to provisions of humanitarian and human rights law applied here; that no military exigencies justified exceptions to some of the relevant provisions of the Hague Regulations and the Fourth Geneva Convention; that no such exigencies existed in the context of other provisions in ways that might allow acts regularly prohibited, and that the violation of those human rights that might be limited in the name of national security or public order do not conform with the principle of proportionality required for their limitation.[31] Moreover, in this particular case, no viable 'state of necessity' argument could be used to protect Israel's actions, since the ICJ was not convinced that the construction of the barrier along the chosen route was the only means of safeguarding the Israeli interests at stake.[32] The ICJ also rejected

---

26. Ibid., para. 122.
27. Ibid. The ICJ noted that these demographic changes might result from Palestinians being forced to depart from certain areas as a result of the barrier. Ibid., para. 133. For a comprehensive discussion of self-determination in this context see J. F. Gareau, 'Shouting at the Wall: Self-Determination and the Legal Consequences of the Construction of a Wall in the Occupied Palestinian Territory', (2005) 18 LJIL 489.
28. The ICJ confined its analysis to provisions that continue to apply after the cut-off date, namely one year after the general closure of military operations, interpreting Art. 6 of the Fourth Geneva Convention to imply that only these provisions are applicable in the OPT. For a powerful critique of this position see Ben-Naftali, *supra* note 8. On this point, see also Imseis, *supra* note 8, at 105–9.
29. Advisory Opinion, *supra* note 1, paras. 123–37.
30. Ibid., para. 133.
31. Ibid., paras. 135–7.
32. Ibid., paras. 140–1.

the applicability of the self-defence argument to this case, and concluded that Israel could not rely on Article 51 of the United Nations Charter.[33]

This is the least satisfactory section of the ICJ Advisory Opinion. Concerning the handling of such issues as military exigency, proportionality of the limitation of rights in the name of national security and public order, and the question of 'necessity', hardly any explanation can be found for the ICJ's conclusions on these matters other than the repeated mantra that the ICJ is 'not convinced'[34] that any of these doctrines can justify Israel's actions, without any explanation as to *why* it is not convinced.[35]

The insufficient analysis of the self-defence question in the Advisory Opinion merits further discussion.[36] The ICJ rejected the argument offered by Israel in various fora stating that the building of the barrier was consistent with the right of states to use force in self-defence, as enshrined in Article 51 of the UN Charter. The ICJ dismissed this argument in a brief paragraph, noting that Article 51 recognizes the right of self-defence in the case of an armed attack by one state against another and that Israel does not claim that the attacks against it are imputable to a foreign state. The ICJ further noted that Israel exercised control over the OPT and that the threat originated from within this territory, so that the situation was different from that contemplated in Security Council Resolutions 1368 and 1373 following the 11 September 2001 terrorist attacks on the United States, and Israel could not therefore invoke these resolutions in support of its claim to be exercising a right to self-defence.[37]

Insofar as the ICJ meant that the doctrine of self-defence applies only to an armed attack by one state against another, I consider it to be wrong.[38] Yet the ICJ's attempt to distinguish the situation that led to the Security Council resolutions recognizing the United States' right to self-defence from the situation of Israel vis-à-vis Palestinian terror indicates that the ICJ might have admitted that self-defence *can* be invoked against non-state actors as well, though not when the attacks originate in a territory controlled by the party that claims to be acting in self-defence. This reasoning appears to be sensible, since granting an occupying power a right to self-defence shifts the structure of the occupation regime and gives the military commander in the occupied territory more powers than the law of occupation had intended. Military commanders have authority to take the actions needed to maintain security in the occupied territory and this, rather than the doctrine of self-defence, is the proper context for examining their conduct.[39]

---

33. Ibid., paras. 138–9.
34. Ibid., paras. 135, 137, 140.
35. For such critiques, see Advisory Opinion (Buergenthal), *supra* note 1. See also Watson, *supra* note 5, at 24; Shany, 'Capacities and Inadequacies', *supra* note 5, at 230–6; Kretzmer, 'The Light Treatment', *supra* note 5, at 98–9. Imseis, *supra* note 8, at 110–15, discusses in detail what he considers to be the ICJ's patent failure to give substantive reasons for its finding that Israel's construction of the barrier cannot be justified by military necessity, and offers reasons of his own.
36. For a comprehensive discussion see Scobbie, *supra* note 8.
37. Advisory Opinion, *supra* note 1, paras. 138–40.
38. Judge Higgins was critical of this view in her concurring opinion, but accepted this is a statement of the law as it stands. Advisory Opinion (Higgins), *supra* note 1, para. 33. In my view the law on this question at this time does not require an attack by a state.
39. For such a reading see also Scobbie, *supra* note 8. About the confusion between self-defence as a legal doctrine and the broader notions of security concerns see ibid., at 84. Thus I agree with the position taken by Judge

The ICJ (including the judges giving separate opinions) also erred in neglecting to note that the building of the barrier, even if conceived as a military action, should be examined in the context of *jus in bello* rather than *jus ad bellum*.[40] The situation in the OPT is one of belligerent occupation. The question of the barrier is not whether to oppose terror but through what means, a problem definitely within the purview of a military commander's authority in a belligerent occupation. Some characterize the situation in the OPT as one of 'armed conflict short of war' and consider that the laws of warfare have applied since the beginning of occupation or, at least, certainly since the outbreak of the Second Intifada. In their decisions on the barrier, both the ICJ and the HCJ failed to rule explicitly on this point and on the possible applicability of the laws of warfare. Determining that these laws apply might muddle the picture, granting the military commander greater authority than that possessed by him according to the law of belligerent occupation.[41] Although the Advisory Opinion seems to imply that the laws of warfare do not apply, the ICJ stopped short of fully addressing the issue.

Even if we were to assume that the laws of armed conflict rather than (or in addition to) those of belligerent occupation apply to this case at this time, the question of the barrier is still not one of *jus ad bellum* but one of *jus in bello*. The doctrine of self-defence is relevant only to the question of *jus ad bellum* and regulates the initial use of force. Examining the measures used by the belligerents through the prism of the self-defence doctrine and using it to justify specific acts is a highly

---

Kooijmans in his separate opinion (Advisory Opinion (Kooijmans), *supra* note 1, paras. 35–6) that the ICJ was wrong insofar as it stated that self-defence can only be a response to an armed attack by a state, but right in rejecting the application of the doctrine to an attack from a territory under a state's control. Judge Higgins found the ICJ's reasoning on the issue of self-defence unconvincing and described it as 'formalism of an unevenhanded sort'. She wondered why an occupying power loses the right to defend its own civilian citizens at home if the attack emanates from the occupied territory (Advisory Opinion (Higgins), *supra* note 1, para. 34). I would argue that the occupying power does have such a right but that, *within* the occupied territory it controls, it may only invoke the security needs of an occupying power rather than the right to self-defence. See Scobbie, *supra* note 10, paras. 51–2, 57–9. Alternatively, if we were to read the situation as one of ongoing armed conflict and maintain that the law of armed conflict applies, then, as noted in the text, self-defence will regulate the initial use of force rather than the legality of specific actions within it. One may also question Judge Higgins's determination whereby, if Palestine is enough of an entity to be part of the ICJ's proceedings and to benefit from humanitarian law, it is also enough of an entity for the prohibition of armed attack against others to apply (ibid., para. 34). The enjoyment of humanitarian law is not dependent on Palestine being or not being an entity but rather on the rights of human beings to enjoy this law. As to its invitation to the proceedings, I would say that here it is actually Higgins who is taking the side of formalism. To argue that since Palestine is enough of an entity for this purpose it is also an independent entity for the purpose of applying the law of self-defence is a formal conceptual position ignoring that, in placing Palestine in legal categories, it is proper to consider the purpose and the context of the classification.

    Judge Buergenthal in his Declaration (Advisory Opinion (Buergenthal), *supra* note 1, para. 6) also disagreed with the ICJ's determinations and expressed the view that the question of Israel's control is irrelevant, and that Israel can exercise the right to self-defence – if the conditions of necessity and proportionality are met – as long as the attacks come from outside Israel proper. For a view that the originating locus of an attack does not diminish a right of self-defence see also Wedgwood, *supra* note 7, at 57–9.

40. See Scobbie, *supra* note 8, at 83–4. For a discussion of the complex relationship between *jus ad bellum* and *jus in bello* in this context see also S. Murphy, 'Self-Defense and the Israeli Wall Advisory Opinion: An Ipse Dixit from the ICJ?', (2005) 99 AJIL 62; I. Canor, 'When *Jus ad Bellum* Meets *Jus in Bello*: The Occupier's Right of Self-Defence against Terrorism Stemming from Occupied Territories', (2006) 19 LJIL 129.

41. For an outline of the positions on this issue see Harvard Program on Humanitarian Policy and Conflict Research, 'The Separation Barrier and IHL', July 2004, available at http://www.ihlresearch.org/opt/feature.php?a=36.

dangerous course that blurs the distinction between *jus ad bellum* and *jus in bello* and serves to legitimize any act that a military force may seek to take.[42]

In sum, the ICJ's determination of illegality is founded on two pillars. The first is a structural analysis of the barrier's place in the broader context of the occupation. The barrier, like the settlements, is perceived as part of an impending de facto annexation of the territory that also entails changing its demographic structure, violating the Palestinians' right to self-determination and prejudging the result of further negotiations. The second is a humanitarian and human rights analysis of the violation of specific provisions within the law of occupation and IHL and within human rights law. The two are obviously connected, since the ICJ assumes that violating the rights of Palestinians living in the 'seam zone' may force them to leave the area, so that the barrier and its associated regime will entail consequences for the demography of the occupied territory.

3. JERUSALEM: *EX ANTE* AND *EX POST*

Both in the *Beit Sourik* and in the later *Mara'abe* rulings, the HCJ discussed questions involving the structural nature of the barrier as well as the violation of specific rights. In both decisions its answers concerning the nature of the barrier are very different from and less satisfactory than those of the ICJ, whereas its answers concerning the violation of rights tend to resemble those of the ICJ but, at least ostensibly, rely on far more solid reasoning.

3.1. HCJ *ex ante: Beit Sourik*

The HCJ ruling, issued several days before the ICJ opinion, deals with the challenge of the *Beit Sourik* village council, as well as other village councils and affected landowners, to the legality of the orders to seize plots in eight villages for the purpose of erecting the separation barrier.[43] The HCJ examined the issue within the framework of the law of belligerent occupation, applying the Hague Regulations, the Fourth Geneva Convention (applied de facto[44]), and Israeli administrative law.[45]

The judgment, like others issued by the HCJ after the beginning of the Second Intifada, offers an account of the events leading to the erection of the barrier. After

---

42. For a discussion of the importance of maintaining the distinction between *jus ad bellum* and *jus in bello* see section 3.1.2, *infra*. Scobbie joins some of the critiques of the ICJ's determination on self-defence, but agrees with the ICJ's rejection of Israel's claims on this matter, partly out of agreement with Judge Higgins's scepticism about the applicability of the doctrine to non-forcible measures. Without taking a position on this complex question, I agree with Scobbie's determination that 'to state the proposition that measures taken in self-defence may exculpate a State from responsibility for violations of IHL is to demonstrate both the fallacy and danger at the heart of the Israeli argument. It is to claim that the law designed to restrain the exercise of force does not apply when force is being exercised.' Scobbie, *supra* note 10, paras. 44–59.

43. *Beit Sourik, supra* note 3, para. 9.

44. The HCJ noted that it will examine the matter under the Fourth Geneva Convention, notwithstanding the controversy about its applicability in the OPT, 'since the parties agree that the humanitarian rules of the Fourth Geneva Convention apply to the issue under review' (ibid., para. 23). On the question of the status of the Fourth Geneva Convention in Israeli Courts see notes 137 and 211–216 and accompanying text, *infra*.

45. *Beit Sourik, supra* note 3, paras. 23–4.

briefly mentioning that Israel had been holding the area in belligerent occupation since 1967, and following a short description of the Oslo process and the failure of the Camp David negotiations in 2000, the HCJ said that it learned from the respondent's affidavit that 'a short time after the failure of the Camp David talks ... in September 2000, the Palestinian side began a campaign of terror against Israel and Israelis'. As of April 2004, noted the HCJ, the conflict had claimed the lives of 900 Israeli citizens and residents, while more than 6,000 had been injured. The HCJ also noted that 'the armed conflict has left many dead and wounded on the Palestinian side as well'.[46] This description of the background to the establishment of the barrier portrays what happened at the beginning of the Second Intifada as a campaign of terror against Israel and Israelis. Alternative narratives, however, are obviously possible. Notably, the Second Intifada broke out as an immediate reaction to a visit to Temple Mount/Haram al-Sharif by then opposition leader Ariel Sharon. During the following days, as a response to stones thrown at Jewish worshippers from the el-Aqsa mosque, Israeli security forces entered the area around the mosque and fired at the crowd, killing five Palestinians and injuring 200 more. These events sparked a cycle of violence.[47]

Not only are there different perspectives on the background, reasons, and course of the Intifada,[48] but the actual circumstances of its beginning (Palestinians killed by Israelis rather than the opposite) are excluded from the HCJ's discourse. This exclusion is important to the eventual framing of the issue as one of Israeli security versus Palestinian terror rather than of Palestinian security versus Israeli military violence. Moreover, the Palestinian toll of victims, not cited by the HCJ, has been significantly higher than that of Israelis and, as of November 2005, amounted to 3,366 dead and over 29,000 wounded.[49]

In adopting this narrative the HCJ placed its discussion in the context of the need to defend Israel and Israelis from a terrorist campaign launched by the Palestinians rather than in the context of the occupation and the settlements.[50] The process of establishing the barrier is thus described as a link in the chain of events described in this narrative. The government decision to establish the barrier cited by the HCJ describes it as a 'security measure for the prevention of terror attacks [which] does not mark a national border or any other border'.[51]

---

46. Ibid., para. 1.
47. See O. Ben-Naftali and K. R. Michaeli, '"We Must Not make a Scarecrow of the Law": A Legal Analysis of the Israeli Policy of Targeted Killings', (2003) 36 *Cornell International Law Journal* 233, at 241, and the sources cited therein.
48. Ibid., at 241–7 (where they discuss the Rashomon quality of the Second Intifada), and the sources cited therein.
49. All data taken from B'Tselem, the Israeli Centre for Human Rights in the Occupied Territories, available at http://www.btselem.org/English/Statistics/Index.asp.
50. As opposed to graphic descriptions of Palestinian terror, mention of the Israeli occupation is confined in the HCJ's Hebrew original to the term '*tefisah lohmatit*' (belligerent occupation), a technical legal term lacking any of the overtones attached to the Hebrew word for occupation (*kibbush*). Ibid., citing a previous ruling (HCJ 7015/02 *Ajuri v. The IDF Commander of the West Bank* 56(6) P.D. 352 (2002), English translation available at http://elyon1.court.gov.il/files_eng/02/150/070/a15/02070150.a15.pdf), which includes this description and was later canonized by the HCJ through recurrent quoting.
51. Cited in *Beit-Sourik, supra* note 3, para. 6. Interestingly, the emphasis on the statement that the barrier is not a border was probably included in the government decision in order to conciliate the Israeli right wing that

As for its effect on the Palestinians, the petition described how the barrier would prevent access to agricultural lands. It stated that tens of thousands of olive trees and fruit trees would be uprooted, and the petitioners' ability to move from place to place would become dependent on a labyrinthine, complex, and burdensome permit regime. It further described the barrier's negative effects on the livelihood of residents of these villages and on their access to urban areas, including medical, educational, and other services.[52]

The HCJ addressed the argument that the military orders are illegal because building the barrier within the occupied territory alters the borders of the West Bank without express legal authority, annexing areas to Israel in violation of international law using a smokescreen of security arguments,[53] and because it violates many rights of the local residents, specifically the rights to property, freedom of movement, and freedom of occupation and livelihood. Violations of access to education and of freedom of religion were also cited.[54]

Beyond its proximity to the ICJ hearings, the *Beit Sourik* litigation was unique in at least two more ways. The first was an *amici curiae* brief submitted by members of the Council for Peace and Security (CPS), a non-governmental organization comprising retired high-ranking officers of the Israeli army. The brief criticized the route chosen for the barrier, stating that its proximity to the houses in the Palestinian villages was not only unnecessary from a security perspective but, due to the serious injury to the local population and the consequent friction, actually detrimental to security.[55] The second is that the petitioners were joined by Israeli-Jewish residents from Mevaseret Zion, a nearby town, who claimed that the barrier's route should be coextensive with the Green Line so as to allow Beit Sourik villagers to work their land, and noted that the building of the barrier had led to a deterioration in their relationship with the Palestinian residents.[56]

The HCJ thus considered two questions: whether the military commander was authorized to build the barrier in the occupied territory and, if so, the legality of the barrier's location, although it noted that the parties had focused mainly on the second question.

3.1.1. Beit Sourik: *the HCJ on the legality of building the barrier in the occupied territory*
Addressing the first question,[57] the HCJ accepted the petitioners' argument that the military commander could not order the construction of the barrier if his reasons were political. The HCJ determined that the military commander in a belligerent occupation had to balance the army's needs against those of the local inhabitants and

---

has traditionally opposed the barrier as a potential border for Israel that would leave out much of the West Bank. On the link between the barrier's route and Israel's permanent borders see note 152 and accompanying text, *infra*.

52. *Beit Sourik, supra* note 3, para. 9.
53. Ibid., para. 10.
54. Ibid., para. 11.
55. *Beit Sourik, supra* note 3, paras. 18, 54, 64, 71, 78.
56. Ibid., para. 22. Another Israeli citizen appearing before the HCJ argued the opposite: bringing the barrier close to the homes of the Jewish residents would endanger them.
57. While noting it does not 'exhaust' it. Ibid., para. 25.

there was no room for additional considerations, be they political views, territorial annexation, or establishing the country's permanent borders. The HCJ determined that the belligerent occupation was temporary and the authority of the military commander was temporary,[58] concluding that the decision to build the barrier had been driven by security rather than political motives and accepting the government's statement that the barrier's course had not been meant to delimit the country's borders.[59] The HCJ thus held that, in principle, seizing land to build the barrier might fit the relevant provision of international law, which allows taking property for permitted military needs as long as the needs of the local population are taken into account.[60] Having determined this, the HCJ proceeded to discuss the second question, dealing with the chosen route per se.

On the first question, therefore, involving the authority to build the barrier in the OPT, the HCJ took a very different view from that of the ICJ. The petitioners' arguments in *Beit Sourik*, which the HCJ rejected, resembled the claims on which the Advisory Opinion had relied when dealing with the establishment of the barrier. The ICJ had seen the barrier's route as overlapping the settlements, creating a 'fait accompli' that might become permanent and tantamount to de facto annexation. The HCJ rejected this position, not only because it adopted a different perspective on the issues at stake but because it confined its discussion to a specific section of the barrier that, for the most part, involved no settlements.[61] The logic of the ICJ Advisory Opinion, winding a course from the Israeli occupation through de facto annexation and up to the denial of Palestinian self-determination that results from the settlements, is absent from the *Beit Sourik* judgment. Hence the HCJ could focus in its holding on specific violations of the residents' rights and avoid the larger issue. On these specific issues, its conclusions were close to those of the ICJ.

3.1.2. Beit Sourik: *the HCJ on the violations of humanitarian norms resulting from the barrier*

In discussing the route of the barrier the HCJ strove to strike a balance between the military commander's authority to maintain security in the area and protect the security of his country and its citizens, and the rights, needs, and interests of the local population.[62] A foundational principle in this balance, said the HCJ, was proportionality: individual liberty can be limited on condition that the restriction is proportionate to the objective. The HCJ viewed this as a significant principle of international law (and specifically of the law of belligerent occupation) and as

---

58. Ibid., paras. 26–7.
59. Whereas the petitioners argued that a security barrier should have been constructed on the Green Line, the HCJ said the opposite was true: the barrier's route must be determined by security considerations rather than by the location of the Green Line (ibid., paras. 28–31).
60. Ibid., paras. 32–3.
61. The HCJ mentioned in passing an area within a West Bank settlement as deserving the barrier's defence, without even mentioning that it is beyond the Green Line. Ibid., para. 80.
62. Ibid., para. 34.

a central standard of Israeli administrative law, which applies to the area under belligerent occupation.[63]

The HCJ's discussion of proportionality in IHL rested on sources pointing to its importance within humanitarian law (i.e., within *jus in bello*) and focusing on the prohibition on the disproportionate use of force:[64] 'Belligerents shall not inflict harm on their adversaries out of proportion with the object of warfare, which is to destroy or weaken the strength of the enemy.'[65] I will argue that this notion of proportionality, as a humanitarian principle of *jus in bello*, is different from that applied in the *Beit Sourik* judgment. Contrary to the demand that the use of force be regulated by principles of proportionality at both the *jus ad bellum* and *jus in bello* levels, the HCJ ruling transplants[66] these principles to the relationship between the military commander and the people under occupation.

Proportionality has a place in both *jus ad bellum* and *jus in bello* in constraining the use of force. Its meaning in each of these contexts, however, is very different. In *jus ad bellum*, it sets limits on a belligerent's overall response to a grievance. In *jus in bello*, currently culminating in IHL, it determines the balance to be struck between the achievement of a military goal and its cost in terms of lives and destruction of civilian property. Regarding combatants, who are legitimate targets in armed conflict, IHL rules on proportionality are intended to prevent unnecessary suffering or superfluous injury. Regarding civilians, who are not legitimate objects of attack, proportionality seeks to protect them from the collateral effects of armed conflict.[67] In *jus ad bellum*, then, it considers whether an act of force in self-defence is a proportional response to an attack. In *jus in bello*, regarding civilians, it determines to what extent they are entitled to protection from the collateral effects of armed conflict, and examines the acts in question vis-à-vis the legitimate object to be achieved.[68]

---

63. Ibid., para. 36. Although Israeli law does not apply to the OPT as such, the HCJ has repeatedly ruled in the past that it would examine the actions of the Israeli army in the OPT according to Israeli administrative law as well, since this law is binding on Israeli army authorities. See HCJ 393/82 *Jamait Askan v. The IDF Commander in Judea and Samaria*, 37(4) P.D. 785, 810 ('Every Israeli soldier carries in his backpack the norms of public and customary international law, which regard the rules of war, as well as the basic norms of Israeli administrative law.')

64. *Beit Sourik, supra* note 3, para. 37.

65. J. Pictet, *Developments and Principles of International Humanitarian Law* (1985), at 62.

66. The term is borrowed from A. Watson, *Legal Transplants: An Approach to Comparative Law* (1993).

67. J. Gardam, 'Proportionality as a Restraint on the Use of Force', (1999) 20 *Australian Yearbook of International Law* 161, at 162, 164–5. The latter meaning of proportionality is currently incorporated into Protocol 1 of the Fourth Geneva Convention, to which Israel is not a party (ibid., at 165). For a detailed discussion of the history of proportionality in international law and problems inherent in the concept see E. Jaworski, '"Military Necessity" and "Civilian Immunity": Where is the Balance?', (2003) 2 CJIL 175. For a historical account of proportionality in international law on the use of force see also J. Gardam, 'Proportionality and Force in International Law', (1993) 87 AJIL 391.

68. Gardam, 'Proportionality as a Restraint', *supra* note 67, at 164–5; R. Higgins, *Problems and Process: International Law and How We Use It* (1994), at 231. Gardam argues that only proportionality in the *jus in bello* derived traditionally from humanitarian considerations, whereas in *jus ad bellum* the limitations of proportionality related to the minimization of the disruption of international peace and security. At present, however, proportionality in the context of the *jus ad bellum* has a humanitarian component, namely to achieve a reasonable balance between the achievement of the legitimate goals of the state claiming self-defence and the anticipated loss of life and suffering of those involved, especially civilians. Gardam, 'Proportionality as a Restraint', *supra* note 67, at 166. See also J. Gardam, 'Legal Restraints on Security Council Military Enforcement Action', (1995) 17 *Michigan Journal of International Law* 285, at 308. For a discussion of the use of the concept of proportionality in the ICJ's Advisory Opinion on The Legality of the Threat or Use of Nuclear Weapons,

The HCJ discussion of proportionality here does not distinguish between the two. Presumably, what should apply here is the proportionality of *jus in bello* or international humanitarian law,[69] which is the linchpin of modern humanitarian law.[70] Yet, beyond failing to make this distinction, the HCJ also determined that included in the military commander's security considerations were not only the security of the area but also the security of his country and its citizens, and then applies proportionality criteria to this issue.

Even more inadequate is the HCJ's transplant of proportionality principles from municipal administrative law. The HCJ referred to the pivotal role of the proportionality principle in Israeli constitutional and administrative law which governs the action of the Israeli army and thus applies to the duties of the military authority.[71] This move, however, is of questionable relevance. Proportionality is a valuable tool because it allows us to weigh conflicting considerations through a means–ends test. It is a consideration to be used with caution, however, because it shifts the human rights discourse to an analysis consistently focused on their infringement and on the extent to which violations are still 'proportional'. The use of this administrative principle in the context of a military occupation is particularly problematic. When used to review administrative action, the principle of proportionality assumes an accountable democratic government committed to the collective good of its citizens, but occasionally forced to violate the rights of whole or part of the population in order to attain legitimate ends. The benefits to the population are then weighed against the infringement of their rights, the point being that the benefits accrue to the *same* population whose rights were violated. But it is questionable whether this logic can apply when the government is a military occupier promoting the collective security interests of its *own* citizens while violating the rights of the people it occupies. Even more questionable is the applicability of this principle to Israel's military occupation: the establishment of settlements that channelled land, water, and rule of law resources to their own inhabitants at the expense of, and by means of the dispossession of, the Palestinian residents[72] makes the use of a proportionality perspective a dubious proposition indeed.

The notion of proportionality in administrative law developed as part of the idea of a free democracy, when the state's very attempt to maximize freedom can have the opposite effect of minimizing the freedom of the citizens. In this equation, the rule of proportionality is that one should only interfere with individual rights if and insofar as it is necessary to satisfy a compelling public interest.[73]

---

see J. Gardam, 'Necessity and Proportionality in *jus ad bellum* and *jus in bello*', in L. Boisson de Chazournes and P. Sands (eds.), *International Law, the International Court of Justice and Nuclear Weapons* (1999), 275.

69. On the relevance of *jus in bello* rather than *jus ad bellum* to the examination of the barrier, see notes 40–2 and accompanying text, *supra*.

70. Gardam, 'Proportionality as a Restraint', *supra* note 67, at 172.

71. *Beit Sourik*, *supra* note 3, para. 38.

72. On these policies as creating a breach of trust by the military commander see O. Ben-Naftali, A. Gross, and K. Michaeli, 'Illegal Occupation: Framing the Occupied Palestinian Territory', (2005) 23 *Berkeley Journal of International Law* 551, at 579–92.

73. N. Emiliou, *The Principle of Proportionality in European Law: A Comparative Study* (1996), 40–3. Emiliou points to this rationale for proportionality in his discussion of the principle as developed in German public law. The inadequacy of transplanting this framework to an occupation context is evident in Moshe

In its discussion of proportionality, then, the HCJ relied on sources that had developed this notion in different contexts and with different meanings, with dubious relevance to a military government engaged in a long-term occupation. Even if a proper distinction had been drawn between the two contexts of proportionality in international law and if we were to relate this only to the part dealing with IHL, we should still question its synthesis with domestic administrative law to create a rule of proportionality applicable to the military commander in a situation of belligerent occupation. In such a context a discourse on proportionality could serve to justify restrictions on the rights of the occupied population in the name of illegitimate goals, as is indeed discussed throughout this article, while actually validating acts banned by international law. If proportionality is measured, in Rosalyn Higgins's words, 'in

---

Cohen-Eliya's analysis of the use of proportionality in the *Beit Sourik* judgment. Cohen-Eliya distinguishes between 'formal' and 'substantive' meanings of proportionality: the former deals with an analysis of the logical and empirical connections between the declared purpose and the means chosen, while the latter deals with the balance between the realization of the declared purpose and the extent to which fundamental rights are infringed. He argues that a focus on the formal meaning of proportionality accords better with the skills of courts, and complies more fully with the democratic principle whereby decisions are determined by representatives expressing the will of a majority of the citizens. In his view, applying the substantive sense of the proportionality test in a limited manner is only justified when fundamental rights are violated, and only after a strict application of formal proportionality has not led to the striking down of the government policy. His argument is that the HCJ erred in *Beit Sourik* when basing its decision on the substantive sense of the proportionality tests, in violation of the democratic principle whereby decisions should be determined by the people's elected representatives. See M. Cohen-Eliya, 'The Formal and the Substantive Meanings of Proportionality in the Supreme Court's Decision Regarding the Security Fence', (2005) 38 *Israel Law Review* 262. This line of analysis illustrates the problem of transplanting the concept of proportionality from a context of administrative law to that of a belligerent occupation. Clearly, the people under occupation whose rights are violated by the barrier do not elect the Israeli government and the military commander making the decisions that affect their lives. The idea that courts should apply a restrained model of proportionality for democratic reasons is thus inconceivable in this context. His critique of the HCJ's reasoning as lacking democratic legitimacy (ibid., at 290) is striking given that the occupation regime is lacking in the basic principle of democratic legitimacy – the consent of the ruled. Although my critique of Cohen-Eliya might be read as suggesting that, in the context of the occupation, the HCJ should apply a strict, or what he calls 'substantive', proportionality analysis, I would rather suggest that it points to the inadequacy of this transplant and to the paradoxical places to which it may lead us. For an analysis that questions the appropriateness of applying another administrative law doctrine outside the context of an accountable democracy, see the discussion of the HCJ's use of reasonableness in the occupied territories in D. Kretzmer, *The Occupation of Justice: The Supreme Court of Israel and the Occupied Territories* (2002), at 69–70.

The problems entailed in analysing the HCJ's and ICJ's decisions on the barrier as if they involved the review of a legitimate democratic government's actions are also apparent in Yehudah Mirsky's critique of the Advisory Opinion. In Mirsky's view, the ICJ failed to distinguish between democratic and non-democratic regimes. It ignored the fact that Israel is a functioning democracy with a robust practice of judicial review and a state that has internalized democratic processes and values. Y. Mirsky, 'Human Rights, Democracy and the Inescapability of Politics: Or, Human Dignity Thick and Thin', (2005) 38 *Israel Law Review* 358. Mirsky contrasts the Advisory Opinion with the *Beit Sourik* judgment, where the HCJ was able to invalidate portions of the wall causing disproportionate injury to the local Palestinian population without denying the security context that brought 'a fundamentally law-abiding democracy to undertake actions that test the limits of legality' (ibid., at 367). Emanuel Gross, too, examines the question from the perspective of a democratic state's right to defend itself against terror, ignoring the fact that the issue is Israel's right to build the barrier in an occupied territory rather than a democracy's right to defend itself. See E. Gross, 'Combating Terrorism: Does Self-Defense Include the Security Barrier? The Answer Depends on Who You Ask', (2005) 38 *Cornell International Law Journal* 569, at 578, 582. This analysis is oblivious to the fact that Israel's rule over the Palestinians has created a non-democratic regime in the West Bank. The length of the occupation, the establishment of settlements, and the reliance on ethnicity criteria make it impossible to describe Israel's actions in this context as the defence of a democracy. In fact, this regime raises questions not only about the occupation but, more generally, about Israeli democracy itself. On this question see Ben-Naftali, Gross, and Michaeli, *supra* note 72, at 611, n. 329. In any event, Israel's long occupation of the West Bank can hardly be described as an internalization of democratic processes and values, and its actions there are hardly those of a law-abiding democracy.

respect of the object legitimately to be achieved,[74] it is clear that 'No conduct that fails to meet the specific requirements of the substantive *jus in bello* can be justified on grounds that it is still "proportionate".'[75] Indeed, proportionality is a limiting element of otherwise *permitted* harm.[76] Thus, insofar as building the barrier is viewed as a military action subject to the proportionality of IHL, we distort IHL, which forbids, as discussed throughout this article, the situation enabling the building of the barrier in the OPT in the first place. And insofar as it is viewed as subject to the proportionality of domestic law, we distort administrative law, which is structured around the concept of a government acting for the benefit of its citizens. The purported synthesis of the two when reviewing the actions of the military commander in an occupation, and especially in a long-term occupation where the military commander assumes many governmental duties, blurs and distorts their respective functions and objects, thereby casting a garb of legitimacy on an illegal endeavour, as is evident in the context of the Israeli occupation of the OPT. Proportionality may be a useful tool for examining the acts of the military commander when he exercises his authority for *legitimate* security causes, and when dealing with actions that IHL does not forbid *in toto*. For instance, IHL absolutely prohibits population transfers to the occupied territory or the deportation of protected persons from it,[77] but allows the destruction of civilian property if an absolute military need is present.[78] Proportionality thus may be used only in the latter of these contexts. One should be careful when developing even this limited doctrine, however, since the transplant of principles used to examine democratic governments to the context of an occupation leads to a slanted discourse about balance, when those who enjoy the benefits are not those whose rights are violated. The discourse is distorted even further by making the settlements part of the military commander's legitimate security concerns.

On closer scrutiny the proportionality analysis pursued by the HCJ in *Beit Sourik* reveals further limitations. The HCJ emphasized that it would not examine the military considerations of the military commander, an examination which requires professional expertise, and would only 'determine whether a reasonable military commander would have set out the route as this military commander did'.[79] Available to the HCJ, however, were the contradictory opinions of recognized military experts, in the *amici curiae* brief submitted by the CPS. Addressing this discrepancy, the HCJ said it would give special weight to the military opinion of the official responsible for security, and thus could not adopt the options proposed by the Council.[80] The HCJ made this determination when discussing the barrier's route, focusing on the authority of the military authority to erect it and defining it as a matter separate from the proportionality of the barrier's route. The distinction between these two issues, however, may not be as blunt as the HCJ indicated. The HCJ stated that the proportionality issue raised no military problems but dealt

---

74. Higgins, *supra* note 68, at 232 (emphasis in the original).
75. Ibid., at 234.
76. Ibid., at 232.
77. Fourth Geneva Convention, Art. 49.
78. Ibid., Art. 53.
79. *Beit Sourik, supra* note 3, para. 46.
80. Ibid., para. 47.

instead with the severity of the injury the route inflicts on the local residents: 'In the framework of this question we are dealing not with military considerations but rather with humanitarian considerations', and '[t]he question is the proportionality between the military consideration and the humanitarian consideration' that, as the HCJ emphasized, was a legal matter within its realm of expertise.[81]

Within this analysis the HCJ determined that three out of five segments of the barrier discussed in this case cause Palestinians disproportional injury.[82] It reached its conclusion on the basis of a segment-by-segment analysis, but also on an evaluation of the entire section of the barrier comprising these segments and of its effect on people's lives in general.[83]

The separation between issues of military and issues of legal expertise adopted by the HCJ, however, is far from convincing. The determination that the injury caused to the inhabitants by the barrier's route is not proportional must assume the existence of other options. As the HCJ itself noted, the question of proportionality required it to answer whether security considerations could have been met by building the barrier on a route causing less (and thus proportionate) injury to the local inhabitants.[84] Notwithstanding its reasoning, then, the HCJ's conclusion can only be interpreted as a rejection of the army's security argument, for the security argument is the one that justifies the current route and cannot be disentangled from the question of its proportionality.[85] It is hard to imagine that the HCJ could have reached this conclusion without taking into account the brief filed by the CPS. In deciding that segments of the barrier were not 'proportional', the HCJ cited the army's argument about the military need for choosing this route, the arguments about the route's effect on the local inhabitants, and the arguments of the CPS about alternative routes that would not only be less detrimental to local residents but also better from a security perspective. By dividing its inquiry concerning each segment into two, the HCJ was able to deal first with the military considerations and, on this matter, accepted the arguments of the army. It then proceeded to deal with the proportionality question and determined that the barrier's route did not fulfil the part of the proportionality requirement requiring that the injury caused to local inhabitants be proportionate to the security benefits accruing from the barrier in the chosen route.[86] The HCJ held that the relationship between the security benefits and the injury to the local inhabitants is not proportionate due to the severe injury

---

81. Ibid., para. 48.
82. Ibid., paras. 49–81.
83. Ibid., para. 82.
84. Ibid., para. 49.
85. Thus I agree with Cohen-Eliya that, notwithstanding its discourse to the contrary, the HCJ did examine the relative effectiveness of the current route vis-à-vis the proposed ones. Cohen-Eliya, *supra* note 73, at 285–6. I also agree with his observation that the HCJ did suspect that the true purpose of the barrier's route was not security, although it did not openly cast doubt on the state's motives (ibid., at 290).
86. This test, of 'proportionality in the narrow sense', which examines the proportionality between the injury to the Palestinians and the security benefit of the barrier, is the third prong of the proportionality test that the HCJ applies generally, and specifically in this case. The other two are the rational means test, which examines whether there is a rational connection between the barrier's route and the goal of its construction, and the 'least injurious' test, which examines whether the chosen route is the least injurious. *Beit Sourik, supra* note 3, para. 44.

they would suffer, and described in great detail the drastic changes to the farmers' lives and the hindrances to their livelihood, property, and freedom of movement.[87] When stating that these injuries were not proportionate, the HCJ noted that they could be substantially decreased by an alternate route – either the one presented by the CPS experts or another set out by the military commander. 'Such an alternate route exists', said the HCJ. 'It is not a figment of the imagination. It was presented before us.' The security advantages to be reaped from the current route as opposed to the proposed ones did not stand in any reasonable proportion to the injury to the local inhabitants. The gap between the security benefits ensured by these two alternatives was minute as opposed to the vast difference between a barrier that separated the local inhabitants from their land and one that did not.[88]

For the HCJ to follow this line of reasoning – supporting an alternate route and, more specifically, stating that the existing one had no justified security advantages – it must do what it said it was not doing: it must assume that, despite the army's declaration, an alternative route is possible from a security perspective, and that the chosen route, contrary to the army's view, is not a military imperative. The HCJ's ruling, then, dismisses the army's security argument and replaces it with its own conviction about security requirements, obviously influenced by the CPS brief. This is one of the most welcome elements in the *Beit Sourik* ruling: it is one of the first major cases in the HCJ's long history of adjudicating claims brought by Palestinians from the OPT in which it rejected the army's security arguments. Its decision to do so after a detailed analysis and recognition of the harm done to Palestinians is a significant and welcome development. This time, the HCJ pierced the veil of security arguments and offered alternatives less injurious to the Palestinian population. But this laudable move actually requires the HCJ not to be convinced of the military exigency behind the barrier's current route. Although the HCJ explained why the army's claim was not convincing, its attempt to do so without questioning the army's security arguments and judgments is unpersuasive. Moreover, the reading I propose of the HCJ's proportionality discussion as implying a rejection of the security argument casts doubts on the HCJ's determination in the first part of its analysis, stating that the sole motive for building the barrier is a legitimate security need. The limits of the proportionality discourse as structured by the HCJ, divorced from the question of military necessity, become immediately evident. The HCJ fails to demonstrate that the separation between the authority and proportionality arguments is possible, given that its explicit determination regarding proportionality relies on the existence of alternatives capable of meeting security needs. The implications of this failure on the role of the security and proportionality analysis in IHL will be further examined below, in section 3.2.2.

3.2. HCJ *ex post: Mara'abe*
Fifteen months after the ICJ's Advisory Opinion and its own *Beit Sourik* decision, the HCJ again issued a landmark ruling on the barrier. The September 2005 decision in

---

87.   Ibid., paras. 59–60.
88.   Ibid., para. 61. See also paras. 71, 76, 80.

Mara'abe v. *The Prime Minister of Israel*[89] continues *Beit Sourik* in many respects but involves two major innovations: it discusses the link between the barrier's route and the settlements, and it engages the ICJ Advisory Opinion.

The *Mara'abe* case dealt with five villages in the so-called 'Alphei Menasheh enclave'. As described by the HCJ, the barrier in this area surrounds the settlement of Alphei Menasheh (which the HCJ describes as 'an Israeli town in the Samaria area') from all sides, leaving a road connecting it to Israel. Several Palestinian villages were included within the barrier and were thus cut off from the rest of the West Bank area, and '[a]n enclave of Palestinian villages on the "Israeli" side of the fence has been created.'[90]

The HCJ's narrative in this case is similar to the one in *Beit Sourik*, and the HCJ again describes the terrorism that 'landed' on Israel as the Second Intifada broke out in September 2000.[91] This time, however, the HCJ's factual background mentioned the changes in the route after its own *Beit Sourik* judgment, noting that the data submitted show that about 19.7 per cent of the barrier is inside Israel or on the Green Line.[92] The HCJ did not note the clear meaning of this data, namely that about 80.3 per cent of the barrier is built beyond the Green Line and inside the West Bank. The HCJ further mentioned that the data submitted show that the barrier's route leaves about 7.8 per cent of the West Bank area on what it calls 'the "Israeli" (western) side of the fence'. The use of the term 'Israeli', albeit in quotation marks, is telling.[93] The HCJ also referred to the regulations applying to the area known as the 'seam zone', including the associated permits regime and the requirement for Palestinians who are not permanent residents of the area to provide a reason for entering.[94]

Living in the five villages within the Alphei Menasheh enclave are about 1,200 Palestinians inhabitants, who can enter the West Bank through several gates that open at different times. The enclave is connected to Israel, however, without a checkpoint.[95] The petitioners pointed to the destructive effects of the barrier[96] and noted, for instance, that doctors can only pass through the gates during opening hours, requiring them to prearrange medical visits, and that no arrangements had been made for medical emergencies.[97]

Petitioners argued both that the barrier was built *ultra vires* and that it was not proportional. Relying, *inter alia*, on the Advisory Opinion, they argued that the enclave was intended to put Alphei Menasheh west of the fence to make it territorially contiguous with the state of Israel, effectively moving the border. The barrier thus created a long-term change, actually annexing the enclave without serving any military need. Defending the residents of Jewish settlements is not, according to the

---

89. *Supra* note 6.
90. Ibid., para. 1
91. Ibid., para. 2.
92. Ibid., para. 6.
93. Ibid.
94. Ibid., para. 7. The HCJ notes that this is true regarding 'Phase A' of the barrier, of which the barrier around Alphei Menasheh was part. See note 22 and accompanying text, *supra*.
95. Ibid., para. 9.
96. Ibid., paras. 76–80.
97. Ibid., para. 104.

petitioners, a military need.[98] The second argument was that the impingement on the rights of Palestinians was disproportionate.[99] The third concerned the permits regime within the enclave, which they argued was discriminatory.[100]

3.2.1. Mara'abe: *The HCJ on the legality of building the barrier in the occupied territory*

The HCJ set for its discussion a legal framework resembling that in *Beit Sourik* – belligerent occupation and the pertinent laws: the Hague Regulations, Israeli administrative law, and the de facto application of the Fourth Geneva Convention.[101] The HCJ also repeated its determination that the military commander was authorized to order the construction of the barrier on security and military grounds, but not if motivated by a political goal of 'annexing' territories to Israel and determining its political borders.[102] Based on the state's response,[103] the HCJ rejected the petitioner's first argument and held that security considerations were behind the decision to erect the barrier, which was a temporary structure as evident from the changes that were made in it following the *Beit Sourik* ruling. The reduction in the number of terrorist attacks proved the barrier's effectiveness as a security measure.[104] Regarding the barrier section before the HCJ, the state's submissions indicated that it acted as a significant obstacle, hindering the terrorists' ability to enter Israel. After examining it and hearing detailed explanations, the HCJ concluded that the route was chosen for security rather than political reasons, and the decision to erect it was thus within the authority of the military commander.[105]

The HCJ determined in its ruling that, if the barrier fulfils military needs, the military commander might take possession of land belonging to Palestinian residents in order to build it.[106] The HCJ emphasized that these measures were temporary: the military commander's authority to erect a security barrier but not to annex territory derived from the fact that his authority was inherently temporary, as was the belligerent occupation. Seizing land in this case was not a prohibited expropriation or a confiscation but a temporary taking of possession.[107] Turning to the needs that required these measures, the HCJ cited three security and military reasons: (i) the

---

98. Ibid., para. 80.
99. Ibid., para. 81.
100. Ibid., para. 82.
101. Ibid., para. 14.
102. Ibid., para. 15.
103. The State cited three reasons for not building the barrier on the Green Line: (i) topography; (ii) the proximity of Israeli towns and villages to the Green Line, which would require building the barrier on their actual limits, leaving no space for an alert zone that would allow security forces to arrive prior to a terrorist infiltration; and (iii) the need to protect Israelis living in the West Bank as well as other 'important locations' such as roads and high-voltage lines. Ibid., para. 99.
104. Ibid., para. 100.
105. Ibid., para. 101.
106. Ibid., para. 16. The HCJ anchored this authority in Arts. 43 and 52 of the Hague Regulations and Art. 53 of the Fourth Geneva Convention. By relying on these sources the HCJ sidestepped the question concerning Art. 23(g) of the Hague Regulations it had applied in *Beit Sourik*, which the ICJ had found was inapplicable and relevant only during hostilities. Although the HCJ questioned the ICJ's reading of the article's applicability, it chose to leave the discussion for another opportunity (ibid., para. 17). The differences between the courts on this matter reflects the controversy about whether the applicable law in the OPT includes the law of warfare. See notes 41–2 and accompanying text, *supra*.
107. Ibid., paras. 15–16.

need to protect the army in the territory under occupation; (ii) the defence of the state of Israel itself; and (iii) the protection of the life and safety of Israelis living in what it called 'Israeli communities in the Judea and Samaria area'.[108] Although reason (ii) is also in dispute,[109] it is the third that emerges as the most controversial determination of *Mara'abe*. The HCJ held that Israelis living in the occupied area were not 'protected persons' per the meaning of this term in Article 4 of the Fourth Geneva Convention. Nevertheless, it stated that the military commander was authorized to protect their lives and defend their safety, and anchored its answer in both international and Israeli law.

The first reason for the HCJ's determination concerning the settlers rests on the military commander's general authority as set out in Article 43 of the Hague Regulations, which grants the commander the authority to 'take all the measures in his power to restore, and ensure, as far as possible, public order and safety, while respecting, unless absolutely prevented, the laws in force in the country'.[110] This authority, said the HCJ, covers any person present in the territory held under belligerent occupation, whose safety must be preserved by the military commander. The protection of the Israeli settlers is called for in the light of every individual's human dignity. For the purpose of this conclusion, held the HCJ, it was not relevant whether settlement activity conformed with or defied international law, as determined in the Advisory Opinion: 'For this reason, we shall express no position regarding that question.' Through this statement the HCJ continued its tradition of refusing to rule directly on the legality of the settlements according to international law, while legitimizing them through decisions that allow the use of land in the OPT for their establishment.[111] Even if a person were located in the area illegally, said the HCJ, he was not outlawed:

---

108. Ibid., paras. 18–19.
109. Imseis argues that military necessity can operate 'only to protect the security interests of the occupying power's military forces, and then only within the occupied territory'. Imseis, *supra* note 8, at 112. Including the security needs of the occupying power's home state under Art. 43 thus remains controversial. Given that a state may use its army to protect its own legitimate borders, I will not enter here the debate on whether this prerogative is part of the military commander's authority.
110. The language of the official French version of Art. 43 of the Hague Regulations refers to 'l'ordre et la vie publique', and thus the term 'civil life' is more accurate and appropriate than the term 'safety' used in the English version. See E. Benvenisti, *The International Law of Occupation* (2004), 7, n. 1 and the references therein.
111. *Mara'abe, supra* note 6, para. 19. For a detailed discussion of the case law on this question, see Kretzmer, *supra* note 73, at 77–9. By refusing to rule on the legality of the settlements and generally choosing not to interfere in decisions connected with the use of land for settlements, the HCJ's case law on this matter served to legitimize government actions. An exhaustive discussion of the HCJ's case law on settlements is beyond the scope of this article, and I will only point to a number of avoidance mechanisms in use by the HCJ. One technique, when dealing with specific settlements, is to hold that arguments made in accordance with Art. 49(6) of the Geneva Convention are not justiciable in Israeli courts because the Convention has not been incorporated into domestic law (see, e.g., HCJ 608/78 *Ayub v. Minister of Defense* 33(2) P.D. 112 (1978), English summary available at (1979) 9 *Israeli Yearbook of Human Rights* 337). Another is to reject petitions brought against settlement policy as too general and abstract, as well as raising non-justiciable political questions (see, e.g., HCJ 4481/91 *Bargil v. Government of Israel*, 47(4) P.D. 210 (1991)). Concerning the use of land for settlements, the HCJ has held that civilian settlements can fulfil military goals and can be temporary, and are thus within the authority of the military commander (see *Ayub v. Minister of Defense, supra*). For a famous exception, which as Kretzmer puts it proves the rule and is the HCJ's sole intervention in these matters, see HCJ 390/79 *Dweikat v. Government of Israel*, 34(1) P.D. 1 (1979), English summary available at (1979) 9 *Israeli Yearbook of Human Rights* 345. For an overview, discussion, and critique of these and other cases see Kretzmer, *supra* note 73, at 75–99.

Even if the military commander acted in a manner that conflicted with the law of belligerent occupation at the time he agreed to the establishment of this or that settlement – and that issue is not before us, and we shall express no opinion on it – that does not release him from his duty according to the law of belligerent occupation itself, to preserve the lives, safety and dignity of every one of the Israeli settlers.[112]

The second justification for the HCJ decision that the military commander was authorized to order the construction of a barrier intended to protect the lives and security of Israeli settlers in the area was that they were Israeli citizens, and that the state of Israel had a duty – grounded in Israel's Basic Law: Human Dignity and Liberty – to defend their lives, safety, and well-being. The constitutional rights granted under the Basic Law were also granted to citizens located in the territory under belligerent occupation that was controlled by Israel.[113] Concerning human rights, Israelis living in these areas enjoyed a different scope and level of protection of human rights from those of Israelis living in Israel, since Israeli law did not apply in these areas and people lived there under a regime of belligerent occupation that was inherently temporary. The rights granted to Israelis living in these areas, said the HCJ, came to them from the military commander, and they had no more than he had – *nemo dat quod non habet.*[114]

The determination that protecting the settlers is within the authority, if not the duty, of the military commander is crucial to the rest of the judgment. The HCJ's further determinations concerning the military commander's considerations, and the need for proportionality when balancing security needs against the rights of the local inhabitants, rest on the determination that building the barrier so as to protect the *settlements* is a legitimate security concern for the military commander. In this specific case, the Palestinian villages in question were saved from what the HCJ called the 'chokehold' placed on their necks, but the question was left open as to what would have been the result had no alternative route been found to protect Alphei Menasheh without such an effect on the Palestinian villages. The HCJ, then, permitted in principle (and in some of its case law on the OPT in actual fact) the violation of Palestinian rights for the sake of the settlers' security.[115]

The logic of this determination, however, is flawed at several levels. First, the HCJ determination granting authority to the military commander to protect the settlers and as a matter of fact the settlements themselves up-ends the logic of Article 43. The rationale of Article 43, which is indeed the basic norm of the law of

---

112. *Mara'abe, supra* note 6, para. 20. The HCJ also cited Art. 3 of the Fourth Geneva Convention to support its conclusion, as well as the Israeli–Palestinian Interim Agreement on the West Bank and the Gaza Strip, which provides that the issue of Israeli settlements in the area will be discussed in the negotiations over the final status, and that Israel shall bear responsibility for the overall security of Israelis and the settlements. For a discussion of the latter see notes 123–5 and accompanying text, *infra.*

113. *Mara'abe, supra* note 6, para. 21.

114. Ibid., para. 22. Though critical of the ICJ's determination on self-defence, the HCJ does not examine the matter and does not make a positive determination as to whether the law of self-defence and Art. 51 of the UN Charter also grant authority to erect the barrier. Ibid., para. 23.

115. For a case where settlers' security justified limiting Palestinians' rights see, e.g., HCJ 10356/02, *Hess v. Commander of the IDF Forces in the West Bank,* 58(3) P.D. 443 (2003). In this case, the rationale stated in the text was accepted by the HCJ as a basis for authorizing the Israeli army to seize land owned by Palestinians and destroy structures in Hebron for the purpose of allowing the settlers safe access to the Cave of the Patriarchs.

occupation,[116] is that the military commander should preserve existing laws 'unless absolutely prevented', that his duty is of temporary duration, and that his role is to manage the territory in a manner that protects civil life, exercising authority as a trustee of the sovereign.[117] Article 43, then, does not confer sovereign powers on the occupant; rather, it limits the occupant's authority to the maintenance of public order and civil life.[118] A reading of Article 43 giving the military commander the right to protect the settlers by way of protecting the settlements, which in the occupation of the West Bank are the most manifest breach of this very article, takes the law of occupation intended to prevent the military commander from changing the nature of the territory under occupation and turns it on its head. The settlements were built in violation of Article 49(6) of the Fourth Geneva Convention, which prohibits occupants to transfer part of their own civilian population into the territory under occupation.[119] The military commander was the one who formally erected the settlements and, as the HCJ held in a ruling on the Gaza withdrawal,[120] has the authority to dismantle them. It is thus inconceivable to determine that, as a matter of international law, it is now his duty to protect the settlers by building yet another structure in the West Bank – this time the barrier – in order to protect the settlements and especially given the structure's indisputable effects on protected persons. Moreover, the HCJ ruling confuses here the settlers and the settlements. The discourse about the need to protect the life of the settlers and not 'outlaw' them in international or Israeli constitutional law takes a prodigious leap and is transformed into a determination that a barrier used to incorporate the settlements is legal.[121]

All this was made possible by the HCJ's choice to sidestep, yet again, the question of the settlements' legality. Although the HCJ said that the question was not before it, the petitioners' argument in this case rested on the illegality of the settlements. The HCJ's reasoning that this question is inconsequential to its judgment is thus misleading, since, if the settlements are illegal, the military commander should obviously consider ways of protecting the settlers without reinforcing this illegality or, at the very least, in the 'least illegal' manner. One option would be to move the settlers to Israel, thereby ending the illegality of the settlements.[122] Moreover, if the

---

116. See Benvenisti, *supra* note 110, at 7–31.
117. Under contemporary international law, and in view of the principle of self-determination, sovereignty is vested in the population under occupation. See Ben-Naftali, Gross, and Michaeli, *supra* note 72, at 554.
118. Ibid., at 563, 575–9.
119. For an elaborate discussion of the application of this prohibition to the settlements, ibid., at 581–2.
120. HCJ 1661/05 *Hof Azah Regional Council v. The Knesset* (not yet published, 2005).
121. See, in this context, Kretzmer's argument about the need to protect settlers who are civilians as grounded in IHL. Kretzmer, 'The Light Treatment', *supra* note 5, at 93. But Kretzmer emphasizes that the need is to protect civilians rather than the settlements in which they live. This begs the question of why, then, the HCJ found it logical (basing itself partly on Kretzmer's argument – see *Mara'abe*, *supra* note 6, para. 20) to infer from this the justification for a barrier that in fact protects the settlements, rather than requiring the military commander to protect the settlers in another way. Indeed, even according to Kretzmer's position, whereby the illegality of the settlements does not per se affect the legality of the barrier, the HCJ should have taken into account, as part of a detailed examination of the barrier's route and the evaluation of its legality, the illegality of the settlements and the consequent duty of the occupying power to return its civilians in those settlements to its own territory. Kretzmer, 'The Light Treatment', *supra* note 5, at 94.
122. Yuval Shany suggests that the illegality of the settlements is an important factor in assessing the legality of the barrier but cannot be the determining element, given the need grounded in human rights law to protect the settlers, the material unfeasibility of a quick dismantling of the settlements, and the fact that

settlers cannot have more than the military commander has, as the HCJ notes, how can the military commander approve their move to the occupied territory (as the HCJ notes he did) when he lacks the authority to allow them to settle there in the first place? The discussion again slides from the need to protect the settlers' lives to conclusions about protecting the settlements, in a way that obscures the need to address these questions.

It has been argued that the illegality of the settlements is no longer an issue given the agreement in the Oslo accords that their future will be decided in the final status negotiations and, until then, Israel is responsible for their security.[123] The HCJ also relied on this position.[124] But this argument is invalid because, when it signed the Oslo accords, the Palestine Liberation Organization (PLO) could not waive the humanitarian rights to which protected people are entitled, including the right enshrined in Article 49(6) of the Fourth Geneva Convention not to have civilian population from the occupying power transferred into their territory.[125]

The principle of *ex injuria jus non oritor*[126] is of relevance here.[127] According to this principle, acts contrary to international law cannot become a source of legal rights for the wrongdoer, so that once a situation is ruled illegal, states for which this finding is binding are obliged to end it.[128] Israel, then, cannot argue that it is allowed to take steps to meet the military need of protecting the settlements which

---

their status is yet to be determined in a final status agreement. Shany, 'Head against the Wall', *supra* note 5. But this argument is problematic given that, notwithstanding the pull-out from Gaza and the dismantling of the settlements there, Israel is not taking any steps to dismantle settlements in the West Bank. Had Israel shown that it is working bona fide and with all deliberate speed to undo the illegality of the settlements, the temporal issues raised by Shany could have become more credible. At this time facts on the ground point rather to the opposite, creating a link between the barrier and plans for settlement expansion. See notes 146–50 and accompanying text, *infra*. As for the question of final status agreement, given that the settlements and the barrier create facts on the ground that may prejudge the final status, it would not make sense to justify the barrier by claiming that final status talks are yet to take place.

123. Interim Agreement on the West Bank and the Gaza Strip (Israel/PLO), 28 September 1995, Art. XII(1), 36 ILM (1997) 551 ('Israel shall continue to carry the responsibility for defence against external threats, including the responsibility for protecting the Egyptian and Jordanian borders, and for defence against external threats from the sea and from the air, as well as the responsibility for overall security of Israelis and Settlements, for the purpose of safeguarding their internal security and public order, and will have all the powers to take the steps necessary to meet this responsibility'); ibid., Art. XXXI(5) ('It is understood that [the permanent status] negotiations shall cover remaining issues, including: Jerusalem, refugees, settlements, security arrangements, borders, relations and cooperation with other neighbours, and other issues of common interest').

124. *Mara'abe, supra* note 6, para 20.

125. See Fourth Geneva Convention, Arts. 7, 8, and 47. For an argument as to why the determination in the Oslo accords implies that the legality of the barrier does not depend on the legality of the settlements, see R. Lapidoth, 'The Advisory Opinion and the Jewish Settlements', (205) 38 *Israel Law Review* 292, at 293–4; Wedgwood, *supra* note 7, at 60–1. Kretzmer, 'The Light Treatment', *supra* note 5, at note 41. For a discussion of the possible effect of the Oslo accords on this issue see Shany, 'Head against the Wall', *supra* note 5.

126. In the words of the ICJ in another context: 'One of the fundamental principles governing the international relationships thus established is that a party which disowns or does not fulfil its own obligations cannot be recognized as retaining the rights which it claims to derive from the relationship'. Legal Consequences for States of the Continued Presence of South Africa in Namibia (South West Africa) notwithstanding Security Council Resolution (Advisory Opinion), (1971) ICJ Rep. 16, at 46.

127. Judge Elaraby mentioned the principle in his Separate Opinion in the Advisory Opinion (Advisory Opinion (Elaraby), *supra* note 1, para. 3.1) but without elaborating precisely on its applicability in this case. To the extent that he intended to imply, as may be apparent from the context of his reference, that states may not acquire land by use of force, this may be a problematic use of the principle, since contemporary international law prohibits such acquisition regardless of whether use of force was illegal, or a legal resort to self-defence.

128. See R. Jennings and A. Watts (eds.), *Oppenheim's International Law* (1992), I, at 183–4 and the references cited therein.

it built illegally in the first place.[129] If the settlements are illegal, a barrier built to protect them that aggravates violations of the local residents' rights for the settlers' benefit is illegal too. The HCJ justifies this violation by relying on Article 43, while it should have determined, at the very least, that the settlers cannot be protected in any way that violates the Palestinians' rights.

Making illegal settlements part of the security considerations to be balanced against the rights of the protected people under occupation places an additional burden on these rights, unanticipated in international law. Even if in this specific case the results ultimately favoured the Palestinians, this additional burden upsets and distorts the law of occupation and humanitarian law and the 'delicate balance', as the HCJ itself calls it,[130] struck between them, leading instead to an *imbalance* of security.[131] When the HCJ discusses the relativity of human rights and the possibility of restricting such rights as freedom of movement due to national security needs, public order, or the rights and freedom of others, as developed in IHL and human rights law,[132] we must consider the problematic application of the concept in this context: IHL does not anticipate placing the onus of balancing the settlers' rights on the protected people. The rights in whose name the Palestinians' rights are limited are those of the settlers, who not only live in the OPT illegally but also enjoy a set of rights and privileges different from those enjoyed by the Palestinians,[133] as the permits regime alone will attest. The regime associated with the barrier, then, is not built on an equal allocation of rights and a fair balance between all the citizens electing a government that makes the decisions. By a special statutory arrangement, Israelis living in the West Bank can vote in Israeli elections and choose the government making decisions about the territory, while the Palestinians have no such right.[134]

A significant element in the HCJ's analysis is that the interests of the people under occupation are defined as rights, while the interests of the settlers are defined as security interests. These security interests, comprising all Israelis and the state of Israel itself, can now be invoked to restrict the rights of the people under occupation, in a conceptual framework that distorts the IHL balance of security versus rights. Striving for proportionality in this framework, then, could lead to strong imbalances, justifying extensive restrictions to the rights of protected people, particularly given the tendency of courts to defer to security arguments adduced by military authorities.

---

129. For a similar position see Imseis, *supra* note 8, at 112. For an elaboration of this position see Shany, 'Head against the Wall', *supra* note 8. As Shany notes, Art. 25(2)(b) of the ILC Draft Articles on State Responsibility would bar states that have contributed to the situation of illegality from invoking the defence of necessity. See ILC Draft Articles on Responsibility of States for Internationally Wrongful Acts, 51, UN Doc. A/CN.4/L.602/Rev.1 (2001). For an argument on why *ex injuria jus nor oritur* may not be relevant here, see Kretzmer, 'The Light Treatment', *supra* note 5, at note 41.

130. *Mara'abe*, *supra* note 6, para. 28.

131. On the (im)balance of security as part of the breach of trust entailed in the Israeli occupation, see Ben-Naftali, Gross, and Michaeli, *supra* note 72, at 590–2.

132. *Mara'abe*, *supra* note 6, paras. 24–5.

133. See Ben-Naftali, Gross, and Michaeli, *supra* note 72, at 581–8.

134. Although Israel generally does not have an absentee ballot and voting can only take place within Israel. See Knesset Elections Law (Consolidated Version) 5729–1969, 23 L.S.I. 110 (1969), Arts. 6 and 147. See on this Ben-Naftali, Gross, and Michaeli, *supra* note 72, at 584–5.

Although in the specific cases of *Beit Sourik* and *Mara'abe* the balance was struck in favour of the people under occupation, the structure of the occupation and many HCJ rulings attest to frequent restrictions of Palestinians' rights, such as freedom of movement, in order to protect the security of the settlers.

The effects of the HCJ's consistent refusal to consider the overall legality of the settlements must be considered in this context. The declaration that the issue is irrelevant to the matter at hand allows the military commander to use his authority to seize land for the purpose of building the barrier as a security measure. At the same time, however, he is not restricted in one of the major prohibitions incumbent on a military commander in the context of a belligerent occupation, which is not to transfer civilian population from his own country to the territory under occupation.[135] Not only does this decision distort the balance of security anticipated in IHL but it also allows Israel to act in the occupied territory as both occupier (enjoying the authority vested in an occupying power) and sovereign (establishing towns and cities, applying its laws to their residents,[136] and protecting its citizens who settle in the territory at the expense of the local population). In turn, the local Palestinian population cannot enjoy the rights of people under occupation or the rights of citizens in a sovereign state. Significantly, although in recent cases the HCJ has examined the violations of Palestinians' rights on the basis of the Fourth Geneva Convention, it has stopped short of determining that the Convention applies *de jure* to the situation.[137]

Throughout the history of the occupation, the Palestinians have been denied most of the rights accorded to people under occupation.[138] Making the settlements part of the military commander's security concerns has tilted the balance against Palestinian rights even further. The HCJ rulings in *Beit Sourik* and *Mara'abe* concerning Israeli violations of humanitarian law may mitigate this situation, but do not change the matrix of Israel's legal control in the OPT.[139] Hence, by refraining from discussing the settlements' legality, the HCJ has conferred legitimacy on an illegal situation.[140]

3.2.2. Mara'abe: *the HCJ on the violations of humanitarian norms resulting from the barrier*

Relying on this framework, the HCJ decided in *Mara'abe* that the military commander had the authority to build the barrier partly in the Alphei Menashe enclave, but that it was not clear whether the barrier passed the 'least injurious means' prong

---

135. See Kretzmer's discussion of what he calls 'a convenient system of control', whereby the government relates to the occupied territories as colonies at the political level while resorting to the law of belligerent occupation at the legal level. Kretzmer, *supra* note 73, at 197. This is a valid analysis, but, as discussed in the text, it is the contradictions between occupation and sovereignty within the legal level itself that structure the matrix of Israeli control in the OPT. See notes 136–9 and accompanying text, *infra*.
136. On the means by which Israeli law is applied to the settlers and the settlements see Ben-Naftali, Gross, and Michaeli, *supra* note 72, at 584–5.
137. For a discussion of Israeli objections to the application of the Fourth Geneva Convention in the OPT and for the rejection of these arguments see ibid., at 567–70.
138. See generally Kretzmer, *supra* note 73; Ben-Naftali, Gross, and Michaeli, *supra* note 72.
139. For a discussion of this matrix see Ben-Naftali, Gross and Michaeli, *supra* note 72, at 609–12.
140. On the illegality of this occupation see ibid.

of the proportionality test.[141] Wondering why the barrier was not planned in a manner that could indeed pass such a test, the HCJ wrote, 'Indeed, based upon the factual basis as presented to us, the existing route of the fence seems strange.' Referring to the south-western section of the enclave, the HCJ said that it was 'by no means' persuaded of any definitive security–military reason for building the barrier in its current route and wondered why it could not be changed so as to ensure that all or most of the Palestinian villages now within the enclave would remain outside it. Referring to the north-western section, the HCJ said that it was 'by no means convinced that it is necessary for security–military reasons' to preserve it.[142] The barrier, then, failed the proportionality test: the HCJ's impression was that no effort had been invested in finding an alternative route able to ensure security with lesser injury to the local residents, as required. In its ruling the HCJ ordered a reconsideration of the current route according to these guidelines, the dismantling of the existing barrier, and the building of a new one.[143] What if the examination of alternatives leads to the conclusion that the current route is the only one meeting minimum security requirements, notwithstanding its severe injury to the residents? The HCJ described this as the hardest of all questions, but stated that the time to confront it had not yet arrived and, indeed, might never come.[144]

This is a perplexing ruling. The HCJ held that the barrier is justified on security grounds, and rejected the argument that building the barrier in the OPT was forbidden since it constituted a politically motivated de facto annexation.[145] It also included – wrongly, in my view – the protection of the settlers and thus the settlements in the category of 'security–military needs'. In its discussion of proportionality, however, the HCJ held that the chosen route was 'strange', and that it was 'by no means' convinced that it could be justified on security–military grounds. An unexplainable gap divides the HCJ's determination that legitimate security considerations motivated the establishment of the barrier from its finding that no security–military explanation justified its 'strange' route. This gap is especially striking given the HCJ's recognition of extreme violations of the Palestinians' rights: if the HCJ cannot find a security–military explanation for a route that causes such serious violations, how can it determine that the barrier is driven by security considerations and merely lacks proportionality?

One line in the HCJ judgment hints that it may indeed have harboured some doubts in this regard. When wondering why the barrier's route was not drawn so as to leave out the Palestinian villages, the HCJ noted,

> There is a planning scheme, which has been filed, for the development of Alfei Menashe in the direction of the southwestern part of the enclave. But as Mr Tirza [the Israeli

---

141. *Mara'abe, supra* note 6, paras. 111–12. On the three prongs of proportionality see note 86, *supra.*
142. *Mara'abe, supra* note 6, para. 113.
143. Ibid., para. 114. Unlike *Beit Sourik,* which had dealt with a planned section of the barrier, the novel feature in *Mara'abe* is that the HCJ ordered changes in a section of the barrier that had already been built.
144. Ibid., para. 116.
145. The rejection of this argument was part of the HCJ's rejection of these sections in the ICJ Advisory Opinion. See notes 176–83 and accompanying text, *infra.*

official in charge of the construction of the barrier], who presented the enclave map to us, stated before us, that is not a consideration which should be taken into account.[146]

The link between the barrier and not only the settlements but also their expansion plans, however, is crucial. In several briefs submitted to the HCJ in pending cases involving other parts of the barrier, the state explicitly argued that the route's course was intended to protect not only built-up areas but also planned expansions. Their protection, said the state, is a legitimate consideration of the military commander.[147] The brief filed by the state in one of these cases argued that the military commander's considerations are confined to security, showing that 'security' is defined by the Israeli government as including not only the protection but also the expansion of existing settlements.[148] In a pending petition, the barrier's route was changed to a course less injurious to Palestinians but later reversed to the original route due to the objection of an existing Jewish settlement. The settlement relied for its objection on, *inter alia*, the claim of a real-estate company stating that the change would hinder a building project in which it had already made a large investment.[149] The barrier's route, then, is affected by plans for expanding the settlements and by the financial interests of the real-estate companies involved, neither of which is a legitimate concern of the military commander.[150]

In *Mara'abe* itself, the HCJ's baffling statement on this matter both points to and denies the connection between the barrier's route and the plans to expand the settlement. The HCJ stops short of addressing the legitimacy of this connection but, by hinting at it, undermines its own decision even further: beyond its problematic

---

146. *Mara'abe, supra* note 6, para. 113.
147. HCJ 8414/05 *Head of the Village Council Bil'in v. The Government of Israel*, Respondent's Brief (17 November 2005), paras. 20–9, 76–84. In this brief the government also noted that some of the settlement construction conducted in the area was at the time illegal even by Israeli law. Ibid., para 25. See on this case Akiva Eldar, 'State Turns Blind Eye to Illegal Construction at Ultra-Orthodox West Bank Settlement', *Ha'aretz*, 14 Dec. 2005, a1. For a discussion of the barrier in Bil'in and the various expansionist and economic interests involved see G. Algazi, 'Matrix in Bil'in' (Hebrew), available at http://www.hagada.org.il/hagada/html/modules.php?name=Newsandfile=articleandsid=4143. In a decision in another pending case, the HCJ issued an interim order prohibiting the construction of the barrier in segments where it was meant to protect 'unauthorized outposts'. HCJ 5139/05 *Falech Mizlach Achmed Shaib v. State of Israel* (unpublished, 26 Dec. 2005), available at http://elyon1.court.gov.il/Files/05/390/051/a10/05051390.a10.HTM. If eventually in its ruling in this case the HCJ determines that the illegality, under Israeli law, of this 'outpost' determines the illegality of building the barrier which is meant to protect it, this will beg the question as to why the same rationale does not apply to the connections between the question of the legality of the settlements themselves and the legality of the barrier meant to protect them.
148. *Head of the Village Council Bil'in v. The Government of Israel, supra* note 147, para 85. For another case where the state indicated that it had taken the settlement's building plans into account when planning the barrier's route see HCJ 2732/05 *The Head of the Azun Council v. The Government of Israel*, Respondent's Brief (30 June 2005), paras. 17–19, 35.
149. HCJ 2577/04 *Taha El Chawaga v. The Prime Minister of Israel*, Corrected Petition filed 2 June 2004 (pending). In an HCJ decision issued on this case on 18 Aug. 2005, the Court added the real estate company in question as a respondent in the petition.
150. For an elaborate discussion of the way in which plans to expand settlements affect the route chosen for the barrier see B'Tselem – The Israeli Information Centre for Human Rights in the Occupied Territories, *Under the Guise of Security: Routing the Separation Barrier to Enable Israeli Settlements Expansion in the West Bank* (2005), available at http://www.btselem.org/english/publications/summaries/200509_under_the_guise_of_security.asp. For a discussion of the economic interests involved, see Algazi, *supra* note 147; G. Algazi, The Upper-Class Fence, available at http://www.kibush.co.il/show_file.asp?num=5086. For a discussion of the economic effects of the barrier see also A. Vitullo, 'The Long Economic Shadow of the Wall', in M. Sorkin (ed.), *Against the Wall* (2005), 100.

determination that the military commander can take into account the protection of settlements, regardless of the question of their legality, it implies that the military commander may also have taken into account, though without admitting it, plans already filed for the settlements' expansion. The HCJ's determination that security grounds cannot explain the chosen route appears to confirm the ICJ's insight in defining the barrier's course as part of Israel's settlement policy. It is not thereby suggested that the barrier serves no security purposes; as a matter of fact it does. Moreover, the proportionality analysis included in the HCJ's decision could be read as an attempt to amend the barrier so as to bring it closer to its security objectives. But erecting the barrier inside the West Bank, in clear violation of Palestinian rights, and admitting that the barrier is also meant to protect the settlements, along a route whose security rationale the HCJ itself rejects, brazenly defies this attempt.

Indeed, several separations in the HCJ analysis – between security and political considerations, and between authority and proportionality – create the possibility of its decision. A critical reading, however, reveals the failure of these separations.

When it determines that the barrier is built for security rather than political–annexational reasons, the HCJ appears to overlook that 'security' interests are politically defined.[151] The HCJ ruling that the barrier is established *intra vires* because its purpose is security, contrary to the ICJ's determination, ignores the question of what is perceived as 'security': when Israel makes the protection of the occupation and of the settlements part of its security interests, these interests become indistinguishable from its political–annexational purposes. Similarly, the HCJ separates authority from proportionality – it determines that the military commander had the authority to build the barrier because of the security concern, and then states that the injury to the Palestinians was not proportionate because the security grounds for the chosen route are not really understandable. Evidence has surfaced in the interim proving the annexational purpose of the barrier, relying not only on the barrier's actual route and its connections to existing and future settlements but also on statements such as that issued by the Israeli Minister of Justice, who proclaimed the barrier as the future border of Israel.[152] While it is possible that this evidence will affect future HCJ rulings in some of the cases that are currently pending, especially in cases where the

---

151. For a discussion of the relationship between 'professional' and 'political' considerations in *Beit Sourik* and in the Advisory Opinion, see Shany, 'Head against the Wall', *supra* note 5. While Shany's position is similar to mine in that he finds the distinction between 'political considerations' and 'professional "security considerations"' to be unrealistic, I cannot agree with his suggestion that instead of judging the barrier in accordance with this division, 'the question which should have been properly placed before the HCJ and ICJ is, then, whether the barrier can be justified in terms of military necessity'. Military necessity could again be based on politically defined security needs, such as the protection of the settlements.

152. See Y. Yoaz, 'Justice Minister: West Bank Fence is Future Border', *Ha'aretz*, 1 Dec. 2005, 3. In the quotation from Minister Tzipi Livni, she further said that the HCJ in its rulings over the barrier 'is drawing the country's borders'. See also Kretzmer, 'The Light Treatment', *supra* note 5, at note 32 and accompanying text. For the argument that Ariel Sharon's political programme for Israel's future borders is identical to the barrier's route, and the barrier thus aims to determine Israel's permanent borders by annexing maximum territory, settlements, and settlers and creating a territorial continuum with the Green Line while annexing a minimum of Palestinians and Palestinian villages, see S. Arieli, 'Between the Completeness of the Land and a Jewish State We Chose the Jewish State', in F. Raday and Y. Shani (eds.), *The Separation Barrier: An Interdisciplinary Analysis* (2004), 25 at 28–9 (Hebrew). Shaul Arieli is a reserve colonel in the Israeli army and formerly the chair of the Office in Charge of Negotiations with Palestinians in the Prime Minster's Office.

connection between the barrier's route and settlement expansion plans is clear, it is doubtful that it will undermine the rationale of *Mara'abe* and its separations. These separations, then, joined by a separation of the barrier into segments examined separately, lead to a discourse that blurs the reality of the barrier and its role within Israel's expansionist policy, in a pattern that has characterized the jurisprudence of the occupation from the start: allowing the military commander to establish civilian settlements, allowing permanent settlements on land 'temporarily' seized by a military commander whose duties are temporary, and allowing a 'temporary' barrier as part of this process. The result is a language game of humanitarian law being played ever since the Israeli HCJ legitimized land use for settlements many years ago, supposedly for security reasons, currently continued in the definition of the barrier as meant only for 'security' purposes.

4. JERUSALEM VERSUS THE HAGUE

Several of the petitions against the barrier submitted to the HCJ, including that in the *Mara'abe* case, rely on ICJ determinations in the Advisory Opinion. In its *Mara'abe* ruling, the HCJ outlined for the first time its own stance on the Advisory Opinion and the way in which it should affect its decision, dividing the discussion into two parts. In the first it described in detail the factual basis that was before the ICJ in the dossier filed by the UN Secretary-General, which included reports by the Secretary-General and by special rapporteurs. In the second, it offered a comparative perspective on the Advisory Opinion and on its own *Beit Sourik* judgment, offering explanations for the differences between them.

The HCJ's discussion is a rare instance of a domestic court offering an elaborate analysis of an opinion issued by the ICJ on the same matter.[153] Noting that the opinion was advisory and not binding, the HCJ nevertheless stated that it was 'an interpretation of international law, performed by the highest judicial body in international law' that 'should be given its full appropriate weight'.[154]

The HCJ read its own and the ICJ decisions as based on a shared normative foundation but reaching different conclusions. Both courts, said the HCJ, agreed that Israel holds the West Bank pursuant to the law of belligerent occupation; that an occupier state is not permitted to annex the occupied territory; that it must act in accordance with the Hague Regulations and the Fourth Geneva Convention (although in regard to the latter the HCJ did not determine the *de jure* status of the Fourth Geneva Convention in the light of Israel's declaration that it would act in accordance with its humanitarian part); that the barrier hinders the rights of Palestinian residents, and that the harm to the Palestinian residents would not

---

153. For a discussion of the attitude of national courts towards ICJ decisions, see M. Bedjaoui, 'The Reception by National Courts of Decisions of International Tribunals', in T. M. Franck and G. H. Fox (eds.), *International Law Decisions in National Courts* (1995), 21 at 21–35; S. Ordonez and D. Reilly, 'The Effect of the Jurisprudence of the International Court of Justice on National Courts', in T. M. Franck and G. H. Fox (eds.), *International Law Decisions in National Courts* (1995), 335, at 335–71. Ordonez and Reilly point out that domestic courts have received ICJ decisions and advisory opinions in various ways, along a spectrum of more or less deferential treatment. Specifically concerning advisory opinions see ibid., at 357–9, 364.

154. *Mara'abe, supra* note 6, para. 56.

be a violation of international law if resulting from military necessity, national security requirements, or public order. The ICJ also determined that human rights conventions apply. This issue, noted the HCJ, did not arise in *Beit Sourik*, but for the purpose of the current judgment it was willing to assume that these conventions do apply.[155]

As for the differences in their conclusions, the HCJ indicated that the ICJ had held that the building of the barrier and its associated regime were contrary to international law, whereas the HCJ held that no particular route should sweepingly be proclaimed a breach of international law. Instead, each segment should be examined separately to clarify whether it impinged on the rights of Palestinians in disproportionate ways.[156] Thus the HCJ held that some segments violated international law while others did not.[157] The HCJ noted that the ICJ was not convinced that the route of the barrier, which severely injures the rights of the Palestinian residents, was necessary for achieving the security objectives pursued by Israel. In its own holding in *Beit Sourik*, the HCJ argued that erecting the barrier was a military necessity, although some of the segments discussed involved a disproportionate violation of the Palestinian residents' rights.[158]

The HCJ explained this difference in the legal conclusions of the two courts as mainly a function of the factual basis made available to them that, in turn, was affected by the way in which the proceedings were conducted and by the legal problems brought before them.[159] To support this determination, the HCJ closely scrutinized the factual basis put before the two courts and noted that the ICJ had relied on the report of the Secretary-General, on his written statement, and on the rapporteurs' accounts, whereas the HCJ had relied on data submitted by the Palestinian petitioners, by the state, and by the military experts who had submitted the *amici curiae* brief in *Beit Sourik*.[160] The main difference in the data before the courts focused on 'the security–military necessity to erect the fence'. It was the evidence regarding terrorism, the failure of other measures to stop it, and the need to find solutions, said the HCJ, that had led it to conclude that the decision to build the barrier resulted from security–military considerations and necessity rather than from a political decision to annex occupied territory to Israel.[161] By contrast, this security–military necessity was mentioned only minimally in the sources before

---

155. Ibid., para. 57. For a critical discussion of the ICJ's application of human rights treaties in the Advisory Opinion see M. J. Dennis, 'Application of Human Rights Treaties Extraterritorially in Times of Armed Conflict and Military Occupation', (2005) 99 AJIL 119. For an extensive discussion of this topic and an evaluation of the ICJ's position see O. Ben-Naftali and Y. Shany, 'Living in Denial: The Application of Human Rights in the Occupied Territories', (2003) 37 *Israel Law Review* 17.

156. The HCJ in *Mara'abe* said, 'Despite this common normative foundation, the two courts reached different conclusions. The ICJ held that the building of the wall, and the regime accompanying it, are contrary to international law ... In contrast, the Supreme Court in the *Beit Sourik* Case held that it is not to be sweepingly said that any route of the fence is a breach of international law' (ibid., para. 58). This statement somewhat obscures the fact that the ICJ's opinion was limited to the part of the barrier being built in the OPT and did not deal with the entire barrier as such. See Advisory Opinion, *supra* note 1, paras. 67, 83.

157. *Mara'abe*, *supra* note 6, para. 58.

158. Ibid., para. 59.

159. Ibid., para. 60.

160. Ibid., para. 61.

161. Ibid., para. 62.

the ICJ. Although the Advisory Opinion recorded the Israeli claim that the barrier's objective was to enable an effective struggle against terrorist attacks originating in the West Bank, the HCJ pointed to the brevity of this discussion.[162] It also stated that the ICJ had relied on a factual basis regarding the barrier's violations of the Palestinians' rights but, unlike its own ruling in *Beit Sourik*, the ICJ had lacked a factual basis regarding the security–military grounds for these violations.[163] The HCJ also claimed that the information before the ICJ was deficient not only regarding Israel's security–military needs but also regarding the scope of the impingement on the rights of the local residents. Whereas both the petitioners and the state had submitted data concerning violations in *Beit Sourik*, the ICJ had relied for its conclusions on the report of the Secretary-General and his supplemental documents, and on special reports that the state counsel arguing before the HCJ in *Mara'abe* claimed had been 'far from precise'.[164]

The HCJ stated that its own access to the facts, which it attributed *inter alia* to an exchange process that was part of the adversarial nature of the proceedings conducted before it,[165] and its differences on this account with the ICJ, were of 'decisive significance'. According to international law, the legality of the barrier route depended on an appropriate balance between security needs and the impingement on the rights of the local residents. The appropriate solution resulted from a '[d]elicate and sensitive balancing between the two sides of the scale'. Its own *Beit Sourik* ruling, claimed the HCJ, struck this balance, unlike the ICJ ruling, which placed great weight on the infringement of rights and none on security–military needs, thus altogether disregarding the question of proportionality.[166]

Besides the differences in the factual basis available to each of the courts as an explanation of their different conclusions, the HCJ also noted that they differed in the scope of their examination. The ICJ looked at the entire route of the barrier, and this 'cast an unbearable task upon the ICJ', which could not embark on the necessary detailed analysis of each segment.[167] By contrast, the HCJ dealt with five segments in *Beit Sourik* and discussed others in various petitions. The HCJ mentioned that about 90 petitions had been submitted since the construction of the barrier began. Hearings on 44 had been completed and in most of them the parties reached a compromise

---

162. Ibid., para. 63.
163. While noting that it did not need to and could not determine the cause for what it called 'this severe oversight', the HCJ listed a few possibilities: the dossier of documents submitted to the ICJ, Israel's neglecting to provide information, the ICJ's unwillingness to use the data Israel did submit as well as the information in the public domain, and the method used by the ICJ, focusing on the barrier in general rather than on specific segments. Ibid., para. 65.
164. The HCJ points to four issues attesting to such imprecision: (i) the area of agricultural land that was seized – the state argued that it was significantly smaller than the data relayed to the ICJ; (ii) freedom of movement – the state argued that a regime of permits allowed entry and exit from the 'seam zone', contrary to the reports before the ICJ describing a split between the residents of this area and the rest of the West Bank; (iii) the water question – the state argued that data before the ICJ according to which Israel is annexing most of the western aquifer system were completely baseless; (iv) information regarding entry into and exit from the city of Qalqilia and the barrier's effect on life in the city. Ibid., paras. 66–7.
165. Ibid., para. 69.
166. Ibid., para. 68.
167. Ibid., para. 70.

after negotiations, usually after amendments were made to the route, while 43 were still pending.[168]

In the light of this analysis, the HCJ concluded that it would give full and appropriate weight to norms of international law as developed and interpreted by the ICJ in its Advisory Opinion. The ICJ's conclusion, however, relying on a different factual basis from the one before the HCJ, was not *res judicata* and did not obligate the HCJ to rule that each and every segment of the barrier violated international law. The HCJ would continue to examine each segment of the barrier as it was brought to its attention, asking whether it represented a proportional balance between security–military needs and the rights of the local population, although each segment would still be viewed as part of a whole.[169]

The rationale of the HCJ, attributing the differences between its own conclusions and those of the ICJ to discrepancies in their factual backgrounds, is not convincing, particularly after the HCJ's analysis in *Mara'abe*. As noted, the HCJ's determination that the barrier was a security measure is undermined by its own discussion of the proportionality question. Moreover, this conclusion is possible only because the HCJ ignored the settlements' expansionism and because it leapt over the question of their legality. The separations the HCJ made between security and political considerations on the one hand, and between the authority and proportionality issues on the other, blur the reality created by the barrier and are part of the background to the differences between the two courts.

The HCJ took pride in the fact that its examination of the barrier segment by segment (though keeping in mind the larger picture) enabled it to reach more nuanced decisions and was another reason for the gap between its conclusions and those of the ICJ.[170] But it is precisely this specific separation as well as the neglect of the larger picture, despite the dictum in *Mara'abe*, that allowed the HCJ to ignore the fact that the barrier is part of an existing de facto annexation and the related attempt to entrench it by drawing up a new border for Israel, incorporating major settlement blocs. Both stages of this process are illegal. The HCJ itself speaks of the side of the barrier including the enclave as 'the "Israeli" side' and, notwithstanding the quotation marks, this description suits a widespread perception of the barrier as a new border.[171]

Critics of the ICJ decision question the legal basis for its sweeping conclusion that the very construction of the barrier on occupied territory violates international law, regardless of whether it involves an attempted annexation or a specific violation of international humanitarian or human rights law. Kretzmer wonders, for instance, whether the barrier would be considered illegal under international law had it been built a few metres from the border in an uninhabited deserted area of the

---

168. Ibid., para. 72.
169. Ibid., para. 74.
170. Along a similar line, Kretzmer criticizes the sweeping conclusions of the ICJ concerning the barrier in its entirety. Kretzmer, 'The Light Treatment', *supra* note 5, at 100–2. Alberto de Puy also seems to find that the HCJ's analysis of each segment of the barrier's route leads to a more persuasive result than that of the ICJ. De Puy, *supra* note 5, at 299.
171. See note 152 and accompanying text, *supra*.

OPT.[172] Although this example is telling, it fails to appreciate that the structural analysis endorsed by the ICJ in the Advisory Opinion looks at the bigger picture. Its determination that building the barrier in the occupied territory is illegal should be read in the context of this specific barrier – the settlements, the dispossession, the de facto annexation, and the violations of human rights and humanitarian law. The ICJ looked at the forest, and not only at the trees. Had it been presented with another barrier built in the West Bank fitting the circumstances of Kretzmer's hypothetical example, its conclusion might have been different.[173]

Shany argues in his analysis of *Beit Sourik* and the Advisory Opinion that the HCJ judgment seems superior to that of the ICJ in its style and methodology,[174] but lacks a comprehensive legal analysis taking into account the link between the legality of the settlements and the legality of the barrier,[175] and attributes these differences to the institutional capacities of the two courts. But although the HCJ does, as noted, provide the detailed analysis missing from the ICJ's brushstroke discussion, it ultimately fails to convince on its own terms, largely because of its failure to address the actual context of the settlements and the de facto annexation.[176] This is precisely what the ICJ did through its appreciation that the whole is bigger than the parts. Indeed, the HCJ says in its judgment,

> *prima facie*, the ICJ could have determined, that on the basis of the examination of the totality of the fence, it had reached the conclusion that the motivation behind its construction is political and not security-based, and that the intention of the government of Israel in erecting the fence was its desire to annex parts of the West Bank which lay on the 'Israeli' side of the fences. The ICJ did not, however, do so; nor was a factual basis placed before it, which would have enabled it to do so.[177]

But the HCJ does note that the ICJ 'came extremely close to such an approach',[178] when pointing to the following statement by the ICJ:

> Whilst the Court notes the assurance given by Israel that the construction of the wall does not amount to annexation and that the wall is of a temporary nature . . . it nevertheless cannot remain indifferent to certain fears expressed to it that the route of the wall will prejudge the future frontier between Israel and Palestine, and the fear that Israel may integrate the settlements and their means of access. The Court considers that the construction of the wall and its associated regime create a 'fait accompli' on the ground that could well become permanent, in which case, and notwithstanding the formal characterization of the wall by Israel, it would be tantamount to de facto annexation.[179]

---

172. Kretzmer, 'The Light Treatment', *supra* note 5, at 100–2.
173. Thus, as Shany points out (Shany, 'Capacities and Inadequacies', *supra* note 5, at 238 and n. 33), although some parts of the barrier in the West Bank cannot definitely be linked to the location of settlements, this does not detract from the general picture as seen by the ICJ.
174. Shany, 'Capacities and Inadequacies', *supra* note 5, at 233–4.
175. Ibid., at 242–5.
176. Ben-Naftali argues that the ICJ failed to consider the legality of the barrier in the context of the legality of the occupation. As she notes, however, although the ICJ did not consider the legality of the occupation, it did consider the issue of the barrier as part of the greater whole of the occupation. Ben-Naftali, *supra* note 8, at 227–9.
177. *Mara'abe*, *supra* note 6, para. 71. For a similar critique see Kretzmer, 'The Light Treatment', *supra* note 5, at 92.
178. *Mara'abe*, *supra* note 6, para. 71.
179. Advisory Opinion, *supra* note 1, para. 121, cited in *Mara'abe*, *supra* note 6, para 71.

The ICJ speaks here of 'fears' of a possible de facto annexation while it should have pointed to an existing one.[180] The ICJ may have, in fact, understated its point.[181] Not least, its discussion of a 'fait accompli' is in the present, not future, tense. Of course, saying that there is a fait accompli does not mean that, given the political will, things could not be reversed, but rather amounts to a description of the current situation as one in which facts have been established on the ground. This paragraph should be read together with the ICJ's determination that the route of the barrier 'gives expression *in loco* to the illegal measures taken by Israel with regard to Jerusalem and the settlements' and that there is 'a risk of further alterations to the demographic composition of the Occupied Palestinian Territory resulting from the construction of the wall'. These measures, stated the ICJ, 'severely impede[s] the exercise by the Palestinian people of its right to self-determination'.[182] John Dugard, the Special Rapporteur of the UN Commission on Human Rights on the situation of human rights in the OPT, was much more explicit: 'what we are presently witnessing in the West Bank is a visible annexation under the guise of security'.[183]

The HCJ's decisions on the barrier ignore the reality of de facto annexation that Dugard explicitly points out and the ICJ cautiously hints at. For instance, the HCJ fails to notice how, in ruling that Israeli civilian towns built in the OPT were entitled to the defence of the Israeli army[184] and their residents to *in personam* application of Israel's Basic Laws, its own rulings become part of the de facto annexation that the barrier only continues. This de facto annexation may entail a greater violation of international law than a 'formal' one. It ensures for Israel the benefits of annexation without requiring it to grant Israeli citizenship and its concomitant rights and privileges to the Palestinians under occupation, while shielding it from sanctions for having annexed the territory illegally. The result is the current regime in the OPT that could, under the guise of a belligerent occupation, appear to resemble apartheid.[185]

Separating the wall into different segments does allow the HCJ a more careful consideration of the damages to Palestinians in the specific communities in question.

---

180. See Ben-Naftali, Gross, and Michaeli, *supra* note 72, at 602.
181. Jean-Francois Gareau indicates that the ICJ's view was not that a de facto annexation has already crystallized, but that it could be a violation *in statu nascendi*. In his view, however, the mere possibility of annexation places Israel in breach of its obligation to respect the Palestinians' right of self-determination, as the acts signalling this possibility are unilateral actions that tend to prejudice or impede the process. Gareau, *supra* note 27, at 513–16. He argues that the very fluidity of the final result compounds the obligation placed on Israel not to perform unilateral changes in the composition of the territory before an agreement is reached. Ibid., at 518. Yet if the barrier's construction is deemed essential to protect (illegal) settlements populated by Israeli citizens who are owed protection by the state, the incorporation of those settlements into Israel's self-defence zone signals that the territory is considered part of Israel and that the construction of the barrier represents an annexation. Ibid., at 521.
182. Advisory Opinion, *supra* note 1, para. 122.
183. J. Dugard, 'Question of the Violation of Human Rights in the Occupied Arab Territories, Including Palestine', Report of the Special Rapporteur of the Commission on Human Rights on the situation of human rights in the Palestinian territories occupied by Israel since 1967, Commission on Human Rights, Sixtieth Session, E/CN.4/2004/6, 8 Sept. 2003, paras. 6–16, available at http://daccessdds.un.org/doc/UNDOC/GEN/G03/160/82/PDF/G0316082.pdf?OpenElement.
184. See Gareau, *supra* note 27, at 521 (on Israel's argument for defence of the settlements as part of its self-defence as implying annexation).
185. See Ben-Naftali, Gross, and Michaeli, *supra* note 72, at 586–8.

But it also allows it to determine that building the barrier in the West Bank is in principle legal even when intended to protect the settlements, while leaving open the question of what would happen were such protection to require a grave violation of Palestinian rights in the absence of an alternative route.

The HCJ was wrong, then, when it determined that its differences with the ICJ could be attributed to the factual backgrounds before them. True, had the ICJ been better informed about Israel's security needs and the barrier's importance in the prevention of terror, it might also have been more sympathetic to some of the purposes behind it.[186] And yet the ICJ would probably have reached the same conclusion even if presented with a different factual background because it insisted on looking at the big picture and considering the structure of the occupation. The ICJ did mention Israel's authority and duty to protect its citizens,[187] but understood that building the barrier in the occupied territory is part of an annexation in the making. The HCJ criticized the ICJ for its failure to preserve the 'delicate and sensitive' balance that should govern the issues at stake, and was supposedly more persuasive because its proportionality analysis was much more detailed and accurate. The HCJ's new formula, however, making the settlements part of Israel's legitimate security interests rather than seeing them as part of a prohibited de facto annexation, besides the other noted contradictions in its reasoning, also upset the purported 'delicate balance'.

The HCJ's discussion of the violation of specific rights, then, is also unsatisfactory. Although both courts found that the violation of humanitarian norms by Israel could not be justified, neither one managed to support this with a convincing rationale, be it due to problems with their reasoning or with their respective doctrines of proportionality and their application to this specific context. The ICJ's answer seems more convincing concerning the larger picture, although its failure to give sufficient weight to the legitimate security purpose of the barrier (if properly built along the Green Line) is unfortunate. The HCJ expressed satisfaction with the fact that both courts operated within the same legal framework, but, had this *really* been the case, it could not have ignored the significant sections of international law forbidding settlements and annexation. The wall separating international law as read in The Hague from the rulings issued in Jerusalem is therefore much higher than the HCJ is willing to admit.

An institutional analysis tracing the limits constraining each court might note that the HCJ went as far as it could.[188] The very fact that it acknowledged the grievances caused to Palestinians, pierced the veil of security, and ordered a rerouting of the barrier is itself a great achievement for international law and human rights. This is probably true, but while in the next section I address the relationship between the legal processes in The Hague and the ones taking place in Jerusalem, my main focus in this article is on an interpretation of what courts actually do rather than on

---

186. On the ICJ's lack of empathy with Israeli society in general and terror victims in particular, see Shany, 'Capacities and Inadequacies', *supra* note 5, at 239–40. The ICJ could have relied here on open information or on the limited input on this issue in Israel's submission.

187. Advisory Opinion, *supra* note 1, para. 141.

188. For an excellent institutional analysis see Shany, 'Capacities and Inadequacies', *supra* note 5.

why they do it or on what they can do. In the next section, I consider the effects of both courts' determinations.

5. A TALE OF TWO COURTS, ONE OCCUPATION

Comparisons made between the Advisory Opinion and the *Beit Sourik* judgment point out that the HCJ's analysis is more specific and meticulous, providing more full-bodied, reasoned arguments,[189] while the ICJ's discussion of humanitarian law suffers from what has rightly been called 'light treatment'.[190] Yet, although well reasoned, the HCJ's discussion in both *Beit Sourik* and *Mara'abe* is not only oblivious of the bigger picture but also marked by internal contradictions on issues of security and military need and the extent of their judicial review, as noted throughout this article. True, the HCJ's two major rulings on the barrier are significant decisions, and give Palestinians a remedy on crucial material issues of humanitarian concern. However, given that they neither undermine nor question the structure of the occupation and its fundamental illegalities, they position the HCJ as a court of regulation of the occupation. The novelty in these two rulings is that the HCJ's regulatory decisions had hitherto been confined largely to procedural issues, whereas here they also extend to substantive matters.

To understand this change, evident also in the HCJ's unprecedented willingness to pierce the veil of security, we cannot ignore the shadow that The Hague cast over Jerusalem.[191] In 2002, prior to the UN General Assembly's request for an Advisory Opinion, the HCJ rejected a number of petitions raising issues similar to those discussed in *Beit Sourik*, usually in brief judgments deferring to the army's security arguments.[192] Different circumstances in the new petitions, as well as the growing reality of the barrier on the ground and the visibility of its effects, together with the accumulation of internal and external pressures in the course of time, may have led to the change in the HCJ's attitude. The change may be also considered as part of a broader context in which the HCJ is becoming more sensitive to international law, especially in the shadow of international criminal law. Specifically in the context of

---

189. Watson, *supra* note 5, at 24–5.
190. Kretzmer, 'The Light Treatment', *supra* note 5, at 88–9. Kretzmer further points to problems in the ICJ's application of the Hague Regulations on the seizure of land and destruction of property (ibid., at 95–100), which point to a lacuna in the ICJ's opinion concerning the question of whether it sees the situation in the West Bank as one of occupation, or one of an occupation in which hostilities amounting to armed conflict are taking place, and thus the laws regulating armed conflict also apply. On this issue see notes 41–42 and 106, and accompanying text, *supra*.
191. G. Levy notes in 'Cry, Our Beloved Country', *Ha'aretz*, 11 Jan. 2004, that the General Assembly's request for the Advisory Opinion is what prompted Israel to discover the wrongs of the barrier and to start considering changes in it.
192. See, e.g., HCJ 8172/02 *Ibrahim v. The IDF Commander in the West Bank* (unpublished, 2002), where the HCJ, in a two-page decision, rejected a petition from Palestinians who were severely affected by the barrier. The HCJ discussed the military commander's authority to seize land but did not discuss any humanitarian or human rights norms and determined that, although the local residents were injured by the actions taken by the military commander, these were security measures 'and, as is well known, this court tends not to intervene in operative security measures'. Other brief decisions issued prior to the General Assembly's referral rejecting arguments against the barrier without elaborate discussion include HCJ 3771/02 *The Local Council of A-Ras Village v. The Military Commander of Judea and Samaria* (unpublished, 2002); HCJ 3325/02 *Rashin Chasan (Kraos) v. The Military Commander of Judea and Samaria* (unpublished, 2002).

the barrier, the opinion of the CPS and the support of the Jewish neighbours in *Beit Sourik* may also have had an important effect. Nevertheless, and although isolating these various elements is not simple, the ICJ's looming shadow appears to have been critical in changing the HCJ's attitude towards the issue.[193]

The interaction between the ICJ and the HCJ can be seen as a case of synergy between national and international judiciaries.[194] Formally, the *Beit Sourik* judgment and the Advisory Opinion ignored each other, and the *Mara'abe* judgment rejected the Advisory Opinion's findings, while supposedly sharing its legal framework. Informally, the HCJ's rejection of Israel's security claims, however limited, is unusual when compared with the HCJ's jurisprudence in cases involving the OPT in general and the barrier in particular before the decision of the General Assembly to refer the matter to the ICJ.[195] The history of the HCJ's involvement in cases dealing with the rights of Palestinians shows that the court had intervened in substantial matters mainly in cases that had been at the forefront of international attention. By the time the HCJ ruled that the interrogation methods used by Israel's General Security Services, which some argued amounted to torture, were illegal,[196] the case had attracted worldwide media interest and gained the attention of the international legal community. The HCJ views itself as part of a cosmopolitan, human-rights community of jurists, and making the issue a matter of international law would not allow it to dismiss the petition outright, as it had often done in similar cases previously.[197]

The actions of both courts and the interactions between them may be viewed, in a phrase borrowed from Harold Koh, as a 'transnational legal process' of 'complex enforcement', in which the decisions of specific courts are not the final stop but only 'way stations'.[198] Koh asserts that nations must eventually interact with one another, and this interaction creates a complex process whereby international legal norms step into domestic processes, both legal and political.[199] For Koh, this process is a key

---

193. Kretzmer rightly notes that we do not know to what extent the pending ICJ proceedings influenced the HCJ's decision in *Beit Sourik*. Kretzmer, 'Introduction', *supra* note 5, at 10. Nevertheless, it seems plausible to assume, given the HCJ's unprecedented intervention in security considerations, that international law or at least its shadow did play a role here. An interesting question is also whether the HCJ's proceedings influenced the ICJ. Kretzmer notes that the Advisory Opinion was not influenced by the *Beit Sourik* ruling, and that the ICJ judges had already voted on the Opinion when the HCJ delivered its judgment and were not prepared to review their position in its light. Ibid. On this issue see also Shany, 'Capacities and Inadequacies', *supra* note 5, at 246.

194. T. M. Franck and G. H. Fox, 'Introduction: Transnational Judicial Synergy', in Thomas M. Franck and Gregory H. Fox (eds.), *International Law Decisions in National Courts* (1996) 1, at 1–11. For an argument on the need for both courts to co-operate within a framework of mutual comity formulated in the context of the separation barrier, see Shany, 'Capacities and Inadequacies', *supra* note 5, at 245–6.

195. Thus I agree with Kretzmer's description of *Beit Sourik* as signalling 'a radical departure' from the HCJ's tendency not to interfere in operational security considerations. Kretzmer, 'Introduction', *supra* note 5, at 8.

196. HCJ 5100/94 *The Israeli Committee Against Torture v. The State of Israel*, 53(4) P.D. 817 (1997).

197. For a few suggestions as to why the ICJ proceedings may have prompted the HCJ to give a substantial decision on the barrier see Shany, 'Capacities and Inadequacies', *supra* note 5, at 232 and note 6. For a discussion of the way the HCJ may have been affected by international legal developments, as part of a system of 'global deliberation', in the context of its scrutiny of Israel's interrogation methods, see A. Reichman, '"When We Sit To Judge We Are Being Judged": The Israeli GSS Case, Ex Parte Pinochet and Domestic/Global Deliberation', (2001) 9 *Cardozo Journal of Internationall and Comparative Law* 41.

198. H. Koh, 'Transnational Legal Process', (1996) 75 *Nebraska Law Review* 181, at 199.

199. Ibid., at 205.

factor in the internalization of norms that, ultimately, is the reason why states obey international law.[200] Although the legal proceedings in the ICJ and the HCJ were independent, the HCJ's request from the parties in subsequent cases involving the barrier to submit their positions concerning the Advisory Opinion is significant.[201] In terms of Koh's model, this request could be viewed as an instance of Israeli law partly internalizing the ICJ's judicial interpretation in its Advisory Opinion, whereby Israel was violating international law.[202] And yet the case of the separation barrier illustrates the need to modify the model: the HCJ internalized the ICJ's interpretation of international law only partly, while rejecting significant sections of it. The HCJ adopted this position before the ICJ rendered its Advisory Opinion (although ostensibly influenced by its expected contents), and reiterated it after the Advisory Opinion was published. The overall effect of the HCJ partly accepting and partly rejecting the ICJ's determination was to lighten the burden of some of the people under occupation, but also to grant further legitimation to Israeli policies that, according to the ICJ, are in violation of international law. Many explanations for the wide divergence between the conclusions of the HCJ and those of the ICJ are possible.[203] For our purposes, what is important is that this case proves the need to rethink 'transnational legal process' as a model that is about the internalization of international law. This model may suitably describe cases such as the litigation on the barrier in the two courts, but this case illustrates that such transnational legal process may sometimes lead to greater enforcement of international law in the service of humanity but at the same time may also result in greater legitimation of military action in violation of humanitarian values.[204]

Incidentally, the effects of this internationalization were evident not only in the HCJ. As soon as the matter was referred to the ICJ and before it rendered its Advisory

---

200. H. Koh, 'Transnational Legal Process After September 11th', (2004) 22 *Berkeley Journal of International Law* 337, at 339–49. See also H. Koh, 'Why Do Nations Obey International Law?', (1977) 106 *Yale Law Journal* 2599, at 2602–3, 2645–58.
201. See Shany, 'Head against the Wall', *supra* note 5.
202. Compare with Koh's discussion of the Nicaragua case in the ICJ and its impact on US domestic law. Koh, 'September 11', *supra* note 200, at 340.
203. For a comprehensive discussion see Shany, 'Capacities and Inadequacies', *supra* note 5.
204. One should also consider in this context Anne-Marie Slaughter's concept of a 'New World Order', in which judges are one of the groups of sub-state actors who interact independently from the states in networks that create a disaggregated world order. In her terminology, the relationship between the HCJ and the ICJ is one of a vertical government network, between national officials, in this case judges, and their supranational counterparts. A.-M. Slaughter, *A New World Order* (2004), 1–35, 131–65. On the role of judges in this order, see ibid., at 65–103. See also A.-M. Slaughter, 'A Typology of Transjudicial Communication', (1994) 29 *University of Richmond Law Review* 99. For our purpose, the relevant factors may not be those concerning judges creating transnational networks and connections, but rather the idea that judges share the recognition of one another as participants in a common judicial enterprise and view themselves as fellow members of a profession that transcends national borders. Ibid., at 68. Although it is not clear from the HCJ's judgment whether it sees the ICJ in this light, the issues on which the HCJ chose to support the ICJ seem to suggest that it may have been partly motivated by this perception of a partnership in a common judicial enterprise. While Slaughter's insights are important to understand sub-state-level dialogues and influences between different actors, such as judges and courts, her description of this 'new world order' does not seem sufficiently inclusive of a variety of possible situations: courts may talk at each other rather than to each other, and the division of labour between courts may sometimes serve to conceal lack of enforcement rather than guarantee a more comprehensive and just legal order. The dynamic between the ICJ and the HCJ may represent a complex case, whereby the HCJ is to some extent affected by the ICJ and even resorts to a deferential discourse in its decision, but rejects many of the ICJ's findings.

Opinion, public debate flared up in Israel on the need to modify the barrier's route. These internal pressures were certainly reinforced by those ensuing externally from the process in The Hague. The result was the two HCJ rulings, which did not fully abide by the logic of the Advisory Opinion and did not examine the barrier as part of the structure of the occupation, but did present the HCJ as a reasoned mediator of security and humanitarian considerations rather than as the bête noire of the international legal community. If synergy means the concerted efforts of two systems to improve the enforcement of international law, the result here is mixed: the barrier as a feature of the occupation ultimately gained judicial legitimacy, but the restrictions imposed on it could help to reduce the onus on the Palestinians and lead to changes in its overall structure. The question whether the cumulative effect of the HCJ's activity will merely be that of regulation or rather that of structural changes in the barrier and its associated regime is still pending. Notwithstanding the novelty these rulings entail, as noted, they still keep the court in its overall role of regulating (now mostly through proportionality), and even legitimizing, the occupation and its illegalities. The court's discourse on humanitarian law and proportionality, together with the army's responses, should be seen in the broader context of the current relationship between humanitarianism and force. As David Kennedy elaborates, humanitarianism and military strategy currently speak the same language, since modern humanitarian law provides a professional vocabulary about objectives and means that civilized people can use to discuss military violence. Military commanders and humanitarians, says Kennedy, assess acts of violence from a similar vantage point, and thus reinforce one another's professionalism. In a way, humanitarian law becomes a blueprint for professional efficiency on behalf of the military: it regulates how the military would best achieve its objectives without unnecessary or disproportional use of force.[205] Kennedy's analysis pertains to the place of humanitarian lawyers and advocates vis-à-vis the military. In petitions against the barrier, humanitarian lawyers do not confine their arguments to proportionality but point to its illegality and to the specific occupation regime it reinforces and creates. The HCJ's judgments, however, could be seen as an instance of the humanitarianism Kennedy describes, sharing the language of proportionality with the military without attempting to look in depth at the structure of the occupation and without questioning the nature and the legitimacy of the concept of 'security' used by the army, but rather regulating within it. This humanitarianism, to borrow from Kennedy's analysis, participates in the occupation machine.[206] Through this regulation policy, the HCJ may rescue thousands of Palestinian villagers from the unbearable conditions the barrier has created for them, which is indeed significant, but it also legitimizes the occupation and the place of the barrier within it. Unlike the HCJ, the ICJ's Advisory Opinion, even if it does not go so far as to call the occupation illegal, does attempt to delegitimize the occupation and the barrier. That it often

---

205. D. Kennedy, *The Dark Side of Virtue: Reassessing International Humanitarianism* (2004), 235–323.
206. For an understanding of various alleviations in the name of humanitarianism as being part of the structure of the regime of the occupation in general and the barrier in particular, see A. Azoulay and A. Ophir, 'The Monster's Tail', in M. Sorkin (ed.), *Against the Wall* (2005), 2 at 23.

does so in an under-reasoned way is unfortunate. That it has no *direct* effect on the reality of people's lives is a well-known reality in international law.

As discussed above, in the HCJ's analysis, the Palestinians' rights are defined as rights, while the settlers' rights are tantamount to security interests. When these definitions are used in the context of applying proportionality in the OPT, Palestinians may enjoy occasional victories in specific cases, but, overall, they find their rights restricted in the name of security in ways that create imbalance.

An interesting phenomenon deserves note in this context. In the OPT, the Israeli army has resorted to practices considered forbidden by most of the international law community but allowed by the HCJ with few if any limitations, including punitive home demolitions[207] and deportations.[208] Eventually, use of these measures was interrupted. Demolitions were stopped when the army judged them to be ineffective as deterrents, and deportations were discontinued when it was understood that their legality under international law, although sanctioned by Israeli courts, is dubious.[209] By contrast, reliance on other heavily regulated practices, such as the barrier, has continued.[210] Allowing a practice in its full horror, then, may eventually lead to its dismissal, perhaps out of fear of international sanctions, especially in the era of international criminal law, while attempts to regulate it through proportionality endow it with an aura of legitimacy. Apparently, these are the rules of the proportionality game.

The jury is still out on whether the HCJ's ruling on the barrier continues or breaks with its previous endeavour concerning the enforcement of humanitarian law in the OPT. The HCJ had not ruled before on the applicability of the Fourth Geneva Convention in the OPT, stating that it was not justiciable in Israeli courts. When it did examine Israeli military activity in the OPT in the light of the Convention, it chose to interpret it in a way that made it meaningless.[211] The few cases where the HCJ did intervene were mostly 'landmark cases' dealing with procedure and due process and hardly affecting the life of the Palestinians.[212] In recent years, the court has scrutinized military actions in light of the Geneva Convention without deciding on its applicability or changing its doctrine on the Convention's justiciability, relying instead on the declaration that Israel abides *ex gratia* by the Convention's

---

207. See Kretzmer, *supra* note 73, at 145–63. See, e.g., HCJ 2006/97 *Ghanimat v. Officer Commanding Central Command*, 51(2) P.D. 651 (1997) (the plausibility of the deterrence objective prevents intervention in the considerations of the military commander concerning home demolitions).

208. See Kretzmer, *supra* note 73, 165–86. See especially HCJ 785/87 *Afu v. IDF Commander of the West Bank*, 42(1) PD 4 (1990), trans. in (1990) 29 ILM 139.

209. On home demolitions see A. Harel, 'IDF Panel Recommends Ending Punitive House Demolitions for Terrorists' Families', *Ha'aretz* 17 Feb. 2005. On deportations see D. Barak-Erez, 'The International Law of Human Rights and Constitutional Law: A Case Study of an Expanding Dialogue', (2004) 2 *International Journal of Constitutional Law* 611, 630–1.

210. Another interesting example is the use of physical force, which some argue amounts to torture, in the investigations of the General Security Services, prohibited by the HCJ in *The Israeli Committee Against Torture v. The State of Israel* (*supra* note 196), but which, according to some reports, continues by other means. See Public Committee Against Torture in Israel, 'Back to a Routine of Torture' (April 2003), available at http://www.stoptorture.org.il//eng/images/uploaded/publications/58.pdf; Public Committee Against Torture in Israel, 'Flawed Defense' (September 2001), available at http://www.stoptorture.org.il//eng/images/uploaded/publications/13.pdf.

211. Kretzmer, *supra* note 73, 43–56.

212. R. Shamir, 'Landmark Cases and the Reproduction of Legitimacy', (1990) 24(3) *Law and Society Review* 781.

humanitarian provisions.[213] In most cases, however, this use of the Convention has served to legitimize Israeli army practices,[214] to deal with issues of due process and procedure[215] or in judgments that are mostly declaratory.[216] The *Beit Sourik* and *Mara'abe* rulings are novel in that, although the HCJ denies this, they pierce the veil of security considerations, reject them, and apply humanitarian law (including the Geneva Conventions) on a matter that may have a significant effect on the life of Palestinians. In this sense these rulings constitute a breakthrough.[217] In a larger context, however, they legitimize the structure of the Israeli occupation and address only specific segments of the barrier, and their overall impact on these specific segments and on the barrier in general remains unclear. After the *Mara'abe* decision the HCJ issued orders in pending barrier cases requesting the parties to express their updated positions on the matter before it in the light of the *Mara'abe* decision,[218] suggesting that this ruling could affect other segments currently under judicial scrutiny. Indeed, the HCJ's requests that the parties to the various pending barrier cases submit positions, first concerning the Advisory Opinion, and later concerning its own major decisions on the issue, may be an indication of a complex trans/national legal process, which is still not over.

On 20 February 2005, in response to the *Beit Sourik* ruling, the Israeli government decided on a new route for the barrier that was purported to be less injurious to Palestinians, reducing the numbers of Palestinians living in the 'seam zone' between the barrier and the Green Line from 93,200 to 49,400.[219] And yet, more than a year after *Beit Sourik*, a decision was still needed in *Mara'abe*, and many new petitions

---

213. For an understanding of these decisions in the broader context of the role of international law within the Israeli legal system see Barak-Erez, *supra* note 209; see especially the discussion of cases concerning the OPT, ibid., at 615–17, 618–23.

214. *Ajuri v. IDF Commander of the West Bank, supra* note 50 (allowing the 'assigned residence' of Palestinians who assisted terrorist activities, while restricting the use of this mechanism through the doctrine of proportionality). See O. Ben-Naftali and K. Michaeli, 'The Call of Abraham – Between Deportation and Assigned Residence: A Critique of the Ajuri Case', (2002) 15 *Hamishpat* 56 (Hebrew). For a reading of this decision as establishing an important role for IHL in the HCJ's jurisprudence see E. Benvenisiti, 'Case Review: *Ajuri et al. v. IDF Commander in the West Bank et al.*', (2003) 9 *European Public Law* 481. On this case see also D. Barak-Erez, 'Assigned Residence in Israel's Administered Territories: The Judicial Review of Security Measures', (2003) 33 *Israel Yearbook on Human Rights* 303.

215. HCJ 3239/02 *Marab v. The IDF Commander in Judea and Samaria*, 57(2) P.D. 349 (2002) (repealing orders enabling detainment of Palestinians for up to 18 days without judicial review).

216. HCJ 4764/04 *PHR v. The IDF Commander in Gaza*, 58(5) P.D. 385 (2004) (declaring the army's obligation to abide by humanitarian law during an operation in the town of Rafiah).

217. A significant decision in another context is the recent judgment concerning the 'early warning' procedure: in this case the HCJ held that the procedure, according to which Israeli soldiers wishing to arrest a Palestinian suspected of terrorist activity may be aided by a local Palestinian resident, who gives the suspect prior warning of possible injury to the suspect or to those with him during the arrest, is illegal. See HCJ 3799/02 *Adalah – The Legal Centre for Arab Minority Rights in Israel v. GOC Central Command* (not yet published, 2005), available at http://elyon1.court.gov.il/Files_ENG/02/990/037/a32/02037990.a32.HTM.

218. See, e.g., HCJ 2577/04 *Taha El Chawaga v. The Prime Minster*, decision issued by the Court on 19 Sept. 2005; HCJ 6336/04 *Head of the Local Council Dir-Balut v. The Prime Minister*, decision issued by the Court on 19 Sept. 2005.

219. For a discussion of the new route and a map comparing it with the previous one see The Humanitarian Impact of the West Bank Barrier on Palestinian Communities, March 2005, Update No. 5, A Report to the Humanitarian Emergency Policy Group (HEPG), compiled by the United Nations Office for Coordination on Humanitarian Affairs (OCHA) and the United Nations Relief and Works Agency for Palestinian Refugees (UNRWA) in the occupied Palestinian Territory, available at http://www.humanitarianinfo.org/opt/docs/UN/OCHA/OCHABarRprt05_Full.pdf. See also the official 'seam zone' website of the Israeli Ministry of Defence: http://www.seamzone.mod.gov.il/Pages/ENG/default.htm.

are constantly being submitted to the HCJ, even after *Mara'abe*, addressing similar circumstances. This situation attests that, despite the judicial pronouncements, the barrier's construction still raises the same problems described back in *Beit Sourik*.[220] As a matter of fact, a new *Beit Sourik* petition is now pending, arguing that the new route in this very area did not solve the problem of the Palestinian residents.[221] On the other hand, in some areas the rerouting of the barrier, following the *Beit Sourik* judgment, to a route proximate to the Green Line, led to changes significant enough to be held by the HCJ as reducing the infringement of the rights of Palestinians in a way that strikes a valid balance between rights and security.[222]

Will *Beit Sourik* and *Mara'abe* become 'landmark cases' that in reality will have little influence on the life of Palestinians? Given that they go beyond the procedural issues handled in previous OPT landmark cases,[223] they do have a potential for truly affecting the lives of Palestinians. Nevertheless, they do confer on the occupation and the barrier the legitimacy of the rule of law while many daily grievances of Palestinians, including injuries associated with the barrier that attracted less judicial and public attention, are still awaiting address. As noted above, there are many petitions concerning the barrier before the HCJ,[224] and obviously even those do not cover the full range of grievances associated with it. In other cases dealing with serious violations of rights in the OPT, the HCJ often still gives the actions of the Israeli army its stamp of approval. Consider, for instance, a petition briefly rejected by the HCJ involving the city of Hebron, where two Palestinians were prevented from returning to homes they had left because of harassment from neighbouring Jewish settlers. The house of one petitioner was in an area outside Hebron where the Jewish settlement of Kiryat Arba was later built. In 1987, a barbed-wire fence – yet another barrier – was built around her house, preventing the family's access. A gate was later installed, to which they were given a key, but the army later replaced the lock and refused to give her the new keys. The HCJ ruled that the arrangement suggested by the army, stating that the gate would be opened within minutes following prior co-ordination by phone, was satisfactory and was required from a security perspective, dismissing the petitioner's fears that opening the gate would each time turn into a protracted affair. In rejecting the petition, the HCJ again accepted the paradigm that Palestinian rights can be restricted to protect the settlers, that only settlers can invoke 'security' arguments, and that an arrangement requiring a person to co-ordinate every entry to her home with the occupying

---

220. See, e.g., the petition in HCJ 1348/05 *Mayor of Salfit v. State of Israel* (pending), describing situations comparable with those discussed in the *Beit Sourik* case, which were not amended following this judgment and required additional petitions. The petition at HCJ 10905/05 *The Major of Jayus v. The Prime Minister*, filed 23 Nov. 2005 (after the *Mara'abe* decision), also outlines problems affecting Palestinians of the type discussed in the two major cases already decided by the HCJ.
221. HCJ 426/05 *Bido Village Council v. The Government of Israel* (pending).
222. HCJ 5683/04 *Beit Sira Village Council v. The Government of Israel* (not yet published, 9 Jan. 2006), available at http://elyon1.court.gov.il/Files/04/830/056/a19/04056830.a19.HTM. For another case where the HCJ held that a significant rerouting of the barrier following its principled rulings resulted in a route which strikes a valid balance see HCJ 6336/04 *Kamal Yosef Mahmud Moussa v. The Prime Minister* (not yet published, 4 Jan. 2006), available at http://elyon1.court.gov.il/Files/04/360/063/a14/04063360.a14.HTM.
223. See Shamir, *supra* note 212.
224. See note 168 and accompanying text, *supra*.

army, all to protect the security of settlements whose legality is never questioned, is acceptable.[225] Unlike the *Beit Sourik* and *Mara'abe* decisions, this one-page ruling was not placed in English translation on the HCJ's website and was not the subject of extensive discussions in international law journals, but is as much a part of the occupation's legal structure as the decisions discussed in this and other articles.

Whether the recent developments in the HCJ's jurisprudence are about the enforcement of humanitarian law or about a *fata morgana* of humanitarian law is, therefore, still to be determined. They may attest to the limits of humanitarian law, including the doctrine of proportionality as applied by the HCJ and its enforcement as discussed throughout the article, particularly by domestic courts. The limits could be inherent in humanitarian law, or reflect its misapplication by the courts or the limits of courts, or all of the above. Indeed, the limited institutional capacity of the courts, both international and domestic, should not be disregarded.[226] Does international humanitarian law, then, serve as a mechanism of legitimation or of emancipation? The answer is both. Whether the HCJ's involvement has contributed more to the legitimation of the occupation or to the improvement of the Palestinians' lives is a recurring question that may never be answered.[227]

6. Conclusion

The barrier can be understood as a physical structure set up in order to ensure the security of Israelis and, as such, part of the system restricting freedom of movement for Palestinians in the OPT. These restrictions are a salient feature of the occupation and play a central role in denying the Palestinians the possibility of conducting a full human life. Not only do they violate their access to health care, education, work, and family life, but they touch on a much deeper issue, concerning the very idea that individuals need to convince someone else that they have a legitimate reason for moving and have procured a special permit for doing so.[228] The barrier continues the checkpoints system restricting freedom of movement within the OPT, whose harsh consequences have been widely documented.[229]

---

225. HCJ 4547/03 *Chlabi v. The Prime Minister* (not yet published, 2005). Some of the facts of this case are not detailed in the HCJ's verdict but in the petition itself. Significantly, the HCJ did not mention in its decision that while the petitioners were outside the house they could not enter, their house was set on fire and destroyed.

226. See Shany, 'Capacities and Inadequacies', *supra* note 5.

227. Kretzmer reminds us that 'however critical one may be of many of the Court's decisions . . . One must also consider what the position would have been if the Court had declined to assume jurisdiction in such petitions.' He further speculates that 'in the short term, the lack of formal external constraints would have resulted in more arbitrariness . . . Is it possible that in the medium or long term, the very lack of restraint . . . would have made the occupation less palatable for Israel's elite, and that the pressure to end the occupation . . . would have been felt much earlier?' (Kretzmer, *supra* note 73, at 198).

228. For a description of such a regime see J. M. Coetzee, *The Life and Times of Michael K* (1983).

229. See Machsomwatch, 'A Counterview: Checkpoints 2004' (2004), available at http://www.machsomwatch.org/docs/Counterview.pdf; B'Tselem – The Israeli Information Center for Human Rights in the Occupied Territories, 'Forbidden Roads: The Discriminatory West Bank Road Regime' (2004), available at http://www.btselem.org/download/200408_Forbidden_Roads_Eng.pdf; B'Tselem – The Israeli Information Center for Human Rights in the Occupied Territories, 'No Way Out' (2001), available at http://www.btselem.org/Download/200106_No_Way_Out_Eng.doc; Physicians for Human Rights, 'The

These restrictions, as noted, rest on the assumption that the rights of Israelis are a security concern justifying a 'proportionate' limitation of rights of Palestinians. While rights may sometimes override these security concerns, the basic structure remains in place: the freedom of Jewish settlers to live in the OPT safely and travel freely is apparently hardly ever challenged, resulting in a regime that regulates people and their movements on the basis of ethnicity. The HCJ noted that this structure has been likened by some to apartheid,[230] but Dugard, the special rapporteur who is also one of South Africa's leading international lawyers, notes in his report that, although the term 'Apartheid Wall' is frequently used in Palestine, 'Strictly speaking, this historical metaphor is inaccurate as no wall of this kind was erected between Black and White in apartheid South Africa.'[231]

The barrier, however, is not only a physical structure. It is part of the structure of the occupation. It represents de facto annexation, confining security concerns to one side, restricting freedom of movement to the point of denying realization of basic aspects of human life, dissecting the occupied territory, branding people, regulating their bodies, their location, and their movements, and allocating their rights on the basis of their ethnicity.[232] Restraining people's access to the barrier to specific hours, only for specific goals such as work or school, and only through specific gates,[233] denies the humanity of the Palestinian residents of the 'seam zone' and others who wish to enter this area: from people who should be able to make choices about their daily life, they become prisoners of the Israeli occupation. When considering the legal questions and the ways in which courts have addressed the barrier, we should recall its effects on people's lives. Arguably, we should also recall its stated purpose, which is to save the lives of Israelis threatened by Palestinian terrorists. This purpose, however, flies in the face of the barrier's route, which often separates Palestinians from Palestinians rather than Palestinians from Israelis. The absence of a barrier between Palestinian villages in the 'seam zone' and Israel, and the existing barrier separating them from the rest of the West Bank, attest that the barrier is not only about 'security', and, indeed, its route may even sacrifice security in the name of other interests. Allowing Palestinians to cross the barrier and enter the 'seam zone' to work, as is required given the barrier's location within the West Bank,

Bureaucracy of Occupation' (2004), available at http://www.phr.org.il/phr/files/articlefile_1108316859979. pdf. See also the film *Checkpoint* (Machsomim), directed by Y. Shamir (Israel, 2004).

230. *Mara'abe, supra* note 6, para. 45.

231. Dugard, *supra* note 183, note 1.

232. Thus the barrier and the permits regimes associated with it can be examined from the perspective of Foucault's notion of 'bio-power' as a form of power which achieves the subjugation of bodies and the control of populations, and of Agamben's idea of 'bare-life'. See respectively M. Foucault, *The History of Sexuality, Volume 1: An Introduction* (1990), at 135–45, and G. Agamben, *Homo Sacer: Sovereign Power and Bare Life* (1998). For discussions which address this perspective, as well as the spatial implications of the barrier and its place within the logic of 'separation' in the Israeli–Palestinian context see Azoulay and Ophir, *supra* note 206; M. Sorkin, 'Introduction: Up Against the Wall', in M. Sorkin (ed.), *Against the Wall* (2005), vi; O. Yiftachel and H. Yacobi, 'Barriers, Walls and Dialectics: The Shaping of "Creeping Apartheid" in Israel/Palestine', in M. Sorkin (ed.), *Against the Wall* (2005), 138; S. Hanafi, 'Spacio-cide and Bio-Politics: The Israeli Colonial Project from 1947 to the Wall', in M. Sorkin (ed.), *Against the Wall* (2005), 158; R. Marton and D. Baum, 'Transparent Wall, Opaque Gates', in M. Sorkin (ed.), *Against the Wall* (2005), 212; E. Weizman, 'Hollow Land: The Barrier Archipelago and the Impossible Politics of Separation', in M. Sorkin (ed.), *Against the Wall* (2005), 224; N. Ouroussoff, 'A Line in the Sand: Architects and Israel's Barrier', *New York Times*, 1 Jan. 2006.

233. See *supra* note 22.

creates 'holes' through which potential terrorists may enter Israel.[234] Rather than building the barrier so as to protect Israel, then, security is sacrificed to maintain the settlements. All of this attests to the gap between the 'fantasy of separation'[235] which the barrier represents, and the complex reality, both separated and not separated, in which Israelis and Palestinians live.

The barrier, however, is also a site of resistance to this persistent breach of Palestinians' rights in the name of perceived Israeli security. It is the site for joint Palestinian–Israeli resistance in the form of demonstrations and sit-ins, but also of violent military reactions to it.[236] One of the movements leading this resistance is an Israeli group called 'Anarchists against the Wall' and the related group 'One Struggle', which is active on both human and animal rights.[237] These groups came to the forefront of public attention after a demonstrator was shot by the Israeli army.[238] The activities of groups seeking to abolish structures of hierarchy while resisting the barrier are a significant development. Another context for considering the barrier are walls between Jewish and Arab neighbourhoods within Israel proper, built supposedly for crime protection but sometimes claimed to represent racist–segregationist ideology, which are currently being litigated in Israeli courts.[239] Although still limited and local, this phenomenon attests to the insidiousness of the separation logic and its effect on the lives of Israelis and Palestinians in Israel and in the OPT.[240]

In one of the many petitions on the barrier submitted to the HCJ, the State Attorney's office argued in its submission that the 'barrier' is a 'natural and required measure, in the spirit of the saying "high fences make good neighbours"',[241] thus twisting the familiar saying 'good fences make good neighbours'. The 'good fences' saying was immortalized in Robert Frost's poem 'Mending Wall',[242] written in 1914.

---

234. Dan Rubinstein, 'The Fence Will Not Block the Next Suicide Bomber', *Ha'aretz*, 9 Dec. 2005, b5 (Hebrew).
235. The term 'fantasy of separation' is used by Weizman in his analysis of the barrier; see Weizman, *supra* note 232, at 225.
236. M. Rapaport, 'Without *Shaids*', *Ha'aretz*, 10 June 2005; G. Lasky, 'Bilin: A Test Case for Immunity – The Culture of Violence and Deception among the Israeli "Security Forces"' (2005), available at http://www.adalah.org/newsletter/eng/octo5/ar1.pdf.
237. See http://www.onestuggle.com.
238. L. Galili, 'Fringe Benefits', *Ha'aretz*, 2 Jan. 2004 (Hebrew); R. Kupperboim, 'Hero Anti', *Ha'ir*, 1 Jan. 2004 (Hebrew).
239. See Administrative Petition (Tel-Aviv) 1252/05 *Aaref Mucharab v. The National Council for Planning and Building – Central District* (pending), which deals with the plan to erect a wall 1,600 metres long and 4 metres high between the Arab neighbourhood of Pardes Snir in Lod and the nearby Jewish village of Nir Zvi. On this case see A. Dayan, 'Wall-Eyed', *Ha'aretz*, 22 July 2003. On walls now being built between Jews and Arabs in Israel see the Arab Association for Human Rights, 'Behind the Walls: Separation Walls Between Arabs and Jews in Mixed Cities and Neighborhoods in Israel' (2005), available at http://www.arabhra.org/publications/reports/Word/SeperationWallsReport_English.doc; L. Galili, 'Long Division', *Ha'aretz* 19 Dec. 2003, which discusses three such walls in detail. For more information on the issue see http://www.bimkom.org/publicationView.asp?publicationId=51 (Hebrew).
    For a discussion of the barrier as part of regimes which are structured around economic and ethnic separations see Algazi, *supra* note 150; see also Ronen Shamir, 'Without Borders? Notes on Globalization as a Mobility Regime', (2005) 23 *Sociological Theory* 197, at 204–5.
240. For a suggestion to look at Israel's land policies in the West Bank as a continuation of its domestic land policies see Ben-Naftali, Gross, and Michaeli, *supra* note 72, at 611, n. 329. On the logic of separation in the Israeli–Palestinian context, see A. Gross, 'The Constitution, Reconciliation and Transitional Justice: Lessons from South Africa and Israel', (2004) 40 *Stanford Journal of International Law*, 47, at 100–2.
241. HCJ 9961/03 *Hamoked – The Center for the Defense of the Individual v. The Government of Israel*, Respondent's Brief (1 Jan. 2004), para. 33.
242. R. Frost, 'Mending Wall', in *The Poetry of Robert Frost*, ed. E. C. Lathem (1979), at 33.

Its origin, however, is older, and some ascribe it to a mention in a 1640 letter from Reverend Rowley to Massachusetts Governor John Winthrop, admitting a that good fence will keep peace between neighbours but cautioning against high stone walls that would preclude them from meeting.[243] A high wall, then, is not a good fence.

Robert Frost's poem actually begins by saying, 'Something there is that doesn't love a wall', describing the speaker and his neighbour walking together to mend a wall between them. The neighbour recurrently says, 'Good fences make good neighbours', but the speaker wonders if he could make his neighbour consider: 'Why do they make good neighbors? . . . /Before I built a wall I'd ask to know/What I was walling in or walling out,/And to whom I was like to give offence.' The neighbour, however, 'moves in darkness as it seems to me –/Not of woods only and the shade of trees./He will not go behind his father's saying,/And he likes having thought of it so well/He says again, "Good fences make good neighbors."'

At first, like the neighbour in the poem, the Israeli government moved in darkness and failed to answer in its submission to the courts why it is building the wall along the present route. Later, answers came. First strategic–security answers, and then answers pertaining to the protection of the settlements themselves, as well as to their expansion. The petitioners in the various cases, like the speaker in the poem, want to bring the government and the courts to consider why the barrier is good and to enquire carefully into what is being walled in or walled out, and to whom the barrier is likely to give offence. The answers to these questions are already well known. The barrier will give offence to many. Its implications for the daily lives of tens of thousands of Palestinians and their freedom of movement, housing, education, health, and family life have been widely reported.[244] All know that the barrier often separates Palestinians from Palestinians rather than Palestinians from Israelis. It divides families, separating people from their workplace, children from their schools, patients from doctors. It turns tens of thousands of Palestinians into illegal residents in their own homes, requiring them to obtain a special permit to stay in the 'seam zone'. Facing a reality in which the barrier is part of the settlements and of the de facto annexation regime entailed by them, international law could shed light on the illegal regime that this barrier is part of rather than move in darkness ignoring its illegality. The structural analysis in the Advisory Opinion could move us in this direction, though its potential and influence are undermined by the many flaws in parts of the ICJ's reasoning. In turn, the HCJ's problematic application of IHL to the barrier, although it might improve on the original planning, also serves to confer legitimacy on this structure and its regime while being unable to dismantle it.

---

243. Wolfgang Mieder, '"Good Fences Make Good Neighbours": History and Significance of an American Proverb', (2003) 114 *Folklore* 155 at 158, available at http://taylorandfrancis.metapress.com/media/988tvgryundke6tvxceg/contributions/5/x/f/g/5xfgtwckwdpm3nxx.pdf.

244. For a detailed report on the violations of human rights deriving from the barrier see B'Tselem – The Israeli Information Centre for Human Rights in the Occupied Territories, 'Behind The Barrier: Human Rights Violations as a Result of Israel's Separation Barrier' (April 2003), available at http://www.btselem.org/Download/200304_Behind_The_Barrier_Eng.pdf; B'Tselem – The Israeli Information Center for Human Rights in the Occupied Territories, 'Not All It Seems: Preventing Palestinians Access to their Lands West of the Separation Barrier in the Tulkarm-Qalqiliya Area' (June 2004), available at http://www.btselem.org/Download/200406_Qalqiliya_Tulkarm_Barrier_Eng.pdf. See also the information from the UN Office for the Coordination of Humanitarian Affairs (OCHA – OPT) at http://www.humanitarianinfo.org/opt/.

The Legality of the West Bank Wall: Israel's High Court of Justice v. the International Court of Justice

*Victor Kattan**

ABSTRACT

This Article offers a critique of the decision reached by Israel's High Court of Justice in the Mara'abe Case (2005) as well as some aspects of the International Court of Justice's Advisory Opinion on the Legal Consequences of the Construction of a Wall in the Occupied Palestinian Territory (2004). The Article takes a socio-legal and facts-based approach to analyzing the decisions' discussions of settlements, self-determination, and self-defense, examining all three topics in light of several recent legal and political developments.

TABLE OF CONTENTS

* LL. B (Hons.) Brunel University, 2001; LL. M Leiden University, 2002; Research Fellow at the British Institute of International and Comparative Law. The Author attended the oral pleadings before the ICJ in The Hague in February 2004 in his personal capacity. He also worked in the Occupied Palestinian Territories as a U.N. Development Programme TOKTEN (transfer of knowledge through expatriate nationals) consultant in 2003-4, where he witnessed the construction of the wall first-hand in Bethlehem, Jerusalem, and Qalqilya. He would like to thank John Dugard, D.W. Greig, William V.G. Kattan, Stephanie Koury, John McHugo, Panos Merkouris, Nigel Parker, Gillian Triggs, John B. Quigley, and Iain Scobbie for their comments. The views expressed here and any mistakes therein are of course attributable to the Author alone. He can be contacted at the following email address: v.kattan@biicl.org.

"Is the separation fence legal? That is the question before us."

–Judge Barak, *Mara'abe v. The Prime Minister of Israel,*
introductory paragraph.

I. INTRODUCTION

On September 15, 2005, the Israel Supreme Court, sitting as the High Court of Justice (HCJ), rendered its decision in *Mara'abe v. The Prime Minister of Israel,*[1] in which it questioned a number of points of law arising from the Advisory Opinion of the International Court of Justice (ICJ) on the *Legal Consequences of the Construction of a Wall in the Occupied Palestinian Territory.*[2] The case in Israel arose as a

---

1.   HCJ 7957/04 [2005] (Isr.), *translated in* 45 I.L.M. 202 (2006).
2.   Legal Consequences of the Construction of a Wall in the Occupied Palestinian Territory, Advisory Opinion, 2004 I.C.J. 131 (July 9), *reprinted in* 43 I.L.M. 1009 (2004) [hereinafter ICJ Wall Advisory Opinion].   For further commentary on this Advisory Opinion, see generally Susan Akram & Michael Link, *The Wall and the Law: A Tale of Two Judgments* (2006); Aeyal M. Gross, *The Construction of a Wall Between The Hague and Jerusalem: The Enforcement and Limits of Humanitarian Law and the Structure of Occupation,* 19 LEIDEN J. INT'L L. 1 (2006); *Agora: ICJ Advisory Opinion on Construction of a Wall in the Occupied Palestinian Territory,* 99 AM. J. INT'L L. 1 (2005) (including contributions from Watson, Pomerance, Falk, Wedgwood, Murphy, Scobbie, Kretzmer, Imseis and Dennis); Pieter H.F. Bekker, *The World Court's Ruling Regarding Israel's West Bank Barrier and the Primacy of International Law: An Insider's Perspective,* 38 CORNELL INT'L L.J. 553 (2005); Paul J. I. M. De Waart, *International Court of Justice Firmly Walled in the Law of Power in the Israeli-Palestinian Peace Process,* 18 LEIDEN J. INT'L L. 467 (2005); Jean-François Gareau, *Shouting at the Wall: Self-Determination and the Legal Consequences of the Construction of a Wall in the Occupied Palestinian Territory,* 18 LEIDEN J. INT'L L. 489 (2005); Andrea Bianchi, *Dismantling the Wall: The ICJ's Advisory Opinion and Its Likely Impact on International Law,* 47 GERMAN Y.B. INT'L L. 343 (2004); and Marco Pertile, *Legal Consequences of the Construction of a Wall in the Occupied Palestinian Territory: A Missed Opportunity for International Law?,* 4 ITALIAN Y.B. INT'L L. 121 (2004). *See also* 39 ISR. L. REV. (2006) (dedicating a special double issue to discuss the

result of a number of petitions filed against the Prime Minister of Israel, the Minister of Defence, the Commander of the Israeli army, the "separation fence" authority, and the *Alfe Menashe* local council.[3] The petitioners, Palestinian residents of a number of villages affected by the route of the wall, argued that in light of the ICJ's Advisory Opinion, Israel's actions in continuing its construction were unlawful.[4] On July 9, 2004, the ICJ concluded that the wall and its *associated régime* of settlements, checkpoints, and closed military zones are contrary to international law.[5] The HCJ therefore had to rule on the legality of the wall that its government has been building in Occupied Palestinian Territory (OPT) of the West Bank since June 2002, while taking into account the advice of the principal judicial organ of the United Nations (U.N.).[6]

The terminology used by the ICJ and the HCJ to describe Israel's vast concrete-and-wire barrier differed. The HCJ referred to it as the "separation fence," and the ICJ simply called it the "wall," as this was the language the General Assembly used in its request for an Advisory Opinion.[7] In deference to the ICJ and the world organization, the terminology they employed will be used throughout

---

domestic and international legal issues arising from the construction of the "separation barrier"); 13 PALESTINE Y.B. INT'L L. 337 (2004–2005) (reprinting the Advisory Opinion, Palestine's written statement to the Court, and several articles).

3. *Alfe Menashe* is an Israeli settlement situated close to the Palestinian town of *Qalqilya* in the West Bank.

4. Interestingly, the HCJ issued simultaneous versions of the judgment in both English and Hebrew, something it does not normally do. The other time it issued versions in both languages was in the *Beit Sourik* case. Iain Scobbie notes that neither decision has been issued in an official Arabic text. Unlike English, Arabic is one of the High Court's official languages and is the tongue spoken by the principle petitioners in both cases. Iain Scobbie, *Regarding/Disregarding: The Judicial Rhetoric of President Barak and the International Court of Justice's Wall Advisory Opinion*, 5 CHINESE J. INT'L L. 269, 287 (2006).

5. As Roger O'Keefe writes:

What is meant . . . by its '*associated régime*' is to be found among paragraphs 114 to 137. One aspect of this régime is obviously the range of legislative and regulatory measures associated with the Wall, from the requisitions of land to the restrictions imposed on the Palestinian populace by the declaration of the Closed Area. . . . In short, the opinion finds not only the construction of the Wall to be illegal but with it the policy and practice of Israeli settlements in the occupied territories, considered as part of its '*associated régime*.'

It follows that the checkpoints and the closed military zones associated with the Wall are also *per se* unlawful. Roger O'Keefe, *Legal Consequences of the Construction of a Wall in the Occupied Palestinian Territory: A Commentary*, 37 REV. BELGE DROIT INT'L 92, 133 (2004).

6. The Advisory Opinion was acknowledged by the U.N. General Assembly on 2 August 2004. G.A. Res. 10/15, U.N. GAOR, 10th Sess., U.N. Doc. A/RES/ES-10/15 (Aug. 2, 2004).

7. ICJ Wall Advisory Opinion, *supra* note 2, at 1029, para. 67.

the remainder of this Article.[8] This Article employs a socio-legal and facts-based approach in analyzing the decisions reached by the HCJ and the ICJ on the legality of the wall, since it is usually the facts of the Israeli-Palestinian conflict rather than the substance of the law that prove to be a point of contention. After all, it was on the basis of "the facts" that Israel's HCJ would ultimately reject the ICJ's Advisory Opinion.[9] In the following pages, the ICJ's opinion and the decisions of the HCJ will be compared and contrasted, concentrating on three areas of controversy: (a) Israeli civilian settlement activity, (b) self-determination, and (c) self-defense. These inter-related topics have been chosen for further analysis because they are at the core of the Israel-Palestine conflict. The right of self-defense cannot be debated without an understanding of why there is a conflict in the first place, and an understanding of why there is a conflict between Israelis and Palestinians cannot be comprehended without taking into account the question of self-determination. Correspondingly, it will be necessary to refer to the Israeli civilian settlements constructed in and around East Jerusalem and scattered throughout the West Bank because they are of direct relevance to any discussion of self-determination. Special attention has been devoted to the issue of self-defense, as the ICJ's opinion on this issue has proved to be particularly contentious. To date, the Israeli government has said that it will not abide by the ICJ's Advisory Opinion, but will only adhere to the decisions reached by its HCJ.[10] It is therefore essential to clarify some of the substantive issues that arose in these cases, especially as Israel is still building the wall. Therefore, the final

---

8.   Although it should be said that structure only takes the form of eight-meter-high-concrete slabs when it passes through areas densely populated by Palestinians such as Qalqilya, Tulkarem, Bethlehem, and East Jerusalem. The remainder of the structure is a fenced complex with electronic sensors and surveillance cameras surrounded by rolls of barbed wire, accompanied by ditches, an earth-covered tracer road (so footprints can be seen), patrol roads and "closed military zones" approximately 40-100 meters wide. For a description of the wall, see generally the U.N. Econ. & Soc. Council [ECOSOC], Comm'n on Human Rights, *Report on the Situation of Human Rights in the Palestinian Territories Occupied by Israel Since 1967*, U.N. Doc. E/CN.4/2004/6 (Sept. 8, 2003) (*prepared by* John Dugard).

9.   *See* HCJ 2056/04 Beit Sourik Village Council v. Israel [2004] (Isr.), *translated in* 43 I.L.M. 1099, ¶ 28 (2004).

> [T]he Fence is motivated by security concerns. As we have seen in the government decisions concerning the construction of the Fence, the government has emphasized, numerous times, that 'the Fence, like the additional obstacles, is a security measure. Its construction does not express a political border, or any other border.

Id.

10.   "Israel vowed to press on with the construction of the West Bank separation fence after the General Assembly overwhelmingly adopted a resolution condemning the barrier late Tuesday." Shlomo Shamir, *Israel Summons EU Envoys Over Support for Anti-fence Ruling*, HA'ARETZ (Jerusalem), July 21, 2004.

section of this Article will be devoted to the debate over the legal effect of Advisory Opinions generally, and particularly the effect of the Advisory Opinion on the wall as a guide for the U.N. in its quest for peace in the Middle East.

Although the Israeli Government's written statement to the ICJ was replete with references to Palestinian terrorism,[11] it is noteworthy that the statement did not justify the building of the West Bank wall as necessary to stop Palestinian terrorist attacks against its nationals in Israel and in West Bank settlements.[12] This is because Israel did not raise the merits of the case in its written statement, which was solely concerned with issues of jurisdiction and propriety.[13] Palestine's written statement argued that the wall is tantamount to annexation because it is being constructed primarily in occupied territory rather than in Israeli territory, which circumvents Israeli civilian settlement blocs, by-passes roads and land designated for their future construction and expansion, and encompasses underground aquifers and water wells.[14] In other words, the issue is the not the wall itself, but its *route* through OPT.[15] This concern was reflected in the question submitted by the U.N. General Assembly to the ICJ in December 2003, which asked:

---

11.   *See* Written Statement of the Government of Israel on Jurisdiction and Propriety, ¶¶ 3.53–.86 (Jan. 30, 2004), *available at* http://www.icj-cij.org/docket/files/131/1579.pdf (last visited Oct. 16, 2007); Letter from Alan Baker, Ambassador, Deputy Dir. and Legal Advisor, Isr. Ministry of Foreign Affairs, to the Int'l Court of Justice (Jan. 29, 2004), *available at* http://www.icj-cij.org/docket/files/131/1579.pdf (accompanying the Written Statement of the Government of Israel on Jurisdiction and Propriety to the ICJ).

12.   According to Israel, the purpose of including factual information on Palestinian terrorist attacks in its written statement was to assist the ICJ "properly to exercise its discretion under Article 65 (1) of the Statute and decide whether or not to answer the question referred to it." Written Statement of the Government of Israel on Jurisdiction and Propriety, *supra* note 11, ¶ 3.54.

13.   Written Statement of the Government of Israel on Jurisdiction and Propriety, *supra* note 11.

14.   Legal Consequences of the Construction of a Wall in the Occupied Palestinian Territory, Written Statement, Submitted by Palestine, ¶¶ 280–297 (Jan. 30, 2004), *available at* http://www.icj-cij.org/docket/files/131/1555.pdf (last visited Oct. 16, 2007).

15.   As pointed out by Vaughan Lowe in his oral pleadings:

The issue here is not whether Israel has a right to build a Wall: it is whether it has a right to build the Wall in the Occupied Palestinian Territory. Palestine's main point is that whatever security effects the Wall might have could be secured by building the Wall along the Green Line, on Israeli territory, so that there is no legal justification for building it in the Occupied Palestinian Territory.

Legal Consequences of the Construction of a Wall in the Occupied Palestinian Territory, Public Sitting, at 47 (Req. for Advisory Op.) (Feb. 23, 2004), *available at* http://www.icj-cij.org/docket/files/131/1503.pdf (last visited Oct. 16, 2007) [hereinafter Request for Wall Advisory Opinion].

What are the legal consequences arising from the construction of the wall being built by Israel, the Occupying Power, *in the Occupied Palestinian Territory, including in and around East Jerusalem,* as described in the report of the Secretary-General, considering the rules and principles of international law, including the Fourth Geneva Convention of 1949, and relevant Security Council and General Assembly resolutions?[16]

II. THE HCJ AND THE WALL

The HCJ has handed down two principal decisions concerning the legality of the wall. On June 30, 2004, some nine days before the ICJ rendered its Advisory Opinion, the HCJ first ruled in *Beit Sourik Village Council v. the Government of Israel*[17] that the wall could be built in the West Bank, in and around occupied East Jerusalem, but that in a number of sections the wall's route did not satisfy the proportionality test established by the court.[18] In response to the petitioner's argument that the route of the wall was motivated by political reasons (i.e. to incorporate into Israel certain Israeli civilian settlements established inside the West Bank), the HCJ held: "[I]t is the security perspective—and not the political one—which must examine a route based on its security merits alone, *without regard for the location of the Green Line.*"[19] Of course the HCJ could only reach this conclusion by not addressing the applicability to the West Bank of Article 49(6) of the Fourth Geneva Convention Relative to the Protection of Civilian Persons in Times of War of 1949 (hereafter Geneva Convention IV).[20] This is because that article prohibits an occupying power from transferring its civilian population to the

---

16.   G.A. Res. 10/14, U.N. GAOR, 10th Sess., U.N. Doc. A/RES/ES-10/14 (Dec. 8, 2003) (emphasis added).

17.   HCJ 2056/04 [2004] (Isr.), *translated in* 43 I.L.M. 1099 (2004).

18.   This begs one to ask what is, and what is not, proportional, from an Israeli-security perspective. Alain Pellet has observed:

[P]roportionality seems more a general directive than a criterion in the proper sense of the word; its appraisal rests on the subjective judgment of those involved and, for this reason, it is ill-suited to serve as a means of distinguishing that which is lawful from that which is not, a process which is the *raison d'être* of a criterion.

Alain Pellet, *The Destruction of Troy Will Not Take Place, in* INTERNATIONAL LAW AND THE ADMINISTRATION OF OCCUPIED TERRITORIES 169, 173 (Emma Playfair ed., 1992); *see generally* Gross, *supra* note 2 (detailing criticisms of the ICJ's application of the proportionality principle).

19.   HCJ 2056/04 Beit Sourik Village Council v. Israel [2004] (Isr.), *translated in* 43 I.L.M. 1099, ¶ 30 (2004) (emphasis added).

20.   Geneva Convention Relative to the Protection of Civilian Persons in Time of War, Aug. 12, 1949, 6 U.S.T. 3516, 75 U.N.T.S. 287 [hereinafter Geneva Convention IV].

territory it occupies.[21] Had the HCJ examined the legality of the Israeli settlements in East Jerusalem and the West Bank by applying the relevant provisions of Geneva Convention IV, it would have been difficult for the HCJ to have reached the conclusion that the wall was a lawful measure to protect the settlements. Instead, the HCJ uncritically accepted the Israeli government's position that the wall is not a political measure, even though most of it is being constructed in territory over which it has no sovereignty.[22] This may also explain why there was so little reference to international law in its judgment, particularly on the question of self-determination and human rights law.[23] Instead, the HCJ decided that there was a lawful basis for constructing the wall according to its interpretation of the law of belligerent occupation and Israeli administrative law.[24] On this basis the HCJ found that a small section of the wall (approximately 30 kilometers) should be re-routed because it inflicted disproportionate harm upon Palestinian residents and could not be justified by Israel's security needs.[25] It was up to the individual military commander in the occupied territories to balance Israel's security needs with the needs of the local inhabitants. As the HCJ's decision in *Beit Sourik* was delivered before the ICJ's Advisory Opinion, the remainder of this article will focus on the *Mara'abe* case, which challenged the ICJ's Advisory Opinion on both factual and legal grounds.

In *Mara'abe*, the HCJ chose to avoid the question of the applicability of Geneva Convention IV as it did in the *Beit Sourik* case[26]—and as it had done several times in earlier decisions—by relaying the position of its government, which has declared that it practices the "humanitarian parts" of the Convention:

> In light of that declaration on the part of the government of Israel, we see no need to re-examine the government's position. We are aware that the Advisory Opinion of the International Court of Justice determined that *The Fourth Geneva Convention* applies in the Judea and Samaria area [that is, the West Bank], and that its application is not conditional upon the willingness of the State of Israel to uphold its provisions. As mentioned, seeing as the government of Israel accepts that the humanitarian aspects of the *Fourth Geneva Convention* apply

---

21.   *Id.*
22.   HCJ 2056/04 *Beit Sourik*, ¶ 28.
23.   See *infra* notes 140, 464–65 and accompanying text for a discussion of this lack of reference to international law by the ICJ.
24.   *See* HCJ 2056/04 *Beit Sourik*, ¶¶ 26–32 ("Regarding the central question raised before us, our opinion is that the military commander is authorized—by the international law applicable to an area under belligerent occupation—to take possession of land, if this is necessary for the needs of the army.").
25.   *Id.* ¶ 80.
26.   *Id.* ¶ 24.

in the *area*, we are not of the opinion that we must take a stand on that issue in the petition before us.[27]

It may fairly be asked what parts of Geneva Convention IV the HCJ does not consider to be "humanitarian." As it has never taken a stance on its applicability to the OPT, this issue will remain a mystery.[28] Yet on the day the Israeli army took over the West Bank on June 7, 1967, the military commander of the Israeli army issued a proclamation that he had assumed all governmental powers in the area, and that the prevailing law would remain in force subject to any orders that he would promulgate.[29] Attached to this proclamation was the Security Provisions Order that contained detailed provisions for Israeli rule in the occupied areas.[30] According to these provisions,

> [a] military tribunal and the administration of a military tribunal shall observe the provisions of the Geneva Convention of August 12, 1949 . . . with respect to legal proceedings, and in case of conflict between this Order and the said Convention, the provisions of the Convention shall prevail.[31]

David Kretzmer writes that after the 1967 war ended, it became clear to the Israeli political establishment that the Israeli army's perception of the territories during that war as "occupied territories" was incompatible with their political stance because they viewed the territories as "liberated."[32] He opines that this was most probably the reason why the above provision was revoked soon after the war.[33] Michael Lynk notes that the HCJ shares a common narrative with the Israeli government and military on the origins and principal features of the Israel-Palestine conflict: "It accepts that the state is under attack, that the occupation has been largely benign, that the military and the government are motivated by security concerns and

---

27.   HCJ 7957/04 Mara'abe v. Prime Minister of Isr. [2005] (Isr.), *translated in* 45 I.L.M. 202, ¶ 14 (2006).

28.   *See* U.S. Dep't of State [USDOS], Bureau of Democracy, Human Rights, and Labor, *Israel and the Occupied Territories* (Feb. 25, 2005), *available at* http://www.state.gov/g/drl/rls/hrrpt/2003/27929.htm (describing, in its section on "The occupied territories," disagreement between the Israeli government and other groups over how the Hague Regulations and Geneva Convention applied to Israel's authority in OPT, and whether Israel "largely observed the Geneva Convention's humanitarian provisions").

29.   DAVID KRETZMER, THE OCCUPATION OF JUSTICE: THE SUPREME COURT OF ISRAEL AND THE OCCUPIED TERRITORIES 32 (2002).

30.   *Id.*

31.   *Id.* (emphasis added); ICJ Wall Advisory Opinion, *supra* note 2, at 1035–36, para. 93; *see also* Mazen Qupty, *The Application of International Law in the Occupied Territories as Reflected in the Judgments of the High Court of Justice in Israel, in* INTERNATIONAL LAW AND THE ADMINISTRATION OF OCCUPIED TERRITORIES, *supra* note 18, at 119–20 n.126 (citing *Booklet No. 1* (1967), 5, at 12). Kretzmer cites in footnote 2 the Proclamation Regarding the Taking of Power by the IDF (7.6.1967) in 1 *Proclamations, Orders and Appointments of the Judea and Samaria Command* at 3.

32.   KRETZMER, *supra* note 29, at 32–33.

33.   *Id.*

guided by human values, and that the benefit of any judicial doubt should be given to the military unless the minimal legal restraints on the occupation have been unmistakably ignored."[34] That the HCJ is security-minded and government-oriented in its decisions relating to the OPT is also a view endorsed by Israeli lawyers and academics in Israeli universities.[35]

The HCJ is well aware that the position of the Israeli government on Geneva Convention IV is at odds with the views of the international community and the International Committee of the Red Cross (ICRC), the body charged with the task of monitoring the Convention[36] and the application of International Humanitarian Law (IHL).[37] In 1990, the U.N. Security Council adopted a resolution that called on the Geneva Convention IV parties to make sure that Israel respects its obligations, in accordance with Article 1 of the Convention.[38] The U.N. Security Council has reaffirmed that Geneva Convention IV is applicable to the Palestinian and other Arab territories occupied by Israel since June 1967, and has called upon Israel to "abide scrupulously by its legal obligations and responsibilities" under that Convention.[39] The U.N. General Assembly has adopted several resolutions to the same effect.[40]

---

34.   Michael Lynk, *Down by Law: The High Court of Israel, International Law, and the Separation Wall*, 35 J. PALESTINE STUD. 6, 8–9 (2005).

35.   *See generally* KRETZMER, *supra* note 29, at 196.   For a more recent exposition of his views, see David Kretzmer, *The Supreme Court of Israel: Judicial Review During Armed Conflict*, 47 GERMAN Y.B. INT'L L. 392 (2005). *See also* Yoav Dotan, *Judicial Rhetoric, Government Lawyers, and Human Rights: The Case of the Israeli High Court of Justice During the Intifada*, 33 L. & SOC'Y REV. 319, 322–24 (1999).

36.   *See* Statutes of the International Committee of the Red Cross, art. 4(c), http://www.icrc.org/Web/Eng/siteeng0.nsf/html/icrc-statutes-080503 (last visited Oct. 17, 2007) (providing that the ICRC shall "undertake the tasks incumbent upon it under the Geneva Conventions, to work for the faithful application of international humanitarian law applicable in armed conflicts and to take cognizance of any complaints based on alleged breaches of that law").

37.   *See* Declaration of the Conference of the High Contracting Parties to the Fourth Geneva Convention and Statement of the ICRC, Dec. 5, 2001, http://www.icrc.org/web/eng/siteeng0.nsf/html/5FLDPJ (last visited Oct. 17, 2007) (discussing the applicability of Geneva Convention IV to the OPT); *United Kingdom Materials on International Law 2002*, 73 BRIT. Y.B. INT'L L. 942 (2002) (discussing British State practice). *See also* Matthew Happold, *The Conference of High Contracting Parties to the Fourth Geneva Convention*, 4 Y.B. INT'L HUM. L. 389 (2004); Ardi Imseis, *On the Fourth Geneva Convention and the Occupied Palestinian Territory*, 44 HARV. INT'L L.J. 65–138 (2003); Hussein A. Hassouna, *The Enforcement of the Fourth Geneva Convention in the Occupied Palestinian Territory, Including Jerusalem*, 7 ILSA J. INT'L & COMP. L. 461 (2001).

38.   S.C. Res. 681, ¶¶ 1–8, U.N. Doc. S/RES/681 (Dec. 20, 1990).

39.   S.C. Res. 1322, ¶ 3, U.N. Doc. S/RES/1322 (Oct. 7, 2000); S.C. Res. 605, ¶ 2, U.N. Doc. S/RES/605 (Dec. 22, 1987).

40.   *See* G.A. Res. 43/21, ¶ 4, U.N. GAOR, 43d Sess., 45th plen. mtg., U.N. Doc. A/RES/43/21 (Nov. 3, 1988) ("*Demands* that Israel, the occupying Power, abide immediately and scrupulously by the Geneva Convention relative to the Protection of

Common Article 1 to the Geneva Conventions requires the Contracting Parties "to respect and *to ensure respect* for the present Convention *in all circumstances.*"   The ICJ held in *Nicaragua v. United States of America* that this requirement derives not only from the Conventions, "but from the general principles of humanitarian law to which the Conventions merely give specific expression."[41]

III. THE WALL AND ISRAELI CIVILIAN SETTLEMENT ACTIVITY

On the question of the legality of Israeli civilian settlement activity in the OPT, Judge Barak, the President of the HCJ who presided over the hearings and wrote the unanimous decision for the three-judge panel, declared:

> Our conclusion is, therefore, that the military commander is authorized to construct a separation fence in the *area* for the purpose of defending the lives and safety of the Israeli settlers in the *area*. It is not relevant whatsoever to this conclusion to examine whether this settlement activity conforms to international law or defies it, as determined in the Advisory Opinion of the International Court of Justice at The Hague. For this reason, we shall express no position regarding that question.[42]

With the benefit of hindsight and with the availability of an array of literature published on the topic, including Pictet's official commentary (which was published *before* Israel occupied the West Bank in 1967),[43] Judge Barak was in an ideal position to examine the legality of Israeli civilian settlements in the OPTs. It is therefore perplexing that he chose to avoid addressing the issue.[44]   This is

Civilian Persons in Time of War."); G.A. Res. 38/180A, ¶ 6, U.N. GAOR, 38th Sess., 102d plen. mtg., U.N. Doc. A/RES/38/180 (A-E) (Dec. 19, 1983) (*"Reaffirms its determination* that all relevant provisions of the Regulations annexed to the Hague Convention IV of 1907, and the Geneva Convention relative to the Protection of Civilian Persons in Time of War, of 12 August 1949, continue to apply to the Syrian territory occupied by Israel since 1967.); G.A. Res. 37/123A, ¶ 6, U.N. GAOR, 37th Sess., 108th plen. mtg., U.N. Doc. A/RES/37/123 (A-F) (Dec. 16, 1982) (*"Reaffirms its determination* that all the provisions of the Hague Convention of 1907 and the Geneva Convention relative to the Protection of Civilian Persons in Time of War, of 12 August 1949, continue to apply to the Syrian territory occupied by Israel since 1967."); G.A. Res. 32/91A, ¶ 3, U.N. GAOR, 32d Sess., 101st plen. mtg., U.N. Doc. A/RES/32/91(A-C) (Dec. 13, 1977) (*"Calls again upon* Israel to acknowledge and to comply with the provisions of that Convention in all the Arab territories it has occupied since 1967.").

    41.   Geneva Convention IV, *supra* note 20, art. 1 (emphasis added); Military and Paramilitary Activities (Nicar. v. U.S.), 1986 I.C.J. 14, para. 220 (June 27).

    42.   HCJ 7957/04 Mara'abe v. Prime Minister of Isr. [2005] (Isr.), *translated in* 45 I.L.M. 202, ¶ 19 (2006).

    43.   COMMENTARY ON THE GENEVA CONVENTIONS OF 12 AUGUST 1949: IV GENEVA CONVENTION RELATIVE TO THE PROTECTION OF CIVILIAN PERSONS IN TIME OF WAR (Jean S. Pictet ed., 1958).

    44.   One reason may be that Barak was seeking to avoid a clash with the legislature. Since the HCJ's jurisdiction over acts of the Israeli military in the OPTs rests on an interpretation of an Israeli statute, the Knesset (Israel's parliament) can

especially true because the settlements violate not only international law, but also, to the extent that they are built on private Palestinian property, Israeli municipal law.[45] Instead, Judge Barak (who recently retired as President of the Supreme Court) concluded that the military commander of the West Bank is authorized to construct the wall for the purpose of defending the lives and safety of the Israeli settlers.[46] In reaching this conclusion, the HCJ in effect directly challenged the ICJ, which was unanimous on this finding of law.[47] Judge Buergenthal (who dissented from the decision to hear the case) agreed with his colleagues when it came to the settlement issue in his Declaration.   Referring to Article 49, paragraph 6 of Geneva Convention IV, he wrote:

> I agree that this provision applies to the Israeli settlements in the West Bank and that their existence violates Article 49, paragraph 6. It follows that the segments of the wall being built by Israel to protect the settlements are *ipso facto* in violation of international humanitarian law.[48]

Note the use of terminology by Judge Buergenthal: where the wall is being built to protect the settlements, it is in violation of IHL by its very existence. In other words, one of the consequences of the illegality of the settlement enterprise is that any measures undertaken to protect settlers must also be considered unlawful. In this respect, it should be said that the illegality of Israeli civilian settlement activity has never been in any doubt, not even in Israel.

---

always redefine the court's jurisdiction so as to limit its review over decisions relating to the occupied territories. This is because Israel has no formal constitution, and, thus, judicial rulings on any subject can be overruled by legislation. *See* Yoav Dotan, *Judicial Review and Political Accountability: The Case of the High Court of Justice in Israel*, 32 ISR. L. REV. 448, 469 (1998) (suggesting that "unlike other systems with entrenched constitutions (such as the United States), the fear of 'judicial tyranny' is far from being real").

45.   *See* Talia Sasson Report, Summary of the Opinion Concerning Unauthorized Outposts, http://www.fmep.org/documents/sassonreport.html (last visited Oct. 18, 2007) [hereinafter Sasson Report] (explaining that the summary opinion has been prepared at the request of the Prime Minister's bureau). According to the report, written by Talia Sasson, a former State prosecutor: "It is absolutely prohibited to establish outposts on private Palestinian property. Such an action may in certain circumstances become a felony." In this regard, Sasson cites the HCJ ruling in the case of Elon Moreh, HCJ 390/79 Dweikat et al. v. Israel [1979] IsrSc 34(1) 1. *See* 9 ISR. Y.B. HUM. RTS. 345 (1979) (offering an English summary of the case); *see also* Steven Erlanger, *West Bank Settlements on Private Land, Data Shows*, INT'L HERALD TRIB., Mar. 14, 2007, *available at* http://www.iht.com/articles/2007/03/14/africa/web-0314israel.php ("An up-to-date Israeli government register shows that 32.4 percent of the property held by Israeli settlements in the occupied West Bank is private, according to the advocacy group that sued the government to obtain the data.").

46.   For a recent commentary on Judge Barak's legacy, see Nimer Sultany, *The Legacy of Justice Aharon Barak: A Critical Review*, 48 HARV. INT'L L.J. ONLINE 83 (2007), http://www.harvardilj.org/online/113.

47.   ICJ Wall Advisory Opinion, *supra* note 2, at 1055, 1080–81.

48.   *Id.* at 1080–81, para. 9 (declaration of Judge Buergenthal).

In fact, in 1967, Theodor Meron, who was then working as the legal counsel to Israel's Foreign Ministry, wrote in a "Top Secret" Memorandum: "My conclusion is that civilian settlement in the administered territories contravenes the explicit provisions of the Fourth Geneva Convention."[49]   In contrast, Judge Barak advanced two principal reasons that the wall could protect the settlements (although he refrained from ruling on their legality): (1) "The authority to construct the wall for the purpose of defending the lives and safety of Israeli settlers is derived from the need to preserve 'public order and safety,' as mentioned in Article 43 of the Hague Regulations;"[50] and (2) "Israelis living in the area are Israeli citizens. The State of Israel has a duty to defend their lives, safety, and well-being."[51]

Judge Barak then qualified this last point by holding that "the scope of the human right of the Israelis living in the *area*, and the level of protection of the right, are different from the scope of the human right of an Israeli living in Israel and the level of protection of that right."[52]   This was because the area in question (a part of the West Bank between *Qalqilya* and the *Alfe Menashe* settlement) "is not part of the State of Israel."[53]   Consequently, Israeli law does not apply there, and those who live in the area "live under the regime of belligerent occupation."[54]   However, according to a leaked EU document, the HCJ (in an important decision relating to the Gaza Disengagement Plan that has not been translated)[55] reiterated the distinction[56] it makes between the legal status of occupied East

---

49.   GERSHOM GORENBERG, THE ACCIDENTAL EMPIRE: ISRAEL AND THE BIRTH OF THE SETTLEMENTS, 1967–1977, at 99–102 (2006). Since the 1970s, legal advisors at the U.S. State Department have accepted that the settlements contravene Article 49(6) of Geneva Convention IV. *See* Letter of H. J. Hansell, Legal Advisor, USDOS to House Comm. on International Relations, Apr. 21, 1978, *in* 17 I.L.M. 777 (1978) (giving advice on the illegality of Israeli civilian settlement activity).

50.   Hague Convention (IV) Respecting the Laws and Customs of War on Land, and Its Annex: Regulations Respecting the Laws and Customs of War on Land, art. 43, Oct. 18, 1907, U.S.T.S. 539 [hereinafter 1907 Hague Regulations]; HCJ 7957/04 Mara'abe v. Prime Minister of Isr. [2005] (Isr.), *translated in* 45 I.L.M. 202, ¶¶ 18–20 (2006).

51.   HCJ 7957/04 *Mara'abe*, ¶ 21.

52.   *Id.*

53.   *Id.*

54.   *Id.*

55.   *See* Disengagement Plan of Prime Minister Ariel Sharon, April 16, 2004, *available at* http://www.knesset.gov.il/process/docs/DisengageSharon_eng.htm (last visited Oct. 18 2007) (containing an outline of the Gaza Disengagement Plan and links to related documents).

56.   *See* Muhammad Abdullah Iwad & Zeev Shimshon Maches v. Military Court, Hebron District & Military Prosecutor for the West Bank Region, *reprinted in* 48 INT'L L. REP. 63 (1975) (making a distinction between the legal status of East Jerusalem and other Palestinian cities in the West Bank); *see also infra* note 111 (discussing the court's decisions in *Hanzalis* and elsewhere).

Jerusalem and the West Bank and Gaza.[57] Apparently, the HCJ ruled that it was legal to take into account political considerations, in addition to security considerations, for the routing of the wall in East Jerusalem because that part of the city has been "Israeli territory" since its annexation in 1967.[58] The Court thus clarified its earlier ruling in the *Beit Sourik* case, in which it had found that the military commander could not construct the wall in the West Bank if his reasons were political.[59]

If this is indeed the case, then the HCJ seems to have drawn a distinction between East Jerusalem, which the Israeli government considers part of Israel under its municipal law, and the West Bank and Gaza, which under IHL is classified as occupied territory.[60] However, it should be emphasized that this finding of law is at complete odds with international law.[61] Even in a war of self-defense, the acquisition and annexation of territory by forcible means is illegitimate.[62] Although the question of whether an international law

---

57.   *See* SEPARATION BARRIER/WALL, JERUSALEM AND RAMALLAH HEADS OF MISSION, REPORT ON EAST JERUSALEM (2005), http://www.passia.org/jerusalem/meetings/2005/EU-Report-Jerusalem.htm (discussing the separation barrier that separates most of East Jerusalem from the West Bank, separating Palestinians from other Palestinians). The suppressed report was an internal EU document written by British staff at that country's consulate in East Jerusalem and was leaked to the press.

58.   *Id.*

59.   HCJ 2056/04 Beit Sourik Village Council v. Israel [2004] (Isr.), *translated in* 43 I.L.M. 1099, ¶ 27 (2004).

60.   *See* Law and Administration Ordinance—Amendment No. 11- Law, 5727-1967, 13 LSI 75, 75 (1967) (Isr.) ("The law, jurisdiction and administration of the State shall extend to any area of Eretz Israel designated by the Government by order."); Sabri Jiryis, *Israeli Laws as Regards Jerusalem, in* THE LEGAL ASPECTS OF THE PALESTINE PROBLEM WITH SPECIAL REGARD TO THE QUESTION OF JERUSALEM 182 (Hans Kochler ed., 1981) (citing Official Gazette (*Kovetz Ha-Takanot*), No. 2064, 28 June, 1967, at 2690–91 (Hebrew)).

61.   *See* S.C. Res. 478, para. 3, U.N. Doc. S/RES/478 (Aug. 20, 1980) (determining "that all legislative and administrative measures and actions taken by Israel, the Occupying Power, which have altered or purport to alter the character and status of the Holy City of Jerusalem, and in particular the recent 'basic law' on Jerusalem, are null and void and must be rescinded forthwith"); LORD MCNAIR & A.D. WATTS, THE LEGAL EFFECTS OF WAR 369 n.2 (1966); S.C. Res. 298, para. 3, U.N. Doc. S/RES/298 (Sept. 25, 1971) ("[A]ll legislative and administrative actions taken by Israel to change the status of the City of Jerusalem . . . are totally invalid and cannot change that status."); S.C. Res. 446, para. 3, U.N. Doc. S/RES/446 (Mar. 22, 1979) ("*Calls once more upon* Israel, as the occupying Power . . . to desist from taking any action which would result in changing the legal status and geographical nature and materially affecting the demographic composition of the Arab territories occupied since 1967, including Jerusalem."); S.C. Res. 452, para. 3, U.N. Doc. S/RES/452 (July 20, 1979) ("*Calls upon* the Government and people of Israel to cease, on an urgent basis, the establishment, construction and planning of settlements in the Arab territories occupied since 1967, including Jerusalem.").

62.   See the first principle to the 1970 Declaration on Principles of International Law Concerning Friendly Relations and Cooperation among States in accordance with the Charter of the United Nations, approved by the General Assembly—with the assent of Israel—in G.A. Res. 2625, at 121, U.N. GAOR, 25th Sess., U.N. Doc. A/8082

overrides a municipal law when the two conflict will depend exclusively (at the municipal level) on the constitutional law of that state, it is interesting to note that Judge Barak, in his latest treatise, has written that "the theoretical principle of rule of law leads to a number of presumptions," which include "the need to ensure rule of law on the international plane by making sure domestic law is compatible with public international law."[63] Evidently, there is a difference between Judge Barak's decisions on the judicial level and his scholarly work, and in this respect his scholarly writings seem to be a more accurate reflection of the law as it should be, especially since, for the purposes of state responsibility, a state may not rely on the provisions of its internal law to justify a failure to comply with international law.[64] It is important to stress this inability on the part of the state to rely on its internal law because declarative statements of customary international law by the ICJ could be viewed by some Israeli judges as part of domestic Israeli law. Some judges could take this view because, in Israel, customary international law (as opposed to treaty law) automatically becomes part of municipal law, with no need for an act of the Israeli legislature to make it binding.[65] Although Geneva Convention IV is a treaty, certain of its provisions reflect customary international law.[66] According to a recent ICRC study, state practice establishes that Article 49(6) is a norm of customary international law.[67] Presumably then, this provision is binding in Israeli law and could be invoked by Israeli judges to outlaw those settlements established in the occupied territories.

A. *The Settlements and Article 43 of the Hague Regulations*

The HCJ's finding that the need to preserve "public order and safety" in the OPT—as mentioned in Article 43 of the 1907 Hague

---

(1970). *See also* ROBERT YEWDALL JENNINGS, THE ACQUISITION OF TERRITORY IN INTERNATIONAL LAW 55 (1963) (writing four years before Israel captured East Jerusalem, the West Bank, Gaza, the Golan Heights and the Sinai Peninsula that "it would be a curious law of self-defence that permitted the defender in the course of his defence to seize and keep the resources and territory of the attacker"); D. W. Bowett, *International Law Relating to Occupied Territory: A Rejoinder*, 87 LAW Q. REV. 473 (1971) (conceding that "states cannot acquire territory by resort to force").

63.   AHARON BARAK, PURPOSIVE INTERPRETATION IN LAW: TRANSLATED FROM THE HEBREW BY SARI BASHI 360 (2005) (citing M. HUNT, USING HUMAN RIGHTS LAW IN ENGLISH COURTS (1997)).

64.   JAMES CRAWFORD, INTERNATIONAL LAW COMMISSION, DRAFT ARTICLES ON RESPONSIBILITY OF STATES FOR INTERNATIONALLY WRONGFUL ACTS art. 32 (2002).

65.   *See, e.g.*, Ruth Lapidoth, *International Law Within the Israeli Legal System*, 24 ISR. L. REV 451, 452 (1990) (noting that in Israel, international custom is part of municipal law and that this position was adopted very early in Israel's history by the Supreme Court).

66.   *See* Geneva Convention IV, *supra* note 20, art. 49.

67.   *See* JEAN-MARIE HENCKAERTS & LOUIS DOSWALD-BECK, CUSTOMARY INTERNATIONAL HUMANITARIAN LAW: VOLUME 1 RULES 462–63, rule 130 (2005).

Regulations—gives the military commander the authority to construct the wall for the purpose of defending the lives and safety of Israeli settlers in the West Bank is also unpersuasive.[68] Article 43 provides:

> The authority of the legitimate power having *in fact* passed into the hands of the occupant, that latter shall take all the measures in his power *to restore and ensure*, as far as possible, public order and safety, while respecting, unless absolutely prevented, the laws in force in the country.[69]

In 1967, the legitimate power in East Jerusalem and the West Bank was Jordan, which claimed that its title rested not on conquest but on the consent of the inhabitants.[70] Even if Jordan was not viewed as the "legitimate" power, it still had the rights and duties of an occupying power before it annexed those territories.[71] Article 31 of the Vienna Convention on the Law of Treaties of 1969 (VCLT) provides that, as a general rule of interpretation, a treaty should be interpreted in good faith in accordance with the ordinary meaning to be given to the terms of the treaty in light of its object and purpose.[72]

---

68.   HCJ 7957/04 Mara'abe v. Prime Minister of Isr. [2005] (Isr.), *translated in* 45 I.L.M. 202, ¶¶ 18–19 (2006).

69.   1907 Hague Regulations, *supra* note 50, art. 43 (emphasis added).

70.   The United Kingdom granted de jure recognition to the union, but most states withheld de jure recognition (although they may have granted de facto recognition). In particular, the other Arab states denounced the union as a betrayal of the Palestinian cause and as a breach of a resolution passed by the Arab League prohibiting the annexation of any part of Palestine. *See The Policy of the Arab States Towards the Question of Palestine, Resolution 320-Sess.12—Sched.6, Apr. 13, 1950, in* MUHAMMAD KHALIL, THE ARAB STATES AND THE ARAB LEAGUE: A DOCUMENTARY RECORD VOLUME II 166 (1962). Eventually a compromise was reached; Jordan declared that the annexation of the West Bank was without prejudice to the final settlement of the Palestine issue, which the other Arab states accepted. *See* Michael Akehurst, *The Place of the Palestinians in an Arab-Israeli Peace Settlement*, 70 ROUND TABLE 443 (1980) (discussing Resolution 242, which outlined the terms of the settlement).

71.   Jordan incorporated East Jerusalem and the West Bank into its Kingdom in 1950 after overrunning the territory in the 1948 war and subsequently occupying it. It did this in collusion with the Provisional Government of Israel. *See generally* AVI SHLAIM, COLLUSION ACROSS THE JORDAN: KING ABDULLAH, THE ZIONIST MOVEMENT, AND THE PARTITION OF PALESTINE (1988).

72.   *See* Vienna Convention on the Law of Treaties art. 4, May 23, 1969, 1155 U.N.T.S. 331 (providing that "the Convention applies only to treaties which are concluded by States after the entry into force of the present Convention with regard to such States"). Although the ICJ has held that Articles 31 and 32 reflect customary international law, and although there is evidence to indicate that this represented the law in the mid-1950s, it has been argued that there is less evidence to suggest that this was reflective of international law in 1907 at the time of the Hague Peace Conference. However, in the *Iron Rhine Arbitration, Between Belgium and the Netherlands*, Permanent Court of Arbitration (May 24, 2005), *available at* http://www.pca-cpa.org/showpage.asp?pag_id=1155, the Arbitral Tribunal, which included three ICJ judges (Judges Higgins, Simma, and Tomka) and two Professors (Alfred H.A. Soons and Guy Schrans), held at paragraph 45 that Articles 31 and 32 of the VCLT reflect pre-existing customary international law, and thus may be (unless there are particular

1440   *VANDERBILT JOURNAL OF TRANSNATIONAL LAW*   *[VOL. 40:1425*

Assuming that when Article 43 was drafted its authors envisaged the possibility of a prolonged occupation, it is clear from the plain and ordinary meaning of Article 43's text that it is concerned with restoring and ensuring—as far as possible—public order and safety, while respecting the laws *already in force* in the country.[73] After all, "good faith," as Judge Barak has recently written, "is a fundamental principle that permeates the objective purpose of every statute."[74] Evidently, one can only restore and ensure public order and *life* (the word "safety" was a mistranslation from the original, official, and authoritative French text) for those persons who already inhabit the area in question.[75] Those Israeli civilian settlements established in the OPTs *after* those territories were captured by Israel in June 1967 necessarily violated Article 49(6) of Geneva Convention IV, which prohibits an occupying power from transferring its civilian population into the territory it occupies.[76] The settlements have also violated Article 43 of the Hague Regulations because Israel changed its laws to facilitate the settlement enterprise.[77] Moreover, Jordan ratified Geneva Convention IV on May 29, 1951. Consequently, the laws embodied in Geneva Convention IV were part of Jordanian law when

---

indications to the contrary) applied to treaties concluded before the entry into force of the Vienna Convention in 1980. They reached this conclusion by referring to the ICJ's jurisprudence in the *Kasikili/Sedudu Island* and *Pulau Ligitan/Sipadan* cases which concerned treaties concluded in the 19th century. *Id.*

73.   Some have argued that this refers to the status quo ante (i.e. the situation in the OPTs before its capture by Israeli forces on 4 June 1967). *See, e.g.,* HCJ 337/71 Christian Soc'y for the Holy Places v. Minister of Def. et al., *translated in* 2 ISR. Y.B. HUM. RTS. 354 (1972) (Cohn, J., dissenting) (arguing that the intention of the words to restore and ensure public order and life in Article 43 is concerned with "the status quo ante . . . to ensure their continued existence").

74.   BARAK, *supra* note 55, at 361. *See also* Robert Kolb, *Principles as Sources of International Law (With Special Reference to Good Faith)*, 53 NETH. INT'L L. REV. 1, 13–25 (2006) (discussing good faith in depth).

75.   According to Edmund Schewnk, a comparison of the original French text of the Hague Regulations with the English translation of "la vie publique" has been translated into "safety." The literal translation of "la vie publique" is "public life." Edmund Schewnk, *Legislative Power of the Military Occupant Under Article 43, Hague Regulations*, 54 YALE L.J. 393, 393 n.1 (1945).

76.   *See* COMMENTARY ON THE GENEVA CONVENTIONS, *supra* note 43, at 283.

It is intended to prevent a practice adopted during the Second World War by certain Powers, which transferred portions of their own population to *occupied territory* for political and racial reasons or in order, as they claimed, *to colonize those territories*. Such transfers worsened the economic situation of the *native population* and endangered their separate existence as a race.

Id. (emphasis added).

77.   In his seminal study, Raja Shehadeh describes the various legal tools Israel has used to facilitate its settlement policy in the occupied territories by declaring Palestinian land to be "State land," "State property," "abandoned"; requisitioning it for "military purposes"; expropriating it for "public purposes"; and acquiring it for "Jewish purchase." RAJA SHEHADEH, OCCUPIER'S LAW: ISRAEL AND THE WEST BANK 15–59 (1985).

Israel captured the West Bank from Jordan in the June 1967 war. Israel is bound by that Convention not only because it has ratified it,[78] but also because it is the occupying power under Article 43 of the Hague Regulations, which reflected customary international law years before Israel occupied the West Bank.[79] Thus Geneva Convention IV was, prior to Israel's occupation, one of the "laws in force in the country," which Israel was obliged to respect.[80]

Because Article 4 restricts the scope of Geneva Convention IV to "protected persons," the HCJ has sought to rely on the Hague Regulations where there are no such restrictions.[81] However, this still does not change the fact that the settlements, which the HCJ has admitted the wall is designed to protect, are contrary to Article 49(6) of Geneva Convention IV.[82] It is therefore hardly surprising that the HCJ refuses to address its applicability. Yet the Hague Regulations are supposed to be supplemented by the relevant provisions of Geneva Convention IV, as well as the Additional Protocols of 1977 (which Israel has not ratified, although Additional Protocol 1 (AP1) may be said to represent customary international law, and was even mentioned in the General Assembly's December 2003 resolution

---

78.   Israel signed the Convention on December 8, 1949, and ratified it on July 6, 1951. Geneva Conventions of 12 August 1949, http://www.icrc.org/ihl.nsf/WebSign?ReadForm&id=375&ps=P (last visited Oct. 19, 2007).

79.   Article 43 was considered as reflecting customary international law before Israel captured the West Bank in the 1967 war. *See Trial of the German major war criminals*, 41 AM. J INT'L L. 248–249 (1947) ("[B]y 1939 these rules laid down in the [Hague] Convention were recognized by all civilized nations, and were regarded as being declaratory of the laws and customs of war. . . ."); *Cessation of vessels and tugs for navigation on the Danube* case, 1 R.I.A.A. 104 (1921). In fact, almost identical words to Article 43 of the Hague Regulations had been used in previous Conventions. *See* Convention (II) with Respect to the Laws and Customs of War on Land and Its Annex: Regulations Concerning the Laws and Customs of War on Land art. 43, July 29, 1899; The Laws of War on Land arts. 43–44, Sept. 9, 1880; Project of an International Declaration Concerning the Laws and Customs of War arts. 2–3, Aug. 27, 1874. For a survey of this legislation, see DORIS APPEL GRABER, THE DEVELOPMENT OF THE LAW OF BELLIGERENT OCCUPATION 1863–1914 (1949).

80.   Geneva Convention IV, *supra* note 20. With regard to the first part of Article 43, one highly-respected jurist in Israel has noted that it "must not be seen as a source of supplementary rights and authority for the Occupying Power, transcending the limits determined by the constraints of discharging its duty. *See* Yoram Dinstein, *The Israel HCJ and the Law of Belligerent Occupation: Article 43 of the Hague Regulations*, 27 ISR. Y.B. HUM. RTS. 1, 16 (1995).

81.   Geneva Convention IV, *supra* note 20, art. 4. Article 4 of Geneva Convention IV provides that it only applies to "protected persons" who are defined as "those who, at a given moment and in any manner whatsoever, find themselves, in case of a conflict or occupation, in the hands of a Party to the conflict or Occupying Power of which they are not nationals." This obviously cannot include nationals of the State of Israel, the occupying power.

82.   HCJ 7957/04 Mara'abe v. Prime Minister of Isr. [2005] (Isr.), *translated in* 45 I.L.M. 202, ¶ 19 (2006).

requesting the Advisory Opinion from the ICJ).[83] Thus, contrary to
the findings of the HCJ, Article 43 cannot be construed as providing
the Israeli military commander with the obligation to defend the lives
and safety of Israelis living in illegal settlements by constructing a
wall.   Article 43 was never drafted to accommodate a settler
population; rather, it was intended to safeguard the interests of the
local population who found itself under belligerent occupation.
Hence, the whole of Article 43 is written in the past tense.[84]

It may also be queried whether establishing Israeli civilian
settlements amidst a Palestinian population struggling for
independence and statehood in East Jerusalem, the West Bank, and
the Gaza Strip for nearly four decades is likely to restore and ensure
public order and life.[85] Indeed, it would seem that the very presence
of the Israeli settlements contributes to acts of violence, riots, and
civil disturbance.[86] Some would even argue that the continued
construction of the settlements was one of the primary factors that
led to the collapse of the "Oslo Peace Process."[87]   Therefore,

---

83.   *See* G.A. Res. ES-10/14, *supra* note 16 (reaffirming in the preamble "the
applicability of the Fourth Geneva Convention *as well as Additional Protocol 1 to the
Geneva Conventions* to Occupied Palestinian Territory, including East Jerusalem"
(emphasis added)). On the customary status of some of AP1's provisions, see Fausto
Pocar, *Protocol 1 Additional to the 1949 Geneva Conventions and Customary
International Law*, 31 ISR. Y.B. HUM. RTS. 145 (2002).

84.   1907 Hague Regulations, *supra* note 50, art. 43.

85.   There have been numerous studies on the impact of population transfers on
the communities affected by the transfer. *See, e.g.*, U.N. Comm'n on Human Rights,
Sub-Comm'n on Prevention of Discrimination & Prot. of Minorities, *Final Report of the
Special Rapporteur on human rights and population transfer*, U.N. Doc.
E/CN.4/Sub.2/1997/23 (June 27, 1997). This report was preceded by a Preliminary
Report UN doc. E/CN.5.Sub.2/1993/17 and Corr.1 and a Progress Report UN Doc.
E/CN.4/Sub.2/1994/19 and Corr.1.   For criticisms of the Draft Declaration on
Population Transfer and Implantation of Settlers, see Emily Haslam, *Unlawful
Population Transfer and the Limits of International Criminal Law*, 61 C.L.J. 66 (2002).
On population transfer generally, see, for example, Eric Kolodner, *Population Transfer:
The Effects of Settler Infusion Policies on a Host Population's Right to Self-
Determination*, 27 N.Y.U. J. INT'L L. & POL. 159 (1994). *See also* Christa Meindersma,
Population Exchanges: International Law and State Practice- Part 1, 9 INT'L J.
REFUGEE L. 335 (1997) (examining the human rights implications of population
exchange agreements); Christa Meindersma, *Legal Issues Surrounding Population
Transfer in Conflict Situations*, 41 NETH. INT'L L. REV. 31 (1994) (providing an
overview of existing and emerging legal standards relevant to ongoing situations of
population transfer).

86.   *See generally* Settler Violence, B'Tselem, Israeli Information Center for
Human Rights in the Occupied Territories, http://www.btselem.org/english/
Settler_Violence/ (last visited Oct. 19, 2007) (documenting settler violence against
Palestinians).

87.   Ron Pundak, Director-General of Israel's Peres Peace Centre in Tel Aviv
who was a key player in the 1993 Oslo negotiations, attributes its failures to the
Netanyahu years of government (1996–1999), as well as to the "patronizing Israeli
attitude towards the Palestinians—one of occupier to occupied—[which] continued
unabated." Ron Pundak, *From Oslo to Taba: What Went Wrong?*, 43 SURVIVAL 31, 33
(2001).

encouraging one's nationals to emigrate to the occupied territory might, according to Israeli lawyer Eyal Benvenisti, "impinge on the local 'public order and civil life' and therefore be proscribed by international law, particularly by Article 43."[88]

B. *The Settlers, the Settlements, and Human-Rights Law*

It is submitted that Israeli settlers may not invoke human rights law to justify their living in the OPTs for the following four reasons: (1) IHL prohibits establishing settlements in occupied territories and is the *lex specialis* in situations of belligerent occupation; (2) human rights law does not give the settlers the right to live wherever they like; (3) the provisions of the 1995 Israeli-Palestinian Interim Agreement on the West Bank and the Gaza Strip[89] regarding the settlements are irrelevant to the matter at hand, and cannot derogate from Geneva Convention IV; and (4) the law of self-determination as a norm of customary international law, as the primordial human right and as a *jus cogens* norm, trumps any rights the settlers may have under general human rights law.

The ICJ has held, in accordance with the long-established position of the U.N. Commission of Human Rights and the practice of the European Court of Human Rights (as reflected in a series of cases concerning Turkey's occupation of northern Cyprus), that international humanitarian and human rights law applies where the occupying power has effective control of the occupied territory.[90] As a result, the indigenous Palestinian population of the West Bank is also entitled to the protection of human rights law.[91] It is therefore clear that Palestinians inhabiting the OPTs are covered by both international humanitarian and human rights law.[92] However, in cases of conflict between these two branches of law, it has been

---

88.   EYAL BENVENISTI, THE INTERNATIONAL LAW OF OCCUPATION 21 (1993) (emphasis added).

89.   Israel-Palestinian Interim Agreement on the West Bank and Gaza Strip, Isr.-Palestine, Sept. 28, 1995, 36 I.L.M. 557 (1997).

90.   *See* Loizidou v. Turkey, Eur. Ct. H.R. App. No. 40/1993/435/514, ¶ 56 (1996) ("Those affected by such policies or actions therefore come within the 'jurisdiction' of Turkey for the purposes of Article 1 of the Convention (art. 1). Her obligation to secure to the applicant the rights and freedoms set out in the Convention therefore extends to the northern part of Cyprus."); *see also* Decision as to the Admissibility of *Banković v. Belgium*, Application No. 52207/99, 41 I.L.M. 517, paras. 70–71 (2002) (finding an obligation to secure an area outside its national territory under its effective control). Turkey has occupied northern Cyprus since July 20, 1974.

91.   *See* HCJ 7957/04 Mara'abe v. Prime Minister of Isr. [2005] (Isr.), *translated in* 45 I.L.M. 202, ¶ 27 (2006) (stating that the HCJ "shall assume—without deciding the matter—that the international conventions on human rights apply in the area").

92.   *See* ICJ Wall Advisory Opinion, *supra* note 2, at 1040, paras. 111, 113 (discussing the applicability of human rights law to the OPTs). Israel ratified the Covenants on Human Rights on January 3, 1992.

suggested that the latter should be interpreted in light of the former as the law specific to belligerent occupation.[93]

In its Advisory Opinion on the *Legality of the Threat or Use of Nuclear Weapons*, the ICJ held that the protection of the International Covenant of Civil and Political Rights[94] (ICCPR) does not cease in times of war unless a state has derogated from certain of its provisions in a time of national emergency.[95]   The Advisory Opinion notes, however, that respect for the right to life is not a provision that can be derogated from, and that the right not to be arbitrarily deprived of one's life applies also in hostilities.[96]   The ICJ then held: "The test of what is an arbitrary deprivation of life . . . *then falls to be determined by the applicable lex specialis, namely, the law applicable in armed conflict which is designed to regulate the conduct of hostilities.*"[97]   In its Advisory Opinion in *Wall*, the ICJ cited its opinion in *Nuclear Weapons*, stipulating that there are three possible situations with regard to the relationship between international humanitarian and human rights law:

> Some rights may be exclusively matters of international humanitarian law; others may be exclusively matters of human rights law; yet others may be matters of both these branches of international law. In order to answer the question put to it, the Court will have to take into consideration both these branches of international law, namely human rights law and, as *lex specialis*, international humanitarian law.[98]

In other words, both of these branches of law may, depending on the circumstances, be applicable to situations of belligerent occupation, which the ICJ recently affirmed in its decision in *Armed activity in the Congo*.[99]   However, where there is a clash between human rights

---

93.   *See* ECOSOC, Sub-Comm. on the Promotion & Prot. of Human Rights, Comm'n on Human Rights, *Working Paper on the Relationship Between Human Rights Law and International Humanitarian Law*, para. 76, U.N. Doc. E/CN.4/Sub.2/2005/14 (Jun. 21, 2005) (*prepared by* Françoise Hampson & Ibrahim Salama) (noting that the case law strongly suggests that human rights bodies should interpret the norms of human rights law in light of international humanitarian law). *See also id.* paras. 57, 69, where the authors conclude that *lex specialis* was not being used by the ICJ in its Wall Advisory Opinion to displace human rights law and that whether IHL/human rights law is applicable is not a question of "either . . . or." They conclude that the case law of the European Court of Human Rights and Inter-American Commission and Court of Human Rights strongly suggests that in situations of conflict, human rights bodies should interpret the norms of human rights law in light of the law of armed conflict and IHL, as the *lex specialis*.

94.   International Covenant on Civil and Political Rights, Dec. 19, 1966, 999 U.N.T.S. 171.

95.   Legality of the Threat of Use of Nuclear Weapons, Advisory Opinion, 1996 I.C.J. 226, ¶¶ 25, 35 (July 8).

96.   *Id.*

97.   *Id.* (emphasis added).

98.   ICJ Wall Advisory Opinion, *supra* note 2, at 1038–39, para. 106.

99.   Armed Activities on the Territory of the Congo (Congo v. Uganda), 2005 I.C.J. 215 (Dec. 19).

and humanitarian law, it would seem that IHL would prevail in situations of armed conflict.[100] Although the ICJ in its *Nuclear Weapons* Advisory Opinion was discussing the test of what is an arbitrary deprivation of life, its finding that IHL is the *lex specialis* in the course of armed conflict would in principle apply to all conflict situations.[101] It would therefore seem that in case of dispute, international humanitarian law as embodied in The Hague Regulations, Geneva Convention IV, and the Additional Protocols— insofar as they reflect customary international law[102]—would prevail over human rights law. Thus, even though Israeli settlers are protected by the law of human rights, this cannot preclude the wrongfulness of breaching specific rules of international humanitarian law such as Article 49(6) of Geneva Convention IV.

The conclusion to be drawn from this is that while Israelis are entitled to have their human rights respected, the settlements in which they live are unlawful. The government of Israel must therefore cease construction of the settlements and refrain from encouraging its nationals to settle in them.[103] The fact that the settlers have human rights under international law should also not prevent them from being relocated from occupied territory.[104] The settlers cannot invoke human rights law to reside wherever they like, as Article 12 of the ICCPR provides: "Everyone *lawfully* within the

---

100.   In other words, human rights law remains applicable in situations of armed conflict, except when it is in direct conflict with the law of armed conflict. *See generally* CHARLES GARRAWAY, CHATHAM HOUSE, THE "WAR ON TERROR": DO THE RULES NEED CHANGING? (2006), *available at* http://www.chathamhouse.org.uk/publications/papers/ download/-/id/384/file/4019_bpwaronterror.pdf (last visited Sept. 8, 2006) (analyzing the relationship between human rights law in the "War on Terror").

101.   *See, e.g.*, Int'l Law Comm'n, *Fragmentation of International Law: Difficulties Arising from the Diversification and Expansion of International Law*, U.N. Doc. A/CN.4/L.682 (Apr. 13, 2006) (*finalized by* Martti Koskenniemi) (discussing *lex specialis* generally).

102.   *See* HENCKAERTS, *supra* note 67 (clarifying and elucidating this reflection of customary international law in this recent ICRC study).

103.   Various financial incentives are used to encourage people to move into settlements. *See generally* B'TSELEM, LAND GRAB: ISRAEL'S SETTLEMENT POLICY IN THE WEST BANK (2002), http://www.btselem.org/Download/200205_Land_Grab_Eng.pdf [hereinafter LAND GRAB] (discussing a number of methods the Israeli government used). Although during Israel's Gaza disengagement plan in September 2005, 8500 Israeli settlers were forced to evacuate Gaza, 14,000 Israeli settlers moved into settlements in the West Bank. Chris McGreal, *Israel Redraws the Roadmap, Building Quietly and Quickly*, GUARDIAN (London), Oct. 18, 2005, at 17.

104.   *See* HCJ 1661/05 Regional Council of Gaza Beach v. Knesset (not translated); *see also* Chatham House, *Disengagement From Gaza—Legal Issues*, *available at* http://www.chathamhouse.org.uk/publications/papers/download/-/id/286/ file/3922_ilp200605.pdf (last visited Oct. 19, 2007) (providing a summary of highlights from the case in English). In this case, Israel's High Court of Justice rejected the claims advanced by the Gaza settlers that their human rights would be breached if they were forced to relocate from the Gaza Strip. Paradoxically, many of these settlers moved to the West Bank, as noted in McGreal, *supra* note 103, at 17.

territory of a *State* shall, *within that territory*, have the right to liberty of movement and freedom to choose his residence."[105] Palestine, as long as it remains OPT, is clearly not a state.[106] Secondly, the settlements are not situated in the State of Israel, but in the occupied territories.[107] Moreover, their presence in those territories is unlawful, and Article 12 is consequently inapplicable.[108] Israel may therefore not invoke human rights law to defend the settlers and the settlements in which they live.[109]

Nor may Israel invoke the security provisions of the Interim Agreement it concluded with the PLO, as Judge Barak did in *Mara'abe*.[110] Although Article XII (1) of the Interim Agreement provides Israel with the responsibility for "overall security of Israelis and settlements," this article does not necessarily make the settlements lawful, as it is only concerned with security and public order. Even if one were to interpret these provisions as "legalizing" the settlements, such legalization would be prohibited by Article 47 of Geneva Convention IV, which provides:

> Protected persons who are in occupied territory shall not be deprived, in any case or in any manner whatsoever, of the benefits of the present Convention by any change introduced, as the result of the occupation of a territory, into the institutions or government of the said territory, *nor by any agreement concluded between the authorities of the occupied territories and the Occupying Power, nor by an annexation by the latter of the whole or part of the occupied territory*."[111]

---

105.   International Covenant on Civil and Political Rights, *supra* note 94, at 176 (emphasis added).

106.   *See* Efrat Ungar v. Palestine Liberation Org., 402 F.3d 274, 292 (1st Cir. 2005) ("We recognize that the status of the Palestinian territories is in many ways sui generis. Here, however, the defendants have not carried their burden of showing that Palestine satisfied the requirements for statehood under the applicable principles of international law at any point in time."). For articles on the question of Palestinian statehood, see Francis A. Boyle, *The Creation of the State of Palestine*, 1 EUR. J. INT'L L. 301 (1990); James Crawford, *The Creation of the State of Palestine: Too Much Too Soon?*, 1 EUR. J. INT'L L. 307 (1990); and Jean Salmon, *Declaration of the State of Palestine*, 5 PALESTINE Y.B. INT'L L. 48 (1989), *translated in* 33 ANNUAIRE FRANÇAIS DE DROIT INT'L 37–62 (1988).

107.   LAND GRAB, *supra* note 103, at 7.

108.   *Id.*

109.   Nor may Israel benefit from its own wrongdoing. This derives from the principle of *ex injuria non jus oritur*. As Judge Elaraby noted in his separate opinion in *Wall*: "The general principle that an illegal act cannot produce legal rights—*ex injuria jus non oritur*—is well recognized in international law." ICJ Wall Advisory Opinion, *supra* note 2, at 1087, para. 3.1 (declaration of Judge Elaraby). *See generally* R.Y. Jennings, *Nullity and Effectiveness in International Law*, in CAMBRIDGE ESSAYS IN INTERNATIONAL LAW: ESSAYS IN HONOUR OF LORD MCNAIR 64, 72–74 (1965) (discussing the principle of *ex injuria non oritur jus*).

110.   HCJ 7957/04 Mara'abe v. Prime Minister of Isr. [2005] (Isr.), *translated in* 45 I.L.M. 202, ¶ 14 (2006).

111.   Geneva Convention IV, *supra* note 20, art. 47 (emphasis added).

Pictet notes that "[a]greements concluded with the authorities of the occupied territory represent a more subtle means by which the Occupying Power may try to free itself from the obligations incumbent on it under occupation law."[112]   In this regard, it is important to note that Article XXXI (7) of the Interim Agreement on Final Clauses provides, "Neither side shall initiate or take any step that will change the status of the West Bank and the Gaza Strip pending the outcome of the permanent status negotiations."[113] This article clearly prohibits any new settlement activity as such activity would affect the status of the West Bank before the outcome of the permanent status negotiations as well as any measures taken to incorporate them within Israel itself. Effectively, Israel is prohibited by Geneva Convention IV from any settlement activity per se, while the Interim Agreement prohibits the creation of any new settlements and the expansion of existing settlements.   Thus two separate treaties (Geneva Convention IV and the Interim Agreement) prohibit Israeli civilian settlement activity in the OPTs, as does Israeli municipal law where the settlements are built on private Palestinian property.[114]   It could therefore be argued that any measures undertaken by Israel to protect the settlements, which are in themselves unlawful, are contrary to international law.[115]

Finally, common Article 1 to both the ICCPR and the International Covenant on Economic, Social, and Cultural Rights[116] (ICESCR) provides: "All peoples have the right of self-determination. By virtue of that right they freely determine their political status and freely pursue their economic, social and cultural development."[117] Evidently, this is the preeminent human right from which all other human rights flow. It is also widely regarded to be a peremptory norm of international law, as reflected in both custom and treaty law, and is therefore presumably binding under Israeli law.[118] Therefore, even if general human rights law is applicable to the settlers, the Palestinian people's right of self-determination takes precedence, especially as the Israeli settlements established after 1967 directly

---

112.   COMMENTARY ON THE GENEVA CONVENTIONS, *supra* note 43, at 274.

113.   Israel-Palestinian Interim Agreement, *supra* note 89.

114.   *See generally* Sasson Report, *supra* note 45 (discussing the settlements and Israeli municipal law).

115.   This was indeed argued by counsel for Jordan and it seems to have been accepted by the ICJ. *See* Request for Wall Advisory Opinion, *supra* note 15, para. 9 (pleading by Sir Arthur Watts, Senior Legal Advisor to Jordan).

116.   International Covenant on Economic, Social and Cultural Rights art. 1, Dec. 16, 1966, 993 U.N.T.S. 3.

117.   *See infra* Part IV (addressing in detail what underlies the Palestinian right of self-determination).

118.   Customary law as opposed to treaty law is binding upon domestic courts in Israel. *See* Lapidoth, *supra* note 65, at 452 (noting that "[a]s in most states, in Israel, too, international custom is automatically part of municipal law, with no need for an act of transformation" from the legislature to make the law binding on the courts).

conflict with their right of self-determination. The Palestinian people cannot pursue this internationally recognized right when the settlers, the soldiers, and the Israeli government are interfering with their economic, social, and cultural development.[119]

C. *The Settlements as De Facto Annexation*

Despite claims to the contrary,[120] Israel's construction of the wall in the West Bank (in and around East Jerusalem) and its enclosure of the large settlement blocs located there are acts that in their very essence amount to de facto annexation.   Indeed, Judge Barak's repetition in his judgment in *Mara'abe* of the assertion he had made in *Beit Sourik*, that "the military commander is not authorized to order the construction of a separation fence if the reason behind the fence is a political goal of 'annexing' territories of the area to the State of Israel and to determine Israel's political border," is undoubtedly correct.[121] However, after making this statement, Judge Barak went on to conclude that the wall's route was not politically motivated, and that it is therefore not tantamount to de facto annexation.[122] This conclusion is, however, a very odd one to reach, especially since state representatives from the government of Israel had previously admitted, in a public session concerning the wall in another case, that "political considerations" did dictate to a certain extent the wall's route.[123]   Surely, therefore, the only logical conclusion is that those sections of the wall that incorporate the large Israeli settlement blocs into Israel are acts tantamount to de facto annexation, according to Judge Barak's statement in *Beit Sourik*.

It may be true that Israel has not in fact annexed the territories de jure because it did not purport to annex East Jerusalem through

---

119.   For example, one major issue is the utilization of natural resources in the West Bank by the settlers and private Israeli companies. *See, e.g.*, G.A. Res. 3171 (XXVIII), U.N. GAOR, 28th Sess., Supp. No. 30, U.N. Doc. A/9400 (Dec. 17, 1973); G.A. Res. 1803 (XVII), ¶ 5, U.N. GAOR, 17th Sess., Supp. No. 17, U.N. Doc. A/5217 (Dec. 14, 1962) (General Assembly resolutions on Permanent Sovereignty over Natural Resources). In the context of natural resources in Palestine and the Golan Heights, see G.A. Res. 57/269, U.N. Doc. A/RES/57/269 (Mar. 5, 2003). *See also* NICO SCHRIJVER, SOVEREIGNTY OVER NATURAL RESOURCES: BALANCING RIGHTS AND DUTIES 152–56 (1997) (discussing permanent sovereignty over the OPTs).

120.   *See* HCJ 7957/04 Mara'abe v. Prime Minister of Isr. [2005] (Isr.), *translated in* 45 I.L.M. 202, ¶ 14 (2006) (arguing that the areas have not been "annexed" and thus are not governed by Israeli law, but instead by public international law regarding belligerent occupation).

121.   *Id.* ¶ 15.

122.   *Id.* ¶ 98.

123.   *See* Yuval Yoaz, *State Prosecution Concedes Political Aim for Jerusalem Fence*, HA'ARETZ (Jerusalem), June 21, 2005, *available at* http://www.christusrex.org/www1/news/haaretz-6-21-05a.html (concerning construction of a separation fence in northern Jerusalem).

the act of its legislature until 1980.[124] But for all intents and purposes, Israel effectively annexed that city soon after its capture in 1967, an action that was condemned by the U.N. Security Council on several occasions.[125] This condemnation was even acknowledged by the HCJ in a number of decisions from the late 1960s and early 1970s.[126] Israel may, in fact, refrain from any de jure act of annexation precisely to avoid condemnation from the U.N. Security Council. But is it not annexation in all but name for Israel to incorporate the settlement blocs by widening the municipal boundaries[127] of Jerusalem, to expand already existing settlements so that they protrude further into occupied territory (such as the proposed E-1 settlement abutting *Ma'aleh Adumim,* see map 3 in Appendix), and to administer these territories as a part of the state of Israel? This logic must have swayed the ICJ, which found that it could not "remain indifferent to certain fears expressed to it that the route of the wall will prejudge the future frontier between Israel and Palestine, and the fear that Israel may integrate the settlements and their means of access."[128] It then held:

---

124. Basic Law: Jerusalem, Capital of Israel, 5740-1980, 34 LSI 209 (1979–1980) (Isr.). *See* S.C. Res. 478, ¶ 5(b), U.N. Doc. S/RES/478 (Aug. 20, 1980) (calling on "those States that ha[d] established diplomatic missions in Jerusalem to withdraw" them); *see also* S.C Res. 476, U.N. Doc. S/RES/476 (June 30, 1980) (holding an emergency session to discuss the legal consequences of building the wall). At present, Jerusalem is not recognized as Israel's capital by any country in the world. *See* Israel Science and Technology, Embassies and Consulates in Israel, http://www.science.co.il/ Embassies.asp (last visited Oct. 19, 2007) (showing all foreign embassies in Israel are located in Tel Aviv, not Jerusalem). Costa Rica and El Salvador, the only countries to have had embassies in Jerusalem, moved them to Tel Aviv in August 2006. *See* Gil Hoffman, *Costa Rica to Relocate Embassy to TA,* JERUSALEM POST, Aug. 17, 2006, *available at* http://www.jpost.com/servlet/Satellite?pagename=JPost%2FJPArticle%2F ShowFull&cid=1154525889070; *El Salvador To Move Embassy From Jerusalem,* YNETNEWS.COM, Aug. 25, 2006, http://www.ynetnews.com/articles/0,7340,L-3295745,00.html.

125. *See* S.C. Res. 298, U.N. Doc. S/RES/298 (Sept. 25, 1971); S.C. Res. 271, U.N. Doc. S/RES/271 (Sept. 15, 1969); S.C. Res. 267, U.N. Doc. S/RES/267 (July 3, 1969); S.C. Res. 252, U.N. Doc. S/RES/252 (May 21, 1968); G.A. Res. 2254 (ES-V), U.N. GAOR, 5th Emer. Spec. Sess., Supp. No. 1, U.N. Doc. A/6798 (July 14, 1967); G.A. Res. 2253 (ES-V), U.N. GAOR, 5th Emer. Spec. Sess., Supp. No. 1, U.N. Doc. A/6798 (July 4, 1967).

126. *See* Muhammad Abdullah Iwad & Zeev Shimshon Maches v. Military Court, Hebron District, *supra* note 49; Golan Heights Law, 5742-1981, 36 LSI 7 (1981) (Isr.); Jurisdiction and Administration Order (No.1), 5727-1967 (1967) (Isr.). The HCJ has stated that from the date of the 1967 Order, "united Jerusalem became an inseparable part of Israel." HCJ 171/68 Hanzalis v. Greek Orthodox Patriarchal Church [1968] (Isr.), *translated in* 48 INT'L L. REP. 93 (1970).

127. For an article examining the various measures Israel has used to expand its control over East Jerusalem by expropriating Palestinian land, constructing Jewish settlements, zoning Palestinian lands as "green areas," developing town planning schemes, demolishing Palestinian homes, and revoking Palestinian residency permits, see Ardi Imseis, *Facts on the Ground: An Examination of Israeli Municipal Policy in East Jerusalem,* 15 AM. U. INT'L L. REV. 1039 (2000).

128. ICJ Wall Advisory Opinion, *supra* note 2, at 1042, para. 121.

> The Court considers that the construction of the wall and its associated régime create a "fait accompli" on the ground that could well become permanent, in which case, *and notwithstanding the formal characterization of the wall by Israel*, it would be tantamount to *de facto* annexation.[129]

Indeed, the prognosis of the ICJ, as well as that of the U.N. Special Rapporteur (who—in his periodic reports to the Human Rights Commission—had defined as de facto annexation Israel's actions in constructing the wall around East Jerusalem), proved to be correct.[130] In February 2006, *B'Tselem*—the Israeli Information Center for Human Rights in the Occupied Territories—reported that Israel had effectively annexed the Jordan Valley by barring almost all Palestinians from entering the region.[131] The Jordan Valley accounts for a third of the West Bank.[132] The result of this annexation is that Palestinians in the West Bank are hemmed in on all sides: by the wall in the north, west, and south, and by the "security corridor" in the Jordan Valley to the east (see map 2 in Appendix).[133]

Ehud Olmert, Israel's acting Prime Minister, told the Knesset (Israel's Parliament) on February 12, 2006, that "the first objective of the next Knesset will be to fix the permanent borders of Israel."[134] Prior to this statement, Condoleezza Rice, the U.S. Secretary of State, had been quoted by *Agence France-Presse* as saying, "[U]nder no circumstances should anyone try and do that [set borders] in a preemptive or predetermined way, because these are issues for negotiation at final status."[135] And even before Secretary Rice's statement, Tzipi Livni, who was then Israel's Minister of Justice, was quoted by an Israeli newspaper as saying that the wall would serve

---

129.   *Id.* (emphasis added).

130.   *See, e.g.,* ECOSOC, Comm'n on Human Rights, *Report of the Special Rapporteur of the Commission on Human Rights, John Dugard, on the Situation of Human Rights in the Palestinian Territories Occupied by Israel Since 1967,* ¶ 14, U.N. Doc. E/CN.4/2004/6 (Sept. 8, 2003). In April 2006, the Human Rights Commission was replaced by a new Human Rights Council. *See* G.A. Res. 60/251, U.N. A/RES/60/251 (Apr. 3, 2006) (establishing the new Human Rights Council to be based in Geneva).

131.   *Israel Has De Facto Annexed the Jordan Valley,* B'TSELEM, Feb. 13, 2006, *available at* http://www.btselem.org/English/Settlements/20060213_Annexation_of_the_Jordan_Valley.asp. According to a report, Ehud Olmert, Israel's acting Prime Minister, said that Israel intends to keep control of the Valley, even after it pulls out of other parts of the West Bank and draws new borders—as a defensive move. Chris McGreal, *Israel Excludes Palestinians from Fertile Valley,* GUARDIAN (London), Feb. 14, 2006, at 22 ("It is impossible to abandon control of the eastern border of Israel." (quoting Olmert)).

132.   McGreal, *supra* note 131, at 22.

133.   For a recent and in-depth study of the effect of the Wall in combination with Israel's prolonged 40-year occupation, see AMNESTY INT'L, ENDURING OCCUPATION: PALESTINIANS UNDER SIEGE IN THE WEST BANK, (2007), *available at* http://www.amnesty.org/resources/pdf/Israelreport.pdf.

134.   Marius Schattner, *Fixing borders is Israel's top priority: Olmert,* LEBANONWIRE, Feb. 13, 2006.

135.   *Id.*

as "the future border of the State of Israel" and that the HCJ in its rulings "is drawing the country's borders."[136]

Even if Israel does at some future date incorporate the West Bank settlements into Israel by passing a law in the Knesset, the ICJ in its Advisory Opinion made it clear that all territory to the east of the 1949 Israel-Jordan armistice line is occupied territory in which Israel only has the status of an occupying power.[137] This, of course, includes East Jerusalem and the settlements surrounding it. The laws of occupation therefore remain applicable to that territory, regardless of what Israel's municipal laws may say.

IV. THE WALL AND SELF-DETERMINATION

The cumulative impact of the wall (its route, scale, and composition), its associated régime (checkpoints, military laws, and closed military zones), the "security corridor" in the Jordan Valley (a no-go area for Palestinians), and the discriminatory road system[138] linking Israeli civilian settlements in the West Bank to each other and to nearby military bases, substantially reduces the territorial sphere in which the Palestinian people seek to exercise their right of self-determination.[139] In its discussion of the wall's route and the regime associated with the wall in both the *Beit Sourik* and *Mara'abe* cases, the HCJ hardly mentioned these so-called "facts on the ground" or the recognition that the Palestinian people have a right of self-determination as a matter of international law.[140] It was also

---

136. Yuval Yoaz, *Justice Minister: West Bank Fence Is Israel's Future Border*, HA'ARETZ (Jerusalem), Dec. 1, 2005.

137. ICJ Wall Advisory Opinion, *supra* note 2, at 1031, para. 78.

138. *See* B'TSELEM, INFORMATION SHEET, FORBIDDEN ROADS: THE DISCRIMINATORY WEST BANK ROAD REGIME (2004), *available at* http://www.btselem. org/Download/200408_Forbidden_Roads_Eng.pdf (analyzing the forbidden roads regime from an international law perspective). *See also* Samira Shah, *On the Road to Apartheid: The Bypass Road Network in the West Bank*, 29 COLUM. HUM. RTS. L. REV 221 (1997–8).

139. According to the *Report of the Special Rapporteur of the Commission on Human Rights*, *supra* note 130, ¶ 15, the right of self-determination is closely linked to the notion of territorial sovereignty. A people can only exercise the right of self-determination within a territory. *Id.* The amputation of Palestinian territory by the Wall seriously interferes with the right of self-determination of the Palestinian people as it substantially reduces the size of the self-determination unit (already small) within which that right is to be exercised." *Id.* *See also* Written Statement Submitted by Palestine, paras. 548–549, Legal Consequences of the Construction of a Wall in the Occupied Palestinian Territory (Req. for Advisory Op.) *available at* http://www.icj-cij.org/docket/files/131/1555.pdf (last visited Oct. 19, 2007) (naming several ways in which the Palestinians claimed the wall interfered with the people's self-determination).

140. HCJ 7957/04 Mara'abe v. Prime Minister of Isr. [2005] (Isr.), *translated in* 45 I.L.M. 202, ¶¶ 48–49 (2006); HCJ 2056/04 Beit Sourik Village Council v. Israel [2004] (Isr.), *translated in* 43 I.L.M. 1099 (2004).

inadequately addressed by the ICJ in its Advisory Opinion.[141]   For instance, the ICJ's historical résumé in paragraphs 70 through 78, which touches upon the origins of the question of self-determination, was not faultless—as Judge Kooijmans noted.[142] Therefore, a much more rigorous assessment of how the construction of the wall adversely affects the right of self-determination would have been appropriate, especially as the ICJ accepted that the wall "severely impedes the exercise by the Palestinian people of [their] right of self-determination."[143]   The question of self-determination lies at the heart of the Israel-Palestine conflict and is linked to the controversy concerning Israel's right of self-defense from attacks emanating from occupied territory, which will be addressed in Part V.

It is submitted that the manner in which the ICJ dealt with the question of self-determination was rather formulaic. The Court first

---

141.   ICJ Wall Advisory Opinion, *supra* note 2, at 1034–53, paras. 88, 115, 118, 122, 155, 159. Judge Higgins also chastised the court for implicitly adopting a "post-colonial view of self-determination" without any particular legal analysis. Whilst she "approves of the principle invoked," she is "puzzled as to its application in the present case." *Id.* at 1062–63, paras. 29–30 (separate opinion of Judge Higgins). So is the author of this Article. For further criticism, see *id.* at 1071–72, paras. 31–33 (separate opinion of Judge Kooijmans).

142.   *Id.* at 1067, para. 7 (separate opinion of Judge Kooijmans). For example, in paragraph 71, the ICJ recalls that the Arab population of Palestine and the Arab States rejected the partition plan, contending that it was unbalanced, and that on May 14, 1948, Israel declared its independence whereupon armed conflict broke out between Israel and a number of Arab States. However, the court does not point out that armed conflict broke out between the Zionists and the Palestine Arabs immediately after the adoption of the partition plan on November 29, 1947, whereupon the Zionists conquered territory in excess of the limits established in the partition resolution before it declared its independence at midnight on May 15, 1948. Nor does the court refer to the mass exodus of the Palestinian population between November 1947 and May 1948 (when some of the biggest expulsions took place), or to the fact that British troops remained in effective control of Palestine until June 29, 1948, when they completed their evacuation. *See Progress Report of the United Nations Mediator on Palestine, submitted to the Secretary-General for Transmission to the Members of the United Nations*, U.N. Doc. A/648 (Sept. 16, 1948) *(prepared by* Count Folke Bernadotte) (discussing the mass Palestinian exodus of over 300,000 Arabs and the termination of the Mandate of partition on May 15, 1948). For historical analysis, see Benny Morris, *Revisiting the Palestinian Exodus of 1948, in* THE WAR FOR PALESTINE: REWRITING THE HISTORY OF 1948, at 37–59 (Eugene L. Rogan & Avi Shlaim eds., 2002).

143.   As the ICJ noted,

the route chosen for the Wall gives expression *in loco* to the illegal measures taken by Israel with regard to Jerusalem and the settlements, as deplored by the Security Council . . . . There is also a risk of further alterations to the demographic composition of the Occupied Palestinian Territory resulting from the construction of the Wall inasmuch as it is contributing . . . to the departure of Palestinian populations from certain areas. That construction, along with measures taken previously, *thus severely impedes the exercise by the Palestinian people of [their] right of self-determination*, and is therefore a breach of Israel's obligation to respect that right

ICJ Wall Advisory Opinion, *supra* note 2, at 1042–43, para. 122 (emphasis added).

mentions self-determination in paragraph 88 of its Advisory Opinion, noting that self-determination is "enshrined in the U.N. Charter and reaffirmed by the General Assembly in Resolution 2625 (XXV)."[144] It then cites Article 1 common to the ICCPR and the ICESCR, as well as its jurisprudence in *Namibia* and *East Timor*.[145] In paragraph 118, the ICJ observed that "as regards the principle of the right of peoples to self-determination . . . the existence of a 'Palestinian people' is no longer in issue."[146] Actually, the existence of "a Palestinian people" has never really been an issue, for Palestinians had been recognized as "a people" during the time of the League of Nations.[147] Already in 1922, the British government had recognized "the people of Palestine," who were specifically mentioned no fewer than six times in an exchange of correspondence between the Palestine Arab Delegation and J.E. Shuckburgh, who was instructed to write on behalf of Winston Churchill, then Secretary of State for the Colonies.[148] Moreover, Britain was prepared to create an Arab agency to occupy a position exactly analogous to that accorded to the Jewish agency under Article 4 of the Mandate. That is, it was to be recognized as a public body for the purpose of advising and cooperating with the administration in such economic, social, and other matters as may affect the interests of the non-Jewish population, and, subject to the control of the administration, of assisting and taking part in the development of the country. Upon the establishment of the Arab Agency, Britain, as the Mandatory Power, intended to approach the League of Nations to seek its approval and place these changes upon "a formal footing."[149] However, this offer was unanimously declined by the Arab leaders of the day on the ground that "it would not satisfy the aspirations of the Arab people."[150] Evidently, the leaders of Palestine's Arab

---

144. *Id.* at 1034, para. 88.

145. *Id.*

146. *Id.* at 1041–42, para. 118.

147. *Palestine: Correspondence with the Palestine Arab Delegation and the Zionist Organisation*, Presented to Parliament by Command of His Majesty, June, 1922 (His Majesty's Stationary Office 1922).

148. *See id.* at No. 2, para. 2 ("It is the object of providing *the people of Palestine* with a constitutional channel for the expression of their opinions and wishes that the draft constitution has been framed." (emphasis added)); *id.* at No. 2, para. 4 ("There is no question of treating *the people of Palestine* as less advanced than their neighbours in Iraq and Syria." (emphasis added)); *id.* at No. 2, para. 5 ("His Majesty's Government are ready and willing to grant to *the people of Palestine* the greatest measure of independence consistent with the pledges referred to." (emphasis added)). Thus, the Palestinian people were recognized as a people from 1922 onwards.

149. *Report of the Palestine Royal Commission Presented by the Secretary of State for the Colonies to the United Kingdom Parliament*, League of Nations Doc. C.495.M.336.1937.VI, ch. VI (1937).

150. Musa Kazem Pasha, on behalf of a group of Arab notables which included Ragheb Bey Nashashibi, Haj Amin al Husseini and Khalil Effendi Sakakini, added that the Arabs, "having never recognized the status of the Jewish Agency, have no

community therefore had legal and political rights that were recognized and acknowledged by Great Britain.[151] It would therefore have been prudent for the ICJ to have, at the very least, noted that the right of the Palestinian people to self-determination had its genesis in the Covenant of the League of Nations and in the period in which Palestine was placed under the tutelage of Britain during the Mandate.[152] "Although decolonization [wa]s not explicitly referred to, the overall concept behind Article 22 of the Covenant may be regarded as the first manifestation of the ultimate goal to abrogate . . . colonial system[s], [a goal] that was still being pursued by many European states" at the time.[153] After all, the Mandate system—like the U.N. Charter system—did not explicitly promote continued or new colonial power.[154] And it was the idea underlying the concept of the Mandate and its "sacred trust" that would

---

desire for the establishment of an Arab Agency on the same basis." *See Palestine: Proposed Formation of an Arab Agency, Correspondence with the High Commissioner for Palestine*, Presented to Parliament by Command of His Majesty, Nov. 1923 (His Majesty's Stationary Office 1923). *See also* U.N. Special Comm. on Palestine, *Report to the General Assembly*, ¶ 101, U.N. Doc. A/364 (Sept. 3, 1947) (noting a past comparison of a proposal to establish an Arab Agency with analogous position to that of the Jewish Agency).

    151.   See, for example, the paper annexed to a "Top Secret" memorandum by Ernest Bevin, Britain's Secretary of State for Foreign Affairs dated January 13, 1947. The Legal Advisers of the Foreign Office and the Colonial Office prepared a paper "on the legal position of His Majesty's Government, in relation to the United Nations, in the event of their deciding either to partition Palestine or to introduce a system of provisional autonomy." In the annexed paper, the Legal Advisers contended that the word "position" in Article 6 of the Mandate included the political position of the Arabs in Palestine. The "Top Secret" seven page memorandum is entitled "Palestine: Reference to the United Nations," dated January 13, 1947. File no. C.P. (47) 28. This document is available in the National Archives in Kew. *See* FOREIGN OFFICE LIST AND DIPLOMATIC AND CONSULAR YEARBOOK 11 (Godfrey E.P. Hertslet ed., 1947) (stating that at the time William Eric Beckett, Gerald Gray Fitzmaurice, Richard Samuel Berrington Best, James Edmund Fawcett and Francis Aime Vallat were legal advisers at the Foreign Office in London and in Britain's Washington Embassy).

    152.   *See* ICJ Wall Advisory Opinion, *supra* note 2, at 1026–54, paras. 49, 71, 129, 162 (referring briefly to the 1947 partition plan and British Mandate, although these references were not in the context of self-determination). For further discussion on the question of self-determination, see League of Nations Covenant art. 22, and British Mandate for Palestine, Annex 391, 3 LEAGUE OF NATIONS—OFFICIAL J. 1007 (1922). Although in 1920 there was no general right of self-determination in international law, that principle was applied by way of exception to mandated territories at the Versailles Conference. JAMES CRAWFORD, THE CREATION OF STATES IN INTERNATIONAL LAW 428–29 (2006).

    153.   Nele Matz, *Civilization and the Mandate System Under the League of Nations as Origin of Trusteeship*, 9 MAX PLANCK Y.B. U.N. 47, 55 (2005).

    154.   *Id.* For further discussion of mandates, see Norman Bentwich, *Le Systèm Des Mandats*, 29(IV) RACUEIL DES COURS 115–86 (1968); NORMAN BENTWICH, THE MANDATES SYSTEM (Arnold D. McNair ed., 1930); and JACOB STOYANOVSKY, THE MANDATE FOR PALESTINE: A CONTRIBUTION TO THE THEORY AND PRACTICE OF INTERNATIONAL MANDATES (1928); QUINCY WRIGHT, MANDATES UNDER THE LEAGUE OF NATIONS (1930); R.N. CHOWDURI, INTERNATIONAL MANDATES AND TRUSTEESHIP SYSTEMS: A COMPARATIVE STUDY (1955).

eventually work its way into the Trusteeship System of the United Nations.[155]

The ICJ then went on to note that the 1995 Israel-Palestinian Interim Agreement refers a number of times to the Palestinian people and their "legitimate rights" (citing the preamble; paragraphs 4, 7, and 8; Article II, paragraph 2; Article III, paragraphs 1 and 2; and Article XXXII, paragraph 2).[156] It therefore considered that these legitimate rights "include the right of self-determination."[157] However, it should be noted that although the Palestinian people's right of self-determination is not dependent upon its recognition by Israel, the occupying power, Israel implicitly recognized this by being party to the Interim Agreement. Moreover, the British Mandate provided both Jews and Arabs with the right of self-determination in Palestine, which was given recognition by the 1947 U.N. partition plan[158] and the effort to establish a U.N. Trusteeship.[159] Their right of self-determination was also confirmed by state practice in the period preceding the adoption of the U.N. Charter as provided for by Article 22 of the Covenant of the League of Nations. In this regard it is telling that all "A-class" Mandates would become independent states, the exception being Palestine.[160] It would therefore be nonsensical for Israel to deny de jure recognition of the right of the Palestinian people to self-determination when the basis for its own right has its origins with that of the very people with whom it is

---

155. In fact, the principle of the "sacred trust," which was enshrined in the Covenant, had its origins in the 1885 Conference of Berlin and was intimately connected with "the duty of civilisation." Charles H. Alexandrowicz, Notes and Commentary, *The Juridical Expression of the Sacred Trust of Civilisation*, 65 AM. J. INT'L L. 149, 154 (1971).

156. ICJ Wall Advisory Opinion, *supra* note 2, at 1041–42, para. 118.

157. *Id.*

158. G.A. Res. 181 (II), U.N. GAOR, 1st Spec. Sess., Supp. No. 1, U.N. Doc. A/310 (Nov. 29, 1947). For the voting record, see U.N. GAOR, 1st Sess., 128th plen. mtg., U.N. Doc. A/PV.128 (Nov. 29, 1947).

159. U.S. Delegation to the U.N., *Draft Trusteeship Agreement for Palestine: Working Paper Circulated by the U.S. Delegation*, art. 4, U.N. Doc. A/C.1/277 (Apr. 20, 1948). For the political debate surrounding the trusteeship decision see MICHAEL J. COHEN, PALESTINE AND THE GREAT POWERS 1945–1948 345 (1982). It is noteworthy that Article 5 of the Draft Trusteeship, which was proposed by the US, provided that the territorial integrity of Palestine would be assured by the U.N. For further reading, see PHILIP JESSUP, THE BIRTH OF NATIONS 255–303 (1974). Jessup was the author of the draft trusteeship agreement for Palestine, which he discusses in this memoir.

160. Although the other Arab countries achieved independence during the time of the League, Trans-Jordan became an independent state *after* the dissolution of the League of Nations in 1946. *See* Treaty of London, U.K.–Trans-Jordan, Mar. 22, 1946, 6 U.N.T.S. 143 (giving Trans-Jordan its independence). This is further precedent indicating, perhaps, that Palestine could have, and should have, become an independent unitary state, encompassing a Jewish national home within its borders. *See* Mary C. Wilson, *King Abdullah and Palestine*, 14 BRIT. SOC'Y MIDDLE E. STUD. 37, 40 (1987) (discussing the independence of Trans-Jordan in 1946 and the reigning ideology of Arab nationalism).

destined to share that land. Thus, when the ICJ affirmed the right of self-determination as an obligation *erga omnes*, this would apply to both Jews and Arabs. However, in this particular instance, it is Israel who is depriving the Palestinians of the exercise of this right, by building a wall through territory in which they aspire to create their state. As the ICJ observed:

> [T]he obligations violated by Israel include certain obligations *erga omnes*. As the Court indicated in the *Barcelona Traction* case, such obligations are by their very nature "the concern of all States" and, "[i]n view of the importance of the rights involved, all States can be held to have a legal interest in their protection." (*Barcelona Traction, Light and Power Company, Limited, Second Phase, Judgment, I.C.J. Reports 1970*, p. 32, para. 33.) The obligations *erga omnes* violated by Israel are the obligation to respect the right of the Palestinian people to self-determination. . . .
>
> [I]n the *East Timor* case, [the Court] described as "irreproachable" the assertion that "the right of peoples to self-determination, as it evolved from the Charter and from United Nations practice, has an *erga omnes* character" (*I.C.J. Reports 1995*, p. 102, para. 29). The Court would also recall that under the terms of General Assembly resolution 2625 (XXV). . . .
>
> 'Every State has the duty to promote, through joint and separate action, realization of the principle of equal rights and self-determination of peoples, in accordance with the provisions of the Charter, and to render assistance to the United Nations in carrying out the responsibilities entrusted to it by the Charter regarding the implementation of the principle. . . .'[161]

The HCJ only mentioned the right of self-determination in passing in the *Mara'abe* case.[162] It merely noted that Judges Higgins and Kooijmans criticized in their separate opinions certain aspects of the ICJ's finding that the wall impinges upon the Palestinian people's right of self-determination.[163] In fact, only six ICJ judges (in five separate opinions and one declaration) referred to the question of the impact of the wall on Palestinian self-determination.[164] Judge Koroma cited the U.N. partition resolution and noted that the construction of the wall would prevent the Palestinian people from creating a state.[165] Judge Al-Khasawneh was of the opinion that it was Israel's prolonged military occupation and its policy of creating fait accomplis on the ground (which presumably also includes the construction of the wall) that prevented the Palestinian people from

---

161.   ICJ Wall Advisory Opinion, *supra* note 2, at 1053, paras. 155–156.

162.   HCJ 7957/04 Mara'abe v. Prime Minister of Isr. [2005] (Isr.), *translated in* 45 I.L.M. 202, ¶¶ 48–49 (2006).

163.   *Id.* ¶ 49.

164.   Judges Koroma, Higgins, Kooijmans, Al-Khasawneh, Elaraby, and Owada issued separate opinions. Judge Buergenthal issued a declaration. ICJ Wall Advisory Opinion, *supra* note 2, at 1054–56, para. 163.

165.   *Id.* at 1056, para. 5 (separate opinion of Judge Koroma).

exercising their right of self-determination.[166] Judge Elaraby simply repeated some of the relevant passages from the ICJ's Advisory Opinion on self-determination.[167] Judge Kooijmans thought that it would have been better if the Court had left the issue of self-determination to the political process.[168] However, he admitted that "the mere existence of a structure that separates the Palestinians from each other makes the realization of their right to self-determination far more difficult."[169] In his Declaration, Judge Buergenthal also agreed with the court's findings that the wall severely impedes the Palestinian people's exercise of their right of self-determination and that Israel was breaching this right.[170] However, he did not necessarily believe that the issue was relevant "to the case before us" and thought that Israel's right of self-defense could have precluded any wrongfulness in this regard (which is discussed more in Part V).[171] Judge Higgins considered the ICJ's finding that the construction of the wall "severely impedes the exercise by the Palestinian people of its right of self-determination, and is therefore a breach of Israel's obligation to respect that right" a non sequitur. She then elaborated upon this point:

> The real impediment is the apparent inability and/or unwillingness of both Israel and Palestine to move in parallel to secure the necessary conditions—that is, at one and the same time, for Israel to withdraw from Arab occupied territory and *for Palestine to provide the conditions to allow Israel to feel secure in so doing. The simple point is underscored by the fact that if the wall had never been built, the Palestinians would still not yet have exercised their right of self-determination.* It seems to me both unrealistic and unbalanced for the Court to find that the wall (rather than "the larger problem," which is beyond the question put to the Court for an opinion) is a serious obstacle to self-determination.[172]

This passage is illuminating. Judge Higgins is correct to note that the actual exercise of the right of self-determination is usually accomplished through a political process, although it has been accomplished through the use of force, such as in Bosnia, Croatia, Bangladesh, Slovenia, southern Sudan, and elsewhere.[173] The

---

166. *Id.* at 1075–76, para. 9 (separate opinion of Judge Al-Khasawneh).

167. *Id.* at 1089–90, para. 3.4 (separate opinion of Judge Elaraby).

168. *Id.* at 1071, para. 31 (separate opinion Judge Kooijmans).

169. *Id.* The current trajectory of the wall loops around the settlement *Ariel,* which is located deep inside occupied territory. It may also loop around the projected E-1 extension to *Ma'ale Adumim.* This would effectively segregate and dissect the West Bank into cantons. See the Map in the Annex.

170. *Id.* at 1078–79, para 4 (declaration of Judge Buergenthal).

171. *Id.*

172. *Id.* at 1063, para. 30 (emphasis added) (separate opinion of Judge Higgins).

173. *See* LAURA SILBER & ALLAN LITTLE, THE DEATH OF YUGOSLAVIA (1996) (discussing Yugoslavia); Ved P. Nanda, *Self-Determination in International Law: The Tragic Tale of Two Cities—Islamabad (West Pakistan) and Dacca (East Pakistan),* 66 AM. J. INT'L L. 321 (1972) (discussing Bangladesh); Machakos Protocol, § B(2.5), July

Zionists also implicitly invoked this right when they created Israel in 1948.[174] One may therefore question whether it is necessary for the Palestinian people—subject to almost four decades of military occupation—to provide the conditions that allow the occupying power to feel secure in withdrawing from Occupied Arab Territory. Whenever attempts have been made to establish a U.N. observer force to maintain law and order between Israelis and Palestinians, which could provide Israel with the conditions necessary to enable it to feel secure in withdrawing from the territories, those attempts have been vetoed at the U.N. Security Council.[175] The reality is that many in Israel oppose a withdrawal because they consider that territory as belonging to Israel (for ideological and other reasons) regardless of its status under international law, and some Israeli lawyers have even advanced technical legal arguments to justify Israel's retention of those territories.[176] This is also the situation with respect to the Syrian Golan Heights, where there has been "peace and quiet" for the last four decades. Yet despite this, Israel

---

20, 2002, *reprinted in* 10 Y.B. ISLAMIC & MIDDLE E. L. 303 (2003–2004) (referring to the possible secession of southern Sudan); *see also* James Crawford, *State Practice and International Law in Relation to Secession*, 69 BRIT. Y.B. INT'L L. 85 (1998) (noting that states are extremely reluctant to recognize or accept unilateral secession outside the colonial context; and John Dugard, *A Legal Basis for Secession: Relevant Principles and Rules, in* SECESSION AND INTERNATIONAL LAW 89–96 (Julie Dahltiz ed., 2003) (discussing secession generally).

174.   *See* Declaration of the Establishment of the State of Israel, 1948–5708, 1 LSI 3–5 (1948) (Isr.) (declaring that the right to a sovereign nation state is a natural right to the Jewish people to be masters of their own fate); *see generally* John A. Collins, Note, *Self-Determination in International Law: The Palestinians*, 12 CASE W. RES. J. INT'L L. 137 (1980) (discussing Israel, Palestine, and self-determination). *See also,* Evan M. Wilson, DECISION ON PALESTINE: HOW THE U.S. CAME TO RECOGNIZE ISRAEL (1979) (discussing in great detail the politics behind the Truman's decision to recognize Israel and how this left the State Department and the US Department of Defense in the cold).

175.   *See* S.C. Draft Res., ¶ 5, UN. Doc. S/2001/1199 (Dec. 14, 2001) (co-sponsored by Egypt and Tunisia) (would have encouraged "all concerned to establish a monitoring mechanism to help the parties implement the recommendations of the Report of the Sharm El-Sheikh Fact-Finding Committee (Mitchell Report) and to help create a better situation in the occupied Palestinian territories"); S.C. Draft Res., ¶ 8, U.N. Doc. S/2001/270 (Mar. 26, 2001) (drafted by Bangladesh, Colombia, Jamaica, Mali, Mauritius, Singapore and Tunisia). The latter would have requested

> the Secretary-General to consult the parties on immediate and substantive steps to implement this resolution and to report to the Council within one month of the adoption of this resolution and expresses the readiness of the Council to act upon receipt of the report to set up an appropriate mechanism to protect Palestinian civilians, including through the establishment of a United Nations observer force.

Id.

176.   *See* Yehuda Z. Blum, *The Missing Reversioner: Reflections on the Status of Judea and Samaria*, 3 ISR. L. REV. 279 (1968); Meir Shamgar, *The Observance of International Law in the Administered Territories*, 1 ISR. Y.B. HUM. RTS. 262 (1971).

has still to withdraw from that territory.[177] Instead, Israel has annexed the territory and established several settlements there.[178] All attempts by the Syrian government to make peace with Israel based upon a full withdrawal from all occupied Arab territory, an approach that was endorsed by the Arab League twice in Beirut in 2002 and in Algiers in 2005 and has been reiterated several times since, have fallen on deaf ears.[179] Moreover, Israel unilaterally withdrew from the Gaza Strip in a matter of days during September 2005, even though the conditions in the strip were, from an Israeli security perspective, probably worse than they had been at any time in its history.[180] Israel's unilateral withdrawal had little to do with whether the Palestinians had provided the necessary conditions for Israel to feel secure in doing this. Rather, it had everything to do with power, territory and demography.[181] As Judge Elaraby opined:

> [N]otwithstanding the general prohibition against annexing occupied territories . . . on 14 April 2004, the Prime Minister of Israel addressed a letter to the President of the United States. Attached to the letter is a Disengagement Plan which one has to interpret as authoritatively reflecting Israel's intention to annex Palestinian territories. The Disengagement Plan provides that

---

177. *See* S.C. Res. 497, U.N. Doc. S/RES/497 (Dec. 17, 1981) (rejecting Israel's decision to impose its laws in Syrian Golan Heights); S.C. Res. 338, U.N. Doc. S/RES/338 (Oct. 22, 1973) (calling for a cease-fire in the Middle East); S.C. Res. 242, U.N. Doc. S/RES/242 (Nov. 22, 1967) (reaffirming the need for peace in the Middle East).

178. Golan Heights Law, 5742-1981, 36 LSI 7 (1981) (Isr.); *see also Golan Settlement Plan Under Fire*, BBC NEWS, Dec. 31, 2003, *available at* http://news.bbc.co.uk/1/hi/world/middle_east/3360085.stm (discussing Israel's settlement activity plans). The Security Council condemned Israel for its decision to impose its laws, jurisdiction, and administration in the occupied Syrian Golan Heights which it considered "null and void and without international legal effect." S.C. Res. 497, *supra* note 177, ¶ 1.

179. *See Letter Dated 24 April 2002 from the Chargé d'Affaires a.i. of the Permanent Mission of Lebanon to the United Nations Addressed to the Secretary-General, Annex II*, U.N. Doc. S/2002/932, A/56/1026 (Aug. 15, 2002) (relaying to the U.N. the resolutions of the Arab Peace Initiative at the Summit-level Council of the League of Arab States in Beirut). According to a 2006 Ha'aretz report, the Arab initiative proposes a new mechanism for furthering talks between Israel, the Palestinians, Lebanon, and Syria. Akiva Eldar, *Arab League Floats New Initiative for Resuming the Peace Process*, HA'ARETZ (Jerusalem), Aug. 31 2006. This report proposes that the Security Council manage and oversee the negotiations, and that the results of these talks be brought before the U.N. in a year. *Id.* The proposal suggests that during the period of negotiations, all hostilities cease and the U.N. is permitted to impose sanctions on cease-fire violators. Israeli PM Tzipi Livni told Annan that Israel intends to oppose the new Arab initiative. *Id.* Prime Minister Ehud Olmert has publicly described the Heights as "an integral part of the State of Israel," saying that he would never hand it back to Syria. AGENCE FRANCE-PRESSE, Sept. 26, 2006.

180. *See* Disengagement Plan of Prime Minister Ariel Sharon, *supra* note 48 (detailing the disengagement of Israel from the Gaza Strip).

181. On the impact of Israel's withdrawal from the Gaza Strip in its immediate aftermath, see *Special Report: Palestinians in Gaza, Will They Sink or Swim?*, ECONOMIST, Sept. 22, 2005, at 29–31. "Israel's withdrawal has left Gaza seething, lawless, poor, cut off from the outside world." *Id.*

> 'it is clear that in the West Bank, there are areas which will be part of the State of Israel, including cities, towns and villages, security areas and installations, and other places of special interest to Israel.'

> The clear undertakings to withdraw and to respect the integrity and status of the West Bank and Gaza legally debar Israel from infringing upon or altering the international legal status of the Palestinian territory.[182]

The Oslo Accords viewed the West Bank and Gaza as one territorial unit which is to be preserved for the final-status negotiations.[183] Judge Elaraby was of the view that it would have been appropriate "to refer to the implications of the letter of the Prime Minister of Israel and its attachments [regarding the Gaza Disengagement Plan] and to underline that what it purports to declare is a breach of Israel's obligations and contrary to international law."[184] When Israel invaded and occupied the Gaza Strip in the 1956 Suez War, it refused to withdraw from that territory and was called upon to do so by the General Assembly.[185] Israel insisted on firm guarantees from the international community before it would agree to a withdrawal. In response, U.S. President Dwight Eisenhower said:

> This raises a basic question of principle. Should a nation which attacks and occupies foreign territory in the face of United Nations disapproval be allowed to impose conditions on its own withdrawal?

> If we agree that armed attack can properly achieve the purposes of the assailant, then I fear we will have turned back the clock of international order. We will, in effect, have countenanced the use of force as a means of settling international differences and through this gaining national advantages.[186]

Judge Higgins is correct to note that if the wall had never been built, the Palestinians would still not have exercised their right of self-determination. But this is precisely because Israel refuses to withdraw (or make a *commitment* to withdraw) from the territories it

---

182.   ICJ Wall Advisory Opinion, *supra* note 2, at 1086, para. 2.5 (separate opinion of Judge Elaraby).

183.   *See* Israel-Palestinian Interim Agreement, *supra* note 89, art. XXXI.7; *see also* Iain Scobbie, *An Intimate Disengagement: Israel's Withdrawal From Gaza, the Law of Occupation and of Self-Determination*, 11 Y.B. ISLAMIC & MIDDLE E. L. 3 (2004–2005) (arguing that Israel's Gaza disengagement plan was inconsistent with the Oslo Accords and international law).

184.   ICJ Wall Advisory Opinion, *supra* note 2, at 1086, para. 2.5 (separate opinion of Judge Elaraby).

185.   A draft U.N. Security Council was vetoed by the UK and France. *But see* G.A. Res. 1120 (XI), ¶ 1, U.N. GAOR, 1st Emer. Spec. Sess., U.N. Doc. A/Res/1120 (Nov. 24, 1956) ("not[ing] with regret that . . . no Israel forces have been withdrawn behind the armistice line although a considerable time has elapsed since the adoption of the relevant General Assembly resolutions." (omission of emphasis)).

186.   *Address by President Eisenhower on the Situation in the Middle East, Feb. 20, 1957*, 36 DEP'T ST. BULL. 387 (1957), *reprinted in* THE ARAB-ISRAELI CONFLICT VOLUME III: DOCUMENTS 643, 647 (John Norton Moore ed., 1974).

occupied in June 1967.[187] Israel's refusal stands even though the Arab world has made it clear that it would be prepared to terminate its state of belligerency with Israel and to recognize Israel's sovereignty, territorial integrity, and political independence—as Egypt did in 1979 and Jordan did in 1994—if Israel were to withdraw.[188] Moreover, according to U.N. Security Council Resolution 242, Israel is obliged to negotiate a withdrawal from the territories it captured in the June 1967 War.[189] The onus to secure the necessary conditions for negotiations is upon Israel, not upon the Palestinian people (who are not even mentioned in that resolution).[190]

---

187. *See, e.g., Israel Hints at Jerusalem Talks*, BBC NEWS, Oct. 8, 2007, *available at* http://news.bbc.co.uk/2/hi/middle_east/7033450.stm (noting that since its occupation in 1967 Israel has claimed the entire city of Jerusalem as an "eternal, indivisible capital").

188. *See* Treaty of Peace, Egypt-Isr., art. III(1), Mar. 26, 1979, *reprinted in* 18 I.L,M. 362 (1979) [hereinafter Egypt-Israel Treaty of Peace] (declaring that the parties will "recognize and . . . respect each other's sovereignty, territorial integrity and political independence"); Treaty of Peace, Isr.-Jordan, art. 2.1, Oct. 26, 1994, *reprinted in* 34 I.L.M. 46 (1995) (also declaring that the parties will "recognize and . . . respect each other's sovereignty, territorial integrity and political independence").

189. *See* S.C. Res. 242, U.N. Doc. S/RES/242 (Nov. 22, 1967) (calling for the "[w]ithdrawal of Israel armed forces from territories occupied in the recent conflict"); *see also* G.A. Res. 2799 (XXVI) (Dec. 13, 1971) (reaffirming the same call for withdrawal); G.A. Res. 2628 (XXV) (Nov. 4, 1970) (reaffirming the same call for withdrawal); *see also* G.A. Res. 3414 (XXX) (Dec. 5, 1975) ("request[ing] the Security Council . . . to take all necessary measures for the speedy implementation . . . of all relevant resolutions of the General Assembly and the Security Council . . . which ensures complete Israeli withdrawal from all the occupied Arab territories"); *see also* G.A. Res. 36/226, U.N. Doc. A/RES/36/226 (Dec. 17, 1981) (condemning Israel's continued occupation); G.A. Res. 35/169, U.N. Doc. A/RES/35/169 (Dec. 15, 1980) (same); G.A. Res. 34/70, U.N. Doc. A/RES/34/70 (Dec. 6, 1979) (same); G.A. Res. 32/20, U.N. Doc. A/RES/32/20 (Nov. 25, 1977) (same); G.A. Res. 31/61, U.N. Doc. A/RES/31/61 (Dec. 9, 1976) (same).

190. U.N. Security Council Resolution 242 only calls upon Israel (not the Arab States) to withdraw its forces from those territories. S.C. Res. 242, *supra* note 189, ¶ 1. The withdrawal phrase of resolution 242 provides for "[w]ithdrawal of Israel armed forces from territories occupied in the recent conflict." *Id.* Arthur J. Goldberg, the U.S. Ambassador to the U.N. said this "refers, and was always intended to refer, to the armed forces of Israel." U.N. SCOR, ¶ 63, UN Doc. S/PV.1377 (Nov. 15, 1967). According to the "right-wing," Israeli interpretation of that phrase, Israel is not obliged to withdraw from all territories it captured in 1967 because the English text of resolution 242 does not include the definitive article "the" or the adjective "all" before the phrase "territories occupied in the recent conflict," as it does in the French text which is equally authoritative. *See* Michla Pomerance, *A Court of 'UN Law,'* 38 ISR. L.R. 134, 149 (2005) (citing with approval Eugene V. Rostow's, *Legal Aspects of the Search for Peace in the Middle East*, 64 AM. SOC'Y INT'L L. PROC 64, 68–69 (1970)). Rostow, interestingly, does not provide any authority for this logic, which is clearly incorrect. *See* John McHugo, *Resolution 242: A Legal Reappraisal of the Right-Wing Israeli Interpretation of the Withdrawal Phrase with Reference to the Conflict Between Israel and the Palestinians*, 51 INT'L & COMP. L. Q. 851 (2002). For an Arab view, which it is submitted is correct in this instance, see the late Musa E. Mazzawi's thorough analysis in MUSA E MAZZAWI, PALESTINE AND THE LAW: GUIDELINES FOR THE RESOLUTION OF THE ARAB-ISRAEL CONFLICT 199–238 (1997). However, the plain meaning of the withdrawal phrase is clear. The text refers *specifically* to "Israel armed

918   *The Palestine Question in International Law*

This principle was subsequently reaffirmed in Resolution 338, which was passed after Israel managed to keep hold of those territories in the October 1973 War.[191] Israel is thus obliged to *negotiate* an end to its occupation of Arab territories, including Palestine, meaning that it cannot postpone negotiations indefinitely by refusing to negotiate, creating obstacles on the ground that would hinder a full withdrawal, or by claiming that it has nobody with whom to negotiate.[192]   The

---

forces" and to no one else. S.C. Res. 242, *supra* note 189, ¶ 1. It then refers to "territories occupied in the recent conflict." *Id.* This obviously refers to territories Israel captured in June 1967, and not to territories the pre-1948 *Yishuv* (the Jewish settler community then living in Palestine) and their militias captured in 1947–1949. *See* McHugo, *supra* note 189, at 880. Indeed, this interpretation was how Abba Eban, Israel's Ambassador to the U.N., understood it at the time. In a diplomatic note, Eban wrote: "The words 'in the recent conflict' convert the principle of eliminating occupation into a mathematically precise formula for restoring the June 4 Map." *See id.* at 875 n.62 (citing 'Comment by Foreign Minister of Israel' and Telegram 3164, UK Mission in New York to Foreign Office, 12 Nov 1967. FO 961/24). The ICJ noted in its 1950 Advisory Opinion on South-West Africa that interpretations placed upon legal instruments by the parties to them have considerable probative value when they contain recognition by a party of its own obligations under an instrument. *See* International Status of South-West Africa, Advisory Opinion, 1950 I.C.J. 135 (July 11); *see also* SYDNEY D. BAILEY, THE MAKING OF RESOLUTION 242, at 155 (1985) (arguing that resolution 242 requires a full withdrawal).

    191.   S.C. Res. 338, U.N. Doc. S/RES/338 (Oct. 22, 1973).

    192.   U.N. Security Council Resolution 338 calls upon all the parties concerned "to start immediately after the cease-fire the *implementation* of Security Council resolution 242 (of 1967) in all of its parts." *Id.* ¶ 2 (emphasis added). Although this Resolution does not expressly refer to any of the provisions of Chapter VII of the U.N. Charter (such as Article 39), it was evident that the situation in the Middle East amounted to a threat to international peace and security, and the situation was referred to as such throughout the debates both preceding the adoption of Resolution 338 and afterwards. *See* U.N. SCOR, 28th Sess., 1747th mtg., U.N. Doc. S/PV.1747 (Oct. 22, 1973) (including statements made by Mr. Scali (United States) and Mr. Malik (U.S.S.R.)). Although Resolution 338 does not invoke Chapter VII, it "*decides* that, immediately and concurrently with the cease-fire, *negotiations* shall start between the parties concerned under appropriate auspices aimed at establishing a just and durable peace in the Middle East." S.C. Res. 338, *supra* note 191, ¶ 3 (emphasis added). In its 1971 Advisory Opinion on *Namibia*, the ICJ said that it is for member states to comply with *decisions* adopted under Article 25, which would include even those members of the Security Council who voted against them and those members of the United Nations who are not members of the Council. *See* U.N. Charter art. 5; Legal Consequences for States of the Continued Presence of South Africa in Namibia (South West Africa) Notwithstanding Security Council Resolution 276, 1971 I.C.J. 52 (June 21) [hereinafter Namibia Advisory Opinion] (discussing S.C. Res. 276, U.N. Doc. S/RES/2706 (Jan. 30, 1970)). Many of the delegates participating in the Security Council debate in October 1973, including those ambassadors representing France, the United States, and the U.S.S.R., expressly referred to Resolution 338 as a "decision" as opposed to a "recommendation." U.N. SCOR, U.N. Doc. S/PV.1747, *supra* note 192. In explaining his country's vote in favor of Resolution 338, Mr. Perez de Cuellar said that it was "binding," and that Peru would fully cooperate in the Council "so that it can discharge its duty in *enforcing* its resolutions." *Id.* ¶¶ 136–37. The representative of Yugoslavia thought that the Council had an "obligation" and a "duty" under the Charter to make Israel stop its firing and to immediately implement Resolution 242. *Id.* ¶ 89. The U.S.S.R. warned Israel of "very serious consequences" if it continued with its

point is that even as Israel prepares for a partial withdrawal, it is preemptively building a wall which it knows will hinder the exercise of that right. Even if Israel withdraws from parts of the West Bank—and it is still unclear whether it will actually do so—the Palestinian people would still not be able to exercise their right of self-determination (which, in this case, would be to create a sovereign, viable, and independent state in East Jerusalem, the West Bank, and the Gaza Strip) because what will remain will be *less* than a state (see the maps in the Appendix). Although what remains of the West Bank and the Gaza Strip may amount to a self-determination unit, it is highly unlikely that it will amount to a state that would be truly independent of Israel, viable, or contiguous.[193] As Prime Minister Yitzhak Rabin told the Knesset upon ratification of the Israeli-Palestinian Interim Agreement on October 5, 1995:

> We view the permanent solution in the framework of State of Israel [*sic*] which will include most of the area of the Land of Israel as it was under the rule of the British Mandate and alongside it a Palestinian *entity* which will be a home to most of the Palestinian residents living in the Gaza Strip and the West Bank.
>
> We would like this to be an entity *which is less than a State* and which will independently run the lives of the Palestinians under its authority. The borders of the State of Israel, during the permanent solution, will be *beyond* the lines which existed before the Six Day War. *We will not return to the 4 June 1967 lines.*[194]

---

campaigns against the Egyptian and Syrian Arab Republics. *Id.* ¶ 108 (statement of Mr. Malik). Subsequently, the U.S.S.R. expressed its satisfaction that the Council had taken "effective measures" for the "immediate dispatch" of observers to the cease-fire line, "so as to *compel* Israel" to respect its decisions. *Id.* Several African countries immediately severed their diplomatic relations with Israel. In Resolution 339, the Security Council confirmed its *decision* "on an immediate cessation of all kinds of firing and of all military action . . . ." S.C. Res. 339, ¶ 1, U.N. Doc. S/RES/ 339 (Oct. 23, 1973) (emphasis added). In referring to U.N. resolutions on the Namibia question, Rosalyn Higgins observes: "The binding or non-binding nature of those resolutions turns not upon whether they are to be regarded as 'Chapter VI' or 'Chapter VII' resolutions . . . but upon whether the parties intended them to be 'decisions' or 'recommendations.'" Rosalyn Higgins, *The Advisory Opinion on Namibia: Which UN Resolutions Are Binding Under Article 25 of the Charter?*, 21 INT'L & COMP. L.Q. 270, 281–82 (1972). In this regard, reference must also be made to the European Court of First Instance, which recently ruled that "Article 39 of the Charter of the United Nations draws a distinction between 'recommendations,' which are not 'binding,' and 'decisions,' which are." Case T-253/02 Chafiq Ayadi v. Council of the European Union, para. 156, (Jul. 12, 2006), para. 156, *available at* Westlaw UK.

193. For further reading on the question of Palestinian statehood, see James Crawford, *Israel (1948-1949) and Palestine (1998-1999): Two Studies in the Creation of States, in* THE REALITY OF INTERNATIONAL LAW: ESSAYS IN HONOUR OF IAN BROWNLIE 95 (Guy S. Goodwin-Gill & Stefan Talmon eds., 1999); Omar M. Dajani, Note, *Stalled Between Seasons: The International Legal Status of Palestine During the Interim Period*, 26 DENV. J. INT'L L. & POL'Y 27 (1997).

194. Yitzhak Rabin, Prime Minister of Israel, Address to the Knesset on the Israel-Palestinian Interim Agreement, Oct. 5, 1995, *reprinted in* 15 ISRAEL'S FOREIGN

Likewise, Prime Minister Ehud Barak was quoted as saying something along the same lines on May 18, 1999, the night of his election victory:

> We will move quickly toward separation from the Palestinians within four security red lines: a *united Jerusalem under our sovereignty* as the capital of Israel for eternity, period; under *no conditions will we return to the 1967 borders*; no foreign army west of the Jordan River; and *most of the settlers in Judaea and Samaria will be in settlement blocs under our sovereignty*. As I undertook, any permanent arrangement will be put to a national referendum. In the long run, you, the people of Israel, will decide.[195]

With regard to Israel's Gaza Disengagement Plan, which, as Judge Elaraby points out, must be seen in the context of the wall and settler expansionism in the West Bank, the question of control over the territory is measured by the extent to which the occupying power is limiting the right of self-determination of the occupied population.[196] In other words, it is the wall *and its associated régime* that is hindering the exercise, by the Palestinian people, of their right of self-determination.   Indeed, the combined effect of the wall, the checkpoints, the settlements and the settlement roads, the permit system, and the economic stranglehold Israel has over the territories has a direct impact upon the right of the Palestinian people to pursue their economic, social, and cultural development. This is because the Palestinian Authority (PA) is unable to function as an independent political entity when it is completely dependent on the international community and Israel to accomplish the basic tasks associated with statehood, and when almost every aspect of the daily lives of the Palestinian people from whom the PA derives its legitimacy is affected by the occupation. The Palestinians cannot be free and independent or pursue their right of self-determination culturally, economically, and socially when they are ruled by another people.

RELATIONS: SELECTED DOCUMENTS 1995–1996, at 322, 323 (Meron Medzini ed., Isr. Ministry of Foreign Affairs 1995–1996) (emphasis added).

195.   *See Barak's Victory Speech*, May 18, 1999, BBC NEWS, *available at* http://news.bbc.co.uk/1/hi/world/monitoring/346507.stm (including excerpts of the victory speech of Ehud Barak, Prime Minister of Israel, given at the Dan Hotel in Tel Aviv).

196.   As a Policy Brief on the Gaza Disengagement Plan, prepared by the Harvard Program on Humanitarian Policy and Conflict Research notes: "The test is not per se the military presence of the occupying forces in all areas of the territory, but the extent to which the Occupying Power, through its military presence, is exerting effective control over the territory and limiting the right of self-determination of the occupied population."   CLAUDE BRUDERLEIN, LEGAL ASPECTS OF ISRAEL'S DISENGAGEMENT PLAN UNDER INTERNATIONAL HUMANITARIAN LAW 8 (2004), *available at* http://www.ihlresearch.org/opt/pdfs/briefing3466.pdf. This paper was initially issued in, and is dated, November 2004, but at some later point it was revised, modifying the original analysis of "effective military control." The paper does not indicate that it has been amended and, moreover, it retains its original date. *See* Iain Scobbie, *supra* note 183.

Had Israel simply withdrawn from the occupied territories to the 1949 armistice lines without constructing the wall along its current route and relocated the settlers as it has done in Gaza, there would have been no obstacle to the exercise of that right.

It is important to note that the "Performance-Based Roadmap to a Permanent Two-State Solution to the Israel-Palestine Conflict," which was mentioned by the ICJ in the final paragraph of its Advisory Opinion, does speak of an "independent, democratic, and *viable*" Palestinian state.[197] And yet when Israel accepted the Roadmap, it submitted fourteen separate reservations that rendered the Roadmap practically devoid of its object and purpose.[198] Of the fourteen reservations Israel submitted when it accepted the Road Map, the fifth reservation is of particular relevance:

> The character of the *provisional* Palestinian State will be determined through negotiations between the Palestinian Authority and Israel. The provisional state will have *provisional borders* and *certain aspects of sovereignty*, be *fully demilitarized with no military forces*, but only with police and internal security forces of limited scope and armaments, be *without the authority* to undertake defense alliances or military cooperation, and *Israeli control over the entry and exit of all persons and cargo, as well as of its air space and electromagnetic spectrum*.[199]

Under these conditions, it is difficult to see how a "provisional Palestinian state" can really be a state at all when it will have no sovereignty, security, or control over its borders, airspace, or electromagnetic spectrum. Surely the real impediment to peace and stability in the Middle East is Israel's apparent unwillingness to move in parallel with those countries in the Arab world that have repeatedly stated they are prepared to recognize it in exchange for a full Israeli withdrawal from Arab occupied territory.

Judge Kooijmans agreed with his colleagues in his separate opinion "that the wall and its associated régime impede[d] the exercise by the Palestinian people of its right of self-determination" because it "establishes a physical separation of the people entitled to enjoy this right."[200] But the wall and its associated régime not only separate Israelis from Palestinians, but also Palestinians from each

---

197. ICJ Wall Advisory Opinion, *supra* note 2, at 1054, para. 162 (emphasis added); *see also Letter Dated 7 May 2003 From the Secretary-General Addressed to the President of the Security Council,* U.N. Doc. S/2003/529/Annex (May 7, 2003) (containing the same language).

198. *See* Israel's Response to the Road Map, ¶¶ 5–6, 9–10 (May 25, 2003), http://www.knesset.gov.il/process/docs/roadmap_response_eng.htm (setting forth all 14 reservations).

199. *Id.* ¶ 5 (emphasis added).

200. ICJ Wall Advisory Opinion, *supra* note 2, at 1071–72, para. 32 (separate opinion of Judge Kooijmans).

other.[201] The wall segregates their land and the natural resources below that land and repartitions the territory into cantons for the benefit of the settlers.[202] The Palestinian people cannot freely pursue their economic, social, and cultural development if they are dependent on Israel for tax rebates, trade, water, security, and the movement of people, among other things.[203] As Catriona Drew observed in relation to the Israeli settlements (writing before Israel began constructing a wall around those settlements):

> Once the right of self-determination has been conceptually stripped of its core entitlements to territory and resources, it becomes possible—for states, institutions and commentators alike [and it should also be added judges]—to assert both the *inalienable, jus cogens* character of the Palestinian right to self-determination, *and* declare the future of Israeli settlements as a matter for political negotiation; to affirm the primacy of the right of self-determination, including the option of a state, and envisage a future for Israeli settlements on the West Bank.[204]

If self-determination is viewed not just as a one-off right of a people to participate in a political process, but is viewed as a *substantive* right—to territory, resources, and demography—it becomes immediately apparent why a wall that prevents, among other things, farmers from accessing their land, doctors from visiting their patients, children from going to school, and the faithful from reaching their places of worship (as well as a future Palestinian government from having access to its own natural resources and control over its economy, borders, sea, and airspace) is problematic.[205] Judge

---

201. Not only are Gazans and West Bankers separated physically from each other (by Israel), but West Bankers are also separated (by the *Ma'ale Adumim* settlement bloc which will effectively partition the West Bank into two separate parts) and East Jerusalemites are separated from their kindred in the West Bank.

202. *See, e.g.*, B'TSELEM, GROUND TO A HALT: DENIAL OF PALESTINIANS' FREEDOM OF MOVEMENT IN THE WEST BANK 26–57 (2007), *available at* http://www.btselem.org/Download/20070805_Ground_to_a_Halt_Eng.pdf.

203. For an interesting book looking at the economics of state formation in Palestine during the Oslo period in the mid to late 1990s, see STATE FORMATION IN PALESTINE: VIABILITY AND GOVERNANCE DURING A SOCIAL TRANSFORMATION (Mushtaq H. Khan, George Giacaman & Inge Amundsen eds., 2004); *see also* Victor Kattan, *State Formation in Palestine*, 4 BORDERLANDS E-J. (2005), http://www.borderlandsejournal. adelaide.edu.au/vol4no1_2005/kattan_stateformation.htm.

204. Catriona Drew, *The East Timor Story: International Law on Trial*, 12 EUR. J. INT'L L. 651, 666–67 (2001) (footnotes omitted).

205. On the impact of Israeli settlements on the Palestinian people's right of self-determination more generally, see Catriona Drew, *Self-Determination, Population Transfer and the Middle East Peace Accords*, in HUMAN RIGHTS, SELF-DETERMINATION AND POLITICAL CHANGE IN THE OCCUPIED PALESTINIAN TERRITORIES 119 (Stephen Bowen ed., 1997). That self-determination is also mentioned in common Article 1 to the International Covenant on Economic, Social, and Cultural Rights could be construed as granting an economic as well as a political right of self-determination. MATTHEW C. R. CRAVEN, THE INTERNATIONAL COVENANT ON ECONOMIC, SOCIAL, AND CULTURAL RIGHTS: A PERSPECTIVE ON ITS DEVELOPMENT 24–25 (1998).

Kooijmans seemed to suggest that it is the "terror" attacks that are impeding the Palestinian people's right of self-determination rather than the wall and the regime associated with it.[206] In other words, if the Palestinian Authority stops the "terror," then Palestinians will be able to exercise their right of self-determination (presumably because Israel will agree to withdraw its armed forces from the occupied territories). However, there is simply no evidence to support this proposition. As Alexander Orakhelashvili aptly highlights:

> Judge Kooijmans failed to distinguish between acts that harm the cause of self-determination and the specific and purposive action by the state, in this case the occupying power, that impedes the exercise of the right of self-determination. With regard to the latter category, it can be safely affirmed that every kind of impediment towards the exercise of self-determination amounts to the breach of this principle.[207]

Ultimately, the ICJ should have dealt with the question of Palestinian self-determination in a more forthright fashion, especially as it found that the wall directly interferes with the exercise of that right.[208] It is, perhaps, understandable that the HCJ would not want to deal with this issue in any great detail. However, self-determination can provide a useful tool through which a common narrative can be forged, as both peoples—Israelis and Palestinians—are destined to share that land together in one way or another.

V. THE WALL AND SELF-DEFENSE

Of all the issues that arose in the ICJ's *Wall* Advisory Opinion, none attracted more attention and criticism than the tersely worded three-paragraph statement on the question concerning Israel's right of self-defense under Article 51 of the U.N. Charter. Judges Buergenthal, Higgins, and Kooijmans all expressed serious reservations regarding the way in which their colleagues had dealt with the matter.[209] Nevertheless, it should be said that, with the exception of Judge Buergenthal, the judges ultimately agreed with

---

206. Judge Kooijmans writes: "As was said by the Quartet in its statement of 16 July 2002, the terrorist attacks (and the failure of the Palestinian Authority to prevent them) cause also great harm to the legitimate aspirations of the Palestinian people and thus seriously impede the realization of the right of self-determination." ICJ Wall Advisory Opinion, *supra* note 2, at 1071, para. 32 (separate opinion of Judge Kooijmans).

207. Alexander Orakhelashvili, *Legal Consequences of the Construction of a Wall in the Occupied Palestinian Territory: Opinion and Reaction*, 11 J. CONFLICT & SEC. L. 119, 122–23 (2006).

208. ICJ Wall Advisory Opinion, *supra* note 2, at 1042–43, para. 122.

209. *Id.* at 1079, paras. 5–6 (declaration of Judge Buergenthal); *id.* at 1063, paras. 33–34 (separate opinion of Judge Higgins); *id.* at 1072, para. 35 (separate opinion of Judge Kooijmans).

1468   *VANDERBILT JOURNAL OF TRANSNATIONAL LAW*   *[VOL. 40:1425*

the rest of their colleagues in finding that Israel could not rely on Article 51 to construct the wall in the West Bank.[210] If any further criticism is warranted, it is in the way the ICJ refrained from elaborating upon *why* it considered Article 51 irrelevant to the matter at hand.[211] In the following pages, the question of self-defense and the construction of the wall will be examined in more depth, and an attempt will be made to explain why the ICJ was ultimately correct in concluding that Article 51 was, in fact, irrelevant.

It will be recalled that Israel did not argue the case on the merits, and therefore the ICJ had to deduce Israel's justifications from its statement before the U.N. Security Council and from the dossier prepared for the Court by the U.N.[212] Thus far, the debate has concerned four issues: (1) whether Article 51 has no relevance to the present situation because it only applies to armed attacks emanating from states, (2) whether the ICJ was correct to conclude that Israel does not have a right of self-defense from attacks originating from occupied territory according to Article 51 of the U.N. Charter, (3) whether Palestinian attacks can be characterized as international in terms of the U.N. resolutions cited, and (4) whether the law of state responsibility precludes any wrongfulness on the part of Israel in building a wall in a territory over which it has no sovereignty.

Of course, Israel, like all states, has a right to defend itself in accordance with international law by referring to Article 51 of the U.N. Charter. No one has ever questioned this right—neither the judges at the ICJ nor counsel for the Palestinians.[213] However, there are good grounds for questioning the extent and the scope of that right and its applicability to the century-long conflict between Israel and those Palestinians inhabiting East Jerusalem, the West Bank, and the Gaza Strip. In a situation of prolonged belligerent occupation, the answer to Israel's security concerns vis-à-vis those *people* (as opposed to a conflict with another state) lies in the law of belligerent occupation and not in the law of self-defense.[214]

---

210.   *Id.* at 1063, para. 35 (separate opinion of Judge Higgins); *id.* at 1072, para. 36 (separate opinion of Judge Kooijmans).

211.   *Id.* at 1049–50, para. 139.

212.   *See* U.N. GAOR, 58th Sess., 21st mtg., at 6, U.N. Doc. A/ES-10/PV.21 (Oct. 20, 2003); The Secretary-General, *Report of the Secretary-General Prepared Pursuant to General Assembly Resolution ES-10/*13, ¶ 6, *delivered to the Security Council and the General Assembly*, UN Doc. A/ES-10/248/Annex I (Nov. 24, 2003).

213.   The following lawyers acted as counsel for Palestine and made oral submission before the ICJ: Professors James Crawford, Georges Abi-Saab, Vaughan Lowe, and Jean Salmon.

214.   *See* Jean Cohen, *The Role of International Law in Post Conflict Constitution Making: Toward a* Jus Post Bellum *for "Interim Occupations,"* 51 N.Y.L. SCH. L. REV. 497, 504 (2006) (discussing the law of belligerent occupation).

One should also bear in mind that Israel frequently resorts to justifying its actions as defensive, even when they are, by all objective accounts, punitive.[215] It was therefore, perhaps, hardly surprising that it chose to justify constructing the wall in occupied territory by claiming that the construction was consistent with Article 51 of the U.N. Charter, its inherent right of self-defense, and Security Council Resolutions 1368 (2001) and 1373 (2001).[216] Israel did so without providing any explanation as to why those provisions were relevant to a situation in which it exercised effective control over the territory from which the terrorist attacks it complained of came.[217]

Article 51 of the U.N. Charter provides in part:

> Nothing in the present Charter shall impair the inherent right of individual or collective self-defense if an armed attack *occurs* against a *Member of the United Nations*, until the Security Council has taken measures necessary to maintain international peace and security.[218]

Article 2 (4) of the U.N. Charter provides:

> All Members shall refrain in their international relations from the threat or use of force against the *territorial* integrity or political independence of any *State*, or in any other manner inconsistent with the Purposes of the United Nations.[219]

Article 4 (1) provides:

> Membership in the United Nations is open to all . . . peace-loving *States* which accept the obligations contained in the present Charter and, in the judgment of the Organization, are able and willing to carry out these obligations.[220]

In order to make a legitimate claim of self-defense according to a strictly textual analysis of Article 51, three conditions must be satisfied: (1) the state must be actually acting in self-defense, meaning that its territorial integrity or political independence is under threat; (2) it must have been the subject of an armed attack (i.e. "if an armed attack *occurs*");[221] and (3) an armed attack[222] must

---

215. On Israel's claims of self-defense and their rejection by the Security Council, see STANIMIR A. ALEXANDROV, SELF-DEFENSE AGAINST THE USE OF FORCE IN INTERNATIONAL LAW 172–79 (1996).

216. ICJ Wall Advisory Opinion, *supra* note 2, at 1021, para. 35.

217. *Id.*

218. U.N. Charter art. 51 (emphasis added).

219. *Id.* art. 2, para. 4.

220. *Id.* art. 4, para. 1.

221. Yoram Dinstein writes that such a restrictive reading of Article 51 is required (i.e., that it permits self-defense solely when an armed attack occurs), as in his opinion any other interpretation would be "counter-textual, counter-factual and counter-logical." YORAM DINSTEIN, WAR, AGGRESSION AND SELF-DEFENCE 182–87 (2005). In his view, the most that can be said is that if a state knows—on the basis of hard intelligence available at the time—that an attack is in the process of being mounted, it may "intercept the armed attack with a view to blunting its edge." *Id. Cf.*

occur against a member of the U.N. (in other words, it must be an attack on a state). Resorting to Article 51 to defend Israeli settlements can therefore be dismissed. Under international law, Israel has no sovereignty over East Jerusalem and the West Bank settlements, and they are thus not considered Israeli "territory" by the international community.[223] Even assuming that the terrorist attacks against the settlements meet the threshold of an "armed attack" for the purposes of Article 51, as opposed to a frontier incident,[224] they cannot be considered armed attacks against a member of the U.N.[225] The Israeli civilian settlements, which are in any event illegal, cannot be assimilated to a foreign embassy, for example, or a state's armed forces.[226] In any event, the Israeli

---

The Secretary-General's High-level Panel on Threats, Challenges & Change, *A More Secure World: Our Shared Responsibility* (2004) (reporting a somewhat different view of the high-level panel on threats, challenges, and change). The report concluded that "a threatened State . . . can take military action [in self-defense] as long as the threatened attack is *imminent*, no other means would deflect it and the action is proportionate." *Id.* ¶ 188. For criticisms of the report of the high-level panel on threats, challenges, and change on self-defense, see Christine Gray, *A Crisis of Legitimacy for the UN Collective Security System?*, 56 INT'L COMP. L. Q. 157, 160–64 (2007).

222.   *See* Norman Menachem Feder, *Reading the UN Charter Connotatively: Toward a New Definition of Armed Attack*, 19 N.Y.U. J. INT'L L. & POL. 395 (1987) (discussing the problems associated with the term "armed attack" and the accumulation of events or *Nadelstichtaktik* theories).

223.   *See* S.C. Res. 471, U.N. Doc. S/RES/471 (June 5, 1980) (stating that under the Geneva Convention, the occupied territories have no legal validity); S.C. Res. 465, U.N. Doc. S/RES/465 (Mar. 1, 1980) (same); S.C. Res. 452, U.N. Doc. S/RES/452 (July 20, 1979) (same); S.C. Res. 446, U.N. Doc. S/RES/446 (Mar. 22, 1979) (same); S.C. Res. 298, U.N. Doc. S/RES/298 (Sept. 25, 1971) (same); S.C. Res. 267, U.N. Doc. S/RES/267 (July 3, 1969) (same); S.C. Res. 252, ¶ 2, U.N. Doc. S/RES/252 (May 21, 1968) (same) .

224.   Although many academic commentators have criticized the distinction between armed attacks and frontier incidents, Christine Gray notes that the reason behind this distinction concerned collective self-defense, as the ICJ in *Nicaragua* wanted to limit third-state involvement. CHRISTINE GRAY, INTERNATIONAL LAW AND THE USE OF FORCE 148 (2004) ("Its insistence on a high threshold for armed attack would serve to limit third party involvement. If there was no armed attack, there could be no collective self-defence. The use of necessity and proportionality alone would not exclude third party involvement, merely limit the scope of their permissible response.").

225.   For pre-Charter authority that small border incidents cannot give rise to a claim of self-defense because there is no unequivocal intention to commit an armed attack, see *Arbitrage entre Le Portugal et L'Allemagne, Sentence arbitrale du 31 juillet 1928 concernant la responsabilité de L'Allemagne à raison des dommages causés dans les colonies portugaises du Sud de L'Afrique* (*Naulilaa Case*), (*Germany v. Portugal*), July 31, 1928, *reprinted in* 2 R. INT'L ARBITRAL AWARDS 1011, 1026–28 (1949).

226.   The Definition of Aggression annexed to the General Assembly Resolution 3314 (XXIX) on December 14, 1974, mentions in Article 3(d) that an attack by the armed forces of a state on the land, sea or air forces, or marine and air fleets of another state is as an act of aggression. G.A. Res. 3314 (XXIX) Annex, 2319th Sess., U.N. Doc A/3314 (Dec. 14, 1974) [hereinafter Definition of Aggression]. With regard to embassies, it could be argued that they are an emanation of statehood as they represent the capacity of a state to enter into international relations. *See* 1933 Montevideo Convention on Rights and Duties of States art.1(d), Dec. 26, 1933, 165

settlements in the OPT are populated by civilians as opposed to military personnel; it is therefore difficult to see how they could be considered a representation of statehood or a component of the Israeli armed forces.[227] To do so would conflict with Article 2(4) of the Charter and Article 49(6) of Geneva Convention IV. Israel, therefore, cannot justify defending its settlements on the basis of Article 51, which may explain why Judge Barak relied on Article 43 of the Hague Regulations.[228] Consequently, building a wall to defend the settlements must *a fortiori* be illegal.

Moreover, even if Israel had invoked a right of self-defense or a right of "humanitarian intervention" to protect its *nationals* in the West Bank settlements, Israel would have been required to *repatriate* them *into* Israel (i.e., behind the 1949 ceasefire lines in territory internationally recognized as belonging to Israel).[229] It could not

---

L.N.T.S. 19. It is, however, not entirely clear whether an armed attack against an embassy can be assimilated to an armed attack upon a state. Although the ICJ in the *Tehran Hostages* case used the terminology "armed attack" twice to describe the actions by Iranian militants in seizing the U.S. Embassy and staff in Tehran, it did not address the legality of the failed American military rescue operation, which was justified as an act of self-defense. Case Concerning United States Diplomatic and Consular Staff in Tehran (U.S. v. Iran), 1980 I.C.J. 3, paras. 32, 57, 64, 93–94 (May 24). Nor, for that matter, did the Security Council characterize the attacks upon the U.S. Embassies in Nairobi, Kenya and Dar-es-Salaam as "armed attacks." S.C. Res. 118, U.N. Doc. S/RES/1189 (Aug. 13, 1998). It would seem that today the doctrine of extraterritoriality does not apply to embassies. *See* EILEEN DENZA, DIPLOMATIC LAW: A COMMENTARY ON THE VIENNA CONVENTION ON DIPLOMATIC RELATIONS 113–14 (1998) (citing a number of cases including *Tietz et al. v. People's Republic of Bulgaria*, in which the Supreme Restitution Court for Berlin held that the doctrine is "an artificial legal fiction which does not appear to be accepted as sound law anywhere in the world today"). However, Ruth Wedgewood considers the bombings of the U.S. embassies in Africa an "armed attack," although she does not address the issue as to whether an embassy can be considered extra-territorial. Ruth Wedgewood, *Responding to Terrorism: The Strikes against Bin Laden*, 24 YALE J. INT'L L. 559, 564 (1999). Instead, she writes that "Article 51 recognises the inherent right of self-defense in the face of an armed attack, and declares that a *victimized nation* is entitled to engage in unilateral or collective self-defense until and unless the Security Council has addressed the issue." *Id.* (emphasis added). Article 51 of the U.N. Charter actually refers to "Members of the United Nations" and not to "victimized nations." In other words, the attack has to be against a state. This is an objective factor and not a subjective factor. It is irrelevant whether a state does or does not consider itself a victim.

227. *See Israel Hints at Jerusalem Talks, supra* note 187 (reporting that Israel has settled hundreds of thousands of citizens in Jerusalem since its 1967 victory in the Arab-Israeli war).

228. *See* Christopher Greenwood, *The Administration of Occupied Territory in International Law, in* INTERNATIONAL LAW AND THE ADMINISTRATION OF OCCUPIED TERRITORIES, *supra* note 18, at 247 (arguing that that the Occupying Power is free to take such measures are as necessary for the protection of its armed forces, but that this license would not necessarily apply to civilian settlers).

229. Examples of this controversial doctrine include the U.S.-Belgian Stanleyville Rescue Operation in the Congo on November 24, 1964 and Israel's rescue mission in Entebbe, Uganda on July 4, 1976. In both instances, the rescued nationals were repatriated to their countries of origin. In the case of the Congo, Belgium and the United States acted with the permission of the Congolese government, whereas

claim a right to protect its nationals by sending its military to remain in the occupied territory indefinitely or by building a semi-permanent structure around the settlements.   Addressing Israel's security justifications, the ICJ abruptly concluded:

> Article 51 of the Charter thus recognises the inherent right of self-defence in the case of armed attack by one State against another State. However, Israel does not claim that the attacks against it are imputable to a foreign State. . . .
>
> The Court also notes that Israel exercises control in the Occupied Palestinian Territory and that, as Israel itself states, the threat which it regards as justifying the construction of the wall originates within, and not outside, that territory. The situation is thus different from that contemplated by Security Council resolutions 1368 (2001) and 1373 (2001), and therefore Israel could not in any event invoke those resolutions in support of its claim to be exercising a right of self-defense. . . .
>
> Consequently, the Court concludes that Article 51 of the Charter has no relevance in this case.[230]

Although this paragraph has been subject to criticism, it will be recalled that Israel did not enter a plea on the merits of the case in its written statement.[231] Nor did Israel participate in the oral pleadings before the Court.[232] Moreover, none of the states that submitted written statements or made oral pleadings before the Court "supported Israel's claim that the construction of the wall was justified as a measure of self-defense under Article 51 of the U.N. Charter."[233] In fact, many argued that it was inapplicable. Perhaps the reason why the ICJ's interpretation of Article 51 was so brief was because self-defense was not pleaded before it as an exculpatory justification for building the wall, although this would not have prevented the Court from engaging with this issue in more depth.

A. *Self-Defense, Self-Determination, and State Attacks*

In the *Mara'abe* case, the HCJ expressed its bewilderment that Article 51 of the U.N. Charter only applies when one state militarily attacks another state.[234] As Judge Higgins duly noted, "There is . . .

Uganda assisted the hijackers in Entebbe.   *See* LOUIS B. SOHN & THOMAS BUERGENTHAL, INTERNATIONAL PROTECTION OF HUMAN RIGHTS 195–211 (1973) (discussing the situation in the Congo and U.S. and Belgian intervention); Leslie C. Green, *Rescue at Entebbe: Legal Aspects*, 6 ISR. Y.B. HUM. RTS. 312 (1976) (discussing the situation in Uganda).

230.   ICJ Wall Advisory Opinion, *supra* note 2, at 1049–50, para. 139.

231.   *Id.* at 1028, para. 57.

232.   *Id.* at 1015–16, para. 12.

233.   Iain Scobbie, *Words My Mother Never Taught Me—"In Defense of the International Court,"* 99 AM. J. INT'L L. 76, 77 (2005).

234.   HCJ 7957/04 Mara'abe v. Prime Minister of Isr. [2005] (Isr.), *translated in* 45 I.L.M. 202, 213, ¶ 23 (2006).

nothing in the text of Article 51 that *thus* stipulates that self-defence is available only when an armed attack is made by a State."[235] Rather, this qualification is a result of the ICJ so determining in *Nicaragua*, which based this finding of law upon the consensus interpretation placed upon the *Definition of Aggression* annexed to General Assembly resolution 3314.   Article 3 of the *Definition* stipulates that an act of aggression must originate from another state, which stipulation the ICJ assimilated to an armed attack for the purposes of its discussion of Article 3(g).[236] That an armed attack must originate from a State is also, according to one study, a reflection of the majority interpretation advanced by international lawyers.[237] As the ICJ held in its *Nicaragua* ruling:

> The Court sees no reason to deny that, in customary law, the prohibition of armed attacks may apply to the sending *by a State* of armed bands to the territory of another State, if such an operation, because of its scale and effects, would have been classified as an armed attack rather than as a mere frontier incident had it been carried out by regular armed forces.[238]

The ICJ's opinion on this point of law has been subject to intense criticism because, some argue, the practice of states since the late 1990s allows them to invoke the right of self-defense under Article 51 in the event of an attack by a non-state actor.[239] There may also be difficulties in ascertaining how much force is necessary before an attack amounts to an *armed* attack as opposed to "a mere frontier incident."[240] Taking its cue from a number of critical commentaries in the *American Journal of International Law*, the HCJ in *Mara'abe*

---

235.   ICJ Wall Advisory Opinion, *supra* note 2, at 1063, para. 33 (separate opinion of Judge Higgins); *see also* HCJ 7957/04 Mara'abe, ¶ 23 ("[Article] 51 of the Charter of the United Nations recognizes the right of self-defense, when one state military attacks another state.").

236.   Definition of Aggression, *supra* note 226. *See also*, Military and Paramilitary Activities (Nicar. v. U.S.), *supra* note 41, para. 195.

237.   The issue is succinctly discussed by Jörg Kammerhofer, *Uncertainties of the Law of Self-Defence in the United Nations Charter*, 35 NETH. Y.B. INT'L L. 143, 178–87 (2004).

238.   Military and Paramilitary Activities (Nicar. v. U.S.), *supra* note 41, para. 195 (emphasis added).

239.   For support for this view, see Matthew Scott King, *The Legality of the United States War on Terror: Is Article 51 a Legitimate Vehicle for the War in Afghanistan or Just a Blanket to Cover-Up International War Crimes?*, 9 ILSA J. INT'L & COMP. L. 457 (2002–2003); and Sean D. Murphy, *Terrorism and the Concept of "Armed Attack" in Article 51 of the UN Charter*, 43 HARV. INT'L L.J. 41 (2002). *See also* Carsten Stahn, *Terrorist Acts as 'Armed Attack': The Right to Self-Defense, Article 51 (1/2) of the UN Charter, and International Terrorism*, 27 FLETCHER F. WORLD AFF. 35, 35–54 (2003) (generally discussing U.S. intervention in Iraq following September 11, 2001).

240.   *See* ROSALYN HIGGINS, PROBLEMS AND PROCESS: INTERNATIONAL LAW AND HOW WE USE IT 251 (1994) (examining the difficulties with ascertaining how much force is necessary for an attack to amount to an "armed attack").

found the ICJ's reasoning regarding Article 51 of the U.N. Charter "hard to come to terms with," and doubted whether it "fits the needs of democracy in the struggle against terrorism."[241] Without entering into a debate over definitions of democracy and terrorism, since the definitions of both are rather controversial in the Middle East,[242] it is fair to say that the reasoning of the ICJ on the scope of Article 51 leaves something to be desired.[243] But it is arguable that the ICJ summarily dismissed Israel's plea, because when Article 51 is looked at in its entirety (meaning when one considers it in the context of the U.N. Charter as a whole), it is evidently inapplicable to the facts at hand; the U.N. Charter only applies to its members, with membership of the organization restricted to "peace-loving States."[244] Furthermore, Article 51 is an exception to the prohibition of aggression contained in Article 2(4), which only applies to states, and which, when coupled with Article 2(3), requires them to settle their disputes peacefully with one another.[245] This also tallies with the principles of sovereign equality mentioned in Article 2(1) and the doctrine of non-intervention.[246] The law on the threat or use of force

---

241.   HCJ 7957/04 Mara'abe v. Prime Minister of Isr. [2005] (Isr.), *translated in* 45 I.L.M. 202, 213, ¶ 23 (2006).

242.   It is highly questionable whether all forms of Palestinian resistance can be labeled "terrorism." Certainly, Palestinian groups do engage in "acts of terror," as does the Israeli military on occasion. Therefore, if this term is to be used at all, it should be used to describe both Israeli and Palestinian actions. *See* Jörg Friederichs, *Defining the International Public Enemy: The Political Struggle Behind the Legal Debate on International Terrorism*, 19 LEIDEN J. INT'L L. 69 (2006) (discussing terrorism and international law generally); BEN SAUL, DEFINING TERRORISM IN INTERNATIONAL LAW (2006) (studying terrorism and international law).

243.   For a critique of the ICJ's determinations of the scope of Article 51, see Sean D. Murphy, *Self-defense and the Israeli Wall Advisory Opinion: An Ipse Dixit From the ICJ?*, 99 AM. J. INT'L L. 62 (2005), and Ruth Wedgwood, *The ICJ Advisory Opinion on the Israeli Security Fence and the Limits of Self-Defense*, 99 AM. J. INT'L L. 52, 57–61 (2005).

244.   The traditional view is probably best expressed by Josef Kunz: "Art. 51 must be interpreted with regard to the doctrine of non-intervention and Art. 2, par. 7, of the Charter. 'Armed attack' gives the right of self-defense if directed against a member of the U.N.; how it is done, on land, by sea, in the air, by invasion of territory by armed forces, or by long-range guided missiles, and so on, is legally irrelevant." Josef L. Kunz, *Individual and Collective Self-Defense in Article 51 of the Charter of the United Nations*, 41 AM. J. INT'L L. 872, 878 (1947) (footnote omitted).

245.   This also addresses the fear that an expansive interpretation of Article 51 could create a loophole enabling states to rationalize military adventurism. *See* U.N. Charter art. 2, para. 3 ("This provides: 'All Members shall settle their international disputes by peaceful means in such a manner that international security and justice, are not endangered.'").

246.   Article 2(7) of the U.N. Charter provides: "Nothing contained in the present Charter shall authorize the United Nations to intervene in matters which are essentially within the domestic jurisdiction of any state or shall require the Members to submit such matters to settlement under the present Charter; but this principle shall not prejudice the application of enforcement measures under Chapter VII." U.N. Charter art. 2, para. 7. In other words, self-defense under the Charter is only

in the Charter is state-orientated. Whether the law has changed in the aftermath of the September 11 attacks on the United States so that it can apply to armed attacks carried out by non-state actors is still open to debate[247] and will depend somewhat on the nature of the non-state actor (as not all non-state actors are considered terrorist organizations).[248] Moreover, the practices of states such as Israel and the United States (and even the United Kingdom) in the "global war on terror" are not universally accepted as representing the current state of international law on the use of force and self-defense.[249] In order to determine whether the law has indeed changed, one would have to consider the Charter provisions as interpreted through both state practice and *opinio juris.*[250] Although there has been a definite trend since September 11, with most members of the Security Council (as well as NATO) invoking the right of self-defense against non-state actors,[251] this is not necessarily universally accepted as reflecting the

---

concerned with conflict between states and not within states or in those areas where it exercises domestic jurisdiction as it may do in occupied territories.

247.   *See* Gray, *supra* note 221, at 160–64 (setting forth and analyzing the debate about armed attack against non-state actors after 9/11); Said Mahmoudi, *Self-Defence and International Terrorism,* 48 SCANDINAVIAN STUD. L. 203 (2005) (arguing that the right to self-defense against international terrorism cannot be challenged after the September 11 attacks).

248.   The current debate over whether to keep the *Mujahideen al-Khalq* (commonly known as the People's Mujahadeen Organisation of Iran) on the proscribed list of terrorist organizations in the EU is of interest. *See, e.g.,* Constant Brand, *European Court Overturns EU Decision to Add Iranian Resistance Movement to Terror List,* ASSOCIATED PRESS, Dec. 12, 2006 (reporting on the EU ruling).

249.   In order to assess state practice, one must look beyond American, British, and Israeli practice. *See generally* Mary Ellen O'Connell, *Taking* Opinio Juris *Seriously: A Classical Approach to International Law and the Use of Force, in* CUSTOMARY INTERNATIONAL LAW ON THE USE OF FORCE: A METHODOLOGICAL APPROACH 9, 30 (Enzo Cannizzaro & Paolo Palchetti eds., 2005) (proposing that it is not enough to just look at state practice on issues of customary law formation and treaty interpretation, the scholar must also "pay careful attention to the legal opinion of international actors in connection with that practice").

250.   Ruys and Verhoeven at the University of Leuven have undertaken one recent study. Tom Ruys & Sten Verhoeven, *Attacks by Private Actors and the Right of Self-Defence,* 10 J. CONFLICT & SEC. L. 89 (2005). They write:

In the end, the present authors are of the opinion that this extreme position [that attacks by private actors always trigger the right of self-defense] must be rejected, not only because legal literature traditionally confirms the need for state involvement in private attacks, but mostly because state practice has consistently upheld the need for a certain link with a state.

Id. at 312.

251.   For instance, Wood cites a statement made by the Russian Defense Minister in the context of its struggle with Chechnya to the effect that Article 51 does not stipulate that an armed attack must emanate from a state. Michael C. Wood, *Towards New Circumstances in Which the Use of Force May be Authorized? The Cases of Humanitarian Intervention, Counter-Terrorism, and Weapons of Mass Destruction, in* THE SECURITY COUNCIL AND THE USE OF FORCE: THEORY AND REALITY—A NEED FOR CHANGE? 87 (Niels Blokker & Nico Schrijver eds., 2005).

law in parts of Africa and the Islamic world (or amongst the non-aligned movement).[252] For instance, while there may be agreement that attacks by terrorist organizations fall within the scope of Article 51, depending on the severity of the attack, there may be disagreement as to whether a state can use force in "self-defense" against a people struggling to exercise their right of self-determination (such as in Kashmir, Western Sahara, and elsewhere).[253] From the statements made in various international forums,[254] it is evident that many states do not view Israeli attacks against Palestinians in the OPTs as legitimate acts of "self-defense," and they do not view Palestinian attacks against Israel as "terrorism," although many such actions could be described as such.[255] For example, the Charter of the Organization of the Islamic Conference provides that its objectives include, among other things, "to co-ordinate efforts for the safeguard of the Holy Places and support of the struggle of the people of Palestine, to help them regain their rights and liberate their land," as well as "to strengthen the struggle of all Moslem peoples with a view to safeguarding their dignity, independence and national rights."[256] One should therefore be careful in assessing state practice, especially because some sixty states in the world today (which is almost a third of the entire

---

252.   For a discussion about Islamic 'perceptions' of the use of force, see Said Mahmoudi, *The Islamic Perception of the Use of Force in the Contemporary World*, 7 J. HIST. INT'L L. 55 (2005). Mahmoudi concludes that the recent practice of Islamic States with respect to the use of force seems not to have been influenced by their character as Islamic countries. However, condemnation of Israel's occupation of Palestine is a permanent issue in the statements of all Arab countries in the debates of the General Assembly. *Id.*

253.   For example, when the Islamic Republic of Iran acceded to the International Convention Against the Taking of Hostages on November 20, 2006, it issued an interpretative declaration to the effect that fighting terrorism should not affect the legitimate struggle of peoples under foreign occupation in the exercise of their right of self-determination. International Convention Against the Taking of Hostages, Accession: Iran, Nov. 20, 2006, C.N.1105.2006.TREATIES-5 (Depositary Notification).

254.   For example, in the Security Council debate over Israel's assassination of Salah Shehahdeh in Gaza City, which resulted in the deaths of fifteen other Palestinians, including several children, terms like "extra-judicial execution," "terrorism," and "state terrorism" were all used by a number of delegates to describe Israeli and Palestinian actions. *See* U.N. SCOR, 57th Sess., 4588th mtg., U.N. Doc S/PV.4588 (July 24, 2002) (including these terms by several of the delegates).

255.   Richard Falk aptly made the point when he expressed his view that "[i]t is profoundly misleading to criminalize Palestinian terrorism while simultaneously treating state terrorism associated with Israeli military operations as 'security' or as 'anti-terrorism.'" Richard Falk, *International Law and Palestinian Resistance*, *in* THE STRUGGLE FOR SOVEREIGNTY: PALESTINE AND ISRAEL, 1993–2005, at 315, 323 (Joel Beinin & Rebecca L. Stein eds., 2006).

256.   Charter of the Organization of the Islamic Conference art. 2, paras. 5–6, Mar. 4, 1972, 914 U.N.T.S. 103, 104–110.

membership of the General Assembly) have majority Muslim populations.[257] As Christine Gray writes:

> [T]he natural focus of writers on controversial cases where states invoke self-defence in protection of nationals, anticipatory or pre-emptive self-defence, and response to terrorism inevitably gives an unbalanced picture or distorts our perception of state practice; it helps to give the impression that the far-reaching claims of states like the USA and Israel are normal rather than exceptional.[258]

Critics[259] of the paragraph on the inapplicability of self-defense in the ICJ's *Wall* Advisory Opinion have also cited the *Caroline* precedent[260] as a case in which a state used force against a non-state actor. However, the *Caroline* precedent should be used with the utmost caution, for it emanates from an era when there was no prohibition on the use of force by states.[261] If it is at all relevant today, it is regarding the question of *necessity* and not self-defense. Moreover, the *Caroline* case can hardly be compared to the present conflict between Israel and the Palestinians. The U.S. was not an occupied territory but a sovereign state when the *Caroline* incident occurred.[262] Moreover, at the time, both Upper and Lower Canada were British colonies (hence the protest by Great Britain over the

---

257.   There are currently fifty-six member states of the Organization of the Islamic Conference (OIC), including Palestine, though it is not technically a state. Other countries with significant Muslim populations (35-50% of the population) who do not have membership in the OIC include Bosnia-Herzegovina, Eritrea, Ethiopia, and Tanzania (Zanzibar is 99% Muslim). Ghana, India, Kenya, the Philippines, Singapore, and Sri Lanka also have relatively large Muslim minorities (ranging from 5-15% of the population).   *See* U.S. CENT. INTELLIGENCE AGENCY, WORLD FACTBOOK, https://www.cia.gov/library/publications/the-world-factbook/index.html (last visited Oct. 19, 2007).

258.   Gray, *supra* note 221, at 97.

259.   *See, e.g.*, Murphy, *supra* note 239, at 43–44 (criticizing the conclusions of governments, scholars, and the ICJ about the issue of self-defense in this context).

260.   *See* Letter from Daniel Webster, U.S. Sec'y of State, to Henry Fox, British Minister in Washington, D.C. (Apr. 24, 1841), *in* 29 BRIT. & FOREIGN ST. PAPERS 1129 (1840–1841) (discussing the *Caroline* decision); *see also* Werner Ming, *The Caroline*, 1 ENCYCLOPEDIA PUB. INT'L L. 537–38 (1992) (including a very brief synopsis of the facts in the *Caroline*); R. Y. Jennings, *The Caroline and McLeod Cases*, 32 AM. J. INT'L L. 82 (1938) (including commentary on the *Caroline*).

261.   This is because back then the concept of self-defense did not exist. Rather, it was used interchangeably with terms like "self-preservation" and "self-help," which are no longer recognized as lawful justifications for using force. *See* Ian Brownlie, *The Use of Force in Self-Defence*, 37 BRIT. Y.B. INT'L L. 183, 241 (1961).

> [T]o regard any form of action formerly held to be self-defence, at a time when self-defence was a phrase regarded as interchangeable with 'self-preservation' and 'necessity,' as within a surviving 'customary right,' is a very arbitrary process. To go further, and assert that the Charter obligations are qualified by this vague customary right, is indefensible.

Id.

262.   The United States declared independence on July 4, 1776.   THE DECLARATION OF INDEPENDENCE (U.S. 1776).

arrest of Alexander McLeod, as it claimed that the destruction of the *Caroline* was the public act of persons on Her Majesty's service and that, as a consequence, individuals acting under such authority were not personally responsible for executing the orders of their government).[263] The same certainly could not be said about Israel's relationship with the Palestinians, which could hardly be described as peaceful (or as a relationship between equals).[264] Of course, this also took place before the U.N. Charter was drafted and before self-determination was established as a legal right and an obligation *erga omnes.*[265] Citing the *Caroline* as a precedent for acting in self-defense—as opposed to its continuing relevancy to the question of necessity—also ignores the development of customary international law prior to the adoption of the U.N. Charter and afterwards.[266] Moreover, the *Caroline* criterion can be abused all too easily if it is not used with caution.[267] Although it has been suggested that Article 51 of the U.N. Charter can apply to non-state actors because the threat in the *Caroline* came from a non-state entity,[268] this surely would not make any difference today because, at the time, the legal status of the entity that carried out that attack was irrelevant. Rather, the dispute between Great Britain and the United States during the *Caroline* debacle arose on an *interpretation* of the law: the circumstances and conditions under which the concept of what they understood at the time to be "self-defense" could serve as a proper justification for the use of force by one nation against another.[269] In

---

263.   *See* Martin A. Rogoff & Edward Collins, Jr., *The Caroline Incident and the Development of International Law,* 16 BROOK. J. INT'L L. 493 (1990).

264.   It should be added that the rebels took refuge in the territory of the United States and not in occupied territory. Israel controls the occupied territories, and therefore the situation is not analogous to the case of the *Caroline,* which involved a violation of U.S. territory.

265.   The U.N. Charter was officially adopted on June 26, 1945. U.N. Charter art.111, para. 3.

266.   *See* Ian Brownlie, *International Law and the Use of Force by States Revisited,* 1 CHINESE J. INT'L L. 1, 4–8 (2002) (making this point forcefully).

267.   For example, Saddam Hussein's government relied on it in order to justify their invasion of Iran in September 1980. *See* R.K. Ramazani, *Who Started the Iraq-Iran War?: A Commentary,* 33 VA. J. INT'L L. 69, 78 (1992) (noting the comparison Saddam Hussein and his Foreign Ministry made between the preventative strikes against Iran and the *Caroline* case); Erik B. Wang, *The Iran-Iraq War Revisited: Some Reflections on the Role of International Law,* 32 CAN. Y.B. INT'L L. 83, 88 (1994) (discussing Iraq's justifications in light of the *Caroline* case).

268.   *See* CHRISTOPHER GREENWOOD, *War, Terrorism and International Law,* in ESSAYS ON WAR IN INTERNATIONAL LAW 409, 420 (2006).

> The threat in the *Caroline* came from a non-state group of the kind most would probably call terrorist today . . . . [N]owhere in the correspondence . . . is it suggested that this fact might make a difference and that the Webster formula might not apply to armed attacks that did not emanate from a State.

Id.

269.   *See supra* notes 260, 263 and accompanying text.

1840, the question as to whether a state could only act in self-defense against another state was not an issue; it only became relevant after the adoption of the U.N. Charter in San Francisco in 1945, which only applies to its constituent states.[270] Furthermore, it is even doubtful whether Israel could justify building the wall as a legitimate act of self-defense along its present trajectory according to the *Caroline* criteria because the Israeli government would have to show a "*necessity* of self-defense, instant, overwhelming, leaving no choice of means, and no moment of deliberation."[271] In other words, Israel would have to prove that it was absolutely *necessary* to build the wall in occupied territory as opposed to building it within its own territory or along the 1949-ceasefire lines. To date, Israel has provided no valid justification for building the wall where it is.[272]

Admittedly, this may be a conservative analysis of Article 51 and the customary international law rules on the recourse to armed force. It is also true that the world is a very different place today than it was when the Charter was drafted in 1945.[273] Yet one must not forget that the struggles in the Middle East are not new. Any difficulties that have arisen with the Charter's interpretation in light of the Israeli-Palestinian conflict are not the fault of the draftsmen. In this particular instance, it is the result of Israel's refusal to withdraw from the territories it occupied in 1967. In so doing, it is forcibly depriving the Palestinian people of their right to exercise self-determination and stretching the limits of self-defense into uncharted waters—for belligerent occupation is supposed to be a relatively temporary phenomenon.[274] Forcibly depriving a people of their right

---

270. Edward Stettinius, the U.S. Secretary of State in 1945 and one of the chief architects of the U.N. Charter, opposed the British Foreign Secretary Anthony Eden's request for an expansionist interpretation of the term "armed attack" that would appear in Article 51 of the U.N. Charter. Eden wanted a phrase that would have permitted action against every sort of aggression, direct or indirect. However, Stettinius refused to budge, contending that a broader phraseology would allow states too great a leeway, including the right of preventative actions, which could legally wreck the organization. He said that World Wars I and II, after all, had begun with preventative attacks. The British backed down. *See* STEPHEN C. SCHLESINGER, ACT OF CREATION: THE FOUNDING OF THE UNITED NATIONS 184–85 (2003).

271. Letter from Daniel Webster, *supra* note 260, at 1138 (emphasis added).

272. *See generally* Press Release, United Nations Information Service, International Meeting on Impact of Wall Built by Israel in Occupied Palestinian Territory Enters Second Day, U.N. Doc. GA/PAL/952 (Apr. 19, 2004) (discussing the Wall's location).

273. Nevertheless, it is submitted that the rules are robust enough to withstand the times even if it seems as though states behave with little regard for the law. For instance, see Oscar Schacter, *In Defense of International Rules on the Use of Force*, 53 U. CHI. L. REV. 113 (1986).

274. *See* Andrew Roberts, *Prolonged Military Occupations: The Israeli-Occupied Territories Since 1967*, 84 AM. J. INT'L L. 44 (1990) (discussing prolonged occupations); Ardi Imseis, *Critical Reflections on the International Humanitarian Law Aspects of the ICJ Wall Advisory Opinion*, 99 AM. J. INT'L L. 102, 105–09 (2005) (criticizing the ICJ's Advisory Opinion on Article 6 of Geneva Convention IV).

to exercise self-determination is considered a breach of an obligation *erga omnes* by the ICJ, and is in itself a violation of international law.[275] In such circumstances, resistance is inevitable. The United Nation's *Definition of Aggression* provides:

> Nothing in this Definition, and in particular article 3, could in any way prejudice the right of self-determination, freedom and independence, as derived from the Charter, of peoples forcibly deprived of that right . . . particularly peoples under colonial and racist regimes or other forms of alien domination: nor the right of these peoples to struggle to that end and to seek and receive support, in accordance with the principles of the Charter and in conformity with the above-mentioned Declaration.[276]

It is well known that all peoples subjected to colonial and racist regimes or other forms of alien domination have resisted such injustices at one time or another.[277] In his separate opinion in the *Namibia* case, Judge Ammoun considered that "the struggle of peoples in general has been one, if not indeed the primary, factor in the formation of the customary rule whereby the right of peoples to self-determination is recognized."[278] Although positive international law provides no explicit basis for a people struggling for freedom and independence to achieve this, no rule of international law prohibits this either (it only proscribes the conduct of those struggling for this right). In fact, such resistance need not necessarily be violent. For instance, non-violent resistance is reflected in the terminology employed by the *Definition of Aggression* ("struggle" as opposed to "armed struggle") and exemplified by Mahatma Gandhi's revolt against the British in India, the struggle of black South Africans against the minority white apartheid government in Pretoria, and even the Palestinian people's struggle for freedom against Israeli occupation from 1987 until 1993.[279] Of course, any quasi-military

---

275. *See* HEATHER A. WILSON, INTERNATIONAL LAW AND THE USE OF FORCE BY NATIONAL LIBERATION MOVEMENTS 91–103 (1988).

276. Definition of Aggression, *supra* note 226.

277. An example is the struggle against Nazi Germany by the Dutch, French, Polish, and Yugoslav partisans. *See* W. J. Ford, *Resistance Movements and International Law*, 7 INT'L REV. RED CROSS 579 (1967) (providing a useful survey of resistance during the Boer War, the Russo-Japanese War, World War I, and World War II). Yasser Arafat in his famous "gun and olive branch" speech before the General Assembly in 1974 recalled that there are just causes where people fight for the freedom and liberation of their land "from the invaders, the settlers and the colonialists." Yasser Arafat, Question of Palestine, U.N. GAOR, at 48, 29th Sess., 2282d mtg., UN Doc. A/PV. 2282 (Nov. 13, 1974).

278. Namibia Advisory Opinion, *supra* note 192, at 70 (separate opinion of Vice-President Ammoun).

279. In fact, contrary to popular belief, most Palestinian resistance to Israeli occupation remains non-violent. This can take the form of ignoring curfews (which can sometimes last for weeks) at great risk to one's personal well-being, or throwing stones and Molotov cocktails. *See* Richard A. Falk & Burns H. Weston, *The Relevance of International Law to Palestinian Rights in the West Bank and Gaza: In Legal Defence*

actions taken by Palestinian organizations against Israel would be subject to the customary rules of IHL, and in particular Article 48 of Additional Protocol 1, which provides as a basic rule that the belligerents "shall at all times distinguish between the civilian population and combatants and between civilian objects and military objectives and accordingly shall direct their operations only against military objectives."[280] Islamic international law also proscribes the conduct of belligerents: "Those non-combatants who are unable to participate in hostilities are classed as protected persons and cannot be attacked, killed or otherwise molested."[281] It should be added that as the Charter's provisions on self-defense only apply to its members, and as there is no Palestinian state at present with membership in that organization, it is arguable that they are not bound by its constraints—such as a prior armed attack—but only by the customary law principles of proportionality and necessity. Consequently, the Palestinians could claim that they have an "inherent" right to protect themselves from Israeli aggression.[282] Since the occupation of foreign territory, even if it resulted from an act of justifiable self-defense, could constitute by itself an act of armed aggression,[283] the Palestinians could always argue that they have a right to respond and to *anticipate* future Israeli attacks. In this respect, those in Israel who advocate an expansive interpretation of self-defense should be aware that such arguments could be used against them.[284] However, it is submitted that the conflict between

---

of the Intifada, 32 HARV. INT'L L.J. 129 (1991) (discussing the first Palestinian and mostly non-violent *intifada*). According to one recent study, it is only violent actions such as suicide bombings that make the headlines in the West. Most forms of non-violent resistance are not deemed newsworthy. GREG PHILO & MIKE BERRY, BAD NEWS FROM ISRAEL (2004).

280. Protocol Additional to the Geneva Conventions of 12 August 1949, and relating to the Protection of Victims of International Armed Conflict art. 48, June 8, 1977, 1125 U.N.T.S. 609; *see also* Pocar, *supra* note 83, at 153 (discussing the status of Article 48 as a customary rule of international law).

281. *See* Shaheen Sardar Ali & Javaid Rehman, *The Concept of Jihad in Islamic International Law,* 10 J. CONFLICT & SEC. L. 321, 338 (2005).

282. *See, e.g.,* E.C. UDECHUKU, LIBERATION OF DEPENDENT PEOPLES IN INTERNATIONAL LAW 22 (2d ed. 1978).

That the Charter did not purport to abolish the inherent right of self-defence of all peoples and confer it only on U.N. Members can be seen from the fact that during the Korean War in 1950 several U.N. Members took the position that the action taken under U.N. auspices against North Korea was in pursuance of the right of collective self-defence of South Korea, even though South Korea was not a Member of the United Nations.

Id.

283. *See* AHMED M. RIFAAT, INTERNATIONAL AGGRESSION: A STUDY OF THE LEGAL CONCEPT: ITS DEVELOPMENT AND DEFINITION IN INTERNATIONAL LAW 127 (1979) (arguing that occupation of foreign territory constitutes an act of armed aggression).

284. *See, e.g.,* Yehuda Z. Blum, *State Response to Acts of Terrorism,* 19 GERMAN Y.B. INT'L L. 223, 235 (1976) ("In fact, it would appear that it is extremely difficult—to

Israel and the Palestinian people within the occupied territories is not a question to be determined according to the *jus ad bellum*, but rather by the *jus in bello*, and that consequently the question of self-defense is not really relevant to this debate.[285] Widening the scope of self-defense so that it can be invoked by both Israelis and Palestinians is likely to lead to further conflict contrary to the spirit of the U.N. Charter, which is "to save succeeding generations from the scourge of war, which twice in our lifetime has brought untold sorrow to mankind."

But perhaps the debate on the nature of the attacker is all really "beside the point" as Judge Kooijmans noted, since Israel was not claiming that the terrorist attacks against its civilian population emanated from another state.[286] Even if it is accepted that state practice has changed since September 11 and Article 51 can apply to non-state actors,[287] Israel would still be precluded from invoking Article 51 because it exercises effective control in the OPT as the occupying power, and therefore the situation, as the ICJ noted, is different from that contemplated by Security Council resolutions 1368 (2001) and 1373 (2001), which speak of international terrorism.[288]

B. *Self-Defense and Occupied Territory*

An occupying power may not invoke self-defense under Article 51 of the U.N. Charter to respond to attacks coming from occupied territory because it has effective control there.[289] In this regard, it would be nonsensical for a state to claim such a right, as attacks that come from a territory and a population over which it exercises effective control is equivalent to an attack emanating from its own territory and population. In this respect, a state would not invoke self-defense to attack itself. Furthermore, jurisprudence from World War II provides support for the view that occupying powers cannot claim a right of self-defense to attack rebels situated in a territory under its effective control. This is because self-defense does not

---

the point of being almost impossible—to apply the traditional concept of proportionality to acts of terrorism.").

285.   "*Jus in Bello*" (justice in war) is a theory identifying a moral framework during the conduction of war, while "*Jus ad Bellum*," (just war theory) identifies the concept that some wars are "morally and legally justifiable, such as those against a totalitarian (or) aggressive regime." BLACK'S LAW DICTIONARY (8th ed. 2004).

286.   ICJ Wall Advisory Opinion, *supra* note 2, at 1072, para. 35 (separate opinion of Judge Kooijmans).

287.   This argument was offered forcibly by Greenwood before the ICJ rendered its Advisory Opinion on the Wall. *See* CHRISTOPHER GREENWOOD, *International Law and the Pre-Emptive Use of Force: Afghanistan, Al-Qaida and Iraq*, in ESSAYS ON WAR IN INTERNATIONAL LAW, *supra* note 268, at 667-700.

288.   S.C. Res 1368, U.N. Doc. S/RES/1368 (Dec. 21, 2001); S.C. Res 1373, U.N. Doc S/RES/1373 (Sept. 28, 2001).

289.   U.N. Charter art. 51.

belong to the rules regarding the conduct of hostilities (the *jus in bello*) but instead to the rules governing the recourse to armed force (the *jus ad bellum*). The only possible justification for using force against an occupied people is provided by the rules regulating the conduct of belligerent reprisals, not the law of self-defense.[290]

The fact that Israel is an occupying power in the West Bank (which includes East Jerusalem) is significant precisely because Israel, as the ICJ noted, exercises effective control there.[291] Israel is consequently caught in a legal limbo: on the one hand it has no sovereignty over the territory, but on the other hand it exercises effective control as the occupying power with the concomitant responsibilities set out in the Geneva Conventions. The simple fact is that Israel cannot have it both ways. Either, it must withdraw from the territories and give the Palestinians the opportunity to create a viable and independent state, or it must accept its responsibilities as the occupying power and abide by the rules of belligerent occupation. Israel evidently desires the territory but not the people who inhabit it, which is precisely why it has never annexed the West Bank or Gaza, an act that would trigger its obligation to grant citizenship rights to the native population.[292] The whole question of the Israel-Palestine conflict, the use of force, and self-defense are inextricably tied up with the question of self-determination. Until this is resolved in a satisfactory manner in accordance with international law, these problems will remain.

It should be recalled that Israel was not created in a territorial vacuum.[293] The Palestinian Arabs have every right to be there as the

---

290. The Geneva Convention codified the current law of belligerent reprisals. Convention Relative to the Protection Civilian Persons in Time of War art. 33, para. 3. Aug. 12, 1949, 75 U.N.T.S. 287.

291. *See* HCJ 593/82 Leah Tsemel, Att'y v. Minister of Def. and Commander of the Ansar Camp [1983] IsrSC 37(3) 365, *translated in* 1 PALESTINE Y.B. INT'L L. 164 (1984) (concerning Israel's occupation of southern Lebanon, in which the HCJ accepted that Geneva Convention IV was applicable). Presumably if Geneva Convention IV was applicable there—where Israel exercised effective control—then it should also be applicable to the OPTs.

292. *See* Geneva Convention IV, *supra* note 20, art. 67.

> The courts shall apply only those provisions of law which were applicable prior to the offence, and which are in accordance with general principles of law, in particular the principle that the penalty shall be proportionate to the offence. *They shall take into consideration the fact the accused is not a national of the Occupying Power.* (emphasis added)

Hague Regulations, *supra* note 50, art. 45 ("It is forbidden to compel the inhabitants of *occupied territory* to swear allegiance to the hostile Power.").

293. The Palestinian Arabs already lived in Palestine at the time that it was promised by a third party, the British, to another third party, the Zionists, in November 1917. Had the land been empty, there would have been little opposition or conflict today. *See generally* GEORGE ANTONIUS, THE ARAB AWAKENING: THE STORY OF

indigenous population of any territory. They are not "foreign" to Israel. Therefore, one cannot invoke their "foreign nationality" as an external link or basis for invoking the right of self-defense.[294] Rather, their statelessness, meaning their lack of nationality, is a direct consequence of actions taken by the Israeli legislature, which unlawfully denationalized them (that is, stripped them of their prior nationality status) in 1952.[295] The passage of time does not cure that illegality.[296]   Therefore, it is arguable that Palestinian attacks against Israel come very close to domestic forms of violence, and that Article 51 is therefore inapplicable.[297] However, the situation is more complex. The Palestinians have stated that they want to establish an independent Palestinian state in the OPTs, from which Israel refuses to withdraw.[298] As with most self-determination disputes, the conflict has both international and domestic characteristics.[299] The ICJ is therefore not being inconsistent when it ruled that Article 51 is inapplicable because Palestine is not a state;[300] this is a matter of fact. The rules of belligerent occupation continue to apply because

---

THE ARAB NATIONAL MOVEMENT (1938) (discussing the rise of Arab nationalism in Palestine).

294.   *See* Iris Canor, *When* Jus ad Bellum *Meet* Jus in Bello*: The Occupier's Right of Self-Defence Against Terrorism Stemming From Occupied Territories*, 19 LEIDEN J. INT'L L. 129, 137 (2006) (discussing the "foreign national" issue).

295.   Nationality Law, 5712–1952, 11 LSI 50 (1952) (Isr.), *reprinted in* FUNDAMENTAL LAWS OF THE STATE OF ISRAEL 254 (Joseph Badi ed., 1961).

296.   *See* Victor Kattan, *The Nationality of Denationalized Palestinians*, 74 NORDIC J. INT'L L. 67, 90–93 (2005).

297.   This would, of course, not preclude an individual defending himself in case of attack, but this would not, strictly speaking, be a question of international law but of a state's criminal laws and, possibly, human rights law. The only exception to this may be in the case of self-defense in relation to war crimes. *See* Timothy L.H. McCormack, *Self-Defence in International Criminal Law*, *in* THE DYNAMICS OF INTERNATIONAL CRIMINAL JUSTICE: ESSAYS IN HONOUR OF SIR RICHARD MAY 231, 232–39 (Hirad Abtahi & Gideon Boas eds., 2006).

298.   *See* ECOSOC, Comm'n on Human Rights, *Statement Submitted by the Palestinian Center for Human Rights*, U.N. DOC. E/CN.4/2002/NGO/161 (2002) ("The internationally recognised right of the Palestinian people to self-determination includes the establishment of a viable and independent state on territories occupied by Israel in 1967. Yet under the Oslo accords, 82% of the OPT remains under direct Israeli military control.").

299.   Article 1(4) of Additional Protocol 1 to the Geneva Conventions which deals with international armed conflicts includes

> armed conflicts which peoples are fighting against colonial domination and alien occupation and against racist regimes in the exercise of their right of self-determination, as enshrined in the Charter of the United Nations and the Declaration on Principles of International Law concerning Friendly Relations and Co-operation among States in accordance with the Charter of the United Nations.

Protocol Additional to the Geneva Conventions, *supra* note 280, art. 1, para. 4.

300.   *See* ICJ Wall Advisory Opinion, *supra* note 2, at 1050, para. 139 (concluding that Article 51 is irrelevant in the case).

when that territory was captured in 1967, it was Jordanian territory (even though its annexation was only recognized by three states), and the inhabitants of the West Bank had Jordanian nationality (though many lost it in 1988, when Jordan gave up its territorial claims).[301] The conflict has therefore evolved *politically* from one between Israel and Jordan to one between Israelis and Palestinians. Geneva Convention IV remains applicable, however. That Jordan claimed sovereignty over the West Bank until 1988 "only strengthens the argument in favour of the applicability of the Fourth Geneva Convention right from the moment of its occupation by Israel in June 1967."[302] In fact, Jordan was, at the time of the June 1967 war, a "High Contracting Party" within the meaning of Article 2 of Geneva Convention IV.[303] To claim that certain Palestinian organizations are somehow alien to the territory and part of a "shadowy network of foreign fighters" is a fallacy unsupported by the facts.[304] Any analogy with the United States' "global war on terror" is simply inappropriate to the question of Palestine, which has been on the U.N. agenda longer than the existence of the Jewish state.[305]

As long as Israel exercises effective control over the OPTs, it remains (for the purposes of legal responsibility) equivalent to its own territory. Therefore, Israel's claim of a right of self-defense to respond to attacks that come from the OPTs (over which it exercises effective control) is equivalent to Israel claiming a right of self-defense from an attack emanating from its own territory and population. In other words, there is no right of self-defense against a civilian population under belligerent occupation; there is only the right to enforce the law in accordance with the laws of belligerent occupation.[306] The question is not one of allegiance, as an occupied people owe no allegiance to an occupying power other than to obey

---

301. *See* His Majesty King Hussein of Jordan, Statement Concerning Disengagement from the West Bank and Palestinian Self-Determination, Address to the Nation (July 31, 1988), *reprinted in* 27 I.L.M. 1637 (1988).

302. ICJ Wall Advisory Opinion, *supra* note 2, at 1067, para. 9 (separate opinion of Judge Kooijmans).

303. Convention Relative to the Protection Civilian Persons in Time of War, *supra* note 290, art. 2.

304. *But see* Rebecca Kahan, *Building a Protective Wall Around Terrorists—How the International Court of Justice's Ruling in the* Legal Consequences of the Construction of the Wall in the Occupied Palestinian Territory *Made the World Safer for Terrorists and More Dangerous for Member States of the United Nations*, 28 FORDHAM INT'L L.J. 827 (2005) (arguing the contrary).

305. *See Question of Palestine, Letter from the United Kingdom Delegation at the United Nations to the Acting Secretary-General of the United Nations*, UN Doc. A/286 (Apr. 2, 1947) (requesting the question of Palestine be put on the Agenda of the General Assembly annual session).

306. *See* HCJ 769/02 Pub. Comm. Against Torture in Isr. v. Israel [2005] (Isr.) para. 4., *available at* http://elyon1.court.gov.il/Files_ENG/02/690/007/a34/02007690. a34.pdf (noting that petitioners made this same argument, although in this case it was not specifically addressed by the court).

legitimate orders issued by it.[307] However, according to Article 43 of the Hague Regulations, just because a population under belligerent occupation owes no allegiance to the occupying power does not mean that it has no responsibility for ensuring public order and life in the occupied territory.[308] Nor can the Palestinian civilian population be compelled to accept living under the yoke of Israeli occupation indefinitely. Indeed, due to the length of the Israeli occupation and the extent of the settlement enterprise, some Israeli lawyers are now openly referring to the situation in the OPTs as an "illegal occupation."[309]

During World War II, Danish, Dutch, Greek, Italian, Swedish, and Yugoslavian partisans fought the Nazis by concealing their weapons, mingling with the local population, and killing and torturing members of the occupying power.[310] Indeed, many of their actions, grotesque as they were, were not too dissimilar to many of

---

307.   *See* Convention Relative to the Protection Civilian Persons in Time of War, *supra* note 290, art. 68(3) ("The death penalty may not be pronounced against a protected person unless the attention of the court has been particularly called to the fact that, since the accused is not a national of the Occupying Power, he is not bound to it by any duty of allegiance."); *see also* COMMENTARY ON THE GENEVA CONVENTIONS OF 12 AUGUST 1949, *supra* note 43, at 346.

> [t]he accused is not a national of the Occupying Power, but on the contrary the inhabitant of a country which is suffering as a result of its invasion and occupation by its enemies . . . . The words 'duty of allegiance' constitute an acknowledgment of the fundamental principle according to which the occupation does not sever the bond existing between the inhabitants and the conquered State.

Maj. Richard R. Baxter, *The Duty of Obedience to the Belligerent Occupant*, 27 BRIT. Y.B. INT'L L. 235 (1950) (discussing the complexities of duties of inhabitants of occupied territories).

308.   1907 Hague Regulations, *supra* note 50, art. 43.

309.   *See, e.g.*, Orna Ben-Naftali, Aeyal M. Gross & Keren Michaeli, *Illegal Occupation: Framing the Occupied Palestinian Territory*, 23 BERKELEY J. INT'L L. 551 (2005) (exploring the question of whether the continued Israeli occupation of Palestinian territory conquered in 1967 is legal or illegal).

310.   *See In re* List and Others (Hostages Trial), [1948] 15 A.D.I.L. 632, 638–39 (Nuremberg Trib.) (describing these facts in detail); *see also* Varrone v. S.U.R.C.I.S., Trib., 14 Jan. 1950, 75 Foro It. 1950, I, 946 (holding that partisans are to be regarded as lawful belligerents for the purpose of international law as well as of Italian municipal law); Baffico v. Calleri, Corte app., 5 Jan. 1948, 70 Foro It. 1947, I, 1016 (discussing this same issue of whether to regard partisans as lawful belligerents; *see also In re* Weizsaecker and Others (Ministries Trial), [1949] 16 A.D.I.L. 354, 354–56 (Nuremberg Trib.) (discussing the role played by Norwegian, Finnish, Danish and Swedish guerrillas; *In re* Kniest, [1949] 16 A.D.I.L. 507, 507–08 (Den.) (setting forth the fact that the accused, the German police, occupying that country tried to justify their ill treatment of the Danish resistance as an act of "self-defense," and holding in response that the treatment could be not justified on this basis and was contrary to international law and the customs of war); *In re* Hoffman, [1949] 16 A.D.I.L. 508 (Den. E. Provincial Ct.) (coming to the same conclusion that the German armed forces could not justify their acts as self-defense even if their actions were undertaken to protect their own soldiers).

the disturbances in the OPTs today.[311] Although the partisans were not generally considered lawful combatants[312] because they concealed their identities and their weapons, the actions of the German Armed Forces were not considered as lawful measures of self-defense either.[313] Self-defense is not available to an occupying power when it has already subdued its enemy and taken control of its territory; it is only available at the start of hostilities, not when they come to an end.[314] Once the occupied territory is under the effective control of the occupying power, the right of self-defense is no longer applicable. An occupying power also does not have the right to determine for itself whether its actions amount to self-defense; only an authorized tribunal or a competent body, such as the Security Council, can validly make the determination.[315] For example, at Nuremberg, the Tribunal found that the question as to whether Germany's actions could be justified as self-defense or whether the manner in which it acquired those territories was legal was ultimately irrelevant, as it could not make that determination for itself.[316] In Tokyo, the International Military Tribunal for the Far East held: "Under the most liberal interpretation of the Kellog-Briand pact, the right of self-defence does not confer upon the State resorting to war the authority to make a final determination upon the justification of its action."[317]

Jurisprudence from World War II also provides support for the view that self-defense does not belong to the rules regarding the conduct of hostilities (the *jus in bello*) but to the rules governing the recourse to armed force (the *jus ad bellum*).[318] This distinction was made at Nuremberg in *In re List and others*,[319] when it pointed out that there is no reciprocal connection between the manner of the military occupation of territory (i.e., whether this entailed a violation

---

311. *See* Joseph Massad, *Palestinians and Jewish History*, 30 J. PALESTINIAN STUD. 1, 56–59 (2000) (describing disturbances in the occupied territories throughout recent history). For extensive accounts of Palestinian "terrorist" acts, see Israeli Ministry of Foreign Affairs, *Terrorism since 2000, available at* http://www.mfa.gov.il/MFA/Terrorism-+Obstacle+to+Peace/Palestinian+terror+since+2000.

312. Though there were exceptions. *See, e.g., Varrone*, 75 Foro It. at 946; *Baffico*, 70 Foro It. at 1016 (both providing examples where the Italian Courts concluded that the partisans were not unlawful under international law or Italian municipal law).

313. *See, e.g.,* In re *Weizsaecker*, 16 A.D.I.L. at 349 (concluding that "the doctrine of self-defence and military necessity was never available to Germany as a matter of international law, in view of its prior violation of that law").

314. U.N. Charter art. 51.

315. *Id.* art. 39.

316. In re *Weizsaecker*, 16 A.D.I.L. at 349.

317. *In re* Hirota, [1948] 15 A.D.I.L 356, 364 (Int'l Military Trib. for the Far East, Tokyo).

318. *See* BLACK'S LAW DICTIONARY, *supra* note 285 and accompanying text (defining and comparing *jus in bello* and *jus ad bellum*).

319. *See In re* List and Others (Hostages Trial), [1948] 15 A.D.I.L. 632 (Nuremberg Trib.).

of the *jus ad bellum*) and the rights and duties of the occupant and population to each other after the relationship has in fact been established (the *jus in bello*).[320] In other words, a distinction is made between the *jus ad bellum* and the *jus in bello*, so that a violation of the former does not affect the applicability of the latter.[321] It is a cardinal principle of humanitarian law that *jus ad bellum* applies to all conflict situations irrespective of the justifications advanced in support of military action.[322] In fact, this principle was considered so important that it was subsequently drafted in the preamble to AP1 and is regarded as one of the foundations of the law of armed conflict.[323] Consequently, one must conclude that the law of self-defense has no relevancy to the law of occupation.[324] As Georges Abi-Saab elucidated in his oral pleading before the ICJ on behalf of Palestine regarding the question of self-defense and the laws which regulate the conduct of hostilities in occupied territories:

> One of the justifications, self-defence, does not belong to international humanitarian law or the *jus in bello*, but to the *jus ad bellum*. Israel makes here an impermissible confusion between the two branches of the law of war that have to be kept radically apart. Once an armed conflict is brought into being, the *jus in bello* (or international

---

320.   *Id.* at 637.

321.   *See* PETER MALANCZUK, AKEHURST'S MODERN INTRODUCTION TO INTERNATIONAL LAW 306 (Routledge, 7th ed. 1997) (1970) ("It is reasonable to treat both areas separately [i.e. the *ius in bello* and the *ius ad bellum*], because of the recognized principle that *ius in bello* is applicable in cases of armed conflict whether the conflict is lawful or unlawful under *ius ad bellum*.").

322.   *See* MARCO SASSÒLI & ANTOINE A. BOUVIER, HOW DOES LAW PROTECT IN WAR: CASES, DOCUMENTS, AND TEACHING MATERIALS ON CONTEMPORARY PRACTICE IN INTERNATIONAL HUMANITARIAN LAW 84 (1999).

> [F]rom a humanitarian point of view, the victims of the conflict on both sides need the same protection, and they are not necessarily responsible for the violation of the *ius ad bellum* committed by 'their' party. IHL has therefore to be respected independently of any argument of *ius ad bellum* and has to be completely distinguished from *ius ad bellum*.

Id.

323.   *See* Protocol Additional to the Geneva Conventions, *supra* note 280, pmbl.

> Further that the provisions of the Geneva Conventions of 12 August 1949 and of this Protocol must be fully applied in all circumstances to all persons who are protected by those instruments, without any adverse distinction based on the nature or origin of the armed conflict or on the causes espoused by or attributed to the Parties to the conflict.

Id.

324.   *See* DOCUMENTS ON THE LAWS OF WAR 1 n.1 (Adam Roberts & Richard Guelff eds., 2d ed. 1989) (noting conflicts in the past between Israel and its neighbors where the uses of force may have constituted self-defense).

humanitarian law) comes into play, as the *lex specialis* governing the ensuing situation regardless of the rules of the jus ad bellum.[325]

Consequently, occupying powers cannot rely on Article 51, which belongs to the *jus ad bellum,* once major combat operations end.[326] Rather, the law is to be governed by the rules of belligerent occupation, the *jus in bello.*[327] For an occupying power, the issue is one of maintaining law and order in the occupied territory, which is not, strictly speaking, a question of self-defense. As one prominent international lawyer has noted, it would be odd to conclude that Israel could rely on self-defense to justify its response to acts that denote a breakdown of the same law and order for which it bears responsibility under international law.[328]

It would therefore seem that Israel is using the concept of "self-defense" as a subterfuge for undertaking belligerent reprisals, which is permitted in the law of armed conflict but only in exceptional circumstances.[329] It is noteworthy that Israel has not signed or acceded to AP1, which severely curtails the targets a state may attack in response to a prior violation of international law by those it perceives to be its "enemies."[330] However, even then, the reprisal must be directed at those persons responsible for the prior violation, and it must be undertaken for the purpose of putting an end to that violation or preventing further violations, rather than for revenge.[331] Reprisals must also be proportionate and necessary, in the sense that their purpose is to prevent future unlawful conduct and to seek

---

325.   Georges Abi-Saab, Oral Pleading, Advisory Opinion on the Construction of a Wall in the Occupied Palestinian Territory 44 (Feb. 23, 2004), *available at* http://www.icj-cij.org/docket/files/131/1503.pdf.

326.   *See* Christian J. Tams, *Light Treatment of a Complex Problem: The Law of Self-Defence in the* Wall *Case,* 16 EUR. J. INT'L L. 963, 970 (2005) (noting that the law of belligerent occupation essentially derogates from the right of self-defense in Article 51 of the U.N. Charter).

327.   *See* L. C. GREEN, THE CONTEMPORARY LAW OF ARMED CONFLICT 320 (1993) (stating that Article 51 "relates to the *jus ad bellum,* the right to resort to war, and has nothing to do with the *jus in bello,* what may be done during a war undertaken by way of self-defence").

328.   Scobbie, *supra* note 233 at 83.

329.   *See* Shane Darcy, *What Future for the Doctrine of Belligerent Reprisals?,* 5 Y.B. INT'L HUMANITARIAN L. 107 (2002) (critiquing of the concept of "belligerent reprisals").

330.   *See* C. Greenwood, *The Twilight of the Law of Belligerent Reprisals,* 20 NETH. Y.B. INT'L L. 35, 51–54 (1989) (discussing the impact of API on the law of belligerent reprisals).

331.   *See* Darcy, *supra* note 329, at 112.

Belligerent reprisals by their very nature rely on a principle of collective responsibility, whereby an enemy's military, government and civilian population are treated as a single group, and measures directed at certain members of that collective will, in theory, coerce the actual guilty members of the group to cease in their unlawful conduct.

Id.

redress rather than to exact retribution.[332]   However, as one commentator notes: "The notion of collective responsibility upon which the taking of reprisals is based [i.e., that an enemy's military, government, and civilian population may be targeted] has become increasingly at odds with the rules and spirit of contemporary international humanitarian law."[333]

C. *Self-Defense and International Terrorism*

The ICJ was correct to conclude that Security Council Resolutions 1368 (2001) and 1373 (2001) do not apply to Israel's struggle with "Palestine" because Palestine is not a state, and the Resolutions refer to "*international* terrorism."[334]   The Resolutions thus require some form of *trans-boundary* violence to trigger the right of self-defense under Article 51. It is not by accident that official Israeli maps do not include the 1949 armistice line between Israel and Jordan or the 1967 cease-fire line (known as the "Green Line").[335] For example, the map produced by Israel's Ministry of Defense to show the route of the wall does not include the Green Line, which is usually portrayed on international maps.[336]   The line is omitted because the 1949 cease-fire lines are not political boundaries.[337] Border crossings for Israelis between the West Bank and Israel also do not exist (the new crossings currently being constructed along the

---

332.   For the classic 1971 text on belligerent reprisals by Frits Kalshoven, which recently has been republished, see FRITS KALSHOVEN, BELLIGERENT REPRISALS (Brill 2005) (1971).

333.   Darcy, *supra* note 329, at 113.

334.   See ICJ Wall Advisory Opinion, *supra* note 2, at 1050, para. 139 (determining that the situation is different from that contemplated in the Security Council resolutions); *see generally* S.C. Res 1368, *supra* note 288; S.C. Res 1373, *supra* note 288.

335.   *See* Israel's Security Fence, Israel Ministry of Defence, http://www.securityfence.mod.gov.il/Pages/ENG/route.htm (displaying a map of Israel's revised route of the security fence as of April 30, 2006).

336.   *Id.*

337.   *See* The Acting Mediator to the Secretary General, *Text of the Egyptian-Israeli General Armistice Agreement*, art. XI, *delivered to the Security Council*, U.N. Doc. S/1264/Corr.1 (Mar. 11, 1949) (noting that no provision of the agreement prejudices the rights and claims of the parties); The Acting Mediator to the Secretary General, *Text of the Jordan-Israel General Armistice Agreement*, art. II(2), *delivered to the Security Council*, U.N. Doc. S/1302/Rev.1 (Apr. 3, 1949) (recognizing that the agreement is "dictated exclusively by military and not by political considerations"); The Acting Mediator to the Secretary General, *Text of the Lebanese-Israeli General Armistice Agreement*, art. II(2), *delivered to the Security Council*, U.N. Doc. S/1296 (Mar. 23, 1949) (recognizing that the agreement is "dictated exclusively by military considerations"); The Acting Mediator on Palestine to the Acting Secretary General, *Text of the Israeli-Syrian General Armistice Agreement*, art. II(2), *delivered to the Security Council*, U.N. Doc. S/1353 (July 20, 1949) (recognizing that the agreement is "dictated exclusively by military and not by political considerations").

route of the wall are for Palestinians only).[338] It would therefore seem that the legal significance of the armistice line is simply to delineate the starting point of Israel's occupation of non-Israeli territory.[339] There is consequently nothing international about the acts of terror committed by Israelis against Palestinians and vice-versa; they are endemic to a self-determination dispute. As Professor Yoram Dinstein of Tel Aviv University writes (while specifically referring to the *Wall* Advisory Opinion):

> Of course, when non-State actors attack a State from within—and no other State is involved—this is a case of an internal armed conflict or domestic terrorism. In neither instance does Article 51 come into play at all. An armed attack against a State, in the meaning of Article 51, posits some element external to the victim State. Non-State actors must strike at a State from the outside.[340]

Similarly, the Chatham House Principles of International Law on the Use of Force in Self-Defence provide that

> [a]n armed attack is an attack directed from outside the territory controlled by the State. In its *Advisory Opinion on the Legal Consequences of the Construction of a Wall in the Occupied Palestinian Territory*, the ICJ's observations may be read as reflecting the obvious point that unless an attack is directed from outside territory under the control of the defending State, the question of self-defence in the sense of Article 51 does not normally arise.[341]

By characterizing the September 11 attacks as "terrorist," the Security Council's intent seemed to have been to subject the perpetrators to the ordinary criminal law and process, as the relevant international conventions on terrorism—referred to in Resolutions 1368 and 1373—require.[342] This would, therefore, not give Israel carte blanche to go after the Palestinians in the name of the "global

---

338.   Moreover, maps in Israeli schoolbooks make no reference to the 1949 armistice lines. Currently, schoolbooks in Israel show its territorial conquests in the 1967 war—the West Bank, Gaza, East Jerusalem and the Golan Heights—as part of Israel. *But see Row Erupts Over Israeli Textbooks*, BBC NEWS, Dec. 5, 2006, *available at* http://news.bbc.co.uk/1/hi/world/middle_east/6210144.stm (reporting that Israel's new Education Minister, Yuli Tamir, has vowed to change this, which prompted sharp criticism from the settler movement).

339.   ICJ Wall Advisory Opinion, *supra* note 2, at 1077, para. 11 (separate opinion of Judge Al-Khasawneh). For an interesting commentary on the significance of the 1949 line from an Israeli perspective, see Robbie Sabel, *The International Court of Justice Decision on the Separation Barrier and the Green Line*, 38 ISR. L. REV. 316 (2005).

340.   *See* DINSTEIN, *supra* note 221, at 204–05.

341.   *See The Chatham House Principles of International Law on the Use of Force in Self-Defence*, 55 INT'L & COMP. L.Q. 963 (2006) (noting participants Sir Franklin Berman QC, James Gow, Christopher Greenwood QC, Vaughan Lowe, Sir Adam Roberts, Phillipe Sands QC, Malcolm Shaw QC, Gerry Simpson, Colin Warbrick, Nicholas Wheeler, Elizabeth Wilmhurst and Sir Michael Wood).

342.   *See generally,* PHILLIP SANDS, LAWLESS WORLD: MAKING AND BREAKING GLOBAL RULES 155 (2005).

war on terror" and to act as though there is no military occupation in the OPT by freeing itself from the constraints imposed by the relevant rules of IHL.[343] As Judge Buergenthal acknowledged in his separate opinion, "I agree that the means used to defend against terrorism must conform to all applicable rules of international law and that a State which is the victim of terrorism may not defend itself against this scourge by resorting to measures international law prohibits."[344]

It will be recalled that the Israeli-Palestinian conflict is no longer solely international in character (the P.L.O. having abandoned such methods as hijackings, kidnappings, and holding foreign governments to ransom), and has not been so since the mid-1980s.[345] The conflict between Israelis and Palestinians in the OPTs is therefore not an international armed conflict between two states, but one between an occupying power and an occupied people (although this could change rapidly, and will to a certain extent depend on outside factors). This was essentially the finding of the March 2001 Report of the U.N. Human Rights Inquiry Commission into violations of Human Rights in the Occupied Arab Territories, including Palestine. The Commission found that

> there is no international armed conflict in the region, as Palestine, despite widespread recognition, still falls short of the accepted criteria of statehood. The question then arises as to whether there is a *non-international armed conflict*, defined by the Appeals Chamber of the International Criminal Tribunal for the Former Yugoslavia in the *Tadic* case, as "protracted armed violence between governmental authorities and organized armed groups.[346]

As this Commission stressed, Palestine is not a state for international law purposes and it is therefore not a member of the U.N.; instead, it has observer status.[347] Israel has no sovereignty over the West Bank

---

343.   *See* Chris McGreal, *Sacred Right to Fight Terror Overrides Court, Says Sharon*, GUARDIAN (London), July 12, 2004 (reporting Sharon having said, "On Friday, the sacred right of the war on terrorism received a slap in the face by the ICJ after it decided that the terrorism-prevention fence is illegal and that Israel must dismantle it.").

344.   ICJ Advisory Opinion, *supra* note 2, at 1078, para. 2 (separate opinion of Judge Buergenthal).

345.   This is when the last major international act of terrorism by a P.L.O. faction took place, on the cruise ship Achille Lauro. Gregory V. Gooding, *Fighting Terrorism in the 1980s: The Interception of the Achille Lauro Hijackers*, 12 YALE J. INT'L L. 158 (1987).

346.   ECOSOC, Comm'n on Human Rights, *Question of the Violation of Human Rights in the Occupied Arab Territories, Including Palestine*, ¶ 39, UN Doc. E/CN.4/2001/121 (Mar. 16, 2001) (emphasis added).

347.   *See* G.A. Res. 52/250, U.N. Doc. A/RES/52/250 (July 13, 1998) (recalling Palestine's "[o]bserver status"); G.A. Res. 43/177, U.N. Doc. 43/177 (Dec. 15, 1988) (recalling the P.L.O.'s "observer status"); G.A. Res. 43/160, U.N. Doc. A/RES/43/160 (Dec. 9, 1988) (recalling the P.L.O.'s "observer status"); G.A. Res. 3237, ¶ 2, U.N. Doc.

(or over East and West Jerusalem, the Gaza Strip, and Syria's Golan Heights). Resolutions 1368 and 1373 do not apply in circumstances where attacks on the territory of the occupant emanate from the territory of the occupied—as there is no international dimension to it (although wars of national liberation are considered international conflicts for the purposes of Geneva Convention IV).[348] And it was this consideration, as Judge Kooijmans noted in his separate opinion, that proved decisive in determining those resolutions irrelevant:

> The right of self-defence as contained in the Charter is a rule of international law and thus relates to international phenomena. Resolutions 1368 and 1373 refer to acts of *international* terrorism as constituting a threat to *international* peace and security; they therefore have no immediate bearing on terrorist acts originating within a territory which is under control of the State which is also the victim of these acts. And Israel does not claim that these acts have their origin elsewhere. The Court therefore rightly concludes that the situation is different from that contemplated by resolutions 1368 and 1373 and that consequently Article 51 of the Charter cannot be invoked by Israel.[349]

It may even be questioned whether the Charter's rules on the use of force and self-defense have any application to this situation at all. Judge Higgins, for instance, was unconvinced that non-forcible measures such as building a wall would fall within the scope of Article 51 (although it would seem that the violence accompanying the wall's construction, such as demolishing houses and firing on demonstrators with rubber-coated-metal bullets, is a use of force).[350] Furthermore, it is plainly evident from reading the Charter that these rules are state-oriented.[351] One is therefore not dealing with the *jus ad bellum*, since major combat operations ended in the West Bank after Israel captured it in 1967.[352] Instead, the rules of

---

A/RES/3237 (Nov. 22, 1974) (noting that the U.N. the P.L.O. had been invited to participate as an observer in various conferences).

348.   Protocol Additional to the Geneva Conventions, *supra* note 280, art. 1, para. 4.

349.   ICJ Wall Advisory Opinion, *supra* note 2, at 1072, para. 36 (separate opinion of Judge Kooijmans).

350.   ICJ Wall Advisory Opinion, *supra* note 2, at 1063, para. 35 (separate opinion of Judge Higgins). However, in a recent lecture, Kooijmans (who recently retired from the bench) made the point that non-forcible measures are covered by resolutions 1368 and 1373 (although not by Article 51). Judge Pieter H. Kooijmans, Annual Grotius Lecture, British Institute of International and Comparative Law, London House, Mecklenburgh Square (Dec. 11, 2006). Israel has resorted to the use of force on numerous occasions when clearing land for the wall's construction. For examples of this use of force, see *Security Forces Fired Live Ammo at Anti-fence Protest*, HA'ARETZ (Jerusalem), Nov. 6, 2006, *available at* http://www.haaretz.com/hasen/spages/783632.html; and *6 Protestors, Officer Injured in Fence Protest*, YNETNEWS.COM, June 6, 2006, *available at* http://www.ynetnews.com/articles/0,7340,L-3258049,00.html.

351.   *See* U.N. Charter art. 2, para. 1 (stating that the basis for the U.N. itself is the sovereign control each member has over its territory due to its status as a state).

352.   The Six Days War ended with a cease fire on June 11, 1967, enforced by the United Nations. S.C. Res. 242, U.N. Doc. S/RES/242 (Nov. 22, 1967).

international humanitarian law, those governing the conduct of hostilities known as the *jus in bello,* are more appropriate, as discussed above.[353]

D. *Circumstances Precluding Wrongfulness*

Article 21 of the International Law Commission's Draft Articles on State Responsibility provides: "The wrongfulness of an act of a State is precluded if the act constitutes a *lawful* measure of self-defence taken in conformity with the Charter of the United Nations."[354] According to the Commentary, "the term 'lawful' implies that the action taken respects those obligations of total restraint applicable in international armed conflict, as well as compliance with the requirements of proportionality and of necessity inherent in the notion of self-defense."[355] Moreover, the action in self-defense must be taken in conformity with the principles and purposes of the U.N. Charter.[356]

It would be difficult to describe Israel's actions in constructing the wall in OPT as in conformity with the Charter, especially because the ICJ has accepted that Israel's actions amount to de facto annexation.[357] The wall interferes with the Palestinian people's right of self-determination mentioned in Articles 1(2) and 55 of the Charter, and elaborated upon in the *Friendly Relations Declaration.*[358] Its construction would also seem to be contrary to the maintenance of international peace and security, which is mentioned in the first article and paragraph of the Charter.[359] Nor could it be said that Israel is settling its dispute with the Palestinian people through "peaceful means" or "in such a manner that international

---

353.   *Id.*
354.   G.A. Res. 56/83, art. 21, U.N. Doc. A/RES/56/83 (Jan. 28, 2002) (emphasis added).   The Articles were approved, without vote, by the General Assembly in Resolution 56/83, 12 December 2001. *Id.*
355.   CRAWFORD, *supra* note 64, at 167.
356.   *Id.*
357.   *See* U.N. Charter art. 2, para. 4 (setting forth provisions that directly conflict with Israel's actions).
358.   *See* G.A. Res. 2625 (XXV), U.N. GAOR, 25th Sess., Supp. No. 18, U.N. Doc A/8018 (Oct. 24, 1970) (explaining that States have a duty to co-operate with one another as stipulated by the U.N. Charter).
359.   *See* U.N. Charter art. 1, para. 1.

To maintain international peace and security, and to that end: to take effective collective measures for the prevention and removal of threats to the peace, and for the suppression of acts of aggression or other breaches of the peace, and to bring about by peaceful means, and in conformity with the principles of justice and international law, adjustment or settlement of international disputes or situations which might lead to a breach of the peace.

Id.

peace and security, and justice, are not endangered."[360] Rather, it would seem as though it is the Palestinians who are attempting, in this instance, to settle their dispute peacefully with Israel.

On the question of necessity and proportionality, the ICJ, in its Advisory Opinion on the *Legality of the Threat or Use of Nuclear Weapons*, recalled its ruling in *Nicaragua*, in which it held: "'there is a specific rule whereby self-defence would warrant only measures which are proportional to the armed attack and necessary to respond to it, a rule well established in customary international law.'"[361] The Court then ruled: "This dual condition applies equally to Article 51 of the Charter, whatever the means of force employed."[362] On the question of proportionality and Article 51 of the Charter, it is worth quoting the opinions of a number of judges from the ICJ in the *Wall* opinion. None of them accepted that building a wall through the OPT was a necessary or proportionate measure to respond to the terrorist attacks emanating from there.[363] Judge Higgins acknowledged, "[E]ven if it were an act of self-defence, properly so called, it would need to be justified as necessary and proportionate."[364] She continued, "While the wall does seem to have resulted in a diminution of attacks on Israeli civilians, the necessity and proportionality for the *particular route selected*, with its attendant hardships for Palestinians uninvolved in these attacks, has not been explained."[365] This may indeed be the case, but surely the point is that Israel could have ensured its security by withdrawing from the OPT and building a wall on what is internationally recognized as its territory (i.e., within the 1949 armistice lines).[366] Judge Buergenthal stated that,

> given the demonstrable great hardship to which the affected Palestinian population is being subjected *in and around the enclaves* created by those segments of the wall, I seriously doubt that the wall

---

360. *Id.* art. 2, para. 3.

361. Legality of the Threat of Use of Nuclear Weapons, ICJ Advisory Opinion, *supra* note 95, ¶ 41.

362. *Id.*

363. *See id.* (explaining that building wall was not a necessary and proportionate measure).

364. ICJ Wall Advisory Opinion, *supra* note 2, at 1063, para. 35 (separate opinion of Judge Higgins).

365. *Id.* (emphasis added).

366. It would seem that if one builds a series of eight-meter-high concrete walls and fences with electronic sensors, accompanied by dirt tracks, trenches and armed watch-towers, accompanied by regular military incursions into the OPT with the attendant extra-judicial assassinations, there will inevitably be a diminution on attacks on Israeli civilians from there simply because its inhabitants have effectively been "imprisoned," making it all but impossible to escape into Israel. For a description of the situation in the occupied West Bank along the route of the Wall, see ECOSOC, Comm'n on Human Rights, *Question of the Violation of Human Rights in the Occupied Arab Territories, Including Palestine*, U.N. Doc. E/CN.4/2004/6/Add.1 (Feb. 27, 2004) (*prepared by* John Dugard).

> would *here* satisfy the proportionality requirement to qualify as a legitimate measure of self-defence.[367]

Judge Kooijmans opined:

> [I]n my view it is of decisive importance that, even if the construction of the wall and its associated régime could be justified as measures necessary to protect the legitimate rights of Israeli citizens, these measures would not pass the proportionality test. The *route chosen* for the construction of the wall and the ensuing disturbing consequences for the inhabitants of the Occupied Palestinian Territory are manifestly disproportionate to interests which Israel seeks to protect, as seems to be recognized also in recent decisions of the Israeli Supreme Court.[368]

The Court as whole ruled that it was not convinced

> that the construction of the wall *along the route chosen* was the only means to safeguard the interests of Israel against the peril which it has invoked as justification for that construction . . . Israel cannot rely on a right of self-defence or on a state of necessity in order to preclude the wrongfulness of the construction of the wall.[369]

It is evident from these quotations that the learned judges cited above only considered the wall disproportionate and unnecessary because of the particular route chosen. As the late Sir Arthur Watts observed in his oral pleading before the ICJ on behalf of Jordan:

> Had Israel built a wall wholly within its own territory, we would not all be here today. And I would just observe that the Court has been given no cogent reasons why it was *necessary* to build this Wall in Occupied Territory, and why a wall built within Israel's own territory would not have met the security concerns which are alleged to have provoked it.[370]

What is of particular interest is whether a wall of the kind Israel is constructing in the OPT could be considered necessary or proportionate if it was constructed solely within Israeli territory.[371] It is evident that such a wall would not be contrary to the U.N. Charter, as it would not amount to acquiring territory by force or in violation of IHL or the law of self-determination if it was *accompanied* by a full-Israeli withdrawal.[372]   But could a 721

---

367.   ICJ Wall Advisory Opinion, *supra* note 2, at 1081, para. 9 (separate opinion of Judge Buergenthal) (emphasis added).

368.   *Id.* at 1072, para. 34 (separate opinion of Judge Kooijmans) (emphasis added).

369.   *Id.* at 1050, paras. 140, 142 (emphasis added).

370.   Legal Consequences of the Construction of a Wall in Occupied Palestinian Territory (Req. for Advisory Op.) (Order of Feb. 24, 2004), *available at* http://www.icj-cij.org/docket/files/131/1511.pdf at 57 (last visited Sept. 25, 2007).

371.   *See* THE BERLIN WALL: A DEFIANCE OF HUMAN RIGHTS (Int'l Comm'n of Jurists 1962) (finding that the Berlin Wall violated several provisions in the Universal Declaration of Human Rights on free movement and the right of residency).

372.   U.N. Charter art. 2, para. 3.

kilometer (448 mile) wall[373] be considered proportionate to Palestinian terrorist attacks if Israel maintained the occupation? How would one determine proportionality in such a situation?

It is submitted that if Israel was serious about pursuing peace with the Palestinians in the wider Middle East, it could start by entering into negotiations with a view to concluding peace treaties with Iraq, Lebanon, and Syria—countries from the 1948 conflict with which it has still not made peace—while implementing Resolutions 242 and 338.[374] This would, of course, require a full Israeli withdrawal from the occupied territories, which could lead to full peace and normalization with the entire Muslim world (assuming that these countries are acting in good faith when they say they are prepared to make peace with Israel).[375] In order to ensure the mutual security of both Israelis and Palestinians, security arrangements could be created between Israel and the West Bank (including East Jerusalem), Gaza, and the Golan Heights that are similar to those provided for in Article 4 of the Israel-Egypt and the Israel-Jordan Peace Treaties.[376] These security arrangements would

---

373.   On April 30, 2006, the Israeli cabinet approved a revised route of the wall and published a map on the Ministry of Defence website. The previous map was released on February 20, 2005. Based on this revised map, the total length of the wall's route will be 703 kilometers long, compared to 670 kilometers of length envisioned in the previous route. *See* U.N. Office for the Coordination of Humanitarian Affairs, Occupied Palestinian Territory, *Preliminary Analysis of the Humanitarian Implications of the April 2006 Barrier Projections* (July 2006), http://www.ochaopt.org/documents/OCHABarrierProj_6jul06.pdf. *But see* U.N. Office for the Coordination of Humanitarian Affairs, Occupied Palestinian Territory, *Three Years Later: The Humanitarian Impact of the Barrier Since the International Court of Justice Opinion* (July 9, 2007), http://www.ochaopt.org/documents/ICJ3_Special_Focus_July2007.pdf (according to the most recent assessment, Israel's barrier will be 721 kilometers long).

374.   For further reading on the 1948 conflict between Israel and the Arab world, see Avi Shlaim, The Iron Wall: Israel and the Arab World (2000). For its consequences and further insights, see Benny Morris, The Birth of the Palestinian Refugee Problem Revisited (2004); Ilan Pappé, The Ethnic Cleansing of Palestine (2006); Henry Cattan, Palestine, The Arabs and Israel: The Search for Justice (1969); Michael Palumbo, The Palestinian Catastrophe: The 1948 Expulsion of a People from their Homeland (1987); Lt. Colonel Netanel Lorch, The Edge of the Sword: Israel's War of Independence, 1947–1949 (1961); Walid Khalidi, Why Did the Palestinians Leave? An Examination of the Zionist Version of the Exodus of 1948 (1963); Walid Khalidi, All That Remains: The Palestinian Villages Occupied and Depopulated by Israel in 1948 (1993); and Norman G. Finkelstein, Image and Reality of the Israel-Palestine Conflict (2003).

375.   Relevant Muslim countries include Bangladesh, Indonesia, Malaysia, Pakistan, and others that have not yet established diplomatic relations with Israel. When Israel withdrew its armed forces from southern Lebanon after its 34-day war with Hezbollah in the summer of 2006, it complained about the presence of peacekeepers in that country with whom it did not have diplomatic relations. *Israel Puts Demands on Peacekeepers*, Associated Press, Aug. 21, 2006.

376.   Egypt-Israel Treaty of Peace, *supra* note 187, art. 4. For discussion of the Israel-Egypt treaty, see generally Michael Akehurst, *The Peace Treaty Between Egypt and Israel*, 7 Int'l Relations 1035 (1981).

be without prejudice to the parties' inherent right of self-defense in accordance with the U.N. Charter. In the event that a Palestinian state is created, there would be no question concerning Israel's right recognized by Article 51 of the Charter to defend itself.[377] A Palestinian government would also be obliged to prevent hostile attacks emanating from territories over which it has effective control.[378]

VI. THE LEGAL SIGNIFICANCE OF THE ADVISORY OPINION

Since the ICJ rendered its opinion on the legal consequences of the construction of the wall in the OPTs on July 9, 2004, Israel has adopted a posture of defiance by ignoring the opinion and continuing with the construction process.[379] Although the U.N. has established a register of damage for all natural and legal persons affected by the wall's route, little has been done to urge compliance by Israel with international law. The Arab group did not attempt to lobby the U.N. Security Council for a resolution imposing countermeasures against Israel, nor did it get the U.N. General Assembly to pass a series of non-binding resolutions[380] in the Emergency Special Session[381] calling on third states to undertake countermeasures.[382] In fact, a draft resolution demanding that all U.N. members comply with their legal obligations as identified in the opinion was defeated.[383] The EU, for its part, still allows Israeli companies to benefit from preferential trade with it, even though this is conditional upon respect for human

---

377.   U.N. Charter art. 51.

378.   *But see* The Corfu Channel Case (U.K. v. Alb.), 1949 I.C.J. 1, at 22 (Apr. 9) (determining that the international responsibility of a state will only be engaged if it *knowingly* allows its territory to be used to attack another state).

379.   *See Sharon Defies Court Over Barrier*, BBC NEWS ONLINE, July 11, 2004, http://news.bbc.co.uk/1/hi/world/middle_east/3884887.stm (reporting that the Israeli government continued to build barrier in the West Bank after World Court held that such a barrier is illegal).

380.   Francis Aimé Vallat, *The Competence of the United Nations General Assembly*, 97 RECUEIL DES COURS 207 (1959). However, the view of Francis Aimé Vallat, a former Legal Adviser to the British Foreign Office, who in his lecture before the Hague Academy of International Law said that the legal effect of a U.N. General Assembly resolution would be of the "greatest significance" in the context of the maintenance of peace and security, if the Security Council fails to take any action to deal with a breach of the peace, and the Assembly recommends measures, for the purpose of restoring the peace, to be taken by member states against one and in support of the other party to a conflict.

381.   *See* G.A. Res. 377(V), 5th Sess. (Nov. 3, 1950) (adopting a "uniting for peace" resolution).

382.   *See* G.A. Res. ES-10/L.18/Rev.1, U.N. Doc. A/ES-10/L.18/Rev.1 (July 20, 2004) (demanding merely that Israel, the occupying power, comply with its legal obligations as mentioned in the advisory opinion).

383.   *Id.*

rights, democracy, and the rule of law.[384] Looking at the way in which the Advisory Opinion has been received by the international community in the three years since it was rendered, one might therefore conclude that the opinion has little, if any, legal significance. However, to hold this position would be imprudent. Although a number of countries expressed reservations with the Advisory Opinion's paragraph on the question of self-defense, they did not question the court's findings of law in the other 162 paragraphs.[385] In the present political climate, there are many reasons that may explain why the international community has failed to enforce international law on the rules regarding the recourse to force, from the invasion of Iraq without prior U.N. Security Council authorization to Israel's invasion of Lebanon in July 2006.[386] However, just because some states get away with breaching their international legal obligations does not mean that those legal obligations are not binding upon them in the first place.

---

384. Victor Kattan, *The Wall, Obligations* Erga Omnes *and Human Rights: The Case for Withdrawing the European Community's Terms of Preferential Trade With Israel*, 13 PALESTINE Y.B. INT'L L. 71, 87 (2004–2005). It is noteworthy in this respect that in the case of Zimbabwe, the European Council implemented a series of targeted sanctions. *See* 2002 O.J. (L 50) 1, 4.

385. *See, e.g.*, U.N. GAOR, Emer. Spec. Sess., 25th mtg., U.N. Doc. A/ES-10/PV.25 (July, 16 2004) (including the statement made by Mr. Danforth (United States) in the debate on the General Assembly resolution following the rendering of the Advisory Opinion:

> The judicial process is not the political process, and the International Court of Justice was not the appropriate forum to resolve this conflict. . . . So the Court opinion . . . seems to say that the right of a State to defend itself exists only when it is attacked by another State, and that the right of self-defense does not exist against non-State actors. It does not exist when terrorists hijack planes and fly them into buildings, or bomb train stations or bus stops, or put poison gas into subways. . . . I would suggest that, if this were the meaning of Article 51, then the United Nations Charter could be irrelevant at a time when the major threats to peace are not from States but from terrorists.

Id.

386. *See generally* Lord Alexander of Weedon QC, *Iraq: The Pax Americana and the Law*, 9 Y.B. ISLAMIC & MIDDLE E. L. 3 (2002–2003) (discussing the legality of the invasion of Iraq); *see also* Sean D. Murphy, *Assessing the Legality of Invading Iraq*, 92 GEO. L.J. 173 (2003–2004) (arguing that the invasion of Iraq in 2003 was illegal); Richard A. Falk, *What Future for the UN Charter System of War Prevention?*, 97 AM. J. INT'L L. 590 (2003) (providing an argument that the war was contrary to international law); Christopher Greenwood, *Britain's War on Saddam Had the Law on Its Side*, 9 Y.B. ISLAMIC & MIDDLE E. L. 3 (2002–2003) (arguing that the invasion of Iraq in 2003 was legal). For an examination of the legality of Israel's invasion of Lebanon in 2006, see Victor Kattan, *The Use and Abuse of Self-Defense in International Law: The Israel-Hezbollah Conflict as a Case Study*, 12 Y.B. ISLAMIC & MIDDLE E. L. (2005–2006). *See also Israel, Hezbollah and the Conflict in Lebanon: An Act of Aggression or Self-Defense?*, 14 HUM. RTS. BRIEF 26 (2006), *available at* http://www.wcl.american.edu/hrbrief/14/1kattan.pdf?rd=1 (providing a shorter version of the Kattan article). *See also* Georgina Redsell, *Illegitimate, Unnecessary and Disproportionate: Israel's Use of Force in Lebanon*, 3 CAMBRIDGE STUDENT L. REV. 70 (2007).

Of course, this will also depend on what one means by "binding." In this respect, it is submitted that a distinction should be made between what is "binding" in the sense that a state, a group of states, or an international organization is obliged to comply with a particular rule, and what is enforceable (i.e., what is politically acceptable to the permanent five countries in the Security Council in the sense that one of them will not exercise its right to veto a resolution imposing countermeasures against a delinquent state). It would, therefore, be advisable for international lawyers, including judges before municipal courts, to make a distinction between politics, the law, and its enforcement.

For instance, after citing a passage from the ICJ's Advisory Opinion concerning the proprietary of giving its advice to the U.N. General Assembly on the legal consequences of constructing the *Wall*, the HCJ in *Mara'abe* ruled that the ICJ's opinion is not binding upon states.[387] However, this statement, which was based upon an erroneous citation,[388] misses the point. No state that submitted a written statement or made an oral submission before the Court claimed that the opinion was binding upon them.[389] Indeed, it was the members of the U.N. General Assembly acting collectively who requested the opinion and not its individual member states.[390] In other words, the ICJ's advice is rendered to the U.N. General Assembly, and the Assembly ultimately decides whether to accept the ICJ's advice.[391] It is not up to states A, B, or C to ignore the collective will of the international community.[392] No state can prevent the ICJ

---

387. HCJ 7957/04 Mara'abe v. Prime Minister of Isr. [2005] (Isr.), *translated in* 45 I.L.M. 202, ¶ 56 (2006) ("As the ICJ itself noted in its opinion (paragraph 31), it does not bind the States.").

388. *See* Interpretation of Peace Treaties with Bulgaria, Hungary and Romania, Advisory Opinion, 1950 I.C.J. 65, 71 (Mar. 30) (recalling its jurisprudence); Western Sahara, Advisory Opinion, 1975 I.C.J. 12, at 24 (Oct. 16) (quoting 1950 I.C.J. 71).

389. *See* HCJ 7957/04 *Mara'abe, translated in* 45 I.L.M. 202 (listing petitioners bringing the case, which includes no nation-states).

390. This is because the U.N. is a separate legal person from its members. It has international personality, and is a subject of international law. Its constituent members have clothed it with the competence required to enable it to effectively discharge its functions, duties, and responsibilities. As the ICJ ruled,

[t]he functions of the Organization are of such a character that they could not be effectively discharged if they involved concurrent action, on the international plane of fifty-eight or more Foreign Offices, and the court concludes that the Members have endowed the organization with the capacity to bring international claims when necessitated by the discharge of its functions.

Reparation of Injuries Suffered in the Service of the United Nations, Advisory Opinion, 1949 I.C.J. 178, 180 (Apr. 11).

391. And indeed, it did precisely this, acknowledging the opinion in G.A. Res. ES-10/L.18/Rev.1, *supra* note 382.

392. The principle of "persistent objection" only applies to the creation of new rules of international law. However, the ICJ was not dealing with any new rules of

from giving an Advisory Opinion, and no state can declare that the ICJ's findings of law are without legal effect.[393] A state that seeks to argue that a considered opinion of the Court does not represent the correct state of the law (particularly where the Court's findings, as in the *Wall* opinion, verge on unanimity) will be in a weak position.[394] The HCJ in *Mara'abe* seemed to be confusing three separate issues: the nature of Advisory Opinions, the role of the U.N. General Assembly, and the irrelevance of res judicata, which only applies when there are parties to a case.[395]

The purpose of Advisory Opinions is to provide authoritative guidance on points of law arising from the functions of organs and specialized agencies of the U.N. But one cannot simply assume that because of the word "advisory" the ICJ's advice is without legal significance altogether. As ICJ noted itself in its Advisory Opinions concerning the *Peace Treaties in Bulgaria, Hungary and Romania* and on the status of *Western Sahara*, "The Court's reply is only of an advisory character: *as such*, it has no binding force."[396] Thus, there may be situations and circumstances under which its opinions will have legal consequences. For instance, in the *Wall* opinion, the ICJ ruled: "The obligations *erga omnes* violated by Israel are the obligation to respect the right of the Palestinian people to self-determination, and certain of its obligations under international humanitarian law."[397] *Erga omnes* obligations are, by their very definition, binding.[398] They are concerned with the enforcement of international law, the violation of which is deemed to be an offense not only against the state or entity in question, but against all members of the international community.[399] Whether these norms

---

international law in its Advisory Opinion on the wall. *See generally* Ted L. Stein, *The Approach of the Different Drummer: The Principle of the Persistent Objector in International Law*, 26 HARV. INT'L L.J. 457 (1985) (discussing this principle in depth).

393. *See* ADAM BASAK, DECISIONS OF THE UNITED NATIONS ORGANS IN THE JUDGMENTS AND OPINIONS OF THE INTERNATIONAL COURT OF JUSTICE 35 (1969) ("[N]o State can cancel the legal effects of a decisions [sic] in which an organ of the UN has decided to ask for an opinion. One must then acknowledge that in the opinion of the Court such a decision is in this sense indirectly binding on all member States.").

394. Hugh Thirlway, *The International Court of Justice*, in INTERNATIONAL LAW 561, 582–83 (Malcolm Evans ed., 2003).

395. *See* Scobbie, *supra* note 4, at 269, 289–91 (discussing the fact that *res judicata* does not attach to an advisory opinion if there are no parties).

396. Interpretation of Peace Treaties with Bulgaria, Hungary and Romania, *supra* note 388, at 71 (emphasis added).

397. ICJ Wall Advisory Opinion, *supra* note 2, at 1053, para. 155.

398. *See* Peter D. Coffman, *Obligations Erga Omnes and the Absent Third State*, 39 GERMAN Y.B. INT'L L. 285, 285 (1996) (discussing the binding nature of *erga omnes* obligations).

399. For discussion on obligations *erga omnes*, see Coffman, *supra* note 398, at 285–333; Michael Byers, *Conceptualising the Relationship between Jus Cogens and Erga Omnes Rules*, 66 NORDIC J. INT'L L. 211, 211–39 (1997); and Karl Zemanek, *New*

are actually *enforced* or not is an entirely different matter and has little to do, strictly speaking, with the law. This is the difference between domestic and international law: the latter is not self-executing (if the law ever is). But this is not the same as saying that the law is not binding. As Sir Gerald Fitzmaurice once wrote:

> The law is not binding because it is enforced: it is enforced because it is already binding. Enforcement presupposes the existence of a legal obligation incumbent on those concerned. The prospect of enforcement is in fact little more than a factor or motive inclining people to obey rules that they are in any case under an obligation to obey: but it is not itself the source of the obligation.[400]

Even before the ascendancy of so-called peremptory norms of international law and obligations *erga omnes*, it was argued by some international lawyers that the difference between Advisory Opinions and contentious decisions of the ICJ was minimal.[401] In fact, some went so far as to write that there was, in reality, no fundamental difference between a "non-binding" Advisory Opinion and a "binding" judgment.[402] For instance, Blaine Sloane, a former director of the U.N. General Legal Division, made the point in an article he wrote in 1950: "While in a formal sense it may be true that an opinion does not have the binding force of a judgement, practically, it does, as an authoritative statement of law, have almost the same legal effect."[403] In other words, the ICJ states what the law is in both its advisory capacity and when there is a contentious case between states. André Gros, formerly a French judge at the ICJ, took a similar view:

> The distinction habitually drawn between Advisory Opinions and judgments, whereby the former do not have the binding character of the latter, is not an absolute one. In the first place, it is only the operative part of a judgment that is distinct from an Advisory Opinion as to its obligatory force. As regards the reasoning, this, in both cases, represents the Court's legal conclusions concerning the situation which is being dealt with, and its weight is the same in both cases: there are no two ways of declaring the law. Second, even advisory proceedings

---

Trends in the Enforcement of Erga Omnes Obligations, 4 MAX PLANCK Y.B. UN L. 1, 1–52 (2000).

400. Gerald Fitzmaurice, *The Foundations of the Authority of International Law and the Problem of Enforcement*, 19 MOD. L. REV. 1, 2 (1956).

401. F. Blaine Sloan, *Advisory Jurisdiction of the International Court of Justice*, 38 CAL. L. REV. 830, 855 (1950) (discussing the fact that advisory opinions and decisions of the ICJ have the same legal effect).

402. *Id.*

403. *Id.*; *see also* Blaine Sloan, *General Assembly Resolutions Revisited (Forty Years Later)*, 58 BRIT. Y.B. INT'L L. 39 (1988) (looking back at the more than 6,000 General Assembly resolutions over the past forty years and discussing the unresolved legal status of such resolutions); F. Blaine Sloan, *The Binding Force of a 'Recommendation' of the General Assembly of the United Nations*, 25 BRIT. Y.B. INT'L L. 1 (1948) (discussing whether U.N. resolutions possess any binding force on Member states).

may involve acts that operate with finality both for the Court itself and for the participating states or organizations.[404]

It could be argued that even if this had been a contentious case between Israel and "Palestine," or between a third state such as Jordan (doing what Ethiopia and Liberia tried to do regarding South-West Africa in the 1960s), the result would have been the same—although in a contentious case, Israel would probably have put in full evidence and arguments on the merits.[405] However, in the present circumstances, this would probably not be possible because Israel has withdrawn its consent to the compulsory jurisdiction of the ICJ.[406] Although Assembly resolutions are only recommendatory according to Articles 10-14 of the Charter, this does not affect the legal quality of an Advisory Opinion; it is still a contemporary statement of the law

---

404.   André Gros, *Concerning the Advisory Role of the International Court of Justice, in* TRANSNATIONAL LAW IN A CHANGING SOCIETY: ESSAYS IN HONOR OF PHILIP C. JESSUP 313, 315 (Wolfgang Friedmann et al. eds., 1972).

405.   Of course, in a contentious case, the losing State would be in violation of the U.N. Charter if it did not comply. From 1949 to 1971, the case of South-West Africa (now Namibia) engaged the International Court of Justice's attention. This resulted in four Advisory Opinions (1950, 1955, 1956 and 1971) and two judgments (1962 and 1966). From 1949 to 1962, South Africa did its best to thwart the supervisory role assigned to the U.N. General Assembly, and just like Israel, it ignored the ICJ's advisory opinions. But by the 1960s, with many new African states as members of the U.N., a new idea took root: to explore the possibility of contentious litigation through a judgment from the ICJ. However, South-West Africa was not a State in the 1960s (it did not attain independence as the state of Namibia until 1990), and it had to rely on Ethiopia and Liberia (who were both members of the League of Nations) to bring the case to the ICJ on its behalf. In 1966, "the white man's court" held that Ethiopia and Liberia were not entitled to receive judgment on the merits of the case, because they had not "established any legal right or interest appertaining to them in the subject matter" of the claims. This judgment came as a surprise to many, and it is generally thought that were it not for the death of Judge Badawi, the illness of Judge Bustamante, and the withdrawal of Judge Zafrullah Khan, the outcome might have been very different. For a commentary by one of the lawyers who participated in that case, see Richard A. Falk, *The South West Africa Cases: An Appraisal, in* RICHARD A. FALK, THE STATUS OF LAW IN INTERNATIONAL SOCIETY 378-402 (1970). Today, the matter seems to be settled as Article 42 of the International Law Commission's Draft Articles on State Responsibility (2001) allows an injured state to invoke the responsibility of another state if the obligation breached is owed to that state, a group of states, or to the international community as a whole. INTERNATIONAL LAW COMMISSION'S DRAFT ARTICLES ON STATE RESPONSIBILITY art. 42 (2001).

406.   Israel followed the US in withdrawing its consent from the compulsory jurisdiction of the ICJ in the aftermath of the *Nicaragua* judgment. The notification of termination of the declaration of 17 October 1956, received from the Government of Israel on 21 November 1985 reads as follows: "On behalf of the Government of Israel, I have the honour to inform you that the Government of Israel has decided to terminate, with effect as of today, its declaration of 17 October 1956 as amended, concerning the acceptance of the compulsory jurisdiction of the International Court of Justice." This statement was signed by Benjamin Netanyahu. *See Declarations Recognizing Jurisdiction*, 38-40 I.C.J. Y.B. 79, 79–80 (1983–1986) (including the statement signed by Golda Meir showing Israel's acceptance of the compulsory jurisdiction of the ICJ in the years before 1985).

by the principal judicial organ of the U.N. Judge Elias went so far as to advance his view that:

> If there is unanimity in the Assembly during the vote, all are bound. . . . If the vote is divided, then those states that vote for a particular resolution by the requisite majority are bound on the grounds of consent and of estoppel. Those that abstain are also bound on the ground of acquiescence and tacit consent, since an abstention is not a negative vote; while those that vote against the resolutions should be regarded as bound by the democratic principles that the majority view should always prevail when the vote has been truly free and fair and the requisite majority has been secured.[407]

Resolution ES-10/L.18/Rev.1, passed in the Advisory Opinion's aftermath, demanded that Israel comply with its legal obligations in the Advisory Opinion.[408] This Resolution differs substantially from resolution ES-10/13.[409] The latter was adopted on October 27, 2003 (i.e., before the Assembly petitioned the ICJ), and demanded that "Israel stop and reverse the construction of the Wall in the Occupied Palestinian Territory, including in and around East Jerusalem, which is in departure of the Armistice Line of 1949 and is in contradiction to relevant provisions of international law."[410] Not only is Israel now obliged to stop and reverse construction of the wall, but according to resolution ES-10/L.18/Rev.1, the Secretary-General is to establish a register of damage caused to all natural or legal persons.[411]

It should not be forgotten that there is no higher judicial authority that can rule on the legal issues involved in this case. The issues addressed in the ICJ's opinion on the *Wall* formed the corpus of law that *guides* the U.N. on the question of Palestine. After all, by analogizing to the ICJ's Advisory Opinions in the South-West Africa cases, one could argue that the U.N., as a successor to the League of Nations, has assumed a supervisory role over the Palestinian territories, which Israel has been effectively administering since June 1967. The "sacred trust" as encapsulated in Article 22 of the Covenant of the League of Nations, as preserved by Article 80 of the U.N. Charter,[412] would render relevant Judge Sir Hersch

---

407.   T. Olawale Elias, *Modern Sources of International Law*, *in* TRANSNATIONAL LAW IN A CHANGING SOCIETY: ESSAYS IN HONOR OF PHILIP C. JESSUP, *supra* note 404, at 34, 51.

408.   G.A. Res. ES-10/L.18/Rev.1, *supra* note 382.

409.   *See* G.A. Res. ES-10/13, U.N. Doc. A/RES/ES-10/13 (Oct. 27, 2003) (discussing illegal Israeli actions in Occupied East Jerusalem and the rest of the OPTs).

410.   *Id.*

411.   *See* The Secretary-General, *Report of the Secretary-General Pursuant to General Assembly Resolution ES-10/15*, para. 4, *delivered to the General Assembly*, U.N. Doc. A/ES-10/361 (Oct. 17, 2006) (discussing the purpose and legal nature of the register of damage).

412.   U.N. Charter art. 80, para. 1.

Lauterpacht's classic statement in the *Voting Procedure Case*.[413] As he noted in his separate opinion while commenting upon the legal effect of Assembly resolutions on South-West Africa:

> Whatever may be the content of the recommendation and whatever may be the nature and the circumstances of the majority by which it has been reached, it is nevertheless a legal act of the principal organ of the United Nations which members of the United Nations are under a duty to treat with a degree of respect appropriate to a resolution of the General Assembly . . . Although there is no automatic obligation to accept fully a particular recommendation or series of recommendations, there is a legal obligation to act in good faith in accordance with the principles of the Charter and the System of Trusteeship. An administering State may not be acting illegally by declining to act upon a recommendation or series of recommendations on the same subject. But in doing so it acts at its peril when a point is reached when the cumulative effect of the persistent disregard of the articulate opinion of the Organization is such as to foster the conviction that the State in question has become guilty of disloyalty to the Principles and Purposes of the Charter. Thus an Administering State which consistently sets itself above the solemnly and repeatedly expressed judgment of the Organization, in particular in proportion as that judgment approximates to unanimity, may find that it has overstepped the imperceptible line between impropriety and illegality, between discretion and arbitrariness, between the exercise of the legal right to disregard the recommendation and the abuse of that right, and that it has exposed itself to consequences legitimately following as a legal sanction.[414]

Resolution ES-10/L.18/Rev.1 was adopted on the basis of an Advisory Opinion and is thus distinct from political rhetoric. Linguistically, this Resolution is of a legal and not of a moral quality.[415] Certain mechanisms have been established to monitor compliance by Israel.

> Except as may be agreed upon in individual trusteeship agreements, made under Articles 77, 79, and 81, placing each territory under the trusteeship system, and until such agreements have been concluded, nothing in this Chapter shall be construed in or of itself to alter in any manner the rights whatsoever of any states or any peoples or the terms of existing international instruments to which Members of the United Nations may respectively be parties.

Id.

413.   Voting Procedures on Questions Relating to Reports and Petitions Concerning the Territory of South-West Africa, Advisory Opinion, 1955 I.C.J. 67 (June 7).

414.   *Id.* at 120 (separate opinion of Judge Lauterpacht).

415.   Richard A. Falk, Comment, *On the Quasi-Legislative Competence of the General Assembly*, 60 AM. J. INT'L L. 782, 787 (1966).

> If the resolution enters a political process that looks toward implementation, then the legislative nature of the claim is more clear-cut, that is, there seems to be some explicit connection between the status of the claim as legislative and the prospects for *effective* implementation: the better the prospects, the more appropriate the label 'legislative.'

Id.

Operative paragraph 6 "calls upon both the Government of Israel and the Palestinian Authority to immediately implement their obligations under the Roadmap, in cooperation with the Quartet, as endorsed by Security Council Resolution 1515 (2003), to achieve the vision of two states living side by side in peace and security, and emphasizes that both Israel and the Palestinian Authority are under an obligation scrupulously to observe the rules of international humanitarian law."[416] Operative paragraph 7 "calls upon all States parties to the Fourth Geneva Convention of 1949 *to ensure respect* by Israel for the Convention, and invites Switzerland, in its capacity as the depositary of the Geneva Conventions, to conduct consultations and to report to the General Assembly on the matter, including with regard to the possibility of resuming the Conference of High Contracting Parties to the Fourth Geneva Convention."[417] The Assembly has clearly taken steps towards ensuring the effective implementation of this Resolution, emphasizing that the political process should lead to a vision of two states living in peace and security.

It is important to distinguish between the ICJ, the U.N.'s principal judicial organ, and the U.N. General Assembly and U.N. Security Council, which are political bodies. According to the U.N. Charter, only the Council can take legally binding decisions under Article 25 of the Charter, directing member states to impose economic sanctions or use force to maintain international peace.[418] But this is a political decision made by a political body subject to the possibility of a veto by one of its permanent members. Politics and law, though closely intertwined in international relations, are fundamentally different. Interestingly, Judge Higgins wrote in her separate opinion that the Court's finding that an act or situation is illegal is the same as a binding decision of a U.N. organ (such as the Security Council) acting under Chapter VI and VII of the Charter.[419] She wrote:

> Although in the present case it is the Court, rather than a United Nations organ acting under Articles 24 and 25, that has found the illegality; and although it is found in the context of an Advisory Opinion rather than in a contentious case, the Court's position as the principal judicial organ of the United Nations suggests that the legal consequence for a finding that an act or situation is illegal *is the same.*[420]

It may therefore be concluded that the obligations that the ICJ outlined are binding upon the U.N., which is estopped from undertaking measures that would conflict with the Advisory Opinion. As Judge Gros stated in *Western Sahara*:

---

416.   G.A. Res. ES-10/L.18/Rev.1, *supra* note 382, para 6.
417.   *Id.* para. 7 (emphasis added).
418.   U.N. Charter art. 25.
419.   ICJ Wall Advisory Opinion, *supra* note 2, at 1064, para. 38.
420.   *Id.* (emphasis added).

The advisory opinion determines the law applicable to the question put; it is possible for the body which sought the opinion not to follow it in its action, but that body is aware that no position adopted contrary to the Court's pronouncement will have any effectiveness whatsoever in the legal sphere.[421]

Whether or not the Palestinians are successful in persuading the international community to urge compliance by Israel with its legal obligations at some future point in time will depend upon geopolitical considerations.[422] Of course this is not, technically speaking, a legal issue, but a question of politics. After all, states can always ignore international law, or dismiss it when it is politically inconvenient.[423]

VII. CONCLUDING REMARKS

It is evident from comparing the ICJ's Advisory Opinion on *Wall* to the HCJ's decisions in the *Beit Sourik* and *Mara'abe* cases that there was little agreement on the substantive issues relating to Israeli civilian settlement activity, self-determination, and self-defense. On the legality of the wall, the Courts were at complete loggerheads: the HCJ ruled that the wall was a *lawful* measure to defend the Israeli civilian settlements established inside the West Bank including in and around East Jerusalem without actually

---

421. Voting Procedures, Advisory Opinion, 1955 I.C.J., *supra* note 413, at 73, para. 6.

422. In this respect, the PLO might want to consider lobbying friendly states in the General Assembly to petition the ICJ for a further Advisory Opinion, as suggested by the U.N. Special Rapporteur. For a discussion, see U.N. Human Rights Council, *Implementation of General Assembly Resolution 60/251 of 15 March 2006 Entitled "Human Rights Council,"* U.N. Doc. A/HRC/4/17 (Jan. 29, 2007) (*prepared by* John Dugard). Indeed, further recourse to the ICJ for Advisory Opinions on legal questions connected to the question of Palestine, and in particular on the legal consequences of prolonged occupations more generally, will be of particular use for third states who may refrain from taking coercive measures against Israel without an explicit legal mandate to do so. In this respect, it could be argued that the Advisory Opinion on the wall already provides a legal mandate to call for countermeasures (such as imposing a comprehensive arms embargo) against Israel, as was done against apartheid South Africa. *See* S.C. Res. 418, U.N. Doc. S/RES/418 (Nov. 4, 1977) (condemning the South African government for its massive violence and further recognizing the arms embargo against the nation to prevent further aggravation of the situation). Of course, that Resolution explicitly referred to Chapter VII of the U.N. Charter, which is unlikely to be accomplished in the case of Israel. In this regard, it would have been preferable if the ICJ could have explicitly enumerated the consequences for states, either in the opinion itself or in the separate opinions of the judges participating in the case, as was done, for example, by Vice-President Ammoun. Namibia Advisory Opinion, *supra* note 192, at 70 (separate opinion of Vice-President Ammoun).

423. *See* Oliver Burkeman & Julian Borger, *War Critic Astonished as US Hawk Admits Invasion was Illegal*, GUARDIAN (London), Nov. 20, 2003, *available at* http://www.guardian.co.uk/Iraq/Story/0,2763,1089158,00.html (noting that when asked about the legality of the invasion of Iraq, Richard Perle said, "I think in this case international law stood in the way of doing the right thing.").

addressing their illegality, whereas the ICJ found that the wall was *unlawful* precisely because it encloses those settlements, which already breach Article 49(6) of Geneva Convention IV.[424]   As examined in Section IV, the way in which both Courts dealt with the question of Palestinian self-determination was at best peripheral and ultimately unsatisfactory, although the ICJ did at least address the issue in some depth.[425]   However, the ICJ should have established more clearly what states should do to ensure Israel's compliance with international law.   It also should have elaborated further upon the question of self-defense, particularly as to whether the law has changed in the aftermath of September 11, although its reluctance to engage in a discussion of this issue was probably because the parties did not adequately argue self-defense before the court.[426]

In its Advisory Opinion, the ICJ considered the wall's route as a whole, whereas the HCJ only dealt with certain sections of it in a piecemeal fashion.[427]   This has allowed the HCJ to obfuscate the fact that the wall's route is in fact segmenting the already miniscule territorial area in which the Palestinian people desire to create a contiguous, sovereign, and viable state as envisaged by the "Performance-Based Road Map to a Two-State Solution to the Israeli-Palestinian Conflict."[428]   The wall's route has a direct impact upon the question of self-determination for the Palestinians, as it affects their economic, social and cultural development.   As is clearly evident

---

424.   Daphne Barak-Erez, *Israel: The Security Barrier–Between International Law, Constitutional Law, and Domestic Judicial Review*, 4 INT'L J. CON. L. 540, 547–48 (2006) ("Paradoxically, the two courts have something in common—namely, a narrow view of the motivations behind the construction of the barrier. The ICJ held that the barrier was a political move and, therefore, refused to acknowledge its security purposes. By contrast, the Israeli Supreme Court firmly held that the barrier was not politically motivated, and that its sole concern was security. The two courts were not open to the possibility that, in fact, both motivations were inseparably linked in the considerations inspiring the barrier's construction.").

425.   *See* U.N. GAOR, *Advisory Opinion of the International Court of Justice on the Legal Consequences of the Construction of the Wall in the Occupied Palestinian Territory*, U.N. Doc. A/ES-10/273 (July 13, 2004) (discussing the International Court of Justice opinion regarding the wall).

426.   *Id.*

427.   *Id.*

428.   *See* Press Release, USDOS, A Performance-Based Roadmap to a Permanent Two-State Solution to the Israeli-Palestinian Conflict (Apr. 30, 2003), http://www.state.gov/r/pa/prs/ps/2003/20062.htm (stating that "[a] settlement, negotiated between the parties, will result in the emergence of an independent, democratic, and viable Palestinian state living side by side in peace and security with Israel and its other neighbors"); ICJ Wall Advisory Opinion, *supra* note 2, at 1054, para. 162 ("Illegal actions and unilateral decisions have been taken on all sides, whereas, in the Court's view, this tragic situation can be brought to an end only through implementation in good faith of all relevant Security Council resolutions, in particular resolutions 242 (1967) and 338 (1973). The 'Roadmap' approved by Security Council resolution 1515 (2003) represents the most recent of efforts to initiate negotiations to this end.").

from examining the various maps of the wall's route (the latest route is shown in map 4 in the Appendix), the adjustments made to the wall's route after the HCJ's rulings in *Beit Sourik* and *Mara'abe* are cosmetic only.[429] In this respect, it should not be forgotten that there are still hundreds of checkpoints scattered throughout the West Bank as well as so-called "flying checkpoints."[430]   Not all of these checkpoints—which are more akin to military barricades—separate Israelis from Palestinians. Some of them separate Palestinians from each other, and in these cases, it is difficult to see what the security rationale for their existence is.[431] Moreover, many parts of the West Bank—an area that is itself designated for a future Palestinian state—are off limits for Palestinians and are accessible to the settlers only.[432] Palestinians are also prohibited from traveling on many of the roads within the West Bank (different types of number plates distinguish Palestinian vehicles from those driven by the settlers and the military), and they need security permits to visit relatives inhabiting other Palestinian cities, towns, and villages in East Jerusalem, the West Bank, and Gaza, as well as in Israel.[433] By analyzing only a small section of the wall's route in *Beit Sourik* and *Mara'abe*, the HCJ was able to ignore the "bigger picture," whereas the ICJ at least took some of these factors into account (although inadequately in the opinion of the author).   In this respect, the "bigger picture" is that after Israel has carved out its most valuable land and resources through constructing the wall, all that remains of the West Bank is a rump entity that will not satisfy Palestinian aspirations for independence and statehood. As a result, Palestinians are likely to remain in a state of permanent dependence upon Israel, unable to pursue their right of self-determination through their economic, social, and cultural development. And the sad thing is that all this has the stamp of approval of the highest Court of law in Israel (the Supreme Court, which was acting as a HCJ in this case). Having said this, as legal precedents, there is little doubt that despite some of the criticisms leveled at the ICJ in academic writings (it should be said, mostly in the United States), the ICJ's Advisory Opinion, outside Israel, has been a persuasive authority.[434]   It has, for

---

429.   *See* Appendix 4.

430.   *See* U.N. Office for the Coordination of Human Affairs [OCHA], *OCHA Closure Update occupied Palestinian Territory* (Apr. 2007), http://www.ochaopt.org/documents/Closure%20Apr07_2.pdf (discussing flying checkpoint positions and limits on Palestinian access to different parts of Israel).

431.   *Id.*

432.   *Id.*

433.   *Id.*

434.   *See, e.g.,* Orakhelashvili, *supra* note 207, at 134–39 (favoring the ICJ's Advisory Opinion over that of the HCJ).

instance, galvanised the international NGO community and Palestinian civil society.[435]

In the *Mara'abe* case, Vice-President M. Cheshin said he found the ICJ's decision "objectionable."[436] He criticized the factual basis upon which the ICJ built its opinion, which he termed a "ramshackle one."[437] He failed to mention that whatever "defects" there were concerning the facts, Israel did not furnish the Court with any additional information for what he claims would have affected the legal outcome (and it is noteworthy that in the three years since the Advisory Opinion was rendered on July 9, 2004, over 80 percent of the wall continues to pass through occupied territory).[438] Although Israel has alleged that the wall it is building in the West Bank is *solely* a protective measure, it still has not accounted for its route in a satisfactory manner or explained why the wall "just happens" to loop around all the major Israeli civilian settlement blocs established in the West Bank. Presumably Israel is not building the wall in a haphazard manner, but deliberately and carefully. According to Judge Barak,

> [t]he only reason for the route beyond the Green Line is a professional reason related to topography, the ability to control the immediate surroundings, and other similar military reasons. Upon which rules of international law can it be said that such a route violates international law?[439]

The ICJ, in its 163-paragraph opinion, has already examined the rules of international law that Israel is violating in constructing the wall in the OPT, and this will not be elaborated upon here.[440] It is interesting to note that a "professional reason related to topography," presumably determined by the Israeli military, just happens to coincide with the Israeli civilian settlements scattered on practically every major hill top around East Jerusalem. Surely, this cannot be a matter of sheer coincidence? A journalist writing for the Israeli newspaper *Ha'aretz* has since written that the wall's route in the

---

435.   *See, e.g.*, Palestinian Civil Soc'y, *Calls for Boycott, Divestment and Sanction against Israel Until It Complies with International Law and Universal Principles of Human Rights*, July 9, 2005, *available at* http://www.stopthewall.org/downloads/pdf/BDSEnglish.pdf (calling on civil organizations and people around the world to impose sanctions against Israel similar to those imposed upon South Africa during Apartheid); BADIL, The Electronic Intifada, *Palestinians Attend World Social Forum*, Jan. 20, 2007, http://wsf2007.org/info/media-articles-online/palestinians-attend-world-social-forum (reporting that a Palestinian delegation supporting this initiative attended the World Social Forum in Nairobi in January 2007).

436.   HCJ 7957/04 Mara'abe v. Prime Minister of Isr. [2005] (Isr.), *translated in* 45 I.L.M. 202, 244 (2006).

437.   *Id.* at 245, para. 4.

438.   *Id.*

439.   *Id.* at 231, para. 70.

440.   ICJ Wall Advisory Opinion, *supra* note 2, at 1054–55, para. 163.

Jerusalem area is "suspiciously congruent" with the master plan of the adjacent settlements:

> When Shaul Arieli of the Council for Peace and Security examined the Defense Ministry's route close to the northernmost neighbourhood of the capital, Neveh Yaakov [an Israeli settlement located in northeast Jerusalem], he could not understand why, contrary to the basic rules of planning a security fence, the fence wound along at the foot of the ridge. Why and for what purpose did the planner decide to deviate at that particular place nearly a kilometre and a half from the eastern border of the neighborhood and go out of the municipal area of Jerusalem into the territories of the West Bank? The riddle was solved when Arieli obtained Master Plan number 240.3 for the establishment of a new neighbourhood/Jewish settlement, by the name of Geva. According to the plan, Geva is to link up via a bridge with the settlement of Geva Binyamin (Adam) to the east.[441]

The HCJ has since castigated the Israeli government for misleading it as to the reasons underlying its route.[442] In a recent decision, the HCJ ruled that "a complete picture was not presented" after what the Court referred to as a "grave phenomenon" was revealed (i.e., that the route of the wall is linked to Israeli civilian settlement activity).[443] Nevertheless, Judge Barak ruled that "our words are not intended to express a position as to the lawfulness of the new route now being considered by the Respondents, nor to express a position as regards other petitions concerning the route of the fence in the Northern and Southern sections."[444] With respect, it is still submitted that, for the HCJ to have even suggested that that the factual basis had changed since July 2004 (as Judge Barak implicitly did in paragraphs 59-72 of his decision in *Mara'abe*, where he cited statements by the State's counsel that called the findings in a number of U.N. reports "far from precise," "exaggerated," and "completely baseless"), and that ICJ's opinion was consequently outdated and irrelevant, was disingenuous.[445] The HCJ should not have accepted the government's contentions so uncritically in the first place, when it

---

441.   Eldar Akiva, *Pulling Out Phase Two of the Road Map*, HA'ARETZ (Jerusalem), June 14, 2006, *available at* http://www.haaretz.com/hasen/objects/pages/PrintArticleEn.jhtml?itemNo=726062.

442.   I would like to thank John Dugard and Aeyal Gross for drawing this to my attention. Ha'aretz reported that Justices Aharon Barak, Dorit Beinisch, and Ayala Procaccia severely criticized the government for concealing in earlier High Court hearings that the existing route was determined partly by a master plan for expanding the settlements, and not solely for security considerations. *See* Yuval Yoaz, *Court Orders Section of Separation Fence Torn Down*, HA'ARETZ (Jerusalem), June 16, 2006, *available at* http://www.haaretz.com/hasen/pages/ShArt.jhtml?itemNo=727626.

443.   HCJ 2732/05 Hassin and Radwan v. Israel [2005] (Isr.), translation provided courtesy of Michael Sfard, Adv. (on file with author).

444.   *Id.*

445.   HCJ 7957/04 Mara'abe v. Prime Minister of Isr. [2005] (Isr.), *translated in* 45 I.L.M. 202, 230, para. 67 (2006).

was evident to all and sundry that something was amiss. As James Crawford pleaded in his oral statement before the ICJ:

> Israel cannot plead lack of facts as a ground to have the Court refuse to decide, when any deficiency in the facts could have been corrected by Israel itself. . . . Anyway the basic facts are perfectly clear. The dominant fact is the US$2billion fact of the Wall, growing daily and dividing Palestinian communities from each other and from their lands and water. That is the essential fact, this US$2billion so-called "temporary" edifice. So much is now known about the Wall, and what is not known can be deduced from its route, its size, its cost, its régime, its effects, and the avowed intentions of those who are building it to impose a unilateral settlement.[446]

Although Crawford was speaking *before* the ICJ rendered its Advisory Opinion, events since that time have only strengthened this argument.[447] Israel is still building the wall in direct contravention of international law as determined by the ICJ, its cost has increased, Palestinians have been displaced, the settlements continue to grow unabated, Israel imposes a unilateral settlement in Gaza, and the conflict continues.[448] Many people can confirm the deterioration of the situation; there are no shortages of NGOs, journalists and U.N. personnel on the ground in Israel and the surrounding areas who are able to travel there and examine the situation for themselves (although things have become more difficult in recent years, particularly in the OPTs). There is also an abundance of information from international, Israeli, and Palestinian human-rights organizations.[449] Judge Owada thought it reasonable to conclude "that the political, social, economic, and humanitarian impacts of the construction of the wall, as substantiated by ample evidence supplied and documented in the course of the present proceedings, is such that the construction of the wall would constitute a violation of international obligations under various international instruments to which Israel is a party."[450] It will be recalled that in *Nicaragua*, the ICJ ruled that it could consider factual material "in the public

---

446.   Legal Consequence of Construction of a Wall in Occupied Palestinian Territory, Advisory Opinion, 2004 I.C.J. 36, paras. 28–29 (Feb. 23).

447.   ICJ Wall Advisory Opinion, *supra* note 2, at 1028, paras. 55–58 (stating the facts and events).

448.   For monthly reports on the situation in the OPT, see the Reports From the Palestinian Monitoring Group (2006), http://www.nad-plo.org/main.php?view= pmg_pmg. *See also* UNDER THE GUISE OF SECURITY: ROUTING THE SEPARATION BARRIER TO ENABLE THE EXPANSION OF ISRAELI SETTLEMENTS IN THE WEST BANK (2005), *available at* http://www.btselem.org/Download/200512_Under_the_Guise_of_ Security_Eng.pdf (examining the connection between the settlements and the separation barrier's route).

449.   *See* Amnesty Int'l, Links to Israeli and Palestinian (Human Rights) Organizations, http://web.amnesty.org/pages/isr-links-eng (providing a list of 45 organizations that are dedicated to human rights work in Israel and Palestine).

450.   ICJ Wall Advisory Opinion, *supra* note 2, at 1097, para. 24 (separate opinion of Judge Owada).

domain," whether or not the parties refer to them.[451] After citing the *Brazilian Loans* case by the Permanent Court of International Justice and its own jurisprudence in the *Nuclear Test* cases, it ruled: "As to the facts of the case, in principle the Court is not bound to confine its consideration to the material formally submitted to it by the parties."[452] Evidently, the ICJ may therefore take other material into consideration. Although, according to the ICJ's Practice Direction XII, information submitted by international NGOs are not considered to be part of the case file, "[s]uch statements and/or documents shall be treated as publications readily available and may accordingly be referred to by States and intergovernmental organizations presenting written and oral statements."[453] Because the ICJ's judgments and Advisory Opinions are not known for their comprehensive references to the sources relied upon for its legal conclusions, it could consider NGO *amicus* briefs without explicitly saying it has done so.[454] The HCJ therefore cannot assume that the ICJ did not take Israel's security justifications into consideration. The ICJ did recognize that "Israel has to face numerous indiscriminate and deadly acts of violence against its civilian population" and it ruled that it has "the right, and indeed the duty, to respond in order to protect the life of its citizens."[455] However, it said, "[t]he measures taken are bound nonetheless to remain in conformity with applicable international law."[456] Several judges also made reference to this in their separate opinions.[457] Therefore, to attack the ICJ's Advisory Opinion on the ground that the facts have changed is perhaps a demonstration of the desperation on the part of the HCJ. It cannot attack the opinion on the law, which is clear, so it goes for the facts—which only Israel could have "corrected" had it taken part in the oral pleadings or submitted a written statement addressing the merits of the case.

Vice-President M. Cheshin also claimed that "the opinion was colored by a political hue" and that it almost completely ignored "the horrible terrorism and security problems which have plagued Israel" without mentioning any of the terrible atrocities committed by the Israeli army in the OPT since 1967 (which were also hardly

---

451. *See* Military and Paramilitary Activities (Nicar. v. U.S.), *supra* note 41, paras. 29–31 (explaining that I.C.J. is not bound to confine its consideration just to the facts that have been submitted).

452. *Id.* para. 30.

453. ICJ, *Practice Directions* (Dec. 6, 2006), http://www.icj-cij.org/documents/index.php?p1=4&p2=4&p3=0.

454. For this view, see Lance Bartholomeusz, *The Amicus Curiae before International Courts and Tribunals*, 5 NON-STATE ACTORS & INT'L L. 209, 223–24 (2005).

455. ICJ Wall Advisory Opinion, *supra* note 2, at 1050, para. 141.

456. *Id.*

457. *See id.* at 1066, paras. 4–5 (separate opinion of Judge Kooijmans); *id.* at 1079, para. 5 (declaration of Judge Beurgenthal); *id.* at 1097–98, paras. 30–31 (separate opinion of Judge Owada).

addressed by the HCJ in either the *Beit Sourik* or *Mara'abe* cases).[458] He called the "silence" over the terrorist attacks on Israel "foreign and strange" before emotionally concluding, "I am sorry, but the decision of the ICJ cannot light my path. Its light is too dim for me to guide myself by it to law, truth and justice in the way a judge does."[459]

There is no doubt that Palestinian attacks against Israeli civilians (or civilians anywhere for that matter) contravene international humanitarian and human rights law as well as domestic criminal law. It would be both hypocritical and ultimately self-defeating for the Palestinian leadership to invoke international law in support of their claims to self-determination and statehood and then breach it by deliberately attacking civilians.[460] But for Israel to react by imprisoning an entire nation for the actions of a minority will not solve its security dilemma either. As Vaughan Lowe declared in his oral pleading before the ICJ on behalf of Palestine:

> The Palestinian Authority has consistently condemned terrorist attacks on Israeli civilians; and it is as absurd as it is offensive to imply that all Palestinians are engaged in a murderous conspiracy to attack Israel. To impose the Wall, and all the consequent restrictions on movement and access to property, jobs, welfare, education and families, as a punishment on the whole Palestinian population is unfair, unprincipled, and illegal.[461]

No one is questioning the legitimacy of a people's right to resist occupation, particularly if it is prolonged and protracted, but there are rules and boundaries that should not be crossed. In this respect, it is worth heeding the words of wisdom of Justice Albie Sachs from a very moving and thought-provoking lecture he gave on terrorism and the African National Congress's struggle against apartheid South Africa on 26 April 2006.[462] Simply put, terrorism, whether committed

---

458.   *See id.* at 1050, para. 141 (addressing the terrorist attacks on Israel). Interestingly, neither the *Beit Sourik* court nor the *Mara'abe* court addressed the question of Israeli attacks on Palestinians.

459.   HCJ 7957/04 Mara'abe v. Prime Minister of Isr. [2005] (Isr.), *translated in* 45 I.L.M. 202, 245, para. 4 (2006).

460.   *See* ICJ Wall Advisory Opinion, *supra* note 2, at 1035, para. 91 (ICJ acknowledging the P.L.O.'s request to unilaterally accede to the Geneva Conventions in 1982). *But see Application to Accede to the Geneva Convention*, 5 PALESTINE Y.B. INT'L L. 318, 319 (1989) (ICJ failing to mention that this effort to accede was opposed by both the United States and Israel).

461.   *See* Geneva Convention IV, *supra* note 20, art. 147 (prohibiting collective punishments under Article 147 of Geneva Convention IV and Article 75 of Additional Protocol I); Legal Consequence of Construction, ICJ Advisory Opinion, *supra* note 446, at 51, para. 23 (oral pleadings of Vaughan Lowe).

462.   Albie Sachs, Justice of the S. Afr. Constitutional Court, Talk at Logan Hall, Institute of Education: Tales of Terrorism: I Was Thirty-Nine Years Old and Quietly Teaching at Southampton University When I Discovered I Was a Terrorist (Apr. 26, 2006) (author attended). This talk was organized and sponsored by the Sir Joseph Hotung Programme in Law, Human Rights and Peace Building in the Middle East at

by states or non-state actors, is immoral, self-defeating, and ultimately harms the legitimacy of the cause in whose names such acts are undertaken.[463]

The HCJ in both *Beit Sourik* and *Mara'abe* looked at the legality of the wall from a very narrow perspective related to Israeli administrative law, military law, and proportionality as defined and determined by Israel.[464] The HCJ thus completely ignored crucial issues such as the legality of the vast settlement enterprise, possibly the biggest obstacle to peace in the Middle East, and the nature of a prolonged occupation which has approached its fourth decade (it is worth bearing in mind that most Palestinians currently living in the OPT, born after 1967, have never experienced freedom). The question of self-determination, which is integral to the Israel-Palestine conflict, was completely marginalized, and the role of the U.N., which has a continuing responsibility towards the Palestinian people until a permanent solution is found, was hardly considered by the HCJ apart from when it addressed the ICJ's Advisory Opinion and the reports of the U.N. Special Rapporteurs.[465] The ICJ could have addressed the question of self-defense and prolonged occupations in far more detail, as the law is not entirely clear in this area. Grappling with this issue, probably one of the most controversial areas in international law, may have given the opinion more credibility. The ICJ could have also provided more of an analysis as to why the construction of the

---

the School of Oriental and African Studies, University of London. Sachs was severely injured in a terrorist attack (a bomb was placed under his car) and carried out by a secret agent working for the apartheid government in the late 1980s.

463.   *See* EQBAL AHMAD, *PLO and ANC: Painful Contrasts*, *in* THE SELECTED WRITINGS OF EQBAL AHMAD 76 (Carollee Bengelsdorf, Margaret Cerullo, & Yogesh Chandrani eds., 2006) (discussing the difference in tactics between the PLO and the ANC).

464.   HCJ 2056/04 Beit Sourik Village Council v. Israel [2004] (Isr.), *translated in* 43 I.L.M. 1099 (2004); HCJ 7957/04 Mara'abe v. Prime Minister of Isr. [2005] (Isr.), *translated in* 45 I.L.M. 202, ¶ 14 (2006).

465.   Having said this, the ICJ's cursory treatment of Palestinian self-determination was dealt with in a similar fashion in the East Timor and Western Sahara cases. For instance, in its decision on East Timor, the ICJ merely repeated the relevant U.N. resolutions recognising that the East Timorese have a right of self-determination. It did not actually elaborate on the norm in much detail in the context of the specific circumstances in East Timor. Instead, it simply discussed the issue in a very general manner. *See* Case Concerning East Timor (Port. v. Austl.), 1995 I.C.J. 90 (June 30) (failing to, as Judge Weeramantry noted in his dissent, "examine such seminal issues as the duties flowing to Australia from the right to self-determination of the people of East Timor or from their right to permanent sovereignty over their natural resources"). The fact is that the ICJ could probably have spent more time examining the issue since Australia's objections as to the admissibility of Portugal's application "were inextricably linked to the merits and should therefore be determined within the framework of the merits." *Id.* at 98, para. 19. For commentaries on East Timor, see generally Iain G.M. Scobbie & Catriona Drew, *Self-determination Undetermined: The Case of East Timor*, 9 LEIDEN J. INT'L L. 185 (1996); and Drew, *supra* note 204.

wall along its current route is unreasonable, justifying its decisions by legal argument.

Although Israel has said that it will not abide by the ICJ's Advisory Opinion (nor for that matter most of the U.N. resolutions adopted during the course of the conflict), the Palestinians have embraced it, including the Hamas and Fatah hardliners in the so-called "prisoners document."[466]　This must surely be a positive development.　Rather than acting unilaterally and aggressively, the Palestinians have attempted to solve their international dispute with Israel peacefully, through non-violent means.[467]　Whether Israel will reciprocate is another matter.　In challenging the authority of the ICJ in reaching a decision that blatantly ignores the settlement issue and by sidelining the Geneva Conventions yet again, it is difficult to see how it can be said that the HCJ is acting independently from the Israeli government when it comes to policy in the OPT.　The questions of self-defense, the wall, and the settlements would have been better discussed in the paradigm of self-determination had more attention been paid to this issue as one of the "legal consequences of the construction of the wall in the Occupied Palestinian Territory," as ultimately this conflict is about much more than just wire and concrete.[468]　It is apparent that the ICJ did itself no favors in refraining from elaborating upon why it found Israel's self-defense arguments based on Article 51 of the Charter irrelevant to the matter at hand; this has given ample ammunition to those persons who are not inclined in favor of international law to attack the court.[469] Having said this, the ICJ was able to produce a concise and coherent

---

466.　*See Full text: The Palestinian Two-State Blueprint*, TIMES ONLINE, May 25, 2006, para. 18, http://www.timesonline.co.uk/article/0251-2196956.html.

> To work on expanding the role and presence of the international solidarity committees and the peace loving groups that support our people in their just struggle against the occupation, settlements, the apartheid Wall politically and locally and to work towards the implementation of the International Court of Justice decision at The Hague pertaining to the removal of the Wall and settlements and their illegitimate presence.

Id.

467.　Recourse to conciliatory methods of dispute resolution is something the Palestinians have tried before. In 1947, they lobbied Egypt and Syria to muster support in the General Assembly to petition the ICJ for an Advisory Opinion which ultimately failed. *See* U.N. Ad Hoc Committee on the Palestinian Question, 32d Sess., U.N. Doc. A/AC.14/SR.32 (Nov. 25, 1947) (*prepared by* Thor Thors).

468.　*See generally* Pertile, *supra* note 2 (discussing the legal consequences of constructing the wall).

469.　*See, e.g.*, Charles Krauthammer, *Travesty at The Hague*, WASH. POST, July 16, 2004, at A21 (describing the ICJ as a "kangaroo court"); Alan Dershowitz, *Israel Follows Its Own Law, Not Bigoted Hague Decision*, JERUSALEM POST, July 11, 2004, at 1 (reporting an unfavorable view of the ICJ as of "questionable status" and deserving of no deference from Israel).

opinion in a relatively short period of time that could provide a framework for negotiations between Israelis and Palestinians when a more enlightened leadership is in a position to assert itself.

VIII. APPENDIX[470]
MAP 1

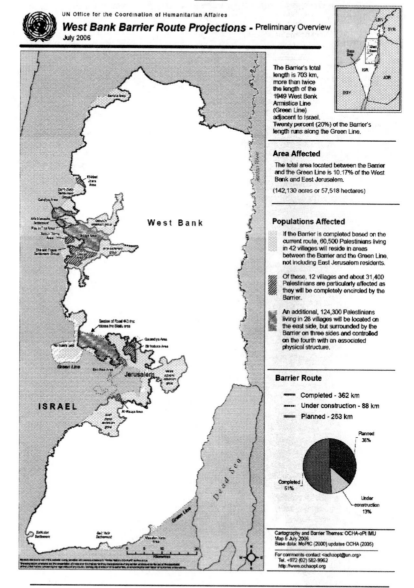

470.   All maps obtained from the Office for the Coordination of Humanitarian Affairs, Occupied Palestinian Territory, Map Center, http://www.ochaopt.org/.

MAP 2

Fragmentation of the West Bank

Israeli settlements, roads primarily for settler use, closed military zones and other measures fragment the West Bank. Checkpoints, underpasses and permits regulate much of Palestinian movement.

MAP 3

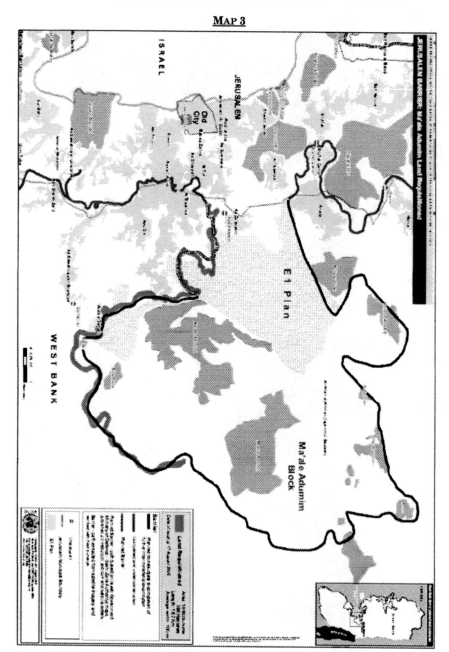

MAP 4

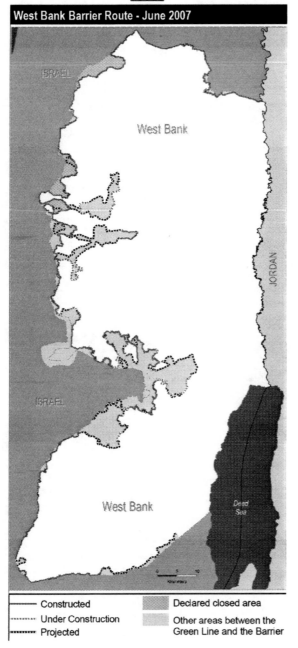

West Bank Barrier Route - June 2007

Part X

PALESTINIAN–ISRAELI NEGOTIATIONS

THE YALE JOURNAL
OF INTERNATIONAL LAW

Shadow or Shade?
The Roles of International Law in
Palestinian-Israeli Peace Talks

by
Omar M. Dajani

32 YALE J. INT'L L. 61

WINTER 2007   VOLUME 32, NUMBER 1

Article

Shadow or Shade? The Roles of International Law in Palestinian-Israeli Peace Talks

Omar M. Dajani[†]

        † Assistant Professor of Law, University of the Pacific, McGeorge School of Law. J.D.,
Yale Law School, 1997; B.A., Northwestern University, 1991. As a political adviser to United Nations
Middle East envoy Terje Roed-Larson from 2001 to 2003, the author was involved in developing the
"Roadmap" peace initiative. Prior to joining the United Nations, he served as legal adviser to the
Palestinian negotiating team in peace talks with Israel. In that capacity, he participated in negotiations of
borders, security, and economic issues, including summits at Camp David and Taba.
        This Article is dedicated, in loving memory, to Ninon Sakr Dajani (1933-2006). The author
gratefully acknowledges the thoughtful comments on earlier drafts offered by George Bisharat, Ron
Dudai, Stephanie Koury, Brian Landsberg, Stephen McCaffrey, John Murray, and participants in
workshops conducted by Pacific McGeorge and the Sir James Hotung Programme at the University of
London's School of Oriental and African Studies. He also acknowledges, with appreciation, the
excellent research assistance provided by John Adams, Judeh Bahnan, Chad Couchot, Alec Gibbs,
Matthew Koski, Kendra Pavkovic, Eric Ritigstein, Andrew Schouten, and Lauren Tipton. He
emphasizes that responsibility for errors and omissions is his alone. Finally, the author is grateful to the
Palestine Liberation Organization's Negotiations Affairs Department and Negotiations Support Unit for
facilitating his access to unpublished materials from the Palestinian-Israeli peace talks.

62 THE YALE JOURNAL OF INTERNATIONAL LAW [Vol. 32: 61

> With what faith
> Can stars
> Sparkle?
> And naked trees
> Cast shade?[1]

I. INTRODUCTION

Pacta sunt servanda, the cardinal rule of international law, prohibits the breaking of agreements. But what role should international law play in the making of agreements? In *How Nations Behave*, Louis Henkin challenges lawyers "to think beyond the substantive rules of law to the function of law, to the nature of its influence, the opportunities it offers, the limitations it imposes—as well as to understand the limits of its influence in a society of sovereign nations."[2] In that spirit, international law scholars have redoubled efforts during the last decade to measure the influence of law on international politics, drawing on theoretical and methodological frameworks developed by political scientists.[3] Relatively little attention, however, has been directed to explaining how law functions in international peace negotiations,[4] in part, perhaps, because it is difficult to find satisfying answers to this question within the framework of a single discipline. While contract and negotiation theorists have examined how parties make use of, and are constrained by, legal rules when engaged in private ordering, their analysis has tended not to address the peculiarities of the international setting—in particular, the relative indeterminacy of international legal norms and the relative unavailability of recourse to third-party adjudication and enforcement. Conversely, because studies by international law and international relations scholars have tended to focus on compliance with multilateral treaty regimes and adjudications by international tribunals, they overlook the unique roles that law plays in the context of international bargaining.

---

1. Muhammad al-As'ad, *The Earth Also Dies*, in ANTHOLOGY OF MODERN PALESTINIAN LITERATURE 123 (Salma Khadra Jayyusi ed., May Jayyusi & Jack Collom trans., 1992).
2. LOUIS HENKIN, HOW NATIONS BEHAVE 4-5 (2d ed. 1979).
3. For a survey of recent work in this area, see MARKUS BURGSTALLER, THEORIES OF COMPLIANCE WITH INTERNATIONAL LAW (2005); Anthony Clark Arend, *Do Legal Rules Matter? International Law and International Politics*, 38 VA. J. INT'L L. 107 (1998); Oona A. Hathaway, *Do Human Rights Treaties Make a Difference?*, 111 YALE L.J. 1935 (2002); Harold Hongju Koh, *Why Do Nations Obey International Law?*, 106 YALE L.J. 2599 (1997); Anne-Marie Slaughter, *International Law and International Relations Theory: A New Generation of Interdisciplinary Scholarship*, 92 AM. J. INT'L L. 367 (1998).
4. A notable exception is Joaquin Tacsan's study of the Central American peace process in the 1980s. *See generally* JOAQUIN TACSAN, THE DYNAMICS OF INTERNATIONAL LAW IN CONFLICT RESOLUTION (1992).

The nature of these roles is of more than academic concern. When Palestinian and Israeli officials undertook from late 1999 to early 2001 to negotiate a "permanent status"[5] agreement in an effort to bring their century-long conflict to an end, they expressed sharply differing views not only about their respective rights and obligations under international law, but also, more fundamentally, about the relevance of international legal norms to the bilateral negotiation process in which they were engaged. Although their failure, ultimately, to conclude a peace agreement is undoubtedly attributable to a variety of factors, I submit that their differences regarding the role of international law in the peace talks form an important, and as yet insufficiently documented, part of the picture. Understanding the nature and consequences of those differences is valuable for the contribution it offers not only to research on the influence of law on international politics, but also, more importantly, to efforts to ensure that when Palestinians and Israelis eventually return to the negotiating table they have more success.

To be sure, the Palestinian-Israeli conflict and peace process are the focus of a voluminous body of academic literature. Political accounts of the peace talks have proliferated since the suspension of negotiations in January 2001.[6] In addition, legal scholars and advocates have explored in some depth both the substantive legal issues implicated by the underlying conflict and an array of process questions presented by the talks.[7] What continues to be

---

5.   In 1993 Palestinians and Israelis agreed to establish interim self-government arrangements for the Palestinian population in the West Bank and Gaza Strip and to commence "negotiations on the permanent status" of the Palestinian territories following a transitional period of five years. Declaration of Principles on Interim Self-Government Arrangements between Israel and the Palestine Liberation Organization, art. 1 (Sept. 13, 1993), *in* 2 DOCUMENTS ON THE ARAB-ISRAELI CONFLICT: THE PALESTINIANS AND THE ISRAELI-PALESTINIAN PEACE PROCESS 890, 890 (M. Cherif Bassiouni ed., 2005) [hereinafter 2 DOCUMENTS ON THE ARAB-ISRAELI CONFLICT].

6.   *See, e.g.*, SHLOMO BEN-AMI, SCARS OF WAR, WOUNDS OF PEACE: THE ISRAELI-ARAB TRAGEDY (2005); CHARLES ENDERLIN, SHATTERED DREAMS: THE FAILURE OF THE PEACE PROCESS IN THE MIDDLE EAST, 1995-2002 (Susan Fairfield trans., Other Press 2003); WILLIAM B. QUANDT, PEACE PROCESS: AMERICAN DIPLOMACY AND THE ARAB-ISRAELI CONFLICT SINCE 1967 (rev. ed. 2001); DENNIS ROSS, THE MISSING PEACE: THE INSIDE STORY OF THE FIGHT FOR MIDDLE EAST PEACE (2004); CLAYTON E. SWISHER, THE TRUTH ABOUT CAMP DAVID: THE UNTOLD STORY ABOUT THE COLLAPSE OF THE MIDDLE EAST PEACE PROCESS (2004); Hussein Agha & Robert Malley, *Camp David: The Tragedy of Errors*, NEW YORK REVIEW OF BOOKS, Aug. 9, 2001, at 59.

7.   Recent contributions to this literature include: JOHN QUIGLEY, THE CASE FOR PALESTINE: AN INTERNATIONAL LAW PERSPECTIVE (2d ed. 2005); GEOFFREY R. WATSON, THE OSLO ACCORDS: INTERNATIONAL LAW AND THE ISRAELI-PALESTINIAN PEACE AGREEMENTS (2000); Susan M. Akram & Terry Rempel, *Temporary Protection as an Instrument for Implementing the Right of Return for Palestinian Refugees*, 22 B.U. INT'L L.J. 1 (2004); Roy Balleste, *The International Status of Jerusalem: The Legacy of Lasting Peace*, 43 REV. DER. P.R. 249 (2004); Kathleen A. Cavanaugh, *Selective Justice: The Case of Israel and the Occupied Territories*, 26 FORDHAM INT'L L.J. 934 (2003); Dr. Fadia Daibes, *A Progressive Multidisciplinary Approach for Resolving the Palestinian-Israel Conflict Over the Shared Transboundary Groundwater: What Lessons Learned From International Law?*, 8 U. DENV. WATER L. REV. 93 (2004); Allison Beth Hodgkins, *Beyond Two-States: Alternative Visions of Self-Determination for the People of Palestine*, 28 FLETCHER F. WORLD AFF. 109 (2004); Ardi Imseis, *On the Fourth Geneva Convention and the Occupied Palestinian Territory*, 44 HARV. INT'L L.J. 65 (2003); Orde F. Kittrie, *More Process Than Peace: Legitimacy, Compliance, and the Oslo Accords*, 101 MICH. L. REV. 1661 (2003) (reviewing THE ISRAELI-PALESTINIAN PEACE PROCESS: OSLO AND THE LESSONS OF FAILURE—PERSPECTIVES, PREDICAMENTS, AND PROSPECTS (Robert L. Rothstein, Moshe Ma'oz & Khalil Shikaki eds. 2002) and MICHAEL WATKINS & SUSAN ROSEGRANT, BREAKTHROUGH INTERNATIONAL NEGOTIATION: HOW GREAT NEGOTIATORS TRANSFORMED THE WORLD'S TOUGHEST POST-COLD WAR CONFLICTS (2001)); Russell Korobkin & Jonathan Zasloff, *Roadblocks to the Road Map: A Negotiation Theory Perspective on the Israeli-Palestinian Conflict After Yasser Arafat*, 30 YALE J. INT'L L. 1 (2005);

missing from the discussion, however, is both a theoretical framework for explaining the functions of law in international peace negotiations and a detailed retrospective analysis of the functions international law actually served—and failed to serve—in Palestinian-Israeli peace talks.[8]

This Article is intended to help fill both of these gaps. Part II of the Article introduces a theoretical framework for analyzing the functions of law in international bargaining. I begin by revisiting the critical insight, offered by Robert Mnookin and Lewis Kornhauser in their influential 1979 article, that parties bargain "in the shadow of the law."[9] As they explain, "the outcome that the law will impose if no agreement is reached gives each [party] certain bargaining chips" in negotiations, even if the parties choose to order their relations in a manner that departs from the outcome that law would otherwise prescribe.[10] Drawing on more recent scholarship by contract and negotiation theorists, I examine how legal rules function to promote efficiency and fairness by narrowing the scope of bargaining, framing trade-offs, providing objective standards for evaluating competing claims, and filling in gaps in an agreement.

I then turn to exploring how these functions translate to the international setting. As I describe, "the shadow of the law"—the influence law exerts on bargaining as a result of the possible imposition of a legal remedy if negotiations fail—is diminished at the international level, where norms are often under-developed and the adjudication and enforcement of legal rights tends to be a remote prospect at best. I argue, however, that the "shadow" metaphor fails to capture an important function of law in international bargaining. As a growing body of international law and international relations literature suggests, the influence of legal rules does not turn solely on the

---

Randolph "Michael" Nacol II, *Negotiating on Un-Holy Land: The Road from Israel to Palestine*, 4 PEPP. DISP. RESOL. L.J. 87 (2003); Jonathan W. Reitman, *Ten Principles to Aid the Quest for Peace in the Middle East*, DISP. RESOL. J., Feb./Apr. 2002, at 50; Lewis Saideman, *Do Palestinian Refugees Have a Right of Return to Israel? An Examination of the Scope of and Limitations on the Right of Return*, 44 VA. J. INT'L L. 829 (2004).

8. There is no lack of interest in the topic. In 1999, Case Western Reserve University School of Law convened a discontinuous symposium entitled "The Legal Foundations of Peace and Prosperity in the Middle East," contributions to which were subsequently published by the Case Western Reserve Journal of International Law. *See, e.g.*, John Quigley, *The Role of Law in a Palestinian-Israeli Accommodation*, 31 CASE W. RES. J. INT'L L. 351 (1999); Shimon Shetreet, *Negotiations and Agreements Are Better Than Legal Resolutions: A Response to Professor John Quigley*, 32 CASE W. RES. J. INT'L L. 259 (2000). Because the symposium took place prior to the resumption of permanent status negotiations in September 1999, however, the participants were unable to offer analysis of the negotiations themselves. More recently, the role of the law in resolving the Palestinian-Israeli conflict was the topic of a symposium sponsored by the Toda Institute for Global Peace and Policy Research, contributions to which were published by the Hastings International and Comparative Law Review. *See* George E. Bisharat, *Facts, Rights, and Remedies: Implementing International Law in the Israel/Palestine Conflict*, 28 HASTINGS INT'L & COMP. L. REV. 319 (2005). This was also the topic of a panel during the 2005 annual conference of the American Society of International Law. *See* Georges Abi Saab, Remarks, *Is There a Role for International Law in the Middle East Peace Process?*, in 99 AM. SOC'Y INT'L L. PROC. 215 (2005). Although participants in both events offered important insights, they did not undertake either to define a theoretical framework for analyzing how law functions in international bargaining processes or to examine in detail how it functioned in Palestinian-Israeli peace talks.

9. Robert H. Mnookin & Lewis Kornhauser, *Bargaining in the Shadow of the Law: The Case of Divorce*, 88 YALE L.J. 950, 950 (1979).

10. *Id.* at 968.

possibility of third-party enforcement; international law's influence also derives from the normative force of the ideas it embodies and its capacity to legitimize negotiated outcomes in the eyes of other international actors and domestic constituencies. In this respect, I submit, international law may influence the process and outcome of peace negotiations not only as a result of the shadow it casts, but also as a result of the shade it offers—i.e., the attributes of legal rules that *pull* parties to align a negotiated outcome with them, even when their ultimate enforcement is unlikely.

Applying this framework, I then turn, in Part III, to describing how law functioned—and failed to function—during Palestinian-Israeli permanent status negotiations. My analysis draws not only on published first- and third-party accounts of the negotiations, but also on unpublished draft texts, memoranda, and minutes prepared by and for the Palestinian negotiating team during the talks.[11]

In Part IV, I assess the factors that constrained the functioning of legal rules in Palestinian-Israeli peace talks, analyzing the consequences of the parties' disagreements about the applicability and determinacy of legal rules and about the efficacy of the outcomes they were claimed to prescribe, as well as the lack of recourse to external adjudication and enforcement. I conclude by suggesting steps that may be taken by the parties and the international community to address these factors. Ultimately, I argue neither that international law provides answers to all of the questions presented by the Palestinian-Israeli conflict, nor that it offers no answers at all. Instead, I submit that by understanding how law functions in international negotiations, and its limitations in that context, it is possible to use law more effectively to advance the cause of peacemaking—both as a tool for efficient resolution of disputed issues and as a means of promoting compliance with international standards of fairness.

II.   THE FUNCTIONS OF LAW IN INTERNATIONAL PEACE NEGOTIATIONS: AN INTERDISCIPLINARY THEORETICAL FRAMEWORK

How do international legal norms influence peace negotiations? What functions can and should law serve in that setting? To answer these questions, this Part introduces a new theoretical framework, synthesizing efforts by contract and negotiation theorists to describe how law functions in the context of private ordering and studies by international law and international relations

---

11.   As legal adviser to the Palestinian negotiating team from September 1999 to June 2001, I was involved in the preparation of some of these documents, and I was subsequently given access to other Palestinian records during my research on this project. Most of the materials I used were drawn from the electronic files of the Negotiations Support Unit (NSU) of the Negotiations Affairs Department. Having worked at the NSU during the period I describe in this Article, I am able to confirm the authenticity of the documents cited. Because the files are electronic and are not uniformly write-protected, however, it is possible (though unlikely) that minor alterations were made to them in the years since they were first prepared.

Although I have drawn upon published accounts by Israeli and American officials involved in the negotiations, I did not seek access to Israeli or United States government records. It is my hope that a fuller analysis of law's roles in the talks will be possible when these records enter the public domain.

scholars regarding the factors influencing compliance with legal rules[12] at the international level.

A.   *The Functions of Legal Rules in Private Ordering*

Law is not, of course, the only factor that shapes the preferences and positions of participants in a bargaining process. Often, it is not even a primary factor: Summarizing a series of empirical studies of contracting behavior, Jay Feinman observes that, "when 'contracting,' people do not usually consciously shape their conduct to conform to the requirements of the law or to achieve certain legal effects; . . . often [parties] are unlikely to know of the content of the law or of the legal consequences of their actions."[13] Indeed, many factors, other than legal rights and obligations, have been found to influence bargaining behavior, including the economic costs and benefits of reaching agreement[14] and of continuing to negotiate;[15] interests in maintaining an ongoing relationship with the other party; [16] social norms; [17] cultural difference;[18] power disparities;[19] even spite or distrust.[20]

To acknowledge that legal rules are not the only—or even the primary— determinant of negotiated outcomes is not to suggest that they lack effect entirely. But how does law influence negotiations? In their article, *Bargaining in the Shadow of the Law: The Case of Divorce*, Robert Mnookin and Lewis Kornhauser examined how the formal legal system affects dispute settlement outside of court in the context of divorce settlement negotiations. As Professor Mnookin later explained, their "core idea is encapsulated by the 'shadow' metaphor: expectations about what might happen in court affect resolutions negotiated outside of court. The law's shadow is cast by legal rules and procedures, as well as by other institutional features of the formal legal

---

12.   In this Article, I use the terms "legal norms" and "legal rules" interchangeably, as is the convention in American international law literature. I do not treat them as the terms of art they represent in regime theory literature. *See, e.g.*, ROBERT KEOHANE, AFTER HEGEMONY: COOPERATION AND DISCORD IN THE WORLD POLITICAL ECONOMY 57 (1984) (defining "norms" as "standards of behavior defined in terms of rights and obligations," and "rules" as "specific prescriptions or proscriptions for action").

13.   Jay M. Feinman, *The Significance of Contract Theory*, 58 U. CIN. L. REV. 1283, 1305-06 (1990).

14.   Such analysis is the stock and trade of Law and Economics scholars. For a recent treatment, see generally Russell Korobkin, *A Positive Theory of Legal Negotiation*, 88 GEO. L.J. 1789 (2000) (proposing a framework for analyzing negotiation processes based on economic choices parties face at each stage of bargaining).

15.   *See* Mnookin & Kornhauser, *supra* note 9, at 971-72.

16.   *See, e.g.*, Ian Macneil, THE NEW SOCIAL CONTRACT (1980) (describing non-legal mechanisms employed by parties to enforce obligations in ongoing relationships involving repeat transactions).

17.   *See* Herbert Jacob, *The Elusive Shadow of the Law*, 26 LAW & SOC'Y REV. 565, 566-72 (1992).

18.   *See generally* RAYMOND COHEN, NEGOTIATING ACROSS CULTURES: INTERNATIONAL COMMUNICATION IN AN INTERDEPENDENT WORLD (1992) (examining the effect of cultural difference on negotiating styles).

19.   *See generally* Richard H. Steinberg, *In the Shadow of Law or Power? Consensus-Based Bargaining and Outcomes in the GATT/WTO*, 56 INT'L ORG. 339 (2002) (reflecting on the differences between law-based and power-based bargaining in GATT and WTO legislative forums).

20.   *See* Jack Hirshleifer & Evan Osborne, *Truth, Effort, and the Legal Battle*, in THE DARK SIDE OF THE FORCE: ECONOMIC FOUNDATIONS OF CONFLICT THEORY 131, 133 (Jack Hirshleifer ed., 2001); Mnookin & Kornhauser, *supra* note 9, at 974-75.

system."[21] Drawing on sociological data, Mnookin and Kornhauser found that parties' negotiating behavior is influenced by "the bargaining endowments created by legal rules that indicate the particular allocation a court will impose if the parties fail to reach agreement."[22] While parties may choose to conclude an agreement that departs from the allocation of rights and obligations that the law would prescribe if they litigated instead of negotiating, the anticipated results of that potential litigation give parties "bargaining chips"[23] that shape their preferences and positions. The value of these bargaining chips is affected by "the degree of uncertainty concerning the legal outcome if the parties go to court" and "the parties' attitudes towards risk."[24] Thus, because legal rules "cast a shadow" over negotiations to the extent that they are likely to be imposed by a court if negotiations fail, the length of their shadow derives from the probability of such enforcement, which, in turn, depends on the determinacy of the rules in question and the costs of seeking enforcement.

Mnookin and Kornhauser acknowledged that legal rules also serve other functions in the bargaining process—determining, for example, who is entitled to participate and the form an agreement must take[25] and defining minimum standards with which an agreement must conform.[26] They argued, however, that "the primary purpose of the legal . . . system should be to provide a framework for private ordering."[27] "After all," they asked, "who can better evaluate the comparative advantages of alternative arrangements than the parties themselves?"[28]

Law's role in facilitating and constraining private ordering by bargaining parties has been further elaborated in more recent studies by contract and negotiation scholars. In one recent article, Russell Korobkin offers a framework and vocabulary for analyzing bargaining processes that are particularly useful for understanding the functions of law. He suggests that negotiations comprise two distinct (though at times sequentially overlapping) phases: "zone definition" and "surplus allocation."[29] During the former, negotiating parties undertake to identify the substantive "bargaining zone" within which a deal is possible—i.e., "the distance between the reservation points (or 'walkaway' points) of the two parties."[30] To put it in simple commercial terms, if the highest price one party is willing to pay is lower than the lowest price at which the other party is willing to sell, the parties lack a bargaining zone, and they both will prefer to walk away from the deal. On the other hand, if the parties' bargaining zone comprises a number of different potential "deal points," they then engage in a process of allocating the

---

21.   Fred R. Shapiro, *The Most Cited Articles from the Yale Law Journal*, 100 YALE L.J. 1449, 1494 (1991) (quoting commentary by Prof. Mnookin).

22.   Mnookin & Kornhauser, *supra* note 9, at 966.

23.   *Id.* at 968.

24.   *Id.* at 966.

25.   *See id.* at 951.

26.   *See id.* at 955, 957.

27.   Shapiro, *supra* note 21, at 1494 (quoting commentary by Prof. Mnookin).

28.   Mnookin & Kornhauser, *supra* note 9, at 957.

29.   Korobkin, *supra* note 14, at 1791-92.

30.   *Id.*

economic "surplus," undertaking to persuade each other of the merits of their respective preferred outcomes.[31]

Legal rules may influence the parties' attempts both to determine whether they share a bargaining zone ("zone definition") and to persuade each other of the merits of their respective preferred outcomes within that zone ("surplus allocation"). Legal rules contribute to zone definition insofar as each party's reservation point is determined by the party's "best alternative to a negotiated agreement" (BATNA),[32] because the BATNA is shaped, in part, by the perceived availability, costs and contours of a legal remedy.[33] In other words, a party will walk away from a deal that is more costly to her than the result that the law is likely to provide if no deal is reached. This kind of influence is essentially the "shadow of the law" that Mnookin and Kornhauser described.[34]

Legal rules, like other "community norms of either procedural or substantive fairness," may also be invoked by the parties during the process of surplus allocation as part of their effort to persuade their counterpart of the virtues of a specific negotiated outcome.[35] Two characteristics of legal rules make them well suited to serve this function. First, because legal rules often are based on majority practices,[36] they provide bargaining parties with an indication of *best practices* in similar circumstances and, accordingly, a standard on which to base arguments for or against various potential deal points within their bargaining zone.[37] Second, because legal rules are defined "independent of each side's will," they provide an *objective* basis for evaluating the merits of various proposed deal points.[38] Both of these characteristics of legal rules make them potentially powerful tools for persuading an adversary of the virtues of a particular deal.

In addition to influencing what the parties choose to put into an agreement, legal rules may influence what they omit from it. As Allan Farnsworth explains, "It has become common in English to refer to [certain] rules as *default* rules, by analogy to the default settings on a computer, since they are subject to contrary agreement but apply by default absent such agreement."[39] Because parties to an agreement cannot foresee every contingency that may arise (and may find it excessively costly to negotiate in

---

31.　*Id.*

32.　The expression was coined by Roger Fisher and William Ury. *See* ROGER FISHER ET AL., GETTING TO YES: NEGOTIATING AGREEMENT WITHOUT GIVING IN 97-106 (2d ed. 1991).

33.　*See* Korobkin, *supra* note 14, at 1800-01.

34.　*See* Mnookin and Kornhauser, *supra* note 9.

35.　Korobkin, *supra* note 14, at 1792.

36.　*See* Randy E. Barnett, *The Sound of Silence: Default Rules and Contractual Consent*, 78 VA. L. REV. 821, 821-26 (1992).

37.　*See* Tamar Frankel, *Trusting and Non-Trusting on the Internet*, 81 B.U. L. REV. 457, 476 (2001) (discussing how contract law may have to adapt specifically for internet business and use default rules that follow fiduciary law to reflect the best practices of industries conducting business on the internet); Cass R. Sunstein, *Symposium: Switching the Default Rule*, 77 N.Y.U. L. REV. 106, 117 (2002) (discussing the benefits of having default rules that reflect best practices in the employment context).

38.　*See* FISHER ET AL., *supra* note 32, at 85.

39.　ALLAN FARNSWORTH, CONTRACTS § 1.10, at 36 (3d ed. 1999). Examples of default rules in the domestic context include the rule in many states providing for maternal custody of the children in the event of divorce and the rule, under the Uniform Commercial Code, that an offeree respond to an offer within a reasonable time.

advance how to address even those they do foresee), all agreements are to some extent incomplete; and default rules provide some indication of how a court will fill in the gaps.[40] Accordingly, parties may decide as much by failing to—or choosing not to—address a particular issue in an agreement as by addressing it, at least insofar as legal rules are available to serve as gap-fillers and recourse is available to a forum capable of interpreting the agreement and the relevant law.

All three of the functions of legal rules described above—facilitating zone definition by helping each party to determine its BATNA, providing a persuasive standard for surplus allocation, and filling in gaps in the parties' agreement—are based on an essentially instrumental view of the law. Legal rules, in this conception, are relevant only to the extent that they are useful to the parties. What is at issue here is efficiency: even though legal rules may be designed to provide for an outcome that is fair or sensible, their value in the bargaining process derives not from their fairness or good sense but, instead, from their potential to reduce transaction costs—either by helping parties to predict the outcome of litigation or by providing ready, tested solutions to issues on the table, making it unnecessary for the parties to incur the costs of negotiating solutions to them. Insofar as law exists to facilitate private ordering, parties are free to agree to terms in accordance with legal rules or to terms that depart from them, if they so prefer. The assumption in both cases is that the parties themselves are in the best position to determine how to allocate costs and benefits between them.

What this emphasis on facilitating efficient private ordering overlooks, however, is the normative function of law. Contracts theorists recognize a distinction between "default" rules and "mandatory" rules[41] (sometimes called "immutable" rules).[42] Unlike default rules, mandatory rules may not be varied or waived by negotiating parties, even if both would choose to do so. Because the law of contracts is a system generally designed to permit, even encourage, parties to order their legal relations according to their own perceived interests and priorities, mandatory rules are rare.[43] Their primary purpose is not, like default rules, to facilitate efficient choices by bargaining parties. Instead, they operate forcibly to inject standards of procedural or substantive fairness into the bargaining process. According to Ian Ayres, these constraints may be "justified either by 'externalities' or 'paternalism' in that lawmakers might make rules mandatory to protect people not in contractual privity (e.g., as in the mandatory prohibition of criminal conspiracies) or to protect people who are parties to the contract itself (e.g., as in the mandatory prohibition against

---

40. *See* Barnett, *supra* note 36, at 821-26.

41. The term "mandatory rules" has a more specialized definition in the conflict of laws context than the one applied here. *See* Mohammad Reza Baniassadi, *Do Mandatory Rules of Public Law Limit Choice of Law in International Commercial Arbitration?*, 10 INT'L TAX & BUS. LAW. 59, 62-63 (1992).

42. *See* Ian Ayres & Robert Gertner, *Filling Gaps in Incomplete Contracts: An Economic Theory of Default Rules*, 99 YALE L.J. 87, 88 (1989).

43. *See* FARNSWORTH, *supra* note 39, § 1.10, at 36. Examples of mandatory rules in the domestic context include the implied obligation of good faith and the warranty of habitability.

contracting with infants)." [44] Thus, whereas default rules are concerned primarily with efficiency, mandatory rules are concerned primarily with fairness. Whereas default rules inform parties' choices about where the soft borders of their bargaining zone should be, mandatory rules comprise the hard borders of what may be called the "zone of lawfulness." Deal points outside that zone, while potentially acceptable to both parties, are not sanctioned by law.

It is consequently the case that the existence of mandatory rules forecloses certain deals that parties may otherwise have found it in their common interest to reach. Indeed, as Ayres observes, the enforcement of mandatory rules may serve in individual cases to leave the very parties the rules are intended to protect worse off, depriving them of the benefits that even a poor deal would offer. [45] As described in the next Section, this tension between the desire to promote adherence to legal rules that represent collective standards of fairness, on the one hand, and the desire to support any deal that will bring a dispute to an end, on the other, has been particularly acute in peacemaking efforts.

Taking this body of theory as a whole, legal norms serve one or more of the following functions in a bargaining process. Norms considered mandatory rules define a zone of lawfulness for negotiations, i.e., standards of procedural and substantive fairness that the parties may not lawfully contravene, even if they would prefer to do so. Norms not considered mandatory rules—i.e., default rules—may in turn serve several functions. First, they may help parties to define their bargaining zone; depending on their determinacy, these rules allow parties to anticipate the contours of a legal remedy should negotiations fail, facilitating definition of their respective BATNAs and, accordingly, their reservation points. Second, these norms may contribute to efficient surplus allocation by providing the parties with objective standards for choosing among potential deals. And, third, they may help a court to fill in gaps that the parties intentionally or unintentionally failed to resolve.

B. *International Bargaining: Analogies and Contrasts*

Does law play the same roles in public international negotiations that it plays in private ordering at the domestic level? The analogy between the two contexts, while inexact, is not incidental. In 1946, Hans Morgenthau observed (with some dismay) that "[t]he application of domestic legal experience to international law is really the main stock in trade of modern international thought." [46] And, indeed, when the drafters of the Vienna Convention on the Law of Treaties (hereinafter "Vienna Convention") undertook to codify customary international norms governing the making and breaking of

---

44.   Ian Ayres, *Empire or Residue: Competing Visions of the Contractual Canon*, 26 FLA. ST. U. L. REV. 897, 901 (1999).

45.   Ayres notes, for example, that the "mandatory prohibition against usurious interest rates might limit the ability of high-risk consumers to borrow money or might induce sellers with bargaining power to extract their profits in a less efficient manner." *Id.* at 901-02.

46.   HANS MORGENTHAU, SCIENTIFIC MAN VS. POWER POLITICS 113 (1946). As discussed further below, the conviction that the analogy between the domestic and international order is false lies at the center of the political philosophy articulated by Morgenthau and other Realists.

agreements between states, they drew substantially upon general principles of domestic contract law.[47] Accordingly, like a domestic contract, a treaty is voidable if conceived through fraud[48] or mistake,[49] and void if consent to it is procured through coercion.[50]

Although each of the functions served by legal rules in domestic bargaining have analogues in public international negotiations, the aptness of the analogy has been challenged. Skeptics ask how law can cast a shadow over negotiations when its content is unclear and its enforcement is unlikely. This Section examines both the analogies and the differences between law's roles in domestic and international bargaining. I conclude by arguing that the function of law in international negotiations is not confined to "casting a shadow" over talks—i.e., its influence is not simply a function of the legal sanction that will follow if no deal is reached. Drawing on recent international law and international relations scholarship, I suggest that law's influence is also a consequence of the *shade* it offers. By this I mean the attributes of legal rules that pull parties to reach an agreement in conformity with them even when enforcement is unlikely.

1. *Analogies*

Analogies may be drawn between each of the functions legal rules serve in the domestic setting and their roles in public international bargaining.

As in the domestic setting, mandatory rules of international law are rare. Under the Vienna Convention, a treaty is unenforceable if it conflicts with a peremptory norm of international law, which is defined as "a norm accepted and recognized by the international community of States as a whole as a norm from which no derogation is permitted . . . ."[51] Thus, an international agreement may not contravene certain legal rules—rules embodying the international community's most fundamental notions of fairness—even if both parties to the agreement would otherwise consent to do so.[52] In theory at least, jus cogens norms therefore represent the mandatory rules of international

---

47.   *See* A. Mark Weisburd, *The Emptiness of the Concept of* Jus Cogens, *as Illustrated by the War in Bosnia-Herzegovina*, 17 MICH. J. INT'L L. 1, 13 (1995). Indeed, delegations to the Conference raised the concern that elements of the International Law Commission's draft text were "based on 'the mechanical and unconsidered application of rules of internal private law to public international law . . . '" IAN SINCLAIR, THE VIENNA CONVENTION ON THE LAW OF TREATIES 174 (2d ed. 1984) (quoting U.N. Conference on the Law of Treaties, 1st Sess., 45th mtg. at 256, U.N. Doc. A/CONF.39/11 (Apr. 30, 1968)).

48.   VIENNA CONVENTION ON THE LAW OF TREATIES art. 49, May 23, 1969, 1155 U.N.T.S. 331, 8 I.L.M. 679 [hereinafter VIENNA CONVENTION].

49.   *Id.* art. 48.

50.   *Id.* art. 52. *See also* Benedetto Conforti & Angelo Labella, *Invalidity and Termination of Treaties: The Role of National Courts*, 1 EUR. J. INT'L L. 44, 50-52 (1990) (citing decisions of three Netherlands courts that concluded that the German-Czechoslovak Nationality Treaty was void because it was concluded under unlawful duress).

51.   VIENNA CONVENTION, *supra* note 48, art. 53.

52.   *See* RESTATEMENT (THIRD) FOREIGN RELATIONS LAW OF THE UNITED STATES § 331 (2), cmt. e (noting that while the U.S. has not ratified the Vienna Convention, "it is generally accepted that there are some peremptory rules of international law that are of superior status and cannot be affected by treaty").

law[53] and may be seen to form the hard edges of the zone of lawfulness within which states may negotiate. Although state practice in this area is extremely limited,[54] most international jurists "have accepted the principle that there may exist norms of international law so fundamental to the maintenance of an international legal order that a treaty concluded in violation of them is a nullity."[55] It is difficult, for example, to conceive of a judicial tribunal's enforcing an agreement that provided for rendition to torture, transfer of slave labor, or cooperation in perpetrating genocide.[56] And even outside of the human rights context, judges of the International Court of Justice have suggested that a treaty reservation contrary to a jus cogens norm would be void.[57]

The function of international law in international negotiation processes is not, however, limited to defining the boundaries of what is lawfully negotiable. In addition, legal rules may contribute to zone definition by helping a party to define its reservation point. As Roger Fisher observes, "law cannot restrain a government from doing what they [sic] want, but law affects what they [sic] want."[58] Examining the actions of the United States and the Soviet Union during the Cuban missile crisis, Fisher suggests that "[i]nternational law affected what the United States decided to try for": while American military authorities likely would have preferred to acquire and study Soviet missiles, "the United States had no legal right to seize those missiles, or even to destroy them." As a consequence, Fisher argues, the United States settled on a set of narrower objectives, including removal of existing missiles from Cuba, commitment not to install additional missiles there, and verification.[59] Louis Henkin reaches similar conclusions in his own analysis of the Cuban Missile Crisis. While acknowledging that "[n]o one can say exactly what factors, in what degree, weighed in the decision" between a ground invasion of Cuba, bombing of Soviet bases, and the "quarantine" ultimately chosen, he suggests that "legal considerations were not insignificant," [60]

53.   For a thoughtful discussion of the domestic analogue to jus cogens rules, see SINCLAIR, *supra* note 47, at 204-07.

54.   *Id.* at 215, 222.

55.   *Id.* at 222; *see also* Jochen Abr. Frowein, *Jus Cogens, in* 7 ENCYCLOPEDIA OF PUBLIC INTERNATIONAL LAW 327 (Rudolf Bernhardt ed., 1984).

56.   *Cf.* United States v. Alfred Krupp, *reprinted in* 9 TRIALS OF WAR CRIMINALS BEFORE THE NUREMBERG MILITARY TRIBUNALS UNDER CONTROL COUNCIL LAW 10, 1395 (1950) (finding that agreement providing for use of French prisoners of war as slave labor in German armament factories was *contra bonus mores* and consequently void); John Dugard & Christine Van Den Wyngaert, *Reconciling Extradition with Human Rights*, 92 AM. J. INT'L L. 187, 198 (1998) (arguing that a party to an extradition agreement may refuse to extradite a person likely to be tortured by the receiving state because prohibition of torture is a jus cogens norm).

57.   *See* North Sea Continental Shelf Cases (F.R.G. v. Den.; F.R.G. v. Neth.) 1968 I.C.J. 3, 182 (Oct. 12) (separate opinion of Judge Tanaka) (concluding that a reservation contrary to a jus cogens norm, such as the "essential principle of the continental shelf institution" would be void); *id.* at 97 (dissenting opinion of Judge Padilla Nervo) (concluding that jus cogens norms cannot be subject to unilateral reservations).

58.   ROGER FISHER, INTERNATIONAL CONFLICT FOR BEGINNERS 163 (1969).

59.   *Id.*; *see also* HENKIN, *supra* note 2, at 282-83.

60.   HENKIN, *supra* note 2, at 286. Similarly, Abram Chayes argues that it is possible to determine "how" law influences decision-making, but not "how much," observing, "It is no more possible to demonstrate 'proximate' causation [in U.S. decision making during the Cuban missile crisis] . . . than in any other human process. The weight and consequence of legal advice in the final decision, like the weight and consequence of military judgment or Kennedy's machismo or the bureaucratic

explaining that concerns about the perceived legitimacy of the U.S. response among Latin American countries affected the choice among these options.[61] Thus, although a variety of political and security factors influenced American decision-making (not least, Soviet nuclear weapons), it seems likely that U.S. officials' assessment of what international law permitted, and of the cost of pursuing a remedy that would be regarded as a violation of international law, informed their definition of the United States's reservation point.

Legal rules may also contribute to zone definition by affecting the credibility of an adversary's reservation point. Fisher's analysis of the Cuban missile crisis is again instructive. Fisher argues that the United States's decisions to involve international institutions and to invoke international norms in support of its proposed blockade of Cuba gave it bargaining chips in its negotiations with the Soviet Union; he observes:

> By making offers and threats more legitimate, the law not only made them more acceptable; it also made them more credible . . . . The stronger the United States's legal case, the more credible each of these threats [became], and the less costly it would have been to the United States to carry them out. The international procedures followed and the legal rhetoric advanced in support of the United States position thus operated to make the threats more influential.[62]

Fisher's account suggests that by rendering its alternative to a negotiated outcome (its BATNA) more credible, the United States's invocation of legal norms also made its declared reservation point—the minimum it would accept from the Soviet Union—more credible. In essence, the message conveyed by American officials to their Soviet counterparts was the following: "The law entitles us to the fulfillment of certain minimum demands; if you are unwilling to accept them, we will walk away from the deal and pursue an alternative remedy." Of course, the United States's alternative remedy was not recourse to an adjudicative tribunal with enforcement capacity, as might be the case in the domestic setting, but rather, its own use of force.[63] By obtaining the imprimatur of international norms and institutions, however, the United States made its own use of force a more potent threat than it otherwise is likely to

---

rigidity of the Air Force are, and must remain, unknowable." ABRAM CHAYES, THE CUBAN MISSILE CRISIS: INTERNATIONAL CRISES AND THE ROLE OF LAW 4-5 (1974).

61.   HENKIN, *supra* note 2, at 287-88. Henkin argues that while American concerns about Latin American perceptions of the crisis were political in nature, they "merely vindicate[d] the international norm and reflect[ed] the interests that [led] nations to accept it." *Id.* at 287. Indeed, as Henkin observes, the choice of the word "quarantine" also points to a U.S. desire to bolster the perceived legal legitimacy of its action: "The use of the word 'quarantine,' a legally neutral term, also suggests the lawyer's influence; it . . . emphasized that the action was limited and 'pacific,' while 'blockade' might have suggested war and belligerency." *Id.* at 289, n.†. Henkin's and Fisher's assessments are supported by evidence made available as a result of the declassification of executive branch materials on the missile crisis. *See* Timothy J. McKeown, *Plans and Routines, Bureaucratic Bargaining, and the Cuban Missile Crisis*, 63 J. POL. 1163, 1167-69 (2001) (describing discussion among executive branch officials about anticipated legal consequences of blockade of Cuba); Norbert A. Schlei, *Anticipatory Self-Defense*, 6 GREEN BAG 2d 195, 201 (2003) (reproducing memorandum from Department of Justice's Office of Legal Counsel examining international legal implications of various responses to potential establishment of missile bases in Cuba by the Soviet Union and recommending measures consistent with international law—some of which were adopted by Kennedy administration).

62.   FISHER, *supra* note 58, at 171; *see also* HENKIN, *supra* note 2, at 290-93 (describing U.S. international law arguments before the Organization of American States).

63.   *See* HENKIN, *supra* note 2, at 286.

have been. Thus, even though the avenues of enforcement of international legal rules are different than those in the domestic setting (a difference addressed further below), the effect on bargaining of their potential enforcement—"the shadow of the law" described by Mnookin and Kornhauser—is qualitatively the same.

In addition to facilitating zone definition, legal norms may provide standards for surplus allocation. As Joaquin Tacsan points out, "[t]hough parties to international disputes have certainly been known to manipulate international law in decidedly non-legal ways, such parties often enough choose to bargain on legal grounds because international law permits less of a range of manipulative calculation than other types of bargaining."[64] In his study of the Central American peace process in the 1980s, Tacsan observes that the parties sought to base their agenda on "absolute respect for the principles of self-determination and nonintervention," using these principles "as the common conflict-resolution criteria to guide the negotiations."[65]

The use of legal concepts may also obviate the need for parties to define every aspect of their relationship in their agreement. The relative precision of legal language—the possibility of "conveying a great deal of meaning" with relative economy through reference to established norms and standardized terms—makes it a valuable vehicle of communication between governments, both during negotiations and in agreements.[66] For example, an agreement delimiting the maritime boundary between two sovereign states need not include an exhaustive description of each state's rights on its side of the boundary. Because those rights are defined by international law, the parties can confine their bargaining to the issues with respect to which a departure from the norm is sought.[67] International legal rules therefore may offer negotiating parties a starting-point for bargaining or, alternatively, a default position with which gaps in their agreement may subsequently be filled.

As these examples suggest, legal rules serve functions in international negotiations that, in many ways, are analogous to those they serve in domestic bargaining. But how far does the analogy go? In what ways do the idiosyncrasies of international law and institutions alter the roles that legal norms play in international bargaining?

2.   Contrasts

Skeptics submit that the analogy between the international and domestic settings is false or, at best, misleading. They highlight two primary differences between the two contexts. First, they argue that the influence of law on

---

64.   TACSAN, *supra* note 4, at 187.

65.   *Id.* at 189. Tacsan argues that the indeterminacy of these norms limited their usefulness as standards. *Id.* at 189-90. The challenge presented by the indeterminacy of international legal rules is addressed further below.

66.   FISHER, *supra* note 58, at 167.

67.   *See* Faraz Sanei, *The Caspian Sea Legal Regime, Pipeline Diplomacy, and the Prospects for Iran's Isolation from the Oil and Gas Frenzy: Reconciling Tehran's Legal Options with Its Geopolitical Realities*, 34 VAND. J. TRANSNAT'L L. 681, 800-01 (2001) (suggesting that application of U.N. Convention on the Law of the Sea as a framework for resolving Caspian Sea resource disputes would facilitate clear definition of littoral states' rights within their respective exclusive economic zones).

bargaining between governments is constrained by the indeterminacy of international legal rules, suggesting that international law's relative lack of development makes it difficult for negotiating parties to discern its meaning and implications and, accordingly, to use it effectively as a tool in negotiations. Second, they argue that the influence of law in domestic settings derives largely from the availability of some form of legal recourse, pointing out that enforcement of claimed legal rights at the international level is usually a remote prospect. I consider each of these arguments in turn.

a.   *Indeterminacy of International Norms*

A rule's "determinacy" is the extent to which it "convey[s] a clear message" such that "one can see through the language of a law to its essential meaning."[68] According to Thomas Franck, the determinacy of a legal rule is "[t]he pre-eminent literary property affecting legitimacy."[69] Determinacy enables "states or persons to whose conduct the rule is directed [to] know more precisely what is expected of them, which is a necessary first step toward compliance."[70] Conversely, indeterminacy renders a rule so malleable that it is easier for a party to justify non-compliance with it.[71] In the context of bargaining, indeterminacy constrains the capacity of legal rules to serve the functions described above: It undermines their usefulness as predictors of the remedy a court (or other tribunal) would impose, making it more difficult for parties to assess the costs and benefits of a non-negotiated resolution of their conflict;[72] and it erodes the persuasive force of rules as objective standards for surplus allocation, resulting in differences between negotiating parties about how a given rule bears on an issue in contention.[73]

Are international legal rules sufficiently determinate to give them influence over international negotiations? Skeptics point out that even the mandatory rules of international law—jus cogens norms—are indeterminate in important respects.[74] Though hardly a skeptic himself, Ian Brownlie acknowledges that "more authority exists for the category of jus cogens than exists for its particular content."[75] Indeed, the Vienna Convention is silent about which rules are jus cogens norms, its drafters apparently having sought to avoid both "misunderstanding as to the position concerning other cases not mentioned in the article" and "prolonged study of matters which fall outside the scope of the present articles."[76] In its commentary to Article 50 of the

---

68.   THOMAS M. FRANCK, FAIRNESS IN INTERNATIONAL LAW AND INSTITUTIONS 30 (1995) [hereinafter FAIRNESS].

69.   THOMAS M. FRANCK, THE POWER OF LEGITIMACY AMONG NATIONS 52 (1990).

70.   *Id.*

71.   *See id.* at 54.

72.   *See* Mnookin & Kornhauser, *supra* note 9, at 969 (explaining that the "lack of precision" of legal rules in the divorce context provides "a bargaining backdrop clouded by uncertainty").

73.   *See* TACSAN, *supra* note 4, at 190-94 (observing that "ambiguity of legal norms" can result in manipulation of legal arguments by the parties, diminishing their value as objective standards).

74.   *See, e.g.*, Weisburd, *supra* note 47, at 21-22.

75.   IAN BROWNLIE, PRINCIPLES OF PUBLIC INTERNATIONAL LAW 515 (3d ed. 1979).

76.   *Reports of the International Law Commission on the Second Part of its Seventeenth Session and on its Eighteenth Session*, 21 U.N. GAOR Supp. (No. 9), U.N. Doc. A/6309/Rev.1 (1966), *reprinted in* [1966] 2 Y.B. Int'l L. Comm'n 169, 248, U.N. Doc. A/CN.4/SER.A/1966/Add.1.

Vienna Convention, the International Law Commission did provide one illustration, characterizing "the law of the Charter concerning the prohibition of the use of force" as "a conspicuous example of a rule in international law having the character of jus cogens."[77] Other norms suggested for inclusion by various state delegations to the Vienna Conference included "the right to self-determination, human rights norms, rules of humanitarian law in warfare, and prohibitions of genocide, racial discrimination, and unequal treaties."[78] None of these rules, however, obtained the universal recognition of delegations to the Conference.[79]

This lack of consensus among the conferees in Vienna points to a larger tension in the international legal system. In addition to still unresolved questions about which international rules are non-derogable, and which may be negotiated around, the substantive contours of recognized peremptory norms remain a subject of controversy. For example, the norm of self-determination, to which the jus cogens label has been attached,[80] has proved to be difficult to apply with any coherence. As Cherif Bassiouni explains:

> "Self-determination" is a catch-all concept which exists as a principle, develops into a right under certain circumstances, unfolds as a process and results in a remedy. As an abstract principle it can be enunciated without reference to a specific context; as a right it is operative only in a relative context; and as a remedy, its equitable application is limited by the rights of others and the potential injuries it may inflict as weighed against the potential benefits it may generate.[81]

Some scholars submit that the indeterminacy of the norm of self-determination and the international community's failure to provide guidance as to its meaning in various contexts have prevented the rule from contributing constructively to resolution of the conflicts in which it has been invoked.[82]

The application of even clearly defined jus cogens norms has also proven difficult in some cases, particularly when strict adherence to the norm has been seen to undermine competing values. Thus, although the rule against the acquisition of territory by force has universally recognized jus cogens status, the international community, in the interest of bringing an end to armed hostilities, has endorsed agreements whose terms arguably derogated significantly from the rule.[83] Similarly, questions have arisen about the lawfulness, in the context of a peace agreement, of granting amnesty to

---

77. *Id.* at 247.

78. Weisburd, *supra* note 47, at 16. *See also* Colm Campbell, *Peace and the laws of war: The role of international humanitarian law in the post-conflict environment*, 839 INT'L REV. RED CROSS 627, 632 (2000) (suggesting that a peace agreement granting formal amnesty to perpetrators of grave breaches of humanitarian law would be unlawful).

79. Weisburd, *supra* note 47, at 16.

80. *See* BROWNLIE, *supra* note 75, at 513; LAURI HANNIKAINEN, PEREMPTORY NORMS 'JUS COGENS' IN INTERNATIONAL LAW: HISTORICAL DEVELOPMENT, CRITERIA, PRESENT STATUS 424 (1988) (recognizing self-determination as a peremptory norm insofar as applied to "colonial-type domination").

81. M. Cherif Bassiouni, *"Self-Determination" and the Palestinians*, 65 AM. SOC'Y INT'L L. PROC. 31, 33 (1971).

82. CHRISTINE BELL, PEACE AGREEMENTS AND HUMAN RIGHTS 176-187 (2000) (examining Palestinian-Israeli and Balkan conflicts); TACSAN, *supra* note 4, at 81, 107-09 (examining Contadora process); WATSON, *supra* note 7, at 270-72 (examining Palestinian-Israeli conflict).

83. *See also* Francis A. Boyle, *Negating Human Rights in Peace Negotiations*, 18 HUM. RTS. Q. 515, 515-16 (1996); Weisburd, *supra* note 47, at 42-43 (pointing out that Dayton Peace Accord sanctioned forcible acquisition of territory by Serbia and Montenegro).

perpetrators of grave breaches of humanitarian law or violations of fundamental human rights.[84] Because international law is derived in part from state practice, efforts to address equitable concerns in peace agreements by departing from the outcome that legal norms would appear to prescribe arguably serve to render the norms less determinate (at least at their margins), further constraining their influence on international negotiations.

The case, however, should not be overstated. Determinacy, after all, is relative and situational: Although international legal rules may often prove indeterminate at their margins, the basic precepts of some rules are sufficiently determinate to allow parties to identify conduct that clearly contravenes them. Thomas Franck offers the following example from the litigation between the United States and Nicaragua in the International Court of Justice in the 1980s: Although the United States's reservation to its acceptance of the International Court of Justice's compulsory jurisdiction barred the Court from adjudicating any case involving "domestic" matters, as determined by the United States, the United States refrained from claiming that the mining of Nicaragua's harbors was a domestic matter, though doing so would have brought an immediate end to Nicaragua's suit against it.[85] Even though the definition of the term "domestic" was undoubtedly elastic at its margins, and subject to interpretation only by the United States, it was sufficiently determinate for certain conduct—the mining of another state's harbors—to fall clearly outside its scope.[86]

Moreover, the existence of differences between bargaining parties regarding the interpretation of rules does not necessarily indicate that the rules in question are indeterminate. As in the domestic setting, parties to international negotiations may adopt an interpretation of a rule that is at odds with a widely accepted understanding of its meaning. But whereas in the domestic setting recourse is available to a judicial tribunal capable of resolving the alleged ambiguity in the rule, the lack of robust international adjudicative and enforcement mechanisms can make it difficult to resolve even spurious claims of indeterminacy. Accordingly, it may be unclear what is prompting non-compliance—the rule's indeterminacy or the lack of recourse to a third party capable of interpreting and enforcing it. It is to the latter that I turn next.

b.   *Lack of International Adjudicative and Enforcement Mechanisms*

Of the four functions of legal rules in negotiations that are described in the Sections above, three assume the availability of recourse to a forum capable of adjudicating and enforcing legal claims: mandatory rules will only appear credibly mandatory if transgressions are likely to elicit some form of sanction; and the usefulness of default rules, either as predictors of the

---

84.   *See* Campbell, *supra* note 78, at 632; Ellen L. Lutz, Eileen F. Babbitt & Hurst Hannum, *Human Rights and Conflict Resolution from the Practitioner's Perspectives*, 27 FLETCHER F. OF WORLD AFF. 173 (2003).

85.   *See* FAIRNESS, *supra* note 68, at 32.

86.   *Id.*

contours of a non-negotiated outcome or as gap-fillers, turns on the expectation that some forum is positioned to impose a legal remedy if the parties fail to reach agreement on some or all of the issues in dispute. But if no such forum is available, or if recourse to it is unavailable, is law's role in negotiations limited to its persuasive power? And, if so, can a government be persuaded to accept a legal rule as a standard for prioritizing competing claims if it perceives compliance with the rule to be at odds with other interests?

The influence of international law on state behavior has been the focus of considerable attention by international relations and international law scholars. Realist scholars like Hans Morgenthau answer these questions in no uncertain terms. Characterizing the international system as "a competitive quest for power," Morgenthau expressed profound skepticism about the influence of international law on the decisions of states.[87] From the Realist perspective, international law is "epiphenomenal"[88]: The effectiveness of legal rules is contingent upon the threat of enforcement or sanction when the rule is violated; if such enforcement is left to individual states, as it is at the international level, the effectiveness of law is a function merely of states' relative power to sanction one another and their respective interests in doing so.[89] Accordingly, governments will not be constrained—or persuaded—by the invocation of legal rules to accept negotiated outcomes that they do not judge otherwise to be in their interests. Absent the threat of enforcement, law has no influence.

The response to the "Realist challenge" has been manifold.[90] Some scholars assert that Realists begin from the wrong starting-point by overstating the influence of enforcement in the domestic setting. Roger Fisher, for example, points out that "[f]or those in whose conduct we are interested—national governments—domestic law is backed up by less force than is international law,"[91] observing that governments "regularly comply with court decisions" even though courts lack the power independently to enforce their judgments against governments.[92] Governments do so because courts are "respected and disinterested," because judicial rulings take the form of "narrow and explicit demand[s]" rather than general rules, and because a decision to defy a court "would establish a disastrous precedent which others

---

87.   Hans Morgenthau, *Positivism, Functionalism and International Law*, 34 AM. J. INT'L L. 260, 283 (1941).

88.   Hathaway, *supra* note 3, at 1945-46 (observing that according to the Realist approach, "if compliance with international law occurs, it is not because the law is effective, but merely because compliance is coincident with the path dictated by self-interest in a world governed by anarchy and relative state power").

89.   *See* Morgenthau, *supra* note 87, at 276-78; *see also* Joseph M. Grieco, *Anarchy and the Limits of Cooperation: A Realist Critique of the Newest Liberal Institutionalism*, 42 INT'L ORG. 485, 488 (1988) (identifying five propositions that form the "core" of Realism, one of which is that international institutions will have only marginal effects on cooperation between states).

90.   *See* Anne-Marie Slaughter Burley, *International Law and International Relations Theory: A Dual Agenda*, 87 AM. J. INT'L. L 205, 207-220 (1993) (describing "Realist challenge" and cataloguing responses to it from different schools of international law and international relations theory).

91.   FISHER, *supra* note 58, at 152.

92.   *Id.* at 154.

might follow."[93] Fisher suggests that the decisions of international courts and other international tribunals elicit compliance for similar reasons.[94]

Other responses to the Realist challenge have focused on the normative force of international legal norms, on the benefits of participation in international regimes, on the attitudes of domestic constituencies, or on the interaction of these factors. While it is not the purpose of this Article to assess the merits of the various perspectives advanced by compliance theorists, their central propositions, taken together, provide a useful framework for analyzing how the influence of legal rules in international negotiations differs from its influence in the domestic setting.

Oona Hathaway categorizes international law compliance theories into two primary models: "rational-actor" models and "normative" models.[95] Rational-actor models, she explains, "have at their heart a shared belief that states and the individuals who guide them are rational, self-interested actors who calculate the costs and benefits of alternative courses of action in the international realm and act accordingly."[96] The role of international law, from this perspective, is defined in instrumental terms—as one of a number of tools through which parties pursue their self-interest.[97]

Some rational-actor models, however, depart from the Realist assertion that law is effective only to justify decisions that would have been taken for other reasons.[98] Institutionalists, for example, argue that states comply with international law because participation in international institutions is useful to them, providing a means of achieving long-term goals that require at least a certain degree of cooperation with other international actors.[99] Thus, international law influences behavior insofar as failure to comply with it leads to reputational costs that diminish access to the benefits of participating in international regimes. "[B]y clustering issues together in the same forums over a long period of time, [international regimes] help to bring governments into continuing interaction with one another, reducing incentives to cheat and enhancing the value of reputation."[100] Liberal theorists, on the other hand, depart from the conception of the state as a unitary actor, submitting that a central factor in a government's compliance decisions is the existence of pressure from their domestic constituencies.[101] Accordingly, it is the internalization of international rules by persons and institutions *within* the

---

93.   *Id.* at 156.

94.   *See id.* at 158-59.

95.   *See* Hathaway, *supra* note 3, at 1944-62.

96.   *Id.* at 1944.

97.   *See id.*

98.   *See* Arend, *supra* note 3, at 115-16.

99.   *See, e.g.*, KEOHANE, *supra* note 12, at 244-45; Andrew T. Guzman, *A Compliance-Based Theory of International Law*, 90 CAL. L. REV. 1823, 1826-27 (2002).

100.   KEOHANE, *supra* note 12, at 244-45. *See also* Hathaway, *supra* note 3, at 1950; Arend, *supra* note 3, at 120.

101.   *See* Andrew Moravcsik, *Taking Preferences Seriously: A Liberal Theory of International Politics*, 51 INT'L. ORG. 513, 513 (1997) (arguing that, particularly in democratic states, their very nature dictates that domestic societal preferences and pressures must shape the state preferences that are projected internationally). *See generally* Anne-Marie Slaughter, *International Law in a World of Liberal States*, 6 EUR. J. INT'L. L. 503 (1995) (offering an overview of liberal theory and its implications for international law).

state and the pressure they exert that influence state behavior, not merely the threat of enforcement by external actors.

Normative theorists approach the question of compliance from a different angle entirely. As Hathaway explains, "Scholars adopting this approach argue that state decisions cannot be explained simply by calculations of geopolitical or economic interests or even the relative power of domestic political groups. A complete description of state action in the international realm, they argue, requires an understanding of the influence and importance of ideas."[102] From this perspective, compliance with law is not driven solely by the threat of enforcement; law also has influence because it is perceived to be legitimate and just.[103] Thomas Franck suggests that a number of factors affect the legitimacy of rules, including their determinacy and what he calls their "symbolic validation."[104] As he explains, "Determinacy communicates meaning. Symbolic validation communicates authority. Both affect the legitimacy of a rule or a rule-making or implementing process, its capacity to pull toward compliance." [105] Symbols, such as the rituals observed in diplomatic practice, bolster legitimacy by signaling "that authority is being exercised in accordance with right process, that it is institutionally recognized and validated."[106] Non-compliance with legal rules may be corrected through interaction and persuasive discourse at both the international level and the transnational level,[107] through the development of compliance capacity among governments, and through efforts to bolster the transparency and fairness of the international processes through which law is made.[108] Through this "transnational legal process," as Harold Koh has called it, state and non-state actors "interact in a variety of public and private, domestic and international fora to make, interpret, enforce, and ultimately, internalize rules of transnational law."[109]

Thus, although the paucity of enforcement avenues undoubtedly shortens the shadow cast by international norms on public international bargaining, the shadow metaphor fails to capture important functions of law in bargaining between international actors. Legal rules may exert a "pull towards compliance"[110] as a result of a variety of factors other than the threat of enforcement. They may influence bargaining behavior because of their perceived fairness, at least insofar as they were developed pursuant to processes perceived to be legitimate. They may influence bargaining because of the reputational costs of non-compliance with them—costs that may hinder access to beneficial international regimes. And they may influence bargaining because domestic constituencies demand adherence to them.

---

102. Hathaway, *supra* note 3, at 1955.
103. *See* Koh, *supra* note 3, at 2602.
104. FAIRNESS, *supra* note 68, at 34.
105. *Id.*
106. *Id.*
107. *See* Koh, *supra* note 3, at 2645-58.
108. *Id.* at 2645.
109. Harold Hongju Koh, *Transnational Legal Process*, 75 NEB. L. REV. 181, 183-84 (1996).
110. FAIRNESS, *supra* note 68, at 34.

3.　*The Shade of the Law*

Taken together, these theoretical approaches suggest that international law may exert influence not only as a result of the *shadow* it casts over bargaining, but also by virtue of the *shade* it offers—that is, its perceived value, independent of the threat of enforcement, as an objective and legitimate standard for resolving disputed issues.

Two examples of state practice illustrate these functions. In a recent study of early settlement in GATT and WTO disputes, Marc Busch and Eric Reinhardt found that a majority of concessions by defendants took place prior to the issuance of a formal ruling by a GATT or WTO panel.[111] Observing that "[n]either GATT nor the WTO possess centralized enforcement power, the upshot being that both have relied on the complainant itself to implement any retaliatory measures that may be authorized,"[112] and that the threat of such enforcement alone is "obviously insufficient" to induce concessions in a majority of cases,[113] Busch and Reinhardt offer several explanations for the tendency of states to settle their disputes prior to a formal ruling. They acknowledge that "the defendant's uncertainty about the complainant's willingness to implement retaliatory measures (if called upon to do so) is absolutely necessary to give recalcitrant defendants some interest, however slight, in cutting a deal in the first place."[114] They suggest, however, that a number of other factors are also influential:

> A panel ruling carries weight to the extent that it delivers a timely and coherent normative statement on the matter. Even without a credible threat by a complainant to seek authorization to retaliate, a definitive legal opinion from the institution may empower groups in the defendant state who oppose the disputed measure. Alternatively, a ruling may enable the defendant's executive to "tie hands," making concessions more politically palatable by citing the need to be a "good citizen" of GATT/WTO. A well-reasoned report may also set a *de facto* (if not formal) precedent that . . . may adversely affect the defendant's positions in ongoing multilateral trade round talks.[115]

Thus, even though an adverse ruling is often unlikely to be followed by effective enforcement, the threat of a ruling nevertheless may suffice to prompt a state to offer concessions in pre-ruling negotiations—because of the normative force of the ruling (the normativist view), the effect of resulting reputational costs on the state's participation in the international trade regime (the institutionalist view), and the likelihood that it will result in domestic challenges to the disputed practice (the liberal view). As far as these factors are concerned, it is the shade of the law—not its shadow—that influences bargaining behavior.[116]

---

111. Marc L. Busch & Eric Reinhardt, *Bargaining in the Shadow of the Law: Early Settlement in GATT/WTO Disputes*, 24 FORDHAM INT'L L.J. 158, 162 (2000).

112. *Id.* at 163.

113. *Id.* at 164.

114. *Id.*, at 166.

115. *Id.* at 165 (citations omitted).

116. Of course, differences between negotiations conducted within the framework of an international trading regime and those conducted in the context of a peace process may affect the influence of legal rules in each. For example, a state's voluntary commitment to participation in the WTO (and the elaborate process by which that commitment is made) may signal a firmer embrace of the regime's rules – and, accordingly, a greater inclination to comply with them – than the near-automatic

A second example further illustrates the role that international legal rules and institutions can play in insulating government actions from domestic challenges. In 1982, the International Court of Justice accepted a request from the United States and Canada to establish a special chamber to resolve a dispute about the two states' maritime boundary in the Gulf of Maine, pursuant to a boundary treaty that entered into force in 1979.[117] Earlier efforts to resolve the countries' contentious dispute over fishing rights in the Gulf had proven unsuccessful, a fisheries treaty failing to earn ratification in the United States Senate due to fierce opposition by fishermen and members of Congress from affected northeastern states.[118] Ultimately, the boundary devised by the ICJ Chamber split the difference between the two sides.[119] By shifting the decision to the World Court, however, the political leaders on each side of the dispute were able to insulate themselves from the dissatisfaction of their constituents;[120] as the legal adviser who represented the United States at the ICJ later recounted:

> Georges Bank is no longer on the agenda of meetings between the President and the Prime Minister. So "throwing the matter to the lawyers" was a success in this regard. That is, a controversy that proved incapable of a compromise negotiated by diplomats was instead compromised by five judges, allowing the political bosses of both States to place any dissatisfaction with the result at the feet of the Chamber rather than at their own. This then is the "realpolitic" point of conjunction between international tribunals and diplomacy where mutual desperation proved such a potent internal political force in both States that our masters decided to grant the legal establishment the opportunity to "do its thing." So, that is what we did and the problem went away.[121]

Although the Gulf of Maine dispute culminated in joint consent by the parties to adjudication by an international tribunal, a step that few governments are prepared to contemplate,[122] it nevertheless demonstrates that international law and institutions can make unpopular political decisions easier by shifting some of the responsibility for them away from political leaders.[123]

Indeed, in an international order in which enforcement continues to be more often the exception than the rule, persuading a negotiating partner to seek the shade of the law may often be a better strategy than attempting to invoke its elusive shadow. Such a strategy may take a variety of forms.

---

membership of states in the United Nations. In addition, the subject matter of the norms implicated in each context may affect states' willingness to conform their behavior to them. As John Yoo has observed, Realist scholars "reject[] the notion that international law can govern the use of force because security is too dear an interest to states." John Yoo, *Using Force*, 71 U. CHI. L. REV. 729, 731 (2004).

117. *See* Delimitation of the Maritime Boundary in the Gulf of Maine Area (Can. v. U.S.) 1984 I.C.J. 246, 252 (Oct. 12).

118. *See* Davis R. Robinson, *The Convergence of Law and Diplomacy in United States-Canada Relations: The Precedent of* The Gulf of Maine Case, 26 CAN.-U.S. L.J. 37, 43 (2000).

119. *Id.* at 44.

120. *Id.*

121. *Id.*

122. *See id.* at 41-42 (observing that governments generally prefer to retain discretion to resolve disputes themselves, rather than "rolling the dice" by placing disputes before international tribunals).

123. According to William Ury, the decision by the governments of Peru and Ecuador to seek arbitration of their border conflict by the guarantors of a prior treaty between them was motivated by similar concerns: "With nationalist passions still running strong, political leaders felt it easier to accept a ruling by others than to make direct concessions to the enemy." WILLIAM L. URY, THE THIRD SIDE: WHY WE FIGHT AND HOW WE CAN STOP 152 (2000).

Institutionalist theory suggests that international legal rules are likely to be more persuasive—and, consequently, more effective tools for surplus allocation—if they are linked to participation in an international regime that offers concrete benefits to participants and imposes costs (even costs short of formal sanctions) for non-compliance. Liberal theory reveals the importance of directing efforts at persuasion not just at the government officials who are the immediate participants in international negotiations, but also at their domestic constituencies, which are likely to be particularly influential in democratic states. And normative theory demonstrates both that discourse about the fairness of legal rules is likely to be more persuasive than rote recitation of norms and that clarification of the content and implication of norms by authoritative actors in the international system may increase their influence even if enforcement capacity is wanting.

As I discuss in Part IV of this Article, these theoretical approaches offer lessons that may usefully inform future efforts to achieve a negotiated settlement of the Palestinian-Israeli conflict. In the next Part, however, I undertake not to look forward, but to look back—at how Palestinians and Israelis actually used international law during their abortive attempt to conclude a permanent status agreement between 1999 and 2001.

III. BARGAINING AT THE SHADOW'S EDGE: LEGAL DISCOURSE DURING PALESTINIAN-ISRAELI PERMANENT STATUS NEGOTIATIONS

In a recent forum on the Middle East peace process convened by the World Council of Churches, Professor Richard Falk and the former speaker of the Israeli Knesset, Avraam Burg, sparred regarding the appropriate role of law in Palestinian-Israeli peace efforts. Falk suggested that "The principal flaw in the Oslo peace process—and the problem with the Geneva Accord—is that both exclude the relevance of international law from the process."[124] Burg "asserted that peace would only succeed if peace negotiators focus directly on the practical concerns of ordinary citizens, rather than 'theoretical' international norms." [125] These disparate assessments of the utility and limitations of international law in Palestinian-Israeli negotiations, delivered several years after the suspension of the peace talks, mirror a persistent debate between the parties themselves. It is beyond the scope of this Article to trace the specific substantive contours of the parties' legal positions regarding each of the issues they were negotiating. Instead, drawing upon the theoretical framework defined in Part II, I undertake here to examine *how* the parties used international legal rules during their negotiation process. I begin by sketching the agreed legal framework and agreed structure of the negotiation process that the parties defined prior to the commencement of permanent status negotiations. I then proceed to analyze the functions served by international norms during the talks.

---

124. Press Release, World Council of Churches, *Panelists at odds over role of international law in Palestinian-Israeli peace efforts* (Nov. 13, 2003), *at* http://www2.wcc-coe.org/pressreleasesen.nsf/index/pu-03-43.html (last visited Nov. 9, 2006).
125. *Id.*

A.   The "Agreed" Legal Framework

In order to place the legal discourse during permanent status negotiations in context, it is useful to begin by assessing the extent to which the parties had agreed upon a legal framework for the talks: Had they reached an understanding about the zone of lawfulness within which they were bargaining? Did international legal norms help them to define their reservation points and the credibility of their counterpart's reservation points? Had they identified a body of norms that might serve as standards for resolving differences between them? Had they agreed on an institution or third party that could use law to fill in gaps in their agreement?

To the extent the parties had defined a legal framework, it was spare: The Declaration of Principles ("DOP"),[126] the foundational agreement that set the basic terms for the negotiation process that ensued, refers to only a few legal parameters. It defines the ultimate aim of the negotiations as follows:

> The aim of the Israeli-Palestinian negotiations within the current Middle East peace process is, among other things, to establish a Palestinian Interim Self-Government Authority . . . for a transitional period not exceeding five years, *leading to a permanent settlement based on Security Council Resolutions 242 and 338.*
>
> It is understood that the interim arrangements are an integral part of the whole peace process and that *the negotiations on the permanent status will lead to the implementation of Security Council Resolution 242 and 338.*[127]

Reflecting the inability of the parties to resolve a longstanding debate about whether Security Council resolutions 242 and 338 are self-executing or require further elaboration through negotiations,[128] the DOP simply incorporates the debate into its terms, providing in one clause that negotiations were to lead to a permanent settlement "based on" Security Council Resolutions 242 and 338 and, in another, that they would lead "to the implementation" of those resolutions.[129] The DOP, moreover, does nothing to articulate a common understanding of Resolution 242, the interpretation of which would become a major dispute when the parties commenced permanent status negotiations.[130]

---

126. *See* Declaration of Principles on Interim Self-Government Arrangements between Israel and the Palestinian Liberation Organization (Sept. 13, 1993), *in* 2 DOCUMENTS ON THE ARAB-ISRAELI CONFLICT, *supra* note 5, at 890 [hereinafter DOP].

127. *Id.* art. 1 (emphasis added). U.N. Security Council Resolution 242 was adopted six months after the June 1967 Arab-Israeli war, see QUANDT, *supra* note 6, at 46, during which Israel seized the West Bank (then occupied and claimed by Jordan), the Gaza Strip (which was administered by Egypt), the Sinai Peninsula (Egyptian territory), and the Golan Heights (Syrian territory). In Resolution 242, the Security Council "emphasiz[ed] the inadmissibility of the acquisition of territory by war and the need to work for a just and lasting peace in which every State in the region can live in security;" and it called, *inter alia*, for the "[w]ithdrawal of Israel armed forced from territories occupied" during the war, and the "[t]ermination of all claims or states of belligerency and respect for and acknowledgement of the sovereignty, territorial integrity and political independence of every State in the area and their right to live in peace within secure and recognized boundaries free from threats or acts of force." S.C. Res. 242, ¶¶ 2 & 4, U.N. Doc. S/RES/242 (Nov. 22, 1967). In Resolution 338, adopted in October 1973 during the Yom Kippur War, the Council called, *inter alia*, for the commencement of negotiations "between the parties concerned under appropriate auspices aimed at establishing a just and durable peace in the Middle East." S.C. Res. 338, ¶ 3, U.N. Doc. S/RES/508 (Oct. 22, 1973).

128. *See* ROSS, *supra* note 6, at 43-44.

129. DOP, *supra* note 126, at 890.

130. *See infra* notes 164-166, 180, 191-195 and accompanying text.

The DOP's few other references to international legal rules are even more oblique. The document's preamble states that the parties "recognize their mutual legitimate and political rights."[131] It does not, however, elaborate on the content of those rights or on their bearing on permanent status issues; and the letters of recognition exchanged by the parties prior to the DOP's signing provide only limited guidance.[132] The DOP does define a general substantive agenda for permanent status negotiations, which is to include "Jerusalem, refugees, settlements, security arrangements, borders, relations and cooperation with their neighbors, and other issues of common interest;"[133] but, with one exception,[134] it does not set out rules or principles to guide resolution of those issues other than through its references to Resolutions 242 and 338. According to Joel Singer, the legal adviser to the Israeli team that negotiated the DOP, the agreement's minimal definition of legal parameters was intentional, reflecting "the principle that all options should be left open."[135]

This "principle" is also apparent in the DOP provisions defining the process by which subsequent agreements, including the permanent status agreement, would be negotiated and disputes about them would be resolved. The PLO officials who negotiated the DOP sought "to retain the option of outside arbitration . . . to guarantee that the agreement would be fulfilled."[136] The DOP makes clear, however, that all disputes "arising out of the application or interpretation" of its terms would be resolved, in the first instance, through negotiations, with recourse to conciliation and arbitration only with the consent of both parties.[137] Reference of disputes to arbitration, moreover, would be limited to "disputes relating to the interim period."[138] Singer writes that this provision was intended to ensure that "[d]isputes relating to the permanent status agreement shall be resolved only through negotiations."[139] Indeed, the DOP leaves little doubt about the approach to conflict resolution it embodies: As declared in its preamble, the agreement set

---

131. DOP, preamble, *supra* note 126, at 890.

132. The PLO recognizes "the right of the State of Israel to exist in peace and security." Letter from Yasser Arafat, Chairman, Palestine Liberation Organization, to Yitzhak Rabin, Prime Minister of Israel (Sept. 9, 1993), *in* 2 DOCUMENTS ON THE ARAB-ISRAELI CONFLICT, *supra* note 5, at 889. Israel, in turn, recognizes "the PLO as the representative of the Palestinian people . . . ." Letter from Yitzhak Rabin to Yasser Arafat (Sept. 9, 1993), *in* 2 DOCUMENTS ON THE ARAB-ISRAELI CONFLICT, *supra* note 5, at 889.

133. DOP, art. 5, *supra* note 126, at 890-91. Agreed minutes appended to the DOP add two issues to this list: "military locations" and "Israelis." Agreed Minutes, Declaration of Principles on Interim Self-Government (Sept. 13, 1993), sec. B, art. IV, *in id.* at 896-97.

134. The one exception appears in an annex to the agreement addressing cooperation in economic and development programs. It provides, "Cooperation in the field of water . . . will include proposals for studies and plans . . . on *equitable utilization of joint water resources* for implementation in and *beyond the interim period.*" DOP, Annex 3, *supra* note 126, at 894-95 (emphasis added). This reference to the norm of equitable utilization would also be a focus of dispute during permanent status negotiations between the parties.

135. Joel Singer, *The Declaration of Principles on Interim Self-Government Arrangements: Some Legal Aspects,* JUST., Winter 1994, at 13.

136. URI SAVIR, THE PROCESS: 1,100 DAYS THAT CHANGED THE MIDDLE EAST 39 (1998).

137. DOP, art. 15, *supra* note 126, at 892-93.

138. *Id.*

139. Singer, *supra* note 135, at 6.

the parties on a path toward peace and reconciliation "through the *agreed political* process"—not through a legal process imposed by others.[140]

A broad cross-section of the international community undertook on various occasions to articulate additional parameters to guide the Palestinian-Israeli peace process. The United Nations General Assembly, for example, passed a series of resolutions during the decade before the commencement of permanent status negotiations that defined "principles for the achievement of comprehensive peace," including:

> *(a)* The withdrawal of Israel from the Palestinian territory occupied since 1967, including Jerusalem, and from the other occupied Arab territories;
>
> *(b)* Guaranteeing arrangements for security of all States in the region, including those named in resolution 181 (II) of 29 November 1947, within secure and internationally recognized boundaries;
>
> *(c)* Resolving the problem of the Palestine refugees in conformity with General Assembly resolution 194 (III) of 11 December 1948, and subsequent relevant resolutions;
>
> *(d)* Dismantling the Israeli settlements in the territories occupied since 1967;
>
> *(e)* Guaranteeing freedom of access to Holy Places, religious buildings and sites.[141]

Although resolutions of this kind received broad support within the General Assembly, Israel and the United States declined to sign on to them.[142]

Indeed, the United States made clear in a letter of assurances to the Palestinians in the run-up to the Madrid Peace Conference in 1991 that, so long as negotiations between the parties were underway, it would not support "a competing or parallel process" in the United Nations.[143] The U.S. maintained this position throughout the Oslo process.[144] In September 1999,

---

140. DOP, preamble, *supra* note 126, at 890 (emphasis added).

141. G.A. Res. 44/42, U.N. Doc. A/RES/44/42 (Dec. 6, 1989); *see also* G.A. Res. 45/68, U.N. Doc. A/RES/45/68 (Dec. 6, 1990). U.N. General Assembly Resolution 194 (III), to which the cited resolutions refer, provides that Palestinian refugees "wishing to return to their homes and live at peace with their neighbours should be permitted to do so . . . and that compensation should be paid for the property of those choosing not to return . . . ." G.A. Res. 194 (III), at 24, U.N. Doc. A/194 (Dec. 11, 1948).

142. The 1989 and 1990 resolutions received nearly universal support, with only Israel, the United States, and Dominica voting against them. Support for these resolutions among European states and the U.S.S.R. trailed off in 1991, however, after the convocation of the Madrid Peace Conference. *See, e.g.,* G.A. Res. 46/75 (Dec. 11, 1991). From 1993 to 1995, the text of this series of resolutions was altered, expressing support for the peace process then underway, while omitting the references to the guiding principles expressed earlier. *See, e.g.,* G.A. Res. 46/75, U.N. Doc. A/RES/46/75 (Dec. 11, 1993). This formulation won the support of Israel and the United States. Resolutions reintroducing the principles (though omitting the reference to dismantling settlements) were again passed with broad support from 1997 through 1999, but these again were opposed by Israel and the United States. *See, e.g.,* G.A. Res. 52/52, U.N. Doc. A/RES/52/52 (Dec. 9, 1997).

143. Letter from James Baker, U.S. Secretary of State, to Palestinians (Oct. 18, 1991), *in* 2 DOCUMENTS ON THE ARAB-ISRAELI CONFLICT, *supra* note 5, at 881, 882.

144. For example, although President Clinton reassured Chairman Arafat in April 1999 that the United States "knows how destructive settlement activities . . . are to the pursuit of Palestinian-Israeli peace" and "will continue to exert maximum efforts to help both parties avoid unilateral steps or actions designed to change the status of the West Bank or Gaza or to prejudge or preempt issues reserved for permanent status negotiations," Letter from Bill Clinton, President, United States of America, to Yasser Arafat, President, Palestinian Authority (Apr. 26, 1999), *in* 2 DOCUMENTS ON THE ARAB-ISRAELI CONFLICT, *supra* note 5, at 1145, the Clinton Administration declined even to allow censure of settlement activity in the Security Council, vetoing two resolutions that called on Israel to halt

shortly before the commencement of permanent status negotiations, the European Union's Minister of Foreign Affairs sent a letter to Chairman Arafat reaffirming "the continuing and unqualified Palestinian right to self-determination including the option of a state," and appealing to the parties "to strive in good faith for a negotiated solution on the basis of the existing agreements, without prejudice to this right, which is not subject to any veto."[145] Although the U.S. Secretary of State also conveyed a letter of assurances to the Palestinians in September 1999, the U.S. letter did not speak of an "unqualified" right to self-determination—or of legal rights and obligations at all. Secretary Albright did express concern about ongoing Israeli settlement activity, but her concerns were framed not in terms of the illegality of settlement construction but, rather, of its effect on the political environment within which negotiations were taking place.[146] Indeed, as it had emphasized in its 1991 letter of assurances to the Palestinians, which stated that it would "accept any outcome agreed by the parties," the U.S. government showed little inclination to recognize any legal constraint on the outcome of the Palestinian-Israeli peace process—other than the necessity that the outcome be negotiated.[147]

In sum, the parties entered permanent status negotiations in 1999 without first having agreed on a clear set of legal principles to guide their talks. Not only had they defined a legal framework of extremely limited scope (just how limited would become clear on the eve of the negotiations), they also had failed to establish any mechanisms—or to agree on any institutions—that could elaborate on it. And the third party that had assumed the lead role in mediating the peace process, the United States, expressed unwillingness to constrain the substantive direction of the talks through parallel action in the United Nations or pronouncements of its own understanding of applicable legal norms. The cumulative effect of these decisions was that a number of questions with important implications for the parties' negotiating positions and strategies remained unresolved upon the commencement of negotiations: Did any mandatory rules of international law narrow the range of negotiated outcomes the parties could reach? Did the parties share a bargaining zone—i.e., was there any overlap between the minimum each would accept? Which criteria, legal or otherwise, would be used to evaluate competing preferences? What principles or bodies of law could be used to fill in the unavoidable gaps

---

construction of the settlement of Har Homa near Jerusalem. *See* Press Release, Security Council, Security Council Again Fails to Adopt Resolution on Israeli Settlement, U.N. Doc. SC/6345 (Mar. 21, 1997). The U.S. ambassador to the United Nations, Bill Richardson, explained the U.S. position during discussion of a similar resolution in the General Assembly, stating, "we must take great care to respond to developments in a constructive way that will bolster the negotiating process, not limit prospects for the successful conclusion of permanent status talks. We have never believed, despite the useful role the United Nations can play and has played in working for Middle East peace, that it is an appropriate forum for addressing the issues now under negotiation between the parties." U.N. GAOR, 51st Sess., 93d mtg., U.N. Doc. A/51/PV.93 (Mar. 13, 1997).

145. Letter from Taria Halonen, Minister of Foreign Affairs, Gov't of Finland, to Yasser Arafat, President, Palestinian Authority (Sept. 4, 1999) (on file with PLO Negotiations Affairs Dep't).

146. *See* SWISHER, *supra* note 6, at 152.

147. For example, in a letter from President Clinton to Chairman Arafat in May 1999, Clinton asks Arafat to "continue to rely on the peace process as the way to fulfill the aspirations of your people," adding that "negotiations are the only realistic way to fulfill those aspirations . . . ." ENDERLIN, *supra* note 6, at 108.

in an agreement? And what institutions or mechanisms could be employed to undertake that process of gap filling after the conclusion of an agreement? As will be seen, most of these questions remained unresolved through the duration of the negotiation process.

B. *The Agreed Structure of the Negotiation Process*

In the DOP, Israel and the PLO resolved to begin permanent status negotiations "as soon as possible, but not later than the beginning of the third year of the interim period,"[148]—i.e., in 1996.[149] Although a ceremonial session was held in May 1996, negotiations were suspended immediately thereafter, following the election of Benjamin Netanyahu as prime minister of Israel that June. Three years later, when Ehud Barak assumed office after decisively defeating Netanyahu, Israeli, Palestinian, and American peace advocates anticipated a prompt resumption—and resolution—of peace talks.[150] At a summit at the Egyptian resort of Sharm el-Sheikh in September 1999, this optimism found expression in an ambitious timetable for the negotiations. The parties agreed to "make a determined effort" to negotiate a permanent status agreement in two phases: First, they would conclude "a Framework Agreement on all Permanent Status issues" ("FAPS") within five months;[151] they would then conclude a comprehensive agreement ("CAPS") seven months later.[152] As discussed below, the vagueness of the parties' agreed legal framework placed severe pressure on their capacity to achieve either of these goals.

The bifurcated process agreed at Sharm—defining a framework of principles that would be elaborated later in a comprehensive treaty—mirrored the processes that had led both to Israel's peace treaties with Egypt and Jordan and to its agreements with the PLO within the Oslo framework.[153] These two sets of precedents, however, pointed in different directions in an important respect. The Camp David Accords of 1978, and the Israel-Jordan Common Agenda of 1993, not only invoked U.N. Security Council Resolution 242 as the basis for the treaties the parties were preparing to negotiate, but also clarified the parties' common understanding of the resolution: essentially, that Egypt and Jordan, respectively, would resume the exercise of full sovereignty up to their internationally recognized borders with Palestine[154] and that the parties would establish relations normal to states at peace.[155] The Camp David

---

148. DOP, art. 5(1), *supra* note 126, at 890-91.

149. By the terms of the agreement, the interim period commenced upon Israel's withdrawal from the Gaza Strip, *id.*, which took place in May 1994.

150. *See* ENDERLIN, *supra* note 6, at 109-111; SWISHER, *supra* note 6, at 13-16.

151. Sharm el-Sheikh Memorandum, para. 1(c), *in* 2 DOCUMENTS ON THE ARAB-ISRAELI CONFLICT, *supra* note 5, at 1149.

152. *Id.* para. 1(d).

153. In both cases, negotiations of a comprehensive treaty commenced after the conclusion of a framework agreement. *See* Camp David Accords between Israel and Egypt [hereinafter Camp David Accords] (Sept. 17, 1978), *in* 2 DOCUMENTS ON THE ARAB-ISRAELI CONFLICT, *supra* note 5, at 865-869; Common Agenda between Israel and Jordan [hereinafter Common Agenda] (Sept. 14, 1993), *in* 2 DOCUMENTS ON THE ARAB-ISRAELI CONFLICT, *supra* note 5, at 889-90.

154. Camp David Accords, *supra* note 153, at 868; Common Agenda, *supra* note 153, at 889.

155. Camp David Accords, *supra* note 153, at 869; Common Agenda, *supra* note 153, at 889.

Accords also defined in somewhat greater detail the establishment of demilitarized zones in the Sinai Peninsula[156] and provided for free passage of Israeli ships through the Suez Canal "on the basis of the Constantinople Convention of 1888."[157]

Four aspects of these framework agreements bear emphasizing. First, they are brief documents, outlining in spare terms the principles that would guide negotiations over more comprehensive treaties. Second, despite their brevity, they define a bargaining zone for subsequent talks, at least with regard to key issues. Third, they incorporate international legal rules by reference to fill in gaps in the texts, such as provisions of the Constantinople Convention and international norms defining sovereignty and peaceful relations. Fourth, they provide detail regarding only the issues on which they depart from the default that international law would provide, such as the establishment of demilitarized zones in the Sinai.

In contrast, the DOP not only offered few substantive parameters for the permanent status negotiations that were to take place some years later,[158] it also failed to define clear principles to guide negotiations over arrangements for the interim period, outlining proposed arrangements in often ambiguous terms [159] and entirely without reference to international norms. These ambiguities, which some had hoped would be resolved in good faith by the parties as their mutual confidence grew,[160] instead resulted in protracted debates about a number of critical issues and substantial delays in the negotiation process.[161] They also made it difficult for the parties to assess whether they actually shared a bargaining zone: Although they had signed an agreement, the ambiguities in it left unclear whether the parties were actually in agreement regarding a range of specific issues—and even whether such agreement was possible.

Which of these models would the FAPS follow? The Palestinian leadership approached permanent status negotiations with the express intention of reaching a FAPS modeled on Israel's framework agreements with Egypt and Jordan, rather than on the DOP. Their popular legitimacy challenged by the perceived failure of the Oslo accords to deliver improvements in Palestinians' lives,[162] the leadership sought to effect a qualitative change in the relationship with Israel that had been established for the interim period and to emphasize that the Palestinians expected the same status and treatment as Israel's other neighbors. Accordingly, the Palestinian position paper on borders and security issues prepared prior to the commencement of negotiations states that the goal of permanent status

---

156. Camp David Accords, *supra* note 153, at 869.
157. *Id.* at 868.
158. See *supra* notes 127-134 and accompanying text.
159. *See* Kittrie, *supra* note 7, at 1700.
160. *Id.* at 1670.
161. *See generally* AHARON KLIEMAN, CONSTRUCTIVE AMBIGUITY IN MIDDLE EAST PEACE-MAKING (1999) (describing various instances of constructive ambiguity in Oslo Accords and disputes arising from them).
162. *See* Omar M. Dajani, *Surviving Opportunities: Palestinian Negotiating Patterns in Peace Talks with Israel, in* HOW ISRAELIS AND PALESTINIANS NEGOTIATE: A CROSS CULTURAL ANALYSIS OF THE OSLO PEACE PROCESS 39, 56 (Tamara Coffman Wittes ed. 2005).

negotiations is to implement U.N. Security Council Resolutions 242 and 338, explaining that "[t]he essence of implementation is reflected in the complete withdrawal of the Israeli military forces from the occupied Palestinian territories, terminating the Israeli security, military and economic control on the elements of the Palestinian life in some regions, removing all negative effects resulted from the Israeli occupation."[163]

The day before the first round of permanent status negotiations commenced, however, Prime Minister Barak articulated a very different understanding of the implications of Resolution 242. While attending the International Socialist conference in Paris, Barak announced to reporters that Resolutions 242 and 338 did not apply to Israeli-Palestinian negotiations, explaining:

> In the case of Jordan, Egypt, Syria, and Lebanon, we are talking about states that have recognized, agreed borders with us. In the past, on that same border there was belligerent action, the results of which led to Israel holding onto territory. Resolution 242 refers to these territories. There is no such border on the West Bank.[164]

In a later clarification, Barak stated that while Resolution 242 was indeed applicable to the negotiations, "its context with regard to negotiations with the Palestinians is different from the context with regard to the other fronts."[165] These statements "created misgivings about Israel's intentions,"[166] provoking a fiery response from Yasser Arafat, who declared in his own speech, "Our Palestinian Arab people are still knocking on the door of international legality . . . . International legality is pivotal in the search for a just and comprehensive peace."[167]

This disagreement about how Resolution 242 applied to the Palestinian-Israeli conflict not only foreshadowed a normative dispute that re-emerged once negotiations began, it also challenged the logic behind the bifurcated process and short timetable to which the parties had agreed at Sharm el-Sheikh. The brief timeframe initially allocated to negotiating the FAPS[168] was based on the expectation that the parties would conclude a relatively brief agreement—"a thin FAPS," as they called it—that, as its name suggested, would define the framework for a comprehensive agreement.

In order to conclude a thin FAPS, however, the parties needed either to agree on principles that were clear and robust enough to establish their bargaining zone (the Egypt/Jordan model), to rely on good faith in interpreting more ambiguous formulations (the DOP model), and/or to provide for a third party mechanism to resolve interpretive differences (as Egypt and Israel had done to resolve a border dispute about Taba). The public scrape over

---

163. Palestinian Committee on Borders and Security, A Position and Concept Paper about Borders and Security in the Final Status Negotiations (October 1999) (on file with PLO Negotiations Affairs Dep't).
164. YOSSI BEILIN, THE PATH TO GENEVA: THE QUEST FOR A PERMANENT AGREEMENT, 1996-2004 115 (2004).
165. *Id.*
166. *Id.* at 115-16.
167. *See* Jocelyn Noveck, *Israeli, Palestinian Leaders Disagree on U.N. Resolutions*, AKRON BEACON, Nov. 10, 1999, at A2.
168. Already brief, the time available for negotiation was shortened by Israel's decision to focus on negotiating a peace agreement with Syria during the same period.

Resolution 242 just before negotiations began raised questions about the parties' ability to agree on clear principles, and the lingering recriminations about the scope of and compliance with their respective obligations under the Oslo accords challenged each side's confidence in the other's good faith. Moreover, Israel had made clear in negotiations regarding interim issues that it regarded the strictly bilateral structure of the negotiations process as a "red line" and would not countenance third party involvement.[169] As discussed in the next section, these obstacles to concluding a thin FAPS ultimately proved insurmountable. As an Israeli legal adviser commented to me during a break in one of the early negotiation sessions, "Why is it only clear to the lawyers in the room that a thin FAPS is impossible? Where you want thin, we want fat, and where we want thin, you want fat!"

C.   Competing Visions of Law's Role in Permanent Status Negotiations

Once permanent status negotiations eventually began in November 1999, the parties were confronted with a challenge of formidable proportions. Having committed to "make a determined effort to conclude a Framework Agreement on all Permanent Status issues" by February 13, 2000,[170] their first deadline loomed only 100 days ahead. Because the parties had reached agreement upon so little prior to the commencement of talks, however, the substantive questions they had yet to resolve were numerous, including:

- Would a Palestinian state be established in the West Bank and Gaza Strip?
- What course would the borders between Israel and the "Palestinian entity"[171] take? Would a territorial link between the West Bank and the Gaza Strip be established?
- How would sovereignty and control over the city of Jerusalem be allocated?
- What would happen to Israeli settlements in the West Bank, East Jerusalem, and the Gaza Strip and their residents?
- How would strategic and tactical security arrangements be structured in the future? Would Israel maintain military/security assets in or access to the West Bank and Gaza Strip and their airspace? Would limitations be placed on Palestinian military or security capacity?
- What would be the fate of the Palestinian refugees who fled or were expelled from territory in what is now the State of Israel? Would they be permitted to return to Israel? What would happen to their real property and other assets in Israel?

---

169. *See* Omar M. Dajani, *Understanding Barriers to Peace: A Palestinian Response*, 20 NEG. J. 401, 404–05 (2004).

170. Sharm el-Sheikh Memorandum, para. 1(c), *in* 2 DOCUMENTS ON THE ARAB-ISRAELI CONFLICT, *supra* note 5, at 1150.

171. Until May 2000, when Israeli negotiators began to acknowledge that a Palestinian state would be established in the West Bank and Gaza Strip in the context of a permanent status agreement, they tended to refer only to the "Palestinian entity" that would be established. *See infra* note 248 and accompanying text.

- How would sovereignty and control over critical resources such as water and the electromagnetic sphere be allocated and coordinated?
- What kind of economic relationship would the parties establish in the future? Would the modified customs union established by the Oslo Accords be replaced by a free trade area?

These questions, in turn, raised a range of difficult process questions: Which issues should be negotiated first? Which issues should be negotiated in tandem? Which, if any, were not subject to negotiation at all? Which issues should be addressed in the FAPS and which in the CAPS? Which should be addressed in other ways, such as through side agreements, unilateral declarations, or commitments to third parties? What effect would commitments in the FAPS have pending negotiation of the CAPS? With which Palestinian entity would each agreement be concluded—the PLO or the government of a Palestinian state? In what order would each side perform its obligations? Would a new set of transitional arrangements be defined? For what duration? How—and by whom—would disputes regarding interpretation or implementation of the agreements be resolved?

Presented with such a dizzying agenda and such a short deadline, each of the parties arrived at the table with ideas about how to simplify the task before them. Their ideas, however, differed, and one of the issues with respect to which they differed most was the role that international law should play in resolving the substantive and procedural questions the parties faced. In his memoir of the peace process, United States mediator Dennis Ross observes:

> Over time, the negotiations that emerged from the Madrid and Oslo processes were very detailed on all issues. But the points of departure were very different. The Arabs and Palestinians always sought acceptance of their principles while the Israelis always sought recognition of the practicalities. The gaps on the issues bore not just disagreements but very different attitudes about the negotiations, their purpose, and the tactics that should be employed.[172]

Even if one puts aside Ambassador Ross's implicit judgment about the reasonableness of the parties' respective approaches (*"their* principles" vs. *"the* practicalities"), I submit that his account misapprehends the core difference between them. As discussed below, both parties undertook to confirm that they shared a bargaining zone by seeking agreement to a set of guiding principles. Both parties also articulated principles on the basis of which, they argued, prospective deal points should be evaluated. What they differed about was which principles to use. Whereas the principles urged by the Palestinians tended to be defined in relation to international legal norms (at least initially), the principles advanced by the Israelis tended to be defined in relation to Israel's national security concept, domestic public opinion, and, toward the end of the negotiation process, American proposals.

In this Section, I undertake to explain those differences by examining how the parties used, or attempted to use, international law and their discourse about its value and relevance to their negotiation process. Although it is difficult to generalize about a process that ultimately spanned thirteen months

---

172. Ross, *supra* note 6, at 44-45.

and scores of meetings among changing teams of negotiators from each side, I suggest that the parties attempted to use international legal rules during the negotiations in four different ways: (1) to facilitate definition of either a zone of lawfulness or a bargaining zone; (2) as objective standards for choosing between competing positions; (3) to fill in gaps in the agreement; and (4) to challenge the legitimacy of non-legal criteria for resolving disputed issues. Each of these patterns is considered below.

1.   *Use of Legal Rules to Facilitate Zone Definition*

During early negotiation rounds in the winter of 1999-2000, the parties dedicated considerable effort to discussing how to structure an agenda for the negotiation process—which issues would be addressed and in what order they would be negotiated. These discussions were sometimes contentious, often implicating the parties' substantive positions, and they never produced a lasting decision, the negotiations instead proceeding in an ad hoc manner. Indeed, debates about the sequence and content of the parties' substantive agenda persisted until well into June 2000 [173]—seven months after the commencement of the talks. To a significant extent, as described below, the parties' disputes about how and what to negotiate arose from disputes about guiding principles.

Particularly during early rounds, the Palestinian team argued that negotiations should begin with an effort to reach a common understanding regarding the legal principles that would guide resolution of disputed issues. Their arguments took two forms. Initially, the Palestinian negotiating team took the position that international norms were *mandatory rules* that required resolution of disputed issues in particular ways, declining to discuss Israeli proposals until the parties reached consensus about the boundaries of the zone of lawfulness within which they were operating. Over time, however, Palestinian negotiators began invoking law in a different way, treating international norms as *default rules*. While acknowledging that the parties could depart from the default if they so agreed, the Palestinians turned to arguing that the rules established certain principles that should serve as a starting point for negotiations, in essence invoking the "shadow of the law" to bolster the credibility of their declared reservation points. The Israeli response to both kinds of arguments was to challenge the applicability and efficacy of international legal norms, as well as the Palestinians' interpretations of them.

a.   *Mandatory Rules*

The Palestinians' initial approach is well-illustrated by their positions in early negotiation sessions on refugees, security, and territorial issues. In their first presentation of their "concept" for resolution of the refugee issue, for example, they argued that U.N. General Assembly Resolution 194, which provides, inter alia, that "the refugees wishing to return to their homes and

---

173. *See* Minutes, Palestinian-Israeli Negotiations, Bolling Air Force Base, Washington, D.C. (June 13, 2000) (transcribed by PLO Negotiations Support Unit) (on file with PLO Negotiations Affairs Dep't).

live in peace with their neighbours should be permitted to do so,"[174] simply "restated and reaffirmed a well-established norm in international customary law."[175] Accordingly, they submitted, "the Framework Agreement must give full recognition to the right of every refugee to return to his or her home" and provide for the implementation of that right.[176] Although the Palestinians' presentation also cited a range of non-legal justifications for refugee return,[177] the central thrust of their argument was that Palestinian refugees have a sacrosanct individual legal right to return and that negotiations should be confined to defining a process for its realization.[178]

The Palestinians' opening presentation on borders and security issues also undertook to narrow the scope of negotiations through reference to mandatory rules. This passage from the speech, a virtual paean to international law, is illustrative:

> We are convinced that the strongest and most durable foundation for peace between us is international law. In the wake of the Second World War, the international community united in an effort to prevent that terrible human tragedy from ever occurring again. That effort yielded two legal instruments that represent the international consensus regarding how we must conduct ourselves during times of peace and during times of war: the Charter of the United Nations and the Geneva Conventions of 1949. To be sure, these two legal instruments do not provide detailed answers to all of the questions presently before us . . . . They do, however, codify many of the principles essential to the orderly conduct of international relations—principles that must guide both our present deliberations and our relationship in the future.
>
> Central among these principles is the rule against the acquisition of territory by threat or use of force. As the United Nations Security Council recognized in Resolution 242, a just and lasting peace in the Middle East is contingent upon faithful application of that rule. Thus, although we believe that every State in the region is indeed entitled to live in peace within secure and recognized borders, we also believe that an unjust border can never be secure. Accordingly, a settlement involving anything less than Israeli withdrawal to 1967 borders and the realization of the civil, political, and economic rights of the Palestinian people will serve neither the interests of peace nor the interests of security.[179]

In this presentation, the Palestinians were not simply citing international norms as evidence of the fairness of their position; they were arguing that international norms mandated a particular result—i.e., that the "rule against the acquisition of territory by force" required nothing less than "Israeli withdrawal to 1967 borders." As Shlomo Ben Ami later recounted, "For the

---

174. G.A. Res. 194 (III), 11 U.N. Doc. A/RES/194 (III) (Dec. 11, 1949).

175. Yasser Abed-Rabbo, Palestinian Authority Minister of Culture and Information, Palestinian Presentation on Refugees at the Palestinian-Israeli Permanent Status Negotiations, Neve Ilan Hotel, Jerusalem (Dec. 9, 1999) (on file with PLO Negotiations Affairs Dep't).

176. *Id.*

177. Other justifications offered in the presentation included Israel's moral obligation "to shoulder the responsibility" for "the creation and perpetuation of the refugee problem over the past fifty years," the interest in "generating public confidence in peace," and interest in minimizing the threat to security represented by "keeping a population of refugees by force out of their places of origin." *Id.*

178. *Id.* At the conclusion of this presentation, the Israeli negotiating team declined to discuss the legal basis for refugee return, and the issue of refugees appears not to have been taken up again by the parties until March 2000. *See* ENDERLIN, *supra* note 6, at 143 (describing U.S.-moderated brainstorming session on refugees).

179. General Abdel Razzaq el-Yahya, Chairman of Palestinian Borders and Security Committee, The Palestinian Vision for Peace and Security, Presentation at the Palestinian-Israeli Permanent Status Negotiations, Neve Ilan Hotel, Jerusalem (Nov. 29, 1999) (on file with PLO Negotiations Affairs Dep't).

Palestinians, this was a simple, clear-cut process of decolonisation based on 'international legitimacy' and 'UN relevant resolutions.'"[180]

The Israeli team began from a very different starting point.[181] At a ceremony on September 13, 1999, marking the formal resumption of permanent status negotiations, Israel's then-Foreign Minister David Levy announced that "Israel is guided by four basic principles in negotiating a permanent status agreement: we will not return to the 1967 lines; united Jerusalem will remain the capital of Israel; settlement blocs will remain under Israeli sovereignty; there will be no foreign army west of the Jordan River."[182] The Israeli negotiating team's proposals during early rounds of negotiations conformed to these principles.[183] On December 20, 1999, for example, the Israeli team presented its "concept" for the "land basket" (i.e., issues with a territorial dimension).[184] Suggesting that "[t]he issue of settlements must be resolved in a permanent and realistic way—and we emphasize 'realistic,'" Israel's head of delegation, Ambassador Oded Eran, explained that there were 175,000 Israeli settlers in the West Bank[185] and that "[i]t would be unrealistic to expect that this number will be removed from where they live today."[186] Accordingly, he proposed, three categories of settlements were envisioned: those "in blocs under Israeli sovereignty"; "other individual settlements . . . under Israeli sovereignty"; and other settlements "not under Israeli sovereignty whose status will be negotiated."[187] With respect to the individual settlements to be placed under Israeli sovereignty, Eran stated that "four principles must be provided for in the agreement: (1) viability and future development of settlements[;] (2) means of livelihood and necessary infrastructure[;] (3) safety and security[; and] (4) free and secure movement and access."[188] In addition, Eran also proposed that a number of security zones—some under Israeli sovereignty, some under Israeli control—be established or maintained in the West Bank and Gaza Strip.[189]

When smaller teams from each side convened the next day to discuss territorial issues in greater detail, the differences between their approaches came into sharper focus. According to a report of the meeting prepared by the PLO's legal unit, the Palestinians continued to argue that international law mandated Israeli withdrawal to 1967 lines: "the Palestinian side emphasized that international law—specifically, the rule against the acquisition of territory by force—and the 'land for peace' formula promoted in Resolution 242

---

180. BEN AMI, *supra* note 6, at 246.

181. *See id.* at 247.

182. David Levy, Minister of Foreign Affairs, Address at the Ceremony Marking the Resumption of Permanent Status Negotiations, Erez Crossing Point (Sept. 13, 1999).

183. ROSS, *supra* note 6, at 624–25 (describing "the red lines that had governed the Israeli approach in the negotiations").

184. Ambassador Oded Eran, Presentation at Negotiation Session, Best Eastern Hotel, Ramallah (Dec. 20, 1999) (transcribed by PLO Negotiations Support Unit) (on file with PLO Negotiations Affairs Dep't).

185. Throughout the negotiations process, the parties disagreed about whether Israeli residents of East Jerusalem were appropriately considered settlers. Reflecting Israel's position, Eran refers here only to Israeli settlers outside of the municipal boundaries of Jerusalem established by Israel.

186. *See* Eran, *supra* note 184.

187. *Id.*

188. *Id.*

189. *Id.*

required Israeli withdrawal to the armistice cease-fire lines in force on June 4, 1967."[190] With respect to the Israeli presentation the day before, "[t]he Palestinian side asked a number of questions intended to probe the legal basis (or lack thereof) for the Israeli proposals," but the Palestinians declined to discuss the issues of borders, settlements, and security arrangements in detail unless "the Israeli side . . . agreed to withdrawal."[191]

The Israeli side, as the Palestinians perceived it, "appeared hesitant to discuss the legal basis for its proposals and sought, throughout the meeting, to shift the discussion to the concrete proposals they presented at the plenary session."[192] When pressed to respond to Palestinian questions about the applicable legal framework, "[t]he Israeli side suggested that international law can be useful in negotiations *only* if both sides agree that it is applicable and agree on its interpretation. They made clear . . . that they did not think there is agreement regarding either the applicability or the interpretation of international law in the present negotiations."[193] According to the Palestinians, the Israeli team responded to their specific legal arguments as follows:

> *Resolution 242.* The Israeli side argued that 242 simply requires a compromise between territory and security. They stated that, while the rule against the acquisition of territory by force was applicable, it was somehow applicable only to a limited extent in the context of the West Bank/Gaza. What 242 did require, they claimed, was the establishment, for each State, of "secure and defensible borders". It is unclear to what extent they regard this requirement as applicable to a state of Palestine, however: they reiterated that Palestine was not mentioned in 242 and that the [sic] Palestinian peoplehood had not received international recognition in 1967.
>
> *Fourth Geneva Convention.* The Israeli side refused to acknowledge that the Convention is applicable, arguing that Israel is not a belligerent occupant. They claimed that occupation presupposes the prior existence of a State and that "nobody knows" the status of the West Bank and Gaza Strip prior to 1967. . . . Although they acknowledged that Israel's views on this issue place it in the extreme minority, they asserted that "no one can force Israel to adopt another interpretation."
>
> *Peace treaties with Egypt and Jordan.* The Israeli side argued, without elaboration, that these peace treaties do not provide useful precedents because the factual contexts were different.[194]

In sum, the Israeli team argued that the legal rules cited by the Palestinians did little to define a zone of lawfulness for the talks: they were either inapplicable or indeterminate with respect to disposition of the issues on the table. They also maintained that Israel could not be obliged to accept the Palestinians' interpretation of norms, even if it was shared by the majority of the international community. Because legal norms were not "useful," the parties should resolve their disputes on the basis of other, more "realistic" grounds.

At virtually the same time that Palestinians and Israelis were debating these issues around the negotiation table, a very similar discussion unfolded among delegates to the sixty-eighth plenary meeting of the U.N. General

---

190. PLO Negotiations Affairs Dep't Legal Unit, Report on Permanent Status Negotiations: Special Session on Borders Issues, December 21, 1999, Ramallah (Dec. 23, 1999) (on file with PLO Negotiations Affairs Dep't) (emphasis added).
191. *Id.*
192. *Id.*
193. *Id.*
194. *Id.*

Assembly. As in previous years, the General Assembly considered a battery of draft resolutions relating to the question of Palestine.[195] In one of these resolutions, entitled "Peaceful settlement of the question of Palestine," the General Assembly noted "with satisfaction . . . the commencement of the negotiations on the final settlement," [196] and emphasized the need for: "realization of the inalienable rights of the Palestinian people, primarily the right to self-determination;" [197] "withdrawal of Israel from the Palestinian territory occupied since 1967;"[198] and "resolving the problem of the Palestine refugees in conformity with its resolution 194 (III) of December 1948."[199]

The resolution was adopted by an overwhelming majority (149 votes to 3, with 2 abstentions), but the delegates' explanations for their votes are more illuminating than the final tally. The Palestinian and Israeli delegates, unsurprisingly, expressed very different views about the appropriate role for the international community in their negotiations. The Israeli delegate reaffirmed Israel's insistence on the strict bilateralism of the peace talks, explaining that Israel had chosen to vote against the resolution because it "openly seeks to predetermine the issues to be resolved by . . . negotiations, even as Israel and the Palestinians commit themselves to the permanent status talks that are now under way." [200] He argued, moreover, that a bilateral approach was explicitly mandated by the parties' earlier agreements.[201] The Palestinian delegate, in contrast, argued for a robust international role in ensuring that the talks were guided by international legal norms. He stated that the broad support for the resolution reflected "the commitment by the international community . . . to continue the efforts that we made to attain peace on the basis of international law and the principles of the Charter of the United Nations," expressing hope "that the Israeli side will abandon its present policy and positions and will start complying with requirements of international legitimacy" and calling on the international community "to take the necessary steps to end [Israel's] misguided conduct."[202]

The other delegates' speeches addressed the role of international law—and of the international community—in constraining the outcome of the peace talks in a number of different ways. A first group, comprised of representatives of Arab and Muslim countries and the Islamic Conference, spoke in the language of mandatory rules. Indonesia's delegate, for example, asserted that "everlasting peace can be established *only* with the full and unfettered exercise of the *inalienable* rights of the Palestinians and the *complete* withdrawal of Israel from all occupied Arab lands," and that "[t]he United Nations continues to bear a historical and moral responsibility for

---

195. *See supra* notes 141-142 and accompanying text.
196. G.A. Res. 54/42, ¶ 3, U.N. Doc. A/RES/54/42 (Jan. 21, 2000).
197. *Id.* ¶ 5.
198. *Id.*
199. *Id.* ¶ 6.
200. U.N. GAOR, 54th Sess., 68th plen. mtg. at 16, U.N. Doc. A/54/PV.68 (Dec. 1, 1999).
201. *Id.*
202. *Id.* at 20.

resolving this intractable conflict in all its aspects."[203] A second group, which included the delegates of Chile and Argentina, expressed support for strict application of international norms and UN resolutions to the resolution of the issues in dispute, but stopped short either of explaining what result that mandated or of demanding an international role in assuring it.[204] The Republic of Korea expressed support for the principles embraced by the resolution but seemed to suggest that the international community should focus on "endeavour[ing] to create the most propitious environment for peace to be realized" by facilitating Palestinian economic development.[205] The European Union simply "reiterate[d] its firm commitment to a just, lasting and comprehensive settlement in the Middle East based on the Madrid and Oslo Accords," leaving the support of its members for the resolution to speak for itself.[206] Finally, the United States, which joined Israel (and the Marshall Islands) in voting against the resolution, lent its support to Israel's bilateralist position, arguing that "[b]y adopting this . . . resolution, the General Assembly would seek to inappropriately interject its views into these negotiations," which "complicate[s] . . . the efforts of the parties themselves to achieve a settlement."[207]

It is risky to extrapolate too much about states' attitudes regarding the role of international law in peace negotiations from votes on resolutions of this kind and the speeches explaining them. The legal effect of General Assembly resolutions in general is a matter of some contention.[208] And when a resolution presumes to apply international law to a specific conflict, it is particularly hard to distinguish a commitment to a given norm from an effort to advance a narrower political agenda (e.g., supporting an ally, seeking a precedent that will advance a government's own interests in a separate (or related) context, or satisfying domestic constituencies with brave words in a setting that presents few costs). Moreover, the speeches offered in support of Resolution 54/42 express so many different rationales at such varying levels of abstraction that a prevailing "international community" position regarding the legal parameters—the zone of lawfulness—for a Palestinian-Israeli peace settlement is difficult to discern.[209]

What the discourse in the General Assembly in December 1999 does illustrate, however, is the challenges Palestinians were likely to face if they sought third-party adjudication or enforcement of the legal norms they were invoking at the negotiating table. Notwithstanding the near universal expression of support for their positions on key issues, the United States's opposition to even a limited normative statement by the international

---

203. *Id.* at 2 (emphasis added). This position was also taken by the delegates from Lebanon, *id.* at 4; Oman, *id.* at 5; the Syrian Arab Republic, *id.* at 6-7; Qatar, *id.* at 10; and the Organization of the Islamic Conference, *id.* at 11.

204. *Id.* at 1 (Chile); *id.* at 9 (Argentina).

205. *Id.* at 8.

206. *Id.* at 13-14.

207. *Id.* at 16.

208. *See* JAN KLABBERS, AN INTRODUCTION TO INTERNATIONAL INSTITUTIONAL LAW 207-211 (2002) (describing various theories regarding the General Assembly's law-making powers).

209. That said, the resolution arguably goes a good distance toward defining a prevailing international conception of the appropriate *political* contours of a peace settlement.

community did not bode well for the Palestinians' argument that the contours of a final settlement were constrained by mandatory rules of international law. Indeed, it foreshadowed the position that United States officials would take at Camp David a few months later.

For a time, however, the normative debate ended there. In January 2000, the parties shifted to negotiating the scope of still unfulfilled interim commitments, [210] and the Barak government focused its attention on negotiating a peace agreement with Syria.[211] The February 13, 2000, deadline for concluding the FAPS passed without fanfare—and without an agreement.

b.   *Default Rules*

During the spring and summer of 2000, Palestinian negotiators began to change the way they used international law in negotiations. They continued to seek Israeli acknowledgement that international legal rules entitled the Palestinian people to certain benefits, but they expressed increasing willingness to exchange those benefits for others—essentially, to bargain in the shadow of the law.

This shift in approach first appeared during a round of "back channel" talks convened in late April and early May 2000 in Jerusalem and Stockholm as part of an effort to jump-start the moribund Palestinian-Israeli track.[212] During these talks, Palestinian negotiators for the first time "acknowledged that settlement areas like Gush Etzion, Ramot, and Gilo could become part of Israel given either their contiguity or their significance in terms of historical Jewish presence[,]"[213] but they continued to state that they "preferred to build the map from concepts rather than to build the concepts from the map."[214] These concepts included recognition of "the inadmissibility of the acquisition of territory by war and the obligation of states to conduct themselves in conformity with the U.N. Charter and the norms of international law, and the right of the Palestinian people to self-determination," norms the Palestinians sought to reference explicitly in the agreement.[215]

The Palestinian negotiators involved in the Stockholm round disclaimed their concessions when their talks were leaked to the public,[216] and Mahmoud Abbas, then head of the Palestinian Negotiations Affairs Department, made clear that Palestinians "could only accept the full implementation of the U.N.

---

210. In the parties' earlier agreements, Israel had committed to undertake a series of redeployments from West Bank territory (territory over which the Palestinian Authority would assume jurisdiction), the last two of which had yet to be completed. The scale of these redeployments, along with other issues, was the focus of negotiation during this period. *See* ENDERLIN, *supra* note 6, at 138-40; *see also* ROSS, *supra* note 6, at 591-99.

211. *See* ENDERLIN, *supra* note 6, at 140-42.

212. These talks were held in secret, with the knowledge only of the participants and their principals, at the same time that "front channel" talks proceeded in the Israeli resort town of Eilat. For a detailed description of the Stockholm round, see ROSS, *supra* note 6, at 603-620; ENDERLIN, *supra* note 6, at 147-158.

213. ROSS, *supra* note 6, at 614.

214. *Id.*

215. ENDERLIN, *supra* note 6, at 154.

216. *Id.* at 158 (noting that Palestinian negotiator Ahmad Qurei' described the Stockholm paper as an "Israeli document").

resolutions now—on both territory and refugees." [217] Nevertheless, the Palestinians reverted to the approach they had taken at Stockholm when they arrived at Camp David two months later. The following exchange regarding territorial issues on July 12, 2000, the second day of the summit, illustrates this shift:

> *Abu Ala [Ahmad Qurei']*: Will you accept the June 4 border [as the basis of discussion]? Will you accept the principle of the exchange of territories?
> *Shlomo Ben Ami*: The Palestinian State will be created in the context of the agreement. This will be the solution to the refugee and Jerusalem problems. It will create a new situation, including various elements [that could play a role in the] exchange of territories.
> *Mohammed Dahlan (with Saeb Erekat translating from Arabic to English)*: We're entering the final week of a negotiation that has lasted five years. I know time isn't on our side. Will you accept Abu Ala's position on the subject of the line of June 4, 1967? We don't trust the way the Israelis are approaching the negotiation. You demand positions in Palestinian territory, we accept, and when all is said and done we wind up as strangers in this territory. We know what you want, but I don't think we can go further if you don't recognize the June 4 line. *After that, it will be possible to discuss modifications of the border and raise the question of the settlements. But this can't be done unless there's an agreement on the '67 line and [recognition of] the concept of an exchange of territories.*
> *Ben Ami*: We'll see that on the maps. But we've always taken the '67 line as a basis. The percentages of territory [that must be evacuated by the Israeli army] in the framework of the interim accord are on the West Bank, that is, on the basis of the '67 line.
> *Dahlan*: We're claiming the '67 line as a reality; it's not just a slogan for us. I reject on principle any agreement that will then be torpedoed in its implementation.
> *Madeleine Albright*: The Palestinians aren't clearly explaining their demands in the negotiation, and that makes the Israelis' task difficult. There has to be more depth in the presentation of your demands. [218]

Although the Palestinian negotiators in this exchange were not explicitly using the language of law, their statements treated the June 4, 1967 line not as a physical fact but as a legal construct. By seeking recognition of the 1967 line as the basis for negotiation, they were in effect claiming legal entitlement to the West Bank. Unlike in their early presentations, however, the Palestinian negotiators expressed willingness at Camp David to "discuss modifications of the border and raise the question of settlements," on the condition that they would receive compensation in the form of land exchange for any negotiated modifications to the 1967 line. Thus, they ceased to present Israeli withdrawal to the 1967 line as a mandatory rule that could not be varied, treating it instead as the default provided by law—a default that could be bargained around if commensurate benefits were offered.

The Palestinians' approach appears to have represented an attempt both to establish a "bargaining endowment"—i.e., to invoke the shadow of the law to bolster the credibility of their claimed reservation point (establishing a Palestinian state on territory equivalent in size to the West Bank and Gaza Strip)—and to narrow the range of outcomes that could emerge from the negotiations, to obtain reassurance that there was a bargaining zone within which a deal acceptable to them could be reached. Colonel Dahlan's expression of concern that a lack of recognition of the 1967 line as a basis for

---

217. ROSS, *supra* note 6, at 624.
218. ENDERLIN, *supra* note 6, at 185 (emphasis added) (citation omitted).

negotiation would yield an agreement that would leave the Palestinians "strangers in the territory" and could be "torpedoed in implementation" was a direct reference to the DOP and other interim agreements, which left Israel wide latitude in determining how much territory Palestinians would control during the interim period.[219] The Palestinians' demand for recognition of their entitlement to the 1967 line at the beginning of the summit seems to have been an attempt to ensure that permanent status talks would not proceed along the same path.

At Camp David, however, the Palestinians' attempt to make international norms the starting point for bargaining encountered resistance not only from the Israeli team,[220] but also from the Americans, as reflected in Secretary Albright's intervention during the initial round of territory negotiations at Camp David. [221] American impatience grew even more pronounced as the summit progressed (or failed to). On July 15, when asked by President Clinton to comment on a map presented by the Israelis, Palestinian negotiator Ahmad Qurei' refused, stating, "The Israelis must first accept the principle of the exchange of territories. Besides, for the Palestinians, international legitimacy means Israeli retreat to the border of June 4, 1967." Clinton's response reportedly was explosive; he shouted, "Sir, I know you'd like the whole map to be yellow [sovereign Palestinian territory]. But that's not possible. This isn't the Security Council here. This isn't the UN General Assembly. If you want to give a lecture, go over there and don't make me waste my time. . . .You're obstructing the negotiation. You're not acting in good faith."[222] In an attempt to clarify their position, the Palestinians conveyed a letter to Clinton the next day, explaining, "The aim of the negotiations is the implementation of Resolutions 242 and 338 . . . that is, Israel's withdrawal to the line of June 4, 1967. We are willing to accept adjustments of the border between the two countries, on condition that they be equivalent in value and importance."[223] According to then-National Security Advisor Sandy Berger, the ensuing discussion between Clinton and Arafat was "very difficult," Clinton threatening to bring an early end to the summit unless the Palestinians responded to Israel's demands for annexation of settlement blocs containing 80% of Israeli settlers, for an Israeli military presence on the West Bank border with Jordan, and a stipulation that the FAPS would "signify the end of the conflict."[224]

The Palestinians' legal arguments did not fall entirely on deaf ears. Describing internal deliberations regarding the formulation of an American proposal on territory in September 2000, Dennis Ross writes:

> Aaron [Miller] was always arguing for a just and fair proposal. I was not against a fair proposal. But I felt that the very concept of "fairness" was, by definition, subjective.

---

219. See Omar M. Dajani, *Stalled Between Seasons: The International Legal Status of Palestine During the Interim Period*, 26 DENV. J. INT'L L. & POL'Y 27, 61-66 (1997).

220. Israelis continued to argue that discussion should focus on the arrangements to be put in place, not on legal rights. *See, e.g.,* ENDERLIN, *supra* note 6, at 201-03.

221. *See supra* note 218 and accompanying text.

222. ENDERLIN, *supra* note 6, at 202; *see also* ROSS, *supra* note 6, at 668-69 (describing same episode).

223. ENDERLIN, *supra* note 6, at 212.

224. *Id.* at 212-13.

> Similarly, both Rob [Malley] and Gamal [Hilal] believed that the Palestinians were entitled to 100 percent of the territory. Swaps should thus be equal. *They believed this was a Palestinian right.* Aaron tended to agree with them not on the basis of right, but on the basis that every other Arab negotiating partner had gotten 100 percent. Why should the Palestinians be different?
>
> I disagreed. I was focused not on reconciling rights but on addressing needs. In negotiations, one side's principle or "right" is usually the other side's impossibility. Of course, there are irreducible rights. I wanted to address what each side needed, not what they wanted and not what they felt they were entitled to.[225]

But while the Palestinians' invocation of legal rights at Camp David does appear to have persuaded some members of the American peace team, Ross's perspective ultimately prevailed, the U.S. government expressing no explicit position on the parties' legal rights during the remainder of the negotiation process.

Even so, the Palestinians attempted to obtain agreement on legal rules as guiding principles with respect to other issues as well. In negotiations regarding water, conducted over a number of sessions during the summer of 2000, similar dynamics emerged. At the opening session on water on June 26, 2000, the Palestinians began by presenting a list of principles "under which we would like to negotiate."[226] These principles included, *inter alia*, "the principle of equality between States," "[s]overeignty over unshared watercourses," and "[e]quitable utilization of international watercourses."[227] In response, the lead Israeli negotiator on water issues stated, "As for underlying principles: our approach should be pragmatic and practical;"[228] and argued, *inter alia*, that the agreement should be based "on existing water uses in existing aquifers and the development of new water sources, primarily through desalination."[229] After the Israeli presentation, the Palestinian team insisted that negotiations not go forward until the parties had reached agreement on guiding principles, and the following exchange ensued:

> *Dr. Erekat*: Before that [sic][discussing quantities to be allocated], we need to establish principles.
>
> *Amb. Eran*: We cannot have an answer to your question in isolation from the rest of the picture.
>
> *Dr. Erekat*: A working relationship must be based on the principle of equality. Separatism and pragmatism do not work. We say, "Be fair to us." Once you establish this principle, only at that point can we talk about joint needs.
>
> *Amb. Eran*: If I may add my own statement, the angle from which we are coming is that we do not doubt that you will have sovereignty over your resources.
> This is not the issue. Since we are dealing with present needs and future needs, if we are going to apply the principles of sovereignty, then we can harm ourselves.
>
> *Dr. Erekat*: We are a nation state, our needs do not mean a disregard of the other party.
> . . . .
> *Amb. Eran*: I want to [sic] the experts to sit down together, and I want to give them a time limit, then ask them to come back to us next time, with whatever they have.

---

225. Ross, *supra* note 6, at 726 (emphasis added). Ross does not explain which rights, in his view, are "irreducible" or on what basis the needs of the parties should be objectively assessed.

226. Minutes, State-to-State Relations Committee, Sheraton Plaza Hotel, Jerusalem (June 26, 2000) (transcribed by PLO Negotiations Support Unit) (on file with PLO Negotiations Affairs Dep't).

227. *Id.*

228. *Id.*

229. *Id.*

We need them to put their agreement into writing, with I's and P's [designating differences in position].

    Dr. Erekat: Why start with this approach without agreeing on the principles?

    . . . .

    Amb. Eran: I am not willing to accept a principle without knowing what the implications are. I suggest that we let them sit with the principles and translate into a document. I don't want to trap them.

    Dr. Sharif: Mr. Noah [Kinnarti, Israeli water negotiator] has repeated pragmatism many times. There is no separation between pragmatism and ideology. The pragmatism is in the implementation.

    Amb.Eran: You cannot drink ideology.[230]

This exchange during the first round of water talks shows that, in this context as well, the Palestinian team sought Israeli acceptance of guiding legal principles—equality of states, sovereignty over endogenous watercourses, equitable utilization of shared watercourses—before it would agree to discuss specific allocations. Although the Israeli team acknowledged that Palestinians would possess sovereign rights to water resources, it expressed doubts about both the determinacy of the rules cited by Palestinians ("I am not willing to accept a principle without knowing what the implications are") and the efficacy of the rules as standards ("if we are going to apply the principles of sovereignty, then we can harm ourselves").

At the next session on water, held in Emmitsburg, Maryland, concurrent with the Camp David summit, the Israeli team again urged that discussion focus on the quantities of water the Palestinians sought to be allocated in the future.[231] The Palestinians again responded that "at that point in time, it was more important to agree on principles than on quantities," but they acquiesced and gave a presentation regarding their projected needs.[232] The Israeli offer made in response to this presentation, however, was "seen as woefully inadequate"[233] and prompted the Palestinian legal adviser in attendance to write to Sa'eb Ereikat, who headed the committee overseeing talks on future bilateral relations, complaining, "[T]he Israelis are negotiating in bad faith. They promised us that they would negotiate on the basis of relations between two sovereign states, but what they are proposing in many areas is a continuation of the interim agreement."[234]

When the parties resumed water talks in Jerusalem a few weeks later, the Palestinians demanded that legal advisers from each side meet to discuss the legal framework for the negotiations, and, after again expressing doubts about the value of such discourse, the Israeli team agreed.[235] During the next meeting, the Palestinians elaborated upon the legal framework that, they argued, governed resolution of water issues. They concluded their presentation by stating, "There is no difference between being practical and

---

230. *Id.*

231. Memorandum from Gamal Abouali, PLO Legal Adviser, to Palestinian Water Auth. & Negotiations Affairs Dep't (July 18, 2000) (on file with PLO Negotiations Affairs Dep't).

232. *Id.*

233. *Id.*

234. Memorandum from Gamal Abouali, PLO Legal Adviser, to Sa'eb Ereikat, Head, Palestinian Side, Monitoring and Steering Comm. (July 18, 2000) (on file with PLO Negotiations Affairs Dep't).

235. Minutes, Water Comm. (Under State-to-State Relations Comm.), Neve Ilan (Aug. 20, 2000) (transcribed by PLO Negotiations Support Unit) (on file with PLO Negotiations Affairs Dep't).

following [international law]. It is a recognition of the development of the law, practice, uses, etc. We do not think that it shouldn't be applied to the Palestine-Israel situation." [236] What then proceeded was one of the few instances of explicit discourse between the parties about the role and relevance of international law to the talks between them. Once again, the Israeli team challenged the determinacy of the norms cited by the Palestinians, observing that, "The principle of sovereignty underwent a lot of changes in the past 50 years. No one knows how to define it anymore." The Israeli team argued that the principle of equitable utilization of international watercourses, on which the Palestinians sought to base water allocations, had not yet achieved the status of binding customary law. [237] In addition, the Israeli legal adviser challenged the utility of legal norms as a basis for resolving the issues under consideration, declaring at the conclusion of his presentation that "international law is vague, not pragmatic, and unrealistic—but that is our position." [238]

Ultimately, the parties were unable to agree on a set of guiding principles for resolution of the issues in dispute. As described above, Israelis rejected Palestinian attempts to obtain their acceptance of certain legal norms as parameters for the talks, a position supported by the United States. And, as described in Section 4, below, Palestinians were unwilling to accept non-legal guiding principles offered by Israel and the United States. Indeed, the parties' inability even at the end of the talks to come to a common understanding regarding the principles that should guide their negotiations raised questions on both sides about whether they shared a bargaining zone at all.

2. Use of Legal Rules as Objective Standards

The American response to the Palestinian legal arguments in the first days of the Camp David summit did not prompt them to cease invoking international law entirely. But the normative debate shifted from the beginning of the discussion to the middle of it: Palestinian negotiators for the most part stopped insisting that the Israeli team recognize Palestinian legal rights as a pre-condition for negotiation, but they continued to cite legal norms in support of their arguments for particular outcomes. For example, in two sessions on security issues in September 2000, the parties debated whether Israel or Palestine would control the Palestinian electromagnetic sphere. In his opening presentation, Israeli negotiator Gilead Sher stated, "we're not interested in any commercial use of the sphere. And whatever needs you may have in it, we shall do our best to accommodate—before signing the agreement." [239] When Palestinian negotiator Mohammad Dahlan responded to Sher the next day, he expressed willingness to construct a cooperative

---

236. Minutes, Water Comm. (Under State-to-State Relations Comm.), Neve Ilan (Aug. 24, 2000) (transcribed by PLO Negotiations Support Unit) (on file with PLO Negotiations Affairs Dep't).

237. *Id.*

238. *Id.*

239. Minutes, Palestinian-Israeli Permanent Status Negotiations, King David Hotel, Jerusalem (Sept. 17, 2000) (transcribed by PLO Negotiations Support Unit) (on file with PLO Negotiations Affairs Dep't).

framework for managing the electromagnetic sphere but rejected Israeli control on legal grounds:

> Regarding the [electromagnetic sphere], you use a phrase which I don't like—that you'll take care of my commercial needs. I'm talking about my rights. Give me your security concerns, and let's discuss it. The [electromagnetic] sphere . . . will be under our sovereignty and control. . . . Let the technical experts of both sides deal with these issues in coordination.[240]

Palestinians took the same approach to addressing control over airspace: while recognizing that there would be a need for close coordination between Palestinian and Israeli air traffic controllers, they rejected the Israeli demand for overriding control over Palestinian airspace, arguing that "it is Palestinian by right, and we will accommodate Israeli needs, not the other way around." [241] Similarly, in the last meeting between the parties and the American peace team before the outbreak of the intifada, Palestinian negotiators, who had earlier expressed willingness to accept Israeli annexation of certain areas of East Jerusalem, [242] argued that contiguity between Palestinian areas of East Jerusalem should trump contiguity between Israeli areas, stating, "the starting point should be that East Jerusalem is under Palestinian sovereignty and is Palestinian by right."[243]

3.   *Use of Legal Rules as Gap-Fillers*

As described above, the bifurcated structure of the permanent status negotiation process was based on the expectation that the parties would conclude a relatively brief framework agreement—a "thin FAPS." As the negotiations proceeded, however, the parties came to recognize the need for a far more detailed agreement than was originally envisaged.[244] The need for detail arose from the parties' inability to agree on guiding principles: the Israelis had declined to embrace the legal norms urged by the Palestinians;[245] and the Palestinians were unwilling to accept principles that gave Israel wide discretion in defining the scale of its commitments.[246]

To a limited extent, however, the parties did use legal rules as gap-fillers. The issue of Palestinian sovereignty is illustrative. In the first months of permanent status negotiations, the Israeli negotiating team declined officially to acknowledge that a Palestinian state would be established in the context of a permanent status agreement. Until May 2000, they insisted on referring to the "Palestinian entity (PE)" that would emerge, instead of a

---

240. Minutes, Palestinian-Israeli Permanent Status Negotiations, King David Hotel, Jerusalem (Sept. 18, 2000) (transcribed by PLO Negotiations Support Unit) (on file with PLO Negotiations Affairs Dep't).

241. inutes, Consultations with United States Officials, Washington, D.C. (Sept. 27, 2000) (transcribed by PLO Negotiations Support Unit) (on file with PLO Negotiations Affairs Dep't).

242. ENDERLIN, *supra* note 6, at 269-70.

243. Minutes, Consultations with United States Officials, Washington, D.C. (Sept. 27, 2000) (transcribed by PLO Negotiations Support Unit) (on file with PLO Negotiations Affairs Dep't).

244. *See* ROSS, *supra* note 6, at 616-18 (describing Israeli support for a "fat FAPS" and Palestinian insistence on "clear" agreement with "no ambiguity").

245. *See supra* Subsection III.C.1.b.

246. *See* ROSS, *supra* note 6, at 616.

Palestinian state;[247] and they undertook to define the rights and obligations of this "entity" from the ground up. For example, an Israeli outline of the structure of a permanent status agreement, presented at talks in Eilat in early May 2000, included headings such as "Foreign relations of the PE," "Territorial regime of areas under PE control and other areas," and "Israelis—Movement."[248] Thus, in the same way that the Oslo Accords had defined the powers delegated by Israel to the Palestinian Authority,[249] the Israelis' initial proposals for a permanent status agreement would have regulated the capacity of the "PE" to engage in foreign relations, its functional jurisdiction in various areas of the West Bank, and its personal jurisdiction over Israeli residents of settlements deep in Palestinian territory.

The parties' discourse changed, however, after Israelis began negotiating from the express assumption that the Palestinians would establish a state in the West Bank and Gaza Strip.[250] A number of the rights attached to statehood ceased to be topics of negotiation, such as Palestine's power to conduct foreign relations, its jurisdiction over all persons within Palestinian territory, and its right to control endogenous watercourses. Rather than defining the Palestinian state's powers from the ground up, the discussion shifted to reaching agreement on the specific derogations from sovereignty sought by the Israelis: assurance that Palestine would not enter into military or security alliances with states hostile to Israel; provision for Israeli military access to Palestinian territory in the event of an emergency; acceptance of monitoring of movement of persons and goods across Palestine's borders for a transitional period; and permission for Israel to apprehend unidentified and/or hostile aircraft approaching the two states and to conduct training exercises in Palestinian airspace. To be sure, some of the derogations sought by the Israelis were substantial, and Palestinians expressed concern that the exceptions would swallow the rule, constraining their sovereignty in ways that would challenge the economic or political viability of their new state.[251] It bears emphasizing, however, that the parties' point of departure had changed. By agreeing that the "Palestinian entity" would be a state, the "submerged" norms[252] of international law that define the rights and duties of states operated as both default rules and as gap-fillers, narrowing the scope of bargaining and helping to frame trade-offs.[253]

---

247. During a negotiation round in Eilat, Israel, in late April 2000, Palestinian and Israeli legal advisers met in an effort to define a "structure" for the FAPS. Even at this time, five months after negotiations commenced, the draft presented by the Israeli side referred to "The Palestinian Entity (PE)," not to a Palestinian state. Daniel Reisner, Israeli Legal Adviser, Draft FAPS Structure (Bolling II round) (Apr. 29, 2000) (presentation to Ghaith al-Omari, PLO Legal Adviser) (on file with PLO Negotiations Affairs Dep't).

248. *Id.*

249. *See* Dajani, *supra* note 219, at 61-69.

250. *See* ROSS, *supra* note 6, at 609 (describing meeting at which Israeli negotiators "conceded statehood as a principle").

251. *See* Official Palestinian Response to the Clinton Parameters (and Letter to the International Community) (Jan. 1, 2001), *in* 2 DOCUMENTS ON THE ARAB-ISRAELI CONFLICT, *supra* note 5, at 1162-67.

252. *See* HENKIN, *supra* note 2, at 21.

253. For example, in return for Palestinian consent to Israeli military access to Palestinian airspace, Israeli negotiators offered to make Palestine "the only sovereign state in the world that will have a specific, particular, privileged air corridor for your needs through Israeli skies." Minutes,

4.   *Challenges to Non-Legal Standards*

In addition to urging that principles of international law guide the negotiations and serve as standards for choosing between competing positions, Palestinian negotiators used legal rules to challenge the legitimacy of non-legal standards proposed by Israeli negotiators and American officials for resolving disputed issues. As described above, Palestinians raised questions about the legal basis of the principles urged by Israelis from the outset of the negotiations.[254] When three of the four principles articulated by David Levy in September 1999 were incorporated into the "ideas" suggested by President Clinton in December 2000,[255] moreover, Palestinians undertook to challenge the Clinton ideas on both legal and non-legal grounds.

During the last rounds of negotiations in January 2001, the Israeli team invoked the principles outlined by Clinton in much the same way that the Palestinians had invoked international legal norms in earlier negotiation sessions. At the Taba talks, for example, the Israeli team challenged the "basis" of Palestinian proposals for border modifications, arguing that they were inconsistent with Clinton's proposal that Israel annex 4-6% of West Bank territory, including 80% of the settlers in blocs. As Shlomo Ben-Ami explained:

> With regards to territory we do welcome the fact that we have a map from your side that assumes the concept of annexing settlement blocks. We have the principle, but not the necessary quantity. According to our calculations your map represents . . . essentially 2.2%. . . . It does not correspond to the parameters of President Clinton. It does not address the major issues of stability, security, and political viability. This is why we included the 80% requirements. I cannot have an agreement that does not incorporate 80% of the settlers—it's more or less the concept, not a math thing. It is necessary for the stability of our borders and for the public to accept the deal.[256]

Thus, like the Palestinians' use of the 1967 line at Camp David, Israeli negotiators treated percentages of territory and settlers as a construct—a "concept" against which to evaluate Palestinian proposals. Like the Palestinians, Israeli negotiators also cited practical and political concerns (border security and domestic public opinion) in support of the principles they were advocating. For legitimacy, however, the Israelis turned not to "the international legality," as the Palestinians had, but instead to the proposals of the President of the United States.

Palestinian-Israeli Permanent Status Negotiations, King David Hotel, Jerusalem (Sept. 18, 2000) (transcribed by PLO Negotiations Support Unit) (on file with PLO Negotiations Affairs Dep't). Similarly, Israeli negotiator Gilad Sher acknowledged: "If I want to have control in the [electromagnetic] sphere for my security needs, I may have to compensate you in a completely different issue." *Id.*

254. *See supra* note 191 and accompanying text.

255. Like the principles articulated by Levy, the Clinton Parameters, *inter alia*, provided for Israel's annexation of settlement blocs, made no reference to the 1967 line, and proposed that Palestine be a "non-militarized state." The sole departure from Levy's principles in the parameters was Clinton's proposal for shared sovereignty in Jerusalem. *See* Clinton Parameters to Palestinian and Israeli Negotiators (Dec. 23, 2000), *in* 2 DOCUMENTS ON THE ARAB-ISRAELI CONFLICT, *supra* note 5, at 1160-62.

256. Minutes, Palestinian-Israeli Permanent Status Negotiations, Hilton Taba Hotel, Taba, Egypt (Jan. 25, 2001) (transcribed by the PLO's Negotiations Support Unit) (on file with PLO Negotiations Affairs Dep't).

Ultimately, the Israelis' attempt to focus discourse on the "Clinton ideas" had little more success than the Palestinians' earlier attempt to focus it on international law. In a reversal of roles, it was the Palestinians at talks in January 2001 who were urging discussion of the "practicalities":

> *Ahmad Qurei'*: [W]e don't want to discuss principles and parameters[. L]et's see the maps, the practicalities[,] and discuss.
> *Gilad Sher*: Do you agree[,] with C[linton], that [the Palestinian allocation of West Bank] territory is between 94% and 96%?
> *Qurei'*: We don't agree, but show us the maps and then we may be convinced.
> *Sher*: Do you agree we need to meet re[garding] territory [on] somewhere in the mid-90s?
> *Qurei'*: Let me see how you designed it, and then I can give a response. Let's see the maps. Let's see the maps.[257]

As part of their effort to shift discourse away from the Clinton "parameters," the Palestinians also argued—as their Israeli counterparts had regarding international law—that the "parameters" were fatally indeterminate. In a memorandum presenting their official response to Clinton, which was distributed to the international diplomatic and press corps on January 1, 2001, they expressed concern that "[t]he United States proposals were couched in general terms that in some instances lack clarity and detail," arguing that "a general, vague agreement at this advanced stage of the peace process will be counter-productive."[258] They also argued that Clinton's failure to offer a proposed map and to define the basis for the percentages of land it allocates to each side makes it "difficult to imagine how the percentages presented can be reconciled with the goal of Palestinian contiguity."[259]

In addition, the Palestinians raised questions about the legitimacy of the legal framework for Clinton's proposals. In the same memorandum, they argued that his use of "'settlement blocs' as a guiding principle" would "subordinate[] Palestinian interests in the contiguity of their state and control over their natural resources to Israeli interests regarding the contiguity of the settlements, *recognized as illegal by the international community*."[260] They complained that Clinton's proposal on refugees "reflects a wholesale adoption of the Israeli position that the implementation of the right of return be subject entirely to Israel's discretion," emphasizing that "[U.N. General Assembly] Resolution 194, long regarded as the basis for a just settlement of the refugee problem, calls for the return of Palestinian refugees to 'their homes,' wherever located—not to their 'homeland' or 'historic Palestine,'" as suggested by Clinton.[261] And they concluded the memorandum by reiterating "that we remain committed to a peaceful resolution of the Palestinian-Israeli conflict in

---

257. Minutes, Palestinian-Israeli Permanent Status Negotiations, Isrotel Tower and Hotel, West Jerusalem (Jan. 16, 2001) (transcribed by the PLO's Negotiations Support Unit) (on file with PLO Negotiations Affairs Dep't).

258. Official Palestinian Response to the Clinton Parameters (and Letter to the International Community) (Jan. 1, 2001), *in* 2 DOCUMENTS ON THE ARAB-ISRAELI CONFLICT, *supra* note 5, at 1163-64..

259. *Id.* at 1164.

260. *Id.* (emphasis added).

261. *Id.* at 1166.

accordance with UN Security Council Resolutions 242 and 338 and international law."[262]

Four weeks after the Palestinians' official response to the Clinton ideas was delivered, President Clinton left office, Ariel Sharon was elected Prime Minister of Israel, and permanent status negotiations were suspended—permanently.

                              *   *   *

In sum, during the course of permanent status negotiations, international legal norms were invoked in a number of different ways: as guiding principles for the talks, as persuasive standards, as gap-fillers, and as a means of challenging non-legal standards on the basis of which resolution of disputed issues was urged. In the third and final Part of this Article, I undertake to explain why international law, for the most part, failed to serve those functions and to identify steps that may be taken to address the factors that constrained its effectiveness during the parties' abortive peace talks.

IV.   CASTING SHADOWS, PROVIDING SHADE: ROLES FOR INTERNATIONAL

LAW IN FUTURE PALESTINIAN-ISRAELI NEGOTIATIONS

The reasons for the failure of Palestinians and Israelis to achieve a negotiated settlement of their dispute have been the focus of sustained debate since the negotiations were suspended in January 2001. Although no consensus has emerged, many factors likely contributed to the parties' impasse, including: mutual mistrust arising not only from more than a century of conflict, but also from the perception that obligations established by previous agreements went unfulfilled; insufficient effort by each party to understand and respond to the other's national narrative; perceptions of bias on the part of American mediators; domestic political pressures and institutional dysfunctions on both sides; and a lack of clarity and frank discourse regarding the essential needs of each. The parties' differences regarding the content and role of international law consequently offer only a partial explanation for their inability to conclude an agreement. As Daniel Bethlehem observed in a recent forum on the role of law in the Middle East peace process:

> [O]ne of the questions we must ask ourselves is whether it was the presence or absence, or the sufficiency or insufficiency, of law that brought us either to the hopeful moments over the past twelve years or to the moments of despair. In my view, the answer to this is that one cannot place at the doorstep of the law either praise for the positive developments or castigation for the negative. The law provides context to the dispute. It is to be found to a greater or lesser extent in the engine room, either giving momentum to

---

262. *Id.* at 1167.

initiatives towards peace or holding such initiatives back as it crystallizes the position of the parties at the furthest extremes of the debate.[263]

To be sure, the parties' legal disputes are part of a larger dynamic in which law is only one variable. As Bethlehem goes on to suggest, moreover, the Palestinian-Israeli conflict presents a number of issues that cannot be resolved simply through reference to international legal rights and obligations.[264] Law, simply put, does not provide all of the answers.

Even so, it can and should provide some of them. I submit that an understanding of how law functions "in the engine room" offers clues about how it might be made to function better—to provide not only "context to the dispute," but also tools that can help to resolve it. Accordingly, in this final Part, I examine the factors that constrained the functioning of international legal norms in the Palestinian-Israeli negotiations. I then turn to offering suggestions as to how the parties and the international community can make international legal rules more effective in negotiations like those undertaken by Palestinians and Israelis, both as tools of conflict resolution and as normative standards to guide the functioning of international relations.

A.   Why Didn't Law Help?

The analysis presented in Part III of this Article suggests that several factors constrained the functioning of legal rules in Palestinian-Israeli negotiations: disagreements about the applicability and determinacy of legal rules; skepticism about the efficacy of solutions prescribed by legal rules; and the perceived lack of recourse to third-party adjudication and enforcement of legal rules. As discussed below, these factors served both to diminish international law's shadow over the negotiations and to deter efforts to seek its shade.

1.   Disagreements about Applicability and Determinacy of Legal Rules

Explicit discourse between the parties about the substantive contours and implications of international law was rare during permanent status negotiations, occurring in only a handful of instances. To the extent it did occur, however, it provides some sense of at least the stated rationales for Israeli negotiators' reluctance to use legal rules as guiding principles, standards, or gap-fillers. Two kinds of *legal* arguments were advanced. First, Israelis argued that the legal norms on the basis of which Palestinians urged

---

263. Daniel Bethlehem, Remarks, *Is There a Role for International Law in the Middle East Peace Process?*, 99 AM. SOC'Y INT'L L. PROC. 217, 218 (2005).

264. The need to devise arrangements through which Palestinian laborers can work in Israel, Israeli Jews can worship at holy sites in Palestinian territory (and Palestinian Christians and Muslims can do the same in Israel), and Palestinians can travel securely and in an unimpeded manner between the West Bank and Gaza Strip, for example, will oblige the parties to move beyond strict application of principles of territorial sovereignty. *See id.* Indeed, even advocates of a "rights-based approach" to resolving the Palestinian-Israeli conflict acknowledge the limitations of law. *See* Bisharat, *supra* note 8, at 330 ("[International law] will never provide all the answers. In respect to some issues, water, the status of Jerusalem, and perhaps others, international law may provide only the broadest parameters for equitable resolutions. Negotiations are thus crucial, and inevitable.").

resolution of many disputed issues were inapplicable to the Palestinian-Israeli conflict. For example, they argued that the principle of the inadmissibility of the acquisition of territory by force, affirmed in U.N. Security Council Resolution 242, was inapplicable to the West Bank and Gaza Strip because there was no recognized border between Israel and the occupied territory prior to 1967; and they rejected the argument that Israel's peace agreements with Jordan and Egypt established precedents with respect to the applicability and content of the norm because of this claimed difference in the factual contexts.[265] They advanced similar arguments with respect to the applicability of the Fourth Geneva Convention, claiming that Israel was not a belligerent occupant in the West Bank and Gaza Strip because they were not recognized as the sovereign territory of a state prior to 1967.[266] In the context of water negotiations, moreover, Israelis argued against the applicability of the principle of equitable utilization of international watercourses, asserting that the norm had yet to achieve customary law status and consequently was not binding upon Israel.[267]

Second, arguments about the applicability of international norms were closely linked to questions about their determinacy. In water negotiations, indeterminacy was raised explicitly: Israeli negotiators expressed unwillingness to agree to legal principles the implications of which, they argued, were unclear; and they took the position that international law is too "vague" to provide a useful framework for resolution of water issues. The disputes, in border negotiations, about the applicability of the principle of the inadmissibility of territory by force and the Fourth Geneva Convention may also be seen as arguments about the determinacy of these norms. Israelis were arguing, after all, that it was unclear how these norms applied in the context of the Palestinian-Israeli conflict. Implicit in their argument was the idea that, if Palestinians and Israelis each came to the table with different views about the applicability of the norms, the norms themselves were insufficiently determinate to guide resolution of disputed issues.

Of course, disagreement about the applicability or determinacy of legal rules does not, in itself, render the rules inapplicable or indeterminate. Whether offered in good faith or in bad faith, claims of inapplicability or indeterminacy are simply claims. In the domestic setting, the validity of those claims can be tested fairly readily, through recourse to a judicial forum. When that recourse is available, clearly frivolous legal claims will have only limited effect on bargaining: both parties will anticipate how they are likely to be received by a court and devise their negotiating positions accordingly. Because the influence of law on international bargaining is wielded through means more diffuse and less predictable than in the domestic setting, however, it is more difficult to trace. And, accordingly, it is more difficult to ascertain the effect of disagreements about the law on bargaining.

At a basic level, at least, disputes between Palestinians and Israelis about the applicability and determinacy of legal rules do seem to have constrained

---

265. *See supra* note 194 and accompanying text.
266. *See id.*
267. *See supra* note 237 and accompanying text.

their influence on the negotiations in a number of ways. In the absence of efforts by authoritative members of the international community to weigh in on the matter (an issue explored further below), the parties' disagreement blurred the lines of the zone of lawfulness within which they were bargaining. Thus, although international law's prohibition of acquiring territory by force is a jus cogens norm, that norm could not operate to rule out certain deal points, to narrow the scope of bargaining, if its applicability and interpretation were in dispute. Moreover, to the extent that influential third parties (like American officials) were persuaded that norms were inapplicable or indeterminate, it made invoking the norms an ineffective means of bolstering the credibility of a party's reservation point because uncertainty about whether or how the norms applied made it less likely they would be imposed on the parties in the absence of a negotiated agreement—the norms cast a minimal shadow over bargaining.

But were they perceived nevertheless to offer shade? The record is less clear on this point. On the one hand, allegations of inapplicability and indeterminacy did likely diminish the persuasive force of legal rules: because the parties could not agree on what the rules provided—or even whether they applied in given circumstances—the rules could neither serve as standards for resolving disputed issues (such as the allocation of sovereignty over Jerusalem) nor as an agreed means of filling in gaps in a "thin FAPS." In this way, claims of inapplicability and indeterminacy appear to have reduced the "compliance pull" of legal rules—the shade they were perceived to offer.

That analysis, however, arguably oversimplifies the picture. Notwithstanding its challenges to the applicability and determinacy of certain rules, over time Israel's positions on some issues moved closer to the outcome that Palestinians had argued the rules prescribed. For example, even though Israeli officials had made clear at the outset that they would not accept "return to the 1967 line," an EU paper on the final round of negotiations at Taba in January 2001 reports that "[t]he two sides agreed that in accordance with U.N. Security Council Resolution 242, the June 4[,] 1967 lines would be the basis for the borders between Israel and the state of Palestine."[268] Although the Israeli team at Taba continued to demand significant alterations to the 1967 line to permit annexation of settlement blocs,[269] their position represented a substantial departure from their earlier demands for annexation of much larger swathes of West Bank land and of isolated settlements.

A number of theories may explain this shift in position: that the Israeli team's stated opening position (or closing position) did not reflect its actual position; that the Israelis' assessment of the strategic, economic and political value of certain settlements changed over the course of the talks; or that other benefits presented by a peace agreement (either with respect to specific issues or the larger goal of ending the conflict) were perceived to outweigh the benefits of maintaining settlements. But one cannot rule out the possibility that legal rules influenced the decision—by virtue of the perceived

---

268. European Union Non-Paper on the Taba Conference, 2001, *in* 2 DOCUMENTS ON THE ARAB-ISRAELI CONFLICT, *supra* note 5, at 1169.
269. *See id.*

reputational costs of sticking to a position at odds with them or even, simply, by virtue of the normative force of repeated declarations by authoritative international institutions that the rules are applicable and controlling. Indeed, in view of the tremendous disparity in the parties' political, economic, and military power, it is worth considering whether settlements would even have been an item on the agenda of permanent status negotiations if the Palestinians were not perceived to have a legal basis for challenging them. In sum, although claims of inapplicability and indeterminacy reduced the instrumental value of legal rules as means of bolstering the efficiency of negotiations, it is not at all clear that they eliminated the rules' normative influence.

2.   *Disagreement about the Efficacy of Legal Rules*

The parties' dispute about the role and relevance of international law was not confined to disagreement about the applicability and determinacy of legal rules; they also expressed differing views about the efficacy, as a matter of policy, of outcomes prescribed by legal norms. Arguments of this kind were advanced with respect to a number of issues, sometimes in tandem with legal arguments about applicability and indeterminacy, and sometimes independent of them.[270]

The parties' negotiations over future security arrangements offer a particularly good illustration of this kind of debate. By September 2001, Israeli negotiators had acknowledged that a Palestinian state would be established in the West Bank and Gaza Strip and that it would have sovereign powers in many spheres.[271] They sought, however, to obtain the Palestinians' agreement to a number of significant derogations from their sovereignty.[272] The Israeli team was not, by this stage, challenging the Palestinians' entitlement to territorial sovereignty; instead, they were arguing that structuring the agreement solely around sovereign rights would produce an undesirable outcome. Their position, they explained, was animated in part by practical considerations (such as the difficulty of dividing control over civil aviation in view of the size and idiosyncratic contours of the two states' territories).[273] It was also motivated, they said, by two elements of Israel's "national security concept": skepticism about the capacity of a peace agreement with the Palestinians to eliminate security threats from elsewhere in

---

270. Israelis argued, for example, that the dismantlement of settlements was "unrealistic." *See supra* note 186 and accompanying text. They also argued against using sovereignty as a guiding principle for determining allocations of water because to do so, they claimed, would harm both parties. *See supra* note 230 and accompanying text. And while declining to concede Palestinian refugees' legal right of return, their arguments against it were framed primarily in terms of practical considerations—in particular, the possibility that its realization would eliminate the Jewish majority within the State of Israel.

271. *See supra* note 250 and accompanying text.

272. *See* Minutes, Permanent Status Negotiations, King David Hotel, Jerusalem (Sept. 17, 2000) (transcribed by PLO Negotiations Support Unit) (on file with PLO Negotiations Affairs Dep't). These derogations included demilitarization of the Palestinian state, the maintenance of Israeli military bases and early warning stations in Palestinian territory, the right to use Palestinian airspace for military training and operations, and the right to deploy Israeli forces in Palestinian territory during emergency situations. *Id.*

273. *See* Minutes, Permanent Status Negotiations, Hilton Taba Hotel, Taba (Jan. 23, 2001) (transcribed by PLO Negotiations Support Unit) (on file with PLO Negotiations Affairs Dep't).

the region and an unwillingness to compromise Israel's independent defensive capacity—to place Israel's security in the hands of others.[274]

Policy concerns of this kind made it difficult for the parties to agree that a set of norms, such as those defining the sovereign rights of states, would serve as guiding principles for the talks. They also limited the persuasive force of the legal rules invoked by the Palestinians, the Israelis questioning the extent to which the rules were responsive to the geo-political context in which the parties were negotiating. What was in dispute in this context, however, was not the content of the norms, but the value of the ideas they embodied. By challenging the efficacy of the norms, the Israelis were asserting that international law offers little shade.

3.   Lack of Recourse to Third-Party Adjudication and Enforcement

As described in Part III, a broad cross-section of the international community undertook on a number of occasions to define a substantive framework for the resolution of permanent status issues, often through reference to international legal norms. From the beginning of the peace process, however, the United States declined to participate in such efforts, insisting that the Palestinian-Israeli conflict could be solved only through bilateral negotiations and refusing to support (or, indeed, permit) "a competing or parallel process" in the United Nations.[275] Once permanent status negotiations commenced, moreover, American officials expressed impatience with appeals by the Palestinians to weigh in on legal disputes. When President Clinton did eventually offer a set of "ideas" for resolution of key issues in December 2000, he referred to the parties' legal terms of reference only briefly—and in instrumental rather than prescriptive terms.[276]

To be sure, American officials were not entirely unwilling to wield the United States's influence, even beyond the articulation of "ideas" for resolution of the conflict. As Dennis Ross argues in the concluding chapter of his memoir:

> Almost by definition, the best measure of whether the parties are ready to conclude the conflict is whether they are prepared to make historic decisions. . . . We can offer guarantees on security; financial assistance to demonstrate the material benefits of hard decisions; and political and international support to bolster the legitimacy of the decisions, all of which may be important in helping each side cross historic thresholds.

---

274. *See* Minutes, Permanent Status Negotiations, King David Hotel, Jerusalem (Sept. 18, 2000) (on file with PLO Negotiations Affairs Dep't).

275. *See supra* note 143 and accompanying text.

276. Clinton suggests that the parties "agree" that his proposed resolution of the refugee issue "implements [UN General Assembly] Resolution 194" and proposes that, upon conclusion of an agreement, the Security Council pass a resolution noting "that Resolutions 242 and 338 have been implemented." Clinton Parameters to Palestinian and Israeli Negotiators (Dec. 23, 2000), *in* 2 DOCUMENTS ON THE ARAB-ISRAELI CONFLICT, *supra* note 5, at 1160, 1162. This approach to addressing Resolution 242 was suggested by Prime Minister Barak at Camp David to "allow Barak to hold to his earlier claim that a settlement would fulfill 242, even if it was not based on 242." SWISHER, *supra* note 6, at 269.

But we cannot create the will for such decisions. . . . Imposed decisions will not endure.[277]

As he describes it, Ross's vision is one of carrots rather than sticks, of offering incentives rather than imposing costs. It is a vision in which the enforcement of legal rules has no place. Indeed, Ross sees third-party intervention as a means of allowing leaders to escape responsibility for political decisions: "[T]he United States may make its greatest contribution to peace by standing against efforts to impose solutions and standing for the principle that regional leaders must finally exercise their responsibilities to confront history and mythology."[278] The American role, from Ross's perspective, is to facilitate negotiations, not to constrain their outcome.

Whether the United States actually played this role during Palestinian-Israeli peace talks is, of course, open to question. American officials, after all, did not limit themselves to providing a forum for the talks or to transmitting messages between the parties. On a number of occasions, they offered their own assessment of the reasonableness of the parties' positions, sometimes even characterizing Israeli proposals as American ideas.[279] Aaron Miller, who served with Ross on the American peace team, suggests that Israel more often than not was the beneficiary of American interventions:

> With the best of motives and intentions, we listened to and followed Israel's lead without critically examining what that would mean for our own interests, for those on the Arab side and for the overall success of the negotiations. The "no surprises" policy, under which we had to run everything by Israel first, stripped our policy of the independence and flexibility required for serious peacemaking. If we couldn't put proposals on the table without checking with the Israelis first, and refused to push back when they said no, how effective could our mediation be? Far too often, particularly when it came to Israeli-Palestinian diplomacy, our departure point was not what was needed to reach an agreement acceptable to both sides but what would pass with only one—Israel.[280]

On the other hand, American officials did not hesitate to "push back" when it came to the Palestinians. Near the conclusion of the Camp David summit, for example, President Clinton warned Chairman Arafat that a failure to offer further concessions would be costly: "You won't have a state, and relations between America and the Palestinians will be over. Congress will vote to stop the aid you've been allocated, and you'll be treated as a terrorist organization."[281]

Although Israeli negotiators had responded dismissively to Palestinian legal arguments in the first rounds of negotiations, stating explicitly that "no one can force Israel to adopt another interpretation" of disputed norms,[282] the American response to them challenged the Palestinian approach in a more fundamental way. The United States, after all, was not simply a mediator. Its tremendous international influence and its Security Council veto rendered it capable of blocking almost any effort to impose terms (or some form of

---

277. ROSS, *supra* note 6, at 772.
278. *Id.*
279. *See* SWISHER, *supra* note 6, at 297.
280. Aaron David Miller, *Israel's Lawyer*, WASH. POST, May 23, 2005, at A19.
281. ENDERLIN, *supra* note 6, at 253.
282. *See supra* note 194 and accompanying text.

censure) on the parties if they failed to reach agreement, as it had demonstrated repeatedly during the decade leading up to the Camp David summit.[283] Indeed, in a unipolar world, the shadow of the law is shaped by—if not coextensive with—the shadow of American power.[284] Accordingly, the unwillingness of the Clinton team to entertain Palestinian legal claims at Camp David, and the indication it provided of the attitude the United States was likely to assume if the parties failed to reach agreement, seriously eroded the credibility of the Palestinians' invocation of "international legality"; it shortened the shadow of the legal norms on which the Palestinians were basing their positions. It is consequently unsurprising that, following President Clinton's angry rebuke of Palestinian negotiators at Camp David, the Palestinians turned increasingly to citing legal norms as persuasive standards in negotiations rather than demanding agreement on them as a pre-condition for further talks. It is also unsurprising that the Palestinians increasingly based their arguments on non-legal grounds, both political and practical.

Of course, the United States is not—and was not then—the only actor on the international stage. On a number of occasions, Palestinians sought the involvement of others, particularly Arab and Muslim states and the European Union.[285] In this regard, it is not incidental that the Palestinians' January 1, 2001 memorandum explaining their concerns about the Clinton "ideas" was circulated widely to international diplomatic personnel rather than only to the Americans. But the Palestinians recognized that no other international actor had influence over Israel's actions comparable to that of the United States and that, consequently, appeals to others were unlikely to cast much of a shadow over the peace talks.[286]

B.   How Can Law Help in the Future?

Future efforts to achieve a negotiated peace between Palestinians and Israelis must be informed by an appreciation of both the opportunities offered by law and the factors that constrained its effectiveness in the past. As described in Part II of this Article, law has the potential to facilitate bargaining in a number of different ways. It can operate to shape negotiating parties' bargaining zone, both disallowing certain outcomes and defining defaults that help each side to identify its own reservation point and assess the credibility of its adversary's. It can serve to fill in gaps in an agreement, obviating the

283. *See supra* notes 141-144 and accompanying text.
284. *See generally* Jose E. Alvarez, *Hegemonic International Law Revisited*, 97 AM. J. INT'L L. 873 (2003) (describing United States's "hegemonic" influence over development and enforcement of international law within U.N. Security Council).
285. *See* ENDERLIN, *supra* note 6, at 180; SWISHER, *supra* note 6, at 175-76.
286. *See* Miller, *supra* note 280, at A19 ("I believe in the importance of a strong U.S.-Israeli relationship. Paradoxically, it is our intimacy with the Israelis that gives America—only America—the capacity to be an honest and effective broker. Arab governments have come to accept this reality. That is why—even now—when our credibility is so diminished in the region, they continue to press for U.S. engagement."); *see also* INT'L CRISIS GROUP, MIDDLE EAST ENDGAME I: GETTING TO A COMPREHENSIVE ARAB-ISRAELI PEACE SETTLEMENT 9 (2002) (observing that "unique relationship between Washington and Jerusalem" and "America's unmatched ability to provide logistical backing to a peace deal" make American involvement in Middle East peacemaking essential); SWISHER, *supra* note 6, at 147-48 (noting Palestinian perception that pleas to the U.N. General Assembly were unlikely to affect course of negotiations if American support was wanting).

need to negotiate, in detail, every aspect of the parties' future relations. As an expression of best practices or by virtue of its objectiveness, it can provide a standard with which to evaluate the efficacy or fairness of a particular proposal. And it can provide legitimacy, a means of validating proposals (and negotiated outcomes) in the eyes of domestic constituencies and other international actors whose support is critical to the success of an agreement.

Each of these functions might have served Palestinian and Israeli negotiators well during the peace talks. Greater clarity from the outset regarding the legal framework for the talks might have helped to prevent the extreme divergence between the parties' respective opening positions—a divergence that not only generated misgivings on each side about the other's intentions, but also made it difficult for the parties to assess what kind of deal was possible, greatly slowing the pace of negotiations. In addition, in a process constrained politically by the short deadlines defined by the parties, consensus about guiding legal principles might have enabled the parties to make constructive use of legal norms as gap-fillers and as a means of framing tradeoffs. To cite one example, a shared acknowledgement of the applicability of the Fourth Geneva Convention to the West Bank and Gaza Strip—and of the fact (recognized by the Security Council[287] and the International Court of Justice[288]) that Israel's settlements in occupied territory contravene Article 49 of the Convention—would not have foreclosed a range of negotiated solutions to the issue of settlements, including some combination of annexation by Israel, dismantlement, long-term leasing, desegregation, and territory exchange. It would, however, have framed the trade-offs that a territorial compromise would require and offered both a standard for prioritizing competing Israeli and Palestinian claims to contiguity in the West Bank and East Jerusalem and a default with which to fill in gaps (and resolve ambiguities) in proposals like those presented by President Clinton in December 2000. Moreover, clearer alignment between the Clinton "ideas" and recognized international norms may well have bolstered their legitimacy in the eyes of Palestinians and of other governments called upon to convince Chairman Arafat to accept them.

Of course, arguing that law might have helped the parties in the past simply begs a larger question: How can law be made a more effective tool in the future? In order for legal rules to function better when Palestinians and Israelis try again to resolve their dispute at the negotiating table, efforts must be undertaken to address the factors that constrained their capacity to bolster the efficiency and fairness of the parties' last attempt to negotiate a peace agreement. Potential responses to those factors are described briefly below.

---

287.   *See* S.C. Res. 465, U.N. Doc. S/RES/465 (March 1, 1980).
288.   *See* Legal Consequences of the Construction of a Wall in the Occupied Palestinian Territory, Advisory Opinion, 2004 I.C.J. 131, para. 134, at 54 (July 9), *available at* http://www.icj-cij.org/icjwww/docket/imwp/imwpframe.htm [hereinafter I.C.J. Advisory Opinion on Construction of a Wall].

1. *Clarifying Rules*

The parties' disagreements about the applicability and determinacy of legal rules, as they bear on the issues in dispute, oblige a response on several levels. At a basic level, there continues to be a need for further development of international legal rules to ensure that they are responsive to recent transformations in the international system, including evolving conceptions of state sovereignty, global security, and the relationship of both to individual rights.[289] That process, however, is likely to be slow; and the need for flexibility in international rules—both to garner support for them from ever-reluctant governments and to ensure that the rules have the capacity to accommodate equitable concerns—will limit the determinacy of even those rules that are embraced by the international community.

What is more critical—and more feasible—at this juncture is a concerted effort by states and international institutions to articulate a common understanding regarding the applicability and implications of existing norms in the Palestinian-Israeli context. Such an effort could serve to increase the compliance-pull of the relevant norms—the shade they offer—by rendering them more determinate and bolstering their perceived legitimacy. It could also serve to facilitate the imposition of costs on the parties for failure to comply with the norms, extending the norms' shadow over future bargaining.

The advisory opinion of the International Court of Justice on the Legal Consequences of the Construction of a Wall in the Occupied Palestinian Territory goes some of this distance, establishing, *inter alia*, that "the [Fourth Geneva] Convention is applicable in the Palestinian territories,"[290] and that "the Israeli settlements in the Occupied Palestinian Territory (including East Jerusalem) have been established in breach of international law."[291] (Both of these conclusions received the unanimous support of the Court.)[292] Although the World Court does not offer any judgments regarding the bearing of the Fourth Geneva Convention on the *disposition* of settlements, confining itself to encouraging peace efforts "with a view to achieving as soon as possible, on the basis of international law, a negotiated solution to the outstanding problems,"[293] its opinion does resolve at least one of the normative disputes that divided Palestinians and Israelis during permanent status negotiations.

The World Court's advisory opinion and other efforts by international institutions to clarify normative standards are unlikely to have a direct influence[294] on future negotiations, however, unless authoritative members of

---

289. *See* High-level Panel on Threats, Challenges and Change, *A more secure world: our shared responsibility*, ¶¶ 29-30, U.N. Doc. A/59/565 (Dec. 1, 2004) (declaring that sovereignty "carries with it the obligation of a State to protect the welfare of its own peoples and meet its obligations to the wider international community"). Such efforts may help to address challenges to the efficacy of international legal rules like those raised in the security talks described above. *See supra* notes 273-274 and accompanying text.

290. *I.C.J. Advisory Opinion on Construction of a Wall*, para. 101, 2004 I.C.J. at 40.

291. *Id.* para. 120, at 46-47.

292. *Id.* paras. 2 & 9, at 1 & 4 (declaration of Judge Buergenthal).

293. *Id.* para. 162, at 62.

294. The litigation before the World Court arguably has already had an indirect influence on Israel's legal posture. *See* YOSSI ALPHER, U.S. INST. FOR PEACE: SPECIAL REPORT NO. 149, *THE FUTURE OF THE ISRAELI-PALESTINIAN CONFLICT: CRITICAL TRENDS AFFECTING ISRAEL*, 9 (Sept. 2005), *available at*

the international community both embrace their conclusions and take the additional step of reaching consensus regarding their basic implications vis-à-vis permanent status issues. In this regard, a number of commentators have suggested that the parties' impasse will only be overcome if the international community, led by the United States, articulates clearer parameters to guide future negotiations. For example, in a recent article, Russell Korobkin and Jonathan Zasloff argue that the United States should present the parties "with a detailed set of agreement terms that it considers fair and reasonable to both sides,"[295] a conclusion also reached by the International Crisis Group ("ICG").[296] Korobkin and Zasloff take no position, however, regarding the content of these terms or their relation to international legal norms; indeed, "[f]rom the perspective of [their] theoretical approach, the substance of the terms proposed is irrelevant. What matters is only that the set of terms falls inside the bargaining zone . . . so that both parties will prefer agreement on the terms included in the initiative to the impossibility of reaching any agreement."[297] Although the ICG does offer suggestions regarding the substantive content of the proposed parameters, it also is silent with respect to their relationship to international legal norms.[298]

What these proposals underestimate, however, is the importance of making clear that proposed parameters are in alignment with established international norms. As described in Part III, the influence of the Clinton "ideas" during the last weeks of permanent status negotiations was undermined by the Palestinians' perception that the ideas were the product of pro-Israel bias on the part of the American team and represented a departure from their recognized rights—perceptions that arguably reinforced each other. An effort to demonstrate the consistency of new parameters for the negotiations with international norms is likely to bolster their persuasiveness not only among Palestinians (and perhaps also Israelis), but also among other members of the international community, whose support for the parameters would provide a critical indication of their legitimacy.[299]

---

http://www.usip.org/pubs/specialreports/sr/49.pdf (suggesting that Israel High Court of Justice opinion in *Beit Sourik Village Council v. Gov't of Israel* was decided "partly in anticipation of the ICJ ruling"). The Court's decision is also likely to shape future Israeli court decisions, which could, in turn, affect Israel's position in future negotiations with the Palestinians. Moshe Hirsch, *The Impact of the Advisory Opinion on Israel's Future Policy: International Relations Perspective*, 1 J. INT'L L. & INT'L REL. 319, 334-35 (2005).

295. Korobkin & Zasloff, *supra* note 7, at 46.
296. *See* INT'L CRISIS GROUP, *supra* note 286, at 12.
297. Korobkin & Zasloff, *supra* note 7, at 47-48.
298. *See* INT'L CRISIS GROUP, *supra* note 286, at 14-17.
299. The inattention of Korobkin and Zasloff and the ICG to the value of linking proposed parameters to established international norms is surprising in view of the emphasis placed by both on the importance of obtaining broad international support for the parameters. *See* Korobkin & Zasloff, *supra* note 7, at 46-47 ("The support of the international community for the U.S. proposal, perhaps in the form of a U.N. Security Council resolution, would have important benefits," including "undermin[ing] likely claims that the United States is biased in favor of Israel"; diminishing the credibility of the "Palestinian claim that an unlimited right of return for refugees is required by international law"; bolstering the credibility of the United States refusal to accept further negotiation of the proposal's terms; and "providing political cover to the Arab states and allowing them to support the proposal without appearing to have succumbed to U.S. pressure."); INT'L CRISIS GROUP, *supra* note 286, at 10 (calling for international backing of parameters).

To be sure, not all of the parties' disputes regarding the determinacy of international legal rules can be resolved by the international community. As Abram Chayes observes:

> International law, in its normative sense, must be seen as indeterminate with respect to much of the array of concrete choices open in a particular situation. Often the rules have no authoritative formulation in words. Even when they do, the terms are open to a broad range of interpretation and emphasis. They do not dictate conduct so much as orient deliberation, order priorities, guide within broad limits.[300]

But even if the most that international law can do with respect to some issues is to "orient deliberation, order priorities, [and] guide within broad limits," that is no small contribution in the highly politicized context of peacemaking—particularly when even the broad limits are in dispute. Indeterminacy, moreover, need not foreclose legal discourse. Indeed, the flexibility created by a certain degree of indeterminacy may serve to facilitate discourse about fairness: As Thomas Franck suggests, "the legitimacy costs of introducing less determinate elements of distributive justice into the text of a rule . . . are more than balanced by the gains achieved when that law's standard opens a more generous fairness discourse."[301] Thus, while the incorporation of equitable standards into legal rules (such as those discussed by the parties during their water negotiations)[302] may serve to make the rules less useful in defining predictable outcomes, it also increases their perceived fairness—and, consequently, the willingness of parties to resolve disputes within the framework of law. Put another way, while equity shortens the shadow of the law, it may make the shade it does offer more attractive.

2. Focusing on Persuasion

The perceived inefficacy of solutions prescribed by international legal norms is in some ways a more difficult challenge to overcome. To a certain extent, it can be addressed through persuasive discourse—by moving beyond simply reciting norms to explaining how the other party's equitable concerns can be addressed within the framework of law. As the Israelis made clear during negotiations over water issues, a party will hesitate to embrace a norm as a guiding principle for talks without some idea of its implications and without confidence that the proposed legal framework is responsive to the party's needs. Although it may seem to be putting the cart before the horse, a detailed explanation of the practical consequences of accepting particular legal rules as standards for the resolution of disputed issues may be necessary to persuade the other party to embrace them. In an international system that continues to be built on consent, adversarial legal arguments devised for the courtroom are unlikely to be effective in the negotiating room, even if they are emotionally satisfying.

Discourse about the responsiveness of legal norms to equitable concerns should not, moreover, be confined to the negotiating room. As Harold Koh

---

300. CHAYES, *supra* note 60, at 101-02.
301. FAIRNESS, *supra* note 68, at 33.
302. *See supra* note 227 and accompanying text.

has argued, governments' internalization of international norms is often the product of interaction at the transnational level—among a range of governmental and non-governmental actors—rather than solely at the intergovernmental level.[303] This is not simply a matter of public relations, though outreach of that kind is important; it is also a matter of making the case in the myriad of forums where government officials, judges, academics, and technical experts interact. While the general public in Israel, Palestine, and elsewhere may have little appetite for a disquisition on the finer points of the United Nations Convention on the Non-Navigational Uses of International Watercourses, for example, second-track negotiations, academic conferences, and meetings of (and with) international institutions provide rich opportunities for exploring how the concerns and interests of both parties can be addressed within bodies of law. The fact that the influence of these forums on governmental decisions is difficult to anticipate and measure does not make its influence less real.

As the parties' disagreements in security talks make clear, however, it is particularly challenging to overcome skepticism about the efficacy of international law-based solutions when it is animated by skepticism about the international system itself. Convincing a nation still haunted by the Holocaust to abandon a security concept built upon independent defensive capacity in favor of a model based on cooperation, sovereign rights, and international guarantees is not an easy task in the best of circumstances. When it is undertaken only a few years after the international community again failed—twice—to prevent genocide, it becomes even more difficult. To acknowledge this difficulty is not to suggest that Israel's current security concept is either effective or sustainable, or that the Palestinians and others should cease to urge a different approach. The credibility of such persuasive efforts, however, is inextricably linked to the perceived strengths and frailties of international institutions and processes. The international community's failure to prevent and respond effectively to international crises will have implications far beyond the specific crisis in question, and attempts to promote compliance with international law by restricting access to or participation in international institutions will have little effect if the institutions themselves are not perceived to offer real benefits. Simply put, a naked tree will not be seen to offer much shade.

3.   *Exerting Third-Party Influence*

It is difficult to conceive of the circumstances that would prompt the international community to intervene militarily to end the Palestinian-Israeli conflict, even if such intervention were likely to be effective. Despite the lack of recourse to police action, however, third parties are not without means to influence the negotiating positions and preferences of Palestinians and Israelis. As noted above, they have an important role to play in helping to clarify the content and implications of international law. In this regard, third party governments should explicitly link both peace proposals (like the

---

303. Koh, *supra* note 3, at 2648-49.

Clinton "ideas" or the "Roadmap") and expressions of censure (such as the condemnation of settlement construction or the refusal of many states to deal with the Palestinian Authority's Hamas-led government) to relevant international norms. Conversely, discourse in intergovernmental forums like the United Nations should move beyond rote citation of norms to a broader discourse about what law does *not* address—and the opportunities that silence offers for addressing equitable concerns (like the factors supporting border modifications) within a legal framework. Third parties also can contribute much by building the capacity of international institutions to provide forums and tools for resolving disputed issues. Indeed, because so many of the issues on the table in Palestinian-Israeli negotiations demand cooperative solutions requiring substantial technical expertise—such as the management of cross-border trade and movement of persons, control over and allocation of electromagnetic frequencies, the management of the two countries' airspace and of infrastructure in shared spaces such as Jerusalem, and even ongoing responses to low-level security threats—international and regional organizations have much to offer the parties as vehicles both for the exchange of information about best practices and for involving other interested parties in solving specific problems.[304]

These kinds of efforts can increase the compliance pull of legal rules[305]—the shade of the law—which, in turn, may bolster their effectiveness as persuasive standards and gap-fillers. In addition, third parties can extend the shadow of international law by taking steps that impose costs on the parties for non-compliance. As others have observed, such steps may include withholding or constraining trade privileges,[306] suspending economic assistance,[307] facilitating criminal prosecution in domestic and international forums of officials accused of war crimes and related offenses,[308] and economic sanctions.[309]

It is beyond the scope of this Article to assess the merits or feasibility of these kinds of measures, but two points bear emphasizing. First, although it is undoubtedly advantageous to all concerned to allow Palestinians and Israelis

---

304. These organizations may include international bodies such as the International Telecommunications Union (which has expertise in addressing electromagnetic sphere issues), the International Civil Aviation Organization, and the World Trade Organization, as well as regional bodies such as NATO and the Organization for Security Cooperation in Europe. *See generally* Robert O. Keohane, *The demand for international regimes, in* INTERNATIONAL REGIMES 141, 170 (Stephen Krasner ed., 1983) (describing how international regimes facilitate substantive agreements between states).

305. *See generally* Hirsch, *supra* note 294, at 332-43 (assessing, from liberal and constructivist viewpoints, the likely impact of the I.C.J. advisory opinion on Israeli policy).

306. *See* Quigley, *supra* note 8, at 378-79 (describing, with approval, efforts to enforce human rights provisions within agreements between the European Union and Israel).

307. *See* Korobkin & Zasloff, *supra* note 7, at 60-61 (suggesting economic assistance to Israelis and Palestinians be made contingent on acceptance of U.S.-proposed parameters).

308. *See MP's call for sanctions against Israel for shootings,* TELEGRAPH (U.K.) (Apr. 4, 2006), *available at* http://www.telegraph.co.uk/news/main.jhtml?xml=/news/2006/04/11/usanctions.xml (last visited Apr. 22, 2006).

309. *See* John Quigley, *The Oslo Accords: International Law and the Palestinian-Israeli Peace Process,* 25 SUFFOLK TRANSNAT'L L. Rev. 73, 88 (2002) (suggesting sanctions as one potential means of encouraging Israel to adhere to international-law based solutions); Carlos Ortiz, Note, *Does a Double Standard Exist at the United Nations?: A Focus on Iraq, Israel and the Influence of the United States on the UN,* 22 WISC. INT'L L.J. 393, 395-96 (2004) (same).

maximum flexibility to structure their future relationship according to terms that they deem mutually beneficial and sustainable, the international community has a responsibility to ensure that their agreement falls within the broad limits defined by mandatory rules of international law—the zone of lawfulness. The functions served by mandatory rules in domestic settings—compensating for distortions in the bargaining process resulting from gross inequality between the parties and ensuring that a negotiated agreement does not violate important public policies or the rights of those unrepresented at the negotiating table—are no less important at the international level. Indeed, they are of particular relevance when the negotiating process takes place in the context of military occupation.[310] When the norms in question are central to the proper functioning of the international system, moreover, the entire international community has a stake in compliance with them, if only because non-compliance creates a precedent that may encourage illegal behavior by others and may compromise the legitimacy of international efforts in other contexts to respond to it.

Second, clarification by the international community of the content and implications of legal rules and of the costs of failing to reach an agreement in accordance with them may bolster not only the fairness of a negotiated outcome, but also the efficiency of the negotiation process. In addition to narrowing the scope of bargaining, framing trade-offs, and providing defaults with which to fill in gaps, such clarification may help to reduce the domestic political costs to the parties' respective leaderships of making a deal, as illustrated by the Gulf of Maine litigation. Ultimately, the compromises necessary to bring the Palestinian-Israeli conflict to an end will, as Dennis Ross observes, require the leadership of both sides to "exercise their responsibilities to confront history and mythology,"[311] an effort that inevitably will invite opposition within both communities even if majorities on both sides favor compromise. To require Palestinian and Israeli leaders to bear that responsibility alone in the fragile, fragmented political context in which both operate is to make peace contingent upon visionary, self-sacrificing political leadership that is as rare in Palestine and Israel as it is in the rest of the world.

V.   CONCLUSION

Palestinian poet Muhammad al-As'ad asks, "With what faith can . . . naked trees cast shade?"[312] In an international legal order that remains "inchoate, unformed and only just discernible,"[313] and in which the enforcement of legal norms is rare, the value of international law in peacemaking is to some extent a question of faith—faith in the power of ideas, in the effectiveness of institutions, and in the commitments of others. In the

---

310. Humanitarian law acknowledges the potential for coercion inherent in negotiations between an occupying power and "the authorities of the occupied territories." Geneva Convention Relative to the Protection of Civilian Persons in Time of War art. 47, Aug. 12, 1949, 6 U.S.T. 3516, 75 U.N.T.S. 287; *see also* Quigley, *supra* note 8, at 377-78; Imseis, *supra* note 7, at 126-27.

311. ROSS, *supra* note 6, at 772.

312. al-As'ad, *supra* note 1, at 123.

313. SINCLAIR, *supra* note 47, at 223.

continuing struggle over the fate of the Holy Land, however, these kinds of faith have failed to command enough believers.

As I have undertaken to demonstrate in this Article, the capacity of law to facilitate and guide negotiations rests on the perception by bargaining parties that legal rules either cast a shadow or offer shade. Norms whose enforcement appears remote or whose fairness or capacity to deliver benefits is in question will exert minimal influence over bargaining. Indeed, in the context of Palestinian-Israeli negotiations, international law too often was perceived as a naked tree. The reluctance of the United States to constrain the substantive direction of the peace talks or to permit censure of Israel for non-compliance with international law substantially shortened the perceived shadow of the law. At the same time, the shade of the law—its "compliance pull" independent of the prospect of enforcement—was diminished by a number of factors: the tendency of Palestinian negotiators, particularly early in the negotiations, to cite legal norms as dictates that require strict adherence, without undertaking to persuade Israeli negotiators about the responsiveness of the legal framework they invoked to Israeli equitable concerns; disputes between the parties about the applicability and determinacy of relevant norms; and a prevailing skepticism among Israeli political and military elites about the capacity of international law and institutions to offer benefits and security to Israel, in view of their impotence in addressing many of the crises of the twentieth century.

What I hope this Article also demonstrates, however, is that international law need not be a naked tree. Efforts by the international community to clarify the content and implications of international legal rules, at least as they apply to the Palestinian-Israeli conflict—and to impose costs on the parties for non-compliance—can do much to extend law's influence. In addition, such efforts should be complemented by persuasive discourse regarding the fairness and efficacy of resolving disputed issues within a legal framework: Although the recognition of legal rights should inform the framework for negotiations, it neither obviates the need to explain the legitimacy and justness of the rights invoked nor should it foreclose discussion of equitable interests that may justify a departure from the remedy prescribed by law. This kind of persuasive effort, moreover, should not be confined to discussions between legal counsel across the negotiating table, and it need not await the formal resumption of negotiations. Indeed, if international law is to embody the international community's values and ideals—if it is to provide shade from the glare of political conflict—then broad-based discourse about its content, its demands, and its limitations should be an integral component of efforts to build popular support for peace.